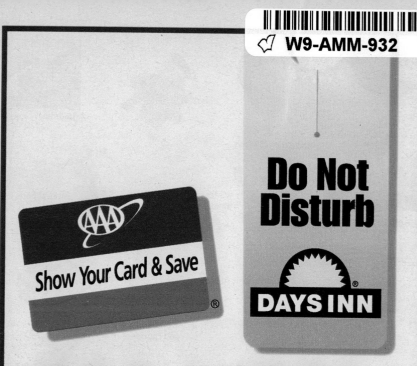

New York

Published by:
AAA Publishing
1000 AAA Drive
Heathrow, FL 32746-5063
Copyright AAA 2000

Send Written Comments to:
AAA Member Comments
1000 AAA Drive, Box 61
Heathrow, FL 32746-5063

**Advertising Rate and Circulation
Information**
Call: (407) 444-8280

Printed in the USA by Quebecor
Printing, Buffalo, NY

New York

TourBook Navigator
Follow our simple guide to make the most of this member benefit 7-23

Comprehensive City Index
Alphabetical list for the entire book 515

■ New York

Historical Timeline 30

Fast Facts 33

AAA Starred Attractions 36

Recreation Areas Chart 42

Temperature Chart 46

Exploring New York 47

POINTS OF INTEREST 54-186

　　Buffalo 64-72

　　New York 106-141

　　Niagara Falls (including
　　　　Niagara Falls, Ontario) .. 142-156

MAPS
New York Orientation 34

Downtown Albany 55

Buffalo Destination Area 67

Buffalo 68

New York Destination Area 110

Lower Manhattan 114

Midtown Manhattan 120

Upper Manhattan 127

Greenwich Village Walking Tour 133

Theater Map Key 136

Niagara Falls Destination Area 145

Niagara Falls
(New York & Ontario) 146

Rochester 166

ACCOMMODATIONS 187-495

   Buffalo 210-228

   New York 318-379

   Niagara Falls (including
       Niagara Falls, Ontario) 380-438

MAPS

   New York Orientation 188

   Adirondacks Area 190

   Albany 193

   Buffalo Destination Area 210

   Buffalo 213

   Finger Lakes Area 255

   Long Island 305

   New York Destination Area 318

   Lower Manhattan 326

Featured Information

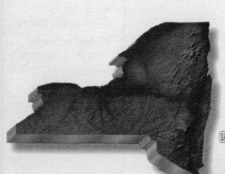

ⓒ *Offices* 496

Driving Distances Map 497

Metric Chart 498

Border Information 499

NEW Bed & Breakfast
  Advertising Section 500

Bed & Breakfast Lodgings Index 500

Country Inns Index 501

Historical Lodgings & Restaurants Index 501

Resorts Index 502

Points of Interest Index 503

SAVE Attraction Admission Discount Index 514

Comprehensive City Index 515

Photo Credit Index 517

MAPS *continued*

Midtown Manhattan 328

New York City 330

Niagara Falls Destination Area 380

Niagara Falls (New York) 384

Niagara Falls (Ontario) 385

Rochester 456

Syracuse 478

When it comes to personal trip planning, nobody beats trained AAA travel counselors.

O ur highly trained counselors can assist you with all facets of planning your trip, from designing the route to making reservations. In addition, only AAA travel counselors can provide our exclusive collection of travel materials selected especially for you.

TourBook® guides are comprehensive travel guides listing AAA Approved attractions, lodgings and restaurants. In addition to the coveted Diamond Ratings, you'll find descriptions of towns and cities and information on discounts available only to AAA members. TourBooks are updated annually and cover every state and province in the United States and Canada.

TripTik® routings trace your route mile-by-mile and are clearly marked with the vital information you need while on the road, such as highway exits and rest stops. These handy maps are custom-configured by your AAA travel counselor and can highlight the quickest, shortest or most scenic routes, as well as highway construction projects along the way.

Sheet maps are updated annually and cover every state and province, plus regional areas throughout North America. An extensive network of road reporters and club staff works with AAA cartographers to ensure that AAA maps are the most detailed and accurate maps available.

O nly AAA offers an integrated travel information system that is tailored to your individual needs.

CampBook® guides list AAA Approved camping and RV facilities, both public and private, throughout the United States and Canada.

So the next time you're planning a trip, remember to visit your local AAA travel counselor.

Travel With Someone You Trust®

Trust

the AAA TourBook for objective travel information. Follow the pages of TourBook Navigator to thoroughly understand this unique member benefit.

Making Your Way Through the AAA Listings

Attractions, lodgings and restaurants are listed on the basis of merit alone after careful evaluation, approval and rating by one of our full-time inspectors or, in rare cases, a designated representative. Annual lodging inspections are unannounced and conducted on site by random room sample.

Those lodgings and restaurants listed with an 〔fyi〕 icon have not gone through the same inspection process as other rated properties. Individual listings will denote the reason why this icon appears. Bulleted attraction listings are not inspected but are included for member information.

An establishment's decision to advertise in the TourBooks has no bearing on its inspection, evaluation or rating. Advertising for services or products does not imply AAA endorsement.

All information in this TourBook was reviewed for accuracy before publication. However, since changes inevitably occur between annual editions, we suggest you contact establishments directly to confirm prices and schedules.

How the TourBook is

Organized

Geographic listing is used for accuracy and consistency. This means attractions, lodgings and restaurants are listed under the city in which they physically are located—or in some cases under the nearest recognized city. A comprehensive TourBook City Index located in the back of the book contains an A-to-Z list of cities. Most listings are alphabetically organized by state or province, city, and establishment name. A color is assigned to each state so that you can match the color bars at the top of the page to switch from Points of Interest to Lodgings and Restaurants.

Destination Cities and Destination Areas

The TourBook also groups information by destination city and destination area. If a city is grouped in a destination vicinity section, the city name will appear at its alphabetical location in the book, and a handy cross reference will give the exact page on which listings for that city begin. Maps are placed at the beginning of these sections to orient you to the destinations.

Destination cities, established based on government models and local expertise, are comprised of metropolitan areas plus nearby vicinity cities.

Destination areas are regions with broad tourist appeal. Several cities will comprise the area.

Points of Interest Section

Orientation maps

near the start of each Attractions section show only those places we call points of interest. Coordinates included with the city listings depict the locations of those cities on the map. Stars accent towns with "must see" attractions. And the black ovals with white numerals locate items listed in the nearby Recreation Areas chart.

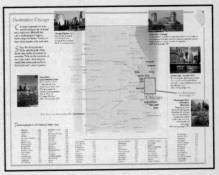

Destination area maps

illustrate key travel areas defined by local travel experts. Communities shown have listings for AAA approved attractions.

National park maps

represent the area in and around the park. Some campground sites and lodges spotted on the maps do not meet AAA/CAA criteria, but are shown for members who nevertheless wish to stay close to the park area.

Walking or self-guiding tour maps

correspond to specific routes described in TourBook text.

City maps

show areas where numerous points of interest are concentrated and indicate their location in relation to major roads, parks, airports and other landmarks.

Featured Information Section

Driving distance maps

are intended to be used only for trip-distance and driving-time planning.

Lodgings & Restaurants Section

State or province orientation maps appear before the property listings in the Lodgings & Restaurants section of selected TourBooks and show the relative positions of major metropolitan areas and the vicinity towns in those areas.

Area maps denote large geographical areas in which there are many towns containing lodgings and/or restaurants. Due to these maps' small scale, lodgings and restaurants are not shown; towns with lodgings and/or restaurants are printed in magenta type.

Destination area maps illustrate key travel areas defined by local travel experts. Communities shown have listings for AAA-RATED® lodgings and/or restaurants.

Spotting maps show the location of lodgings and restaurants. Lodgings are spotted with a black-background (**22** for example); restaurants are spotted with a white-background (**23** for example). Spotting map indexes have been placed after the main city heading to provide the user with a convenient method to identify what an area has to offer at a glance. The index references the map page number where the property is spotted, indicates if a property is an Official Appointment and contains an advertising reference if applicable. It also lists the property's diamond rating, high season rate range and listing page number.

Downtown/city spotting maps are provided when spotted facilities are very concentrated. Starred points of interest also appear on these maps.

Vicinity spotting maps spot those properties that are outside the downtown or city area. Major roads, landmarks, airports and starred points of interest are shown on vicinity spotting maps as well. The names of suburban communities that have AAA-RATED® accommodations are shown in magenta type.

Sample Attraction Listing

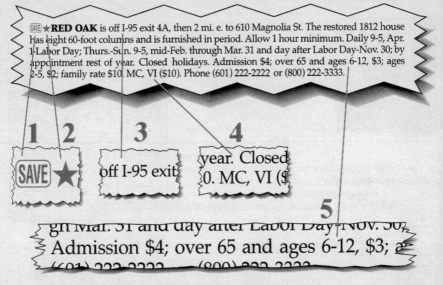

SAVE ★**RED OAK** is off I-95 exit 4A, then 2 mi. e. to 610 Magnolia St. The restored 1812 house has eight 60-foot columns and is furnished in period. Allow 1 hour minimum. Daily 9-5, Apr. 1-Labor Day; Thurs.-Sun. 9-5, mid-Feb. through Mar. 31 and day after Labor Day-Nov. 30; by appointment rest of year. Closed holidays. Admission $4; over 65 and ages 6-12, $3; ages 2-5, $2; family rate $10. MC, VI ($10). Phone (601) 222-2222 or (800) 222-3333.

1   2   3   4

SAVE ★   off I-95 exit   year. Closed 0. MC, VI ($

5

gh Mar. 31 and day after Labor Day-Nov. 30;

Admission $4; over 65 and ages 6-12, $3; a

(601) 222-2222   (800) 222-3333

1 SAVE Participating attractions offer AAA/CAA cardholders or holders of a AAA MasterCard or AAA Visa Card and up to six family members at least 10% off admission for the validity period of the TourBook. Present your card at the admissions desk. A list of participating attractions appears in the Indexes section of the book. The SAVE discount may not be used in conjunction with other discounts. Attractions that already provide a reduced senior rate may not honor the SAVE discount for this age group. Discounts may not apply during special events or particular days or seasons.

2 ★ Attraction is of exceptional interest and quality.

3 Unless otherwise specified, directions are given from the center of town, using the following highway designations: I (interstate highway), US (federal highway), Hwy. (Canadian highway), SR (state route), CR (county road), FM (farm to market road), FR (forest road), MM (mile marker)

4
AE=American Express	JC=Japanese Credit Bureau
CB=Carte Blanche	MC=MasterCard
DI=Diners Club	VI=VISA
DS=Discover	

Minimum amounts that may be charged appear in parentheses when applicable.

5 Admission prices are quoted without sales tax. Children under the lowest age specified are admitted free when accompanied by an adult. Days, months and age groups written with a hyphen are inclusive. Prices pertaining to attractions in the United States are quoted in U.S. dollars; Canadian province and territory attraction prices are quoted in Canadian dollars.

Bulleted Listings: Casino gambling establishments not contained within hotels are visited by club personnel to ensure safety. Recreational activities of a participatory nature (requiring physical exertion or special skills) are not inspected. Both are presented in a bulleted format for informational purposes.

Attraction Partners

These Show Your Card & Save® attraction partners provide the listed member benefits. Admission tickets that offer greater discounts may be available for purchase at the local AAA club. A maximum of six tickets is available at the discount price.

Universal Studios Escape
Universal Studios Hollywood

[SAVE] Save $3 on 1-day admission, $4 on 2-day admission, and $5 on 3-day admission at the gate (Universal Studios Florida and Hollywood)

[SAVE] Save 10% on selected souvenirs and dining

SeaWorld/Busch Gardens

Save at SeaWorld, Busch Gardens, Sesame Place, Water Country USA and Adventure Island.

[SAVE] Save 10% on general admission

Six Flags Adventure Parks

[SAVE] Save $4 on admission at the gate

[SAVE] Save $12 on admission at the gate each Wednesday

[SAVE] Save 10% on selected souvenirs and dining

Citizens or permanent residents of the United States who are 62 and older can obtain Golden Age Passports for a one-time $10 fee. Golden Access Passports are free to citizens or permanent residents of the United States (regardless of age) who are medically blind or permanently disabled. Both cover entrance fees for the holder and accompanying private party to all national parks, historic sites, monuments and battlefields within the U.S. national park system, plus half off camping and other fees. Apply in person at most federally operated areas. The Golden Eagle Passport is available to everyone, despite country of origin. It costs $50 annually and covers entrance fees for the holder and accompanying private party to all federally operated areas. Obtain the pass in person at any national park or regional office of the U.S. park service or forest service.

Golden Passports

Sample Lodging Listing

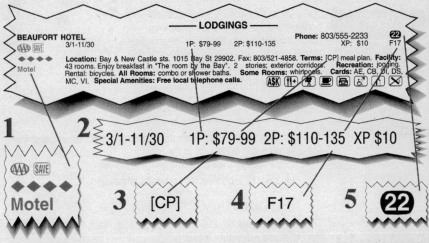

1 🔺🔺🔺 or 🔺 indicates our Official Appointment (OA) lodgings. The OA Program permits properties to display and advertise the 🔺 or 🔺 emblem. We highlight these properties with red diamonds and classification. Some OA listings include special amenities such as free breakfast; early check-in/late check-out; free room upgrade or preferred room, such as ocean view or poolside (subject to availability); free local phone calls; and free daily newspaper. This does not imply that only these properties offer these amenities. The 🔺 or 🔺 sign helps traveling members find accommodations that want member business.

◆◆◆ or ◆◆◆ The number of diamonds—not the color—informs you of the overall level of quality in a lodging's amenities and service. More diamond details appear on page 14.

Motel or Motel: Diamond ratings are applied in the context of lodging type, or classification. See pages 20-21 for our Lodging Classifications.

Discounts

(SAVE) Official Appointment properties guarantee members a minimum 10% discount off the published TourBook rates.

(SAVE) AAA's Show Your Card & Save® chain partners provide special values to our members: Select Choice Hotels, Days Inn, Hilton, Hyatt, and La Quinta . Individual properties in these chains appearing in the TourBook have been inspected and approved by AAA. Be sure to read How to Get the Best Room Rates on page 19.

(S•D) Establishments offer a minimum senior discount of 10% off the listed rates. This discount is available to members 60 or older.

(ASK) Many TourBook properties offer discounts to members even though the lodgings do not participate in a formal discount program. The (ASK) is another reminder to inquire about available discounts when making your reservations or at check-in.

> Discounts normally offered at some lodgings may not apply during special events or holiday periods. Special rates and discounts may not apply to all room types.

To obtain published rates or discounts, you must identify yourself as a AAA or CAA member and request AAA rates when making reservations. The SAVE or senior discount may not be used in conjunction with other discounts. Be sure to show your card at registration and verify the room rate.

The rates listed for approved properties are provided to AAA by each lodging and represent the regular (rack) rate for a standard room. Printed rates, based on rack rates and last room availability, are rounded to the nearest dollar. Rates do not include taxes and discounts. U.S. rates are in U.S. dollars; rates for Canadian lodgings are in Canadian dollars.

2 Rate Lines

Shown from left to right: dates the rates are effective; rates for 1 person or 2 persons; extra person charge (XP); and any applicable family plan indicator.

Rates Guaranteed

AAA members are guaranteed that they will not be charged more than the maximum regular rate printed in each rate range for a standard room. Rates may vary within the range depending on season and room type. Listed rates are based on last standard room availability.

Exceptions

Lodgings may temporarily increase room rates, not recognize discounts or modify pricing policies during special events. Examples of special events range from Mardi Gras and Kentucky Derby (including pre-Derby events) to college football games, holidays, holiday periods and state fairs. Although some special events are listed in AAA TourBook guides, it is always wise to check, in advance, with AAA travel counselors for specific dates.

Discounts

Member discounts will apply to rates quoted, within the rate range, applicable at the time of booking. Special rates used in advertising, and special short-term, promotional rates lower than the lowest listed rate in the range, are not subject to additional member discounts.

3 Meal Plan Indicators

The following types of meal plans may be available in the listed room rate:

AP = American Plan of three meals daily
BP = Breakfast Plan of full hot breakfast
CP = Continental Plan of pastry, juice and another beverage
ECP = Expanded Continental Plan, which offers a wider variety of breakfast items
EP = European Plan, where rate includes only room
MAP = Modified American Plan of two meals daily

> **Check-in times are shown in the listing only if they are after 3 p.m.; check-out times are shown only if they are before 10 a.m. Parking is on the premises and free unless otherwise noted.**

4 Family Plan Indicators

F17 = Children 17 and under stay free (age displayed will reflect property's policy)
D17 = Discount for children 17 and under
F = Children stay free
D = Discounts for children

5 Lodging Locators

Numerals are used to locate, or "spot," lodgings on maps we provide for larger cities.

The few lodgings with fyi in place of diamonds are included as an "informational only" service for members. The icon indicates that a property has not been rated for one or more of the following reasons: too new to rate; under construction; under major renovation; not inspected; or may not meet all AAA requirements. Listing prose will give insight as to why the fyi rating was assigned.

The Lodging Diamond Ratings

AAA field inspectors evaluate and rate each lodging based on the overall quality and services offered at a property. The size, age and overall appeal of an establishment are considered as well as regional decorating and architectural differences.

While guest services are an important part of all diamond ratings, they are particularly critical at the four and five diamond levels. A property must provide a high level of service, on a consistent basis, to obtain and support the four and five diamond rating.

Properties are world-class by definition, exhibiting an exceptionally high degree of service as well as striking, luxurious facilities and many extra amenities. Guest services are executed and presented in a flawless manner. The guest is pampered by a professional, attentive staff. The properties' facilities and operation help set industry standards in hospitality and service.

Properties are excellent and display a high level of service and hospitality. They offer a wide variety of amenities and upscale facilities in the guest rooms, on the grounds and in the public areas.

Properties offer a degree of sophistication. Additional amenities, services and facilities may be offered. There is a noticeable upgrade in physical attributes, services and comfort.

Properties maintain the attributes offered at the one diamond level, while showing marked enhancements in decor and furnishings. They may be recently constructed or older properties, both targeting the needs of a budget-oriented traveler.

Properties offer good but modest accommodations. Establishments are functional, emphasizing clean and comfortable rooms. They must meet the basic needs of comfort and cleanliness.

Guest Safety

Room Security

In order to be approved for listing in AAA/CAA TourBook® guides for the United States and Canada, all lodgings must comply with AAA's guest room security requirements.

In response to AAA/CAA members' concern about their safety at properties, AAA-RATED® accommodations must have deadbolt locks on all guest room entry doors and connecting room doors.

If the area outside the guest room door is not visible from inside the room through a window or door panel, viewports must be installed on all guest room entry doors. Bed and breakfast properties and country inns are not required to have viewports. Ground floor and easily accessible sliding doors must be equipped with some other type of secondary security locks.

Field inspectors view a percentage of rooms at each property since it is not feasible to evaluate every room in every lodging establishment. Therefore, AAA cannot guarantee that there are working locks on all doors and windows in all guest rooms.

Fire Safety

Because of the highly specialized skills needed to conduct professional fire safety inspections, AAA/CAA inspectors cannot assess fire safety.

All U.S. and Canadian lodging properties must be equipped with an operational, single-station smoke detector, and all public areas must have operational smoke detectors or an automatic sprinkler system. A AAA/CAA inspector has evaluated a sampling of the rooms to verify this equipment is in place.

For additional fire safety information read the page posted on the back of your guest room door, or write:

**National Fire Protection Association
1 Batterymarch Park, P.O. Box 9101
Quincy, MA 02269-9101**

Access for Travelers with Disabilities

Qualified properties listed in this book have symbols indicating they are fully accessible, semi-accessible or meet the needs of the hearing-impaired. This two-tiered mobility standard was developed to meet members' varying degrees of accessibility needs.

(&) Fully accessible properties meet the needs of those that are significantly disabled and utilize a wheelchair or scooter. A fully accessible lodging will provide at least one guest room meeting the designated criteria. A traveler with these disabilities will be able to park and access public areas, including restrooms, check-in facilities and at least one food and beverage outlet. A fully accessible restaurant indicates that parking, dining rooms and restrooms are accessible.

(⼈) Semi-accessible properties meet the needs of those that are disabled but do have some mobility. Such travelers would include people using a cane or walker, or a disabled individual with good mobility but a limited arm or hand range of motion. A Semi-accessible lodging will provide at least one guest room meeting the designated criteria. A traveler with these disabilities will be able to park and access public areas, including restrooms, check-in facilities and at least one food and beverage outlet. A semi-accessible restaurant indicates that parking, dining rooms and restrooms are accessible.

(🕭) This symbol indicates a property with the following equipment available for hearing impaired travelers: TDD at front desk or switchboard; visual notification of fire alarm, incoming telephone calls, door knock or bell; closed caption decoder available; text telephone or TDD available for guest room use; telephone amplification device available, with shelf and electric outlet next to guest room telephone.

The criteria used by AAA/CAA do not represent the full scope of the Americans With Disabilities Act of 1990 Accessibility Guidelines (ADAAG); they are, however, consistent with the ADAAG. Members can obtain from their local AAA/CAA club the AAA brochure, "AAA Accessibility Criteria for Travelers with Disabilities", which describes the specific criteria pertaining to the fully accessible, semi-accessible and hearing-impaired standards.

The Americans With Disabilities Act (ADA) prohibits businesses that serve the public from discriminating against persons with disabilities who are aided by service animals. Some businesses have mistakenly denied access to their properties to persons with disabilities who use service animals. ADA has priority over all state and local laws, as well as a business owner's standard of business, that might bar animals from the premises. Businesses must permit guests and their service animal entry, as well as allow service animals to accompany guests to all public areas of a property. A property is permitted to ask whether the animal is a service animal or a pet, or whether a guest has a disability. The property may not, however, ask questions about the nature of a disability or require proof of one.

No fees or deposits (even those normally charged for pets) may be charged for the service animal.

AAA/CAA urges members with disabilities to always phone ahead to fully understand the accommodation's offerings. Some properties do not fully comply with AAA/CAA's exacting accessibility standards but may offer some property design standards that meet the needs of some guests with disabilities.

AAA/CAA does not evaluate recreational facilities, banquet rooms or convention and meeting facilities for accessibility. Call a property directly to inquire about your needs for these areas.

What The Icons Mean

Member Values

ⒶⒶⒶ or ⒶⒶ Official Appointment

🆂 Offers minimum 10% discount

🆂 SYC&S chain partners

🅰🆂🅺 May offer discount

🆂 Offers senior discount

🆔 Informational listing only

Member Services

✈ Airport transportation

🐾 Pets allowed

🍽 Restaurant on premises

🍽 Restaurant off premises
(walking distance)

🕐 24-hour room service

🍸 Cocktail lounge

Special Features

🖥 Business services

🅿 Valet parking

🧺 Laundry service

👶 Child care

♿ Fully accessible

🛗 Semi-accessible

🚿 Roll-in showers

👂 Hearing impaired

In-Room Amenities

✖ Non-smoking rooms

🅐🅒 No air conditioning

☎ No telephones

📺 No cable TV

🎬 Movies

[VCR] VCR

📻 Radio

☕ Coffee maker

🔲 Microwave

🔌 Refrigerator

[DATA PORT] Data port/modem line

Sports/Recreation

🏊 Outdoor pool

🏊 Indoor pool

🏊 Indoor/outdoor pool

🏋 Fitness center

⊠ Recreational facilities

Please see listing prose for specific details regarding any item represented by an icon.

Additional Fees

Fees may be charged for some of the services represented by the icons listed here; please refer to the listing text and inquire when making reservations.

If a pet icon is not present, assume that the property does not accept pets; although deposits and fees are stated in the listing, check policies and restrictions when making reservations.

Preferred Lodging Partners

 Call the member-only toll-free numbers below or your club to get these member benefits. Have your membership card on hand when calling.

Show Your Card & Save

GUARANTEED RATES - Lowest public rate available for dates of stay when booked in advance via the toll-free numbers listed below.
SATISFACTION GUARANTEE - If you're not satisfied with your stay, it's free. *Member must provide opportunity for lodging to correct any problem.*

Save 10%.   Save 10%.   Save 10%.   Save 20%.*   Save 10%.   Save 10%.
Satisfaction Guarantee. Children under 18 stay free.   *(most Clarion & Carriage House Inns)

(800) 228-1222

Guaranteed Rates. Satisfaction Guarantee. Children under 12 stay free.
(800) 432-9755

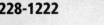

Guaranteed Rates. Satisfaction Guarantee. Children under 18 and spouse stay free.
(800) 221-4731

Guaranteed Rates. Satisfaction Guarantee. Children under 18 stay free.
Receive second entree at half price when staying in hotel.
(800) 532-1496

Hilton
Guaranteed Rates. Satisfaction Guarantee. Children under 18 stay free. Save up to 25%
(800) 916-2221

Lowest Public Rate. Satisfaction Guarantee. Children 18 and under stay free.
(800) 456-7793

Making Reservations

Give Proper Identification

When making reservations, you must identify yourself as a AAA/CAA member. Give all pertinent information about your planned stay. Request written confirmation to guarantee: type of room, rate, dates of stay, and cancellation and refund policies. Note: Age restrictions may apply.

Confirm Deposit, Refund and Cancellation Policies

Most establishments give full deposit refunds if they have been notified at least 48 hours before the normal check-in time. Listing prose will note if more than 48 hours notice is required for cancellation. However, when making reservations, confirm the property's deposit, cancellation and refund policies. Some properties may charge a cancellation or handling fee.

When this applies, "cancellation fee imposed" will appear in the listing. If you cancel too late, you have little recourse if a refund is denied.

When an establishment requires a full or partial payment in advance, and your trip is cut short, a refund may not be given.

When canceling reservations, call the lodging immediately. Make a note of the date and time you called, the cancellation number if there is one, and the name of the person who handled the cancellation. If your AAA/CAA club made your reservation, allow them to make the cancellation for you as well so you will have proof of cancellation.

Review Charges for Appropriate Rates

When you are charged more than the maximum rate listed in the TourBook, question the additional charge. If management refuses to adhere to the published rate, pay for the room and submit your receipt and membership number to AAA/CAA within 30 days. Include all pertinent information: dates of stay, rate paid, itemized paid receipts, number of persons in your party, the room number you occupied, and list any extra room equipment used. A refund of the amount paid in excess of the stated maximum will be made if our investigation indicates that unjustified charging has occurred.

Get the Room You Reserved

When you find your room is not as specified, and you have written confirmation of reservations for a certain type of accommodation, you should be given the option of choosing a different room or finding one elsewhere. Should you choose to go elsewhere and a refund is refused or resisted, submit the matter to AAA/CAA within 30 days along with complete documentation, including your reasons for refusing the room and copies of your written confirmation and any receipts or canceled checks associated with this problem.

How to Get the Best Room Rates

You'll find the best room rate if you book your reservation in advance with the help of a travel counselor or agent at your local AAA/CAA office.

If you're not yet ready to make firm vacation plans or if you prefer a more spontaneous trip, take advantage of the partnerships that preferred hotel chains have arranged with AAA. Call the toll-free numbers on the previous page that have been set up exclusively for members for the purpose of reserving with these Show Your Card & Save® chain partners.

Even if you were unable to make a reservation, be sure to show your membership card at the desk and ask if you're being offered the lowest rate available for that time. Many lodgings offer reduced rates to members.

Lodging Classifications

AAA inspectors evaluate lodgings based on classification, since all lodging types by definition do not provide the same level of service and facilities. Thus, hotels are rated in comparison to other hotels, resorts to other resorts—and so on. A lodging's classification appears beneath its diamond rating in the listing.

Hotel — *full service*
Usually high-rise establishments, offering a wide range of services and on-premise food/beverage outlets, shops, conference facilities and recreational activities.

Motel — *limited service*
Low-rise or multi-story establishment offering limited public and recreational facilities.

Country Inn — *moderate service*
Similar in definition to a bed and breakfast, but usually larger in size, with a dining facility that serves at least breakfast and dinner.

Resort — *full service*
Offers a variety of food/beverage outlets, and an extensive range of recreational and entertainment programs - geared to vacation travelers.

Bed & Breakfast — *limited service*
Usually smaller, owner-operated establishments emphasizing an "at home" feeling. A continental or full, hot breakfast is served and included in the room rate.

Condominium — *limited service*
Apartment-style units or homes primarily owned by individuals and available for rent. A variety of room styles and décor treatments, as well as limited housekeeping service, is typical.

Motor Inn — *moderate service*
Single or multi-story establishment offering on-premise food/ beverage service, meeting and banquet facilities and some recreational facilities.

Complex — *service varies*
A combination of two or more types of lodging classifications.

Lodge — *moderate service*
Typically two or more stories with all facilities in one building. Rustic décor is common. Usually has food/beverage service.

Apartment — *limited service*
Primarily offers temporary guest accommodations with one or more bedrooms, a living room, a full kitchen and an eating area. Studio apartments may combine the sleeping and living areas into one room.

Cottage — *limited service*
Primarily individual housing units that may offer one or more separate sleeping areas, a living room and cooking facilities.

Ranch — *moderate service*
Often offers rustic décor treatments and food/beverage facilities. Entertainment and recreational activities are geared to a Western theme.

Subclassifications

The following are subclassifications that may appear along with the classifications listed above to provide a more specific description of the lodging.

Suite
One or more bedrooms and a living room/sitting area, closed off by a full wall. Note: May not have a partition bedroom door.

Extended Stay
Properties catering to longer-term guest stays. Will have kitchens or efficiencies and may have a separate living room area, evening office closure and limited housekeeping services.

Historic
Accommodations in restored structures built prior to 1920, with décor reflecting the ambiance of yesteryear. Rooms may lack some modern amenities and may have shared bathrooms.

Classic
Renowned and landmark properties, older than 50 years, known for their unique style and ambiance.

Sample Restaurant Listing

CAFE TERRA COTTA   **Lunch:** $5-14   **Dinner;** $14-22   **Phone:** 520/299-1759
Location: SE corner Campbell Ave & River Rd in St Phillips Plaza. 4613 N Campbell Ave   85758. **Hours:** 11 am-9:30 pm, Fri & Sat-10:30 pm. Closed:11/25 & 12/25. **Reservations:** suggested. **Features:** children's menu; carryout; cocktails; a la carte. Casual indoor or outdoor patio dining **Cards:** AE, CB, DI, DS, MC.

Italian

1

Italian

2 **Dinner $14-22**

3 **Cards:** AE, CB, DI,

4

1 ⒶⒶⒶ or ⓄⒶ indicates our Official Appointment (OA) restaurants. The OA Program permits properties to display and advertise the ⒶⒶⒶ or ⓄⒶ emblem. We highlight these properties with red diamonds and cuisine type. The ⒶⒶⒶ or ⓄⒶ sign helps traveling members find restaurants that want member business.

◆◆◆ or ◆◆◆ The number of diamonds—not the color—informs you of the overall level of quality for food and presentation, service and ambiance. Restaurants also are classified by cuisine type.

2 The dinner price range is approximate and includes a salad or appetizer, an entrée, a vegetable and a non-alcoholic beverage for one person. Taxes and tip are not included. Some listings include additional information such as the availability of a senior citizen menu, children's menu or "early bird specials," if offered at least 5 days a week.

3 AE=American Express   JC=Japanese Credit Bureau
CB=Carte Blanche   MC=MasterCard
DI=Diners Club*   VI=VISA
DS=Discover

Minimum amounts that may be charged appear in parentheses when applicable.

4 This icon indicates that the restaurant has a designated non-smoking section or is entirely smoke-free.

The restaurants with ⓕⓨⓘ in place of diamonds are included as an "informational only" service for members. This designation indicates that the restaurant has not been inspected.

The Restaurant Diamond Ratings

AAA field inspectors evaluate and rate each restaurant on the overall quality of food, service, décor and ambiance—with extra emphasis given to food and service.

The ratings represent a range of member dining needs and expectations. A one diamond rating indicates simple, family or specialty meals, while a five diamond rating indicates an ultimate dining experience that is truly a memorable occasion.

A memorable occasion—the ultimate in adult dining. Food shows the highest culinary skills, evident in all areas of preparation and presentation. An extensive wine list is available. A professional staff—often in formal attire—provides flawless and pampering service. The decor has classic details, often formal, and reflects comfort and luxury.

A high degree of sophistication, thus creating an adult dining experience. Complex food is creatively presented. An extensive wine list is offered. The service staff, often formally attired, is professionally trained. The decor is distinctive, stylish and elegant; some establishments are casual while still offering refinement or formality.

An upscale or special family dining experience. Food is cooked to order and creatively prepared with quality ingredients. A wine list is available. A skilled, often uniformed staff provides service. The usually professional and inviting decor projects a trendy, upbeat, casual or formal atmosphere.

More extensive menus for family or adult dining. Food is prepared with standard ingredients. Service is attentive but may be informal, casual, limited or self-serve. The decor presents a unified theme that is comfortable but also may be trendy, casual or upbeat.

Provides a simple, family or specialty meal in clean, pleasant surroundings. Food is basic and wholesome. Service is casual, limited or self-serve. Decor is informal.

Note: Major restaurant chains are not listed due to their widespread recognition.

The Smart Choice for Your Family's Financial Future

Your family's financial needs change throughout life. Now you can trust AAA to bring you a full array of financial products and services to meet those financial needs at every stage. With AAA Financial Services' great rates and hassle-free service, you're covered for life. Call us today!

Exclusively for AAA members

- AAA *Platinum Plus*[sm] Visa® Credit Card

1-800-523-7666

- Market Rate Checking
- Money Market Accounts
- Auto Loans & Leases
- Home Equity Loans & Lines of Credit[1]
- Certificates of Deposit[2]
- Education Loans

1-800-680-AAA4

AAA Financial Services

Make The Most Of Your Membership.[SM]

24 Hours A Day. 7 Days A Week.

www.financial.aaa.com

For AAA members, it's easy to find no-fee American Express® Travelers Cheques. Just visit your nearest AAA office. American Express Travelers Cheques are the most recognized worldwide, and if lost or stolen can usually be replaced in a day. So whether your travels take you across the state or across the world, first come in for your American Express Travelers Cheques. It's one more way your AAA membership brings you added value and peace of mind. For no fee.

©1999 American Express. Payment methods vary from club to club.

You don't have to travel back in

time for old-fashioned hospitality.

Just across America.

Whether it's our free breakfast, clean, comfortable rooms, fair rates or our 100% Satisfaction Guarantee, there's nothing we like more than seeing a smile on your face. For reservations call 1-800-HAMPTON or visit us at www.hampton-inn.com.

Hampton Inn **Hampton Inn & Suites**

One of the few nice places still around.℠

New York

The Big Apple

Skyscrapers, theater, museums, shopping, bustling crowds—New York City

Take a Sip

New York state's wines compare with the world's finest

Niagara Falls

The power of Mother Nature is awesome

Historic Canals

When the Great Lakes met the Hudson River, commerce flowed

Explore the Outdoors

Raft, hike, boat, fish, bike, canoe, ski—you can do it all in New York

an
intriguing
collage

Take an escalator to an observation floor in Manhattan's towering Empire State Building, and you'll view a busy panorama of asphalt and skyscrapers.

As spectacular as that sight may be, it's a one-dimensional snapshot of the state of New York. The broader picture encompasses much more.

A rich maritime and farming heritage characterizes Long Island, a resort playground with pristine beaches, breathtaking mansions and quaint lighthouses.

The Catskills and the Adirondacks give you adventure—by water, by land and by air.

The past is the draw in the Hudson Valley, in which Franklin D. Roosevelt's ancestral home is counted among the many historic sites.

Albany, the state capital, is noted for its art and architecture, while vineyards are the trademark in the fertile Finger Lakes region.

You'll find romance at Niagara Falls and in the Thousand Islands, an area with scenic trails and warm beaches.

History and sports are the focus in the Leatherstocking region where the Erie Canal system and baseball and soccer legends are celebrated.

And varied cultures— American Indian and Amish—in Chautauqua-Allegheny grant you the opportunity to expand your horizons.

Its many images and varied attractions make New York an intriguing collage.

Brazilian. Chinese. German. Irish. Italian. Korean. Mexican. Polish. Russian. South African. Vietnamese.

These nationalities represent a mere handful of the full shelf of ethnic spices that add zest to the New York City melting pot. The city's cultural stew is an epicurean *piéce de résistance*.

Similarly, the tantalizing attractions of the state as a whole combine in a recipe equally appetizing.

Among the most savory ingredients is history, and you'll find it in several flavors.

One traces the turmoil and strife of the Revolutionary War. Nearly a third of the war's battles were fought on New York soil—at such places as Johnstown, Saratoga, Schuylerville and White Plains. Weapons, uniforms, paintings and documents relating to the struggle for independence fill a museum at Fort Ticonderoga.

The story of the underground railroad is another. Many slaves found freedom taking cover in the safe houses along the route. Among those preserved sites are the Harriet Tubman Home in Auburn; the H. Lee White Marine Museum in Oswego; and the John Brown Farm State Historic Site in Lake Placid. Displays in Fenton History Center in Jamestown provide a wealth of information about the abolitionist network.

Yet a third recounts America's love of sports. In addition to being the home of numerous professional teams, the Empire State boasts halls of fame for several sports, including boxing, horse racing and soccer. Most notable, though, is Cooperstown's National Baseball Hall of Fame and Museum, which pays homage to the national pastime.

Architectural Smorgasbord

Add to this historical stock samples of diverse styles of architecture.

Albany's Capitol, one of few such buildings without a dome, bears intricate carvings that give it a decidedly French feel. The Beaux-Arts style characterizes the Vanderbilt Mansion National Historic Site in Hyde Park. A Greek Revival flair marks the Rose Hill Mansion in Geneva.

Fold in a rich dollop of art. Renowned museums in Albany, Buffalo and New York show off the talents of such artists as Willem de Kooning, Pablo Picasso, Auguste Rodin and Andy Warhol. Exquisite

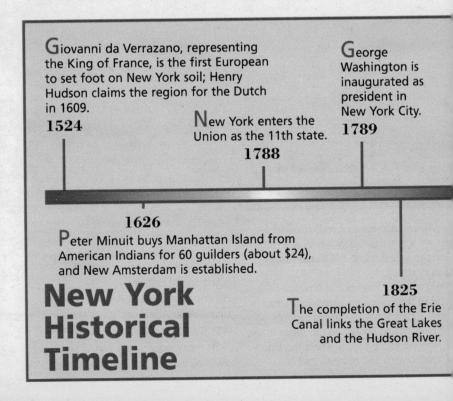

Giovanni da Verrazano, representing the King of France, is the first European to set foot on New York soil; Henry Hudson claims the region for the Dutch in 1609.
1524

New York enters the Union as the 11th state.
1788

George Washington is inaugurated as president in New York City.
1789

1626
Peter Minuit buys Manhattan Island from American Indians for 60 guilders (about $24), and New Amsterdam is established.

1825
The completion of the Erie Canal links the Great Lakes and the Hudson River.

New York Historical Timeline

glass is the centerpiece at Corning Glass Center.

The Statue of Liberty, equal parts architecture and art, rises up from Liberty Island as a 151-foot tall symbol of freedom on a 154-foot high pedestal.

Pour in plenty of water. Hugging varied borders are the Atlantic Ocean, Long Island Sound, lakes Champlain, Erie and Ontario, and the Delaware and St. Lawrence rivers. The aptly named Finger Lakes, 11 glacial lakes, gash vertical blue streaks in the landscape south of the stretch of I-90 linking Rochester and Syracuse.

Breathtaking waterfalls—including 215-foot Taughannock Falls in Ithaca, Rainbow Falls in Watkins Glen and the honeymooner's paradise of Niagara Falls—cascade and plummet all over the state.

The Canal Connection

Constructed to link major waterways and thereby open trade west of the Appalachians, the famed Cayuga-Seneca, Champlain, Erie and Oswego canals occupy their own niche in New York lore.

Sprinkle in a pinch of nature's other treasures. Brick walkways weave through the stalactites and stalagmites in Howe Caverns in Howes Cave. Huge outcroppings comprise the Panama Rocks in Panama. Follow along through the three interesting tunnels in Table Rock Complex in the Niagara Falls area, and you'll be rewarded with a spectacular vantage point for viewing Horseshoe Falls and the Niagara River.

Top it all off with a heaping spoonful of presidential homesteads. Millard Fillmore, Franklin D. Roosevelt, Theodore Roosevelt and Martin Van Buren all were New York natives.

Accompany each course with a glass of premium wine from one of six major viticultural regions: Cayuga Lake, the Finger Lakes, Hudson River, Lake Erie, the Long Island Hamptons and the Long Island North Fork. More than 100 vineyards produce upwards of 20 million gallons of such varieties as chardonnay, pinot noir and cabernet sauvignon each year.

Bon appetit!

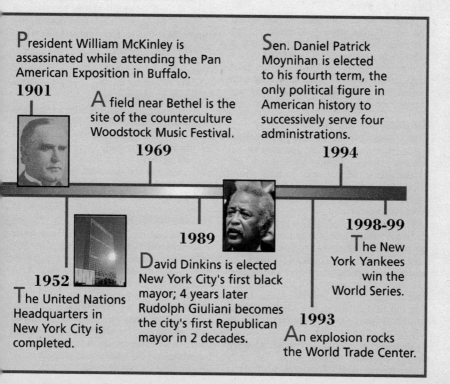

President William McKinley is assassinated while attending the Pan American Exposition in Buffalo.
1901

A field near Bethel is the site of the counterculture Woodstock Music Festival.
1969

Sen. Daniel Patrick Moynihan is elected to his fourth term, the only political figure in American history to successively serve four administrations.
1994

1952
The United Nations Headquarters in New York City is completed.

1989
David Dinkins is elected New York City's first black mayor; 4 years later Rudolph Giuliani becomes the city's first Republican mayor in 2 decades.

1993
An explosion rocks the World Trade Center.

1998-99
The New York Yankees win the World Series.

Recreation

Forests. Mountains. Valleys. Waterways. If you're looking for fun in the great outdoors, New York has it all.

From the heights of the rugged Adirondacks to the pine barrens of Long Island, New York entices explorers of all stripes with miles upon miles of **hiking** trails. Notable among them are the Appalachian, Erie Canal, Finger Lakes and Northville-Lake Placid trails; the Long Island Greenbelt; and the Long Path, which links New York City with the Adirondacks. In winter many of these routes are popular for cross-country skiing.

Get a different perspective while **spelunking** alongside the subterranean river in Howe Caverns, in Howes Cave.

Steady yourself on two wheels and go **bicycling** along the 35-mile Mohawk-Hudson Bikeway, near Albany; through the 32 miles of trails in Old Erie Canal State Park, east of Syracuse; and on the 60-mile Barge Canal Recreationway, which traverses Monroe and Orleans counties.

If **horseback riding** is your thing, visit Allegany State Park, Connetquot State Park Preserve or Rockefeller State Park Preserve. Nearly 100 miles of trails are divided between the three.

Looking to go **canoeing** or **kayaking?** The Adirondacks are a good place to start. The range boasts 2,800 lakes and ponds in addition to thousands of miles of rivers. Explore the scenic wilderness in the Saint Regis canoe area—57 lakes and ponds near Saranac Lake—or head for Old Forge and navigate the Adirondack Canoe Route.

Running on the River

If you're new to **white-water rafting,** try a run on the Delaware, Genesee or Sacandaga rivers. Thrills abound on the feistier Black, Moose and Salmon rivers. Combine spectacular scenery and turbulent waters and you get the Hudson River, a perennial favorite.

There are plenty of other ways to play in the water. More than 4,000 lakes—including two of the Great Lakes and the Finger Lakes—add up to scores of options for **boating, swimming** and **water skiing.** The 524 miles of waterways in the New York State Canal System link the Great Lakes with the Hudson River and other northeastern inland waters to form another prime locale for pleasure boating.

Shipwrecks off the coast of Oswego County in Lake Ontario make for great **scuba diving.** Also of interest to divers is

Lake George, where the well-preserved *Land Tortoise* sank; Lake Champlain, home of a legendary beast akin to the Loch Ness Monster; Long Island Sound; and the crystal-clear waters of the Thousand Islands-Seaway region.

Cast a line in one of New York's bodies of water, and you're in for a **fishing** adventure. Fresh waters yield bass, trout, perch, muskie, salmon and panfish. Bluefish, fluke, striper and weakfish swim in the surf. Long Island is noted for its cod, blackfish and flounder.

Three outstanding fishing streams—Beaver Kill, Neversink and Willowemoc—are within Catskill Forest Preserve in Catskill.

Playing on the Edge

For a rush of adrenaline, try **rock climbing** in the Adirondack, Catskill, Shawangunk or Taconic mountains; **parasailing** over Lake George; or **hang gliding** over the Rondout River near Ellenville. You'll also feel that excitement while **surfing** in the ocean off Long Island, **windsurfing** on the Finger Lakes or **snowmobiling** through Finger Lakes National Forest.

Exhilaration also is the name of the game at such **downhill skiing** hot spots as Belleayre Mountain, near Highmount; Big Tupper Ski Area in Big Tupper Lake; Gore Mountain in North Creek; Holiday Valley, near Ellicottville; Hunter Mountain in Hunter; Lake Placid/Whiteface in Wilmington; Ski Windham in Windham; and Titus Mountain in Malone.

A **camping** excursion is sure to free you from the rigors of everyday life. The state's more than 500 campgrounds are all over the place: in backwoods spots reached only by boat or foot, along the shores of lakes and rivers, on the beautiful Atlantic coast. For detailed camping information, *see the AAA Northeastern CampBook.*

Recreational Activities

Throughout the TourBook, you may notice a Recreational Activities heading with bulleted listings of recreation-oriented establishments listed underneath. Since normal AAA inspection criteria cannot be applied, these establishments are presented for information only. Age, height and weight restrictions may apply. Reservations are often recommended and sometimes required. Visitors should phone or write the attraction for additional information, and the address and phone number are provided for this purpose.

Fast Facts

POPULATION: 18,137,200.

AREA: 49,576 square miles; ranks 30th.

CAPITAL: Albany.

HIGHEST POINT: 5,344 ft., Mount Marcy.

LOWEST POINT: Sea level, Atlantic Ocean.

TIME ZONE: Eastern. DST.

MINIMUM AGE FOR DRIVERS: Minimum driving age is 16 with restrictions, 18 without. In New York City no one under 18 may drive.

MINIMUM AGE FOR GAMBLING: 18.

SEAT BELT/CHILD RESTRAINT LAWS: Seat belts required for driver, front-seat passengers and back-seat passengers ages 4-9. Child restraints required for under 4.

HELMETS FOR MOTORCYCLISTS: Required.

RADAR DETECTORS: Permitted.

FIREARMS LAWS: Vary by state and/or county. Contact the New York State Police Headquarters, Building 22, State Campus, Albany, NY 12226; phone (518) 457-6811.

HOLIDAYS: Jan. 1; Martin Luther King Jr.'s Birthday, Jan. (3rd Mon.); Lincoln's Birthday, Feb. (1st Mon.); Washington's Birthday, Feb. (3rd Mon.); Memorial Day, May (last Mon.); July 4; Labor Day, Sept. (1st Mon.); Columbus Day, Oct. (2nd Mon.); Election Day, Nov.; Veterans Day, Nov. 11; Thanksgiving; Dec. 25.

TAXES: New York's statewide sales tax is 4 percent, with local options for additional increments of up to 4.5 percent. Localities may impose taxes on lodgings, admissions or restaurant meals. New York City imposes a 13.25 percent plus $2 room tax as well as additional sums depending on the room rate.

STATE INFORMATION CENTERS: On/near the New York State Thruway (I-87) open daily year-round: Sloatsburg N.; Harriman exit 16; Catskill exit 21; New Baltimore N. and S.; Utica exit 31; Seneca W.; and Grand Island Blvd. exit 18A N. Centers open daily, May-Oct.: Newburgh exit 17; Plattekill N.; westbound Pattersonville, Warners, Schuyler and Clarence; Angola E. and W.; Westfield exit 60; Ripley exit 61; and Pembroke E. State Gateway Information Centers open daily year-round: Binghamton rest area (I-81) N.; Thousand Island International Bridge S. and Beekmantown rest area (Adirondack Northway) S.

FURTHER INFORMATION FOR VISITORS:

Department of Economic Development
Division of Tourism
One Commerce Plaza
Albany, NY 12245
(518) 474-4116
(800) 225-5697 (50 states and possessions)

New York Convention and Visitors Bureau
810 Seventh Ave.
New York, NY 10019
(212) 484-1200
(800) 692-8474

RECREATION INFORMATION:

New York State Office of Parks, Recreation and Historic Preservation
Agency Building #1
Empire State Plaza
Albany, NY 12238
(518) 474-0456

FISHING AND HUNTING REGULATIONS:

Division of Fish and Wildlife
State Environmental Conservation Department
50 Wolf Rd.
Albany, NY 12233
(518) 457-3521

NATIONAL FOREST INFORMATION:

Forest Supervisor
Finger Lakes National Forest
5218 State Route 414
Hector, NY 14841
(607) 546-4470
(877) 444-6777 (reservations)

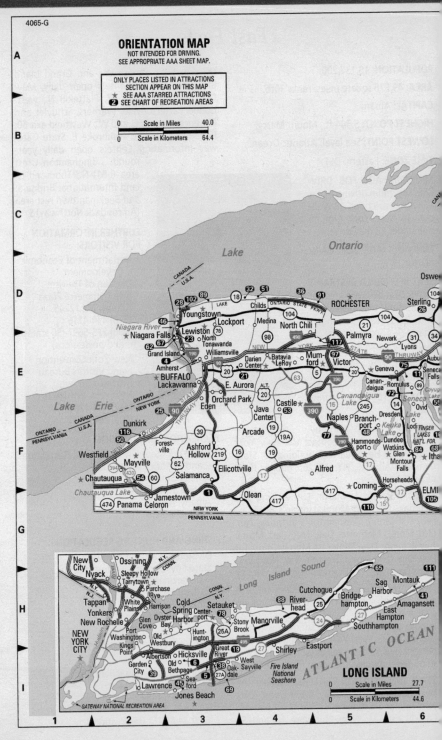

4065-G

ORIENTATION MAP
NOT INTENDED FOR DRIVING.
SEE APPROPRIATE AAA SHEET MAP.

ONLY PLACES LISTED IN ATTRACTIONS
SECTION APPEAR ON THIS MAP
★ SEE AAA STARRED ATTRACTIONS
2 SEE CHART OF RECREATION AREAS

Scale in Miles 40.0
Scale in Kilometers 64.4

Lake Ontario

CANADA U.S.A.

Oswego

Youngstown
Lewiston
★ Niagara Falls
Grand Island
Amherst
★ BUFFALO
Lackawanna

Lockport
North
Tonawanda
Williamsville

Childs
Medina
North Chili
ROCHESTER
Sterling

Palmyra
Newark
Lyons
Batavia
LeRoy
Mum-
ford
Victor
Geneva
Seneca
Falls
Romulus

Darien
Center

E. Aurora
Orchard Park
Eden
Java
Center
Arcade

Castile
Canan-
daigua
Canandaigua
Lake
Naples
Branch-
port
Dresden
Lodi
Ovid
Dundee
Hammonds-
port
Watkins
Glen
Montour
Falls

Lake Erie

ONTARIO
NEW YORK
CANADA
U.S.A.
ONTARIO
PENNSYLVANIA

Dunkirk
Forest-
ville
Westfield
Mayville
★ Chautauqua
Chautauqua Lake
Jamestown
Panama Celoron

Ashford
Hollow
Ellicottville
Salamanca

Alfred
Corning
Horseheads
ELMI

Olean

NEW YORK
PENNSYLVANIA

New
City
Nyack
Ossining
Sleepy Hollow
Tarrytown
Purchase
Rye
White
Plains
Harrison

N.Y.
CONN.

Long Island Sound

Sag
Harbor
Montauk
Cutchogue
Bridge-
hampton
Amagansett
East
Hampton
Southampton

Tappan
Yonkers
New Rochelle
Cold
Spring
Center-
port
Setauket
Riverhead
Glen
Cove
Oyster
Bay
Stony
Brook
Manorville
Port
Washington
Kings
Point
Old
Westbury
Hunt-
ington
NEW
YORK
CITY
Albertson
Old
Bethpage
Hicksville
Great
River
West
Sayville
Oak-
dale
Shirley
Eastport
Garden
City
Sea-
ford
Lawrence
Jones Beach
Fire Island
National
Seashore

ATLANTIC OCEAN

LONG ISLAND
Scale in Miles 27.7
Scale in Kilometers 44.6

GATEWAY NATIONAL RECREATION AREA

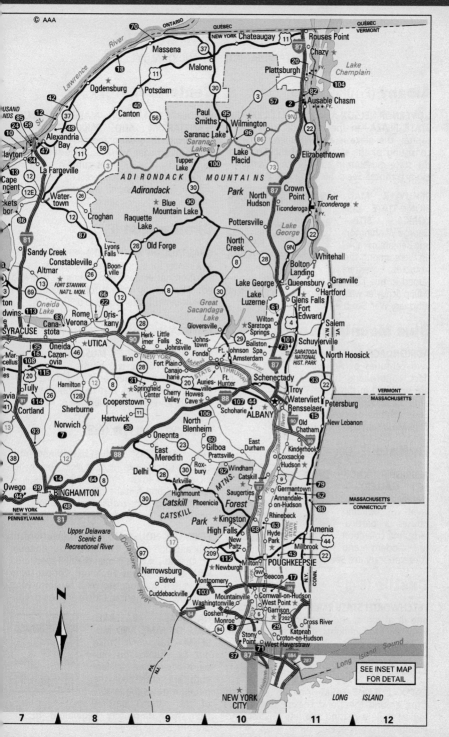

© AAA

ONTARIO
QUÉBEC
QUÉBEC VERMONT

Lawrence River

NEW YORK
70
Massena
Chateaugay
Rouses Point
11
87
Chazy

18
Malone
37
Plattsburgh
20
Lake Champlain

Ogdensburg
11
Potsdam
30
3
57
2
Ausable Chasm
104
82
FY.

42
Canton
40
95
Paul Smiths
9N

USAND NDS
85
59
37
56
Wilmington
22
FY.

24
10
49
Saranac Lake
96
86

Clayton
58
Saranac Lakes
Lake Placid
Elizabethtown

34
13
La Fargeville
11
3
Tupper Lake
100
73

Cape ncent
12
12E
ADIRONDACK   MOUNTAINS   Park
30
North Hudson
87
Crown Point
Fort Ticonderoga

ckets bor
86
Watertown
26
Adirondack
Blue Mountain Lake
90
Ticonderoga
FY.

81
Sandy Creek
12
Croghan
Raquette Lake
Pottersville
Lake George
22

69
Constableville
Altmar
87
Lyons Falls
28
Old Forge
North Creek
Whitehall

3
13
FORT STANWIX NAT'L. MON.
66
Boonville
8
28
9N
Bolton Landing
Granville

ton
dwins
113
Rome Verona
22
12
8
Lake George
Queensbury
Hartford

SYRACUSE
83
Cana-stota
Oris-kany
Great Sacandaga Lake
Lake Luzerne
61
Glens Falls

35
Oneida
UTICA
28
Herk-imer
Little Falls
St. Johnsville
Gloversville
Wilton
4
Fort Edward
Salem

16
Cazen-ovia
46
Ilion
Johns-town
29
Saratoga Springs
101
Schuylerville
N.Y.

108
115
90
Fort Plain
Fonda
Ft. Johnson
73
SARATOGA NATIONAL HIST. PARK
North Hoosick

20
Tully
Hamilton
12B
28
Canajo-harie
Amsterdam
Schenectady
33
22

81
114
Cortland
26
8
31
Springfield Center
20
Auries-ville
Ft. Hunter
88
107
44
Troy
Watervliet
Rensselaer
Petersburg
VERMONT
MASSACHUSETTS

13
93
Norwich
Sherburne
Cooperstown
Cherry Valley
Howes Cave
106
Schoharie
ALBANY
15
Old Chatham
New Lebanon

Hartwick
11
North Blenheim
East Durham
90
Kinderhook
90

38
12
Oneonta
23
60
Gilboa
Coxsackie
Hudson
79

Owego
99
BINGHAMTON
East Meredith
Prattsville
92
Windham
Catskill
Germantown
52
MASSACHUSETTS
CONNECTICUT

94
98
Delhi
28
Arkville
Rox-bury
Saugerties
Annandale-on-Hudson
80

NEW YORK
PENNSYLVANIA
81
Highmount
Catskill
Phoenicia
Forest
Kingston
Rhinebeck
63
Amenia

14
64
8
Catskill
Park
High Falls
58
Hyde Park
43
Millbrook
44

97
Narrowsburg
Eldred
17
New Paltz
112
Milton
POUGHKEEPSIE
22

103
Montgomery
209
Newburgh
9W
Beacon
17
N.Y. CONN.

Cuddebackville
Mountainville
Cornwall-on-Hudson
84

94
Washingtonville
West Point
202
Cross River

Goshen
Monroe
8
Garrison
29
Katonah

3
Stony Point
Croton-on-Hudson

37
87
71
West Haverstraw
684
287

PA
N.Y.
Long Island Sound

NEW YORK CITY
LONG   ISLAND

SEE INSET MAP FOR DETAIL

7   8   9   10   11   12

AAA Starred Attractions

EXCEPTIONAL INTEREST AND QUALITY

Albany (F-10)

GOVERNOR NELSON A. ROCKEFELLER EMPIRE STATE PLAZA—In the heart of New York's capital, the plaza is a government complex consisting of the state capitol building and the state museum in addition to a performing arts center. See p. 56.

SCHUYLER MANSION STATE HISTORIC SITE— George Washington and Benjamin Franklin were among the notables enter-

tained in this 1761 Georgian home; its owner Phillip Schuyler was a general during the Revolutionary War. See p. 174.

Blue Mountain Lake (C-9)

ADIRONDACK MUSEUM— Two centuries of Adirondack culture and history are explored in this museum's 22 indoor and outdoor exhibits overlooking Blue Mountain Lake. See p. 62.

Buffalo (E-3)

ALBRIGHT- KNOX ART GALLERY—A stately Greek Revival building houses a particularly fine collection of modern and contemporary art. See p. 69.

Castile (E-4)

LETCHWORTH STATE PARK—Three waterfalls, one lit at night, and scenic roads, trails and views are the highlights of this state park. See p. 74.

Catskill (F-10)

CATSKILL GAME FARM—Animals and birds from around the world coexist in this zoological park; a petting zoo lets children and young animals meet each other. See p. 74.

Centerport (H-3)

VANDERBILT MANSION, MARINE MUSEUM, PLANETARIUM AND PARK—William K. Vanderbilt II, great-grandson of Cornelius Vanderbilt, began work on his estate in the early 1900s; the 43 acres contain a marine museum, reflecting his interest in the sea and marine life, his home, a planetarium and landscaped grounds. See p. 75.

Chautauqua (F-2)

CHAUTAUQUA INSTITUTION—Begun in 1874 as a center for Sunday-school teachers, the institution has evolved into a summer arts and education center known for its lectures and entertainment offerings. See p. 75.

Chazy (A-11)

THE ALICE T. MINER MUSEUM—This gray stone Colonial Revival house museum contains glass, porcelain, prints, paintings, carpets, furniture and textiles, primarily from the 18th and 19th centuries. See p. 76.

Cooperstown (F-8)

THE FARMERS' MUSEUM—Nineteenth-century rural life in upstate New York is depicted here in a restored 1845 village, a farmstead and a stone dairy barn now used to house exhibits; craftspeople in period attire practice their trades. See p. 77.

FENIMORE HOUSE MUSEUM—Collections of folk and fine art are exhibited in this museum on Otsego Lake, as is memorabilia associated with author James Fenimore Cooper, who was raised in Cooperstown; a separate wing is devoted to American Indian art. See p. 78.

NATIONAL BASEBALL HALL OF FAME AND MUSEUM—You won't strike out by visiting this museum where baseball legends are enshrined; the museum traces the history of the nation's pastime

from its 19th-century beginnings to the present. See p. 78.

AAA Starred Attractions (continued)

Corning (G-5)

CORNING GLASS CEN-
TER—The artistry and his-
tory of glass, its uses and
its manufacturing process
are explained through
museum exhibits and
glassblowing demonstrations. See p. 78.

THE ROCKWELL
MANSION— West-
ern art is the focus
here, pardner, but
you also can see
glass designed by
the founder of
Steuben Glass Works and a collection of antique toys. See p. 79.

Darien Center (E-4)

DARIEN LAKE THEME PARK & CAMPING RE-
SORT—You will definitely be entertained at
this complex where roller coasters, water
parks, stage shows and thrill rides are all part
of the fun. See p. 80.

Fort Stanwix National Monument (D-8)

FORT STANWIX NATIONAL MONUMENT—
Built in 1758, the original fort protected the
Mohawk Valley during the French and Indian
and Revolutionary wars; its reconstruction
contains archeological exhibits and living history demonstrations. See p. 86.

Fort Ticonderoga (C-11)

FORT TICONDEROGA—The fort's strategic position on Lake Champlain led to its constant
changes in ownership—from the French to
the British to the Americans and back to the
British; now restored, it has a museum with
period artifacts. See p. 86.

Garrison (H-10)

BOSCOBEL—Saved from destruction in the
mid-1900s, this restored 1804 Federal-style
mansion is on a bluff overlooking the Hudson
River. See p. 138.

Geneva (E-6)

ROSE HILL MAN-
SION—The 1839
Greek Revival man-
sion overlooking
Seneca Lake has 21
rooms furnished in
period that can be
seen on guided tours. See p. 87.

Glens Falls (D-11)

THE HYDE COLLEC-
TION ART MU-
SEUM—An Italian
Renaissance- style
villa is the setting
for an extensive
collection of 15th- to 20th-century art which
includes works by European old masters and
American artists as well as European antiques. See p. 88.

Hammondsport (F-5)

PLEASANT VALLEY WINE CO.—The cellars
carved into the hillside and the wooden and
stone structures of this winery date to its
1860 founding, adding to its Old World feeling; the Great Western Winery Visitor Center
features tours, tastings and exhibits. See
p. 90.

Howes Cave (E-9)

HOWE CAVERNS—Tours of the prehistoric
cave proceed through chambers of stalagmites and stalactites and end with a quarter-
mile boat ride on underground Lake of
Venus. See p. 91.

Hudson (F-11)

AMERICAN MU-
SEUM OF FIRE-
FIGHTING— The
history of firefight-
ing in America is
examined from its
early 18th-century
origins to the present. See p. 91.

AAA Starred Attractions (continued)

Hyde Park (G-10)

FRANKLIN D. ROOSEVELT MUSEUM AND LIBRARY—Home of the first presidential library, the museum includes family possessions as well as photographs, speeches and gifts from heads of state; a section is devoted to FDR's wife Eleanor. See p. 92.

HOME OF FRANKLIN D. ROOSEVELT NATIONAL HISTORIC SITE—FDR's home has been maintained as it was when he died in 1945; the graves of the president and his wife are in a rose garden. See p. 93.

MILLS MANSION STATE HISTORIC SITE—A 65-room mansion, built in 1832 and enlarged in 1895, sits on a 900-acre site; elaborately decorated, the house has marble fireplaces, ornate furniture and artifacts from around the world. See p. 93.

VANDERBILT MANSION NATIONAL HISTORIC SITE—Frederic Vanderbilt's elegant mansion, built during the "Gilded Age" of the late 19th-century, contains original furnishings; the grounds afford scenic views of the Hudson River and the Catskill Mountains. See p. 93.

Ithaca (F-6)

TAUGHANNOCK FALLS STATE PARK—The waterfall for which the park is named cascades 215 feet between 400-foot-tall rocky cliffs; trails offer a choice of views from either above or below the falls. See p. 94.

Jones Beach (I-3)

JONES BEACH STATE PARK—The attraction here is swimming—at ocean-front beaches, a bay beach or in two pools; a 2-mile-long boardwalk follows part of the shoreline. See p. 95.

Kingston (G-10)

SENATE HOUSE STATE HISTORIC SITE—This stone house belonging to Abraham Van Gaasbeek was where the governmental system of New York state was adopted in 1777; a museum contains works by area artists. See p. 96.

Lewiston (E-3)

EARL W. BRYDGES ARTPARK—A hybrid, this 200-acre state park along the Niagara River gorge is both a performing arts complex and a recreational facility; visitors flock here for dance, opera and music concerts as well as for hiking and nature trails. See p. 151.

Massena (A-9)

MOSES-SAUNDERS POWER DAM—Part of Robert Moses State Park, the dam is jointly owned by the New York Power Authority and Ontario Hydro; a visitor center has maps, an audiovisual presentation and computerized exhibits. See p. 102.

Mayville (F-2)

CHAUTAUQUA BELLE—This replica of an old-fashioned steam-powered stern-wheeler transports guests on tours of Chautauqua Lake. See p. 103.

Mumford (E-5)

GENESEE COUNTRY VILLAGE AND MUSEUM— Craftspeople and guides in period costume portray life in a typical 19th-century country village; nature trails and a gallery of sporting and wildlife art complete the complex. See p. 104.

AAA Starred Attractions (continued)

Newburgh (H-10)

WASHINGTON'S HEADQUARTERS STATE HISTORIC SITE—The general had his headquarters in this house 1782-83 as he di-rected troops during the Revolutionary War; a museum contains exhibits about the Continental Army. See p. 105.

New York (I-10)

AMERICAN MUSEUM OF NATURAL HISTORY—A freestanding dinosaur greets visitors in the rotunda; his relatives and other fossil displays are the highlights of this natural history museum. See p. 118.

BRONX ZOO/WILDLIFE CONSERVATION PARK—The animals in this 265-acre park, a landmark since 1899, reside in natural habitats; its children's zoo was one of the first in the country. See p. 129.

BROOKLYN BOTANIC GARDEN—A 52-acre garden grows in Brooklyn; formal and informal gardens include a fragrance garden for the blind, a Japanese garden, a conservatory and a bonsai museum. See p. 130.

CENTRAL PARK—An oasis in the middle of bustling Manhattan, the park's 840 acres contain lakes, skating rinks, an Egyptian obelisk, a wildlife conservation center, gardens and a theater; see it all by buggy ride, horse-drawn hansom cab or a walking tour conducted by a park ranger. Seep. 119.

CHINATOWN—This little bit of China in New York City's Lower East Side is an exotic ethnic neighborhood of Asian restaurants, street vendors and shops stocked with everything Oriental. See p. 113.

THE CLOISTERS—A branch of the Metropolitan Museum of Art, The Cloisters is known for medieval art; five French cloisters, gardens, 15th-century tapestries and illuminated manuscripts carry out the theme. See p. 126.

EMPIRE STATE BUILDING—This 1931 Art Deco building has long symbolized New York City; its two observatories afford panoramic views, one from the 86th floor, the other from the 102nd. See p. 119.

FEDERAL HALL NATIONAL MEMORIAL—This historic site was where our fledgling nation protested "taxation without representation," where the first Congress met and where George Washington was inaugurated; a museum contains exhibits pertaining to these events. See p. 113.

LINCOLN CENTER FOR THE PERFORMING ARTS—This 14-acre complex encompasses the halls and theater where the New York Philharmonic, the Metropolitan Opera, the New York Ballet and the New York City Opera perform. See p. 122.

METROPOLITAN MUSEUM OF ART—One of the world's great museums, the Metropolitan's collections span 500 years of art history. See p. 124.

THE MUSEUM OF MODERN ART—More than 100,000 pieces of modern art, including paintings, sculptures, drawings, prints and photographs, comprise MoMA's comprehensive collection of 20th-century works. See p. 124.

NEW YORK BOTANICAL GARDEN—Stop and smell the roses here, and also visit a glass palacelike conservatory and specialty gardens featuring mountain flowers, plants native to the eastern United States, day lilies, perennials and herbs. See p. 129.

NEW YORK STOCK EXCHANGE—This cornerstone of the nation's financial community has a visitor's gallery above the trading floor; as tickets are limited, it's best to arrive early. See p. 115.

RIVERSIDE CHURCH—The 74 bronze bells of its carillon ring out three times each Sunday at this interdenominational church. See p. 128.

AAA Starred Attractions (continued)

ROCKEFELLER CENTER—A "city within a city," Rockefeller Center is well-known as the home of Radio City Music Hall and the "Today" show. See p. 124.

ST. PATRICK'S CATHEDRAL—Surrounded by skyscrapers, the twin spires of St. Patrick's have been a Manhattan landmark since 1879. See p. 125.

SOLOMON R. GUGGENHEIM MUSEUM—Frank Lloyd Wright's circular design for the museum is a perfect complement for the modern art collection hung along its sloping walkway. See p. 128.

STATUE OF LIBERTY NATIONAL MONUMENT AND ELLIS ISLAND—Lady Liberty, a gift from France in 1884, has welcomed millions of immigrants to America's shores; a symbol of the country's freedoms, the statue has an immigration museum in its base. See p. 117.

UNITED NATIONS HEADQUARTERS—Flags of all 185 member nations mark this complex of buildings where the countries of the world meet to discuss global problems. See p. 126.

WORLD TRADE CENTER—This 16-acre office complex is known for its two 110-story towers, among the world's tallest; an observation deck on the 107th floor offers a simulated helicopter tour of Manhattan, while the 110th floor has an open-air rooftop platform. See p. 118.

Niagara Falls, New York (D-3)

CAVE OF THE WINDS TRIP—Get a topsy-turvy view of the falls from this interesting cave. See p. 148.

GOAT ISLAND—Skirt the edges of both the Canadian and American falls from midstream. See p. 148.

MAID OF THE MIST—Rides on these boats take visitors directly in front of the powerful falls. See p. 148.

NIAGARA POWER PROJECT VISITOR CENTER—The story of the harnessing of the falls' power is electrifying. See p. 148.

Niagara Falls, Ontario (D-3)

GREAT GORGE ADVENTURE—You'll be swept away by this close-up view of the rolling Niagara River rapids. See p. 151.

LOUIS TUSSAUD'S WAXWORKS—Get up-close and personal with the famous and the infamous. See p. 152.

MAID OF THE MIST—You'll be grateful for the waterproof clothing provided on this boat trip in front of the falls. See p. 152.

MARINELAND—After you've seen the spectacular shows, make a spectacle of yourself on the roller coaster. See p. 152.

NIAGARA FALLS IMAX THEATRE AND DAREDEVIL ADVENTURE—Learn about the thrill seekers who challenged the falls. See p. 153.

NIAGARA SPANISH AERO CAR—Get a bird's-eye view of the Niagara Gorge and the whirlpool from this cable car. See p. 154.

QUEEN VICTORIA PARK—If the falls have dampened your spirit, let these fine floral displays perk you up. See p. 155.

RIPLEY'S BELIEVE IT OR NOT! MUSEUM—Explore the outer limits of reality at this museum of the unusual. See p. 155.

TABLE ROCK COMPLEX—Get a behind and bottom-up view of Horseshoe Falls from this unusual vantage point. See p. 156.

Ogdensburg (A-8)

FREDERIC REMINGTON ART MUSEUM—Paintings, bronzes, watercolors and drawings by the great artist of the American West are exhibited in this museum near his birthplace. See p. 158.

Oyster Bay (H-3)

PLANTING FIELDS ARBORETUM STATE HISTORIC PARK—In addition to 409 acres of greenhouses, gardens and natural habitats, the historic site's grounds are graced with a 65-room Tudor Revival mansion with 16th- and 17th-century furnishings. See p. 161.

AAA Starred Attractions (continued)

Rochester (D-5)

GEORGE EASTMAN HOUSE—The estate of the founder of Eastman Kodak Co., restored to its early 20th-century appearance, contains gardens and the International Museum of Photography and Film. See p. 167.

ROCHESTER MUSEUM & SCIENCE CENTER—This museum, which specializes in science, technology and the environment, also presents star and laser sound-and-light shows in its planetarium. See p. 167.

THE STRONG MUSEUM—The story of everyday life in America is related through collections of items dating from 1820—toys, housewares and home furnishings, clothing and advertising materials. See p. 168.

Saratoga Springs (D-10)

LAKE GEORGE OPERA FESTIVAL—Operas are presented by a regional repertory company late June to early August; the company strives to develop young American artists and provide a combination of new and traditional works. See p. 172.

Springfield Center (E-9)

GLIMMERGLASS OPERA—Opera is performed in repertory on the shores of Otsego Lake in a theater whose walls open to reveal views of the countryside. See p. 176.

Tarrytown (H-2)

SUNNYSIDE—Washington Irving's estate on the banks of the Hudson River is a charming stone mansion that still has the wisteria Irving planted at its entranceway; interpreters in period costume conduct tours. See p. 141.

Utica (E-8)

MUNSON-WILLIAMS-PROCTOR INSTITUTE—The institute, which consists of an art museum, a performing arts program and an art school, has fine collections of American and European art. See p. 181.

Watkins Glen (F-6)

WATKINS GLEN STATE PARK—Scenic gorges sculpted by nature, waterfalls, rocky cliffs and a bridge over the chasm are high points at this popular state park. See p. 183.

West Point (H-10)

UNITED STATES MILITARY ACADEMY—Many of America's military heroes were trained at this venerable academy overlooking the Hudson River. See p. 184.

WEST POINT MUSEUM—This museum at the military academy contains exhibits about military and academy history and extensive collections of artifacts from Revolutionary War days to the present. See p. 184.

Wilmington (B-10)

WHITEFACE MOUNTAIN VETERANS' MEMORIAL HIGHWAY—Constructed 1929-35 as a tribute to New Yorkers killed in World War I, the 6-mile road provides numerous scenic mountain and lake viewpoints. See p. 185.

Youngstown (D-3)

OLD FORT NIAGARA—On the grounds of Fort Niagara State Park, the fort was constructed by the French and has served under the flags of three nations. See p. 151.

RECREATION AREAS

	MAP LOCATION	CAMPING	PICNICKING	NATURE TRAILS	BOATING	BOAT RAMP	BOAT RENTAL	FISHING	SWIMMING	PETS ON LEASH	BICYCLE TRAILS	WINTER SPORTS	VISITOR CENTER	LODGE/CABINS	FOOD SERVICE
NATIONAL RECREATION AREA *(See place listing)*															
Gateway															
Breezy Point District (I-2)			•	•				•	•		•		•		•
Jamaica Bay District (I-2) Horse rental.			•	•	•	•		•			•	•	•		•
Staten Island Unit (I-2)			•	•	•	•		•	•	•	•		•		•
NATIONAL FOREST *(See place listing)*															
Finger Lakes (F-6) 16,000 acres in north-central New York on a ridge between Seneca and Cayuga lakes, via I-90, I-81 and SR 17.		•	•	•				•		•		•			
NATIONAL SEASHORE *(See place listing)*															
Fire Island (I-4) 6,220 acres on Fire Island, off the s. shore of Long Island.		•	•	•				•	•	•			•		
STATE															
Allan H. Treman Marine (F-6) 1 mi. n. of Ithaca on SR 89.	109		•		•	•		•	•						
Allegany (G-3) 60,398 acres (two areas) s. of Salamanca on State Park Rd. 1. Cross-country skiing; horse rental.	1	•	•	•	•	•	•	•	•	•	•	•	•	•	•
Ausable Point (B-11) 500 acres 12 mi. s. of Plattsburgh on US 9.	2	•	•		•			•	•						•
Bear Mountain (H-10) 5,067 acres 5 mi. s. of West Point off US 9W. Museum, nature trails, zoo. *(See West Point p. 184)*	3		•	•	•	•	•	•	•	•		•	•	•	•
Beaver Island (E-3) 1,081 acres 8 mi. w. of Buffalo on southern tip of Grand Island. Snowmobiling.	4		•	•				•	•	•	•	•			•
Belmont Lake (I-3) 459 acres 4 mi. n. of Babylon off Southern State Pkwy. exit 38. Bridle paths.	5		•	•	•		•	•		•		•			•
Bethpage (I-3) 1,475 acres 1 mi. n. of Farmingdale. Cross-country skiing, golf, tennis, tobogganing; bridle paths.	6		•	•						•	•	•			
Bowman Lake (F-8) 653 acres 8 mi. n.w. of Oxford off SR 220. Nature trails.	7	•	•	•	•		•	•	•	•		•			•
Burnham Point (B-7) 12 acres 3 mi. e. of Cape Vincent on SR 12E.	8	•	•		•	•		•		•					
Buttermilk Falls (F-6) 751 acres s. of Ithaca on SR 13. Cross-country skiing.	9	•	•	•				•	•	•		•		•	•
Canoe-Picnic Point (B-7) 70 acres on southern tip of Grindstone Island; access is by boat only.	10	•	•		•			•		•					
Cayuga Lake (E-6) 141 acres 3 mi. e. of Seneca Falls on SR 89. Sledding; recreation building.	11	•	•		•	•		•	•	•		•			•
Cedar Island (B-7) 10 acres on Cedar Island w. of Chippewa Bay; access is by boat only.	12	•	•		•			•		•					
Cedar Point (B-7) 48 acres 6 mi. w. of Clayton on SR 12E.	13	•	•		•	•	•	•	•	•					•
Chenango Valley (C-7) 1,071 acres 13 mi. n.e. of Binghamton on SR 369. Nature trails.	14	•	•	•	•		•	•	•	•		•	•	•	•
Cherry Plain (F-11) 175 acres 2 mi. n. of Stephentown on Miller Rd.	15		•	•	•	•	•	•	•	•					
Chittenango Falls (E-7) 192 acres 4 mi. n. of Cazenovia on SR 13.	16	•	•	•				•		•					
Clarence Fahnestock Memorial (H-11) 6,800 acres 11 mi. w. of Carmel on SR 301. Cross-country skiing.	17	•	•	•	•	•	•	•	•	•		•	•		•
Clark Reservation (E-7) 310 acres 3 mi. s.e. of Syracuse on SR 173. Playground.	108		•	•				•		•					
Coles Creek (A-8) 1,800 acres 5 mi. e. of Waddington on SR 37.	18	•	•		•	•		•	•	•					•
Connetquot Preserve (I-3) 3,473 acres near Oakdale/ Bohemia on SR 27. Historic. Cross-country skiing; bridle paths.	19			•				•				•			
Cumberland Bay (A-11) 350 acres 1 mi. n. of Plattsburgh off US 9.	20	•	•					•	•	•					•
Darien Lake (E-4) 1,845 acres 2 mi. w. of Darien Center on US 20. Cross-country skiing, snowmobiling.	21	•	•	•	•	•		•	•			•			

RECREATION AREAS

Recreation Area	MAP LOCATION	CAMPING	PICNICKING	NATURE TRAILS	BOATING	BOAT RAMP	BOAT RENTAL	FISHING	SWIMMING	PETS ON LEASH	BICYCLE TRAILS	WINTER SPORTS	VISITOR CENTER	LODGE/CABINS	FOOD SERVICE
Delta Lake (D-8) 400 acres 6 mi. n.e. of Rome on SR 46. Snowmobiling.	22	•	•	•	•	•	•	•	•	•	•	•			•
Devil's Hole (E-3) 42 acres 4.5 mi. n. of Niagara Falls. Scenic. Nature trails.	23		•	•				•		•					
DeWolf Point (B-7) 13 acres on Wellesley Island in the St. Lawrence River.	24	•			•	•		•		•			•		
Evangola (F-2) 733 acres 5 mi. s.w. of Angola on SR 5.	25	•	•	•				•	•			•			•
Fair Haven Beach (D-6) 865 acres 1 mi. n. of Fair Haven off SR 104A. Cross-country skiing, snowmobiling; nature trails.	26	•	•	•	•	•	•	•	•	•		•			•
Fillmore Glen (F-7) 939 acres 1 mi. s. of Moravia on SR 38.	27	•	•	•				•	•	•		•			
Fort Niagara (D-3) 504 acres at the mouth of the Niagara River off SR 18F. Snowmobiling, tobogganing. *(See Youngstown p. 151)*	28		•	•	•	•	•	•		•		•			•
Four Mile Creek (D-3) 248 acres 4 mi. e. of Youngstown on SR 18.	102	•	•					•		•					
Franklin Delano Roosevelt (H-10) 952 acres w. of Yorktown Heights off the Taconic State Pkwy. Snowmobiling.	29		•	•	•		•	•	•	•		•			•
Gilbert Lake (F-8) 1,569 acres 12 mi. n.w. of Oneonta off SR 205. Cross-country skiing.	30	•	•	•	•	•	•	•	•	•		•		•	•
Glimmerglass (E-9) 593 acres 4 mi. s. of East Springfield. Snowmobiling.	31	•	•	•	•	•		•	•	•		•			•
Golden Hill (D-4) 510 acres 5 mi. n.e. of Barker off SR 148. Snowmobiling.	32	•		•	•	•		•		•		•			
Grafton Lakes (E-11) 2,357 acres .5 mi. s. of Grafton off SR 2. Cross-country skiing; nature trails.	33		•	•	•	•	•	•	•	•		•			•
Grass Point (B-7) 66 acres 5 mi. s. of Alexandria Bay off SR 12.	34	•	•		•	•		•	•	•					
Green Lakes (E-7) 1,700 acres 4 mi. n.e. of Fayetteville on SR 290. Cross-country skiing.	35	•	•	•	•		•	•	•	•		•	•		•
Hamlin Beach (D-4) 1,243 acres 5 mi. n. of Hamlin on Lake Ontario. Cross-country skiing; nature trails.	36	•	•	•				•	•	•		•			•
Harriman (I-10) 46,613 acres 5 mi. w. of Stony Point on SR 210. Cross-country skiing; nature trails.	37	•	•	•	•	•	•	•	•			•			•
Heckscher (I-3) 1,657 acres 1 mi. s. of East Islip off Southern State Pkwy. Cross-country skiing; bridle paths.	38	•	•	•	•	•		•	•	•		•	•		•
Hempstead Lake (I-2) 775 acres 2 mi. s. of Hempstead. Tennis; bridle paths, nature trails.	39		•	•				•		•		•			•
Higley Flow (B-9) 1,200 acres 2 mi. w. of South Colton off SR 56. Cross-country skiing; nature trails.	40	•	•	•	•	•		•	•	•		•			•
Hither Hill (H-6) 1,755 acres 8 mi. w. of Montauk on SR 27.	41	•	•	•				•	•	•					•
Jacques Cartier (B-7) 461 acres 2 mi. w. of Morristown off SR 12. Cross-country skiing.	42	•	•		•	•		•	•	•		•			•
James Baird (G-11) 590 acres 11 mi. e. of Poughkeepsie on Taconic State Pkwy. Cross-country skiing, golf.	43		•	•					•	•		•			•
John Boyd Thacher (E-10) 2,000 acres 4 mi. n. of New Salem on SR 157. Nature trails.	44		•	•					•	•	•		•		
Jones Beach (I-3) 2,413 acres on the ocean shore of Long Island off Meadowbrook or Wantagh Pkwy. Golf. *(See Jones Beach p. 95)*	45		•		•			•	•	•	•				•
Joseph Davis (D-3) 388 acres 2.5 mi. s. of Youngstown off Robert Moses Pkwy.	46		•	•				•	•	•		•			
Keewaydin (B-7) 180 acres 1 mi. w. of Alexandria Bay on SR 12.	47	•	•		•	•	•	•	•	•			•		
Keuka Lake (F-5) 621 acres 6 mi. s.w. of Penn Yan off SR 54A. Snowmobiling.	48	•	•	•	•	•		•	•	•		•			•
Kring Point (B-8) 51 acres 10 mi. n.e. of Alexandria Bay.	49	•	•		•	•		•	•	•				•	
Lake Erie (F-2) 355 acres 2 mi. n. of Brocton on SR 380. Snowmobiling, tobogganing.	50	•	•	•				•	•	•		•		•	

RECREATION AREAS

Recreation Area	Map Location	Camping	Picnicking	Nature Trails	Boating	Boat Ramp	Boat Rental	Fishing	Swimming	Pets on Leash	Bicycle Trails	Winter Sports	Visitor Center	Lodge/Cabins	Food Service
Lakeside Beach (D-4) 734 acres 1.5 mi. e. of Kuckville on SR 18. Cross-country skiing.	51	•	•					•		•	•	•			•
Lake Taghkanic (G-11) 1,568 acres 12 mi. s.e. of Hudson on SR 82. Cross-country skiing, snowmobiling.	52	•	•	•	•	•	•	•	•	•			•	•	•
Letchworth (F-4) 14,336 acres 2 mi. n. on SR 19A to Denton's Corners, then 2 mi. e. Scenic. Cross-country skiing; nature trails. *(See Castile p. 74)*	53	•	•	•				•	•	•	•	•	•		•
Long Point (E-6) 108 acres 4 mi. s. of Aurora off SR 90 to Lake Rd.	55		•		•	•		•	•						
Long Point (C-7) 23 acres 11 mi. s.w. of Three Mile Bay off SR 12E.	56	•	•			•		•							
Long Point on Lake Chautauqua (F-2) 360 acres 1 mi. s. of Maple Springs off SR 17. Snowmobiling.	54		•		•	•	•	•	•	•		•			
Macomb Reservation (B-10) 600 acres 3 mi. w. of Schuyler Falls off SR 22B. Cross-country skiing.	57	•	•	•				•	•	•		•			
Margaret Lewis Norrie (G-10) 329 acres 3 mi. n. of Hyde Park on US 9.	58		•										•	•	
Mary Island (B-7) 13 acres at n.e. end of Wellesley Island; access is by boat only.	59	•	•		•			•							
Max V. Shaul (F-9) 15 acres 5 mi. s. of Middleburgh on SR 30.	106	•	•					•	•	•					
Mine Kill (F-10) 15 mi. s. of Middleburgh via SR 30.	60		•	•	•	•		•	•	•			•		
Minnewaska State Park (G-10) 10 mi. w. of New Paltz via US 44/SR 55. Cross-country skiing.	112		•	•			•	•	•			•			
Montauk Point (H-6) 724 acres 4 mi. e. of Montauk on SR 27. Nature Trails.	111		•	•				•							
Moreau Lake (D-10) 645 acres 4 mi. s. of Glens Falls off US 9. Cross-country skiing; nature trails.	61	•	•	•	•			•	•	•		•			•
Newton Battlefield Reservation (G-6) 330 acres 5 mi. e. of Elmira via SR 7.	105	•	•									•	•		
Niagara Reservation (E-2) 433 acres at foot of Falls St. in Niagara Falls. Scenic. Nature trails, recreation programs. *(See Niagara Falls p. 148)*	62		•					•		•	•		•		•
Ogden and Ruth Livingston Mills Memorial (G-10) 575 acres 5 mi. n. on US 9 to Old Post Rd. Cross-country skiing, golf.	63		•					•				•			
Oquaga Creek (F-8) 1,482 acres 9 mi. s. of Sidney off SR 206.	64	•	•	•	•			•	•	•		•			•
Orient Beach (H-5) 357 acres 3.5 mi. e. of Orient off SR 25.	65		•	•				•							•
Pinnacle (G-5) 2 mi. s. of Addison off Ackerson Rd. Golf.	110		•									•			
Pixley Falls (D-8) 375 acres 6 mi. s. of Boonville off SR 46.	66		•					•		•					
Point Au Roche (A-11) 850 acres 4 mi. n. of Plattsburgh e. of SR 9. Cross-country skiing; nature center.	104		•	•	•	•		•	•	•		•	•		
Reservoir (E-3) 132 acres 2 mi. n. of Niagara Falls at jct. SRs 265 and 31.	67		•	•				•		•	•				
Robert H. Treman (F-6) 1,025 acres 5 mi. s.w. of Ithaca off SR 327.	68	•	•	•				•	•	•		•		•	•
Robert Moses (I-3) 1,000 acres on the w. end of Fire Island on the Atlantic Ocean, accessible via the Robert Moses Causeway from Captree State Park. *(See Fire Island National Seashore p. 85)*	69		•	•				•	•						
Robert Moses (A-8) 4,122 acres 2 mi. n.e. of SR 37 on Barnhart Island. Scenic. Downhill skiing; nature trails. *(See Massena p. 102)*	70	•	•	•	•	•		•	•	•		•	•		•
Rockland Lake (I-10) 1,079 acres 3 mi. n. of Nyack on US 9W. Cross-country skiing; nature trails.	71		•	•	•		•	•	•	•		•			•
Sampson (E-6) 1,853 acres 5 mi. n. of Ovid on SR 96A. Recreation building.	72	•	•	•	•	•		•	•	•		•	•		•
Saratoga Spa (E-11) 2,002 acres n. of I-87 exit 13N in Saratoga Springs. Cross-country skiing, snowmobiling. *(See Saratoga Springs p. 172)*	73		•					•	•	•	•	•	•	•	•

RECREATION AREAS

	MAP LOCATION	CAMPING	PICNICKING	NATURE TRAILS	BOATING	BOAT RAMP	BOAT RENTAL	FISHING	SWIMMING	PETS ON LEASH	BICYCLE TRAILS	WINTER SPORTS	VISITOR CENTER	LODGE/CABINS	FOOD SERVICE
Selkirk Shores (D-7) 980 acres 5 mi. w. of Pulaski on SR 3. Snowmobiling.	74	•	•	•	•	•		•	•	•	•	•		•	•
Seneca Lake (E-6) 141 acres 1 mi. e. of Geneva off US 20.	75		•		•	•	•	•	•	•					
Southwick Beach (C-7) 313 acres 32 mi. s.w. of Watertown off SR 3. Nature trails.	76	•	•	•				•	•	•		•			•
Stony Brook (F-5) 577 acres 3 mi. s. of Dansville on SR 36. Snowmobiling.	77	•	•	•				•	•	•		•			•
Sunken Meadow/Governor Alfred E. Smith (H-3) 1,266 acres 1 mi. n. of Kings Park. Cross-country skiing, golf, sledding; bridle paths.	78		•	•				•	•		•	•	•		•
Taconic-Copake Falls (F-11) 4,647 acres 1 mi. e. of Copake Falls on SR 344. Nature trail.	79	•	•	•				•	•			•		•	
Taconic-Rudd Pond (G-11) 210 acres 3 mi. n. of Millerton.	80	•	•	•	•	•	•	•	•			•			•
Taughannock Falls (F-6) 783 acres 8 mi. n. of Ithaca on SR 89. *(See Ithaca p. 94)*	81	•	•	•	•	•		•	•	•		•		•	•
Thompson's Lake (E-10) 50 acres 3 mi. s.w. of East Berne on SR 157A.	107	•	•					•	•	•					
Valcour Landing (B-11) 4 mi. s. of Plattsburgh off US 9.	82	•	•		•			•							
Verona Beach (D-8) 1,735 acres 1 mi. s. of Sylvan Beach off SR 13. Cross-country skiing, snowmobiling.	83	•	•	•	•			•	•	•		•			•
Watkins Glen (F-6) 1,000 acres adjoining Watkins Glen at the s. end of Seneca Lake. Recreation building. *(See Watkins Glen p. 183)*	84	•	•	•				•	•	•		•		•	•
Wellesley Island (B-7) 2,636 acres 2 mi. n. of Alexandria Bay via the Thousand Islands Bridge.	85	•	•	•	•	•	•	•	•	•		•	•	•	•
Westcott Beach (C-7) 319 acres 4 mi. s.w. of Sackets Harbor off SR 3.	86	•	•					•	•	•		•			•
Whetstone Gulf (C-8) 1,902 acres 3 mi. s. of Martinsburg off SR 26. Nature trails.	87	•	•	•				•	•			•			•
Wildwood (H-4) 769 acres 3 mi. e. of Wading River off SR 25A. Cross-country skiing.	88	•	•					•	•	•		•			•
Wilson-Tuscarora (D-3) 390 acres 1 mi. w. of Wilson on SR 18.	89		•	•				•	•						
OTHER															
Adirondack Park (C-9) 6,000,000 acres in upstate New York. Horse rental. *(See place listing p. 54)*	90	•	•	•	•	•	•	•	•		•	•	•	•	•
Braddock Bay (D-5) 2,295 acres 10 mi. w. of Rochester on Lake Ontario. Nature trails.	91		•	•				•			•	•			
Catskill Forest Preserve (F-10) 287,989 acres in the Catskill Mountains. *(See Catskill p. 74)*	92	•		•	•	•		•	•				•		
Dorchester (F-7) 1,242 acres 2 mi. n. of Whitney Point on SR 26.	93	•	•		•	•	•	•	•	•					
Genesee Vally Park (D-5) 2.5 mi. s.w. of Rochester on Elmwood Ave. Golf (18-hole), ice skating, tennis.	117		•	•				•							
Greenwood Park (G-7) 440 acres 13 mi. n. of Endicott on SR 26.	94	•	•		•			•	•	•		•			
Highland Forest (E-7) 2,700 acres 4 mi. e. of Fabius on SR 80.	114		•	•				•			•	•	•	•	
Jamesville Beach Park (E-7) 250 acres off SR 173 on Apulia Rd. in Jamesville.	115		•	•				•	•	•					•
Lake Colby (B-10) 1 mi. n. of Saranac Lake Village on SR 86.	95		•		•	•	•	•	•				•		
Lake Flower (B-10) in Saranac Lake Village on SR 86. Canoeing, tennis.	96		•		•	•		•	•					•	•
Mendon Ponds (E-5) 2,462 acres 12 mi. s.e. of Rochester on SR 65. Nature trails.	97		•	•	•			•	•	•		•	•	•	
Nathaniel Cole (G-8) 370 acres 5 mi. e. of Kirkwood on Colesville Rd.	98	•	•				•	•	•	•					
Oneida Shores Park (D-7) 390 acres on Bartell Rd. off I-81 exit 31 in Brewerton.	113	•	•		•	•		•	•	•		•			
Otsiningo (G-7) 84 acres 1 mi. n. of Binghamton on US 11.	99		•	•				•		•	•	•			

RECREATION AREAS

	MAP LOCATION	CAMPING	PICNICKING	NATURE TRAILS	BOATING	BOAT RAMP	BOAT RENTAL	FISHING	SWIMMING	PETS ON LEASH	BICYCLE TRAILS	WINTER SPORTS	VISITOR CENTER	LODGE/CABINS	FOOD SERVICE
Point Gratiot (F-2) 75 acres on Lake Shore Dr. W. in Dunkirk.	116	•						•	•	•	•				
Saranac Lakes (B-10) Three lakes.	100														
Lower Saranac Lake .5 mi. w. of Saranac Lake off SR 3W. Horse rental.		•	•	•	•	•	•	•	•	•			•	•	
Middle Saranac Lake 3 mi. w. of Saranac Lake off SR 3W.		•	•	•	•			•	•				•		
Upper Saranac Lake 11 mi. w. of Saranac Lake off SR 3W. Horse rental.		•	•	•	•	•	•	•	•	•			•	•	
Saratoga Lake (E-11) 3 mi. e. of Saratoga Springs via SR 9P.	101	•	•		•	•	•	•	•				•	•	•
Thomas Bull Memorial Park (H-9) 652 acres s.w. of Montgomery on SR 416. Golf, tennis.	103		•		•		•	•				•	•	•	•

New York Temperature Averages
Maximum/Minimum
From the records of the National Weather Service

	JAN	FEB	MAR	APR	MAY	JUN	JUL	AUG	SEP	OCT	NOV	DEC
Albany	31 / 14	33 / 15	42 / 24	57 / 36	70 / 46	79 / 56	84 / 61	81 / 59	73 / 50	62 / 40	48 / 31	35 / 19
Binghamton	30 / 15	31 / 15	39 / 23	53 / 34	65 / 45	74 / 55	79 / 60	77 / 58	70 / 50	59 / 40	45 / 30	33 / 19
Buffalo	30 / 17	30 / 16	38 / 23	52 / 34	65 / 44	75 / 55	80 / 59	79 / 58	72 / 51	60 / 44	46 / 32	33 / 21
New York	40 / 28	40 / 27	48 / 34	59 / 43	71 / 53	80 / 63	85 / 69	83 / 68	76 / 61	66 / 51	54 / 41	42 / 30
Rochester	33 / 18	33 / 17	40 / 24	55 / 36	67 / 46	78 / 56	83 / 61	80 / 59	73 / 52	62 / 42	48 / 33	36 / 22
Syracuse	32 / 17	32 / 17	40 / 25	55 / 37	68 / 47	78 / 57	82 / 62	81 / 60	72 / 52	61 / 42	47 / 33	35 / 21

Exploring New York

For descriptions of places in bold type, see individual listings.

Adirondack Mountains

Stretching over 6 million acres and consisting of 46 peaks more than 4,000 feet tall, the Adirondack Mountains encompass thousands of miles of rivers and streams and more than 2,000 lakes and ponds. Low winter temperatures and heavy snowfall create excellent conditions for winter sports.

Lakes Champlain and George form the region's eastern border, while the Mohawk and St. Lawrence river valleys define its southern and northern limits.

Providing access to the region's mountainous interior are SRs 9N/86 and 73 from I-87; and SRs 30 and 12/28 from I-90. A popular spot for hot-air balloonists between the Hudson River and Lake George, **Glens Falls** features the Hyde Collection of fine arts in a Florentine-style mansion. Cruise boats depart from the village of **Lake George** to explore the 365 islands of 32-mile-long Lake George.

The village also serves as a base for exploring lakeshore recreational facilities and historical sites. Scenic Lakeshore Drive links the village to **Fort Ticonderoga**, which controlled the narrow isthmus between lakes Champlain and George during Colonial times.

Extending southward 120 miles from Canada, Lake Champlain varies in width from one-quarter of a mile to 12 miles. From **Plattsburgh,** Port Kent and Essex, ferries reach Vermont.

Escape to the Empire State

Off I-87, **Ausable Chasm** has a series of waterfalls and rapids. Plattsburgh, near the Canadian border, played a strategic role in the the War of 1812.

SRs 9N/86 and 73 wind through about 50 miles of small farms, resort communities and rugged mountains before joining near **Lake Placid.** East of town is **Wilmington,** where 4,867-foot Whiteface Mountain ranks as the highest skiing peak in the East. West of Lake Placid is the town of **Saranac Lake,** where author Robert Louis Stevenson sought relief from tuberculosis and wrote extensively.

Blue Mountain Lake, at the junction of SRs 30 and 28, features the Adirondack Museum, which provides a thorough background on the region; summer concerts take place at the Adirondack Lakes Center for the Arts. Along Raquette Lake near the town of **Tupper Lake** lie the extravagant "Great Camps" of the Victorian-era industrialists.

Catskill Mountains

American Indians called this heavily forested section of the Appalachian escarpment *Onteora,* or "land in the sky." With its trout-filled streams and established resorts, the Catskill region is popular among artists and entertainers.

Four routes reach the Catskills from the Hudson River Valley. From the town of **Catskill,** scenic SR 23 and SR 23A climb the steep 1,000-foot wall of the Catskills' eastern edge. SR 23 reaches the ski resort of **Windham** and continues on to **Oneonta.**

Before joining SR 23 at **Prattsville,** SR 23A winds upward through scenic Kaaterskill Clove to the mountain ski resort of Hunter. From **Kingston,** SR 28 passes Ashokan Reservoir and heads into the heart of the 278,000-acre Catskill Forest Preserve. From there, SR 28 crosses one of the least developed sections of the Catskills.

SR 17 between Harriman State Park/I-87 and **Binghamton** allows access to resort towns. Monticello serves as a base for exploring the headwaters of the Delaware River.

Winter recreational opportunities in the Catskills include hiking and snowshoeing. For ski enthusiasts, the Catskills offer snowmaking capacity for more than 1,100 acres, a combined vertical drop in excess of 8,890 feet and more than 200 trails. For additional information phone the Ski the Catskills association at (800) 882-2287. Cross-country skiing is available in state parks, the Catskill Forest Preserve and at area ski centers.

Mohawk Valley

The Mohawk Valley Heritage Corridor is a mosaic of picturesque landscapes and legendary places where great events shaped the history of America. Homeland to the Iroquois Confederacy, the region stretches 130 miles from the Hudson River to Oneida Lake, and includes Albany, Herkimer, Fulton, Montgomery, Oneida, Saratoga, Schenectady and Schoharie counties as well as the Oneida Indian Nation.

Heroic battles fought and won in the area became the turning point in the Revolutionary War. Once one of the busiest thoroughfares from the Atlantic seaboard, waves of settlers traversed the area heading westward through the Adirondack and Appalachian mountains. Many settled along the Erie Canal, creating a vibrant 19th century center of industrial innovation and commerce.

The primary east-west route is the I-90/NYS Thruway toll road from **Albany** to **Utica.** Albany was the site of the first general congress of all the Colonies in 1754. Northwest of Albany, Schenectady displays its Dutch heritage in the restored Stockade District. With the opening of the Erie Canal in 1825, **Amsterdam,** just west of **Schenectady,** became an important industrial town.

Nearby **Johnstown** remains a glove-making center and contains the site of one of the last battles of the Revolution. Utica, 60 miles west, developed with the canal. **Rome,** a portage station that connected the Hudson River to the Great Lakes before the Erie Canal, grew up around the site of **Fort Stanwix,** which played an important role in the Revolutionary War.

Central

Pivotal in the growth of water-powered industry and the opening of the West via the Erie Canal, central New York consists of rolling hills, dense forests and ample rivers. The region is demarcated by the Hudson River to the east; the Adirondacks, Mohawk River and Oneida Lake to the north; the Finger Lakes to the west; and the Catskills to the south.

James Fenimore Cooper's novels chronicled the area's pioneer days and gave the region its nickname, Leatherstocking Country. As the Erie Canal system became obsolete, many of the towns declined; except for scattered dairy farms, much of the countryside has reverted to its natural state.

From Schenectady, I-88 heads southwest across rolling farmland to Binghamton. Two scenic routes offer access to the southern portion of the region: SR 12 runs from Binghamton to Utica, and SR 28 runs from Oneonta to **Cooperstown.**

Beginning with the collection of salt from Onondaga Lake, **Syracuse** blossomed into a leading industrial and university city. Chittanango Falls State Park to the southeast contains one of the state's most beautiful waterfalls.

Binghamton developed after the opening of the Chenango Canal, which created a direct route between Pennsylvania coal fields and the Erie Canal. At the turn of the 20th century Eastern European immigrants sought work in shoe factories, leaving their mark in golden, onion-domed churches.

From Oneonta, home of the National Soccer Hall of Fame, SR 28 heads to Cooperstown, the home of the National Baseball Hall of Fame and the setting for James Fenimore Cooper's novels. Near the town of **Howes Cave** are caverns that contain a river, a lake and the floor of an ancient ocean.

Finger Lakes

Glaciers carved 11 deep, narrow finger-shaped lakes and the distinctive drumlin ridges and left a landscape bearing names reminiscent of the Iroquois Indian civilization. Artistic retreats, wineries and parkland are a few of the region's attractions. The **Finger Lakes** lie south of I-90 between Syracuse and **Rochester,** northeast of SR 17/I-390 between Binghamton and Rochester, and west of I-81 between Syracuse and Binghamton.

The following routes allow access to the shorelines of the principal lakes: SR 13 between

Cortland, Ithaca and **Elmira;** scenic SR 89 along Cayuga Lake between Ithaca and the Montezuma National Wildlife Refuge; and SR 14 along Seneca Lake from **Geneva** via **Watkins Glen** to Elmira. The region's most popular wineries line SRs 89, 14 and 54 at Keuka Lake.

At the northern end of Owasco Lake, **Auburn** is an agricultural center with fine Victorian houses. **Seneca Falls,** at the head of Cayuga Lake, was the birthplace of the women's rights movement. At the southern end of the lake, Ithaca boasts Cornell University. Nearby Taughannock Falls plunges 215 feet.

In Geneva, at the northern tip of Seneca Lake, are the Greek Revival-style Rose Hill estate and Richardsonian-style Belhurst Castle. Watkins Glen, at the southern end of the lake, is known for auto racing and a state park where a stream has cut unusual patterns in the rocks as it drops 700 feet in a series of 18 waterfalls.

South of Seneca and Keuka lakes is Elmira, where Mark Twain spent his summers. **Corning,** synonymous with glass manufacturing, displays its products at the Corning Glass Center. Northwest of Corning via SR 54 is **Hammondsport,** associated with the state's grape and wine industry. **Canandaigua,** at the north end of Canandaigua Lake, serves as a performing arts and grape-growing center.

Home of the Eastman Kodak Co., Rochester is known for its parks, gardens and estates. South off I-390, Mount Morris provides access to Letchworth State Park's "Grand Canyon of the East."

The Hamptons

When city streets begin to bake in the summer sun—an event that occurs with increasing regularity after Memorial Day—thousands of New Yorkers head for the cooler retreats

of Long Island Sound and the Atlantic Ocean. Poshness seems to increase as one travels eastward on **Long Island.**

Generally speaking, the working class heads for such closer spots as Coney Island and **Jones**

Beach. Free spirits trek to Fire Island Pines on the **Fire Island National Seashore.** Young professionals splurging on group house rentals migrate to Westhampton. The truly rich and famous, however, congregate in multimillion-dollar beach houses in an area of summer colonies known as the Hamptons.

SR 27 winds through this area of vineyards, marinas, farmlands and sandy beaches. Luxurious resort communities dot the landscape. At the junction of SRs 114 and 27 are the magnificent estates of **East Hampton.**

In **Montauk,** Montauk Lighthouse—commissioned by President George Washington in 1796—stands at the easternmost tip of Long Island. From Montauk a ferry departs for Block Island, R.I., during the summer. The season also is enlivened by numerous fishing tournaments.

Perhaps the best-known and most exclusive Hampton is **Southampton,** east on SR 80 from SR 27. Settled in 1640 and named after the aristocratic Earl of Southampton, the town's social distinctions and conservative politics are firmly rooted.

According to one story, satires printed in a neighboring village's newspaper stating that the town council had voted to ban cars more than 3 years old and to reserve parking for vehicles worth more than $30,000 were reputedly accepted at face value by some Southamptonites. Twelve-foot hedges acting as green sentries shield the huge mansions on Gin Lane from the roadway.

Culture manages to maintain a foothold in Southampton even amid the rusticity of sand and salt spray. In the summer there is some sort of festival—wine, antique, art, theater—held almost every week.

Contrary to popular belief, the Hamptons region is not all high society glitter. Tucked among the fashionable enclaves are such towns as **Sag Harbor,** once one of the world's largest whaling centers. Other communities on Long Island Sound's south fork include **Amagansett, Bridgehampton** and Quogue.

Hudson River Valley

The size of the Hudson River estuary led explorer Henry Hudson to believe he had discovered a passage to the Orient. Because of its navigability, the river developed into a strategic waterway that attracted invading armies, facilitated exploration and trade westward, sustained the Industrial Revolution and guaranteed the growth of New York City as an international port.

Breathtaking bridges span 400-foot cliffs; farms and estates line the valley; and recreational possibilities abound in the Catskills and Taconic mountains to the west and east.

Primary routes paralleling the Hudson from **New York City** include the spectacular Palisades Interstate Parkway and US 9W on the west bank via the George Washington toll bridge; the faster New York Thruway toll road (I-87), via the Tappan Zee toll bridge; the scenic Henry Hudson Parkway/US 9/SR 9D/SR 9G route on the east bank; and the faster Saw Mill River Parkway/Taconic State Parkway road farther east.

Just north of New York City on the east bank off SR 9A is **Yonkers,** a major industrial town containing the Georgian-style Philipse Manor Hall. **Tarrytown** occupies a cove under the Tappan Zee Bridge on SR 9. Washington Irving's "Legend of Sleepy Hollow" described the town; Sunnyside was the author's home.

Sleepy Hollow, formerly North Tarrytown, contains the 18th-century Dutch-style Philipsburg Manor. **Ossining's** claim to fame is the infamous maximum-security prison Sing Sing. Nearby **Croton-on-Hudson** contains the Van Cortlandts, the 80,000-acre estate of a Colonial Dutch patroon.

At the Bear Mountain Bridge north of Peekskill, scenic SR 9D follows the Hudson River, which narrows at the rugged cliffs of the Hudson Highlands. In the shadow of 1,000-foot Storm King Mountain, **Garrison** features the Boscobel mansion, an example of Federal architecture. **Poughkeepsie** is built on rocky terraces rising

250 feet above the Hudson and is home to Vassar College.

Just north, **Hyde Park** has the Home of Franklin D. Roosevelt National Historic Site, Eleanor Roosevelt's Val-Kill retreat and the FDR Library. Nearby **Rhinebeck** contains Beekman Arms, said to be the oldest hotel in the United States, and the Old Rhinebeck Aerodrome, known for vintage aircraft and summer air shows.

Finally, the former whaling town of **Hudson,** the northernmost point of interest along the river's east bank, features unusual Olana, a blend of castle and mosque designed by painter Frederick Church.

On the Hudson's west bank about 41 miles north of New York City is Bear Mountain State Park, where the river begins slicing through the Appalachian mountain chain. An observation deck provides views of four states—New York, New Jersey, Connecticut and Massachusetts. Guarding this narrow stretch is **West Point,** home of the vast United States Military Academy. **Newburgh** served as Gen. George Washington's headquarters during the Revolutionary War from April 1782 until August 1783.

New Paltz, established by French Huguenots in the 17th century, boasts some of the oldest neighborhoods in America. **Kingston,** a Dutch trading post, lies at the mouth of the Delaware and Hudson Canal, which transported Pennsylvania coal and the Catskill Mountain bluestone that was destined to be the curbing and sidewalks of Manhattan.

Rip Van Winkle's legendary nap took place in the town of **Catskill,** which also is the beginning of scenic SR 23 northwest over East Windham Mountain.

As home to the United States' second largest state government, Albany provides diverse architecture ranging from the original Dutch settlement of Quackenbush and the Schuyler Mansion State Historic Site to the sleek high-rises of the Empire State Plaza complex of government buildings.

At the nearby confluence of the Mohawk and Hudson rivers lies industrial **Troy.** Along with neighboring communities, Troy forms the Hudson-Mohawk Urban Cultural Park, which commemorates the area's crucial role in 19th-century commerce and industry.

The northern end of the Hudson Valley is celebrated for horse racing and the health-giving properties of its springs. **Saratoga Springs** developed into a premier Victorian horse racing resort. It also is the summer home of the New York City Ballet and the Philadelphia Orchestra. Although summer activities center on Thoroughbred races and the arts, the town also is becoming a year-round sports and convention center.

Southeast via SR 29 and US 4 is **Saratoga National Historical Park,** which commemorates the Battles of Saratoga, fought on Sept. 19 and Oct. 7, 1777, and considered the turning point of the American Revolution.

center of the island. The Atlantic Ocean continues to shape the dune-covered barrier islands of the South Shore.

Most of Long Island is less than a 2-hour drive from Midtown Manhattan. The Long Island Expressway, I-495, runs east-west through the center of the island, allowing convenient access to most points of interest.

once served as the estate of industrialist John S. Phipps.

Sagamore Hill National Historic Site, near **Oyster Bay,** was Theodore Roosevelt's summer White House. The 1885 house displays his family memorabilia. From this point SR 25A leads to **Centerport,** where the Vanderbilt Mansion stands overlooking Northport Harbor. The Spanish

Long Island

A bedroom community of Manhattan, the westernmost portion of Long Island is truly an extension of New York City, since it contains Brooklyn and Queens, two of the city's boroughs.

As Long Island extends eastward about 125 miles, the most densely populated areas give way to farms, vineyards, posh resorts and old whaling ports.

Glaciers scraped this low-lying extension of the New England coastal plain to produce the low bluffs of the North Shore along Long Island Sound and the moraines in the

Highlights of the island include 20th-century mansions and 17th-century saltbox houses.

SR 25A offers a more leisurely, scenic route along the North Shore, while the Southern State Parkway and Sunrise Highway, SR 27, provide access to the South Shore.

As an alternative to driving, the Long Island Railroad links Manhattan to most major towns on Long Island.

The elegant estates that inspired F. Scott Fitzgerald's novel "The Great Gatsby" line the western half of the North Shore, also called the Gold Coast. Old Westbury Gardens, in the town of **Old Westbury,**

Revival home is furnished with period pieces.

The eastern terminus of I-495 is at **Riverhead,** where Long Island separates into two peninsulas, the North and South Forks. SR 25 skirts the farms of the North Fork to Orient Point, where the Cross Sound Ferry sails to New London, Conn. From Riverhead, SR 24 merges with scenic SR 27 to follow the South Fork to its eastern terminus, also called The Hamptons.

Along the South Shore of Long Island heading west, SR 27 parallels undeveloped Fire Island National Seashore and the more commercialized Jones Beach, both popular recreation spots for New York City residents.

New York City

New York City is indebted to the tough bedrock that anchors the lofty skyscrapers of **Manhattan**, heart of the culturally rich, energetic "Big Apple."

With one of the highest traffic densities in the nation, as well as scarce and expensive parking, Manhattan poses problems for the motorist. For those driving between Upper, Mid-town and Lower Manhattan, take the route consisting of controlled-access sections of FDR Drive, East River Drive, Harlem River Drive, I-95, the West Side Elevated Highway and the Henry Hudson Parkway (SR 9A).

The outlying boroughs of New York City also have much to offer. From Upper Manhattan, the Cross-Bronx Expressway (I-95) and the Major Deegan Expressway (I-87) reach **The Bronx**. Highlights here include the New York Botanical Garden covering some 250 acres and featuring 28 specialty gardens, and the Bronx Zoo/Wildlife Conservation Park, one of the country's largest urban zoos.

From Midtown Manhattan the Long Island Expressway (I-495) via the Queens Midtown toll tunnel reaches **Queens**, which has Flushing Meadows-Corona Park, site of the 1939-40 and 1964-65 New York's World Fairs.

From Lower Manhattan, **Brooklyn** is reached via the Brooklyn Battery toll tunnel and the Prospect Expressway; the Brooklyn and Manhattan bridges also link Manhattan to the borough. Brooklyn contains the Brooklyn Botanic Garden, Brighton Beach and the vintage Coney Island Boardwalk.

Richmond (Staten Island), reached from Brooklyn via the Verrazano Narrows toll bridge or by the Staten Island Ferry, is home to Historic Richmond Town, a restored 100-acre village re-creating 3 centuries of local history.

Thousand Islands-St. Lawrence River

Called the "jewels in the crown of the Empire State," the **Thousand Islands** range in size from 2 square feet to 20 square miles and are a paradise for anglers, boaters and swimmers. Although the region was the scene of some of the bloodiest battles of the War of 1812, Canada and the United States now cooperate along their "Fourth Seacoast" in operating the **Great Lakes-St. Lawrence Seaway System** and in generating electricity.

A principal route through the region is I-81, between Syracuse and the Thousand Islands International toll bridge. A scenic combination of SRs 12E and 12 then follows the St. Lawrence southwest to Lake Ontario. In the opposite direction SRs 12 and 37 lead to **Massena.**

Along I-81 in wooded, gently rolling farmland is **Watertown,** the birthplace of the Woolworth five-and-dime store chain. **Sackets Harbor,** a nearby lakeside resort, saw a U.S. victory against British warships during the War of 1812. From Fishers Landing the Thousand Islands International Bridge to Ontario offers a perspective of some of the rocky, pine-covered islands.

Boat tours from **Alexandria Bay** or **Clayton** offer a closer perspective of such attractions as Boldt Castle on Heart Island, a 1900 turreted stone castle.

SR 12/37 crosses semi-wooded farmland to **Ogdensburg,** the oldest settlement in upstate New York and the boyhood home of artist Frederic Remington. A museum displays some of his American West themed paintings.

Farther northeast, a 90-foot drop in the river marks the location of Massena, the U.S. end of the Moses-Saunders Power Dam, which generates 2 million kilowatts for Ontario and New York state. The town lies on the St. Lawrence Seaway, a series of connecting locks, lakes and rivers that compensate for rapids and the 602-foot change in altitude from the mouth of the St. Lawrence to the Great Lakes.

Western

Thundering Niagara Falls and the Allegheny Mountains draw visitors to New York's western region, which is bordered by the Niagara River and Lake Erie to the west, the Pennsylvania border to the south, Lake Ontario to the north and the Finger Lakes to the east.

The principal routes include I-90 between Rochester via **Buffalo** and the Pennsylvania border and I-290/190 around Buffalo to **Niagara Falls** and Lake Ontario. From its junction with I-390, SR 17 traverses the Allegheny Mountains and merges with SR 430 near Bemus Point and Chautauqua Lake.

New York's second largest city, Buffalo serves as a major international port and manufacturing center. It also has strong ethnic neighborhoods and such architectural treasures as the Albright-Knox Art Gallery and the Guaranty Building skyscraper. The Peace toll bridge provides access to Canada. Just east off US 20 amid rolling farm country is **Darien Center,** where there is an amusement park complex.

From Buffalo I-190 leads to Niagara Falls via **Grand Island,** a residential community in the middle of the Niagara River.

For a spray-catching close-up of the falls themselves—which consist of the massive American Falls, tiny Bridal Veil Falls and the magnificent Canadian Horseshoe Falls—ride the *Maid of the Mist* around the base of the falls, or hike near the Cave of the Winds on Goat Island, where walkways bring you to within 25 feet of the American Falls.

The falls power one of North America's largest hydroelectric projects, which is the focus of the Niagara Power Project Visitor Center. An observation building affords wonderful views of the falls, while working models and displays explain how the generators operate. The Rainbow and Whirlpool Rapids toll bridges lead into Canada.

From Niagara Falls, follow the Robert Moses Parkway or SR 18F north along the Niagara River, which churns through the breathtaking Niagara Escarpment. Fort Niagara, outside of **Youngstown,** guards the strategic mouth of the Niagara River on Lake Ontario.

Built by the French in 1726, the fort played an important role during Colonial times.

Between Pennsylvania and Buffalo, I-90 parallels a section of the old underground railroad through rolling vineyards and fruit orchards within sight of Lake Erie. **Chautauqua,** a Victorian-style summer resort and center of a wine-producing region on the shores of Chautauqua Lake, offers a variety of arts- and education-related

activities. The Chautauqua Institution offers activities for all in the arts, education, religion and recreation.

Near the southeastern end of the lake is **Jamestown,** known for its furniture and wood products. From Jamestown, SR 17 heads eastward through forested mountains to 60,398-acre Allegany State Park, New York's largest state park.

Farther east, **Salamanca** is the home of the Seneca-Iroquois National Museum. The collection portrays the life and culture of the Iroquois.

Rock City Park in nearby **Olean** allows hikers to examine 500-million-year-old quartz boulders that project from the edge of the Allegheny Mountains.

Points of Interest

ADIRONDACK PARK (C-9)

Adirondack Park encompasses about two-thirds of upstate New York, embracing some 6 million acres of both private and state land. Nearly half of it is wilderness. Physical features range from rugged mountains and sheer cliffs to low rolling uplands, beaver meadows, swamps and a grassy plain.

Among the 42 mountains that exceed 4,000 feet in elevation is 5,344-foot Mount Marcy, the highest in the state. Some 2,800 lakes and ponds, 1,200 miles of rivers and more than 30,000 miles of brooks and streams cover the landscape, allowing a mere 1,100 miles of highway and 120 miles of railroad to squeeze between the park's southwest border at Remsen and the northeast border at Lake Placid.

The park's geologic base reveals the contrasts of eons of change. Part of the main mountain chain is an outcropping of the Laurentian, or Canadian, Shield, a rare surfacing of some of the oldest and hardest known rock forged in the Earth's interior. Other areas contain fossil-rich strata formed millions of years later at the bottom of prehistoric seas.

Ecosystems, which range from alpine and sub-alpine to boreal and lowland lake to wetland, present an overlapping of northern and southern forest types with an occasional stand of virgin timber. With the exception of small areas near lakes George and Champlain, the park harbors no poisonous snakes.

The area was named after the Algonquin Indians. The Iroquois Indians called Algonquin *Ha-De-Ron-Dah* or "bark eaters" because they ate certain kinds of tree bark. The domain of hunters and loggers during the 18th and early 19th centuries, the Adirondacks were not "discovered" until after the Civil War. They evolved into a woodland retreat for the wealthy, who built luxurious resorts, private camps *(see Raquette Lake p. 165)* and summer homes on the lakes.

The area is being preserved for recreation in a wild and peaceful setting. There are scenic views at every turn, some still bearing the vestiges of logging activity and the stubborn scars left by the forest fires of 1899, 1903 and 1908, and the hurricane of 1950.

Recreational possibilities span the seasons; boating, birdwatching, camping, canoeing, fishing, horseback riding, downhill and cross-country skiing, snowmobiling and snowshoeing are available. Areas with major development include Blue Mountain Lake, Lake George and Lake Placid *(see place listings pp. 63, 97 and 98).*

Two interpretive visitor centers provide indoor and outdoor exhibits and programming about the park. Both centers offer a surfaced trail system with interpretive signage.

The visitor center at Paul Smiths, 1 mile north of SR 86 on SR 30, provides information about the history, people and ecology of the Adirondack Park region. Features of the Newcomb Center, 14 miles east of Long Lake on SR 28N, include an exhibit about the birth and development of the conservation and preservation movements and the 20-minute multi-image presentation "Adirondack Passages." Comprehensive information about the park and its outdoor recreation opportunities can be obtained by contacting the Department of Environmental Conservation, P.O. Box 296, SR 86, Ray Brook, NY 12977; phone (518) 897-1200.

The visitor centers are open daily 9-5; closed Thanksgiving and Dec. 25. Free. Phone (518) 327-3000. *See Recreation Chart the AAA Northeastern CampBook. See color ad.*

ALBANY (F-10)

pop. 101,100, elev. 30′

See map page 55.

Albany is the state capital. The city's modern governmental complex, construction of which

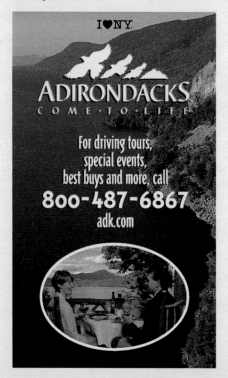

began in 1962, contrasts with its pastoral surroundings along the Hudson River.

Although French trappers were in the area in the mid-1500s, it was not until 1609 that Dutch fur traders arrived and established a trading center and fort. The first permanent settlement was founded in 1624 by 18 Walloon families, French Protestants who left the Spanish Netherlands seeking religious freedom. The settlement was called Beverwyck until it was transferred to England and renamed in honor of the Duke of York and Albany.

Albany was chartered in 1686 with Pieter Schuyler as the first mayor. By 1750 it had become an important trading center. Robert Fulton's *North River Steamboat* made the first successful steamboat run from New York to Albany in 1807. The opening of the Erie Canal between Buffalo and Albany in 1825 and the city's growth as a major railroad terminus greatly increased its importance.

Albany's notable citizens have included U.S. presidents Martin Van Buren, Millard Fillmore and Theodore and Franklin Roosevelt, as well as authors Herman Melville and Henry James.

Albany is an expanding cultural center with museums, theaters and historic buildings. Governor Nelson A. Rockefeller Empire State Plaza *(see attraction listing),* a 98.5-acre, 11-building complex that comprises state government offices and cultural and convention facilities, commands downtown Albany.

Other cultural showcases include the Palace Theatre, home of the Albany Symphony Orchestra, and Park Playhouse, one of the larger outdoor theaters on the East Coast. The Capital Repertory Theatre, the area's resident professional equity theater, presents a variety of plays year round.

The Albany Urban Cultural Park Visitor Center, at the intersection of Broadway and Clinton avenues at 25 Quackenbush Sq., has hands-on exhibits tracing the history of Albany. The Henry Hudson Planetarium within the visitor center presents shows Saturdays.

Nestled along the Hudson River waterfront in downtown Albany is the Corning Preserve, a narrow strip of land several miles long that has nature trails popular for jogging, walking, bicycling and inline skating. The site also beckons picnickers and is frequently used for concerts and festivals.

Albany County Convention and Visitors Bureau: 25 Quackenbush Sq., Albany, NY 12207; phone (518) 434-1217 or (800) 258-3582.

Self-guiding tours: The Albany Heritage Area Visitor Center has self-guiding walking and driving tour information; phone (518) 434-0405.

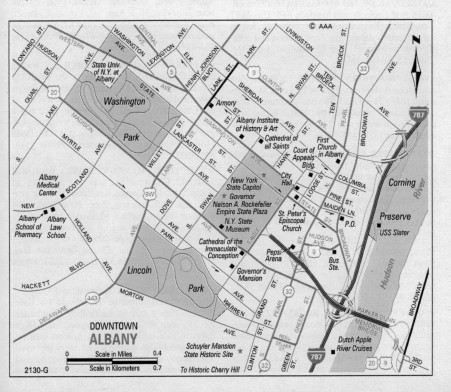

Shopping areas: Colonie Center, Wolf Road and Central Avenue, has Macy's and Sears as its anchor stores, while Crossgates Mall, on Crossgates Mall Road, counts Filene's, JCPenney, Lord & Taylor and Macy's among its more than 230 stores.

[SAVE] **ALBANY INSTITUTE OF HISTORY AND ART,** 125 Washington Ave., presents permanent and changing exhibits about the art, culture and history of Albany and the Hudson Valley region. Collections include Hudson River School landscapes, early Dutch limner portraits, Albany silver, 18th- and 19th-century New York furniture, sculpture, pewter, ceramics and decorative arts, as well as an Egyptian collection. The museum also houses the McKinney Library. **Note:** The museum is undergoing renovations and will reopen Spring 2001. A temporary location, at 63 State St., houses changing exhibits.

Allow 1 hour minimum. Mon.-Fri. 11-6; closed holidays. Free. Phone (518) 463-4478.

CATHEDRAL OF ALL SAINTS is at 62 S. Swan St. This 1884 Gothic Revival Episcopal church has stained glass, mosaics, stone carvings, 17th-century choir stalls carved in Belgium and historic and artistic objects. Guided tours are available by appointment. Allow 30 minutes minimum. Mon.-Fri. 7:30-3, Sat. 8-11, Sun. 7-1. Donations. Phone (518) 465-1342.

CATHEDRAL OF THE IMMACULATE CONCEPTION is at Eagle St. and Madison Ave. This 1852 Neo-Gothic Revival Catholic cathedral has a carved pulpit, stained glass and historic and artistic objects. Mon.-Fri. 7-5:30, Sat.-Sun. 8-6. Free. Phone (518) 463-4447.

COURT OF APPEALS BUILDING, Eagle and Pine sts. opposite Academy Park at 20 Eagle St., dates from 1842. This Greek Revival structure houses a courtroom designed by H.H. Richardson. Mon.-Fri. 10-noon and 2-4, or by appointment. Free. Phone (518) 455-7711.

DUTCH APPLE RIVER CRUISES, Broadway and Quay sts. adjoining the U-Haul building, offers 2-hour narrated cruises on the Hudson River. Lunch, dinner and hors d'oeuvre cruises also are available. Departures Wed.-Sat. at 11 and 2, May-Oct. Fare $10; ages 5-12, $6. Departures require a minimum of 20 persons. MC, VI. Phone (518) 463-0220.

FIRST CHURCH IN ALBANY(Reformed), 110 N. Pearl St., was founded in 1642. Its pulpit and weather vane both date from 1656. Self-guiding tours Mon.-Fri. 8:30-3. Donations. Phone (518) 463-4449.

★ **GOVERNOR NELSON A. ROCKEFELLER EMPIRE STATE PLAZA,** downtown between Madison Ave. and State St., houses a governmental center, a performing arts center, a meeting center, the New York State Museum of Art and a collection of modern American art. Phone (518)

473-7521 to arrange a free tour of the art collection. Allow 1 hour minimum. The observation deck of the 42-story Corning Tower Building is open daily 10-3:45; closed Jan. 1, Easter, Thanksgiving and Dec. 25. Free. Phone (518) 474-2418.

New York State Capitol, bounded by Washington Ave. and Swan, State and Eagle sts., was built in the late 1800s and the governor's office and the New York State Senate and Assembly. Carvings on the Million Dollar Staircase depict famous people in American history as well as friends and relatives of the sculptors. Guided 1-hour tours daily at 10, noon, 2 and 3; closed Jan. 1, Easter, Thanksgiving and Dec. 25. Free. Phone (518) 474-2418.

New York State Museum is in the Empire State Plaza. Multimedia exhibits focus on the Adirondacks, the New York City metropolis and American Indians of the state. Participatory programs about art, history, science and technology are offered. Allow 1 hour, 30 minutes minimum. Daily 10-5; closed Jan. 1, Thanksgiving and Dec. 25. Donations. Phone (518) 474-5877.

[SAVE] **HISTORIC CHERRY HILL** is between First and McCarty aves. at 523½ S. Pearl St. The 1787 Georgian-style house, once the center of a Colonial farm, contains furniture, silver, china, glass, letters and clothing from five generations. Allow 1 hour minimum. Guided tours on the hour Tues.-Sat. 10-3, Sun. 1-3, Feb.-Dec.; closed major holidays. Tour $3.50; over 61, $3; college students with ID $2; ages 6-17, $1. Phone (518) 434-4791.

ST. PETER'S EPISCOPAL CHURCH is 1 blk. e. of the Capitol at State and Lodge sts. The 1859 French Gothic church contains stained-glass windows and elaborate floor mosaics, a replica of the Queen Anne silver presented in 1712 and a British general's grave beneath the vestibule. Organ recitals are offered Fridays at 12:30. Open Mon.-Fri. 11:30-1:15. Donations. Phone (518) 434-3502.

★ **SCHUYLER MANSION STATE HISTORIC SITE,** 32 Catherine St., was the residence of Philip Schuyler, a noted Revolutionary War general and U.S. senator from New York. His daughter Betsy married Alexander Hamilton in the house. Guided tours on the hour Wed.-Sat. 10-4, Sun. 1-4, mid-Apr. through Oct. 31; by appointment rest of year. Closed Columbus Day. Tour $3; senior citizens $2; ages 5-12, $1. Phone (518) 434-0834.

USS SLATER, I-787 exit 2, then n. to 1 Quay St., is in the Corning Preserve. This World War II destroyer offers a look at the floating environment for 216 men aboard this renovated ship. Highlights include the bunk rooms, officers quarters, galley and bridge area. Guided tours are available. Some steep stair climbing is required. Allow 30 minutes minimum. Thurs.-Sun. 11-4,

Apr.-Nov.; closed major holidays. Admission $5; over 62 and ages 6-18, $3. Phone (518) 439-1943.

ALBERTSON (I-2)
pop. 5,200, elev. 140'

CLARK BOTANIC GARDEN, 193 I.U. Willetts Rd., is reached from the Northern State Pkwy. and Long Island Expwy. via Willis Ave. S. exits. Rose, wildflower, vegetable and herb gardens as well as woodlands are available. Allow 1 hour minimum. Daily 10-4:30. Guided tours are given Sun. at 2, mid-Apr. through Sept. 30. Closed Jan.

1, Thanksgiving and Dec. 25. Free. Phone (516) 484-8600.

ALEXANDRIA BAY (B-8)
pop. 1,200, elev. 274'

ALEX BAY BOAT TOURS departs from 5 Fuller St. (Upper Harbor). Narrated sightseeing tours cover the Thousand Island region and the area around Alex Bay, including such sights as the shortest international bridge and Boldt Castle. Dinner cruises also are available.

Allow 1 hour, 30 minutes minimum. Tours depart daily at 10, noon, 2 and 4, June 2-Labor

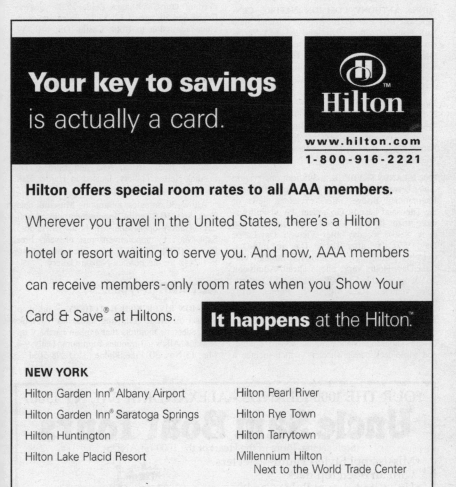

Day; Sat.-Sun. at 10, noon, 2 and 4, May 15-June 1 and day after Labor Day-Oct. 15. Fare $11.50, under 12 free. Reservations are recommended. AE, MC, VI. Phone (315) 482-8687.

BOLDT CASTLE, on Heart Island, is accessible by ferry service or boat tours. Construction of the turreted stone castle began in 1900, but the nearly completed castle was abandoned and never lived in. It has been under restoration since 1977. The Boldt Yacht House, accessible only by shuttle boat, contains antique boats. Allow 1 hour minimum. Daily 10-6:30, mid-May to mid-Oct. Admission $4.25; ages 6-12, $2. Boldt Yacht House $2; ages 6-12, $1. Phone (800) 847-5263.

MINNA ANTHONY COMMON NATURE CENTER, off I-81 exit 51 in Wellesley Island State Park *(see Recreation Chart and the AAA Northeastern CampBook),* is a 600-acre wildlife sanctuary with 8 miles of trails. The interpretive visitor center has nature exhibits. Trails for cross-country skiing are available.

Allow 30 minutes minimum. Center open Mon.-Sat. 8:30-8:30, Sun. 8:30-4:30, July-Aug.; Mon.-Sat. 8:30-4:30, Sun. 10-4:30, rest of year. Trails open daily dawn-dusk. Admission to sanctuary $5 per private vehicle, Memorial Day-Labor Day; free rest of year. Phone (315) 482-2479.

1000 ISLANDS SKYDECK, a 395-foot observation tower between the spans of the Thousand Islands International Bridge, offers excellent views of the Thousand Islands. On a clear day visibility is more than 40 miles. Food is available. Open daily 8:30-8:30, day after Victoria Day-Labor Day; 9-7, day after Labor Day to mid-Oct. (weather permitting); 9-6 mid-Apr. through Victoria Day. Hours vary; phone ahead. Admission $6.95; ages 6-12, $3.95. Bridge toll $2 per private vehicle. AE, MC, VI. Phone (613) 659-2335.

UNCLE SAM BOAT TOURS, I-81 exit 50N to foot of James St., offers 2.25-hour sightseeing cruises of the Thousand Islands region aboard double- and triple-deck paddlewheelers, which include a stop at Boldt Castle *(see attraction listing)* in season. A ferry to Boldt Castle also is available. Lunch and dinner cruises are available in summer.

Sightseeing cruise departs daily every hour 9-4:30, May-Sept.; schedule varies in Apr. and Oct. Ferry departs daily every 30 minutes 10-6, July-Aug.; every hour 10-5, mid-May through June 30 and Sept. 1 to mid-Oct. One-hour evening cruise departs daily at 7, mid-May through Labor Day. Three-hour Seaway Island Cruise departs daily late June-Labor Day. Sightseeing cruise $13; over 65, $12; ages 4-12, $6.50. Ferry $6.75; ages 4-12, $4.25. One-hour evening cruise $9; ages 4-12, $5.25. Seaway Cruise $14.50; ages 4-12, $7.75. Fares do not include admission to Boldt Castle. DS, MC, VI. Phone (315) 482-2611 or (800) 253-9229. *See ad.*

ALFRED (F-5) pop. 4,600, elev. 1,671'

THE INTERNATIONAL MUSEUM OF CERAMIC ART AT ALFRED, in the Ceramic Corridor Innovation Center on CR 244 at the New York State College of Ceramics at Alfred University, houses contemporary American ceramics and ceramic technology, pottery of the ancient Americas and ceramics from Africa, Asia and Europe. The Fosdick-Nelson Gallery, located in Harder Hall, presents changing exhibits.

Allow 30 minutes minimum. Museum open Tues.-Sun. 10-5 and by appointment; closed holidays. Gallery open Mon.-Fri. 11-4, Sat. noon-5, Sept.-May; by appointment rest of year. Free. Phone (607) 871-2421 for the museum or 871-2442 for the Fosdick-Nelson Gallery.

ALTMAR (D-7) pop. 300

SALMON RIVER FISH HATCHERY, 7 mi. e. of Pulaski off SR 13 following signs, has fish tanks and videotape monitors that explain hatchery operations. Allow 30 minutes minimum. Daily 9-4, Mar. 15-Nov. 30. Free. Phone (315) 298-5051.

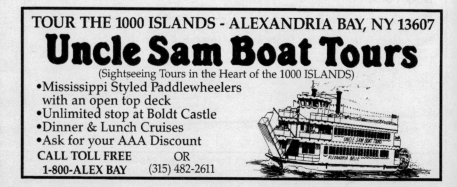

AMAGANSETT (H-6) elev. 64'

Despite its lack of a natural harbor, Amagansett has been a fishing village since it was settled in 1690. In the 18th and early 19th centuries the whaling industry was one of the town's most important sources of commerce and employment as well as the basis for an enduring folklore immortalizing old salts and the big ones that got away. *Also see Long Island p. 100.*

EAST HAMPTON TOWN MARINE MUSEUM is .5 mi. s. of jct. SR 27 and Atlantic Ave. on Bluff Rd. Dioramas and exhibits depict early whaling and modern fishing industries. A gunning shanty display with bird decoys, a children's discovery room and a garden also are on the grounds. Allow 1 hour minimum. Daily 10-5, July-Aug.; Sat.-Sun. 10-5 in June and Sept. Admission $4, over 64 and children $2. Phone (631) 267-6544 or 324-6850.

AMENIA (G-11) pop. 5,200

WINERIES

- **Cascade Mountain Winery**, 3 mi. n. on SR 22, then 3.5 mi. w. on Webutuck School Rd., following signs. Thurs.-Tues. 10-5. Phone (914) 373-9021.

AMHERST—*see Buffalo p. 71.*

AMSTERDAM (E-10)
pop. 20,700, elev. 275'

Amsterdam, settled in 1783, became an important industrial center with the opening of the Erie Canal in 1825. After the Utica & Schenectady Railroad came through 11 years later, the town entered its commercial heyday with more than 100 industrial plants manufacturing such goods as carpets, brooms, buttons, clothing and linseed oil.

Montgomery County Chamber of Commerce: 366 W. Main St., P.O. Box 309, Amsterdam, NY 12010; phone (518) 842-8200.

FORT JOHNSON—*see place listing p. 85.*

WALTER ELWOOD MUSEUM AND ART GALLERY is reached via I-90 exit 27, w. on SR 5, 3 blks. n. on Evelyn St., then w. to 300 Guy Park Ave. This museum has a gallery with changing art exhibits and artifacts relating to U.S. history. Permanent displays include a blacksmith shop, a Cherokee Indian tepee, a nature room, a local history room, a cabin dating from the time the first European settlers arrived in America, Victorian furnishings, and exhibits about Eskimos, the USS *Amsterdam,* natural history, the Iroquois Indians and Thomas Edison.

Allow 1 hour minimum. Mon.-Fri. 8:30-4, Sept.-June; Mon.-Thurs. 8:30-3:30, Fri. 8:30-1,

rest of year. Closed legal holidays, Good Friday, the day after Easter and the day after Thanksgiving. Donations. Phone (518) 843-5151.

ANNANDALE-ON-HUDSON (G-11)

MONTGOMERY PLACE, .2 mi. off SR 9G, then 3 mi. n. of SR 199, was built in 1805. Later additions transformed the Federal mansion to Classical Revival style. Other buildings, gardens and grounds can be seen on a self-guiding tour. Guided tours Wed.-Mon. 10-5, Apr.-Oct.; Sat.-Sun. 10-5, Nov.-Dec. Guided tour $6; over 60, $5; ages 6-17, $3. Self-guiding grounds tour $3. AE, MC, VI. Phone (914) 758-5461.

ARCADE (F-4) pop. 2,100, elev. 1,455'

ARCADE AND ATTICA RAILROAD, on SR 39 at 278 Main St., offers a historical and educational 15-mile steam locomotive passenger train ride. Various themed excursions are held throughout the year, including a trip to Beaver Meadow sanctuary in March, a Civil War trip the third weekend in August and Santa runs in December.

Allow 3 hours minimum. Departures Wed. and Sat.-Sun. at 12:30 and 3, Fri. at 1, July-Aug.; Sat.-Sun. at 12:30 and 3, in June, Sept. and the last weekend in Oct.; Fri. at 1, Sat.-Sun. at noon, 2 and 4, first 3 weekends in Oct.; Sat.-Sun. at noon and 2, first 3 weekends in Dec. Fare $8.50; ages 3-11, $5; under 3 on lap free. Reservations are highly recommended for themed tours. MC, VI. Phone (716) 496-9877 or 492-3100.

ARKVILLE (F-9) elev. 1,373'

SAVE **DELAWARE AND ULSTER RAIL RIDE,** on SR 28, offers 1- and 1.75-hour round-trip train rides through the scenic Catskill Mountains. The depot displays railroad memorabilia. Departures Wed.-Sun. at 10:30, 1 and 2:30, July 5-Labor Day; Sat.-Sun. at 11, 1 and 3, Memorial Day weekend-July 3 and day after Labor Day-Oct. 30. Fare $7-$10; over 63, $5.50-$7.50; ages 3-12, $4-$5. MC, VI. To verify price and schedule phone (914) 586-3877 or (800) 225-4132 in New York.

ASHFORD HOLLOW (F-3)

GRIFFIS SCULPTURE PARK, off SR 219 on Ahrens Rd., displays 200 steel, aluminum and bronze sculptures in meadows overlooking the rolling countryside. The park, which is in a 400-acre nature preserve, offers 10 miles of hiking trails. Picnicking is permitted. Daily 9-dusk, May-Oct. Donations. Phone (761) 257-9344.

AUBURN (E-6) pop. 31,300, elev. 694'

In 1793 Auburn's location at the northern tip of Owasco Lake attracted its first settler, surveyor and Revolutionary War hero Col. John

Hardenbergh. He built a cabin and a mill on the site. In 1805 the town was named for a locale in Oliver Goldsmith's poem "Deserted Village." Five years later the community boasted 90 dwellings and 17 mills.

The opening in 1817 of the state prison, built on land donated by citizens, and the establishment in 1829 of a theological seminary, which is affiliated with Union Theological Seminary, stimulated additional growth. Prison labor was cheap and, until 1882, legal. By the early 1920s the town was firmly entrenched as an industrial center and market for the region's agricultural products.

Fort Hill Cemetery, 19 Fort St., contains part of a hill thought to have been erected by Moundbuilders as well as the graves of William Seward, secretary of state under Presidents Lincoln and Andrew Johnson, and Logan, a Mingo Indian orator who led a war party in 1774 in retaliation for the murder of his family. *Also see Finger Lakes p. 84.*

Chamber of Commerce of Auburn and Cayuga County: 36 South St., P.O. Box 675, Auburn, NY 13021; phone (315) 252-7291.

CAYUGA MUSEUM/CASE RESEARCH LAB MUSEUM, 203 Genesee St., has changing and permanent Cayuga County history displays, including 19th-century furnishings. The Case Research Laboratory, site of the invention of early sound motion pictures, is on the grounds. Tues.-Sun. and Mon. holidays noon-5, Feb.-Dec.; closed Easter, Thanksgiving and Dec. 25. Donations. Phone (315) 253-8051.

DID YOU KNOW

Approximately
one-third of
all battles fought
during the
Revolutionary War were
fought on
New York soil.

EMERSON PARK, 2.5 mi. s. via SR 38A on Owasco Lake, covers 133 acres and contains the Cayuga County Agricultural Museum. Owasco Teyatasta offers Northeast Woodland Native American collections. Boating, fishing, picnicking and swimming are permitted. Food is available. Museum open Wed.-Sun. 1-5, Memorial Day weekend-Labor Day. Park open daily 6 a.m.-dusk, mid-May through Labor Day. Museum by donation. Park admission $2 per private vehicle. Phone (315) 253-5611.

HARRIETT TUBMAN HOME, 1.5 mi. s. on SR 34 at 180 South St., features a 25-minute videotape about the life of the former slave who delivered more than 300 slaves from the South on the underground railroad. During the Civil War Tubman rendered invaluable service to the Union Army as a nurse, scout and spy. A guided tour includes her simple house and the home for the aged built and run in her honor. Allow 1 hour minimum. Tues.-Fri. 10-4, Sat. by appointment, Feb.-Oct.; by appointment rest of year. Donations. Phone (315) 252-2081.

HOOPES MEMORIAL PARK, 1.2 mi. e. on US 20 at E. Genesee St., contains a miniature lake and rose gardens. Daily 7 a.m.-9 p.m. Free. Phone (315) 252-9300.

SCHWEINFURTH MEMORIAL ART CENTER, 205 W. Genesee St., houses changing exhibits featuring works by area children, senior citizens and contemporary New York artists as well as a yearly exhibit of quilts. Tours, lectures, art classes, workshops and videotapes supplement the exhibits. Allow 1 hour minimum. Tues.-Sat. 10-5, Sun. 1-5, Feb.-Dec.; closed Thanksgiving and Dec. 25. Admission $3, children free. A fee may be charged for certain exhibits. Phone (315) 255-1553.

WILLARD MEMORIAL CHAPEL, 2 blks. e. of SR 34 at 17 Nelson St., is an example of the interior design work of Louis Comfort Tiffany and the Tiffany Decorating and Glass Co. The 1892 Romanesque Revival chapel has carved wooden pews, stained-glass windows, leaded-glass chandeliers, mosaic floors, and oak wainscotting and furnishings.

Allow 1 hour minimum. Guided tours Tues.-Fri. 10-4. Chapel open Tues.-Fri. 10-4; closed holidays. Admission $2, under 11 free. Phone (315) 252-0339.

SAVE **WILLIAM H. SEWARD HOUSE,** 33 South St. on SR 34, was the home of the secretary of state under Presidents Abraham Lincoln and Andrew Johnson. It contains original family furnishings, clothing, antique toys and mementos of Seward's career. A painting by Emanuel Leutze depicts Seward's negotiations for the purchase of Alaska. Allow 1 hour minimum. Tues.-Sat. 10-4, Sun. 1-4, July 1-Oct. 14; Tues.-Sat. 1-4, Oct. 15-Dec. 31 and Feb.-June. Closed major holidays. Admission $3.25; over 59 and ages 12-18, $2.75. Phone (315) 252-1283.

AURIESVILLE (E-9) elev. 304'

NATIONAL SHRINE OF NORTH AMERICAN MARTYRS, off I-90 exits 27 or 28, on SR 5S, marks the site of the Mohawk village of Ossernenon, where Father Isaac Jogues and his companions were killed in the 1640s. They were later canonized as martyrs. It also is the birthplace of the Blessed Kateri Tekakwitha, a Mohawk Indian who is being canonized.

Also on the grounds are an Indian museum and the Big Round Church, which seats 6,500. Picnicking is permitted. Food is available. Allow 2 hours minimum. Shrine daily dawn-dusk. Information center daily 10-4, May-Oct. Free. Phone (518) 853-3033.

AUSABLE CHASM (B-11)

SAVE AUSABLE CHASM is reached via I-87 exit 34. The 1.5-mile-long gorge has waterfalls and rapids formed by the Ausable River; in places the rocky walls rise perpendicularly 200 feet above the river. The tour includes a participatory raft ride and a .75-mile self-guiding walking tour with many stairs and a return-trip bus ride. Wear comfortable shoes. A walking tour also is available. Picnicking is permitted.

Allow 2 hours minimum. Daily 9:30-5, July 1-Labor Day; 9:30-4, Memorial Day-June 30 and day after Labor Day-Columbus Day. Fare $19; over 54, military with ID and ages 5-11, $17. Walking tour only $13; over 54, military with ID and ages 5-11, $11. AE, DI, MC, VI. Phone (518) 834-7454.

BALDWINSVILLE (D-7)
pop. 6,600, elev. 389'

BEAVER LAKE NATURE CENTER, 8477 E. Mud Lake Rd., covers 550 acres, including 238-acre Beaver Lake. Up to 10,000 geese stop in the area during spring migration, and many return in the fall. Eight trails traverse forest, meadows, lakeshore and wetlands. Trail highlights include boardwalks, an observation tower, interpretive signs, telescopes and a bog with orchids and insect-eating plants. Guided canoe trips are offered in summer; cross-country skiing and snowshoeing are available in winter. Daily 7:30-dusk; closed Dec. 25. Admission $1 per private vehicle. Phone (315) 638-2519.

BALLSTON SPA (E-10)
pop. 4,900, elev. 288'

NATIONAL BOTTLE MUSEUM, 76 Milton Ave., promotes the study, appreciation and preservation of the American bottle industry. Exhibits include permanent and changing displays of bottles, containers and glass-blowing tools. A videotape describes glassmaking and molding. The museum also has a research library. Allow 30 minutes minimum. Daily 10-4, June-Sept.; Mon.-Fri. 10-4, rest of year. Admission $2; ages 6-12, $1. Phone (518) 885-7589.

BATAVIA (E-4)
pop. 16,300, elev. 956'

Batavia was only a junction of the old Genesee Road and Tonawanda Creek Indian trails when Robert Morris bought more than 3 million acres in western New York from Massachusetts in 1797. Having obtained the Indian title to the land by the Big Tree Treaty, Morris sold most of his holdings to the Dutch Holland Land Co. The town is named for the Netherlands republic from which the owners originated.

Genesee County Chamber of Commerce: 210 E. Main St., Batavia, NY 14020; phone (716) 343-7440 or (800) 622-2686. See color ad p. 202.

HOLLAND LAND OFFICE MUSEUM, 131 W. Main St., is the original 1815 Holland Land Co. office. Allow 30 minutes minimum. Tues.-Sat. 10-4; closed county holidays. Donations. Phone (716) 343-4727.

BEACON (H-10)
pop. 13,200, elev. 150'

In 1663 Francis Rombout bought all the land he could see from the top of Mount Beacon from the native inhabitants. Catharyna Brett inherited the property and managed the holdings until her death in 1764. During the Revolutionary War fires burning on the summit of Mount Beacon to warn Gen. George Washington of British movements up the Hudson River gave the mountain and the city their names.

Madame Brett's Homestead, 50 Van Nydeck Ave., has been the residence of seven generations of the family and is said to be the oldest house in Dutchess County. The 1709 building is open the first Sunday of each month May through December; phone (914) 831-6533.

BINGHAMTON (G-8)
pop. 53,000, elev. 866'

The site of Binghamton was bought by Philadelphia merchant William Bingham in 1786 and was settled by Joseph Leonard and other pioneers the following year. Originally called Chenango for the river it bordered, the settlement was renamed Binghamton in honor of the man whose donations of land allowed it to grow into a village and later into a full-fledged town.

Railroads, photography equipment and cigar making were the town's major industries before 1900, but shoe manufacturing became the dominant enterprise in the early 20th century. Such high tech corporations as Universal Instruments and Link Flight Simulation, which manufactures aerospace equipment, have now come to the forefront. IBM established its first plant in nearby Endicott.

Gold- and onion-domed churches of various Eastern European cultures are found throughout Broome County. Binghamton also includes among its cultural assets a branch of the State University of New York. The Anderson Center for the Performing Arts at SUNY Binghamton presents performing artists of national and international acclaim. The Forum on Washington Street hosts cultural productions.

The Binghamton area has six antique wood-carved carousels that visitors can ride from Memorial Day through Labor Day (weather permitting). George F. Johnson, who donated the carousels to local parks, stipulated that the municipalities never charge a fee for a ride. The carousels are at C. Fred Johnson Park in Johnson City; George W. Johnson Park in Endicott; Highland Park in Endwell; Recreation Park in Binghamton; Ross Park Zoo in Binghamton *(see attraction listing)*; and West Endicott Park in Endicott.

Broome County Chamber of Commerce: Metro Center, 49 Court St., P.O. Box 995, Binghamton, NY 13902; phone (607) 772-8860 or (800) 836-6740.

Self-guiding tours: Brochures outlining walking and driving tours of scenic and historic attrac-

tions in the Triple Cities—Binghamton, Endicott and Johnson City—are available at the chamber of commerce.

Shopping areas: Oakdale Mall, 3 miles west on Reynolds Road (SR 17 exit 70N), has JCPenney, Montgomery Ward and Sears among its 126 stores.

ROBERSON MUSEUM AND SCIENCE CENTER, 30 Front St., is a regional museum of 19th- and 20th-century art, history, folk life, science and natural history. It is composed of the historic 1907 Roberson Mansion, a museum, planetarium and science gallery. Also on site is the Binghamton Visitor Center which features permanent and changing heritage displays and a slide presentation. The mansion includes the Broome County Historical Society Research Library.

Allow 2 hours minimum. Complex open Mon.-Sat. 10-5 (also last Fri. of the month 5-9), Sun. noon-5; closed major holidays. Planetarium shows are offered Sat.-Sun. at 2, last Fri. of the month at 7:30. Research library open Tues.-Fri. 10-4. Admission $5; over 61 and ages 5-16, $3. Planetarium $1. Phone (607) 772-0660.

ROSS PARK ZOO, 60 Morgan Rd., is a 25-acre facility. Animals exhibited include eastern timber wolves and red wolves, otters and golden lion tamarins. Signs explain each animal's habitat, diet and social structure. A 1919 carousel operates daily Memorial Day through Labor Day.

Picnicking is permitted. Allow 1 hour, 30 minutes minimum. Daily 10-5, Apr.-Nov. Admission $3.50; senior citizens and ages 3-12, $2.75. Carousel free. Phone (607) 724-5454.

BLUE MOUNTAIN LAKE (C-9)
elev. 1,789'

To the north of Blue Mountain Lake, Blue Mountain rises 3,759 feet. Splendid views of the region are available from the summit, reached by a 3-mile trail. *Also see Adirondack Park p. 63.*

Blue Mountain Lake Association: Main Street, Blue Mountain Lake, NY 12812; phone (518) 352-7659.

[SAVE] ★**ADIRONDACK MUSEUM,** on SR 30, explores the culture, environment and history of the Adirondack region. The museum, on 32 acres overlooking Blue Mountain Lake, has indoor and outdoor exhibits about logging, boating, outdoor recreation and mining. Visitors also can enjoy an elegant private railroad car, a hermit's camp and a Bull Cottage enhanced by rustic furniture. Food is available.

Allow 3 hours minimum. Daily 9:30-5:30, mid-June to mid-Oct. Admission $10; over 62, $9; ages 7-16, $6. AE, DS, MC, VI. Phone (518) 352-7311.

BOLTON LANDING (D-11)

A resort area on the west shore of Lake George, Bolton Landing originated as an American Indian encampment on a wilderness trail. It later became the Bolton Landing stage stop on the Great Road. Wealthy families made the area their summer home. Scenic Route 9N runs north and south and is part of a lake shore route through the Adirondack Mountains.

Bolton Chamber of Commerce: P.O. Box 368, Bolton Landing, NY 12814; phone (518) 644-3831.

MARCELLA SEMBRICH MEMORIAL STUDIO, .5 mi. s. on SR 9N to 4800 Lakeshore Dr., contains mementos of the early 20th-century opera star's career. Allow 30 minutes minimum. Daily 10-12:30 and 2-5:30, June 15-Sept. 15. Admission $2, under 12 free. Phone (518) 644-9839 or 644-2492.

BOONVILLE (D-8)
pop. 2,200, elev. 1,135'

Boonville was named for Garret Boon, an agent of the Holland Land Co. The company owned property in the region at the end of the 18th century. The Black River Canal and the Black River Railroad brought prosperity to the town in the mid-1800s. Many of the grand houses of that period are on Schuyler Street. Hulbert House, a Georgian coach inn, was built in 1812.

Boonville Area Chamber of Commerce: P.O. Box 163, Boonville, NY 13309; phone (315) 942-5112.

BRANCHPORT (F-5) elev. 736'

WINERIES

- **Hunt Country Vineyards,** off SR 54A at 4021 Italy Hill Rd. Mon.-Sat. 10-6, Sun. noon-6, July-Oct.; Mon.-Sat. 10-5, Sun. noon-5, rest of year. Phone (315) 595-2812 or (800) 946-3289.

BRIDGEHAMPTON (H-5)
pop. 2,000, elev. 50'

BRIDGEHAMPTON HISTORICAL MUSEUM is at Montauk Hwy. and Corwith Ave. The early 19th-century Greek Revival Corwith House displays local artifacts and is furnished in various periods dating from the late 18th century. The Hildreth-Simons Machine Shop contains working antique engines and farm machines; the George W. Strong Wheelwright Shop displays tools used in wagon repair. Guided tours Thurs.-Sat. noon-4, mid-June through Labor Day. Donations. Phone (631) 537-1088.

Buffalo

How Buffalo was named remains a mystery, although the site has never been called anything else. Ironically there have never been buffalo in Buffalo; even the shaggy beasts at the Buffalo Zoological Gardens are technically North American bison. One theory blames the misnomer on a mispronunciation of the French *beau fleuve,* or "beautiful river." The river in question is the Niagara.

The French explorer Robert La Salle paddled his canoe down the Niagara in 1628. A small French settlement was established in 1758. It was burned by the British the following year, but the settlers held fast. Joseph Ellicott informed them in 1800 that the Holland Land Co. had bought the land. Ellicott mapped out plans for a town to be called New Amsterdam and patterned after Washington, D.C.

The town was built, but residents insisted on calling it Buffalo. Put to the torch again by the British during the War of 1812, the town was quickly reconstructed. In 1818 the first Great Lakes steamboat, *Walk-on-the-Water,* was built, the first of two major events that turned a small village into a major city in only 16 years.

The second event was the opening of the Erie Canal in 1825. By connecting numerous trade and transportation routes, the canal made Buffalo the nucleus of the shipping trade between the Great Lakes region, Canada and the eastern United States. Ten years later the addition of railroads to Buffalo's transportation network boosted the city's growth potential even higher.

Buffalo's major industries include glass, rubber, plastics, electronics and airplane and automobile manufacturing. High-technology has emerged as a viable successor to the city's imperiled heavy industries. Agriculture also plays an important economic role, particularly the growing of fruits and vegetables. Grain distribution and flour and feed production have been part of the local economy since the 1950s. The city also is the home of the only player piano roll manufacturer in the world.

Buffalo has produced important people as well. Two of its residents, Millard Fillmore and Grover Cleveland, became president. Fillmore is buried in Forest Lawn Cemetery. Theodore Roosevelt was sworn in at the Wilcox Mansion on Delaware Avenue after President William McKinley's assassination at the city's Pan-American Exposition in 1901.

Other former Buffalo residents include William G. Fargo of the Wells Fargo stagecoach line, as well as the inventors of the windshield wiper, the pacemaker and the electric chair. Ellsworth Statler opened the

first Hotel Statler on Delaware Avenue in 1908 with the slogan "A room with a bath for a dollar and a half."

Samuel Clemens, a resident in the 1870s, was editor of the *Buffalo Express*. Author Taylor Caldwell also called Buffalo home. Such musical classics as "When Irish Eyes Are Smiling," "My Wild Irish Rose" and "Over the Rainbow" were penned by Buffalo composers. Edwin P. (Ned) Christy launched the Christy Minstrels show in Buffalo.

Buffalo can aptly be called a college town; its 18 higher educational facilities range in curriculum from liberal arts to business to vocational training. The State University of New York at Buffalo is the largest university in the state; D'Youville College on Porter Avenue is noted for its nursing program.

The Albright-Knox Art Gallery *(see attraction listing p. 69)*, Kleinhans Music Hall and other cultural centers balance industrial practicality with aesthetic appreciation. At the stadiums and arenas cheering the local teams is almost a prerequisite for citizenship in a town known for its high attendance at sporting events.

Approaches

By Car

From Rochester and other points east I-90 approaches Buffalo's northeast corner. It then joins I-190 and travels south, paralleling the city's eastern boundary before continuing west along the Lake Erie shoreline. The segment of I-290 that connects I-90 from the east and I-290 going north to Niagara Falls is called the Youngmann Expressway.

I-190 approaches the city from the northwest, passing through the west side before cutting across town and joining I-90 to the east. Toll barriers along I-190 are inbound only and are found between the Scajaquada Expressway (SR 198) and the Peace Bridge and between I-90 and Ogden Street. Travelers using I-90 from the west can either go northwest through the city via I-190 or northeast via I-90. Both I-90 and I-190 are part of the New York State Thruway.

Entering the area from the south are US 219 (Southern Expressway) from Springville and SR 400 (Aurora Expressway) from South Wales. Both join I-90 headed northeast. SR 5 from Dunkirk joins I-190 just below Seneca Street; SR 5 then becomes Main Street, cutting northeast. US 62 (Bailey Avenue), going north and south, bisects Buffalo.

The Kensington Expressway (SR 33) comes in from the east; the Scajaquada Expressway (SR 198) enters from the west off I-190. At the intersection of these two expressways, the Scajaquada ends; the Kensington Expressway continues south to downtown and east to Buffalo-Niagara Falls International Airport on Genesee Street.

(continued on page 68)

The Informed Traveler

City Population: 310,500

Elevation: 680 ft.

Sales Tax: The sales tax in Buffalo is 8 percent. There also is a 7 percent tax levied on lodgings and a 5 percent tax on rental cars.

WHOM TO CALL

Emergency: 911

Police (non-emergency): (716) 853-2222

Time: (716) 844-1717

Weather: (716) 844-4444

Hospitals: Buffalo General, (716) 859-5600; Mercy Hospital, (716) 826-7000; Millard Fillmore Health System, (716) 887-4600; Sisters of Charity Hospital, (716) 862-1000.

WHERE TO LOOK

Newspapers

The *Buffalo News* is the local daily newspaper. Also available are more than 40 weekly and special-interest publications.

Radio and TV

Buffalo radio station WEBR (970 AM) is an all-news/weather station; WBFO (88.7 FM) is a member of National Public Radio. The major TV channels are 2 (NBC), 4 (CBS), 7 (ABC), 17 (PBS) and 29 (FOX).

Visitor Information

Information is available from the Greater Buffalo Convention and Visitors Bureau, 617 Main St., Buffalo, NY 14203; phone (716) 852-2356 or (800) 283-3256. For parks information phone (716) 851-5806.

TRANSPORTATION

Air Travel

Airport Taxi Service provides limousine transportation to the airport from major hotels and the Ellicott Street Bus Terminal daily 6 a.m.-11 p.m.; phone (716) 633-8294.

The Niagara Shuttle runs to major hotels in Niagara Falls daily; phone (800) 551-9369.

Rental Cars

Hertz, (716) 632-4772 or (800) 654-3080, offers discounts to AAA members. For listings of other agencies check the telephone directory.

Rail Service

Amtrak has two connecting stations: one at Exchange Street near the junction of Main and Seneca streets and another on Dick Road, in the Cheektowaga area.

Buses

Greyhound Lines Inc. operates out of the Ellicott Street Bus Terminal downtown; phone (800) 231-2222. For Empire Trailways information phone (800) 295-5555.

Taxis

Cab companies include Airport Taxi Service, (716) 633-8294; Broadway, (716) 896-4600; and City Service, (716) 852-4000. The rate is $1.80 per mile. For a complete list of taxi services check the telephone directory.

Public Transport

The major Metro bus routes operate daily 5 a.m. to midnight. Service varies by route, but buses generally run every 20 minutes on weekdays. The base fare is $1.25; exact fare is required. Zone charges apply in the suburbs; transfers 25c. Tokens can be purchased at Metro offices and local banks.

A light rail rapid transit system runs from Memorial Auditorium at the base of Main Street through Buffalo Place and the theater district, ending at the State University of New York at Buffalo campus. Rail fares are the same as bus fares, with free transfers available between the two systems. Route maps are available at the Transportation Center at 181 Ellicott St.; phone (716) 855-7211.

Destination Buffalo

*T*he "Queen City" has something for everyone. Travel back in time to the days of the dinosaurs at the Buffalo Museum of Science or watch history come alive at the Naval and Military Park.

*C*heer on football's Bills or watch hockey's Sabres slice the ice. For a taste of Buffalo, sample its spicy chicken wings or visit the Buffalo and Erie County Historical Society where more than 700 Buffalo-made products include Cheerios.

Albright-Knox Art Gallery, Buffalo. Matisse, Monet, Picasso, Renoir and Van Gogh–all can be discovered behind these columns. (See listing page 69)

Buffalo and Erie County Botanical Gardens. Noted landscape architect Frederick Law Olmsted clearly left his mark on these 11.3-acre gardens. (See listing page 69)

North Tonawanda

Grand Island *Amherst* *Williamsville*

Buffalo

Lackawanna

See Vicinity map page 68

Naval and Military Park, Buffalo. Saluting one of the nation's largest inland naval parks, board the USS *Croaker* and see what life was like on a World War II submarine or tour the guided-missile cruiser USS *Little Rock*. (See listing page 69)

Orchard Park *East Aurora*

Eden

*P*laces included in this AAA Destination City:

Amherst	71	Lackawanna	72
East Aurora	71	North Tonawanda	72
Eden	72	Orchard Park	72
Grand Island	72	Williamsville	72

Buffalo Zoological Gardens. Come visit these shaggy critters as well as more than 1,000 other wild and exotic animals. (See listing page 69)

Getting Around

Street System

Buffalo's major streets branch off from its central business district in a radial pattern. Because Lake Erie borders the city's southwest side, most roads begin downtown and branch out to the north and east. Niagara Square is the primary downtown intersection. From the square Delaware Avenue runs north and south; Niagara Street goes diagonally northwest to the Black Rock Canal and then heads north. Genesee Street extends northeast from Niagara Square to the airport.

Main Street, 2 blocks east of Delaware Avenue, runs north and south downtown but branches off to the northeast at Ferry Street. Main Street downtown and to the northeast is SR 5; however, to the south SR 5 is known as Fuhrmann Boulevard and then Hamburg Turnpike as it goes farther south down the Lake Erie shoreline.

Because of the creation of Buffalo Place, a pedestrian mall downtown, Main Street has been permanently closed to traffic from the theater district to the foot of Main Street. To maintain traffic flow, two sets of one-way streets are on either side of the mall. To the east, Elm Street runs north and Oak Street runs south; to the west, Franklin Street runs north and Pearl Street runs south. Buffalo's metro rail line also traverses this area.

Seneca Street and Abbott Road are two main east-west routes connecting downtown and the southeast suburbs. Clinton Street begins 4 blocks east of Niagara Square at Lafayette Square and heads alternately south and east, detouring the two-block section from Michigan Avenue to Pine Street.

The downtown speed limit is 30 mph. Unless otherwise posted, right turns at red lights are permitted after a complete stop; left turns at red lights from a one-way street to another one-way street are permitted after a complete stop. Rush hours, 7-9 a.m. and 4-6 p.m., should be avoided.

Parking

Metered parking is available downtown, but spaces fill quickly. With patience, unmetered

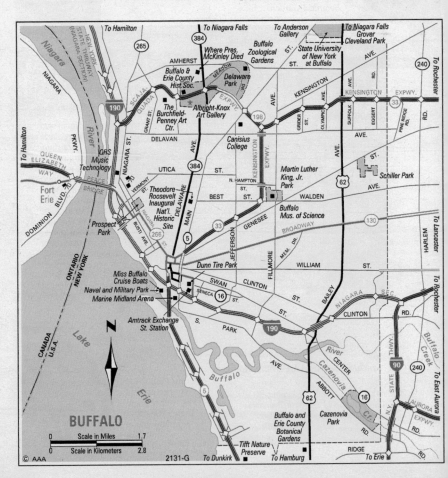

spaces also can be found. Many parking garages are available at $4-$5 per day. Underground parking is offered at Main Place, One M&T Plaza and One Marine Midland Center.

What To See

★ **ALBRIGHT-KNOX ART GALLERY,** just s. of jct. SR 198 on Elmwood Ave., is a Greek Revival building housing paintings and sculptures dating from 3000 B.C. to the present. The contemporary collection of American and European art is especially notable and includes works by Willem de Kooning, Henri Matisse, Pablo Picasso and Jackson Pollock. Food is available.

Allow 2 hours minimum. Tues.-Sat. 11-5, Sun. noon-5; closed Jan. 1, Thanksgiving and Dec. 25. Admission $4, over 62 and students with ID $3, under 12 free, family rate $8. Parking $1.50 for first hour, 75c each additional hour. Phone (716) 882-8700.

ANDERSON GALLERY, SR 33W (Main St. exit), then n. on Englewood Ave. to Martha Jackson Pl., offers changing exhibits of post-World War II art, many with a regional theme. Display media range from paintings and photographs to sculpture. Tues.-Sat. 11:30-5, Sun. noon-5. Free. Phone (716) 834-2579.

BUFFALO AND ERIE COUNTY BOTANICAL GARDENS, US 62 and McKinley Pkwy. at 2655 South Park Ave., displays identified plants in 12 greenhouses. Allow 1 hour minimum. Mon.-Fri. 9-4 (also Wed. 4-6), Sat.-Sun. 9-5. Donations. Phone (716) 696-3555.

BUFFALO MUSEUM OF SCIENCE, 1020 Humboldt Pkwy. at Northampton St. (Best St. exit from SR 33), has exhibits about dinosaurs, insects, space, endangered species and human beings, as well as a children's discovery room. The Kellogg Observatory offers sun shows in the summer.

Allow 2 hours minimum for the museum. Museum open Tues.-Sun. 10-5 (also Fri. 5-10, Sept.-May); closed Jan. 1, July 4, Thanksgiving and Dec. 25. Observatory open Tues.-Fri. 11-1, June-Aug.; Fri. dusk-9:30 p.m., Sept.-May (weather permitting). Admission $5.25; over 61, college students with ID and ages 3-17, $3.25. AE, MC, VI. Phone (716) 896-5200.

THE BURCHFIELD-PENNEY ART CENTER, in Rockwell Hall on Elmwood Ave. on the Buffalo State College campus, has a variety of changing exhibits and presentations. Concerts, lectures, recitals, films and classes are held; an archive also is available. Featured is a collection of watercolor paintings by Charles E. Burchfield. Allow 30 minutes minimum. Tues.-Sat. 10-5, Sun. 1-5. Donations. Phone (716) 878-6011.

DELAWARE PARK, 2 mi. n. on Elmwood Ave., then e. on Iroquois Dr., offers tennis, bicycling and golf.

Buffalo and Erie County Historical Society, 25 Nottingham Ct., is housed in the only remaining building from the 1901 Pan-American Exposition. Exhibits highlight the commercial and industrial development of the Buffalo area. An archive library is available. Allow 1 hour minimum.

Exhibits Tues.-Sat. 10-5, Sun. noon-5. Library Wed.-Fri. 10-5, Sat. noon-5. Closed Jan. 1, Thanksgiving and Dec. 25. Admission $3.50; over 60, $2; ages 7-15, $1.50; students with ID free; family rate (two adults and two children) $7.50. Library $3.50. MC, VI. Phone (716) 873-9644.

Buffalo Zoological Gardens has indoor and outdoor displays of more than 1,000 animals and birds on 23.5 acres, including a greater one-horned rhinoceros. Special exhibits include a World of Wildlife Building, a lion and tiger outdoor habitat, gorilla rain forest exhibit and a children's zoo. Carousel and train rides also are available in season. Food is available.

Allow 1 hour, 30 minutes minimum. Gates open daily 10-5, June 1-Labor Day; daily 10-4, rest of year. Grounds remain open 1 hour later. Admission $7; ages 3-14, $3.50; over 62, $3. Parking $3. DS, MC, VI. Phone (716) 837-3900.

SAVE **NAVAL AND MILITARY PARK,** on Lake Erie at the foot of Pearl and Main sts. at 1 Naval Park Cove, is one of the few inland naval parks in the country. Visitors can board fighting ships, the guided-missile cruiser USS *Little Rock*, the destroyer USS *The Sullivans* and the World War II submarine USS *Croaker*. Displays include aircraft, scale models of ships and airplanes and a videotape about the park's features and history. Daily 10-5, Apr.-Oct.; Sat.-Sun. 10-4, in Nov. Admission $6; over 61 and ages 6-16, $3.50. Phone (716) 847-1773.

THEODORE ROOSEVELT INAUGURAL NATIONAL HISTORIC SITE (Wilcox Mansion), 641 Delaware Ave., is an 1838 Greek Revival structure. Theodore Roosevelt was sworn in as the 26th president in the library. Displays include items relating to President William McKinley's assassination and President Roosevelt's inauguration, a slide presentation and changing art exhibits.

Allow 1 hour minimum. Mon.-Fri. 9-5, Sat.-Sun. noon-5; closed Jan. 1, Memorial Day, July 4, Labor Day, Thanksgiving and Dec. 25. Admission $3; over 61, $2; ages 6-14, $1; family rate $6.50. Phone (716) 884-0095.

TIFFT NATURE PRESERVE is w. on SR 5 to 1200 Fuhrmann Blvd. The park encompasses 264 acres, including nature trails, a wildflower garden and a 75-acre cattail marsh. The visitor center contains mounted specimens of local wildlife and displays detailing the preserve's development. Guided walks are offered Sundays at 2. Picnicking, fishing, cross-country skiing and snowshoeing are permitted.

Park open daily dawn-dusk. Visitor center open Tues.-Sun. 9-5; closed Jan. 1, Thanksgiving and Dec. 24-25. Donations. Phone (716) 825-6397.

What To Do

Sightseeing

Those unfamiliar with Buffalo may wish to begin their sightseeing with an aerial view of the city from the observation deck on the 28th floor of City Hall at Niagara Square downtown; phone (716) 851-4200. The deck is open Mon.-Fri. 9-3; closed holidays.

Many of Buffalo's historic structures have been renovated or restored; Allentown, a historic preservation district just south of North Street between Elmwood Avenue and Main Street, has Victorian buildings, ethnic restaurants, art galleries and boutiques. Information about tours of Allentown is available from the Allentown Association, 235 Allen St., Buffalo, NY 14201; phone (716) 881-1024.

Boat Tours

MISS BUFFALO CRUISE BOATS depart from the area adjacent to the Erie Basin Marina at Marine Dr. and Erie St. The 2-hour narrated tours of Buffalo Harbor travel from Lake Erie down the Niagara River to Squaw Island, returning through the locks of Black Rock Canal. Food is available. Tours depart Tues.-Fri. at 3, Sat.-Sun. at 12:30 and 3, July 1-Labor Day; Sat.-Sun. at 3, day after Labor Day-Sept. 30. Fare $10; ages 5-12, $7. AE, DS, MC, VI. Phone (716) 856-6696.

Bus Tours

Bus tours of Buffalo are offered by AFT Tours Inc., phone (716) 646-4682; Apex Transportation Services, phone (716) 632-4666; Bedore Tours Inc., (716) 285-7550; [SAVE] Gray Line of Buffalo & Niagara Falls, (716) 694-3600, 695-1603 or (800) 695-1603; and Motherland Connextions Inc., (716) 282-1028.

Industrial Tours

QRS MUSIC TECHNOLOGY .5 mi. n. of the Peace Bridge at 1026 Niagara St., offers guided tours of the world's only manufacturer of player piano rolls. The tour's group size is limited to 15 persons and is not recommended for small children. Mon.-Fri. at 10 and 2; closed Jan. 1, Good Friday, Memorial Day, July 4, Labor Day, Thanksgiving and Dec. 24-25 and 31. Fee $2; under 12, $1. Phone (716) 885-4600.

Walking Tours

Guided 30-minute to 2-hour walking tours of Allentown, Main and N. Pearl streets or Delaware Avenue depart from the Wilcox Mansion, 641 Delaware Ave. Parking is available in the rear of the building. A tour of the downtown area departs near the library. Guided tours run April through October; a minimum of six persons is required. Fee $5; ages 5-12, $2.50. Phone (716) 884-0095 for tour schedule; reservations must be made 2 weeks in advance.

Self-guiding tours of the same areas are available year-round; there is a $5 fee for the use of an audio cassette. A refundable $25 deposit for cassette and player is required.

Forest Lawn Cemetery, 1411 Delaware Ave., offers bird-watching and sculpture on its 267 acres. A brochure outlining a self-guiding tour map is available at the cemetery office inside the Delaware Avenue entrance Mon.-Fri. 8:30-4:30, Sat. 8:30-4; phone (716) 885-1600.

For information about other self-guiding tours contact the Greater Buffalo Convention and Visitors Bureau *(see The Informed Traveler box).*

Sports and Recreation

Buffalo has an extensive municipal park system where sports enthusiasts can find ample playing space. More than 100 **baseball** and **softball** diamonds are available, as are 84 **tennis** courts and three **soccer** fields. Sports such as **lawn bowling** and **cricket** also are offered. **Swimming** can be enjoyed at local pools and beaches.

Running tracks are available for walkers, joggers and runners. **Basketball** courts and **football** fields are scattered throughout town; six indoor ice rinks permit year-round **ice skating**.

Skiing is very popular in the region. Nine major areas with chair lifts, T-bars and other facilities are within close driving distance of the city; Kissing Bridge and Holiday Valley are less than an hour away. Other winter sports such as **tobogganing, sledding** and **snowmobiling** are permitted in public parks.

Those who consider spectating a sport in its own right will find plenty of company in Buffalo, where stadiums and arenas are filled with professional fans. Football lovers can see the Buffalo Bills in The Ralph Wilson Stadium; phone (716) 649-0015. The Buffalo Bisons play baseball at Dunn Tire Park; phone (716) 878-8488. Slicing the ice in the Marine Midland Arena every winter is the Buffalo Sabres **hockey** team; phone (716) 855-4100. Buffalo's numerous colleges and universities also offer a wide variety of sporting events.

Four-legged athletes offer their share of excitement to **horse racing** buffs as well. **Harness racing** is held at the Buffalo Raceway in Hamburg; phone (716) 649-1280 for schedule.

Note: Policies concerning admittance of children to pari-mutuel betting facilities vary. Phone for information.

Shopping

The variety of stores offering fashions, fads and foods for every taste and budget make shopping in Buffalo an adventure. The downtown shopping area extends from Main and Church streets north to Main and Chippewa streets, and west along Elmwood and Delaware avenues. Buffalo Place offers a wide variety of shops. Main Place Mall stretches along Main Street from Swan to Goodell streets. Boutiques line Delaware Avenue as well.

The Bon-Ton and Kaufmann's are two major department stores. Antique and specialty gift shops are found in the Allentown area, Buffalo's version of Greenwich Village. Bargain hunters will appreciate the Ammex Tax & Duty Free Shop at The Peace Bridge.

Broadway Market at Broadway and Fillmore streets is an indoor marketplace in an Old World setting offering fresh produce, baked goods, crafts and specialty items. The Hertel, North Main Street and Riverside commercial areas also offer a wide range of shops.

Walden Galleria, at I-90 and Walden Avenue, offers more than 200 stores including The Bon-Ton, JCPenney, Kaufmann's, Lord & Taylor and Sears.

Theater and Concerts

Shea's Performing Arts Center, an ornate 1926 theater at 646 Main St., presents performances year-round. For information about schedules and tickets phone (716) 847-0850.

Across the street at 681 Main St. is the Pfeifer Theatre. Professional performances are presented September through May; phone (716) 847-6461. The Theatre of Youth (TOY) Company performs children's shows in its Franklin Street Theatre; phone (716) 856-4410.

The rejuvenated theater district also includes The New Phoenix Theatre at 95 Johnson Pkwy., phone (716) 855-2225; Studio Arena Theater at 710 Main St., phone (716) 856-5650; and Ujima Theatre at 545 Elmwood Ave., phone (716)

883-0380. Plays and musicals are presented September through early June.

The Alleyway Theatre, at One Curtain Up Alley, is a professional theater company dedicated to performing new plays in off-Broadway style; phone (716) 852-2600. The Irish Classical Theatre Co. performs international classics and plays from Irish literature at 625 Main St.; phone (716) 853-4282. Just outside of downtown at 320 Porter Ave. is the Kavinoky Theatre-D'Youville College; phone (716) 881-7668.

Special Events

In March the city unfurls one of the country's largest St. Patrick's Day parades. May is enlivened by the Hellenic Festival, offering cultural displays, folk dancing and Greek food. During the second weekend in June the Allentown Art Festival in the historic Allentown district displays the works of local artisans.

July 1-4, Buffalo and Fort Erie, Ontario, celebrate brotherhood during the Friendship Festival. Festivities include an air show, arts and crafts exhibits, a cultural parade, equestrian jumping, concerts and fireworks. Buffalo's best restaurants prepare epicurean delights from chicken wings to cheesecakes for the second weekend of July's Taste of Buffalo festival.

At the Erie County Fairgrounds, 12 miles south off I-90 exit 56 in Hamburg, one of the nation's oldest and largest county fairs takes place in mid-August. The second week in August brings the Lake Erie Can Am Challenge Walleye Tournament, in which anglers from Canada and the United States vie to catch the largest total weight of walleye perch. Buffalo's Winterfest, celebrated from December to January, is highlighted by ice skating, snow sculpture competitions and other activities.

The Buffalo Vicinity

AMHERST (E-3)
pop. 111,700, elev. 260'

Amherst borders Buffalo-Niagara Falls International Airport, which is the focus of major air service to the Buffalo-Niagara Falls area. In the center of town is one of two campuses belonging to the State University of New York at Buffalo.

Amherst Chamber of Commerce: 325 Essjay Rd., Suite 200, Amherst, NY 14221; phone (716) 632-6905.

AMHERST MUSEUM is reached from I-990 to SR 263, then n. on New Rd. to 3755 Tonawanda Creek Rd. Featured are 12 restored 19th-century buildings. Indoor exhibits include displays featuring local history, costumes, a children's discovery room and hands-on exhibits.

Allow 2 hours minimum. Museum open Tues.-Fri. 9:30-4:30, Sat.-Sun. 12:30-4:30, Apr.-Oct.; Tues.-Fri. 9:30-4:30, rest of year. Buildings open May 15-Oct. 15. Closed holidays. Admission $4; ages 5-12, $1.50; family rate $10. DS, MC, VI. Phone (716) 689-1440.

EAST AURORA (E-4) pop. 6,600

East Aurora is home to Roycroft Campus, an art community founded in 1895 by Elbert Hubbard, a former salesman and marketing genius turned artist, writer, publisher and craftsman. Hubbard, a leader in the American Arts and Crafts movement, went on to design a simple, straight-line style of furniture that remains popular.

Greater East Aurora Chamber of Commerce: 431 Main St., East Aurora, NY 14052; phone (716) 652-8444.

Self-guiding tours: A brochure outlining the 14 historic buildings, including the Roycroft Inn, on Roycroft Campus is available at the chamber.

TOY TOWN MUSEUM, 1.1 mi. e. of SR 16/78 to 636 Girard Ave., is dedicated to preserving the heritage of toys and is home to items from the early 1900s to the present. Toy Works, designed for children over 7, is the museum's interactive learning lab. Allow 30 minutes minimum. Mon.-Sat. 10-4. Free. Phone (716) 687-5151.

EDEN (E-3) pop. 3,100, elev. 797'

THE ORIGINAL AMERICAN KAZOO CO., 8703 S. Main St., is a factory that produces metal kazoos. The factory floor is closed to visitors, but there is a special area for viewing the production process. Exhibits depict the musical toy's West African origins as well as modern production methods. Guided tours are available by reservation. Allow 30 minutes minimum. Mon.-Sat. 10-5, Sun. noon-5; closed holidays. Free. Phone (716) 992-3960.

GRAND ISLAND (E-2) pop. 17,600

MARTIN'S FANTASY ISLAND, off I-190 exit 19N, is a theme park with rides, shows and attractions. A water park, miniature golf course and canoes are available. Picnicking is permitted. Allow 4 hours minimum. Tues.-Sun. 11:30-8:30, mid-June through Labor Day; Sat.-Sun. 11:30-8:30, mid-May to mid-June. Admission $15.95; under 48 inches tall $11.95; over age 65, $9.95; under age 2 free. AE, DS, MC, VI. Phone (716) 773-7591.

LACKAWANNA (E-3)
pop. 20,600, elev. 592'

Just south of Buffalo's city limits, Lackawanna is the site of the country's second oldest basilica, Our Lady of Victory Basilica and National Shrine. The Italian Renaissance church, built in 1921, contains ornate altars, statues and a grotto shrine. For further information contact the chamber of commerce.

Lackawanna Area Chamber of Commerce: 638 Ridge Rd., Lackawanna, NY 14218; phone (716) 823-8841.

NORTH TONAWANDA (E-3)
pop. 35,000

The Erie Canal spurred the development of North Tonawanda and its neighbor Tonawanda with a flourishing lumber industry. Today, the canal provides numerous recreational opportunities, including walking and biking along the Canalway Trail.

Chamber of Commerce of the Tonawandas: 15 Webster St., North Tonawanda, NY 14120; phone (716) 692-5120.

[SAVE] **THE HERSCHELL CARROUSEL FACTORY MUSEUM,** 180 Thompson St., preserves one of several local factories that produced carousels and band organs. Exhibits detail the process of hand-carving the various carousel animals and other objects. Of special note is a restored and working 1916 carousel. A children's carousel also is available. Self-guiding tours are available. Daily 11-5, July-Aug.; Wed.-Sun. 1-5, Apr.-June and Sept.-Dec. Admission $4; over 59, $3; ages 2-12, $1.50. Phone (716) 693-1885.

ORCHARD PARK (E-3)
pop. 3,300, elev. 886'

Founded by Quakers in the early 1800s, Orchard Park now is home to the NFL's Buffalo Bills who play in Ralph Wilson Stadium. An outdoor lovers dream, the area offers 1,500-acre Chestnut Ridge Park, complete with hiking trails and picnicking areas. Winter brings snow to the hills, perfect for tobogganing and sledding.

Orchard Park Chamber of Commerce: 4211 N. Buffalo Rd., Suite 14, Orchard Park, NY 14127; phone (716) 662-3366.

PEDALING HISTORY BICYCLE MUSEUM, 3943 N. Buffalo Rd., with more than 300 bicycles including antiques, originals and reproductions, is said to be the country's largest museum of its kind. Displays include a collection of children's wheeled vehicles, dating from the 1890s; boneshakers, built during the 1860s and so named because of the jarring riders experienced; wooden highwheels; an 1881 Marine bicycle; and folding paratrooper bicycles, used during World War II. Changing exhibits and programs also are featured.

Allow 1 hour minimum. Mon.-Sat. 11-5, Sun. 1:30-5, Apr. 2-Jan. 14; Mon. and Fri.-Sat. 11-5, Sun. 1:30-5, rest of year. Closed Jan. 1, Thanksgiving and Dec. 25. Admission $4.50; over 61, $4; ages 7-15, $2.50; family rate $12.50. MC, VI. Phone (716) 662-3853.

WILLIAMSVILLE (E-3) pop. 5,600

In 1804, Jonas Williams built a mill along Ellicott Creek and expanded his businesses which included several grist mills, a sawmill, a tannery, a distillery, and dams and raceways to power his mills. He owned and operated so much of the area that it became know as Williams Mills, and later Williamsville. Present-day Williamsville Water Mills continues the operation began in 1811.

Surrounded on all sides by the larger town of Amherst, the Village of Williamsville maintains geographic and political independence.

Amherst Chamber of Commerce: 325 Essjay Rd., Suite 200, Williamsville, NY 14221; phone (716) 632-6905.

WILLIAMSVILLE WATER MILLS, 56 Spring St., is a restored 1811 water-powered mill. The site offers historical exhibits, and cider is made early September through March 31. Mon.-Sat. 10-5:30, Sun.11-4:30. Free. Phone (716) 632-1162.

**The previous listings were for the Buffalo Vicinity.
This page resumes the alphabetical listings of cities in New York.**

CANAJOHARIE (E-9)
pop. 2,300, elev. 317'

In an area settled by Dutch and Germans in the early 1700s, Canajoharie gets its name from an American Indian expression meaning "the washed pot." The pot is a large pothole in the nearby Canajoharie Creek Gorge. A 45-foot waterfall can be seen at the gorge from Wintergreen Park.

The surrounding area is part of the historic Mohawk Valley Heritage Corridor, home of the Iroquois Confederacy. *See Exploring New York p. 48.* Phone (518) 673-1045 for information.

CANAJOHARIE LIBRARY AND ART GALLERY, s.w. off New York Thruway exit 29 at Church St. and Erie Blvd., contains watercolors and oils by such American painters as John Singleton Copley, Winslow Homer, George Inness, Albert Pinkham Ryder, John Singer Sargent and Gilbert Stuart. Other displays feature local history; industry, including the Beech-Nut and Life Savers companies; and genealogy. Guided tours are available by appointment.

Allow 30 minutes minimum. Mon.-Wed. and Fri. 10-4:45, Thurs. 10-8:30, Sat. 10-1:30; closed holidays. Free. Phone (518) 673-2314.

CANANDAIGUA (E-5)
pop. 10,700, elev. 685'

Canandaigua stands on the shore of the lake that shares its name. The town is on the site of the Seneca Indian village *Kan-an-dar-gue*, destroyed by Gen. John Sullivan in 1779. Considered to be one of the most beautiful of the Finger Lakes, Canandaigua Lake is 17 miles long and averages about a mile wide. It harbors bass, pickerel, pike and trout. Around the lake are thousands of acres of vineyards. *Also see Finger Lakes p. 84.*

Thoroughbred horse racing takes place Friday through Tuesday, early April through early December, at Finger Lakes Race Track, 8 miles north on SR 96 just east of its junction with SR 332; for information phone (716) 924-3232.

Note: Policies concerning admittance of children to pari-mutuel betting facilities vary. Phone for information.

Canandaigua Chamber of Commerce: 113 S. Main St., Canandaigua, NY 14424; phone (716) 394-4400.

CAPTAIN GRAY'S BOAT TOURS, 770 S. Main St., offers 1-, 2- and 3-hour narrated cruises around Lake Canandaigua. One-hour cruises depart daily at 11, 1, 3, 5 and 7, July-Oct. Cruises also are available Sat.-Sun., May-June. Fare $7.50; under 13, $4. Two-hour cruise $12; under 13, $7. Three-hour cruise $17.50; under 13, $11. Phone (716) 394-5270.

SAVE **GRANGER HOMESTEAD AND CARRIAGE MUSEUM** is at 295 N. Main St. This restored 1816 Federal-style homestead was built by Gideon Granger, U.S. postmaster general under Presidents Thomas Jefferson and James Madison. The Carriage Museum has 44 horse-drawn vehicles made or used in the region 1810-1920.

Guided tours of the house and museum are given on the hour Tues.-Sun. 1-4, June-Aug.; Tues.-Fri. 1-4, mid-May through May 31 and Sept. 1 to mid-Oct. Admission $4; over 61, $3; ages 7-16, $1. Phone (716) 394-1472.

ONTARIO COUNTY HISTORICAL SOCIETY MUSEUM, 55 N. Main St., features Civil War displays, changing exhibits about local history, archives and a genealogical library. Allow 1 hour minimum. Tues.-Sat. 10-4:30 (also Wed. 4:30-9); closed holidays. Museum admission $2; ages 12-17, 50c. Library $5. Phone (716) 394-4975.

SONNENBERG GARDENS, n. off SR 21 (Gibson St.) at 151 Charlotte St., near New York State Thruway (US 90) exits 43 and 44, is a 50-acre estate with gardens and an 1887 Victorian mansion with period furnishings. Fountains, streams, ponds and statues accent rose, Italian, Colonial, Japanese, rock and other themed gardens. A greenhouse complex includes a palm house, an orchid house and a desert house. Food is available.

Allow 1 hour minimum. Gardens open daily 9:30-5:30, mid-May to mid-Oct. Guided tours are given daily at 10 and 2. Admission $7.50; over 64, $6.50; ages 6-16, $3. MC, VI. Phone (716) 394-4922.

CANASTOTA (D-7)
pop. 4,700, elev. 436'

CANASTOTA CANAL TOWN MUSEUM, 122 Canal St., is in an 1874 house. Displayed are antiques, Erie Canal historical items and local memorabilia including photographs, maps, dolls, a water pump at an old-fashioned kitchen sink and examples of the handmade crystal for which Canastota was well-known in the early 1900s. Allow 30 minutes minimum. Mon.-Fri. 10-4, Sat. 10-1, June-Aug.; Tues.-Fri. 11-3, Apr.-May and Sept.-Oct. Also open by appointment. Closed holidays. Donations. Phone (315) 697-3451.

INTERNATIONAL BOXING HALL OF FAME, off New York State Thruway (I-90) exit 34 at 1 Hall of Fame Dr., offers displays of such boxing memorabilia as robes, gloves, videotapes and ticket stubs. Allow 30 minutes minimum. Mon.-Sat. 9-5, Sun. 9-4; closed Easter, Thanksgiving and Dec. 25. Admission $4; over 65 and ages 7-15, $3. MC, VI. Phone (315) 697-7095.

CANTON (B-8) pop. 6,400, elev. 375'

Canton was settled by Vermonters in the early 1800s. The names for this town and nine others in the county were chosen from the world atlas in the hope that familiar names would help the land sell more easily. In 1861 Frederic Remington, sculptor and painter of the American West, was born in Canton, where his father was editor of the newspaper. Canton is home to St. Lawrence University, a liberal arts institution of about 2,000 students which was founded in 1856.

Canton Chamber of Commerce: P.O. Box 369, Canton, NY 13617; phone (315) 386-8255.

ST. LAWRENCE COUNTY MUSEUM, 3 E. Main St., was the home of U.S. senator and New York governor Silas Wright. The exterior and first-floor interior have been restored to the 1830-50 period. Permanent and changing exhibits relate to St. Lawrence County history; a research library is available. Allow 1 hour minimum. Museum and library open Tues.-Sat. noon-4 (also Fri. 4-8); closed holidays. Museum free; fee charged for library. Phone (315) 386-8133.

CAPE VINCENT (C-7)
pop. 700, elev. 253'

CAPE VINCENT HISTORICAL MUSEUM, downtown adjacent to Horns Ferry Dock on lower James St., features displays depicting area history. A genealogy room is available by appointment. Allow 30 minutes minimum. Daily 10-4, July-Aug. Donations. Phone (315) 654-4400.

CASTILE (E-4)
pop. 1,100, elev. 1,397'

★ **LETTCHWORTH STATE PARK,** 2 mi. n. on SR 19A to Denton's Corners, then 2 mi. e., is noted for the three waterfalls of the Genesee River Gorge. Middle Falls, a 107-foot cascade, is lighted nightly until 11. The walls of the 17-mile gorge reach heights up to 600 feet, offering views of the river and surrounding area. Scenic roads and trails pass through the park. Food is available.

Allow 4 hours minimum. Daily 6 a.m.-11 p.m. Admission $5 per private vehicle, mid-May through Oct. 31; free rest of year. Phone (716) 493-3600. *See Recreation Chart.*

William Pryor Letchworth Pioneer and Indian Museum, in Letchworth State Park, has a varied display of artifacts. Allow 3 hours minimum. Daily 10-5, mid-May to mid-Oct. Free. Phone (716) 493-2760.

CATSKILL (F-10)
pop. 4,700, elev. 67'

Near Catskill is the scene of Rip Van Winkle's legendary nap. The area affords a number of scenic drives, such as the section of SR 23 northwest over East Windham Mountain and SR 23B over Hunter Mountain.

Greene County Promotional Department: P.O. Box 527, Catskill, NY 12414; phone (518) 943-3223.

CATSKILL FOREST PRESERVE, comprising 287,989 acres in the Catskill Mountains, is particularly beautiful in June when the laurel blooms and in October when the leaves turn. Slide Mountain, with a height of 4,180 feet, is the highest point in the preserve. The preserve also is the location of Beaver Kill, Neversink and Willowemoc, three of the best fishing streams in the state. For more information contact the Department of Environmental Conservation, 21 S. Putt Corners Rd., New Platz, NY 12561. Daily 24 hours. Free. Phone (914) 256-3000. *See Recreation Chart.*

★ **CATSKILL GAME FARM** is off I-87 exit 21, w. 6.5 mi. on SR 23, then 5.5 mi. s. on SR 32. This farm has animals and birds from around the world, including rare or threatened species. Animal shows are presented daily, Memorial Day weekend-Labor Day. Amusement rides, recreation facilities and a petting zoo are available. Food is available. Allow 2 hours minimum. Mon.-Fri. 9-5, Sat.-Sun. 9-6, May-Oct. Admission $13.95; ages 4-11, $9.95. MC, VI. Phone (518) 678-9595.

CLYDE PEELING'S REPTILAND, 6.5 mi. w. of I-87 exit 21 on SR 23, then 3.5 mi. s. on SR 32, following signs, displays reptiles including snakes, alligators and crocodiles. A 1-hour educational show is offered, and an animal trainer answers questions and brings out various animals for visitors to touch. Allow 1 hour, 30 minutes minimum. Daily 10-6, Memorial Day-Labor Day. Shows are offered at 10:30, noon, 1:30, 3 and 4:30. Admission $6; ages 4-11, $4. Phone (518) 678-3557.

CAZENOVIA (E-7)
pop. 3,000, elev. 1,205'

Cazenovia embraces the end of Cazenovia Lake, originally called *Ho-wah-ge-neh* (lake where the yellow perch swim) by American Indians. In 1793 John Lincklaen, a land agent for the Holland Land Co., settled in this area and renamed the site for Theophile Cazenove, the general agent for the company. The village first prospered as the economic crossroads of the region.

The invention of the modern game of football is credited to Cazenovia native Gerrit Smith Miller, who adapted it from a form of rugby in 1860-62.

Greater Cazenovia Area Chamber of Commerce: 51 ½ Albany St., P.O. Box 66, Cazenovia, NY 13035; phone (315) 655-9243 or (888) 218-6305.

LORENZO STATE HISTORIC SITE is off SR 13, .2 mi. s. of US 20 at 17 Rippleton Rd. The 1807 mansion, overlooking Cazenovia Lake, contains original furnishings and a formal garden and houses a carriage collection. Allow 1 hour minimum. Open Wed.-Sun. 10-4:30. Guided tours are available mid-May through Oct. 31, otherwise by appointment. Admission $3; senior citizens $2; under 12, $1. Phone (315) 655-3200.

CELORON (G-2) pop. 1,200

SAVE *SUMMER WIND* RIVER AND LAKE CRUISES depart from the Paradise Yacht Club in Lucille Ball Memorial Park 1 mi. n. of SR 394. Two-hour sightseeing cruises on Chautauqua Lake are given. Food cruises also are offered. Sightseeing cruises depart daily beginning at 12:30, May-Oct. Fare $11.95; ages 3-12, $8.95. Reservations are recommended. MC, VI. Phone (716) 763-7447.

CENTERPORT (H-3)
pop. 5,300, elev. 50'

★**VANDERBILT MANSION, MARINE MUSEUM, PLANETARIUM AND PARK** is 1.5 mi. n. of SR 25A on Little Neck Rd. Overlooking Northport Harbor, this Spanish Revival-style mansion contains period pieces, antiques and original furnishings. The mansion and museum also contain marine and wildlife specimens. Guided tours are available.

Tues.-Fri. 10-5, Memorial Day-Labor Day; Tues.-Fri. noon-5, rest of year. Closed Jan. 1, Thanksgiving and Dec. 25. Admission $8; senior citizens and students with ID $6; under 12, $4. Mansion tour $3. Phone (631) 854-5555.

Planetarium, on Little Neck Rd., contains astronomy and science exhibits, telescopes, an observatory and a sky theater with a 60-foot-diameter dome. The Goto projector creates special effects with multiple projections of stars, moon, planets, twilights and dawns. Laser shows also are featured. Children's programs are available. Sky shows Sat. at 11, 1, 2:30, 4 and 8, Sun. at 1, 2:30 and 4. Admission $3 (in addition to park admission). Phone (631) 854-5544,, or 854-5533 for laser show information.

CHATEAUGAY (A-10)
pop. 800, elev. 1,010'

HIGH FALLS PARK, 1 mi. w. on SR 11 following signs, features a 120-foot waterfall, which is reached by nature trails through a wooded area. Signs identify trees and plants; picnic facilities adjoin a playground. Daily 9-9, May 15-Sept. 30; 3-8, Oct. 1-15. Admission $2; over 64, students

with ID and ages 6-11, $1. Phone (518) 497-3156.

CHAUTAUQUA (F-2)
pop. 4,600, elev. 1,427'

A summer arts and education center bordering Chautauqua Lake, Chautauqua Institution is a secluded community whose population reaches as high as 7,500 during the summer. Victorian cottages line narrow wooded streets that slope down to the water; boating, fishing and swimming are among the activities available on the lake.

★**CHAUTAUQUA INSTITUTION** is on SR 394. Founded in 1874 as an educational center for Sunday-school teachers, the institution became known for its concept of presenting lectures and entertainment to large groups. Chautauqua Institution offers activities for all ages in the arts, education, religion and recreation, including symphony, opera, theater and dance. For further information contact Chautauqua Institution, Box 28, Chautauqua, NY 14722.

Lectures and popular entertainment are presented in the amphitheater June 24-Aug. 27. Daily gate ticket prices range between $11 and $36. AE, MC, VI. Phone (800) 836-2787.

CHAZY (A-11) pop. 3,900, elev. 151'

Chazy was founded in 1763 by Jean Fromboise. During the Revolution the British forces

Combination Tickets

Individual admission and combination tickets are available for The Farmers' Museum, Fenimore Art Museum and the National Baseball Hall of Fame and Museum *(see attraction listings).*

Combination admission for all attractions $22; ages 7-12, $9.50. National Baseball Hall of Fame and Museum and either The Farmers' Museum or Fenimore Art Museum $15; ages 7-12, $6.50. Fenimore Art Museum and The Farmers' Museum $14.50; ages 7-12, $6.50. Phone (607) 547-1400.

DID YOU KNOW

New York's motto "The Empire State" is derived from George Washington's comment during a 1784 visit that the state was the "Seat of Empire."

---

of Gen. John Burgoyne overran the area, and Fromboise was forced to flee. After the war Fromboise returned to Chazy, where he planted the region's first apple orchard. The McIntosh orchards in Chazy are some of the larger in the world.

Another notable area resident was William H. Miner, an 1800s railroad industrialist and philanthropist. One of his gifts to the city is the Miner Institute, an agricultural and environmental science center that offers self-guiding tours of its facilities.

★ **THE ALICE T. MINER MUSEUM** is reached via I-87 exit 41, 1 mi. e. on US 191, then .5 mi. s. on US 9. The Colonial Revival gray stone house museum contains collections of arts primarily from the 18th and 19th centuries. Included are prints, paintings, porcelain, glass, carpets, furniture and textiles. Gardens are on the grounds. Allow 1 hour, 30 minutes minimum. Tues.-Sat. 10-4, Feb. 1-Dec. 22. Tours are given at 10, 11:30, 1 and 2:30 and by appointment. Tour $3; over 61, $2; students $1; under 5 free. Phone (518) 846-7336.

CHERRY VALLEY (E-9)
pop. 600, elev. 1,326'

Settled in 1740, Cherry Valley was an important stagecoach stop on the Cherry Valley Turnpike, now US 20. A large stone monument in the village cemetery commemorates the victims of the Massacre of 1778, when 700 American Indians and Tories killed or captured most of the residents.

CHERRY VALLEY MUSEUM, 49 Main St., exhibits household articles, Civil War memorabilia, books and documents, pumpers, clothing and farm implements. Allow 1 hour minimum. Daily 10-5, Memorial Day weekend-Oct. 15; by appointment rest of year. Admission $2; over 59, $1.50; under 11 free. Phone (607) 264-3303 or 264-3060.

CHILDS (D-4)

COBBLESTONE SOCIETY MUSEUM is at jct. SRs 104 and 98 at 14393 Ridge Rd. This collection of seven historic buildings includes three cobblestone structures: an 1834 church, an 1840 parsonage once owned by Horace Greeley and a one-room schoolhouse built in 1849. Four frame buildings house a blacksmith shop, a harness shop and a print shop as well as Farmers Hall, which displays 19th- and 20th-century farming tools and implements. Guided tours are available.

Allow 1 hour, 30 minutes minimum. Tues.-Sat. 11-5, Sun. 1-5, June 23-Labor Day; Sun. 1-5, day after Labor Day-Oct. 31. Admission $3.50; over 54, $3; ages 5-17, $2. Phone (716) 589-9013.

CLAYTON (B-7) pop. 2,200, elev. 276'

The Thousand Islands extend more than 10 miles above and below the village of Clayton on the St. Lawrence River. The Thousand IslandsCraft School offers workshops in folk arts and crafts.

Clayton Area Chamber of Commerce: 510 Riverside Dr., Clayton, NY 13624; phone (315) 86-3771 or (800) 252-9806.

ANTIQUE BOAT MUSEUM is 6 mi. s.w. of 1000 Islands Bridge (I-81) on SR 12N at 750 Mary St. This collection of freshwater wooden boats includes American Indian dugout and birch bark canoes, St. Lawrence skiffs, early 20th-century speedboats, launches and pleasure craft. Featured are the *Dixie II*, the *Miss Canada III* and other Gold Cup boats and the personal boats of Presidents Ulysses S. Grant and James Garfield.

Allow 1 hour, 30 minutes minimum. Daily 9-5, mid-May to mid-Oct. Admission $6; over 64, $5; ages 6-17, $2. MC, VI. Phone (315) 686-4104.

THE THOUSAND ISLANDS MUSEUM is at 403 Riverside Dr. in the historic Town Hall/Opera House. The museum has artifacts from the Golden Age along the St. Lawrence River set in a replica village square. Among the displays are record muskies and award-winning decoys. Daily 10-4, mid-May to mid-Oct. Admission $2, students $1, under 6 free. Phone (315) 686-5794.

UNCLE SAM BOAT TOURS depart from the Riverside Dr. dock. Three-hour narrated Seaway Island tours aboard double- and triple-deck boats are offered. Cruises include an optional stop at Boldt Castle *(see Alexandria Bay p. 57)*. Tours depart daily at 9:30, 12:30 and 3:30, July-Aug. Fare are $14.75; ages 4-12, $7.75. Fare does not include admission to Boldt Castle. DS, MC, VI. Phone (315) 686-3511 or (800) 253-9229 for departure times. *See ad p. 58.*

COLD SPRING HARBOR (H-3)
pop. 4,800, elev. 100′

COLD SPRING HARBOR WHALING MUSEUM, on Main St. (SR 25A), offers self-guiding tours and audio cassette guides which tell the story of the whaling industry and its impact on the local area as well as the significance of whaling in general. Displays include a fully equipped whaleboat, whaling implements, marine paintings, ships models and a diorama of Cold Spring Harbor in 1850. Changing exhibits and a family activity room also are offered. Daily 11-5, Memorial Day-Labor Day; Tues.-Sun. 11-5, rest of year. Admission $2; over 64 and ages 6-12, $1.50. Phone (516) 367-3418.

CONSTABLEVILLE (D-8) pop. 300

CONSTABLE HALL, .5 mi. e. of SR 26, is an 1819 Georgian mansion. The house contains original furnishings, artifacts and a library. The grounds include a garden. Allow 1 hour minimum. Guided tours Tues.-Sat. and Mon. holidays 10-4, Sun. 1-4, June 1-Oct. 15. Last tour begins 30 minutes before closing. Admission $3; ages 6-13, $1.50. Phone (315) 397-2323.

COOPERSTOWN (F-8)
pop. 2,200, elev. 1,270′

Cooperstown was founded in 1786 by Judge William Cooper, father of James Fenimore Cooper, who wrote "The Last of the Mohicans" and other tales. Nine-mile-long Otsego Lake, set among hills and forests, is the "Glimmerglass" of Cooper's stories. The original appearances of many of the town's picturesque buildings and houses have been carefully maintained.

Another renowned Cooperstown resident was Gen. Abner Doubleday, who, by official decree of the National Baseball Commission in 1908, was credited with founding the game of baseball in 1839 while a student at a military academy. However, more recent research indicates that credit also is due to the man who devised the playing field and many of the rules, New York City resident Alexander Joy Cartwright.

Cooperstown Chamber of Commerce: 31 Chestnut St., Cooperstown, NY 13326; phone (607) 547-9983.

★ THE FARMERS' MUSEUM, 1 mi. n. on SR 80 on Lake Rd., is a living-history museum of 19th-century rural life. Craftspersons demonstrate rural trades and skills in the restored buildings of

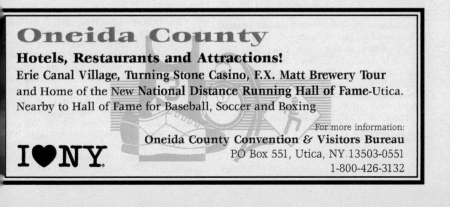

an 1845 village which includes a general store, blacksmith shop and a tavern. The working farmstead with animals, exhibits in the main barn and the hands-on activities are of particular interest. Food is available.

Allow 2 hours minimum. Daily 10-5, June-Sept.; Tues.-Sun. 10-4, Apr.-May and Oct.-Nov. Closed Thanksgiving. Admission $9; ages 7-12, $4. A combination ticket with the Fenimore Art Museum and National Baseball Hall of Fame and Museum is available. AE, DS, MC, VI. Phone (607) 547-1450, or 547-1500 for recorded information. *See color ad p. 241.*

★ FENIMORE ART MUSEUM is 1 mi. n. on SR 80. This museum features fine collections of American art in a neo-Georgian structure with terraced gardens overlooking Otsego Lake. James Fenimore Cooper memorabilia, historic photographs and changing exhibitions of folk art and fine art are presented. Of particular interest is the Eugene and Clare Thaw Collection of American Indian Art in the American Indian wing. Food is available.

Daily 9-5, June-Sept.; Tues.-Sun. 10-4, Apr.-May and Oct.-Dec. Closed Thanksgiving and Dec. 25. Admission $9; ages 7-12, $4. A combination ticket with The Farmers' Museum and National Baseball Hall of Fame and Museum is available. AE, MC, VI. Phone (607) 547-1450, or 547-1500 for recorded information. *See color ad p. 241.*

SAVE LAKE OTSEGO BOAT TOURS depart from the southern tip of Lake Otsego at the foot of Fair St. Narrated 1-hour tours are conducted aboard a 60-foot 1912 boat. Departures daily at 10, 11, 1, 2, 3, 4 and 6, mid-June through Labor Day; at 1, 2, 3 and 4, late May to mid-June and day after Labor Day-Columbus Day (weather permitting). Fare $9.50; ages 3-12, $5. Departures require a minimum of eight passengers. Phone (607) 547-5295.

★ NATIONAL BASEBALL HALL OF FAME AND MUSEUM, on Main St., chronicles the history of baseball through photographs, memorabilia and video and interactive terminals. Included among the many exhibit areas are the World Series, Women In Baseball, Ballparks, the Babe Ruth Room, Grandstand Theatre and Pride & Passion: The African American Baseball Experience. The centerpiece of the museum is the Gallery which features a plaque representing each Hall of Famer.

Daily 9-9, May-Sept.; Sun.-Thurs. 9-5, Fri.-Sat. 9-8 in Apr. and Oct.-Dec.; daily 9-5, rest of year. Closed Jan. 1, Thanksgiving and Dec. 25. Admission $9.50; over 65, $8; ages 7-12, $4. A combination ticket with The Farmers' Museum and Fenimore Art Museum is available. AE, MC, VI. Phone (607) 547-7200. *See color ad p. 241.*

CORNING (G-5)
pop. 11,900, elev. 938'

Corning, on a plateau divided by the Chemung River, traces its economic origins to the manu-facture of glass. After the completion of the Chemung Canal in 1833, Erastus Corning of Albany bought real estate in the area and built a railroad from Pennsylvania to the canal. In 186? the Flint Glass Co. of Brooklyn relocated to Corning and reorganized, selling two-fifths of the company to local residents. Home to the Corning Glass Center, Corning is recognized as one of the world's glass centers.

Historic Market Street, the main commercial district, has been restored to its late 19th-century appearance with tree-lined brick sidewalks, shops and restaurants. A shuttle bus provides transportation from the Corning Glass Center to Market Street every 20 minutes. *Also see Finger Lakes p. 84.* Visitors can view glass making in progress along Market Street at several glass galleries. *See color ad p. 243.*

The Spence Crest Nature Center, off Denison Pkwy. on Powderhouse Rd., is situated on 200 acres of rolling wooded grounds and includes miles of nature trails and interpretative displays. Opportunities for hiking, fishing, picnicking, cross-country skiing and snowshoeing are available. Phone (607) 962-2169.

Greater Corning Area Chamber of Commerce: 42 E. Market St., Corning, NY 14830; phone (607) 936-4686. *See color ad p. 243.*

★ CORNING GLASS CENTER, off SR 17 exit 46, following signs to 151 Centerway, is home to one of the world's most comprehensive glass collections. The Art and History Galleries display 3,500 years of glassmaking. The Hot Glass Show, set in a working glass factory, presents narrated demonstrations in the art of glassblowing. The Glass Innovation Center uses interactive exhibits and a videotape presentation to introduce the technology that make glass a part of everyday life. The Sculpture Gallery showcases contemporary glass art. Food is available.

Allow 3 hours minimum. Daily 9-8, July-Aug.; 9-5, rest of year. Closed Jan. 1, Thanksgiving and Dec. 24-25. Admission mid-June through Dec. $9; senior citizens $8; ages 6-17, $7. Admission rest of year $6; senior citizens $5; ages 6-17, $4. AE, DS, MC, VI. Phone (607) 974-5371 or (800) 732-6845. *See color ad p. 79 & p. 243.*

SAVE THE CORNING-PAINTED POST HISTORICAL SOCIETY MUSEUM COMPLEX, 59 W. Pulteney St., is home to various restored buildings representing the area's history. The Benjamin Patterson Inn is a restored 1796 inn containing 19th-century furniture and crafts. Guided tours and craft demonstrations are offered. The Browntown Schoolhouse retains the flavor of the late 19th century schooldays, while the 1860s Starr Barn contains an agricultural exhibit. The complex also features a blacksmith shop and a 178? log cabin. Allow 1 hour minimum. Mon.-Fri. 10-4, Mar. 16-Dec. 15; closed major holidays. Admission $3.50; over 59, $3; ages 6-17, $1.50; family rate $10. Phone (607) 937-5281.

SAVE ★ **ROCKWELL MUSEUM**, 111 Cedar St., is in the Market Street Historic District. The museum displays a comprehensive collection of Western paintings and sculptures, more than 2,000 examples of early Steuben glass designed by Frederick Carder and antique toys. Other exhibits include antique firearms and a hands-on art room for children. Until the 1970s, the Romanesque revival style brick building served as Corning's city hall, fire station and jail. Guided tours are available.

Allow 1 hour minimum. Mon.-Sat. 9-5, Sun. noon-5; closed Jan. 1, Thanksgiving and Dec. 24-25. Admission $5; over 59, $4.50; ages 6-17, $2.50; family rate $12.50. AE, DI, DS, MC, VI. Phone (607) 937-5386. *See color ad & p. 243.*

WEST END GALLERY, 12 W. Market St., showcases original oils and watercolors by regional artists. Exhibits change every 6 to 8 weeks. Allow 30 minutes minimum. Mon.-Fri. 10-5:30, Sat. 10-4, Sun. noon-5. Free. Phone (607) 936-2011.

CORNWALL-ON-HUDSON (H-10)
pop. 3,100, elev. 12'

MUSEUM OF THE HUDSON HIGHLANDS, .7 mi. s.w. off SR 218 on The Boulevard, is devoted to the natural and cultural history of the Hudson Valley. The natural history wing has live native animals; the Ogden Gallery presents changing art exhibits, films and lectures; and the central wing has changing exhibits. Self-guiding nature trails explore the 75-acre grounds.

Tues.-Sun. noon-5; closed Jan. 1, Easter, July 4, Thanksgiving and Dec. 24-25 and 31. Admission $2. MC, VI. Phone (914) 534-7781.

CORTLAND (F-7)
pop. 19,800, elev. 1,130'

Established in 1808, Cortland was named for Gen. Pierre Van Cortlandt, New York's first lieutenant governor. The Cortland Repertory Theatre presents five main-stage productions mid-June through August in the turn-of-the-20th century Pavilion Theatre. The theater is in Dwyer Memorial Park on Little York Lake, 8 miles north on SR 281. Further information is available from the Cortland Repertory Theatre Business Office, 37 Franklin St., Cortland, NY 13045; phone (607) 756-2627.

Cortland County Convention and Visitors Bureau: 34 Tompkins St., Cortland, NY 13045; phone (607) 753-8463 or (800) 859-2227.

THE 1890 HOUSE MUSEUM, 1 blk. s.w. on SR 13 at 37 Tompkins St., is a Victorian mansion with period furnishings, cherry and oak woodwork, elaborate wall stenciling and stained glass. A slide presentation is available in the orientation room. Tues.-Sun. 1-4; closed major holidays. Admission $3.50, senior citizens and students with ID $2.50, under 12 free. Phone (607) 756-7551.

COXSACKIE (F-11)
pop. 2,800, elev. 139'

Named for an American Indian word meaning "hoot of an owl," Coxsackie was an exclusively Dutch settlement from the late 1600s until 1790, when other settlers arrived. In 1775, 225 of the villagers wrote and signed a declaration of independence protesting "arbitrary and oppressive acts of the British Parliament"—a year before their counterparts farther south drafted their own declaration.

The village, situated along the banks of the Hudson River, features Colonial and Victorian houses. Riverside Park offers a panorama of the Hudson River and the Berkshire Mountains.

SAVE BRONCK MUSEUM is off US 9W to Pieter Bronck Rd. Dutch Hudson Valley history is reflected in the main houses of stone and brick, the oldest dating from 1663. Buildings include a New World Dutch barn. Allow 1 hour minimum. Tues.-Sat. 10-4, Memorial Day-Oct. 15. Admission $4; over 64, $3.50; ages 12-15, $2; ages 5-11, $1. Phone (518) 731-8862 or 731-6490.

CROGHAN (C-8) pop. 700, elev. 847'

AMERICAN MAPLE MUSEUM, on Main St. (SR 812), illustrates the history of maple production through displays of lumbering and syrup-making equipment. The museum also contains the Maple Industry Hall of Fame. Museum open Mon.-Sat. 11-4, July 1-Labor Day; Fri.-Sat. and Mon. 11-4, mid-May through June 30 and day after Labor Day-early Oct. Phone to verify schedule. Admission $2; ages 5-12, $1. Phone (315) 346-1107.

CROSS RIVER—see New York p. 138.

CROTON-ON-HUDSON—
see New York p. 138.

CROWN POINT (C-11)
pop. 2,000, elev. 126'

CHAMPLAIN MEMORIAL LIGHTHOUSE is 7.5 mi. n.e. following SR 9N/22, then e. on CR 903 to the New York end of the Lake Champlain Bridge. The original light station was constructed in 1858. A new light and memorial were erected by Vermont and New York in 1912 to honor Samuel de Champlain, who discovered the lake in 1609. The bas-relief "La Belle France" by Auguste Rodin was a gift from France. Picnicking and camping are permitted.

Allow 30 minutes minimum. Mon.-Fri. 10-4, Memorial Day-Labor Day (weather permitting). Admission $3. Phone (518) 597-3603.

CROWN POINT STATE HISTORIC SITE is 7.5 mi. n.e. at the New York end of the Lake Champlain Bridge. The site contains the preserved ruins of fortifications occupied during the French and Indian and Revolutionary wars. A visitor center has history and archeology exhibits that focus on the 1734 French Fort St. Frederic and the 1759 British Fort Crown Point. An orientation film and self-guiding tours are offered.

Allow 2 hours minimum. Wed.-Sat. 10-5, Sun. 1-5, mid-May to late Oct. Admission $4 per private vehicle Sat.-Sun. and Mon. holidays. Free weekdays. Phone (518) 597-3666.

THE PENFIELD HOMESTEAD HISTORICAL MUSEUM, off I-87 exit 28, 12 mi. e. on SR 74, then 3 mi. n. on Corduroy Rd., is a complex of 19th-century buildings covering more than 500 acres in the Ironville Historic District. Structures include the Crown Point Iron Co. works, said to have been the first industrial operation to use electricity. Allow 2 hours minimum. Daily 10-4, July-Aug.; Wed.-Sun. 10-4, May 15-June 30 and Sept. 1-Oct. 15. Donations. Phone (518) 597-3804.

CUDDEBACKVILLE (H-9)

SAVE NEVERSINK VALLEY AREA MUSEUM is on Hoag Rd. in the D&H Canal Park, a 300-acre historical park that includes a 1-mile portion of the D&H Canal. The museum contains exhibits and photographs as well as miniature replicas and artifacts pertaining to area history and the canal's importance to community development. A self-guiding canal walking tour is available. Allow 1 hour, 30 minutes minimum. Thurs.-Sun. noon-4, Apr.-Dec. Admission $2; ages 6-17, $1. Phone (914) 754-8870.

CUTCHOGUE (H-5)
pop. 2,600, elev. 40'

The Corchaug Indian word Cutchogue means "it splits off land." The Old House, built in 1649 and one of the nation's earliest buildings, was moved to Cutchogue's Village Green in 1661 from nearby Southold. Exposed sections inside show construction features. Also on the Village Green are the 1700 Wickham Farmhouse and the 1840 Old Schoolhouse. *Also see Long Island p. 100.*

Cutchogue-New Suffolk Chamber of Commerce: P.O. Box 610, Cutchogue, NY 11935; phone (631) 298-5757.

WINERIES

• **Hargrave Vineyard**, on North Country Rd. (CR 48). Mon.-Fri. 10-5, Sat.-Sun. 11-6, May-Dec. Phone (631) 734-5111 or 734-5158.

DARIEN CENTER (E-4) elev. 931'

SAVE ★ SIX FLAGS DARIEN LAKE is 5 mi. s. of I-90 exit 48A at 9993 Allegheny Rd. This entertainment complex features more than 100 rides, including five roller coasters, and live shows. Highlights include Looney Tunes Seaport kids area, Superman-Ride of Steel, Batman Thrill Spectacular stunt show, and Barracuda Bay and Hook's Lagoon water parks. National recording artists appear throughout the season at the 20,000-seat Darien Lake Performing Arts Center. Also on the grounds are camping facilities. Picnicking is permitted. Food is available.

Daily 10-10, June 17-Sept. 3; Sat.-Sun. 10-10, May 1-June 16 and Sept. 4-Oct. 31; schedule varies, phone ahead. Admission $28.99; reduced rate for under 48 inches tall. Parking $6. AE, DS, MC, VI. Phone (716) 599-4641. *See color ad p. 202.*

DELHI (F-9) pop. 3,000, elev. 1,360'

DELAWARE COUNTY HISTORICAL ASSOCIATION MUSEUM, 2 mi. n.e. on SR 10, offers seven restored rural buildings. Buildings include the 1790s Frisbee House, a schoolhouse, a blacksmith shop, a gun shop, timber-frame barn and an exhibit about area farming. Also featured are changing art and history exhibits. Picnicking is permitted.

Allow 1 hour minimum. Museum open Tues.-Sun. 11-4:30, Memorial Day weekend-Oct. 15. Research library open Mon.-Tues. 10-3, year-round. Admission $3; under 12, $1.50. Phone (607) 746-3849.

DRESDEN (F-6) pop. 300

ROBERT INGERSOLL MUSEUM is e. of SR 14 at 61 Main St. The birthplace of Robert Ingersoll, a mid-1880s lawyer, politician and writer, houses a collection of his speeches and writings. Ingersoll was a controversial advocate for separation of church and state. Guided tours are available. Allow 30 minutes minimum. Fri.-Sun. noon-5, Memorial Day-Oct. 30. Donations. Phone (315) 536-1074 to verify schedule.

DUNDEE (F-5) pop. 1,600, elev. 994'

WINERIES

• **Glenora Wine Cellars,** on SR 14. Daily 10-8, July-Aug.; daily 10-6, May-June and Sept.-Oct.; Mon.-Sat. 10-5, Sun. noon-5, rest of year. Closed Jan. 1, Easter, Thanksgiving and Dec. 25. Phone (800) 243-5513.

DUNKIRK (F-2)
pop. 14,000, elev. 613'

Founded as Chadwick's Bay in 1805, Dunkirk was renamed in 1817 because its harbor was said to resemble that of Dunkerque, France. On Thanksgiving 1946 the citizens of Dunkirk aided their war-impoverished namesake with a shipment of more than $100,000 worth of emergency supplies.

Dunkirk's harbor, which has been a key factor in the town's commercial growth, offers numerous recreational opportunities, including fishing, boating, swimming and water skiing. Lake Erie State Park is 7 miles west *(see Recreation Chart).* The Lily Dale Assembly, 8 miles south of US 90 exit 59, offers a diversified summer program of lectures and workshops about spiritualism.

Northern Chautauqua Chamber of Commerce: 212 Lake Shore Dr. W., Dunkirk, NY 14048; phone (716) 366-6200.

DUNKIRK HISTORICAL LIGHTHOUSE AND VETERANS PARK MUSEUM is n. on Lighthouse Point Dr. off SR 5. The lighthouse was built in 1875 on the site of the first Point Gratiot lighthouse, established in 1827. The museum, housed in the keeper's quarters, displays armed services and war memorabilia, and exhibits related to the lighthouse and its keepers. Also on the grounds is a Coast Guard and submarine exhibit room.

Allow 1 hour minimum. Thurs.-Tues. 10-4, July-Aug.; Mon.-Tues. and Thurs.-Sat. 10-2, Apr.-June and Sept.-Nov.; by appointment in Dec. Schedule may vary; phone ahead. Museum and grounds admission $4.50; ages 4-12, $1. Grounds only $1. Phone (716) 366-5050.

DUNKIRK HISTORICAL MUSEUM, .5 mi. s. of SR 5 at 513 Washington Ave., contains permanent and changing exhibits about local businesses, schools and veterans as well as paintings by local artists. In addition to the displays, the museum offers a small library and information about local attractions. Allow 30 minutes minimum. Mon.-Fri. noon-4 and by appointment; closed holidays. Donations. Phone (716) 366-3797.

WINERIES

• **Woodbury Vineyards Winery**, .5 mi. s. off I-90 exit 59, 1 mi. e. on US 20, then 1 mi. s. on Roberts Rd. Mon.-Sat. 9-8, Sun. noon-8, late June-Labor Day; Mon.-Sat. 9-5, Sun. noon-5, rest of year. Closed major holidays. Phone (716) 679-9463.

EAST AURORA—*see Buffalo p. 71.*

EAST DURHAM (F-10)

IRISH-AMERICAN HERITAGE MUSEUM, on SR 145, has changing exhibits about Irish-American culture and history. Featured is "Fire upon the Hearth," an exhibit celebrating Irish-American women, a 7-minute film providing background information about the museum and an audio-visual reading library for research purposes.

Allow 1 hour minimum. Wed.-Sat. and holidays 11-5, Sun. noon-5, Memorial Day weekend-Labor Day; Fri.-Sat. and holidays 11-5, Sun. noon-5, day after Labor Day-Columbus Day. Admission $3.50; over 64, students with ID and under 12, $2; family rate $9. Phone (518) 634-7497, or 432-6598 in the off-season.

EAST HAMPTON (H-6)
pop. 1,400, elev. 55'

This section of Long Island's south shore has many fashionable summer colonies and estates. The Clinton Academy, the first chartered academy in the state, has changing local history exhibits; phone (631) 324-1850.

East Hampton Chamber of Commerce: 79A Main St., East Hampton, NY 11937; phone (631) 324-0362.

EAST HAMPTON TOWN MARINE MUSEUM— *see Amagansett p. 59.*

GUILD HALL OF EAST HAMPTON, 158 Main St., is a cultural center with changing art exhibits and theater presentations. Daily 11-5, Memorial Day-Labor Day; Wed.-Sat. 11-5, Sun. noon-5, rest of year. Admission $3. Phone (631) 324-0806.

"HOME SWEET HOME" is across the village green from SR 27 at 14 James Ln. This was the childhood home of playwright, actor and diplomat John Howard Payne. The house contains 17th- and 18th-century furniture and a collection of English ceramics and lusterware. An herb garden and the 1804 Pantigo Windmill also are on the grounds. Allow 30 minutes minimum. Mon.-Sat. 10-4, Sun. 2-4; closed Jan. 1, Nov. 1, Thanksgiving and Dec. 25. Admission $4; ages 2-12, $2. Phone (631) 324-0713.

THE MULFORD FARMHOUSE, across the village green from SR 27 at 10 James Ln., is a 4-acre site that preserves the original 17th-century settlement of Maidstone. Highlights include decorative arts exhibits, information about East Hampton's architectural styles and tours by costumed interpreters. Daily 10-5, June-Aug. Admission $4; senior citizens $2. Phone (631) 324-6869.

EAST MEREDITH (F-9) elev. 1,353'

[SAVE] **HANFORD MILLS MUSEUM,** on CRs 10 and 12, is a restored 19th-century water-powered milling complex. Exhibits and demonstrations are featured at the sawmill and gristmill. Other buildings include a feed mill, barn, hardware store, wagon and lumber shed, garage and shingle mill. Guided tours are available. Allow 1 hour minimum. Daily 10-5, May-Oct. Admission $5; ages 6-12, $3. MC, VI. Phone (607) 278-5744 or (800) 295-4992.

EASTPORT (I-5) elev. 25'

SHRINE OF OUR LADY OF THE ISLAND is midway between Long Island Expwy. (I-495) exit 70 and Sunrise Hwy. (SR 27) exit 61 on Eastport Manor Rd. The 70-acre site includes wooded walkways, the stations of the cross, gardens, statues and chapels. Picnicking is permitted. Grounds open daily 10-4. Chapels open daily 10-7. Free. Phone (631) 325-0661.

EDEN—*see Buffalo p. 72.*

ELDRED (H-9) pop. 700, elev. 1,000'

On the edge of the Catskills, Eldred is home to the Eldred WWII Museum at 201 Main St. Dedicated to preserving the history of the war, the museum contains various displays as well as a videotape presentation. Phone (814) 225-2220.

ELIZABETHTOWN (B-11)
pop. 1,300, elev. 550'

One of the most picturesque drives in northern New York is US 9, which extends through the Boquet River Valley to the south.

ADIRONDACK HISTORY CENTER, jct. US 9 and Church St., offers a sound-and-light show about the history of the Champlain Valley as well as a forest fire observation tower and a formal garden. Additional displays feature pioneer settlement, wilderness exploration, mining, transportation and the local community. Allow 1 hour minimum. Mon.-Sat. 9-5, Sun. 1-5, mid-May to mid-Oct. Admission $3.50; over 59, $2.50; ages 6-18, $1.50. Phone (518) 873-6466.

ELLICOTTVILLE (F-3)
pop. 500, elev. 1,549'

In winter Ellicottville's snow festooned evergreens lure skiing enthusiasts. The 60,398 acres of nearby Allegany State Park *(see Recreation Chart and the AAA Northeastern CampBook)* provide cold-weather devotees with opportunities for cross-country skiing, snowmobiling and ice

DID YOU KNOW

Kingston, Poughkeepsie and New York City all served as the state's capital before the honor went to Albany in 1797.

fishing, while those who prefer the summer sunshine can hike and bike, fish and swim, camp and ride horseback.

For an unusual site, view a herd of buffaloes on the hill adjacent to the ski slopes at the B&B Buffalo Ranch on Horn Hill Road.

Ellicottville Chamber of Commerce: P.O. Box 456, Ellicottville, NY 14731; phone (716) 699-5046 or (800) 349-9099.

Shopping areas: Washington Street is home to various antiques and specialty shops.

RECREATIONAL ACTIVITIES

Skiing

- **Holiday Valley Resort**, s. on US 219. Write Holiday Valley Rd., Ellicottville, NY 14731. Other activities are available. Mon.-Thurs. 9 a.m.-10 p.m., Fri.-Sun. 8:30 a.m.-10:30 p.m. late Nov.-Easter (weather permitting). Phone (716) 699-2345.

ELMIRA (G-6) pop. 33,700, elev. 854'

Nine years after the decisive battle of Newton in 1779 the first permanent settlers built their cabins on the site that is now Elmira. The name of the city was derived in 1808, according to local tradition, from the name of a neighborhood child who wandered into a meeting where local politicians were trying to decide on a name for the town.

Samuel Clemens, better known as Mark Twain, married Elmira native Olivia Langdon in 1870; thereafter the Clemens family spent its summers at Olivia's sister's farm. It was in Elmira that Twain wrote "The Adventures of Huckleberry Finn" and other classic works.

Woodlawn National Cemetery contains more than 3,000 graves of Confederate soldiers who died in the local prisoner of war camp. Year-round entertainment is available at the Clemens Performing Arts Center at Clemens Center Parkway and Gray Street. From July through Labor Day, 90-minute trolley tours depart from the chamber of commerce.

Sailplane rides are available at Schweizer Soaring School at the Elmira-Corning Regional Airport and from Harris Hill Soaring Corporation *(see attraction listing). Also see Finger Lakes p. 84.*

Chemung County Chamber of Commerce: 215 E. Church St., Elmira, NY 14901; phone (607) 734-5137 or (800) 627-5892. *See color ad p. 256.*

Self-guiding tours: Maps and brochures outlining a self-guiding tour of the Near Westside historic neighborhood are available from the chamber of commerce or the Near Westside Neighborhood Association at W. Church and Davis streets; phone (607) 733-4924.

Shopping areas: Arnot Mall, exit 51 off SR 17 between Elmira and Corning, has 117 stores, including The Bon-Ton, JCPenney, Kaufmans and Sears.

ARNOT ART MUSEUM, 235 Lake St., is in an 1833 Greek Revival mansion. The museum's collection includes 17th-, 18- and 19th-century Dutch, Flemish, French and German paintings as well as 19th- and 20th-century American art, bronze sculpture and changing exhibits. Allow 30 minutes minimum. Tues.-Sat. 10-5, Sun. 1-5; closed major holidays. Admission $2, over 64 and students with ID $1, children 50c. Phone (607) 734-3697.

CHEMUNG VALLEY HISTORICAL MUSEUM, 415 E. Water St., contains local and state historical artifacts. Among the displays are items once belonging to Mark Twain as well as seasonal exhibits. Allow 1 hour minimum. Tues.-Sat. 10-5, Sun. 1-5; closed holidays. Admission $2; senior citizens and under 13, $1. Phone (607) 734-4167.

GRAVE OF MARK TWAIN, facing East Hill in Woodlawn Cemetery at the n. end of Walnut St., is identified by a monument that is 12 feet high or "mark twain." The expression, which Samuel Clemens adopted as his byline, refers to the 2-fathom (12-foot) water depth necessary for riverboats to pass through a river.

Clemens' son-in-law, the distinguished musician Ossip Gabrilowitsch, is buried at his request at Clemens' feet. Grave markers bear quotes from the author's works. Daily dawn-dusk. Free.

HARRIS HILL SOARING CORPORATION, SR 417 exit 51 s., then w. on CR 64 on Harris Hill Park, features flights in modern high-performance sailplanes above the scenic Chemung Valley. Allow 1 hour minimum. Daily 10-6, June 15-Labor Day weekend; Sat.-Sun. and holidays 10-6, Apr. 1-Jun. 14. Fare $60. MC, VI. Phone (607) 734-0641.

MARK TWAIN STUDY, on the Elmira College campus, is an octagonal study built in the form of a Mississippi riverboat pilothouse. The study, built for Clemens by his sister-in-law, once overlooked the city from atop East Hill and contains some of its original furniture. Guided tours of the study and Hamilton Hall's Mark Twain exhibit are available. Daily 9-5, mid-June through Aug. 31; by appointment rest of year. Free. Phone (607) 735-1941.

SAVE **NATIONAL SOARING MUSEUM**, Harris Hill, SR 17 exit 51 following signs to 51 Soaring Hill Dr., has movies and exhibits about gliding, including classic and contemporary sailplanes. Interactive computer programs include a sailplane cockpit simulator. Allow 1 hour minimum. Daily 10-5; closed Jan. 1, Thanksgiving and Dec. 25. Admission $5; over 59, $4; students with ID and ages 7-17, $3; under 7 free with an adult. MC, VI ($10). Phone (607) 734-3128.

SULLIVAN'S MONUMENT AT NEWTOWN BATTLEFIELD, 3 mi. e. on SR 17, was the site of a Revolutionary War campaign staged by Gen.

John Sullivan and Brig. Gen. James Clinton. Occasional battle re-enactments are presented throughout the year. Hiking and biking trails are available as well as campsites, cabins, playgrounds and picnic areas. Allow 30 minutes minimum. Daily 10-dusk, Fri. before Memorial Day-Columbus Day. Free. Phone (607) 732-6067.

FINGER LAKES

American Indian folklore holds that the Finger Lakes were formed when God placed his handprint on some of the most beautiful land ever created. There are actually 11 finger-shaped lakes beginning just east of I-390 and extending east almost to I-81 south of Syracuse; the northern boundary straddles I-90, with SR 17 defining the southern edge.

The lakes are named for the tribes of the Six Nations of the Iroquois: the Cayugas, Mohawks, Onondagas, Oneidas, Senecas and Tuscaroras. SRs 14 and 89, which parallel the western shores of Seneca and Cayuga lakes, respectively, are major north-south routes cutting through the center of the region. Seneca and Cayuga are the largest lakes. Boating, fishing and swimming are popular area recreational pastimes.

Information about regional attractions can be found in place listings for Auburn, Branchport, Canandaigua, Corning, Elmira, Geneva, Glenora, Hammondsport, Horseheads, Ithaca, Lodi, Montour Falls, Moravia, Naples, Palmyra, Seneca Falls, Skaneateles and Watkins Glen.

FINGER LAKES NATIONAL FOREST (F-6)

Elevations in the forest range from 1,400 ft. at the southeast corner near Reynoldsville to 1,860 ft. at Hector Backbone. Refer to AAA maps for additional elevation information.

On a ridge between Seneca and Cayuga lakes, via I-90, I-81 and SR 17, lies the only national forest in New York. Officially designated as such in October 1985, the Finger Lakes National Forest comprises just 16,000 acres and is one of the smallest of the country's 76 national forests.

More than one-third of the land provides pasture for beef and dairy cattle. The remaining area is used for camping, hiking on the 33-mile trail system, horseback riding, fishing and hunting. Midsummer draws blueberry pickers, and winter cross-country skiers and snowmobilers, to the gentle, rolling hillsides. The Forest Service office is about 9 miles north of Watkins Glen on SR 414; the office is open weekdays 8-4:30. Free.

For further information contact the District Ranger, Finger Lakes National Forest, 5218 SR 414, Hector, NY 14841. Phone (607) 546-4470. *See Recreation Chart.*

FIRE ISLAND NATIONAL SEASHORE (I-4)

Fire Island National Seashore encompasses most of the lands between Robert Moses State Park *(see attraction listing)* and Smith Point County Park off the south shore of Long Island. Low shrubs and beach grass along the Atlantic shore protect sand from erosion; in sheltered portions, high thickets and groves of pitch pine are common.

Wildlife is abundant along the seashore. Anglers can find bass, blowfish, bluefish, fluke, mackerel, weakfish and winter flounder. Waterfowls are numerous October through March; white-tailed deer, red foxes and rabbits also can be seen.

The seashore is accessible by car near its eastern end at Smith Point County Park or by mainland ferry lines that leave Bay Shore, Sayville and Patchogue in summer. A visitor center at Smith Point West next to Smith Point County Park has exhibits and visitor information; a ranger is on duty year-round. A national wilderness area extends west for 7 miles.

The lightkeeper's quarters of the mid-19th-century Fire Island Lighthouse is a visitor center

with exhibits about the history of the site. To reach the lighthouse, park at the east end of Robert Moses State Park *(see attraction listing)* and walk about a quarter-mile over a dirt trail. Physically impaired persons can park at the lighthouse; phone (631) 289-4810.

Sailors Haven, 1 mile west of the private community of Cherry Grove, offers a marina, beach and picnic areas. A self-guiding nature trail leads through the Sunken Forest.

Access to Sailors Haven is by boat or walk-on ferry from Sayville or Patchogue; phone (631) 589-8980 or 475-1665, respectively. Round-trip fare to Sailor's Haven is $8; ages 2-11, $4.50. Visitor services are offered during the summer.

The William Floyd Estate is at 245 Park Dr. in Mastic Beach. The preserved house of one of the signers of the Declaration of Independence reflects the changes in styles during the 250 years of Floyd family ownership. Guided house tours and self-guiding grounds tours are available; phone (631) 399-2030.

For further information contact the Superintendent, Fire Island National Seashore, 120 Laurel St., Patchogue, Long Island, NY 11772. Phone (631) 289-4810. *See Recreation Chart and the AAA Northeastern CampBook. Also see Long Island p. 100.*

ROBERT MOSES STATE PARK is on the w. end of Fire Island on the Atlantic Ocean, accessible via the Robert Moses Cswy. from the Long Island Expwy. or the Southern State Pkwy. Recreational facilities include a pitch-and-putt golf course, boat anchorages, fishing pier and bathhouses. Picnicking is permitted. Daily dawn-dusk, Memorial Day-Labor Day; Sat.-Sun. dawn-dusk, day after Labor Day-Oct. 31. Free. Parking $7, Memorial Day-Labor Day; $5, rest of year. Phone (631) 669-0449. *See Recreation Chart.*

FONDA (E-9) pop. 1,000, elev. 291'

THE NATIONAL SHRINE OF BLESSED KATERI TEKAKWITHA AND NATIVE AMERICAN EXHIBIT is .5 mi. w. on SR 5. The shrine honors the place where this American Indian girl was baptized and lived almost half her life. Also included is the 1663 Caughnawaga Indian village Mohawk, an excavated and staked-out Iroquois village, and American Indian artifacts exhibits. Picnicking is permitted. Allow 2 hours minimum. Daily 9-4, May 1-Nov. 1. Donations. Phone (518) 853-3646.

FORESTVILLE (F-3)
pop. 700, elev. 928'

WINERIES

• **Merritt Estate Winery**, 2264 King Rd. Mon.-Sat. 10-5, Sun. noon-5. Phone (716) 965-4800.

FORT EDWARD (D-11)
pop. 3,600, elev. 144'

On the portage trail between the Hudson River and Lake Champlain, Fort Edward was fortified throughout the French and Indian and Revolutionary wars. During the Revolutionary War, local citizen Jane McCrea was murdered on the way to see her fiance in the British Army. Her grave can be seen at Union Cemetery on Broadway.

Fort Edward Chamber of Commerce: P.O. Box 267, Fort Edward, NY 12828; phone (518) 747-3000.

OLD FORT HOUSE MUSEUM (Smythe House), .5 mi. s. on US 4 to 29 Lower Broadway, was built in 1772. A tavern and courthouse under British rule, it was the Revolutionary War headquarters for Gens. Philip Schuyler, John Burgoyne and John Stark. On the grounds are a 19th-century tollhouse, a 19th-century schoolhouse, the 1870 Washington County Fair building, the Baldwin Barn Gallery, the A. Dallas Wait Law Office and the John P. Burke Research Center.

Allow 1 hour, 30 minutes minimum. Daily 1-5, June 1-Sept. 1; 1-4, first Sat. in Dec.-Dec. 22. Closed July 4. Admission $2, under 18 free. Phone (518) 747-9600.

FORT HUNTER (E-10)

Alongside the Erie Canal in Fort Hunter is Schoharie Crossing, a 3-mile nature trail with interpretive signage and picnic facilities.

Vestiges of the original Erie Canal locks, as well as structures from two other phases of canal construction, can be seen at Schoharie Crossing State Historic Site on Schoharie Street. The site preserves the six remaining arches from the Schoharie Aqueduct, built in the late 1830s to carry the Erie Canal over Schoharie Creek as well as a restored 1850 canal store. A visitor center is open Wednesday through Saturday 10 to 5, Sunday 1 to 5, May 15 through the last weekend in October. The site also offers nature and bike trails; phone (518) 829-7516.

FORT JOHNSON (E-10) pop. 600

FORT JOHNSON, on SR 5 w. of SR 67, was built in 1749 by Sir William Johnson. During the American Revolution it was confiscated and sold at auction. The fort has been restored to the 1749-75 period and contains original furnishings and exhibits about regional history and the Mohawk Valley Indians. Wed.-Sun. 1-5, May 15-Oct. 15. Admission $2, under 12 free. Phone (518) 843-0300.

FORT NIAGARA—
see Youngstown p. 151.

FORT PLAIN (E-9)
pop. 2,400, elev. 317'

FORT PLAIN MUSEUM, from jct. SRs 80 and 5S, w. on SR 5S to 389 Upper Canal St., is the site of a Revolutionary War fort that was the headquarters for the western defense. Exhibits include an extensive collection of American Indian artifacts, an Erie Canal room and information about area agriculture. Guided tours are available. Allow 1 hour minimum. Wed.-Sun. noon-5, mid-May through mid-Sept.; by appointment rest of year. Donations. Phone (518) 993-3419.

★ FORT STANWIX NATIONAL MONUMENT (D-8)

Fort Stanwix, off SR 26 in Rome, was built during the French and Indian War. In 1776, at the outbreak of the Revolution, the fort was repaired and restored by American rebels. Attacked by a force of British, Tories and American Indians in 1777, it successfully withstood a 3-week siege. The fort contains exhibits. Costumed interpreters re-enact 18th-century life in a military outpost June through August.

Open daily 9-5, Apr.-Dec.; closed Thanksgiving and Dec. 25. Admission $2, under 16 free with an adult. Phone (315) 336-2090.

★ FORT TICONDEROGA (C-11)

Fort Ticonderoga, 1 mile northeast of Ticonderoga on SR 74, was built in 1755 by the French, who named it Fort Carillon. Bordering Lake Champlain, the fort controlled the connecting waterway between Canada and the American Colonies. In 1758 the French successfully defended Fort Carillon against the British, but in 1759 British general Jeffery Amherst captured, rebuilt and renamed the fort.

Ethan Allen and his Green Mountain Boys took the fort in a bloodless surprise attack in 1775; the next year Benedict Arnold assembled the first American fleet at this site. In 1777 Gen. John Burgoyne captured the fort for the British. Later that year they abandoned the fortification and burned all buildings on both sides of the lake. The fort was never garrisoned again.

Fort Ticonderoga has been restored on the original foundations according to the French plans. The museum contains collections of weapons, utensils, paintings and papers dealing with the Colonial and Revolutionary periods. A well-marked battleground surrounding the fort was the site of the British and Colonial defeat in 1758 by the French under the Marquis de Montcalm.

Fort open daily 9-6, July-Aug.; 9-5, early May-June 30 and Sept. 1-late Oct. Guided tours, cannon-firing demonstrations and fife-and-drum music are offered July-Aug. Admission $10; over 60, $8; ages 7-12, $6. AE, MC, VI. Phone (518) 585-2821. *See color ad p. 179.*

SAVE **MOUNT DEFIANCE,** 1 mi. s.e. off SR 22/74, is reached by a blacktop road. British cannon mounted at this point forced Gen. Arthur St. Clair to surrender American-held Fort Ticonderoga in 1777. At an elevation of 853 feet, the overlook provides a panorama of Lake Champlain, the valley and the Green Mountains. Daily 9-5, July-Aug.; 9-4, early May-June 30 and Sept. 1 to mid-Oct. Free. Phone (518) 585-2821.

FULTON (D-7) pop. 12,900, elev. 393'

Fulton lies along the Oswego River about 11 miles south of Lake Ontario. The town was founded in the late 18th century by Dutch settlers from the Hudson and Mohawk valleys.

In the 1820s the Oswego Canal between the Erie Canal and Lake Ontario opened, boosting Fulton's economy. Locks enabled boats to negotiate the falls of the Oswego River, which drop 14 feet, and a series of rapids to the north, which drop another 30 feet. An observation area in Canal Park overlooks the lower locks. Recreation Park, on Lake Neahtahwanta at the west end of town, offers sports facilities.

Exhibits related to Fulton's history can be seen at the Pratt House, 177 S. First St.; phone (315) 593-7796.

Greater Fulton Chamber of Commerce: 41 S. 2nd St., P.O. Box 148, Fulton, NY 13069; phone (315) 598-4231.

GARDEN CITY (I-2)
pop. 21,700, elev. 88'

Near Garden City is Roosevelt Field, where Charles A. Lindbergh began his historic transatlantic flight in 1927. *Also see Long Island p. 100.*

Garden City Chamber of Commerce: 230 7th St., Garden City, NY 11530; phone (516) 746-7724.

Shopping areas: Roosevelt Field Shopping Center, off Meadowbrook Parkway exit M2W, is near Garden City. Among its 185 stores are JCPenney and Macy's.

CATHEDRAL OF THE INCARNATION (Episcopal), Cathedral Ave. at 6th St., is of 13th-century Gothic style. The 1885 church is noted for its hand-carved mahogany woodwork and rare marble. Fri.-Tues. 9-4. Hours may vary; phone ahead. Free. Phone (516) 746-2955.

GARRISON—*see New York p. 138.*

GATEWAY NATIONAL RECREATION AREA (I-2)

Gateway National Recreation Area comprises the Sandy Hook Unit in New Jersey and three units in New York City, offering urban residents and visitors a chance to enjoy nature and the sea.

The Breezy Point Unit, on Rockaway Peninsula, includes Jacob Riis Beach, historic Fort Tilden and the westernmost point of the peninsula. The Jamaica Bay Unit includes Jamaica Bay Wildlife Refuge in Queens *(see New York p. 131)*, Canarsie Pier, Plumb Beach and Floyd Bennett Field in Brooklyn. The Staten Island Unit consists of Great Kills Park and Miller Field. The Sandy Hook Unit in Highlands, N.J., includes a beach, a lighthouse and Fort Hancock.

Historical, educational, cultural and recreational events are presented throughout the year. The beaches are open daily, Memorial Day weekend-Labor Day. For further information contact the Public Affairs Office, Gateway National Recreation Area, Headquarters, Bldg. 69, Floyd Bennett Field, Brooklyn, NY 11234. Phone (718) 338-3687 or 338-3688. *See Recreation Chart.*

GENEVA (E-6) pop. 14,100, elev. 671'

On Seneca Lake, largest of the Finger Lakes, Geneva is the center of a rich agricultural and nursery region. A local wine research and development center explores new ways of growing grapes and making wine; numerous vineyards are found in the area. The historical society museum, 543 S. Main St. (SR 14), has permanent and changing exhibits about local history; phone (315) 789-5151. *Also see Finger Lakes p. 84.*

Geneva Area Chamber of Commerce: 1 Lakeside Dr., P.O. Box 587, Geneva, NY 14456; phone (315) 789-1776.

Self-guiding tours: A brochure outlining a self-guiding walking tour of Geneva's historic S. Main Street is available from the Geneva Historical Society.

Self-guiding walking tours of the Hobart and William Smith College campus are detailed in a brochure available at the Alumni House, 615 S. Main St.; phone (315) 781-3700.

THE MIKE WEAVER DRAIN TILE MUSEUM is on SR 96A, 1.5 mi. s. jct. SR 5 and US 20; visi-

tors should go to the nearby Rose Hill Mansion for an escort to the museum. The museum displays 350 styles of tile dating from 100 B.C. to the present. Mon.-Sat. 10-3, Sun. 1-4, May-Oct. Admission $1. Phone (315) 789-3848 or 789-5151.

★**ROSE HILL MANSION** is 3 mi. e. on SR 96A, 1 mi. s. of jct. US 20/SR 5. This beautifully restored 1839 mansion, on 30 acres of land, overlooks Seneca Lake. Furnished in the Empire style of the period, the house is one of America's finest examples of Greek Revival architecture. Many furnishings are original to the Swan family, who occupied the mansion 1850-90. Twenty-one rooms are open to the public.

Guides provide detailed explanations of furnishings and demonstrations of how items of that period were used in daily life. Paint colors, wallpaper and textiles in the house are typical of the period as is the extensive use of wall-to-wall carpeting. Allow 1 hour, 30 minutes minimum. Mon.-Sat. 10-4, Sun. 1-5, May-Oct. Admission $3; over 62 and ages 10-18, $2. Phone (315) 789-3848. *See ad.*

GERMANTOWN (G-11)
pop. 2,000, elev. 11'

CLERMONT STATE HISTORIC SITE, 4 mi. s. on SR 9G, then 1 mi. w. on CR 6 following signs to 1 Clermont Ave., comprises the 490-acre Hudson River estate of Chancellor Robert R. Livingston, delegate to the second Continental Congress and member of the committee to draft the Declaration of Independence. The original circa 1730 mansion was burned by the British in 1777 and rebuilt 1779-82. The grounds contain historical nature trails and restored formal gardens.

Guided tours of the mansion and visitor center are available Tues.-Sun. and Mon. holidays 11-5, Apr.-Oct. Grounds open daily 8:30-dusk. Grounds and visitor center free. Guided tour $3; senior citizens $2; ages 5-12, $1. Phone (518) 537-4240.

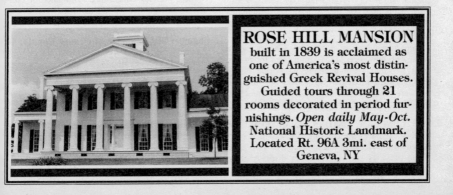

GILBOA (F-10) pop. 1,200, elev. 960'

Off SR 342 just west of the Schoharie Creek bridge is a group of fossil tree stumps that represent the oldest known species of trees on Earth. Known as *eospermatopteris*, they were seed-bearing tree ferns which grew in the shore muds of an ancient Devonian sea that lay west of the present Catskill Mountains. The fossils are identified by a historical marker.

GLEN COVE (H-2)
pop. 24,100, elev. 115'

GARVIES POINT MUSEUM AND PRESERVE, Glen Cove Rd. n. to the fire station, then following signs to Barry Dr., is a 62-acre preserve overlooking Hempstead Harbor with 5 miles of nature trails. The museum has regional archeology and geology exhibits and changing displays. Tues.-Sun. 10-4; closed some holidays. Admission $1; ages 5-12, 50c. Phone (516) 571-8010.

GLENS FALLS (D-11)
pop. 15,000, elev. 376'

Part of a land grant settlement founded in 1759, Glens Falls grew up around the power-producing 60-foot falls on the Hudson River—a site known to the indigenous population as *Chepontuo*, "a difficult place to get around." The village was destroyed by the British in 1780 and resettled in 1788 by Col. John Glen. His mills established the town as an industrial center.

Adirondack Regional Chamber of Commerce: P.O. Box 158, Glens Falls, NY 12801; phone (518) 798-1761.

Shopping Areas: Aviation Mall, a quarter-mile east of I-87 exit 19, is a major local shopping center. Among its 80 stores are JCPenney and Sears. A series of factory outlet stores are located off I-87 exit 20.

[SAVE] **ADIRONDACK BALLOON FLIGHTS** offers hot-air balloon rides departing off I-87 (Adirondack Northway) exit 19. Balloon takeoff and landing sites vary with wind conditions. Rides offer panoramas of the Adirondack Mountains and the rural countryside. Flying time is approximately 1 hour.

Departures daily at dawn and 3 hours before dusk, Apr.-Nov. Fee $185; group rates for two to eight passengers are available. The ride is not recommended for under 10 or over 80. Reservations are required. AE, DS, MC, VI. Phone (518) 793-6342.

THE CHAPMAN HISTORICAL MUSEUM, 348 Glen St., features the DeLong House which is restored to its Victorian-era appearance. Two exhibition galleries contain changing displays about the history of the Southern Adirondacks. The Seneca Ray Stoddard photographs of the Adiron-

dacks are on display. Tues.-Sat. 10-5; closed major holidays. Admission $2, senior citizens and students with ID $1, under 12 free. Phone (518) 793-2826.

★ **THE HYDE COLLECTION ART MUSEUM,** 161 Warren St., is displayed in a furnished Florentine Renaissance mansion. The collection includes changing and permanent art exhibits from the 4th century B.C. to the 20th century. Among the pieces displayed are paintings, sculpture, tapestries and period furniture.

Allow 1 hour, 30 minutes minimum. Tues.-Sat. 10-5 (also Thurs. 5-7), Sun. noon-5; closed national holidays. Guided tours are offered Tues.-Sun. 1-4. Free. Phone (518) 792-1761.

GLOVERSVILLE (D-9)
pop. 16,700, elev. 796'

FULTON COUNTY MUSEUM, 2.5 mi. w. of SR 30A at 237 Kingsboro Ave., offers historical displays, with emphasis on the manufacture of leather and gloves, for which the city was named. Also exhibited are Victorian clothing, regional 19th-century folk art and memorabilia of the Sacandaga Amusement Park, which was flooded when the dam that created Great Sacandaga Lake was built.

Allow 1 hour minimum. Tues.-Sun. 10-4, July-Aug.; Tues.-Sat. noon-4, late Apr.-June 30 and Sept.-Oct. Donations. Phone (518) 725-2203.

GOSHEN (H-10)
pop. 5,300, elev. 431'

The Goshen Public Library, (914) 294-7741, contains the signatures of Alexander Hamilton and Benedict Arnold among its historical artifacts. The collection and a genealogical library are available by appointment only.

The Historic Goshen Track is one of the oldest harness racetracks in the United States and the sporting world's first national historic landmark. Self-guiding walking tours of the barn and blacksmith shop are offered; phone (914) 294-5357.

Note: Policies concerning admittance of children to pari-mutuel betting facilities vary. Phone for information.

Chamber of Commerce of Orange County: 40 Matthews St., Suite 103, Goshen, NY 10924; phone (914) 294-8080.

[SAVE] **HARNESS RACING MUSEUM & HALL OF FAME,** 240 Main St., honors the sport of harness racing. The Tudor-style building, originally a stable, houses a collection of Currier & Ives trotting prints, a timeline tracing the sport's history, trotting memorabilia and interactive exhibits. A 3-D simulator takes visitor for a ride. The Hall of Fame showcases the people and horses who have contributed to the sport. Allow 1 hour minimum. Daily 10-6; closed Jan. 1, Thanksgiving and Dec. 25. Admission $7.50; senior citizens $6.50; ages 6-12, $4; under 6, $3.50. MC, VI. Phone (914) 294-6330. *See color ad p. 492.*

GRAND ISLAND—*see Buffalo p. 72.*

GRANVILLE (D-11)
pop. 2,600, elev. 403'

THE PEMBER MUSEUM OF NATURAL HISTORY, 33 W. Main St., is a Victorian-period museum housing specimens of birds and mammals, rocks and minerals, shells, eggs and other objects related to natural history. Hiking trails are open year-round at the Pember Nature Preserve; trail maps are available at the museum. Programs and guided nature hikes are available by appointment. Allow 1 hour minimum. Tues.-Fri. 1-5, Sat. 10-3. Admission $2.50; senior citizens and under 18, $1. Phone (518) 642-1515.

GREAT LAKES-ST. LAWRENCE SEAWAY SYSTEM

The Great Lakes-St. Lawrence Seaway System consists of a 2,342-mile marine highway that extends from the Atlantic Ocean to the headwaters of the Great Lakes. It was completed in 1959 as a joint venture between the United States and Canada. The United States dredged the Thousand Islands section and constructed the Wiley-Dondero Ship Channel and the two locks with auxiliary facilities near Massena.

Canada built canals and four locks in territorial waters between Cornwall, Ontario, and Montréal, Québec; built a canal and lock at Iroquois, Ontario; and deepened channels of the Welland Canal. For information about points of interest in the St. Lawrence Seaway area, *see Alexandria Bay, Clayton, Massena, Ogdensburg and Thousand Islands pp. 57, 76, 102, 158 and 178.*

GREAT RIVER (I-3) elev. 21'

BAYARD CUTTING ARBORETUM, on SR 27A (Montauk Hwy.), covers 697 acres, more than 140 acres of which are accessible to the public. The grounds are planted with a wide variety of plants, including azaleas, evergreens, hollies, rhododendrons and wildflowers.

The former Cutting residence, a 68-room Tudor-style house with lavish woodwork, stained-glass windows and large fireplaces, contains a natural history museum with a collection of mounted birds and American Indian artifacts. Food is available mid-April through Labor Day. Allow 2 hours, 30 minutes minimum. Arboretum open Tues.-Sun. 10-dusk. Cutting House and museum Tues.-Sun. 10-5, Apr.-Oct.; Sat.-Sun. 10-4, rest of year. Admission (includes Cutting House) $5 per private vehicle. Phone (631) 581-1002.

HAMILTON (E-8)
pop. 3,800, elev. 1,109'

Colgate University is on SR 12B. The Case Library houses exhibits and rare books, Alumni Hall displays archeological and ethnological materials and the Dana Arts Center contains the Picker Art Gallery and the University Theater. Free guided campus tours can be arranged through the admissions office; phone (315) 228-7401.

Southern Madison County Chamber of Commerce: 10 Utica St., P.O. Box 303, Hamilton, NY 13346; phone (315) 824-8213.

HAMMONDSPORT (F-5)
pop. 900, elev. 740'

The Keuka Lake community of Hammondsport is the center of the state's grape and wine industry as well as the home of aviation pioneer Glenn H. Curtiss. *Also see Finger Lakes p. 84.*

GLENN H. CURTISS MUSEUM, .5 mi. s. on SR 54, exhibits early aircraft, motorcycles and engines. Other displays include china dolls, turn-of-the-20th-century life and winemaking. Allow 1 hour, 30 minutes minimum. Mon.-Sat. 9-5, Sun. 11-5, May-Oct.; Mon.-Sat. 10-4, Sun. noon-5, in Apr. and Nov.-Dec.; Thurs.-Sat. 10-4, Sun. noon-5, rest of year. Closed Jan. 1, Thanksgiving and Dec. 25. Admission $5; over 65, $3.50; ages 7-18, $2.50. MC, VI. Phone (607) 569-2160.

KEUKA MAID DINNER BOAT departs from the Hammondsport town dock on SR 54, .2 mi. n. of SR 54A. The ship is a 500-passenger, three-deck vessel that operates on Keuka Lake.

Allow 2 hours, 30 minutes minimum. Tues.-Sat. at 12:30 and 6:30, Sun. at 1 and 5, May-Oct. Boarding begins 30 minutes before departure. Fare (without meals) $12; ages 3-12, $6. Reservations are required 1 day in advance. AE, DS, MC, VI. Phone (607) 569-2628 or (888) 372-2628.

THE WINE AND GRAPE MUSEUM OF GREYTON H. TAYLOR is off SR 54A, 1 mi. n. on Greyton H. Taylor Memorial Dr., next to Bully Hill Vineyards. Displays trace the process of wine production. The wood and stone building dates from the late 19th century and houses antique equipment used in tending the vineyards and producing wines and brandy; coopers' tools and local historical memorabilia also are displayed. Mon.-Sat. 9-5, Sun. noon-5, May-Oct. Donations. Phone (607) 868-4814.

WINERIES

- **Bully Hill Vineyards**, off SR 54A, then 2 mi. up the hill on Bully Hill Rd. Tours are offered on the hour Mon.-Sat. 10-4, mid-May through Oct. 31; Sat. 10-4, Sun. noon-5, rest of year. Phone (607) 868-3610 or 868-3210.

- ★ **PLEASANT VALLEY WINE CO.**, off SR 54 and CR 88 following signs. Daily 10-5, Apr.-Dec.; Tues.-Sat. 10-4, rest of year. Closed Jan. 1, Easter, Thanksgiving and Dec. 25. Phone (607) 569-6111.

HARRISON—see New York p. 138.

HARTFORD (D-11) pop. 2,000

THE LOG VILLAGE GRIST MILL AND MUSEUM, 2 mi. e. of SR 40 on CR 30 in East Hartford, is a restored and working 1810 gristmill with original equipment. Also on the grounds are a museum of antique farm equipment and household items, gas and steam engines, an 1894 cider mill and press, a machine shed and a library. A guide service is available.

Allow 2 hours minimum. Sat. and holidays 10-6, Sun. noon-6, Mon.-Fri. by appointment, Memorial Day-Oct. 31. Admission $2.50; ages 5-16, 50c; family rate $6. Phone (518) 632-5237.

HARTWICK (F-8)
pop. 2,000, elev. 1,339'

LOLLYPOP PETTING ZOO is 2 mi. w. on CR 11 (Hartwick-Index Rd.). The zoo is home to exotic and miniature animals, including camels and cougars, and is designed as a hands-on petting experience. Allow 1 hour minimum. Daily 9-5, May 15-Oct. 15. Admission $5; over 59, $4; ages 3-12, $3. DS, MC, VI. Phone (607) 293-7766.

HERKIMER (E-9)
pop. 7,900, elev. 398'

Settled in 1725 by German Palatines, Herkimer began as a dairying center, then became a focus of state politics and conventions during the early 1800s. In 1865 Warner Miller perfected the process of making paper from wood pulp, which cut the cost of newsprint and caused a huge increase in newspaper, magazine and book publishing.

A trial at the Herkimer County Courthouse inspired Theodore Dreiser's novel "An American Tragedy." More recent local activities include digging for "Herkimer Diamonds," which are actually rare, exceptionally clear, double-terminated quartz crystals. An open-pit mine and museum can be found on SR 5; phone (315) 891-7355.

Herkimer County Chamber of Commerce: 28 W. Main St., Mohawk, NY 13407; phone (315) 866-7820 or (877) 984-4636.

HERKIMER COUNTY HISTORICAL SOCIETY, 400 N. Main St., provides an overview of the agriculture, industry and domestic life of Herkimer County from the 1700s to the 1990s. A guided tour of the old county jail and a self-guiding tour of the doll house collection are available. Allow 1 hour minimum.

Mon.-Fri. 10-4; closed holidays. Museum free. Jail tour $1, family rate $2.50. Doll house tour $1.50, family rate $3.50. Combination jail and doll house tours $2, family rate $5. Phone (315) 866-6413.

HICKSVILLE (I-3)
pop. 40,200, elev. 149'

HICKSVILLE GREGORY MUSEUM, at Heitz Pl. and Bay Ave., is in the 1895 Heitz Place Courthouse. The museum's mineral collection features specimens from throughout the world. A butterfly and moth collection emphasizes species native to Long Island. Visitors can see the 1915 jail, where inmates were supervised by a constable who resided in quarters above the courtroom. Audio-visual programs and traveling displays also are available.

Allow 1 hour minimum. Tues.-Fri. 9:30-4:30, Sat.-Sun. 1-5; closed major holidays. Admission $3; over 59 and ages 6-16, $1.50; family rate $8.50. Phone (516) 822-7505.

LONG ISLAND REPTILE MUSEUM, 70 Broadway, contains some 3,000 live reptiles and amphibians from around the world housed in exhibit areas closed to their natural habitat. A movie about the animals is featured. Allow 1 hour minimum. Daily 10-6 (also Fri. 6-8 p.m.); closed Jan. 1, Thanksgiving and Dec. 25. Admission $9.95; over 55 and ages 3-12, $7.95. CB, DS, MC, VI. Phone (516) 931-1500.

HIGH FALLS (G-10) elev. 256'

DELAWARE & HUDSON CANAL MUSEUM, .5 mi. s. of SR 213 on Mohonk Rd., is devoted to the history of a 108-mile canal that linked the company's coal fields to the Hudson River at Kingston 1828-98. Exhibits depict 19th-century life along the canal and activity on the canal boats and include photographs, artifacts, dioramas and working models of a lock and gravity railroad car. A self-guiding tour of the nearby "Five Locks Walk" also is available.

Allow 1 hour minimum. Thurs.-Sat. and Mon. 11-5, Sun. 1-5, Memorial Day-Labor Day; Sat. 11-5, Sun. 1-5, May 1-day before Memorial Day and day after Labor Day-Oct. 31. Admission $2; under 12, $1; family rate $5. Phone (914) 687-9311.

HIGHMOUNT (G-9) elev. 795'

A winter sports center, Highmount is near Belleayre Mountain, said to have the highest base elevation in the Northeast. Downhill and cross-country skiing are popular.

HORSEHEADS (F-6)
pop. 6,800, elev. 915'

Horseheads is named for the remains of the pack horses Gen. John Sullivan used to transport his men from Pennsylvania to western New York to fight the Six Nations of the Iroquois. On the return trip the horses collapsed, and Sullivan destroyed an estimated 300 of them at this site. Their sun-bleached skulls were all that remained when the first European settlers arrived in 1789. The Horseheads Historical Society Museum houses local historical artifacts in addition to works by early 20th-century political cartoonist Eugene "Zim" Zimmerman. *Also see Finger Lakes p. 84.*

NATIONAL WARPLANE MUSEUM, off SR 17 exit 51 following signs to 17 Aviation Dr. at Elmira-Corning Regional Airport, traces aviation history from 1919 to the present with an emphasis on aircraft from World War II, Korea and Vietnam. The collection features transport, sea, fighter and scout planes—including a flying-condition B-17 Flying Fortress—as well as aviation memorabilia and model airplanes. A hangar shows restoration work in progress.

Allow 1 hour minimum. Mon.-Sat. 9-5, Sun. 11-5; closed Jan. 1, Thanksgiving and Dec. 25. Admission $5; over 64, $4; ages 6-17, $3; family rate $13. AE, DS, MC, VI. Phone (607) 739-8200.

HOWES CAVE (E-9) elev. 795'

★ **HOWE CAVERNS** is off I-88 exit 22, 1.7 mi. e. on SR 7, then 1.5 mi. n. following signs. The guided tour begins as elevators descend into the prehistoric caverns, 160 to 200 feet underground. Follow the brick walkways along the subterranean river through chambers with stalactites and stalagmites to the departure point for a boat ride on the underground Lake of Venus. The caverns have a constant temperature of 52 degrees Fahrenheit (12 C). Geode cutting and gemstone mining are available all year. Horseback trail rides and pony rides are available (weather permitting). Food is available.

Allow 2 hours minimum. Daily 9-6; closed Jan. 1, Thanksgiving and Dec. 25. Guided tour $12; over 64, $10.50; ages 7-12, $6; under 7 free with an adult. DS, MC, VI. Phone (518) 296-8990.

IROQUOIS INDIAN MUSEUM, off I-88 exit 22, 1.7 mi. e. on SR 7, then 1 mi. n. on Caverns Rd., is devoted to the Iroquois people, their culture and the preservation of their heritage. The museum houses a collection of contemporary Iroquois artwork. Archeological and historical exhibits also are displayed. A children's museum contains hands-on exhibits. Nature trails through a 45-acre park are available.

Allow 1 hour minimum. Tues.-Sat. 10-5, Sun. noon-5, Apr.-Dec.; closed Easter, Thanksgiving and Dec. 24-25. Admission $7; senior citizens and ages 13-17, $5.50; ages 5-12, $4. MC, VI. Phone (518) 296-8949.

HUDSON (F-11) pop. 8,000, elev. 67'

Named after Henry Hudson, who landed at this site in 1609, Hudson was chartered in 1785 and missed being the state capital by just one vote. This once booming whaling port and port of entry is rich in architectural as well as cultural heritage: Hudson has one of the country's largest assortments of 19th-century architecture.

The 1811 Robert Jenkins House and Museum contains Hudson River School paintings, local artifacts, whaling lore and a genealogical library. Several antique shops line Warren Street in the business district. Promenade Hill overlooks the Hudson River and the Catskills.

Columbia County Chamber of Commerce: 507 Warren St., Hudson, NY 12534; phone (518) 828-4417.

★ **AMERICAN MUSEUM OF FIREFIGHTING,** at the Firemen's Home at 125 Harry Howard Ave., was founded in 1925. One of the oldest museums of its type in the country, it contains more than 60 firefighting machines, one of which dates from 1725, fire-related paintings and firefighting memorabilia. Allow 30 minutes minimum. Daily 9-4:30; closed major holidays. Free. Phone (518) 828-7695.

OLANA STATE HISTORIC SITE is off New York State Thruway (US 87) exit 21 to SR 23E, then 1 mi. s. on SR 9G. The Victorian Estate was the home of Frederic Edwin Church, landscape painter of the Hudson River School. The mansion, built 1870-76 in the Persian style, commands a view of the Hudson River Valley and the Catskills. The visitor center offers a film and exhibit about Church. Recreational opportunities include hiking and cross-country skiing. Picnicking is permitted.

Allow 1 hour minimum. House tours every half-hour Wed.-Sun. 10-5, Apr. 2-Oct. 31. Grounds open daily 8-dusk. Tour $3; over 62, $2; children $1. Grounds free. Tours are limited to 12 persons; reservations are suggested. Phone (518) 828-0135.

HUNTINGTON (H-3)
pop. 18,200, elev. 205'

Huntington is the birthplace of poet Walt Whitman and the place where patriot Nathan Hale was arrested. Situated on Long Island's North Shore, Huntington is characterized by rolling hills, bluffs and picturesque harbors. The John Lloyd Manor House, built 1766-67, is a restored local historic site. The Lloyd Neck Black Oak, measuring 19 feet, 7 inches in circumference, is the largest known black oak in the United States and is north from SR 25A on West Neck Road.

Huntington Township Chamber of Commerce: 151 W. Carver St., Huntington, NY 11743; phone (631) 423-6100.

Shopping areas: Walt Whitman Mall, 2 miles north of I-495 exit 49N on the east side of SR 110, serves the Huntington area. Macy's is among its 100 stores.

HECKSCHER MUSEUM, in Heckscher Park at Prime Ave. and Main St., contains a permanent collection of European and American paintings and sculpture from the 16th century to the present as well as changing exhibits. Allow 30 minutes minimum. Tues.-Fri. 10-5 (also first Fri. of the month 5-8:30), Sat.-Sun. 1-5; closed major holidays. Admission $3, children $1. Phone (631) 351-3250.

SAVE **HUNTINGTON HISTORICAL SOCIETY,** in the 1750 David Conklin House at High St. and New York Ave. and in the Daniel Whitehead Kissam House at 434 Park Ave., maintains a museum of historic furnishings. Allow 30 minutes minimum. Conklin House open Tues.-Fri. and Sun. 1-4. Kissam House open Sun. 1-4, May-Oct.; otherwise by appointment. Admission $2.50; over 61, $2; under 13, $1; family rate $5. Phone (631) 427-7045.

NATHAN HALE MEMORIAL MONUMENT, 1 mi. n. of SR 25A on SR 110 and Mill Dam Rd., marks the spot where the patriot spy was captured. Daily 24 hours. Free.

SAVE **WALT WHITMAN BIRTHPLACE STATE HISTORIC SITE** is off SR 110 at 246 Old Walt Whitman Rd. The 1819 farmhouse is where Walt Whitman spent his early childhood years. At the Interpretive Center visitors can delve into Whitman's life and poetry through a series of exhibits that trace the poet's development from his boyhood on Long Island to his international prominence as one of the country's visionaries.

The exhibits incorporate more than 130 portraits of Whitman as well as original letters, manuscripts and artifacts. Among the more important artifacts are a writing desk used by Whitman as a young teacher, and first editions of his epic book of poetry "Leaves of Grass," and his autobiographical work, "Specimen Days." The Interpretive Center also features Whitman's voice on tape and an orientation film. Guided tours, picnic facilities and maps for a combined auto-hiking tour of Whitman-related sites in historic West Hills are available. Picnicking is permitted.

Allow 30 minutes minimum. Daily 11-4, last week in June-Labor Day; Wed.-Fri. 1-4, Sat.-Sun. 11-4, rest of year. Closed major holidays. Admission $3; over 62 and students with ID $2; ages 7-12, $1. Phone (631) 427-5240.

HYDE PARK (G-10)
pop. 21,200, elev. 8′

Hyde Park is the home of the Culinary Institute of America, a vocational training school for aspiring chefs. The school was founded in 1946 with 16 students; its most recent enrollment is about 1,800. The institute occupies a former Jesuit seminary on US 9 overlooking the Hudson River. The institute's four restaurants are open to the public by reservation.

Hyde Park Chamber of Commerce: 629 Albany Post Rd., P.O. Box 17, Hyde Park, NY 12538; phone (914) 229-8612.

ELEANOR ROOSEVELT NATIONAL HISTORIC SITE is off SR 9G, .5 mi. n. of St. Andrews Rd. Val-Kill, the main cottage, was Mrs. Roosevelt's weekend and holiday retreat from her hectic public duties during her husband's presidency. After President Franklin D. Roosevelt died in 1945, she lived in the cottage until her death in 1962. The grounds include gardens, outbuildings, woodland trails and a pond. The site's access road is unpaved and narrow; check locally for road conditions. Guided tours are available.

Allow 1 hour minimum. Daily 9-5, May-Oct.; Sat.-Sun. 9-5, Mar.-Apr. and Nov.-Dec. Closed Thanksgiving and Dec. 25. Admission $5, under 17 free. Combination ticket $18 (includes the Franklin D. Roosevelt Museum and Library, Home of Franklin D. Roosevelt National Historic Site, and Vanderbilt Mansion National Historic Site). MC, VI. Phone (914) 229-9115, or 229-2501 Sat.-Sun.

★ **FRANKLIN D. ROOSEVELT MUSEUM AND LIBRARY,** next to the Home of Franklin D. Roosevelt National Historic Site, was the first

presidential library. The museum's displays of photographs, artworks, official documents and speeches, gifts from admirers and heads of state, and family possessions and letters chronicle the lives and careers of President and Mrs. Roosevelt.

Allow 1 hour, 30 minutes minimum. Daily 9-6; closed Jan. 1, Thanksgiving and Dec. 25. Admission $10, under 17 free. Combination ticket $18 (includes the Eleanor Roosevelt National Historic Site, Home of Franklin D. Roosevelt National Historic Site, and Vanderbilt Mansion National Historic Site). MC, VI. Phone (914) 229-8114.

★ HOME OF FRANKLIN D. ROOSEVELT NATIONAL HISTORIC SITE, 2 mi. s. on US 9, consists of more than 200 acres and includes the home and graves of President and Mrs. Roosevelt. The 1826 house remains almost exactly as it was at the time of the president's death in 1945. The estate includes stables, icehouses, a walking trail and a tourist information center. The graves, marked by a plain white marble monument, are in the Rose Garden, northeast of the house.

Allow 1 hour, 30 minutes minimum. Daily 9-5; closed Jan. 1, Thanksgiving and Dec. 25. Admission $10, under 17 free. Combination ticket $18 (includes the Eleanor Roosevelt National Historic Site, Franklin D. Roosevelt Museum and Library, and Vanderbilt Mansion National Historic Site). MC, VI. Phone (914) 229-9115, or 229-2501 Sat.-Sun.

★ MILLS MANSION STATE HISTORIC SITE is 5 mi. n. on US 9 to Old Post Rd. This 65-room mansion, built in 1832 and remodeled and enlarged in 1895 by architect Stanford White, contains marble fireplaces, wood paneling, gilded plaster work, ornate furniture and art objects from around the world. The Ogden and Ruth Livingston Mills Memorial Park has recreational facilities (see Recreation Chart).

Allow 1 hour minimum for tour. Mansion open Wed.-Sat. 10-5, Sun. noon-5, May 1-Labor Day; Wed.-Sun. noon-5, day after Labor Day-Oct. 31. Guided house tours are conducted every half-hour. Last tour begins 30 minutes before closing. Grounds open daily 8-dusk. Admission $3; over 62, $2; ages 5-12, $1. Phone (914) 889-8851.

★ VANDERBILT MANSION NATIONAL HISTORIC SITE is 2 mi. n. on US 9. This 1898 mansion exemplifies the Beaux-Arts architecture of the late 19th-century "Gilded Age." The French and Italian furnishings are original pieces. Also exhibited are Flemish and French tapestries and Oriental rugs. The grounds afford views of the Hudson River.

Allow 1 hour minimum. Daily 9-5, May-Oct.; Thurs.-Mon. 9-5, rest of year. Closed Jan. 1, Thanksgiving and Dec. 25. Admission $8, under 17 free. Combination ticket $18 (includes Eleanor Roosevelt National Historic Site, Franklin D. Roosevelt Museum and Library, and Home

of Franklin D. Roosevelt National Historic Site). MC, VI. Phone (914) 229-9115.

ILION (E-8) pop. 8,900, elev. 392'

REMINGTON PLANT TOUR, off SR 5S on Catherine St., walks visitors 1.5 miles through the gun-making process. No cameras, backpacks or strollers allowed on the tour. Allow 1 hour minimum. Tours depart Mon.-Fri. at 10 and 1. Free. Phone (315) 895-3301.

Remington Museum offers a display of firearms ranging from flintlock rifles to rare pistols and revolvers. Other Remington products from the past include a 19th-century typewriter and a 1900s bicycle. A videotape presentation is offered. Allow 30 minutes minimum. Mon.-Fri. 9-5, Sat. 10-4, June 1-Sept. 1; Mon.-Fri. 9-5, rest of year.

ITHACA (F-6) pop. 29,500, elev. 836'

Ithaca is at the southern tip of Cayuga Lake. Buttermilk Falls (see Recreation Chart), Taughannock Falls (see attraction listing) and Robert H. Treman (see Recreation Chart) state parks offer recreational opportunities. The Cayuga Wine Trail begins at this point and continues north on scenic SR 89, passing several wineries along the western shore of the lake.

Founded in 1892 as a conservatory of music, Ithaca College, atop South Hill off SR 96B, offers drama and music presentations and a public art gallery. Campus tours are available through the admissions office; phone (800) 429-4274. Also see Finger Lakes p. 84.

Ithaca/Tompkins County Convention and Visitors Bureau: 904 E. Shore Dr., Ithaca, NY 14850; phone (607) 272-1313 or (800) 284-8422.

CORNELL UNIVERSITY is on the n.e. side of town. The Herbert F. Johnson Museum of Art is open Tues.-Sun. 10-5. Chimes at the University Clock Tower are played regularly when school is in session. Other places of interest on the campus include Triphammer Bridge, with its view of Fall Creek Gorge, Triphammer Falls and Beebe Lake; the Olin Library; Anabel Taylor Hall; and the Lua A. Minns Memorial Gardens.

Central campus tours depart from the main lobby of Day Hall Mon.-Fri. at 9, 11, 1 and 3, Sat. at 9 and 1, Sun. at 1, Apr.-Nov.; daily at 1, rest of year. Closed Jan. 1 and Dec. 24-25. Phone (607) 254-4636.

Cornell Plantations, 2.5 mi. n. on SRs 79 and 366 at One Plantation Rd., lie along the Cascadilla and Fall Creek gorges. The plantations contain trails, botanical gardens, ponds, streams, woodlands, swamps, a lake and an arboretum. Picnicking is permitted. Allow 1 hour minimum. Daily dawn-dusk. Free. Phone (607) 255-3020.

Sapsucker Woods, 3 mi. n.e. of the main campus at 159 Sapsucker Woods Rd., is the home of the Cornell Laboratory of Ornithology research center. Four miles of sanctuary trails wind through woodlands and swamps filled with nesting and migrating birds. In the Lyman K. Stuart Observatory a picture window overlooks a bird-feeding garden and a 10-acre pond. Displayed is a collection of paintings by ornithological painter Louis Agassiz Fuertes.

Allow 1 hour minimum. Observatory open Mon.-Thurs. 8-5, Fri. 8-4, Sat. 10-4; closed Jan. 1 and Dec. 25. Trails open daily 24 hours. Donations. Phone (607) 254-2473.

[SAVE] **SCIENCENTER** is off SR 13 downtown following signs at 601 First St. This interactive science museum features numerous hands-on displays that allow visitors to explore scientific principles while having fun. Among the exhibits are "whisper dishes" that project a voice over a long distance, a hydraulic raceway, a two-story-high ball machine and a giant walk-in camera.

Allow 2 hours minimum. Tues.-Sat. and some national holidays 10-5, Sun. noon-5. Admission $4.50; over 64, $4; ages 4-12, $3.50. Phone (607) 272-0600.

STEWART PARK, on Cayuga Lake .5 mi. n. on Meadow St., has a carousel, a goldfish pond and a rose garden. Adjoining the park are the Fuertes Wild Fowl Preserve and the Renwick Bird Sanctuary. Picnicking is permitted. Allow 30 minutes minimum. Daily 8 a.m.-10 p.m. Free.

★ **TAUGHANNOCK FALLS STATE PARK** is 8 mi. n. on SR 89. The 215-foot Taughannock Falls is in a .75-mile-long glen with sides rising from 350 to 400 feet. Trails follow the edge of the gorge. Camping and swimming are permitted in season.

Park open daily 8 a.m.-dusk. Trails open mid-May to mid-Oct. Admission $5 per private vehicle, June 1-Labor Day; $4, day after Labor Day-Columbus Day; free rest of year. Phone (607) 387-6739. *See Recreation Chart and the AAA Northeastern CampBook.*

TOMPKINS COUNTY MUSEUM AND DEWITT HISTORICAL SOCIETY, 401 E. State St., presents seasonal exhibits focusing on local industries, arts and ethnic groups. A reference room is available Tuesdays, Thursdays and Saturdays. Museum open Tues.-Sat. 11-5; closed Jan. 1, July 4, Thanksgiving and Dec. 25. Donations. Phone (607) 273-8284.

JAMESTOWN (G-2)
pop. 34,700, elev. 1,323'

Jamestown's founder, James Prendergast, built the town's first dam and sawmill in 1811, taking advantage of the vast white pine forests on the hills overlooking the southeast tip of Chautauqua Lake. By the mid-1800s Jamestown was one of the state's leading producers of furniture and wood products. Locally produced "pearl ash"

was used to make glass, and the town was nicknamed Pearl City.

Old-fashioned family fun can be found at Midway Park, on SR 430 in nearby Maple Springs. Highlights include a beach for swimming, picnic areas and several amusement rides, including bumper boats and go-carts. Phone (716) 386-3165.

Jamestown Area Chamber of Commerce: 101 W. 5th St., Jamestown, NY 14701; phone (716) 484-1101.

Self-guiding tours: Jamestown is the site of many 19th-century commercial and industrial buildings, churches and private houses. Brochures detailing self-guiding walking tours are available from the Fenton History Center-Museum & Library *(see attraction listing).*

Shopping areas: Chautauqua Mall, 3 miles west on SR 394, includes The Bon-Ton, JCPenney and Sears among its 60 stores.

ART GALLERY, in the James Prendergast Library at 509 Cherry St., contains 19th- and 20th-century French, German and American paintings as well as changing exhibits. Allow 30 minutes minimum. Mon.-Fri. 9-8:30, Sat. 9-5, Sun. 1-3:30, Nov.-Apr.; Mon.-Fri. 9-8:30, Sat. 9-4:30, rest of year. Free. Phone (716) 484-7135.

★ *CHAUTAUQUA BELLE—see Mayville p. 103.*

FENTON HISTORY CENTER-MUSEUM & LIBRARY, at 67 Washington St. (SR 60), just s. of Washington St. bridge, is in the 1863 Italian villa-style mansion of New York Gov. Reuben E. Fenton. The center features a restored Renaissance Revival drawing room, other period rooms, changing topical exhibits and a reference/genealogy library. An annual holiday exhibit highlights historic and ethnic observances and celebrations. Guided tours are available.

Allow 1 hour minimum. Mon.-Sat. 10-4, Sun. 1-4, day after Thanksgiving-Jan. 6; Mon.-Sat. 10-4, rest of year. Admission $2.50; over 64, $2; ages 4-16, $1. Phone (716) 664-6256.

JAMESTOWN AUDUBON NATURE CENTER is 2 mi. s. on SR 60, 3 mi. s. on US 62, then .5 mi. e. to 1600 Riverside Rd. The Roger Tory Peterson Nature Interpretive Building offers educational and environmental exhibits, mounted bird specimens, a viewing area on the third floor and prints by Peterson, noted American wildlife artist. The 600-acre wildlife sanctuary features nature trails, an arboretum, an herb and butterfly garden and several habitats, as well as being home to area wildlife, especially wetland species.

Allow 1 hour minimum. Sanctuary open daily dawn-dusk. Interpretive building open Tues.-Sat. 10-5, Sun. 1-5; closed holidays. Donations. Phone (716) 569-2345.

[SAVE] **LUCY-DESI MUSEUM,** 212 Pine St., houses exhibits describing the lives and entertainment careers of Desi Arnaz and Jamestown-native Lucille Ball. Interactive exhibits recount the history of comedy and the couple's impact on the television industry. Several items that once belonged to the two performers are on display. Changing exhibits chronicle different aspects of their personal and professional lives.

Mon.-Sat. 10-5:30, Sun. 1-5, May-Oct.; Sat. 10-5:30, Sun. 1-5, rest of year. Closed Jan. 1, Easter and Dec. 25. Admission $5; over 55 and ages 6-18, $3.50. DS, MC, VI. Phone (716) 484-7070.

ROGER TORY PETERSON INSTITUTE OF NATURAL HISTORY, 311 Curtis St., is a national center for nature education named for the award-winning naturalist and author of a popular series of natural history field guides. The institute features wildlife art and nature photography exhibits, trails and a butterfly garden on 27 wooded acres. Tues.-Sat. 10-4, Sun. 1-5. Admission $3, students with ID and children $2. Phone (716) 665-2473.

JAVA CENTER (F-4) pop. 200

BEAVER MEADOW NATURE CENTER, 1610 Welch Rd., features several nature trails including one that passes near a couple of old farmsteads and others that follow the edge of Beaver Pond. A visitor center contains exhibits. Allow 1 hour minimum. Tues.-Sat. 10-5, Sun. 1-5; closed Jan. 1, July 4, Thanksgiving and Dec. 25. Donations. Phone (716) 457-3228.

JOHNSTOWN (E-9)
pop. 9,100, elev. 650'

Johnstown was founded by and named for Sir William Johnson, a British general and Superintendent of Indian Affairs during the mid-1700s. Johnstown has been a center of the glove-making industry since its earliest days, as has the adjoining city of Gloversville *(see place listing p. 88)*. Elizabeth Cady Stanton, a pioneer of women's rights, was born in Johnstown in 1815.

Johnstown Battlefield preserves the site of what was probably the Revolutionary War's last battle, fought Oct. 25, 1781, 6 days after Gen. Charles Cornwallis surrendered at Yorktown.

The Tryon County Court House, on W. Main Street between N. William and N. Melcher streets, was erected in 1774 and is the only Colonial courthouse standing in the state.

JOHNSON HALL STATE HISTORIC SITE, .2 mi. w. off SR 29 on Hall Ave., is a 1763 Georgian mansion. The house was a center for American Indian trade and negotiations prior to the Revolution. Diorama and period exhibits are in the original stone house flanking the main house. Picnicking is permitted. Allow 1 hour minimum. Guided tours Wed.-Sat. 10-5, Sun. 1-5, mid-May through Oct. 31. Tour $3; over 65, $2; ages 6-12, $1. Phone (518) 762-8712.

JONES BEACH (I-3)

★ **JONES BEACH STATE PARK,** covering 2,413 acres on the ocean shore of Long Island off Meadowbrook or Wantagh Pkwy., offers supervised swimming in Zach's Bay, ocean-front beaches and two pools. Bathhouses are available; a boardwalk follows part of the shoreline. Facilities at Field 4 include a pitch-and-putt golf course and court games. Free events include softball games and outdoor dancing. Planned programs are presented weekends.

Park open daily dawn-midnight, second weekend in June-Labor Day; dawn-dusk, rest of year. Parking $4, Memorial Day-Labor Day; free, rest of year. *See Recreation Chart.*

KATONAH—*see New York p. 138.*

KINDERHOOK (F-11)
pop. 1,300, elev. 288'

COLUMBIA COUNTY MUSEUM, 5 Albany Ave., has a genealogical library, regional art gallery and changing exhibits of historical artifacts. Allow 30 minutes minimum. Mon.-Fri. 10-4, May-Nov.; Mon., Wed. and Fri. 10-4, rest of year. Phone ahead for Sat. hours. Closed federal holidays. Admission $3; over 54 and ages 12-18, $2. Phone (518) 758-9265.

JAMES VANDERPOEL HOUSE, 16 Broad St., has guided tours of the 1820 Federal-style house containing period furniture and decorative arts. Allow 1 hour minimum. Thurs.-Sat. 11-5, Sun. 1-5, Memorial Day weekend-Labor Day weekend; closed federal holidays. Tour $3; over 54 and ages 12-18, $2. Combination with the Luykas Van Alen House $5; over 54 and ages 12-18, $3. Phone (518) 758-9265.

LUYKAS VAN ALEN HOUSE AND ICHABOD CRANE SCHOOLHOUSE are 1 mi. s. on SR 9H. The 1737 farmhouse is furnished with period furniture and 18th-century decorative arts. The 1850 one-room schoolhouse has been restored to its 1920s appearance and displays Columbia County school artifacts. Allow 1 hour minimum. Guided tours Thurs.-Sat. 11-5, Sun. 1-5, Memorial Day weekend-Labor Day weekend; closed federal holidays. Admission $3; over 54 and ages 12-18, $2. Combination with the James Vanderpoel House $5; over 54 and ages 12-18, $3. Phone (518) 758-9265.

MARTIN VAN BUREN NATIONAL HISTORIC SITE, 2 mi. s. on SR 9H, is the estate of the eighth U.S. president. The 1797 mansion was remodeled in the Italianate style. Guided tours are available. Allow 1 hour, 30 minutes minimum. Daily 9-4, mid-May through Oct. 31; Sat.-Sun. 9-4, rest of year. Admission $2, under 17 free. Phone (518) 758-9689.

KINGS POINT (H-2) pop. 4,800

U.S. MERCHANT MARINE ACADEMY, on Steamboat Rd. facing Long Island Sound, trains and educates officers for the Merchant Marine and Naval Reserve. The grounds include the estate of automobile manufacturer Walter Chrysler, the American Merchant Marine Museum and the U.S. Merchant Marine Memorial Chapel. Allow 1 hour minimum. Campus open to visitors daily 9-4:30, Aug.-June. Museum open Tues.-Fri. 10-3, Sat.-Sun. 1-4:30. Closed federal holidays. Free. Phone (516) 773-5000.

KINGSTON (G-10)
pop. 23,100, elev. 295′

Established as a Dutch trading post in 1614, Kingston became a permanent settlement in 1652. The first state constitution was drafted and adopted in Kingston in 1777, when the city became the first capital. Several Colonial houses are in the Kingston area; one of the most notable is the Bevier House, which serves as the Ulster County Historical Society Headquarters and Museum.

Chamber of Commerce of Ulster County: 7 Albany Ave., #G3, Kingston, NY 12401; phone (914) 338-5100.

Self-guiding tours: Brochures outlining a walking tour of the historic Uptown Stockade area, Midtown and Rondout Creek corridor are available at the Urban Cultural Park's Visitor Center, 20 Broadway; phone (914) 331-7517. Brochures also are available from the visitor center at 308 Clinton Ave., (800) 331-1518, and at Kingston's city hall, 1 Garraghan Dr., (914) 331-0080.

ASHOKAN RESERVOIR lies w. in the Catskills; it is encircled by a picturesque 40-mi. drive (SRs 28 and 28A). The reservoir provides New York City with more than 500 million gallons of water daily when full. Phone (914) 657-2304.

SAVE **HUDSON RIVER CRUISES** depart from Rondout Landing on Broadway in the Historic Rondout District aboard the MV *Rip Van Winkle.* The 2-hour narrated cruise passes several lighthouses and magnificent Hudson River mansions. A music cruise also is available. Allow 2 hours minimum. Two-hour cruise departs Tues.-Sun. at 11:30 and 2, July-Aug.; schedule varies rest of season. Fare $13; over 60, $12; ages 4-11, $6. DS, MC, VI. For schedule phone (914) 255-6515 or (800) 843-7472.

OLD DUTCH CHURCH AND CEMETERY is on Main St. between Wall and Fair sts. The church was established in 1659; the cemetery dates from 1661. The cemetery contains the grave of George Clinton, first governor of the state. Mon.-Fri. 9-4 and by appointment. Free. Phone (914) 338-6759.

★ **SENATE HOUSE STATE HISTORIC SITE,** 312 Fair St., was the meeting site of the first New York State Senate. A museum features Hudson Valley furnishings and art exhibits relating to John Vanderlyn and other Hudson Valley artists. Rooms in the Senate House are furnished as they would have appeared in 1777 when the New York State Senate met in the home of Abraham Van Gaasbeek.

Allow 30 minutes minimum. Guided tours Wed.-Sat. 10-5, Sun. 1-5, mid-Apr. to Oct. 31. Tour $3; over 62, $2; ages 5-12, $1. Phone (914) 338-2786.

VOLUNTEER FIREMEN'S HALL AND MUSEUM OF KINGSTON, 265 Fair St., houses a parade carriage, a display of 1800s fire convention badges and a collection of souvenir mugs. The museum has a functioning fire alarm system and a fire company parlor, complete with a working player piano and ornately carved furniture with the fire company's initials on each piece. Wed.-Fri. 11-3, Sat. 10-4, Apr.-Oct. Donations. Phone (914) 331-0866 or 331-4065.

LACKAWANNA—*see Buffalo p. 72.*

LA FARGEVILLE (C-7) elev. 375′

AGRICULTURAL MUSEUM, 6 mi. s. on SR 180, illustrates the development of agriculture in the region. The complex includes a one-room schoolhouse, a church/meetinghouse and a cheese factory. Guided tours daily 9-4, June-Sept.; by appointment only in May. Admission $3. Phone (315) 658-2353.

LAKE CHAMPLAIN (A-11)

Extending from Canada southward for 120 miles, Lake Champlain varies from a quarter-mile to 12 miles wide. Two-thirds of its cubic area lies in Vermont; the rest, except for a small Canadian portion, is in New York. Lake Champlain accommodates large vessels and, with its Hudson River connector, the Champlain Canal, makes navigation possible from New York City to Montréal and the Great Lakes.

Legends of Lake Champlain's own version of the Loch Ness Monster have persisted since Samuel de Champlain sighted what he described as a serpentine creature 20 feet long, as thick as a barrel and with a head like a horse. Occasional sightings of the elusive creature, affectionately named "Champ," still occur, but whether or not a distant cousin of the Scottish sea serpent really resides in the lake remains a matter of speculation.

LAKE CHAMPLAIN FERRIES offer scenic links between Vermont and New York via three separate crossings: Burlington to Port Kent, N.Y. (crossing time 1 hour); Charlotte to Essex, N.Y. (crossing time 20 minutes); Grand Isle to Plattsburgh, N.Y. (crossing time 12 minutes). The Grand Isle ferry operates 24-hours year-round. AAA clubs have schedules and fares. Contact the

Lake Champlain Transportation Co., King Street Dock, Burlington, VT 05401; phone (802) 864-9804.

LAKE GEORGE (VILLAGE)
(D-10) pop. 900, elev. 325'

The village of Lake George is at the southern end of the 32-mile-long lake. Of the 365 islands dotting the lake, 92 have been developed for camping (see Adirondack Park p. 54 and the AAA Northeastern CampBook). On the southern shore along Beach Drive are a public beach, departure points for steamboat and cruise boat rides and areas where speedboats, parasails and horse-drawn carriages may be rented.

Million Dollar Beach, east of US 9 on Beach Road, is a popular swimming beach with a bathhouse, lifeguard, lockers, picnic facilities and volleyball courts. It is open Memorial Day through Labor Day; phone (518) 668-3352 to verify hours and prices. Scenic Lake Shore Drive (SR 9N) follows the west shore between the towns of Lake George and Ticonderoga (see place listing p. 179).

Lake George Chamber of Commerce: P.O. Box 272, Lake George, NY 12845; phone (518) 668-5755.

Shopping areas: Several factory outlet centers are located along "Million-Dollar-Half-A-Mile" in the Lake George area, including Adirondack Factory, French Mountain Commons, Lake George Plaza and Log Jam, all on SR 9 off I-87 exit 20.

FORT WILLIAM HENRY MUSEUM is on US 9 (Canada St.) in the center of town. This 1757 British fort was the subject of James Fenimore Cooper's "The Last of the Mohicans." The replica contains barracks, stockades and dungeons and fort artifacts. An audiovisual program recounts fort history. The Living History tour includes musket firing, a bomb toss and musket ball molding. The Archeological Hall contains an exhibit about the 1997 archeological dig and the original Fort Well excavation. Free parking is behind the building.

Allow 2 hours minimum. Daily 9 a.m.-10 p.m., July-Aug.; 10-5, May-June and Sept. 1 to mid-Oct. Tour $8.50; over 59 and ages 3-11, $6.50. AE, DS, MC, VI. Phone (518) 668-5471.

THE GREAT ESCAPE FUN PARK— see Queensbury p. 164.

LAKE GEORGE BATTLEFIELD PARK, .5 mi. s. off US 9, contains the ruins of Fort George, an American Indian monument and a memorial to Jesuit missionary Father Jogues. Picnicking is permitted. Daily 9-8, mid-June through Labor Day; Sat.-Sun. 9-8, early May to mid-June. Park free. Parking $3. Phone (518) 668-3352. See the AAA Northeastern CampBook.

★LAKE GEORGE OPERA FESTIVAL— see Saratoga Springs p. 172.

LAKE GEORGE STEAMBOAT CO., with cruises departing from Steel Pier, offers a narrated 4.5-hour Discovery Tour and 2.25-hour Paradise Bay cruises aboard the Mohican. One-hour paddlewheel cruises are available aboard the Minne-ha-ha. Two-hour moonlight cruises also are available. Two-hour excursions aboard the Lac du Saint Sacrement can be cruise only or can include lunch or dinner.

Discovery Tour departs daily at 9, June 26-Labor Day. Paradise Bay cruise departs daily at 2:15, Memorial Day-Columbus Day. Paddlewheel cruise departs daily at 9:30, 11:30, 1:30, 3, 4:30, 6 and 7:30, June 19-Labor Day; Sat.-Sun. at 10, 11:30, 1:30, 3 and 4:30, Memorial Day weekend-June 18 and day after Labor Day-Columbus Day. Cruises on the Lac du Saint Sacrement depart daily at noon and 6:30, June 19-Labor Day; at noon, May 8-June 18 and day after Labor Day-Oct. 24.

Round-trip Discovery Tour $16.50; ages 3-11, $8.50. Paradise Bay cruise $13.50; ages 3-11, $6.75. Paddlewheel cruise $8.50; ages 3-11, $5.50. Cruise only on the Lac du Saint Sacrement cruise $12.75; ages 3-11, $6.50. Reservations are recommended for lunch and dinner cruises. AE, DS, MC, VI. Phone (518) 668-5777 or (800) 553-2628.

PROSPECT MOUNTAIN VETERANS MEMORIAL HIGHWAY, I-87 exit 21, then 1 mi. n. on US 9, provides a scenic 5.5-mile drive to a crest overlooking Lake George. The summit is reached via free view-mobiles or a hiking trail. Picnicking is permitted. Allow 1 hour minimum. Daily 9-5, Memorial Day-late Oct. Admission $5 per private vehicle. Phone (518) 668-5198 in season or 668-3352 rest of year.

SHORELINE CRUISES OF LAKE GEORGE leave from the lake front at 2 Kurosaka Ln. Narrated tours explain the scenic and historic sites along the shore. One-hour sightseeing cruises depart every 30 minutes daily 9:30-7:30, Memorial Day-Labor Day; at 10, noon, 2 and 4, May 1-day before Memorial Day and day after Labor Day-Oct. 31. Two-and-a-half-hour Horicon Paradise Bay cruises depart daily at 1, Memorial Day-Labor Day; Sat.-Sun. at 1, May 1-day before Memorial Day and day after Labor Day-Oct. 31. Midnight entertainment and happy hour cruises also are available.

One-hour cruise $8; over 64, $7; ages 3-11, $4.50. Horicon Paradise Bay cruise $11; over 64, $10; ages 3-11, $5.50. MC, VI. Phone (518) 668-4644, or (800) 894-2427 in N.Y.

LAKE LUZERNE (D-10)
pop. 2,800, elev. 624'

RECREATIONAL ACTIVITIES
White-water Rafting
- **Hudson River Rafting Co.** departs from the company's headquarters downtown on Main

St. off SR 9N. Write P.O. Box 47, North Creek, NY 12853. Departures daily June 1-Labor Day; Sat.-Sun. Memorial Day-May 31 and day after Labor Day-Columbus Day. Phone (518) 696-2964.

LAKE PLACID (B-10)
pop. 2,500, elev. 1,864'

The village of Lake Placid lies on the shores of Mirror Lake and Lake Placid; the former provides a backdrop for the Main Street commercial district. Host of the 1932 and 1980 Winter Olympics, the area boasts downhill skiing at Whiteface Mountain, 8 miles north, as well as other competitive and recreational sports activities at both state-operated and private facilities.

Summer recreational facilities include bridle and bicycle paths, private and public beaches, tennis courts, six golf courses, hiking trails and the indoor Olympic Arena for summer ice skating. Boats can be rented at both lakes. Whiteface Mountain provides chairlift rides over grassy ski slopes, and the Whiteface Mountain Veterans' Memorial Highway *(see Wilmington p. 185)* runs almost to the summit.

The United States Olympic Training Center, 421 Old Military Rd., offers self-guiding tours of its facilities; phone (518) 523-2600. The Uihlein-Cornell Sugar House on Bear Cub Road contains maple sugar exhibits and demonstrations.

Lake Placid/Essex County Chamber and Visitors Bureau: Olympic Center, 216 Main St., Lake Placid, NY 12946; phone (518) 523-2445 or (800) 447-5224.

HIGH FALLS GORGE—*see Wilmington p. 185.*

JOHN BROWN FARM STATE HISTORIC SITE is 2 mi. s. on SR 73, then .7 mi. s. on John Brown Rd. A monument and restored farmhouse mark the burial spot of abolitionist John Brown. A self-guiding trail passes through the grounds, which are accessible all year. Cross-country trails also are available. A guided tour of the farmhouse also is available. Allow 30 minutes minimum. House open Wed.-Sat. 10-5, Sun. 1-5 (also 10-5, Memorial Day, July 4 and Labor Day), May 1-late Oct. Free. Phone (518) 523-3900.

LAKE PLACID BOAT RIDES, 1 mi. n. on Mirror Lake Dr. at Lake Placid Marina, offers narrated 1-hour cruises that depart daily at 10:30, 1, 2:30 and 4, June 20-Labor Day; Mon.-Fri. at 10:30 and 2:30, Sat.-Sun. at 10:30, 2:30 and 4, May 16-June 19; daily at 10:30, 1:30 and 3, day after Labor Day-Oct. 18. Fare $6.75; over 62, $5.75; ages 3-12, $4.75. MC, VI. Phone (518) 523-9704 to verify schedule and prices.

LAKE PLACID/NORTH ELBA HISTORICAL SOCIETY MUSEUM, 2 blks. from SRs 73 and 86 on Averyville Rd., chronicles Lake Placid's history over the last 200 years. The waiting room and the baggage room of this former train station now house displays of primitive farm implements, musical instruments, period photographs and memorabilia and 1932 and 1980 Olympic material. A train engine also is featured. Allow 30 minutes minimum. Tues.-Sun. noon-4, June-Sept. Donations. Phone (518) 523-1608.

LAKE PLACID SIGHTSEEING TOURS departs from all major hotels and motels in town. The 2 hour, 30 minute bus tours highlight local historic and Olympic sites. Tours depart daily at 1, June-Oct. Other tours and times are available by appointment. Fare $20; over 60, $18; ages 6-12, $15. Fare includes admission to the Intervale Ski Jumping Complex. Reservations are required. MC, VI. Phone (518) 523-4431.

OLYMPIC CENTER, 218 Main St. off SR 86, is a multipurpose facility hosting numerous world and national class events, including hockey games, ice shows, public skating, concerts and curling. Originally built for the ice events of the 1932 Winter Olympic Games, the center received an additional wing to host the 1980 Winter Olympic Game—providing a total of four indoor ice rinks. A guided tour of the center is available.

The center houses the main office of the New York Olympic Regional Development Authority, created in 1981 to preserve Lake Placid's Olympic heritage. Other sites include the Whiteface Mountain facilities, off SR 86 in Wilmington, and the Olympic Jumping complex and Olympic Sports Complex, both off SR 73. During the summer months, the complex features gondola rides to the top of Little Whiteface and Whiteface Mountain Veterans' Memorial Highway, an 8-mile long toll road to the summit.

The Summer Olympic Site Passport is a self-guiding tour that includes admission to all summer venues, while the Total Winter Experience package includes participation in many of the winter sports including a bobsled ride, cross-country skiing at Mount Van Hoevenberg or ice skating

Allow 4 hours minimum. Center open daily 9-5. Guided tour offered on the hour daily 10-3, July 1-Labor Day. Summer Olympic Site Passport offered daily 9-5, mid-June to mid-Oct. Total Winter Experience available Dec. 26 to mid-Mar. Center free. Guided tour $4; senior citizens $3; ages 5-12, $2. Summer Olympic Site Passport $16-$18. Total Winter Experience $39. Phone (518) 523-1655. *See color ad p. 99.*

1932 & 1980 Lake Placid Winter Olympic Museum, within the Olympic Center at 218 Main St., explores the legacy of the 1932 and 1980 Olympic Games. A videotape presentation, displays of athletes' uniforms and equipment, and a model of the entire Olympic complex are featured. Allow 30 minutes minimum. Daily 10-5; closed Dec. 25. Admission $3; over 62, $2; ages 7-12, $1. Phone (518) 523-1655.

Olympic Jumping Complex, 2 mi. s.e. of the village on SR 73, is the training ski jump for the U.S. Olympic teams. The Kodak Sports Park is a freestyle skiing training center. In the winter the site is home to international competition and training; in summer plastic matting is used to simulate snow. Featured is a 295-foot tower with a glass-enclosed elevator and a view of Mount Marcy.

Daily 9-4. Admission $4; with chairlift pass and elevator to top of ski jump $8; over 61 and ages 5-12, $6. Phone (518) 523-1655 or 523-2202.

Olympic Sports Complex at Mount Van Hoevenberg, 7 mi. s.e. on SR 73, offers more than 50 miles of groomed cross-country ski trails. The Bobsled Finnish Building presents films and a slide show about the sledding sports in summer. The Nordic Lodge rents ski equipment in winter. Picnicking is permitted.

Open daily 9-4. A bobsled ride is offered Wed.-Mon. 10-4, in winter (weather permitting). Day-use fees (special events excluded) $2. Cross-country ski area $12; senior citizens and under 12, $10. Bobsled ride $30. Phone (800) 462-6236 or (518) 523-4436.

SANTA'S WORKSHOP—*see Wilmington p. 185.*

LAWRENCE (I-2)
pop. 6,500, elev. 30′

ROCK HALL MUSEUM, 199 Broadway, is a restored, 1767 Georgian Colonial mansion furnished in the style of the late 18th century. A garden and picnic area are on the grounds. Wed.-Sat. 10-4, Sun. noon-4; closed holidays. Free. Phone (516) 239-1157.

LE ROY (E-5) pop. 5,000, elev. 863′

LE ROY HOUSE MUSEUM AND JELL-O GALLERY, I-90 exit 47, s. on SR 19 to 23 E. Main St., was built in the early 19th century. Seven rooms are furnished in period, including a basement kitchen and a children's playroom. An exhibit about Jell-O, the dessert invented in Le Roy in 1897, is presented. Allow 30 minutes minimum. Mon.-Sat. 10-4, Sun. 1-4, Memorial Day-Labor Day. Admission $3; ages 6-12, $1.50. MC, VI. Phone (716) 768-7433. *See color ad p. 202.*

LEWISTON—*see Niagara Falls p. 151.*

LITTLE FALLS (E-9)
pop. 5,800, elev. 370′

Water has always been a factor in the development of the city of Little Falls. Although in the city's earliest days the falls may have created a navigational problem, they soon became a natural blessing; their presence spurred the onset of settlement in the gorge and became a source of water power. Lock #17, with a drop of 40 feet, is the largest lock on the Barge Canal. As transportation improved, trade increased, and Little Falls soon became a stopping point between New York City and the western part of the state.

Historic Canal Place is a revitalized industrial area that includes two refurbished 19th-century stone mill buildings set amidst two parks along the Mohawk River. The area includes antique and art galleries as well as other shops and restaurants and a visual and performing arts center. An underground walkway connects Historic Canal Place with Main Street.

Of interest is the Little Falls Historical Society Museum at 319 S. Ann St. Housed in the restored 1833 bank building, exhibits include local memorabilia, genealogical files, a bank vault and Victorian clothing. Phone (315) 823-0643.

Self-guiding tours: Brochures detailing self-guiding tours of the city's landmarks, historic areas and natural wonders are available at the Little Falls Historical Society Museum or at the Urban Renewal Office on Main St., phone (315) 823-3560.

Shopping areas: Little Falls Antique Center, 25 W. Mill St. in Historic Canal Place, offers two floors of antiques and decorative arts displayed in an 1855 stone mill building. Several art galleries also call this area home.

HERKIMER HOME STATE HISTORIC SITE, 3 mi. e. on SR 169 at interchange 29A, was the home of American Revolutionary War general Nicholas Herkimer. The 1764 house contains historic furnishings, artifacts and memorabilia. The site includes a Colonial herb and vegetable garden. A visitor center presents an audiovisual program about late 18th-century Colonial life.

Allow 1 hour minimum. Guided tours begin on the half-hour Wed.-Sat. 10-5, Sun. 1-5, mid-May through Oct. 31. Tour $3; over 62, $2; ages 5-12, $1. Phone (315) 823-0398.

LOCKPORT (D-3)
pop. 24,400, elev. 544'

Lockport derived its name from the locks that overcome the difference in elevation along the Niagara Escarpment. The "Old 5" Locks built in 1840, can be seen from an observation point on Pine Street Bridge or from the boats that offer narrated cruises along the canal. The town also boasts one of the widest bridges in the world, located downtown within walking distance from the locks. The Canal Museum displays canal construction photographs and other canal memorabilia; phone (716) 434-3140.

Eastern Niagara Chamber of Commerce: Canal Terrace, 151 W. Genesee St., Lockport, NY 14094-3686; phone (716) 433-3828.

Shopping areas: Lockport Mall, 5737 S. Transit Rd., includes Ames and The Bon-Ton.

KENAN CENTER, 433 Locust St., is a community cultural and recreational complex on a 25-acre estate. The Taylor Theater is in a restored carriage house. Kenan House is a restored 1859 Victorian mansion with an art gallery and formal gardens. Special events and theater productions are held throughout the year. Allow 1 hour minimum. Art gallery open daily 2-5, Sept.-June; Sun.-Fri. 2-5, rest of year. Formal gardens open daily dawn-dusk. Donations. Admission charged during special events. Phone (716) 433-2617.

[SAVE] **LOCKPORT CAVE AND UNDERGROUND BOAT RIDE** offers an historical tour departing from the ticket office at 21 Main St. at the corner of Pine. A combination walking and .5-mile underground boat tour of an industrial section of the Erie Canal explores locks, early 1800s manufacturing buildings and a 1,600-foot tunnel blasted 1858-59 to supply water power to mills and plants. Allow 1 hour, 30 minutes minimum. Tours depart daily every hour 10-6, May 27-Sept. 4; Sat.-Sun. at 10, noon, 2 and 4, Sept. 5-24. Fare $7.75; ages 4-12, $5.25. AE, MC, VI. Phone (716) 438-0174.

LOCKPORT LOCKS AND ERIE CANAL CRUISES depart from a restored 1840s stone warehouse at 210 Market St. off SR 31. Two-hour narrated cruises along the Erie Canal are offered where boats are raised 50 feet to overcome the difference in elevation of the Niagara Escarpment. Passengers cruise past historic sites and five of the original 1825 locks. The Canal Heritage Interpretive Center also is in the warehouse and offers canal exhibits. Food and picnic facilities are available. Trips depart daily at 10, 12:30 and 3, May-Nov.; schedule varies; phone ahead. Fare $11.50; ages 4-12, $7. MC, VI. Phone (716) 433-6155 or (800) 378-0352.

NIAGARA COUNTY HISTORICAL SOCIETY, 215 Niagara St., is a complex devoted to county history. Exhibits include businesses, farm equipment, Civil War items, medical memorabilia and Iroquois Indian artifacts. The Transportation Building displays a Junior R—a locally produced aluminum automobile—and a 1954 Pontiac, the first General Motors car to be air conditioned. Allow 1 hour, 30 minutes minimum. Thurs.-Sun. 1-5, May-Dec.; Wed.-Sat. 1-5, rest of year. Closed holidays. Donations. Phone (716) 434-7433.

Col. William M. Bond House, 143 Ontario St., is an 1824 brick house featuring 12 period rooms used as backdrops for changing exhibits. Allow 1 hour minimum. Sat.-Sun. and Thurs. 1-5, May-Dec. Donations. Phone (716) 434-7433.

LODI (F-6) pop. 400

WINERIES

• **Wagner Vineyards and Micro Brewery,** just s. of SR 96A on SR 414. Daily 10-5. Brewery open Mon.-Sat. 10-5, Sun. noon-5. Closed Jan. 1, Thanksgiving and Dec. 25. Phone (607) 582-6450.

LONG ISLAND

Ask both a New Yorker and a geography student to define Long Island, and you will get two different answers. Geographically speaking, the island encompasses 1,723 square miles within its boundaries, which extend 125 miles to the east of Manhattan.

A New Yorker pictures the island a bit differently, however. Because two counties—Queens and Kings (Brooklyn)—of the island's four are boroughs of New York City, only the remaining Nassau and Suffolk counties form Long Island in the minds of many city dwellers. Queens and Brooklyn account for more than 5 million of the island's total population of 6,861,500.

Nassau is populated mostly by commuters. The northern side of the county forms the island's Gold Coast, whose beautiful gardens and elegant estates were the aspirations of Jay Gatsby in F. Scott Fitzgerald's novel "The Great Gatsby." Some of New York's most well-known beaches extend from western Nassau County along the southern shore through Suffolk County. These include Jones Beach State Park *(see Jones Beach p. 95)* and Fire Island National Seashore *(see place listing p. 84)*.

Suffolk County, along the island's north shore where Suffolk meets Nassau, is the site of some of New York's most productive farmland. At the eastern end of Suffolk County are the North and South Forks. The more urban South Fork also is known as the Hamptons. The populations of these quiet towns swell each summer with the wealthy, the famous and others who wish to escape the hectic and humid city.

From such 20th-century mansions as Old Westbury House in Nassau County to the 17th-century saltboxes of Sag Harbor in Suffolk County, carefully preserved buildings and houses dot Long Island.

Places and towns on Long Island with individual place listings are (clockwise around the island from the northwest) King's Point, Glen Cove, Oyster Bay, Cold Spring Harbor, Lloyd Harbor, Centerport, Stony Brook, Setauket, Riverhead, Cutchogue, Bridgehampton, Sag Harbor, Montauk, Amagansett, East Hampton, Southampton, Eastport, Manorville, Shirley, Fire Island National Seashore, West Sayville, Oakdale, Great River, Jones Beach, Old Bethpage, Old Westbury, Albertson, Lawrence and Garden City.

Long Island Convention and Visitors Bureau: 350 Motor Pkwy., Hauppauge, NY 11788. The Suffolk County branch office is on the Long Island Expressway between exits 51 and 52 eastbound, and the Nassau County branch office is off the Southern State Parkway between exits 12 and 13 eastbound; phone (631) 951-3440 or (800) 441-4601.

LYONS (E-6) pop. 4,300, elev. 406′

WAYNE COUNTY HISTORICAL SOCIETY MUSEUM, 2 blks. w. of the County Court House at Butternut and Church sts., is housed in a brick mansion and an attached stone jail built in 1854. Displays include antiques, farm implements, ships artifacts and exhibits depicting the area's early judicial process. The restored horse barn contains transportation artifacts and agricultural and domestic equipment. Guided tours are offered by appointment.

Allow 1 hour minimum. Tues.-Fri. 10-noon and 12:30-3:30, Sat.-Sun. by appointment; closed holidays. Donations. Phone (315) 946-4943.

LYONS FALLS (C-8) pop. 700

LEWIS COUNTY HISTORICAL SOCIETY MUSEUM (GOULD MANSION), off SR 12 on High St. following signs, is a partially restored 1902 Richardsonian Romanesque house furnished to illustrate gracious living in the early 20th century. A permanent exhibit focuses on Franklin B. Hough, the father of American forestry. The museum's changing exhibits highlight Lewis County history. Guided tours are available.

Allow 1 hour minimum. Tues.-Sat. 10-4, June 1 to mid-Oct. A research room is available Tues.-Fri. 10-3, June 1 to mid-Oct.; Wed. 10-3, rest of year. Donations. Phone (315) 348-8089.

MALONE (A-10)
pop. 6,800, elev. 756′

FRANKLIN COUNTY HOUSE OF HISTORY, 51 Milwaukee St., features guided tours of an 1850s home complete with period furniture, photographs and household items. There also are displays about weaving, spinning and broommaking. A geneological library is available. Allow 30 minutes minimum. Tues.-Sat. 1-4, June 1-Sept. 4; Sat. 1-4, rest of year or by appointment. Closed holidays. Donations. Phone (518) 483-2750.

WILDER FARM—BOYHOOD HOME OF ALMANZO WILDER is 2.5 mi. e. of SR 30 on US 11, 1 mi. s. on CR 23, then 1 mi. s. on Donahue and Stacy rds. following signs. Visitors can take guided tours of Wilder's boyhood home, the setting for Laura Ingalls Wilder's novel "Farmer Boy," based on her husband's boyhood. Included is period furniture and Wilder family memorabilia. A visitor center and museum displays family photographs and a model of the farm as described in the book. Special events are occasionally offered; phone for details. Picnicking is permitted.

Tours Tues.-Sat. 11-4, Sun. 1-4, Memorial Day weekend-Labor Day and by appointment. Admission $3, students with ID $1.50. Phone (518) 483-1207 or 483-4516.

MANORVILLE (H-4) pop. 6,200

THE ANIMAL FARM, .2 mi. n. off SR 27 exit 59 or 3 mi. s. of I-495 (Long Island Expwy.) exit 69 to 184A Wading River Rd., is a refuge for neglected and unwanted animals. The petting zoo is designed so children may touch, feed and have close contact with farm and exotic animals. Picnicking is permitted. Food is available. Mon.-Fri. 10-5, Sat.-Sun. 10-6, Apr.-Oct. Admission $10; over 65 and ages 2-16, $7. MC, VI. Phone (631) 878-1785.

LONG ISLAND GAME FARM AND FAMILY RIDE PARK, off I-495 (Long Island Expwy.) exit 70, then 2.2 mi. s. on Chapman Blvd. following signs, has a wildlife collection, a petting zoo and performing animal shows. Themed nature trails and several rides also are available. Picnicking is permitted.

Allow 2 hours, 30 minutes minimum. Mon.-Fri. 10-5, Sat. Sun. and holidays 10-6, mid-Apr. to mid-Oct. Admission $11.95; ages 2-11, $9.95; over 60, $6.95. DS, MC, VI. Phone (631) 878-6644.

MARCELLUS (E-7)
pop. 1,800, elev. 492'

CENTERS FOR NATURE EDUCATION/BALTIMORE WOODS is .4 mi. n. on Bishop Hill Rd. from SR 175. Seven trails wind around a re-created pioneer homestead, herb garden, open fields, two spring-fed streams and undisturbed hillside forests of mixed hardwood and old growth timber. Interpreted programs about the ecology of the area are offered all year. Allow 2 hours minimum. Daily dawn-dusk. Free. Phone (315) 673-1350.

MASSENA (A-9)
pop. 11,700, elev. 24'

An 80-foot drop in the St. Lawrence River along the Great Lakes-St. Lawrence Seaway System *(see place listing p. 89)* has been a two-fold boon to Massena. Two locks, the Bertrand Snell and Dwight D. Eisenhower, were built to overcome the descent, while the Moses-Saunders Power Dam was constructed to take advantage of it.

From the parking lot on SR 131 just north of Massena, ships can be seen passing through the Dwight D. Eisenhower Lock. Visitor facilities, including viewing decks and parking, are available in summer. Picnicking is permitted. Recorded information about shipping traffic is available by phoning (315) 769-2422.

Greater Massena Chamber of Commerce: 50 Main St., P.O. Box 387, Massena, NY 13662; phone (315) 769-3525 or 769-5000.

Shopping areas: St. Lawrence Centre Mall on SR 37 features more than 100 stores, including Hills, JCPenney and Sears, as well as specialty shops. An Ammex Tax & Duty Free Shop is at the American Bridge Plaza in Rooseveltown, northeast off SR 37.

MASSENA MUSEUM, 200 E. Orvis, contains items of local interest, including an 1882 hotel book signed by President Chester A. Arthur, a carved Victorian hearse adapted for winter with sled runners and Victorian furnishings. A town historian is available mornings. Allow 30 minutes minimum. Mon.-Fri. 10-4; closed major holidays. Free. Phone (315) 769-8571.

ROBERT MOSES STATE PARK is 2 mi. n.e. of SR 37 on Barnhart Island. This 4,122-acre park overlooks lock operations and affords access to the Moses-Saunders Power Dam. An information center provides seaway brochures. A marina offers a boat ramp and boat rentals. Park open daily dawn-dusk, mid-May through Columbus Day. A beach is available June through Labor Day. Information center open 8-4:30, mid-May through Columbus Day. Park free. Beach $6; after 4, $4. Phone (315) 769-8663. *See Recreation Chart and the AAA Northeastern CampBook.*

★ **Moses-Saunders Power Dam**, owned jointly by the New York Power Authority and Ontario Hydro, generates almost 2 million kilowatts of power. Flags mark the boundary in the center of the dam. A visitor center has a hand-carved wooden map showing the voyages of Jacques Cartier, discoverer of the St. Lawrence River; a terrain map of the power project; a film presentation; and computerized exhibits that explain how electricity is produced and used.

Allow 1 hour minimum. Visitor center open daily 9:30-6, Memorial Day-Labor Day; daily 9-4:30, day after Labor Day-Columbus Day; Mon.-Fri. 9-4:30, rest of year. Closed holidays, Columbus Day-day before Memorial Day. Free. Phone (315) 764-0226, ext. 304.

MAYVILLE (F-2)
pop. 1,600, elev. 1,303'

Located on the northwest shore of Chautauqua Lake, Mayville began as a portage point between Lake Erie and the Allegheny and Ohio rivers. Boating, hiking, bicycling and fishing are among the recreational opportunities available nearby.

Mayville/Chautauqua Chamber of Commerce: P.O. Box 22, Mayville, NY 14757; phone (716) 753-3113.

★ *CHAUTAUQUA BELLE*, on SR 394 on the Chautauqua Lake waterfront, is a replica of an old-fashioned, steam-powered stern-wheeler offering 1 hour, 30 minute cruises. Cruises depart daily at 11, 1:15 and 3, Memorial Day-Labor Day. Fare $15; over 54, $13; ages 6-12, $6. AE, DS, MC, VI. Phone (716) 753-2403 to confirm schedule.

MEDINA (D-4) pop. 6,700, elev. 543'

MISS APPLE GROVE, departing from the Apple Grove Inn dock 1.5 mi. w. on SR 31E, is a replica of a 19th-century Erie Canal packet boat. A 2-hour trip aboard the mule-drawn boat provides a narration describing life on the canal during the 1840s. Entertainment is provided. A luncheon cruise also is available. Two-hour cruise departs Sun. at 1, mid-May to mid-Oct. Two-hour cruise $10; ages 5-12, $7.50; under 5, $3. Reservations are required. To confirm daily schedules phone (716) 798-2323.

MILLBROOK (G-11)
pop. 1,300, elev. 567'

WINERIES
* **Millbrook Vineyards & Winery**, 3.5 mi. n. on SR 82 to Shunpike Rd. (CR 57), then 3 mi. e. following signs. Daily noon-5; closed major holidays. Phone (914) 677-8383 or (800) 662-9463.

MILTON (G-10) pop. 1,100

WINERIES
* **Royal Kedem Winery**, on Dock Rd. Sun.-Thurs. 9:30-4:30; closed Jewish holidays. Phone (914) 236-4281.

MONROE (H-10)
pop. 6,700, elev. 607'

MUSEUM VILLAGE is 1.2 mi. w. on SR 17M or off SR 17 exit 129. This 17-acre outdoor museum has exhibit buildings with collections of 19th-century Americana and includes a drugstore, schoolhouse and natural history museum. Demonstrations of 19th-century crafts, family workshops and farm animals also are featured. Food is available.

Wed.-Fri. 10-5, Sat.-Sun. and holidays 11-5, July-Aug.; Wed.-Fri. 10-2, Sat.-Sun. and holidays 11-4, May-June and Sept.-Dec. Admission $8; over 59, $6; ages 3-15, $5. MC, VI. Phone (914) 782-8247. *See color ad p. 492.*

MONTAUK (H-6) pop. 3,000, elev. 9'

Once inhabited by the Montaukett Indians, Montauk is a resort on a peninsula along the south shore of extreme eastern Long Island. The "cod ledge" off the banks of Montauk is one of the most renowned fishing areas in the world.

Hither Hill State Park *(see Recreation Chart and the AAA Northeastern CampBook)* and Montauk Point State Park *(see Recreation Chart)* provide various recreational facilities. Montauk County Park also offers recreational facilities as well as the 1799 Third House Museum. *Also see Long Island p. 100.*

A ferry to Block Island, R.I., departs from Viking Landing daily at 9, late May-Columbus Day; Sat.-Sun. at 9, mid- to late May. The ferry returns at 4:30; phone (631) 668-5700.

MONTAUK POINT LIGHTHOUSE MUSEUM, on Montauk Point 6 mi. e. on SR 27, is in one of the oldest active lighthouses in the country. The 1796 lighthouse was commissioned by George Washington. Visitors may climb the 137 steps to the top of the tower. Exhibits about maritime history and a videotape are available.

Allow 1 hour minimum. Open daily at 10:30, Memorial Day-Columbus Day; closing times vary. Phone for winter schedule. Admission $4; senior citizens $3.50; 41 inches tall to age 12, $2.50. Parking $5. Under 41 inches tall are not permitted in the tower. Phone (631) 668-2544 or (888) 685-7646.

SECOND HOUSE MUSEUM is .5 mi. w. at e. jct. of Old Montauk Hwy. and SR 27. This late 18th-century house contains period artifacts and a one-room school. Allow 1 hour minimum. Thurs.-Tues. 10-4, Memorial Day-Columbus Day. Admission $2; ages 6-12, $1. Phone (631) 668-5340.

MONTGOMERY (H-10)
pop. 2,700, elev. 388'

SAVE HILL-HOLD MUSEUM, n.e. on SR 416, re-creates life on an 1830s Hudson Valley farm. The grounds contain an herb garden, a one-room schoolhouse and barnyards with livestock. Some original furnishings remain, including pieces that were crafted on the farm. Allow 1 hour minimum. Wed.-Sun. 10-4:30, early May to mid-Oct.; phone for December holiday schedule. Admission $2.50; under 16, $1.50; family rate $6. Phone (914) 291-2404 or 457-4905.

MONTOUR FALLS (F-6)
pop. 1,800, elev. 456'

Montour Falls occupies the site of Catharines Town, a village ruled by and named for Queen

Catharine Montour of the Iroquois Nation. A score of waterfalls flow through the seven glens that surround the town.

Havana Glen has hiking trails past numerous waterfalls, pools and cascades, as well as camping facilities. Picnicking is permitted. Chequagua Falls, 156 feet high, is at the head of Main Street; the falls are illuminated at night. Seneca Lake is immediately north of the village; a marina is open daily from mid-April to mid-October. Recreational activities available include boating, camping and fishing. Picnicking is permitted.

Nearby Catharine Creek is known for its rainbow and brown trout fishing, which is at its best April through December. *Also see Finger Lakes p. 84.*

SCHUYLER COUNTY HISTORICAL SOCIETY MUSEUM, 108 N. Catharine St., is housed in the 1830 Old Brick Tavern, the county's oldest brick building. The Georgian-style building displays period artifacts that characterize 19th-century life in rural upstate New York.

Among the exhibits are antique farm implements and tools of various trades, American Indian relics, ladies' fashions, antique toys and medical memorabilia. The bedrooms are furnished in period. Allow 1 hour minimum. Mon.-Thurs. and Sat. 10-4; closed major holidays. Donations. Phone (607) 535-9741.

MORAVIA (E-7) pop. 1,600, elev. 802'

MILLARD FILLMORE CABIN is 1 mi. s. on SR 38 in Fillmore Glen State Park. The cabin is a replica of the cabin in which the 13th president was born. The Fillmore birthplace, designated by markers within Fillmore Glen State Park *(see Recreation Chart and the AAA Northeastern CampBook),* is 4 miles east via Skinner Hill Road. Park open daily dawn-dusk. Cabin open daily 8 a.m.-dusk, early May-early Oct. Admission $6 per car, late June-Labor Day; $5 per car, rest of year. Phone (315) 497-0130.

MOUNTAINVILLE (H-10)

STORM KING ART CENTER, off SR 32 on Old Pleasant Hill Rd., is a 500-acre outdoor sculpture park museum with more than 120 outdoor sculptures. Its permanent collection contains sculptures by Magdalena Abakanowicz, Siah Armajani, Alexander Calder, Mark di Suvero, Louise Nevelson, Isamu Noguchi and David Smith; exhibitions change annually. Allow 2 hours minimum. Daily 11-5:30, Apr.-Oct. Admission $7, senior citizens $5, students with ID $3, under 5 free. MC, VI. Phone (914) 534-3115.

MUMFORD (E-5) elev. 617'

SAVE ★ **GENESEE COUNTY VILLAGE & MUSEUM,** 1.2 mi. w. of SR 36 on Flint Hill Rd. (George St.), has more than 57 structures that re-

create life 1797-1870. The buildings have been moved from their original sites, restored and authentically furnished. Costumed villagers portray life in the 19th century. Craftspeople demonstrate spinning, weaving, cooking and other crafts. The Gallery of Sporting Art displays some 700 works by nationally-acclaimed artists. The Genesee Country Nature Center features more than 5 miles of interpretive trails. Picnicking is permitted. Food is available. A trolley runs throughout the area daily in July and August.

Wear comfortable walking shoes; a tour of the grounds takes 3-4 hours. Tues.-Sun. and holidays 10-5, mid-May to mid-Oct. Last admission 1 hour before closing. Combined admission to museum, nature center and art gallery $11; over 61, $9.50; ages 4-16, $6.50. Gallery of Sporting Art admission $5; over 61, $4; ages 4-16, $3. Nature center admission $2.50; over 61, $2; ages 4-16, $1.50. No pets permitted. AE, MC, VI. Phone (716) 538-6822.

NAPLES (F-5) pop. 1,200, elev. 818'

Near the southern end of Canandaigua Lake, Naples is in the vicinity of three scenic glens, Parrish, Tannery and Grimes, with many waterfalls. Rainbow trout fishing is popular. *Also see Finger Lakes p. 84.*

SAVE **CUMMING NATURE CENTER** is 1.2 mi. w. on Clark St., then 7 mi. n. on Gulick Rd. to 6472 Gulick Rd. Part of the Rochester Museum & Science Center *(see Rochester p. 167),* this 900-acre environmental center in Bristol Hills has 6 miles of thematic trails for nature walks and cross-country skiing and snowshoeing in the winter; equipment rentals are available. Featured are natural history programs, exhibits and seasonal events.

Wed.-Sun. 9-5. Admission $4; over 61 and college students with ID $3; grades K-12, $1.50. Phone (716) 374-6160.

WINERIES

- **Widmer's Wine Cellars Inc.,** 1 Lake Niagara Ln. Mon.-Sat. 10-4, Sun. 11:30-4, May-Oct.; daily 1-4, rest of year. Closed Jan. 1, Easter, Thanksgiving and Dec. 25. Phone (716) 374-6311 or (800) 836-5253.

NARROWSBURG (H-9) elev. 716'

SAVE **FORT DELAWARE—MUSEUM OF COLONIAL HISTORY,** .7 mi. n. on SR 97, is an 18th-century stockade with blockhouses, three log cabins, a gun platform, storehouses, a blacksmith shop, an armory, an animal yard and an herb garden. The fort is patterned after the mid-1700s Cushetunk settlement. Guides in period dress present lectures, demonstrations and slide and videotape shows about Colonial arts and crafts.

Allow 1 hour minimum. Daily 10-5:30, June 30-Labor Day; Sat.-Sun. 10-5:30, May 29-June

26. Admission $3.50; over 54, $2.50; ages 6-16, $1.75; under 6 free with an adult; family rate (up to five) $10. Phone (914) 252-6660.

NEWARK (E-5) pop. 9,800, elev. 457'

HOFFMAN CLOCK MUSEUM, 2 blks. s. of SR 31 in the Newark Public Library at 121 High St., displays antique clocks. Allow 1 hour minimum. Mon. noon-9, Tues.-Fri. 9:30-9, Sat. 10-3. Free. Phone (315) 331-4370.

NEWBURGH (H-10)
pop. 26,500, elev. 164'

The site of George Washington's headquarters for more than a year during the Revolutionary War, Newburgh later based its economy on a thriving whaling industry. With the demise of whaling the town successfully turned its ships to other trade in the late 1800s; its seafaring tradition is still evident.

Downtown Newburgh is the site of several historic buildings dating from the late 18th through 19th centuries. Guided tours of the 455-acre historic district depart Sunday afternoons and by appointment; phone (914) 561-2585.

The Chamber of Commerce, Inc.: 47 Grand St., Newburgh, NY 12550; phone (914) 562-5100.

NEW WINDSOR CANTONMENT STATE HISTORIC SITE, 1 mi. s. of I-84 on Temple Hill Rd. (SR 300), is the site of the last winter encampment of Gen. George Washington's Continental Army. Costumed interpreters demonstrate 18th-century military life, including musket and artillery drills, woodworking and blacksmithing.

A visitor center has exhibits about the Revolutionary War in the Hudson Highlands and on the cantonment. Picnicking is permitted. Wed.-Sat. 10-5, Sun. 1-5, Apr. 15-Oct. 31. Admission $3; ages 5-12, $1. Phone (914) 561-1765.

★ WASHINGTON'S HEADQUARTERS STATE HISTORIC SITE, Liberty and Washington sts., was Gen. George Washington's headquarters from April 1782 until August 1783 and the place from which Washington ordered the end of the Revolutionary War. The 1750 Hasbrouck House is furnished as a military headquarters. The nearby museum contains exhibits relating to the Continental Army. A 6-acre park includes the 1887 Tower of Victory monument. Wed.-Sat. 10-5, Sun. 1-5, mid-Apr. to late Oct. Admission $3; senior citizens $2; ages 5-12, $1. Phone (914) 562-1195.

NEW CITY—see New York p. 138.

NEW LEBANON (F-11)

MOUNT LEBANON SHAKER VILLAGE, s. of US 20 on Shaker Rd., was the home of the Shakers 1785-1947. Known for their celibate lifestyle and community living, the Shakers designated this village the "Center of Union," a site of spiritual importance equivalent to that of the Vatican for Catholics or Mecca for Muslims. Self-guiding and guided tours offer a glimpse into the lifestyle, furniture and architecture of the sect. Numerous trails wander throughout the village.

Allow 1 hour, 30 minutes minimum. Fri.-Sun. 9:30-5, Memorial Day-Columbus Day weekend. Admission $4, children $2, under 5 free, family rate $10. MC, VI. Phone (518) 794-9500.

NEW PALTZ (G-10)
pop. 5,500, elev. 252'

New Paltz was established by French Huguenots. Six stone houses built 1692-1712 stand on Huguenot Street as reminders of the original settlement.

New Paltz Chamber of Commerce: 259 Main St., New Paltz, NY 12561; phone (914) 255-0243.

SAVE HUGUENOT HISTORICAL SOCIETY TOURS, beginning at Deyo Hall, 6 Broadhead Ave., visit all Huguenot Street houses and a 1717 stone church. The guided tour takes 3 hours. A 1.25-hour tour including two houses and the church and a one-house tour also are available. All-inclusive tour departs Tues.-Sun. at 9 and 1, May-Oct. Tour $10; over 62 and students with ID $9; under 12, $5. Children must be with an adult. MC, VI. Phone (914) 255-1889 or 255-1660.

LOCUST LAWN FEDERAL MANSION AND STONE HOUSE (Col. Josiah Hasbrouck House), 4 mi. s. on SR 32 in Gardiner, dates from 1814 and contains original furnishings. Marbleized plaster embellishes the three-story center hall in the Federal-style mansion. Wed.-Sun. 10-4, June-Sept. Admission $5; over 61, $4; under 12, $2.50. Phone (914) 255-1889 or 255-1660.

NEW ROCHELLE—
see New York p. 139.

New York

New York City is the business, entertainment and publishing capital of the country. The nation's largest city, it is teeming, busy and always rushing. It is the city that most foreigners have in mind when they think of America and a magnet that also draws Americans to its man-made canyons.

Although populated by about 23,320 people per square mile, more than 17 percent of the total land area of New York City is devoted to parks and playgrounds. Museums, art galleries and theaters and millions of people as well as two wildlife refuges and a bird sanctuary coexist in this 314-square-mile city of contrasts.

The first explorers of the area were Giovanni da Verrazano in 1524 and Estevan Gomez a year later. In 1609 Henry Hudson sailed up the Hudson River as far as Albany. Adriaen Block erected four trading houses in 1613, prompting permanent settlement. Governor Peter Minuit is said to have bought Manhattan Island in 1626 from the indigenous peoples for $24 worth of beads and trinkets.

In 1633 the first church was built, soon followed by the establishment of Fort Amsterdam. By 1653 the population of New Amsterdam was 800. Great Britain had previously claimed the Hudson River country, and in 1664 the Duke of York sent a fleet to seize it from the Dutch. The colony became an English possession without bloodshed and was renamed New York. The city was chartered April 27, 1686.

After the Battle of Long Island in 1776, when Sir William Howe's British forces defeated the Colonial forces of Gen. George Washington, the city again passed into English hands and remained in their control until 1783. Congress met in New York City 1785-90, and it was in New York City that Washington was inaugurated president.

In the intervening centuries New York has become a city of superlatives. Its harbor is one of the finest in the world. Dominating the harbor is the Statue of Liberty. The port of New York is the busiest in the world. New York also is a great railroad center and industrial city. As a commercial center it leads the world in the value of goods produced.

New York is composed of five boroughs—The Bronx, Brooklyn, Manhattan, Queens and Richmond (Staten Island). The Bronx was annexed to New York City partly in 1874 and partly in 1895 and is the only borough attached to the mainland. Brooklyn was isolated from the city until the Brooklyn Bridge was completed in 1883. The Act of Consolidation in 1898 made Brooklyn a borough of New York.

Manhattan is the oldest and smallest of the five boroughs. Queens was organized as a county in 1683. Its western section, including Flushing, became a part of the city in 1898, and its eastern section was set apart as Nassau County. Richmond (Staten Island) was originally called Staaten Eyland in honor of the States General, the governing body of the Netherlands.

In most cities, bridges and tunnels are simply means of expediting vehicular traffic. In New York these monuments to a growing city are themselves attractions. They include the Verrazano-Narrows Bridge, the second longest single span bridge in the world, and the Holland Tunnel, a marvel of engineering skill at the time of its completion in 1927.

The Brooklyn Battery Tunnel is one of the longest in the world, and the Bayonne Bridge is one of the longest steel arch bridges in the world. The Brooklyn Bridge is undoubtedly the world's best known—and most purchased—bridge. The ability to sell the Brooklyn Bridge to gullible visitors was long a standard of the worth of a con man.

Approaches
By Car

Entering the city from the north, the New York Thruway (I-87) connects with the Major Deegan Expressway, following the east side of the Harlem River through the Bronx and connecting with the Bruckner Expressway (I-278) at the Triborough Bridge. This route bypasses Manhattan and allows easy access to Brooklyn, Queens and other points on Long Island.

Also from the north, the New England Thruway (I-95) leads through the eastern part of the Bronx to either the Bronx-Whitestone Bridge or to the Throgs Neck Bridge, again bypassing Manhattan and allowing easy access to Long Island. Both routes also connect with the Cross Bronx Expressway (I-95), leading to the Henry Hudson Parkway (SR 9A) and points in Manhattan.

I-80 from the west in New Jersey runs congruently with I-95 as it approaches the George Washington Bridge. Once across the bridge it continues east to connect with roads leading to Long Island or swings south on Henry Hudson Parkway or Harlem River Drive to Franklin D. Roosevelt Drive (East River Drive) and downtown Manhattan.

The New Jersey Turnpike (I-95) is the major southern access road to the city. Motorists traveling to Brooklyn and points east should take exit 10 to SR 440E (the West Shore Expressway on Staten Island) to I-278E, which crosses Staten Island, and use the Verrazano-Narrows Bridge to Brooklyn and Long Island.

Lower Manhattan is best approached from the New Jersey Turnpike via the Holland Tunnel. Motorists heading for mid-Manhattan should continue on the turnpike to exit 16E and the Lincoln Tunnel approach.

(continued on page 109)

The Informed Traveler

City Population: 7,380,900

Elevation: 54 ft.

Sales Tax: The sales tax in New York City is 8.25 percent. The tax on hotel rooms and car rentals is 13.25 percent each.

WHOM TO CALL

Emergency: 911

Police (non-emergency): Use local precinct phone number

Time: (212) 976-1616 or (718) 976-1616

Temperature: (212) 976-1212

Hospitals: Beth Israel, (212) 420-2000; Cabrini, (212) 995-6000; Coney Island, (718) 616-3000; Doctors' Hospital of Staten Island, (718) 390-1400; Elmhurst, (718) 334-4000; Jamaica, (718) 206-6000; Lincoln Medical and Mental Health Center, (718) 579-5700; Maimonides, (718) 283-6000; Mount Sinai, (212) 241-8888; New York University, (212) 263-7300.

WHERE TO LOOK

Newspapers

New York City has 11 English and foreign language dailies. The most popular English language papers are *Newsday, New York Daily News, New York Post* and *New York Times.*

Radio and TV

New York radio station WCBS (880 AM) is an all news/weather station; WNYC (93.9 FM or 820 AM) is a member of National Public Radio.

The major TV channels are 2 (CBS), 4 (NBC), 5 (FOX), 7 (ABC) and 13 (PBS).

Visitor Information

The New York Convention and Visitors Bureau operates an information center at 810 Seventh Ave. Maps in six languages and visitor guides are available free. Phone (212) 484-1200. For visitors literature phone (212) 397-8222 or (800) 692-8474.

TRANSPORTATION

Air Travel

New York City is served by John F. Kennedy and La Guardia airports in Queens and Newark Airport in New Jersey. *See Approaches By Plane for details.*

Rental Cars

Hertz, 310 E. 48th St., offers discounts to AAA members; phone (800) 654-3080. Check the telephone directory for other car rental agencies.

Rail Service

There are two train stations in Manhattan: Pennsylvania, at Seventh Avenue and W. 33rd Street, and Grand Central, at Park Avenue and E. 42nd to 44th streets. Amtrak only runs out of Pennsylvania Station. Phone (212) 582-6875.

Buses

The Port Authority Bus Terminal, Eighth to Ninth avenues between W. 40th and 42nd streets, is the main terminal for the city. Phone (212) 564-8484.

Taxis

Taxi fare is $2 for a pickup and 25c for each additional four blocks; 30c is charged for each 75 seconds of waiting time. Tips are expected. An additional 50c per fare applies between 8 p.m. and 6 a.m. Yellow medallion taxis are the only ones authorized to pick up street hails. Complaints or lost articles can be reported to the Taxi and Limousine Commission; phone (212) 302-8294. When calling, passengers must provide the taxicab identification number.

Public Transport

Subways and buses provide public transportation. *See Getting Around-Public Transportation for details.*

Boats

A leading world seaport, New York accommodates passenger liners of all major companies along the Hudson River piers.

By Plane

The New York City area has three airports. John F. Kennedy and La Guardia, two of the busiest airports in the world, are in Queens; Newark Airport is in New Jersey. John F. Kennedy Airport is undergoing renovation work to improve its terminals, roadways and arrivals buildings. Work is scheduled to be completed by 2002.

Express buses from Newark Airport stop at the Port Authority Bus Terminal at W. 42nd Street and Eighth Avenue in midtown Manhattan; Olympia Trails Bus Service buses depart every 20 minutes from 7 a.m. to 12:40 a.m. and every 30 minutes from 1 a.m. to 3:30 a.m. and from 5 a.m. to 7 a.m. The fare is $10 one-way; phone (908) 354-3330.

New Jersey Transit Airlink bus #302 shuttles between Newark Airport and selected points in Newark, including Newark's Penn Station, where PATH subways depart for Broadway at 34th Street and the World Trade Center in Manhattan. Buses leave Mon.-Sat. every 30 minutes 6:05 a.m. to 1:40 a.m., Sun. every 30 minutes 6:25 a.m. to 1:55 a.m.; the fare is $4.

New York Airport Service provides bus service between La Guardia and JFK airports and Manhattan and the Jamaica, Queens, Long Island Rail Road station. The bus stops in Manhattan at the Port Authority bus terminal, 41st Street and Park Avenue, Grand Central Terminal and most midtown hotels for both airports. Fares are: from Manhattan to La Guardia $10, to JFK $13; from Jamaica to either airport $5; between La Guardia and JFK $11; and from hotels to La Guardia $10, to JFK $13. Buses run frequently; for schedules and other information phone New York Airport Service at (718) 706-9658.

The Port Authority Bus Terminal offers ground transportation to and from New York City area airports; for schedule and other information phone (800) 247-7433.

The Gray Line Air Shuttle, which departs from all La Guardia terminals, drops off passengers anywhere between 29th and 63rd streets. Fare is $13 and the schedule varies according to passenger demand; phone (212) 315-3006. Gray Line also offers shuttle service to all three airports in vans designed to handle wheelchairs; reservations are required. Fares are $19 to Kennedy, $16 to La Guardia and $19 to Newark; phone (212) 397-2620 or (800) 451-0455. *See color ad.*

The subway is another option: Take the A, C or H train directly to the Howard Beach JFK Airport station; the Q10 bus also connects Union Turnpike (E or F train), 121st Street (J or Z train) and Lefferts Boulevard (A train) stations with JFK airport.

La Guardia airport access is via the Q33 bus to Roosevelt Avenue (E, F, G or R train) or 74th Street/Broadway (7 train) stations; the Q48 bus shuttles between the airport and the 111th Street or Main Street (both on 7 train) stations.

Taxis are usually plentiful at all airports, except during inclement weather or at an unusual hour. A taxi ride from Kennedy, La Guardia or Newark to midtown Manhattan costs $30, plus tolls.

Getting Around

Street System

For those unfamiliar with Manhattan traffic, the best driving advice is: DON'T. While rush hours for traffic are 7-9:30 a.m. and 4:30-6:30 p.m., city streets are busy at all times. New York City traffic patterns can be a nightmare for even the most experienced drivers.

If driving is a necessity, be alert at all times. The traffic density of streets in Manhattan is probably the highest in the country. A good street map is helpful. When driving in the other boroughs a street index and map are necessities. **Note:** Drivers should keep car doors locked at all times.

Most avenues are one-way and are alternately northbound and southbound. In general, even-numbered streets are eastbound and odd-numbered streets are westbound. Most downtown streets are one-way. Exceptions are Canal, Houston, 14th, 23rd, 34th, 42nd, 57th, 72nd, 79th and

Destination New York City

F rom classic opera at Lincoln Center to a walk on the wild side at the Bronx Zoo, the Big Apple has something for everyone.

Y ou say you like museums? Well, there are some 150 with exhibits ranging from dinosaurs to Degas. Do you have the theater bug? Stop on Broadway to catch a show. Got your head in the clouds? Check out the diverse architecture of the city's skyscrapers. And if things are moving too swiftly, hop in a buggy for a quiet ride through the city's backyard–Central Park.

Statue of Liberty National Monument and Ellis Island, New York. Proudly she stands, guarding the harbor and greeting all who pass her way. (See listing page 117)

World Trade Center, New York. The city's tallest structure at 110 stories dominates the lower Manhattan skyline. (See listing page 118)

P *laces included in this AAA Destination City:*

Cross River........138	Purchase............139
Croton-On-	Rye...................139
Hudson............138	Sleepy Hollow.....139
Garrison............138	Stony Point........140
Harrison............138	Tappan...............140
Katonah.............138	Tarrytown..........140
New City...........138	West
New Rochelle......139	Haverstraw.......141
North Tarrytown.139	White Plains.......141
Nyack................139	Yonkers..............141
Ossining............139	

Metropolitan Museum of Art, New York.
Climb on up to "the Met," where you
can explore more than 3 million works
of art, including the massive Temple
of Dendur in the Egyptian wing.
(See listing page 124)

**See Midtown Manhattan
map page 120**

**See Upper Manhattan
map page 127**

*Empire State
Building/Chrysler
Building, New York.*
Glimmering at dusk,
these crowning spires
grace midtown
Manhattan's skyline.
(See listing page 119)

New York City

**See Lower Manhattan
map page 114**

Bronx Zoo/Wildlife Conservation Park.
Lions and tigers and bears, and
gorillas too, can all be found at one
of the nation's largest urban zoos.
(See listing page 129)

86th streets, which run both east and west. The city is divided between east and west at Fifth Avenue.

The speed limit on downtown streets is 30 mph, or as posted. Crosstown traffic usually moves faster on 14th, 23rd, 34th, 42nd and 57th streets, because these streets are wide.

Northbound and southbound traffic moves faster, at least during non-rush hours, on one-way avenues: These northbound avenues are First, Third, Madison, Eighth and Avenue of the Americas (Sixth Avenue), while the southbound avenues include Second, Lexington, Fifth, Seventh and Ninth. Gridlock is a particular hazard of driving in the city; it is illegal to stand or stop in the middle of an intersection or to make left turns, except where otherwise indicated.

For those who do not wish to use surface streets to travel, East River Drive and West Side Highway provide elevated, controlled-access roads around the city. **Note:** Avoid the parkways and expressways during rush hours.

No one under 18 is allowed to drive in New York City, even with a valid driver's license from another state.

Parking

Parking is prohibited on most downtown Manhattan streets. Midtown parking lots and garages average about $10 an hour.

Very few accommodations have free parking. Guests staying at a hotel with parking facilities often find it is easiest to leave the car in the lot or garage and use public transportation or taxis.

The best strategy available for those wishing to avoid the heavy traffic and exorbitant parking fees in Manhattan is to "park and ride" with the daily commuters. From Queens, parking is available near the #7 Flushing line at Shea Stadium, 126th Street and Roosevelt Avenue, from 5-5: fee before 11, $3.50; after 11 and after 5 p.m. for NY Mets games $4.50.

Another garage is located at Queens Plaza and Jackson Avenue above the Queens Plaza IND subway line and one block from the Queensboro Plaza IRT subway line. Fee 35c per half-hour; $4.75 maximum per 12 hours.

The Metro North serves Westchester, Putnam and Dutchess counties. For schedules phone (212) 532-4900 in New York City, or (800) 638-7646 elsewhere in New York.

The Long Island Railroad serves Nassau and Suffolk counties. For schedule information phone (516) 822-5477. From New Jersey, the NJ Transit stops every hour at Harmon Meadow Boulevard; phone (201) 762-5100.

Public Transportation

Compared to some cities, public transportation is a good bargain. A $1.50 token allow riders to ride more than 237 miles of subway lines. In Manhattan subways traverse the length of Avenue of the Americas (Sixth Avenue), Broadway, Seventh and Eighth avenues and several portions of both Lexington and Park avenues.

Crosstown subways operate on 14th, 42nd, 53rd and 60th streets. In addition there is a shuttle train from Grand Central Terminal to Times Square (intersection of Seventh Avenue and Broadway from 42nd to 43rd streets) where passengers can transfer free of charge to other lines.

Subways also are fast. Directional signs and maps are posted at each station, and with a little planning, this mode of travel is not difficult. Visitors should note that some stations are served by both local and express trains. Inexperienced subway travelers are advised to avoid the express and take the local trains. Although not as fast as the express, the local trains stop at each station, making missing the correct stop less likely.

It is useful to purchase several tokens at once, as some token booths close before the stations do, and token lines tend to be tedious; tokens also can be used for bus fare. The color of the globe sitting atop the subway's entranceway stanchion indicates whether or not the token booth is open: if white, it is open; if red, it is not.

You can avoid waiting in line for tokens by using a thin plastic fare card called MetroCard,

which is good for 10 rides and costs $15; another option is a 7-day unlimited ride card for $17. The card can be used on all New York City buses and at all subway stations. A Metrocard Fun Pass is good for unlimited rides within a 24 hour period; fare $4.

Subway and bus maps are available at the Grand Central, Pennsylvania and Columbus Circle stations and the New York Convention and Visitors Bureau.

A total of 210 bus lines serves New York City. Buses run uptown on Tenth, Eighth, Sixth, Madison, Third and First avenues and downtown on Ninth, Seventh, Fifth and Second avenues. Some of the major east-west crosstown bus routes are 14th, 23rd, 34th, 42nd, 57th, 65th and 79th streets. Upon boarding, ask the bus driver for a free transfer from an uptown or downtown bus to a crosstown bus, or vice versa.

Most bus stops have Guide-A-Ride signs, showing bus stops and transfer points along that route. Fare on the Manhattan and Bronx lines is $1.50; exact change (no bills) or a token is required. For information concerning the subway and city-operated buses phone the New York Transit Authority at (718) 330-1234.

Note: In the *What To See* section attraction listings will often include the nearest subway (S) station or stations. Consult a subway map to determine which train line is nearest and most direct; not every train runs from each station.

What To See

LOWER MANHATTAN AND NEW YORK HARBOR

BATTERY PARK, s. tip of Manhattan Island (S: South Ferry), was the site of a fort established by the first Dutch settlers in 1624. The park affords views of New York Harbor and the Statue of Liberty. The East Coast War Memorial is inscribed with the names of thousands of American servicemen who died on the seas during World War II. Daily 24 hours. Free.

Castle Clinton National Monument (S: South Ferry, Bowling Green) commemorates the 1811 West Battery Fort built to defend New York Harbor. The fort was U.S. Army headquarters during the War of 1812. Tickets to the Statue of Liberty are available. Daily 8:30-5; closed Dec. 25. Free. Phone (212) 344-7220.

THE BOWERY, extending from Chatham Sq. n. to E. 4th St., was once the city's liveliest district and later the habitat of the homeless.

★ **CHINATOWN,** near Chatham Sq., w. of the Bowery (S: Canal St.), includes Mott, Pell and Doyers streets. Chinese restaurants and shops line these streets and vendors crowd the busy sidewalks.

CITY HALL faces City Hall Park at Chambers St. and Broadway (S: City Hall). Near this spot, in the presence of Gen. George Washington, the Declaration of Independence was read to the Army on July 9, 1776. Mon.-Fri. 10-3:30. Free. Phone (212) 788-4636.

ELLIS ISLAND—*see Statue of Liberty National Monument and Ellis Island p. 117.*

★ **FEDERAL HALL NATIONAL MEMORIAL,** Wall and Nassau sts. (S: Wall St., Rector St.), was built in 1842 and is on the site of the first U.S. Capitol. The museum contains material pertaining to George Washington's inauguration, the Bill of Rights and old Federal Hall. Special events and programs also are available. Mon.-Fri. 9-5; closed major holidays. Free. Phone (212) 825-6888.

FEDERAL RESERVE BANK, 33 Liberty St. (S: Fulton St., Wall St.), offers tours by appointment that include a brief explanation of the Federal Reserve System. Allow 1 hour minimum. Tours are given Mon.-Fri. at 9:30, 10:30, 11:30, 12:30, 1:30 and 2:30. Reservations should be made at least 1 week in advance. Free. Phone (212) 720-6130.

FRAUNCES TAVERN MUSEUM, on the second and third floors of 54 Pearl St. at Broad (S: Whitehall St./South Ferry), was built in 1719 and became a tavern in 1762. In 1783 Gen. George Washington bade farewell to the officers of the Continental Army at the site. It housed the first American War Department. Mon.-Fri. 10-4:45, Sat.-Sun. noon-4; closed major holidays except July 4. Admission $2.50, senior citizens and students with ID $1, under 7 free. Phone (212) 425-1778.

GRAMERCY PARK, E. 20th St. between Third Ave. and Park Ave. S., is a private park surrounded by a high iron fence. The gates are locked at all times. Since 1831 only persons living in the immediate vicinity have had keys to the grounds. In this section of the city are the National Arts Club, The Players Club, a statue of Edwin Booth and a synagogue.

GREENWICH VILLAGE extends from 14th St. s. to Houston St. and Washington Sq. w. to the Hudson River (S: W. 4th St., 8th St., Christopher St., Astor Pl.). Known for many years as the city's Bohemian center, "the Village" is famed for its restaurants, curio shops, bookstores, art shows, coffeehouses and nightclubs. For a walking tour description, *see What To Do, Sightseeing p. 133.*

The Cherry Lane Theater, 38 Commerce St. (S: Christopher St., Houston St.), is the oldest theater in New York. A popular off-Broadway showplace, it offers a wide range of shows; phone (212) 989-2020.

GUGGENHEIM MUSEUM SOHO—
see Solomon R. Guggenheim Museum, Upper Manhattan p. 128.

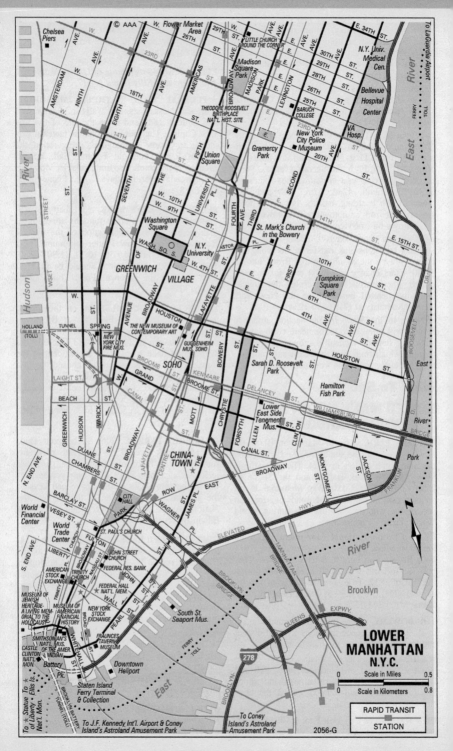

LOWER
MANHATTAN
N.Y.C.

Scale in Miles
0   0.5

Scale in Kilometers
0   0.8

RAPID TRANSIT
STATION

2056-G

HARBOR EXCURSIONS—
see What to Do, Sightseeing p. 132.

JOHN STREET CHURCH (United Methodist), 44 John St. (S: Fulton St., Broadway-Nassau St.), was dedicated as Wesley Chapel in 1768 and is said to be the oldest Methodist society in the United States. The church was torn down and rebuilt in 1817 and 1840. It contains many Methodist relics. Mon., Wed. and Fri. noon-4 and by appointment. Free. Phone (212) 269-0014.

LOWER EAST SIDE TENEMENT MUSEUM, 90 Orchard St. (S: Grand St., Delancey St.), recognizes the nation's urban, working class immigrants. The museum is in an 1863 tenement designed to house 20 families. "Meddling With Peddling: The Pushcart Wars" is an exhibit that traces the history of peddling in the city. "One-Third of a Nation" is a display of Depression-era photographs that portray the conditions of tenement life. The Urban Log Cabin, a scale model of 97 Orchard St., depicts family life in the tenement during 1870 and 1915.

In order to see the museum, visitors must take part in the guided tour. Unescorted visitors are not allowed. For an additional fee the museum also offers walking tours, dramas, a slide show and genealogy services. Allow 1 hour minimum. Guided tours every 30 minutes Mon. 1-3, Tues.-Fri. 12:30-4, Sat.-Sun. 11-4:30; closed Jan. 1, Thanksgiving and Dec. 25. Admission $8, over 65 and students with ID $6, under 5 free. AE, MC, VI. Phone (212) 431-0233.

MUSEUM OF AMERICAN FINANCIAL HISTORY, 28 Broadway (S: Whitehall, Bowling Green) in the heart of the financial district, chronicles the history of American capital and finance including the stock market, business and industry, and finance in politics. Allow 30 minutes minimum. Mon.-Fri. 11:30-3:30; closed major holidays. Donations. Phone (212) 908-4110.

MUSEUM OF JEWISH HERITAGE—A LIVING MEMORIAL TO THE HOLOCAUST, 18 First Pl. in Battery Park City (S: Bowling Green, South Ferry, Whitehall, World Trade Center), chronicles the 20th-century Jewish experience through artifacts, photographs and videotaped personal narratives in three exhibits: "Jewish Life a Century Ago" introduces the Jewish culture; the Holocaust is remembered by survivors in "The War Against the Jews;" and "Jewish Renewal" highlights the post-World War II achievements of the Jewish people. A Torah recovered from the Nazis is displayed in a hexagon-shaped room.

The six-sided building, itself a monument to Jewish heritage, symbolizes the points of the Star of David and the 6 million Jews who died in the Holocaust. An audio tour narrated by actress Meryl Streep and violinist Itzhak Perlman highlights the museum's artifacts. Allow 2 hours minimum. Sun.-Wed. 9-5 (also Thurs. 5-8), Fri. and eve of Jewish holidays 9-3, mid-Apr. to mid-Sept.; Sun.-Thurs. 9-5 (also Thurs. 5-8), Fri. and eve of Jewish holidays 9-2, rest of year. Closed Thanksgiving and Jewish holidays. Last admission is 1 hour before closing. Admission $7, senior citizens and students with ID $5, under 6 free. Advance purchase tickets are available. MC, VI. Phone (212) 968-1800.

THE NEW MUSEUM OF CONTEMPORARY ART, in the Astor Building at 583 Broadway (S: Prince St., Houston St.), displays works focusing on experimental ideas as well as exhibits portraying the development of emerging artists. Wed.-Sun. noon-6 (also Thurs-Sat. 6-8 p.m.); closed holidays. Admission $6, senior citizens and students with ID $3, under 18 free. Phone (212) 219-1222.

NEW YORK CITY FIRE MUSEUM, 1 blk. n. of the Holland Tunnel at 278 Spring St. (S: Spring St.), displays the combined collection of fire memorabilia from the New York City Fire Department and The Home Insurance Co. The 1904 Beaux Arts-style firehouse has firefighting vehicles and tools from Colonial days to the present as well as displays about infamous fires, the firefighter and the history of fire insurance.

Allow 1 hour minimum. Tues.-Sun. 10-4; closed major holidays. Admission $4; under 12, $2. Phone (212) 691-1303.

NEW YORK CITY POLICE MUSEUM, 25 Broadway (S: Whitehall, Bowling Green), houses police memorabilia and emergency service displays. Allow 1 hour, 30 minutes minimum. Mon.-Fri. 9-3; closed major holidays. Free. Phone (212) 301-4440.

★ **NEW YORK STOCK EXCHANGE** is at 20 Broad St. (S: Broad St., Rector St., Wall St.). Outside stands a tree that symbolizes the buttonwood tree where traders once gathered to exchange stock. A visitors' gallery and self-guiding tours are available. Mon.-Fri. 9-4:30; closed major holidays. Free. Tickets are required for tours and are limited, so arrive early. Cameras are not permitted. Phone (212) 656-3000 or 656-5165 for visitors center.

NEW YORK UNIVERSITY, main division, at 50 W. 4th St., dominates the e. and s. sides of Washington Sq. (S: W. 4th St., 8th St., Christopher St., Astor Pl.). Samuel F.B. Morse developed the electric telegraph and John W. Draper took the first photographic portrait at this spot. Guided tours of the campus are available Mon.-Fri. at 11 and 2:30, Sat. by appointment. Free. Phone (212) 998-4500.

ST. MARK'S CHURCH IN THE BOWERY (Episcopal), Second Ave. at 10th St. (S: Astor Place, Broadway, 8th St.), was built in 1795. Peter Stuyvesant, the last Dutch governor of New Netherland, is buried in the church. Mon.-Fri. 10-6. Services are Wed. at 6:30 and Sun. at 10:30. Donations. Phone (212) 674-6377.

The Lincoln Highway

The horseless carriage rolled onto the American landscape in the 1890s. By 1910 there were more than 450,000 registered automobiles, yet the country still lacked a public road system.

Organized movements for better roads brought issues to the attention of the federal government, which had not participated in major road construction since it funded the National Road project in 1806.

But one particular initiative captured the public's support with a unique idea. In 1913 Carl Fisher—the man who built the Indianapolis Motor Speedway in 1909—and automobile industry leaders chartered the Lincoln Highway Association for the purpose of defining a direct coast-to-coast automobile route.

The LHA's first official act was to delineate a 3,389-mile, 12-state continuous route from New York to California—one that would be passable before the opening of the 1915 Panama-Pacific International Exposition in San Francisco. Although not perfect, the throughway was ready as promised, and a motion picture of America's transcontinental highway was shown at the exposition. Over time, the association improved surfaces by using better materials, shortened the driving distance with realignments and published guidebooks about the Lincoln Highway. Automobile touring had never been so good.

Through example, the LHA educated the public as well as state and federal governments about the value of good roads for almost 15 years. The 1919 moving of a military convoy over the "Lincolnway" foretold the utility of an integrated highway system for national defense and interstate commerce.

With the 1921 Federal Highway Act came the funds for states to construct and maintain connecting arteries. Four years later the United States adopted a highway numbering system, and most of the Lincoln route

ST. PAUL'S CHAPEL (Episcopal), Trinity Parish, is at Broadway and Fulton St. (S: Fulton St., Chambers St.). Dedicated in 1766, the church is purported to be the oldest public building in continuous use now standing in Manhattan. George Washington and Gov. George Clinton had designated pews. A 45-minute concert is given on Monday at noon and on Thursday at 1. Mon.-Fri. 9-3, Sun. 7-3; closed holidays. Donations. Concert $2. Phone (212) 602-0874.

SMITHSONIAN'S NATIONAL MUSEUM OF THE AMERICAN INDIAN, adjacent to Battery Park in the Alexander Hamilton U.S. Custom House at One Bowling Green (S: South Ferry), features one of the world's largest collections of Indian artifacts depicting the art, culture and lifestyles of North, Central and South American Indians since prehistoric times.

Collections represent cultures from the United States, Mexico, Canada and Central and South America. Artifacts displayed include tools, weapons, ornaments, clothing, utensils, containers, toys and means of transport as well as changing thematic and temporary displays. Allow 1 hour minimum. Daily 10-5 (also Thurs. 5-8); closed Dec. 25. Free. Phone (212) 668-6624 or 825-6700.

SOHO, an acronym for "south of Houston Street," is 3 blks. s. of Washington Square Park. Avant-garde galleries, shops and eateries line the streets between West Broadway, Houston, Lafayette and Canal streets. SoHo's trademark cast-iron buildings appealed to poor artists, who transformed the area into one of the city's hot spots.

SOUTH STREET SEAPORT MUSEUM is a 12-block historic area bounded by South, John, Pearl and Dover sts. (S: Broadway-Nassau St., Fulton St.). Robert Fulton once docked his steamboat in the vicinity. The Fulton Market, Schermerhorn Row and Museum Block offer shops and restaurants.

At 211 Water St. is Bowne and Co. Stationers, typical of the kind of printing establishment that flourished in the 19th-century seaport; antique presses and a large collection of 19th-century wood and foundry type are displayed.

The Museum Gallery offers changing historical exhibits. The Norway Galleries have exhibitions about New York's maritime heritage; a children's center has special exhibits, programs and workshops. The Maritime Crafts Center feature maritime artisans. The small craft collection is displayed in the Fulton Market Building. Visitors also can see a pilothouse from a 1923 tugboat and a memorial to the victims of the 1912 *Titanic* disaster. Area information is available at the visitor center at 12 Fulton St. Food is available.

Daily 10-6 (also Thurs. 6-8 p.m.), Apr.-Sept.; Wed.-Mon. 10-5, rest of year. Museum and ship admission $6; senior citizens $5; students with ID $4; ages 2-11, $3. AE, MC, VI. Phone (212) 748-8600 or 669-9400.

Museum Ships are docked at Piers 15 and 16 in the East River. Vessels that can be boarded include the 1885 *Wavertree*, the 1908 *Ambrose* and the 1911 *Peking*. Guided tours are available.

★ **STATUE OF LIBERTY NATIONAL MONUMENT AND ELLIS ISLAND** is in Upper New York Bay on Liberty Island (S: South Ferry). The statue was presented to the United States by France in 1884 in commemoration of the two countries' alliance during the American Revolution. Measuring 151 feet high on a 154-foot-high pedestal, it is the tallest statue of modern times. The American Museum of Immigration in the base traces the history of immigration into the United States; also presented is an exhibit about the history of the statue. Nearby Ellis Island *(see attraction listing p. 117)* was the main point of entry into the United States for immigrants 1892-1954.

Liberty Island is only accessible by ferry service, available daily from Battery Park in Lower Manhattan and from Liberty State Park in Jersey City, N.J. A round-trip ticket includes stops at both Liberty Island and Ellis Island. Visitors should arrive at the statue early during the summer to ensure access to the crown viewing area. On peak visitation days the wait and the climb can take more than 3 hours. Picnicking is not permitted. Food is available.

Allow 2 hours minimum. Ferry service from Battery Park daily 9-3:30 (also 3:30-4:30 in summer), with return trips every 30 minutes; phone for schedule. Tickets sold daily 8:30-3:30 (also 3:30-4:30 in summer). Ferry service from Liberty State Park in Jersey City, N.J., runs every 45 minutes daily 8:30-4 (weather permitting); closed Dec. 25. Statue free. Ferry $7; over 62, $6; ages 3-17, $3. Phone (212) 363-3200 for the monument, (201) 915-3400 for Liberty State Park or (212) 269-5755 for the ferry.

★ **Ellis Island**, in New York Harbor near the Statue of Liberty (S: South Ferry), was the nation's main point of entry for millions of immigrants 1892-1954. Exhibits chronicle the history of the processing station and the island. The site also includes the Immigration Library and an oral history studio.

The American Immigrant Wall of Honor is a series of stainless steel panels engraved with the names of nearly 400,000 immigrants. Audiotapes, which relate the history of the island, explain the exhibits and outline a walking tour, are available. Arrive early to avoid crowds.

Ellis Island is only accessible by ferry service, available daily from Battery Park in Lower Manhattan and from Liberty State Park in Jersey City, N.J. A round-trip ticket includes stops at both Liberty Island, the site of the Statue of Liberty National Monument, and Ellis Island.

Allow 4 hours minimum. Museum open daily 9-5; closed Dec. 25. Ferry service from Battery Park daily 9:30-3:30, with return trips every 30 minutes. Ferry service from Liberty State Park in Jersey City, N.J., runs every 45 minutes daily 8:30-4 (weather permitting); closed Dec. 25. Museum free. Ferry $7; over 62, $6; ages 3-17, $3. Phone (212) 269-5755 for general or ferry information, or (212) 363-7772 for the museum.

THEODORE ROOSEVELT BIRTHPLACE NATIONAL HISTORIC SITE, 28 E. 20th St. between Park Ave. S. and Broadway (S: 23rd St., Park Ave. S.), is the

The Lincoln Highway
(continued)

became US 30, 40 and 50. The association disbanded in 1928, but not before it engaged Boy Scout troops across the country to place some 3,000 concrete Lincoln Highway markers along the route in all 12 states: New York, New Jersey, Pennsylvania, Ohio, Indiana, Illinois, Iowa, Nebraska, Wyoming, Utah, Nevada and California. Many of these markers still exist.

Times Square in **New York City** was the official eastern terminus of the Lincoln Highway, which consisted of only 1 mile of road in New York state. From Broadway, motorists departed what Lincoln Highway guidebooks called "one of the most congested thoroughfare points in the world" and drove west on 42nd Street to the Hudson River, then caught a ferry to Weehawken, N.J. The Holland Tunnel, from Canal Street in Lower Manhattan to Jersey City, N.J., was completed about 1927; however, the Weehawken ferry served motorists crossing from Midtown Manhattan until the Lincoln Tunnel was built at 39th Street in the late 1930s. **Look for these New York Lincoln Highway landmark towns in this TourBook guide.**

For more information about the old Lincoln Highway contact the new Lincoln Highway Association, P.O. Box 308, Franklin Grove, IL 61031; phone (815) 456-3030.

NEW YORK

New York City

reconstructed boyhood home of the only United States president born in New York City. It was his home 1858-72. Galleries and 1865-period rooms relate the story of young Teddy. The four floors contain items pertaining to Roosevelt's youth, ranch days, presidency and exploring days.

Guided tours on the hour Wed.-Sun. 9-5; closed federal holidays. Last tour begins 1 hour before closing. Admission $2, National Park Pass holders and under 17 free. Phone (212) 260-1616.

TRINITY CHURCH (Episcopal), Broadway at Wall St. (S: Rector St., Wall St.), was originally built 1696-97. In 1754 it was the first site of King's College (now Columbia University). The present edifice was completed in 1846. Alexander Hamilton and Robert Fulton are buried in the church. Church museum open Mon.-Fri. 9-11:45 and 1-3:45, Sat. 10-3:45, Sun. 11-3:45. Guided tours Mon.-Fri. at 2. Free. Phone (212) 602-0800.

WALL STREET (S: Wall St.), the financial keystone of the country, takes its name from the wooden wall erected by the Dutch burghers in 1653 to protect the colony from attack.

WASHINGTON SQUARE, foot of Fifth Ave., is the scene of art shows in the spring and fall. Washington Arch, designed by Stanford White, stands at the head of the square.

WORLD FINANCIAL CENTER is off West St. between Albany and Vesey sts. (S: Cortlandt St., Chambers St., World Trade Center). The center is the business and commercial hub of Battery Park City. It comprises four major towers integrating office, retail and public space and employing nearly 30,000.

The 300,000 square feet of indoor and outdoor public areas include the Winter Garden, a 120-foot-high vaulted glass and steel structure tiled with marble. It is the primary site of an ongoing series of free music, dance and theater productions; phone (212) 945-0505.

Balconies and canopied gazebos surround the Courtyard, a three-story, glass-roofed piazza housing six international restaurants and specialty shops. Outdoors, the plaza's 3.5 acres of landscaped grounds encompass the North Cove and feature a marina and riverside esplanade providing views of the Statue of Liberty and Ellis Island (*see attraction listings p. 117*). Allow 1 hour minimum.

SAVE ★ **WORLD TRADE CENTER**, on Church St. between Vesey and Liberty sts. (S: Cortlandt St., Chambers St., World Trade Center), is a 16-acre complex of offices and a landscaped plaza. The twin towers, each 110 stories tall, are among the tallest in the world. High-speed elevators run to the observatory on the 107th floor, and escalators take visitors to the open-air rooftop platform on the 110th floor.

The observation deck, known as Top of the World, offers more than just panoramic views of three states. The glass-enclosed 107th floor includes a free simulated helicopter tour of Manhattan. In addition, multilingual, interactive computer stations provide information about New York City history and sites. One of the best times to visit—the bonus is shorter lines and a sunset or evening view—is after 5. The observatory box office is on the second floor of tower 2. Food is available.

Note: Admission lines may be long due to strict security procedures. Daily 9:30 a.m.-11:30 p.m., Memorial Day-Labor Day; 9:30-9:30, rest of year. Observatory admission $13; over 65 and military with ID, $9.50; ages 13-17, $11; ages 6-12, $6.50. MC, VI. Phone (212) 323-2340. *See ad p. 112.*

MIDTOWN MANHATTAN

AMERICAN CRAFT MUSEUM, 40 W. 53rd St. (S: 5th Ave., 53rd St.), exhibits artistic handicrafts in fabrics, ceramics, metals, wood and architecture. Allow 1 hour, 30 minutes minimum. Tues.-Sun. 10-6 (also Thurs. 6-8 p.m.); closed Jan. 1, July 4, Thanksgiving and Dec. 25. Admission $5, over 64 and students with ID $2.50, under 12 free. AE, MC, VI. Phone (212) 956-3535.

★ **AMERICAN MUSEUM OF NATURAL HISTORY**, Central Park West at 79th St. (S: 79th St./Broadway, 81st St./Central Park W.), offers permanent and changing exhibits. Cultures explored include American Indian, Asian, Pacific islanders, South American and the Aztec and Mayan empires.

The Lila Acheson Wallace Wing of Mammals and their Extinct Relatives houses one of the largest fossil displays in the world. The dinosaur halls feature nearly 100 specimens including a Tyrannosaurus rex and Apatosaurus.

The Hall of Human Biology and Evolution educates visitors on the marvels of the human body through the use of models, dioramas, animation and holograms. Other displays include amphibian, bird, gem, mineral, reptile and seashell exhibits as well as memorabilia of John Burroughs, Lincoln Ellsworth and Theodore Roosevelt. An IMAX theater presents films about natural, scientific and anthropological subjects. Food is available.

Allow 3 hours minimum. Daily 10-5:45 (also Fri.-Sat. 5:45-8:45); closed Thanksgiving and Dec. 25. Guided museum tours depart daily at 10:15, 11:15, 1:15, 2:15 and 3:15 (also Sat.-Sun at 12:15) from the African Mammal Hall. IMAX films daily on the half-hour 10:30-4:30 (also Fri.-Sat. at 6 and 7:30 p.m.). Admission $9.50; senior citizens $7.50; under 12, $6. Theater $13; over 59, $9; under 13, $7. AE, MC, VI. Phone (212) 769-5100 or 769-5650. *See ad p. 112.*

ASIA SOCIETY GALLERIES, 725 Park Ave. at 70th St. (S: 68th St.-Hunter College), presents

Asian cultural programs and changing exhibits of Asian art. Tues.-Sat. 11-6 (also Thurs. 6-8 p.m.), Sun. noon-5; closed major holidays. Guided tours Tues.-Sat. at 12:30. Admission $4, senior citizens and students with ID $2; free to all Thurs. 6-8 p.m. Phone (212) 288-6400.

★ **CENTRAL PARK**, extending from 59th to 110th sts. and from Fifth Ave. to Central Park W., was designed as a refuge for New York City residents by its architects, Frederick Law Olmstead and Calvert Vaux. The park contains 840 acres of wooded and landscaped grounds, gardens, woodlands, lakes, two outdoor skating rinks, a swimming pool at 109th Street and a carousel.

Narrated buggy rides offering an overview of the park and the surrounding area are available year-round. The 2.5-acre Strawberry Fields honors John Lennon. Recreational opportunities exist for skating, bicycling, boating, horseback riding, catch-and-release fishing and tennis.

"Cleopatra's Needle," an Egyptian obelisk at E. 81st Street, was presented to the United States by the Khedive of Egypt in 1881. Belvedere Castle and Henry Luce Nature Observatory, at 79th Street, offer nature lovers exhibits about the park's ecosystems and wildlife. The 1872 castle, constructed of white stone, was designed by Calvert Vaux. Among the park's other attractions are free Shakespearean plays presented at the Delacorte Theater during the summer.

The Central Park Zoo and Wildlife Conservation Center at 64th Street displays wildlife in naturalistic surroundings; phone (212) 439-6500 or 861-6030 for information. The formal conservatory gardens are at 105th Street and Fifth Avenue. The Conservatory Water, near 74th Street and Fifth Avenue, is a model boat pond. Horse-drawn hansom cabs are for hire at the Plaza entrance on Central Park South. A Central Park visitor center at 65th Street west of the Central Park Zoo and Wildlife Conservation Center is housed in a restored dairy building that was a 19th-century refreshment center; phone (212) 794-6564.

Park rangers conduct walking tours and provide information about park activities on Saturdays and Sundays. Picnicking is permitted. Food is available. **Note:** Visit the park during daylight hours only. Visitor center Tues.-Sun. 11-5, mid-Apr. through Oct. 15; 11-4, rest of year. Zoo and wildlife conservation center Mon.-Fri. 10-4:30, Sat.-Sun. 10:30-4:30. Park free. Zoo and wildlife conservation center $3.50; over 64, $1.25; ages 3-12, 50c. For schedule information phone (212) 427-4040. Phone (212) 360-3456 or 360-1333 for events information.

SAVE **CHILDREN'S MUSEUM OF MANHATTAN**, in the Tisch Building at 212 W. 83rd St. between Broadway and Amsterdam Ave. (S: 86th St./ Broadway), presents permanent and changing exhibits that teach children about the creative

processes using art, science and nature participatory exhibits and activity stations. Allow 1 hour minimum. Wed.-Sun. and school holidays 10-5; closed Jan. 1, Thanksgiving and Dec. 25. Admission $6, senior citizens $3, under 1 free. AE, MC, VI. Phone (212) 721-1223.

DAHESH MUSEUM, 601 5th Ave., is named for a Lebanese writer and philosopher with a penchant for European art. The museum is home to changing exhibits which focus on 19th- and 20th-century European academic art and include paintings, drawings, watercolors, sculptures, prints and decorative arts. Tues.-Sat. 11-6. Free. Phone (212) 759-0606.

★ **EMPIRE STATE BUILDING**, 350 Fifth Ave. at 34th St. (S: 33rd St., 34th St. Herald Sq.), is one of the world's tallest office buildings. The 1931 Art Deco building, soaring 1,454 feet, has 2 million square feet of office space. Elevators run to the observatory on the 86th floor (1,050 feet) where visitors can see approximately 50 miles. Another elevator takes visitors to the circular glass-enclosed observation tower on the 102nd floor (1,250 feet). Visitors may encounter long lines.

Completed in 1931, the building is made of Indiana limestone and granite trimmed with sparkling stainless steel. The marble in the lobby was imported from Belgium, France, Germany and Italy. The lobby features eight original art works depicting the Seven Wonders of the Ancient

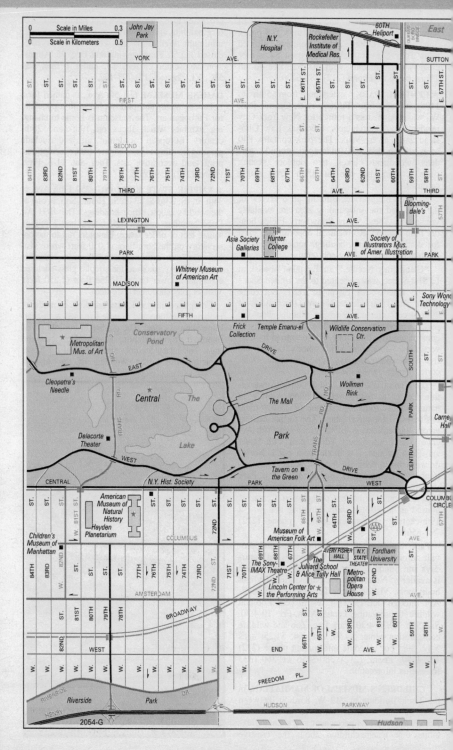

Scale in Miles   0   0.3
Scale in Kilometers   0   0.5

John Jay Park

N.Y. Hospital

Rockefeller Institute of Medical Res.

60TH Heliport

East

YORK   AVE.

SUTTON

E. 66TH ST.
E. 65TH ST.

E. 57TH ST.

ST.

FIRST   AVE.

SECOND   AVE.

84TH
83RD
82ND
81ST
80TH
79TH
78TH
77TH
76TH
75TH
74TH
73RD
72ND
71ST
70TH
69TH
68TH
67TH
66TH
65TH
64TH
63RD
62ND
61ST
60TH
59TH
58TH

THIRD   AVE.   THIRD

Bloomingdale's

LEXINGTON   AVE.

57TH

Asia Society Galleries

Hunter College

Society of Illustrators Mus. of Amer. Illustration

PARK   AVE.   PARK

Whitney Museum of American Art

MADISON   AVE.

E.   E.   E.

E.   E.   E.

Sony Wonder Technology

FIFTH   AVE.

Frick Collection

Temple Emanu-el

Wildlife Conservation Ctr.

Metropolitan Mus. of Art

Conservatory Pond

EAST   DRIVE

Cleopatra's Needle

Central   The

The Mall

Wollman Rink

South ST.

Carne Hall

Delacorte Theater

Lake

Park

WEST   DRIVE   WEST

CENTRAL   N.Y. Hist. Society   PARK

Tavern on the Green

American Museum of Natural History

Hayden Planetarium

N.Y. Hist. Society

COLUMBUS CIRCLE

ST.

57TH

Children's Museum of Manhattan

Museum of American Folk Art

AVE.

84TH
83RD
82ND

77TH
76TH
75TH
74TH
73RD
72ND
71ST
70TH
69TH
68TH
67TH
66TH
65TH
64TH
63RD

62ND
61ST
60TH
59TH
58TH

The Sony-IMAX Theatre

AVERY FISHER HALL

N.Y. STATE THEATER

Fordham University

COLUMBUS

The Juliard School & Alice Tully Hall

Metropolitan Opera House

Lincoln Center for the Performing Arts

AMSTERDAM

81ST
80TH
79TH
78TH

BROADWAY

WEST   END   AVE.

W.   W.   W.

FREEDOM PL.

RIVERSIDE

Riverside   Park   DR.

HUDSON   PARKWAY

HENRY

2054-G

Hudson

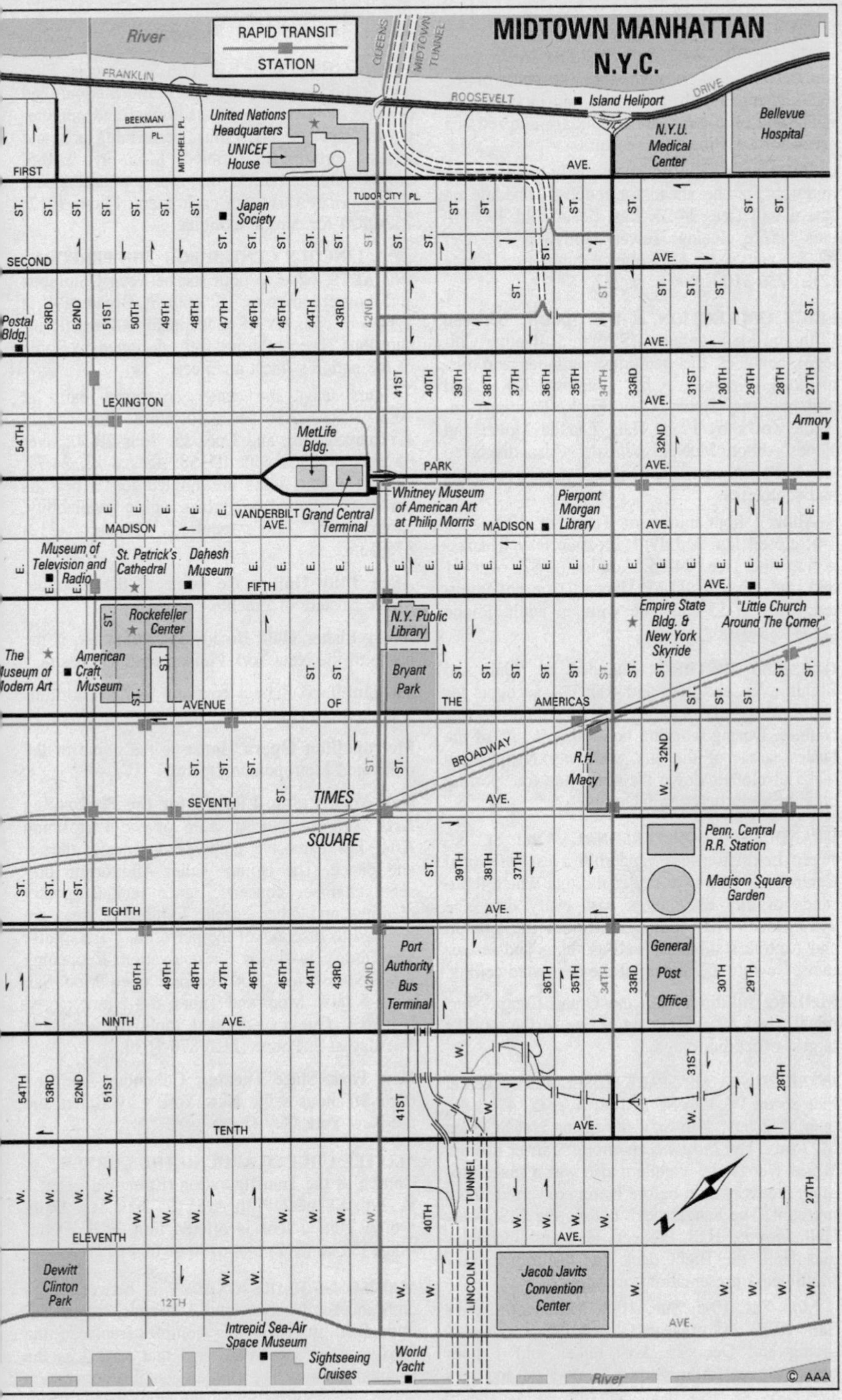

RAPID TRANSIT
STATION

MIDTOWN MANHATTAN N.Y.C.

River

FRANKLIN

QUEENS

MIDTOWN TUNNEL

ROOSEVELT

DRIVE

Island Heliport

BEEKMAN PL.

MITCHELL PL.

United Nations Headquarters
UNICEF House

N.Y.U. Medical Center

Bellevue Hospital

FIRST

Japan Society

TUDOR CITY PL.

SECOND

AVE.

Postal Bldg.

53RD   52ND   51ST   50TH   49TH   48TH   47TH   46TH   45TH   44TH   43RD   42ND

41ST   40TH   39TH   38TH   37TH   36TH   35TH   34TH   33RD

32ND   31ST   30TH   29TH   28TH   27TH

AVE.

LEXINGTON

54TH

Armory

MetLife Bldg.

PARK   AVE.

VANDERBILT AVE.

Grand Central Terminal

Whitney Museum of American Art at Philip Morris

MADISON

Pierpont Morgan Library

AVE.

MADISON

Museum of Television and Radio

St. Patrick's Cathedral

Dahesh Museum

FIFTH

AVE.

The Museum of Modern Art

American Craft Museum

Rockefeller Center

N.Y. Public Library

Bryant Park

Empire State Bldg. & New York Skyride

"Little Church Around The Corner"

AVENUE

OF

THE

AMERICAS

BROADWAY

R.H. Macy

W. 32ND

SEVENTH

ST.

TIMES

AVE.

SQUARE

39TH   38TH   37TH

Penn. Central R.R. Station

Madison Square Garden

EIGHTH

AVE.

Port Authority Bus Terminal

General Post Office

50TH   49TH   48TH   47TH   46TH   45TH   44TH   43RD   42ND

36TH   35TH   34TH   33RD

30TH   29TH

NINTH

AVE.

54TH   53RD   52ND   51ST

41ST

W.

31ST

28TH

TENTH

AVE.

W.

40TH

LINCOLN TUNNEL

27TH

ELEVENTH

AVE.

Dewitt Clinton Park

12TH

Jacob Javits Convention Center

W.

AVE.

Intrepid Sea-Air Space Museum

Sightseeing Cruises

World Yacht

River

© AAA

World as well as the Eighth Wonder of the Modern World—the Empire State Building.

The top 30 floors of the building are lit year-round from dusk to midnight. The color of the lights changes with the season and includes red, white and blue for national holidays and red and green for the Christmas season.

Observation tower open daily 9:30 a.m.-midnight; phone ahead for reduced schedule on Jan. 1 and Dec. 24-25. Last ticket sold 30 minutes before closing. Tower admission $7; over 62, $4; ages 5-12, $3. Lobby exhibits free. Phone (212) 736-3100. *See ad p. 112.*

FRICK COLLECTION, at 1 E. 70th St. between Fifth and Madison aves. (S: 68th St.-Hunter College), includes the paintings, antiques and furnishings owned by industrialist and philanthropist Henry Clay Frick. Paintings include works by Frans Hals, Claude Monet and James Abbott McNeill Whistler. Also displayed are Limoges enamels, Oriental rugs, porcelains and sculptures.

Allow 1 hour minimum. Tues.-Sat. 10-6, Sun. 1-6; closed Jan. 1, July 4, Election Day, Thanksgiving and Dec. 24-25. Admission $7, over 61 and students with ID $5. Under 10 are not admitted; ages 11-15 must be with an adult. Phone (212) 288-0700.

GARMENT DISTRICT, bounded by Sixth and Eighth aves. and 34th and 40th sts., accounts for one-third of the clothes manufactured in this country. During working hours this is one of the busiest areas of the city, with workers pushing racks of clothes down the street and transporting bolts of cloth between factories.

GRAND CENTRAL TERMINAL, 42nd St. between Lexington and Vanderbilt aves. (S: Grand Central), is a 79-acre center through which thousands of city commuters pass every day. The 1913 Beaux Arts terminal includes the Conrail and Amtrak stations as well as shops and restaurants. Be sure to gaze up at the decorated ceiling.

MetLife Building, atop the Grand Central Terminal, rises 59 stories and is one of the world's largest office buildings.

INTREPID SEA-AIR-SPACE MUSEUM is docked at Pier 86 on W. 46th St. at 12th Ave. (S: 42nd St., then M42 bus; 49th St., 50th St. or 51st St., then M27 bus. The *Intrepid,* an aircraft carrier used in World War II and Vietnam, also was a space program recovery ship before being converted into a museum. The hangar deck houses the U.S. Navy Hall, *Intrepid* Hall, Pioneers Hall and Technologies Hall; the flight deck has historic aircraft. Multimedia presentations are offered.

Mon.-Sat. 10-5, Sun. 10-6, May-Sept.; Wed.-Sun. 10-5, rest of year. Closed Jan. 1, Thanksgiving and Dec. 25. Last ticket sold 1 hour before closing. Admission $10; over 64 and ages 12-17, $7.50; ages 6-11, $5; first child under 6

free (each additional child $1). AE, MC, VI. Phone (212) 245-2533. *See ad p. 112.*

JAPAN SOCIETY, 333 E. 47th St. between First and Second aves. (S: Grand Central Station/42nd St.), presents exhibits of traditional and contemporary Japanese art. Films, performing arts and topical lectures are offered. Mon.-Fri. 9:30-5, during exhibits. Hours may vary; phone ahead. Ticket prices vary with each event. Phone (212) 752-0824 for current exhibits.

SAVE ★ **LINCOLN CENTER FOR THE PERFORMING ARTS,** 62nd to 66th sts. between Columbus and Amsterdam aves. (S: 66th St./Broadway), is a 14-acre complex of educational and artistic institutions. The buildings were designed by some of the nation's finest architects.

Tours leave the center concourse daily at 10:30, 12:30, 2:30 and 4:30; closed Jan. 1, July 4, Thanksgiving and Dec. 25. Tour $9.50; over 65 and students with ID $8; ages 3-12, $4.75. Guided 1-hour tours are limited to 19 persons per tour; phone to confirm space availability. Reservations are required. Phone (212) 875-5350.

Alice Tully Hall is the home of the Chamber Music Society of Lincoln Center.

Avery Fisher Hall, Broadway at 65th St., is the home of the New York Philharmonic Orchestra.

The Juilliard School contains four auditoriums and classrooms for music students.

Metropolitan Opera House is the home of the renowned Metropolitan Opera.

New York Public Library for the Performing Arts (Library and Museum of the Performing Arts) has extensive archives on music, theater and dance. The Bruno Walter Auditorium presents chamber concerts, dance recitals, poetry readings and other events. Exhibition areas are devoted to displays of the performing arts. **Note:** The library is closed for renovation. Reopening is scheduled for 2000. Library open Mon.-Sat. noon-6 (also Mon. and Thurs. 6-8 p.m.); closed holidays. One-hour guided tours are available Tuesday at 2. Phone (212) 870-1630.

New York State Theater, Columbus Ave. and 63rd St., houses the New York City Ballet and the New York City Opera.

"LITTLE CHURCH AROUND THE CORNER," or Church of the Transfiguration (Episcopal), is at 1 E. 29th St. near Fifth Ave. (S: 28th St.). Daily 8-6. A guided tour is offered Sun. at 1. Donations. Phone (212) 684-6770 or 684-6771.

MADISON SQUARE GARDEN is between Seventh and Eighth aves. and 31st and 33rd sts. (S: 34th St.). In 1874 this complex replaced the canvas-covered railroad shed that served as the original Garden. The Garden contains convention space and facilities for seven simultaneous major

Key to
Manhattan Street Numbers

Correct use of this formula will locate the cross-street of virtually any address in Manhattan.

NORTH-SOUTH AVENUES

Step A: Cancel the last figure of the house number.

Step B: Divide the remainder by 2.

Step C: Add the key number, or deduct as indicated.

Example: 1165 Third Ave. A: Cancel the last figure—result 116. B: Divide by 2—result 58. C: Add 10 (key number for Third Ave.)—result 68th St.

*On streets or address numbers preceded by an asterisk, omit Step B from the computation.
**On streets or address numbers preceded by two asterisks, omit Steps A and B from the computation and divide the house number by 10.

Ave. A, B, C, D 3	Tenth Ave. 13
First Ave. 3	Eleventh Ave. 15
Second Ave. 3	Amsterdam 59
Third Ave.. 10	Columbus 59
Fourth Ave. 8	Lexington 22
Fifth Ave.:	Madison 27
1—200 13	Park 34
201—400 16	West End 59
401—600 18	**Central Park West 60
601—775 20	**Riverside Dr.:
*776—1286............................ Deduct 18	*1—567 73
Avenue of the Americas............... Deduct 12	*Above 567 78
Seventh Ave.:	Broadway:
1—1800 12	1—754 are below 8th St.
Above 1800 20	754—858................... Deduct 29
Eighth Ave. 9	858—958................... Deduct 25
Ninth Ave. 13	Above 1000 .... Deduct 31

EAST-WEST NUMBERED STREETS

Addresses begin at the streets listed below.

East Side		West Side	
1 .... Fifth Ave.		1 .... Fifth Ave.	
101 ....Park Ave.		101 .... Avenue of the Americas	
201 .... Third Ave.		201 .... Seventh Ave.	
301 .... Second Ave.		301 ....Eighth Ave.	
401 .... First Ave.		401 .... Ninth Ave.	
501 ....York or Ave. A		501 .... Tenth Ave.	
601 .... Ave. B		601 ....Eleventh Ave.	

events. It is the home of the city's basketball and hockey teams. Phone (212) 465-6741.

★ **METROPOLITAN MUSEUM OF ART**, 1000 Fifth Ave. at 82nd St. (S: 86th St./Lexington Ave.), is one of the great museums of the world. Among the collections are Egyptian, Greek and Roman art; Near Eastern art and antiquities; European and Oriental paintings and sculpture; arms and armor; musical instruments; arts from Africa, Oceania and the Americas; 20th-century art; ancient glass; and European and American decorative arts.

The Iris and B. Gerald Cantor Roof Garden provides a vantage point overlooking Central Park and features many modern sculptures including "The Burghers of Calais" by Auguste Rodin.

Allow 3 hours minimum. Tues.-Sun. 9:30-5:15 (also Fri.-Sat. 5:15-8:45); closed Jan. 1, Thanksgiving and Dec. 25. Admission $10, over 64 and students with ID $5, under 12 free. Admission includes The Cloisters in Upper Manhattan *(see attraction listing p. 126)*. Phone (212) 535-7710.

MUSEUM OF AMERICAN FOLK ART, 2 Lincoln Sq. and Columbus Ave. between 65th and 66th sts. (S: 66th St./Broadway), presents six major folk art exhibits per year. Tues.-Sun. 11:30-7:30; closed Jan. 1, July 3-4, Thanksgiving, Dec. 25 and during exhibit installations. Admission $3. Phone (212) 977-7298, 977-7170 or 595-9533 for exhibit information.

★ **THE MUSEUM OF MODERN ART**, 11 W. 53rd St. (S: Fifth Ave./53rd St.), offers a survey of 20th-century paintings, sculptures, drawings, prints, photographs, architectural models and plans, design objects, films and videotapes. Classic, artistic or documentary movies are shown Thursday through Tuesday. Food is available.

Allow 2 hours, 30 minutes minimum. Thurs.-Tues. 10:30-6:30 (also Fri. 6:30-8:15 p.m.); closed Thanksgiving and Dec. 25. Gallery talks are provided Mon.-Tues., Thurs., and Sat.-Sun. at 1 and 3; Fri. at 3, 6 and 7. Admission $10.50, over 65 and students with ID $6.50, under 16 free with an adult, donations Fri. 4:30-8:30. Phone (212) 708-9480. *See ad p. 112.*

MUSEUM OF TELEVISION AND RADIO, 25 W. 52nd St. (S: 5th Ave.), maintains a collection of some 50,000 radio and television program tapes. Visitors can select material from the museum's library, then watch or listen to it at one of 96 radio and television consoles. Tues.-Sun. noon-6 (also Thurs. 6-8 p.m.); closed Jan. 1, July 4, Thanksgiving and Dec. 25. Admission $6; over 64 and students with ID $4; under 14, $3. Phone (212) 621-6800.

NEW YORK HISTORICAL SOCIETY, 170 Central Park W. at 77th St. (S: 79th St./Broadway, 81st St./Central Park W.), houses a museum, print room and reference library. Allow 1 hour, 30 minutes minimum. Tues.-Sun. 11-5; closed Jan. 1, Thanksgiving and Dec. 25. Admission $5; over 64, $3; under 12 free. Phone (212) 873-3400.

NEW YORK PUBLIC LIBRARY, 42nd St. and Fifth Ave. (S: 42nd St./Ave. of Americas, Fifth Ave.), houses a research library that contains more than 5 million volumes, including 21 specialized collections of American history, art, periodicals and Slavic, Jewish and Oriental literature. Main room open Tues.-Wed. 11-7:30, Thurs.-Sat. and Mon. 10-6; closed federal holidays. Free. Phone (212) 930-0800.

NEW YORK SKYRIDE is on the 2nd floor of the Empire State Building, 5th Ave. and 34th St. at 350 5th Ave. (S: 33rd St., 34th St. Herald Sq.). Two 40-seat big-screen flight-simulator theaters feature a "ride" over various city landmarks, including the Statue of Liberty and Times Square. Motion simulators that are computer-synchronized to the film's action move and tilt the seats, giving "passengers" the feel of soaring over the Manhattan skyline, crashing into Wall St. and FAO Schwartz, and riding Coney Island's Cyclone roller coaster.

Allow 30 minutes minimum. Daily 10-10. Admission $11.50; over 61, $9.50; ages 4-12, $8. AE, CB, MC, VI. Phone (212) 279-9777.

PARK AVENUE, between 46th and 60th sts., is the site of major office buildings which incorporate innovative architectural features. Among the most impressive structures are the Seagram Building, 375 Park Ave.; the Lever House, 390 Park Ave.; and the corporate headquarters of Manufacturer's Hanover Bank, 270 Park Ave.

PIERPONT MORGAN LIBRARY, 29 E. 36th St. at Madison Ave. (S: 34th St.), a palazzo-style building of Renaissance architecture, was the private library of J. Pierpont Morgan. Rare editions and illuminated manuscripts are featured as well as art objects, paintings, sculpture and a glass-enclosed garden court. Changing art and literature exhibits also are presented. Food is available.

Tues.-Thurs. 10:30-5, Fri. 10:30-8, Sat. 10:30-6, Sun. noon-6; closed holidays. Admission $7, over 64 and students with ID $5, under 12 free. Phone (212) 685-0610.

★ **ROCKEFELLER CENTER**, Fifth Ave. to Avenue of the Americas (Sixth Ave.) and 48th to 51st sts. (S: 47th St./50th St., 49th St., 50th St., 51st St.), is a model of urban planning and design, housing 24 acres of underground shops and restaurants. A self-guiding tour brochure is available at the information desk. Phone (212) 698-2950, or 632-3975 for information.

NBC Studio Tours gives 1-hour behind-the-scenes tours of the production areas of several television shows. The tours depart every 15 minutes Mon.-Sat. 8:30-5:30, Sun. 9:30-4:30. Ticket sales begin at 7. Tours $17.50; senior citizens and ages 6-16, $15. Under 6 are not permitted. MC, VI. Phone (212) 664-4000 or 664-7174.

Radio City Music Hall is on Ave. of the Americas (Sixth Ave.) between W. 50th and W. 51st sts. This 1932 Art Deco theater presents musical stage spectaculars with the Rockettes, theatrical productions and live concerts. Guided 1-hour tours departing from the lobby are available. Mon.-Sat. 10-5, Sun. 11-5. Tour $13.75; under 12, $9. AE, MC, VI. Phone (212) 247-4777, or 632-4041 for tour reservations.

★**ST. PATRICK'S CATHEDRAL** (Roman Catholic), Fifth Ave. at 50th St. (S: 47th St./50th St., 49th St., 50th St., 51st St.), is one of the largest churches in the United States, with a seating capacity of 2,400. The rose window is 26 feet across, and the pipe organ has more than 7,380 pipes. Twin spires 330 feet high grace the 14th-century-Gothic-style structure.

The foundations of the church were laid before the Civil War, but the church was not open until 14 years after the war ended. Guided tours are available by appointment. Daily 6:30 a.m.-8:45 p.m. Phone (212) 753-2261.

SOCIETY OF ILLUSTRATORS MUSEUM OF AMERICAN ILLUSTRATION, 128 E. 63rd St. (S: 59th St./ Lexington Ave.), displays changing exhibits by noted illustrators of the past and present. Lectures and special demonstrations also are held. Allow 1 hour minimum. Tues.-Fri. 10-5 (also Tues. 5-8), Sat. noon-4. Free. Phone (212) 838-2560.

THE SONY IMAX THEATRE, Broadway and 68th St. (S: 66th St./Broadway), houses one of world's largest IMAX screens. Using 3-D visual and auditory technology, the theater features "Across the Sea of Time: New York 3-D," a film that includes panoramic aerial photography of the city. Allow 1 hour minimum. Daily 10:30 a.m.-10:40 p.m. (also midnight shows Fri.-Sat.). Admission $9.50; over 61, $7.50; under 12, $6. AE, MC, VI. Phone (212) 336-7669.

SONY WONDER TECHNOLOGY LAB, between 55th and 56th sts. at 550 Madison Ave. (S: 53rd St./5th Ave.), is an interactive science and technology museum that emphasizes hands-on state-of-the-art communications technology. Allow 1 hour minimum. Tues.-Sat. 10-6 (also Thurs. 6-8 p.m.), Sun. noon-6. Free. Phone (212) 833-8100.

TEMPLE EMANU-EL, Fifth Ave. and 65th St. (S: 68th St.), was founded in 1845 and is the oldest reform congregation in the city. One of the world's largest Jewish houses of worship, the current sanctuary, built in 1927, has striking architecture, mosaics and stained-glass windows. Visitors are welcome to the festivals and a community service offered on high holy days. Sun.-Thurs. 10-5, Fri. 10-4; closed to visitors prior to Jewish festivals and on high holy days. Free. Phone (212) 744-1400.

UNICEF HOUSE, 3 United Nations Plaza at 44th St. between 1st and 2nd Ave. (S: 42nd St.), offers multimedia presentations about world peace, global devel

Television Show Tickets

If available, tickets to attend the major television shows can be obtained from the networks.

Contact the networks' respective Guest Relations Offices: American Broadcasting Co., 38 W. 66th St., New York, NY 10023, (212) 456-3537; Columbia Broadcasting System, 524 W. 57th St., New York, NY 10019, (212) 975-2476; and National Broadcasting Co., 30 Rockefeller Plaza, New York, NY 10012, (212) 664-3055.

Citypass

CityPass offers savings to those who plan visits to many New York City attractions. The pass covers the price of admission to six sites: American Museum of Natural History, Empire State Building Observatory, *Intrepid* Sea-Air-Space Museum, Metropolitan Museum of Art, The Museum of Modern Art and Top of the World at the World Trade Center.

CityPass ticket booklets can be purchased at visitor information centers, major hotels and at any of the participating attractions. The tickets, valid for 9 days from the first date of use, are $29.75; ages 13-18, $21; over 64, $18.75. *See ad p. 112.*

opment and the future of the world. Allow 1 hour minimum. Mon.-Fri. 10-5. Donations. Phone (212) 326-7000.

★ UNITED NATIONS HEADQUARTERS, on First Ave. between 42nd and 48th sts. (S: Grand Central/42nd St.), is along the East River. The visitors entrance is at First Ave. and 46th St. The complex consists of the majestic Secretariat Building, the domed General Assembly Building, the Conference Building and the Hammarskjold Library. Each building was designed and decorated by celebrated architects and artisans.

Tours lasting 1 hour depart from the public lobby daily 9:15-4:45; closed major holidays and several days around Dec. 25 and Jan. 1. Tour $7.50; over 59, $5.50; students with ID $4.50; grades 1-8, $3.50. Under 5 not permitted on tour. Phone (212) 963-7713 for tour information.

WHITNEY MUSEUM OF AMERICAN ART, 945 Madison Ave. at 75th St. (S: 77th St.), presents modern sculptures, paintings, photographs, drawings, films and videotapes. An inverted pyramid construction allows 30,000 square feet of exhibition space in a building only 97 feet tall.

Allow 1 hour, 30 minutes minimum. Fri.-Sun. and Wed. 11-6, Thurs. 1-8; closed Jan. 1, Thanksgiving and Dec. 25. Admission $12.50, over 61 and college students with ID $10, under 12 free with an adult; free to all Thurs. 6-8 p.m. Phone (212) 570-3676.

WHITNEY MUSEUM OF AMERICAN ART AT PHILIP MORRIS, 120 Park Ave. at 42nd St. (S: 42nd St./Grand Central Station), presents changing exhibits on the ground floor and in the sculpture court. Museum talks are held Wednesday at 1. Gallery open Mon.-Fri. 11-6 (also Thurs. 6-7:30 p.m.); closed holidays. Sculpture court open Mon.-Sat. 7:30 a.m.-9:30 p.m., Sun. 11-7. Free. Phone (917) 663-2453.

UPPER MANHATTAN

AUDUBON TERRACE MUSEUM GROUP, Broadway at 155th St. (S: 157th St./Broadway), houses five museums with varying displays and exhibits. The Children's Museum of the Native American is open only to school groups.

American Academy of Arts and Letters, 633 W. 155 St., with gallery entrance on Audubon Terr., offers three exhibits a year. Tues.-Sun. 1-4, in Mar., mid-May to mid-June and mid-Nov. to mid-Dec.; closed major holidays. Free. Phone (212) 368-5900.

American Numismatic Society, Broadway at 155th St., has more than 600,000 coins and medals; a selected portion is displayed. Library and exhibit rooms open Tues.-Sat. 9-4:30, Sun. 1-4; closed major holidays. Free. Phone (212) 234-3130.

Hispanic Society of America, 613 W. 155th St. between 155th and 156th sts., exhibits Spanish

and Portuguese sculpture, paintings and decorative arts. Tues.-Sat. 10-4:30, Sun. 1-4; closed holidays. Free. Phone (212) 926-2234.

CATHEDRAL OF ST. JOHN THE DIVINE (Episcopal), 112th and Amsterdam Ave. at 1047 Amsterdam Ave. (S: 110th St. Cathedral Pkwy.), was begun in 1892. Built entirely of stone, including Maine granite and Indiana limestone, St. John's is two football fields long and 17 stories high. The Biblical Garden contains more than 100 plants mentioned in Scripture; the Peace Fountain is by Greg Wyatt.

Allow 1 hour minimum. Daily 7-5. Guided tours Tues.-Sat. at 11, Sun. at 1. Guided tour $3. Self-guiding tour $2, senior citizen $1. Phone (212) 316-7490.

★ THE CLOISTERS is in Fort Tryon Park, first exit n. of George Washington Bridge off Henry Hudson Pkwy. (S: 190th St. or M4 bus "Cloisters" on Madison Ave. to end). Devoted to medieval art, this branch of the Metropolitan Museum of Art includes parts of five French cloisters, a Romanesque chapel and extensive gardens. Collections include statues, paintings, stained-glass windows and tapestries.

Tues.-Sun. 9:30-5:15, Mar.-Oct.; 9:30-4:45, rest of year. Closed Jan. 1, Thanksgiving and Dec. 25. Admission $10, over 64 and students with ID $4, under 12 free. Admission includes the Metropolitan Museum of Art in Midtown Manhattan (see attraction listing p. 124). Phone (212) 923-3700.

COLUMBIA UNIVERSITY is in Morningside Heights, between Broadway and Amsterdam Ave. and 114th and 120th sts. (S: 116th St.). Founded in 1754 as King's College, it includes Columbia College, School of Engineering and Applied Sciences, several graduate and professional schools and is affiliated with Teachers College and Barnard College for women. Guided tours are available Mon.-Fri. at 11 and 2. Free. Phone (212) 854-4900.

COOPER-HEWITT NATIONAL DESIGN MUSEUM-SMITHSONIAN INSTITUTION, in the landmark Andrew Carnegie Mansion at 2 E. 91st St. (S: 86th St.), features architectural and ornamental drawings, prints, textiles, ceramics, wallpaper, jewelry, metalwork, woodwork, specialized materials and changing exhibits.

Tues.-Sat. 10-5 (also Tues. 5-9), Sun. noon-5; closed Jan. 1, July 4, Thanksgiving and Dec. 25. Admission $5, senior citizens and students with ID $3, under 12 free; free to all Tues. 5-9. Phone (212) 849-8300 or 849-8386.

DYCKMAN HOUSE, 204th St. and Broadway (S: 207th St.), dates from 1784 and is the only Dutch farmhouse remaining on Manhattan Island. It is furnished in the style typical of wealthy colonists. Tues.-Sun. 11-4; closed Jan. 1, July 4, Thanksgiving and Dec. 25. Hours may vary; phone ahead. Donations. Phone (212) 304-9422.

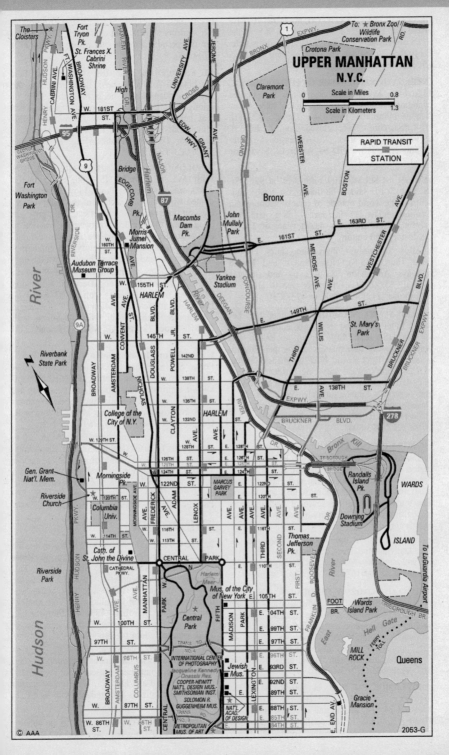

UPPER MANHATTAN
N.Y.C.

Scale in Miles
0   0.8

Scale in Kilometers
0   1.3

RAPID TRANSIT
STATION

To: ★ Bronx Zoo/
Wildlife
Conservation Park

Crotona Park

Claremont
Park

Bronx

Fort
Washington
Park

The
Cloisters

Fort
Tryon
Pk.

St. Frances X.
Cabrini Shrine

High

Bridge

Pk.

Morris
Jumel
Mansion

Audubon Terrace
Museum Group

HARLEM

Macombs
Dam Pk.

John
Mullaly
Park

Yankee
Stadium

E. 163RD   ST.

E.   161ST   ST.

E.   149TH

Riverbank
State Park

College of the
City of N.Y.

HARLEM

St. Mary's
Park

E.   138TH   ST.

BRUCKNER   BLVD.

Gen. Grant
Nat'l. Mem.

Morningside
Pk.

Riverside
Church

Columbia
Univ.

Cath. of
St. John the Divine

Marcus
Garvey
Park

Bronx
Kill

Randalls
Island Pk.

Downing
Stadium

WARDS

ISLAND

Thomas
Jefferson
Pk.

To LaGuardia Airport

Riverside
Park

Harlem
Meer

Mus. of the City
of New York

Central
Park

International Center
Of Photography

Jacqueline Kennedy
Onassis Res.

Cooper-Hewitt
Nat'l. Design Mus.
Smithsonian Inst.

Solomon R.
Guggenheim Mus.

Nat'l. Acad.
Of Design

Metropolitan
Mus. Of Art

Jewish
Mus.

Wards
Island Park

MILL
ROCK

Gracie
Mansion

Queens

Hell Gate

FOOT
BR.

Hudson

River

E. 104TH   ST.

E.   99TH   ST.

E.   97TH   ST.

E. 96TH   ST.

E. 93RD   ST.

E.   92ND   ST.

E.   89TH   ST.

E.   88TH   ST.

E.   84TH   ST.

© AAA

2053-G

GENERAL GRANT NATIONAL MEMORIAL, Riverside Dr. and 122nd St. (S: 116th St.), is the tomb of President Ulysses S. Grant and his wife. Daily 9-5; closed Jan. 1, Thanksgiving and Dec. 25. Free. Phone (212) 666-1640.

INTERNATIONAL CENTER OF PHOTOGRAPHY, 1130 Fifth Ave. at 94th St. (S: 96 St.), houses changing exhibits devoted to photography. Allow 1 hour minimum. Tues. and Thurs. 10-5, Fri. 10-8, Sat.-Sun. 10-6; closed Jan. 1, July 4, Thanksgiving and Dec. 25. Admission $6; over 64 and students with ID $4; under 12, $1. Phone (212) 860-1777.

JEWISH MUSEUM, 1109 Fifth Ave. at 92nd St. (S: 86th St.) is said to be the largest Jewish museum in the world outside of Israel. "Culture and Continuity: The Jewish Journey" is a permanent exhibition that traverses 4,000 years of Jewish art, history and culture.

Allow 1 hour minimum. Sun.-Thurs. 11-5:45 (also Tues. 5:45-8); closed major and Jewish holidays. Admission $8, over 64 and students with ID $5.50, under 12 free; free to all Tues. 5-8. Phone (212) 423-3200 or 423-3230.

MORRIS-JUMEL MANSION, 65 Jumel Terr. between 160th and 162nd sts., .5 blk. e. of St. Nicholas Ave. (S: 163rd St.), served as British and American army headquarters during the Revolutionary War. Built around 1765, the mansion is one of Manhattan's oldest surviving residential structures and it houses Colonial, Revolutionary, Federal and American Empire furniture. Wed.-Sun. 10-4; closed major holidays. Admission $3, over 64 and students with ID $2, under 10 free with an adult. Phone (212) 923-8008.

MUSEUM OF THE CITY OF NEW YORK, Fifth Ave. and 103rd to 104th sts. (S: 103rd St./Lexington Ave.), is devoted to the life and history of the city. Weekend educational and entertainment programs are held in the museum's auditorium. The museum also offers seasonal walking tours to various parts of the city *(see What To Do, Sightseeing).*

Wed.-Sat. 10-5, Sun. noon-5; closed Jan. 1, Thanksgiving and Dec. 25. Admission $5, over 64 and students with ID $4, family rate $10. Phone (212) 534-1672.

NATIONAL ACADEMY OF DESIGN, 1083 Fifth Ave. at 89th St. (S: 86th St.), displays a permanent collection of artworks as well as changing drawing, painting, sculpture and architectural exhibits. Allow 30 minutes minimum. Wed.-Thurs. 10-5, Fri. 10-6, Sat.-Sun. noon-5; closed major holidays. Admission $8; over 64, students with ID and under 16, $4.50. MC, VI. Phone (212) 369-4880.

★**RIVERSIDE CHURCH,** at 490 Riverside Dr. between 120th and 122nd sts. (S: 116th St.), houses a 74-bell carillon that is played Sunday at 10:30, 12:30 and 3. The carillon is the heaviest and the second largest in the world. Bell tower

open Tues.-Sat. 11-4, Sun. 12:30-4. Admission $2; students with ID and ages11-18, $1. Under 6 are not permitted in the bell tower. Phone (212) 870-6700.

ST. FRANCES X. CABRINI SHRINE, 701 Fort Washington Ave. (M4 bus), is dedicated to the first American saint, who is the patron saint of immigrants. Displayed are objects and clothes that belonged to her. Allow 30 minutes minimum. Daily 9-4:30; closed Memorial Day, July 4, Labor Day and Thanksgiving. Free. Phone (212) 923-3536.

★**SOLOMON R. GUGGENHEIM MUSEUM,** 1071 Fifth Ave. at 89th St. (S: 86th St./Lexington Ave.), was designed by Frank Lloyd Wright. The domed white circular section of the building creates an interesting visual effect; paintings are hung along the spiraled walkway. In addition to the permanent collection, the museum exhibits late 19th- and early 20th-century and contemporary paintings and sculpture. Food is available.

Allow 2 hours minimum. Sun.-Wed. 9-6, Fri.-Sat. 9-8; closed Jan. 1 and Dec. 25. Admission $12, over 64 and students with ID $7, under 12 free. Combination admission with Guggenheim Museum SoHo $16, over 64 and students with ID $10, under 12 free. AE, MC, VI. Phone (212) 423-3600.

Guggenheim Museum SoHo, 575 Broadway at Prince St. (S: Prince St.), is in a historic 19th-century structure. The interior, designed by well-known architect Arata Isozaki, contains displays from the permanent collection. Special exhibitions that complement those at the Solomon R. Guggenheim Museum also are featured.

Allow 1 hour minimum. Thurs.-Mon. 10-6; closed Jan. 1, Thanksgiving and Dec. 25. Admission $8, over 64 and students with ID $5, under 12 free. Combination admission with Solomon R. Guggenheim Museum $16, over 64 and students with ID $10, under 12 free. AE, MC, VI. Phone (212) 423-3500. *See ad p. 112.*

THE BRONX

BARTOW-PELL MANSION MUSEUM, e. of the Orchard Beach exit of the Hutchinson River Pkwy., then .5 mi. n. to 895 Shore Rd. (S: Pelham Bay Park), occupies a site bought from the Siwanoy Indians in 1654. The first house was destroyed during the Revolutionary War; the existing mansion was built 1836-42. Furnished in period, it is the only home of its era in this region. Gardens adorn the grounds.

Gardens open Tues.-Sun. 8:30-4:30. Mansion open Wed. and Sat.-Sun. noon-4, Thurs.-Fri. and Tues. by appointment; closed Jan. 1, Thanksgiving weekend and Dec. 25. Mansion admission $2.50, senior citizens and students with ID $1.25, under 12 free. Phone (718) 885-1461.

BRONX COMMUNITY COLLEGE is in University Heights on University Ave. and W. 181st St.

(S: 183rd St.). On campus is the Hall of Fame for Great Americans, open daily 10-5. Free. Phone (718) 289-5100.

★ BRONX ZOO/WILDLIFE CONSERVATION PARK, off the Bronx River Pkwy. at Fordham Rd. (S: Pelham Pkwy., E. Tremont Ave.), displays animals representing more than 600 species in naturalistic indoor environments and large outdoor habitats. Additional attractions, including a camel ride, monorail and shuttle, are available May through October.

Mon.-Fri. 10-5, Sat.-Sun. and holidays 10-5:30, Apr.-Oct.; daily 10-4:30, rest of year. A children's zoo is open Mar.-Oct. Admission Apr.-Oct. $7.75; over 65 and ages 2-12, $4; free to all Wed. Admission Nov. 1-Jan. 3, $6; over 65 and ages 2-12, $3. Admission rest of year $4; over 65 and ages 2-12, $2. Camel ride $3. Children's zoo $2. Monorail $2. Shuttle $2. Parking $6. Phone (718) 367-1010.

FORDHAM UNIVERSITY, Third Ave. at E. Fordham Rd., near n.w. Bronx Park (S: Fordham Rd.), was founded in 1841 as an independent Jesuit university. Fordham's 10 schools have three campuses: Rose Hill, Lincoln Center and Tarrytown. Guided tours are available Mon.-Fri. at 12:30 and 2, Sat.-Sun. by appointment. Free. Phone (718) 817-1000.

★ NEW YORK BOTANICAL GARDEN, 200th St. and Kazimiroff Blvd. (S: Bedford Park Blvd.), was founded in 1891 and is one of the world's largest botanical gardens, covering 250 acres. The garden has 28 specialty gardens and plant collections. The palacelike, glass-enclosed Enid A. Haupt Conservatory contains A World of Plants, an exhibit featuring plants displayed in settings similar to their tropical, subtropical and desert habitats.

Outdoor gardens include the Peggy Rockefeller Rose Garden, the Rock Garden, the Native Plant Garden and the Jane Watson Irwin Perennial Garden as well as 40 acres of original forest that once covered the city. The 12-acre, indoor/outdoor Everett Children's Adventure Garden has 40 hands-on activities for discovering plants and nature, plus mazes and topiaries.

Other features include narrated tram rides; children's activities, such as gardening in the Ruth Rea Howell Family Garden; and guided walking tours. On weekends spring through fall a shuttle departs from the American Museum of Natural History and the Metropolitan Museum of Art (see attraction listings pp. 118 and 124). Food and picnic facilities also are available.

Grounds open Tues.-Sun. 10-6, Apr.-Oct.; 10-4, rest of year. Hours vary for conservatory and children's, rock and native plant gardens; phone ahead. Closed Thanksgiving and Dec. 25.

Grounds $3; over 64 and students with ID $2; ages 2-12, $1; free to all Wed. and Sat. 10-noon, Apr.-Oct. Conservatory $3.50; over 64 and students with ID $2.50; ages 2-12, $2. Children's garden $3; over 64 and students with ID $2; ages 2-12, $1. Rock and native plant gardens $1; over 64, students with ID and ages 2-12, 50c. Combination ticket $9.50; over 64, $7; ages 2-12, $3.50. Tram $1. Parking $4. Phone (718) 817-8700.

NORTH WIND UNDERSEA INSTITUTE, off I-95 exit 8B at 610 City Island Ave. (S: Kingsbridge Rd.), occupies an old sea-captain's home in a quaint little village. The museum offers hands-on exhibits for children and exhibits of nautical items. Allow 30 minutes minimum. Mon.-Fri. noon-4; closed major holidays. Admission $3; over 59 and ages 1-14, $2. Phone (718) 885-0701.

VAN CORTLANDT HOUSE MUSEUM is at Broadway and 246th St. in Van Cortlandt Park. This 1748 mansion features 17th- and 18th-century Dutch, English and American furnishings. Tues.-Fri. 10-3, Sat.-Sun. 11-4; closed holidays. Admission $2, senior citizens and students with ID $1.50, under 12 free. Phone (718) 543-3344.

WAVE HILL, off the Henry Hudson Pkwy. at W. 249 St. and Independence Ave., was built in 1843 and features a 28-acre garden and cultural center overlooking the Hudson River. The Glyndor House presents changing horticultural exhibits. Guided walks among the herb, wildflower and aquatic gardens are held Sunday at 2:15; special events are held periodically.

Allow 1 hour minimum. Tues.-Sun. 9-5:30, mid-Apr. through Oct. 14; Tues.-Sun. 9-4:30, rest of year. Admission $4, senior citizens and students with ID $2, under 6 free; free to all Tues. all day, Sat. 9-noon and Nov. 15-Mar. 14. Phone (718) 549-3200.

WOODLAWN CEMETERY, Webster Ave. at E. 233rd St. (S: Jerome Ave.), was established in 1863 and contains more than 250,000 graves, including those of Duke Ellington, Herman Melville, Joseph Pulitzer and Elizabeth Cady Stanton. Sculpture adorns the landscaped grounds. Musical programs, tours and special events are held regularly. Daily 9-4:30 (weather permitting). Free. Phone (718) 920-0500.

BROOKLYN

AQUARIUM FOR WILDLIFE CONSERVATION, on the Coney Island Boardwalk (S: West 8th St. N.Y. Aquarium, Coney Island Stillwell Ave.), exhibits marine life in outdoor pools and indoor tanks. The Oceanic tank features a Beluga whale. Local species are featured in the Hudson River exhibit. The Gulf Stream Habitat examines the various fish that are swept up the river by the stream during the summer. The Sea Cliffs exhibit is a replica of the rocky Pacific coast and features walruses, sea otters, seals and penguins.

Mon.-Fri. 10-5, Sat.-Sun. and holidays 10-6, Memorial Day-Labor Day; daily 10-5, rest of year. Admission $8.75; over 65 and ages 2-12, $4.50. Parking $6. Phone (718) 265-3474.

★ **BROOKLYN BOTANIC GARDEN** has entrances at Flatbush Ave. and Empire Blvd. and at Washington Ave. and Eastern Pkwy. (S: Eastern Pkwy., Prospect Park). Its 52 acres include the Garden of Fragrance for the blind; the Japanese Garden; the Conservatory, housing tropical plants and a bonsai museum under three glass pavilions.

Allow 1 hour minimum. Garden open Tues.-Fri. 8-6, Sat.-Sun. and holidays 10-6, Apr.-Sept.; Tues.-Fri. 8-4:30, Sat.-Sun. and holidays 10-4:30, rest of year. Conservatory open Tues.-Sun. and holidays 10-5:30, Apr.-Sept.; Tues.-Sun. 10-4, rest of year. Admission $3; over 64 and students with ID $1.50; ages 6-16, 50c. Free to all Tues. all day and Sat. 10-noon. Phone (718) 623-7200.

BROOKLYN CHILDREN'S MUSEUM, 145 Brooklyn Ave. (S: Kingston Ave.), contains more than 77,000 artifacts. Children learn through touching, entering or interacting with exhibits. Arrive early on weekends to avoid crowds. Wed.-Fri. 2-5, Sat.-Sun. and holidays 10-5; closed Jan. 1, Thanksgiving and Dec. 25. Admission $3. Phone (718) 735-4400 or 735-4402.

BROOKLYN HISTORY MUSEUM, 128 Pierrepont St. at Clinton St. (S: Borough Hall/Court St./Jay St.), traces the development of Brooklyn Village in the 1830s through the construction of the Brooklyn Bridge in 1883; the historical significance of Coney Island; and baseball's early roots in Brooklyn with original photographs of the Brooklyn Dodgers. **Note:** the museum is closed for renovation and is scheduled to reopen in 2000.

Allow 1 hour minimum. Tues.-Sat. noon-5. Admission $2.50; over 64 and ages 1-12, $1; free to all Wed. Phone (718) 624-0890 to verify accessibility.

BROOKLYN MUSEUM, Eastern Pkwy. and Washington Ave. at Prospect Park (S: Eastern Pkwy./Bklyn. Museum), houses collections of Egyptian, African, Asian, Oceanic, classical, New World and ancient Middle Eastern art as well as American paintings, 29 Colonial period rooms spanning the 17th-20th centuries and an outdoor sculpture garden.

Wed.-Fri. 10-5, Sat.-Sun. 11-6 (also first Sat. of each month 6-11 p.m.); closed Jan. 1, Thanksgiving and Dec. 25. Admission $4; students with ID $2; over 59, $2 under 12 free with an adult. Parking $6. Phone (718) 638-5000.

CYPRESS HILLS NATIONAL CEMETERY is on Jamaica and Hale aves. (S: Cypress Hills). The original 3,170 graves are casualties received from Civil War hospitals in the New York City vicinity. Daily 9-4:30. Free.

FORT GREENE PARK, at Myrtle and DeKalb aves., and St. Edwards and Cumberland sts. (S: Fulton St./Lafayette Ave.), contains Martyrs' Monument, designed by Stanford White and dedicated to the Continental soldiers who died on British prison ships in Wallabout Bay. Daily dawn-dusk. Free.

NEW YORK CITY TRANSIT MUSEUM, jct. of Boerum Pl. and Schermerhorn St. under the Board of Education building (S: Borough Hall, Court St., Jay St.), has photographs, equipment, artifacts and memorabilia that trace the development of the city's bus and subway systems. Numerous trains and vehicles are displayed, some of which can be entered. Tues.-Fri. 10-4, Sat.-Sun. noon-5; closed major holidays. Admission $3; over 61 and under 17, $1.50. Phone (718) 243-8601, or 243-3060 for information.

PROSPECT PARK, between Prospect Park W. and Prospect Park S.W. and Flatbush and Parkside aves. (S: 7th Ave./Grand Army Plaza), contains a Quaker graveyard, gardens, trails, zoo, boating facilities and historic buildings. Grand Army Plaza, at the north entrance at Flatbush Avenue and Eastern Parkway, has an arch commemorating Civil War heroes and a memorial to John F. Kennedy.

The Ravine, an Adirondack-style gorge, has waterfalls, pools and 24 acres of restored woodlands. Lefferts Homestead, in the park on Flatbush Avenue, is a museum containing early American furnishings and relics, particularly from the 1820s. Park open daily dawn-dusk. Lefferts Homestead open by appointment. Free. Phone (718) 965-8951, 965-8999 24 hours a day, or 965-6505 for the homestead.

ST. JOHN'S EPISCOPAL CHURCH, 9818 Fort Hamilton Pkwy. (S: 95th St.), was founded in 1834. Generals Robert E. Lee and Thomas "Stonewall" Jackson were members of the congregation while at Fort Hamilton. Mon.-Fri. 9-3, Sat. 11-2, Sun. after 8 a.m. and 10:30 a.m. service. Free. Phone (718) 745-2377.

QUEENS

AMERICAN MUSEUM OF THE MOVING IMAGE, 35th Ave. and 36th St. in Astoria (S: Steinway St.), chronicles the art, history, technique and technology of motion pictures, television, video and digital media. The museum occupies a renovated building on the site of the former Astoria Studio, a 1920s facility used by Paramount Pictures. The museum presents interpretive programs, changing exhibitions and screenings. No stollers permitted. Tues.-Fri. noon-5, Sat.-Sun. 11-6. Admission $8.50; over 65 and students with ID $5.50; ages 5-18, $4.50. Phone (718) 784-0077 or 784-4777.

FLUSHING MEADOWS CORONA PARK is bounded by Roosevelt Ave., Van Wyck Expwy., Union Tpke. and 111th St. (S: Willets Point/Shea Stadium). Site of New York's World Fairs 1939-40 and 1964-65, the park has bicycle paths, the Queens Wildlife Conservation Center, a carousel, freshwater fishing, pitch-and-putt golf, an indoor ice-skating rink and a marina. Baseball, cricket, football and softball fields are available as well as boccie courts. The U.S. Tennis Center has indoor and outdoor courts open to the public daily from 8 a.m.-midnight; for rates phone (718) 760-6200.

Paddleboats and rowboats can be rented on Meadow Lake from 9:30-7:30. A special playground for handicapped children is open Mon.-Fri. 1:30-5, Sat.-Sun. 10-5; phone (718) 699-3478. The Willow Lake Nature Area has free urban ranger tours; phone (718) 699-4204. Picnicking is permitted. Daily 9-dusk. Free. Phone (718) 760-6565.

THE ISAMU NOGUCHI GARDEN MUSEUM, 32-37 Vernon Blvd. (S: Broadway), displays sculpture in 12 galleries and an outdoor garden. A shuttle service from midtown Manhattan to the museum is available for $5 round-trip; phone for details. Allow 2 hours minimum. Wed.-Fri. 10-5, Sat.-Sun. 11-6, Apr.-Oct. Guided tours are given at 2. Admission $4, senior citizens and students with ID $2. Phone (718) 204-7088.

JAMAICA BAY WILDLIFE REFUGE is 3 mi. s. on Crossbay Blvd. off Belt Pkwy. exit 17. The 9,155-acre refuge contains varied habitats, including freshwater ponds, marshes, bays, fields, wooded areas and islands. It is a major stopover for migrating birds; some 329 species have been recorded since the mid-1950s. A 1.75-mile walking trail allows visitors to see the early stages of forest development. Comfortable walking shoes are recommended. Allow 2 hours minimum. Refuge daily 8:30-dusk. Visitor center daily 8:30-5. Free. Phone (718) 318-4340.

NEW YORK HALL OF SCIENCE, 111th St. and 46th Ave. in Flushing Meadows Corona Park (S: 111 St.), is a hands-on science and technology center. Many of the exhibits are geared toward making scientific processes understandable for children. The center also has a multimedia library.

Allow 2 hours minimum. Thurs.-Sun. 9:30-5, Mon.-Wed. 9:30-2; closed Jan. 1, Thanksgiving and Dec. 24-25. Admission $7.50; over 61 and ages 4-15, $5; free to all Thurs.-Fri. 2-5. Parking $6. MC, VI. Phone (718) 699-0005.

QUEENS BOTANICAL GARDEN is at 43-50 Main St.; take I-495 (Long Island Expwy.) exit 23 to Main St., then 1 mi. n. to Dahlia Ave. (S: Main St.). Trails and paths wind through rose, rock and formal gardens, and a live beehive is the focal point in a wildflower meadow. Special programs, educational tours and projects are offered throughout the year. Tues.-Fri. 8-6, Sat.-Sun. 8-7, Memorial Day-Sept. 30; daily 8-4:30, rest of year. Donations. Phone (718) 886-3800.

QUEENS MUSEUM OF ART, in the New York City Building at Flushing Meadows Corona Park (S: Willets Point/Shea Stadium) *(see attraction listing)*, offers changing art exhibitions. Allow 1

hour minimum. Wed.-Fri. 10-5, Sat.-Sun. noon-5; closed Jan. 1, Thanksgiving and Dec. 25. Admission $4, senior citizens and students with ID $2, under 5 free. Phone (718) 592-9700.

RICHMOND (STATEN ISLAND)

ALICE AUSTEN HOUSE is off I-278 Bay St. Exit, n. 1 mi. to Hylan Blvd. then e. to 2 Hylan Blvd. This Victorian house, carefully restored to its 1890s appearance, displays photographs taken from the late 1800s through the first half of the 20th century by Alice Austen, who lived here 1866-1929. Allow 1 hour minimum. Thurs.-Sun. noon-5. Admission $2, under 12 free. Phone (718) 816-4506.

HISTORIC RICHMOND TOWN, s. of I-278 via Richmond Rd./Clove Rd. exit following signs, is a restored 100-acre village that re-creates the appearance and lifestyle of 3 centuries of local history. Period furniture, antique toys, craft demonstrations and interpretive exhibits are offered among the buildings, shops and grounds.

Allow 2 hours minimum. Wed.-Fri. 10-5, Sat.-Sun. 1-5, July-Aug.; Wed.-Sun. 1-5, rest of year. Closed Jan. 1, Easter, Thanksgiving and Dec. 25. Admission $4; over 61, students with ID and ages 6-18, $2.50. Phone (718) 351-1611.

JACQUES MARCHAIS MUSEUM OF TIBETAN ART is at 338 Lighthouse Ave.; take I-278W to Richmond Rd., then 5 mi. s. to Lighthouse Ave. Designed like a small Tibetan mountain temple, the museum collects, preserves and displays Tibetan, Tibeto-Chinese, Nepalese and Mongolian art objects and paintings. Terraced sculpture gardens, a lily and fish pond and a view of the Lower Bay provide a serene atmosphere. Lectures, demonstrations and performances are offered on selected Sunday afternoons.

Allow 1 hour minimum. Wed.-Sun. 1-5, Apr.-Nov.; by appointment Wed.-Sun. 1-5, rest of year. Closed Thanksgiving, day after Thanksgiving and Dec. 25. Admission $3; over 64, $2.50; ages 1-12, $1; Sun. programs $3 additional. Phone (718) 987-3500.

SNUG HARBOR CULTURAL CENTER, Clove Rd. exit off I-278, then 3 mi. n. to 1000 Richmond Terr., was founded in 1801 as the nation's first maritime hospital and home for retired sailors. Restored buildings include Main Hall, with its Newhouse Center for Contemporary Art, and Veterans Hall, which showcases jazz, classical, chamber and folk music concerts. Phone (718) 448-2500.

The Staten Island Botanical Garden includes an English perennial garden, formal displays of annuals, a greenhouse display of orchids and other tropical plants and a sensory garden for the disabled. Grounds open daily dawn-dusk. Greenhouses open Mon.-Fri. 9-5, Sat.-Sun. noon-4. Free. Phone (718) 273-8200.

Staten Island Children's Museum, in the Snug Harbor Cultural Center, contains exhibits about art, science and humanities. Hands-on workshops, performances and special events designed for pre-school through eighth grade children are presented throughout the year. Allow 1 hour, 30 minutes minimum. Tues.-Sun. noon-5; closed Jan. 1, July 4, Thanksgiving and Dec. 25. Admission $4, under 2 free. Phone (718) 273-2060.

STATEN ISLAND INSTITUTE OF ARTS AND SCIENCES, 75 Stuyvesant Pl. (5-minute walk from the ferry terminal in St. George), displays art, natural science and history collections and exhibits about Staten Island and its people. Its archives and library have documents dating from the early 1700s. Allow 1 hour minimum. Mon.-Sat. 9-5, Sun. 1-5; closed major holidays. Admission $2.50, over 64 and students with ID $1.25. Phone (718) 727-1135.

Staten Island Ferry Collection, in the Staten Island Ferry waiting room directly off the terminal's large lobby, displays an assortment of ships wheels and whistles, vintage photographs, mechanical drawings and scale models of historical ferries. Allow 30 minutes minimum. Daily 8-1; closed major holidays. Admission $1; under 13, 25c. Phone (718) 727-1135.

STATEN ISLAND ZOO, in Barrett Park, West New Brighton at 614 Broadway, is an educational zoo with mammals, birds, reptiles and tropical fish. Exhibits include a representation of a tropical rain forest, an aquarium, a serpentarium and a children's center emphasizing domestic animals that help man. Allow 1 hour minimum. Daily 10-4:30; closed Jan. 1, Thanksgiving and Dec. 25. Admission $3; ages 3-11, $2; free to all Wed. 2-4:30. Phone (718) 442-3100.

What To Do In New York City
Sightseeing
Boat Tours

Boat tours can make sightseeing even more exciting. From early March through December, SAVE Circle Line Cruises operates a 3-hour, 35-mile narrated tour around Manhattan Island, allowing close up views of the busy New York docks and the skyline; phone (212) 563-3200 for schedules. Fare $22; senior citizens $16; ages 2-12, $12. A Harbor Lights Cruise is offered early Mar.-Oct. 31. The fare is $18; ages 2-12, $10.

The 1885 schooner *Pioneer* offers 2-hour excursions of New York Harbor Tues.-Sun., June 1-Sept. 23; Sat.-Sun., Apr.-May. Tickets are sold at the Pier 16 ticket booth; phone (212) 748-8786.

One of the best sightseeing bargains in the city is a ride on the Staten Island Ferry. Leaving South Ferry in Battery Park every day at least once an hour, the free ride provides views of the Lower Manhattan skyline and the Statue of Liberty. Avoid the ferry during peak commuter hours, Mon.-Fri. 8-10 and 4-6; phone (718) 390-5253.

SPIRIT CRUISES departs from Pier 62, off W. 23rd St. and Weehawken, NJ, at 1500 Harbor Blvd., and offers narrated 2-hour lunch and 2.5-hour Sunday lunch cruises on the East and Hudson rivers. Dinner cruises are available but are not narrated. All cruises include live music and entertainment. Inquire about refund policies.

Lunch cruises Mon.-Sat. at noon, Sun. at 1, mid-Apr. through Oct. 31 and in Dec.; otherwise varies. All tours board 30 minutes before departure. Lunch cruises Mon.-Fri. $29.95, Sat. $33.95, Sun. $37.95. Reservations are strongly recommended. AE, DI, MC, VI. Phone (212) 727-2789.

WORLD YACHT, Pier 81 and W. 41st St. on the Hudson River, offers brunch and dinner cruises of New York harbor. Passengers can experience marvelous views of the Statue of Liberty and the city's skyline. Live entertainment is provided. Allow 3 hours minimum. Dinner cruises depart daily at 7, brunch cruises Sun. at 12:30; closed Jan. 1 and Dec. 25. Boarding is 1 hour prior to departure.

Dinner cruise (jacket required) Sun.-Thurs., $70.47, Fri. $79.13, Sat. $83.46, brunch cruise $39. Parking $15. Reservations are required. AE, MC, VI. Phone (212) 630-8100.

Bus Tours

To see the most in the least amount of time, take a bus tour. The all-day tours visit top tourist attractions. Other tours averaging 2 to 4.5 hours can be combined to satisfy your sightseeing tastes.

There are numerous bus tours that cover all parts of the city; information is available either from your local AAA club or by phoning the bus lines directly.

SAVE Gray Line offers about 20 tours to the general public; phone (212) 397-2620. Number 1 goes to Lower Manhattan; Number 2 visits Harlem and Upper Manhattan; Number 3 encompasses much of the city and is called The Grand Tour; Number 4 includes the Statue of Liberty and Lower Manhattan; and Number 5 includes The Grand Tour plus the Statue of Liberty; Number 6 lasts all day. Short Line, (212) 397-2600, is another tour operator. *See color ad p. 109.*

Walking Tours

An inexpensive way to see the city is by self-guiding walking tours. Various ethnic neighborhoods offer intriguing shops, restaurants and sidewalk fairs best sampled on foot.

Some of the best known communities include Little Italy, centering on Mulberry Street; the Jewish sector, on Essex and Orchard streets; the Middle Eastern enclave, along Atlantic Avenue; and the East Indian neighborhood, on Lexington Avenue. Check with a local AAA club for more information about what other areas would lend themselves to walking tours.

Various guided walking tours are offered daily by the Municipal Art Society, based in the Urban Center at 457 Madison Ave. and 51st Street; phone (212) 935-3960.

The Museum of the City of New York (see attraction listing p. 128) conducts various guided walking tours of Manhattan, Brooklyn and Staten Island one Sunday a month, April through October; the fee is $10, $8 for senior citizens and students with ID. Reservations are required. For a brochure describing the various tours contact the Education Department, Museum of the City of New York, 1220 Fifth Ave., New York, NY 10029; phone (212) 534-1672, ext. 206.

Theme tours of Harlem, including jazz, soul food and art galleries, are available from Harlem, Your Way! Tours Unlimited; phone (800) 382-9363. New York City Cultural Walking Tours, (212) 979-2388, offers guided tours that emphasize Manhattan's architecture and history. The 92nd Street YMCA provides walking tours that center on the art, history and architecture of various neighborhoods; phone (212) 996-1100.

Talk-A-Walk offers tape tours of various Lower Manhattan attractions and the Brooklyn Bridge. The cassettes can be obtained through the mail for $9.95 each (plus $2.90 for postage and shipping for up to six cassettes) by writing Talk-A-Walk, 30 Waterside Plaza, 10D, New York, NY 10010. They also are available at some downtown hotels; for locations phone (212) 686-0356.

GREENWICH VILLAGE WALKING TOUR: The only way to see and feel the tempo of "the Village" is to walk. This walking tour allows visitors to sample a vast range of Village life in about 1 hour (see map). Many, however, will find it hard not to make more leisurely stops at the many points en route.

Start your tour at Washington Square Park, at the bottom of Fifth Avenue. Walk south across the park to W. 4th Street and turn left to La Guardia Place. Turn right and continue south on La Guardia Place. Apartment buildings flank the east side of the street; the Loeb Student Center of New York University (N.Y.U.) is on the west.

Turn right on Bleecker Street. At 147 Bleecker St. is the Bitter End, a restaurant featuring entertainment. In the next block on the southwest corner of Thompson and Bleecker streets is the Village Gate. Top performers in the jazz and folk fields compete with comedians and musical groups at this spot.

At MacDougal Street turn right. The next two blocks of MacDougal and the stretch of W. 4th Street to Seventh Avenue are lined with handicraft shops, clothing shops and cafes.

A right turn onto Seventh Avenue takes you to 178 Seventh Ave. S. (between 11th and Perry streets), site of the Village Vanguard, noted for its jazz presentations. Turn right on Perry to Greenwich Avenue. The three blocks between Perry and Sixth Avenue (Avenue of the Americas) are flanked by numerous small shops offering a variety of handicrafts, clothing and jewelry.

There is an outdoor produce and flower mart at the intersection of Greenwich and Sixth avenues.

Cross the street to W. 8th Street and walk down to MacDougal Street. Both sides of 8th Street have men's and women's clothing shops and various other establishments. Then backtrack along 8th Street to Sixth Avenue. Turn right and go uptown to W. 9th Street. Across the street is Balducci's Market, which offers fresh produce and international foods of all kinds.

Washington Square Park, at the foot of Fifth Avenue, is in a residential section of the Village. Many artists gather and display their works in open-air art shows during the spring and summer. The Washington Arch, a formidable structure designed by Stanford White, stands at the head of the park.

Chess and checkers players can be seen in the southwest corner of the park during every season and in all but the most inclement weather. On Sunday afternoons the site is usually filled with both Villagers and tourists who come to listen to the poetry readings and folk singers or to just hang out.

Sports and Recreation

Beaches listed below, although generally more crowded and not as good as the one at Jones Beach State Park (see Jones Beach p. 95), can be reached by either bus or subway.

Coney Island Beach and Boardwalk and Manhattan Beach, Oriental Boulevard from Ocean Avenue to Mackenzie Street, are both in Brooklyn. Pelham Bay Park and Orchard Beach are in the Bronx. Jacob Riis Park and Jamaica Bay, Beach 149th to Beach 169th streets, and Rockaway Beach and Boardwalk, Beach 9th to Beach 149th streets, are in Queens.

In Richmond (Staten Island) are Great Kills Park, Hylan Boulevard, Great Kills; South Beach

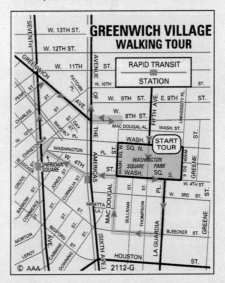

GREENWICH VILLAGE WALKING TOUR

and Boardwalk, Fort Wadsworth to Miller Field, Midland Beach; and Wolfe's Pond Park, Holten and Cornelia avenues, Prince's Bay.

Bicycling in Central Park has become a favorite with visitors and New Yorkers alike. The roadways in the park are closed to motorized traffic Fri. 7 p.m.-Mon. 6 a.m. (also Mon.-Thurs. 10 a.m.-3 p.m. and 7-10 p.m., Fri. 10 a.m.-3 p.m., Apr.-Oct.). However, the transverse roads are always open. Park paths are at 72nd Street and West Drive, south to 59th Street, east to East Drive, and north on East Drive to 72nd Street; at 104th Street crossroad; and at the north end of Center Drive.

Few people would believe you if you claimed to have gone **boating** in the middle of Manhattan, but it is possible. Rowboats are for rent in Central Park at Loeb Boathouse, 72nd Street Lake off East Drive, for $10 an hour and a $30 deposit.

Bowling fans will find numerous tenpin lanes in Manhattan. Some are open all night. Check the phone book for locations.

There are no **golf** courses in Manhattan. However, the Department of Parks does operate 12 18-hole public courses in the other boroughs. On weekends golfers might have to wait as long as 8 hours before they are able to tee off; to find out the waiting times, try the weekend news broadcasts over WNYC (93.9 FM or 820 AM). The following courses accept reservations, but not for same-day playing: Clearview, Dyker Beach, La Tourette, Silver Lake, South Shore and Split Rock.

Most fees are $19 on weekdays and $21 on weekends and holidays; over 61 and under 18, $8 on weekdays and $12.50 on weekends and holidays. Persons under 18 must have a golf permit. Phone the individual courses for exact fees.

The first course listed under each borough is open all year; other courses are open the first weekend in April through the last weekend in November. Phone the individual courses or (718) 225-4653 for reservations.

Brooklyn: Dyker Beach, Seventh Avenue and 86th Street, (718) 836-9722; and Marine Park, Flatbush Avenue between Avenue U and the Belt Parkway, (718) 338-7113.

The Bronx: Pelham and Split Rock courses, Shore Road, Pelham Bay Park, (718) 885-1258; and Van Cortlandt, Van Cortlandt Park South and Bailey Avenue, (718) 543-4595.

Queens: Clearview, 23rd Avenue and Willets Point Boulevard, (718) 229-2570; Douglaston Park, Commonwealth Boulevard and Marathon Parkway, (718) 428-1617; Forest Park, Main Drive and Interboro Parkway, (718) 296-0999; and Kissena, 164-15 Booth Memorial Rd., (718) 939-4594.

Richmond (Staten Island): Silver Lake, 915 Victory Boulevard, (718) 447-5686; La Tourette, Forest Hill and London roads, (718) 351-0326; and South Shore, Hugenot Avenue and Arthur Kill Road, (718) 984-0101.

Horseback riding in Manhattan is confined to trails in Central Park. The Claremont Riding Academy, 175 W. 89th St. between Amsterdam and Columbus avenues, rents horses for $40 an hour and also offers lessons; phone (212) 724-5100. Riders must be experienced in English riding.

Ice skating is popular among spectators and participants, especially at the Rockefeller Plaza Rink and the Wollman Memorial Skating Rink in Central Park, both outdoor rinks. The New York City Building skating rink in Flushing Meadows-Corona Park is open all year and has rentals.

Tennis enthusiasts can play in seven Manhattan locations: Central Park, 93rd Street and West Drive; East River Park at Fort Washington Park, at 172nd street; Fred Johnson Park at W. 151st Street east of Seventh Avenue; Inwood Hill Park, 207th Street and Seaman Avenue; Riverside Park, at 96th and at 119th streets; and Sunken Meadow Randalls Island. The Department of Parks issues permits; phone (212) 360-8133.

The U.S. Open Tennis Championships, played at the Louis Armstrong Memorial Stadium (National Tennis Center) in Flushing Meadows Corona Park, attracts a host of devotees annually in late August and early September.

New Yorkers have many professional teams and games to choose from all year. The New York Knicks play **basketball** in Madison Square Garden; phone (212) 465-6741. The city has two **football, baseball** and **ice hockey** teams. The Giants and the Jets play football in Giants Stadium in East Rutherford, N.J., at the Meadowlands complex; phone (201) 935-8222 (Giants) or (516) 560-8200 (Jets).

Shea Stadium's baseball diamond is home to the Mets; phone (718) 507-6387. The Yankees play at Yankee Stadium in The Bronx; phone (718) 293-6000. On the ice it is the Rangers at Madison Square Garden, (212) 465-6741, and the Islanders at Nassau Coliseum, (516) 794-4100.

Horse racing fans can choose their favorites at the Aqueduct Race Track in Queens, (718) 641-4700; at Belmont Park Race Track in Elmont, (718) 641-4700; and at the Meadowlands in East Rutherford, N.J., (201) 935-3900. Harness racing can be seen at Yonkers Raceway in Yonkers; phone (914) 968-4200.

Note: Policies concerning admittance of children to pari-mutuel betting facilities vary. Phone for information.

Looking for one-stop recreation. Visit Chelsea Piers, a 30-acre sports village located along the Hudson River between 17th and 23rd streets in four renovated shipping piers. Some of the highlights include 52 heated hitting stalls for golfers, a 25-yard swimming pool, an indoor running track, a hockey rink open to ice skaters, an outdoor roller rink, a 40-lane bowling alley and several basketball courts. Sailing, kayaking and speedboat tours of the harbor also are offered.

Various shops and eateries call the historic piers home. Phone (212) 336-6666.

Shopping

For the avid shopper, New York is a nightmare—not because of a lack of goods, but because there is so much from which to choose. From antiques to zircons, there is an outlet that sells whatever you want.

While Peter Minuit got the best trade in the city's history—in 1626 he paid $24 for Manhattan Island, currently worth more than $48 billion—Manhattan is still a borough of bargains. The saying "I can get it for you wholesale" is nowhere more applicable.

The following list does not pretend to be exhaustive; it merely suggests a few of the leading stores and shopping areas for various items. All stores and areas, unless specified, are in Manhattan. For phone numbers consult the telephone directory.

Among New York's leading department stores are Bloomingdale's, Third Avenue at 59th Street; Lord and Taylor, Fifth Avenue at 39th Street; Macy's, known as the largest store in the world, 34th Street and Broadway; Saks, Fifth Avenue at 50th Street; and Sterns, Sixth Avenue at 33rd Street in Sterns Plaza.

Women's clothing is the specialty of Bergdorf Goodman, Fifth Avenue at 57th Street; Lane Bryant, Fifth Avenue at 40th Street; and Wallach's, 555 Fifth Ave. Bolton's, with several locations including 57th Street between Fifth and Sixth avenues, and Loehmann's, in The Bronx, are renowned for their discounted women's apparel.

For men's clothing, try A. Sulka & Co., Park Avenue at 55th Street; Barney's, Seventh Avenue at 17th Street; British American House, 488 Madison Ave.; Brooks Brothers, Madison Avenue at 44th Street; F.R. Tripler & Co., Madison Avenue at 46th Street; and Paul Stuart, Madison Avenue at 45th Street.

Trump Tower, at Fifth Avenue and 56th Street, has an elegant collection of fashion, food and gift shops within its glass, marble and bronze atrium. The building is the tallest concrete structure in New York and includes walkways, hanging gardens and an 80-foot waterfall.

The Market, at Citicorp Center between Lexington and Third avenues and 53rd and 54th streets, is a seven-story building that houses international restaurants and shops. The atrium is an indoor garden cafe with skylights; free entertainment is offered daily.

For something a bit different, try the McDonald's at 160 Broadway in the financial district. Those expecting the usual drive-up window will no doubt be surprised at the elegant look provided by high-tech green and pink neon, miniature spotlights, marble-topped tables and the presence of a grand piano. A gift boutique offers the likes of gold earrings fashioned in the well-known golden arches motif. In Uptown Manhattan at 140 W. 57th Street is Planet Hollywood, where the fascination with all that is Hollywood is captured in souvenirs ranging from designer T-shirts to key chains to leather jackets.

Shoppers looking for more meaningful and personal items than the ashtrays, hats and pennant souvenirs that differ only in city name should consider the United Nations Gift Center, 46th Street and First Avenue. This store handles handicraft items from all over the world.

A little closer to home, a good choice would be the jewelry and handicraft items found in Greenwich Village stores. If you do not see what you want, describe it to the shopkeeper—who often also is the artisan—and he or she will either be able to make it for you or tell you where to obtain it.

Alfred Dunhill of London, 450 Park Ave. at 57th Street, is another haven for gifts. A variety of shops are within the South Street Seaport Museum (see attraction listing p. 116) complex on the East River. Other sources of singular items are the shops in the major art and cultural museums.

Often many shops of the same specialty are found within a radius of several blocks. These informal groupings are a boon for the shopper, who reaps the benefits of convenience and competitive prices. The hunting grounds for antiques are Second and Third avenues, from the upper 40s to the 80s; Madison Avenue; and E. 55th Street and 57th Street.

Art galleries are grouped between Fifth and Madison avenues from 45th to 85th streets; bookstores cluster between Madison and Fifth avenues, 46th to 57th streets, and 57th Street between Seventh and Third avenues. Diamonds are bought and sold on W. 47th Street between Fifth and Sixth avenues. Flower markets adorn the 28th Street and Sixth Avenue area.

Outlets for clothing are found all along Madison and Fifth avenues and along side streets between the Garment District and 85th Street.

The large malls are mostly found outside Manhattan. Kings Plaza Shopping Center is an enclosed mall 1 mile north of Belt Parkway exit 11N in Brooklyn. Elmhurst, in Queens County, has Queens Center, 2 blocks west of the Long Island Expressway (I-495) on Queens Boulevard. Staten Island Mall, 2 miles south of I-278 on Richmond Avenue, has 170 stores, including Macy's and Sears.

Theater and Concerts

Centered on the Times Square area between 41st and 55th streets from Eighth to Sixth avenues are the theaters that have perpetuated the magic of Broadway—only two of these theaters are actually on Broadway. Glittering marquees announce the latest productions.

Not quite as glamorous, but rivaling the popularity of Broadway hits, are the off-Broadway theaters.

Note: The categories of Broadway and off-Broadway indicate the size of the theater—all off-Broadway houses have fewer than 300 seats. This size distinction allows apparent contradictions in that some of the theaters in the Times Square area are classified as off-Broadway; other houses almost next door are described as Broadway theaters.

While the Broadway shows stick to the formula of name stars, writers and directors, the off-Broadway productions are noted for their experimental presentations and revivals. These sometimes equal or surpass the artistry of Broadway and are usually the offerings of young hopefuls, although it is not uncommon for a Broadway "name" to appear in them.

One celebrated off-Broadway theater is the Provincetown Playhouse, 133 MacDougal St. in Greenwich Village. In this theater the early works of Eugene O'Neill, E. E. Cummings, Edna St. Vincent Millay and other literary notables were produced.

Also in the Village are the Sullivan Street Playhouse, 181 Sullivan, where "The Fantasticks" continues to enjoy the distinction of being the longest running show, and the Cherry Lane Theater, 38 Commerce, oldest in the city, where many young actors have gotten their start.

Queens Theatre in the Park, in the New York State Pavilion at Flushing Meadows Corona Park, presents a year-round schedule of plays, children's theater and dance; phone (718) 760-0064.

Current theater listings appear in *New York* and *The New Yorker* magazines, in the newspapers and in *Variety,* a weekly newspaper devoted

to the entertainment world, including off-Broadway theaters in Greenwich Village.

Advance planning is the key to obtaining the best tickets for the best prices. Seats to Broadway shows are on sale anywhere from 3 months to 1 year in advance.

Agencies charge a fee in addition to the price printed on the ticket; they also may charge a service fee for delivery of tickets to the hotel or box office. Inquire at your hotel desk for the names and locations of agencies. If you are unable to purchase tickets to the show of your choice from one agency, try another. Tickets generally are available at theater box offices a few hours before show time, which is usually 8 p.m.

The range and quality of New York musical activity is unequaled. During the course of a year, in the four major concert halls—those with more than 1,000 seats—in the city, you can expect to hear performances by such diverse artists as Al Hirt or the Metropolitan Opera Company.

Carnegie Hall, renowned for its perfect acoustics, is at 57th Street and Seventh Avenue. Tours of the facility are conducted Mon.-Tues. and Thurs.-Fri. at 11:30, 2 and 3. The Rose Museum takes a look at the hall's history. Museum open Thurs.-Tues. 11-4. The tour fee is $6; senior citizens and students with ID $5; under 12, $3. Phone (212) 247-7800.

City Center, the city's largest concert hall, is on 55th Street between Sixth and Seventh avenues; phone (212) 581-1212. Avery Fisher Hall, the only public concert hall of orchestral size to be constructed in the city since 1891, is in the

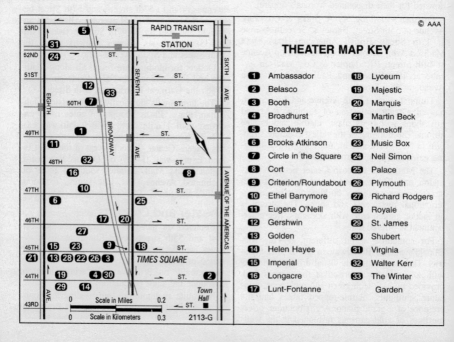

© AAA

THEATER MAP KEY

❶	Ambassador	⑱	Lyceum
❷	Belasco	⑲	Majestic
❸	Booth	⑳	Marquis
❹	Broadhurst	㉑	Martin Beck
❺	Broadway	㉒	Minskoff
❻	Brooks Atkinson	㉓	Music Box
❼	Circle in the Square	㉔	Neil Simon
❽	Cort	㉕	Palace
❾	Criterion/Roundabout	㉖	Plymouth
❿	Ethel Barrymore	㉗	Richard Rodgers
⓫	Eugene O'Neill	㉘	Royale
⓬	Gershwin	㉙	St. James
⓭	Golden	㉚	Shubert
⓮	Helen Hayes	㉛	Virginia
⓯	Imperial	㉜	Walter Kerr
⓰	Longacre	㉝	The Winter
⓱	Lunt-Fontanne		Garden

Lincoln Center Plaza at Broadway and 65th Street; phone (212) 875-5030. Town Hall, noted for its fine acoustics and excellent seating plan, is between Sixth and Seventh avenues on 43rd Street; phone (212) 840-2824.

Special Events

Most ethnic groups in New York City observe at least some of their native holidays with parades, festivals or celebrations. When dates vary for events listed below, only the month in which the event occurs is given. For a listing of special events, contact the New York Convention and Visitors Bureau *(see The Informed Traveler box).*

It is said that everyone loves a parade, and New Yorkers may love them more than most. Spring parades include St. Patrick's Day and Greek Independence Day in March; Easter in March or April; American Ethnic in April; Solidarity Day, Armed Forces Day, Norwegian Constitution Day and Memorial Day in May; and Israeli Day, held in the spring, but the month varies.

Parades the rest of the year include Puerto Rican Day in June; Labor Day, Steuben Day, African-American Day and West Indian-American Day, in September; Pulaski Day, Desfile de la Hispanidad: Columbus Day and Columbus Day in October; Greenwich Village Halloween on Oct. 31; and Veterans Day and Thanksgiving Day in November.

When not parading, New Yorkers attend festivals: Ukrainian and the Ninth Avenue International Food in May; Saint Anthony in June; Shakespeare held June through August; Festa Italiana and Fourth of July Fireworks in July; Greenwich Village Jazz in August and September; and the Feast of San Gennaro, which occurs in September.

Then there are celebrations that cannot be classified as either parades or festivals: Chinese New Year in late January; Lincoln Center Out-of-Doors in May; Museum Mile in June; Harlem Week in August; and the New York is Book Country Day in September.

Other seasonal events include the beginning of the circus engagement in March or April; the annual Egg Rolling contest in Central Park, held the Saturday before Easter; Washington Square Outdoor Art Show from late May through June and August to mid-September; the opening of the Metropolitan Opera season in September; Tree Lighting Ceremony and Christmas Carols at Rockefeller Center in December; and Christmas services throughout the month of December.

Theater Ticket Bargains

Theater tickets for Broadway and off-Broadway shows are sold at half-price on the day of the performance at the TKTS booths at the corner of Broadway and 47th Street and on the mezzanine at 2 World Trade Center. At Broadway and 47th Street, the ticket purchase hours are 3-8 for Mon.-Sat. evening tickets; 10-2 for Wed. and Sat. matinee tickets; and noon-7 for Sun. matinee and evening tickets. At 2 World Trade Center the ticket purchase hours are 11-5:30 for Mon.-Fri.

 evening tickets and 11-3:30 for Sat. tickets. A $2.50 surcharge is added to the ticket price. Cash and travelers checks are accepted.

Caution: lines form early.

Discount theater tickets are available at many newsstands, coffee shops and drugstores. Tickets also are available at the New York Convention and Visitors Bureau *(see The Informed Traveler box).*The coupons offer a 30-percent discount and are seldom valid on weekends. Discounts are not available for all shows; usually those that have had an extra-long run or have not yet caught on are discount material.

The New York Vicinity

CROSS RIVER (H-11)

WARD POUND RIDGE RESERVATION, jct. SRs 35 and 121, is a 4,700-acre park and wildlife sanctuary. Camping shelters and picnic areas are available, as are hiking and skiing trails and a wildflower garden. Plant, animal and American Indian artifacts displays are in the Delaware Indian Resource Center in the Trailside Nature Museum. Park open daily 9-dusk. Museum open Wed.-Sun. 9-4; closed Jan. 1, Thanksgiving and Dec. 25. Admission $7 per private vehicle. Phone (914) 763-3493.

CROTON-ON-HUDSON (H-11)
pop. 7,000, elev. 8'

Croton-on-Hudson, once part of the estate of Van Cortlandt Manor, was founded by Irish and Italian laborers working on the Croton Reservoir dam in the 1840s. During the 1920s the town became a fashionable haven for intellectuals, including poet Edna St. Vincent Millay, feminist Doris Stevens, journalist John Reed and economist Stuart Chase.

VAN CORTLANDT MANOR, off US 9, is a restored 18th-century Dutch-English manor house on 20 acres of what was originally an 86,000-acre estate. The restored Ferry House and Ferry House Kitchen at the east end supplied food and lodging to travelers on the Albany Post Road. Family portraits, furniture, silver and porcelains are exhibited. Guided tours are available.

Allow 1 hour minimum. Wed.-Mon. 10-5, Apr.-Dec.; closed Thanksgiving and Dec. 25. Last tour begins 2 hours before closing Nov.-Dec., 1 hour before closing rest of season. Admission $8; over 59, $7; ages 6-17, $4. AE, DS, MC, VI. Phone (914) 631-8200 or 271-8981.

GARRISON (H-10)

★ **BOSCOBEL** is 8 mi. n. of Bear Mountain Bridge on SR 9D above the Hudson River Valley. The facade of the restored 1804 New York Federal-style mansion has three unusual draperies of carved wood. Other features include *trompe l'oeil* wallpaper, period furniture, china and silver. The grounds offer a panorama of the Hudson Valley and contain a gatehouse, orangery, springhouse and herb garden.

Guided tours are given Wed.-Mon. 10-4:15, Apr.-Oct.; Wed.-Mon. 10-3:15, Nov.-Dec. Closed Thanksgiving and Dec. 25. Tour $7; over 62, $6; ages 6-14, $4. MC, VI. Phone (914) 265-3638.

GRAYMOOR CHRISTIAN UNITY CENTER, US 9 just s. of SR 403, is on a mountaintop overlooking the Hudson River Valley. Home of the Franciscan Friars of the Atonement, the center contains many shrines and chapels. Picnicking is permitted. Grounds open daily 8 a.m.-9:30 p.m. Free. Phone (914) 424-3671.

HARRISON (H-2)
pop. 23,300, elev. 65'

Harrison benefits from the progressive environment fostered by the State University of New York at Purchase. The PepsiCo Sculpture Garden, across the street from the university, includes 40 sculptures on 112 acres landscaped by noted garden designer Russell Page.

Harrison Chamber of Commerce and Civic Association: Municipal Building, 1 Heineman Pl., Harrison, NY 10528; phone (914) 835-2000, ext. 330.

NEUBERGER MUSEUM OF ART is on the campus of Purchase College, SUNY at Purchase, off I-287 exit 8E, off the Hutchinson River Pkwy. exit 28 or off I-684 exit 2 following signs. The museum presents a permanent collection and changing exhibits focusing on 20th-century American and European art as well as African art.

Allow 1 hour minimum. Tues.-Fri. 10-4, Sat.-Sun. 11-5; closed major holidays. Guided gallery talks are conducted Tues.-Fri. at 1, Sun. at 2 and 3, Oct.-June. Admission $4, over 62 and students with ID $2, under 12 free; free to all first Sat. of the month. Phone (914) 251-6100 or 251-6133.

KATONAH (H-11) elev. 226'

JOHN JAY HOMESTEAD STATE HISTORIC SITE, 400 Jay St. (SR 22), was the retirement home of the first chief justice of the United States and second governor of New York. The house has restored period rooms with family memorabilia and portraits by American artists. The grounds include landscape plantings and 19th- and 20th-century farm outbuildings. Guided tours are available on the hour.

Allow 1 hour minimum. Wed.-Sat. 10-4, Sun. noon-4, Apr.-Nov.; phone for Dec. holiday schedule. Admission $3; over 62, $2; under 12, $1. Phone (914) 232-5651.

KATONAH MUSEUM OF ART, SR 22 and Jay St., presents changing exhibits from major museums, artists and private collectors. Allow 30 minutes minimum. Tues.-Fri. and Sun. 1-5, Sat. 10-5; closed major holidays and during the installation of new exhibits. Guided tours are offered Tues.-Sun. at 2:30. Admission $2, under 12 free. Phone (914) 232-9555.

NEW CITY (G-1)
pop. 33,700, elev. 163'

Several farms and orchards in the New City area allow visitors to pick their own strawberries and apples during harvest time.

New City Chamber of Commerce: P.O. Box 2222, New City, NY 10956; phone (914) 638-1395.

HISTORICAL SOCIETY OF ROCKLAND COUNTY is off Palisades Pkwy. exit 11, e. onto New Hempstead Rd., then n. at Main St. to 20 Zukor Rd. The museum presents changing exhibits, including a doll house and furnishings display in December. Guided tours of an 1832 restored Dutch farmhouse are offered Sunday 1-5. Allow 30 minutes minimum. Tues.-Sun. 1-5; closed federal holidays and briefly between exhibits. Admission $4; ages 6-12, $3. Phone (914) 634-9629.

NEW ROCHELLE (H-2)
pop. 67,300, elev. 72′

The New Rochelle area was settled in 1688 by Huguenot refugees who named their community after their old home, La Rochelle, in France. New Rochelle grew quickly due to its healthy shipbuilding industry, its location as a key port of trade with New York City and other nearby harbors and its position on the strategic Boston Post Road, the major route to cities farther north.

In the 1890s the town became a popular retreat for noted actors, artists and authors, including Eddie Foy, Agnes Booth and Frederic Remington. The town still is known as a wealthy suburb of commuters who work in New York City.

The Thomas Paine Cottage, 20 Sicard Ave., was the home of the American political theorist and writer. A museum 100 yards north houses Huguenot and Indian artifacts. Both are open to the public. Phone (914) 632-5376 for Friday through Sunday hours and fees.

New Rochelle Chamber of Commerce: 557 Main St., New Rochelle, NY 10801; phone (518) 297-3040.

NORTH TARRYTOWN—
see Sleepy Hollow p. 139.

NYACK (H-2) pop. 6,600, elev. 100′

Nyack's way of life has always been tied to the Hudson River: The Nyack Indians gathered oysters on its banks, European settlers established a prosperous river landing and today pleasure craft abound. Artist Edward Hopper was born in Nyack in 1882; his boyhood home is now a public art gallery.

For a free 40-page "Guide to Nyack" contact the Art, Craft & Antiques Dealers Association of the Nyacks, P.O. Box 223-3A, Nyack, NY 10960; phone (914) 353-2221.

The Nyacks Chamber of Commerce: P.O. Box 677, Nyack, NY 10960; phone (716) 945-2034.

Self-guiding tours: Brochures outlining several walking tours through historic and scenic areas in Nyack are available for $3 from Friends of the Nyacks, P.O. Box 384, Nyack, NY 10960. Phone (914) 358-4973.

OSSINING (G-2) pop. 22,600, elev. 8′

TEATOWN LAKE RESERVATION, off Taconic Pkwy. onto SR 134 w., then 1 mi. n. to 1600 Spring Valley Rd., is an environmental education center and wildlife sanctuary with 12 miles of nature trails. Changing exhibits relating to mammals, birds, plants and geology are presented in a museum; native birds of prey unable to live in the wild also are displayed.

Guided tours of Wildflower Island, including a display of rare orchids, are available by appointment May 1 through Sept. 15. Nature center open Tues.-Sat. 9-5, Sun. 1-5; closed major holidays. Grounds open daily dawn-dusk. Donations. Phone (914) 762-2912.

PURCHASE (H-2) elev. 355′

DONALD KENDALL SCULPTURE GARDENS, off Anderson Hill Rd. at PepsiCo, is a 114-acre garden with modern sculpture. Highlights include exotic trees and shrubs, a waterlily pool and works by such artists as Henry Moore, Claes Oldenburg and Auguste Rodin. A self-guiding tour brochure is available. Daily dawn-dusk. Free. Phone (914) 253-2000.

RYE (H-2) pop. 14,900, elev. 49′

PLAYLAND, off I-95 exit 19 following signs to Playland Pkwy., is a recreational complex offering rides, a beach and boardwalk, saltwater lake, riverboat excursions, 18-hole miniature golf and a children's park. Playland was among the earliest totally planned amusement parks in the country. Features include original Art Deco buildings, a long grass mall, the Dragon Coaster and a vintage carousel. Free entertainment is provided daily.

Allow 3 hours, 30 minutes minimum. Tues.-Thurs. and Sun. noon-11, Fri.-Sat. and Mon. holidays noon-midnight, June 28-Labor Day; Tues.-Thurs. 10-4, Fri.-Sat. and Mon. holidays noon-midnight, Sun. noon-11, day after Memorial Day-June 27; Sat.-Sun. and Mon. holidays noon-11, early May-Memorial Day. Hours may vary; phone ahead.

Thirty-six ticket book $18; 24 ticket book $14; 12 tickets $7.50. Individual ride tickets 70c. Beach $3.25, senior citizens and under 50 inches tall $1.50, infants free. All rides cost between three and five tickets. Pool $4.50, under 50 inches tall $2.50. Golf $3.50 per person. Parking Sat.-Sun. $5, Tues.-Fri. $3. MC, VI. Phone (914) 925-2700.

SLEEPY HOLLOW (H-2)
pop. 8,200

Sleepy Hollow, North Tarrytown until 1996 when the residents voted to change the town's name, is on the east bank of the Hudson, where the river widens to form the Tappan Zee. In 1680, near where the Pocantico River flows into the Hudson, Frederick Philipse built a stone house, a church and other buildings. The church was popularized by Washington Irving in "The Legend of Sleepy Hollow."

The Rockefellers commissioned several works of art to adorn a small chapel known as the Union Church of Pocantico Hills. Inside is a cycle of stained-glass windows by Marc Chagall and a rose window by Henri Matisse.

HEADLESS HORSEMAN BRIDGE carries US 9 across the Pocantico River where the old bridge once stood from which, in Irving's story, the headless horseman hurled his pumpkin head at Ichabod Crane.

PHILIPSBURG MANOR, on US 9, consists of an early 18th-century Dutch-American manor house, an operating gristmill, an oak-timbered dam and a barn. The stone manor house is furnished with period artifacts. Costumed guides lead tours, and a reception center offers exhibits and a film about the development and restoration of the manor. Food is available. Philipsburg Manor is the departure point for reserved tours to Kykuit, the former home of four generations of Rockefellers.

Allow 1 hour minimum. Wed.-Mon. 10-4, Mar.-Dec.; closed Thanksgiving and Dec. 25. Last tour begins 1 hour before closing. Admission $8; over 60, $7; ages 6-17, $4. AE, DS, MC, VI. Phone (914) 631-8200, or 631-9491 for Kykuit information and reservations.

SLEEPY HOLLOW CEMETERY, on US 9, includes the graves of Washington Irving, Andrew Carnegie, William Rockefeller and Whitelaw Reid. Daily 8-4:30. Free. Phone (914) 631-0081.

STONY POINT (H-10)
pop. 10,600, elev. 32'

STONY POINT BATTLEFIELD STATE HISTORIC SITE is 8 mi. s. of the Bear Mountain bridge off US 9W on Park Rd. This was the location of a successful midnight assault by the American Corps of Light Infantry, commanded by Brig. Gen. Anthony Wayne, against a British garrison in July 1779. A museum presents exhibits and a slide show. Guided tours, self-guiding tours, picnic areas, panoramic river views, and tours of the 1826 lighthouse also are available. Interpreters in period dress offer demonstrations of muskets, artillery, cooking and the usual tasks of camp life.

Allow 1 hour minimum. Grounds open Wed.-Sat. and Memorial Day, July 4 and Labor Day 10-5, Sun. 1-5, Apr. 15-last weekend in Oct. Museum open Wed.-Sat. 10-4:30, Sun. 1-4:30, Apr. 15-last weekend in Oct. Admission $4 per vehicle. A fee is charged for special events. Phone (914) 786-2521.

TAPPAN (H-2) pop. 6,900, elev. 50'

Historically, Tappan is best noted for being the setting for the prologue and denouement of the Benedict Arnold—Maj. John Andre conspiracy. At his DeWint House headquarters, Gen. George Washington gave the command of West Point to Arnold, who arranged to betray the garrison to the British.

However, Arnold's contact, Andre, was captured, and the plans were uncovered. Andre was jailed in the old Seventy-Six House and executed by hanging on what is known as Andre Hill. His body was later traded for that of Gen. Richard Montgomery, who was killed in the Siege of Quebec in 1775. Andre was interred in Westminster Abbey in 1821.

GEORGE WASHINGTON'S HEADQUARTERS AT TAPPAN (The DeWint House), Livingston Ave. and Oak Tree Rd., was built in 1700 and was used on occasion by Gen. George Washington as an army headquarters during the Revolutionary War. This restored house features furnished period rooms. The Carriage House Museum contains Washington artifacts and various memorabilia. Daily 10-4; closed Thanksgiving and Dec. 25. Donations. Phone (914) 359-1359.

TARRYTOWN (H-2)
pop. 10,700, elev. 14'

"In the bosom of one of those spacious coves which indent the eastern shore of the Hudson, at that broad expansion of the river denominated by the Tappan Zee there lies a small market town or rural port, which by some is called Greenburgh, but which is more generally and properly known as Tarry Town."

So Washington Irving described the town nearest the bucolic little glen that figures in "The Legend of Sleepy Hollow." Tarrytown is joined on the south by Irvington and on the north by Sleepy Hollow, formerly North Tarrytown. These three communities form the well-known Sleepy Hollow country.

According to Irving the name of Tarrytown was given by housewives "from the inveterate propensity of their husbands to linger about the village tavern on market days."

Near the boundary of Sleepy Hollow and Tarrytown British spy Maj. John Andre was captured, exposing Benedict Arnold's treachery.

Sleepy Hollow Chamber of Commerce: 54 Main St., Tarrytown, NY 10591; phone (914) 631-1705.

LYNDHURST, .2 mi. e. of jct. US 9 and I-287 at 635 S. Broadway (US 9) overlooking the Hudson River, is an example of an American Hudson River Gothic Revival mansion. The house is furnished in Gothic, Beaux Arts and French 19th-century styles. The interior has ribbed and vaulted ceilings, figured bosses, stained-glass windows and panels, and walls painted to resemble dressed stone. Landscaped grounds surround the mansion.

Allow 1 hour minimum. Tues.-Sun. and Mon. holidays 10-5, Apr. 15-Oct. 31; Sat.-Sun. 10-5, rest of year. Closed Jan. 1, Thanksgiving and Dec. 25. Last tour begins 45 minutes before closing, May-Oct.; last tour begins 1 hour, 30 minutes before closing, rest of year. Admission $9; over 61, $8; ages 12-17, $3. Phone (914) 631-4481.

PATRIOTS' PARK, on US 9, contains Andre Brook, the dividing line between the Tarrytowns. Captors' Monument is topped by a bronze figure of John Paulding, one of the captors of British spy Maj. John Andre. Daily 24 hours. Free. Phone (914) 631-1705.

★ **SUNNYSIDE,** .5 mi. s. of Tappan Zee Bridge on US 9 to W. Sunnyside Ln., was the home of Washington Irving 1835-59. Set at the bottom of a hill next to the Hudson River, this is the home the romantic Irving called his "little snuggery." The house was built in the late 17th century as a tenant farmer's cottage and was occupied in the 18th century by a branch of the Van Tassel family that figures in "The Legend of Sleepy Hollow."

Irving added Urban Dutch-style stepped gables to the main part of the house, attached a Romanesque tower and planted wisteria and ivy vines. The interior has features that were far advanced for their day, such as a bathtub with running water and a hot water tank in the kitchen fed by pipes from the pond that Irving called the "Little Mediterranean." Costumed guides explain the house and its furnishings, which include the author's library. The house is surrounded by grounds that were planned by Irving. Picnicking is permitted.

Allow 1 hour minimum. Wed.-Mon. 10-5, Mar.-Dec.; closed Thanksgiving and Dec. 25. Last tour begins 1 hour before closing. Admission $8; over 59, $7; ages 6-17, $4. AE, DS, MC, VI. Phone (914) 631-8200.

WASHINGTON IRVING MEMORIAL, W. Sunnyside Ln. at Broadway (US 9), is by Daniel Chester French, sculptor of the seated figure in the Lincoln Memorial in Washington, D.C. The memorial consists of a bust of the author with figures of characters from his stories. Daily 24 hours. Free. Phone (914) 631-1705.

WEST HAVERSTRAW (I-11)
pop. 9,200, elev. 100'

MARIAN SHRINE, 2 mi. e. of Palisades Pkwy. exit 14 off Filors Ln., includes among its 200 acres an Italian marble rosary way, a replica of the St. John Bosco birthplace and a 48-foot bronze statue of the Rosary Madonna. Daily 9-5. Donations. Phone (914) 947-2200.

WHITE PLAINS (H-2)
pop. 48,700, elev. 201'

Seat of Westchester County, White Plains was the birthplace of the state; the first Provincial Congress met at this site on July 10, 1776. What is now the Washington's Headquarters Museum (Elijah Miller House) was the General's headquarters during the last phase of the Battle of White Plains; phone (914) 949-1236 for an appointment to tour the site.

County Chamber of Commerce: 235 Mamaroneck Ave., White Plains, NY 10605; phone (914) 948-2110.

Shopping areas: Galleria Mall is 2 blocks east of Bronx River Parkway exit 21 at 100 Main St. Among its 149 stores are JCPenney and Sterns.

WHITE PLAINS NATIONAL BATTLEFIELD SITE consists of three monuments that mark Washington's position during the Battle of White Plains. One is at Chatterton Hill; two are on Battle Avenue. The battle was fought Oct. 28, 1776. Daily 24 hours. Free.

YONKERS (H-2)
pop. 188,100, elev. 300'

Once a village of the Manhattes Indians, the site of Yonkers was part of a parcel of land granted to Adriaen Cornelissen van der Donck by the Dutch West India Co. in 1646. His title, De Jonkheer, became the city's name.

Today the city is a major industrial center, supported by more than 100 different industries. Despite its nearness to New York City, the city is not a bedroom community—most of its breadwinners are employed in Yonkers.

Yonkers Chamber of Commerce: 20 S. Broadway, Suite 1207, Yonkers, NY 10701; phone (914) 963-0332.

Shopping areas: Cross County Shopping Center, south of Cross County Parkway exit 5, has 108 stores, including Sterns and Wanamakers.

THE HUDSON RIVER MUSEUM OF WESTCHESTER, 511 Warburton Ave. overlooking the Hudson River, includes changing exhibitions of 19th- and 20th-century American art from its permanent collection. The elements of art, history and science are combined in a given subject. Within the museum complex are the 19th-century Glenview Mansion and the Andrus Planetarium. Programs for senior citizens and children are offered regularly. Food is available.

Allow 1 hour, 30 minutes minimum. Museum open Wed.-Sun. noon-5 (also Fri. 5-9), May-Sept.; Wed.-Sun. noon-5, rest of year. Closed major holidays. Planetarium shows Fri. at 7, Sat.-Sun. at 1:30, 2:30 and 3:30. Museum $3; over 61 and under 13, $1.50. Planetarium $4; over 61 and under 13, $2; Fri. show free to all. Phone (914) 963-4550, or 963-8558 for the planetarium.

Niagara Falls

(including Niagara Falls, Ontario)

Young in geologic time, Niagara Falls were created by the recession and melting of a mammoth ice sheet. As the ice retreated some 50,000 years ago the land rose behind it, forming such ridges as the Niagara Escarpment. The melting ice formed a vast lake in what is now Lake Erie and its surrounding lowlands; the lake overflowed about 12,000 years ago, creating Niagara Falls.

The falls originally formed 7 miles north in what is now Lewiston. Due to erosion they are currently about midway between lakes Erie and Ontario on the Niagara River, a 37-mile-long strait that is bisected by the international boundary. The cities of Niagara Falls, N.Y., and Niagara Falls, Ontario, are connected by bridges across the river.

The Canadian, or Horseshoe, Falls are 176 feet high with a deeply curving crest of about 2,200 feet. The American Falls, higher at 184 feet, have a shorter, fairly straight crest of about 1,075 feet. The third and smallest of Niagara's falls, Bridal Veil, is separated from the other falls by Luna and Goat islands.

Untouched, the combined flow of the water over the falls would be about 1.5 million gallons per second; however, one-half to three-quarters of the river is diverted for the generation of electricity before it reaches the falls. Most of the siphoning is done at night. The water flow is reduced to about 700,000 gallons per second during the tourist season and to less at other times.

The first people to gaze upon this natural spectacle were ancestors of the Seneca Indians. They were the area's first inhabitants some 2,000 years ago. One of the earliest Europeans to view the falls was French priest Father Louis Hennepin in 1678. History recounts that upon seeing the spectacle Hennepin fell to his knees in prayer, saying of the falls that "the universe does not afford its parallel."

In the next few years the French built and rebuilt several forts at the mouth of the river. Old Fort Niagara *(see Youngstown p. 151)* was to play key roles in the major wars of the next 90 years. In 1759, during the French and Indian War, the British captured the fort. They held it until 1796 when they withdrew to Fort George in Canada.

The War of 1812 was the most devastating to hit Niagara Falls. Many small settlements on both sides of the river were looted and burned. Niagara Falls witnessed the Battle of Lundy's Lane, the war's bloodiest, on July 25, 1814. Neither side could claim victory in that fierce conflict. Five months later the Treaty of Ghent ended 2.5 years of fighting and reinstated the boundary line.

After the war Niagara Falls entered a new era of peace and prosperity. Settlement began in earnest, and by 1892 Niagara Falls was incorporated as a city. With the arrival of steamships in 1820, the Erie Canal in 1825 and the railroad in 1840, the town became accessible to tourists. An old saw predicts that "the love of those who honeymoon here will last as long as the falls themselves."

A different type of romance lured daredevils to the falls in the 1800s and early 1900s. The first stuntster was Sam Patch. He survived two dives into the waters below the falls. The first person to go over the falls in a barrel was Annie Taylor in 1901. William Fitzgerald took the plunge in 1961. He was arrested as soon as he surfaced, because stunts on the river and falls had by then been outlawed.

In 1895 the world's first commercial hydroelectric plant was built at the falls. The Niagara Power Project opened in 1961 with 13 generators and a total installed power of 2,190,000 kilowatts, one of the largest hydroelectric facilities in the world. But the power won't last forever; the falls are eroding about an inch per year. For the next 2,500 years, however, the falls will look much the same as they have since Father Hennepin's visit.

Approaches

By Car

Traffic arriving from the south can connect with a part of the New York State Thruway (I-90), which interchanges with both I-290 and I-190. I-190, an expressway spur, leads across Grand Island to Niagara Falls, connecting with the major arteries to downtown. For the most direct and scenic route to the falls from I-190 take the Robert Moses Parkway and follow the signs to Niagara Reservation State Park (see attraction listing p. 148).

From points east, access is primarily via I-90, which collects traffic from across the state. From the Rochester area, however, SRs 31 and 104 each offer an alternate route to the city.

Approaches from the west are via any of several highways in Canada, with three bridges funnelling traffic stateside: the Rainbow Bridge in the southwest part of the city near Prospect Park; the Whirlpool Rapids Bridge in the northwest just below Whirlpool State Park (see attraction listing p. 149); and the Lewiston-Queenston Bridge in Lewiston, which connects the northern end of I-190 with Canada's Hwy. 405.

(continued on page 147)

The Informed Traveler

City Population: 58,400

Elevation: 571 ft.

Sales Tax: The sales tax in Niagara Falls is 7 percent. An additional 11 percent is levied for hotel/motel rooms, and 12 percent is added for rental cars.

WHOM TO CALL

Emergency: 911

Police (non-emergency): (716) 286-4711

Time and Temperature: (716) 844-1717

Hospitals: Niagara Falls Memorial Medical Center, (716) 278-4000.

WHERE TO LOOK

Newspapers

Niagara Falls has one daily paper, the morning *Niagara Gazette*. The *Buffalo News*, as well as such metropolitan dailies as the *New York Times* and the *New York Daily News* also are available.

Radio and TV

Radio station WEBR (970 AM) is an all-news/weather station; WBFO (88.7 FM) is a member of National Public Radio.

The major TV channels are 2 (NBC), 4 (CBS), 7 (ABC), 17 (PBS) and 29 (FOX).

Visitor Information

Information is available from the Niagara Falls Convention & Visitors Bureau, 310 4th St., Niagara Falls, NY 14303, (716) 285-2400 or (800) 421-5223; the Niagara Falls Information Center, 4th and Niagara streets., (716) 284-2000; or Niagara County Tourism *(see ad p. 147)*, (800) 338-7890. For parks information contact the New York State Parks Commission in Prospect Park at (716) 278-1770.

TRANSPORTATION

Air Travel

The nearest airport offering major domestic and international flight service is the Buffalo-Niagara Falls International Airport at Genesee Street and Cayuga Road. Shuttle buses run between the airport and major hotels; phone (800) 551-9369. Taxi service is available with fares averaging $35. Short- and long-term parking is available at SunPark at 4099 Genesee St.; phone (716) 633-6040.

The Niagara Falls International Airport on Porter Road serves charter and private flights.

Rental Cars

Hertz, (716) 632-4772 or (800) 654-3080, offers discounts to AAA members. For listings of other agencies check the telephone directory.

Rail Service

Passenger rail service is available at the Amtrak station at Hyde Park Boulevard and Lockport Road; phone (716) 285-4224.

Buses

Connections by bus may be made at the Transportation Center at the Niagara Falls Information Center at the corner of 4th and Niagara streets; phone (716) 285-9319.

Taxis

Cab companies include LaSalle Cab Co., (716) 284-8833, and United Cab Co., (716) 285-9331. Rates are $1.50 for the first half-mile, then 75c for each additional sixth of a mile. For a complete list of taxi services check the telephone directory.

Public Transport

The Niagara Frontier Transportation Authority (Metro) offers bus service within the city and outlying areas, including connections to Lockport and Buffalo. Service is generally from 5 a.m. to 10:30 p.m. Fares are $1.25 plus 20c for each additional zone; over 64, ages 5-11 and the physically impaired 55c plus 10c for each additional zone. Phone (716) 285-9319.

Destination Niagara Falls

*W*hile the falls are Niagara's primary diversion, the area offers more than meets the eye.

*S*ee how the river's power is harnessed at the Niagara Power Project Visitor Center. Cross a footbridge and hike wooded Goat Island. Say hello to a colony of Peruvian penguins at the Aquarium of Niagara. Or view some contemporary art at the Castellani Art Museum.

Maid of the Mist, Niagara Falls. Cruise past the base of thundering American Falls and Horseshoe Falls. The exciting 30-minute journey sails past tumbling waters as the mighty falls crash down upon massive rocks. (See listing page 148)

Aquarium of Niagara. Come visit the dolphins and seals and more than 1,500 of their aquatic friends. (See listing page 147)

Niagara Falls

Youngstown

Lewiston

See Vicinity map page 146

Cave of the Winds Trip, Niagara Falls. Don your rain gear and hike along these wooden walkways to the base of Bridal Veil Falls. (See listing page 148)

*P*laces included in this AAA Destination Area:

Lewiston 151
Youngstown 151

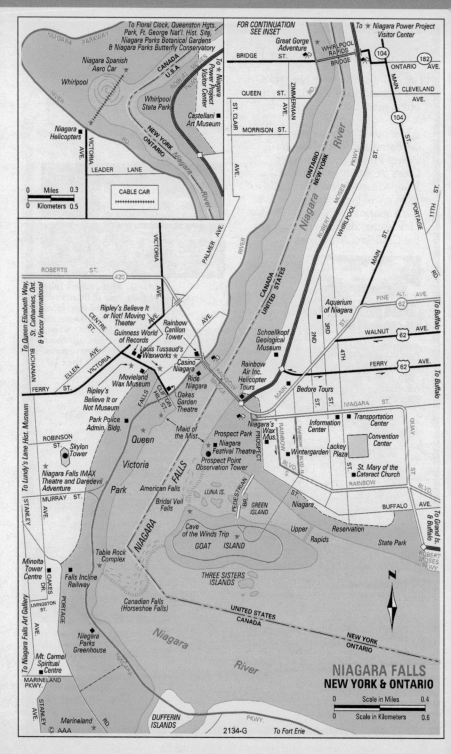

To Floral Clock, Queenston Hgts.
Park, Ft. George Nat'l. Hist. Site,
Niagara Parks Botanical Gardens
& Niagara Parks Butterfly Conservatory

FOR CONTINUATION
SEE INSET

To ★ Niagara Power Project
Visitor Center

NIAGARA PARKWAY

Niagara Spanish
Aero Car

Whirlpool

Whirlpool
State Park

Niagara
Helicopters

VICTORIA AVE.

LEADER LANE

Castellani
Art Museum

To ★ Niagara
Power
Project
Visitor Center

CANADA
U.S.A.

ROBERT MOSES PKWY.

ST. CLAIR AVE.

NEW YORK
ONTARIO

Niagara River

Great Gorge
Adventure

BRIDGE ST.

WHIRLPOOL
RAPIDS
BRIDGE

QUEEN ST.

ZIMMERMAN AVE.

MORRISON ST.

104

ONTARIO AVE.

182

CLEVELAND
AVE.

MAIN ST.

104

Miles 0.3
Kilometers 0.5

CABLE CAR
++++++++++++

VICTORIA AVE.

ROBERTS ST.

420

To Queen Elizabeth Way,
St. Catharines, Ont.
& Vincor International

CENTRE ST.

VICTORIA AVE.

ELLEN AVE.

BUCHANAN AVE.

Ripley's Believe It
or Not! Moving
Theater
Guinness World
of Records
Louis Tussaud's
Waxworks
Casino
Niagara

Movieland
Wax Museum

Ripley's
Believe It or
Not Museum

Park Police
Admin. Bldg.

FERRY ST.

ROBINSON
ST.

To Lundy's Lane Hist. Museum

Skylon
Tower

Niagara Falls IMAX
Theatre and Daredevil
Adventure

MURRAY ST.

STANLEY AVE.

To Niagara Falls Art Gallery

Minolta
Tower
Centre

OAKES DR.

LIVINGSTON
ST.

PORTAGE

Mt. Carmel
Spiritual
Centre

MARINELAND
PKWY.

STANLEY AVE.

Marineland

© AAA

Rainbow
Carillon
Tower

Ride
Niagara

Oakes
Garden
Theatre

Maid of
the Mist

Queen

Victoria

Park

American Falls

Bridal Veil
Falls

NIAGARA FALLS

Table Rock
Complex

Falls Incline
Railway

Canadian Falls
(Horseshoe Falls)

Niagara
Parks
Greenhouse

DUFFERIN
ISLANDS

RD.

PALMER AVE.

RIVER RD.

CANADA
UNITED STATES

ROBERT MOSES PKWY.

WHIRLPOOL ST.

Niagara River

RAINBOW BRIDGE

Aquarium
of Niagara

Schoellkopf
Geological
Museum

Rainbow
Air Inc.
Helicopter
Tours

Bedore Tours

PINE ALT. AVE.
62
To Buffalo

WALNUT
62 AVE.

FERRY
62 AVE.
To Buffalo

2ND ST.
3RD ST.
4TH ST.

MAIN ST.

NIAGARA ST.

Niagara's
Wax Mus.

Prospect Park

Niagara
Festival Theatre

Prospect Point
Observation Tower

LUNA IS.

Cave of
the Winds Trip
GOAT ISLAND

THREE SISTERS
ISLANDS

UNITED STATES
CANADA

Niagara

PROSPECT ST.

RAINBOW BLVD. N.

RAINBOW BLVD. S.

Information
Center

Wintergarden

RAINBOW BLVD.

Transportation
Center

Convention
Center

Lackey
Plaza

St. Mary of the
Cataract Church

BUFFALO AVE.

PEDESTRIAN BR.

GREEN
ISLAND

Upper
Rapids

Reservation

State Park

QUAY

To Grand Is.
& Buffalo

ROBERT
MOSES
PKWY.

N

NEW YORK
ONTARIO

2134-G

To Fort Erie

NIAGARA FALLS
NEW YORK & ONTARIO

0 Scale in Miles 0.4

0 Scale in Kilometers 0.6

Getting Around

Street System

In Niagara Falls, N.Y., the streets are laid out in the traditional grid pattern. Numbered streets run north to south, from 1st Street on the western edge of the city to 102nd Street on the eastern boundary. Named streets generally run east to west. Avenues run east to west, and roads and boulevards run north to south or diagonally.

The Robert Moses Parkway parallels the river as it runs along the extreme western and southern edges of Niagara Falls, while the Niagara Expressway (I-190) bypasses downtown traffic as it hugs the eastern edge before crossing into Canada.

Parking

Parking is plentiful on the U.S. side of the river and ranges from on-street parking to free or pay lots. State-owned lots are in Prospect Park and on the east and west ends of Goat Island; other lots are concentrated in the southwest corner of the city around the convention center. Pay lots average a minimum of $3 per day.

What To See

SAVE **AQUARIUM OF NIAGARA,** 701 Whirlpool St. at Pine Ave. (US 62), displays more than 1,500 aquatic animals ranging from the Great Lakes to the coral reefs and is home to the state's largest collection of Great Lakes fish. Visitors can see California sea lions, sharks, piranha, river otters and more. Highlights include a colony of endangered Peruvian penguins and an outdoor harbor seal pool. The penguins are fed daily at 9:30 and 2:30, the seals at 11 and 3:45; sharks and otters are fed on alternate days at 11:30. The aquarium is the site of the 81st "Whaling Wall" by environmental marinelife artist Wyland.

Daily 9-7, Memorial Day-Labor Day; 9-5, rest of year. Closed Thanksgiving and Dec. 25. Admission $6.50; over 59 and ages 4-12, $4.50. AE, DS, MC, VI. Phone (716) 285-3575 or (800) 500-4609.

BEDORE TOURS, departing from the Howard Johnson at the Falls at 454 Main St., near the Rainbow Bridge and from area hotels, offers the U.S. and Canadian Boat and Van Tour; the All-American Boat and Van Tour; and an evening tour, the Canadian Illumination Tour. Each tour visits the American, Horseshoe and Bridal Veil falls as well as other area attractions. The day tours also include sightseeing directly in front of the falls aboard the *Maid of the Mist* tour boats (*see attraction listing*).

Departures daily May-Oct. Day tours depart at 9 and 2. Illumination tours depart at 7 p.m. Fare

$49.95; ages 5-11, $25; under 5 on lap free. All-American tour $39.95. Combination day and evening tours $84.95. Reservations are required. AE, DS MC, VI. Phone (716) 285-7550 or (800) 538-8433.

CASTELLANI ART MUSEUM is on the Niagara University campus. The museum's permanent collection emphasizes 20th-century and contemporary art and includes works by Jean-Michel Basquiat, Anish Kapoor, Romare Bearden, Joan Mitchell and Cindy Sherman. In addition there are collections of paintings, drawings, photographs, and pre-Columbian ceramics. Changing exhibits also are presented. Wed.-Sat. 11-5, Sun. 1-5, Mon.-Tues. by appointment; closed major holidays. Free. Phone (716) 286-8200.

★ **CAVE OF THE WINDS TRIP**, on Goat Island (*see attraction listing*), follows wooden walkways to within 25 feet of the base of the falls. An elevator takes visitors 175 feet through the Niagara rock escarpment to view the falls from the bottom. Allow 1 hour minimum. Daily 9-8, mid-May through Labor Day; 9-5 (also Sat.-Sun. 5-6), day after Labor Day-late Oct. Schedule may vary; phone ahead. Admission $6; ages 6-12, $5.50. Under age 6 must be at least 42 inches tall. AE, DI, MC, VI. Phone (716) 278-1730.

★ **GOAT ISLAND**, in the Niagara River, separates the Canadian and American falls. Easily accessible by foot or vehicular bridge, this wooded island has paved drives and walks that offer spectacular views from the edges of both falls.

The Three Sisters Islands, which lie in the rapids, are accessible by footbridge, as is Luna Island, which lies between the American and Bridal Veil falls.

★ *MAID OF THE MIST* boats depart from the dock at Prospect Point on the American side and is also listed in Niagara Falls, Ontario, where this information is included. The boats pass directly in front of the falls and enter the Horseshoe Basin.

Trips leave daily starting at 9:15, Memorial Day weekend-Labor Day weekend; at 10 Apr. 1-day before Memorial Day weekend and day after Labor Day-Oct. 24. Closing times vary; phone ahead. **Note:** These hours reflect the American side; the Canadian side runs 15 minutes earlier. Fare (waterproof clothing included) $8.50; ages 6-12, $4.80. Elevator 50c. To confirm daily schedules phone (716) 284-8897 in N.Y. or (905) 358-5781 in Ontario. *See color ad p. 147.*

★ **NIAGARA POWER PROJECT VISITOR CENTER** is 4.5 mi. n. of the falls on US 104; it also can be reached from the Robert Moses Pkwy. following signs. The observation and information building affords a view of the river and gorge. Movies, working models and dioramas explain how the generators operate. A mural by Thomas Hart Benton depicts Father Louis Hennepin viewing the falls for the first time. **Note:** The visitor center is closed for renovation until late

2000. A temporary facility offers hands-on exhibits and videotape presentations about the construction and operation of the plant. Phone ahead for schedule information. Daily 9-5; closed Jan. 1, Thanksgiving and Dec. 24-25 and 31. Free. Phone (716) 286-6661.

NIAGARA RESERVATION STATE PARK, at Prospect Point, covers more than 400 acres. New York's oldest state park, it opened in 1885. The visitor center has displays and electronic exhibits about the falls and information about area attractions. Visitor center open daily 8 a.m.-10:15 p.m., early May-Labor Day; daily 8 a.m.-8:15 p.m., early Apr.-early May and day after Labor Day-late Nov.; Sun.-Thurs. 8 a.m.-8:15 p.m., Fri.-Sat. 8 a.m.-10:15 p.m., late Nov.-early Jan.; daily 8-6:15, rest of year. Park open daily dawn-dusk. Free. Phone (716) 278-1796. *See Recreation Chart.*

Niagara Festival Theater, in the visitor center, presents the film "Niagara Wonders." Filmed using a technique that gives a 3-D effect, the movie provides a birds-eye view of the Niagara Falls region. Shows on the hour Wed.-Sun. 10-8, May 19-Sept. 9; 10-6, Apr. 1-May 18 and Sept. 10-Oct. 7; Wed.-Sun. 9-5, Oct. 8-Nov. 24. Admission $2; ages 6-12, $1. Phone (716) 278-1792.

🅂🅰🆅🅴 **NIAGARA'S WAX MUSEUM,** 303 Prospect St., exhibits figures in scenes depicting the history of the area. Topographic maps and collections of memorabilia from the Niagara frontier also are displayed. Daily 9 a.m.-11 p.m., May-Sept.; 11-9 in Apr. and Oct.-Dec.; 11-5, rest of year. Admission $4.95; over 64, $4.45; ages 13-17, $3.95; ages 6-12, $2.95. MC, VI. Phone (716) 285-1271.

OVER THE FALLS TOURS, departing from all area accommodations, offers three narrated van tours of Niagara Falls, New York and Niagara Falls, Ontario. Each tour includes a ride aboard the *Maid of the Mist.* The American/Canadian Tour also includes the Minolta Tower with a return pass. The American Tour also includes the Cave of the Winds Trip. The Illumination tour allows visitors to see the area's attractions both during the day and at night.

Allow 4 hours, 30 minutes minimum. Tours depart daily from 9-7. Hours may vary; phone ahead. Fare $49.95; ages 6-12, $27.95; under 6 on lap free. Reservations are required. AE, DI, MC, VI. Phone (716) 283-8900 or (877) 783-8900.

PROSPECT POINT OBSERVATION TOWER, at the base of the American Falls in Prospect Park, is a 282-foot structure of aluminum, glass and steel that rises 100 feet above the cliffs. Two elevators descend into the gorge, permitting a close glimpse of the falls. *Maid of the Mist* boats (*see attraction listing*) board near the tower.

Daily 8 a.m.-11 p.m., mid-May through Labor Day; Mon.-Fri. 8 a.m.-9 p.m., Sat.-Sun. 8 a.m.-10 p.m., day after Labor Day-Oct. 24; 9-5, rest of year (weather permitting after Dec. 15). Closed Dec. 25. Admission 50c, under 5 free. Phone (716) 278-1750.

RAINBOW TOURS OF NIAGARA offers pick-up service at local lodgings. This 4-hour bus and boat tour visits both the Canadian and American sides of the falls and includes stops at Luna Island, Three Sisters Islands, the floral clock, Minolta Tower Centre and *Maid of the Mist* boat rides. Other tours are available. Daily 9-6:30. Hours may vary; phone ahead. Fare $49.95; ages 6-12, $25; under 6 on lap free. AE, DS, MC, VI. Phone (716) 282-5317.

ST. MARY OF THE CATARACT CHURCH, 259 4th St., was built in the early 19th century. Highlights include stonework and stained-glass windows. Sun.-Fri. 8-1, Sat. 8-5. Free. Phone (716) 282-0059.

SCHOELLKOPF GEOLOGICAL MUSEUM, .2 mi. n. of the Rainbow Bridge, is accessible from the Robert Moses Pkwy. following signs. This museum offers an audiovisual explanation of the natural history of the Niagara Gorge and the falls. A geological garden and nature trail are on the grounds. Guided trail tours are offered seasonally by reservation.

Daily 9-7, Memorial Day-Labor Day; daily 9-5, Apr. 1-day before Memorial Day and day after Labor Day-Oct. 31. Admission $1, under 6 free. Phone (716) 278-1780.

WHIRLPOOL STATE PARK, on the Robert Moses Pkwy., is on a bluff overlooking the whirlpool that results from the Niagara River's 90-degree turn. Nature trails are available. Ramps and steps wind along the gorge. Daily 8 a.m.-9 p.m. Free. Phone (716) 278-1770.

WINTERGARDEN, downtown on Rainbow Blvd., is a glass-enclosed garden with tropical, semitropical and desert plants and trees, waterfalls, pools and secluded rest areas. Winding pathways, platforms and three-story glass elevators offer a variety of views. The garden is illuminated in the evening. Daily 9 a.m.-11 p.m. Free. Phone (716) 286-4940.

What To Do
Sightseeing

Sightseeing is what Niagara Falls is all about, and there is an amazing array of ways to view the falls. Many of the attractions listed in the What To See section are basically different forms of sightseeing.

For the do-it-yourselfer, excellent views of the falls and river are available from vantage points at the state parks along the Niagara, including Whirlpool State Park, Devil's Hole State Park, and Prospect and Upper Rapids parks and Goat Island in Niagara Reservation State Park. The breathtaking view is further enhanced each night when the falls are illuminated for 2.5 to 3.5 hours after dusk.

Information about guide services and sightseeing companies is available from your local AAA club or from the Niagara Falls Convention and Visitors Bureau (*see The Informed Traveler box*). The New York State Parks Commission, phone (716) 278-1770, also has area sightseeing information.

Bus and Van Tours

Major tour bus companies include Blue Bird, (716) 372-5500; Gavin Travel Service Inc., (716) 282-3715; Grand Island Transit, (716) 433-6777; SAVE Gray Lines of Niagara Falls, (716) 695-1603; SAVE Niagara Majestic Tours, (716) 285-2113; and Niagara Scenic Bus Lines, (716) 648-1500 or (800) 695-0086.

NIAGARA VIEWMOBILES sightseeing trains can be boarded at several locations on Goat Island and near the Prospect Point Observation Tower (*see attraction listings*). The 30-minute tour takes visitors close to the falls and other points of interest, with stopovers at six sites. Daily 9-8, Memorial Day weekend-Labor Day; 9-5, day after Labor Day to mid-Nov. (weather permitting). Fare $4.50; ages 6-12, $3.50. Phone (716) 278-1730.

Helicopter Tours

RAINBOW AIR INC. HELICOPTER TOURS, departing from 454 Main St., offer views of both the American and Canadian falls. Allow 1 hour minimum. Daily 9-dusk. Fare for 10-minute tour $50. MC, VI. Phone (716) 284-2800.

Sports and Recreation

Niagara Falls has several city and state parks that offer recreational opportunities, as do nearby lakes Erie and Ontario. Most parks offer picnicking, scenic views and **nature trails;** several have **fishing, swimming, tennis** courts, **bike trails** and playgrounds. **Boating** and fishing are available at many sites on lakes Erie and Ontario, which also have sandy beaches for swimming.

In the southeast are Griffon, Hennepin, Jayne and LaSalle parks; in the southwest, Niagara Reservation State Park *(see attraction listing p. 148 and Recreation Chart)* comprises Prospect Park, Upper Rapids Park and Goat Island. In the northwest are Devil's Hole and Whirlpool state parks and Centre Court and Unity city parks.

In the center of Niagara Falls at Hyde Park Boulevard and Pine Avenue is Hyde Park, the largest of the city parks. Hyde Park has two nine-hole public **golf** courses and a swimming pool.

During winter several of the nature trails in the area's parks convert to **cross-country skiing** and **snowmobiling** trails. **Downhill skiing** is available within an hour's drive at Kissing Bridge, the Alpine Recreation Area or Tamarack Ridge, all southeast on SR 240.

For further information about recreational facilities phone the state parks commission at (716) 278-1770, or the city parks service at (716) 286-4943.

Shopping

There are almost as many places to shop in the city as there are ways to view the falls. In the Main Street Shopping Area, a few minutes from Rainbow Bridge, there are some 60 variety stores in a five-block area.

Nearby Artisans Alley *(see color ad p. 147)* at 10 Rainbow Blvd. is a shop and gallery featuring works of more than 600 artisans. On Williams Road between SR 384 and US 62 is Summit Park Mall, a complex of more than 100 stores, including Jenss and Sears. At Murphy Orchard, 25 minutes east in Burt, visitors can pick their own fruits and vegetables, choose from jams and jellies ranging from mango-kiwi to hot pepper, pet farm animals and view the doorway of a room that was a stop on the underground railroad.

For those on a budget or just looking for a good deal, the Niagara Factory Outlet Mall at 1900 Military Rd. offers savings on such items as clothing, glassware, jewelry, pottery, shoes and accessories and toys; included is the Wear House, which sells designer clothes at a discount. A block from the American Falls on Rainbow Boulevard is Rainbow Centre Factory Outlet.

Before crossing the Rainbow Bridge back into the United States, visitors to the Canadian side can shop for discounted merchandise at the Niagara Duty Free Shop. *See color ad p. 154.*

Note: Visitors to Niagara Falls, Ontario, should be aware that currency exchange rates vary by merchant and are sometimes lower than the official rate offered by banks. U.S. Customs regulations limit or prohibit the importation of certain goods (such as sealskin products) from Canada; further information is available at customs offices or in the Border Regulations section of the Canadian TourBooks.

Theater and Concerts

The premier showcase for sports events, concerts, trade shows and theater in Niagara Falls is the huge International Convention Center, which overlooks the falls at 305 4th St. For ticket and schedule information phone (716) 286-4769; for credit card purchases phone Ticketmaster at (716) 852-5000.

Other theatrical and musical performances can be found in nearby Buffalo and at Earl W. Brydges Artpark, 7 miles north on the Robert Moses Parkway in Lewiston *(see place listing p. 151).*

Special Events

The big event of the year is the Festival of Lights, held from late November to early January in the convention center/Prospect Park area. Sporting a scenic backdrop of illuminated falls, more than 500,000 holiday lights and life-size storybook characters, the festival includes parades, fireworks, ice skating, entertainment and music. For information contact the Niagara Falls Convention and Visitors Bureau; phone (716) 285-2400.

The Niagara Summer Experience is a series of ethnic festivals and dances, theater and musical performances that are offered in the E. Dent Lackey Plaza of the Niagara Falls International Convention Center on weekends in July and August. The Scarecrow Festival in late September features scarecrow making and pumpkin carving. For details phone the 24-hour Niagara Falls Events Hot Line at (716) 285-8711.

DID YOU KNOW

Forty million gallons of water spill over Niagara Falls every minute.

The Niagara Falls Vicinity

LEWISTON (E-3)
pop. 3,000, elev. 363'

The site of Niagara Falls some 12,000 years ago, the Lewiston area later was home to various tribes, including the Attawandaronk, Hopewell and Seneca, who landed their canoes here to portage around the deadly rapids and falls of the Niagara River. Though also the site of portages by explorers in the late 1600s, the area was not settled until 1796, when the British surrendered nearby Fort Niagara.

Named for Gov. Morgan Lewis, Lewiston quickly grew into a center of trade and transportation; a tramway built by the British is said to have become America's first railroad. Another of Lewiston's innovations is the cocktail, which was invented by a local tavern proprietress who mixed some gin and herb wine in a tankard and stirred the drink with the tail feather of a stuffed cock pheasant.

★ EARL W. BRYDGES ARTPARK, a 200-acre state park along the Niagara River gorge, is a unique concept that combines culture and entertainment with recreation and nature. The park features internationally known singers, dancers and musicians who perform in a 2,400-seat theater, and artists and craftspeople who display their creations throughout the site. Recreational facilities, including nature trails, picnic areas and fishing docks, are part of the complex. ArtPark at the Church offers smaller theater productions seating 150 people April through December.

Park open daily dawn-dusk. Theater performances are presented July-Sept. Hands-on art experiences take place July-Aug. Fee for activities. Parking $5, May-Sept. Phone (800) 659-7275.

NATIONAL SHRINE BASILICA OF OUR LADY OF FATIMA, 1.5 mi. e. on US 104, 2 mi. n. on SR 18, then .5 mi. e. on Swan Rd., is an outdoor cathedral with more than 100 life-size statues, a giant rosary and a translucent domed chapel that has an observation deck on top. Picnicking is permitted. Food is available. Daily 9-5; closed Thanksgiving and Dec. 25. Free. Phone (716) 754-7489.

YOUNGSTOWN (D-3)
pop. 2,100, elev. 301'

FORT NIAGARA STATE PARK covers 504 acres at the mouth of the Niagara River off SR 18F following signs to Robert Moses Pkwy. Tennis, basketball, boating, fishing and swimming facilities are available Memorial Day through Labor Day. Daily dawn-dusk. Free. Parking $5 daily, July 1-Labor Day and Sat.-Sun., Memorial Day weekend-June 30; free, rest of year. Phone (716) 745-7273. *See Recreation Chart.*

SAVE ★ Old Fort Niagara, adjacent to the state park grounds, was begun by the French in 1726. Active under three flags, the fort contains many mounted cannons, a hot shot furnace, a drawbridge and pre-revolution buildings. The site includes the only fortified French castle in the United States; it has been restored and furnished to re-create its stark 18th-century atmosphere. Drills and ceremonies are presented daily, July through Labor Day. Re-enactments are held throughout the year.

Allow 1 hour minimum. Daily 9-7:30, July-Aug.; Mon.-Fri. 9-6:30, Sat.-Sun. 9-7:30, in June; Mon.-Fri. 9-5:30, Sat.-Sun. 9-6:30 in May and Sept.; daily 9-5:30 in Apr. and Oct.; daily 9-4:30, rest of year. Closed Jan. 1, Thanksgiving and Dec. 25. Admission $6.75; over 64, $5.50; ages 6-12, $4.50. AE, DS, MC, VI. Phone (716) 745-7611. *See color ad p. 147.*

Nearby Ontario

NIAGARA FALLS

FALLS INCLINE RAILWAY, next to the Table Rock Complex, operates twin cable-rail cars between the Minolta Tower Centre and Table Rock Complex areas. Daily 9 a.m.-midnight, mid-June through Labour Day; Mon.-Fri. 10-7, Sat.-Sun. 9 a.m.-10 p.m., May 1 to mid-June and day after Labour Day-Sept. 15; Sat.-Sun. 10-7, Easter weekend-Apr. 30 and Sept.16-second Mon. in Oct. One-way fare $1. Phone (905) 356-0943.

FLORAL CLOCK, 10 km (6 mi.) n. on River Rd. at Sir Adam Beck-Niagara Generating Station, is one of the world's largest floral clocks. Approximately 19,000 plants that bloom from early spring to the first frost compose the 12-metre (40-foot) in diameter clock. Westminster chimes ring every 15 minutes. Free.

★ GREAT GORGE ADVENTURE, n. of the Whirlpool Rapids Bridge on the Niagara Pkwy., includes elevator service to the river level. Visitors can stroll along the boardwalk beside the rapids of the lower Niagara River. Daily 9-8, mid-June through Labour Day; daily 9-5, late Apr. to mid-June and day after Labour Day to mid-Oct. Admission $5; ages 6-12, $2.50. Combined admission to Great Gorge Adventure, Niagara Spanish Aero Car and Table Rock Complex, with an all-day People Movers transportation pass, $18.65; ages 6-12, $9.55. AE, DI, MC, VI. Phone (905) 371-0254 to verify prices and schedule. *See color ad p. 155.*

SAVE GUINNESS WORLD OF RECORDS, 4943 Clifton Hill, displays exhibits demonstrating world records in sports, science and nature. Videotapes depict accomplishments in outer space and high-speed travel. Daily 9 a.m.-2 a.m., June-Sept.; daily 10-5, Oct.-Mar.; otherwise varies rest of year. Admission $6.95; over 59 and students with ID $5.95; ages 6-12, $3.95. AE, MC, VI. Phone (905) 356-2299.

SAVE ★LOUIS TUSSAUD'S WAXWORKS, 4915 Clifton Hill at Falls Ave. at the Sheraton Foxhead Inn, displays life-size reproductions of the world's famous and infamous. See King Henry VIII and his wives, ogle Tom Cruise or share chocolate with Forrest Gump. Statesmen, artists, explorers and religious leaders appear in historically accurate costumes and settings. Visitors also can get their hand waxed.

Daily 9 a.m.-1 a.m., May-Aug.; 10 a.m.-11 p.m., Sept.-Dec.; 11-5, rest of year. Admission $7; over 54, $5; ages 6-12, $3.99. AE, MC, VI. Phone (905) 374-6601 or 374-4534.

LUNDY'S LANE HISTORICAL MUSEUM, 1.6 km (.9 mi.) from the falls off Hwy. 420 at 5810 Ferry St., is on the site of one of the fiercest battles of the War of 1812. The 1874 building contains military displays of that conflict and the Fenian Raids as well as Indian artifacts, a collection of art glass and items that portray the life of the region's early settlers. Allow 30 minutes minimum. Daily 9-4, May-Nov.; Mon.-Fri. noon-4, rest of year. Closed Jan. 1 and Dec. 25-26. Admission $1.60; over 64 and students with ID $1; ages 6-12, 50c. Phone (905) 358-5082.

★*MAID OF THE MIST* boats depart from the dock at Clifton Hill and River Rd. on the Canadian side. The boats enter the Horseshoe Basin and pass directly in front of the falls.

Trips depart daily beginning at 9, Memorial Day weekend-Labour Day weekend; daily at 9:45, Apr. 1-day before Memorial Day weekend and day after Labour Day-Oct. 24. Closing times vary; phone ahead. **Note:** These hours reflect the Canadian side; the American side runs 15 minutes later. Fare (waterproof clothing included) $10.65; ages 6-12, $6.55. Elevator cost included. To confirm daily schedules phone (905) 358-5781 in Ontario, or (716) 284-8897 in N.Y. *See color ad p. 147.*

★MARINELAND, 7657 Portage Rd., is known for its marine shows, which feature killer whales, dolphins and sea lions. There also are an aquarium and wildlife displays with bears, elk and buffaloes and a deer petting park. At the interactive Killer Whale Habitat visitors can touch a whale. Several rides are available, including Dragon Mountain, a large steel roller coaster. A few children's rides also are available. Show times vary according to the season.

Daily 9-6, late June-Labour Day; 10-5, Victoria Day-late June and day after Labour Day to mid-Oct. Amusement rides open third weekend in May-second weekend in Oct. Admission late June-late Sept. $26.95; over 59 and ages 5-9, $23.95. Reduced admission late May-late June and late Sept. to mid-Oct. Parents should ask

about height restrictions before paying admission. Phone to verify prices. MC, VI. Phone (905) 356-9565 or 356-8250.

MINOLTA TOWER CENTRE, overlooking the falls at 6732 Oakes Dr., rises 99 metres (325 ft.) above the ground and 203 metres (665 ft.) above the base of the falls, providing a magnificent view of the surrounding area. Three levels at the top include three floors of dining rooms and two floors of indoor/outdoor observation decks. At the base of the tower are amusements such as virtual reality adventures.

Allow 1 hour minimum. Daily 8 a.m.-midnight, May-Oct.; 9-9, rest of year. Admission $6.95; over 64 and ages 6-18, $4.95; under 6 free with an adult. Amusements extra. AE, DS, MC, VI. Phone (905) 356-1501.

MOUNT CARMEL SPIRITUAL CENTRE, n. of McLeod Rd. at 7021 Stanley Ave., just above the falls, was founded in 1894; it is now used for religious retreats. The main altar has woodcarvings and paneling in American white oak. The center contains Our Lady of Peace Church, built in 1827. Daily 9-5, June-Aug.; 10-4, rest of year. Free. Phone (905) 356-4113.

MOVIELAND WAX MUSEUM, on Clifton Hill, displays figures of film and television personalities in scenes that made them famous. Daily 9 a.m.-midnight, May-June and in Sept.; 8 a.m.-2 a.m., July-Aug.; 10-9, rest of year. Admission $5.99; over 59, $4.50; ages 3-11, $3.99. AE, MC, VI. Phone (905) 358-3061.

NIAGARA FALLS ART GALLERY/KURELEK COLLECTION, 1.5 km (.9 mi.) s.e. of QEW exit 27 (McLeod Rd.) at 8058 Oakwood Dr., has an outstanding collection of works by Canadian artist William Kurelek, including the 160-panel tempera work "The Passion of Christ." The gallery also houses the Niagara Children's Museum featuring hands-on art activities.

Also noteworthy are two sculptures: "Pierre Rock," a 10-metric-ton (11-ton) dolomite slab carved with 17 symbols of pioneer achievement, and "Stepova Baba" (Grandmother of the Steppes), a sculpture at least 2,500 years old that was presented to the museum by the Ukrainian government. Mon-Fri. 10-5, Sat. 1-5. Donations. Phone (905) 356-1514.

★ **NIAGARA FALLS IMAX THEATRE AND DAREDEVIL ADVENTURE,** next to the Skylon Tower at 6170 Buchanan Ave., presents "Niagara: Miracles, Myths and Magic" on a screen six stories tall. The Daredevil Adventure features artifacts from those daredevils who have challenged the falls in the past, including boats and barrels, photographs and laser disks. Food is available.

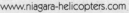

Daily 10-9, July 1-Labour Day; daily 11-8, Apr.-June and day after Labour Day-second Mon. in Oct.; Mon.-Fri. 2-3, Sat. 11-6, Sun. 11-4, rest of year. Admission $7.50; over 64 and ages 12-18, $7; ages 5-11, $5.50. MC, VI. Phone (905) 358-3611.

THE NIAGARA PARKS BOTANICAL GARDENS, 8 km (5 mi.) n. to 2565 Niagara Pkwy., is the home of the Niagara Park School of Horticulture, reputedly the only residential school in Canada for apprentice gardeners. Floral displays and gardens, including 2,300 varieties of roses, are on the 40-hectare (99-acre) campus. Daily dawn-dusk. Free. Phone (905) 356-8554 to verify price and schedule.

Niagara Parks Butterfly Conservatory, 2565 Niagara Pkwy. on the grounds of the Botanical Gardens, is home to some 2,000 butterflies comprising more than 50 species. Waterfalls and various flora line the pathways throughout the conservatory. More than 120 butterfly species can be observed in a native butterfly garden outside the conservatory. Allow 1 hour minimum. Daily 9-9, May 31-Sept. 5; 9-8, May 3-30 and Sept. 6-Oct. 17; 9-6, Mar. 8-May 2; 9-5, rest of year. Closed Dec. 25. Timed-tickets are available. Admission $7.50; ages 6-12, $3.75. MC, VI. Phone (905) 371-2054 to verify prices and schedule. *See color ad p. 155.*

NIAGARA PARKS GREENHOUSES, 5 km (.2 mi.) s. of the Canadian Horseshoe Falls, have seasonal displays of local flowers and foliage, palm trees, more than 75 tropical birds and other tropical plants. There also is an outdoor fragrance garden for the visually impaired.

Daily 9 a.m.-10 p.m., May 3-Labour Day; 9-6, day after Labour Day-day after second Mon. in Oct.; 9-5, rest of year. Extended hours during festivals and holidays. Free. Phone (905) 371-0254 to verify schedule. *See color ad p. 155.*

★**NIAGARA SPANISH AERO CAR,** on the Niagara Pkwy. 3.25 km (2 mi.) below the falls and n. of Horseshoe Falls, is a cable car carrying passengers 76.2 metres (250 feet) above the Niagara Gorge and back on a 549-metre-long (1,800-ft.) cableway. Below the suspended aerocar the churning river backs up into the 24-hectare (60-acre) Whirlpool Basin.

Allow 30 minutes minimum. Daily 9-dusk, Victoria Day-second Mon. in Oct. (weather permitting). Round trip $5.25; ages 6-12, $2.65. Combined admission to Great Gorge Adventure, Niagara Spanish Aero Car and Table Rock Complex, with an all-day People Movers transportation pass, $18.65; ages 6-12, $9.55. AE, DS, JC, MC, VI. Phone (905) 371-0254 to verify prices and schedule. *See color ad p. 155.*

OAKES GARDEN THEATRE, 1 km (.6 mi.) n. on the Niagara Pkwy. at the foot of Clifton Hill, is a

Greco-Roman style amphitheater in a setting of rock gardens, lily ponds, terraces and promenades overlooking the American Falls. Daily 24 hours. Free.

★ QUEEN VICTORIA PARK, on the Niagara Pkwy. at the falls, originated in 1887. It is a 62-hectare (154-acre) landscaped park offering fine views of the falls and beautiful floral displays. The park is illuminated at night. Daily 24 hours. Free.

QUEENSTON HEIGHTS PARK, 11 km (7 mi.) n. of the Horseshoe Falls, commemorates one of the crucial battles of the War of 1812. A small force of British regulars, militia and Indians under Gen. Sir Isaac Brock turned back a larger American invasion force in a stunning victory. A 64-meter-tall (210-ft.) monument honors Brock, who was killed during the battle.

The park is a popular recreation area offering tennis, hiking, picnicking and 3 p.m. Sunday band concerts from the third Sunday in June through August. For the younger crowd there is a playground and a wading pool.

Sweeping vistas of the surrounding countryside can be seen from the top of the Niagara Escarpment, which dominates the park. Queenston Heights also is the eastern terminus of the 720-kilometre (447-mi.) Bruce Trail, which follows the escarpment to Tobermory and the Niagara River Recreational Trail, which runs from Fort Erie to Niagara-on-the-Lake. Food is available. Park open daily 9-dusk. Free.

RAINBOW CARILLON TOWER, at the terminus of the Rainbow Bridge, presents concerts on its 55 tuned bells Fri.-Sun. at 4 and 7 and before the Friday Fireworks display, early June-Labour Day. Free.

RIDE NIAGARA, 5755 River Rd., features a computerized motion simulator that gives visitors the sensation of being propelled through a tunnel system to emerge above the falls, surging toward the brink. Allow 1 hour minimum. Daily 10 a.m.-11 p.m., mid-June through Labour Day; otherwise varies. Admission $8.95; ages 5-13, $4.50; ages 3-4 free. Under 3 are not permitted. AE, MC, VI. Phone (905) 374-7433.

[SAVE] ★ RIPLEY'S BELIEVE IT OR NOT! MUSEUM, 4960 Clifton Hill, displays bizarre and unusual items. More than 350 exhibits are featured in nine galleries. Daily 9 a.m.-1 a.m., May-Aug.; 10 a.m.-11 p.m., Sept.-Dec.; 11-5, rest of year. Admission $7.50; over 55, $5.50; ages 6-12, $4.50. AE, MC, VI. Phone (905) 356-2238.

[SAVE] Ripley's Believe It Or Not! Moving Theater, 4983 Clifton Hill, offers a 10-minute ride in a motion simulator while watching a virtual reality movie. Note: Persons with back or neck problems may find the ride uncomfortable. Daily

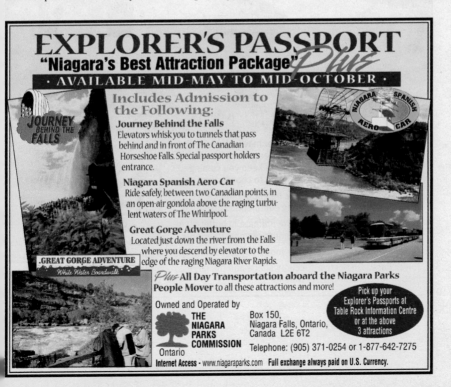

9 a.m.-1 a.m., May-Aug.; 10-8, Sept.-Dec.; 11-5, rest of year. Double feature $10.95; single show $7. Phone (905) 356-2261.

SAVE **SKYLON TOWER,** overlooking the falls at 5200 Robinson St., rises 160 meters (525 ft.) above the ground and 244 meters (800 ft.) above the base of the falls, providing a magnificent view of the surrounding area. Three levels at the top include a revolving dining room, a summit suite buffet and an indoor/outdoor observation deck. Daily 8 a.m.-midnight, May 1 to mid-Oct.; otherwise varies. Admission $8.50; over 64, $7.50; ages 6-12, $4.25; family rate $22.95. AE, DI, DS, JC, MC, VI. Phone (905) 356-2651 to verify prices. *See color ad and p. 437.*

★ **TABLE ROCK COMPLEX** (Journey Behind the Falls), 1 mi. s. of Rainbow Bridge on Niagara Pkwy., contains an elevator that descends for a close-up view of Horseshoe Falls and the Niagara River. Three tunnels lead from the elevator

and provide excellent vantage points. The observation plaza is about 38 meters (125 ft.) below the gorge embankment and 8 meters (26 ft.) above the river's edge. Saturdays and Sundays in July and August a Mountie in ceremonial uniform is posted near the brink of the falls.

Complex opens daily at 9; closing times vary. Tunnels close 30 minutes before complex closing; phone ahead for closing times. Closed Dec. 25. Tunnel $6.50; ages 6-12, $3.25. Combined admission to Great Gorge Adventure, Niagara Spanish Aero Car and Table Rock Complex, with an all-day People Movers transportation pass, $18.65; ages 6-12, $9.55. AE, DI, JC, MC, VI. Phone (905) 358-3268 or (877) 642-7275. *See color ad p. 155.*

CASINOS

• **Casino Niagara,** 5705 Falls Ave. Daily 24 hours. Phone (905) 374-3598.

The previous listings were for the Niagara Falls Vicinity.
This page resumes the alphabetical listings of cities in New York.

NORTH BLENHEIM (F-9)

elev. 791'

BLENHEIM-GILBOA PUMPED STORAGE POWER PROJECT, 3 mi. s. on SR 30, has two reservoirs. During the day water is released from the upper reservoir to create electricity, and at night electricity is used to pump water from the lower to the upper reservoir to repeat the process the next day. A 19th-century barn houses a visitor center with energy displays.

Daily 10-6, late June-Labor Day; 10-5, rest of year. Closed Jan. 1, Thanksgiving and Dec. 25. Free. Phone (518) 827-6121, or (800) 724-0309.

Lansing Manor Museum adjoins the power project's visitor center. The 1819 house was part of an 840-acre estate owned by John T. Lansing Jr., an aide to Revolutionary War general Philip Schuyler. The restored manor is furnished in period. Wed.-Mon. 10-5, Memorial Day weekend-Columbus Day. Free. Phone (518) 827-6121 or (800) 724-0309.

OLD BLENHEIM BRIDGE, on SR 30 across Schoharie Creek, was built in 1854 and is said to be the world's longest single-span wooden covered bridge. It is 232 feet long, 26 feet wide and has two driveways. The bridge is open only to pedestrians. Free. For more information, phone the Blenheim-Gilboa Pumped Storage Power Project at (518) 827-6121, or (800) 724-0309.

NORTH CHILI (D-4) elev. 582'

VICTORIAN DOLL MUSEUM AND CHILI DOLL HOSPITAL, 4332 Buffalo Rd. (SR 33), 4.5 mi. w. on SR 33 exit 7B off I-490, has more than 2,000 identified dolls made of bisque, china, wax, tin and vinyl. Also displayed are toys, Victorian memorabilia, a puppet theater, a circus and a Noah's Ark. A doll hospital also is featured. Allow 1 hour minimum. Tues.-Sat. 10-4:30 (also Sun. 1-4, in Dec.), Feb.-Dec.; closed holidays. Admission $2; under 12, $1. Phone (716) 247-0130.

NORTH CREEK (C-10) elev. 1,013'

North Creek is a popular access point for recreation in the surrounding Adirondack Park. Downhill and cross-country skiing are available 5 miles northwest off SR 28 at Gore Mountain, (518) 251-2411, and at Garnet Hill, (518) 251-2821. White-water rafting expeditions depart from downtown.

Gore Mountain Region Chamber of Commerce: Main Street, North Creek, NY 12853; phone (518) 251-2612.

GORE MOUNTAIN GARNET MINE is 4.5 mi. n. on SR 28, then w. 5 mi. on Burton Mines Rd.

One of the largest garnet mines in the world, it was begun in 1878. In 1983, the main mining operation moved to nearby Ruby Mountain. One-hour guided tours feature the original site and include a walk through an open-pit mine 800 feet below the summit of Gore Mountain.

Tours depart the Gore Mountain Mineral Shop on the hour Mon.-Sat. 9-4, Sun. 11-4, late June-Labor Day. Tour $3; over 59 and ages 7-12, $2. Rocks collected cost $1 per pound. Phone (518) 251-2706 to verify schedule and prices.

RECREATIONAL ACTIVITIES

White-water Rafting

- **Hudson River Rafting Co.** departs from Cunningham's Ski Barn off I-87 exit 23, SR 9 onto SR 28. Write P.O. Box 47, North Creek, NY 12853. Departures daily at 9, early Apr.-Aug. 31; Sat.-Sun. and holidays at 9, Sept. 1-Columbus Day. Phone (518) 251-3215 or (800) 888-7238.

NORTH HOOSICK (E-11)

BENNINGTON BATTLEFIELD STATE HISTORIC SITE, 3 mi. e. on SR 67, is the site of one of the earliest decisive Colonial victories of the Revolutionary War. In 1777 Gen. John Stark and his New Hampshire, Vermont and Massachusetts militia captured a British expeditionary force. An interpretive sign explains the course of the battle. A hilltop picnic area overlooks the battlefield.

Allow 1 hour minimum. Daily 10-7, Memorial Day weekend-Labor Day; Sat.-Sun. 10-7, day after Labor Day-Columbus Day (weather permitting). Free. Phone (518) 279-1155.

NORTH HUDSON (C-10) pop. 300

FRONTIER TOWN, Blue Ridge Rd. (I-87 exit 29), is a Western theme park with six separate complexes. Visitors ride a steam locomotive from the admission area to the park. Among the areas are Pioneer Village, an Indian village and Roth's Forge Village. Park attractions also include rodeos, shows and pony, horse and stagecoach rides. Food is available.

Allow 4 hours minimum. Daily 9:30-5, mid-June through Labor Day. Admission $15.95; over 59 and ages 3-12, $13.95. AE, DI, DS, MC, VI. Phone (518) 532-7181 to verify price and schedule.

NORTH TARRYTOWN—

see Sleepy Hollow p. 139.

NORTH TONAWANDA—

see Buffalo p. 72.

NORWICH (F-8)
pop. 7,600, elev. 1,015'

[SAVE] **NORTHEAST CLASSIC CAR MUSEUM,** 24 Rexford St. (SR 23), displays more than 100 restored automobiles dating from the turn of the 20th century to the 1960s. Among the changing exhibits are Auburns, Cord, Duesenbergs, MG's, Packards, Stutz, Pierce Arrow and more as well as an extensive collection of Franklin luxury cars. Other highlights include World War II aircraft engines. Complementing the vehicles are informational placards and mannequins dressed in period clothing.

Allow 1 hour minimum. Daily 10-5; closed Jan. 1, Thanksgiving and Dec. 25. Admission $7; over 65, $6; ages 6-18, $3.50. AE, DS, MC, VI. Phone (607) 334-2886.

NYACK—see New York p. 139.

OAKDALE (I-3) pop. 7,900, elev. 17'

CONNETQUOT RIVER STATE PARK PRESERVE, entered off SR 27, is a 3,400-acre refuge supporting many species of animals and plants. Guided nature walks and interpretive tours are conducted Wednesday through Sunday; reservations are required. Fishing is permitted with a New York license; equestrian permits are available by phoning the preserve.

Tues.-Sun. 6-4:30, Apr.-Sept.; Tues.-Sun. 8-4, rest of year. Free, but a $1 entry permit must be obtained in advance at the preserve or by contacting the Connetquot River State Park Preserve, P.O. Box 505, Oakdale, NY 11769-0505. Parking $4. Phone (631) 581-1005.

OGDENSBURG (A-8)
pop. 13,500, elev. 276'

Situated on the banks of the St. Lawrence River, Ogdensburg was founded as the French Fort La Presentation in 1749 by the Sulpician missionary Abbé François Picquet. The fort, which also served as a mission, trading post and school, was damaged by the French before the British could capture it in 1760. On the ruins of La Presentation the British built Fort Oswegatchie, which was an important military stronghold during the Revolution. A replica of Fort Presentation in in the planning stages.

In 1796 Oswegatchie was turned over to Col. Samuel Ogden, and in 1817 it was incorporated as the village of Ogdensburgh. The village dropped its "h" when incorporated as a city in 1868.

The Custom House, 127 Water St., designated the oldest federal government building in the United States, was built 1809-10. The building offered protection to both American and British soldiers during a battle on Feb. 23, 1813. Battle scars are visible near the roof peak on the north side of the building. It has served as the customhouse since 1928.

The New York State Armory, a massive castellated-style edifice, 225 Elizabeth St., was constructed 1897-98 by architect Isaac Perry. Built for the Fortieth Separate Co., the building has been historically significant due to its association with American military history.

Greater Ogdensburg Chamber of Commerce: 1020 Park St., Ogdensburg, NY 13669; phone (315) 393-3620.

Shopping areas: An Ammex Tax & Duty Free Shop is at Bridge Plaza off SR 37. Gateway Centre also is off SR 37, and Seaway Shopping Center is on Canton Street.

★ **FREDERIC REMINGTON ART MUSEUM,** 303 Washington St., displays bronzes, oil paintings, watercolors and pen-and-ink illustrations by Frederic Remington, known for his depictions of the American West. The artist's tools, library, personal notes and furnishings from his home are on display. In addition the museum presents traveling exhibitions that relate to the artist's style, theme and time period.

Allow 1 hour minimum. Mon.-Sat. 9-5, Sun. 1-5, May-Oct.; Wed.-Sat. 11-5, Sun. 1-5, rest of year. Closed Jan. 1, Easter, Thanksgiving and Dec. 25. Admission $4; over 65 and students age 6-22, $3. Phone (315) 393-2425.

OLD BETHPAGE (I-3) pop. 5,600

OLD BETHPAGE VILLAGE RESTORATION, 1 mi. s. of Long Island Expwy. exit 48S on Round Swamp Rd., is a reconstructed pre-Civil War Long Island working farm village. Buildings include blacksmith shops, a church, homes, a store and a tavern. Costumed guides explain each building and the activities of its owners. Demonstrations are scheduled throughout the year. Self-guided tours begin at the reception center with an introductory film. Picnicking is permitted.

Allow 2 hours minimum. Wed.-Sun. 10-5, Mar. 1-Nov. 15; Wed.-Sun. 10-4, rest of year. Closed holidays, except Memorial Day, July 4, Labor Day and Columbus Day. Last admission 1 hour before closing. Admission $6; over 59 and ages 5-12, $4. Phone (516) 572-8400.

OLD CHATHAM (F-11) elev. 551'

THE SHAKER MUSEUM AND LIBRARY is off Taconic Pkwy. (exit 295) and the N.Y. State Thruway Berkshire Spur exit (exit B-2) to CR 13, following signs to 88 Shaker Museum Rd. Twenty-six exhibit areas include painted shaker furniture, baskets, poplarware, domestic items and pre-1900 tools. Displays span more than 200 years of Shaker history. Thurs.-Mon. 10-5, May-Oct. Admission $8; over 61, $7; under 12, $4. Phone (518) 794-9100, ext. 100.

OLD FORGE (C-9) elev. 1,706′

Originating in Old Forge is a canoe trip through the eight lakes of the Fulton Chain as well as Raquette, Forked, Long and Saranac lakes. McCauley Mountain offers summer and winter recreation.

Central Adirondack Association: P.O. Box 68, Old Forge, NY 13420; phone (315) 369-6983.

ARTS CENTER/OLD FORGE, .3 mi. n. on SR 28, exhibits paintings, pottery, photography and other media as well as works from the permanent collection. Special month-long exhibitions are offered year-round. Workshops and performances also are offered. Allow 30 minutes minimum. Mon.-Sat. 10-4, Sun. noon-4; closed major holidays. Donations. Admission charged for special exhibits. Phone (315) 369-6411.

ENCHANTED FOREST/WATER SAFARI, on SR 28, is a 60-acre family-oriented water theme park featuring 31 heated water rides and attractions. Adirondack Expedition features such rides as Log Jammer, an action river ride; Cascade Falls; the Sawmill's three stories of slides; and Black River, an enclosed tube slide. Circus shows are offered twice daily. Food is available. Daily 9:30-7, July 3-Aug. 15; daily 9:30-6, mid-June through July 2 and Aug. 16-Labor Day; Mon.-Fri. 10-4, Sat.-Sun. 9:30-6, June 11-20. Admission $19.95; ages 2-11, $17.95. DS, MC, VI. Phone (315) 369-6145.

OLD FORGE LAKE CRUISES depart from the SR 28 Dock. Narrated trips include a 2.5-hour cruise, a 2-hour excursion, a 1.5-hour children's cruise and a moonlight cruise with live entertainment.

Cruises depart daily at 11, 1 and 3, June 24-Labor Day; Mon.-Fri. at 1, Sat.-Sun. at 11 and 1, Memorial Day-June 23; Mon.-Fri. at 1, Sat.-Sun. at 11, 1 and 3, day after Labor Day-Columbus Day. Children's cruise departs daily at 6:30, July 4-Labor Day. Moonlight cruise departs daily at 8:30 p.m., July 1-Labor Day. Fare $9.50; under 12, $4.75. MC, VI. Phone (315) 369-6473.

OLD WESTBURY (H-2) pop. 3,900

OLD WESTBURY GARDENS is at 71 Old Westbury Rd. between Long Island Expwy. (SR 495) and Jericho Tpke. (SR 25). The 1906 Westbury House is furnished with antique furniture and art, including paintings by Henry Raeburn, Sir Joshua Reynolds, John Singer Sargent and Richard Wilson. The grounds feature landscaping patterned after the English "Great Parks" of the 18th century. Picnicking is permitted. Food is available.

Allow 2 hours minimum. Guided house and garden tours Wed.-Mon. 10-5, late Apr.-Oct. 31 and Dec. 1 to mid-Dec.; Sat.-Sun. 10-5, in Nov. House and garden tour $10; over 62, $8; ages 6-12, $6. Garden only tour $6; over 62, $5; ages 6-12, $3. Phone (516) 333-0048.

OLEAN (G-4) pop. 16,900, elev. 1,435′

ROCK CITY PARK, 5 mi. s. on SR 16, has paths that wind through 320-million-year-old quartz boulders projecting from the edge of the Allegheny Mountains; the paths provide panoramas. The site reputedly has the world's largest exposure of quartz conglomerate, also known as pudding stone. A stairway into a crevice leads to a .75-mile trail through gigantic boulders. Another stairway is believed to have been built by the Seneca Indians, who used the area as a fortress.

A museum and black mineral display also are featured. Comfortable clothing and shoes are suggested. Picnicking is permitted. Food is available. Allow 1 hour minimum. Daily 9-8, July-Aug.; 9-6, May-June and Sept.-Oct. (weather permitting). Admission $4.50; over 61, $3.75; ages 6-12, $2.50. Phone (716) 372-7790.

ONEIDA (E-7) pop. 10,900, elev. 427′

The Oneida Community was founded nearby in 1848 by John Noyes. A religious and social commune who called themselves Perfectionists, they shared all property and looked for ways of improving their self. The communal way of life was abandoned in 1881. However a joint stock corporation was formed to carry on the manufacturing activities. The present corporation has retained some cooperative features; Oneida Ltd. has factories and home offices in the area as well as in Sherrill, where silverware is made.

Of interest is the Mansion House at 170 Kenwood Ave. Begun in 1860, the home contains some 300 rooms that reflect the needs of the society that lived as one family. Guided tours present family portraits, Empire and Victorian furniture, costumes and historical photographs. Phone (315) 363-0745.

Greater Oneida Chamber of Commerce: 136 Lenox Ave., Oneida, NY 13421-1745; phone (315) 363-4300.

MADISON COUNTY HISTORICAL SOCIETY HEADQUARTERS, 435 Main St., occupies the Gothic Revival mansion "Cottage Lawn." The house offers changing exhibits about local history, a genealogical library and seven period rooms. The carriage barn has an agricultural museum which features a display about hops. Guided tours are available Mon.-Sat. 9-4, May-Sept.; Mon.-Fri. 9-4, rest of year. Closed major holidays. Tour $2; under 12, $1. Phone (315) 363-4136.

ONEONTA (F-8)
pop. 14,000, elev. 1,083′

Oneonta is the Oneida Indian word for "cliffs abound" or "exposed rock in side of hills." The town is on the western edge of the Catskills surrounded by hills.

Oneonta became the site of a major railroad car-building shop for the Albany & Susquehanna line in 1863. Twenty years later a handful of train yard workers formed the Brotherhood of Railroad Brakemen, the embryo of today's Brotherhood of Railroad Trainmen. When first built, the Delaware and Hudson roundhouse was one of the largest turntables in the world.

Otsego County Chamber of Commerce: 12 Carbon St., Oneonta, NY 13820; phone (607) 432-4500. *See color ad p. 240.*

NATIONAL SOCCER HALL OF FAME, I-88 exit 13 to 18 Stadium Cir., tells the story of soccer in the United States through interactive exhibits, historic footage, artifacts and videotape presentations. For an additional fee, soccer buffs can test their skills in the Kick's Game Zone with six different games. Allow 1 hour minimum. Sun.-Thurs. 10-7, Fri.-Sat. 10-9, May 15-Sept. 7; Mon.-Fri. 10-3 (game days 10-8), Sat.-Sun. 10-5, Sept. 8-Nov. 7; Mon. and Thurs.-Fri. 10-3, Sat.-Sun. 10-4, rest of year. Closed Jan. 1, Thanksgiving and Dec. 25. Phone ahead to verify schedule. Admission $7.50; senior citizens $5.50; under 10, $4.50. Kick's Game Zone $2 per game. DI, MC, VI. Phone (607) 432-3351.

SCIENCE DISCOVERY CENTER OF ONEONTA is in the Physical Science Building at State University College on Ravine Pkwy. This center promotes the enjoyment and understanding of science by children and adults through direct, hands-on experiences and educational fun. Allow 1 hour minimum. Mon.-Sat. noon-4, July-Aug.; Thurs.-Sat. noon-4, rest of year. Closed Good Friday, July 4, Thanksgiving and Dec. 25. Free. Phone (607) 436-2011.

YAGER MUSEUM, on the Hartwick College campus, includes the van Ess Gallery, which displays Renaissance and Baroque works, 19th-century paintings and sculpture and 20th-century paintings and drawings. The museum's collections include Upper Susquehanna Native American, Southwestern, pre-Columbian and Mesoamerican collections. Tours, lecture/tours, special programs and changing exhibits are available. Open Tues.-Sat. 11-5 (also Wed. 5-9), Sun. 1-5. Free. Phone (607) 431-4480.

ORCHARD PARK—
see Buffalo p. 72.

ORISKANY (D-8)
pop. 1,500, elev. 423'

ORISKANY MUSEUM, 420 Utica St., exhibits items commemorating the Battle of Oriskany, fought during the Revolutionary War, as well as other military contributions from the area. An airplane and an anchor from the aircraft carrier USS *Oriskany,* which served during the Korean and Vietnam wars, also are displayed. Allow 30 minutes minimum. Tues. and Thurs.-Fri. 1-5, Sat. 4-8; closed Dec. 25. Free. Phone (315) 736-7529.

OSSINING—*see New York p. 139.*

OSWEGO (D-6)
pop. 19,200, elev. 298'

On Lake Ontario at the mouth of the Oswego River, Oswego was fought over by the French, English and Americans during most of the 1700s because of its strategic position at the end of the inland water route. By 1796 Oswego was firmly in U.S. hands, and the town soon became a booming port. Oswego is the largest U.S. port on Lake Ontario and the home of the State University of New York at Oswego.

Greater Oswego Chamber of Commerce: 156 W. 2nd St., Oswego, NY 13126; phone (315) 343-7681.

THE ENERGY CENTER is 2 mi. e. of SR 481 on SR 104, 2 mi. n. on Kosher Rd., then 6 mi. e. on Lake Rd. On a bluff overlooking Lake Ontario, the center has exhibits and a multimedia presentation explaining nuclear power generation and other energy sources. Picnicking is permitted. Allow 1 hour minimum. Daily 10-4, Memorial Day-Labor Day; Mon.-Fri. 10-4, rest of year. Closed Jan. 1, Thanksgiving and Dec. 24-25. Free. Phone (315) 342-4117.

FORT ONTARIO STATE HISTORIC SITE, 3 blks. n. of SR 104 on E. 9th St., overlooks Oswego Harbor and Lake Ontario. The 1755 structure was first fortified during the French and Indian War and remained in use through World War II. It was the only American site to house Jewish refugees during World War II. Barracks, guard houses, powder magazines and two officers' corridors have been restored to the 1868-73 time period. Guided tours are available and costumed guards perform drills daily Memorial Day through Labor Day. Picnicking is permitted.

Allow 1 hour minimum. Wed.-Sat. 10-5, Sun. and holidays 1-5, mid-May through Oct. 31. Admission $3; over 61, $2; under 12, $1. Phone (315) 343-4711.

H. LEE WHITE MARINE MUSEUM, SR 104 to W. 1st St. then .5 mi. to end of pier, houses exhibits covering 300 years of Oswego and Great Lakes history including displays about local American Indians, early settlement, navigation on Lake Ontario and the activities of the underground railroad in the area. Model ships and a restored American Indian canoe are displayed while a World War II tugboat and an Erie Canal barge can by toured.

Allow 1 hour minimum. Daily 10-5, July-Aug.; 1-5, Memorial Day weekend-June 30 and in Sept.; Thurs.-Sun. 1-5, Oct.-Dec. Admission $2; ages 4-12, $1. AE, MC, VI. Phone (315) 342-0480.

RICHARDSON-BATES HOUSE MUSEUM, 135 E. 3rd St., contains period rooms dating from around 1890 with original Victorian pieces, an exhibit about county history and changing exhibits. Allow 1 hour minimum. Tues.-Fri. 10-5, Sat.-Sun. 1-5; closed holidays. Admission $2, over 64 and students (to age 25) with ID $1, under 5 free. Phone (315) 343-1342.

OVID (F-6) pop. 700, elev. 816'

WINERIES

• **Cayuga Ridge Estate Winery** is 4 mi. e. via SR 96A and CR 138, then .5 mi. n. on SR 89. Daily noon-5, mid-May to mid-Nov.; Sat.-Sun. noon-4, rest of year. Guided tours are offered daily at 2:30, mid-May to mid-Nov. Phone (607) 869-5158.

OWEGO (G-7) pop. 4,400

THE TIOGA COUNTY HISTORICAL SOCIETY MUSEUM, 110 Front St., offers permanent and changing interpretive exhibits about local and regional history. Displays include Iroquois Indian artifacts and 19th-century tools, toys and fashions. Area genealogical information dating from 1800 also is available. Allow 30 minutes minimum. Museum open Tues.-Sat. 10-4. Research library open Tues.-Fri. 1-4, Sat. 10-4. Closed holidays. Museum free. Library $5. Phone (607) 687-2460.

OYSTER BAY (H-3)
pop. 6,700, elev. 8'

Oyster Bay, discovered in 1653 by settlers from Massachusetts, found itself in the middle of a tug of war: The Dutch Government in New Amsterdam and the English Colonial government in Hartford were unable to agree on who had jurisdiction over Oyster Bay. The settlers made appeals to both governments for protection.

During the Revolutionary War the village was headquarters for British lieutenant colonel John Graves Simcoe, a close friend of Maj. John Andre, adjutant general of the British Army in North America. As Benedict Arnold's British contact, Andre played an instrumental role in the ensuing scandal and was executed as a British spy in 1780. From 1901 to 1909 Oyster Bay was the site of President Theodore Roosevelt's summer White House. *Also see Long Island p. 100.*

Oyster Bay Chamber of Commerce: P.O. Box 21, Oyster Bay, NY 11771; phone (516) 922-6464.

Self-guiding tours: Brochures detailing self-guiding tours of Oyster Bay are available from the chamber of commerce.

EARLE-WIGHTMAN HOUSE MUSEUM, 20 Summit St., was built in 1720 as a one-room home, with additional rooms added over the following 150 years by successive owners. One room has been renovated to reflect the 18th century, and a second room depicts a 19th-century parlor. Other rooms feature changing exhibits. An 18th-century garden is on the grounds.

Allow 30 minutes minimum. Tues.-Fri. 10-2, Sat. 9-1, Sun. 1-4; closed Jan. 1, July 4, Thanksgiving and Dec. 25. Admission $1.50, senior citizens and students with ID $1, under 12 free. Phone (516) 922-5032.

★**PLANTING FIELDS ARBORETUM STATE HISTORIC PARK,** w. via Mill River and Oyster Bay rds., covers 409 landscaped acres of greenhouses, gardens and natural habitat. Collections include rhododendrons, azaleas, camellias, orchids, ferns and bromeliads. The Synoptic Garden's ornamental shrubs and small trees are arranged alphabetically and are identified by botanical and common name and by family and country of origin.

Allow 1 hour, 30 minutes minimum. Arboretum open daily 9-5; closed Dec. 25. Greenhouses open daily 9-4:30. Camellia house open daily 9-4. Admission free. Parking $4 daily, May-Sept. and Sat.-Sun. and holidays, rest of year. Phone (516) 922-9201 or 922-9200.

Coe Hall, on the arboretum grounds, is a 65-room Tudor Revival mansion furnished with 16th- and 17th-century pieces. Carpets, paintings and tapestries were imported from Europe. Carved oak paneling is found throughout the house. The Buffalo Room contains murals of buffalo and American Indians set against a Western landscape. Allow 30 minutes minimum. Daily noon-3:30, Apr.-Sept.; closed holidays. Admission $5; over 61, $3.50; under 6 free. Parking $5. Phone (516) 922-9210.

DID YOU KNOW

America's first railroad consisted of the 11-mile stretch between Albany and Schenectady.

RAYNHAM HALL MUSEUM, 20 W. Main St., British headquarters during the Revolutionary War, was the home of Samuel Townsend, who was partially responsible for the capture of Maj. John Andre and the exposure of Benedict Arnold's plan to betray West Point. Allow 30 minutes minimum. Tues.-Sun. noon-5, July 1-Labor Day; Tues.-Sun. 1-5, rest of year. Closed Jan. 1, Thanksgiving and Dec. 25. Admission $3; over 65 and ages 6-18, $2. Phone (516) 922-6808.

ROOSEVELT BIRD SANCTUARY AND TRAILSIDE MUSEUM is 2 mi. e. on E. Main St. at Cove Rd. Features include a memorial to President Theodore Roosevelt and a museum with examples of Long Island plant and animal life. Guided tours are available by appointment. Films and nature programs are presented on occasional weekends. Young Memorial Cemetery, next to the sanctuary, contains President Roosevelt's grave.

Allow 30 minutes minimum. Mon.-Fri. 8:30-4:30, Sat.-Sun. 9-5; closed Jan. 1, Thanksgiving and Dec. 25. Donations. Phone (516) 922-3200.

SAGAMORE HILL NATIONAL HISTORIC SITE, 3 mi. e. via E. Main St. and Cove Neck Rd., was the home of President Theodore Roosevelt until his death in 1919. The house served as the "summer White House" during his administration. The 1885 house displays trophies, furniture and other memorabilia. The nearby Old Orchard Museum offers audiovisual programs and exhibits relating to the political career and family life of President Roosevelt.

Guided tours of the house are given daily every hour 9:30-4, May 1-day before Columbus Day; Wed.-Sun. 9-4, rest of year. Closed holidays. Grounds open daily 9:30-dusk. Admission $5, under 16 free. Tour tickets go on sale at 9:15. MC, VI. Phone (516) 922-4447.

PALMYRA (E-5)
pop. 3,600, elev. 442'

Palmyra was the birthplace of Mormonism and the early home of Joseph Smith. The Church of Jesus Christ of Latter-day Saints was organized and the "Book of Mormon" was published nearby in 1830. A visitor center on the Peter Whitmer Farm, where the church was founded, is 5 miles south of Waterloo on SR 96. *Also see Finger Lakes p. 84.*

ALLING COVERLET MUSEUM, 122 William St., has changing 19th-century coverlet and quilt displays. Daily 1-4, June 1-Sept. 15. Free. Phone (315) 597-6737.

BOOK OF MORMON HISTORIC PUBLICATION SITE, 217 E. Main St., is the site where the first 5,000 copies of the "Book of Mormon" were printed by E.B. Grandin. The restored site includes a bindery and the print shop. Allow 1 hour minimum. Forty-minute guided tours are given Mon.-Sat. 9-6, Sun. noon-6. Free. Phone (315) 597-5982 to verify schedule.

HILL CUMORAH, 2 mi. n. of I-90 exit 43, is where Joseph Smith is said to have received from the angel Moroni the golden plates inscribed with the history of ancient Americans, from which he translated the "Book of Mormon." A 40-foot monument crowns the hill. The visitor center has an audiovisual tour centering on Jesus Christ. Twenty-five minute guided tours are given Mon.-Sat. 9-6, Sun. noon-6. Free. Phone (315) 597-5851.

JOSEPH SMITH HOME, 4 mi. s. on SR 21 to Stafford Rd. (a few miles from Hill Cumorah), includes the Smith frame home, a reconstructed log home and the Sacred Grove. Guided tours of the homes are given Mon.-Sat. 9-6, Sun. noon-6. Free. Phone (315) 597-4383.

PANAMA (G-2) pop. 500, elev. 1,548'

PANAMA ROCKS, .2 mi. w. of jct. SR 474 and CR 33, then s. on CR 10, is an outcrop of Paleozoic sea islands compressed into quartzconglomerate rock fractured by earthquakes and unearthed by glaciers. The huge rocks, some more than 60 feet high, extend along a half-mile ridge. Geologic features include cavernous dens, small caves, passageways and crevices. Pets are not allowed. Picnicking facilities are available.

Daily 10-5, May 1 to mid-Oct. Admission $5; over 55 and ages 13-17, $4; ages 6-12, $3. Additional fee charged during special events. Under 18 must be with an adult. Phone (716) 782-2845.

PAUL SMITHS (B-9) pop. 500

⟨SAVE⟩ WHITE PINE CAMP, .5 mi. e. of jct. SRs 86 and 30, following signs, is a complex of 18 buildings constructed in the early 20th century as an Adirondack "Great Camp," or summer retreat. Several prominent people have stayed in the camp including President Calvin Coolidge during the summer of 1926. Visitors see the complex by way of a 2-hour tour. A videotape is shown before the tour.

Allow 2 hours minimum. Tours depart daily at 10 and 1:30, Memorial Day-Columbus Day. Admission $9; over 64, $8; ages 6-15, $4.50. MC, VI. Phone (518) 327-3030.

PETERSBURG (E-11)
pop. 1,500, elev. 684'

⟨SAVE⟩ BERKSHIRE BIRD PARADISE AND SANCTUARY, 2 mi. n. on CR 87 from jct. SR 2 and CR 87, then 1 mi. e. to 43 Red Pond Rd., is dedicated to the conservation of wild birds. The site is home to more than 1,00 birds, including raptors, tropical birds and birds of prey. Allow 1 hour minimum. Daily 9-5, Apr.-Oct. Admission $5; under 10, $3. Phone (518) 279-3801.

PHOENICIA (G-9) elev. 795′

RECREATIONAL ACTIVITIES

Tubing

- **The Town Tinker Tube Rental**, 10 Bridge St., P.O. Box 404, Phoenicia, NY 12464. Daily 9-6, May 15-Sept. 15. Phone (914) 688-5553.

PLATTSBURGH (A-10)
pop. 21,300, elev. 109′

On Lake Champlain, Plattsburgh was the site of the Battle of Plattsburgh on Sept. 11, 1814. While Gen. Alexander Macomb restrained a superior British land force, the Americans, under Cmdr. Thomas Macdonough, scored a decisive naval victory in Plattsburgh Bay.

Plattsburgh North Country Chamber of Commerce: 7061 SR 9, P.O. Box 310, Plattsburgh, NY 12901; phone (518) 563-1000.

Shopping areas: Two major malls serve the Plattsburgh area. Champlain Centers Mall, a quarter-mile east on SR 3 from exit 37 and a half-mile north on Smithfield Boulevard, numbers 90 stores, including Ames, JCPenney and Sears.

CLINTON COUNTY HISTORICAL MUSEUM, 48 Court St., contains a diorama of the 1814 Battle of Plattsburgh and the 1776 Battle of Valcour. Also displayed are domestic and historical artifacts and memorabilia, including a collection of Redford glass. Tues.-Fri. noon-4, Sat. 1-4. Admission $2; over 64, $1.50; students with ID and ages 6-12, $1. Phone (518) 561-0340.

JUNIPER **BOAT TOURS**, foot of Dock St., offers 2-hour narrated cruises on Lake Champlain. Highlights include Valcour Island, the site of a major naval engagement during the American Revolution. A 4-hour sunset dinner cruise with live entertainment also is available. Two-hour cruise departs daily at 1, May-Sept. Fare $7.95; senior citizens $7.50; ages 5-11, $4. Two-hour cruise requires a minimum of 20 persons. Phone (518) 561-8970.

KENT-DELORD HOUSE MUSEUM, 17 Cumberland Ave., overlooks Lake Champlain at the mouth of the Saranac River. The Federal-style structure was commandeered by the British in 1814. They left behind an oak tea chest when they fled. American decorative arts and period furniture also are displayed. Exhibits change in even-numbered years to reflect one of three time periods: 1810-30, 1830-60 and 1860-1910. Guided tours are available.

Tues.-Sat. noon-4, Mar.-Dec.; closed major holidays. Tour $3; over 64, students with ID and ages 12-19, $2; ages 5-11, $1. Phone (518) 561-1035.

LAKE CHAMPLAIN FERRIES—
see Lake Champlain p. 96.

PLATTSBURGH ART MUSEUM, SUNY, in the Myers Fine Arts Gallery/Winkel Sculpture Court/ Rockwell Kent Gallery on the campus of the State University of New York at Plattsburgh, displays a collection of paintings, drawings and books by illustrator Rockwell Kent. The gallery also houses photographs by Ansel Adams, German expressionist prints and prints by Paul Cézanne, Albrecht Dürer, Francisco José de Goya, Pablo Picasso and Peter Paul Rubens.

The Myers Fine Arts Gallery presents changing historical and contemporary exhibitions of mixed media. Next to the gallery is the Winkel Sculpture Court. A "museum without walls" incorporates an outdoor sculpture garden and terrace. Allow 30 minutes minimum. Museum open daily noon-4; closed holidays. Donations. Phone (518) 564-2813.

PORT WASHINGTON (H-2)
pop. 15,400, elev. 140′

Port Washington Chamber of Commerce: 329 Main St., P.O. Box 121, Port Washington, NY 11050; phone (516) 883-6566.

SANDS POINT PRESERVE, 6 mi. n. of I-495 exit 36 on Searingtown Rd./Port Washington Blvd. at 95 Middleneck Rd., contains a 209-acre forest and shoreline preserve. Restored Guggenheim family homes display artifacts and antiques. Revolving nature and science exhibits are on the grounds. Allow 2 hours, 30 minutes minimum. Grounds open daily 10-5. Admission $6; ages 3-12, $3. Special events incur an additional charge. Phone (516) 571-7900.

Castlegould, in Sands Point Preserve, is a huge 1902 stone castle that once served as a stable. It houses a visitor reception center and a main exhibit hall. Allow 1 hour minimum. Tues.-Sun. 10-5, Feb.-Oct. Visitor center free. Main exhibit hall $6; over 59, $4; ages 3-12, $3.

Falaise, in Sands Point Preserve, was built by Capt. Harry F. Guggenheim in 1923. The elegant Normandy-style manor house contains original furnishings and historic memorabilia relating to Guggenheim's support of aeronautical technology. Allow 1 hour minimum. Guided tours Wed.-Sun. noon-3, May-Oct. Last tour begins 1 hour before closing. Tour $5; over 59, $3. Under 10 are not permitted.

Hempstead House, in Sands Point Preserve, was the main residence. The design of the 1912 house includes features of an English Tudor castle. Tours of the main rooms and viewings of the Wedgwood china collection are offered Fri.-Sun. 12:30-4:30, May 1-Oct. 26. Fee $2.

POTSDAM (A-9)
pop. 10,300, elev. 397′

Potsdam was settled in 1803 by land agent Benjamin Raymond. Five years later a post office opened to serve a thriving community of more than 900. The Clarkson family ran a farm and a variety of businesses, built Trinity Church and founded the Thomas Clarkson Memorial College of Technology. Raymond built a schoolhouse, which became part of the state university system in 1949. Sandstone quarried in the area has been used for structures in Ottawa, Syracuse, and New York City.

Potsdam Chamber of Commerce: 71 Market St., P.O. Box 717, Potsdam, NY 13676; phone (315) 265-5440.

GIBSON GALLERY, on SR 56 in Brainerd Hall at the State University of New York, College of Potsdam, presents changing exhibitions featuring student and regional, national and international artists throughout the year and houses a permanent collection and a sculpture park. Allow 1 hour minimum. Mon.-Fri. noon-5 (also Tues.-Thurs. 7-9 p.m.), Sat.-Sun. noon-4 and by appointment; closed school holidays. Free. Phone (315) 267-2245 or 267-2481.

POTSDAM PUBLIC MUSEUM, on SR 11 in the Civic Center, houses the Burnap Collection of English pottery, dating 1700-1870. The collection includes Delft chargers, Wedgwood, lusterware, transfer prints and relief wares. Also displayed are American decorative glassware, furniture and changing exhibits pertaining to local history. Tues.-Sat. 2-5; closed holidays. Free. Phone (315) 265-6910.

POTTERSVILLE (C-10)

[SAVE] **NATURAL STONE BRIDGE AND CAVES** is 1 mi. n. of I-87 exit 26 on US 9, then 2.5 mi. w. following signs. A well-marked path leads through a series of caves, rock formations and underground waterways. Natural paths cover some uneven terrain; wear sturdy shoes. Rental tennis shoes are available. Fishing and picnicking are permitted.

Allow 1 hour minimum. Daily 9-7, Memorial Day weekend-Labor Day; 10-6, day after Labor Day-Columbus Day. Admission $8.50; over 59, $7.50; ages 6-12, $4.50. AE, DI, MC, VI. Phone (518) 494-2283.

POUGHKEEPSIE (G-11)
pop. 28,800, elev. 168′

Originally settled by the Dutch, Poughkeepsie became the state capital in 1777. Eleven years later the state ratified the U.S. Constitution. The city is built on the rocky terraces rising 250 feet above the Hudson River and the level plateau above. The Home of Franklin D. Roosevelt and the Vanderbilt Mansion national historic sites are nearby *(see Hyde Park p. 92)*.

Poughkeepsie Area Chamber of Commerce: 110 Main St., Poughkeepsie, NY 12601; phone (914) 454-1700.

THE FRANCES LEHMAN LOEB ART CENTER, on the campus of Vassar College at 124 Raymond Ave., contains more than 12,500 art objects. Exhibits include works from the permanent collection displayed chronologically in the Main Gallery and selections from the college's significant holdings in Asian art. Among the displays are works by Pieter Brueghel the Younger, Alexander Calder, Paul Cézanne, Georgia O'Keeffe and Jackson Pollock.

Allow 1 hour minimum. Tues.-Sat. 10-5, Sun. 1-5; closed major holidays. Free. Phone (914) 437-5632.

[SAVE] **SAMUEL F.B. MORSE HISTORIC SITE, LOCUST GROVE,** 2 mi. s. of Mid-Hudson Bridge at 370 South Rd. (US 9), was the home of artist, educator and telegraph inventor Samuel F.B. Morse 1847-72. Designed by A.J. Davis, the house contains period furnishings, china, art, original telegraph equipment and other Hudson Valley memorabilia. The 150-acre site includes hiking trails and historic formal gardens, carriage and ice houses, a picnic grove and a visitor center.

Allow 1 hour, 30 minutes minimum. Home open daily 10-4, May 1-Thanksgiving; by appointment Mar.-Apr. and day after Thanksgiving-Dec. 31. Grounds open daily 8 a.m.-dusk. Last tour begins 30 minutes before closing. Fee $5; over 59, $4; ages 6-12, $2. MC, VI. Phone (914) 454-4500.

PRATTSVILLE (F-10)
pop. 800, elev. 1,165′

ZADOCK PRATT MUSEUM, on SR 23 (Main St.), was the home of Prattsville's founder and U.S. representative Zadock Pratt. The 1828 house contains original and period furnishings; exhibits pertain to Pratt's lively and varied occupations, as well as to town and regional history. Wed.-Sun. 1-5, Memorial Day-Columbus Day. Admission $2; under 13, $1. Phone (518) 299-3395 to verify schedule.

PURCHASE—*see New York p. 139.*

QUEENSBURY (D-11)
pop. 800, elev. 293′

[SAVE] **THE GREAT ESCAPE AND SPLASHWATER KINGDOM,** 3.7 mi. n. on US 9, just e. of I-87 Northway via exits 19 or 20, is one of the state's largest theme parks with more than 125 rides, live shows and attractions. Features include a full water park, five roller coasters and a variety of shows for children.

Allow 6 hours minimum. Park opens daily at 9:30 Memorial Day weekend-late Oct.; closing times vary. Admission $28.99, under 48 inches tall $14.50. Two-day passes are available. AE, DS, MC, VI. Phone (518) 792-3500. *See ad p. 281.*

★LAKE GEORGE OPERA FESTIVAL—
see Saratoga Springs p. 172.

RAQUETTE LAKE (C-9)
elev. 1,810'

GREAT CAMP SAGAMORE, 4 mi. s. from SR 28 following signs via a dirt road, was a rustic summer retreat built in 1897 and expanded in 1901. Exemplifying the 19th century's Great Camps, the lake-side main lodge features log and bark siding. Other buildings include the caretakers' quarters, a bowling alley and a dining hall.

A 2-hour guided tour is offered daily at 10 and 1:30, July 4th-Labor Day; Sat.-Sun., day after Labor Day-Columbus Day. Admission $8, children $3. MC, VI. Phone (315) 354-5311 to verify schedule and prices.

RENSSELAER (F-11)
pop. 8,300, elev. 21'

Across the Hudson from Albany, Rensselaer was founded in 1631 by Dutch settlers sent by wealthy patron Killean Van Rensselaer. Fort Crailo was built in 1704 for protection against the indigenous inhabitants. It is said that "Yankee Doodle" was composed in Rensselaer in 1758 as a satire of the Provincial troops.

CRAILO STATE HISTORIC SITE is 1.5 blks. s. of jct. US 9 and US 20 at 9 ½ Riverside Ave. The museum houses exhibits that explain the history, development, culture and influence of Dutch settlements in the Upper Hudson Valley area. Allow 1 hour minimum. Guided tours are given every half-hour. Wed.-Sat. 10-5, Sun. 1-5, mid-Apr. through Oct. 31; closed holidays, except Memorial Day, July 4 and Labor Day. Last tour begins 1 hour before closing. Tour $3; ages 5-12, $1. Phone (518) 463-8738.

RHINEBECK (G-10)
pop. 2,700, elev. 203'

OLD RHINEBECK AERODROME, .5 mi. n. on US 9 off SR 9G, then 1.5 mi. e. to 42 Stone Church Rd., presents antique airplanes from 1908-37. Fifteen-minute rides in a 1929 open cockpit airplane are available weekends before and after air shows. Daily 10-5, May 15-Oct. 31. Air shows are presented mid-June to mid-Oct. Aerodrome $5; ages 6-10, $2. Air shows $10; ages 6-10, $5. Plane rides $30. Phone (914) 758-8610.

RIVERHEAD (H-4)
pop. 8,800, elev. 25'

SPLISH SPLASH WATER PARK is .5 mi. w. of jct. I-495 and SR 25 at 2549 Splish Splash Dr. The 40-acre park contains such water rides as Splash Landing, Lazy River and Giant Twisters.

Children's areas and tropical bird and sea lion shows also are featured. Food is available.

Allow a full day. Daily 9:30-7, mid-June through Labor Day; Sat.-Sun. 9:30-5, Memorial Day to mid-June. Over 48 inches tall $22.95, over age 62 and children under 48 inches tall $16.95, under age 3 free. Parking $5. AE, DS, MC, VI. Phone (631) 727-3600.

SUFFOLK COUNTY HISTORICAL SOCIETY, on SR 25 at 300 W. Main St., has permanent and changing exhibits about the history of Suffolk County, including early crafts, textiles, china, whaling and American Indian artifacts and a research library. Allow 1 hour minimum. Tues.-Sat. 12:30-4:30; closed holidays. Library open Wed.-Sat. 12:30-4:30. Donations. Library $2. Phone (631) 727-2881.

ROCHESTER (D-5)
pop. 231,600, elev. 660'
See map page 166.

Originally called the "Flour City" because of its milling industries, Rochester also became known as the "Flower City" because of its nurseries, parks and fruit and garden areas. Rochester leads in the manufacture of optical, surgical, dental, check-protecting and gear-cutting goods.

Some of the local parks preserve historical sites; others were created especially for recreation. Cobb's Hill Park between Highland Avenue and Culver Road contains Lake Riley, the old Erie Canal turning basin; phone (716) 428-6909. The city can be viewed from the hilltop. Upper Falls Park, on the Genesee River off St. Paul Street, has a 100-foot waterfall; phone (716) 325-2030. Originally used to power the city's flour mills, the falls continue to generate electricity.

Manhattan Square Park at Chestnut and Broad streets has a 100-foot observation tower; phone (716) 428-7541. Mendon Ponds Park at Clover Street and Pond Road is a 550-acre natural preserve with several self-guiding trails and a visitor center; phone (716) 334-3780.

City Hall at Church and Fitzhugh streets presents exhibits in its central atrium; phone (716) 428-6690. Another landmark is Mount Hope Cemetery on Mount Hope Avenue. One of the oldest Victorian cemeteries in the nation, it contains the graves of Susan B. Anthony and Frederick Douglass; phone (716) 473-2755.

Rochester's contribution to education and technology is evident at the University of Rochester's Laboratory of Laser Energetics, where nuclear fusion research takes place. The Rochester Institute of Technology has the School for American Craftsmen and the National Technical Institute for the Deaf.

The Rochester Philharmonic Orchestra performs at the Eastman Theater; phone (716) 222-5000. The GEVA Theatre, 75 Woodbury

Blvd., offers performances throughout the year; phone (716) 232-1363. Local theater and musical companies and touring Broadway shows also offer productions. The Eastman School of Music is said to produce more professional musicians than any other conservatory in the country.

One of the most popular recreational pursuits is fishing. Lake Ontario and its tributaries offer ice fishing in winter and warm-water angling in summer. Abundant species include coho and giant chinook salmon, smelt, bass, pike and steelhead, rainbow and brown trout. Hiking and biking are popular along the Barge Canal Trail recreation area.

Greater Rochester Visitors Association, Inc.: 126 Andrews St., Rochester, NY 14604; phone (716) 546-3070 or (800) 677-7282.

Shopping areas: Several major enclosed malls serve the Rochester area. Near Greece in Rochester's northwest suburbs is The Mall at Greece Ridge Center, with 100 stores 1 mile west of

I-390 at West Ridge Road; anchor stores are JCPenney, Kaufmann's and Sears.

Eastview Mall, on SR 96 near I-490 in Victor, has a JCPenney, Kaufmann's and Sears among its 106 stores. Northeast on SR 104 is the Irondequoit Mall, which has JCPenney and Sears. Marketplace Mall, at W. Henrietta and Jefferson roads in Henrietta, has a JCPenney and 147 other stores.

Discounted merchandise can be found at the 70 stores of the Outlet Centre at Southtown Plaza, 3333 W. Henrietta Rd. at Jefferson Road, and the 27 stores at the Panorama Outlet Mall and Plaza, 3 miles east of I-490 on Penfield Road in Penfield.

Antiques and crafts are the specialty at Craft Company No. 6, 785 University Ave., and Village Gate Square, housed in a renovated 1800s printing factory at 274 N. Goodman St.

CAMPBELL-WHITTLESEY HOUSE MUSEUM, 123 S. Fitzhugh St., is an example of Greek Revival architecture. The house has been restored

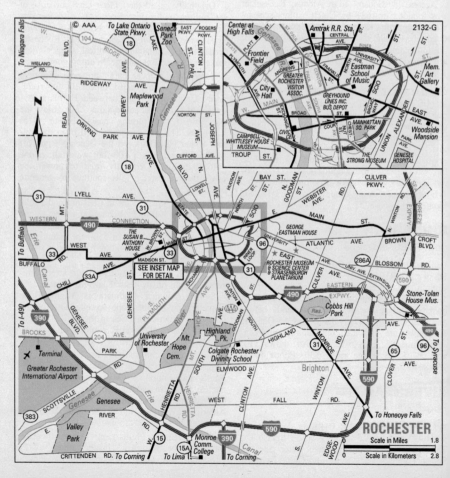

and furnished to illustrate life in a flour miller's household during the early 19th-century Erie Canal "boom-town" period. The 1840 Hoyt-Potter House holds an exhibit gallery.

Allow 1 hour minimum. Guided tours Fri.-Sun. noon-4, Mar.-Dec.; closed major holidays. Last tour begins 1 hour before closing. Admission $3; ages 8-18, $1. Combination admission with the Stone-Tolan House Museum $5; ages 8-18, $1.50. Phone (716) 546-7029.

CENTER AT HIGH FALLS, 60 Browns Race, is downtown along the Genesee River. An educational and entertainment complex, the Center's neighborhood was once the country's flour milling center. Interactive 3-D exhibits trace Rochester's development, an art gallery presents works by local artists, and visitors can walk three stories beneath street level through Triphammer Forge, the ruins of an 1816 factory. A pedestrian bridge provides scenic views of High Falls, while a short hike leads to an observation deck.

The Laser, Light & Fireworks Spectacular floods the 96-foot falls with dancing lights mid-May to early October (weather permitting); phone ahead for schedule. Guided tours are available by appointment. Food is available. Allow 1 hour, 30 minutes minimum. Tues.-Sat. 10-4, Sun. noon-4; closed major holidays. Schedule and hours are extended mid-May to early Oct.; phone ahead. Free. Phone (716) 325-2030.

DURAND-EASTMAN PARK, 7 mi. n. off I-590, has a 2-mile frontage on Lake Ontario. Part of the Monroe County Arboretum, the park contains an 18-hole golf course and a large collection of flowering wild crab apples. Daily 10 a.m.-11 p.m. Free. Phone (716) 342-9810.

★**GENESEE COUNTRY VILLAGE AND MUSEUM**—*see Mumford p. 104.*

★**GEORGE EASTMAN HOUSE** is at 900 East Ave. This 50-room mansion, once occupied by George Eastman, founder of Eastman Kodak Co., has been restored to its early 1900s appearance. Formal gardens surround the mansion. The International Museum of Photography and Film houses changing displays of photography, film, technology and related literature. The Dryden Theater presents evening film programs Wednesday through Saturday at 8.

Allow 2 hours minimum. Daily 10-4:30, in May; Tues.-Sat. 10-4:30 (also Thurs. 4:30-8), Sun. 1-4:30, rest of year. Closed Jan. 1, Thanksgiving and Dec. 25. Garden tours are given Tues.-Sat. at 10:30 and 2, Sun. at 2, May-Sept. Admission $6.50; over 59 and students with ID $5; ages 5-12, $2.50. Film programs $5. AE, MC, VI. Phone (716) 271-3361.

HIGHLAND PARK, off I-490 exit 12 or 14 following signs to entrance, contains botanic gardens, a conservatory and a collection of more than 1,200 lilac bushes. Allow 1 hour, 30 minutes minimum. Park open daily 10 a.m.-11 p.m. Conservatory open Wed.-Sun. 10-6 (also Wed. 6-8 p.m.), May-Oct.; Wed.-Sun. 10-4, rest of year. Free. Phone (716) 244-8079.

MAPLEWOOD PARK, Lake Ave., contains one of the nation's largest municipal rose gardens. Allow 1 hour minimum. Daily 10 a.m.-11 p.m. Free. Phone (716) 647-2379.

MEMORIAL ART GALLERY, 500 University Ave., features art works spanning 50 centuries. Notable artists whose works are displayed include Mary Cassatt, Paul Cézanne, Winslow Homer, Henri Matisse and Claude Monet. Changing exhibitions also are featured. Food is available. Wed.-Fri. 10-4, Sat. 10-5, Sun. noon-5, Tues. noon-9; closed major holidays. Admission $5; over 61 and college students with ID $4; ages 6-18, $3. All admissions $2 Tues. after 5. MC, VI. Phone (716) 473-7720, or TDD (716) 473-6152.

[SAVE] ★**ROCHESTER MUSEUM & SCIENCE CENTER,** 657 East Ave., provides visitors the opportunity to explore science and technology, the natural environment and the cultural heritage of the region. The museum has family-oriented activities and permanent and changing exhibits. Highlights include a Haudenosaunee (Iroquois) collection of artifacts. Family programs and activities for children are offered on weekends and school holidays. Food is available.

Allow 2 hours, 30 minutes minimum. Mon.-Sat. 9-5, Sun. noon-5; closed Thanksgiving and Dec. 25. Admission $6; senior citizens and college students with ID $5; ages 3-18, $4. DS, MC, VI. Phone (716) 271-1880.

CUMMING NATURE CENTER— *see Naples p. 104.*

Strasenburgh Planetarium, 657 East Ave., presents large-format science/nature films in the Star Theater. Family oriented, current events star shows, and laser sound-light shows also are presented. "I See the Sky" is designed for children ages 3-5 and is offered Saturdays at 10. The observatory is open May-Oct.; phone for schedule. Shows are presented daily; phone for times. Closed Thanksgiving and Dec. 25. Admission $6; college students with ID $5; over 59 and under 18, $3. Prices vary with type of show. Under 5 are not admitted to evening shows. DS, MC, VI. Phone (716) 271-1880 or 271-4552, ext. 411.

SEABREEZE PARK/RAGING RIVERS WATER PARK, off I-590 and SR 104 at Culver Rd., is an amusement and water park with roller coasters, water slides, children's rides, a classic wooden carousel and a log flume. Live shows are presented.

Allow 4 hours minimum. Daily noon-10, mid-June through Labor Day; Sat.-Sun. noon-10, May 1 to mid-June. Ride and slide pass $14.50, under 48 inches tall $10.50. Admission after 5 p.m. $8.95. Admission Plus Pass includes two ride tickets $5.95, under age 2 free. DS, MC, VI. Phone (716) 323-1900.

SENECA PARK ZOO, 2222 St. Paul St., along the Genesee River Gorge, features a Rocky Coasts Exhibit which offers underwater viewing of polar bears, sea lions and penguins. The zoo also houses African elephants and Bornean orangutans. Allow 1 hour minimum. Mon.-Fri. 10-5, Sat.-Sun. 10-5, Memorial Day-Labor Day; daily 10-4, rest of year. The grounds are open 1 hour later. Admission $4; over 59, $3; ages 4-12, $2. Phone (716) 467-9453.

STONE-TOLAN HOUSE MUSEUM, 2370 East Ave., is an early 19th-century rural tavern and farmhouse, furnished to reflect frontier life. Guided tours Fri.-Sun. noon-4, Mar.-Dec. Last tour begins 1 hour before closing. Admission $3; ages 8-18, $1. Combination admission with the Campbell-Whittlesey House Museum $5; ages 8-18, $1.50. Phone (716) 546-7029.

SAVE ★ **THE STRONG MUSEUM**, One Manhattan Sq., features a variety of interactive learning environments including a "Sesame Street" exhibit where visitors can appear on a television screen with characters from the show. Children can scan groceries, climb the food pyramid in a child-sized supermarket or visit an old-fashioned ice-cream fountain. The museum's collections include dollhouses, toys, miniatures, home furnishings and a comprehensive doll collection. A glass atrium features a historic street scene, vintage operating diner and a 1918 carousel.

Allow 3 hours minimum. Mon.-Sat. 10-5 (also Fri. 5-8), Sun. noon-5; closed Jan. 1, Thanksgiving and Dec. 25. Admission $6; over 62 and students with ID $5; ages 3-17, $4. DS, MC, VI. Phone (716) 263-2702 or TDD (716) 712-2702.

SAVE **THE SUSAN B. ANTHONY HOUSE**, 17 Madison St., was the home of the well-known civil rights leader during the most politically active period of her life. It also was the site of her famous arrest for voting in 1872. Guided tours of the red brick Victorian house feature personal items and a collection of suffrage material. A visitor center provides additional exhibits.

Tues.-Sun. 11-5, Memorial Day-Labor Day; Wed.-Sun. 11-4, rest of year. Admission $6; over 65, $4.50; students with ID $3; under 13, $2. DS, MC, VI. Phone (716) 235-6124.

VICTORIAN DOLL MUSEUM AND CHILI DOLL HOSPITAL—*see North Chili p. 157.*

WOODSIDE MANSION is at 485 East Ave. The Greek Revival mansion, built in 1840, now serves as headquarters of the Rochester Historical Society. A distinctive feature is the house's round, glazed cupola set on a square pedestal surrounded by balustrades. Rooms display portraits, period furnishings and costumes. An enclosed perennial garden laid out in parterres is beyond the rear veranda. The collections include a reference library, archives and genealogical information.

Allow 1 hour minimum. Mon.-Fri. 10-4 or by appointment; closed holidays. Admission $2; over 59 and students age 18-21 with ID $1.50; high school students with ID $1; ages 8-15, 50c; under 8, 25c. Phone (716) 271-2705.

ROME (D-8) pop. 44,400, elev. 435'

Long before the Europeans discovered Rome, it was called *De-O-Wain-Sta*, an American Indian term meaning "the carrying place." In the city's center is a portage on the only practical water route south of the St. Lawrence River, which connected the Great Lakes with the Hudson River.

Francis Bellamy, author of the "Pledge of Allegiance to the Flag," is buried in the Rome cemetery. The Tomb of the Unknown Soldiers of the American Revolution is next to the city hall at 207 N. James St. It was designed by Lirimer Rich, who also planned the Tomb of the Unknown Soldier in Arlington National Cemetery in Virginia.

The Tug Hill plateau north of Rome receives up to 200 inches of snow a year. This region is renowned for its skiing, snowmobiling and year-round hunting and fishing.

Rome Chamber of Commerce: 139 W. Dominick St., Rome, NY 13440; phone (315) 337-1700.

ERIE CANAL VILLAGE, 3 mi. w. on SR 49 at 5789 Rome-New London Rd., is a restoration of an 1840 community with museums and restored buildings. Demonstrations, audiovisual programs and farm, canal and Americana exhibits are featured. A 30-minute horse-drawn packet boat ride along a restored part of the canal also is offered. Allow 1 hour, 30 minutes minimum.

Tues.-Thurs. 10-5, Fri.-Sun. 10-6, Memorial Day-Labor Day; Sat.-Sun. 10-5, day after Labor Day-Oct. 31. Admission $6; over 61, $5; ages 4-17, $4. Boat ride $3. AE, MC, VI. Phone (315) 337-3999.

FORT RICKEY CHILDREN'S DISCOVERY ZOO is 3 mi. w. on SRs 46 and 49. Hands-on presentations and two petting areas allow children to interact with animals. Displayed are such animals as bobcats, spider monkeys, llamas, bison and owls. A reptile building includes pythons, lizards and a boa constrictor. Children also can enjoy pony rides, pedal boats, a playground, a wet play fountain, a "ball crawl" and a catfish feeding area. Picnicking is permitted. Food is available.

Allow 1 hour, 30 minutes minimum. Daily 10-5:30, mid-June through Labor Day; Sat.-Sun. 10-5, mid-May to mid-June. Admission $7.50; over 64 and ages 2-12, $5.50. MC, VI. Phone (315) 336-1930.

FORT STANWIX NATIONAL MONUMENT—*see place listing p. 86.*

RISKANY BATTLEFIELD, 6 mi. e. on SR 69, is marked by a granite shaft. On Aug. 6, 1777, in the "bloodiest battle of the Revolution," a force of Mohawk Valley militiamen en route to relieve Fort Stanwix was ambushed by a large force of Tories and Indians. The Colonists, under Gen. Nicholas Herkimer and their Oneida Indian Nation allies, were badly mauled in the 6-hour battle. Guided tours and a good view of the valley are available.

Allow 30 minutes minimum. Wed.-Sat. and Mon. holidays 9-5, Sun. 1-5, Memorial Day-Columbus Day. Free. Phone (315) 768-7224.

ROME-BOONVILLE GORGE, traversed by SR 46, is a narrow valley from Rome to North Western and a gorge from North Western to Boonville. Portions of the Black River Canal can be seen along the drive.

ROMULUS (E-6)
pop. 2,500, elev. 717'

MISTY MEADOW FARM is off New York State Thruway (I-90) exit 41, 15 mi. s. on SR 414, then 2 mi. e. to 2828 Vineyard Rd. Misty Meadow is a working farm where visitors learn first-hand about agriculture. Hundreds of farm animals can be held and fed. Guided barn tours, narrated haywagon rides and a hay jump also are available. A sunflower maze and the picking of sunflowers can be enjoyed in season. Food is available.

Allow 1 hour minimum. Tues.-Sat. 11-4, last week of June-Labor Day; closed July 4. Admission $4.50; under 12, $3.50. Phone (607) 869-9243.

WINERIES

Goose Watch Winery is 2.5 mi. s. of jct. CR 124 at 5480 SR 89. Open daily 10-5:30. Tours Sat.-Sun. at 1 and 3. Phone (315) 549-2599.

Swedish Hill Vineyard and Winery is .5 mi. s. of jct. SR 336 at 4565 SR 414. Tours are given Mon.-Fri. at 1 and 3, Sat.-Sun. at noon, 2 and 4, May-Oct. Phone (315) 549-8326.

ROUSES POINT (A-11)
pop. 2,400, elev. 117'

Rouses Point is less than a mile south of the Canadian border; a U.S. Customs and Immigration Service office is in the village. At nearby Island Point are the ruins of Fort Montgomery, which replaced Fort Blunder. The construction of Fort Blunder was abandoned in 1818 when it was learned that the land belonged to Canada. Vermont can be reached via the Korean Veterans Memorial Bridge.

Northern Tier Chamber of Commerce: P.O. Box 44, Rouses Point, NY 12979; phone (518) 297-3040.

Shopping areas: An Ammex Tax & Duty Free Shop is on Five Lake Street and SR 9B.

ROXBURY (F-9) elev. 1,495'

RECREATIONAL ACTIVITIES
Skiing

- **Ski Plattekill**, Plattekill Mountain Rd., P.O. Box 187, Roxbury, NY 12474. Other activities are available. Daily Dec.-Apr. Phone (607) 326-3500 or (800) 633-3275.

RYE—see New York p. 139.

SACKETS HARBOR (C-7)
pop. 1,300, elev. 255'

A resort on eastern Lake Ontario, Sackets Harbor saw one of the first battles in the War of 1812, when five British battleships were repelled by one U.S. ship and a group of farmers on shore with a single cannon. The only British shot to land near the farmers was loaded into the cannon and returned; it took down the mast of the British flagship.

The Old Military Cemetery on Broad Avenue has graves of soldiers from the War of 1812, including that of Gen. Zebulon Pike, discoverer of Pikes Peak.

Self-guiding tours: A pamphlet describing a combination walking and driving tour past the historic buildings and sites of Sackets Harbor is available for a fee at the Sackets Harbor Visitors Center in the Sacket Mansion on West Main Street.

SACKETS HARBOR BATTLEFIELD STATE HISTORIC SITE, at the village, was the site of two battles in the War of 1812, during which Sackets Harbor served as headquarters for the Army of the Northern Frontier and the Navy of the Great Lakes. The restored commandant's house dates from 1850. Behind the house the 1812 Navy Exhibit depicts a sailor's life aboard the *Jefferson* during the war. Thursday through Sunday in June and July an 1812 living-history encampment features an army squad demonstrating such tasks as musket firing and cooking.

Guided and self-guiding walking tours and lectures about building restoration are offered. An archeological walking tour brochure is available. Allow 1 hour minimum. Battlefield open daily 8-dusk. Museums open Wed.-Sat. 10-5, Sun. 1-5, mid-May through Labor Day. Last tour begins 1 hour before closing. Admission $1, under 12 free. Phone (315) 646-3634.

SAG HARBOR (H-5)
pop. 2,100, elev. 10'

Sag Harbor's sheltered position between the North and South Forks of Long Island made it important from its earliest days. As early as 1707 it had assumed such stature as a port that the British Crown appointed an officer to stop the "running of illicit cargos into Sagg Harbour, the principal port of Long Island." The town was one of the first two ports of entry created by Congress in 1789.

The whaling industry was of primary importance to Sag Harbor's development. During this period the town was the source of many real and imagined heroes, including those of the sea stories of James Fenimore Cooper, who began his first novel in this area in 1824. Sag Harbor ranked as one of the largest whaling ports in the world before the industry died in 1871.

Antique hunters have long since replaced whale hunters. The streets of the town's historic district contain interesting buildings ranging from simple weathered saltbox cottages to the more ornate houses of its wealthy past. *Also see Long Island p. 100.*

Sag Harbor Chamber of Commerce: 459 Main St., P.O. Box 116, Sag Harbor, NY 11963; phone (631) 725-0011.

CUSTOM HOUSE, Main and Garden sts., is the restored home of a customs officer and postmaster of Sag Harbor in the late 1700s and early 1800s. Original and restored furnishings and artifacts are displayed. Allow 30 minutes minimum. Tues.-Sun. 10-5, July-Aug.; Sat.-Sun. 10-5, May-June and Sept.-Oct. Admission $3; senior citizens and ages 7-14, $1.50. Phone (631) 692-4664.

SAG HARBOR WHALING MUSEUM is on Main St. opposite the library. Exhibits include whaling equipment, scrimshaw, oil paintings, ships models, fishing gear, logbooks and other objects connected with Colonial eastern Long Island. Allow 30 minutes minimum. Mon.-Sat. 10-5, Sun. 1-5, May 15-Sept. 30. Admission $3; over 59, $2;

DID YOU KNOW

The Stars and Stripes
was flown in battle
for the first time
at Fort Stanwix
in Rome.

---

ages 6-13, $1; physically impaired free. Phone (631) 725-0770.

ST. JOHNSVILLE (E-9) pop. 1,800

Situated in the Mohawk Valley, St. Johnsville was first home to the Dutch in the mid-1600s, followed by the Palatine who were driven from their home along the Rhine River in Germany. They called their new home "the Promised Land" because the area resembled their homeland.

FORT KLOCK HISTORIC RESTORATION, 2 mi. e. on SR 5, is a fortified 1750 farmhouse built for trading and defense purposes. Partially furnished with antiques, the main house contains exhibits relating to rural 18th-century life. A schoolhouse, Dutch barn and blacksmith shop are next to the house. Picnicking is permitted. Allow 1 hour minimum. Tues.-Sun. 9-5, Memorial Day to mid-Oct. Admission $1; ages 10-15, 50c. Phone (518) 568-7779.

MARGARET REANEY MEMORIAL LIBRARY AND MUSEUM, 3 blks. e. of Main St. at 19 Kingsbury Ave., was built in 1909. Among the many historical displays are Civil War items, period rooms and farm and trade tools. The library contains approximately 25,000 volumes. Allow 1 hour minimum. Mon. and Fri. 9:30-5 and 6:30-8:30, Tues.-Wed. 9:30-5, Thurs. 1-5, Sat. 9:30-noon. Free. Phone (518) 568-7822.

SALAMANCA (F-3)
pop. 6,600, elev. 1,389'

Salamanca's Iroquois heritage is evident in the abundance of local artisans who create traditional arts and crafts.

Salamanca Area Chamber of Commerce: 784 Broad St., Salamanca, NY 14779; phone (716) 945-2034.

SALAMANCA RAIL MUSEUM, 170 Main St., is a restored 1912 Buffalo, Rochester and Pittsburgh Railway passenger depot. Artifacts, photographs and videotapes depict the role railroads played in area history. Mon.-Sat. 10-5, Sun. noon-5, May-Sept.; Tues.-Sat. 10-5, Sun. noon-5, in Apr. and Oct.-Dec. Closed Thanksgiving and Dec. 25. Donations. Phone (716) 945-3133.

SENECA-IROQUOIS NATIONAL MUSEUM is off US 17 exit 20 on the Allegany Indian Reservation, Broad St. extension. The museum's collection portrays the life and culture of the Iroquois Indians, with emphasis on the Seneca Nation. Guided tours are available by reservation; reservations must be made 2 weeks in advance. Allow 30 minutes minimum.

Tues.-Sat. 10-5, Sun. noon-5, Apr. 1 to mid-Oct.; Mon.-Fri. 10-5, rest of year; closed major holidays. Hours may vary, phone ahead. Admission $4; senior citizens and students with ID $3; ages 7-13, $2. Phone (716) 945-1738 or 945-1760.

SALEM (D-11) pop. 1,000, elev. 490'

THE BATTEN KILL RAMBLER SCENIC TRAIN departs from Salem Station at 223 Main St./SR 22 and the Cambridge Station at 6 Broad St. The train takes passengers on 2- to 3-hour excursions through the scenic countryside along the Batten Kill River. The train also can be boarded at Cambridge. A fall foliage trip and other special events tours also are available.

Allow 2 hours, 30 minutes minimum. Train departs Thurs. at 10:30 and 1:30, Sat. at 11:30 and 2:30, Sun. at 1, July 1-Sept. 5; Sat. at 11:30, Sun. at 1, May 29-June 30. Fare $10; over 59, $9; ages 3-12, $6. Phone (518) 692-2191.

SANDY CREEK (D-7) pop. 800

RAIL CITY HISTORICAL MUSEUM, 4.4 mi. n. on SR 3 (Seaway Tr.), focuses on the history of railroading and Rail City. A 1950s museum, one of the first in the country, is devoted to preserving historic railroad structures, steam locomotives and rolling stock. The museum features a rebuilt 1873 railroad station, steam-era photographs and displays of rail memorabilia.

Allow 30 minutes minimum. Mon.-Sat. 10-5, Sun. 11-5, June 24-day before Labor Day; Sat. 10-5, Sun. 11-5, June 3-23 and day after Labor Day-Oct. 21. Admission $3; over 55, $2; under 12 free. Phone (315) 387-2932 or 387-5720.

SARANAC LAKE (B-9)
pop. 5,400, elev. 1,535'

First settled in 1819, Saranac Lake was a major tuberculosis treatment center during the late 1800s and early 1900s. The area's mountains and lakes make it a popular vacation site. Many cottages, inns and treatment centers from the late 1800s and early 1900s still stand along Saranac Lake's winding streets.

Saranac Lake Area Chamber of Commerce: 30 Main St., Saranac Lake, NY 12983; phone (518) 891-1990 or (800) 347-1992.

CHARLES DICKERT WILDLIFE MUSEUM, in the library on Main St., exhibits mounted specimens of species native to the Adirondacks. Wed.-Fri. 11-3, July-Aug. Free. Phone (518) 891-4190.

ROBERT LOUIS STEVENSON COTTAGE, off jct. SRs 3 and 86 on Stevenson Ln. via Church and Main sts., was the author's home during the winter of 1887-88. The cottage and original furniture have been preserved. The museum reputedly holds the world's largest collection of Stevenson memorabilia. Tues.-Sun. 9:30-noon and 1-4:30, July 1 to mid-Sept.; by appointment rest of year. Admission $5, under 12 free. Phone (518) 891-1462.

SARATOGA NATIONAL HISTORICAL PARK (E-11)

Saratoga National Historical Park is 8 miles south of Schuylerville on US 4 and embraces partially wooded country along the west side of the Hudson River. The 2,800-acre park is made up of three areas: The Battlefield in Stillwater, the Schuyler House in Schuylerville and the Saratoga Monument in Victory. The park commemorates the Battles of Saratoga, fought on Sept. 19 and Oct. 7, 1777, in which Gen. Horatio Gates' American forces defeated Gen. John Burgoyne's British forces.

On Oct. 17, 1777, Burgoyne surrendered to the Americans near Schuylerville (Old Saratoga), thus preventing British control of the Hudson and the north-south split of the Colonies that would have ensued. Some historians consider this victory to be the turning point of the Revolution. Eight miles from the battlefield stands the Saratoga Monument commemorating Burgoyne's surrender *(see Schuylerville p. 174)*. A 155-foot stone obelisk marks the approximate location where the British army was encamped the week before their surrender. The monument is currently closed for renovations; reopening is scheduled for fall 2000 or spring 2001.

Ironically, the strategic planning and bravery of Benedict Arnold helped to secure an American victory at Saratoga. Just 3 years later he would attempt to turn West Point over to the British; but at the Breymann Redoubt he valiantly galloped through cross-fire and received his second bullet wound in the same leg for the rebel cause. A marble boot, epaulets and an inscription document Arnold's heroics, but tactfully neglect to mention his name.

A visitor center on Fraser Hill, the highest point in the park, affords a view of the battlefield and surrounding area. Theater programs are available daily. Costumed interpreters present living history programs.

A 9.5-mile scenic driving tour has 10 stops in the park. Costumed guides are available July through August at the Nielson House. There is a $4 per private vehicle fee for the tour. Bicycles are permitted on the driving tour roads for $2 per person. Hiking trails also are available for $2 per person; trails are free with the driving tour. Tour and trail charges are good for 7 days. An annual pass is available for $10. The tour road is closed from mid-November through early April due to the harsh weather conditions. **Note:** In 2000, the battlefield's driving tour road, as well as the hiking and riding trails, will be undergoing reconstruction and will be closed. Picnicking is permitted. Allow a full day. Daily 9-5; closed Jan. 1, Thanksgiving and Dec. 25. Park admission and visitor center free. Phone (518) 664-9821, ext. 224.

THE PHILIP SCHUYLER HOUSE, 8 mi. n. of the visitor center on US 4 in Schuylerville, is the restored summer house of Revolutionary War general Philip Schuyler. The rooms of the two-story wooden house are furnished in period. Guided tours are available. Allow 1 hour minimum. Wed.-Sun. 10-4:30, mid-June through Labor Day. Free. Phone (518) 664-9821, ext. 224.

SARATOGA SPRINGS (D-10)
pop. 25,000, elev. 312'

Saratoga Springs is renowned for the beauty of its setting, the reputed health-giving properties of its waters and the gaiety of its summer life. The resort also is gaining popularity as a year-round sports and convention center. Many of the large Victorian homes in the area were built by wealthy horse racing patrons.

Summer activities center on the racetracks. Harness races are held from mid-April to mid-November at Saratoga Harness Racing off Nelson Avenue; phone (518) 584-2110. In August spectators can watch the Thoroughbred races at Saratoga Race Course on Union Avenue; phone (518) 584-6200.

Note: Policies concerning admittance of children to pari-mutuel betting facilities vary. Phone for information.

Winter events focus on Saratoga Springs' many alpine and cross-country skiing facilities and ice skating and snowshoeing areas. The Saratoga Springs Heritage Area and Visitor Center, across from Congress Park, is open all year; phone (518) 587-3241.

Saratoga County Chamber of Commerce: 28 Clinton St., Saratoga Springs, NY 12866; phone (518) 584-3255.

Self-guiding tours: Brochures with maps detailing the points of interest downtown and in the surrounding area are available from the chamber of commerce.

Shopping areas: On SR 50 is the Wilton Mall, which includes JCPenney and Sears.

CASINO AND CONGRESS PARK, off Broadway (US 9), contains an 1870 casino, Italian sculpture gardens, and sculptures by Daniel Chester French, who created the seated Lincoln in the Washington, D.C., memorial. The Historical Society of Saratoga Springs Museum traces Saratoga Springs' growth from a rural village to a flamboyant resort. The Walworth Memorial Museum chronicles the saga of a Saratoga family whose members included authors, lawyers and a murderer.

Allow 30 minutes minimum. Mon.-Sat. 10-4, Sun. 1-4, June-Sept.; Wed.-Sat. 10-4, Sun. 1-4, rest of year. Admission $3, over 59 and students with ID $2, under 12 free. Phone (518) 584-6920.

★**LAKE GEORGE OPERA FESTIVAL** presents performances at the Spa Little Theatre in Saratoga Spa State Park. This regional repertory opera company presents two to four main stage performances each season. The company is committed to the development of young American performers and strives to present a combination of new works as well as traditional musical theater.

Resident performers and guest artists of the American Lyric Theatre also perform concerts. For reservations contact Lake George Opera Festival, P.O. Box 2172, Glens Falls, NY 12801. The season runs late June-early July. Admission $18-$50, with reduced rates for senior citizens and students. MC, VI. Phone (518) 793-3858.

NATIONAL MUSEUM OF DANCE, 1 mi. s. on Broadway (US 9), presents changing exhibits about professional dance. The museum also includes the Dance Hall of Fame. Dance classes can be observed in the Lewis A. Sawyer Studio. Allow 1 hour minimum. Tues.-Sun. 10-5. Admission $3.50; senior citizens and students with ID $2.50; under 12, $1. Phone (518) 584-2225.

NATIONAL MUSEUM OF RACING AND HALL OF FAME, Union Ave. and Ludlow St., contains exhibits about the past, present and future of Thoroughbred racing in America. Displays include paintings and sculptures. The Hall of Fame honors horses, jockeys and trainers. Photographs, videotapes and a skeleton illustrate selective breeding and anatomy. In a simulated racetrack, videotapes of well-known trainers and jockeys explain training and racing techniques. **Note:** The museum will be undergoing renovations and reopening spring 2000.

Allow 1 hour minimum. Daily 9-5, late July-Labor Day; Mon.-Sat. 10-4:30, Sun. noon-4:30, rest of year. Closed Jan. 1, Easter, Thanksgiving and Dec. 25. Admission $5, over 54 and students with ID $3. Phone (518) 584-0400.

SARATOGA SPA STATE PARK, n. of I-87 exit 13N, features bathhouses, mineral springs, walking trails, golf courses and picnic pavilions. The park also includes the Saratoga Performing Arts Center and the Spa Little Theatre. Allow 4 hours minimum. Daily 8 a.m.-dusk. Free. Parking $4, Memorial Day-Labor Day; free rest of year. Phone (518) 584-2535, or 587-3330 for program and ticket information. *See Recreation Chart.*

YADDO, just w. of I-87 Northway exit 14 on Union Ave., is a private estate made available as a working community for visual artists, writers, filmmakers, choreographers and composers. Although the estate is private, the rose gardens are open to visitors daily 8-dusk. Free. Phone (518) 584-0746.

SAUGERTIES (G-10)
pop. 3,900, elev. 159'

Saugerties has changed little since the days when riverboats stopped at its port on the Hudson. Victorian houses and small shops help to maintain the town's rural atmosphere.

OPUS 40 AND QUARRYMAN'S MUSEUM is 6 mi. w. on SR 212 from I-87 exit 20 to Glasco Tpke. following signs. Opus 40 consists of curvilinear pathways, pools and fountains of bluestone fitted to the contour of the land and surrounding a 9-ton monolith. The Quarryman's Museum houses 19th-century tools and household furnishings of the quarryman and other tradesmen.

Allow 1 hour minimum. Fri., Sun., most Sats. and Mon. holidays noon-5, Memorial Day-Oct. 31. Admission $5, over 61 and students with ID $4, under 12 free. Phone (914) 246-3400.

SCHENECTADY (E-10)
pop. 65,600, elev. 246′

On the Mohawk River at the eastern side of the scenic Mohawk Valley, Schenectady was founded in 1661 by Dutch pioneers under the leadership of Arendt Van Curler. The Dutch influence is visible in much of the architecture of the historic Stockade District; this Front and Union streets area includes more than 66 homes and buildings built 1700-1850.

The G.E. Realty Plot historic district, bounded by Lenox Road, Nott Street, West Alley and Union Avenue, has some 130 homes dating from the early 1900s when the neighborhood was created as an exclusive residential community.

Schenectady's downtown renaissance is apparent in such urban revitalization projects as Canal Square, a shopping/office complex; Jay Street, a pedestrian mall with shops and outdoor cafes; and Center City, an indoor ice-skating rink and exhibit hall. Proctor's Theater, a restored 1926 vaudeville house at 432 State St., presents touring Broadway shows, dance and music events and classic films; phone (518) 382-1083.

Scenic attractions include the rose garden in Central Park. Jackson's Garden, 8 acres of formal gardens and woodland, is on the Union College campus; phone (518) 370-6098. Opened in 1795, the college purportedly was the first architecturally-designed campus in the country.

Guided trolley tours of downtown are available by appointment. For further information contact the Schenectady Heritage Area, Tues.-Fri. noon-4, Sat. 9-1; phone (518) 382-5147.

Schenectady County Chamber of Commerce: 306 State St., Schenectady, NY 12305; phone (800) 962-8007.

Self-guiding tours: Brochures detailing self-guiding tours of the city's historic areas are available at the Schenectady County Historical Society Museum or the Schenectady Museum *(see attraction listings)* or the chamber of commerce.

Shopping areas: Mohawk Mall, on SR 5 (State Street), contains 85 stores including Marshall's and Montgomery Ward. Rotterdam Square, off I-890 exit 2A on Campbell Road, has Filene's

and Sears. Specialty stores can be found within a three-block area along Upper Union Street. The Jay Street Pedestrian Walkway is home to numerous shops and eateries.

SCHENECTADY COUNTY HISTORICAL SOCIETY MUSEUM, 32 Washington Ave., is housed in the 1895 Dora Jackson house. The museum contains 18th- and 19th-century furnishings, artifacts of Dutch heritage, oil paintings, an 1834 doll house and a genealogy library. Allow 1 hour minimum. Mon.-Fri. 1-5, every 2nd Sat. 9-1; closed holidays. Admission $2, under 14 with adult $1, family rate $5. Library $5. Phone (518) 374-0263.

SCHENECTADY MUSEUM AND SCHENECTADY HERITAGE AREA VISITORS CENTER, downtown at Nott Terrace Heights between SR 5 and Union St., features a planetarium, a hands-on science exploration area, live reptiles and exhibits about art, regional history and the history of the electrical industry.

Allow 2 hours minimum. Tues.-Fri. 10-4:30, Sat.-Sun. noon-5; closed major holidays. Planetarium shows Sat.-Sun. at 1:30, 2:30 and 3:30. Museum $3.50; ages 4-12, $2. Museum and planetarium $5.50; ages 4-12, $3; family rate $17 (two adults and two children under 18). MC, VI. Phone (518) 382-7890.

SCHOHARIE (F-10)
pop. 1,000, elev. 611′

Schoharie, one of the oldest villages in upstate New York, was called Brunnen Dorf when it was settled in 1712. Many of the town's original buildings remain, including the 1770 George Mann House, the 1772 Swartz Tavern and the 1795 Lasell Hall. One of the oldest buildings in Schoharie County, the restored 1743 Palatine House on Spring Street is known as the Old Lutheran Parsonage; the house serves as a museum.

The old Middleburgh-Schoharie Railroad Complex on Depot Lane has been restored and is a historic cultural center open weekends. It has original buildings and an 1890 passenger/baggage train car that houses a small museum.

Schoharie County Chamber of Commerce: P.O. Box 400, Schoharie, NY 12157; phone (518) 295-7033.

OLD STONE FORT MUSEUM COMPLEX, 1 mi. n. on N. Main St., is a 1772 Dutch Reformed church, stockaded as a fort during the American Revolution. Other buildings include a 1740 Palatine house, an 18th-century Dutch barn, an 1850 law office, an 1860 schoolhouse and a historical and genealogy library. Furnishings, weaponry, automobiles, tools and farm implements are displayed.

Mon.-Sat. 10-5, Sun. noon-5, July-Aug.; Tues.-Sat. 10-5, Sun. noon-5, May-June and Sept.-Oct. Admission $5; over 62, $4.50; ages 6-18, $1.50. MC, VI. Phone (518) 295-7192.

SCHUYLERVILLE (E-11)
pop. 1,400, elev. 146'

Schuylerville, originally a Native American camping ground, was settled by French refugees in 1688 and named Saratoga. In 1831 it was renamed Schuylerville after Revolutionary War general Philip Schuyler.

The turning point of the Revolutionary War took place in Schuylerville in 1777; the British army was trapped after retreating from the Battle of Saratoga *(see Saratoga National Historical Park p. 171).* The field of grounded arms is in the area. The Saratoga Monument commemorates British general John Burgoyne's surrender. The monument is currently closed for renovations; it is expected to reopen in 2000 or 2001.

SEAFORD (I-3) pop. 15,600, elev. 9'

TACKAPAUSHA MUSEUM AND PRESERVE, off Seaford-Oyster Bay Expwy. exit 2E, .5 mi. e. on Sunrise Hwy., then .5 mi. s. on Washington Ave., occupies an 80-acre glacial outwash plain. Museum exhibits focus on the habitats and the life cycles of Long Island animals and plants. Changing videotapes and programs cover a variety of natural history topics. Nature trails traverse the wildlife sanctuary.

Tues.-Sat. 10-4, Sun. 1-4; closed major holidays. Admission $1; under 12, 50c; under 5 free with an adult. Phone (516) 571-7443.

SENECA FALLS (E-6)
pop. 7,400, elev. 473'

Seneca Falls is known as the birthplace of the women's rights movement. Notable former residents include Amelia Bloomer, who popularized the undergarments that bore her name, and Elizabeth Cady Stanton, organizer of the first Women's Rights Convention and an early feminist leader. The nation's first women's rights convention was held in Seneca Falls in 1848.

Several wineries lie within a 20-mile area of scenic SR 89, known as the Cayuga Wine Trail, that skirts the western shore of Cayuga Lake. As its name suggests, the Cayuga-Seneca Canal connects Cayuga and Seneca lakes and passes through diverse landscapes. The double locks at Seneca Falls create a 49-foot change in elevation. Houseboat rentals by the week are available locally; contact the chamber of commerce. *Also see Finger Lakes p. 84.*

Seneca County Chamber of Commerce: P.O. Box 294, Seneca Falls, NY 13148; phone (315) 568-2906 or (800) 732-1848. *See color ad p. 84.*

MONTEZUMA NATIONAL WILDLIFE REFUGE, with its headquarters 5 mi. e. on US 20 and SR 5, covers more than 7,000 acres. A link in the Atlantic flyway, the refuge is a nesting and resting spot for migratory waterfowls and other birds. Visitors can see geese and ducks during the fall and spring migrations. Shorebirds also are numerous in the fall. The refuge also has a resident population of bald eagles.

Facilities include a visitor center, two observation towers, a nature trail, a boat launch and three public fishing sites. A self-guiding automobile tour also is available. Bicycling is not permitted. Daily dawn-dusk. Free. Phone (315) 568-5987.

NATIONAL WOMEN'S HALL OF FAME, 76 Fall St., honors and celebrates the achievements of distinguished American women who have made contributions to the arts, athletics, business, government, philanthropy, humanities, science and education. The stories of its honorees are told through portraits and photographs, biographies, memorabilia and soundtracks. Among the women enshrined in the hall are Susan B. Anthony, Amelia Earhart, Sandra Day O'Connor, Georgia O'Keeffe, Rosa Parks and Eleanor Roosevelt.

Allow 30 minutes minimum. Mon.-Sat. 9:30-5, Sun. noon-4, May-Oct.; Wed.-Sat. 10-4, Sun. noon-4, Feb.-Apr. and Nov.-Dec. Closed major holidays. Admission $3, senior citizens and students with ID $1.50, family rate $7. Phone (315) 568-8060.

SAVE SENECA FALLS HISTORICAL SOCIETY, 55 Cayuga St., was founded in 1896 and occupies an imposing 1880 Queen Anne style mansion called The Becker House Museum. It features Victorian period rooms, exhibits of local history and the Civil War as well as an extensive research library with archives and genealogical records. The society also owns a collection of glass plate negatives relating to the Women's Rights Movement, which many historians consider to have begun in the town. An outdoor garden is home to an 1895 Seth Thomas town clock and a Victorian outbuilding called the Beehive which is set-up as a period general store. Guided tours are available.

Allow 1 hour minimum. Mon.-Fri. 9-5, (also Sat.-Sun. 1-4, June-Sept.); closed most holidays. Admission $3, students with ID $1.50, under 5 free, family rate $7.50. Phone (315) 568-8412.

WOMEN'S RIGHTS NATIONAL HISTORICAL PARK, 136 Fall St., chronicles the development of the women's rights movement. Highlights include changing exhibits, films and summer interpretive talks. Guided tours of the restored 1836 Elizabeth Cady Stanton Home at 32 Washington St. are offered on a varying schedule. Walking tours of Seneca Falls also are available.

Allow 1 hour minimum. Park and visitor center open daily 9-5; closed Jan. 1, Martin Luther King Jr.'s Birthday, Presidents Day, Thanksgiving and Dec. 25. Admission $2, under 16 free. Phone (315) 568-2991.

SETAUKET (H-3)
pop. 13,600, elev. 189'

Setauket is part of a region called The Three Villages, which encompasses Setauket, Stony Brook and Old Field. Revolutionary War spies used the town as a headquarters; the town later became known for shipbuilding. William Sidney Mount captured the area's post-Revolutionary lifestyle on canvas in the mid-1800s from his mobile art studio.

The 1729 Caroline Church of Brookhaven is open on request for a fee; phone (631) 941-4245. Open by appointment from Memorial Day to mid-October, the Sherwood-Jayne House contains a varied furniture collection and hand-painted wall frescoes; phone (631) 692-4664. *Also see Long Island p. 100.*

Self-guiding tours: A brochure outlining a walking and driving tour of Setauket and the surrounding area is available from The Three Village Historical Society office at 93 North Country Rd., P.O. Box 76, East Setauket, NY 11733; phone (631) 751-3730.

THOMPSON HOUSE, 1 mi. n.e. of Stony Brook Station on N. Country Rd., is a typical 17th-century saltbox house with period furnishings. Allow 30 minutes minimum. Fri.-Sun. 1-5, Memorial Day to mid-Oct. Admission $1.50; over 64 and ages 7-14, $1. Phone (631) 692-4664.

SHERBURNE (E-8)
pop. 1,500, elev. 1,048'

ROGERS ENVIRONMENTAL EDUCATION CENTER, 1 mi. w. on SR 80 off SR 12, provides 571 acres of habitat for plants and animals in a variety of aquatic, woodland and field environments. Short nature trails begin at the visitor center. Mounted North American birds are displayed. Six miles of trails are open year-round for hiking, cross-country skiing and snowshoeing. Educational programs are offered on Saturday. Picnicking is permitted.

Allow 1 hour minimum. Visitor center open Mon.-Fri. 8:30-4:45, Sat.-Sun. 1-4:45, June-Aug.; Mon.-Fri. 8:30-4:45, Sat. 1-4:45, rest of year. Grounds and trails open daily dawn-dusk. Free. Phone (607) 674-4017.

SHIRLEY (I-4) pop. 22,900

LONG ISLAND NATIONAL WILDLIFE REFUGE COMPLEX has its headquarters in Wertheim National Wildlife Refuge, .5 mi. s. on Smith St. off Montauk Hwy. Wertheim offers boating, crabbing, fishing and a nature trail which is accessible only by boat.

Morton National Wildlife Refuge is east on SR 27 to exit 9, 2.5 miles north on N. Sea Road (SR 38), then 5 miles east on Noyack Road *(see Southampton p. 175).* Target Rock National Wildlife Refuge is 4.5 miles north on W. Neck Road off SR 25A in Huntington village, then 3 miles east on Lloyd Harbor Road and Target Rock Road to the refuge entrance. Walking trails travel through hardwood forests and formal gardens and past a pond and Huntington Bay.

Refuges open daily 30 minutes before dawn-30 minutes after dusk. Admission to Target Rock and Morton refuges $4 per private vehicle, $2 each for persons on bicycles or on foot, over 61 free. Admission to Wertheim refuge free. Phone (631) 286-0485.

MANOR OF ST. GEORGE is off SR 27 (Sunrise Hwy.), 3.2 mi. s. on William Floyd Pkwy. On a 127-acre site overlooking Great South Bay, the three-story manor house displays furnishings from the early 1800s and paintings and documents concerning the estate, which was granted to Col. William Tangier Smith by the British Crown in 1693. Allow 30 minutes minimum. Wed.-Sun. 9-5, May-Oct. Free. Phone (631) 281-5034.

SKANEATELES (E-7)
pop. 2,700, elev. 903'

MID-LAKES NAVIGATION CO., 1 blk. w. of jct. SRs 321 and 20 at 11 Jordan St., offers sightseeing cruises. Dinner, lunch and wine tasting cruises also are available. A mailboat cruise leaves daily at 10 a.m., July-Aug. Mailboat cruise $16; under 12, $10. AE, MC, VI. Phone (315) 685-8500 or (800) 545-4318.

SLEEPY HOLLOW—
see New York p. 139.

SOUTHAMPTON (H-5)
pop. 4,000, elev. 45'

Settled in 1640 by English colonists from Massachusetts, Southampton is one of the oldest English settlements in New York. In the mid-19th century the proximity of its scenery and beaches to New York City began to draw summer visitors, who boarded with farmers and fishermen. The coming of the railroad to Southampton in 1870 brought thousands more persons, who began to buy land and build estates.

Soon the "Hamptons" gained the reputation as one of the East Coast's principal resorts for the wealthy and famous. The residents of the luxurious beachfront homes along Gin and Meadow lanes rub elbows with tourists and young professionals from the city as they shop at the boutiques and local branches of New York City stores along Job's Lane and Main Street.

In spite of the modern lines of some of the luxurious beach "cottages," Southampton Village has managed to retain much of its past. Roads with names like Ox Pasture and Meeting House

Lane are lined with pleasant houses ranging in style from Colonial cedar shake to Victorian gingerbread.

The descendants of the Shinnecock Indians, who welcomed the first settlers, have a reservation next to the town off SR 27A. *Also see Long Island p. 100.*

Southampton Chamber of Commerce: 76 Main St., Southampton, NY 11968; phone (631) 283-0402.

Self-guiding tours: Information about self-guiding tours of Southampton by car, bicycle or foot is available from the chamber of commerce. Information also is available from the Southampton Historical Museum and Colonial Society *(see attraction listing).*

MORTON NATIONAL WILDLIFE REFUGE, e. on SR 27 to exit 9, 2.5 mi. n. on N. Sea Rd. (SR 38), then 5 mi. e. on Noyack Rd., is a feeding, resting and nesting area for migratory birds on the Atlantic flyway, particularly for endangered piping plovers, least terns and ospreys. The refuge offers bird-watching, fishing, hiking and a visitor center. A nature trail traverses a forest and field, past wetlands and onto a bay beach. For further information contact the Refuge Manager, Wertheim National Wildlife Refuge, Box 21, Shirley, NY 11967.

Daily 30 minutes before dawn-30 minutes after dusk; public access is sometimes restricted. Admission $4 per private vehicle, $2 each for persons on bicycles or on foot, over 61 free. Phone (631) 286-0485. *See also Long Island National Wildlife Refuge Complex attraction listing in Shirley p. 175.*

THE OLDE HALSEY HOUSE, .5 mi. s. on S. Main St., is a restored two-story 1648 house that is deemed the oldest frame house in the state. Built by one of the original settlers, Thomas Halsey, it contains 17th- and 18th-century furnishings. Behind the house is a Colonial herb garden. Allow 30 minutes minimum. Tues.-Sun. 11-4:30, mid-June to mid-Sept. Admission $2; under 12, 50c. Phone (631) 283-3527 or 283-1612.

PARRISH ART MUSEUM AND ARBORETUM, 25 Job's Ln., displays 19th- and 20th-century American art, including a collection of William Merritt Chase and Fairfield Porter. The grounds include an arboretum and statuary. Allow 1 hour minimum. Mon.-Tues. and Thurs.-Sat. 11-5, Sun. 1-5, mid-June to mid-Sept.; Thurs.-Sat. and Mon. 11-5, Sun. 1-5, rest of year. Admission $2, senior citizens $1, students with ID and under 12 free. Phone (631) 283-2118.

SOUTHAMPTON HISTORICAL MUSEUM AND COLONIAL SOCIETY, off Main St. at 17 Meeting House Ln., consists of an 1843 whaling captain's home and 11 other buildings, including blacksmith, carpentry, cobbler and harness shops, a drugstore, a carriage house, an 1890s saloon

and a country store housed in a pre-Revolutionary barn. A whaling exhibit, one-room schoolhouse and two original outhouses also are displayed.

Allow 1 hour minimum. Tues.-Sun. 11-5, June 12 to mid-Sept. Admission $3; under 12, 50c. Phone (631) 283-2494, 283-0605 or 283-1612.

SPRINGFIELD CENTER (E-9)

★ **GLIMMERGLASS OPERA,** on Lake Otsego, 2 mi. s.w. on SR 80, features four operas performed in repertory at the Alice Busch Opera Theater. The theater has side walls that open to the landscape. Theater tours are given by appointment; donations are requested. Opera previews are given 1 hour before performances. For further information contact Glimmerglass Opera, P.O. Box 191, Cooperstown, NY 13326.

Allow 1 hour minimum for tour; 2 hours, 30 minutes to 3 hours for performances. Performances July-Aug. Tickets $20-$80; previews are free. AE, DS, MC, VI. Phone (607) 547-2255.

STERLING (D-6)
pop. 3,000, elev. 320'

STERLING RENAISSANCE FESTIVAL is held off SR 104A at 15431 Farden Rd., following festival signs. The festival presents costumed minstrels and players, jousting, street theater, plays, games, madrigals, food and puppet shows, and crafts reminiscent of Renaissance England. Allow 3 hours minimum. Sat.-Sun. 10-7, July 1-Aug. 13. Admission $12.99; ages 6-12, $5.99. AE, MC, VI. Phone (315) 947-5783.

STONY BROOK (H-4) pop. 13,700

Settled by New Englanders in 1665, Stony Brook developed into a prosperous farming community whose economy was supplemented in the early 1800s by shipping and shipbuilding.

In 1940 Ward Melville sponsored the rehabilitation of Stony Brook's Main Street. The crescent-shaped shopping center was designed around a Republican-style post office overlooking a 2-acre village green on Stony Brook Harbor. Visitors can watch a mechanical, carved wooden eagle atop the building flap its wings on the hour. *Also see Long Island p. 100.*

Self-guiding tours: Free brochures outlining a walking tour of Stony Brook's historic district are available in the shops at the Stony Brook Village Center on Main Street or by contacting the Ward Melville Heritage Organization, Box 572, Stony Brook, NY 11790; phone (631) 751-2244.

DISCOVERY WETLANDS CRUISE, departing from the waterfront dock on Shore Rd., offers a 90-minute pontoon boat cruise through the wetlands off the historic village of Stony Brook. Highlights include views of area cottages and estates, birds and waterfowl in addition to insights into the area's history, geology and ecology. Trips depart daily at high tide, May-Oct.; closed holidays. Fare $15; under 13, $9. MC, VI. Phone (631) 751-2244.

THE MUSEUMS AT STONY BROOK, Main St. and SR 25A at 1208 SR 25A, is a 9-acre complex with exhibits of 19th- and 20th-century American art and history. In addition to museums and historic buildings, the complex also encompasses gardens and a family burial ground dating from 1796.

Allow 2 hours, 30 minutes minimum. Mon.-Sat. 10-5, Sun. noon-5, July-Aug. and in Dec.; Wed.-Sat. and Mon. holidays 10-5, Sun. noon-5, rest of year. Closed Jan. 1, Thanksgiving and Dec. 24-25. Admission $4; over 59, $3; students with ID and ages 6-17, $2. Phone (631) 751-0066.

Art Museum presents changing exhibits of works by 19th- and 20th-century American artists.

Carriage Museum has eight galleries displaying approximately 90 horse-drawn wagons and sleighs, including European royal coaches, firefighting equipment and gypsy wagons.

History Museum, in a renovated lumber mill, has the Antique Decoy and Miniature Room galleries, and changing exhibits about American history.

Historic Buildings include the blacksmith shop, one-room schoolhouse, a 1794 barn and an 1867 carriage shed.

STONY BROOK GRIST MILL, on Harbor Rd. off Main St., is a working 1751 grist mill. A rare example of Dutch framing, the site is run by a miller as it was in the 18th and 19th centuries. Allow 30 minutes minimum. Wed.-Sun. noon-4:30; June-Aug.; Sat.-Sun. noon-4:30, Apr.-May and Sept.-Nov. Admission $1; under 12, 50c. Phone (631) 751-2244.

STONY POINT—
see New York p. 140.

SYRACUSE (E-7)
pop. 163,900, elev. 522′

The growth of Syracuse as a prominent city is due to its geographic location and geologic wealth. In 1570 the Onondagas Indian chief Hiawatha chose the site as the location of the capital of the Iroquois Confederacy. The Jesuits founded a mission and fort called Fort Ste. Marie de Gannentaha in the area in 1656. Indian hostility caused the fort to be abandoned after 2 years.

Salt first brought the Indians and the French to the shores of Onondaga Lake; the first Anglo-American settlers came to boil the brine in 1788. The city of Syracuse was founded in 1805 and for many years supplied the bulk of the salt used in America.

Syracuse's American Indian population is concentrated south of the city in Nedrow at the Onondaga Indian Reservation, which is the seat of the Iroquois Confederacy.

Syracuse University, founded in 1870, occupies a 640-acre campus; its most outstanding feature is the Carrier Dome.

Greater Syracuse Chamber of Commerce: 572 S. Salina St., Syracuse, NY 13202; phone (315) 470-1800.

Self-guiding tours: Brochures detailing a walking tour of the downtown area are available through the Syracuse Urban Cultural Park Visitor Center at the Erie Canal Museum *(see attraction listing).* Interpretive signs are located throughout the downtown area, describing the history of the city and the people who built it.

Shopping areas: Downtown Syracuse offers the historic Armory Square District with quaint shops and restaurants. Six major shopping malls serve Syracuse's outlying suburbs. Camillus Mall, 5301 W. Genesee St. in Camillus, has 75 stores including Ames, The Bon-Ton and Sears. Carousel Center, off I-81 exit 23, features more than 170 stores and shops including JCPenney, Kaufmann's and Lord & Taylor as well as cinemas and restaurants.

Fayetteville Mall, at the intersection of SR 5, E. Genesee and N. Burdick streets in Fayetteville, features Royal Discount Books, The Avenue Plus and T.J. Maxx as well as a merry-go-round and a food court. Great Northern Mall, at the intersection of SRs 481 and 31, has The Bon-Ton, Dick's Clothing and Sporting Goods, Kaufmann's, Sears, specialty shops, cinemas and a food court.

BURNETT PARK ZOO is off I-90 exit 36, then take I-81 s. to exit 22; from the e. take I-690 exit 10, following signs; from the w., take I-690 exit 8, following signs. The zoo displays domestic and exotic animals in simulated natural settings. Elephants are exhibited daily (weather permitting) and there is a Siberian tiger exhibit. The veterinary clinic and kitchen can be viewed through windows.

Allow 2 hours minimum. Daily 10-4:30; closed Jan. 1, Thanksgiving and Dec. 25. Admission $5; over 61 $3; ages 5-14, $2. Phone (315) 435-8511.

ERIE CANAL MUSEUM, 318 Erie Blvd. E., is in the 1850 Weighlock Building. Designed to weigh 100-foot-long canal boats, this is believed the only surviving building of its kind. The museum features the canal boat *Frank Thomson,* changing exhibits and the Urban Cultural Park Visitor Center *(see Self-guiding tours).* Flash photography is not permitted. Allow 1 hour minimum. Daily 10-5; closed major holidays. Donations. Phone (315) 471-0593.

EVERSON MUSEUM OF ART, 401 Harrison St., displays American paintings and sculpture from

Colonial times to the present, and a large ceramics collection. The museum also displays changing exhibits. Food is available. Tues.-Sun. noon-5. Donations. Phone (315) 474-6064.

MID-LAKES NAVIGATION CO. LTD. cruises depart from Dutchman's Landing, 3 mi. w. of Liverpool; take I-90 to exit 38 (SR 57N) to John Glen Blvd., w. to SR 370, then w. on River Road to Hillside Rd. All-day Erie Canal cruises aboard the *City of Syracuse* offer good views of the city along the tree-lined Onondaga Lake portion of the canal. Jazz, brunch, lunch, dinner and sightseeing cruises are available.

Dinner cruises depart daily at 6. All-day cruise $38. Two-hour cruise $13. One-hour cruise $8. Reservations are required. AE, MC, VI. Phone (315) 685-8500 or (800) 545-4318.

MILTON J. RUBENSTEIN MUSEUM OF SCIENCE AND TECHNOLOGY, Franklin St. at W. Jefferson St., is a hands-on science museum with exhibits that explain scientific and technological phenomena. Displays address topics such as animals, chemistry, color, computers, gravity, light, sound and the stars. Demonstrations are offered. The Bristol Omnitheater offers showings on a six-story-high, domed screen.

Museum open Sun.-Thurs. 11-5, Fri.-Sat. 9:30-5. The Silverman Planetarium offers sky shows daily at 11:30, 2:15 and 4:15; special shows for under age 5 are held Sat.-Sun. at 10:30. Phone for Omnitheater schedule. Museum admission $4.75; senior citizens and ages 2-11, $3.75. Planetarium shows $1. Museum and Omnitheater$9.75; senior citizens and ages 2-11, $7.75. DS, MC, VI. Phone (315) 425-9068.

SAVE **THE MUSEUM OF AUTOMOBILE HISTORY,** I-81 exit 19 to 321 N. Clinton St., takes visitors on a ride through history with more than 10,000 displays of automobile memorabilia. Allow 1 hour minimum. Wed.-Sun. 10-5. Admission $4.75; over 65, $3.75; under 16, $2.75. MC, VI. Phone (315) 478-2277.

ONONDAGA HISTORICAL ASSOCIATION MUSEUM, 321 Montgomery St., features a permanent collection of items, paintings, photographs and memorabilia documenting 300 years of Onondaga history. The museum also has changing exhibits. Allow 1 hour minimum. Tues.-Fri. noon-4, Sat. 11-4; closed holidays. Donations. Phone (315) 428-1864.

ONONDAGA LAKE PARK, off I-81 Liverpool exit 24, then 1.5 mi. w. on SR 370W to Onondaga Pkwy., extends 6 mi. along the eastern shore. The park has a marina, a boat launch and athletic fields as well as the original Salt Spring and the Jesuit Well. Tram rides, inline skate rentals and bicycle rentals are available Memorial Day weekend through Columbus Day. The park's Salt Museum contains a replica of a 19th-century salt boiling block and other artifacts. Picnicking is permitted. Food is available.

Park open daily dawn-dusk. Museum open Tues.-Sun. and Mon. holidays noon-5, May-Oct. Free. Phone (315) 453-6712, or 451-7275.

SAINTE MARIE AMONG THE IROQUOIS is off I-81 Liverpool exit 24A, then 1.5 mi. w. on SR 370W to Onondaga Lake Pkwy. This re-creation of a 17th-century Jesuit mission features costumed interpreters who demonstrate traditional cooking, building and harvesting techniques. A re-created Iroquois fishing village is presented. Seasonal programming occurs throughout the year. An orientation center has environmental and American Indian related exhibits.

Allow 1 hour minimum. Wed.-Sat. 10-5, Sun. 12:30-5. Admission $3.50; over 61, $3; ages 5-14, $1.50; family rate $10. A modified schedule with reduced prices is offered Labor Day through Memorial Day; phone for details. DS, MC, VI. Phone (315) 453-6767.

TAPPAN—*see New York p. 140.*

TARRYTOWN—
see New York p. 140.

THOUSAND ISLANDS (B-7)

A French explorer called this region "Thousand Islands," although the islands number more than 1,700. Some of these islands in the St. Lawrence River are mere points of rocks and others are village size, but most can accommodate only a home or summer camp. Numerous stone castles and summer homes dot the islands, and many historical markers commemorate the arrival of the Loyalists to British North America.

The best way to see the islands is to take a boat tour offered by the boat lines described under Alexandria Bay and Clayton *(see place listings pp. 57 and 76)*. Between the spans of the Thousand Islands Bridge is the 1000 Islands Skydeck *(see Alexandria Bay p. 58)*.

ST. LAWRENCE ISLANDS NATIONAL PARK is in the St. Lawrence River between Kingston and Brockville, Ontario, and a 96-acre (39-hectare) area at Mallorytown Landing on the mainland. Part of the Canadian park system, the site consists of 21 widely scattered units of the Thousand Islands. Mallorytown Landing contains the park headquarters, picnic areas, a campground and a beach. A visitor center has displays about the natural history and settlement of the Thousand Islands.

General Information and Activities

Access to the park by private vehicle is available only at the Mallorytown Landing entrance.

The visitor center, staffed by park naturalists, is open daily mid-May through mid-Oct.; phone for hours. Interpretive programs and hikes are conducted periodically on the mainland and on the islands. Provincial fishing licenses are required; visitors must hire or supply their own boats. Semi-primitive campsites are available on a first-come-first-served basis.

ADMISSION is by daily pass $5 per private vehicle, $10 per private vehicle and trailer; annual pass for this park only $30. Seasonal car and trailer pass $60. Island camping (accessible by private boat only) $10. Rates apply mid-May through mid-October and are in Canadian dollars. Phone to verify rates.

PETS are permitted in the park only if they are leashed or otherwise physically restricted; they are not permitted in the beach area.

ADDRESS inquiries to the Superintendent's Office, St. Lawrence Islands National Park, 2 CR 5, RR 3, Mallorytown, ON, Canada K0E 1R0; phone (613) 923-5261.

TICONDEROGA (C-11)
pop. 2,800, elev. 277'

FORT TICONDEROGA—see place listing p. 86.

TICONDEROGA HISTORICAL SOCIETY LIBRARY AND MUSEUM, SR 9N at Montcalm St., is in a reproduction of John Hancock's Boston home. Displays include original and reproduction American furniture, Redford glass and historic own memorabilia. Facing the house is the bronze Liberty Monument by Charles Keck. Wed.-Sat. 10-4. Donations. Phone (518) 585-7868.

TROY (E-11) pop. 54,300, elev. 35'

Troy, an industrial city at the head of Hudson River navigation, was home to the man who inspired the national symbol of Uncle Sam. In the early 1800s meatpacker Sam Wilson's "U.S. Beef" meat stamp was jokingly interpreted as "Uncle Sam's Beef." Life became legend, and the character of Uncle Sam was born.

Troy's Rensselaer Polytechnic Institute is one of the nation's foremost technological institutions of higher learning and one of the oldest engineering schools in the English-speaking world. The school owns and operates Rensselaer Technology Park, the site of a growing number of Troy's high-tech companies.

Troy and neighboring communities form the Hudson-Mohawk Urban Cultural Park, which preserves the historical features at the confluence of the Hudson and Mohawk rivers. Included in the park are waterfalls, 19th-century mill districts and workers' houses, river fronts, canals, warehouses, music halls, churches and merchants' mansions. A 26-mile heritage trail links the various features of the park, and 2nd Street features many fine examples of 19th-century architecture.

An audiovisual program, exhibits and computerized area information kiosks are available Tues.-Sat. 11-6 (also Thurs. 6-8), from the River-Spark Visitor Center, 251 River St., Troy, NY 12180; phone (518) 270-8667.

Rensselaer County Regional Chamber of Commerce: 31 2nd St., Troy, NY 12180; phone (518) 274-7020.

Self-guiding tours: A brochure detailing a self-guiding tour of the Hudson-Mohawk Urban Cultural Park and a brochure detailing a self-guiding walking tour through downtown historic districts and neighborhoods can be obtained at the River-Spark Visitor Center.

HART-CLUETT MANSION, 59 Second St., was built in 1827. The Federal-style mansion contains original and period furnishings, many of which were made locally. The adjoining Carr Building houses changing exhibits, and a research library containing historical information about Rensselaer County. Allow 1 hour minimum. Mansion open Tues.-Sat. 10-4. Research library open Tues.-Fri. 1-4, Sat. 10-4, Feb.-Dec. Closed holidays and Christmas week. Admission $3. Phone (518) 272-7232.

JUNIOR MUSEUM is in North Troy at 282 Fifth Ave., at the corner of 106th St. This hands-on children's museum has changing and participatory exhibits relating to science, history and the

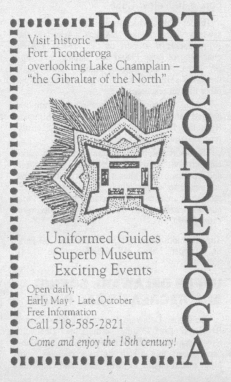

arts. Allow 1 hour minimum. Wed.-Sun. noon-5; closed major holidays. Admission Sat.-Sun. $4, Wed-Fri. $3. under 2 free. Phone (518) 235-2120.

UNCLE SAM TABLET, in Oakwood Cemetery, marks the grave of Samuel Wilson, the original "Uncle Sam." He was an Army beef contractor in the War of 1812; his trademark and caricature eventually became a national symbol. Daily 9-4:30. Free. Phone (518) 272-7520.

TULLY (E-7) pop. 900, elev. 1,251'

SONG MOUNTAIN ALPINE SLIDE, 3 mi. w. of I-81 exit 14, ascends to the summit via chairlift and returns by a 3,000-foot alpine slide for plastic sleds. Water slides, go-carts and miniature golf also are available. Ski facilities and equipment rentals are available in season.

Mon.-Fri. 10-10, Sat. and holidays 9 a.m.-10 p.m., Sun. 9-8, mid-May through Labor Day. All-day, all-inclusive pass $15, under 5 free with an adult on alpine slide. Three-hour all-inclusive pass $12, under 5 free with an adult on alpine slide. One ride $3, under 5 free with an adult. Water slide $2. Go-carts $2. Miniature golf $1. AE, DS, MC, VI. Phone (315) 696-5711 or (800) 677-7664.

TUPPER LAKE (B-9)
pop. 4,100, elev. 1,556'

Tupper Lake, which began as a lumber and sawmill village in the 1890s, is a resort in the Adirondacks; it is part of the Tri-Lakes Area consisting of Lake Placid and Saranac and Tupper lakes. As the logging industry diminished, the town shifted its commercial interests to its other natural resources.

Fishing, swimming and boating opportunities abound at Big Tupper Lake, Lake Simond, Raquette River and Raquette Pond, easily reached from Tupper Lake.

The resort also boasts a municipal beach, park, campground, tennis courts, 18-hole golf course and boat-launching sites. The nearby mountains are suited to skiing, climbing and hiking. Other recreation areas can be found in Adirondack Park (*see Recreation Chart and the AAA Northeastern CampBook*).

Tupper Lake Chamber of Commerce: 60 Park St., Tupper Lake, NY 12986; phone (518) 359-3328.

UPPER DELAWARE SCENIC AND RECREATIONAL RIVER

The Upper Delaware Scenic and Recreational River comprises 73 miles of the Upper Delaware River from just north of Port Jervis, Pa., to Hancock. Along this stretch the river changes from long, placid eddies to swift water and challenging rapids. It is paralleled on the New York side by SR 97, which has several scenic overlooks.

Almost all land along the river is privately owned; public river access areas are located on both the Pennsylvania and New York shores. Private campgrounds and canoe liveries are available near the river.

The Upper Delaware was an important transportation route for American Indians and early settlers. In 1828 the Delaware and Hudson Canal opened, bringing coal-laden boats from the Pennsylvania interior to the port of New York. However, problems soon developed at the point where the canal crossed the river: Slow-moving boats being towed across the river were constantly colliding with the huge log and timber rafts that were coursing down the river to sawmills and shipyards in Trenton, N.J., and Philadelphia. To solve the problem the canal company approved a plan to "build the canal above the water."

John Roebling, who later designed the Brooklyn Bridge, built the Delaware Aqueduct. The aqueduct is considered to be the oldest wire suspension bridge in America. The adjacent tollhouse contains exhibits interpreting the history of the Delaware and Hudson Canal, John Roebling and the Delaware Aqueduct. It is open Saturdays and Sundays, Memorial Day to mid-October.

Area wildlife includes bears, white-tail deer, beavers, otters, muskrats, minks, squirrels and rabbits. Birds include bald eagles, ospreys, great egrets, great blue herons, turkey vultures, Canada geese and several varieties of hawks and ducks.

Recreational opportunities include rafting, canoeing, boating and fishing. National Park Service programs are offered in the summer. Included are cultural and natural history walks, canoeing demonstrations and guided canoe tours

Information stations are located at the public boating access sites in Ten Mile River, Narrowsburg and at Skinner's Falls, as well as in Lackawaxen, Pa.

An information center/bookstore on Main Street in Narrowsburg generally is open daily 9:30-4:30, Memorial Day-Labor Day; Sat.-Sun. 9:30-4:30, mid-Apr. through day before Memorial Day and day after Labor Day to mid-Nov. Phone (914) 252-3947 or (717) 729-7134.

UTICA (E-8) pop. 68,600, elev. 452'

Built on land granted to William Crosby in 1734, Utica was the site of Old Fort Schuyler, erected in 1758. Sparsely settled for many years, Utica did not begin to develop until after the Revolution; its real growth as a commercial and industrial center dates from the completion of the Erie Canal in 1825. Edward A. Hanna Park, downtown, is known for its scenic landscaping.

Mohawk Valley Chamber of Commerce: 520 Seneca St., Utica, NY 13502; phone (315) 724-3151.

THE MATT BREWING CO., Court and Varick sts., demonstrates the process of beer manufacturing and offers trolley rides June through August to the 1888 Tavern, where samples are served. Allow 1 hour minimum. Guided tours daily 10-4, June-Aug.; Mon.-Fri. at 1 and 3, Sat. at 11, 1 and 3, rest of year. Closed major holidays. Tour $3; ages 6-11, $1. Reservations are required Sept.-May. Phone (315) 732-0022.

★ MUNSON-WILLIAMS-PROCTOR ARTS INSTITUTE, 310 Genesee St., is a fine arts center with programs in the visual and performing arts and an art museum. The museum's collections include American art from the Colonial period to the present, with an emphasis on 19th- and 20th-century paintings and sculpture. Works by European artists are displayed, as are examples of graphic and decorative arts. Nearby is Fountain Elms Museum which is housed in an 1850 building. Allow 1 hour, 30 minutes minimum. Tues.-Sat. 10-5, Sun. 1-5. Free. Phone (315) 797-0000.

ONEIDA COUNTY HISTORICAL SOCIETY, 1608 Genesee St., has exhibits about Utica, Oneida County and Mohawk Valley history. A reference library also is available. Allow 1 hour minimum. Tues.-Fri. 10-4:30, Sat. 11-3. Exhibits free; library $5 per day. Phone (315) 735-3642.

UTICA ZOO, Steele Hill Rd., has a variety of animals. Primates are in one building; reptiles and amphibians are in another. The children's zoo has a petting area. Sea lion feedings and demonstrations are held Wed.-Mon. at noon and 3. A playground is on the premises. Food is available. Allow 1 hour, 30 minutes minimum. Daily 10-5; closed Jan. 1, Thanksgiving and Dec. 25. Admission $4.25; over 60, $3.75; ages 4-12, $2.50; free to all Nov.-Feb. Phone (315) 738-0472.

VERONA (E-8) pop. 700

CASINOS

• **Turning Stone Casino** is .5 mi s. on I-90 exit 33 at 5218 Patrick Rd. Daily 24 hours. Phone (315) 361-7711.

VICTOR (E-5) pop. 7,200

GANONDAGAN STATE HISTORIC SITE is w. on CR 41 (Boughton Hill Rd.) to Victor-Bloomfield Rd. On the site of a 17th-century Seneca village are interpretive trails and a visitor center with displays and a half-hour videotape. An exhibit by Seneca artist Carson Waterman focuses on the Iroquois clan system. Allow 1 hour minimum. Trails open daily 8 a.m.-dusk (weather permitting). Visitor center open Wed.-Sun. 9-5, May 15-Oct. 31. Long house open Wed.-Sun. 10-noon and 1-4. Free. Phone (716) 924-5848.

WASHINGTONVILLE (H-10)
pop. 4,900, elev. 310'

WINERIES

• **Brotherhood Winery** (America's Oldest Winery), 2 blks. e. on SR 94 to Brotherhood Plaza Dr. Daily 11-5, May-Oct.; Sat.-Sun. 11-5, rest of year. Closed Jan. 1, Thanksgiving and Dec. 25. Hours may vary; phone ahead to verify schedule. Phone (914) 496-3661.

WATERTOWN (C-7)
pop. 29,400, elev. 454'

During an 1878 county fair F.W. Woolworth tested the idea of selling a fixed-price line of merchandise in a department store. The result of his experiment was the Woolworth store chain. Watertown also is noted as the home of Fort Drum.

Greater Watertown Chamber of Commerce: 230 Franklin St., Watertown, NY 13601; phone (315) 788-4400.

JEFFERSON COUNTY HISTORICAL SOCIETY, 228 Washington St. in the 1878 Paddock Mansion, contains high-Victorian furnishings and decorative art, American Indian artifacts from Jefferson County, historic water turbines, Civil War memorabilia, coverlets and special exhibits. A re-created Victorian garden and a carriage barn with antique automobiles and farm implements also are on the premises. Guided tours available by appointment. Allow 30 minutes minimum. Tues.-Fri. 10-5, Sat. noon-5, May-Nov.; Tues.-Fri. noon-5, rest of year. Closed major holidays. Donations. Phone (315) 782-3491.

THE SCI-TECH CENTER OF NORTHERN NEW YORK, 154 Stone St., is a hands-on science museum. Exhibits focus on light, sound and electricity. Guided tours are available by appointment. Allow 1 hour minimum. Tues.-Sat. 10-4; closed Jan. 1, July 4, Thanksgiving and Dec. 25. Admission $3; ages 3-18, $2; senior citizens $1.50; family rate $10. Phone (315) 788-1340.

THOMPSON PARK, just e. off SR 12, has playground, swimming and tennis facilities. A 35-acre zoo featuring North American species also is featured. Picnicking is permitted. Daily 10-5; closed Thanksgiving and Dec. 25. Park free. Zoo $3; students with ID $2; senior citizens and ages 4-12, $1.50. MC, VI. Phone (315) 782-6180.

RECREATIONAL ACTIVITIES
White-water Rafting

• SAVE **ARO Adventures**, departs from various locations for 4-hour white-water raft trips on the Black River. Write P.O. Box 649, Old Forge, NY 13420. Trips depart Wed.-Mon. in Aug. and Wed.-Sun. in July; weekend trips are available May-June and Sept.-Oct. Phone

MAGICAL THINGS HAPPEN
IN THE LAND OF LIVING COLOUR.

34 parks

Brookies,
Browns, and
Bass

55 golf courses

I t's one of those undiscovered countries – a land of living colour. It's Central New York, and it's all here. Relive America's history at Revolutionary War Fort Stanwix and along the Erie Canal. Dig for diamonds, visit the home of Oz, or learn the heritage of the tenacious Oneida People. Explore our glacier-carved outdoors and cast a fly for a rainbow (trout that is), or visit fabulous Turning Stone Casino Resort.

Season by season, Central New York offers more than you can imagine. Call 1-888-889-6968 or visit us at www.tourismcny.com and we'll send our free travel and accommodations guides along with a little magic.

LIVING COLOUR
CENTRAL NEW YORK

The Oneida Indian Nation   Oneida   Madison   Herkimer   Onondaga   Counties

(315) 369-3536 for reservations, or (800) 525-7238 for information.

Hudson River Rafting Co., departing from the office off I-81 exit 46 (Coffeen St.) to 424 Newell St. Write P.O. Box 47, North Creek, NY 12853. Trips depart Wed.-Fri. and Mon. at 11, Sat.-Sun. at 10 and 1, in Aug.; Wed.-Fri. at 11, Sat.-Sun. at 10 and 1, in July; Fri.-Sun. at 11 (also at 11, Labor Day) in June and Sept.; Sat. at 10 and 1, Fri. and Sun. at 11 (also at 11, Columbus Day) in May and Oct. Phone (315) 782-7881 or (800) 888-7238.

WATERVLIET (E-11)
pop. 11,100, elev. 50′

WATERVLIET ARSENAL MUSEUM, I-787 exit 887, then 1.5 mi. n. to Broadway/SR 32, is the nation's oldest continuously running arsenal. Built in 1813, the arsenal is owned by the government and continues to produce large caliber weapons. Housed in the 1859 cast-iron storehouse, the museum displays cannon and other military equipment from the 19th century through the present. Mon.-Thurs. 10-3. Free. Phone (518) 266-5805

WATKINS GLEN (F-6)
pop. 2,200, elev. 1,008′

At the southern tip of Seneca Lake, Watkins Glen is renowned for its summer auto racing at Watkins Glen International. Long before the roar of cars, this small town's most notable features were the nearby salt wells, which made this region one of the state's major salt producers. *Also see Finger Lakes p. 84.*

Several wineries are located in the area. They are located on either side of Seneca Lake off SRs 14 and 414.

Schuyler County Chamber of Commerce: 100 N. Franklin St., Watkins Glen, NY 14891; phone (607) 535-4300. *See color ad p. 258.*

CAPTAIN BILL'S SENECA LAKE CRUISES depart from the foot of Franklin St. Scenic 10-mile trips are offered; lunch, brunch, dinner and other cruises also are available. Sightseeing departures daily on the hour 10-8, July 1-early Sept.; daily on the hour 11-4, early Sept.-Oct. 15; Mon.-Fri. on the hour 11-4, Sat.-Sun. and holidays on the hour 10-8, May 15-June 30. Sightseeing fare $7.50; under 13, $3.50. AE, DS, MC, VI. Phone (607) 535-4541 or 535-4680.

FARM SANCTUARY is at 3100 Aikens Rd.; take CR 409W (4th St.) 1.5 mi. to SR 23, then w. 8 mi. to Aikens Rd., following signs. This 175-acre working farm is home to hundreds of cows, pigs, turkeys, and goats rescued from slaughterhouses and stockyards and nursed back to health. One-hour guided tours encourage visitors to pet the animals. A visitor center contains two videotapes and photographs.

Tours on the hour Wed.-Sun. 10-4, June-Aug.; Sat.-Sun. 10-4, in May and Sept.-Oct. Tour $2; ages 4-12, $1. Phone (607) 583-2225.

★**WATKINS GLEN STATE PARK** adjoins the village at the s. end of Seneca Lake. The scenic glen, which drops about 400 feet in 2 miles, is highlighted by rock formations and 18 waterfalls; Rainbow Falls is especially lovely. Cliffs rise 300 feet above the stream; a bridge 165 feet above the water spans the glen. Buses to the head of the glen are available for those who wish to avoid climbing.

Allow 1 hour, 30 minutes minimum. Daily 8 a.m.-dusk, mid-May to mid-Oct. Park admission free. Parking $6, mid-June through Labor Day; $5, rest of season. Phone (607) 535-4511. *See Recreation Chart and the AAA Northeastern CampBook.*

WINERIES

- **Chateau Lafayette Reneau**, 7 mi. n. on SR 414. Mon.-Sat. 10-6, Sun. 11-6, Apr.-Oct.; Mon.-Sat. 10-5, Sun. noon-5, rest of year. Phone (607) 546-2062.

WESTFIELD (F-2)
pop. 3,500, elev. 728′

Those who like to walk will find plenty of room in which to travel in Westfield. The Chautauqua Gorge extends 7 miles along a 100-foot-deep gorge between Westfield and Mayville. Barcelona Harbor offers fishing and a boat launch. It is the site of a historical lighthouse. Westfield is part of Chautauqua wine country, and several small wineries west of the city off US 20 offer wine tastings and guided tours in season.

Shopping areas: The Westfield streets are lined with various antiques shops, including Landmark Acres and Priscilla Nixon Antiques on W. Main Rd., Militello Antiques at 31 Jefferson St. and Antique Marketplace, Eley Place, Monroe's Mini Mall, Saraf's Emporium and W.B. Mollard Antiques all on E. Main St.

THE MCCLURG MANSION, jct. US 20 and US 394, was built in 1820 and contains period furniture, a pioneer kitchen, Colonial farm implements, American Indian artifacts and a military exhibit. Tues.-Sat. 10-5; closed most holidays. Admission $1.50; over 59 and students with ID $1; under 12, 50c. Phone (716) 326-2977.

WINERIES

- **Johnson Estate Winery** is 2 mi. w. on US 20 (E. Main Rd.) Guided tours daily on the half-hour 10-5, July-Aug. Phone (716) 326-2191 or (800) 374-6569.
- **Vetter Vineyards** is 3 mi. e. to Prospect Rd., then right .5 mi. to US 20 (E. Main Rd.). Tastings Mon.-Sat. 11-5, Sun. noon-5. Phone (716) 326-3100.

WEST HAVERSTRAW—

see New York p. 141.

WEST POINT (H-10)
pop. 8,000, elev. 10′

BEAR MOUNTAIN STATE PARK is 5 mi. s. off US 9W. The George W. Perkins Memorial Drive winds to the 1,305-foot summit of Bear Mountain, where a tower and observation deck provide views of four states and the Hudson River Valley. Picnicking is permitted. Food is available. Park open daily dawn-dusk. Drive open daily 8-dusk (weather permitting), Apr.-Nov. Tower daily 9-4. Park admission free. Parking $4 Sat.-Sun. in winter. Phone (914) 786-2701. *See Recreation Chart.*

Trailside Museum and Zoo is s. on US 9W near the park entrance. A nature trail leads to animal enclosures, museums, trail-side exhibits, the outer breastworks of Fort Clinton and a statue of Walt Whitman. The museums feature animal habitat displays as well as geological, historical and natural exhibits. Allow 3 hours minimum. Daily 9-5:30, Memorial Day-Labor Day; 9-4:30, rest of year (weather permitting). Admission daily May 1-Labor Day, Sat.-Sun. and holidays rest of year $1, children 50c; otherwise free.

★**UNITED STATES MILITARY ACADEMY** is on the w. bank of the Hudson River off scenic Old Storm King Hwy. (SR 218); the academy also can be reached from US 9W. The post is open daily, but the cadet barracks, mess hall, academic and administration buildings are closed to visitors; driving and parking are permitted in designated areas only. Cadet parades are held on varying days in spring and fall (weather permitting). Guided bus tours *(see color ad p. 492)* are available.

A visitor center (Building 2107) just outside Thayer Gate (South Post) is open daily 9-4:45; closed Jan. 1, Thanksgiving and Dec. 25. Guided 1-hour bus tour Mon.-Sat. 10-3:30, Sun. 11-3:30; 2-hour tour at 11:15 and 1:15, May-Oct. Tours begin at the visitor center, except during home football Sat. and graduation week. One-hour tour $5; under 12, $2.50. Two-hour tour, $7; under 12, $5. Phone the visitor center at (914) 938-2638 for parade dates, or 446-4996 for athletic schedules.

Cadet Chapel contains stained-glass windows and one of the largest church organs in the world. The organ contains more than 18,000 pipes, which range in size from smaller than a pencil to 32 feet long. Allow 30 minutes minimum. Mon.-Sat. 8-4:15, Sun. 1-4:15; closed during special events. Phone (914) 938-2308.

Chapel of the Most Holy Trinity (Catholic) is Norman Gothic in style and is patterned after the St. Ethelred's Carthusian abbey church in England. Daily 9-9; closed during special events. Phone (914) 938-8760.

Jewish Chapel, dedicated in 1984, reflects the Gothic architecture of West Point. Mon.-Fri. 9-4, Sat.-Sun. noon-4; closed during special events. Phone (914) 938-2710.

Old Cadet Chapel is in the Post Cemetery. On the 1836 building's walls are battle flags and marble shields commemorating the American generals of the Revolutionary War, including one for Benedict Arnold. Daily 8-4; closed during special events. Phone (914) 938-2433.

The Site of Fort Clinton is n.e. of the parade ground, The Plain. On the east front of Fort Clinton is a monument to the Polish general Thaddeus Kosciuszko who fought for the Patriot cause in the American Revolution. Phone (914) 938-2638.

Trophy Point, off Washington Rd., displays numerous relics of wars dating from the American Revolution. Included are links from the great barrier chain stretched across the Hudson River during the Revolution. Battle Monument is dedicated to men of the Regular Army who were killed in the Civil War. Allow 30 minutes minimum. Daily dawn-dusk. Phone (914) 938-2638.

★**West Point Museum** is in Olmsted Hall at Pershing Center. The museum contains a large collection of military artifacts from antiquity to modern times. The collection includes flags, jeeps, paintings, tanks, uniforms and weapons. Allow 1 hour minimum. Daily 10:30-4:15; closed Jan. 1, Thanksgiving and Dec. 25. Free. Phone (914) 938-2203.

WEST SAYVILLE (I-4)
pop. 4,700, elev. 28′

LONG ISLAND MARITIME MUSEUM, e. on Montauk Hwy. on the grounds of the West Sayville Golf Course at 86 West Ave., displays ships models, paintings and artifacts. Allow 1 hour minimum. Wed.-Sat. 10-3, Sun. noon-4; closed Jan. 1, Easter, Election Day, Thanksgiving and Dec. 25. Donations. Phone (631) 854-4974.

WHITEHALL (D-11)
pop. 3,100, elev. 123′

Settled by Capt. Philip Skene and about 30 other British families in 1759, Whitehall was originally named Skenesborough in the captain's honor. After the Revolutionary War, during which Skene supported the British, the town changed its name.

Whitehall Chamber of Commerce: 259 Broadway, Whitehall, NY 12887; phone (518) 499-2292.

Self-guiding tours: Historic buildings dating from 1824 are in a downtown area bounded by Broadway, Williams, Saunders and Clinton streets. A brochure detailing self-guiding walking and driving tours of Whitehall's historic areas is available at the Skenesborough Museum.

SKENESBOROUGH MUSEUM, just n. of US 4 on SR 22 in the center of town, includes a Navy room with models of 1776 and 1812 shipyards and ships models, a doll room, a military room and local historical artifacts. Mon.-Sat. 10-4, Sun. noon-4, mid-June through Labor Day; Sat. 10-3, Sun. noon-3, day after Labor Day to mid-Oct. Admission $2, senior citizens $1, students with ID 50c, family rate $5. Phone (518) 499-0716.

WHITE PLAINS—
see New York p. 141.

WILLIAMSVILLE—*see Buffalo p. 72.*

WILMINGTON (B-10)
pop. 1,000, elev. 1,019'

HIGH FALLS GORGE, 4.5 mi. s.w. on SR 86, is a deep ravine cut into the base of Whiteface Mountain by the Ausable River. A colorful variety of strata, rapids, falls and potholes can be seen from a network of well-constructed bridges and paths. The center of the gorge can be reached without climbing stairs. The main building features mineral displays. Downhill ski and snowshoe rentals are available. Picnicking is permitted. Food is available.

Allow 1 hour minimum. Daily 8:30-4:45, July 1-Labor Day; 9-4:15, Memorial Day-June 30 and day after Labor Day-Columbus Day. Hours vary Thanksgiving-Easter; phone ahead. Admission $5.50; over 60, $4.50; ages 12-17, $3.50; ages 4-11, $1.50. DS, MC, VI. Phone (518) 946-2278.

SANTA'S WORKSHOP, 1.5 mi. w. on SR 431 at North Pole, has Santa Claus, live reindeer, craft shops, live entertainment, children's rides and storybook characters. Rides are available only late June through August and fall weekends.

Allow 3 hours, 30 minutes minimum. Daily 9:30-4:30, late June-Labor Day; daily 10-3:30, mid-June to late June; Mon.-Fri. 10-3:30, Sat.-Sun. 9:30-4, day after Labor Day to mid-Oct.; Sat.-Sun. 10-3:30, weekend before Thanksgiving-weekend before Dec. 25. Admission $9.95-$11.95; ages 3-17, $6.95-$7.95. DS, MC, VI. Phone (518) 946-2211 or 946-2212.

[SAVE] ★ **WHITEFACE MOUNTAIN VETERANS' MEMORIAL HIGHWAY,** 3.5 mi. w. via SR 431, is a 6-mile macadam road leading to a parking area near the summit of Whiteface Mountain. The 4,867-foot summit is reached by a .2-mile hiking trail or by an unusual electric elevator set in the cone of the peak. Wear proper footwear and warm clothing. On a clear day the summit house affords a view across more than 100 miles, including the St. Lawrence River and lakes Champlain and Placid.

Allow 1 hour minimum. Daily 9-6, late June-Labor Day; 9-4, mid-May to late June and day after Labor Day to mid-Oct. (weather permitting). Admission per private vehicle (including driver) $8, each passenger $4; motorcycle (including driver) $5, passenger $4. Maximum private vehicle rate $25. Phone (518) 523-1655 or 946-7175.

RECREATIONAL ACTIVITIES
Skiing
• **Whiteface Mountain Ski Center**, 3 mi. s. on SR 86. Write P.O. Box 1980, Wilmington, NY 12997. Other activities are offered. Lifts operate daily 8:30-4, mid-Nov. to mid-Apr. (weather permitting). Phone (518) 946-2223.

WILTON (D-10)

GRANT COTTAGE STATE HISTORIC SITE is on the grounds of the Mount McGregor Correctional Facility; take exit 16 off I-87 and follow signs. This summer cottage is where Gen. Ulysses S. Grant spent his last days and completed his memoirs in 1885. The cottage has been left largely as it was the day he died. Wed.-Sun. 10-4, Memorial Day-Labor Day; Sat.-Sun. 10-4, day after Labor Day-second weekend in Oct. Admission $2.50; over 59, $2; ages 5-16, $1. Phone (518) 587-8277 or 584-4768.

WINDHAM (F-10) pop. 1,700

RECREATIONAL ACTIVITIES
Skiing
• **Ski Windham**, off SR 23 following signs. Write P.O. Box 459, Windham, NY 12496. Other activities are available. Mon.-Fri. 9-4, Nov.-Mar. Phone (518) 734-4300.

YONKERS—*see New York p. 141.*

YOUNGSTOWN—
see Niagara Falls p. 151.

Everything you need.

Clean comfortable rooms.

Free breakfast.

Free local phone calls.*

Great Priority Club® rewards.

Everywhere you go.

Over 900 convenient locations

worldwide.

Holiday Inn EXPRESS

www.hiexpress.com

Stay Smart®

Call 1-800-HOLIDAY.

1-800-238-5544 (TDD only)

or call your travel professional

New York

Albany 191

Buffalo 211

Finger Lakes ... 255

New York 320

Niagara Falls
    New York 381

Niagara Falls
    Ontario 397

Rochester 454

Syracuse........ 476

New York Orientation Map to Destinations

Buffalo (see p. 211)   The Buffalo Vicinity (see p. 219)

Akron...........219	Cheektowaga . 221	Elma 225	Tonawanda....226
Amherst........219	Clarence........223	Grand Island...225	Williamsville...226
Blasdell.........221	Depew..........224	Hamburg.......225	
Bowmansville . 221	East Aurora....224		

Niagara Falls (see p. 381)   The Niagara Vicinity (see p. 396)

Lewiston...................................396	Wheatfield................................396
Newfane...................................396	Youngstown..............................397
Sanborn...................................396	Niagara Falls, Ontario 397

New York (see p. 320)

New York (Lower Manhattan) 331	New York (Midtown Manhattan).......336
New York 363	

The New York Vicinity (see p. 370)

Armonk 370	Elmsford 372	Nyack............374	Rye...............376
Brooklyn 370	Hartsdale........372	Orangeburg 374	Rye Brook.......376
Carmel..........371	Hawthorne 372	Ossining.........374	Staten Island ...377
Chappaqua 371	Jamaica..........372	Pearl River 375	Suffern 377
Congers 371	Mount Kisco ...373	Peekskill.........375	Tarrytown.......377
Croton-on-	Nanuet 373	Port Chester 375	White Plains 378
Hudson 371	New Rochelle ..373	Pound Ridge....375	Yonkers..........379

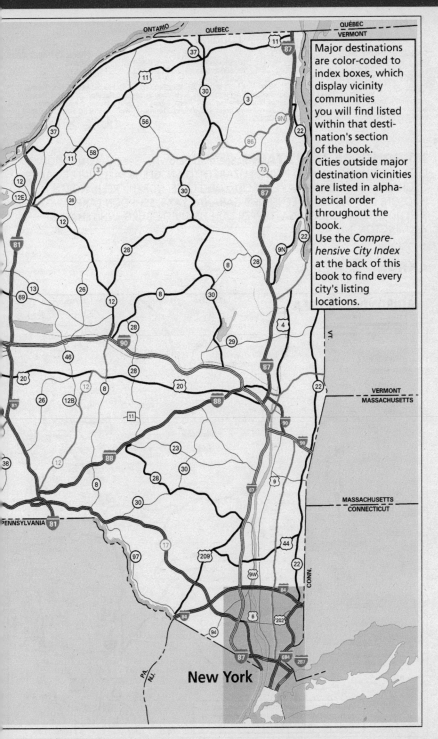

Major destinations are color-coded to index boxes, which display vicinity communities you will find listed within that destination's section of the book. Cities outside major destination vicinities are listed in alphabetical order throughout the book. Use the *Comprehensive City Index* at the back of this book to find every city's listing locations.

ACRA pop. 600

--- LODGING ---

LANGE'S GROVE SIDE
Phone: (518)622-3393

11/23-4/30	1P: $50-$90	2P: $60-$90	XP: $15
7/1-9/3	1P: $50-$75	2P: $65-$75	XP: $10
5/1-6/30 & 9/4-11/22	1P: $34-$40	2P: $55-$75	XP: $5

Motor Inn **Location:** 5 mi w on SR 23, 12 mi w of I-87, exit 21. SR 23 12405 (Box 79). Fax: 518/622-3393. **Terms:** [CP] meal plan; 7 day cancellation notice; 2 night min stay, weekends in season. **Facility:** 23 rooms. Peaceful location on extensive landscaped grounds. Small brook runs out back. Picnic tables set up in summer. 2 two-bedroom units. 1 story; exterior corridors; heated pool, whirlpool; 1 tennis court; playground. **Dining:** Dining room; 8:30 am-10 & 5:30-7 pm; 6/29-9/2; $11-$14; cocktails. **Cards:** AE, CB, DI, DS, MC, VI.

ADIRONDACK MOUNTAINS (See map below) — See BOLTON LANDING, CHESTERTOWN, DIAMOND POINT, ELIZABETHTOWN, GLENS FALLS, INLET, LAKE GEORGE, LAKE LUZERNE, LAKE PLACID, LONG LAKE, NORTH CREEK, NORTH HUDSON, OLD FORGE, QUEENSBURY, SARANAC LAKE, SCHROON LAKE, SPECULATOR, TICONDEROGA, TUPPER LAKE, WARRENSBURG, WHITEHALL & WILMINGTON.

AKRON —See Buffalo p. 219.

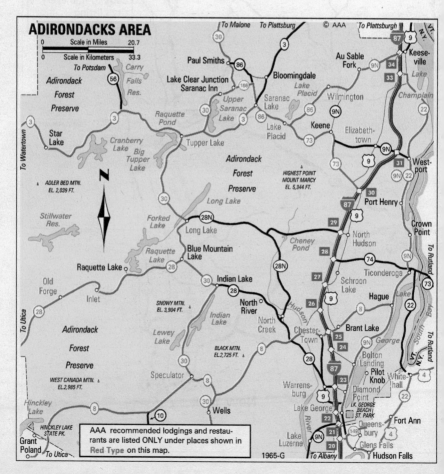

ADIRONDACKS AREA

© AAA

AAA recommended lodgings and restaurants are listed ONLY under places shown in Red Type on this map.

1965-G

ALBANY pop. 101,100   (See map p. 193; index below)

This index helps you "spot" where approved accommodations are located on the detailed maps that follow. Rate ranges are for comparison only and show the property's high season. Turn to the listing page for more detailed rate information and consult display ads for special promotions. Restaurant rate range is for dinner unless only lunch (L) is served.

✈ Airport Accommodations

Spotter/Map Page Number	OA	ALBANY	Diamond Rating	Rate Range High Season	Listing Page
19 / p. 193		Albany Marriott, 2 mi se of airport	◆◆◆	Failed to provide	236
20 / p. 193		Best Western Albany Airport Inn, 2 mi se of airport	◆◆	$109	236
23 / p. 193		Courtyard by Marriott, 2 mi se of airport	◆◆◆	$109-$129	236
22 / p. 193	◆◆◆	The Desmond Hotel, 1.5 mi e of airport	◆◆◆	$99-$219	236
25 / p. 193	◆◆◆	Hilton Garden Inn-Albany Airport, just w of terminal	◆◆◆	$89-$129	237
17 / p. 193	◆◆◆	Holiday Inn Turf on Wolf Road, 2 mi se of airport	◆◆◆	$89-$139	237
15 / p. 193	◆◆◆	Red Roof Inn, 2 mi se of airport	◆◆	$58-$88	237
28 / p. 193	◆◆◆	Comfort Inn At Albany Airport, 0.5 mi n of airport	◆◆◆	$79-$99	301

ALBANY

Spotter/Map Page Number	OA	ALBANY - Lodgings	Diamond Rating	Rate Range High Season	Listing Page
1 / p. 193	◆◆◆	Crowne Plaza Albany	◆◆◆	$89	196
2 / p. 193	◆◆◆	Albany Mansion Hill Inn & Restaurant	◆◆◆	$125-$165	194
3 / p. 193	◆◆◆	Albany Quality Inn	◆◆	$75-$95	194
4 / p. 193	◆◆◆	Albany Ramada Inn	◆◆	$92-$125	194
5 / p. 193		The Albany Thruway Courtyard	◆◆◆	$119	196
6 / p. 193		Extended Stay America	◆◆	Failed to provide	196
		ALBANY - Restaurants			
1 / p. 193		La Serre Restaurant	◆◆◆	$13-$24	196
3 / p. 193	◆◆◆	Jack's Oyster House	◆◆◆	$11-$20	196
4 / p. 193		Thatcher's Restaurant	◆◆	$12-$18	196
5 / p. 193		Ogden's	◆◆◆	$15-$25	196
6 / p. 193		Albany Mansion Hill Inn Restaurant	◆◆◆	$13-$22	196
7 / p. 193		Nicole's Bistro At Quackenbush House	◆◆◆	$17-$22	196

Nearby Accommodations

Spotter/Map Page Number	OA	COLONIE - Lodgings	Diamond Rating	Rate Range High Season	Listing Page
11 / p. 193	◆◆◆	Ambassador Motor Inn	◆◆	$55-$88	236
12 / p. 193	◆◆◆	Comfort Inn & Business Center	◆◆◆	$71-$119	236
15 / p. 193	◆◆◆	Red Roof Inn	◆◆	$58-$88	237
16 / p. 193		Days Inn Airport - see color ad p 195	◆◆	Failed to provide	236
17 / p. 193	◆◆◆	Holiday Inn Turf on Wolf Road	◆◆◆	$89-$139	237
18 / p. 193		Albany Marriott	◆◆◆	Failed to provide	236
20 / p. 193		Best Western Albany Airport Inn - see color ad p 195	◆◆	$109	236
21 / p. 193	◆◆◆	Econo Lodge Albany	◆◆	$68-$75	237
22 / p. 193	◆◆◆	The Desmond Hotel	◆◆◆	$99-$219	236
23 / p. 193		Courtyard by Marriott	◆◆◆	$109-$129	236
24 / p. 193	◆◆◆	Ramada Limited	◆◆	$80-$85	237
25 / p. 193	◆◆◆	Hilton Garden Inn-Albany Airport - see color ad p 57, p 195	◆◆◆	$89-$129	237
		COLONIE - Restaurants			
12 / p. 193	◆◆◆	The Cranberry Bog	◆◆	$14-$22	238
13 / p. 193		Butcher Block Steak & Seafood Restaurant	◆◆	$13-$19	237
14 / p. 193		Bangkok Thai Restaurant	◆◆	$10-$17	237
15 / p. 193		Grandma's Country Restaurant	◆◆	$8-$15	238

Spotter/Map Page Number	OA	COLONIE - Restaurants (continued)	Diamond Rating	Rate Range High Season	Listing Page
⑰ / p. 193		Scrimshaw	◆◆◆	$18-$30	238
⑱ / p. 193	AAA	**Ashley's**	◆◆◆◆	$17-$28	237
⑲ / p. 193		Garcia's Mexican Restaurant	◆◆	$5-$10	238
⑳ / p. 193		Veeder's Restaurant Inc	◆	$7-$16	238
		LATHAM - Lodgings			
㉗ / p. 193		Residence Inn by Marriott Albany Airport	◆◆◆	$155-$205	301
㉘ / p. 193	AAA	**Comfort Inn At Albany Airport**	◆◆◆	$79-$99 [SAVE]	301
㉙ / p. 193		Wingate Inn	◆◆◆	$125-$135	301
㉚ / p. 193	AAA	**Century House Restaurant & Hotel**	◆◆◆	$109-$129	301
㉜ / p. 193		Hampton Inn-Latham	◆◆◆	$109-$134	301
㉞ / p. 193	AAA	**Microtel Inn - see ad p 194**	◆◆	$47-$80 [SAVE]	301
		LATHAM - Restaurants			
㉔ / p. 193	AAA	**Dakota**	◆◆	$9-$18	302
㉕ / p. 193		Century House	◆◆	$14-$20	301
		GLENMONT - Lodgings			
㉟ / p. 193		Days Inn Albany	◆◆	Failed to provide	263
		GLENMONT - Restaurant			
㉖ / p. 193	AAA	**Alteri's Restaurant**	◆◆	$9-$16	263
		EAST GREENBUSH - Lodgings			
㊴ / p. 193	AAA	**Econo Lodge**	◆◆	$49-$89 [SAVE]	249
		TROY - Lodgings			
㊷ / p. 193		Super 8 Motel-Troy	◆◆	$55-$80	482
㊸ / p. 193	AAA	**Best Western-Rensselaer Inn**	◆◆	$59-$89 [SAVE]	482
		TROY - Restaurant			
㉜ / p. 193		Holmes & Watson, Ltd	◆	$8-$12	482
		GUILDERLAND - Lodgings			
㊺ / p. 193		Holiday Inn Express Turf on Western Ave	◆◆◆	$89-$130	266
		GUILDERLAND - Restaurant			
㊱ / p. 193		Bavarian Chalet	◆◆	$11-$16	266
		LOUDONVILLE - Restaurant			
㊵ / p. 193		Pearl of the Orient	◆◆	$7-$17	307

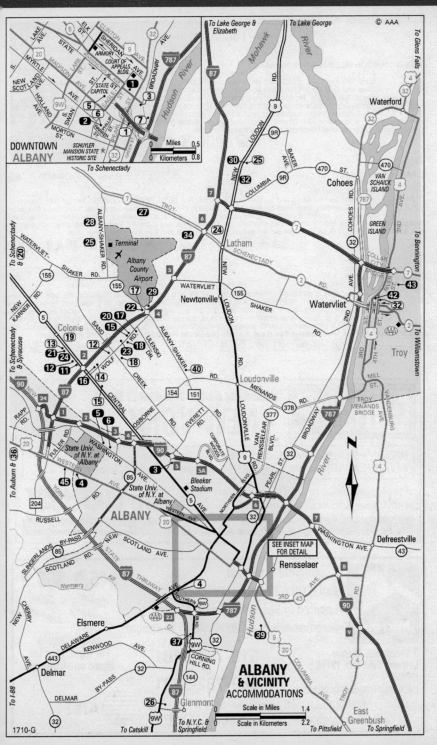

© AAA

DOWNTOWN ALBANY

ALBANY & VICINITY
ACCOMMODATIONS

1710-G

ALBANY pop. 101,100 (See map p. 193; index p. 191)

———— LODGINGS ————

ALBANY MANSION HILL INN & RESTAURANT
Phone: (518)465-2038 **2**

(AAA) (SAVE)
◆◆◆
Historic Bed & Breakfast

All Year   1P: $125-$155   2P: $135-$165
Location: From I-90 to I-787 s to Madison Ave exit (US 20 W), to Philip St, then s; from I-87 to I-787 to downtown exit (US 20 W), Madison to Philip St, then s. 115 Philip St at Park Ave 12202 (45 Park Ave). Fax: 518/434-2313. **Terms:** [BP] meal plan; 5 day cancellation notice; $10 service charge; pets. **Facility:** 8 rooms. Original buildings date back to 1860 and 1913, nicely appointed rooms; all with hair dryer. A Downtown inn. 2 stories; interior/exterior corridors. **Dining:** Restaurant; restaurant, see separate listing. **Services:** area transportation, train & bus depot. **All Rooms:** extended cable TV. **Some Rooms:** Fee: VCR. **Cards:** AE, DI, DS, MC, VI. **Special Amenities:** Free local telephone calls and free newspaper.

ALBANY QUALITY INN
Phone: (518)438-8431 **3**

(AAA) (SAVE)
◆◆
Motor Inn

7/2-9/1   1P: $75-$95
5/1-7/1 & 9/2-4/30   1P: $65-$85
Location: Jct I-90, exit 5 and Everett Rd. 3 Watervliet Ave 12206. Fax: 518/438-8356. **Terms:** [BP] meal plan; weekly & monthly rates avail; package plans. **Facility:** 215 rooms. Good sized rooms. 13 kitchens $10 extra charge; 2-9 stories; interior corridors; 2 pools, 1 heated, 1 small heated, & non-heated outdoor pool. **Dining:** Dining room; 6:30 am-10 pm; $9-$18; cocktails. **All Rooms:** extended cable TV. **Some Rooms:** Fee: refrigerators, VCR. **Cards:** AE, CB, DI, DS, MC, VI. **Special Amenities:** Free breakfast and free local telephone calls.

ALBANY RAMADA INN
Phone: (518)489-2981 **4**

(AAA) (SAVE)
◆◆
Motor Inn

All Year   1P: $92-$105   2P: $102-$125   XP: $10   F17
Location: 5 mi w on US 20; 0.7 mi se of I-87, exit 24; or 0.7 mi s of I-90 exit 2 (Fuller Rd) westbound; following signs to US 20. 1228 Western Ave 12203. Fax: 518/489-8967. **Terms:** [BP] meal plan; 14 day cancellation notice; package plans; small pets only, $10 extra charge. **Facility:** 195 rooms. Across from the state university. 5 stories; interior corridors; heated pool, sauna. **Dining:** Dining room; 6:30 am-10 pm; $9-$16. **Services:** winter plug-ins. **All Rooms:** combo or shower baths, extended cable TV. **Cards:** AE, CB, DI, DS, JC, MC, VI. **Special Amenities:** Free breakfast and free room upgrade (subject to availability with advanced reservations).

(See map p. 193)

THE ALBANY THRUWAY COURTYARD   Phone: (518)435-1600   **5**
◆◆◆   All Year   1P: $119
Motel   **Location:** I-90, exit 2, just s on Fuller Rd, just e. 1455 Washington Ave 12206. **Fax:** 518/435-1616. **Facility:** 78 rooms. Comfortably furnished spacious guest rooms. 3 stories; interior corridors; small heated indoor pool.
All Rooms: combo or shower baths. **Cards:** AE, DI, DS, MC, VI.

CROWNE PLAZA ALBANY   Phone: (518)462-6611   **1**
(AAA) (SAVE)   All Year   1P: $89
◆◆◆   **Location:** Center; at Ten Eyck Plaza. State & Lodge sts 12207. **Fax:** 518/462-2901. **Terms:** Check-in 4 pm;
Hotel   package plans; pets, $50 extra charge. **Facility:** 354 rooms. 15 stories; interior corridors; heated pool, whirlpool. **Fee:** parking. **Dining:** Dining room; 6:30 am-10 pm; $16-$26; cocktails. **Services:** gift shop; area transportation. **Some Rooms:** Fee: VCR. **Cards:** AE, CB, DI, DS, JC, MC, VI.

EXTENDED STAY AMERICA   Phone: (518)446-0680   **6**
◆◆   Property failed to provide current rates
Motel   **Location:** I-90, exit 2, just s on Fuller Rd, 0.5 mi e. 1395 Washington Ave 12206. **Fax:** m18/446-0779.
Facility: 134 rooms. Good sized efficiencies. 2 stories; interior corridors. **All Rooms:** efficiencies, combo or shower baths. **Cards:** AE, DI, DS, MC, VI.

─────── **RESTAURANTS** ───────

ALBANY MANSION HILL INN RESTAURANT   **Dinner:** $13-$22   Phone: 518/465-2038   **6**
◆◆◆   **Location:** I-90 to I-787 s to Madison Ave (US 20 W), to Philip St, then s; I-87 to I-787 to downtown (US 20
American   W), Madison to Philip St, then s; in Albany Mansion Hill Inn. 115 Philip St at Park Ave 12202. **Hours:** 5 pm-9 pm; summer hrs vary. Closed major holidays & Sun. **Reservations:** suggested. **Features:** dressy casual; carryout; cocktails; a la carte. In a small, intimate setting, the restaurant is decorated in the classic American style. The succulent swordfish has a crusted mustard texture and taste, while the blueberry creme brulee has a different—but very good—flavor. Service is professional. **Cards:** AE, CB, DI, DS, MC, VI.

JACK'S OYSTER HOUSE   **Lunch:** $5-$9   **Dinner:** $11-$20   Phone: 518/465-8854   **3**
(AAA)   **Location:** Downtown; just s of City Hall. 42 State St 12207. **Hours:** 11:30 am-10 pm.
◆◆◆   **Reservations:** suggested. **Features:** casual dress; children's menu; health conscious menu; carryout;
Seafood   cocktails & lounge. In the heart of the downtown business district, the lively, energetic restaurant is a favorite for fine dining. A lovely mural brightens the wall behind a reproduction of a Florentine bar. The menu centers on seafood. The key lime brulee is exquisite. **Cards:** AE, CB, DI, DS, MC, VI.

LA SERRE RESTAURANT   **Lunch:** $7-$13   **Dinner:** $13-$24   Phone: 518/463-6056   **1**
◆◆◆   **Location:** Just s of State St; 3 blks e of State Capitol building. 14 Green St 12207. **Hours:** 11:30 am-2:30 &
Continental   5-9 pm, Fri-9:30 pm, Sat 5 pm-9:30 pm. Closed major holidays. **Reservations:** suggested. **Features:** casual dress; cocktails & lounge; street parking. Chilean sea bass, rack of lamb and lobster ravioli are among specialties on the restaurant's inventive menu. The renovated 1829 white-gabled building resides in the heart of downtown. The atmosphere in the elegant dining room is upscale and intimate. **Cards:** AE, CB, DI, MC, VI.

NICOLE'S BISTRO AT QUACKENBUSH HOUSE   **Lunch:** $6-$13   **Dinner:** $17-$22   Phone: 518/465-1111   **7**
◆◆◆   **Location:** Downtown. 25 Quackenbush Sq 12207. **Hours:** 11:30 am-2:30 & 5-10 pm, Sat from 5 pm. Closed
Nouvelle   major holidays & Sun. **Reservations:** suggested. **Features:** casual dress; health conscious menu; cocktails
American   & lounge; a la carte, buffet. The converted, 17th-century home is decorated in soft tones and charcoal sketches. Flavorful dishes—such as steak au poivre and onion soup gratinee—are prepared with obvious thought to color and texture. The light, sweet chocolate mousse is exquisite. **Cards:** AE, CB, DI, MC, VI.

OGDEN'S   **Lunch:** $6-$12   **Dinner:** $15-$25   Phone: 518/463-6605   **5**
◆◆◆   **Location:** 42 Howard St 12207. **Hours:** 11:30 am-2 & 5:30-9 pm. Closed major holidays & Sun.
Continental   **Reservations:** suggested. **Features:** casual dress; cocktails & lounge. Natural wood, live plants and elegant table settings enhance the tasteful decor of the downtown restaurant. Great care is taken in the attractive presentation of such choices as oysters on the half-shell, yellowfin tuna steak and creme caramel. **Cards:** AE, MC, VI.

THATCHER'S RESTAURANT   **Lunch:** $5-$8   **Dinner:** $12-$18   Phone: 518/465-0115   **4**
◆◆   **Location:** Jct Holland and Delaware aves, 0.3 mi w. 272 Delaware Ave 12209. **Hours:** 11:30 am-4 & 5-10
American   pm, Fri-11 pm, Sat 5 pm-11 pm. Closed: 11/23, 12/25 & Sun. **Reservations:** accepted. **Features:** casual dress; children's menu; carryout; cocktails & lounge. A country farmhouse decor punctuates the informal dining room. Representative of menu offerings is the filet of sole, which is stuffed with sun-dried tomatoes, garlic and parsley. During pleasant weather, seating in the lovely garden is popular. **Cards:** AE, CB, DI, MC, VI.

ALEXANDRIA BAY pop. 1,200

──── LODGINGS ────

OTTER CREEK INN
	7/1-9/4	2P: $65-$89	XP: $7	F5
	9/5-10/9 & 4/15-4/30	2P: $45-$65	XP: $7	F5
Motel	5/1-6/30	2P: $65	XP: $7	F5

Phone: (315)482-5248

Location: Jct Crossmon and Church sts, following signs. 2 Crossmon St Ext 13607. Fax: 315/482-5248. **Terms:** Open 5/1-10/9 & 4/15-4/30; weekly & monthly rates avail; 3 day cancellation notice; 2 night min stay, weekends in season; package plans. **Facility:** 32 rooms. Modern rooms. Pleasant location on Otter Creek. 2 stories; interior/exterior corridors; boat dock, boat ramp. **Recreation:** charter fishing, fishing; picnic tables. **All Rooms:** extended cable TV. **Cards:** DI, DS, MC, VI.

RIVEREDGE RESORT & HOTEL

AAA [SAVE]

♦♦♦♦

Resort

	6/16-9/3	1P: $218-$298	2P: $218-$298	XP: $20	F12
	5/1-6/15 & 9/4-10/29	1P: $148-$238	2P: $148-$238	XP: $20	F12
	10/30-4/30	1P: $98-$178	2P: $98-$178	XP: $20	F12

Phone: (315)482-9917

Location: I-81, exit 50 N, n on SR 12, just ne. 17 Holland St 13607. Fax: 315/482-5010. **Terms:** [AP], [BP] & [MAP] meal plans; weekly rates avail; check-in 4 pm; 14 day cancellation notice; package plans; pets, $10 extra charge. **Facility:** 129 rooms. Well appointed rooms, each with balcony overlooking the St Lawrence River. 2-3 night min stay weekends; 27 whirlpool rooms, $141-$268; 4 stories; interior corridors; 2 heated pools, sauna, whirlpools; boat ramp. Fee: marina. **Dining:** Dining room, restaurant; 6:30 am-10 pm; $24-$32; also, Jacques Cartier Dining Room, see separate listing; entertainment. **Services:** gift shop. Fee: massage. **Recreation:** charter fishing, fishing, ice fishing; cross country skiing. **All Rooms:** extended cable TV. **Cards:** AE, CB, DI, DS, MC, VI. **Special Amenities:** Free room upgrade and preferred room (each subject to availability with advanced reservations). (See color ad p 197)

------- **RESTAURANT** -------

JACQUES CARTIER DINING ROOM

AAA

♦♦♦♦

French

Dinner: $24-$32   **Phone:** 315/482-9917

Location: I-81, exit 50N, n on SR 12, just ne; in Riveredge Resort & Hotel. 17 Holland St 13607. **Hours:** 6 pm-10 pm. Closed: Sun-Thurs 10/15-4/24. **Reservations:** suggested. **Features:** dressy casual; Sunday brunch; children's menu; health conscious menu; cocktails; entertainment; valet parking; a la carte. The dining room affords wonderful views of the St. Lawrence River and Historic Boldt Castle. A harpist adds to the decidedly romantic atmosphere. Such dishes as the veal chop are carefully prepared and flavorful. Service is attentive and unpretentious. **Cards:** AE, CB, DI, DS, MC, VI.

ALFRED pop. 4,600

------- **LODGING** -------

SAXON INN

♦♦♦

Motel

All Year   1P: $85-$110   2P: $95-$110   XP: $10   F12

Phone: 607/871-2600

Location: On Alfred University campus. 1 Park St 14802 (Saxon Dr). Fax: 607/871-2650. **Terms:** [CP] meal plan; cancellation fee imposed. **Facility:** 26 rooms. Elegantly furnished rooms. Historical ceramics displayed in lobby. Closed 11/23 and 12/25. 2 stories; interior corridors. **Services:** winter plug-ins. **Cards:** AE, DI, DS, MC, VI.

AMAGANSETT

—— RESTAURANT ——

LOBSTER ROLL   **Dinner: $6-$18**   **Phone: 631/267-3740**
◆
Seafood   **Location:** 4 mi e on SR 27. **Hours:** Open 5/1-10/15; 11:30 am-10 pm. **Features:** No A/C; casual dress; children's menu; carryout; beer & wine only; a la carte. Known locally as "Lunch"—the sign seen before the name—the large beach road stop delivers its namesake salads, fish burgers and all manner of fresh seafood prepared in a traditional manner. Servers in casual attire race around but get the job done. Smoke free premises. **Cards:** MC, VI.   ⊠

AMHERST —See Buffalo p. 219.

AMITYVILLE   pop. 9,300

—— RESTAURANT ——

ROSE COTTAGE   **Lunch: $7-$11**   **Dinner: $18-$30**   **Phone: 516/691-6881**
◆◆◆
Continental   **Location:** On SR 27A, 0.5 mi e of SR 110. 348 Merrick Rd 11701. **Hours:** 11:30 am-3 & 5-9 pm, Fri & Sat-10 pm, Sun noon-8:30 pm. Closed: 12/25 & Mon. **Reservations:** suggested; weekends. **Features:** casual dress; Sunday brunch; early bird specials; senior's menu; health conscious menu items; cocktails & lounge; a la carte. Enhancing the restaurant's French chalet decor are knotty pine walls, beamed ceilings, dried-flower wreaths and intimate lighting. An extensive wine list complements a menu that centers on steaks and pasta, such as the wonderful Fusilli Riviera. **Cards:** AE, DI, DS, MC, VI.   ⊠

AMSTERDAM   pop. 20,700

—— LODGING ——

SUPER 8 MOTEL   **Phone: (518)843-5888**

◆◆	7/14-9/8	1P: $65-$74	2P: $69-$76	XP: $4	F12
Motel	5/1-7/13	1P: $51-$65	2P: $55-$69	XP: $4	F12
	9/9-10/14	1P: $51-$61	2P: $57-$61	XP: $4	F12
	10/15-4/30	1P: $49-$52	2P: $53-$55	XP: $4	F12

Location: Jct I-90, exit 27 and SR 30 S. Rt 30 S 12010. **Fax:** 518/843-5888. **Terms:** [CP] meal plan. **Facility:** 67 rooms. 2 stories; interior corridors. **Services:** winter plug-ins. **Some Rooms:** Fee: VCR. **Cards:** AE, CB, DI, DS, MC, VI.   ⟨ASK⟩ ⟨S♦⟩ ⟨▮↑⟩ ⟨⊠⟩ ⟨VCR⟩

ANGELICA   pop. 1,000

—— LODGING ——

ANGELICA INN BED & BREAKFAST   **Phone: 716/466-3295**
◆◆◆   All Year   1P: $60-$90   2P: $70-$100   XP: $20   D6
Historic Bed & Breakfast   **Location:** SR 17, exit 31, 0.5 mi w. 64 W Main St 14709. **Terms:** [BP] meal plan; 14 day cancellation notice; cancellation fee imposed; small pets only, in country house only, dogs on premises. **Facility:** 6 rooms. Restored Victorian mansion with individually furnished rooms. 1 three-bedroom unit, 2 two-bedroom units. 3 stories, no elevator; interior corridors. **Services:** gift shop. **All Rooms:** combo or shower baths. **Some Rooms:** kitchen, color TV. **Cards:** AE, DS, MC, VI.   ⟨ASK⟩ ⟨S♦⟩ ⟨🐾⟩ ⟨📶⟩ ⟨⊠⟩ ⟨🔲⟩ ⟨▭⟩ ⟨▭⟩ ⟨🛢⟩

ARMONK —See New York p. 370.

ATHENS   pop. 1,700

—— LODGING ——

THE STEWART HOUSE   **Phone: 518/945-1357**
◆◆   11/1-4/30   1P: $80-$90   2P: $80-$90   XP: $15   F3
Historic Country Inn   5/1-10/31   1P: $90   2P: $90   XP: $15   F3
Location: Center. 2 N Water St 12015. **Fax:** 518/945-1990. **Terms:** [CP] meal plan; 14 day cancellation notice; cancellation fee imposed. **Facility:** 5 rooms. Renovated 1883 hotel. Individually decorated guest rooms, many antiques. 2 stories; interior corridors; smoke free premises; street parking only. **All Rooms:** combo or shower baths. **Cards:** AE, MC, VI.   ⟨▮⟩ ⟨Ƴ⟩ ⟨⊠⟩ ⟨☎⟩

AUBURN   pop. 31,300—See also FINGER LAKES.

—— LODGING ——

HOLIDAY INN   **Phone: (315)253-4531**
◆◆◆   7/1-9/7   1P: $89-$139   2P: $89-$139
Motor Inn   5/1-6/30   1P: $79-$109   2P: $79-$109
   9/8-4/30   1P: $69-$109   2P: $69-$109
Location: SR 34, n of SR 5 and US 20. 75 North St 13021. **Fax:** 315/252-5843. **Terms:** Small pets only. **Facility:** 166 rooms. 5 stories; interior corridors; heated pool. **Services:** winter plug-ins. **Some Rooms:** Fee: refrigerators, microwaves. **Cards:** AE, CB, DI, DS, JC, MC, VI. *(See color ad p 257)*
⟨ASK⟩ ⟨S♦⟩ ⟨🐾⟩ ⟨▮⟩ ⟨Ƴ⟩ ⟨📶⟩ ⟨👕⟩ ⟨⊠⟩ ⟨🔲⟩ ⟨🖥⟩ ⟨▭⟩ ⟨🛢⟩ ⟨DATA PORT⟩ ⟨♿⟩ ⟨🐾⟩

——— RESTAURANT ———

SPRINGSIDE INN Historical   Dinner: $9-$20   Phone: 315/252-7247
(AAA)   **Location:** 3.3 mi s on SR 38 S; in Springside Inn. 41-43 W Lake Rd 13021. **Hours:** 5 pm-9 pm, Fri & Sat-10
◆◆   pm, Sun 10:30 am-7 pm; seasonal hrs may vary. Closed: 12/25 & Mon. **Reservations:** suggested.
American   **Features:** casual dress; Sunday brunch; children's menu; cocktails & lounge. Two fireplaces, high ceilings
                and a collection of world flags add to the charm and cozy ambience of this restored 1850s inn. Such
                specialties as roast duck, cheese souffle, baked scrod and prime rib line the menu. Service is pleasant and
attentive. **Cards:** AE, MC, VI.   ✕

AURORA pop. 700

——— RESTAURANT ———

AURORA INN DINING ROOM Country Inn   **Lunch:** $3-$11   **Dinner:** $4-$42   **Phone:** 315/364-8888
◆◆   **Location:** SR 90. Main St 13026. **Hours:** 11:30 am-2 & 5-8:30 pm, Fri & Sat 5 pm-9 pm. Closed: 1/1, 12/25,
American   Sun & Mon. **Reservations:** suggested. **Features:** casual dress; children's menu; carryout; cocktails &
                lounge; street parking. Overlooking Cayuga Lake, the restaurant delivers a varied menu with flavorful
preparations of steak, seafood, pasta, chicken and game. The pub is a nice spot for homemade soup or a two-handed
sandwich. All of the wonderful desserts are homemade. Smoke free premises. **Cards:** DS, MC, VI.   ✕

AVERILL PARK pop. 2,700

——— LODGING ———

THE GREGORY HOUSE COUNTRY INN   Phone: (518)674-3774
◆◆◆   5/1-10/31   1P: $95-$115   2P: $100-$125   XP: $10
Country Inn   11/1-4/30   2P: $90-$115   XP: $10
               Location: Center. 3016 New York 43 12018 (PO Box 677). Fax: 518/674-8916. **Terms:** [CP] meal plan; age
restrictions may apply; 7 day cancellation notice; cancellation fee imposed; package plans. **Facility:** 12 rooms. Well-kept
rooms, 3 with balcony. 2 stories; interior corridors; smoke free premises. **Cards:** AE, CB, DI, DS, MC, VI.

AVOCA pop. 1,000—*See also FINGER LAKES.*

——— LODGING ———

CABOOSE MOTEL   Phone: 607/566-2216
(AAA)   5/1-10/31   1P: $37   2P: $46-$51   XP: $7
◆   **Location:** I-390, exit 1, 2.2 mi n on SR 415. 8620 SR 415 14809. Fax: 607/566-3817. **Terms:** Open 5/1-10/31;
Motel   3 day cancellation notice; cancellation fee imposed; small pets only. **Facility:** 23 rooms. Quiet location with
               units back from the road. 18 conventional units and 5 separate 1916-1917 restored train cabooses used for
               lodging, each sleeping up to 6 persons. Well-kept grounds also emphasize railroad motif. Caboose rooms, $70
for up to 2 persons, extra person $7; 1 story; exterior corridors; heated pool; playground. **All Rooms:** combo or shower baths,
extended cable TV. **Some Rooms:** Fee: refrigerators. **Cards:** MC, VI.

AVON pop. 3,000—*See FINGER LAKES.*

BABYLON pop. 12,200

——— RESTAURANT ———

DON RICARDO'S MEXICAN RESTAURANT   **Lunch:** $7-$13   **Dinner:** $10-$17   **Phone:** 631/587-0122
◆   **Location:** Between Deer Park Ave and SR 231. 94 E Main St 11702. **Hours:** noon-10 pm, Fri & Sat-11 pm,
Ethnic   Sat & Sun 1 pm-11 pm. Closed: 7/4, 11/23 & 12/25. **Reservations:** suggested. **Features:** children's menu;
               carryout; cocktails; street parking; a la carte. The first two dining rooms have the feel of a Mexican tavern,
while the back room, made up of a brick courtyard with skylights and a stone fountain, exudes a friendly warmth. Menu
offerings center on hearty and tasty Mexican and Spanish fare. Smoke free premises. **Cards:** AE, MC, VI.   ✕

BAINBRIDGE pop. 1,600

——— RESTAURANT ———

OLDE JERICHO TAVERN   **Lunch:** $6-$12   **Dinner:** $12-$16   **Phone:** 607/967-5893
◆◆   **Location:** 4 N Main St 13733. **Hours:** 11:30 am-2 & 5-8 pm, Fri & Sat-8:30 pm, Sun noon-7 pm. Closed:
American   Mon, Tues & 1/1-1/15. **Features:** casual dress; cocktails & lounge. In business since 1793, the stately,
               Colonial tavern has a storied history, which is brought to life in pictures and postcards. Such tempting
choices as ribs, peel-and-eat shrimp and black bean soup line the buffet. Fresh blueberry muffins are delicious. **Cards:** AE,
MC, VI.   ✕

BALLSTON LAKE pop. 700

—— RESTAURANT ——

CARNEY'S TAVERN   **Lunch:** $4-$7   **Dinner:** $8-$16   **Phone:** 518/399-9926
◆   **Location:** Center. 17 Main St 12019. **Hours:** 11 am-9 pm, Tues-Sat to 10 pm, Sun from 11:30 am. Closed:
American   4/23, 11/23 & 12/25. **Features:** casual dress; carryout; cocktails; a la carte. The original tin ceiling and bar
                back add to the authentic feel of the mid-19th-century Colonial tavern. Traditional Irish pub fare, including the
specialty steaks, is at the heart of the menu. The homemade bread pudding is a mouthwatering treat. **Cards:** AE, DS,
MC, VI.

BALLSTON SPA pop. 4,900

—— RESTAURANT ——

SPA BRAUHAUS   **Dinner:** $10-$20   **Phone:** 518/885-4311
◆◆   **Location:** I-87, exit 12, 1.5 mi w on SR 67 to E Line Rd, 2 mi n, 0.3 mi e. 200 E High St 12020. **Hours:** 4
German   pm-10 pm, Sun noon-9 pm. Closed: 12/24, 12/25 & Mon (except 8/1-8/31). **Reservations:** suggested.
                Features: casual dress; children's menu; carryout; cocktails. Sauerbraten, potato pancakes and Wiener
schnitzel are representative of German specialties on the restaurant's menu. Hand-carved statues and a brick fireplace add
inviting warmth to the dining room. Made on the premises, the Black Forest cake is divine. **Cards:** CB, DI, MC, VI.   ⊠

BARNEVELD pop. 300

—— LODGING ——

SUGARBUSH BED AND BREAKFAST   **Phone:** (315)896-6860
(AAA) (SAVE)   All Year   1P: $55-$81   2P: $90-$125   XP: $15   D5
◆◆   **Location:** 0.3 mi se of jct SR 12 and Old Poland Rd. 8451 Old Poland Rd 13304. **Fax:** 315/896-8828.
Bed &   **Terms:** [BP] meal plan; 3 day cancellation notice. **Facility:** 5 rooms. Restored 1800s Colonial home set upon
Breakfast   8 acres, once a boys' boarding school. Family oriented with home-like atmosphere. Small to good sized guest
                rooms. 1 two-bedroom unit. Suites, $125-$145; 2 stories; interior corridors; smoke free premises; playground.
                Recreation: cross country skiing. **All Rooms:** combo or shower baths, extended cable TV.
Some Rooms: color TV. **Cards:** AE, DI, MC, VI. **Special Amenities: Early check-in/late check-out and free local telephone
calls.**   (SD) ⊠ (K) (☎) (🖨) ⊠

BATAVIA pop. 16,300

—— LODGINGS ——

BEST WESTERN BATAVIA INN   **Phone:** (716)343-1000
(AAA) (SAVE)   6/16-9/3   1P: $74-$94   2P: $84-$109   XP: $6   F18
◆◆   5/1-6/15 & 9/4-10/20   1P: $61-$69   2P: $74-$84   XP: $6   F18
Motor Inn   10/21-4/30   1P: $57   2P: $61-$69   XP: $6   F18
                Location: Just sw from jct I-90 and SR 98. 8204 Park Rd 14020. **Fax:** 716/343-8608. **Terms:** Weekly rates
                avail; pets. **Facility:** 75 rooms. Bright rooms with contemporary decor. 2 stories; interior corridors; heated pool,
seasonal outdoor pool. **Dining:** Restaurant; 6:30-11 am, 11:30-1:30 & 5-9 pm, Sat from 7 am, Sun 7:30 am-8:30 pm; $7-$15;
cocktails. **Services:** winter plug-ins. **All Rooms:** extended cable TV. **Cards:** AE, CB, DI, DS, MC, VI. **Special Amenities:**
Early check-in/late check-out and free local telephone calls.   (🛏) (🍽) (🍸) (🐾) (⛱) ⊠ (🎬) (🖨) (DATA PORT) (🏊)

COMFORT INN   **Phone:** (716)344-9999
(AAA) (SAVE)   5/1-9/30   1P: $89-$149   2P: $89-$149   XP: $10   F18
◆◆◆   10/1-4/30   1P: $79-$109   2P: $79-$109
Motel   **Location:** I-90 (New York Thruway), exit 48, just n on SR 98. 4371 Federal Dr 14020. **Fax:** 716/345-7400.
                Terms: [CP] meal plan. **Facility:** 60 rooms. Tastefully appointed guest rooms and inviting public areas. 5 whirl-
                pool rooms, $109-$149; 2 stories; interior corridors. **All Rooms:** combo or shower baths, extended cable TV.
Cards: AE, DI, DS, MC, VI.   (🐾) (⛱) (♿) (🔌) ⊠ (🎬) (🖨) (🍽) (📷) (🚪) (DATA PORT) (🏊) (👷)

CROWN INN

	5/12-10/15	1P: $56-$78	2P: $66-$89	XP: $6 F12
	5/1-5/11 & 10/16-4/30	1P: $46-$56	2P: $52-$62	XP: $6 F12

Phone: (716)343-2311

🆘 SAVE ◆◆ Motel

Location: I-90, exit 48, just sw. 8212 Park Rd 14020. Fax: 716/343-2053. **Terms:** [CP] meal plan; weekly rates avail; pets, $6 extra charge. **Facility:** 20 rooms. Small to medium sized rooms with a light, airy, contemporary scheme. 2 stories; interior corridors. **Dining:** Restaurant nearby. **Services:** winter plug-ins. **All Rooms:** extended cable TV. **Cards:** AE, DI, DS, MC, VI. **Special Amenities:** Free breakfast.

MICROTEL INN & SUITES

	6/24-9/3	1P: $90-$110	2P: $96-$116	XP: $6 F16
	5/12-6/23	1P: $75-$95	2P: $81-$101	XP: $6 F16
	5/1-5/11 & 9/4-4/30	1P: $63-$73	2P: $69-$79	XP: $6 F16

Phone: (716)344-8882

🆘 SAVE ◆◆◆ Motel

Location: I-90, exit 48. 8210 Park Rd 14020. Fax: 716/344-7187. **Terms:** [CP] meal plan. **Facility:** 52 rooms. Spacious guest rooms with dark wood furnishings, 22 suites with appliances. 2 stories; interior corridors; heated pool, whirlpool. **All Rooms:** combo or shower baths, extended cable TV. **Cards:** AE, DI, DS, MC, VI. **Special Amenities:** Free breakfast. *(See ad p 201)*

——— RESTAURANT ———

PONTILLO'S PIZZA & PASTA

Lunch: $4-$7   **Dinner:** $4-$7   **Phone:** 716/343-3303

◆ Italian

Location: Downtown; just e on SR 5 (Main St). 500 E Main St 14020. **Hours:** 11 am-midnight. Closed: 4/23, 11/23 & 12/25. **Features:** casual dress; health conscious menu items; carryout; beer & wine only. Established in 1947, the casual family restaurant delivers traditional Italian and American dishes, such as chicken wings, homemade pasta and tasty pizzas baked in stone hearth ovens. Diners can watch food being prepared in the open kitchen. **Cards:** AE, CB, DI, DS, MC, VI.

BATH pop. 5,800—See also FINGER LAKES.

——— LODGINGS ———

BATH SUPER 8

Phone: (607)776-2187

◆◆ Motel

Property failed to provide current rates

Location: SR 17, exit 38, just n. 333 W Morris St 14810. Fax: 607/776-3206. **Facility:** 50 rooms. 3 stories, no elevator; interior/exterior corridors. **Cards:** AE, CB, DI, DS, JC, MC, VI.

DAYS INN
◆◆
Motor Inn

	6/1-9/30	1P: $60	2P: $95	XP: $5	D18
	10/1-4/30	1P: $60	2P: $75		
	5/1-5/31	1P: $60	2P: $75	XP: $5	D18

Phone: (607)776-7644

Location: SR 17, exit 38, just n. 330 W Morris St 14810. Fax: 607/776-7650. **Terms:** Pets. **Facility:** 104 rooms. Nice looking rooms close to commercial area. 5 stories; interior corridors; heated pool. **Services:** winter plug-ins. **All Rooms:** Fee: safes. **Cards:** AE, CB, DI, DS, JC, MC, VI.

———— RESTAURANT ————

LOAFIN TREE RESTAURANT   Dinner: $6-$13   Phone: 607/776-7734
ⓐⓐⓐ   **Location:** 1 mi n on SR 54 from jct SR 54 and Rt 415. 143 Geneva St 14810. **Hours:** 4 pm-10 pm, Sun
◆   11:30 am-10 pm. Closed: 11/23 & 12/25. **Reservations:** accepted; larger groups. **Features:** casual dress;
American   children's menu; carryout; cocktails & lounge. This family-style restaurant offers good-size portions of
          wholesome, homecooked food. Finger Lakes wines are available by the bottle or the glass. The
          well-coordinated dining room has a pleasant, relaxed atmosphere. Uniformed servers are efficient.
Cards: AE, DS, MC, VI.

BAY SHORE pop. 21,300

———— LODGING ————

SUMMIT MOTOR INN   Phone: (631)666-6000
ⓐⓐⓐ   All Year   1P: $75-$105   2P: $85-$125   XP: $10   F12
◆   **Location:** On SR 27A, exit 42 S of Southern State Pkwy, 1.1 mi e of jct 5th Ave and Main St; I-495, exit 56,
Motel   5.5 mi s to SR 27A, 1.5 mi w. 501 E Main St 11706. Fax: 631/665-7476. **Terms:** Weekly rates avail. **Facility:** 42
         rooms. 1 story; exterior corridors. **Dining:** Restaurant nearby. **All Rooms:** combo or shower baths, extended
         cable TV. **Cards:** AE, CB, DI, DS, MC, VI.

BELLEROSE pop. 1,100

———— RESTAURANT ————

CALLA LARGA-NORTHERN ITALIAN   Lunch: $10-$21   Dinner: $12-$23   Phone: 718/343-2185
◆◆◆   **Location:** Cross Island Pkwy, exit 27 E, just e on Jericho Tpke/Jamaica Ave. 247-63 Jamaica Ave & Jericho
Northern Tpke 11426. **Hours:** noon-3 & 5-10 pm, Fri-11 pm, Sat 5 pm-11 pm, Sun 2 pm-9 pm. Closed: 1/1, 12/25 &
Italian   Mon. **Reservations:** suggested. **Features:** dressy casual; carryout; cocktails; a la carte. A cozy ambience
          prevails in the intimate dining room, which is decorated with attractive art. The menu lists a fairly wide
assortment of seafood, pasta and meat dishes, including innovative specialties from the Dalmatian coast of the Adriatic.
Cards: AE, DI, MC, VI.

BELLPORT pop. 2,600

———— LODGING ————

THE GREAT SOUTH BAY INN   Phone: 631/286-8588
◆◆◆   5/26-9/30   2P: $105-$125   XP: $15
Bed &   5/1-5/25 & 10/1-4/30   2P: $85-$99   XP: $15
Breakfast **Location:** Downtown; on Main St (S Country Rd). 160 S Country Rd 11713. Fax: 631/286-2460. **Terms:** [BP]
          meal plan; age restrictions may apply; 7 day cancellation notice; small pets only, $15 extra charge. **Facility:** 6
rooms. Lovingly restored late 19th century shungle home. Large parlour and sun room. All rooms have original wainscotting
intact. Overflowing gardens. 2 stories; interior corridors; smoke free premises. **Some Rooms:** color TV. **Cards:** MC, VI.

BEMUS POINT pop. 400

———— RESTAURANTS ————

ITALIAN FISHERMAN   Lunch: $7-$14   Dinner: $12-$22   Phone: 716/386-7000
◆◆   **Location:** SR 17, exit 10, 1 mi s on Rt 430; on Lake Chautauqua. 61 Lakeside Dr 14712. **Hours:** Open
American 5/1-9/20; 11:30 am-10 pm, Fri & Sat-midnight. **Reservations:** suggested. **Features:** casual dress; children's
          menu; health conscious menu items; carryout; cocktails & lounge; street parking. The restaurant's outdoor
decks—casual gathering places for families—overlook Lake Chautauqua. The eclectic menu satisfies a wide range of
appetites, whether you crave steak, lemon-pepper tuna or pasta. Service is attentive and inquisitive. **Cards:** AE, DI, MC, VI.

YE HARE N' HOUNDS INN   Dinner: $14-$19   Phone: 716/386-2181
◆◆   **Location:** Opposite Lake Chautauqua, 1 mi s from SR 17, exit 10. 64 Lakeside Dr 14712. **Hours:** 5 pm-10
American pm, Sun 4 pm-9 pm; closing hrs may vary in winter. Closed: 9/4, 12/24 & 12/25. **Reservations:** suggested.
          Features: casual dress; cocktails & lounge. Enjoy lovely views of Lake Chautauqua from the informal, rustic
dining room of the English-style inn. Preparations of seafood, chicken, veal and steak are flavorful. Try the mouthwatering,
deep-fried artichoke hearts and one of the creative pies. **Cards:** AE, DS, MC, VI.

BERLIN pop. 1,900

———— LODGING ————

THE SEDGWICK INN   **Phone:** (518)658-2334
◆◆   Property failed to provide current rates
Country Inn   **Location:** 1 mi s on Rt 22. 17971 Rt 22 12022 (PO Box 250). Fax: 518/658-3998. **Terms:** [BP] meal plan;
cancellation fee imposed; pets, $5 extra charge. **Facility:** 11 rooms. Main inn dates to 1791 with rooms fur-
nished in antiques; also 6 modest motel units. Peaceful location in rural area. Age restrictions may apply for inn rooms. Owner
has pets on premises. 1-2 stories; interior/exterior corridors. **Services:** gift shop. **All Rooms:** combo or shower baths.
Some Rooms: B/W TV, color TV. **Cards:** AE, CB, DI, DS, MC, VI.   🛏 🍴 ⊠ ⱯⱯ VCR 🖨 ▣ 🔒

———— RESTAURANT ————

SEDGWICK INN DINING ROOM   Country Inn   **Lunch:** $5-$8   **Dinner:** $17-$23   **Phone:** 518/658-2334
◆◆◆   **Location:** 1 mi s on Rt 22; in The Sedgwick Inn. 17971 Rt 22 12022. **Hours:** 11:30 am-2 & 5-9 pm, Sun 1
Continental   pm-8 pm. Closed: Mon & Tues. **Reservations:** suggested; req weekends. **Features:** No A/C; dressy casual;
cocktails; a la carte. In a building that dates to 1791, the restaurant has a weekly changing, blackboard
menu that lists an eclectic array of offerings, including delicious homemade soups and desserts. The wine cellar is
well-stocked. A pianist plays on most weekends. **Cards:** AE, CB, DI, DS, MC, VI.   ⊠

BIG FLATS

———— LODGING ————

ECONO LODGE   **Phone:** (607)739-2000
◆◆   7/1-8/31   1P: $59-$126   2P: $72-$126   XP: $7   F18
Motel   5/1-6/30 & 9/1-4/30   1P: $59-$88   2P: $72-$88   XP: $7   F18
Location: SR 17, exit 51, just s. (811 Rt 64, ELMIRA, 14903). Fax: 607/739-3552. **Terms:** [CP] meal plan.
Facility: 48 rooms. 2 stories; interior/exterior corridors. **Services:** area transportation. **Cards:** AE, CB, DI, DS, MC, VI.
SAVE S/D 🔀 🍴 🛏 ⊠ 🏆 🖨 ▣ 🔒 DATA PORT

BINGHAMTON pop. 53,000

———— LODGINGS ————

BEST WESTERN BINGHAMTON REGENCY HOTEL AND CONFERENCE CENTER   **Phone:** (607)722-7575
◆◆◆   All Year   1P: $79-$119   2P: $79-$119   XP: $10   F12
Hotel   **Location:** Front to E Clinton, I-81, exit 5; New York Rt 17, exit 72; to Front St, 1 mi s on Front St, just e on E
Clinton, then just s. 225 Water St 13901. Fax: 607/724-7263. **Terms:** Check-in 4 pm; 2 night min stay, 5/19-
5/21; package plans. **Facility:** 204 rooms. Extensive conference facilities in downtown area. 10 stories; interior corridors;
heated pool. **Services:** gift shop. **Cards:** AE, CB, DI, DS, MC, VI. *(See color ad below)*
ASK S/D 🔀 🍴 🍸 🎿 🛏 🐕 🎣 ⊠ 🖨 ▣ 🔒 DATA PORT 🛏 🧍

COMFORT INN

DAYS INN
◆◆◆
Motel

5/19-9/30	1P: $85	2P: $95	XP: $10 F
5/1-5/18	1P: $75	2P: $95	XP: $10 F
10/1-4/30	1P: $75	2P: $75	XP: $10 F

Phone: (607)724-3297

Location: I-81 S, exit 6, 2 mi s on Rt 11; I-81 N, exit 5 (Front St), 1 mi n on Rt 11. 1000 Front St 13905. **Fax:** 607/771-0206. **Terms:** [CP] meal plan; 90 day cancellation notice; cancellation fee imposed; pets, with advance notice. **Facility:** 105 rooms. Tastefully decorated rooms close to Broome Community College and commercial areas. 4 stories; interior corridors. **Some Rooms:** Fee: refrigerators. **Cards:** AE, CB, DI, DS, JC, MC, VI.

HOLIDAY INN ARENA
◆◆◆
Hotel

All Year 1P: $90 2P: $90

Phone: (607)722-1212

Location: Downtown. 2-8 Hawley St 13901. **Fax:** 607/722-6063. **Terms:** Check-in 4 pm; package plans; pets, $25 extra charge. **Facility:** 240 rooms. Downtown and overlooks river, across from events arena. 11 two-bedroom units. 9 stories; interior corridors; heated pool. **Services:** gift shop. **Cards:** AE, CB, DI, DS, JC, MC, VI.
(See color ad p 205)

MOTEL 6 - 1222
(AAA)
◆ ◆
Motel

5/1-10/11	1P: $39-$49	2P: $45-$55	XP: $3 F17
10/12-4/30	1P: $36-$46	2P: $42-$52	XP: $3 F17

Phone: 607/771-0400

Location: I-81 S, exit 6, 2 mi s on Rt 11; I-81 N, exit 5 (Front St), 1 mi n on Rt 11. 1012 Front St 13905. **Fax:** 607/773-4781. **Terms:** Small pets only. **Facility:** 97 rooms. Comfortable rooms with pleasant appearance close to Broome Community College and commercial areas. 2 stories; interior corridors. **Dining:** Restaurant nearby. **All Rooms:** combo or shower baths, extended cable TV. **Cards:** AE, CB, DI, DS, MC, VI.

RAMADA INN
(AAA) SAVE
◆ ◆
Motor Inn

All Year 1P: $82-$92 2P: $102 XP: $15 F18

Phone: (607)724-2412

Location: I-81, exit 5; SR 17 E, exit 72, 1 mi s. 65 Front St 13905. **Fax:** 607/724-4000. **Terms:** Package plans; pets, $25 dep req. **Facility:** 124 rooms. 3 stories; interior corridors; heated pool, saunas. **Dining:** Restaurant; 7-10 am, 11:30-2 & 5-8 pm; $9-$20. **All Rooms:** extended cable TV. **Cards:** AE, CB, DI, DS, MC, VI. **Special Amenities:** Early check-in/late check-out and free breakfast.

SUPER 8 MOTEL-BINGHAMTON
◆ ◆
Motel

All Year 1P: $35-$105 2P: $35-$105 XP: $5 F17

Phone: (607)773-8111

Location: I-81, exit 5 to access road. 650 Old Front St 13905. **Fax:** 607/773-8111. **Terms:** [CP] meal plan; pets, $35 dep req. **Facility:** 63 rooms. Set near residential area but close access to commercial areas and Broome Community College. 2 stories; interior corridors. **Cards:** AE, CB, DI, DS, JC, MC, VI.

SUPER 8 UPPER COURT STREET
◆
Motor Inn

All Year 1P: $42-$50 2P: $50-$60 XP: $8 F12

Phone: (607)775-3443

Location: I-81 S, exit 3; I-81 N, exit 2 W; SR 17 W, exit 75. 771 Upper Court St 13904-0196 (PO Box 196). **Fax:** 607/775-2368. **Terms:** [CP] meal plan; pets. **Facility:** 104 rooms. Adequate rooms with good access to hwys. 2 stories; exterior corridors. **Some Rooms:** Fee: refrigerators, microwaves. **Cards:** AE, CB, DI, DS, JC, MC, VI.

------ **RESTAURANTS** ------

ARGO RESTAURANT
◆
Greek

Lunch: $4-$7 Dinner: $6-$12 **Phone:** 607/724-4692

Location: 117 Court St 13901. **Hours:** 6 am-9 pm. Closed: 1/1, 11/23 & 12/25. **Features:** carryout; beer & wine only; street parking. Rustic decor adds to the charm of the simple, casual restaurant, which offers counter and table seating. The broad menu includes Greek, Italian and fresh seafood dishes, as well as lunch specials and sandwiches. Breakfast items are served all day. **Cards:** AE, DI, DS, MC, VI.

THE COPPER CRICKET
◆ ◆
Continental

Dinner: $10-$13 **Phone:** 607/729-5620

Location: I-81, exit 5, 1 mi s on Front St, 1 mi w on Main St; SR 17, exit 71, 0.5 mi s on Airport Rd, 0.5 mi s on Glenwood Ave, then w. 266 Main St 13905. **Hours:** 5 pm-10 pm. Closed: 11/23, 12/25, Sun & Mon. **Reservations:** suggested. **Features:** casual dress; health conscious menu items; beer & wine only; a la carte. Old hats hang along the walls and wine bottles line the sills of crank windows in the dining room. Representative of menu selections are baked brie with almonds, pork barbecue and cream of mushroom and amaretto soup. Service is informal but attentive. Smoke free premises. **Cards:** AE, MC, VI.

CORTESE RESTAURANT
(AAA)
◆ ◆
Italian

Lunch: $3-$13 Dinner: $3-$25 **Phone:** 607/723-6477

Location: SR 17/I-81, exit 4, s to Robinson St exit, then e. 117 Robinson St 13904. **Hours:** 11 am-11 pm, Fri & Sat-midnight. Closed: 4/4, 11/23, 12/24 & 12/25. **Reservations:** accepted; suggested wknd. **Features:** casual dress; health conscious menu items; carryout; cocktails & lounge. Family operated since 1947, this family-oriented restaurant boasts a convivial, upbeat atmosphere. The tempting scents of aromatic steaks, chops and pizza hang in the air of the dining room. The entire staff is friendly, cooperative and prompt. **Cards:** AE, CB, DI, DS, MC, VI.

LITTLE VENICE
◆ ◆
Italian

Lunch: $4-$7 Dinner: $7-$18 **Phone:** 607/724-2513

Location: Downtown. 111 Chenango St 13901. **Hours:** 11:30 am-midnight. Closed: Mon. **Reservations:** suggested. **Features:** casual dress; carryout; cocktails & lounge. An area institution since 1946, the restaurant is known for tasty Italian and American cuisine—particularly its spaghetti sauce, which it packages and ships. The dining room walls are covered with original artwork, some of which dates back to the 1800s. **Cards:** DS, MC, VI.

LOST DOG CAFE/COFFEEHOUSE   **Lunch:** $5-$7   **Dinner:** $9-$13   **Phone:** 607/771-6063
◆◆   **Location:** Front to E Clinton, I-81 exit 5; SR 17 exit 72; to Front St, 1 mi s on Front St, just e on E Clinton,
American   just s; across from BW Regency. 222 Water St 13901. **Hours:** 11 am-11 pm, Fri & Sat-midnight, Sun 10
am-4 pm. Closed major holidays. **Features:** No A/C; casual dress; children's menu; health conscious menu;
beer & wine only. The trendy bistro, appointed in a mix of Americana furnishings, has a cafe-style ambience.
Health-conscious diners appreciate the creative menu, which focuses on nouvelle cuisine, much of which is vegetarian.
Chicken muffuletta is particularly tasty. **Cards:** AE, DI, DS, MC, VI.   ⊠

NUMBER 5   Historical   **Dinner:** $13-$24   **Phone:** 607/723-0555
◆◆◆   **Location:** I-81, exit 4 S, to SR 434, just over bridge. 33 S Washington St 13903. **Hours:** 5 pm-10 pm.
American   Closed: 12/25. **Reservations:** suggested. **Features:** casual dress; cocktails & lounge. An extensive wine list
complements traditional preparations of steaks, fish, veal, pasta and chicken, as well as many Greek
entrees. Lots of antiques and old photographs decorate the restored fire station. The atmosphere is warm and comfortable.
Cards: AE, DI, DS, MC, VI.   ⊠

SPOT DINER RESTAURANT   **Lunch:** $5-$12   **Dinner:** $8-$20   **Phone:** 607/723-8149
◆   **Location:** On Hwys 11 and 12, between exits 5 and 6 off I-81. 1062 Front St 13905. **Hours:** 24 hrs.
American   **Reservations:** accepted. **Features:** casual dress; children's menu; carryout; cocktails & lounge. Greek and
Italian dishes—such as gyros and Reubens—are among selections on the casual restaurant's extensive
menu. As you enter, you're tempted by an appealing display of fresh-baked pastries, fluffy cheesecakes and luscious Greek
desserts. **Cards:** AE, DI, DS, MC, VI.   ⊠

BLASDELL —See Buffalo p. 221.

BLOOMFIELD pop. 500—See also FINGER LAKES.

—— **RESTAURANT** ——

THE ORIGINAL HOLLOWAY HOUSE   Historical   **Lunch:** $8-$12   **Dinner:** $15-$20   **Phone:** 716/657-7120
(AAA)   **Location:** 8 mi w of jct 332 on US 20 and SR 5. 29 State St 14443. **Hours:** Open 5/1-12/15 & 4/1-4/30;
11:30 am-2 & 5-9 pm, Sun noon-7:30 pm. Closed: Mon, except 9/4. **Reservations:** suggested.
◆◆◆   **Features:** casual dress; children's menu; early bird specials; cocktails & lounge. The quaint 1808 country inn
American   is decorated in the Early American style, with lace curtains, wreaths and country accents. Home-style
favorites, such as roast turkey dinners with gravy and mashed potatoes, mingle with fresh-baked breads and
desserts. **Cards:** AE, MC, VI.   ⊠

BOLTON LANDING pop. 1,600—See also ADIRONDACK MOUNTAINS.

—— **LODGINGS** ——

BONNIE VIEW RESORT   **Phone:** 518/644-5591
(AAA)   7/14-9/3   1P: $95-$140   2P: $95-$140   XP: $7
       6/19-7/13   1P: $79-$115   2P: $79-$115   XP: $7
◆◆   5/12-6/18 & 9/4-9/18   1P: $53-$72   2P: $53-$72   XP: $3
Complex   **Location:** 1.5 mi s on SR 9 N. 4654 Lake Shore Dr 12814-0330 (PO Box 330, 12814). Fax: 518/644-3611.
Terms: Open 5/12-9/18; weekly rates avail; 28 day cancellation notice; 3 night min stay, 7/1-7/31. **Facility:** 50
rooms. Located on Lake George. Motel rooms and cottages, some with fireplace. Additional charge for housekeeping service
in cottage units. 7 night min stay, housekeeping units, $505-$1200 for up to 6 persons, 7/1-8/30; 3 night min stay, 7/1-7/30; 4
night min stay, 8/1-8/31; 1 story; exterior corridors; beach, heated pool; 1 tennis court; playground. Fee: boat dock.
Recreation: swimming, fishing, row boats; lawn games. **All Rooms:** combo or shower baths, extended cable TV.
Some Rooms: 5 efficiencies. **Cards:** DS, MC, VI. *(See color ad p 282)*   ☎ ▣ ▤ 🏊 ⊠

MELODY MANOR RESORT   **Phone:** (518)644-9750
(AAA)   6/23-9/4   1P: $115-$160   2P: $115-$160   XP: $15   D
       5/5-6/22 & 9/5-10/22   1P: $65-$100   2P: $65-$100   XP: $10   D
◆◆◆   **Location:** 1.8 mi s on SR 9 N. 4610 Lakeshore Dr 12814 (PO Box 366). Fax: 518/644-9750. **Terms:** Open
Motor Inn   5/5-10/22; 15 day cancellation notice; cancellation fee imposed; 3 night min stay, 7/1-8/31. **Facility:** 40 rooms.
Some lakefront units with balcony. Spacious landscaped grounds on inlet of Lake George. 2 stories; exterior
corridors; designated smoking area; lakefront; beach, heated pool; 1 tennis court; playground. Fee: boat dock. **Dining:** Res-
taurant; 8 am-noon & 5-10 pm, 6/24-9/5 & weekends off season; $9-$20; cocktails; also, Villa Napoli, see separate listing.
Recreation: swimming, fishing, paddleboats, rowboats; lawn games. **All Rooms:** extended cable TV. **Some Rooms:** Fee: refrigerators. **Cards:** MC, VI. *(See ad p 290)*   🍴 🍸 ♿ ⊠ 🖨 ▤ 🏊 ⊠

THE SAGAMORE   **Phone:** (518)644-9400
(AAA)   6/23-9/3   2P: $240-$380   XP: $18   F12
       5/1-6/22 & 9/4-11/11   2P: $170-$290   XP: $18   F12
◆◆◆◆   11/12-4/30   2P: $125-$150   XP: $18   F12
Resort   **Location:** Sagamore Island on Lake George; from I-87 Northway, exit 22, 0.7 mi n to jct SR 9 N, 9.4 mi n on
SR 9 N. 110 Sagamore Rd 12814 (PO Box 450). Fax: 518/644-2626. **Terms:** [MAP] meal plan; check-in 4 pm;
14 day cancellation notice, 30 day notice 7/1-8/31; cancellation fee imposed; 3 night min stay, weekends 7/1-8/31; package
plans. **Facility:** 350 rooms. Restored historic Adirondack retreat on private island on Lake George. Hotel and lodge-style
rooms. $5 per person gratuity service charge; 2-3 stories; interior/exterior corridors; miniature golf; beach, heated pool, steam-
rooms, whirlpool; spa. Fee: 18 holes golf; saunas; racquetball court, 7 tennis courts (2 indoor, 5 lighted); boat dock.
Dining: Dining room, 3 restaurants; 7 am-1 am; $12-$30; health conscious menu items; cocktails; also, Trillium, see separate
listing; entertainment. **Services:** gift shop. Fee: massage. **Recreation:** swimming, fishing; cross country skiing, ice skating; bicycles, carriage rides, sightseeing cruise. Fee: charter sailboats, charter fishing, dinner cruises, parasailing. Rental: boats.
All Rooms: safes. **Cards:** AE, CB, DI, DS, MC, VI. *(See ad p 290)*

🈯 🍴 🍸 ♿ 🅿 ⛱ 🛏 🏌 ⊠ 🎿 🖨 ▣ 🖼 ▤ 📊 🏊 ♿ ⊠

VICTORIAN VILLAGE RESORT MOTEL **Phone: 518/644-9401**

◆◆ 6/24-9/4 1P: $72-$80 2P: $72-$80 XP: $12

Motel 5/1-6/23 & 9/5-11/1 1P: $65-$67 2P: $65-$67 XP: $12

Location: 0.8 mi s on SR 9 N. Rt 9 N 12814 (PO Box 12). Fax: 518/644-9401. **Terms:** Open 5/1-11/1; 7 day cancellation notice; 3 night min stay, 7/1-9/8. **Facility:** 30 rooms. Spacious, attractively landscaped grounds in peaceful setting on Lake George. 1 story; exterior corridors; 1 tennis court. Fee: boat dock. **Recreation:** swimming, canoeing, fishing. **All Rooms:** combo or shower baths. **Cards:** MC, VI.

──────── **RESTAURANTS** ────────

ALGONQUIN RESTAURANT **Lunch:** $7-$17 **Dinner:** $17-$23 **Phone:** 518/644-9442

ⒶⒶⒶ **Location:** 1 mi s on SR 9 N. Rt 9 N 12814. **Hours:** Open 5/1-10/12 & 4/19-4/30; noon-9:30 pm.

◆◆ **Reservations:** suggested; for Topside. **Features:** casual dress; children's menu; health conscious menu;

American carryout; cocktails & lounge. Overlooking Lake George, the casual restaurant is especially popular in summer, when diners gather in the Topside room and on the patio to enjoy great views and good food.

MC, VI. Salmon, veal and steak are among well-prepared choices. Desserts are homemade. **Cards:** AE, DI, DS, MC, VI.

TRILLIUM **Dinner:** $17-$30 **Phone:** 518/644-9400

ⒶⒶⒶ **Location:** Sagamore Island on Lake George; from I-87 Northway, exit 22, 0.7 mi n to jct SR 9 N, 9.4 mi n on

◆◆◆◆ SR 9 N; in The Sagamore. 110 Sagamore Rd 12814. **Hours:** 6 pm-9:30 pm. **Reservations:** required.

American **Features:** semi-formal attire; children's menu; health conscious menu; cocktails & lounge; valet parking; a la carte. An impressive selection of wines complements such innovative entrees as ginger-poached halibut with herbed risotto, Thai tomato broth and fresh spinach. The dining room is bathed in a luxurious, sophisticated ambience. Service is gracious and pampering. **Cards:** AE, CB, DI, DS, MC, VI.

VILLA NAPOLI **Dinner:** $10-$20 **Phone:** 518/644-9047

ⒶⒶⒶ **Location:** 1.8 mi s on SR 9 N; in Melody Manor Resort. 46-10 Lakeshore Dr 12814. **Hours:** Open

◆◆◆ 5/15-10/11; 8 am-11:30 am; 5 pm-10 pm, 5/15-10/11; weekends only, 5/20-6/14 & 9/6-10/11.

Italian **Reservations:** suggested. **Features:** casual dress; children's menu; health conscious menu items; carryout; cocktails & lounge; a la carte. Hand-carved marble fireplace and art deco appointments lend to the sophisticated charm of the elegant dining room, which is on the property of a former estate. Braised veal shanks and sauteed, stuffed eggplant are examples of flavorful entrees. **Cards:** AE, MC, VI.

BOONVILLE pop. 2,200

──────── **LODGING** ────────

HEADWATERS MOTOR LODGE **Phone:** (315)942-4493

ⒶⒶⒶ Ⓢⓐⓥⓔ 6/2-9/30 & 12/4-4/30 1P: $45-$49 2P: $59-$65 XP: $8 F12

◆◆ 5/1-6/1 1P: $45-$49 2P: $55-$59 XP: $8 F12

Motel 10/1-12/3 1P: $49 2P: $59 XP: $8 F12

Location: SR 12, 0.7 mi n of jct US 12 and 120. 13524 Rt 12 13309 (PO Box 337). Fax: 315/942-4626. **Terms:** [CP] meal plan; 3 day cancellation notice; package plans; small pets only. **Facility:** 37 rooms. Good sized guest rooms with older colonial decor. 1-2 stories; interior corridors. **Services:** winter plug-ins. **All Rooms:** extended cable TV. **Some Rooms:** efficiency. **Cards:** AE, DS, MC, VI. **Special Amenities: Free breakfast and free local telephone calls.**

──────── **RESTAURANT** ────────

──────── *The following restaurant has not been inspected by AAA* ────────
but is listed for your information only.

HULBERT HOUSE **Phone:** 315/942-4318

[fyi] Not inspected. **Location:** 106 Main St. **Features:** This is a very casual steak and seafood restaurant with an early American atmosphere.

BOWMANSVILLE —*See Buffalo p. 221.*

BREWERTON pop. 3,000

──────── **LODGING** ────────

HOLIDAY INN EXPRESS **Phone:** (315)676-3222

ⒶⒶⒶ Ⓢⓐⓥⓔ All Year 2P: $75-$125 XP: $10 F14

◆◆◆ **Location:** I-81, exit 31 (Bartell Rd), just w. 5552 Bartell Rd 13029. Fax: 315/676-7497. **Terms:** Weekly &

Motel monthly rates avail. **Facility:** 64 rooms. 2 stories; interior corridors. **Dining:** Restaurant nearby. **Services:** winter plug-ins. **All Rooms:** combo or shower baths, extended cable TV. **Cards:** AE, DI, DS, JC, MC, VI. **Special Amenities: Free breakfast and free local telephone calls.**

──────── **RESTAURANT** ────────

SAM'S LAKESIDE RESTAURANT **Lunch:** $3-$6 **Dinner:** $6-$18 **Phone:** 315/668-6110

ⒶⒶⒶ **Location:** I-81, exit 31, nw corner of jct I-81 and Bartell Rd. 5555 Bartell Rd 13029. **Hours:** 11 am-11 pm,

◆◆ Fri & Sat-midnight. Closed: 12/25. **Features:** casual dress; children's menu; early bird specials; senior's

American menu; cocktails & lounge; entertainment. Fresh Boston seafood and Italian home-style fare make up the bulk of the family restaurant's menu. Italian paintings and area maps decorate the walls of the unpretentious dining room. Tempting pies are made on the premises. Servers are friendly. **Cards:** AE, DI, DS, MC, VI.

BRIGHTON pop. 34,500 (See map p. 456; index p. 455)

LODGINGS

COURTYARD BY MARRIOTT BRIGHTON   Phone: (716)292-1000   [18]
♦♦♦   All Year   1P: $89-$114   2P: $89-$114
Motel   **Location:** I-390, exit 16B (E Henrietta Rd) southbound; exit 16 northbound. 33 Corporate Woods 14623.
Fax: 716/292-0905. **Terms:** Check-in 4 pm. **Facility:** 149 rooms. Attractive courtyard area. 3 stories; interior corridors; heated pool. **Cards:** AE, DI, DS, MC, VI.

HAMPTON INN-SOUTH   Phone: (716)272-7800   [16]
♦♦♦   All Year   1P: $99   2P: $99
Motel   **Location:** I-390, exit 16B (Henrietta Rd) southbound; exit 16 northbound. 717 E Henrietta Rd 14623.
Fax: 716/272-1211. **Terms:** [CP] meal plan; small pets only. **Facility:** 113 rooms. Breakfast area in lobby. 4 parlor rooms are more spacious. 5 stories; interior corridors. **Cards:** AE, DI, DS, MC, VI.

TOWPATH MOTEL   Phone: (716)271-2147   [19]
AAA SAVE   All Year   1P: $35-$65   2P: $40-$75   XP: $10   F15
♦   **Location:** I-590, exit 2A, just w on US 31. 2323 Monroe Ave 14618. Fax: 716/271-2147. **Terms:** [CP] meal
Motel   plan; cancellation fee imposed. **Facility:** 20 rooms. Modestly furnished rooms. 2 stories; exterior corridors.
Dining: Restaurant nearby. **All Rooms:** combo or shower baths, extended cable TV. **Some Rooms:** Fee: microwaves. **Cards:** AE, CB, DI, DS, MC, VI.

WELLESLEY INN & SUITES   Phone: (716)427-0130   [17]
AAA SAVE   All Year   1P: $60-$85   2P: $65-$105   XP: $5   F17
♦♦   **Location:** SR 15A, at I-390, exit 16 northbound; exit 16B southbound. 797 E Henrietta Rd 14623.
Motel   Fax: 716/427-0903. **Terms:** [CP] meal plan; pets, $3 extra charge. **Facility:** 96 rooms. Cherry veneer furniture
in rooms. Some suites. A modest size but smartly appointed lobby. 4 stories; interior corridors. **Dining:** Restaurant nearby. **All Rooms:** combo or shower baths, extended cable TV. **Some Rooms:** Fee: refrigerators.
Cards: AE, CB, DI, DS, MC, VI. **Special Amenities:** Free breakfast and free newspaper.
(See color ad p 458 & color ad p 4)

RESTAURANT

MARIO'S VIA ABRUZZI   **Dinner:** $13-$17   Phone: 716/271-1111   [11]
♦♦   **Location:** I-590, exit 2 (Monroe Ave), just w. 2740 Monroe Ave 14618. **Hours:** 5 pm-10 pm, Fri-11 pm, Sat 4
Italian   pm-11 pm, Sun 11 am-2 & 4-9 pm. Closed major holidays. **Reservations:** suggested. **Features:** casual
dress; Sunday brunch; children's menu; carryout; cocktails & lounge; a la carte. Quality ingredients go into the preparation of such entrees as fettuccine Alfredo. An Italian motif, carried out with wall hangings and other decor, weaves through the dining room. To end your meal on a great note, enjoy the creme caramel cappuccino. Smoke free premises. **Cards:** AE, DI, DS, MC, VI.

BRISTOL CENTER pop. 100—See also *FINGER LAKES.*

LODGING

ACORN INN   Phone: (716)229-2834
AAA   5/1-11/30   1P: $115-$205   2P: $115-$205
♦♦♦♦   12/1-4/30   1P: $100-$195   2P: $100-$195
Historic Bed   **Location:** Center. 4508 SR 64 S 14424-9309. Fax: 716/229-5046. **Terms:** [BP] meal plan; weekly & monthly
& Breakfast   rates avail; age restrictions may apply; 14 day cancellation notice; 2 night min stay, weekends 7/1-10/31;
package plans. **Facility:** 4 rooms. Built in 1795 as a stagecoach inn. Beautifully appointed rooms with fine furnishings and many antiques. Lovely gardens and quiet country charm. Whirlpool room; 2 stories; interior corridors; designated smoking area; whirlpool. **All Rooms:** extended cable TV. **Cards:** AE, DS, MC, VI.

BROCKPORT pop. 8,700

LODGING

ECONO LODGE OF BROCKPORT   Phone: (716)637-3157
AAA SAVE   All Year   1P: $50-$75   2P: $53-$90   F18
♦♦   **Location:** Just w on SR 31 from jct SR 19. 6575 4th Section Rd 14420. Fax: 716/637-0434. **Terms:** Pets.
Motel   **Facility:** 39 rooms. Small rooms. 2 stories; exterior corridors; playground. **Dining:** Restaurant nearby.
Some Rooms: 4 efficiencies. **Cards:** AE, CB, DI, DS, JC, MC, VI. **Special Amenities:** Free breakfast and free newspaper.

BROOKLYN —See *New York p. 370.*

Destination Buffalo

*O*ften described as a European-looking city, Buffalo has been sculpted by the hands of architectural greats.

*F*rom the bucolic city park system designed by Frederick Law Olmsted and the handful of Frank Lloyd Wright masterpieces, to Henry Hobson Richardson's Psychiatric Center and the Louis Sullivan Guaranty Building, Buffalo offers a varied palette of architectural styles.

Skyline, Buffalo.
Head across the Buffalo River and become immersed in the "Queen City's" spectacular array of buildings.

Erie County Fair, Hamburg.
Get dizzy on the circular rides at one of the country's oldest and largest fairs held in mid-August.
(See mention page 71)

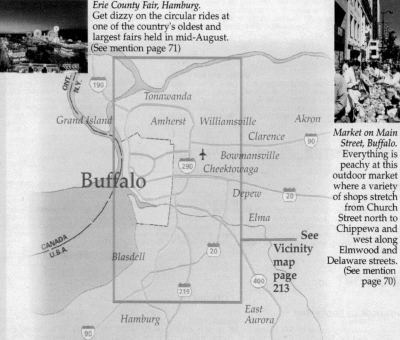

Market on Main Street, Buffalo.
Everything is peachy at this outdoor market where a variety of shops stretch from Church Street north to Chippewa and west along Elmwood and Delaware streets. (See mention page 70)

Skiing.
The sky's the limit on the slopes of the Buffalo area's nine major ski resorts. (See mention page 70)

*P*laces included in this AAA Destination City:

Akron	219	East Aurora	224
Amherst	219	Elma	225
Blasdell	221	Grand Island	225
Bowmansville	221	Hamburg	225
Cheektowaga	221	Tonawanda	226
Clarence	223	Williamsville	226
Depew	224		

Buffalo *pop. 328,100*

This index helps you "spot" where approved accommodations are located on the detailed maps that follow. Rate ranges are for comparison only and show the property's high season. Turn to the listing page for more detailed rate information and consult display ads for special promotions. Restaurant rate range is for dinner unless only lunch (L) is served.

✈ Airport Accommodations

Spotter/Map Page Number	OA	BUFFALO	Diamond Rating	Rate Range High Season	Listing Page
17 / p. 213	⬥	**Comfort Suites-Buffalo Airport, 0.7 mi w of West Terminal**	◆◆◆	$95-$115	221
20 / p. 213		Days Inn-Buffalo Airport, just e of terminal	◆◆	$64-$99	221
16 / p. 213	⬥	**Holiday Inn-Buffalo Airport, Just 0.8 mi e of terminal**	◆◆◆	$99-$149	222
25 / p. 213		Quality Inn-Buffalo Airport, facing Airport Terminal entrance	◆◆	$69-$130	222
22 / p. 213		Radisson Hotel & Suites, facing terminal entrance	◆◆◆	$146-$176	222
21 / p. 213	⬥	**Wellesley Inn & Suites, 0.8 mi e of terminal**	◆◆	$85-$115	223

BUFFALO

Spotter/Map Page Number	OA	BUFFALO - Lodgings	Diamond Rating	Rate Range High Season	Listing Page
1 / p. 213	⬥	**Adam's Mark Hotel - see color ad p 214**	◆◆◆	$109	214
2 / p. 213		Radisson Suite Hotel Buffalo	◆◆◆	$119-$169	216
5 / p. 213	⬥	**Best Western Inn-On The Avenue**	◆◆	$99-$125	215
6 / p. 213		Buffalo/Amherst Courtyard By Marriott	◆◆◆	$49-$149	215
8 / p. 213		Hyatt Regency Buffalo	◆◆◆	$114-$144	216
9 / p. 213	⬥	**Holiday Inn-Downtown**	◆◆	$109-$119	215
10 / p. 213	⬥	**Hampton Inn-Airport/Galleria Mall - see ad p 215**	◆◆◆	$89-$105	215

		BUFFALO - Restaurants			
2 / p. 213		Rue Franklin	◆◆◆	$17-$22	218
3 / p. 213		La Riviera Ristorante	◆◆	$8-$22	218
4 / p. 213		Just Pasta	◆◆	$10-$17	217
5 / p. 213		Ali Baba	◆◆	$4-$15	217
6 / p. 213		Oliver's Restaurant	◆◆◆	$17-$29	218
10 / p. 213		The Hourglass Restaurant	◆◆	$17-$29	217
11 / p. 213		The Park Lane Tavern & Oyster Bar	◆◆◆	$16-$25	218
12 / p. 213		Lord Chumley's	◆◆◆	$30-$50	218
13 / p. 213		The Blackthorn	◆◆	$9-$14	217
14 / p. 213		Breckenridge Brewery	◆◆	$7-$18	217
15 / p. 213		The Coda	◆◆◆	$17-$20	217
17 / p. 213		Colter Bay Grill	◆	$6-$11	217
19 / p. 213		Enchante	◆◆◆	$18-$28	217
20 / p. 213		Fiddle Heads Restaurant	◆◆◆	$12-$22	217
23 / p. 213		Hemingway's	◆◆	$10-$11	217
24 / p. 213		Hutch's	◆◆◆	$11-$19	217
26 / p. 213		Left Bank	◆◆	$8-$19	218
30 / p. 213		Metropolitan	◆◆	$8-$17	218
31 / p. 213		The Steer	◆◆	$9-$15	219
32 / p. 213		Pettibone's Grille	◆◆	$10-$18	218
34 / p. 213		Roseland	◆◆◆	$6-$30	218
37 / p. 213		Saratoga	◆◆◆	$10-$15	218
38 / p. 213		Sequoia	◆◆◆	$15-$20	219

Buffalo Vicinity

Spotter/Map Page Number	OA	CHEEKTOWAGA - Lodgings	Diamond Rating	Rate Range High Season	Listing Page
16 / p. 213	AAA	Holiday Inn-Buffalo Airport	◆◆◆	$99-$149 ▨	222
17 / p. 213	AAA	Comfort Suites-Buffalo Airport - see ad p 214	◆◆◆	$95-$115 ▨	221
18 / p. 213		Homewood Suites Hotel	◆◆◆	$109-$149	222
19 / p. 213		Four Points Hotel Sheraton-Buffalo Airport - see color ad p 222	◆◆◆	$149-$164	221
20 / p. 213		Days Inn-Buffalo Airport	◆◆	$64-$99	221
21 / p. 213	AAA	Wellesley Inn & Suites - see color ad p 4	◆◆	$85-$115 ▨	223
22 / p. 213		Radisson Hotel & Suites - see color ad p 216	◆◆◆	$146-$176	222
23 / p. 213	AAA	Holiday Inn Express Hotel & Suites	◆◆◆	$99-$119 ▨	222
25 / p. 213		Quality Inn-Buffalo Airport	◆◆	$69-$130	222
26 / p. 213		Sleep Inn	◆◆	$75-$109	222
		CHEEKTOWAGA - Restaurants			
47 / p. 213		Jasmine II	◆◆	$8-$17	223
48 / p. 213		Pranzo Ristorante	◆◆◆	$23-$32	223
		AMHERST - Lodgings			
30 / p. 213	AAA	Travelodge	◆◆	$53-$70 ▨	220
31 / p. 213	AAA	Lord Amherst Motor Hotel	◆◆	$59-$85 ▨	220
33 / p. 213	AAA	Holiday Inn Buffalo-Amherst	◆◆◆	$100-$110 ▨	220
34 / p. 213	AAA	Buffalo Marriott-Niagara - see ad p 219	◆◆◆	$99-$159 ▨	219
35 / p. 213		Extended Stay America	◆◆	Failed to provide	219
36 / p. 213	AAA	Red Roof Inn	◆◆	$70-$90	220
37 / p. 213		Super 8 Motel-Amherst	◆◆	$47-$79	220
38 / p. 213		Sleep Inn	◆◆	$69-$99	220
39 / p. 213	AAA	Hampton Inn-Buffalo/Amherst	◆◆◆	$80-$90 ▨	220
		AMHERST - Restaurants			
53 / p. 213		Dakota Grill	◆◆◆	$11-$20	220
55 / p. 213		San Marco	◆◆◆	$12-$21	220
		WILLIAMSVILLE - Lodgings			
42 / p. 213	AAA	Lancaster Motor Inn	◆	$70-$90 ▨	227
43 / p. 213		Microtel-Lancaster	◆◆	$45-$50	228
44 / p. 213		Howard Johnson	◆◆	$69-$109	227
45 / p. 213		Residence Inn by Marriott Buffalo/Amherst	◆◆◆	$120-$150	228
47 / p. 213		Holiday Inn Express - see ad p 214	◆◆◆	$95-$109	227
49 / p. 213		Fairfield Inn-Lancaster	◆◆◆	Failed to provide	226
50 / p. 213		Garden Place Hotel	◆◆◆	$84-$129	227
		WILLIAMSVILLE - Restaurants			
62 / p. 213		Sigmund's Bistro	◆◆◆	$11-$20	228
64 / p. 213		ZuZon American Grille	◆◆	$9-$18	228
66 / p. 213		Hanny's Eagle House Restaurant	◆◆	$10-$20	228
67 / p. 213		Daffodil's	◆◆◆	$13-$30	228
		BOWMANSVILLE - Lodgings			
52 / p. 213	AAA	Red Roof Inn-Buffalo Airport	◆◆	$63-$87	221
		TONAWANDA - Lodgings			
56 / p. 213	AAA	Days Inn	◆◆	$59-$99 ▨	226
57 / p. 213		Microtel-Tonawanda	◆◆	$45-$71	226
59 / p. 213	AAA	Ellicott Park Court Motel	◆◆	$50-$60 ▨	226
60 / p. 213	AAA	Sheridan Park Motor Hotel	◆	$40-$60	226
		BLASDELL - Lodgings			
65 / p. 213	AAA	Econo Lodge South - see ad p 215	◆◆	$40-$99 ▨	221
66 / p. 213	AAA	McKinley Park Inn	◆◆◆	$49-$125 ▨	221
		BLASDELL - Restaurant			
72 / p. 213	AAA	Ilio DiPaolo's Restaurant	◆◆	$7-$18	221

Spotter/Map Page Number	OA	**CLARENCE** - Lodgings	Diamond Rating	Rate Range High Season	Listing Page
68 / below	🏛	Heritage Country Inn - see color ad p 216	◆◆	$50-$150 SAVE	223
70 / below	🏛	Asa Ransom House	◆◆◆	$85-$150 SAVE	223
71 / below	🏛	The Village Haven - see color ad p 216	◆◆◆	$60-$275	223
		CLARENCE - Restaurants			
80 / below		Palermo	◆◆	$7-$15	224
81 / below		Old Red Mill Inn	◆◆	$10-$19	224
83 / below	🏛	Asa Ransom House Dining Room	◆◆◆	$12-$28	223
		ELMA - Lodgings			
76 / below	🏛	Transit Manor Motel	◆	$32-$64 SAVE	225
		DEPEW - Restaurant			
89 / below	🏛	Salvatore's Italian Gardens	◆◆◆◆	$19-$45	224

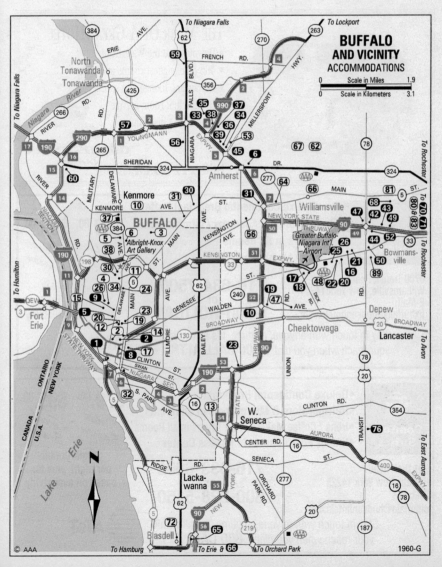

BUFFALO
AND VICINITY
ACCOMMODATIONS

© AAA

1960-G

BUFFALO pop. 328,100 (See map p. 213; index p. 211)

─── LODGINGS ───

ADAM'S MARK HOTEL
Phone: (716)845-5100 ❶
AAA SAVE   All Year   1P: $109   2P: $109
◆◆◆   **Location:** Downtown; I-90, exit 7 at Church and Lower Terrace sts. 120 Church St 14202. Fax: 716/845-5377.
Hotel   **Terms:** Monthly rates avail; package plans. **Facility:** 486 rooms. Most guest rooms are spacious and nicely
             appointed. Whirlpool room; 9 stories; interior corridors; heated pool. Fee: parking. **Dining:** Restaurant; 6:30
             am-11 pm; $7-$26; cocktails. **Services:** gift shop; area transportation, downtown; winter plug-ins.
All Rooms: combo or shower baths, extended cable TV. **Some Rooms:** Fee: refrigerators, VCR. **Cards:** AE, CB, DI, DS, JC, MC, VI. **Special Amenities:** Early check-in/late check-out and preferred room (subject to availability with advanced reservations). *(See color ad below)*

(See map p. 213)

BEST WESTERN INN-ON THE AVENUE   Phone: (716)886-8333 **5**

AAA SAVE	7/1-10/31	1P: $99-$105	2P: $105-$125	XP: $6	F18
	1/1-4/30	1P: $91-$101	2P: $98-$108	XP: $6	F18
◆◆	5/1-6/30 & 11/1-12/31	1P: $88-$98	2P: $95-$105	XP: $6	F18

Motel   **Location:** Downtown; between Virginia and Allen sts. 510 Delaware Ave 14202. Fax: 716/884-3070. **Terms:** [CP] meal plan; small pets only. **Facility:** 61 rooms. Nice rooms with wall of windows overlooking parking. 5 stories; interior corridors. **Dining:** Restaurant nearby. **All Rooms:** extended cable TV. **Cards:** AE, CB, DI, DS, MC, VI. **Special Amenities: Early check-in/late check-out and free breakfast.**

BUFFALO/AMHERST COURTYARD BY MARRIOTT   Phone: (716)626-2300 **6**

◆◆◆	All Year	1P: $49-$149	2P: $49-$149

Motel   **Location:** I-290, exit 6, just ne. 4100 Sheridan Dr 14221. Fax: 716/626-2322. **Terms:** Cancellation fee imposed. **Facility:** 108 rooms. 4 stories; interior corridors; heated pool. **All Rooms:** combo or shower baths. **Cards:** AE, CB, DI, DS, MC, VI.

HAMPTON INN-AIRPORT/GALLERIA MALL   Phone: (716)894-8000 **10**

AAA SAVE	5/1-10/31	1P: $89-$99	2P: $95-$105
◆◆◆	11/1-4/30	1P: $79-$89	2P: $79-$99

Motel   **Location:** 0.3 mi sw of I-90, exit 52 W. 1745 Walden Ave 14225. Fax: 716/894-3554. **Terms:** [CP] meal plan; package plans. **Facility:** 133 rooms. 57 whirlpool rooms; 5 stories; interior corridors; heated pool, whirlpool. **Dining:** Restaurant nearby. **Services:** area transportation, within 5 mi. **Recreation:** sports court. **All Rooms:** combo or shower baths, extended cable TV. **Cards:** AE, CB, DI, DS, JC, MC, VI. **Special Amenities: Free breakfast and free local telephone calls.** *(See ad below)*

HOLIDAY INN-DOWNTOWN   Phone: (716)886-2121 **9**

AAA SAVE	5/1-10/31	1P: $109	2P: $119	XP: $10	F18
◆◆	11/1-4/30	1P: $95	2P: $95	XP: $10	F18

Hotel   **Location:** Downtown; between Allen and North sts. 620 Delaware Ave 14202. Fax: 716/886-7942. **Terms:** [BP] meal plan; 3 day cancellation notice; package plans; small pets only. **Facility:** 168 rooms. Older property with average to better sized rooms. Compact public space. 8 stories; interior corridors; heated pool. **Dining:** Restaurant; 6:30 am-10 pm; $9-$18; cocktails. **Services:** area transportation, bus & train station. **Some Rooms:** Fee: refrigerators. **Cards:** AE, CB, DI, DS, MC, VI.

(See map p. 213)

HYATT REGENCY BUFFALO
◆◆◆ All Year   1P: $114 2P: $144 **Phone:** (716)856-1234 **8**
Hotel   XP: $25   F18
 Location: Downtown; on Pearl St at W Huron St; near the convention center and theater district. 2 Fountain Plaza 14202. **Fax:** 716/852-6157. **Terms:** Cancellation fee imposed; package plans. **Facility:** 395 rooms. Offers spacious guest rooms and some luxury services with in-room fax machine. 16 stories; interior corridors. Fee: parking. **Services:** gift shop. **All Rooms:** combo or shower baths. **Some Rooms:** efficiency. Fee: VCR. **Cards:** AE, CB, DI, DS, JC, MC, VI.

RADISSON SUITE HOTEL BUFFALO
◆◆◆ All Year   1P: $119-$159 2P: $119-$169 **Phone:** (716)854-5500 **2**
Suite Hotel   XP: $10   F18
 Location: Downtown; between Main and Washington sts, at Chippewa St; in the theater district. 601 Main St 14203. **Fax:** 716/854-4836. **Terms:** [BP] meal plan; package plans. **Facility:** 146 rooms. 1-bedroom suites with separate living area and 2 TVs. 7 stories; interior corridors. **Services:** area transportation. **Some Rooms:** Fee: microwaves. **Cards:** AE, DI, DS, JC, MC, VI.

(See map p. 213)

——— RESTAURANTS ———

ALI BABA   Lunch: $4-$15   Dinner: $4-$15   Phone: 716/886-4000   ⑤
◆◆   **Location:** Just s of Forest Avenue. 1116 Elmwood Ave 14222. **Hours:** 11 am-10 pm.
Mexican   **Reservations:** suggested; Fri & Sat. **Features:** casual dress; street parking; a la carte. The contemporary
restaurant is a local favorite for casual dining. Dishes cover a broad spectrum, showing influences from the
Mediterranean to the Red Sea. Kabobs, falafel, pasta and rice dishes and baklava are among healthy, creative choices.
Smoke free premises. **Cards:** DS, MC, VI.   ✕

THE BLACKTHORN   Lunch: $6-$8   Dinner: $9-$14   Phone: 716/825-9327   ⑬
◆◆   **Location:** On SR 16, 1.5 mi w of jct SR 240; at Seneca and Cazenovia. 2134 Seneca St 14210.
Steak and   **Hours:** 11:30 am-11:30 pm, Fri & Sat-12:30 am, Sun noon-11:30 pm. Closed major holidays.
Seafood   **Features:** casual dress; health conscious menu items; carryout; cocktails & lounge. The attractive, nicely
                decorated restaurant welcomes the neighborhood crowd to enjoy an extensive menu of snacks, sandwiches,
soups and entrees. Stop by at lunch to sample the buffet. The Friday fish fry and weekend prime rib specials are popular.
Cards: AE, MC, VI.   ✕

BRECKENRIDGE BREWERY   Lunch: $4-$9   Dinner: $7-$18   Phone: 716/856-2739   ⑭
◆◆   **Location:** In the Market Arcade complex. 623 Main St 14203. **Hours:** 11 am-11 pm, Fri & Sat 1 am. Closed
American   major holidays. **Reservations:** accepted; 8 or more. **Features:** casual dress; cocktails & lounge; fee for
                parking. The 1990s-style stagecoach stop is large but with few tables. Many dishes, which show strong
Southwestern influences, are made with beer and heavy seasoning. The barlike atmosphere is casual and upbeat. Servers
are courteous and efficient. **Cards:** AE, MC, VI.   ✕

THE CODA   Dinner: $17-$20   Phone: 716/886-6647   ⑮
◆◆◆   **Location:** Across the street from Kleinhans Music Hall. 350 Pennsylvania Ave 14201. **Hours:** 5:30 pm-10
French   pm, Fri & Sat-11 pm. Closed: 7/1-8/31. **Reservations:** required. **Features:** health conscious menu items;
               street parking; prix fixe. The converted, mom-and-pop grocery store exudes a homey charm, with pretty lace
tablecloths and well-coordinated decor. The limited menu—which centers on interesting foods cooked with cream, butter and
eggs—has weekly changing selections. Smoke free premises.   ✕

COLTER BAY GRILL   Lunch: $6-$11   Dinner: $6-$11   Phone: 716/882-1330   ⑰
◆   **Location:** Downtown; at jct Delaware and Allen. 561 Delaware Ave 14202. **Hours:** 11:30 am-11 pm, Fri &
American   Sat-midnight. **Features:** casual dress; Sunday brunch; children's menu; health conscious menu items;
                carryout; cocktails & lounge. The trendy, youth-oriented restaurant has a rustic appeal, with national park
pictures hanging on wood walls. Interesting spices punctuates preparations of steak and pasta, as well as homemade
soups, burgers and salads. Many draft beers are available. **Cards:** AE, MC, VI.   ✕

ENCHANTE Historical   Lunch: $7-$12   Dinner: $18-$28   Phone: 716/885-1330   ⑲
◆◆◆   **Location:** 16 Allen St 14202. **Hours:** 11 am-10 pm, Sat from 5:30 pm. Closed: 1/1, 12/25 & Sun.
French   **Reservations:** suggested. **Features:** dressy casual; health conscious menu items; cocktails; street parking.
                Small and charming, in an atmospheric Victorian mansion. French influences and imaginative diverse menu
selections. **Cards:** AE, DI, DS, MC, VI.   ✕

FIDDLE HEADS RESTAURANT   Dinner: $12-$22   Phone: 716/883-4166   ⑳
◆◆◆   **Location:** Corner of Franklin St. 62 Allen St 14202. **Hours:** 11:30 am-3 & 5-10 pm, Sat from 5:30 pm.
American   Closed: 11/23, 12/25, Sun & Mon. **Reservations:** suggested; weekends. **Features:** casual dress; health
                conscious menu items; beer & wine only; street parking. The tiny restaurant plans an interesting menu of
innovative, well-prepared dishes, which are served with unusual sides that complement. Two offerings to try are the pizza
made from real fiddleheads and the steamed sea bass. Servers are friendly. **Cards:** DS, MC, VI.

HEMINGWAY'S   Dinner: $10-$11   Phone: 716/852-1937   ㉓
◆◆   **Location:** In the heart of the theater district. 492 Pearl St 14202. **Hours:** 11:30 am-11 pm, Fri & Sat-1 am,
American   Sun 4 pm-10 pm. Closed: 4/23, 11/23 & 12/25. **Features:** health conscious menu items. Fun and whimsical
                decorations brighten the large dining room, a favorite spot of the theatergoing crowd. The eclectic menu
dabbles in sandwiches and salads, as well as burgers and full entrees. Chocolate cheesecake is a sinful temptation.
Cards: AE, DI, MC, VI.

THE HOURGLASS RESTAURANT   Dinner: $17-$29   Phone: 716/877-8788   ⑩
◆◆   **Location:** 0.8 mi e of SR 384; Kenmore at Hiler. 981 Kenmore Ave 14217. **Hours:** 4 pm-9:30 pm. Closed
Continental   major holidays, Sun, Mon & 6/25-7/14. **Reservations:** suggested. **Features:** casual dress; cocktails. Informal
                dining in an unimposing setting. Features fresh seafood and rack of lamb, but also offers varied selections of
other meat and poultry. Fresh baked dessert highlight talents of owner's wife. **Cards:** AE, MC, VI.   ✕

HUTCH'S   Dinner: $11-$19   Phone: 716/885-0074   ㉔
◆◆◆   **Location:** 1 blk from Gates Circle. 1375 Delaware Ave 14209. **Hours:** 5 pm-10 pm, Fri & Sat-midnight, Sun
American   4 pm-9 pm. Closed major holidays. **Reservations:** suggested. **Features:** casual dress; health conscious
                menu items; cocktails & lounge. Representative of creative dishes are fettuccine pasta with spiced cream,
chicken, shrimp and chorizo and sesame-seed-crusted yellowfin tuna with pickled ginger, wasabi and soy sauce.
Leopard-skin rugs and a brick-walled bar stand out in the dining room. **Cards:** AE, DI, MC, VI.   ✕

JUST PASTA   Lunch: $5-$8   Dinner: $10-$17   Phone: 716/881-1888   ④
◆◆   **Location:** Uptown; just w of jct Bryant St and Elmwood Ave, 0.3 mi w of Delaware Ave. 307 Bryant St
Italian   14222. **Hours:** 11:30 am-4 & 5-10 pm, Fri-11 pm, Sat 5 pm-11 pm. Closed major holidays & Sun.
                Reservations: suggested. **Features:** dressy casual; carryout; cocktails & lounge; a la carte. The moderately
upscale dining room bustles with activity, as artsy types drop in for Northern Italian preparations of pasta, which reflect a
pronounced use of seasonings. For dessert, it's tough to choose from a list of irresistible homemade selections. **Cards:** AE,
DI, MC, VI.   ✕

(See map p. 213)

LA RIVIERA RISTORANTE   **Lunch:** $5-$7   **Dinner:** $8-$22   **Phone:** 716/837-7712   ③
◆◆   **Location:** Uptown; on Hertel Ave at Starin Ave; 0.7 mi w of jct SR 5 (Main St). 1735 Hertel Ave 14216.
Italian   **Hours:** 11 am-11 pm, Sun noon-9 pm. Closed: 12/25. **Reservations:** accepted; Fri & Sat. **Features:** casual dress; early bird specials; carryout; cocktails. "Mama" makes sure everything is just right in the traditional Italian eatery, a favorite spot for family dining. Seafood and steak choices mingle with homemade pasta and Sicilian specialties. The solarium offers a nice seating alternative. Smoke free premises. **Cards:** AE, DS, MC, VI.

LEFT BANK   **Dinner:** $8-$19   **Phone:** 716/882-3509   ㉖
◆◆   **Location:** Near Kleinhans Music Hall. 511 Rhode Island St 14213. **Hours:** 5 pm-11 pm, Fri & Sat-midnight.
American   Closed major holidays. **Reservations:** suggested; Thurs-Sun. **Features:** casual dress; Sunday brunch; health conscious menu items; street parking. The comfortable, bistrolike restaurant offers many tempting and unusual items, such as its signature eggplanets, a large, thick slice of breaded eggplant "steak" sandwiched with ricotta and grilled veggies and topped with fresh mozzarella.

LORD CHUMLEY'S Historical   **Dinner:** $30-$50   **Phone:** 716/886-2220   ⑫
◆◆◆   **Location:** Downtown; just n of jct Virginia St. 481 Delaware Ave 14202. **Hours:** 5 pm-10 pm, Fri & Sat-11
Continental   pm. Closed major holidays. **Reservations:** suggested. **Features:** dressy casual; cocktails; street parking. The turn-of-the-20th-century townhouse reflects the cozy ambience of a cobblestone-street sidewalk cafe. Three-tiered prix fixe menus include dishes prepared with premium ingredients. Turtle cheesecake is representative of delicious desserts. Smoke free premises. **Cards:** DI, DS, MC, VI.

METROPOLITAN   **Dinner:** $8-$17   **Phone:** 716/882-0772   ㉚
◆◆   **Location:** Downtown; between W Ferry and Breckenridge St. 716 Elmwood Ave 14222. **Hours:** 11:30
American   am-11:30 pm, Fri & Sat-1 am, Sun 10:30 am-11 pm. **Reservations:** accepted. **Features:** casual dress; health conscious menu items; carryout; cocktails; street parking. The restaurant delivers large portions of well-prepared pasta and salads, as well as pizza and more elaborate entrees. The decor is contemporary and sleek, featuring a mural of the skylines of major cities. A jazz band plays on the seasonal patio. Smoke free premises. **Cards:** AE, CB, MC, VI.

OLIVER'S RESTAURANT   **Lunch:** $7-$11   **Dinner:** $17-$29   **Phone:** 716/877-9662   ⑥
◆◆◆   **Location:** Uptown; SR 384, 0.5 mi n of jct SR 198 at Delaware and Amherst aves. 2095 Delaware Ave
Continental   14216. **Hours:** 11:30 am-3 & 5-10 pm, Fri & Sat 5 pm-midnight, Sun 4:30 pm-9:30 pm. Closed: 5/31, 7/4 & 9/4. **Reservations:** suggested; weekends. **Features:** dressy casual; cocktails & lounge; a la carte. Elegant table appointments add to the contemporary sophistication of the informal dining room. International influences punctuate innovative, creatively presented dishes. The food and wine sampler menu, available Tuesday through Friday, is a treat. **Cards:** AE, MC, VI.

THE PARK LANE TAVERN & OYSTER BAR   **Lunch:** $7-$11   **Dinner:** $16-$25   **Phone:** 716/881-2603   ⑪
◆◆◆   **Location:** Delaware Ave at Gates Cir. 33 Gates Cir 14209. **Hours:** 11:30 am-3:30 & 5-10:30 pm. Closed:
American   Sun & Mon. **Reservations:** suggested. **Features:** dressy casual; health conscious menu items; cocktails & lounge; valet parking. Risotto, soft-shell crabs and thoughtful preparations of fresh fish stand out on the restaurant's seasonally changing menu. Two fireplaces and oversized wood beams enhance the rustic appeal of the Tudor-style setting. The atmosphere is relaxed. **Cards:** AE, MC, VI.

PETTIBONE'S GRILLE   **Lunch:** $5-$10   **Dinner:** $10-$18   **Phone:** 716/846-2100   ㉜
◆◆   **Location:** At North AmeriCare Park, Swan and Washington sts; I-190, exit 6, Seneca St ramp to Swan St to
American   Washington St; at North Americare Park. 275 Washington St 14203. **Hours:** 11:30 am-3 pm; open evenings for special events; tickets required on game days. Closed: 4/23, 11/23 & 12/25. **Reservations:** suggested; during games. **Features:** casual dress; health conscious menu items; carryout; cocktails & lounge. Perched above the baseball park, the casual restaurant lays out a menu of such dishes as steaks, chops, seafood and pasta. The grilled portobello sandwich is particularly tasty. Plaques commemorate players being inducted in the local hall of fame. **Cards:** AE, MC, VI.

ROSELAND   **Dinner:** $6-$30   **Phone:** 716/882-3328   ㉞
◆◆◆   **Location:** Near Kleinhans Music Hall. 490 Rhode Island St 14213. **Hours:** 4 pm-10 pm, Sat 5 pm-11 pm,
Italian   Sun 3 pm-9 pm. **Reservations:** suggested. **Features:** dressy casual; health conscious menu items; cocktails & lounge; a la carte. The "dinner for two" option is a popular, budget-conscious choice at the intimate restaurant, which focuses its menu on Italian and American fare. The homemade manicotti—topped with sauteed rock shrimp—is an excellent choice. The atmosphere is cozy. **Cards:** AE, DS, MC, VI.

RUE FRANKLIN   **Dinner:** $17-$22   **Phone:** 716/852-4416   ②
◆◆◆   **Location:** Just n of Tupper St. 341 Franklin St 14202. **Hours:** 5:30 pm-10 pm. Closed major holidays, Sun,
French   Mon & 8/22-9/13. **Reservations:** suggested. **Features:** dressy casual; cocktails & lounge; a la carte, also prix fixe. The nicely appointed dining room lets you unwind in refined comfort. The limited, seasonal menu unveils such interesting, contemporary cuisine as green gazpacho with tomato sorbet and curried jumbo shrimp. The homemade blueberry tart is exquisite. Smoke free premises. **Cards:** AE, CB, MC, VI.

SARATOGA   **Lunch:** $5-$8   **Dinner:** $10-$15   **Phone:** 716/875-3015   ㊲
◆◆◆   **Location:** Corner of Delaware and Kenmore aves. 2694 Delaware Ave 14216. **Hours:** 11 am-10 pm, Fri &
Traditional   Sat-1 am, Sun 3 pm-10 pm. Closed: 12/25. **Reservations:** suggested. **Features:** semi-formal attire; health
Steakhouse   conscious menu items; cocktails & lounge. A gentle, horse-racing theme wends through the attractive and comfortable neighborhood restaurant. Italian foods and seafood and beef preparations make up the menu. A delicious choice is the veal piccata, which is served with many artichoke hearts. **Cards:** AE, CB, DI, DS, MC, VI.

(See map p. 213)

SEQUOIA
◆◆◆
American

Lunch: $5-$8   **Dinner:** $15-$20   **Phone:** 716/882-2219   38
Location: Downtown. 718 Elmwood Ave 14222. **Hours:** 11:30 am-3:30 & 5:30-10 pm, Fri & Sat-11 pm, Sun 10:30 am-3:30 & 5-9 pm. **Closed:** 12/25 & Mon. **Reservations:** suggested. **Features:** dressy casual; Sunday brunch; health conscious menu items; cocktails & lounge; street parking. Huge portions of down-home dishes with an original contemporary twist, in a small, attractively decorated place. **Cards:** AE, MC, VI. ✕

THE STEER
◆◆
American

Dinner: $9-$15   **Phone:** 716/838-0478   31
Location: 0.3 mi from University of Buffalo south campus. 3151 Main St 14214. **Hours:** 4 pm-4 am. **Closed:** 11/23 & 12/25. **Reservations:** suggested. **Features:** casual dress; health conscious menu items; cocktails & lounge. A rustic, contemporary atmosphere prevails in the friendly steakhouse. In addition to the requisite prime rib, ribeye and strip steak dinners, offerings include chicken wings and roast beef on a kummelweck roll. The summer deck is breezy and relaxed. **Cards:** AE, MC, VI. ✕

The Buffalo Vicinity

AKRON pop. 2,900

——— RESTAURANT ———

THE AKRON HOUSE   Historical
Ⓐ
◆◆
American

Lunch: $6-$9   **Dinner:** $10-$20   **Phone:** 716/542-2280
Location: Center; on SR 93. 15 Main St 14001. **Hours:** 11 am-9 pm, Sat 3 pm-10 pm, Sun 10 am-8 pm. Closed: 7/4, 12/25 & Mon. **Reservations:** suggested. **Features:** casual dress; children's menu; early bird specials; health conscious menu items; carryout; cocktails; street parking. Representative of tasty choices on a menu that centers on meat, seafood and pasta is chicken stuffed with cashews and drizzled in raspberry sauce. The renovated Victorian hotel is a pleasant spot for informal dining. Servers are friendly and prompt.
Cards: MC, VI. ✕

AMHERST pop. 111,700   (See map p. 213; index p. 212)

——— LODGINGS ———

BUFFALO MARRIOTT-NIAGARA
Ⓐ SAVE
◆◆◆
Hotel

Phone: (716)689-6900   34
5/1-11/16   1P: $99-$149   2P: $99-$159
11/17-4/30   1P: $79-$149   2P: $79-$159
Location: I-290, exit 5B, 0.5 mi n on SR 263 (Millersport Hwy). 1340 Millersport Hwy 14221. Fax: 716/689-0483. **Terms:** [BP] meal plan; package plans; pets, $50 extra charge. **Facility:** 356 rooms. Attractive outdoor courtyard with lush gardens in season. Average sized rooms vary in appointments. Some luxury services avail. Rates for up to 4 persons; 10 stories; interior corridors; heated pool, sauna, whirlpool. **Dining:** Restaurant; 6:30 am-10 pm; $8-$20; cocktails. **Services:** gift shop; area transportation. **All Rooms:** combo or shower baths, extended cable TV. **Some Rooms:** Fee: refrigerators, VCR. **Cards:** AE, DI, DS, JC, MC, VI. *(See ad below)*

🆂🄳 🗲 ⛅ ⊣ ≈ 🛆 🖩 🕎 ✕ 🐾 VCR 🖨 💻 📞 DATA PORT 🛄 👾

EXTENDED STAY AMERICA
◆◆
Extended
Stay Motel
MC, VI.

Phone: 716/564-0620   35
Property failed to provide current rates
Location: I-290, exit 3, just n on Niagara Falls Blvd (US 62) to access road. 125 Inn Keepers Ln 14228. Fax: 716/564-0630. **Facility:** 119 rooms. Designed specifically for long term value conscious business travelers. 3 stories; interior corridors. **All Rooms:** efficiencies, combo or shower baths. **Cards:** AE, DI, DS,

🕎 🛆 🎇 🖩 📺 💻 📞 📞 DATA PORT

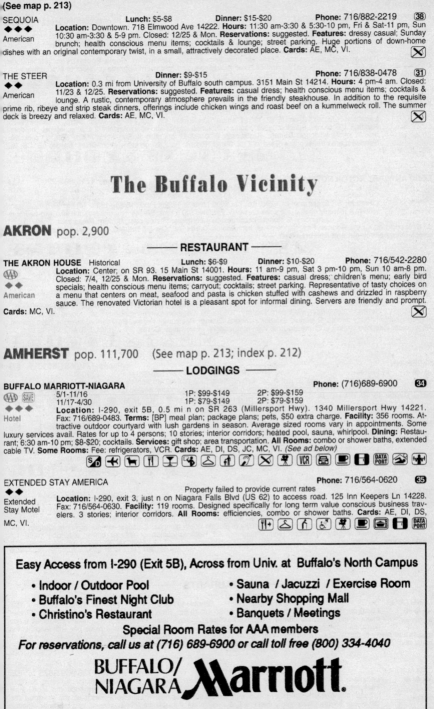

(See map p. 213)

HAMPTON INN-BUFFALO/AMHERST
Phone: (716)689-4414 **39**

[AAA] [SAVE]

◆◆◆
Motel

All Year   1P: $80   2P: $90
Location: I-290, exit 5B, 0.5 mi n on SR 263 (Millersport Hwy). 10 Flint Rd 14226. Fax: 716/689-4382. **Terms:** [CP] meal plan; weekly & monthly rates avail; cancellation fee imposed. **Facility:** 196 rooms. Rooms offer bright, upscale decors. Rates for up to 4 persons; 4 stories; interior corridors; heated pool, whirlpool. **Dining:** Restaurant nearby. **Services:** area transportation, within 5 mi. **Some Rooms:** Fee: refrigerators. **Cards:** AE, CB, DI, DS, MC, VI. **Special Amenities:** Free newspaper and free room upgrade (subject to availability with advanced reservations).

HOLIDAY INN BUFFALO-AMHERST
Phone: (716)691-8181 **33**

[AAA] [SAVE]

◆◆◆
Motor Inn

All Year   1P: $100-$110   2P: $100-$110   XP: $10   F19
Location: I-290, exit 3, on US 62. 1881 Niagara Falls Blvd 14228. Fax: 716/691-4965. **Terms:** Package plans. **Facility:** 199 rooms. Spacious guest rooms with varied decors and appointments. 2 stories; interior corridors; heated pool, whirlpool. **Dining:** Restaurant; 6:30 am-11 pm, Sat & Sun from 7 am; $8-$13; cocktails. **Services:** area transportation, within 2 mi. **Some Rooms:** Fee: refrigerators, microwaves. **Cards:** AE, CB, DI, DS, JC, MC, VI.

LORD AMHERST MOTOR HOTEL
Phone: (716)839-2200 **31**

[AAA] [SAVE]

◆◆
Motor Inn

5/1-10/31   1P: $59-$75   2P: $69-$85   XP: $7   F18
11/1-4/30   1P: $49-$65   2P: $59-$75   XP: $7   F18
Location: SR 5, just w of jct I-290, exit 7A. 5000 Main St 14226. Fax: 716/839-1538. **Terms:** [BP] meal plan; weekly & monthly rates avail; small pets only. **Facility:** 100 rooms. Weekly or monthly rental for 1 two-bedroom apartment and efficiencies; 2 stories; interior/exterior corridors; heated pool. **Dining:** Restaurant; 7 am-10 pm; $6-$15; cocktails. **Some Rooms:** Fee: refrigerators, microwaves. **Cards:** AE, CB, DI, DS, MC, VI. **Special Amenities:** Early check-in/late check-out and free breakfast.

RED ROOF INN
Phone: (716)689-7474 **36**

[AAA]

◆◆
Motel

5/1-8/31   1P: $70-$84   2P: $76-$90   XP: $6   F18
9/1-12/31   1P: $50-$66   2P: $56-$72   XP: $6   F18
1/1-4/30   1P: $42-$50   2P: $48-$56   XP: $6   F18
Location: I-290, exit 5B, 0.5 mi n on SR 263 (Millersport Hwy). 42 Flint Rd 14226. Fax: 716/689-2051. **Terms:** Weekly rates avail; pets. **Facility:** 108 rooms. Compact to more spacious guest rooms with simple furnishings, contemporary decors. 2 stories; exterior corridors. **Dining:** Restaurant nearby. **Recreation:** in-room video games. **All Rooms:** extended cable TV. **Some Rooms:** Fee: refrigerators, microwaves. **Cards:** AE, CB, DI, DS, MC, VI.

SLEEP INN
Phone: (716)691-6510 **38**

◆◆
Motel

All Year   1P: $69-$85   2P: $69-$99   XP: $5   F18
Location: I-290, exit 3, just n on Niagara Falls Blvd (US 62) to access road. 75 Inn Keepers Ln 14228. Fax: 716/691-3454. **Facility:** 92 rooms. 5 stories; interior corridors; heated pool. **All Rooms:** combo or shower baths. **Cards:** AE, DI, DS, MC, VI.

SUPER 8 MOTEL-AMHERST
Phone: (716)688-0811 **37**

◆◆
Motel

5/1-9/30   1P: $47-$74   2P: $52-$79   XP: $5   F12
10/1-4/30   1P: $35-$55   2P: $42-$65   XP: $5   F12
Location: I-290, exit 5B. 1 Flint Rd 14226. Fax: 716/688-2365. **Terms:** [CP] meal plan. **Facility:** 103 rooms. Situated on nice lot close to SUNY Buffalo. 4 stories; interior corridors. **Some Rooms:** Fee: refrigerators, microwaves. **Cards:** AE, DI, DS, MC, VI.

TRAVELODGE
Phone: (716)837-3344 **30**

[AAA] [SAVE]

◆◆
Motel

All Year   1P: $53-$70   2P: $59-$70   XP: $5   F12
Location: SR 5, just w of jct US 62. 3612 Main St 14226. Fax: 716/834-6246. **Terms:** [CP] meal plan; weekly rates avail, 11/1-5/31; cancellation fee imposed. **Facility:** 40 rooms. White wrought iron deck rails outside rooms looking across street to University of Buffalo South campus. 2 stories; exterior corridors. **Dining:** Restaurant nearby. **Services:** winter plug-ins. **All Rooms:** combo or shower baths, extended cable TV. **Some Rooms:** 10 efficiencies. **Cards:** AE, DS, MC, VI.

——— **RESTAURANTS** ———

DAKOTA GRILL
Lunch: $6-$8   **Dinner:** $11-$20   **Phone:** 716/834-6600 **53**

◆◆◆
American

Location: 4224 Maple Rd 14226. **Hours:** 11:30 am-10 pm, Fri & Sat-11 pm, late night menu-1 am. Closed major holidays. **Reservations:** accepted. **Features:** dressy casual; children's menu; health conscious menu items; carryout; cocktails & lounge. The cozy dining room has the ambience of a piano bar, with jazz-themed murals and plenty of bustle. Choices on the menu include Angus steak, a spicy bean dip called "cowboy caviar" and messy, tangy ribs. The young staff is friendly and energetic. **Cards:** AE, DI, DS, MC, VI.

SAN MARCO
Dinner: $12-$21   **Phone:** 716/839-5876 **56**

◆◆◆
Northern
Italian

Location: 2082 Kensington Ave 14226. **Hours:** 5:30 pm-10:30 pm. Closed major holidays & Mon. **Features:** dressy casual; health conscious menu items. A serene ambience envelops the moderately upscale dining room, which is dotted with formal table settings. Preparations—such as the delicious sea bass—are flavored with lightly thickened sauces, rather than the traditional olive oil and balsamic vinegar. **Cards:** AE, MC, VI.

BLASDELL pop. 2,900 (See map p. 213; index p. 212)

—— LODGINGS ——

ECONO LODGE SOUTH
Phone: (716)825-7530 [65]
All Year   1P: $40-$99   2P: $47-$99   XP: $7   F18
Location: SR 179, just e of I-90, exit 56. 4344 Milestrip Rd 14219. Fax: 716/825-7530. **Terms:** 7 day cancellation notice; package plans. **Facility:** 85 rooms. Very attractive furnished rooms. 2 two-bedroom units. 1-2 stories; exterior corridors. **Dining:** Restaurant nearby. **Services:** winter plug-ins. **Cards:** AE, CB, DI, DS, JC, MC, VI. *(See ad p 215)*

MCKINLEY PARK INN
Phone: (716)648-5700 [66]
All Year   1P: $49-$125   2P: $54-$125   XP: $5   F17
Location: I-90, exit 56, 0.4 mi e on SR 179, 0.8 mi s. S 3950 McKinley Pkwy 14219. Fax: 716/648-5700. **Terms:** [CP] meal plan; weekly & monthly rates avail. **Facility:** 78 rooms. Large well furnished rooms. 5 whirlpool rooms, $125; 2 stories; interior corridors. **Dining:** 6-11 am; combined restaurant/lounge/club; health conscious menu items; cocktails. **All Rooms:** combo or shower baths, extended cable TV. **Some Rooms:** efficiency, no utensils. **Cards:** AE, MC, VI. **Special Amenities:** Free breakfast.

—— RESTAURANT ——

ILIO DIPAOLO'S RESTAURANT   **Lunch:** $6-$10   **Dinner:** $7-$18   **Phone:** 716/825-3675 [72]
Location: On US 62, 0.3 mi n of jct SR 179 and 90. 3785 S Park Ave 14219. **Hours:** 11:30 am-10 pm, Fri-midnight, Sat 2 pm-midnight, Sun 1 pm-10 pm. Closed: 4/23, 11/23 & 12/25. **Reservations:** suggested. **Features:** casual dress; children's menu; early bird specials; health conscious menu; carryout; cocktails & lounge. Established in 1965 by a professional wrestler, the family restaurant caters to families. Homemade pasta-such as fettuccine and angel hair-enhance the flavor of well-prepared dishes. A hand-painted mural and photographs of stars brighten the dining room. Smoke free premises. **Cards:** AE, DI, MC, VI.

BOWMANSVILLE pop. 580 (See map p. 213; index p. 212)

—— LODGING ——

RED ROOF INN-BUFFALO AIRPORT
Phone: (716)633-1100 [52]
6/30-9/3	1P: $63-$80	2P: $70-$87	XP: $7	F18
9/4-11/30	1P: $50-$70	2P: $57-$77	XP: $7	F18
5/1-6/29	1P: $43-$60	2P: $50-$67	XP: $7	F18
12/1-4/30	1P: $40-$56	2P: $47-$63	XP: $7	F18

Location: Just e of SR 78, just n of entrance to I-90 (New York Thruway), exit 49; behind Bob Evans Restaurant. 146 Maple Dr 14026. Fax: 716/633-2297. **Terms:** Weekly rates avail; small pets only. **Facility:** 109 rooms. 2 stories; exterior corridors. **Dining:** Restaurant nearby. **Some Rooms:** Fee: refrigerators, microwaves. **Cards:** AE, CB, DI, DS, MC, VI.

CHEEKTOWAGA pop. 84,400 (See map p. 213; index p. 212)

—— LODGINGS ——

COMFORT SUITES-BUFFALO AIRPORT
Phone: (716)633-6000 [17]
5/1-10/31   1P: $95-$105   2P: $95-$115
11/1-4/30   1P: $85-$95   2P: $85-$99
Location: Just sw of jct SR 33 and Dick Rd exit. 901 Dick Rd 14225. Fax: 716/633-6858. **Terms:** [CP] meal plan; package plans. **Facility:** 100 rooms. 1-room suites with separate sleeping and sitting area. 20 whirlpool rooms, $99-$159; 2 stories; interior corridors; small heated indoor pool, whirlpool. **Services:** area transportation, within 5 mi. **Recreation:** Fee: in-room video games. **All Rooms:** extended cable TV. **Cards:** AE, CB, DI, DS, MC, VI. *(See ad p 214)*

DAYS INN-BUFFALO AIRPORT
Phone: (716)631-0800 [20]
All Year   1P: $64-$99   2P: $64-$99
Location: SR 33, 1.6 mi w of jct SR 78. 4345 Genesee St 14225. Fax: 716/631-7589. **Terms:** [CP] meal plan; 2 night min stay, most summer weekends; package plans. **Facility:** 129 rooms. 6 stories; interior corridors; heated pool. **Services:** area transportation. **Some Rooms:** Fee: refrigerators, microwaves. **Cards:** AE, CB, DI, DS, JC, MC, VI.

FOUR POINTS HOTEL SHERATON-BUFFALO AIRPORT
Phone: (716)681-2400 [19]
All Year   1P: $149   2P: $164   XP: $10   F17
Location: I-90, exit 52 E, 0.3 mi e; adjacent to Walden Galleria Mall. 2040 Walden Ave 14225. Fax: 716/681-8067. **Terms:** Package plans. **Facility:** 292 rooms. Spacious guest rooms. 2-8 stories; interior/exterior corridors; heated pool. **Services:** gift shop; area transportation. **Some Rooms:** Fee: refrigerators. **Cards:** AE, DI, DS, MC, VI. *(See color ad p 222)*

(See map p. 213)

HOLIDAY INN-BUFFALO AIRPORT
Phone: (716)634-6969 ⑯

AAA SAVE ◆◆◆ Motor Inn

8/1-8/31	1P: $99-$149	2P: $99-$149
5/1-7/31	1P: $79-$109	2P: $79-$109
9/1-11/15	1P: $69-$99	2P: $69-$99
11/16-4/30	1P: $64-$99	2P: $64-$99

Location: SR 33, 1 mi w of jct SR 78. 4600 Genesee St 14225. Fax: 716/634-0920. **Terms:** 7 day cancellation notice. **Facility:** 207 rooms. Inviting public areas. 4 whirlpool rooms, $99-$159; 2 stories; interior corridors; heated pool, wading pool, whirlpool. **Dining:** Restaurant; 6:30 am-10 pm, Sat & Sun from 7 am; $6-$14; cocktails. **Services:** area transportation, within 5 mi. **All Rooms:** extended cable TV. **Cards:** AE, CB, DI, DS, JC, MC, VI.

HOLIDAY INN EXPRESS HOTEL & SUITES
Phone: (716)896-2900 ㉓

AAA SAVE ◆◆◆ Motor Inn

6/1-8/31	1P: $99-$119	2P: $99-$119	XP: $10	F18
5/1-5/31 & 9/1-10/31	1P: $89-$99	2P: $89-$99	XP: $10	F18
11/1-4/30	1P: $79-$99	2P: $79-$99	XP: $10	F18

Location: 0.3 mi ne of I-190, exit 1; I-90, exit 53. 601 Dingens St 14206. Fax: 716/896-3765. **Terms:** [CP] meal plan; weekly & monthly rates avail; 3 day cancellation notice; cancellation fee imposed. **Facility:** 117 rooms. Some smaller but nicely appointed rooms. 3 whirlpool rooms, $129-$169; 2 stories; interior corridors; heated pool, whirlpool. **Dining:** Restaurant; 10 am-9 pm; $6-$13; cocktails. **Services:** area transportation, bus & train station. **All Rooms:** combo or shower baths. **Cards:** AE, DI, DS, JC, MC, VI. **Special Amenities:** Free breakfast and free local telephone calls.

HOMEWOOD SUITES HOTEL
Phone: 716/685-0700 ⑱

◆◆◆ Suite Motel

All Year — 1P: $109-$149 — 2P: $109-$149

Location: 0.3 mi sw jct of SR 33, Dick Rd exit. 760 Dick Rd 14225. Fax: 716/685-2034. **Terms:** [CP] meal plan; 10 day cancellation notice; package plans; small pets only. **Facility:** 77 rooms. A home away from home; short distance from airport and shopping areas. 9 two-bedroom units. Interior corridors; heated pool. **Services:** area transportation. **All Rooms:** kitchens, combo or shower baths. **Cards:** AE, CB, DI, DS, JC, MC, VI.

QUALITY INN-BUFFALO AIRPORT
Phone: (716)633-5500 ㉕

◆◆ Motel

All Year — 1P: $69-$130 — 2P: $69-$130

Location: SR 33, 1.8 mi e of jct SR 78. 4217 Genesee St 14225. Fax: 716/633-4231. **Terms:** [CP] meal plan; package plans. **Facility:** 104 rooms. Bright spacious rooms with upscale appeal. 1-2 stories; interior corridors. **Services:** area transportation. **Some Rooms:** Fee: refrigerators, microwaves. **Cards:** AE, DI, DS, MC, VI.

RADISSON HOTEL & SUITES
Phone: (716)634-2300 ㉒

◆◆◆ Hotel

All Year — 1P: $146-$156 — 2P: $166-$176 — XP: $10 — F16

Location: SR 33, 1.7 mi w of jct SR 78. 4243 Genesee St 14225. Fax: 716/632-2387. **Terms:** Package plans. **Facility:** 274 rooms. Mix of standard guest rooms and 1-room suites. 2-4 stories; interior corridors; heated pool. **Dining:** nightclub. **Services:** gift shop; area transportation. **Some Rooms:** Fee: refrigerators, microwaves, VCR. **Cards:** AE, CB, DI, DS, JC, MC, VI. (See color ad p 216)

SLEEP INN
Phone: (716)626-4000 ㉖

◆◆ Motel

5/1-9/30	1P: $75-$99	2P: $85-$109	XP: $10	F12
11/1-4/30	1P: $55-$72	2P: $65-$82	XP: $10	F12
10/1-10/31	1P: $55-$75	2P: $65-$75	XP: $10	F12

Location: 1.1 mi w on SR 33 from jct SR 78, just n. 100 Hotlz Rd 14225. Fax: 716/626-3370. **Terms:** [CP] meal plan; check-in 3:30 pm. **Facility:** 62 rooms. Spacious rooms with pleasant visual appeal. 3 stories; interior corridors. **Services:** area transportation. **All Rooms:** combo or shower baths. **Some Rooms:** Fee: refrigerators. **Cards:** AE, DI, DS, JC, MC, VI.

(See map p. 213)

WELLESLEY INN & SUITES
Phone: (716)631-8966 **21**

| | 5/1-10/31 | 1P: $85-$110 | 2P: $90-$115 | XP: $5 | F18 |
| | 11/1-4/30 | 1P: $70-$90 | 2P: $75-$95 | XP: $5 | F18 |

Motel   **Location:** SR 33, 1 mi w of jct SR 78. 4630 Genesee St 14225. Fax: 716/631-8977. **Terms:** [CP] meal plan; small pets only, $5 extra charge. **Facility:** 82 rooms. Pleasantly appointed rooms. 4 stories; interior corridors. **Dining:** Restaurant nearby. **All Rooms:** combo or shower baths. **Cards:** AE, CB, DI, DS, JC, MC, VI.
Special Amenities: Free breakfast and free newspaper. *(See color ad p 4)*

——— RESTAURANTS ———

JASMINE II   **Dinner:** $8-$17   Phone: 716/683-6553 **47**

Location: 3719 Union Rd 14225. **Hours:** 11:30 am-3 & 5-9 pm, Fri & Sat-10 pm. Closed: 7/4, 11/23 & 12/25. **Reservations:** accepted. **Features:** casual dress; health conscious menu items; beer & wine only. The restaurant delivers substantial portions of piquant Thai cuisine, which is seasoned to your preference. Food is excellent in preparation, presentation and especially taste. Masks, dolls and cozy tables give the dining room a warm, intimate ambience. Smoke free premises. **Cards:** AE, DI, DS, MC, VI.

Ethnic

PRANZO RISTORANTE   **Dinner:** $23-$32   Phone: 716/634-2300 **48**

Location: SR 33, 1.7 mi w of jct SR 78; in Radisson Hotel & Suites. 4243 Genesee St 14225. **Hours:** 5 pm-11 pm. Closed major holidays & Sun. **Reservations:** suggested. **Features:** dressy casual; cocktails & lounge; valet parking; a la carte. The contemporary restaurant—an area favorite for upscale dining—delivers exquisite and well-presented cuisine, attentive service and such wonderful desserts as mango-lime ice cream with fruit. The lengthy wine list displays many quality selections. **Cards:** AE, CB, DI, DS, JC, MC, VI.

Nouvelle
Italian

CLARENCE pop. 20,000   (See map p. 213; index p. 213)

——— LODGINGS ———

ASA RANSOM HOUSE
Phone: (716)759-2315 **70**

| | 5/1-12/31 & 2/9-4/30 | 1P: $85-$125 | 2P: $95-$150 | XP: $20 | F7 |

Historic
Country Inn   **Location:** 5.3 mi e on SR 5 from jct SR 78. 10529 Main St 14031. Fax: 716/759-2791. **Terms:** Open 5/1-12/31 & 2/9-4/30; [BP] & [MAP] meal plans; weekly rates avail; 7 day cancellation notice; package plans. **Facility:** 9 rooms. Closed on Fri. Rooms range from spacious and modern to smaller and slightly more rustic. Some with fireplace and/or porch. Each room individually appointed with a country elegance. 2 stories; interior corridors; smoke free premises; pass for guests to use town pool within walking distance. **Dining:** Dining room, see separate listing. **Services:** gift shop. **All Rooms:** extended cable TV. **Cards:** DS, MC, VI. **Special Amenities:** Free breakfast and free room upgrade (subject to availability with advanced reservations).

HERITAGE COUNTRY INN
Phone: (716)633-4900 **68**

	5/1-9/30	1P: $50-$150	2P: $50-$150	XP: $10	F6
	10/1-12/31	1P: $40-$110	2P: $40-$110	XP: $10	F6
	1/1-4/30	1P: $35-$100	2P: $35-$100	XP: $7	F6

Motel   **Location:** 0.6 mi e on SR 5 from jct SR 78. 8261 Main St 14221. Fax: 716/633-4900. **Terms:** [CP] meal plan; weekly rates avail; cancellation fee imposed; package plans. **Facility:** 53 rooms. Tasteful country decor and warm hospitality yield comforting ambiance. 12 efficiencies, $60-$99; 2 stories; interior corridors. **Dining:** Restaurant nearby. **All Rooms:** extended cable TV. **Some Rooms:** Fee: refrigerators, microwaves. **Cards:** AE, MC, VI. **Special Amenities:** Free breakfast and free room upgrade (subject to availability with advanced reservations). *(See color ad p 216)*

THE VILLAGE HAVEN
Phone: 716/759-6845 **71**

	5/1-9/30	1P: $60-$275	2P: $60-$275	XP: $10	F6
	10/1-12/31	1P: $40-$200	2P: $40-$200	XP: $10	F6
	1/1-4/30	1P: $35-$175	2P: $35-$175	XP: $7	F6

Motel   **Location:** SR 5, 3 mi e from jct SR 78. 9370 Main St 14031. Fax: 716/759-6847. **Terms:** [CP] meal plan; weekly rates avail; cancellation fee imposed; package plans. **Facility:** 34 rooms. Set back from hwy on spacious, landscaped grounds. Compact comfortable rooms to large elegant suites, 5 with fireplace. At-door parking. Office hrs 7:30 am-11 pm, Fri and Sat-midnight. 9 whirlpool suites, $99-$290; 1 story; exterior corridors; whirlpool. **Dining:** Restaurant nearby. **Recreation:** basketball. **All Rooms:** combo or shower baths, extended cable TV. **Some Rooms:** 4 efficiencies. **Cards:** AE, MC, VI. *(See color ad p 216)*

——— RESTAURANTS ———

ASA RANSOM HOUSE
DINING ROOM Country Inn   **Lunch:** $7-$14   **Dinner:** $12-$28   Phone: 716/759-2315 **83**

Location: 5.3 mi e on SR 5 from jct SR 78; in Asa Ransom House. 10529 Main St 14031. **Hours:** Open 5/1-12/31 & 2/6-4/30; 4 pm-8 pm, Wed 11:30 am-2 pm; Thurs tea 2 pm-4 pm, Fri & Sat limited seating; 5 course prix fixe menu, $80 per couple, 3 seatings 6 pm, 7 pm & 8 pm. Closed: Mon. **Reservations:** suggested. **Features:** children's menu; early bird specials; health conscious menu items; cocktails. Savor such dishes as grilled chicken, served with raspberry vinaigrette and fresh raspberries, or mango-mustard-glazed salmon, garnished with basil and watercress. A wood-burning fireplace is the focal point of the 1853 village inn's dining room. Smoke free premises. **Cards:** DS, MC, VI.

American

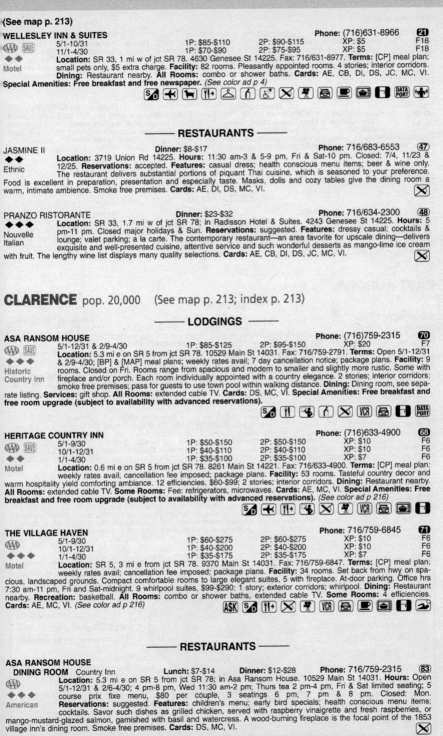

(See map p. 213)

OLD RED MILL INN
◆◆
American

Lunch: $5-$10   **Dinner:** $10-$19   **Phone:** 716/633-7878   81

Location: 0.5 mi e on SR 5 from jct SR 78. 8326 Main St 14221. **Hours:** 11:30 am-9 pm, Fri & Sat-10 pm, Sun 11 am-2 & 3-9 pm. Closed: 12/25 & Mon. **Reservations:** suggested. **Features:** casual dress; Sunday brunch; children's menu; early bird specials; health conscious menu items; carryout; cocktails & lounge. Built in 1858, the bright-red grist mill is appointed in a rustic theme, with farm and railroad motifs prevailing. Meat and seafood selections show subtle, international influences. Warm apple pie is just one great choice from an array of fresh desserts. **Cards:** AE, CB, DI, DS, MC, VI.

PALERMO
◆◆
Italian

Dinner: $7-$15   **Phone:** 716/759-8923   80

Location: SR 5, 3 mi e from jct SR 78. 9780 Main St 14031. **Hours:** 4 pm-9 pm, Sun from 9 pm. Closed major holidays & Mon. **Reservations:** accepted. **Features:** casual dress; senior's menu; health conscious menu items; carryout; cocktails & lounge. The spiffy, little place has a traditional Sicilian menu with such specialties as sausage cacciatore with homemade sausage, pasta con sarde and tripe. A "small appetite" section of the menu caters to those who can't handle the plentiful portions. Smoke free premises. **Cards:** MC, VI.

DEPEW pop. 17,700   (See map p. 213; index p. 213)

———— RESTAURANT ————

SALVATORE'S ITALIAN GARDENS
AAA
◆◆◆◆
Italian

Dinner: $19-$45   **Phone:** 716/683-7990   89

Location: SR 78; just s of jct SR 33. 6461 Transit Rd 14043. **Hours:** 5 pm-10 pm, Fri & Sat-11 pm, Sun 3 pm-10 pm; 11 am-3 pm 12/1-12/31. Closed: 12/24 & 12/25. **Reservations:** suggested. **Features:** children's menu; cocktails & lounge. Imposing architecture, formal gardens, elaborate seasonal decorations and an extensive collection of fine sculptures make this a wonderful place for special occasions. Salmon Wellington is a particularly good choice on a menu of mostly steaks and pasta. **Cards:** AE, CB, DI, MC, VI.

EAST AURORA pop. 6,600

———— LODGING ————

THE ROYCROFT INN
◆◆◆
Historic
Country Inn

All Year   **Phone:** (716)652-5552

1P: $130-$260   2P: $130-$260   XP: $10   F12

Location: Downtown; just s of jct US 20A and SR 16, adjacent to The Roycroft Colony Buildings. 40 S Grove St 14052. Fax: 716/655-5345. **Terms:** [CP] meal plan; cancellation fee imposed; package plans. **Facility:** 22 rooms. Recently restored 1900s era country inn with spacious luxurious public areas and rooms restored to The Roycroft Arts and Crafts period style with multiple rooms and large baths. A National Landmark. 3 stories; interior corridors; smoke free premises. **Services:** winter plug-ins. **Cards:** AE, DI, DS, MC, VI. *(See color ad below)*

———— RESTAURANTS ————

OLD ORCHARD INN   Historical
◆◆◆
American

Lunch: $8-$14   **Dinner:** $14-$22   **Phone:** 716/652-4664

Location: 2.4 mi s on old SR 16 from jct US 20A, go (under SR 400) to Blakely Corner, 0.4 mi w, following signs. 2095 Blakeley Corners Rd 14052. **Hours:** 11:30 am-2:30 & 5-9 pm, Sat-10 pm, Sun noon-9 pm. Closed: 12/25. **Reservations:** suggested. **Features:** dressy casual; cocktails. On manicured grounds overlooking a lake, the restored lodge has a convivial, rustic appeal. Homemade rolls and desserts—particularly the luscious lemon angel—make your mouth water. In season, terrace seating is a nice alternative to the dining room. **Cards:** AE, DS, MC, VI.

THE ROYCROFT INN DINING ROOM   Historical
◆◆◆
American

Lunch: $7-$11   **Dinner:** $12-$24   **Phone:** 716/652-5552

Location: Downtown; just s of jct US 20A and SR 16, adjacent to The Roycroft Colony Buildings; in The Roycroft Inn. 40 S Grove St 14052. **Hours:** 11:30 am-2 & 5-9 pm, Fri & Sat-10 pm. **Reservations:** suggested. **Features:** dressy casual; Sunday brunch; children's menu; health conscious menu items; cocktails & lounge. Reflections of the arts and crafts movement—including pictures dating back to the inn's 1900s origin—are evident in the cozy dining room. Lamb chops, chicken and shrimp pasta, tuna steak and beef tenderloin are examples of well-prepared choices. Smoke free premises. **Cards:** AE, CB, DI, DS, MC, VI.

ELMA pop. 2,400   (See map p. 213; index p. 213)

—— LODGING ——

TRANSIT MANOR MOTEL   Phone: (716)674-7070   **76**
AAA [SAVE]   All Year   1P: $32-$52   2P: $44-$64   XP: $5   F12
◆   **Location:** US 20 and SR 78, 0.8 mi n of jct SR 400. 2831 Transit Rd 14059. **Terms:** Weekly rates avail; 3 day
Motel   cancellation notice. **Facility:** 18 rooms. 1 story; exterior corridors. **Services:** winter plug-ins. **All Rooms:** ex-
           tended cable TV. **Some Rooms:** efficiency. **Cards:** AE, DS, MC, VI. **Special Amenities:** Early check-in/late
           check-out and free local telephone calls.

GRAND ISLAND pop. 17,600

—— LODGINGS ——

BUDGET MOTEL   Phone: (716)773-3902
AAA [SAVE]   All Year   1P: $32-$52   2P: $39-$69   XP: $8   F
◆   **Location:** I-190 N, exit 20, 2 mi se on SR 324; I-190 S, exit 20B just e on SR 324. 3080 Grand Island Blvd
Motel   14072. Fax: 716/773-4972. **Terms:** Weekly rates avail; 3 day cancellation notice. **Facility:** 21 rooms. All rooms
           with contemporary appeal. 2 stories; exterior corridors. **Recreation:** 2 gas barbecue grills. **Cards:** AE, DS,
           MC, VI. **Special Amenities:** Early check-in/late check-out and free local telephone calls.

CHATEAU MOTOR LODGE   Phone: (716)773-2868
AAA   6/1-9/8   1P: $45-$65   2P: $49-$79   XP: $5   F7
       5/1-5/31   1P: $35-$45   2P: $39-$49   XP: $5   F7
◆   9/9-4/30   1P: $30-$39   2P: $35-$49   XP: $5   F7
Motel   **Location:** 0.5 mi w on SR 324 from I-190, exit 18A northbound. 1810 Grand Island Blvd 14072.
           Fax: 716/773-5173. **Terms:** Weekly & monthly rates avail; 3 day cancellation notice; pets, $8 extra charge.
Facility: 17 rooms. Compact rooms with vintage features to larger rooms with contemporary appeal. 1 story; exterior corridors.
Dining: Restaurant nearby. **Services:** winter plug-ins. **All Rooms:** combo or shower baths. **Some Rooms:** 4 efficiencies, no
utensils. **Cards:** AE, DS, MC, VI.

CINDERELLA MOTEL   Phone: (716)773-2872
◆◆   11/1-4/30   1P: $35-$45   2P: $45-$69   XP: $5   F7
Motel 5/1-10/31   1P: $45   2P: $69   XP: $5   F7
           Location: I-190 N, exit 19, 1.3 mi w on SR 324; I-190 S, exit 20B, just e on SR 324. 2797 Grand Island Blvd
14072-1210. **Terms:** 3 day cancellation notice; cancellation fee imposed; pets. **Facility:** 16 rooms. Large, bright rooms with
some upscale appointments. Meticulously well-kept property. Office hrs 7 am-1 am. 1 two-bedroom unit. 1 story; exterior corridors. **Services:** winter plug-ins. **All Rooms:** combo or shower baths. **Some Rooms:** efficiency. **Cards:** AE, DS, MC, VI.

HOLIDAY INN NIAGARA FALLS/GRAND ISLAND RESORT   Phone: (716)773-1111
AAA [SAVE] 5/27-9/5   1P: $80-$164   2P: $80-$164   XP: $10   F
            9/6-4/30   1P: $70-$89   2P: $70-$89   XP: $10   F
◆◆◆   5/1-5/26   1P: $75-$85   2P: $75-$85   XP: $10   F
Motor Inn   **Location:** I-190, exit 19, 4 mi e. 100 Whitehaven Rd 14072. Fax: 716/773-9386. **Terms:** [BP] meal plan;
           monthly rates avail; package plans. **Facility:** 264 rooms. Family oriented facility on very nice Niagara riverfront
setting; also affords extensive conference capabilities. 4-6 stories; interior corridors; 2 heated pools, wading
pool, sauna, whirlpool, Grand Lady boat cruises; 2 tennis courts; boat dock; playground. Fee: 18 holes golf. **Dining:** Restaurant; 6:30 am-10 pm; $13-$19; cocktails. **Services:** gift shop. Fee: massage. **Recreation:** fishing. **All Rooms:** combo or
shower baths. **Some Rooms:** Fee: VCR. **Cards:** AE, CB, DI, DS, JC, MC, VI.

HAMBURG pop. 10,400

—— LODGINGS ——

DAYS INN   Phone: (716)649-8100
◆◆   8/1-9/4   1P: $65-$85   2P: $70-$90   XP: $5   F17
Motel 9/5-4/30   1P: $40-$85   2P: $48-$90   XP: $5   F17
       5/1-7/31   1P: $40-$75   2P: $48-$75   XP: $5   F17
Location: SR 75, just nw of jct I-90, exit 57. 5220 Camp Rd 14075. Fax: 716/648-5213. **Facility:** 59 rooms. Adjoining truck
stop. 2 stories; interior corridors. **All Rooms:** combo or shower baths. Fee: safes. **Some Rooms:** efficiency. **Cards:** AE, CB,
DI, DS, JC, MC, VI.

HOLIDAY INN HAMBURG   Phone: (716)649-0500
AAA [SAVE]   All Year   1P: $69-$109   2P: $69-$109   XP: $10   F19
◆◆◆   **Location:** SR 75, 0.3 mi s e of jct I-90, exit 57. 5440 Camp Rd 14075. Fax: 716/648-2278. **Terms:** Check-in
Motor Inn 4 pm; package plans; small pets only, $10 extra charge. **Facility:** 129 rooms. Tasteful rooms. 2 stories; inte-
           rior corridors; heated pool. **Dining:** Restaurant; 6 am-2 & 5-10 pm, Sat & Sun from 7 am; $9-$17; cocktails.
           All Rooms: combo or shower baths, extended cable TV. **Some Rooms:** Fee: refrigerators, microwaves, VCR.
Cards: AE, CB, DI, DS, JC, MC, VI.

PENNY WISE INN
◆◆ All Year   1P: $32-$85   2P: $38-$95   **Phone:** (716)648-2000
Motel   **Location:** SR 75, just nw of jct I-90, exit 57. 5245 Camp Rd 14075. Fax: 716/648-9718. **Terms:** Check-in 4
         pm; 14 day cancellation notice; pets, $25 dep req. **Facility:** 117 rooms. 1 story; exterior corridors.
Some Rooms: Fee: refrigerators, microwaves. **Cards:** AE, CB, DI, DS, JC, MC, VI.

RED ROOF INN   **Phone:** (716)648-7222
(AAA)   5/1-8/31   1P: $44-$64   2P: $51-$71
         9/1-10/31   1P: $40-$50   2P: $47-$57   XP: $7   F18
◆◆   11/1-4/30   1P: $36-$43   2P: $43-$50   XP: $7   F18
Motel   **Location:** SR 75, just se of jct I-90, exit 57. 5370 Camp Rd 14075. Fax: 716/648-7324. **Terms:** Weekly rates
         avail; small pets only. **Facility:** 108 rooms. King business rooms with work stations. 2 stories; exterior corri-
dors. **Dining:** Restaurant nearby. **Recreation:** Fee: in room video games. **Cards:** AE, CB, DI, DS, MC, VI.

RESTAURANT

DANIEL'S   **Dinner:** $15-$22   **Phone:** 716/648-6554
◆◆◆   **Location:** On US 62 (Buffalo St); across from Hamburg Village Plaza. 174 Buffalo St 14075. **Hours:** 5 pm-9
American pm, Fri & Sat-9:30 pm. Closed major holidays, Sun & Mon. **Reservations:** suggested. **Features:** dressy
         casual; cocktails. Rich sauces and many wines complement lavish dishes of fresh seafood, meats and pasta.
The former house is cozy and inviting, with fresh flowers and piped-in classical music. The decadent dessert sampler platter
is an unquestionable delight. Smoke free premises. **Cards:** AE, MC, VI.

TONAWANDA pop. 65,300   (See map p. 213; index p. 212)

LODGINGS

DAYS INN   **Phone:** (716)835-5916   56
(AAA) [SAVE] 5/1-10/31   1P: $59-$99   2P: $64-$99   XP: $5   F18
         11/1-4/30   1P: $49-$99   2P: $49-$99   XP: $5   F18
◆◆   **Location:** US 62, 1.3 mi s of jct I-290, exit 3 (Niagara Falls Blvd). 1120 Niagara Falls Blvd 14150.
Motel   Fax: 716/835-6030. **Terms:** [CP] meal plan; weekly rates avail. **Facility:** 51 rooms. Adjacent to large shopping
         mall. 2 whirlpool rooms; 2 stories; exterior corridors. **Dining:** Coffee shop nearby. **All Rooms:** extended cable
TV. **Cards:** AE, CB, DI, DS, MC, VI. **Special Amenities:** Free breakfast and free local telephone calls.

ELLICOTT PARK COURT MOTEL   **Phone:** (716)693-6412   59
(AAA) [SAVE] 5/22-9/8   1P: $50-$60   2P: $50-$60   XP: $4   F12
         5/1-5/21 & 9/9-4/30   1P: $44-$54   2P: $44-$54   XP: $4   F12
◆◆   **Location:** US 62, 1.8 mi n of jct I-290, exit 3 (Niagra Falls Blvd). 2740 Niagara Falls Blvd 14150.
Motel   Fax: 716/693-6413. **Terms:** Weekly rates avail, off season; 7 day cancellation notice. **Facility:** 14 rooms. All
         rooms with hair dryer. Well kept with attractive rooms. 4 whirlpool rooms, $90-$125; 1 story; exterior corridors.
Services: gift shop. **All Rooms:** combo or shower baths, extended cable TV. **Cards:** AE, DS, MC, VI. **Special Amenities:**
Early check-in/late check-out and free local telephone calls.

MICROTEL-TONAWANDA   **Phone:** 716/693-8100   57
◆◆   7/1-10/31   1P: $45-$66   2P: $50-$71   XP: $5   F18
Motel   11/1-4/30   1P: $37-$59   2P: $42-$64   XP: $5   F18
         5/1-6/30   1P: $39-$52   2P: $44-$59   XP: $5   F18
Location: Just n on SR 384 (Delaware St) from jct I-290, exit 1, 0.5 mi e on Crestmount Ave. 1 Hospitality Centre Way 14150.
Fax: 716/693-8750. **Terms:** Pets. **Facility:** 100 rooms. Compact rooms with bright, functional furnishings. 2 stories; interior
corridors. **Cards:** AE, CB, DI, DS, MC, VI.

SHERIDAN PARK MOTOR HOTEL   **Phone:** (716)873-8776   60
(AAA)   5/1-9/30   1P: $40-$50   2P: $50-$60   XP: $5
◆   10/1-4/30   1P: $35-$40   2P: $40-$45   XP: $5
Motel   **Location:** SR 324, just e of jct I-190, exit 15 (Sheridan Dr). 40 Grand Island Blvd 14150. **Terms:** Weekly &
         monthly rates avail, in winter; cancellation fee imposed. **Facility:** 17 rooms. Modest rooms with compact decor.
         1 story; exterior corridors. **Dining:** Restaurant nearby. **All Rooms:** combo or shower baths, extended cable TV.
Cards: AE, DS, MC, VI.

WILLIAMSVILLE pop. 5,600   (See map p. 213; index p. 212)

LODGINGS

FAIRFIELD INN-LANCASTER   **Phone:** 716/626-1500   49
◆◆◆   Property failed to provide current rates
Motel   **Location:** Just e on Frontage Road from jct SR 78; 0.3 mi n of jct I-90 (New York Thruway), exit 49. 52
         Freeman Dr 14221. Fax: 716/626-1500. **Terms:** [CP] meal plan. **Facility:** 135 rooms. Compact to medium
sized rooms. 3 stories; interior/exterior corridors; heated pool. **Cards:** AE, CB, DI, DS, MC, VI.

(See map p. 213)

GARDEN PLACE HOTEL
Phone: 716/635-9000 **50**
◆◆◆ All Year 1P: $84-$129 2P: $84-$129 XP: $20
Motel **Location:** SR 78, facing entrance to I-90 (New York Thruway), exit 49. 6615 Transit Rd 14221.
Fax: 716/635-9098. **Terms:** [CP] meal plan; package plans. **Facility:** 119 rooms. Elegantly furnished with extensive public rooms. Comfortable rooms and deluxe suites. 2 stories; interior corridors. **Services:** area transportation.
All Rooms: combo or shower bath. **Cards:** AE, DI, MC, VI.

ASK SD ✈ ⊞ ⊞ ⊞ & ⊠ ⊠ VCR ⊞ ⊞ ⊞ ⊞ DATA/PORT ⊞

HOLIDAY INN EXPRESS
Phone: 716/634-7500 **47**
◆◆◆ 5/1-10/31 1P: $95-$109 2P: $95-$109 XP: $10 F18
Motel 11/1-4/30 1P: $74-$89 2P: $74-$99 XP: $10 F18
Location: SR 78, 0.3 mi n of jct I-90 (New York Thruway), exit 49. 6700 Transit Rd 14221. Fax: 716/634-7502.
Terms: [CP] meal plan. **Facility:** 80 rooms. Compact to more spacious guest rooms. 2 stories; interior corridors; small heated pool. **Services:** area transportation. **Some Rooms:** Fee: refrigerators, microwaves. **Cards:** AE, DI, DS, MC, VI.
(See ad p 214)

ASK SD ✈ ⊞ ⊞ ⊞ ⊠ ⊠ VCR ⊞ ⊞ ⊞ ⊞ DATA/PORT ⊞ ⊞

HOWARD JOHNSON
Phone: (716)633-1011 **44**
◆◆ 5/1-10/31 1P: $69-$89 2P: $79-$109 XP: $10 F18
Motel 11/1-4/30 1P: $59-$79 2P: $69-$99 XP: $10 F18
Location: SR 78; facing entrance to I-90 (New York Thruway), exit 49. 6619 Transit Rd 14221.
Fax: 716/633-1171. **Terms:** [CP] meal plan. **Facility:** 50 rooms. 2 stories; interior corridors. **All Rooms:** combo or shower baths. **Cards:** AE, CB, DI, DS, JC, MC, VI.

ASK SD ⊞ ⊞ ⊠ ⊠ ⊞ ⊞ ⊞ DATA/PORT

LANCASTER MOTOR INN
Phone: (716)634-6560 **42**
AAA SAVE 7/1-9/2 1P: $70 2P: $90 XP: $20
5/1-6/30 1P: $55 2P: $60 XP: $20
◆ 9/3-12/31 1P: $50 2P: $60 XP: $20
Motel 1/1-4/30 1P: $45 2P: $50 XP: $20
Location: SR 78, 0.3 mi n of jct I-90 (New York Thruway), exit 49. 6685 Transit Rd 14221. **Facility:** 15 rooms.
Large well kept rooms. 1 story; exterior corridors. **Dining:** Restaurant nearby. **Services:** winter plug-ins. **All Rooms:** extended cable TV. **Cards:** AE, CB, DI, DS, MC, VI. **Special Amenities:** Early check-in/late check-out and free local telephone calls.

SD ⊞ ⊠ ⊠ VCR ⊞

(See map p. 213)

MICROTEL-LANCASTER   **Phone: 716/633-6200** 43
◆◆   7/1-9/4   1P: $45   2P: $50   XP: $5   F16
Motel   5/1-6/30 & 9/5-10/27   1P: $40   2P: $45   XP: $5   F16
            10/28-4/30   1P: $36   2P: $41   XP: $5   F16
Location: Just e on Frontage Rd from jct SR 78; 0.3 mi n of jct I-90 (New York Thruway), exit 49. 50 Freeman Rd 14221.
Fax: 716/633-1329. **Terms:** Small pets only, $5 extra charge. **Facility:** 100 rooms. Functional rooms. 2 stories; interior corri-
dors. **Services:** winter plug-ins. **Cards:** AE, DI, DS, MC, VI.

RESIDENCE INN BY MARRIOTT BUFFALO/AMHERST   **Phone: (716)632-6622** 45
◆◆◆   All Year   2P: $120-$150
Apartment   **Location:** Just e on Maple Rd from jct SR 263 (Millersport Hwy). 100 Maple Rd 14221. Fax: 716/632-5247.
Terms: [ECP] meal plan; pets, $6 extra charge. **Facility:** 112 rooms. Mixture of 1- and 2-bedded studios and
loft bedroom units in cluster buildings many with fireplace. 2 stories; exterior corridors; heated pool. **Services:** winter plug-ins.
Recreation: sports court. **Some Rooms:** Fee: VCR. **Cards:** AE, CB, DI, DS, MC, VI.

──── RESTAURANTS ────

DAFFODIL'S   **Lunch:** $7-$11   **Dinner:** $13-$30   **Phone:** 716/688-5413   67
◆◆◆   **Location:** 1.8 mi e on Maple Rd from jct SR 263 (Millersport Hwy). 930 Maple Rd 14221. **Hours:** 11:30
Steak and am-2:30 & 5-11 pm, Fri-midnight, Sat 5 pm-midnight, Sun 4 pm-10 pm. Closed: 5/31, 7/4 & 9/6.
Seafood   **Reservations:** suggested. **Features:** dressy casual; health conscious menu items; carryout; cocktails &
lounge. A corner fireplace adds to the cozy, homey ambience of the visually appealing dining room. Creative
menu selections reflect American and Continental influences. Rack of lamb—bathed in an excellent sauce—is the
outstanding dinner specialty. **Cards:** AE, DI, MC, VI.

HANNY'S EAGLE HOUSE
RESTAURANT Historical   **Lunch:** $7-$10   **Dinner:** $10-$20   **Phone:** 716/632-7669   66
◆◆   **Location:** SR 5, in downtown Williamsville; 1 mi e of jct I-290, exit 7. 5578 Main St 14221. **Hours:** 11 am-10
American   pm, Fri & Sat-11 pm, Sun 3 pm-9 pm. Closed: Sun 7/1-8/31. **Reservations:** accepted; except Fri.
Features: casual dress; cocktails & lounge. The two-story, wood-frame building dates back to the
stagecoach era. Most every taste is satisfied from a varied menu that includes homey comfort foods, as well as such local
specialties as broiled scrod. Peach-almond pie is a tasty dessert choice. **Cards:** AE, CB, DS, MC, VI.

SIGMUND'S BISTRO   **Lunch:** $6-$11   **Dinner:** $11-$20   **Phone:** 716/688-2051   62
◆◆◆   **Location:** Corner of Maple and N Forest in the Maple/Forest Plaza; 2 mi e of jct Millersport Hwy. 724 Maple
American   Rd 14221. **Hours:** 11:30 am-3:30 & 4:30-10 pm, Fri-11 pm, Sat 5 pm-11 pm. Closed major holidays & Sun.
Reservations: accepted. **Features:** dressy casual; early bird specials; health conscious menu items;
carryout; cocktails & lounge. The attractive, little restaurant boasts a sophisticated decor and an extensive menu with such
dinner entrees as pistachio-crusted pork tenderloin, salmon bistro, potato-crusted sea bass and orange roughy piccata.
Great attention is paid to eye appeal. **Cards:** AE, DI, DS, MC, VI.

ZUZON AMERICAN GRILLE   **Lunch:** $7-$12   **Dinner:** $9-$18   **Phone:** 716/634-6123   64
◆◆   **Location:** On SR 5 in Warren Center, just e of jct I-290. 5110 Main St 14221. **Hours:** 11:30 am-10 pm, Sun
American   4 pm-10 pm. Closed: 12/25. **Reservations:** accepted. **Features:** casual dress; children's menu; early bird
specials; health conscious menu items; carryout; cocktails & lounge. Large, handsome and informal, the
California-style restaurant is a local favorite for an eclectic menu and occasional live jazz. Selections range from meatloaf
with mashed potatoes to mushroom ragout to salade nicoise with fresh tuna. The pace is swift. Smoke free premises.
Cards: AE, MC, VI.

This ends listings for the Buffalo Vicinity.
The following page resumes the alphabetical listings of
cities in New York.

CAMBRIDGE pop. 1,900

—— LODGING ——

CAMBRIDGE INN BED & BREAKFAST　　　　　　　　　　　　　**Phone:** 518/677-5741
◆　　6/1-9/1　　　　　　　　　1P: $48　　　　2P: $65-$75　　XP: $10　　　F11
Bed &　5/1-5/30　　　　　　　　1P: $45　　　　2P: $58-$68　　XP: $10　　　F11
Breakfast　9/2-4/30　　　　　　　　　　　　　　　2P: $58-$68　　XP: $10　　　F11
　　　　Location: 0.3 mi w of jct rts 22 and 372. 16 W Main St 12816. **Terms:** [CP] meal plan; 3 day cancellation notice; cancellation fee imposed; pets, $10 extra charge. **Facility:** 8 rooms. Small to very large units, each individually decorated. 1 three-bedroom unit, 3 two-bedroom units. 2 stories; interior/exterior corridors. **All Rooms:** combo or shower baths. **Some Rooms:** 4 kitchens.

CAMILLUS pop. 1,200   (See map p. 478; index p. 477)

—— LODGING ——

GREEN GATE INN　　　　　　　　　　　　　　　　　**Phone:** 315/672-9276　　**40**
◆◆　　All Year　　　　　　　1P: $60-$175　　　　XP: $10　　　　　　　　　F
Historic　**Location:** Center; SR 5. 2 Genesee St 13031. Fax: 315/672-9216. **Terms:** [CP] meal plan; 10 day cancella-
Country Inn　tion notice. **Facility:** 6 rooms. 2 stories; interior corridors. **All Rooms:** combo, shower or tub baths. **Cards:** AE,
　　　　DS, MC, VI.

—— RESTAURANTS ——

GREEN GATE INN　　　　　**Lunch:** $5-$7　　**Dinner:** $8-$26　　**Phone:** 315/672-9276　　**20**
◆◆　　**Location:** Center, SR 5; in Green Gate Inn. 2 Genesee St 13031. **Hours:** 11:30 am-3 & 4-10 pm, Sat 4
American　pm-10 pm, Sun 10 am-2 & 3-9 pm, Mon 11:30 am-3 & 4-9 pm. Closed: 7/4, 12/24, 12/25 & Mon.
　　　　Reservations: suggested. **Features:** casual dress; children's menu; early bird specials; carryout; cocktails & lounge. Victorian furnishings decorate the five dining rooms of the 1861 farmhouse. Steaks, seafood, veal, pasta and chicken selections line the menu. Although everyone here is welcomed, the warm, romantic atmosphere is particularly inviting to couples. **Cards:** AE, DI, DS, MC, VI.

INN BETWEEN RESTAURANT　　　　　　　**Dinner:** $18-$22　　　　**Phone:** 315/672-3166　　**19**
◆◆◆　**Location:** 2.3 mi w on SR 5; 10 mi w of Syracuse and 10 mi e of Skaneatles. 2290 Rt 5 W 13031. **Hours:** 5
American　pm-10 pm, Sun 2 pm-8 pm. Closed: 12/24, 12/25 & Mon. **Reservations:** suggested; req weekends.
　　　　Features: casual dress; cocktails & lounge. The 19th-century, Victorian manor house has a sophisticated feel, with crisp linens and elegant table settings. Beef Wellington and roast duckling are among well-prepared entrees of beef, poultry, veal and seafood. Desserts are delicately presented. **Cards:** AE, MC, VI.

CANAAN pop. 1,800

—— LODGING ——

THE INN AT SILVER MAPLE FARM　　　　　　　　　　　　　**Phone:** (518)781-3600
◆◆◆　5/1-10/31　　　　　　　1P: $95-$275　　2P: $95-$275　　XP: $20
Bed &　11/1-4/30　　　　　　　　1P: $75-$250　　2P: $75-$250
Breakfast　**Location:** Just w on Rt 295. Rt 295 12029 (PO Box 358). Fax: 518/781-3883. **Terms:** [BP] meal plan; age re-
　　　　strictions may apply; 7 day cancellation notice; 2 night min stay, some weekends. **Facility:** 11 rooms. Reno-
vated barn in quiet rural area. Small to large guest rooms decorated with a simple country charm. 2 suites with fireplace. 1-2 stories; interior corridors; smoke free premises. **Services:** gift shop. **All Rooms:** combo or shower baths. **Cards:** AE, DS, MC, VI.

CANANDAIGUA pop. 10,700—See also FINGER LAKES.

—— LODGINGS ——

CANANDAIGUA INN ON THE LAKE　　　　　　　　　　　　　**Phone:** (716)394-7800
AAA SAVE　5/1-8/31　　　　　　1P: $104-$134　　2P: $114-$144　　XP: $10　　F17
◆◆◆　9/1-10/31　　　　　　1P: $94-$124　　2P: $104-$134　　XP: $10　　F17
Motor Inn　11/1-4/30　　　　　　1P: $79-$104　　2P: $89-$114　　XP: $10　　F17
　　　　Location: Just s of jct SR 332, US 20 and SR 5. 770 S Main St 14424. Fax: 716/394-5003. **Terms:** Cancel-
lation fee imposed; package plans; pets. **Facility:** 134 rooms. Lovely lakefront location, many rooms with bal-
cony and lake view. Many suites. 10 whirlpool rooms, $179-$350; 2 stories; interior corridors; small heated indoor pool, whirlpool; boat dock, boat ramp. **Dining:** Dining room; 6:30 am-9 pm, Fri & Sat-10 pm; $15-$25; cocktails. **Recreation:** fishing. Fee: in-room video games. **All Rooms:** combo or shower baths, extended cable TV. **Cards:** AE, CB, DI, DS, MC, VI.
(See ad p 230)

ECONO LODGE CANANDAIGUA

Phone: (716)394-9000

(AAA) [SAVE]

◆◆
Motel

5/26-8/31	1P: $61-$75	2P: $61-$75	XP: $5	F18
9/1-10/31	1P: $50-$74	2P: $50-$74	XP: $5	F18
5/1-5/25	1P: $45-$65	2P: $45-$65	XP: $5	F18
11/1-4/30	1P: $40-$64	2P: $40-$64	XP: $5	F18

Location: 0.5 mi e of jct SR 332, SR 5 and US 20. 170 Eastern Blvd 14424. Fax: 716/396-2560. **Terms:** [CP] meal plan; pets. **Facility:** 65 rooms. Spacious guest rooms, some with view of Lake Muar. 2 stories; interior corridors. **Dining:** Restaurant nearby. **Some Rooms:** Fee: VCR. **Cards:** AE, DI, DS, JC, MC, VI. *(See ad below)*

GEORGIAN MOTEL

Phone: 716/394-2321

◆◆
Motel

5/1-12/31	1P: $40	2P: $50	XP: $5
4/1-4/30	1P: $40	2P: $44-$46	XP: $5

Location: 1.5 mi n on SR 332. 2580 Rochester Rd 14424. **Terms:** Open 5/1-12/31 & 4/1-4/30. **Facility:** 11 rooms. Guest rooms with a view of beautifully landscaped lawns. 1 story; exterior corridors. **All Rooms:** combo or shower baths. **Cards:** MC, VI.

SUPER 8

Phone: 716/394-7224

(AAA)

◆◆
Motel

5/1-10/31	1P: $50-$70	2P: $60-$80	XP: $5	F12
11/1-4/30	1P: $45-$65	2P: $55-$75	XP: $5	F12

Location: 0.5 mi e of jct SR 332, SR 5 and US 20. 350 Eastern Blvd 14424. Fax: 716/396-7333. **Terms:** Cancellation fee imposed. **Facility:** 50 rooms. Contemporary accommodations. Rear rooms overlook pond. 4 whirlpool rooms, $60-$80; 2 stories; interior corridors. **Cards:** AE, DI, DS, MC, VI.

SUTHERLAND HOUSE

Phone: (716)396-0375

◆◆◆
Bed &
Breakfast

All Year	1P: $90-$175	2P: $90-$175	XP: $20

Location: I-90 (New York Thruway), Canandaigua exit 44, Rt 332 S into city, w on Bristol (SR 21S). 3179 Rt 21 S 14424. Fax: 716/396-9281. **Terms:** [BP] meal plan; 14 day cancellation notice; cancellation fee imposed. **Facility:** 5 rooms. Uniquely restored house dates back to 1885. Several outdoor sitting areas. 1 two-bedroom unit. 2 stories; interior corridors; designated smoking area. **All Rooms:** combo or shower baths. **Cards:** AE, DS, MC, VI.

RESTAURANTS

BRADLEY'S
◆◆
American

Lunch: $4-$7   Dinner: $5-$16   Phone: 716/396-7280
Location: 0.5 mi n, from jct SR 21. 325 N Main St 14424. **Hours:** 11:30 am-2:30 & 5-9 pm, Fri & Sat-10 pm.
Closed: 1/1, 12/25 & Sun. **Reservations:** accepted; large parties. **Features:** casual dress; beer & wine only.
Seafood is the specialty at the quiet restaurant, which is known for its generous portions and excellent
homemade soups. Old photographs and period antiques lend to the historic feel of the 1884 brick building. Soft jazz plays in
the background. Smoke free premises. **Cards:** MC, VI.

CASA DE PASTA
◆◆
Italian

Dinner: $10-$20   Phone: 716/394-3710
Location: Downtown. 125 Bemis St 14424. **Hours:** 5 pm-9:30 pm, Fri & Sat-10 pm. Closed major holidays.
Features: casual dress; carryout; cocktails & lounge. Quality ingredients go into traditional dishes of pasta,
seafood, veal and beef. An established local clientele frequents the restaurant—in a mid-19th-century
house—for its friendly atmosphere. Soft lighting and background music enhance the ambience. **Cards:** MC, VI.

LINCOLN HILL INN   Historical
◆◆◆
American

Dinner: $12-$24   Phone: 716/394-8254
Location: 1.3 mi s on SR 364. 3365 E Lake Rd 14424. **Hours:** 5 pm-9 pm, Fri & Sat-10 pm, Sun noon-5
pm. Closed: 12/25 & Mon. **Reservations:** suggested. **Features:** casual dress; children's menu; cocktails &
lounge. The restored 1804 farmhouse exudes a warm, casual ambience, in the dining room, as well as on
the three outdoor decks. Such dishes as shrimp scampi and onion soup are flavorful and aesthetically pleasing. Top the
meal with dessert or gourmet coffee. **Cards:** AE, MC, VI.

THENDARA INN & RESTAURANT
◈◈◈
◆◆◆
American

Dinner: $16-$32   Phone: 716/394-4868
Location: 4 mi s on SR 364. 4356 E Lake Rd 14424. **Hours:** Open 5/1-1/1; 5 pm-9 pm. Closed: Mon &
Tues 9/1-10/31 & 5/1-5/31; Mon-Thurs 11/1-12/31. **Reservations:** suggested. **Features:** casual dress;
cocktails & lounge; a la carte. The handsome lakefront property offers seating in the cozy, old great room
and on the enclosed porch, which looks out over the water. Carefully prepared dishes, such as chicken with
prosciutto and mozzarella in a phyllo pastry, are nicely presented. Smoke free premises. **Cards:** AE, MC, VI.

CANASTOTA pop. 4,700

LODGING

DAYS INN
◆◆
Motel

Phone: (315)697-3309
All Year   1P: $59-$80   2P: $64-$89   XP: $10   F12
Location: On SR 13, at jct New York Thruway exit 34. N Peterboro St 13032 (PO Box 655).
Fax: 315/697-5541. **Terms:** [CP] meal plan; package plans; pets. **Facility:** 60 rooms. Smallish attractive guest
rooms. Ground floor rooms have sliding glass doors. 2 stories; interior corridors. **Services:** winter plug-ins. **Cards:** AE, CB, DI,
DS, JC, MC, VI.

CANTON pop. 6,400

LODGINGS

BEST WESTERN UNIVERSITY INN
◆◆
Motor Inn

Phone: (315)386-8522
All Year   1P: $78-$88   2P: $78-$88   XP: $10   F17
Location: 1 mi e on US 11, at jct US 11, 68 and 310. 90 E Main St 13617-1452. Fax: 315/386-1025.
Terms: Package plans; pets, $25 extra charge. **Facility:** 98 rooms. Variety of room styles. 3 stories, no el-
evator; interior corridors; heated pool. **Services:** winter plug-ins. **All Rooms:** combo or shower baths. **Some Rooms:** Fee: re-
frigerators, microwaves. **Cards:** AE, CB, DI, DS, JC, MC, VI.

CANTON/POTSDAM COMFORT SUITES
◆◆◆
Motel

Phone: (315)386-1161
All Year   1P: $85-$169   2P: $85-$169   XP: $10   F18
Location: US 11, just e of jct US 11, 68 and 310. 6000 US Rt 11 13617. Fax: 315/386-2515. **Terms:** [CP] meal
plan; 3 day cancellation notice; cancellation fee imposed. **Facility:** 69 rooms. Comfortable one-room suites. 3
stories; interior corridors; heated pool. **Services:** winter plug-ins. **All Rooms:** combo or shower baths. **Some Rooms:**
Fee: VCR. **Cards:** AE, CB, DI, DS, JC, MC, VI.

RESTAURANT

MCCARTHY'S RESTAURANT
◈◈◈
◆
American

Lunch: $3-$6   Dinner: $8-$15   Phone: 315/386-2564
Location: 0.8 mi s on Rt 11 from SR 68. 5821 US Hwy 11 13617. **Hours:** 7 am-9 pm. Closed major
holidays. **Features:** casual dress; Sunday brunch; children's menu; carryout; salad bar; cocktails; a la carte.
A favorite with the locals, the family restaurant pleases with reliable, home-style cooking—including tasty
chicken and biscuits, plus homemade pies and soups. Casual country decor peppers the tidy dining room.
Pleasant servers are personable and prompt. **Cards:** DS, MC, VI.

CARLE PLACE pop. 5,100

LODGING

HOLIDAY INN
◆◆
Motor Inn

Phone: (516)997-5000
All Year   1P: $150   2P: $150   XP: $15   F18
Location: Meadow Brook Pkwy, exit M1, 0.5 mi e. 369 Old Country Rd 11514. Fax: 516/997-3623.
Facility: 152 rooms. Nicely landscaped courtyard & pool areas. 3 stories; interior corridors. **Services:** gift shop.
Some Rooms: Fee: refrigerators. **Cards:** AE, CB, DI, DS, MC, VI.

CARMEL —See New York p. 371.

CASSADAGA pop. 800

———— RESTAURANT ————

LAZZARONI'S LAKESIDE
◆◆◆
American

Dinner: $11-$28   **Phone:** 716/595-2557
Location: Overlooking Cassadaga Lake. 282 Dale Dr 14718. **Hours:** 5 pm-10 pm, Sun 4 pm-8 pm; winter hrs may vary. Closed: 12/25 & weeknights in winter. **Reservations:** suggested. **Features:** casual dress; health conscious menu items; cocktails. Enjoy romantic dining, whether you're overlooking the lake or warming next to the fireplace. Moroccan overtones punctuate a wide choice of sophisticated dishes. Such splendid desserts as the visually appealing walnut baklava are made in house. **Cards:** AE, MC, VI.

CASTLETON-ON-HUDSON pop. 1,500

———— LODGING ————

ECONO LODGE
AAA SAVE
◆◆
Motel

Phone: (518)477-2606

5/1-10/31	1P: $49-$69	2P: $59-$89	
11/1-4/30	1P: $44-$64	2P: $54-$84	

Location: Just nw on SR 9 and US 20, from I-90 (New York Thruway), exit 11 W. 1666 Columbia Tpke 12033. **Fax:** 518/477-2606. **Terms:** Weekly rates avail, off season. **Facility:** 22 rooms. Large, contemporary style guest rooms. 3 whirlpool rooms, $89-$150; 1 story; exterior corridors. **Services:** winter plug-ins. **All Rooms:** extended cable TV. **Cards:** AE, DI, DS, MC, VI. **Special Amenities:** Early check-in/late check-out and free room upgrade **(subject to availability with advanced reservations).**

CATSKILL pop. 4,700

———— LODGING ————

RED RANCH MOTEL
AAA
◆◆
Motel

Phone: (518)678-3380

6/16-9/4	1P: $45-$60	2P: $48-$70	XP: $5	F14
11/25-4/30	1P: $38-$55	2P: $42-$65	XP: $10	F14
5/1-6/15 & 9/5-11/24	1P: $38-$45	2P: $42-$55	XP: $5	F14

Location: SR 32, 0.5 mi s of jct SR 23A, exit 20; off I-87, New York Thruway, 9 mi n. 4555 Rt 32 12414. **Terms:** Weekly rates avail; 2 night min stay, weekends 7/1-8/31. **Facility:** 39 rooms. Peaceful location on spacious grounds. Seasonal picnic area. 1 two-bedroom unit. 4 efficiencies, $55-$90; $190-$480 weekly for 4-6 persons; 1-2 stories; exterior corridors; kiddie pool avail; playground. **Dining:** Restaurant nearby. **Services:** winter plug-ins. **All Rooms:** combo or shower baths, extended cable TV. **Some Rooms:** Fee: refrigerators. **Cards:** AE, CB, DI, DS, MC, VI.

———— RESTAURANT ————

LA CONCA D'ORO
◆◆
Italian

Lunch: $4-$9   **Dinner:** $9-$25   **Phone:** 518/943-3549
Location: Center. 440 Main St 12414. **Hours:** 11:30 am-10 pm, Fri-11 pm, Sat 3 pm-11 pm, Sun 2 pm-10 pm. Closed: Tues. **Reservations:** required; weekends. **Features:** casual dress; children's menu; carryout; cocktails & lounge; street parking. Representative of tasty choices is the lobster tail Contidinia, which is served with shrimp and clams in a mushroom marinara sauce over fresh linguine. Homemade desserts—such as cheesecake, bread pudding, tarts and tiramisu—quiet the sweet tooth. **Cards:** MC, VI.

CAYUGA HEIGHTS —See also FINGER LAKES.

—— RESTAURANT ——

THE HEIGHTS CAFE & GRILL   **Lunch:** $8-$12   **Dinner:** $15-$30   **Phone:** 607/257-4144
◆◆◆   **Location:** New York Rt 13, Triphammer Rd exit, 0.9 mi e on Triphammer Rd, to Community Corners Plaza.
American   903 Hanshaw Rd 14850. **Hours:** 11:30 am-2:30 & 5-9 pm, Fri & Sat-10 pm. Closed major holidays & Sun.
Reservations: suggested. **Features:** casual dress; children's menu; health conscious menu items; carryout;
cocktails. An extensive wine list complements sophisticated cuisine, which is prepared with fresh ingredients and loads of
imagination. Much attention is paid to artistic plate presentation. Tasteful jazz music plays in the background of the art deco
dining room. Smoke free premises. **Cards:** AE, DI, DS, MC, VI.   ⊠

CAZENOVIA pop. 3,000

—— LODGING ——

BRAE LOCH INN   **Phone:** (315)655-3431
AAA SAVE   All Year   1P: $60-$140   2P: $80-$140   XP: $15   F12
◆◆◆   **Location:** On US 20. 5 Albany St 13035. Fax: 315/655-4844. **Terms:** [CP] meal plan; 10 day cancellation no-
Country Inn   tice; package plans. **Facility:** 12 rooms. 1805 Victorian mansion furnished to period. Attractive rooms with
modern conveniences. 3 stories, no elevator; interior corridors; lake & golf privileges. **Dining:** Restaurant, see
separate listing. **Services:** gift shop. **Cards:** AE, MC, VI. **Special Amenities: Free breakfast and free room
upgrade (subject to availability with advanced reservations).**   ⊽ 🐕 🎦 VCR 📠

—— RESTAURANTS ——

BRAE LOCH INN Country Inn   **Dinner:** $13-$17   **Phone:** 315/655-3431
◆◆◆   **Location:** On US 20; in Brae Loch Inn. 5 Albany St 13035. **Hours:** 5 pm-9:30 pm, Sat-10 pm, Sun 1 pm-9
Ethnic   pm, 12/2-4/14; 11 am-9 pm, 9/3-6/18. Closed: 12/24 & 12/25. **Reservations:** suggested. **Features:** dressy
casual; children's menu; carryout; cocktails & lounge. The prime minister—prime rib served in natural juices
with a side of Yorkshire pudding—stands out on a menu of steak, lamb and seafood choices. A Scottish influence shows in
the memorabilia and tartan carpets of the warm, intimate dining room. **Cards:** AE, DS, MC, VI.   ⊠

THE BREWSTER INN DINING ROOM Country Inn   **Dinner:** $18-$22   **Phone:** 315/655-9232
◆◆◆   **Location:** 0.5 mi w on US 20; in The Brewster Inn. 6 Ledyard Ave 13035. **Hours:** 5 pm-9 pm, Sat from 6
Continental   pm, Sun 11 am-2 & 5-9 pm. Closed: 1/1, 12/24, 12/25 & 12/31. **Reservations:** suggested.
Features: semi-formal attire; Sunday brunch; health conscious menu; cocktails & lounge. On Cazenovia
Lake, the Victorian mansion exudes an upscale charm. Particularly well-prepared is veal Atlantis, a sauteed cut of veal
topped with lobster, served on a bed of wild greens and finished with tarragon beurre blanc sauce. Desserts change daily.
Smoke free premises. **Cards:** DI, MC, VI.   ⊠

WHEATBERRY RESTAURANT   **Lunch:** $5-$8   **Dinner:** $13-$19   **Phone:** 315/655-2102
◆◆◆   **Location:** Center. 63 Albany St 13035. **Hours:** 11:30 am-3 & 6-9 pm, Fri & Sat-10 pm, Sun from 11 am.
Continental   Closed: Mon. **Reservations:** suggested. **Features:** casual dress; Sunday brunch; children's menu; carryout;
beer & wine only; street parking; a la carte. Modern lighting and attractive artwork enhance the sophisticated
ambience of the comfortable restaurant. The frequently changing menu focuses on European peasant cuisine, well-prepared
with fresh ingredients. Homemade desserts are exceptional. **Cards:** MC, VI.   ⊠

CHAPPAQUA —See New York p. 371.

CHAUTAUQUA pop. 4,600

—— LODGING ——

ST ELMO ACCOMMODATIONS   **Phone:** 716/357-3566
◆◆◆   6/24-8/27 Wkly   1P: $1395-$2400   2P: $1595-$2600
Complex   5/1-6/23 & 8/28-4/30 Dly   1P: $65-$105   2P: $65-$165
Location: Main gate off SR 394, left to Ramble, then right. 1 Pratt Ave 14722. Fax: 716/357-3317.
Terms: Check-in 4 pm; 30 day cancellation notice; cancellation fee imposed; 7 night min stay, in summer. **Facility:** 30 rooms.
Apartment style condominiums in the Chautauqua Institution. Reservations for summer should be made months in advance.
3 two-bedroom units. 4 stories; interior corridors; smoke free premises. Fee: parking. **Services:** gift shop; massage.
All Rooms: efficiencies, combo or shower baths. **Cards:** AE, DS, MC, VI.   ⊽ 🐕 👔 ⊠ VCR 📠 🖥 📺 🔌

CHEEKTOWAGA —See Buffalo p. 221.

CHESTERTOWN pop. 9,100—See also ADIRONDACK MOUNTAINS.

———— LODGING ————

FRIENDS LAKE INN
Phone: (518)494-4751
All Year — 1P: $190-$330 — 2P: $235-$375 — XP: $65
Historic
Country Inn
Location: 2 mi n on SR 8 from jct US 9 and SR 8, 2.3 mi w on Friends Lake Rd, 0.8 mi n. 963 Friends Lake Rd 12817. Fax: 518/494-4616. **Terms:** [BP] & [MAP] meal plans; 14 day cancellation notice; 2 night min stay, weekends; package plans. **Facility:** 17 rooms. Owner pet on premises. Peaceful, rural location with very attractive rooms ranging from small to spacious. Patio dining. All rooms with hair dryer, iron and ironing board. 7 whirlpool rooms, $255-$375, 3 stories, no elevator; interior corridors; designated smoking area; beach, sauna, whirlpool. **Dining:** Dining room; 8 am-10 & 5-10 pm; $17-$25; cocktails. **Recreation:** swimming, canoeing; cross country skiing; hiking trails. Fee: cross county equipment & snow shoes. **All Rooms:** combo or shower baths. **Cards:** AE, CB, DI, MC, VI.

———— RESTAURANT ————

MAIN STREET ICE CREAM PARLOR
Lunch: $4-$10 — Dinner: $7-$15 — Phone: 518/494-7940
American
Location: Center. Main St 12817. **Hours:** 10 am-10 pm; 10 am-6 pm, Fri-Sat to 9 pm, Sun-4 pm 10/1-5/31. Closed major holidays. **Features:** No A/C; casual dress; carryout; street parking; a la carte. An air of nostalgia drifts through the 1950s soda fountain, decorated with Coca-Cola antiques and Adirondack memorabilia. The menu focuses on home-style lighter fare: delicious soups, hearty deli sandwiches and ice cream sodas made the old-fashioned way. Smoke free premises. **Cards:** DS, MC, VI.

CICERO pop. 25,600

———— RESTAURANT ————

PLAINVILLE FARMS RESTAURANT
Lunch: $4-$7 — Dinner: $6-$10 — Phone: 315/699-3852
American
Location: 0.3 mi n on US 11; I-81, exit 30. 8450 Brewerton Rd 13039. **Hours:** 11 am-9 pm. Closed: 12/25. **Reservations:** suggested; major holidays. **Features:** casual dress; children's menu; senior's menu; carryout; salad bar; buffet. Hand-painted murals, antique platters and turkey memorabilia decorate the cozy dining room of the friendly, family restaurant. The clear specialty is home-style turkey, which is freshly roasted and prepared in a variety of flavorful dishes. Smoke free premises. **Cards:** DS, MC, VI.

CLARENCE —See Buffalo p. 223.

CLAY

———— LODGING ————

CLAY FAIRFIELD INN
Phone: (315)622-2576
All Year — 1P: $59-$89 — 2P: $59-$89 — XP: $5 — F16
Motel
Location: On SR 31 just w of jct SR 481. (3979 Rt 31, LIVERPOOL, 13090). Fax: 315/622-2576. **Terms:** [CP] meal plan; $12 service charge. **Facility:** 63 rooms. 3 stories; interior corridors; heated pool. **All Rooms:** combo or shower baths. **Cards:** AE, DI, DS, MC, VI.

CLAYTON pop. 2,200

———— LODGINGS ————

BERTRAND'S MOTEL
Phone: (315)686-3641
7/1-10/1 — 1P: $49-$70 — 2P: $65-$75 — XP: $5 — F13
Motel
5/1-6/30 & 10/2-4/30 — 1P: $39-$60 — 2P: $50-$60 — XP: $5 — F13
Location: 0.5 mi n from jct SR 12 N and 12 via James St. 229 James St 13624. Fax: 315/686-3641. **Terms:** 2 night min stay, weekends 7/1-8/31. **Facility:** 28 rooms. Variety of room styles. 1-2 stories; exterior corridors. **Cards:** AE, DI, DS, MC, VI.

FAIRWIND LODGE MOTEL & COTTAGES
Phone: 315/686-5251
6/24-9/4 — 1P: $44-$64 — 2P: $50-$70 — XP: $6 — D18
9/5-10/15 — 1P: $38-$46 — 2P: $40-$52 — XP: $4 — D18
Motel
5/12-6/23 — 1P: $38-$46 — 2P: $40-$52 — XP: $4 — D18
Location: 2.5 mi sw on SR 12 E. 38201 Rt 12 E 13624 (PO Box 276). Fax: 315/686-5253. **Terms:** Open 5/12-10/15; weekly rates avail. **Facility:** 18 rooms. Tranquil setting St. Lawrence River. Modest cabin accommodations. Premium TV channel is avail only in motel rooms. 6 two-bedroom housekeeping cottages $510 weekly, for up to 2 persons; 1 story; exterior corridors; heated pool; boat dock. **Recreation:** fishing. **All Rooms:** combo or shower baths, extended cable TV. **Some Rooms:** Fee: refrigerators. **Cards:** AE, DS, MC, VI.

RESTAURANT

THOUSAND ISLANDS INN
Lunch: $4-$9   **Dinner:** $8-$29   **Phone:** 315/686-3030

🆎🆎🆎
◆◆
American

Location: On St. Lawrence Riverfront. 335 Riverside Dr 13624. **Hours:** Open 5/21-9/30; 7 am-1:30 & 5:30-9 pm, Fri & Sat-10 pm. **Reservations:** suggested. **Features:** casual dress; children's menu; early bird specials; cocktails & lounge. Overlooking the St. Lawrence River, this family restaurant delivers such tasty fare as homemade beef vegetable soup and seafood fettuccine. Thousand Island salad dressing was first served here. Friendly, prompt servers are adept at follow-up. **Cards:** AE, CB, DI, DS, MC, VI.   ⊠

CLIFTON PARK pop. 30,100

LODGING

COMFORT INN
Phone: (518)373-0222

🆎🆎🆎 SAVE
◆◆◆
Motel

7/20-9/9	1P: $119-$139	2P: $129-$149	XP: $10 F18
9/10-4/30	1P: $69-$99	2P: $79-$139	XP: $10 F18
5/1-7/19	1P: $69-$99	2P: $79-$109	XP: $10 F18

Location: Just n of Rt 146; I-87, northbound exit 9; southbound exit 9 E. 41 Fire Rd 12065. Fax: 518/373-0278. **Terms:** [CP] meal plan; weekly & monthly rates avail, off season; small pets only. **Facility:** 60 rooms. Well furnished attractive rooms with country decor. 5 whirlpool rooms, $79-149; 2 stories; interior corridors; heated pool. **Services:** winter plug-ins. **Recreation:** Fee: rental movies. **All Rooms:** extended cable TV. **Some Rooms:** Fee: refrigerators, microwaves. **Cards:** AE, CB, DI, DS, JC, MC, VI.

CLINTON pop. 2,200

LODGINGS

THE ARTFUL LODGER
Phone: (315)853-3672

◆◆◆
Historic Bed
& Breakfast

5/1-10/31 & 4/1-4/30	1P: $65-$105	2P: $75-$115	XP: $15 F12
11/1-3/31	1P: $65-$85	2P: $75-$95	XP: $15 F12

Location: I-90, exit 32. 7 E Park Row 13323. Fax: 315/853-1489. **Terms:** [CP] meal plan; check-in 4 pm; 3 day cancellation notice; cancellation fee imposed. **Facility:** 5 rooms. On National Register of Historic Places on the village green. All rooms with ceiling fan. 2 stories; interior corridors; smoke free premises. **All Rooms:** combo or shower baths. **Cards:** AE, DI, DS, MC, VI.   ASK ⊠ ☎ 🖨

THE HEDGES
Phone: (315)853-3031

◆◆
Bed &
Breakfast

All Year	1P: $65-$125	2P: $75-$125	XP: $10 F5

Location: College St, 0.3 mi n Elm St to Sanford Ave. 180 Sanford Ave 13323. Fax: 315/736-7725. **Terms:** [BP] meal plan; check-in 4 pm; 7 day cancellation notice; cancellation fee imposed; pets, pet on premises. **Facility:** 5 rooms. All original artwork. 2 stories; interior corridors; designated smoking area. **Some Rooms:** kitchen. **Cards:** AE, MC, VI.

CLYMER pop. 1,500

LODGING

PEEK'N PEAK RESORT & CONFERENCE CENTER
Phone: (716)355-4141

🆎🆎 SAVE
◆◆◆
Resort

12/22-4/30	1P: $130-$245	2P: $130-$245	XP: $20 F18
5/26-10/14	1P: $125-$165	2P: $125-$165	XP: $20 F18
10/15-12/21	1P: $100-$135	2P: $100-$135	XP: $20 F18
5/1-5/25	1P: $90-$125	2P: $90-$125	XP: $20 F18

Location: SR 17, exit 4, 5 mi s via SR 426 following signs. 1405 Olde Rd 14724. Fax: 716/355-4542. **Terms:** Weekly & monthly rates avail; check-in 4 pm; 7 day cancellation notice; cancellation fee imposed; 2 night min stay, Fri & Sat; package plans. **Facility:** 144 rooms. Public areas with elegant lodge atmosphere. Large rooms with upscale decor. Some with loft bedrooms, fireplace and balcony. 2- & 3-bedroom suites, $150-$350; 20 whirlpool rooms; 2 stories; interior corridors; 2 pools, 1 indoor heated, sauna, whirlpool; 2 lighted tennis courts (Fee: 1 indoor); playground. Fee: 36 holes golf, miniature golf. **Dining:** Dining room, coffee shop; 6:30 am-9 pm, Fri & Sat-10 pm, Sun 11 am-2 & 5-9 pm; $12-$20; cocktails. **Services:** gift shop. **Recreation:** winter tubing; bicycles, sports court. Fee: downhill & cross country skiing. **All Rooms:** combo or shower baths. **Some Rooms:** 24 efficiencies, 12 kitchens. **Cards:** AE, DI, DS, MC, VI.

COBLESKILL pop. 5,300

LODGING

BEST WESTERN OF COBLESKILL
Phone: (518)234-4321

🆎🆎🆎 SAVE
◆◆
Motor Inn

7/3-9/6	1P: $126-$149	2P: $126-$149
9/7-10/31	1P: $89-$121	2P: $89-$121
5/1-7/2	1P: $86-$121	2P: $86-$121
11/1-4/30	1P: $76-$121	2P: $76-$121

Location: On SR 7, 0.8 mi e of jct SR 10; from I-88, exit 22 westbound; exit 21 eastbound. 12 Campus Dr Extension 12043. Fax: 518/234-3869. **Terms:** [BP] meal plan, off season; package plans; pets, $20 dep req. **Facility:** 76 rooms. On hillside, set back from hwy with panoramic view. Rates for up to 5 persons; 2 stories; interior corridors; heated pool. **Dining:** Restaurant, 7 am-9 pm, Fri & Sat-10 pm; 7 am-10 pm in summer; $8-$17; cocktails; braille menu avail. **Services:** winter plug-ins. **Recreation:** rental movies. Fee: bowling. **All Rooms:** extended cable TV. **Some Rooms:** Fee: refrigerators, microwaves, VCR. **Cards:** AE, DI, DS, MC, VI. **Special Amenities:** Free local telephone calls and free newspaper. (See color ad p 241)

COLLIERSVILLE pop. 400

──── RESTAURANT ────

THE HOMESTEAD RESTAURANT Dinner: $13-$19 Phone: 607/432-0971
(AAA) **Location:** Rt 7, jct Rt 7 and 28. 13747. **Hours:** 3:30 pm-8:30 pm, Sat-10 pm, Sun noon-8 pm. Closed: Mon.
◆◆ **Reservations:** suggested. **Features:** casual dress; children's menu; senior's menu; health conscious menu;
Steak and salad bar; cocktails & lounge. This pleasant restaurant pleases with its Friday seafood buffets, salad and
Seafood sundae bars and such appealing specials as Dijonnaise scallops over linguine. Servers impress with
  excellent attention and care to needs. The atmosphere is welcoming to families. **Cards:** AE, DI, DS, MC, VI.

COLONIE pop. 8,000 (See map p. 193; index p. 191)

──── LODGINGS ────

ALBANY MARRIOTT Phone: 518/458-8444 **18**
◆◆◆ Property failed to provide current rates
Hotel **Location:** 0.3 mi se of I-87 Northway, exit 4. 189 Wolf Rd 12205. Fax: 518/458-7365. **Terms:** Check-in 4 pm;
  package plans; pets. **Facility:** 360 rooms. Attractive public areas. Good sized comfortable guest rooms. 8 stories; interior corridors; 2 heated pools. **Dining:** entertainment. **Services:** gift shop; area transportation. **Some Rooms:** Fee: refrigerators, VCR. **Cards:** AE, CB, DI, DS, JC, MC, VI.

AMBASSADOR MOTOR INN Phone: (518)456-8982 **11**
(AAA) SAVE 6/1-9/1 1P: $55-$77 2P: $66-$88 XP: $7
◆◆ 5/1-5/31 & 9/2-4/30 1P: $55-$65 2P: $60-$70 XP: $7
Motel **Location:** 5.4 mi w on SR 5; 0.8 mi w I-87, exit 2 W. 1600 Central Ave 12205 (1600 Central Ave, ALBANY).
  Fax: 518/456-8982. **Terms:** [CP] meal plan; weekly & monthly rates avail, off season; pets, $50 dep req, cash
only. **Facility:** 56 rooms. Comfortable pleasant rooms. 2 stories; exterior corridors. **Dining:** Restaurant nearby.
All Rooms: extended cable TV. **Cards:** AE, CB, DI, DS, MC, VI. **Special Amenities: Free breakfast and free newspaper.**

BEST WESTERN ALBANY AIRPORT INN Phone: (518)458-1000 **20**
◆◆ 8/1-8/31 1P: $109 2P: $109 XP: $10 F17
Motor Inn 5/1-7/31 & 9/1-4/30 1P: $99 2P: $99 XP: $10 F17
  Location: 0.3 mi se of I-87 Northway, exit 4. 200 Wolf Rd 12205. Fax: 518/458-2807. **Facility:** 153 rooms.
Comfortable rooms with pleasant decor. 2 stories; interior corridors; heated pool. **Services:** winter plug-ins. **Cards:** AE, CB,
DI, DS, MC, VI. *(See color ad p 195)*

COMFORT INN & BUSINESS CENTER Phone: (518)869-5327 **12**
(AAA) SAVE All Year 1P: $71-$119 2P: $71-$119 XP: $7 F18
◆◆◆ **Location:** 5.5 mi w on SR 5; 0.8 mi w of I-87, exit 2 W. 1606 Central Ave 12205. Fax: 518/456-8971.
Motel **Terms:** [CP] meal plan. **Facility:** 108 rooms. Small, but well furnished rooms. Small meeting room. Small busi-
  ness center in lobby. 2 whirlpool rooms, $125-$195; 2 stories; exterior corridors; heated pool, whirlpool.
Dining: Restaurant nearby. **Services:** winter plug-ins. **Recreation:** rental movies. **All Rooms:** extended cable
TV. **Some Rooms:** Fee: refrigerators. **Cards:** AE, CB, DI, DS, MC, VI. **Special Amenities: Free breakfast and free local
telephone calls.**

COURTYARD BY MARRIOTT Phone: 518/482-8800 **23**
◆◆◆ All Year 1P: $109-$129 2P: $109-$129
Motel **Location:** 0.4 mi se of I-87 Northway, exit 4. 168 Wolf Rd 12205. Fax: 518/482-0001. **Terms:** 2 night min stay,
  some weekdays. **Facility:** 78 rooms. Attractive comfortable guest rooms. 3 stories; interior corridors.
All Rooms: combo or shower baths. **Cards:** AE, CB, DI, DS, MC, VI.

DAYS INN AIRPORT Phone: 518/459-3600 **16**
◆◆ Property failed to provide current rates
Motel **Location:** Just n of jct SR 5 and I-87 Northway, exit 2 E; opposite Colonie Shopping Mall. 16 Wolf Rd 12205.
  Fax: 518/459-3677. **Terms:** [CP] meal plan; check-in 4 pm; small pets only, $25 dep req. **Facility:** 167 rooms.
Pleasant rooms. 3 stories; interior corridors. **Services:** area transportation; winter plug-ins. **Cards:** AE, CB, DI, DS, MC, VI.
(See color ad p 195)

THE DESMOND HOTEL Phone: (518)869-8100 **22**
(AAA) SAVE All Year 1P: $99-$219 2P: $99-$219
◆◆◆ **Location:** Jct I-87, exit 4; near airport. 660 Albany Shaker Rd 12211. Fax: 518/869-7659. **Terms:** Check-in 4
Motor Inn pm; package plans. **Facility:** 324 rooms. Variety of room styles, many overlooking attractive court yard. Appealing Colonial decor. Whirlpool room; suites, $149-$219; 3-4 stories; interior corridors; 2 heated pools,
see separate listing. **Services:** gift shop; winter plug-ins. **Recreation:** billard room, exercise equipment. **All Rooms:** combo or
shower baths. **Some Rooms:** Fee: refrigerators. **Cards:** AE, DI, DS, MC, VI.
saunas, whirlpools. **Dining:** Dining room, restaurant; 6:30 am-midnight; $13-$20; cocktails; also, Scrimshaw,

(See map p. 193)

ECONO LODGE ALBANY
Phone: (518)456-8811   **21**

AAA SAVE	5/1-10/31	1P: $68	2P: $75	XP: $6	F18
◆◆	11/1-4/30	1P: $60	2P: $65	XP: $6	F18

Motel   **Location:** 0.8 mi w of I-87 Northway, exit 2 W, just off SR 5. 1632 Central Ave 12205. Fax: 518/456-0811. **Terms:** Pets, with permission. **Facility:** 97 rooms. Well-lighted rooms, all with voice mail. 2 stories; interior corridors; designated smoking area. **Dining:** Restaurant nearby. **All Rooms:** combo or shower baths, extended cable TV. **Cards:** AE, CB, DI, DS, MC, VI. **Special Amenities: Free breakfast and free local telephone calls.**

HILTON GARDEN INN-ALBANY AIRPORT
Phone: (518)464-6666   **25**

AAA SAVE	7/1-10/31	1P: $89-$129	2P: $89-$129
◆◆◆	5/1-6/30	1P: $69-$109	2P: $69-$109
Motor Inn	1/1-4/30	1P: $62-$104	2P: $62-$104
	11/1-12/31	1P: $59-$99	2P: $59-$99

Location: 1.8 mi nw of jct I-87, exit opposite terminal. 800 Albany Shaker Rd 12211. Fax: 518/464-9400. **Terms:** Check-in 4 pm; package plans. **Facility:** 155 rooms. Stylish public areas and guest rooms; all with hair dryer, iron and ironing board. Patio dining avail, also a pantry with microwavable items. 6 stories; interior corridors; designated smoking area; small heated indoor pool, whirlpool. **Recreation:** in-room video games. **Cards:** AE, CB, DI, DS, JC, MC, VI. **Special Amenities: Free local telephone calls and free newspaper.** *(See color ad p 57 & p 195)*

HOLIDAY INN TURF ON WOLF ROAD
Phone: (518)458-7250   **17**

AAA SAVE	All Year	1P: $89-$139	2P: $89-$139

◆◆◆ Motor Inn   **Location:** 0.3 mi se of I-87 Northway, exit 4. 205 Wolf Rd 12205. Fax: 518/458-7377. **Terms:** Check-in 4 pm; package plans. **Facility:** 309 rooms. Large holidome with indoor recreation area. Variety of room styles. 6 whirlpool rooms, $139-$159; suites, $159-$179; 2-6 stories; interior/exterior corridors; 2 pools, 1 indoor heated, sauna, whirlpool; 2 lighted tennis courts. **Dining:** Dining room; 6 am-2:30 & 5-10 pm, Sat 6 am-11:30 & 5-10 pm, Sun 6 am-2 & 5-10 pm; $10-$17; cocktails; nightclub. **Services:** gift shop; area transportation, within 5 mi. **All Rooms:** extended cable TV. **Cards:** AE, CB, DI, DS, JC, MC, VI. **Special Amenities: Free newspaper.**

RAMADA LIMITED
Phone: (518)456-0222   **24**

AAA SAVE	7/24-9/3	1P: $80-$85	2P: $80-$85	XP: $10	F16
◆◆	5/1-7/23 & 9/4-4/30	1P: $62-$85	2P: $72-$85	XP: $10	F16

Motel   **Location:** 5.5 mi w on SR 5, 0.8 mi w of I-87 Northway, exit 2 W. 1630 Cental Ave 12211. Fax: 518/452-1376. **Terms:** [CP] meal plan; pets, $50 dep req. **Facility:** 101 rooms. Large comfortable rooms. Located in busy commercial area. 13 whirlpool rooms, $82-$189; 2 stories; exterior corridors. **Dining:** Restaurant nearby. **Services:** winter plug-ins. **Recreation:** Fee: video rentals. **All Rooms:** extended cable TV. **Some Rooms:** Fee: refrigerators, microwaves. **Cards:** AE, CB, DI, DS, JC, MC, VI.

RED ROOF INN
Phone: (518)459-1971   **15**

AAA	7/1-10/31	1P: $58-$81	2P: $65-$88	XP: $7	F18
◆◆	5/1-6/30	1P: $51-$71	2P: $56-$76	XP: $5	F18
Motel	11/1-4/30	1P: $49-$65	2P: $56-$72	XP: $7	F18

Location: I-87 Northway, exit 4, 0.3 mi e. 188 Wolf Rd 12205. Fax: 518/459-2374. **Terms:** Pets. **Facility:** 115 rooms. 3 stories; exterior corridors. **Dining:** Restaurant nearby. **Recreation:** Fee: in-room video games. **Cards:** AE, CB, DI, DS, MC, VI.

--- **RESTAURANTS** ---

ASHLEY'S
Dinner: $17-$28   Phone: 518/458-8444   **18**

AAA   ◆◆◆◆   Continental   **Location:** 0.3 mi se of I-87 Northway, exit 4; in Albany Marriott. 189 Wolf Rd 12205. **Hours:** 6 pm-10 pm. Closed major holidays & Sun. **Reservations:** suggested. **Features:** casual dress; health conscious menu; cocktails; a la carte. Swans engraved in glass, elegant table settings and a beautiful grand piano in the lobby show an emphasis on sophistication. The cuisine displays a similar focus, particularly in such outstanding desserts as Italian tortes and key lime souffle. Smoke free premises. **Cards:** AE, CB, DI, DS, JC, MC, VI.

BANGKOK THAI RESTAURANT
Lunch: $6-$8   Dinner: $10-$17   Phone: 518/435-1027   **14**

◆◆   Thai   **Location:** Just n of jct SR 5 and I-87 Northway, exit 2 E; opposite Colonie Shopping Mall. 8 Wolf Rd 12205. **Hours:** 11:30 am-10:30 pm, Fri & Sat-11 pm. **Reservations:** accepted. **Features:** casual dress; carryout; cocktails; a la carte. Teak statues and pretty table settings add to the warmth and friendly aura of the relaxed dining room. The menu centers on flavorful preparations of pork, beef, chicken and seafood. Kanon geep—pork and shrimp dumplings—is a nice appetizer choice. **Cards:** AE, DI, MC, VI.

BUTCHER BLOCK STEAK & SEAFOOD RESTAURANT
Lunch: $6-$10   Dinner: $13-$19   Phone: 518/456-1653   **13**

◆◆   Steak and Seafood   **Location:** 0.8 mi w of I-87 Northway, exit 2 W. **Hours:** 11:30 am-10 pm, Sun 3 pm-9 pm. Closed: 11/23 & 12/25. **Reservations:** accepted. **Features:** casual dress; children's menu; early bird specials; carryout; cocktails & lounge. As its name might suggest, the restaurant centers the menu on seafood and steak, particularly the succulent prime rib. The atmosphere of the dining room is rustic and cozy, welcoming to families. Decadent desserts appeal to both eyes and palate. **Cards:** AE, CB, DI, DS, MC, VI.

(See map p. 193)

THE CRANBERRY BOG   Lunch: $6-$13   Dinner: $14-$22   Phone: 518/459-5110   12
[AAA] ◆◆ American — **Location:** 0.5 mi n of I-87 Northway, exit 2 E. 56 Wolf Rd 12205. **Hours:** 11:30 am-11 pm, Fri & Sat-midnight, Sun 10:30 am-11 pm. Closed: 1/1 & 7/4. **Reservations:** suggested. **Features:** casual dress; Sunday brunch; children's menu; early bird specials; carryout; cocktails & lounge. The well-established restaurant is a local favorite for such dishes as cranberry harvest chicken and pasta a la bog. Nautical decor shows reflections of Cape Cod. Relax on the seasonal patio or in the greenhouse, where a menu of lighter fare is available. **Cards:** AE, CB, DI, DS, MC, VI.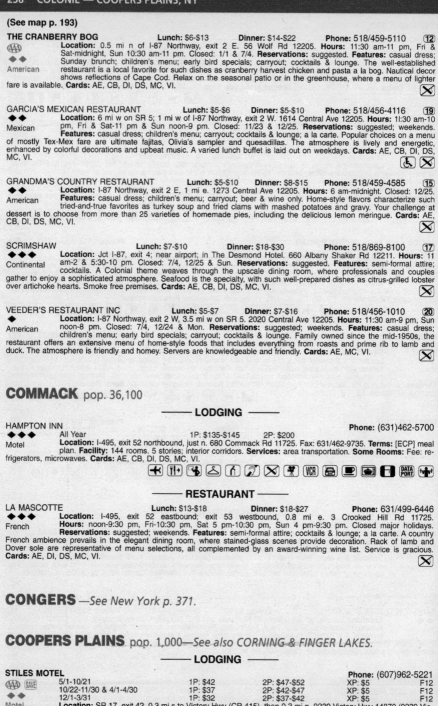

GARCIA'S MEXICAN RESTAURANT   Lunch: $5-$6   Dinner: $5-$10   Phone: 518/456-4116   19
◆◆ Mexican — **Location:** 6 mi w on SR 5; 1 mi w of I-87 Northway, exit 2 W. 1614 Central Ave 12205. **Hours:** 1l:30 am-10 pm, Fri & Sat-11 pm & Sun noon-9 pm. Closed: 11/23 & 12/25. **Reservations:** suggested; weekends. **Features:** casual dress; children's menu; carryout; cocktails & lounge; a la carte. Popular choices on a menu of mostly Tex-Mex fare are ultimate fajitas, Olivia's sampler and quesadillas. The atmosphere is lively and energetic, enhanced by colorful decorations and upbeat music. A varied lunch buffet is laid out on weekdays. **Cards:** AE, CB, DI, DS, MC, VI.

GRANDMA'S COUNTRY RESTAURANT   Lunch: $5-$10   Dinner: $8-$15   Phone: 518/459-4585   15
◆◆ American — **Location:** I-87 Northway, exit 2 E, 1 mi e. 1273 Central Ave 12205. **Hours:** 6 am-midnight. Closed: 12/25. **Features:** casual dress; children's menu; carryout; beer & wine only. Home-style flavors characterize such tried-and-true favorites as turkey soup and fried clams with mashed potatoes and gravy. Your challenge at dessert is to choose from more than 25 varieties of homemade pies, including the delicious lemon meringue. **Cards:** AE, CB, DI, DS, MC, VI.

SCRIMSHAW   Lunch: $7-$10   Dinner: $18-$30   Phone: 518/869-8100   17
◆◆◆ Continental — **Location:** Jct I-87, exit 4; near airport; in The Desmond Hotel. 660 Albany Shaker Rd 12211. **Hours:** 11 am-2 & 5:30-10 pm. Closed: 7/4, 12/25 & Sun. **Reservations:** suggested. **Features:** semi-formal attire; cocktails. A Colonial theme weaves through the upscale dining room, where professionals and couples gather to enjoy a sophisticated atmosphere. Seafood is the specialty, with such well-prepared dishes as citrus-grilled lobster over artichoke hearts. Smoke free premises. **Cards:** AE, CB, DI, DS, MC, VI.

VEEDER'S RESTAURANT INC   Lunch: $5-$7   Dinner: $7-$16   Phone: 518/456-1010   20
◆ American — **Location:** I-87 Northway, exit 2 W, 3.5 mi w on SR 5. 2020 Central Ave 12205. **Hours:** 11:30 am-9 pm, Sun noon-8 pm. Closed: 7/4, 12/24 & Mon. **Reservations:** suggested; weekends. **Features:** casual dress; children's menu; early bird specials; carryout; cocktails & lounge. Family owned since the mid-1950s, the restaurant offers an extensive menu of home-style foods that includes everything from roasts and prime rib to lamb and duck. The atmosphere is friendly and homey. Servers are knowledgeable and friendly. **Cards:** AE, MC, VI.

COMMACK pop. 36,100

—— LODGING ——

HAMPTON INN   Phone: (631)462-5700
◆◆◆ Motel — All Year   1P: $135-$145   2P: $200
Location: I-495, exit 52 northbound, just n. 680 Commack Rd 11725. Fax: 631/462-9735. **Terms:** [ECP] meal plan. **Facility:** 144 rooms. 5 stories; interior corridors. **Services:** area transportation. **Some Rooms:** Fee: refrigerators, microwaves. **Cards:** AE, CB, DI, DS, MC, VI.

—— RESTAURANT ——

LA MASCOTTE   Lunch: $13-$18   Dinner: $18-$27   Phone: 631/499-6446
◆◆◆ French — **Location:** I-495, exit 52 eastbound; exit 53 westbound, 0.8 mi e. 3 Crooked Hill Rd 11725. **Hours:** noon-9:30 pm, Fri-10:30 pm, Sat 5 pm-10:30 pm, Sun 4 pm-9:30 pm. Closed major holidays. **Reservations:** suggested; weekends. **Features:** semi-formal attire; cocktails & lounge; a la carte. A country French ambience prevails in the elegant dining room, where stained-glass scenes provide decoration. Rack of lamb and Dover sole are representative of menu selections, all complemented by an award-winning wine list. Service is gracious. **Cards:** AE, DI, DS, MC, VI.

CONGERS —See New York p. 371.

COOPERS PLAINS pop. 1,000—See also CORNING & FINGER LAKES.

—— LODGING ——

STILES MOTEL   Phone: (607)962-5221

[AAA] [SAVE]	5/1-10/21	1P: $42	2P: $47-$52	XP: $5	F12
◆◆	10/22-11/30 & 4/1-4/30	1P: $37	2P: $42-$47	XP: $5	F12
Motel	12/1-3/31	1P: $32	2P: $37-$42	XP: $5	F12

Location: SR 17, exit 42, 0.3 mi s to Victory Hwy (CR 415), then 0.3 mi n. 9239 Victory Hwy 14870 (9239 Victory Hwy, PAINTED POST). Fax: 607/962-7299. **Terms:** Pets, $3 extra charge. **Facility:** 15 rooms. Quiet residential setting. 1 story; exterior corridors; playground. **Services:** winter plug-ins. **All Rooms:** combo or shower baths. **Cards:** DS, MC, VI. **Special Amenities:** Free local telephone calls. (See ad p 242)

COOPERSTOWN pop. 2,200—

See also HARTWICK SEMINARY, INDEX & SPRINGFIELD CENTER.

—— **LODGINGS** ——

LAKE FRONT MOTEL
Phone: 607/547-9511

⬭⬭⬭⬭	7/1-9/4	1P: $99-$150	2P: $99-$150
◆◆	5/1-6/30	1P: $70-$150	2P: $70-$150
Motor Inn	9/5-10/31	1P: $75-$125	2P: $75-$125
	11/1-4/30	1P: $60-$125	2P: $60-$125

Location: Center; just n. 10 Fair St 13326. **Fax:** 607/547-2792. **Terms:** Weekly rates avail, off season; 3 day cancellation notice; cancellation fee imposed. **Facility:** 44 rooms. Located on Ostego Lake. Limited number of rooms open in winter. 1-2 stories; exterior corridors. Fee: marina. **Dining:** Dining room; 7:30 am-9 pm 5/1-10/20; $10-$15; cocktails. **Recreation:** Fee: boat tours. **All Rooms:** combo or shower baths, extended cable TV. **Cards:** MC, VI. ⬭ ⬭ ⬭ ⬭

TUNNICLIFF INN

7/1-8/31	1P: $125-$145	2P: $125-$145	XP: $10
5/1-6/30	1P: $99-$125	2P: $99-$125	XP: $10
9/1-10/31	1P: $70-$90	2P: $70-$90	XP: $10
11/1-4/30	1P: $50-$70	2P: $50-$70	

Phone: (607)547-9611

Historic Country Inn **Location:** Center; jct Main and Pioneer sts. 34-36 Pioneer St 13326. **Fax:** 607/547-4064. **Facility:** 17 rooms. Limited on-site parking. Restored 1806 Federal townhouse style architecture. Pleasant guest rooms; some very small bathrooms. 3 stories, no elevator; interior corridors; designated smoking area. **Dining:** Dining room; 11 am-4 & 5-9 pm, Fri & Sat-10 pm; formal dining room in summer; casual dining avail in tap room; $15-$19; cocktails. **All Rooms:** combo or shower baths, extended cable TV. **Cards:** AE, DI, DS, MC, VI.

——— RESTAURANTS ———

BLACK BART'S BBQ
Lunch: $6-$16 **Dinner:** $6-$16 **Phone:** 607/547-5656
American **Location:** Center. 64 Main St 13326. **Hours:** Open 5/1-10/31; 11 am-8 pm. **Features:** casual dress; children's menu; carryout; beer & wine only; street parking; a la carte. Barbecue pork, beef and ribs are delicious choices on a menu that also includes Tex-Mex specialties. The casual, homey atmosphere—decorated with a smattering of south-of-the-border accents—is welcoming to families. Service is capable and attentive. **Cards:** DS, MC, VI.

THE DOUBLEDAY CAFE
Lunch: $3-$7 **Dinner:** $5-$13 **Phone:** 607/547-5468
American **Location:** Center. 93 Main St 13326. **Hours:** 7 am-9 pm, Fri & Sat-10 pm; 1 hr later, in summer. Closed: 11/23 & 12/25. **Features:** casual dress; carryout; beer & wine only; street parking. Wholesome food—steaks, salads, sandwiches, burgers and some Mexican choices—makes up the restaurant's menu of familiar fare. Savory soups are particularly noteworthy. The walls of the popular family spot are decorated with baseball memorabilia. **Cards:** DS, MC, VI.

GABRIELLA'S ON THE SQUARE
Lunch: $5-$7 **Dinner:** $16-$24 **Phone:** 607/547-8000
Continental **Location:** At Main and Chestnut sts. 161 Main St 13326. **Hours:** 11:30 am-2 & 5-9:30 pm; seasonal hrs may vary. Closed: 1/1, 11/23, 12/24 & 12/25. **Reservations:** suggested. **Features:** casual dress; health conscious menu; carryout; cocktails & lounge; street parking; a la carte. The four dining rooms—two upstairs and two down—are elegantly appointed in stylish Victorian decor. An excellent selection of wines complements such well-prepared entrees as rack of lamb, chicken penne and salmon. Tempting desserts are delicious. **Cards:** AE, CB, DI, DS, MC, VI.

THE PEPPER MILL
Dinner: $9-$17 **Phone:** 607/547-8550
American **Location:** 0.5 mi s on Rt 28. Lower Chestnut St Rt 28 S 13326. **Hours:** Open 5/1-12/31 & 4/2-4/30; 4 pm-9 pm, Fri & Sat-10 pm. Closed: 12/24-12/25. **Reservations:** suggested. **Features:** casual dress; children's menu; carryout; cocktails. Baseball Hall of Fame pictures on the wall set the scene for casual dining that is far from ballpark style. Wonderful house sauces flavor preparations of steak and chicken. To top off the meal, enjoy a cup of robust coffee with cinnamon bread pudding. **Cards:** AE, DS, MC, VI.

CORNING pop. 11,900—*See also FINGER LAKES.*

——— LODGINGS ———

COMFORT INN

7/1-10/31	1P: $75-$125	2P: $85-$125	XP: $10 F18
5/1-6/30	1P: $65-$125	2P: $75-$125	XP: $10 F18
11/1-4/30	1P: $60-$125	2P: $70-$125	XP: $10 F18

Motel Phone: (607)962-1515
Location: SR 17, exit 46, just s on Rt 414, just w on SR 415. 66 W Pulteney St 14830. **Fax:** 607/962-1899. **Terms:** [ECP] meal plan. **Facility:** 62 rooms. 2 stories; interior corridors; heated pool. **Services:** winter plug-ins. **Cards:** AE, CB, DI, DS, JC, MC, VI.

DISCOVER CORNING
N E W   Y O R K

Corning Museum of Glass

See glass in a new light at The Corning Museum of Glass, where the art, history, and science of glassmaking come to life with daily demonstrations, intriguing exhibits, and fabulous objects.

The totally renovated museum campus includes the Art and History galleries (opening July 2000), Glass Innovation Center, Sculpture Gallery, Hot Glass Show, eight Glass Shops, two eateries, and The Studio for glassmaking instruction.

Open daily 9 a.m. to 5 p.m.,
in July and August, 9 a.m. to 8 p.m.

One Corning Glass Center
Corning, NY 14830-2253
Exit 46 off Route 17 / Interstate 86
800.732.6845 • Fax: 607.974.8270
e-mail: tours@cmog.org • www.cmog.org

ROCKWELL MUSEUM

American Western Art
Native American Artifacts
Carder Steuben Glass
Hands-on Art Room • Museum Shop

Open daily Mon.-Sat.,
9 a.m. to 5 p.m., Sun., 12 to 5 p.m.

111 Cedar Street, Corning, NY 14830
607.937.5386
www.stny.com/rockwellmuseum

Historic MarketStreet

A carefully restored architectural gem, filled with flowers, shops, outlets, galleries, studios and a variety of award-winning restaurants.

Greater Corning Area Chamber of Commerce
42 East Market Street, Corning, NY 14830
607.936.4686 • www.corning-chamber.org

Call today for your Southern Destinations Vacation Package (800) 596-9322

CORNING DAYS INN

AAA
◆◆
Motel

5/1-10/31	1P: $70-$95	2P: $80-$135	XP: $5	F16
11/1-4/30	1P: $50-$75	2P: $75-$95	XP: $5	F16

Phone: (607)936-9370

Location: Center; corner Ferris St and Riverside Dr, just w of Corning Glass Center. 23 Riverside Dr 14830. Fax: 607/936-0513. **Facility:** 56 rooms. 10 efficiencies, $95; 27 whirlpool rooms, $85-$135; 3 stories; interior corridors; heated pool, whirlpool. **All Rooms:** extended cable TV. **Some Rooms:** 10 efficiencies, no utensils. Fee: refrigerators, microwaves. **Cards:** AE, DI, DS, MC, VI.

FAIRFIELD INN BY MARRIOTT CORNING/RIVERSIDE

◆◆◆
Motel

All Year	1P: $84	2P: $84	

Phone: (607)937-9600

Location: SR 17 E, exit 45, just e on 352, just n; SR 17 W, exit 45, just e on Pulteney St, just s. 3 S Buffalo St 14830. Fax: 607/937-3155. **Terms:** [ECP] meal plan. **Facility:** 63 rooms. Spacious guest rooms with well lit work desks. 3 stories; interior corridors; heated pool. **All Rooms:** combo or shower baths. **Cards:** AE, DI, DS, MC, VI.

GATE HOUSE MOTEL

AAA
◆◆
Motel

5/15-11/15	1P: $33-$40	2P: $38-$52	XP: $6	F18
5/1-5/14 & 11/16-4/30	1P: $29-$40	2P: $35-$44	XP: $6	F18

Phone: (607)936-4131

Location: SR 17 E, exit 47 (SR 352), 0.8 mi e; SR 17 W, exit 48 (SR 352), 1.5 mi w. 145 E Corning Rd (SR 352) 14830. **Terms:** 7 day cancellation notice. **Facility:** 20 rooms. Modest, traditional motel design, decor and furnishings. 1 story; interior/exterior corridors. **Dining:** Coffee shop; 6-11:30 am. **Services:** winter plug-ins. **All Rooms:** combo or shower baths, extended cable TV. **Cards:** AE, MC, VI.

RADISSON HOTEL CORNING

◆◆◆
Hotel

5/1-10/31	1P: $109-$165	2P: $109-$165	XP: $10	F18
11/1-4/30	1P: $85-$145	2P: $85-$145	XP: $10	F18

Phone: (607)962-5000

Location: Center; on SR 17. 125 Denison Pkwy E 14830-2786. Fax: 607/962-4166. **Terms:** Package plans; small pets only. **Facility:** 177 rooms. Some elegantly appointed rooms. 3 stories; interior corridors; heated pool. **Dining:** entertainment. **Some Rooms:** honor bars. **Cards:** AE, CB, DI, DS, JC, MC, VI. *(See color ad below)*

ROSEWOOD INN

AAA
◆◆◆
Historic Bed
& Breakfast

5/15-1/1	1P: $125-$165	2P: $135-$185	XP: $35	
5/1-5/14 & 1/2-4/30	1P: $105-$125	2P: $115-$145	XP: $35	

Phone: 607/962-3253

Location: Just off Rt 352, corner of 1st and Chemung sts. 134 E 1st St 14830. **Terms:** [BP] meal plan; age restrictions may apply. **Facility:** 7 rooms. 1855 English Tudor home operated with Victorian elegance. Rooms furnished with antiques. Suite with sitting room & fireplace, $125-$165; 2 stories; interior/exterior corridors; smoke free premises. **Dining:** Afternoon tea. **Services:** winter plug-ins. **All Rooms:** combo or shower baths, extended cable TV. **Some Rooms:** kitchen, color TV. **Cards:** AE, CB, DI, DS, MC, VI.

———— **RESTAURANTS** ————

ICE CREAM WORKS

AAA
◆
American

Lunch: $4-$8   Dinner: $4-$8   Phone: 607/962-8481

Location: Downtown. W Market St & Centerway S 14830-2680. **Hours:** 9 am-5 pm; to 10 pm, 6/1-8/31. Closed: 1/1, 12/25 & Sun off season. **Reservations:** accepted. **Features:** casual dress; children's menu; health conscious menu items; carryout; fee for parking; a la carte. Original furnishings and fixtures decorated the authentically restored 1880s restaurant and ice cream parlor. The menu centers on lighter fare—sandwiches, burgers and wraps—as well as fantastic desserts, such as the melt-in-your-mouth Pyrex sundae. **Cards:** AE, DS, MC, VI.

LONDON UNDERGROUND CAFE

AAA
◆◆◆
Continental

Lunch: $6-$10   Dinner: $13-$23   Phone: 607/962-2345

Location: Downtown; just n of SR 17. 69 E Market St 14830. **Hours:** 11:30 am-11 pm. Closed: 11/23, 12/25 & Sun. **Reservations:** suggested. **Features:** casual dress; children's menu; health conscious menu items; beer & wine only; street parking. Stunning plate presentation and palate-pleasing flavors are consistent characteristics of the gourmet Continental cuisine—especially the memorable New Zealand rack of lamb. The casual, three-level dining room is decorated in a British theme. **Cards:** AE, CB, DI, DS, MC, VI.

PELHAM'S UPSTATE TUNA COMPANY RESTAURANT   **Dinner:** $10-$18   **Phone:** 607/936-8862
◆◆
Steak and
Seafood
Location: Downtown; in historic Market St district. 73-75 E Market St 14830. **Hours:** 5 pm-10 pm. Closed major holidays. **Reservations:** suggested. **Features:** casual dress; children's menu; health conscious menu items; carryout; salad bar; cocktails & lounge; street parking; a la carte. In the historic Market Street district, the restaurant is suitable for moderately upscale dining. The owners specialize in fresh grilled seafood, steak, pasta and poultry—in addition to creative vegetable side dishes and homemade desserts. **Cards:** AE, MC, VI.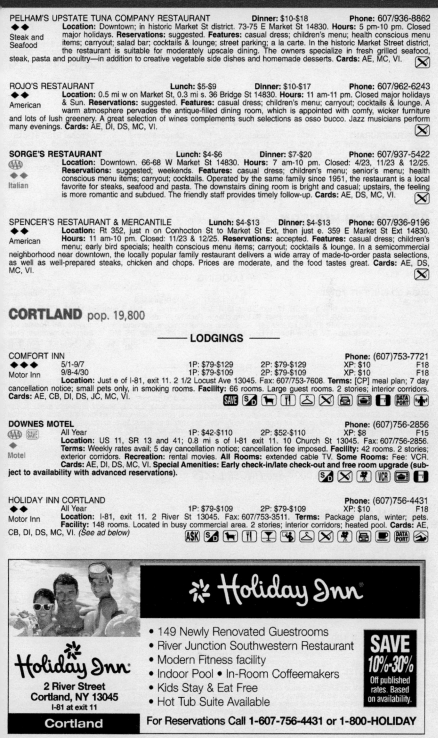

ROJO'S RESTAURANT   **Lunch:** $5-$9   **Dinner:** $10-$17   **Phone:** 607/962-6243
◆◆
American
Location: 0.5 mi w on Market St, 0.3 mi s. 36 Bridge St 14830. **Hours:** 11 am-11 pm. Closed major holidays & Sun. **Reservations:** suggested. **Features:** casual dress; children's menu; carryout; cocktails & lounge. A warm atmosphere pervades the antique-filled dining room, which is appointed with comfy, wicker furniture and lots of lush greenery. A great selection of wines complements such selections as osso bucco. Jazz musicians perform many evenings. **Cards:** AE, DI, DS, MC, VI.

SORGE'S RESTAURANT   **Lunch:** $4-$6   **Dinner:** $7-$20   **Phone:** 607/937-5422
(AAA)
◆◆
Italian
Location: Downtown. 66-68 W Market St 14830. **Hours:** 7 am-10 pm. Closed: 4/23, 11/23 & 12/25. **Reservations:** suggested; weekends. **Features:** casual dress; children's menu; senior's menu; health conscious menu items; carryout; cocktails. Operated by the same family since 1951, the restaurant is a local favorite for steaks, seafood and pasta. The downstairs dining room is bright and casual; upstairs, the feeling is more romantic and subdued. The friendly staff provides timely follow-up. **Cards:** AE, DS, MC, VI.

SPENCER'S RESTAURANT & MERCANTILE   **Lunch:** $4-$13   **Dinner:** $4-$13   **Phone:** 607/936-9196
◆◆
American
Location: Rt 352, just n on Conhocton St to Market St Ext, then just e. 359 E Market St Ext 14830. **Hours:** 11 am-10 pm. Closed: 11/23 & 12/25. **Reservations:** accepted. **Features:** casual dress; children's menu; early bird specials; health conscious menu items; carryout; cocktails & lounge. In a semicommercial neighborhood near downtown, the locally popular family restaurant delivers a wide array of made-to-order pasta selections, as well as well-prepared steaks, chicken and chops. Prices are moderate, and the food tastes great. **Cards:** AE, DS, MC, VI.

CORTLAND pop. 19,800

—— LODGINGS ——

COMFORT INN   **Phone:** (607)753-7721
◆◆◆
Motor Inn

	1P: $79-$129	2P: $79-$129	XP: $10	F18
5/1-9/7	1P: $79-$129	2P: $79-$129	XP: $10	F18
9/8-4/30	1P: $79-$109	2P: $79-$109	XP: $10	F18

Location: Just e of I-81, exit 11. 2 1/2 Locust Ave 13045. Fax: 607/753-7608. **Terms:** [CP] meal plan; 7 day cancellation notice; small pets only, in smoking rooms. **Facility:** 66 rooms. Large guest rooms. 2 stories; interior corridors. **Cards:** AE, CB, DI, DS, JC, MC, VI.

DOWNES MOTEL   **Phone:** (607)756-2856
(AAA) (SAVE)
Motel
All Year   1P: $42-$110   2P: $52-$110   XP: $8   F15
Location: US 11, SR 13 and 41; 0.8 mi s of I-81 exit 11. 10 Church St 13045. Fax: 607/756-2856. **Terms:** Weekly rates avail; 5 day cancellation notice; cancellation fee imposed. **Facility:** 42 rooms. 2 stories; exterior corridors. **Recreation:** rental movies. **All Rooms:** extended cable TV. **Some Rooms:** Fee: VCR. **Cards:** AE, DI, DS, MC, VI. **Special Amenities:** Early check-in/late check-out and free room upgrade (subject to availability with advanced reservations).

HOLIDAY INN CORTLAND   **Phone:** (607)756-4431
◆◆
Motor Inn
All Year   1P: $79-$109   2P: $79-$109   XP: $10   F18
Location: I-81, exit 11. 2 River St 13045. Fax: 607/753-3511. **Terms:** Package plans, winter; pets. **Facility:** 148 rooms. Located in busy commercial area. 2 stories; interior corridors; heated pool. **Cards:** AE, CB, DI, DS, MC, VI. (See ad below)

SUPER 8 MOTEL-CORTLAND
◆◆   5/1-9/7   1P: $58-$98   2P: $58-$98   XP: $5   F12
Motel   9/8-4/30   1P: $58-$88   2P: $58-$88   XP: $5   F12
Phone: (607)756-5622
Location: SR 13 at I-81, exit 11. 188 Clinton Ave Extension 13045. Fax: 607/753-6171. **Terms:** 7 day cancellation notice; pets, $50 dep req. **Facility:** 58 rooms. Well maintained comfortable guest rooms with a country decor. 2 stories; interior corridors. **Cards:** AE, CB, DI, DS, JC, MC, VI.

COXSACKIE pop. 2,800

—— RESTAURANT ——

RED'S RESTAURANT   **Lunch:** $5-$8   **Dinner:** $10-$19   **Phone:** 518/731-8151
◆◆
American
Location: On US 9 W, 1.5 mi s of New York Thruway exit 21B. **Hours:** 11:30 am-9 pm, Fri & Sat to 9:30 pm, Sun 10:30 am-8 pm. Closed: 12/25 & Mon. **Features:** casual dress; Sunday brunch; carryout; cocktails & lounge; a la carte. Established in 1945, the restaurant is decorated in a roadside country style, with knotty pine, pictures of 1950s and '60s movies and lots of plants. Traditional American preparations of seafood and meat combine with soups, salads and sandwiches. **Cards:** AE, CB, DI, DS, MC, VI.

CROTON-ON-HUDSON —See New York p. 371.

CUBA pop. 1,700

—— LODGING ——

CUBA COACHLIGHT MOTEL   **Phone:** (716)968-1992
AAA SAVE   All Year   1P: $39-$44   2P: $49-$55   XP: $3
◆◆
Motel
Location: New York SR 17, exit 28, n to N Branch Rd, then e. 1 N Branch Rd 14727 (PO Box 103). Fax: 716/968-3826. **Terms:** Pets, $5 extra charge. **Facility:** 27 rooms. Nicely decorated and spacious rooms close to NY Rt 17 in rural location. 1-2 stories; interior corridors. **Services:** winter plug-ins. **All Rooms:** extended cable TV. **Some Rooms:** Fee: refrigerators. **Cards:** AE, CB, DI, DS, MC, VI. **Special Amenities:** Free local telephone calls.

—— RESTAURANT ——

MOONWINKS   **Lunch:** $4-$10   **Dinner:** $11-$30   **Phone:** 716/968-1232
◆◆
American
Location: SR 17, exit 28, 1.2 mi n on Rt 305. Rt 305 14727. **Hours:** 5 pm-9 pm, Tues noon-2:30 & 5-9 pm, Wed & Thurs noon-2:30 & 5-9:30 pm, Fri noon-2:30 & 4:30-10 pm, Sat noon-10 pm, Sun 11 am-8 pm. Closed: 12/25. **Reservations:** suggested. **Features:** casual dress; Sunday brunch; children's menu; health conscious menu items; carryout; cocktails & lounge. The pleasant, rural atmosphere welcomes diners to relax and enjoy entrees of pasta, chicken, veal, pork, seafood and beef. Rack of lamb stands out as a particularly flavorful selection. Wonderful desserts are made on the premises. Servers are attentive. **Cards:** AE, DS, MC, VI.

DANSVILLE pop. 5,000—See FINGER LAKES.

DARIEN CENTER pop. 700

—— LODGING ——

SIX FLAGS HOTEL LODGE ON THE LAKE   **Phone:** (716)599-5500
◆◆◆   5/5-10/31   2P: $195   XP: $25
Lodge
Location: I-90, exit 48A, 5 mi s on SR 77. 9993 Alleghney Rd 14040 (PO Box 91). Fax: 716/599-4053. **Terms:** Open 5/5-10/31; [CP] meal plan; 3 day cancellation notice; cancellation fee imposed; 2 night min stay, 7/1-8/31; package plans. **Facility:** 163 rooms. Family oriented facility; all rooms with sofa sleeper. Adjoins amusement park. 3 stories; interior corridors; heated pool. **All Rooms:** combo or shower baths. **Cards:** AE, DS, MC, VI.

DELHI pop. 3,100

—— LODGING ——

BUENA VISTA MOTEL   **Phone:** (607)746-2135
AAA   All Year   1P: $42-$56   2P: $49-$82   XP: $7   F12
◆◆
Motel
Location: SR 28, 0.8 mi e of jct SR 10. Rt 28, Andes Rd 13753 (Box 212). Fax: 607/746-6008. **Terms:** [CP] meal plan; weekly rates avail; 7 day cancellation notice; pets. **Facility:** 33 rooms. Comfortable breakfast area in lobby with fireplace. Large back yard with picnic tables set up in summer. Some smaller rooms. Panoramic valley views. 2 stories; exterior corridors. **Dining:** Breakfast, 7-10:30 am, Sat, Sun & major holidays 8-10:30 am. **Services:** winter plug-ins. **All Rooms:** combo or shower baths, extended cable TV. **Some Rooms:** 2 efficiencies. **Cards:** AE, CB, DI, DS, MC, VI.

DEPEW —See Buffalo p. 224.

DE WITT pop. 8,200   (See map p. 478; index p. 477)

——— RESTAURANTS ———

SARATOGA STEAKS AND SEAFOOD   **Lunch:** $6-$11   **Dinner:** $12-$20   **Phone:** 315/445-1976   [22]
◆◆   **Location:** Rt 481, exit 2 (Jamesville), n on Jamesville Rd, w on Nottingham Rd to 1st stop sign, then right.
American   200 Waring Rd 13224. **Hours:** 4 pm-10 pm, Fri & Sat-11 pm. Closed: 1/1 & 12/25. **Reservations:** accepted.
Features: casual dress; children's menu; carryout; cocktails & lounge. Windows that wrap around the front of the building overlook the golf course. Horse racing prints decorate the walls, and a pit fireplace provides a good focal point. Fresh fish and hand-cut steaks are at the heart of a menu that also offers lighter fare. **Cards:** AE, CB, DI, DS, MC, VI. [X]

SCOTCH N' SIRLOIN   **Dinner:** $10-$30   **Phone:** 315/446-1771   [23]
◆◆   **Location:** 5.5 mi e on SR 5; in Shoppingtown Shopping Centre. 3687 Erie Blvd E 13214. **Hours:** 5
Steak and   pm-10:30 pm, Fri & Sat-11:30 pm, Sun 4 pm-9 pm. Closed major holidays, Sun & 7/1-8/31.
Seafood   **Reservations:** suggested. **Features:** casual dress; children's menu; salad bar; cocktails & lounge; a la carte.
Tools hang on the walls of the rustic steakhouse, which is decidedly Western in feel. Succulent steaks are hand-cut and aged on the premises. Among the delicious homemade desserts, cheesecake and the varied pies are noteworthy. Servers are friendly. **Cards:** AE, CB, DI, DS, MC, VI. [X]

DIAMOND POINT pop. 500—See also ADIRONDACK MOUNTAINS.

——— LODGINGS ———

CAPRI VILLAGE   **Phone:** 518/668-4829
◆   7/1-9/4   2P: $75-$88   XP: $10   F10
Motel   5/15-6/30 & 9/5-9/21   2P: $70-$80   XP: $10   F10
Location: 4.5 mi n on SR 9 N from I-87, exit 22. 3926 Lake Shore Dr 12824. **Fax:** 518/668-0303. **Terms:** Open 5/15-9/21; 56 day cancellation notice; cancellation fee imposed. **Facility:** 58 rooms. On Lake George. Housekeeping units and motel rooms. 21 two-bedroom units. 1-2 stories; interior/exterior corridors; playground. Fee: boat dock. **Recreation:** swimming, fishing. **Cards:** AE, MC, VI.

CHELKA LODGE   **Phone:** 518/668-4677
(AAA)   6/29-9/3   1P: $109-$144   2P: $109-$144   XP: $10
◆◆   5/15-6/28 & 9/4-10/10   1P: $84-$109   2P: $84-$109   XP: $10
Motel   **Location:** 5.8 mi n on SR 9 N from I-87, exit 22. 4204 Lake Shore Dr 12824. **Terms:** Open 5/15-10/10; [CP]
meal plan; weekly rates avail; 15 day cancellation notice; cancellation fee imposed; 3 night min stay, weekends.
Facility: 25 rooms. Located on Lake George with beautiful view. 1 two-bedroom unit. 3 efficiencies, $144; $109 off season; 1-2 stories; interior/exterior corridors; beach; 1 tennis court. Fee: boat dock. **Recreation:** swimming, canoeing, fishing, rowboats; 1 paddle tennis court, ping pong, shuffleboard. **Some Rooms:** 2 kitchens. **Cards:** MC, VI.
(See color ad p 283)

DIAMOND COVE COTTAGES   **Phone:** 518/668-5787
◆◆   7/2-9/15 Wkly   1P: $595-$1650   2P: $595-$1650   XP: $10   F12
Cottage   6/11-7/1 Dly   1P: $70-$110   2P: $70-$175   XP: $10   F12
5/15-6/10 Dly   1P: $65-$90   2P: $65-$150   XP: $10   F12
Location: 3.3 mi n on SR 9 N from I-87, exit 22. 3648 Lake Shore Dr 12824 (PO Box 65). **Terms:** Open 5/15-9/15; 30 day cancellation notice; cancellation fee imposed; 2 night min stay, cabins off season; small pets only, $50 dep req. **Facility:** 39 rooms. Units on lakeside and across street. Family atmosphere. Variety of differently styled, modestly furnished rooms, many with patio and barbecue grill. Some fireplaces. Housekeeping services in cottages, extra charge. 1 story; exterior corridors; miniature golf; heated pool; boat ramp; playground. Fee: boat dock. **Recreation:** swimming, fishing. Rental: canoes, paddleboats. **All Rooms:** combo or shower baths. **Some Rooms:** 6 efficiencies, 25 kitchens. **Cards:** MC, VI. *(See color ad p 284)*

GOLDEN SANDS RESORT   **Phone:** 518/668-2203
◆◆   7/17-8/26   2P: $90-$140   XP: $10
Motel   7/1-7/16 & 8/27-9/4   2P: $80-$125   XP: $10
5/26-6/30   2P: $60-$90   XP: $10
Location: I-87, exit 22, 3.3 mi n on SR 9 N. 3654 Lake Shore Dr 12824 (PO Box 11). **Terms:** Open 5/26-9/4; [CP] meal plan; 59 day cancellation notice; cancellation fee imposed; package plans. **Facility:** 26 rooms. Located on Lake George. Motel rooms and efficiency units. 1-2 stories; exterior corridors; heated pool; playground. Fee: boat dock, boat ramp. **Recreation:** swimming, fishing. **All Rooms:** shower baths. **Cards:** MC, VI.

TREASURE COVE RESORT MOTEL   **Phone:** 518/668-5334
(AAA)   6/30-9/4   1P: $105-$131   2P: $105-$131   XP: $10   F3
◆◆   5/1-6/29 & 9/5-10/16   1P: $65-$70   2P: $65-$70   XP: $8   F3
Motel   **Location:** 5 mi n on SR 9 N from I-87, exit 22. 3940 Lake Shore Dr 12824. **Fax:** 518/668-9027. **Terms:** Open 5/1-10/16; weekly rates avail; 21 day cancellation notice; 2 night min stay. **Facility:** 50 rooms. Located on Lake George. Variety of different room styles. Additional charge for housekeeping services in cottages. 9 two-bedroom units, $1125-$1310 weekly for up to 4 persons; 1 three-bedroom unit, $1185 weekly for up to 5 persons; 1-2 stories; exterior corridors; designated smoking area; beach; 2 pools, 1 heated; boat ramp; playground. Fee: boat dock. **Recreation:** swimming, fishing, rowboats; arcade, grills, picnic tables. Rental: boats. **All Rooms:** combo or shower baths, extended cable TV. **Some Rooms:** 14 efficiencies, 25 kitchens.

------ RESTAURANT ------

MCGOWANS
◆◆
American

Location: 3712 Lakeshore Dr 12845. **Hours:** 7 am-3 pm. **Features:** casual dress; children's menu; carryout. The casual restaurant is a local favorite for generously portioned breakfasts—from simple eggs with toast to the McGowan special breakfast sandwich—as well as hearty brunches and hot and cold lunch sandwiches. Service is quiet and attentive. **Cards:** AE, DS, MC, VI.

Lunch: $4-$8   **Phone:** 518/668-4800

⊠

DOVER PLAINS pop. 1,800

------ LODGING ------

OLD DROVERS INN
◆◆◆
Historic
Country Inn

All Year   2P: $150-$395   **Phone:** (914)832-9311

Location: 3 mi s of village, 0.7 mi e off SR 22 via signs. Old Rt 22 12522 (PO Box 100). Fax: 914/832-6356. **Terms:** [MAP] meal plan; age restrictions may apply; 14 day cancellation notice; cancellation fee imposed; 2 night min stay, weekends; $15 service charge; pets, $20 extra charge, dogs only. **Facility:** 4 rooms. Closed 1/4-1/21, Tues and Wed. 1750 authentic American inn. 2 stories; interior corridors; designated smoking area. **All Rooms:** combo or tub baths. **Cards:** MC, VI.

------ RESTAURANT ------

OLD DROVERS INN   Country Inn   **Lunch:** $9-$25   **Dinner:** $17-$35   **Phone:** 914/832-9311
◆◆◆◆
Continental

Location: 3 mi s of Village, 0.8 mi off SR 22 via signed roads; In Old Drovers Inn. Old Rt 22 12522. **Hours:** 5:30 pm-9 pm, Fri noon-3 & 5-10 pm, Sat noon-10 pm, Sun noon-9 pm. Closed: 12/25, Tues, Wed & 1/4-1/21. **Reservations:** suggested. **Features:** dressy casual; health conscious menu; cocktails; a la carte. The tavern-turned-restaurant reflects an 1800s ambience, much as the state's early herd drovers would have experienced. Seasonally changing selections center on lamb, beef and fowl. Desserts range from decadent cakes and ice creams to light Pavlovas. **Cards:** DI, MC, VI.

⊠

DUNKIRK pop. 14,000

------ LODGINGS ------

COMFORT INN
(AAA) [SAVE]
◆◆◆
Motel

	1P: $70-$80	2P: $70-$80	XP: $10	F17
5/1-9/15	1P: $70-$80	2P: $70-$80	XP: $10	F17
9/16-10/31	1P: $60-$70	2P: $60-$70	XP: $10	F17
4/1-4/30	1P: $55-$65	2P: $55-$65	XP: $10	F17
11/1-3/31	1P: $50-$60	2P: $50-$60	XP: $10	F17

Phone: (716)672-4450

Location: Just w of jct SR 60 and I-90, exit 59. 3925 Vineyard Dr 14048. Fax: 716/672-4446. **Terms:** [CP] meal plan; cancellation fee imposed; pets, $10 extra charge. **Facility:** 61 rooms. 8 whirlpool rooms, $99-$139; 2 stories; interior corridors. **Dining:** Restaurant nearby. **Services:** winter plug-ins. **All Rooms:** combo or shower baths, extended cable TV. **Some Rooms:** Fee: VCR. **Cards:** AE, CB, DI, DS, MC, VI. **Special Amenities:** Free breakfast and free room upgrade (subject to availability with advanced reservations).

DAYS INN
(AAA) [SAVE]
◆◆
Motel

	1P: $61-$71	2P: $71-$81	XP: $10	F17
5/10-9/30	1P: $61-$71	2P: $71-$81	XP: $10	F17
5/1-5/9	1P: $49-$59	2P: $59-$69	XP: $10	F17
10/1-12/31	1P: $47-$57	2P: $57-$67	XP: $10	F17
1/1-4/30	1P: $43-$53	2P: $53-$63	XP: $10	F17

Phone: (716)673-1351

Location: SR 60, just s of jct I-90, exit 59. 10455 Bennett Rd 14063. Fax: 716/672-6909. **Terms:** [CP] meal plan; weekly & monthly rates avail; pets, $10 fee, $50 dep req. **Facility:** 132 rooms. 5 whirlpool rooms, $67-$94; 2 stories; interior/exterior corridors. **Dining:** Restaurant nearby. **Recreation:** grills, picnic tables. **Some Rooms:** Fee: refrigerators. **Cards:** AE, CB, DI, DS, JC, MC, VI.

FOUR POINTS SHERATON HARBORFRONT HOTEL
◆◆◆
Motor Inn

			Phone: (716)366-8350	
5/1-5/11	1P: $69-$99	2P: $69-$199	XP: $10	F18
5/12-9/10	1P: $89-$139	2P: $89-$139	XP: $10	F18
9/11-4/30	1P: $69-$99	2P: $69-$99	XP: $10	F18

Location: SR 5, 0.3 mi w of jct SR 60. 30 Lake Shore Dr E 14048. Fax: 716/366-8899. **Terms:** Package plans; small pets only, $10 extra charge. **Facility:** 132 rooms. All rooms with colonial-style furnishings. Some rooms with wonderful views of Lake Erie and adjacent marina. 4 stories; interior corridors; 2 heated pools. **Some Rooms:** Fee: refrigerators, VCR. **Cards:** AE, CB, DI, DS, JC, MC, VI. *(See color ad p 248)*

SOUTHSHORE MOTOR LODGE
◆
Complex

			Phone: 716/366-2822
5/1-11/1	1P: $49-$98	2P: $49-$98	

Location: SR 5, 4 mi w of jct SR 60. 5040 W Lake Rd (Rt 5) 14048. **Terms:** Open 5/1-11/1; 21 day cancellation notice, for weekly rentals; pets, dogs only. **Facility:** 20 rooms. Sprawling grounds fronting Lake Erie. Offer mix of standard motel units and 1- or 2-bedroom cottages with separate living rooms. 7 two-bedroom units. 1 story; exterior corridors; heated pool. **Some Rooms:** 5 efficiencies, 13 kitchens. **Cards:** MC, VI.

THE VINEYARD MOTEL & RESTAURANT
◆◆
Motor Inn

			Phone: (716)366-4400	
6/1-9/30	1P: $50-$70	2P: $50-$70	XP: $7	F12
5/1-5/31 & 10/1-4/30	1P: $45-$65	2P: $45-$65	XP: $7	F12

Location: Just w of jct SR 60 and I-90, exit 59. 3929 Vineyard Dr 14048. Fax: 716/366-3375. **Terms:** Pets, $5 extra charge. **Facility:** 28 rooms. 1 story; exterior corridors; playground. **Cards:** AE, CB, DI, DS, MC, VI.

EAGLE BAY

—————— **RESTAURANT** ——————

—————— *The following restaurant has not been inspected by AAA* ——————
but is listed for your information only.

BIG MOOSE INN
[fyi]
Not inspected. **Location:** Located on Big Moose Lake. Big Moose Rd 13331. **Features:** This casual Adirondack-style inn, built in early 1900s, is open seasonally and features seafood and prime beef.

EAST AMHERST

—————— **RESTAURANT** ——————

IL FIORENTINO
◆◆◆
Italian

Dinner: $25-$28 **Phone:** 716/625-4250

Location: Just s jct Rt 78 (Transit Rd) and 263 (Millersport Hwy). 8485 Transit Rd 14051. **Hours:** 6 pm-9 pm. Closed: Sun & Mon. **Reservations:** required. **Features:** dressy casual; health conscious menu items; wine only. Representative of upscale Florentine cuisine are such dishes as risotto Nero and spicy, grilled Cornish hen. The restaurant was built to resemble a Tuscan country home, with stucco and tile outside and woodwork inside. A romantic ambience prevails. Smoke free premises. **Cards:** AE, CB, DI, DS, MC, VI.

EAST AURORA —*See Buffalo p. 224.*

EAST DURHAM pop. 700

—————— **LODGINGS** ——————

THE CARRIAGE HOUSE BED AND BREAKFAST
[AAA] [SAVE]
◆◆
Bed &
Breakfast

			Phone: 518/634-2284	
5/25-11/25	1P: $68	2P: $78-$88	XP: $35	D12

Location: 1.5 mi w on Rt 145. 2946 Rt 145 12423 (Box 12A, Rt 145). Fax: 518/634-2284. **Terms:** Open 5/25-11/25; [BP] meal plan; weekly rates avail; 3 day cancellation notice; cancellation fee imposed. **Facility:** 5 rooms. Peaceful location. 255 foot creekside boardwalk leading to on grounds waterfall. Personal checks accepted; 2 stories; interior corridors; swimming hole. **Recreation:** hiking trails. Fee: horse & carriage rides. **All Rooms:** combo or shower baths, extended cable TV. **Cards:** AE, DS, MC, VI.

GAVIN'S GOLDEN HILL RESORT
[AAA]
◆
Motor Inn

			Phone: 518/634-2582	
5/1-10/31	1P: $150-$175	2P: $89-$99	XP: $79	D14

Location: 0.5 mi w from jct Rt 145 and Golden Hill Rd. Golden Hill Rd 12423 (PO Box 6). Fax: 518/634-2531. **Terms:** Open 5/1-10/31; [MAP] meal plan; weekly rates avail; package plans. **Facility:** 60 rooms. Adult resort atmosphere. Relaxing mountain setting variety of room types ranging from compact to large. 1 two-bedroom unit. Personal checks accepted; 2-3 stories, no elevator; exterior corridors. **Dining:** Dining room; 8:30-10 am, 12:30 pm buffet lunch, 6 pm-7 pm seating for dinner. **Services:** area transportation, village. **Recreation:** daily planned activities & lawn games. **All Rooms:** combo or shower baths. **Cards:** AE, MC, VI.

EAST GREENBUSH pop. 3,800 (See map p. 193; index p. 192)

—————— **LODGING** ——————

ECONO LODGE
[AAA] [SAVE]
◆◆
Motel

			Phone: (518)472-1360	**39**
5/1-10/31	1P: $49-$69	2P: $59-$89	XP: $6	F18
11/1-4/30	1P: $44-$64	2P: $54-$84	XP: $6	F18

Location: US 9 and 20, 1.5 mi e of I-787, Renesselaer exit. 110 Columbia Tpk 12144. Fax: 518/427-2926. **Terms:** [CP] meal plan; weekly rates avail, off season. **Facility:** 54 rooms. Pleasant guest rooms. 7 whirlpool rooms, $89-$150; 1 story; interior/exterior corridors. **Services:** winter plug-ins. **All Rooms:** combo or shower baths, extended cable TV. **Cards:** AE, DI, DS, MC, VI. **Special Amenities:** Free breakfast and free newspaper.

EAST HAMPTON pop. 1,400

—— LODGING ——

DUTCH MOTEL   **Phone:** (631)324-4550
AAA SAVE   6/30-9/4   1P: $115-$150   2P: $115-$150   XP: $25   F12
◆◆   5/1-6/29   1P: $80-$115   2P: $80-$115   XP: $15   F12
                9/5-10/31   1P: $80-$90   2P: $80-$90   XP: $15   F12
Motel   11/1-4/30   1P: $63-$73   2P: $63-$73   XP: $15   F12
Location: 1.3 mi e on SR 27 E (Montauk Hwy). 488 Montauk Hwy 11937. Fax: 631/324-2619. **Terms:** Weekly & monthly rates avail; 60 day cancellation notice, 7 days off season; cancellation fee imposed; 3 night min stay, weekends 6/24-9/11; $2 service charge; pets, $10 extra charge. **Facility:** 28 rooms. 6 whirlpool rooms, $84-$190; 2 stories; exterior corridors. **Dining:** Restaurants nearby. **All Rooms:** extended cable TV. **Some Rooms:** 12 efficiencies, no utensils. **Cards:** AE, DS, MC, VI.

—— RESTAURANTS ——

THE PALM IN HUNTTING INN   Country Inn   **Dinner:** $18-$29   **Phone:** 631/324-0411
◆◆   **Location:** Center; in Huntting Inn. 94 Main St 11937. **Hours:** 5 pm-10 pm, Fri & Sat-11 pm; winter hrs may
American   vary. Closed: Tues & Weds in spring, winter & fall. **Features:** casual dress; cocktails & lounge; valet parking; a la carte. On the grounds of Huntting Inn, the Early American landmark is a respected steakhouse, known for succulent porterhouse steaks and huge lobsters. Dark wood accents decorate the upscale dining room. Servers in white aprons are prompt and attentive. Smoke free premises. **Cards:** AE, CB, DI, MC, VI.

PECONIC COAST   **Dinner:** $16-$34   **Phone:** 631/324-6772
◆◆◆   **Location:** Just w on SR 25. 103 Montauk Hwy 11937. **Hours:** 5:30 pm-11 pm, Fri & Sat-midnight. Closed:
American   11/23 & 12/25. **Features:** casual dress; cocktails; a la carte. Warm, red walls contribute to the sleek, modern setting. Contemporary cuisine often shows Mediterranean influences. Choices range from the sophisticated to comfort foods, such as succulent ribs with garlic mashed potatoes. Sour cream brulee is intriguing. Smoke free premises. **Cards:** AE, DI, MC.

EAST MEADOW pop. 36,900

—— LODGING ——

COLISEUM MOTOR INN   **Phone:** (516)794-2100
AAA SAVE   All Year   1P: $95   2P: $110   XP: $10   F12
◆◆   **Location:** Meadowbrook Pkwy, exit M5, 0.3 mi e. 1650 Hempstead Tpke 11554. Fax: 516/794-2278.
Motel   **Terms:** Cancellation fee imposed. **Facility:** 110 rooms. Located close to Nassau Coliseum. Many guest rooms offer contemporary appeal. 2 stories; interior/exterior corridors. **Dining:** Restaurant nearby. **All Rooms:** combo or shower baths. **Cards:** AE, CB, DI, DS, MC, VI. *(See ad p 306)*

—— RESTAURANT ——

ARTHUR AVE   **Lunch:** $7-$10   **Dinner:** $6-$16   **Phone:** 516/520-9447
◆   **Location:** 1.5 mi e of Meadowbrook Pkwy, exit M5. 2367 Hempstead Tpke 11554. **Hours:** 11:45 am-10 pm,
Italian   Fri & Sat-11 pm. Closed: 7/4 & 12/25. **Reservations:** suggested; 4 or more. **Features:** casual dress; children's menu; carryout; cocktails & lounge; a la carte. The restaurant is named for the "Little Italy" section of the Bronx, which is depicted by a mural. Relax in the comfortable, laid-back setting and enjoy home-style Italian fare, including pasta, traditional and gourmet pizzas, and even hero sandwiches. Smoke free premises. **Cards:** AE, CB, DI, DS, MC, VI.

EAST NORWICH pop. 2,700

—— LODGING ——

EAST NORWICH INN   **Phone:** (516)922-1500
AAA SAVE   5/1-10/31 & 4/1-4/30   1P: $115   2P: $130   XP: $10   F16
◆◆   11/1-3/31   1P: $95   2P: $115   XP: $10   F16
Motel   **Location:** SR 25A (N Hempstead Tpke) at jct SR 106 (Oyster Bay Rd), just nw. 6321 Northern Blvd 11732. Fax: 516/922-1089. **Terms:** [ECP] meal plan; weekly & monthly rates avail; 5 day cancellation notice. **Facility:** 72 rooms. Tudor-style building with rich decor in lobby. Rates for up to 4 persons; suites, $185-$260; 2 stories; interior corridors; sauna, small outdoor seasonal pool. **Dining:** Restaurant nearby. **All Rooms:** combo or shower baths, extended cable TV. **Some Rooms:** 2 kitchens. Fee: refrigerators, VCR. **Cards:** AE, CB, DI, DS, MC, VI.

EAST QUOGUE

—— LODGING ——

CAROLE'S BED & BREAKFAST   **Phone:** (631)653-5152
◆◆   5/16-10/15   2P: $135-$160   XP: $40   F8
Bed &   5/1-5/15 & 10/16-4/30   1P: $100-$125 2P: $100-$125   XP: $40   F8
Breakfast   **Location:** Center; just s of St Rosalie's Church. 7 Walnut Ave 11942 (PO Box 1646). **Terms:** [BP] meal plan; 7 day cancellation notice; 2 night min stay, weekends, in summer. **Facility:** 5 rooms. Beautifully restored Victorian home with wrap around porch. Individually appointed guest rooms feature a contemporary decor enhanced with some antiques. 2 stories; interior corridors; smoke free premises. **Services:** area transportation. **All Rooms:** combo or shower baths. **Cards:** AE, MC, VI.

EAST SYRACUSE pop. 3,300 (See map p. 478; index p. 477)—

———— LODGINGS ————

CANDLEWOOD SUITES
Phone: (315)432-1684 **16**
◆◆◆ All Year 1P: $110
Motel **Location:** I-90, exit 35. 6550 Court Street Rd 13057. Fax: 315/433-9959. **Facility:** 92 rooms. All rooms with CD player. 6 two-bedroom units. 3 stories; interior corridors. **All Rooms:** efficiencies, combo or shower baths.
Cards: AE, DI, DS, MC, VI.

COURTYARD BY MARRIOTT
Phone: (315)432-0300 **14**
◆◆◆ 5/1-11/15 & 3/1-4/30 1P: $80-$140
Motor Inn 11/16-2/28 1P: $70-$100
Location: I-90, exit 35 (Carrier Cir), just e to Old Collamer Rd, then 0.5 mi n. 6415 Yorktown Cir 13057. Fax: 315/432-9950. **Facility:** 149 rooms. Comfortably furnished guest rooms. 3 stories; interior corridors; heated pool.
All Rooms: combo or shower baths. **Cards:** AE, DI, DS, MC, VI. *(See color ad 479)*

EAST SYRACUSE SUPER 8
Phone: 315/432-5612 **18**

◆◆	7/1-11/1	1P: $45-$60	2P: $51-$66	XP: $6	F17
Motel	5/1-6/30	1P: $40-$55	2P: $46-$61	XP: $6	F17
	11/2-4/30	1P: $40-$50	2P: $46-$56	XP: $6	F17

Location: I-90, exit 35 (Carrier Cir), just e on SR 298, just n. 6620 Old Collamer Rd 13057. Fax: 315/432-5620. **Terms:** Pets. **Facility:** 53 rooms. 2 stories; interior corridors. **All Rooms:** combo or shower baths. **Some Rooms:** kitchen. Fee: refrigerators. **Cards:** AE, CB, DI, DS, MC, VI.

EMBASSY SUITES
Phone: (315)446-3200 **19**
(AAA) (SAVE) All Year 1P: $149 2P: $169
◆◆◆ **Location:** I-90, exit 35 (Carrier Cir), to Rt 298 E to College Pl. 6646 Old Collamer Rd 13057.
Suite Motor Fax: 315/437-3302. **Terms:** Check-in 4 pm; cancellation fee imposed. **Facility:** 215 rooms. Attractive atrium. 5
Inn two-bedroom units. 5 stories; interior corridors; heated pool, sauna, whirlpool. **Dining:** Dining room; 6:30-9:30 am, 11:30-2:30 & 5-11 pm, Fri & Sat 7-10:30 am, 11:30-2:30 & 5-11 pm. $10-$19; cocktails. **Services:** gift shop; complimentary evening beverages, area transportation, train station. **Some Rooms:** Fee: VCR. **Cards:** AE, CB, DI, DS, MC, VI. **Special Amenities:** Free breakfast. *(See ad p 479)*

HAMPTON INN-CARRIER CIRCLE
Phone: (315)463-6443 **22**

(AAA)	6/16-10/31	1P: $82-$90	2P: $87-$95
◆◆◆	5/12-6/15	1P: $68-$75	2P: $72-$80
	11/1-4/30	1P: $64-$74	2P: $69-$79
Motel	5/1-5/11	1P: $60-$70	2P: $65-$75

Location: I-90, exit 35 (Carrier Cir), just e on 298, just n. 6605 Old Collamer Rd 13057. Fax: 315/432-1080.
Terms: [CP] meal plan; 7 day cancellation notice; cancellation fee imposed. **Facility:** 116 rooms. 4 stories; interior corridors.
Dining: Restaurant nearby. **All Rooms:** extended cable TV. **Cards:** AE, CB, DI, DS, JC, MC, VI. *(See ad p 480)*

HOLIDAY INN EAST-CARRIER CIRCLE
Phone: (315)437-2761 **17**

(AAA) (SAVE)	7/1-10/31	1P: $94-$109	2P: $94-$109
	5/1-6/30	1P: $84-$99	2P: $84-$99
◆◆◆	2/1-4/30	1P: $79-$94	2P: $79-$94
Motor Inn	11/1-1/31	1P: $69-$84	2P: $69-$84

Location: I-90, exit 35 (Carrier Cir), to SR 298 E to College Pl. 6555 Old Collamer Rd 13057.
Fax: 315/463-0028. **Terms:** Small pets only. **Facility:** 203 rooms. Good sized guest rooms. 2-3 stories; interior/exterior corridors; heated pool, saunas, whirlpool. **Dining:** Restaurant; 6 am-2 & 5-10 pm, Sat & Sun from 7 am; $9-$17; cocktails. **Recreation:** Fee: in-room video games. **All Rooms:** extended cable TV. **Some Rooms:** Fee: refrigerators, microwaves.
Cards: AE, CB, DI, DS, JC, MC, VI. **Special Amenities:** Free local telephone calls and free newspaper.
(See color ad p 480)

MICROTEL INN SYRACUSE
Phone: 315/437-3500 **20**
◆◆ 5/1-10/31 1P: $44-$59 2P: $44-$59
Motel 11/1-4/30 1P: $39-$44 2P: $39-$44
Location: I-90, exit 35 (Carrier Cir) to SR 298 E. 6608 Old Collamer Rd 13057. Fax: 315/437-0111.
Terms: Pets. **Facility:** 100 rooms. Compact rooms. 2 stories; interior corridors. **Services:** winter plug-ins. **All Rooms:** combo or shower baths. **Cards:** AE, CB, DI, DS, MC, VI.

RESIDENCE INN BY MARRIOTT
Phone: (315)432-4488 **15**
◆◆◆ All Year 1P: $115 2P: $131
Apartment **Location:** I-90, exit 35; at Carrier Cir. 6420 Yorktown Cir 13057. Fax: 315/432-1042. **Terms:** [CP] meal plan; pets, $5 extra charge, $50-$100 fee. **Facility:** 102 rooms. Complimentary dinner every Wed. 24 two-bedroom units. 2 stories; exterior corridors; heated pool. **Recreation:** sports court. **All Rooms:** kitchens. **Cards:** AE, DI, DS, JC, MC, VI.

WYNDHAM SYRACUSE
Phone: (315)432-0200 **21**
◆◆◆ All Year 1P: $79-$129 XP: $20 F18
Hotel **Location:** I-90, exit 35, 0.5 mi e on SR 298. 6301 Rt 298 13057. Fax: 315/433-1210. **Terms:** Cancellation fee imposed; package plans. **Facility:** 250 rooms. 4-7 stories; interior corridors; heated pool. **Services:** gift shop.
Some Rooms: Fee: refrigerators, VCR. **Cards:** AE, CB, DI, DS, MC, VI. *(See color ad p 479)*

(See map p. 478)

------- **RESTAURANT** -------

CARMELLA'S CAFE   **Lunch:** $5-$11   **Dinner:** $6-$14   **Phone:** 315/445-8733   (13)
◆ ◆   **Location:** New York Thruway, exit 35, 2.4 mi s on Thompson Rd, 0.7 mi e on Erie Blvd, just n. 5840 Bridge
American   St 13124. **Hours:** 11 am-1 am, Sun-midnight. Closed: 11/23 & 12/25. **Features:** casual dress; children's
menu; early bird specials; carryout; cocktails & lounge. A festive mood prevails in the energized dining room,
which is decorated with eclectic antiques. Chicken riggies—which blends rigatoni noodles, charbroiled chicken, mushrooms,
peppers, olives and onions—has long been a favorite dinner selection. **Cards:** AE, DI, DS, MC, VI.   [X]

ELIZABETHTOWN pop. 1,300—*See also ADIRONDACK MOUNTAINS.*

------- **LODGING** -------

PARK MOTOR INN   **Phone:** (518)873-2233
(AAA) [SAVE]   6/17-9/5   1P: $59   2P: $59   XP: $5
◆ ◆   5/1-6/16 & 9/6-10/19   1P: $49   2P: $49   XP: $5
Motel   10/20-4/30   1P: $39   2P: $39   XP: $5
        Location: I-87, exit 31, 4 mi w on SR 9 N, 0.3 mi s of jct US 9 and SR 9 N; on US 9. Court St 12932 (PO Box
786). **Terms:** Cancellation fee imposed. **Facility:** 8 rooms. Well-maintained good sized rooms. 1 story; exterior
corridors. **Services:** winter plug-ins. **All Rooms:** extended cable TV. **Cards:** MC, VI. **Special Amenities: Free local telephone calls and preferred room (subject to availability with advanced reservations).**   [S/D] [X] [Z] [H]

ELLICOTTVILLE pop. 500

------- **LODGINGS** -------

ILEX INN   **Phone:** 716/699-2002
(AAA)   12/25-4/30   1P: $95-$185   2P: $95-$185
◆ ◆ ◆   5/1-12/24   1P: $55-$95   2P: $75-$125
Bed &   **Location:** 0.6 mi e on US 219 and SR 242. 6416 E Washington St 14731-1585 (PO Box 1585).
Breakfast   Fax: 716/699-5539. **Terms:** [BP] meal plan; age restrictions may apply; check-in 4 pm; 14 day cancellation no-
tice; cancellation fee imposed. **Facility:** 7 rooms. Pleasant and charming. All rooms have bathrobes and slip-
pers. Inviting public areas. 2 stories; interior corridors; smoke free premises; heated pool, whirlpool.
Services: winter plug-ins. **All Rooms:** combo or shower baths, extended cable TV. **Some Rooms:** 2 efficiencies, color TV.
Cards: AE, MC, VI.   [X] [♺] [VCR] [≡] [▣] [▦] [H] [≈]

THE INN AT HOLIDAY VALLEY RESORT   **Phone:** (716)699-2336
(AAA) [SAVE]   11/24-3/10   1P: $118-$169   2P: $118-$169   XP: $20   F17
◆ ◆ ◆   5/1-11/23   1P: $92-$115   2P: $92-$115   XP: $20   F17
Resort   3/11-4/30   1P: $84-$96   2P: $84-$96   XP: $20   F17
        Location: 0.8 mi s of jct SR 242 and US 219. Rt 219 & Holiday Valley Rd 14731 (PO Box 370).
Fax: 716/699-5861. **Terms:** [CP] meal plan; 14 day cancellation notice; cancellation fee imposed; package
plans. **Facility:** 102 rooms. Many rooms with mountain view. Many rooms with patio or balcony, all rooms with armoirs. 7 whirl-
pool rooms, $127-$250; 2 stories; interior/exterior corridors; 4 heated pools, sauna, whirlpool. Fee: 18 holes golf. **Dining:** Res-
taurant; 11:30 am-2:30 & 5-9 pm; hrs may vary off season; $7-$20; cocktails. **Services:** gift shop; winter plug-ins.
Fee: massage. **Recreation:** 52 ski trails & slopes for skiing with 12 lifts; hiking trails, extensive recreational facilities.
Fee: downhill & cross country skiing; bicycles. **All Rooms:** combo or shower baths, extended cable TV. **Some Rooms:**
Fee: VCR. **Cards:** AE, CB, DI, DS, MC, VI.
[¶] [Y] [♨] [≋] [f] [♿] [X] [VCR] [≡] [▣] [▦] [H] [DATA PORT] [≈] [≋] [♦] [X]

THE JEFFERSON INN   **Phone:** (716)699-5869
(AAA)   12/13-4/30   2P: $110-$145
◆ ◆   6/30-10/8   2P: $80-$100
Bed &   5/1-6/29 & 10/9-12/12   2P: $75-$90
Breakfast   **Location:** Just n of jct US 219 and SR 242; center. 3 Jefferson St 14731 (PO Box 1566). Fax: 716/699-5758.
        Terms: [BP] meal plan; age restrictions may apply; 30 day cancellation notice; pets, in 2 suites, dog on prem-
ises. **Facility:** 7 rooms. Charming Victorian home with a quiet location walking distance to downtown. Children
permitted in suites; 2 stories; interior corridors; designated smoking area. **Dining:** Restaurant nearby. **Services:** winter plug-
ins. **All Rooms:** extended cable TV. **Some Rooms:** color TV. **Cards:** AE, DI, DS, MC, VI.
[♦] [¶+] [♨] [X] [♺] [VCR] [≡] [▣] [▦] [H] [♦]

------- **RESTAURANTS** -------

DINA'S   **Lunch:** $5-$8   **Dinner:** $8-$21   **Phone:** 716/699-5330
◆ ◆   **Location:** Center; on US 219. 15 Washington St 14731. **Hours:** 7 am-10 pm. Closed: 11/23.
American   **Features:** casual dress; health conscious menu items; carryout; cocktails. In a restored 1840 building, the
        restaurant has the ambience of a cozy bistro. Stop by for breakfast, lunch and dinner selections, many of
which exhibit Italian and Mexican influences. Homemade pastries are among tempting dessert choices. Smoke free
premises. **Cards:** AE, MC, VI.   [X]

TIPS UP-CAFE   **Dinner:** $8-$19   **Phone:** 716/699-2136
◆ ◆   **Location:** Center; SR 242. 32 Washington St 14731. **Hours:** 4 pm-11 pm, Sun-10 pm. Closed: 4/23, 11/23,
Italian   12/24 & 12/25. **Reservations:** accepted. **Features:** carryout; cocktails & lounge; street parking. Popular with
        the locals, this often-busy restaurant is in a restored historical building that's loaded with friendly charm. The
limited menu of well-prepared dishes features Italian and American offerings. The wait staff provide prompt, pleasant service.
Cards: MC, VI.   [X]

ELMA —See Buffalo p. 225.

ELMIRA pop. 33,700

—— LODGING ——

HOLIDAY INN-ELMIRA RIVERVIEW DOWNTOWN

			Phone: (607)734-4211
◆◆◆	7/2-9/3	1P: $95-$129	
Motor Inn	9/4-4/30	1P: $86-$109	
	5/1-7/1	1P: $84-$109	

Location: SR 17, exit 56 (Water St), just s on Church St, 0.4 mi e on Judson, just s; SR 17, exit 57, 0.5 mi s. 760 E Water St 14901. Fax: 607/734-3549. **Terms:** Pets, in smoking rooms. **Facility:** 150 rooms. Long brick building overlooking riverfront and close to downtown area. 2 stories; interior/exterior corridors; 2 pools, 1 indoor heated. **Services:** winter plug-ins. **Some Rooms:** Fee: refrigerators, microwaves. **Cards:** AE, CB, DI, DS, MC, VI.

(ASK) 🛏️🗄️🍴 ☕ 🍽️ △ ✕ 📷 (VCR) 🖨️ 💻 📠 🛗 🏊 🏖️ 🛗

—— RESTAURANT ——

MORETTI'S RESTAURANT   Historical   **Dinner:** $8-$32   **Phone:** 607/734-1535

Italian   **Location:** 0.5 mi n, 0.3 mi e on E Washington Ave, just s. 800 Hatch St 14901. **Hours:** 5 pm-10:30 pm. Closed: 4/23, 11/23, 12/24 & 12/25. **Reservations:** suggested. **Features:** casual dress; children's menu; carryout; cocktails & lounge; a la carte. A regional favorite since 1917, the restaurant delivers many Italian staples, as well as traditional American preparations of veal, steak, chicken and chops. Dining rooms are decorated in a local nostalgic theme. Fish is a popular on Friday and Saturday. **Cards:** AE, DI, DS, MC, VI.   ✕

ELMIRA HEIGHTS pop. 4,400

—— RESTAURANT ——

PIERCE'S 1894 RESTAURANT   **Dinner:** $12-$26   **Phone:** 607/734-2022

AAA   **Location:** 2.5 mi n in Elmira Heights; at 14th St and Oakwood Ave; 2.5 mi s of jct SR 14, 17 and 328; just w of SR 14. 228 Oakwood Ave 14903. **Hours:** 4:30 pm-9:30 pm, Sun 4 pm-8:30 pm. Closed: 11/23, 12/24, ◆◆◆   12/25 & most Mon. **Reservations:** suggested. **Features:** dressy casual; children's menu; carryout; cocktails American   & lounge; a la carte. Gourmet dishes, as well as varied Continental entrees, pepper the innovative menu. Selections in the wine cellar are extensive. Distinctive, well-appointed dining rooms contribute to a sophisticated and relaxing experience. Orange mousse is delightful. **Cards:** AE, DS, MC, VI.   ✕

ELMSFORD —See New York p. 372.

ENDICOTT pop. 13,500

—— LODGING ——

TRAVELODGE AT KINGS INN   **Phone:** (607)754-8020

AAA SAVE	All Year	1P: $55-$67	2P: $65-$110	XP: $8 F13

Location: SR 17 W, exit 69, 1.7 mi w; SR 17 E, exit 67, 1.3 mi e. 2603 E Main St 13760. Fax: 607/754-6768. ◆◆◆   **Terms:** Weekly & monthly rates avail; 14 day cancellation notice. **Facility:** 60 rooms. Lobby in 100 year old Motel   house. 2 stories; exterior corridors; heated pool, sauna. **Dining:** Coffee shop; 7-9:30 am, Sat & Sun-11 am. **Services:** winter plug-ins. **All Rooms:** extended cable TV. **Cards:** AE, CB, DI, DS, MC, VI. **Special Amenities:** Early check-in/late check-out and free newspaper. *(See ad p 205)*

🛏️ 🍴 🎮 △ ✕ 📷 🖨️ 💻 📠 🛗 (DATA PORT) 🏖️ 🛗

―――― RESTAURANT ――――

RUSSELL'S STEAK & SEAFOOD HOUSE   **Dinner:** $13-$22   **Phone:** 607/754-233﹖
♦♦   **Location:** From jct SR 17C and SR 26, 1.2 mi w on 17C (Main St). 1001 W Main St 13760. **Hours:** 4 pm-1﹖
Steak and   pm, Sun noon-8 pm. Closed: 1/1, 11/23, 12/24 & 12/25. **Reservations:** suggested; on weekends
Seafood   **Features:** casual dress; children's menu; early bird specials; health conscious menu items; carryou﹖
   cocktails & lounge. Treat yourself to one of Russell's steaks, which are prepared to your liking. Seafoo﹖
lovers won't be disappointed with touches that bring out the flavors in shrimp, scallops and lobster. The friendly wait sta﹖
contributes to the pleasant atmosphere. **Cards:** AE, CB, DI, DS, MC, VI.   ☒

FAIRPORT pop. 5,900   (See map p. 456; index p. 455)

―――― LODGINGS ――――

THE LODGE AT WOODCLIFF   **Phone:** (716)381-4000   28
♦♦♦   All Year   1P: $99-$135   2P: $99-$135   XP: $4   F12
Motor Inn   **Location:** I-490, exit 27 (Bushnell's Basin), 3.2 mi s on Rt 96 to Woodcliff Dr, just e. 199 Woodcliff Dr 1445﹖
   (PO Box 22850, ROCHESTER, 14692). Fax: 716/381-2673. **Terms:** Package plans. **Facility:** 244 rooms. I﹖
suburban area overlooking Bristol Hills. Few bi level suites. 6 stories; interior corridors; heated pool. Fee: 9 holes golf; 2 tenni﹖
courts. **Dining:** entertainment. **Services:** area transportation. Fee: massage. **Recreation:** cross country skiing; joggin﹖
All Rooms: combo or shower baths, honor bars. **Some Rooms:** Fee: VCR. **Cards:** AE, CB, DI, DS, MC, VI.

(ASK) 🍽 🍸 🐾 (VALET) 🏔 🎣 📷 🚫 📹 (VCR) 📠 🖥 📷 🛎 (DATA PORT) 🏊 ▦ ☒

TRAIL BREAK MOTOR INN   **Phone:** (716)223-1710   29
AAA   5/1-10/31   1P: $35-$49   2P: $59-$69   XP: $5   F1﹖
♦   11/1-4/30   1P: $30-$40   2P: $45-$50
Motel   **Location:** 1.5 mi e of SR 250 on SR 31. 7340 Pittsford-Palmyra Rd 14450. **Terms:** Weekly rates avail; pet﹖
   $2 extra charge. **Facility:** 32 rooms. 1-2 stories; exterior corridors. **Dining:** Restaurant nearby. **All Rooms:** ex﹖
   tended cable TV. **Cards:** AE, DI, DS, MC, VI.   (ASK) 🐾 🏠 🍽 ☒ 📠 🛎

FALCONER pop. 2,700

―――― LODGING ――――

MOTEL 6 - 1215   **Phone:** 716/665-367﹖
AAA   6/15-8/31   1P: $48-$58   2P: $54-$64   XP: $3   F1
♦♦   9/1-4/30   1P: $42-$52   2P: $48-$58   XP: $3   F1
Motel   5/1-6/14   1P: $38-$48   2P: $44-$54   XP: $3   F1
   Location: SR 17, exit 13, just w on SR 394. 1980 E Main St 14733. Fax: 716/664-7651. **Terms:** Weekly rate﹖
   avail; small pets only. **Facility:** 80 rooms. Spacious rooms. 2 stories; interior corridors. **Recreation:** nature wal﹖
adjoining property. **All Rooms:** combo or shower baths. **Some Rooms:** kitchen. **Cards:** AE, CB, DI, DS, MC, VI.

🐾 🏠 🎣 ☒ 📹 🛎

―――― RESTAURANT ――――

HULTMAN'S RESTAURANT & LOUNGE   **Lunch:** $4-$7   **Dinner:** $9-$20   **Phone:** 716/665-683﹖
♦♦   **Location:** 1 mi w on SR 394 from jct SR 17, exit 13. 232 W Main St 14733. **Hours:** 5 pm-9 pm, Wed-F﹖
American   11:45 am-1:30 pm. Closed: 7/4, 11/23, 12/25 & Sun. **Reservations:** suggested. **Features:** casual dres﹖
   cocktails & lounge. Victorian tables and antiques decorate the casual restaurant, a family favorite fo﹖
comfortable dining. A variety of seafood, beef, chicken and pasta preparations lines the menu. Interesting cylindrical lights ﹖
varying sizes hang overhead. **Cards:** AE, DS, MC, VI.

FARMINGTON pop. 10,400—See also FINGER LAKES.

―――― LODGING ――――

BUDGET INN   **Phone:** (716)924-502﹖
AAA (SAVE)   All Year   1P: $36-$54   2P: $43-$70   F﹖
♦♦   **Location:** SR 96 at jct SR 332, 1 mi s of I-90, exit 44. 6001 Rt 96 14425. Fax: 716/924-5020. **Terms:** Weekl﹖
Motel   rates avail, winter only; small pets only, $5 extra charge. **Facility:** 20 rooms. 1 story; exterior corridor﹖
   Dining: Restaurant nearby. **All Rooms:** extended cable TV. **Cards:** AE, DS, MC, VI. **Special Amenities:** Earl﹖
   check-in/late check-out and free local telephone calls.   🐾 🏠 🍽 📹 🛎

FAYETTEVILLE pop. 4,200

―――― LODGING ――――

CRAFTSMAN INN   **Phone:** (315)637-800﹖
AAA (SAVE)   All Year   1P: $74-$79   2P: $84-$89   XP: $10   F1﹖
♦♦♦   **Location:** SR 5 (Genesse St); across from the Fayetteville Shopping Mall. 7300 E Genesee St (SR 5) 1306﹖
Motor Inn   Fax: 315/637-2440. **Terms:** [CP] meal plan; monthly rates avail; cancellation fee imposed; package plan﹖
   Facility: 70 rooms. Beautifully furnished guest rooms individually decorated with either traditional or arts an﹖
crafts. Stickley furniture. 3 whirlpool rooms, $99-$150; 2 stories; interior corridors; smoke free premise﹖
Dining: Restaurant; 11:30 am-2 & 5-10 pm, Sun-9 pm; $7-$18; cocktails. **Services:** winter plug-ins. **All Rooms:** combo ﹖
shower baths, extended cable TV. **Cards:** AE, CB, DI, MC, VI. **Special Amenities:** Free breakfast and free local telephon﹖
calls.

🐾 🍽 🍸 🐾 🏔 🎣 📷 ☒ 📹 (VCR) 📠 📷 🛎 (DATA PORT)

——— RESTAURANTS ———

ARAD EVANS INN Historical   **Dinner:** $17-$24   **Phone:** 315/637-2020
◆◆◆   **Location:** 1.5 mi e of Rt 481 S, 0.5 mi w of Lower Fayetteville. 7206 Genesee St 13066. **Hours:** 5 pm-11
Continental   pm, Sun 4:30 pm-9 pm. Closed major holidays. **Reservations:** suggested. **Features:** dressy casual;
                cocktails & lounge. The renovated, 1840s, Federal-style country house is decorated with period furniture and
attractive, Oriental rugs. Upscale fusion cuisine blends French, Italian and nouveau influences. The signature New Zealand
rack of lamb is memorable. **Cards:** AE, DI, DS, MC, VI.   ✕

KYOKO JAPANESE RESTAURANT   **Dinner:** $7-$22   **Phone:** 315/637-1110
◆◆   **Location:** SR 5, 2.5 mi e of jct 481. 111 Brooklea Pl 13066. **Hours:** 5 pm-9 pm, Fri & Sat-10 pm, Sun 4
Japanese   pm-9 pm. **Reservations:** suggested. **Features:** casual dress; carryout; beer & wine only; a la carte. Fresh,
                high-quality ingredients go into made-to-order selections of traditional Asian food, which is presented in an
American style, with garnishes of parsley and lemon. Table, bar and tatami seating is available. Servers are knowledgeable
and friendly. **Cards:** AE, DI, JC, MC, VI.   ✕

FILLMORE pop. 400

——— LODGING ———

JUST A "PLANE" BED & BREAKFAST   **Phone:** 716/567-8338
◆◆   5/1-11/30 & 3/1-4/30   1P: $50   2P: $62   XP: $15
Bed &   **Location:** Jct Rt 19 and 19A, just n. 11152 Rt 19A 14735. **Terms:** Open 5/1-11/30 & 3/1-4/30; [BP] meal plan;
Breakfast   age restrictions may apply; check-in 4 pm; 14 day cancellation notice; package plans. **Facility:** 4 rooms. Quiet
                rural location with airplane rides available from adjoining grass airstrip; nicely decorated rooms with country
flair. 7 mi to Letchworth State Park. 3 stories, no elevator; interior corridors; designated smoking area. **Recreation:** hiking trails.
All Rooms: combo or shower baths. **Cards:** AE, MC, VI.   🐾 ✕ 🅿 🖨 ✕

FINGER LAKES (See map below)—See AUBURN, AVOCA, AVON, BATH, BLOOMFIELD, BRISTOL CENTER, CANANDAIGUA, CORNING, DANSVILLE, FARMINGTON, GENESEO, GENEVA, GLENORA, GROTON, HAMMONDSPORT, HONEOYE FALLS, HORNELL, HORSEHEADS, ITHACA, MANCHESTER, MONTOUR FALLS, NAPLES, PAINTED POST, SKANEATELES, TRUMANSBURG, VICTOR, WATERLOO, WATKINS GLEN & WEEDSPORT.

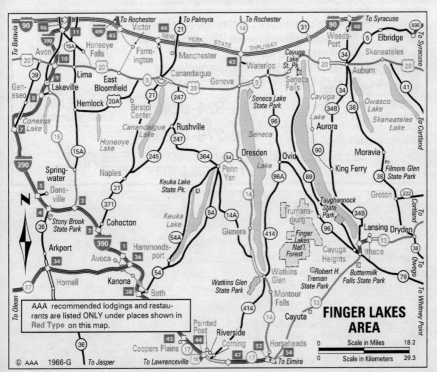

© AAA   1966-G

FISHKILL pop. 2,000

——— LODGINGS ———

COURTYARD BY MARRIOTT
♦♦♦
Motor Inn

Property failed to provide current rates

Phone: 914/897-2400

Location: Just n of I-84, exit 13. 90 Westage Business Center Dr 12524. Fax: 914/897-2274. **Facility:** 152 rooms. Comfortable guest rooms. Small courtyard area with gazebo. 4 stories; interior corridors; designated smoking area; heated pool. **Services:** winter plug-ins. **Some Rooms:** Fee: VCR. **Cards:** AE, CB, DI, DS, MC, VI.

HAMPTON INN FISHKILL
♦♦♦
Motel

Phone: (914)896-4000

4/1-4/30	1P: $95-$115	2P: $95-$115
6/1-11/1	1P: $95-$115	2P: $95-$115
5/1-5/31	1P: $95-$105	2P: $95-$105
11/2-3/31	1P: $79-$105	2P: $79-$105

Location: On US 9, just n of jct I-84, exit 13; behind Holiday Inn. 2515 Rt 9 12524. Fax: 914/896-2799. **Terms:** [CP] meal plan. **Facility:** 99 rooms. New motel. Attractive public area and guest rooms. All rooms with 2 phone lines. 4 stories; interior corridors; designated smoking area; heated pool. **All Rooms:** combo or shower baths. **Cards:** AE, CB, DI, DS, JC, MC, VI.

HOLIDAY INN FISHKILL
♦♦
Motor Inn

Phone: (914)896-6281

5/1-10/31	1P: $109	2P: $109	XP: $10	F19
11/1-4/30	1P: $89	2P: $89	XP: $10	F19

Location: On US 9; just n of jct I-84, exit 13. 542 Rt 9 12524. Fax: 914/896-5410. **Facility:** 156 rooms. Large courtyard area with gazebo. Good sized guest rooms. 2-3 stories; interior/exterior corridors; designated smoking area. **All Rooms:** Fee: safes. **Some Rooms:** Fee: refrigerators, VCR. **Cards:** AE, CB, DI, DS, JC, MC, VI.

MAINSTAY SUITES FISHKILL
(AAA) (SAVE)
♦♦♦
Motel

Phone: (914)897-2800

1/1-4/30	1P: $125-$135	2P: $125-$135
5/1-10/31	1P: $96-$106	2P: $96-$106
11/1-12/31	1P: $90-$100	2P: $90-$100

Location: I-84, exit 13, just n. 25 Merritt Blvd 12524. Fax: 914/897-2616. **Terms:** [CP] meal plan, Mon-Fri; pets, $10 extra charge, after 7 days $100 dep req. **Facility:** 106 rooms. New property. Fully equipped rooms. All rooms with 2 phone lines. Office hrs 8 am-6 pm weekdays; 10 am-4 pm weekends. During non-office hrs check-in requires use of credit card and automated self-serve system. 3 stories; interior corridors; designated smoking area. **Dining:** Restaurant nearby. **Recreation:** sports court. **All Rooms:** kitchens, combo or shower baths. **Cards:** AE, CB, DI, DS, JC, MC, VI. **Special Amenities:** Early check-in/late check-out. *(See color ad below)*

RESIDENCE INN BY MARRIOTT
♦♦♦
Apartment

Phone: (914)896-5210

1/1-4/30	1P: $139-$159	2P: $139-$159	XP: $10	F19
5/1-12/31	1P: $109-$129	2P: $109-$129	XP: $10	F19

Location: On US 9, just n of jct I-84, exit 13. 2481 Rt 9 12524. Fax: 914/896-9689. **Terms:** [CP] meal plan; cancellation fee imposed; package plans; pets, $350 extra charge. **Facility:** 136 rooms. Numerous buildings built in clusters. Studio and 2-level loft units; some with fireplace. 34 two-bedroom units. 2 stories; exterior corridors; designated smoking area; playground. **Recreation:** sports court. **All Rooms:** kitchens. **Cards:** AE, CB, DI, DS, JC, MC, VI.

WELLESLEY INN & SUITES
(AAA) (SAVE)
♦♦
Motel

Phone: (914)896-4995

All Year	1P: $75-$150	2P: $75-$150	XP: $5	F18

Location: Just n of I-84, exit 13. 2477 Rt 9 12524. Fax: 914/896-6631. **Terms:** [CP] meal plan; weekly rates avail; pets. **Facility:** 82 rooms. Modern decor. 4 stories; interior corridors; designated smoking area. **Services:** winter plug-ins. **All Rooms:** combo or shower baths, extended cable TV. **Cards:** AE, CB, DI, DS, MC, VI. **Special Amenities:** Free breakfast and free newspaper. *(See color ad p 4)*

——— RESTAURANT ———

HUDSON'S RIBS & FISH
◆ ◆
Steak and
Seafood

Dinner: $14-$23

Phone: 914/297-5002

Location: 3 mi n. 2014 Rt 9 12524. **Hours:** 4 pm-10 pm, Fri & Sat-11 pm, Sun-9 pm. Closed: 1/1, 11/23 & 12/25. **Reservations:** suggested. **Features:** casual dress; children's menu; carryout; cocktails & lounge. Baby back ribs, prime rib and fresh fish are the focus of the menu. Lacquered tables with maps of New York riverways contribute to the nautical decor. Delicious popovers are served with strawberry honey butter. Service is pleasant and prompt. **Cards:** AE, DI, DS, MC, VI.

FLORAL PARK pop. 15,900 (See map p. 330; index p. 325)

——— LODGING ———

FLORAL PARK MOTOR LODGE
(AAA) [SAVE]
◆ ◆
Motel

Phone: (516)775-7777 [153]

1/1-4/30	1P: $150-$160	2P: $160-$210	XP: $15 F18
5/1-12/31	1P: $140-$150	2P: $150-$184	XP: $15 F18

Location: SR 25 (Jericho Tpke), 0.8 mi e of Cross Island Pkwy (Belt Pkwy), exit 27 E. 30 Jericho Tpke 11001. **Fax:** 516/775-0451. **Terms:** [ECP] meal plan. **Facility:** 107 rooms. 3 stories; interior corridors. **Dining:** Restaurant nearby. **Services:** winter plug-ins. **All Rooms:** combo or shower baths, extended cable TV. **Some Rooms:** Fee: VCR. **Cards:** AE, CB, DI, DS, MC, VI. **Special Amenities:** Free breakfast and free newspaper. *(See color ad p 364)*

——— RESTAURANTS ———

ARTURO'S
◆ ◆
Northern
Italian

Lunch: $13-$28   **Dinner:** $14-$30   **Phone:** 516/352-7418 [209]

Location: Belt Pkwy to Cross Island exit 27, 0.3 mi e on SR 25 (Jericho Tpke). 246-04 Jericho Tpke 11001. **Hours:** noon-3 & 5:30-10 pm, Fri-11 pm, Sat 5 pm-11 pm, Sun 3 pm-9:30 pm. Closed: 11/23, 12/25 & Sun. **Reservations:** suggested. **Features:** casual dress; cocktails & lounge; entertainment; a la carte. Enjoy dinner in the "old school" style. Attentive servers in semiformal attire deliver Northern Italian cuisine, such as chicken penne pasta with olive oil, herbs and garlic. Among delicious desserts are tiramisu, cream puffs and the classic Napoleon. Smoke free premises. **Cards:** AE, DI, DS, MC, VI.

POPPY'S PLACE
◆
Italian

Lunch: $7-$11   **Dinner:** $7-$11   **Phone:** 516/358-2705 [210]

Location: Tulip Ave and the Railroad Station, just e. 12 Verbena Ave 11001. **Hours:** 11 am-3 & 5-10 pm, Fri & Sat-11 pm, Sun 4 pm-10 pm. Closed major holidays & Mon. **Features:** casual dress; health conscious menu items; carryout; cocktails & lounge; street parking; a la carte. The unpretentious restaurant is a local favorite for made-from-scratch American and Italian food. Reasonably priced dishes—such as poached calamari with pasta—are served in generous portions. The dining room can be noisy when it's busy, which is often. **Cards:** AE, DI, DS, MC, VI.

FRANKFORT pop. 2,700

——— RESTAURANT ———

KITLAS RESTAURANT
◆
American

Lunch: $3-$6   **Dinner:** $8-$14   **Phone:** 315/732-9616

Location: SR 5 S, Turner Rd exit, n to Broad St. 2242 Broad St 13340. **Hours:** 11:30 am-2 & 4:30-8:30 pm, Sat 4:30 pm-8:30 pm. Closed major holidays, Sun & for dinner on Mon. **Features:** casual dress; children's menu; carryout; cocktails & lounge. Owned by the same family since 1939, the restaurant delivers classic fare, including the slow-roasted pork loin over herbed mashed potatoes and lemon-horseradish-crusted haddock. The atmosphere is casual and comfy, making the place popular with families. **Cards:** AE, DS, MC, VI.

FREDONIA pop. 10,400

——— LODGING ———

THE WHITE INN
(AAA)
◆ ◆ ◆
Historic
Country Inn

Phone: (716)672-2103

All Year	1P: $79-$179	2P: $79-$179	XP: $10 F12

Location: Center; on US 20, 1.3 mi sw of jct SR 60. 52 E Main St 14063. **Fax:** 716/672-2107. **Terms:** [BP] meal plan; weekly & monthly rates avail; package plans. **Facility:** 24 rooms. Restored residence with large covered veranda and 170-year old, giant maples. Handsomely appointed rooms, some antique, others more contemporary. Few smaller rooms. 2 whirlpool rooms, $139-$179; 3 stories; interior corridors. **Dining:** Dining room, see separate listing. **Services:** gift shop. **All Rooms:** combo or shower baths, extended cable TV. **Some Rooms:** efficiency. **Cards:** AE, DI, DS, MC, VI.

——— RESTAURANT ———

THE WHITE INN DINING ROOM Historical
◆ ◆ ◆
American

Lunch: $5-$10   **Dinner:** $12-$21   **Phone:** 716/672-2103

Location: Center; on US 20, 1.3 mi sw of jct SR 60; in The White Inn. 52 E Main St 14063. **Hours:** 7-10 am, 11:30-2 & 5-8:30 pm, Fri & Sat-9 pm, Sun 8 am-11 & 12:30-8 pm. **Reservations:** suggested. **Features:** dressy casual; cocktails & lounge. The restored historic inn is known for both traditional and imaginative selections that show regional influences and much thought to presentation. The cozy veranda welcomes diners to unwind. Neatly attired servers are prompt and friendly. **Cards:** AE, DI, DS, MC, VI.

FREEPORT pop. 39,900

LODGING

FREEPORT MOTOR INN & BOATEL
Phone: (516)623-9100

(AAA) (SAVE)
All Year
1P: $82-$92
2P: $92-$102
XP: $6
D12
◆ ◆
Motel
Location: 1 mi s from SR 27 (Sunrise Hwy), s on Henry St to S Main. 445 S Main St 11520.
Fax: 516/546-5739. **Terms:** [CP] meal plan; weekly & monthly rates avail. **Facility:** 60 rooms. Quiet neighborhood location overlooking the marina. 2 stories; exterior corridors. Fee: marina. **Dining:** Restaurant nearby.
All Rooms: combo or shower baths, extended cable TV. **Some Rooms:** Fee: refrigerators, microwaves, VCR.
Cards: AE, CB, DI, DS, MC, VI. **Special Amenities:** Early check-in/late check-out and free breakfast. *(See ad below)*

FULTON pop. 12,900

RESTAURANT

LOCK III
Lunch: $4-$6
Dinner: $11-$15
Phone: 315/598-6900
◆ ◆
Continental
Location: Center. 24 S 1st St 13069. **Hours:** 11:30 am-2:30 & 4:30-10:30 pm. Closed: 1/1, 7/4 & 12/25.
Reservations: suggested. **Features:** casual dress; children's menu; early bird specials; carryout; salad bar; cocktails & lounge; a la carte. On the Oswego River overlooking the barge canal, the casual restaurant welcomes a clientele of mostly families. Specialties of steak and fresh seafood mingle with soups, sandwiches and burgers on the lengthy menu. Decor is cohesive and attractive. **Cards:** AE, DI, MC, VI.

GATES pop. 28,600 (See map p. 456; index p. 455)

LODGINGS

COMFORT INN CENTRAL
Phone: (716)436-4400
[14]

(AAA) (SAVE)
5/1-10/31
1P: $64-$74
2P: $69-$79
XP: $8
F18
11/1-4/30
1P: $59-$69
2P: $64-$74
XP: $8
F18
◆ ◆
Motel
Location: SR 204, 0.3 mi w of jct I-390, exit 18B; opposite entrance to Rochester-Monroe County Airport. 395 Buell Rd 14624. Fax: 716/436-6496. **Terms:** [CP] meal plan; weekly & monthly rates avail; 7 day cancellation notice; cancellation fee imposed; pets. **Facility:** 73 rooms. 2 stories; interior corridors. **Dining:** Restaurant nearby. **All Rooms:** extended cable TV. **Some Rooms:** Fee: refrigerators, microwaves. **Cards:** AE, DI, DS, MC, VI.
(See ad below)

(See map p. 456)

FAIRFIELD INN BY MARRIOTT-AIRPORT
◆◆◆
Motel

1/1-4/30	1P: $80-$90		
5/1-6/17	1P: $79-$89		
6/18-12/31	1P: $69-$89		

Phone: (716)529-5000 🔢15

Location: I-390, exit 18B; on grounds of Greater Rochester International Airport. 1200 Brooks Ave 14624. Fax: 716/529-5011. **Terms:** [CP] meal plan. **Facility:** 63 rooms. 3 stories; interior corridors; heated pool. **All Rooms:** combo or shower baths. **Cards:** AE, DI, DS, MC.

HOLIDAY INN-AIRPORT
◆◆◆
Motor Inn

All Year   1P: $115   2P: $115   XP: $10   F12

Phone: (716)328-6000 🔢13

Location: SR 204 at jct I-390, exit 18A. 911 Brooks Ave 14624. Fax: 716/328-1012. **Terms:** Package plans; pets. **Facility:** 280 rooms. 2 stories; interior corridors; heated pool. **Cards:** AE, CB, DI, DS, JC, MC, VI.

(See color ad p 457)

GENESEO pop. 7,200—*See FINGER LAKES.*

GENEVA pop. 14,100—*See also FINGER LAKES.*

—— **LODGINGS** ——

BELHURST CASTLE
🔺
◆◆◆
Historic
Country Inn

5/1-10/31	2P: $105-$315	XP: $30	
11/1-4/30	2P: $70-$265	XP: $30	

Phone: 315/781-0201

Location: 2 mi s on SR 14. Rt 14 S 14456 (PO Box 609). Fax: 315/781-0201. **Terms:** [CP] meal plan; 7 day cancellation notice. **Facility:** 13 rooms. 1885 castle on shore of Seneca Lake. On National Register of Historic Places. Whirlpool room, $295-$315; 3 stories, no elevator; interior corridors; boat dock. **Dining:** Dining room; 11 am-2 & 5-9:30 pm, Sun 11 am-2 & 4-9 pm; $20-$28; cocktails. **Recreation:** fishing. **All Rooms:** combo or shower baths, extended cable TV. **Some Rooms:** honor bars. **Cards:** MC, VI. *(See color ad p 256)*

CHANTICLEER MOTOR INN
🔺
◆◆
Motel

5/1-10/31	1P: $42-$50	2P: $47-$55	XP: $10	F16
11/1-4/30	1P: $32-$40	2P: $37-$45	XP: $6	F16

Phone: (315)789-7600

Location: 1.8 mi w on US 20 and SR 5. 473 Hamilton St 14456. **Terms:** Weekly & monthly rates avail. **Facility:** 79 rooms. Good to very good rooms. 2 stories; interior/exterior corridors. **Some Rooms:** 3 kitchens. Fee: refrigerators, microwaves. **Cards:** AE, CB, DI, DS, MC, VI.

CLARK'S MOTEL
◆◆
Motel

5/17-10/31	1P: $38-$42	2P: $38-$42	XP: $3
11/4-4/30	1P: $28-$32	2P: $28-$32	XP: $3
5/1-5/16	1P: $32	2P: $32	XP: $3

Phone: 315/789-0780

Location: 2 mi w on US 20 and SR 5. 824 Canandaigua Rd 14456. **Facility:** 10 rooms. Large rooms; attractively landscaped grounds. 1 story; exterior corridors. **Some Rooms:** Fee: refrigerators. **Cards:** MC, VI.

GENEVA-ON-THE-LAKE
🔺
◆◆◆
Historic
Country Inn

6/1-10/31	1P: $187-$588	2P: $197-$598	XP: $30	F12
5/1-5/31 & 4/1-4/30	1P: $163-$516	2P: $173-$526	XP: $30	F12
11/1-3/31	1P: $134-$427	2P: $144-$437	XP: $30	F12

Phone: (315)789-7190

Location: 1.5 mi s on SR 14. 1001 Lochland Rd 14456. Fax: 315/789-0322. **Terms:** [CP] & [MAP] meal plans; weekly & monthly rates avail; 15 day cancellation notice; package plans. **Facility:** 30 rooms. Italian Renaissance villa on a bluff overlooking Seneca Lake. Some suites with fireplace, balcony or terrace. 10 two-bedroom units. 3 stories, no elevator; interior corridors; boat dock. **Dining:** Dining room; 9 am-10 & 6-9 pm 11/1-4/30; 8 am-10 & 6-9 pm 5/1-10/31; noon-2 pm in season; $29-$42; cocktails. **Services:** gift shop. Fee: massage. **Recreation:** fishing; bicycles, lawn games. Fee: sailboating, windsurfing, pontoon boat. Rental: canoes, paddleboats. **All Rooms:** kitchens, combo or shower baths, extended cable TV. **Some Rooms:** Fee: VCR. **Cards:** AE, DS, MC, VI. *(See color ad p 256)*

MOTEL 6 - 1216
🔺
◆◆
Motel

6/22-10/22	1P: $50-$60	2P: $56-$66	XP: $3	F17
5/1-6/21	1P: $43-$53	2P: $49-$59	XP: $3	F17
10/23-4/30	1P: $40-$50	2P: $46-$56	XP: $3	F17

Phone: 315/789-4050

Location: 1.5 mi w on US 20 and SR 5. 485 Hamilton St 14456. Fax: 315/781-2338. **Terms:** Small pets only. **Facility:** 61 rooms. 2 stories; interior corridors. **Dining:** Restaurant nearby. **All Rooms:** combo or shower baths, extended cable TV. **Cards:** AE, CB, DI, DS, MC, VI.

RAMADA INN GENEVA LAKEFRONT
◆◆◆
Motor Inn

5/12-10/31	1P: $99-$139	2P: $109-$149	XP: $10	F16
5/1-5/11 & 3/31-4/30	1P: $89-$129	2P: $99-$139	XP: $10	F16
11/1-3/30	1P: $69-$109	2P: $79-$119	XP: $10	F16

Phone: (315)789-0400

Location: I-90, exit 42, 8 mi s on SR 14. 41 Lakefront Dr 14456. Fax: 315/789-4351. **Terms:** Package plans; pets, $10 extra charge. **Facility:** 148 rooms. 6 stories; interior corridors; small heated indoor pool. **All Rooms:** combo or shower baths. **Some Rooms:** Fee: refrigerators, microwaves. **Cards:** AE, CB, DI, DS, MC, VI.

—— RESTAURANTS ——

PASTA ONLY'S COBBLESTONE   **Lunch:** $6-$8   **Dinner:** $9-$17   **Phone:** 315/789-8498
Ⓐ
◆◆
Italian
    Location: 1.5 mi w on US 20 and SR 5. 3610 Pre-Emption Rd at 5 & 20 14456. **Hours:** 11:30 am-2 & 5-9:30 pm, Sat-Mon from 5 pm; closing hours may vary. Closed: 12/24 & 12/25. **Reservations:** suggested. **Features:** casual dress; children's menu; carryout; cocktails. Although the restored 1825 farmhouse delivers a menu of Italian cuisine, wood-grilled steaks, chops and fresh seafood, this place is known for its exquisite desserts. The pastry chef whips up outstanding creations, including the sunken chocolate souffle. **Cards:** AE, CB, DI, DS, MC, VI.

WING TAI ORIENTAL RESTAURANT   **Lunch:** $4-$5   **Dinner:** $6-$9   **Phone:** 315/789-8892
◆
Chinese
    Location: Just off SR 14. 164 Castle St 14456. **Hours:** 11 am-9:30 pm, Fri & Sat-10:30 pm. Closed: 11/23. **Reservations:** suggested; weekends. **Features:** carryout; cocktails; a la carte. In business since the late 1970s, the restaurant is decorated in an Oriental style, with Chinese lanterns and painted wallpaper. Seven star around the moon—a seafood, beef and chicken dish for two—is popular, as is the irresistible flaming cherry desser. **Cards:** AE, DI, DS, MC, VI. ⊠

GHENT pop. 4,800

—— RESTAURANT ——

RED BARN LUNCHEONETTE   **Lunch:** $3-$7   **Dinner:** $3-$7   **Phone:** 518/828-5821
Ⓐ
◆
American
    Location: 2.5 mi n of jct Rt 66 and 9-H. Old Post Rd/Rt 9-H 12075. **Hours:** Open 5/1-11/1 & 4/1-4/30; noon-9 pm; 11:30 am-10 pm in summer. Closed: Wed. **Features:** casual dress; carryout; a la carte. An old-fashioned atmosphere lends to the quaint, homespun charm of the converted barn. Relax in the smoke-free dining room, and enjoy selections from a menu of lighter fare. When it's time for dessert, opt for the delicious, homemade ice cream. Smoke free premises. ⊠

GLEN COVE pop. 24,100

—— RESTAURANT ——

LA PACE   **Lunch:** $12-$18   **Dinner:** $12-$25   **Phone:** 516/671-2970
Ⓐ
◆◆◆
Northern
Italian
    Location: Jct Glen Cove Rd, 0.5 mi e. 51 Cedar Swamp Rd 11542. **Hours:** noon-2:30 & 6-10 pm, Fri-11 pm, Sat 6 pm-11 pm, Sun 4 pm-10 pm. Closed: 4/23 & 12/25. **Reservations:** suggested. **Features:** semi-formal attire; cocktails & lounge; a la carte. A Gold Coast tradition since the late 1970s, the restaurant exudes a sophisticated European ambience that is reflective of an earlier time. The specialty veal chop with wild mushrooms is well-prepared and flavorful. Service is reserved and professional. **Cards:** AE, DI, MC, VI. ⊠

GLENMONT pop. 1,300   (See map p. 193; index p. 192)

—— LODGING ——

DAYS INN ALBANY   **Phone:** (518)465-8811   **37**
◆◆
Motor Inn
  Property failed to provide current rates
    Location: SR 9 W, 0.5 mi s of I-87, exit 23. 37 Rt 9 W 12077 (Box 175). Fax: 518/465-5732. **Facility:** 100 rooms. Good sized rooms. Some background noise from hwy, some with at-door parking. 2 stories; interior corridors. **Cards:** AE, CB, DI, DS, JC, MC, VI. 🍴 🍸 ⊠ 🛁 ⊠ 🐕 🖨 DATA PORT 🛗

—— RESTAURANT ——

ALTERI'S RESTAURANT   **Lunch:** $4-$8   **Dinner:** $9-$16   **Phone:** 518/436-0002   **26**
Ⓐ
◆◆
Italian
    Location: From jct of I-787 (end), 2 mi s on Rt 9 W. 312 Rt 9 W 12077. **Hours:** 11:30 am-9:30 pm, Fri-10 pm, Sat 3 pm-10 pm. Closed: 11/23 & 12/25. **Reservations:** suggested; weekends. **Features:** casual dress; children's menu; carryout; cocktails & lounge. Tiffany-style lamps provide subtle lighting in the casual dining room, which is decorated with turn-of-the-20th-century photographs of the city. The menu centers on American and Italian dishes, with plenty of sandwiches, soups and salads. **Cards:** AE, CB, DI, DS, MC, VI. ⊠

GLENORA pop. 100—See also FINGER LAKES.

—— LODGING ——

SOUTH GLENORA TREE FARM BED & BREAKFAST   **Phone:** 607/243-7414
◆◆◆
Bed &
Breakfast
    All Year   **1P:** $99   **2P:** $129   **XP:** $20
    Location: SR 14, 1 mi w via S Glenora Rd following signs. 546 S Glenora Rd 14837 (546 S Glenora Rd, DUNDEE). **Terms:** [BP] meal plan; 14 day cancellation notice; cancellation fee imposed; 2 night min stay, weekends 5/1-11/30. **Facility:** 5 rooms. Remodeled barn building with cozy country-themed rooms in tranquil setting. 1 story; interior/exterior corridors; designated smoking area. **Recreation:** fishing; hiking trails. **All Rooms:** combo or shower baths. **Some Rooms:** color TV. **Cards:** DS, MC, VI. ⊠ VCR 🖨 ⊠

GLENS FALLS pop. 15,000—
See also ADIRONDACK MOUNTAINS & SOUTH GLENS FALLS.

—— LODGING ——

QUEENSBURY HOTEL   Phone: (518)792-1121

7/26-9/3	1P: $149	2P: $149	XP: $10	F18
5/1-7/25 & 9/4-10/31	1P: $99	2P: $99	XP: $10	F18
11/1-4/30	1P: $74	2P: $74	XP: $10	F18

Hotel **Location:** Center. 88 Ridge St 12801. Fax: 518/792-9259. **Terms:** Cancellation fee imposed; 2 night min stay, some weekends; package plans. **Facility:** 123 rooms. Gracious old redbrick hotel overlooking park. Elegant, traditional decor. 5 stories; interior corridors; heated pool, whirlpool. **Dining:** Cocktails; also, The Crock & Boulle, see separate listing. **Services:** winter plug-ins. Fee: massage. **Recreation:** small exercise room. **All Rooms:** combo or shower baths, extended cable TV. **Some Rooms:** Fee: refrigerators. **Cards:** AE, CB, DI, DS, MC, VI. **Special Amenities:** Free newspaper and free room upgrade (subject to availability with advanced reservations).

—— RESTAURANTS ——

THE CROCK & BOULLE   **Lunch:** $6-$10   **Dinner:** $6-$20   **Phone:** 518/792-1121
American **Location:** Center; in Queensbury Hotel. 88 Ridge St 12801. **Hours:** 6:30 am-9:30 pm. **Reservations:** suggested. **Features:** casual dress; children's menu; health conscious menu; carryout; cocktails & lounge; a la carte. Casual, smoke-free dining room has a garden decor, with floral prints and furniture in the wrought-iron look. Unusual ingredients, such as chickpeas and green olives, add interest to the not-so-standard salad. Dishes are well-presented and flavorful. Smoke free premises. **Cards:** AE, CB, DI, DS, MC, VI.

DAVIDSON BROTHERS RESTAURANT & BREWERY   **Lunch:** $4-$7   **Dinner:** $9-$15   **Phone:** 518/743-9026
American **Location:** Center. 184 Glen St 12801. **Hours:** 11:30 am-10 pm, Fri-11 pm, Sat noon-11 pm, Sun noon-10 pm, lounge-1 am. **Features:** No A/C; casual dress; children's menu; carryout; cocktails & lounge; street parking. Baby back ribs and steamers are among traditional pub foods that are well-complemented by a selection of 12 hand-crafted ales, which are brewed on the premises. The two-story building is decorated with machinery from the city's industrial past. **Cards:** AE, MC, VI.

FIDDLEHEADS   **Lunch:** $6-$12   **Dinner:** $15-$23   **Phone:** 518/793-5789
Continental **Location:** I-87 Northway, exit 18, follow signs toward hospital 2 mi, just beyond to 2nd traffic light, bear left on 9L. 21 Ridge St 12801. **Hours:** 11:30 am-3 & 5-9 pm. Closed major holidays, Sun & Mon. **Reservations:** suggested. **Features:** casual dress; cocktails; street parking. A country ambience is pervasive in the charming restaurant. Maryland crab cakes stand out on a menu of beef, lamb, fowl and seafood preparations, all thoughtfully arranged by the owner-chef. In addition to being delicious, desserts have great eye appeal. Smoke free premises. **Cards:** AE.

GRAND ISLAND —*See Buffalo p. 225.*

GREAT NECK pop. 8,700

—— LODGING ——

INN AT GREAT NECK   Phone: (516)773-2000
All Year   1P: $195-$225   2P: $215-$240   XP: $20   F18
Hotel **Location:** From jct Middleneck Rd, just w. 30 Cutter Mill Rd 10021. Fax: 516/773-2020. **Terms:** Package plans; small pets only, $200 dep req. **Facility:** 85 rooms. Boutique hotel styled to recreate the hotels of the 1920s. Located in the center of small town convenient to shopping and restaurants. All rooms with CD player. 5 stories; interior corridors. **All Rooms:** combo or shower baths, safes, honor bars. **Cards:** AE, DI, DS, MC, VI.

—— RESTAURANT ——

PETER LUGER   **Lunch:** $8-$30   **Dinner:** $13-$59   **Phone:** 516/487-8800
Steakhouse **Location:** I-495, exit 33, 0.8 mi n on Lakeville Rd, then 0.6 mi w. 255 Northern Blvd 11021. **Hours:** 11:30 am-10:15 pm, Fri-11 pm, Sat-11:30 pm, Sun 12:30 pm-10:15 pm. **Reservations:** suggested. **Features:** casual dress; cocktails & lounge; valet parking; a la carte. Succulent prime porterhouse steaks, which are dry-aged on premise, are this sophisticated restaurant's specialty—and they are exceptional. Many by-the-glass selections line the excellent wine list. The dining room exudes an elegant, Old World charm.

GREECE pop. 15,600   (See map p. 456; index p. 455)

—— LODGINGS ——

COMFORT INN-WEST   Phone: (716)621-5700   **21**

5/1-10/31	1P: $74-$79	2P: $84-$89	XP: $8	F18
11/1-4/30	1P: $69-$79	2P: $74-$84	XP: $8	F18

Motel **Location:** SR 104, 0.5 mi e of jct SR 390 and 104 (Ridge Rd). 1501 W Ridge Rd 14615. Fax: 716/621-8446. **Terms:** [CP] meal plan; weekly & monthly rates avail; 7 day cancellation notice; cancellation fee imposed; pets. **Facility:** 83 rooms. 8 whirlpool rooms, $129-$149; 5 stories; interior corridors. **Dining:** Restaurant nearby. **Recreation:** Fee: privileges at a nearby health club. **All Rooms:** extended cable TV. **Cards:** AE, CB, DI, DS, JC, MC, VI.
(See ad p. 457)

(See map p. 456)

COURTYARD BY MARRIOTT-ROCHESTER WEST
◆◆◆ Phone: (716)621-6050 ⓴
Motel All Year 1P: $109 2P: $109
Location: I-390, exit 24, just e on SR 104 (Ridge Rd), just s on Hoover Dr, just w. 400 Paddy Creek Cir 14615. Fax: 716/621-6115. **Facility:** 78 rooms. 3 stories; interior corridors; heated pool, 1 small heated indoor.
All Rooms: combo or shower baths. **Cards:** AE, DI, DS, MC, VI.

HAMPTON INN-ROCHESTER NORTH
◆◆◆ Phone: (716)663-6070 ㉔
Motel All Year 1P: $78-$88 2P: $86-$96
Location: I-390, Ridge Rd E exit, just e on Rt 104, just n on Buckman Rd to Center Place Dr. 500 Center Place Dr 14615. Fax: 716/663-9158. **Terms:** [CP] meal plan; pets. **Facility:** 118 rooms. 4 stories; interior corridors.
All Rooms: combo or shower baths. **Cards:** AE, CB, DI, DS, MC, VI.

MARRIOTT AIRPORT HOTEL
◆◆◆ Phone: (716)225-6880 ㉒
Motor Inn All Year 1P: $160 2P: $160
Location: SR 104, w of jct I-390; 3.5 mi n of I-490. 1890 Ridge Rd W 14615. Fax: 716/225-8188. **Terms:** Package plans. **Facility:** 210 rooms. Attractive pool area and well maintained grounds. 7 stories; interior corridors; heated pool. **Cards:** AE, DI, DS, MC, VI.

RESIDENCE INN BY MARRIOTT-WEST
◆◆◆ Phone: (716)865-2090 ㉕
Extended All Year 2P: $84-$169
Stay Motel Location: I-390, exit 24, just e on SR 104 (Ridge Rd), just s on Hoover Dr, just w. 500 Paddy Creek Cir 14615. Fax: 716/865-2990. **Terms:** [CP] meal plan; pets. **Facility:** 90 rooms. 13 two-bedroom units. 3 stories; interior corridors; heated pool. **Recreation:** sports court. **All Rooms:** kitchens, combo or shower baths. **Cards:** AE, CB, DI, DS, MC, VI.

WELLESLEY INN & SUITES
(AAA) (SAVE) Phone: (716)621-2060 ㉓
◆◆ 5/1-10/31 1P: $60-$105 2P: $60-$105 XP: $10 F18
Motel 11/1-4/30 1P: $50-$85 2P: $50-$85 XP: $10 F18
Location: SR 104, just e of I-390. 1635 W Ridge Rd 14615. Fax: 716/621-7102. **Terms:** [CP] meal plan; pets, $3 extra charge. **Facility:** 97 rooms. 4 stories; interior corridors. **Dining:** Restaurant nearby. **All Rooms:** combo or shower baths, extended cable TV. **Cards:** AE, CB, DI, DS, JC, MC, VI.
Special Amenities: Free breakfast and free newspaper. *(See color ad p 458 & color ad p 4)*

GREENE pop. 6,100

—— LODGING ——

SHERWOOD INN
◆◆ Phone: (607)656-4196
Country Inn All Year 1P: $50-$115 2P: $60-$115 XP: $10 F12
Location: Downtown. 25 Genesee St 13778. Fax: 607/565-9772. **Terms:** 7 day cancellation notice; cancellation fee imposed; pets. **Facility:** 29 rooms. Victorian charm with old fashioned country hospitality. 3 stories; interior/exterior corridors. **All Rooms:** combo or shower baths. **Cards:** AE, DS, MC, VI.

GREENPORT pop. 2,100

—— LODGING ——

THE BARTLETT HOUSE INN
◆◆ Phone: 631/477-0371
Historic Bed 5/26-10/31 1P: $110-$140 2P: $110-$140 XP: $25
& Breakfast 5/1-5/25 1P: $95 2P: $95-$125 XP: $25
11/1-4/30 1P: $75-$95 2P: $75-$125 XP: $25
Location: SR 25 (Front St), 0.5 mi w of center. 503 Front St 11944. **Terms:** [ECP] meal plan; age restrictions may apply; 7 day cancellation notice; 2 night min stay, weekends in season. **Facility:** 10 rooms. Large Victoria cedar shingle home, circa 1908. Interesting wood and plaster work in parlor and large shady porch. 3 stories, no elevator; interior corridors; smoke free premises. **All Rooms:** combo or shower baths. **Cards:** DS, MC, VI.

—— RESTAURANTS ——

CLAUDIO'S RESTAURANT
CLAM BAR & MARINA Historical Lunch: $8-$13 Dinner: $16-$22 Phone: 631/477-0627
◆◆ Location: Rt 25 to corner of Main and Front sts se, just s to water. 111 Main St 11944. **Hours:** Open 5/1-1/2
Steak and & 4/15-4/30; 11:30 am-10 pm, Fri & Sat-11 pm. **Reservations:** suggested. **Features:** casual dress; children's
Seafood menu; health conscious menu items; cocktails & lounge; a la carte. Overlooking the marina and fishing harbor, the established restaurant has been operated by generations of the same family since 1870. Traditional preparations of mostly seafood are wholesome and flavorful. A nautical theme weaves through the dining areas.
Cards: MC, VI.

RHUMB LINE
◆
Steak and
Seafood

Lunch: $8-$14 **Dinner:** $11-$18 **Phone:** 631/477-9883
Location: Downtown; between Main and 1st sts; on SR 25. 36 Front St 11944. **Hours:** 11:30 am-3 & 5-9 pm, Sat 11:30 am-10 pm, Sun 11:30 am-9 pm. Closed: 11/23 & 12/25. **Features:** casual dress; children's menu; health conscious menu items; carryout; cocktails & lounge. Half hulls of sailboats, ropes, ship wheels and stained-glass mermaid windows contribute to the nautical decor of the casual dining room. The menu centers on well-prepared steaks, chops and seafood, as well as a nice offering of soups and sandwiches. **Cards:** AE, DI, DS, MC, VI.

GREENWICH pop. 2,000

——— LODGING ———

SUNSHINE INN
◆◆
Motel

			Phone: 518/692-2997	
7/21-9/7	1P: $90	2P: $95	XP: $10	F10
5/1-7/20 & 9/8-4/30	1P: $50	2P: $55	XP: $5	F10

Location: 0.5 mi n on SR 40. 2624 SR 40 12834. Fax: 518/692-2601. **Terms:** 7 day cancellation notice. **Facility:** 10 rooms. Set on small hill in rural area. Small guest rooms attractively appointed. 1 story; exterior corridors. **Services:** winter plug-ins. **All Rooms:** combo or shower baths. **Cards:** AE, DS, MC, VI.

GROTON pop. 2,400—See also FINGER LAKES.

——— RESTAURANT ———

BENN CONGER INN Historical
◆◆◆
Continental

Dinner: $15-$24 **Phone:** 607/898-5817
Location: Just w. 206 W Cortland St 13073. **Hours:** 6 pm-9 pm, Sun from 5 pm. Closed: Mon & Tues. **Reservations:** required. **Features:** No A/C; semi-formal attire; cocktails & lounge. The 1919 Southern revival mansion is elegantly appointed with upscale table settings including signature china. A delicious menu choice is scallops over spinach fettuccine. Among outstanding desserts are profiterole and blueberry creme brulee. Smoke free premises. **Cards:** AE, DI, MC, VI.

GUILDERLAND pop. 1,900 (See map p. 193; index p. 192)

——— LODGING ———

HOLIDAY INN EXPRESS TURF ON WESTERN AVE
◆◆◆
Motel

			Phone: (518)438-0001	45
7/15-9/6	1P: $89-$130	2P: $89-$130	XP: $5	F19
9/7-4/30	1P: $69-$110	2P: $69-$110	XP: $5	F19
5/1-7/14	1P: $69-$100	2P: $69-$100	XP: $5	F19

Location: 0.5 mi e on US 20 (Western Ave) from jct I-87 Northway and US 20. 1442 Western Ave 12203. Fax: 518/438-0690. **Terms:** Check-in 4 pm; 3 day cancellation notice; cancellation fee imposed. **Facility:** 121 rooms. Very modern, comfortably furnished guest rooms. Attractive public areas. 3-4 stories; interior corridors; heated pool. **Services:** gift shop. **All Rooms:** combo or shower baths, safes. **Some Rooms:** Fee: refrigerators. **Cards:** AE, CB, DI, DS, JC, MC, VI.

——— RESTAURANT ———

BAVARIAN CHALET
◆
German

Dinner: $11-$16 **Phone:** 518/355-8005 36
Location: Center; from jct I-87 Northway and US 20, on US 20, 5.8 mi w. 5060 Western Tpke 12084. **Hours:** 4 pm-9 pm, Sat-10 pm, Sun 3 pm-8 pm; hrs vary in winter. Closed: 7/4, Mon, Tues & 12/24-12/26. **Reservations:** suggested. **Features:** casual dress; children's menu; cocktails & lounge. German selections—such as soup with potatoes, ham and cabbage—are particularly tasty on a menu of veal, game, black Angus steaks and seafood. Bavarian decor lends to the authenticity of the setting. Many imported and microbrewed beers are offered. **Cards:** AE, MC, VI.

HALFMOON pop. 500

——— RESTAURANTS ———

GRECIAN GARDENS PIZZA & RESTAURANT
◆
Italian

Lunch: $4-$9 **Dinner:** $11-$16 **Phone:** 518/373-9950
Location: On Rt 9, 0.9 mi s of jct Rt 146 and 9. 1612 Rt 9 12065. **Hours:** 11 am-11 pm. Closed: 11/23 & 12/25. **Reservations:** accepted. **Features:** casual dress; carryout; cocktails & lounge; a la carte. A fountain is the centerpiece of the family-style restaurant's laid-back dining room. The menu dabbles in Greek, Italian and American cuisine, including particularly tasty pizzas. Tables with colorful umbrellas dot the breezy, seasonal patio. **Cards:** AE, MC, VI.

TAI-PAN
◆◆
Chinese

Lunch: $6-$7 **Dinner:** $8-$14 **Phone:** 518/383-8581
Location: On Rt 9. 1519 Halfmoon Pkwy 12065. **Hours:** 11 am-10 pm, Sat-11 pm. **Reservations:** suggested; weekends. **Features:** casual dress; carryout; cocktails & lounge; a la carte. Next to Clifton Park, the comfortable restaurant has a moderately sophisticated ambience that's welcoming to professionals. The menu centers on Thai and Hong Kong cuisine, such as chili lamb curry. A wonderful dim sum brunch is served on the weekends. **Cards:** AE, DI, MC, VI.

HAMBURG —*See Buffalo p. 225.*

HAMLIN pop. 9,200

———— LODGING ————

SANDY CREEK MANOR HOUSE   **Phone:** (716)964-7528
◆◆   All Year   1P: $60-$76   2P: $70-$95
Bed &   **Location:** 0.3 mi n of SR 18, 2 mi w of SR 19. 1960 Redman Rd 14464-9635. Fax: 716/964-9244. **Terms:** [BP]
Breakfast   meal plan; check-in 4 pm; 10 day cancellation notice; package plans; pets. **Facility:** 4 rooms. Secluded
              wooded 6 acre lot with salmon stream. Small individually decorated guest rooms. Owner pets on premises. 2
stories; interior corridors; smoke free premises. **Services:** gift shop. **Recreation:** fishing. **Cards:** AE, DS, MC, VI.

HAMMONDSPORT pop. 900—*See also FINGER LAKES.*

———— LODGINGS ————

BLUSHING ROSE BED & BREAKFAST   **Phone:** 607/569-3402
(AAA)   All Year   1P: $85-$95   2P: $95-$105   XP: $20
◆◆◆   **Location:** Downtown; just n of SR 54A. 11 William St 14840. Fax: 607/569-2504. **Terms:** [BP] meal plan;
Historic Bed restrictions may apply; 14 day cancellation notice; cancellation fee imposed. **Facility:** 4 rooms. 1843 Victorian
& Breakfast   Italian. Near Keuka Lake. 2 stories; interior corridors; smoke free premises. **All Rooms:** combo or shower
              baths.

HAMMONDSPORT MOTEL   **Phone:** (607)569-2600
(AAA)   5/1-11/13 & 4/1-4/30   1P: $57-$63   2P: $57-$63   XP: $9   F6
◆◆   **Location:** Downtown; just n of SR 54A, on Keuka Lake. William St & Water St 14840 (PO Box 311).
Motel   **Terms:** Open 5/1-11/13 & 4/1-4/30; 7 day cancellation notice. **Facility:** 17 rooms. Shaded grounds. Very well-
              kept. 1 story; exterior corridors; lakefront; Beach & swimming avail at adjacent public park area. Fee: boat
              dock, boat ramp. **Dining:** Restaurant nearby. **Recreation:** fishing. **All Rooms:** extended cable TV.
Cards: MC, VI.

PARK INN   **Phone:** (607)569-9387
◆◆   5/1-10/31   1P: $71-$81   2P: $71-$81   XP: $10
Historic   11/1-4/30   1P: $47-$55   2P: $59   XP: $10
Country Inn   **Location:** Center; on town square. 37-39 Shethar St 14840. **Terms:** [BP] meal plan; 7 day cancellation notice;
              cancellation fee imposed. **Facility:** 5 rooms. All units are 2-room suites in historic hotel overlooking the town
square. 2 stories; interior corridors; designated smoking area; street parking only. **All Rooms:** combo or shower baths.
Cards: DS, MC, VI.

VILLAGE TAVERN INN   **Phone:** 607/569-2528
(AAA)   5/1-11/30   1P: $69-$149   2P: $69-$149
◆◆   12/1-4/30   1P: $69-$129   2P: $69-$129
Historic   **Location:** SR 54A; in Village Square. 30 Mechanic St 14840 (Box 573). Fax: 607/569-3560. **Terms:** Weekly
Country Inn   rates avail; 10 day cancellation notice; cancellation fee imposed. **Facility:** 4 rooms. Quaint
              rooms on village square within walking distance of Keuka Lake. Closed 1/5-1/21. 1 two-bedroom unit. Rates
              for up to 4 persons; 2 stories; interior corridors; street parking only; Keuka Lake nearby. **Dining:** Restaurant;
cocktails; restaurant, see separate listing. **All Rooms:** efficiencies, extended cable TV. **Cards:** AE, DS, MC, VI.

———— RESTAURANT ————

VILLAGE TAVERN   **Lunch:** $5-$7   **Dinner:** $10-$22   **Phone:** 607/569-2528
◆◆◆   **Location:** SR 54A; in Village Tavern Restaurant & Inn. 30 Mechanic St 14840. **Hours:** 11:30 am-3 pm & 5-9
American   pm, Fri & Sat-10 pm. Closed: 11/23, 12/25 & Mon-Wed 1/1-3/31. **Reservations:** suggested.
              Features: casual dress; children's menu; health conscious menu items; carryout; cocktails & lounge; street
parking. An extensive selection of wines and exotic beers matches well with thoughtfully prepared steak, seafood and pasta
dishes. Chilled melon soup with blueberry bits is simply fantastic. Airplane photographs hang on the walls of the comfortable
dining room. **Cards:** AE, DS, MC, VI.

HANCOCK pop. 1,300

———— LODGING ————

SMITHS COLONIAL MOTEL   **Phone:** (607)637-2989
(AAA) (SAVE) 5/1-9/7   1P: $45-$75   2P: $55-$75   XP: $5   F14
             9/8-12/31   1P: $44-$75   2P: $49-$75   XP: $5   F14
◆◆   3/2-4/30   1P: $44-$50   2P: $48-$58   XP: $5   F14
Motel   1/1-3/1   1P: $44-$50   2P: $49-$55   XP: $5   F14
              Location: SR 17, exit 87; or 87A to Rt 97 S. RR 1, Box 172D, Rt 97 13783. **Terms:** Cancellation fee imposed;
pets. **Facility:** 16 rooms. Quaint property in peaceful area on the Delaware River. 1 story; exterior corridors. **Services:** winter
plug-ins. **Recreation:** fishing; basketball, horseshoes. Rental: canoes. **All Rooms:** shower baths, extended cable TV.
Cards: AE, DS, MC, VI. **Special Amenities:** Free local telephone calls.

HARTSDALE —*See New York p. 372.*

HARTWICK SEMINARY pop. 100—*See also COOPERSTOWN.*

———— LODGING ————

BEST WESTERN COOPERSTOWN INN & SUITES　　　　　　　　Phone: (607)547-9439

(AAA) (SAVE)　6/9-9/3　　　　　　　1P: $140-$200　　　2P: $150-$210　　　XP: $8　　　F12
◆◆◆　5/1-6/8 & 9/4-10/28　1P: $95-$160　　　2P: $105-$170　　　XP: $8　　　F12
Motel　10/29-4/30　　　　　1P: $70-$140　　　2P: $80-$150　　　XP: $8　　　F12

Location: Center; on SR 28. 50 Commons Dr, Rt 28 13326. Fax: 607/547-7082. **Terms:** [ECP] meal plan; small pets only. **Facility:** 98 rooms. Weekend rates may be higher; 6 whirlpool rooms; 2 stories; interior corridors; heated pool, whirlpool. **Dining:** Restaurant nearby. **Services:** winter plug-ins. **Recreation:** exercise equipment, game room. Fee: rental movies. **All Rooms:** combo or shower baths, extended cable TV. **Some Rooms:** 36 efficiencies. Fee: VCR. **Cards:** AE, CB, DI, DS, MC, VI. **Special Amenities:** Free breakfast and free local telephone calls. *(See ad p 240)*

HAUPPAUGE pop. 19,800

———— LODGINGS ————

ISLANDIA MARRIOTT LONG ISLAND　　　　　　　　　　　　Phone: (631)232-3000

◆◆◆　All Year　　　　　　1P: $159-$219　　　2P: $159-$219
Hotel　**Location:** I-495, exit 58, 0.3 mi w on n service road. 3635 Express Dr N 11788. Fax: 631/232-3029. **Terms:** Package plans. **Facility:** 277 rooms. 2-floor glass atrium lobby. Concierge level rooms avail. 10 stories; interior corridors; heated pool. **Services:** gift shop. **All Rooms:** combo or shower baths. **Cards:** AE, CB, DI, DS, MC, VI.

WYNDHAM WIND WATCH HOTEL & HAMLET GOLF CLUB　　　Phone: (631)232-9800

◆◆◆　All Year　　　　　　1P: $119-$185　　　　　　　　　　　　　F18
Hotel　**Location:** I-495, exit 57, just n to Motor Pkwy, 1.3 mi ne. 1717 Vanderbilt Motor Pkwy 11788. Fax: 631/232-9853. **Terms:** Cancellation fee imposed; package plans, weekend; pets. **Facility:** 360 rooms. Traditional estate style property nestled among acres of lush greenland. 10 stories; interior corridors; valley view; putting green; 2 heated pools; 2 lighted tennis courts; playground. Fee: 18 holes golf. **Dining:** nightclub. **Services:** gift shop; area transportation. Fee: massage. **Some Rooms:** Fee: VCR. **Cards:** AE, DI, DS, MC, VI. *(See color ad below)*

———— RESTAURANTS ————

KOTOBUKI　　　　　　**Lunch:** $6-$18　　　**Dinner:** $8-$18　　　Phone: 631/360-3969
◆　**Location:** Just w of jct SR 111; in Hauppauge Shopping Center. 372 Nesconset Hwy 11787.
Japanese　**Hours:** noon-2:30 & 5:30-10 pm, Sat 5 pm-10:30 pm, Sun 5 pm-9:30 pm. Closed: Mon. **Features:** casual dress; carryout; beer & wine only; a la carte. Drive up to the unpretentious restaurant, and you'll see "sushi" before you see the name. Among other selections are regionally inspired rolls, sashimi, and nigiri, as well as a variety of savory cooked dishes, such as teriyaki, yakitori and tempura. Smoke free premises. **Cards:** AE, CB, DI, DS, MC, VI.

SEMPRE VIVOLO　　　　**Lunch:** $14-$22　　　**Dinner:** $18-$23　　　Phone: 631/435-1737
◆◆◆　**Location:** I-495 (Long Island Expwy), exit 55, just n. 696 Motor Pkwy 11788. **Hours:** noon-2:30 & 5-9:30
Italian　pm. Closed major holidays & Sun. **Reservations:** suggested. **Features:** dressy casual; health conscious menu items; cocktails & lounge; a la carte. A knowledgeable and attentive wait staff serves diners in the upscale, elegant setting. Sophisticated Italian dishes include delicious roasted salmon and a pasta dish with pancetta and fresh and sun-dried tomatoes. Roman artwork decorates the dining room. Smoke free premises. **Cards:** AE, DI, DS, MC, VI.

HAWTHORNE —*See New York p. 372.*

HENRIETTA pop. 1,300 (See map p. 456; index p. 455)—

——— LODGINGS ———

ECONO LODGE-ROCHESTER SOUTH   **Phone:** (716)427-2700   **32**
AAA SAVE
5/1-10/31   1P: $64-$74   2P: $69-$79   XP: $6   F18
11/1-4/30   1P: $59-$69   2P: $64-$74   XP: $6   F18
Motel   **Location:** Just w on SR 252, I-390, exit 14A. 940 Jefferson Rd 14623. **Fax:** 716/427-8504. **Terms:** [CP] meal plan; 7 day cancellation notice; cancellation fee imposed; pets. **Facility:** 102 rooms. Some "green" rooms with special water filter and superior appointments. 7 whirlpool rooms, $129; 3 stories; interior corridors.
Dining: Restaurant nearby. **All Rooms:** extended cable TV. **Cards:** AE, CB, DI, DS, JC, MC, VI. *(See ad p 458)*

FAIRFIELD INN BY MARRIOTT   **Phone:** (716)334-3350   **31**
All Year   1P: $84   2P: $84
Motel   **Location:** Jct of SR 253 and 15. 4695 W Henrietta Rd 14467. **Fax:** 716/334-2295. **Terms:** [CP] meal plan.
Facility: 63 rooms. 3 stories; interior corridors; heated pool. **All Rooms:** combo or shower baths.
Some Rooms: Fee: refrigerators. **Cards:** AE, DI, DS, MC, VI.

HOLIDAY INN SOUTH   **Phone:** 716/475-1510   **38**
All Year   1P: $116   2P: $116
Motor Inn   **Location:** SR 252, just w of I-390, exit 14. 1111 Jefferson Rd 14623. **Fax:** 716/427-8673. **Terms:** Package plans. **Facility:** 250 rooms. Atrium lobby. 6 stories; interior corridors; heated pool. **Services:** gift shop.
All Rooms: combo or shower baths. **Some Rooms:** Fee: refrigerators, VCR. **Cards:** AE, CB, DI, DS, JC, MC, VI.

MICROTEL   **Phone:** 716/334-3400   **35**
Property failed to provide current rates
Motel   **Location:** SR 253, 0.3 mi e of jct SR 15; I-390, northbound exit 12; southbound exit 12A, just n on SR 253.
905 Lehigh Station Rd 14467. **Fax:** 716/334-5042. **Terms:** Small pets only. **Facility:** 98 rooms. Compact rooms. 2 stories; interior corridors. **All Rooms:** combo or shower baths. **Cards:** AE, CB, DI, DS, MC, VI.

RED ROOF INN-HENRIETTA   **Phone:** (716)359-1100   **39**
AAA
5/1-10/31   1P: $48-$76   2P: $55-$83   XP: $7   F18
3/1-4/30   1P: $46-$64   2P: $53-$71   XP: $7   F18
11/1-2/28   1P: $44-$60   2P: $51-$67   XP: $7   F18
Motel   **Location:** US 15, just s of jct SR 253. 4820 W Henrietta Rd 14467. **Fax:** 716/359-1121. **Terms:** Pets.
Facility: 108 rooms. Some small rooms. 2 stories; exterior corridors. **Dining:** Restaurant nearby. **Cards:** AE, CB, DI, DS, MC, VI.

RESIDENCE INN BY MARRIOTT   **Phone:** (716)272-8850   **40**
All Year   1P: $97-$130   2P: $97-$130
Apartment   **Location:** I-390, exit 14A, 0.5 mi e. 1300 Jefferson Rd 14623. **Fax:** 716/272-7822. **Terms:** [CP] meal plan; cancellation fee imposed; pets, $6 extra charge, $125 cleaning fee. **Facility:** 112 rooms. Studio and loft units with fully equipped kitchens. Most rooms with a fireplace. 28 two-bedroom units. 2 stories; exterior corridors.
Recreation: sports court. **All Rooms:** kitchens. **Cards:** AE, CB, DI, DS, JC, MC, VI. *(See color ad p 458)*

ROCHESTER MARRIOTT THRUWAY HOTEL   **Phone:** (716)359-1800   **37**
All Year   1P: $105   2P: $105
Motor Inn   **Location:** SR 15, I-90, exit 46; I-390 N, Lehigh Station Rd, exit w to SR 15, 0.7 mi s. 5257 W Henrietta Rd 14586 (PO Box 20551, ROCHESTER, 14602). **Fax:** 716/359-1349. **Terms:** Package plans. **Facility:** 305 rooms. Attractive public facilities. 3-5 stories; interior corridors; putting green; heated pool. **Services:** gift shop. **Some Rooms:** Fee: refrigerators. **Cards:** AE, CB, DI, DS, JC, MC, VI.

SUPER 8 MOTEL   **Phone:** (716)359-1630   **36**
AAA SAVE
5/1-9/30 & 4/1-4/30   1P: $50-$60   2P: $59-$67   XP: $5   F17
10/1-3/31   1P: $43-$51   2P: $46-$54   XP: $3   F17
Motel   **Location:** SR 253, 0.3 mi e of jct SR 15, just w of jct I-390, northbound exit 12; southbound exit 12A. 1000 Lehigh Station Rd 14467. **Fax:** 716/359-1630. **Terms:** Package plans. **Facility:** 121 rooms. Large pleasant guest rooms. Some king rooms with exercise equipment and superior furnishings. 8 whirlpool rooms, $95-$105; 2 stories; interior corridors. **Services:** winter plug-ins. **All Rooms:** extended cable TV. **Some Rooms:** kitchen.
Cards: AE, CB, DI, DS, MC, VI. **Special Amenities:** Free breakfast and free newspaper.

HERKIMER pop. 7,900

——— LODGINGS ———

HERKIMER MOTEL
AAA SAVE
◆◆
Motel

				Phone: (315)866-0490
7/1-9/4	1P: $46-$54	2P: $59-$68	XP: $7	F12
5/1-6/30 & 9/5-4/30	1P: $42-$46	2P: $54-$59	XP: $7	F12

Location: Jct SR 28 and I-90 (New York Thruway), exit 30. 100 Marginal Rd 13350. Fax: 315/866-0416. **Terms:** Weekly & monthly rates avail, off season; small pets only. **Facility:** 60 rooms. Picnic tables. Variety of room types and furnishings. Kitchenettes, $73-$83 for up to 4 persons; 2 stories; interior/exterior corridors, heated pool. **Dining:** Restaurant nearby. **Services:** winter plug-ins. **All Rooms:** combo or shower baths, extended cable TV. **Cards:** AE, CB, DI, DS, MC, VI. **Special Amenities:** Free local telephone calls and free room upgrade (subject to availability with advanced reservations).

INN TOWNE MOTEL
AAA SAVE
◆
Motel

| | | | | Phone: (315)866-1101 |
| All Year | 1P: $36-$46 | 2P: $46-$58 | XP: $8 | F12 |

Location: I-90, exit 30, 1 mi n on Rt 28, just w. 227 N Washington St 13350. Fax: 315/866-1101. **Terms:** Weekly & monthly rates avail, winter; small pets only. **Facility:** 33 rooms. Downtown location. Modestly furnished guest rooms. Efficiency rooms, $25 extra charge. $10 phone dep req; 2 stories; exterior corridors. **All Rooms:** extended cable TV. **Some Rooms:** 3 efficiencies, no utensils. **Cards:** AE, DS, MC, VI. **Special Amenities:** Early check-in/late check-out and free local telephone calls.

——— RESTAURANTS ———

BABY BOOMERS COOKERY & LOUNGE   **Lunch:** $4-$6   **Dinner:** $9-$12   **Phone:** 315/866-3183
◆
American

Location: From SR 5, just n on Albany St, then just e. 527 E Albany St 13350. **Hours:** 11 am-9 pm, Fri & Sat-10 pm. Closed major holidays, Sun & Mon. **Features:** casual dress; children's menu; health conscious menu; carryout; cocktails & lounge; a la carte. The menu of primarily lighter fare lists soups, salads and sandwiches, as well as steaks and seafood. Mahogany accents, turn-of-the-20th-century postcards and stained-glass windows add to the attractive decor of the comfortable dining room. **Cards:** AE, DS, MC, VI.

CRYSTAL CHANDELIER RESTAURANT   **Dinner:** $8-$16   **Phone:** 315/891-3366
◆◆◆
American

Location: On SR 28. 4579 SR 28 13350. **Hours:** Open 5/1-1/1 & 4/1-4/30; 5 pm-9:30 pm, Fri & Sat-10 pm. Sun noon-7 pm. Closed: 1/1, 12/24, 12/25, Mon & Tues. **Reservations:** accepted. **Features:** casual dress; children's menu; carryout; cocktails & lounge; a la carte. Smoked baby back ribs stand out on a menu of well-prepared beef, seafood and poultry selections. Flowers and fine artwork decorate the moderately upscale dining room. The restaurant caters to a diverse clientele, ranging from families to professionals. **Cards:** AE, CB, DI, DS, MC, VI.

HICKSVILLE pop. 40,200

——— LODGINGS ———

DAYS INN-HICKSVILLE
AAA SAVE
◆◆
Motel

| | | | | Phone: (516)433-1900 |
| All Year | 1P: $60-$100 | 2P: $70-$120 | XP: $10 | F12 |

Location: I-495, exit 43, Northern State Pkwy exit 36, then 2.5 mi s. 828 S Oyster Bay Rd 11801. Fax: 516/433-0218. **Terms:** [CP] meal plan; weekly & monthly rates avail. **Facility:** 70 rooms. Quiet location. Guest rooms vary in style and size. 10 efficiencies, $5 extra charge; 2 stories; exterior corridors. **Dining:** Restaurant; 11 am-midnight, Sat & Sun 5 pm-midnight; $5-$20; cocktails. **All Rooms:** no utensils. **Cards:** AE, DI, DS, MC, VI. **Special Amenities:** Free breakfast and free newspaper.

ECONO LODGE
AAA SAVE
◆
Motor Inn

| | | | | Phone: (516)433-3900 |
| All Year | 1P: $75-$105 | 2P: $75-$105 | XP: $10 | F18 |

Location: I-495, exit 41 S, 2.5 mi s on SR 106, 1.2 mi w on Old Country Rd. 429 Duffy Ave 11801. Fax: 516/433-3909. **Terms:** [CP] meal plan. **Facility:** 72 rooms. 2 stories; interior corridors. **Dining:** Restaurant nearby. **All Rooms:** combo or shower baths, extended cable TV. **Cards:** AE, CB, DI, DS, MC, VI. *(See color ad below)*

—— **RESTAURANT** ——

SANSAR INDIAN CUISINE **Lunch:** $8-$13 **Dinner:** $8-$13 **Phone:** 516/681-9834
Location: 0.5 mi s of train station. 128 Broadway 11801. **Hours:** 11:30 am-3 & 5-10 pm, Fri & Sat-11 pm.
◆ Northern Italian
Features: casual dress; carryout; cocktails; a la carte. The clay tandoor oven creates wonderful broiled meat and seafood, as well as great breads, including naan and roh. The menu also lists other specialties: bicyanis and vegetarian dishes. Selections on the lunch buffet are laid out in copper kettles. Smoke free premises.
Cards: AE, CB, DI, DS, MC, VI. ✕

HIGH FALLS pop. 600

—— **RESTAURANTS** ——

DEPUY CANAL HOUSE Historical **Lunch:** $12-$24 **Dinner:** $20-$45 **Phone:** 914/687-7700
◆◆◆ American
Location: Center; on SR 213. 1111 E New York Rt 209 12440. **Hours:** 5:30 pm-10 pm, Sun 11:30 am-2 & 4:30-9 pm. Closed: 12/25, Mon-Wed & 1/1-2/13. **Reservations:** suggested. **Features:** casual dress; Sunday brunch; health conscious menu; cocktails & lounge; a la carte. Along the historic Delaware and Hudson Canal, the 1797 landmark has been meticulously restored and is appointed in antiques. Braised veal shoulder stuffed with lean, smoked pork loin is one example of the creative, internationally influenced cuisine. **Cards:** AE, MC, VI. ✕

THE EGG'S NEST **Lunch:** $6-$10 **Dinner:** $8-$14 **Phone:** 914/687-7255
◆◆ American
Location: Center. Rt 213 12440. **Hours:** 11:30 am-11 pm, Fri & Sat-midnight. Closed: 11/23, 12/24 & 12/25.
Features: casual dress; carryout; cocktails & lounge; a la carte. Inventive overstuffed sandwiches—such as the "Thanksgiving feast," which stacks turkey, stuffing and melted cheese on egg-battered bread—are as wonderful as the decor, which brims with such funky finds as toaster lamps and three-dimensional art. ✕

HIGHLAND pop. 4,500

—— **LODGING** ——

ROCKING HORSE RANCH **Phone:** (914)691-2927
AAA 5/26-9/4 1P: $150-$180 2P: $300-$360 XP: $75 F3
◆◆◆ Ranch 5/1-5/25 & 9/5-4/30 1P: $95-$180 2P: $190-$360 XP: $75 F3
Location: I-87 Thruway, exit 18, 2.4 mi e on Rt 299, 0.6 mi s on New Paltz Rd, 3 mi w on Pancake Hollow Rd. 600 Rt 44-55 12528. Fax: 914/691-6434. **Terms:** [MAP] meal plan; check-in 4 pm; 21 day cancellation notice; 2 night min stay, weekends; package plans; 15% service charge. **Facility:** 119 rooms. Ranch resort with extensive recreational facilities. 2 stories; interior/exterior corridors; designated smoking area; miniature golf; 2 heated pools, wading pool, saunas, waterslide, whirlpool; 2 lighted tennis courts; playground. **Dining:** Dining room, deli; 8 am-10:30 & 12:30-1:30 pm; dinner seatings at 5:30 pm & 7:30 pm; cocktails; entertainment; nightclub. **Services:** gift shop; area transportation; winter plug-ins. **Recreation:** fishing, paddleboats, waterskiing, banana boating; downhill skiing, ice skating, ski instruction, sleigh rides, snow tubing; hiking trails, horseback riding, sports court, archery, baseball, beach volleyball, hayrides, indoor laser rifle, petting zoo. **Some Rooms:** Fee: refrigerators, VCR. **Cards:** AE, DI, DS, MC, VI.
🍽 🐾 📶 VCR 🖨 📱 DATA PORT 🏊 🏖 ♨ ✕

HIGHLAND FALLS pop. 3,900

—— **LODGINGS** ——

BEST WESTERN PALISADE MOTEL **Phone:** (914)446-9400
AAA SAVE All Year 1P: $80-$95 2P: $85-$120 XP: $5 F16
◆◆ Motel
Location: SR 218, at jct US 9 W, 2.5 mi s of US Military Academy s gate. 17 Main St 10928. Fax: 914/446-9400. **Terms:** [CP] meal plan; weekly rates avail; pets. **Facility:** 53 rooms. Simple contemporary furnishings; some spacious units. 2 stories; exterior corridors. **Services:** winter plug-ins. **All Rooms:** extended cable TV. **Some Rooms:** 10 efficiencies. **Cards:** AE, DI, DS, MC, VI. **Special Amenities:** Free breakfast and free local telephone calls.
🆓 🐾 🏖 ♨ 🖨 📱

WEST POINT MOTEL **Phone:** (914)446-4180
AAA SAVE 5/1-10/31 & 4/1-4/30 1P: $74-$125 2P: $74-$125 XP: $5 F12
◆ Motel 11/1-3/31 1P: $64-$125 2P: $69-$125 XP: $5 F12
Location: Jct US 9 W and Rt 218, 1 mi n. 156 Main St (SR 218) 10928 (PO Box 301). Fax: 914/446-4180. **Terms:** [CP] meal plan; weekly rates avail; 10 day cancellation notice. **Facility:** 51 rooms. 2 stories; exterior corridors. **Dining:** Restaurant nearby. **All Rooms:** combo or shower baths, extended cable TV. **Cards:** AE, CB, DI, DS, MC, VI. **Special Amenities:** Early check-in/late check-out and free local telephone calls. *(See color ad p 492)*
🆓 🍽 🏖 ✕ ♨ 🖨 📱

—— **RESTAURANT** ——

SCHADES RESTAURANT **Lunch:** $5-$9 **Dinner:** $7-$12 **Phone:** 914/446-2626
◆ American
Location: Downtown. 457 Main St 10928. **Hours:** 11 am-9 pm, Fri & Sat-10 pm. Closed major holidays.
Features: casual dress; carryout; beer & wine only; a la carte. Artwork decorates the clean, well-lighted restaurant, a favorite of locals and tourists alike. The menu delivers a broad variety of entrees, including steak, chicken, pasta, pizza and sandwiches. The family-oriented atmosphere is casual and comfortable. **Cards:** AE, DS, MC, VI. ✕

HILLSDALE pop. 1,800

——— RESTAURANT ———

AUBERGINE Country Inn
◆◆◆◆
French
Dinner: $22-$35
Phone: 518/325-3412
Location: Center; jct SR 22 and 23. Intersection 22 & 23 12529. **Hours:** 5:30 pm-11 pm. Closed: Mon & Tues. **Reservations:** suggested. **Features:** dressy casual; cocktails & lounge; a la carte. The owner-chef prepares superior American country dishes, which are clearly influenced by contemporary French cuisine. The smoke-free dining room has an elegant, but casual, aura. Innovative desserts include the creme brulee with a hint of lemongrass. **Cards:** AE, DI, MC, VI. ⊠

HOBART pop. 400

——— LODGING ———

BREEZY ACRES FARM BED & BREAKFAST
◆◆◆
Historic Bed
& Breakfast
All Year
1P: $45-$75
2P: $60-$90
XP: $15
Phone: 607/538-9338
D18
Location: Jct Rt 23 and 10 (Stamford), 2.2 mi s. Rt 10 13788 (RD 1, Box 191). **Terms:** [BP] meal plan; age restrictions may apply; 14 day cancellation notice; 2 night min stay, summer weekends. **Facility:** 3 rooms. 1840s converted crop farm located on 300 acres of wooded land. Delightful blend of modern comforts with antique accents. Family homemade breakfast with home grown ingredients, featuring own maple products. 2 stories; interior corridors; smoke free premises. **Recreation:** swimming, canoeing, fishing. **Cards:** AE, DS, MC, VI. ⊠ 🐾 ☎ 🖨 ⊠

HOLBROOK pop. 25,300

——— RESTAURANT ———

MAMMA LOMBARDI'S
◆◆◆
Italian
Lunch: $9-$15
Dinner: $13-$22
Phone: 631/737-0774
Location: I-495, exit 61, 0.8 mi s, then just w. 400 Furrows Rd 11741. **Hours:** 11:30 am-10 pm, Fri & Sat-11:30 pm, Sun 1 pm-10 pm. Closed: 11/23 & 12/25. **Features:** casual dress; children's menu; carryout; cocktails & lounge. Burgundy tones and gilded artwork lend an air of sophistication to the cozy dining room. Bow tie pasta with gorgonzola sauce is representative of well-prepared offerings, which are served in abundant portions. Service is professional and attentive. Smoke free premises. **Cards:** AE, DI, DS, MC, VI. ⊠

HOLTSVILLE pop. 5,100

——— LODGING ———

BEST WESTERN MACARTHUR HOTEL
◆◆
Motor Inn
5/1-10/31
1P: $129-$250
2P: $129-$250
Phone: 631/758-2900
11/1-4/30
1P: $119-$199
2P: $119-$199
Location: I-495, exit 63, on sw service road. 1730 N Ocean Ave 11742. Fax: 631/758-2612. **Terms:** [ECP] meal plan; 14 day cancellation notice; package plans. **Facility:** 189 rooms. 3 stories; interior corridors; heated pool. **Services:** area transportation. **All Rooms:** combo or shower baths. **Some Rooms:** Fee: refrigerators. **Cards:** AE, DI, DS, MC, VI.
(A$K) (S🄳) ✈ 🍴 🍸 🐾 🛗 🔍 ⊠ 📷 🖨 🔌 (DATA PORT) 🐾 ✚

HONEOYE pop. 1,000

——— LODGING ———

GREENWOODS BED & BREAKFAST INN
(AAA)
◆◆◆
Bed &
Breakfast
All Year
1P: $70-$125
2P: $95-$145
XP: $15
Phone: 716/229-2111
Location: 2.5 mi e on Rt 20A, just n. 8136 Quayle Rd 14471. Fax: 716/229-2111. **Terms:** [BP] meal plan; age restrictions may apply; 14 day cancellation notice; cancellation fee imposed; package plans; winter; pet on premises. **Facility:** 6 rooms. Attractive individually decorated guest rooms. Quiet country location. 2 stories; interior corridors; smoke free premises; whirlpool. **Cards:** AE, DS, MC, VI. (A$K) ⊠ ☎ 🖨 ⊠

HONEOYE FALLS pop. 2,300—See also FINGER LAKES.

——— RESTAURANT ———

THE SHERWOOD
◆◆
American
Dinner: $10-$25
Phone: 716/624-3580
Location: 0.3 mi s of jct SR 65. 60 W Main St 14472. **Hours:** 4 pm-9 pm, Fri & Sat-10 pm, Sun noon-8 pm. Closed: 1/1, 12/24, 12/25 & Mon. **Reservations:** suggested; weekends. **Features:** casual dress; early bird specials; cocktails & lounge. A scenic creek babbles alongside the comfortable dining room, which is decorated with chandeliers, mirrors and wood accents. The menu centers on seafood, veal and steak. Delicious, homemade breads and pastries are sure to make your mouth water. **Cards:** AE, DI, DS, MC, VI. ⊠

HORNELL pop. 9,900—See also FINGER LAKES.

—— LODGING ——

COMFORT INN
Phone: (607)324-4300

◆◆◆	4/1-4/30	1P: $80	2P: $85	XP: $5	F18
Motor Inn	5/1-11/1	1P: $75	2P: $85	XP: $5	F18
	11/2-3/31	1P: $65	2P: $75	XP: $5	F18

Location: 3 mi s of jct US 36 and SR 17. 1 Canisteo Sq 14843. Fax: 607/324-4311. **Terms:** [CP] meal plan; 7 day cancellation notice; cancellation fee imposed. **Facility:** 62 rooms. Spacious guest rooms tastefully decorated. 2 stories; interior corridors; heated pool. **Services:** winter plug-ins. **All Rooms:** combo or shower baths. **Some Rooms:** Fee: refrigerators, microwaves, VCR. **Cards:** AE, CB, DI, JC, MC, VI.

HORSEHEADS pop. 6,800—See also FINGER LAKES.

—— LODGINGS ——

HOLIDAY INN
Phone: (607)739-3681

◆◆◆	5/1-10/14	1P: $84-$105	2P: $84-$105	
Motor Inn	10/15-4/30	1P: $79-$84	2P: $79-$84	

Location: Jct SR 14, 17 and 328, exit 52 off SR 17. 2666 Corning Rd 14845. Fax: 607/796-6927. **Terms:** 3 day cancellation notice. **Facility:** 100 rooms. Convenient suburban location, with easy access to Corning, Elmira, and Watkins Glen. 2 stories; interior/exterior corridors; heated pool. **Cards:** AE, CB, DI, DS, JC, MC, VI.

MOTEL 6 HORSEHEADS - 1217
Phone: 607/739-2525

ⓐ	6/15-11/1	1P: $42-$52	2P: $48-$58	XP: $3	F17
◆◆	5/1-6/14 & 11/2-4/30	1P: $38-$48	2P: $44-$54	XP: $3	F17

Motel

Location: S side of Hwy 17, 0.5 mi w of jct Rt 17 and 13. 4133 Rt 17 14845. Fax: 607/739-1051. **Terms:** Small pets only. **Facility:** 81 rooms. Nice rooms in a light commercial area. 2 stories; interior/exterior corridors. **All Rooms:** combo or shower baths, extended cable TV. **Cards:** AE, CB, DI, DS, MC, VI.

HOUGHTON pop. 1,700

—— LODGING ——

THE INN AT HOUGHTON CREEK
Phone: 716/567-8400

◆◆◆	All Year	1P: $54-$59	2P: $64	XP: $5	F12

Motel

Location: 3 mi n from jct SR 19A and 243. 9722 Genesee St 14744-8773. Fax: 716/567-4842. **Facility:** 17 rooms. Large rooms with distinctive country elegance. Offers many upgraded amenities. Office closed 11 pm-7 am. 2 stories; interior corridors; smoke free premises. **All Rooms:** combo or shower baths. **Cards:** AE, DS, MC, VI.

HOWES CAVE pop. 200

—— LODGING ——

HOWE CAVERNS MOTEL
Phone: 518-296-8950

ⓐ	7/1-9/4	1P: $78-$100	2P: $78-$100	XP: $10	
	5/1-6/30, 9/5-10/29 & 4/15-4/30	1P: $68-$90	2P: $68-$90	XP: $10	

Motor Inn

Location: I-88, exit 22, 1.2 mi e on Rt 7, 1.3 mi n on CR 8, then e follow signs. Howe Caverns Rd 12092 (Box 107). Fax: 518/296-8992. **Terms:** Open 5/1-10/29 & 4/15-4/30. **Facility:** 21 rooms. Modest guest rooms. Panoramic view. 2 two-bedroom units. Suites, $99-$125; 1 story; exterior corridors. **Dining:** Restaurant; 7:30 am-8 pm; Fri from 4 pm, Sat from 7 am & Sun 7 am-6 pm 9/1-10/26 & 4/15-6/30; $5-$13; cocktails. **Recreation:** Fee: horseback riding, cavern tours, gem stone mining. **All Rooms:** combo or shower baths. **Cards:** DS, MC, VI.

HUDSON pop. 8,000

------ LODGING ------

ST. CHARLES HOTEL
◆◆◆ All Year 1P: $79-$109 2P: $79-$109 XP: $10 F1
Historic Hotel **Location:** Center; on SR 9 (Park Pl), n of jct SR 9G. 16-18 Park Pl 12534. **Fax:** 518/822-0835. **Terms:** [C
meal plan; check-in 4 pm; package plans; pets, $50 dep req. **Facility:** 34 rooms. Recently restored 1868 hot
3 stories; interior corridors. **All Rooms:** combo or shower baths, safes. **Cards:** AE, CB, DI, DS, MC, VI.
Phone: (518)822-990

HUNTER pop. 400

------ LODGINGS ------

HUNTER INN
◆◆◆ 11/24-4/10 1P: $80-$195 2P: $80-$195 XP: $20 F1
Country Inn 6/30-11/23 1P: $80-$125 2P: $80-$125 XP: $10 F1
Location: On Rt 23A. Rt 23A 12442 (PO Box 355). **Fax:** 518/263-3981. **Terms:** Open 6/30-4/10; [ECP] me
plan; 14 day cancellation notice; cancellation fee imposed; package plans; pets, $50 extra charge. **Facility:** 40 rooms. Chal
style building. Close to Hunter Mountain. Some rooms with view of mountain. All rooms with ski racks. 3 stories, no elevato
interior corridors; designated smoking area. **Cards:** AE, DS, MC, VI.
Phone: (518)263-377

SCRIBNER HOLLOW LODGE
◆◆ 11/16-4/30 1P: $150-$250 2P: $200-$500 XP: $60 D1
Motor Inn 5/1-11/15 1P: $120-$200 2P: $160-$450
Location: 0.5 mi e. Rt 23A 12442. **Fax:** 518/263-5266. **Terms:** [MAP] meal plan; 14 day cancellation notic
30 for peak weekends; cancellation fee imposed; 2 night min stay, winter weekends; package plans; 10% service charg
Facility: 38 rooms. Closed 4/15-5/17 and open Thurs-Sun only 5/18-7/1 and 9/12-11/11. Advance reservation suggested. Va
riety of different room styles from modestly furnished to attractive fireplace lofts. 2-3 stories, no elevator; interior corridors;
heated pools; 1 tennis court. **Services:** area transportation. Fee: massage. **Recreation:** cross country skiing. **Cards:** AE, DS
MC, VI.
Phone: (518)263-421

------ RESTAURANT ------

TEQUILLA'S RESTAURANT
◆◆ **Location:** Center. Rt 23A 12442. **Hours:** 4 pm-11 pm; 5 pm-11 pm, Sat & Sun noon-11 pm 6/1-8/31. Close
Mexican 11/23 & Easter. **Reservations:** suggested. **Features:** casual dress; children's menu; carryout; cocktails
lounge; street parking; a la carte. The friendly, laid-back restaurant delivers an extensive menu of Tex-Mex
and Cajun specialties, as well as flavorful Texas barbecue and well-prepared fresh seafood. Service is prompt and pleasan
Homemade desserts satisfy your sweet tooth. **Cards:** AE, DS, MC, VI.
Dinner: $9-$13 **Phone:** 518/263-486

HUNTINGTON

------ RESTAURANT ------

**The following restaurant has not been inspected by AAA
but is listed for your information only.**

PANCHO VILLA'S
[fyi] Not inspected. **Location:** 331 New York Ave. **Features:** This attractive, inviting restaurant offers a variety
authentic Mexican dishes.
Phone: 631/549-002

HUNTINGTON STATION pop. 28,200

------ LODGINGS ------

HUNTINGTON COUNTRY INN
⬟ SAVE All Year 1P: $95-$115 2P: $95-$125
◆◆ **Location:** SR 25 (Jericho Tpke), just w of jct SR 110. 270 W Jericho Tpke 11746. **Fax:** 631/421-5287
Motel **Terms:** [CP] meal plan. **Facility:** 63 rooms. Cozy decor with thoughtful extras in rooms. 43 whirlpool rooms
$126-$135; 2 stories; interior/exterior corridors. **Dining:** Restaurant nearby. **All Rooms:** extended cable TV
Some Rooms: kitchen. **Cards:** AE, CB, DI, DS, MC, VI. **Special Amenities:** Free breakfast and preferre
room (subject to availability with advanced reservations).
Phone: (631)421-390

WHITMAN MOTOR LODGE
⬟ SAVE All Year 1P: $75-$125 2P: $75-$125 XP: $15 F1
◆ **Location:** On SR 25, 0.6 mi e of SR 110. 295 E Jericho Tpke 11746. **Fax:** 516/932-0308. **Terms:** Weekly rate
Motel avail. **Facility:** 44 rooms. Good budget accommodations featuring contemporary guest room decor. 1-2 stories
interior/exterior corridors. **All Rooms:** combo or shower baths, extended cable TV. **Some Rooms:** 13 efficien
cies, 2 kitchens. **Cards:** AE, CB, DI, DS, MC, VI.
Phone: (631)271-280

──── RESTAURANT ────

PANAMA HATTIE'S
♦♦♦
American

Dinner: $58   **Phone:** 631/351-1727

Location: Between SR 110 and Deer Park. 872 E Jericho Tpke 11746. **Hours:** 5:30 pm-10 pm. Closed: 12/25. **Reservations:** suggested. **Features:** dressy casual; health conscious menu items; cocktails & lounge; prix fixe. The three-course, prix fixe menu centers on eclectic cuisine, which is prepared with gourmet ingredients, as well as rare delicacies. Sophisticated dining rooms are appointed in the art deco style. Desserts are not only decadent, but also artful. Smoke free premises. **Cards:** AE, DI, DS, MC, VI.

HYDE PARK pop. 21,200

──── LODGINGS ────

GOLDEN MANOR MOTEL   **Phone:** 914-229-2157

7/1-8/31	1P: $40-$45	2P: $55-$65	XP: $10	F6
5/1-6/30 & 9/1-10/31	1P: $40-$45	2P: $45-$55	XP: $5	F6
11/1-4/30	1P: $35-$40	2P: $40-$45	XP: $5	F6

Motel   **Location:** US 9, 1.5 mi s of jct CR 41. 522 Albany Post Rd 12538. Fax: 914/229-6127. **Terms:** [CP] meal plan; weekly rates avail. **Facility:** 38 rooms. Modest to large size rooms. Rooms with 3 beds, $55-$65; 1 story; exterior corridors; designated smoking area; outdoor pool 5/30-9/7. **Services:** winter plug-ins. **All Rooms:** extended cable TV. **Some Rooms:** 4 efficiencies. **Cards:** AE, DS, MC, VI.

THE ROOSEVELT INN   **Phone:** 914-229-2443

5/1-10/31	1P: $53-$73	2P: $95	XP: $10	F17
11/1-4/30	1P: $43-$63	2P: $75	XP: $10	F17

Motel   **Location:** Center; on US 9, just s of jct CR 41. 616 Albany Post Rd 12538. Fax: 914/229-0026. **Terms:** Weekly rates avail, off season; 2 night min stay, weekends in summer. **Facility:** 26 rooms. Spacious and smaller, modest rooms with knotty pine interiors. 1 two-bedroom unit, $95; $75 off season for up to 4 persons; 1-2 stories; exterior corridors; designated smoking area. **Dining:** Coffee shop; 7-10 am 3/15-11/15. **All Rooms:** combo or shower baths, extended cable TV. **Cards:** AE, DS, MC, VI.

SUPER 8 MOTEL   **Phone:** (914)229-0088

All Year	1P: $49-$95	2P: $49-$110	XP: $8	F12

Motel   **Location:** On US 9, 1 mi s of jct CR 41. 528 Albany Post Rd 12538. Fax: 914/229-8088. **Terms:** [CP] meal plan; weekly rates avail, in winter; 7 day cancellation notice. **Facility:** 61 rooms. Set back on wooded grounds. Small guest rooms. 2 stories; interior corridors; designated smoking area. **All Rooms:** extended cable TV. **Some Rooms:** Fee: refrigerators, microwaves. **Cards:** AE, CB, DI, DS, MC, VI. **Special Amenities:** Free breakfast and free newspaper.

──── RESTAURANTS ────

AMERICAN BOUNTY
♦♦♦
Regional
American

Lunch: $16-$22   **Dinner:** $20-$25   **Phone:** 914/471-6608

Location: In Culinary Institute; 3 mi of Poughkeepsie on US 9. 433 Albany Post Rd (Rt 9) 12538-1499. **Hours:** 11:30 am-1 & 6:30-8:30 pm. Closed major holidays, Sun & Mon. **Reservations:** suggested. **Features:** dressy casual; cocktails & lounge. The menu—well complemented by an impressive selection of domestic wines and beers—brings to life the diversity of America's cultural heritage with regional specialties prepared from local ingredients. The atmosphere is refined and traditional. Smoke free premises. **Cards:** AE, DI, DS, MC, VI.

THE BRASS ANCHOR
♦♦
American

Lunch: $7-$10   **Dinner:** $14-$23   **Phone:** 914/452-3232

Location: 3.4 mi n of Poughkeepsie on Rt 9, just w on Riverpoint Rd, just s. 31 River Point Rd 12601. **Hours:** 11:30 am-10 pm; from 4 pm 11/1-2/28. Closed major holidays. **Reservations:** accepted. **Features:** casual dress; Sunday brunch; cocktails & lounge; a la carte. Green awnings decorate the front of the white, wood-sided building, while nautical decor brightens the dining room, which overlooks the Hudson River. The menu centers on seafood, with such choices as fried clams and fish and chips. Service is responsive. **Cards:** AE, DI, DS, MC, VI.

CATERINA DE MEDICI
♦♦♦
Regional
Italian

Lunch: $22   **Dinner:** $28   **Phone:** 914/471-6608

Location: 3 mi n of Poughkeepsie on US 9; in Culinary Institute. 433 Albany Post Rd (Rt 9) 12538-1499. **Hours:** 11:30 am-1 & 6:30-8:30 pm. Closed major holidays, Sat & Sun. **Reservations:** suggested. **Features:** dressy casual; beer & wine only. Fitting showcases for Italy's diverse culinary traditions, prix-fixe menus center on regional specialties. A broad selection of wines, beefs and aperitifs is available. Service in the warm, comfortable atmosphere is professional and attentive. Smoke free premises. **Cards:** AE, DI, DS, MC, VI.

COPPOLA'S ITALIAN AMERICAN BISTRO
♦♦
Italian

Lunch: $5-$18   **Dinner:** $5-$18   **Phone:** 914/229-9113

Location: On US 9, 1 mi s of jct CR 41. 535 Albany Post Rd 12538. **Hours:** 11:30 am-9:30 pm, Fri & Sat-10 pm, Sun-9 pm. Closed: 11/23 & 12/25. **Reservations:** suggested; for dinner. **Features:** casual dress; children's menu; early bird specials; carryout; cocktails & lounge; a la carte. Traditional preparations of American and Italian foods, including lots of pasta and pizzas, are well-presented and flavorful. The menu also offers a selection of lighter fare. The casual, laid-back atmosphere makes the restaurant a favorite of families. **Cards:** AE, DI, DS, MC, VI.

ESCOFFIER
♦♦♦
French

Lunch: $16-$22   **Dinner:** $20-$25   **Phone:** 914/471-6608

Location: 3 mi n of Poughkeepsie on US 9; in Culinary Institute. 433 Albany Post Rd (Rt 9) 12538-1499. **Hours:** 11:30 am-1 & 6:30-8:30 pm. Closed major holidays, Sun & Mon. **Reservations:** suggested. **Features:** dressy casual; cocktails; a la carte. The dining room exudes elegance with a contemporary flair. Such selections as the casserole of lamb, duck, white beans and sausage are complemented by a good selection of French wines. Tableside preparations enhance the memorable dining experience. Smoke free premises. **Cards:** AE, DI, MC, VI.

ST ANDREW'S CAFE   **Lunch:** $10-$12   **Dinner:** $15-$20   **Phone:** 914/471-6608
◆◆◆   **Location:** 3 mi n of Poughkeepsie on US 9; in Culinary Institute. 433 Albany Post Rd (Rt 9) 12538-1499.
American   **Hours:** 11:30 am-1 & 6:30-8:30 pm. Closed major holidays, Sat & Sun. **Reservations:** suggested.
          Features: casual dress; beer & wine only; a la carte. Exemplary of bold, flavorful fare is the wonderful grilled
salmon with lemon-infused whole-wheat couscous. The [0080] la carte menu lists healthfully prepared wood-fired pizzas,
vegetarian selections and grilled entrees. Service is professional. Smoke free premises. **Cards:** AE, DI, DS, MC, VI. ⊠

INDEX pop. 100—See also COOPERSTOWN.

—— RESTAURANT ——

THE 1819 HOUSE RESTAURANT & TAVERN Historical   **Dinner:** $11-$23   **Phone:** 607/547-1819
◆◆◆   **Location:** Just w of jct Rt 28 on CR 11. **Hours:** 5 pm-9 pm. Closed: 1/1, 12/25 & Sun.
Continental   **Reservations:** accepted. **Features:** children's menu; health conscious menu; cocktails & lounge. The
          unusual, historic setting welcomes diners to relax in casually sophisticated environment. Veal and seafood,
particularly fresh fish, stand out on a menu that also delivers a good array of lighter fare. Service is professional and
attentive. **Cards:** AE, MC, VI. ⊠

INLET pop. 300—See also ADIRONDACK MOUNTAINS.

—— LODGING ——

MARINA MOTEL   **Phone:** (315)357-3883
ⓐⓐⓐ   All Year   1P: $55-$75   2P: $55-$75   XP: $8   F5
◆◆   **Location:** Just s of SR 28. 6 S Shore Rd 13360 (PO Box 480). Fax: 315/357-5629. **Terms:** Weekly rates avail;
Motel   14 day cancellation notice; cancellation fee imposed. **Facility:** 16 rooms. On inlet between 4th and 5th lake,
          atop small hill over looking the village. May be closed 4/1-4/30 and 11/1-11/30, call ahead. 1 story; exterior cor-
ridors; within walking distance to beach. **Dining:** Restaurant nearby. **Recreation:** adjacent to cross country &
snow mobile trails, game room. **Cards:** AE, MC, VI.   ⊞ ⊠ ▣

ISLANDIA pop. 2,800

—— LODGING ——

HAMPTON INN   **Phone:** (631)234-0400
◆◆◆   All Year   1P: $129-$159   2P: $139-$169
Motel   **Location:** I-495, exit 57, just e on S Service Rd. 1600 Veterans Memorial Hwy 11722. Fax: 631/234-0415.
          Terms: [CP] meal plan; 3 day cancellation notice. **Facility:** 121 rooms. Guest rooms feature warm, contempo-
rary decor. 4 stories; interior corridors. **Services:** area transportation. **Some Rooms:** Fee: refrigerators, microwaves.
Cards: AE, CB, DI, DS, MC, VI.   ✈ ▤ ⌂ ⊠ ▣ ▤ ⊡ ▤ ⊟ ▨ ▨

ITHACA pop. 29,500—See also FINGER LAKES.

—— LODGINGS ——

COMFORT INN   **Phone:** (607)272-0100
ⓐⓐⓐ 〔SAVE〕   All Year   1P: $59-$145   2P: $69-$145   XP: $10   F18
◆◆   **Location:** SR 13, 1.5 mi sw of jct SR 96, 89 and 79. 356 Elmira Rd 14850. Fax: 607/272-2405. **Terms:** [CP]
Motel   meal plan; 7 day cancellation notice. **Facility:** 79 rooms. Nice rooms. In commercial area. 2 stories;
$119-$175; 2 stories; interior corridors. **Services:** winter plug-ins. **All Rooms:** extended cable TV. **Cards:** AE,
CB, DI, DS, JC, MC, VI. **Special Amenities:** Free breakfast and free local telephone calls.
          〔Sᴅ〕 ▨ ▤ ⌂ ⊠ ▣ ▤ ⊡ ⊟ ▨

HOLIDAY INN-EXECUTIVE TOWER   **Phone:** (607)272-1000
ⓐⓐⓐ 〔SAVE〕   5/1-11/19   1P: $99-$159   2P: $99-$159   XP: $10   F19
          4/1-4/30   1P: $99-$109   2P: $99-$109   XP: $10   F19
◆◆◆   11/20-3/31   1P: $79-$89   2P: $79-$89   XP: $10   F19
Motor Inn   **Location:** Just n from SR 96B. 222 S Cayuga St 14850. Fax: 607/277-1275. **Terms:** [BP] meal plan; weekly
          & monthly rates avail; 30 day cancellation notice; package plans; small pets only, $15 extra charge.
Facility: 178 rooms. Whirlpool room; 10 stories; interior/exterior corridors; heated pool. **Dining:** Dining room; 6:30 am-11 &
5-10 pm; $6-$14; cocktails. **Services:** area transportation, bus station; winter plug-ins. **Recreation:** Fee: video game room.
Some Rooms: Fee: refrigerators. **Cards:** AE, DI, DS, JC, MC, VI.
          〔Sᴅ〕 ✈ ⌂ ⊟ ⊻ ▨ ▧ ⊘ ⊠ ▣ ▤ ⊡ ⊟ 〔DATA PORT〕 ▨ ▨

LA TOURELLE COUNTRY INN   **Phone:** (607)273-2734
◆◆◆   All Year   1P: $79-$199   2P: $99-$299   XP: $10
Country Inn   **Location:** 3 mi s on SR 96B from Ithaca. 1150 Danby Rd 14850. Fax: 607/273-4821. **Terms:** Cancellation fee
          imposed; package plans; pets, $50 dep req, 2 pet maximum. **Facility:** 36 rooms. Enticing building on Southern
hill overlooking Cayuga Lake. 1-3 stories, no elevator; interior corridors; 4 tennis courts (2 lighted). **Recreation:** fishing.
All Rooms: combo or shower baths, safes. **Cards:** AE, DI, MC, VI.
          〔ASK〕 〔Sᴅ〕 ⌂ ⊟ ⊻ ▤ ⊠ 〔VCR〕 ▤ ⊡ ⊟ ⊟ ⊠

MEADOW COURT INN
Phone: (607)273-3885

6/2-11/15	1P: $75-$125	2P: $85-$150	XP: $5	F12
5/1-6/1	1P: $50-$95	2P: $60-$125	XP: $5	F12
11/16-4/30	1P: $45-$75	2P: $50-$85	XP: $5	F12

Motor Inn   **Location:** 1.5 mi s on SR 13 and 96. 529 S Meadow St 14850. Fax: 607/277-0758. **Terms:** Weekly & monthly rates avail; cancellation fee imposed; pets, $100 dep req. **Facility:** 60 rooms. Modest rooms. In commercial area. 6 three-bedded rooms, $75; whirlpool room, $99-$275; 1-2 stories; interior/exterior corridors. **Dining:** Restaurant; 7 am-9 pm, Sat from 5 pm, closed Sun; $8-$15; cocktails. **All Rooms:** combo or shower baths, extended cable TV. **Some Rooms:** Fee: parking; refrigerators, microwaves, VCR. **Cards:** AE, DI, DS, MC, VI.

PEREGRINE HOUSE VICTORIAN INN
Phone: 607-272-0919

Property failed to provide current rates

Historic Bed & Breakfast   **Location:** Just n of jct SR 79 and 366; just s of Cornell University. 140 College Ave 14850. Fax: 607-272-0919. **Terms:** [BP] meal plan; check-in 4 pm. **Facility:** 8 rooms. 1874 Victorian house, some modest sized rooms. 3 stories, no elevator; interior corridors; designated smoking area. **Cards:** DS, MC, VI.

THE STATLER HOTEL
Phone: (607)257-2500

1/5-4/30	1P: $149-$159	2P: $149-$159	XP: $10
5/1-12/20	1P: $139-$149	2P: $139-$149	XP: $10

Hotel   **Location:** On the campus of Cornell University. 11 East Ave 14853. Fax: 607/257-6432. **Terms:** Open 5/1-12/20 & 1/5-4/30; package plans. **Facility:** 150 rooms. Many staff members are students at the School of Hotel Administration. Closed Thanksgiving weekend. 9 stories; interior corridors; 2 heated pools; racquetball courts, 24 tennis courts (12 indoor). Fee: parking; 18 holes golf. **Services:** gift shop; area transportation. **Recreation:** jogging. **All Rooms:** combo or shower baths. **Some Rooms:** safes. Fee: refrigerators, VCR. **Cards:** AE, CB, DI, DS, MC, VI.

SUPER 8 MOTEL
Phone: (607)273-8088

5/1-11/30	1P: $56-$90	2P: $62-$90	XP: $6	F12
4/1-4/30	1P: $52-$90	2P: $58-$90	XP: $6	F12
12/1-3/31	1P: $46-$80	2P: $54-$80	XP: $6	F12

Motor   **Location:** Just s of jct SR 96B and 13. 400 S Meadow St 14850. Fax: 607/273-4832. **Terms:** 90 day cancellation notice. **Facility:** 63 rooms. Nice rooms in close proximity to downtown and commercial areas. 2 stories; interior corridors. **Cards:** AE, DI, DS, MC, VI.

RESTAURANTS

CHEF YEPPI PRESENTS
Lunch: $6-$14   **Dinner:** $13-$24   **Phone:** 607-272-6484

American   **Location:** On SR 13, 2 mi s of town. 919 Elmira Rd 14850. **Hours:** 11:30 am-3:30 & 4:30-9:30 pm, Sat 4:30 pm-9:30 pm. Closed: 12/25. **Reservations:** suggested. **Features:** casual dress; Sunday brunch; children's menu; early bird specials; cocktails & lounge. Hardwood floors, hanging Tiffany-style lights, artwork and shades of green decorate the comfortable, Victorian-feel dining room. Menu offerings, such as the wonderful wild mushroom soup, are well-prepared and flavorful. Servers are knowledgeable. **Cards:** AE, DI, DS, MC, VI.

GLENWOOD PINES
Lunch: $3-$16   **Dinner:** $4-$16   **Phone:** 607-273-3709

American   **Location:** 2 mi n on SR 89. 1213 Taughannock Blvd 14850. **Hours:** 11 am-11 pm, Fri & Sat-midnight. Closed major holidays & 4/4. **Features:** No A/C; casual dress; children's menu; carryout; cocktails & lounge. Perched atop a slope overlooking Cayuga Lake, the restaurant caters to families. Tasty food—which is reasonably priced—is traditionally prepared with simple ingredients. Casually dressed servers capably handle the generally busy business. **Cards:** DS, MC, VI.

JOE'S RESTAURANT
Dinner: $8-$18   **Phone:** 607-273-2693

Italian   **Location:** SR 13 and Buffalo St. 602 W Buffalo St 14850. **Hours:** 4 pm-10 pm, Fri & Sat-11 pm. Closed: 1/1, 11/23 & 12/25. **Features:** dressy casual; children's menu; health conscious menu items; carryout; cocktails & lounge. A local tradition since 1932, the restaurant offers a crisp but casual atmosphere with a stylish 1950s decor. The place is usually crowded—and with good reason—so phone ahead to be placed on a "table list" to minimize the wait. Pasta portions are huge. Smoke free premises. **Cards:** AE, DI, DS, MC, VI.

JOHN THOMAS STEAKHOUSE
Dinner: $13-$27   **Phone:** 607-273-3464

American   **Location:** 3 mi s on SR 96B; from Ithaca; next to La Tourelle Country Inn. 1152 Danby Rd 14850. **Hours:** 5:30 pm-10 pm, Fri & Sat-11 pm. Closed major holidays. **Reservations:** required; college events. **Features:** dressy casual; cocktails; a la carte. Prime, dry-aged beef-such as the specialty porterhouse steak for two-and fresh seafood are what the restaurant is all about. The mid-1800s farmhouse has beamed ceilings and wide-plank floors. An extensive selection of wines provides a fitting complement. **Cards:** AE, DI, MC, VI.

MANOS DINER
Lunch: $5-$14   **Dinner:** $5-$14   **Phone:** 607-273-1173

American   **Location:** SR 13 S. 357 Elmira Rd 14850. **Hours:** 24 hrs. Closed: 12/25. **Features:** casual dress; children's menu; carryout; cocktail lounge. Good, old comfort foods are at the heart of the restaurant's menu. You can order breakfast at any time, or enjoy Manhattan open-faced sandwiches, steak, seafood, chicken, chops, pasta and pizza, all of which are served in generous portions. **Cards:** AE, MC, VI.

MOOSEWOOD RESTAURANT
Lunch: $5-$6   **Dinner:** $10-$13   **Phone:** 607-273-9610

American   **Location:** Downtown; in Dewitt Mall (old Ithaca High School). 215 N Cayuga St 14850. **Hours:** 11:30 am-2 & 5:30-8:30 pm; later hrs in summer. Closed: 1/1, 12/25 & closed for lunch on Sun. **Features:** casual dress; health conscious menu items; carryout; cocktails & lounge; fee for parking. Acclaimed as a driving force in the world of creative vegetarian cooking, the restaurant delivers an innovative, daily-changing menu that draws on many inspirations, ranging from regional American to many ethnicities. The atmosphere is casual and relaxed. Smoke free premises. **Cards:** MC, VI.

RENEE'S
◆◆◆
American
Dinner: $16-$26
Phone: 607/272-0656
Location: 1 mi n on N Tioga St, at corner of E Falls and N Tioga. 202 E Falls St 14850. **Hours:** 5:30 pm-10 pm. Closed major holidays & Sun. **Reservations:** suggested. **Features:** dressy casual; carryout; beer & wine only. The crisp, upscale bistro delivers a limited, frequently changing menu of gourmet cuisine, which is creatively prepared with only the freshest ingredients. Plate presentation is attractive, and flavors are memorable. Homemade desserts are worth the wait. Smoke free premises. **Cards:** AE, CB, DI, MC, VI.

THE STATION RESTAURANT Historical
AAA
◆◆
American
Dinner: $11-$22
Phone: 607/272-2609
Location: Just w, off SR 79 and 89, 0.3 mi w of SR 13. 806 W Buffalo St 14850. **Hours:** 4 pm-9 pm, Sat-9:30 pm, Sun noon-8 pm. Closed: Mon in fall and winter. **Reservations:** accepted. **Features:** casual dress; children's menu; early bird specials; salad bar; cocktails & lounge. The converted, late-19th-century railroad station and railroad cars provide a fun setting in which for families to enjoy delicious food and nice views of Cayuga Lake. Menu offerings include well-prepared specialties of beef, seafood and pasta.
Cards: DS, MC, VI.

THAI CUISINE
◆◆
Ethnic
Dinner: $9-$20
Phone: 607/273-2031
Location: 1.5 mi s on SR 13 and 96. 501 S Meadow St 14850. **Hours:** 5 pm-9:30 pm, Fri-10 pm, Sat 11:30 am-2:30 & 5-11 pm, Sun 11:30 am-2 & 5-9:30 pm. Closed: Tues. **Reservations:** suggested. **Features:** casual dress; Sunday brunch; carryout; beer & wine only. Authentic Thai cuisine—including many preparations of beef, chicken, pork and seafood—is made from traditional recipes. Dishes are seasoned to suit your tastes, from mild to piquant to hot. Casual servers exhibit good menu knowledge. Smoke free premises. **Cards:** AE, DI, DS, MC, VI.

JAMAICA —See New York p. 372.

JAMESTOWN pop. 34,700

──── **LODGINGS** ────

THE COLONY MOTEL
AAA
◆
Motor Inn
All Year
Phone: 716/488-1904
1P: $45-$55　　2P: $45-$65　　XP: $5
Location: On SR 394, 2 mi w of jct SR 60. 620 Fairmount Ave 14701. **Terms:** 3 day cancellation notice. **Facility:** 45 rooms. Compact to larger rooms; all with vintage decors. 5 two-bedroom units. 2 stories; interior/exterior corridors; heated pool. **Dining:** Restaurant; 7 am-10 & 5-9 pm, Sat & Sun 7:30 am-10:30 am; $5-$13; cocktails. **All Rooms:** combo or shower baths, extended cable TV. **Cards:** AE, CB, DI, DS, JC, MC, VI.

COMFORT INN
AAA SAVE
◆◆◆
Motel
5/15-9/4	1P: $99-$149	2P: $99-$149	XP: $10 F18
9/5-10/29	1P: $79-$129	2P: $79-$129	XP: $10 F18
5/1-5/14 & 10/30-4/30	1P: $69-$129	2P: $69-$129	XP: $10 F18

Phone: (716)664-5920
Location: SR 17, exit 12 (SR 60). 2800 N Main St Extension 14701. Fax: 716/664-3068. **Terms:** [CP] meal plan; package plans; small pets only, in designated rooms. **Facility:** 101 rooms. 6 whirlpool rooms; 2 stories; interior corridors. **Dining:** Cocktails; restaurant nearby. **All Rooms:** extended cable TV. **Cards:** AE, CB, DI, DS, JC, MC, VI.
(See ad below)

HOLIDAY INN
AAA SAVE
◆◆◆
Hotel
7/1-9/1	1P: $99	2P: $99	XP: $10 F18
5/1-6/30	1P: $69	2P: $69	XP: $10 F18
9/2-4/30	1P: $59	2P: $59	XP: $10 F18

Phone: (716)664-3400
Location: Center; 2 mi s of SR 17, exit 12, on SR 60. 150 W 4th St 14701. Fax: 716/484-3304. **Terms:** Package plans. **Facility:** 146 rooms. Average sized rooms with varied decor treatments. 8 stories; interior corridors; heated pool. **Dining:** Restaurant; 6:30 am-2 & 5:30-10 pm; $9-$17; cocktails. **All Rooms:** combo or shower baths, extended cable TV. **Some Rooms:** Fee: refrigerators. **Cards:** AE, CB, DI, DS, JC, MC, VI.

——— RESTAURANTS ———

IRONSTONE RESTAURANT **Lunch:** $4-$8 **Dinner:** $10-$18 **Phone:** 716/487-1516
◆◆ **Location:** 0.5 mi w, off SR 60. 516 W 4th St 14701. **Hours:** 11:30 am-9 pm, Sat from 5 pm; closing hrs may
teak and vary. Closed major holidays & Sun. **Reservations:** suggested; weekends. **Features:** casual dress; health
eafood conscious menu items; cocktails & lounge. Mahogany accents, pretty chandeliers and assorted statues add
to the charm of the quiet restaurant and its open-air courtyard. The menu—which delivers everything from
teaks and seafood to pasta and veal—reflects international influences. **Cards:** AE, DI, DS, MC, VI. ⊠

MACDUFF'S **Dinner:** $17-$26 **Phone:** 716/664-9414
◆◆◆ **Location:** Downtown; just e of Rt 60, at 4th and Pine. 317 Pine St 14701. **Hours:** 5:30 pm-10 pm. Closed
Continental major holidays, 12/24 & Sun. **Reservations:** suggested. **Features:** dressy casual; health conscious menu
items; cocktails & lounge. The intimate restaurant boasts a sophisticated verbal menu that changes nightly.
ersonal service and comfortable surroundings add to the dining experience. Save room for the splendid orange ice cream
with bittersweet chocolate bits in a chocolate shell. **Cards:** AE, MC, VI. ⊠

JAMESVILLE pop. 700   (See map p. 478; index p. 477)

——— RESTAURANT ———

GLEN LOCH RESTAURANT Historical **Dinner:** $11-$20 **Phone:** 315/469-6969 (24)
AAA **Location:** I-481, exit 2, 1.4 mi s. 4626 North St 13078. **Hours:** 5 pm-10 pm, Sun 10 am-9 pm. Closed:
◆◆◆ 12/24, 12/25 & Mon. **Reservations:** suggested. **Features:** Sunday brunch; children's menu;
ontinental carryout; cocktails & lounge. Since the early 1970s, succulent prime rib has been the specialty at the rustic
and laid-back restaurant, which was built in 1827 and overlooks a lovely creek. For dessert, savor the
exquisite torte, which is served warm with vanilla bean ice cream. **Cards:** AE, DS, MC, VI. ⊠

JOHNSON CITY pop. 16,900

——— LODGINGS ———

BEST INNS & SUITES **Phone:** (607)770-9333
◆◆ All Year 1P: $43-$80 2P: $52-$125 XP: $8 F18
otel **Location:** 0.3 mi n of SR 17, exit 70 N; opposite Oakdale Mall. 581 Harry L Dr 13790. **Fax:** 607/770-7526.
Terms: [CP] meal plan. **Facility:** 61 rooms. Spacious nicely decorated rooms in convenient commercial loca-
on. 4 stories; interior corridors. **Some Rooms:** Fee: refrigerators, microwaves. **Cards:** AE, CB, DI, DS, JC, MC, VI.

BEST WESTERN OF JOHNSON CITY **Phone:** (607)729-9194
AAA SAVE All Year 1P: $54-$63 2P: $55-$67 XP: $10 F12
◆◆◆ **Location:** 0.3 mi n of SR 17, exit 70 N; opposite Oakdale Mall. 569 Harry L Dr 13790. **Fax:** 607/729-3205.
otel **Terms:** [ECP] meal plan; weekly & monthly rates avail; pets, $20 extra charge. **Facility:** 102 rooms. Located
in a convenient commercial area. 4 stories; interior corridors; pool privileges at adjacent Court Jester Athletic
Club. **Dining:** Restaurant nearby. **Services:** winter plug-ins. **Recreation:** Fee: off site fitness/exercise facility.
All **Rooms:** extended cable TV. **Some Rooms:** Fee: refrigerators, microwaves, VCR. **Cards:** AE, CB, DI, DS, JC, MC, VI.
Special Amenities: Free breakfast and free local telephone calls.

HAMPTON INN **Phone:** (607)729-9125
◆◆◆ All Year 1P: $72-$80 2P: $76-$86
otel **Location:** SR 17, exit 70 N. 630 Field St 13790. **Fax:** 607/729-9816. **Terms:** [ECP] meal plan; cancellation fee
imposed. **Facility:** 64 rooms. Busy commercial intersection; new construction behind Wegman's Supermarket.
stories; interior corridors. **All Rooms:** combo or shower baths. **Cards:** AE, CB, DI, DS, MC, VI.

RED ROOF INN-BINGHAMTON **Phone:** (607)729-8940
AAA 7/1-12/31 1P: $56-$66 2P: $63-$73 XP: $7 F18
◆◆ 5/1-6/30 1P: $50-$56 2P: $57-$63 XP: $7 F18
otel 1/1-4/30 1P: $46-$50 2P: $53-$57 XP: $7 F18
Location: 0.3 mi n of SR 17, exit 70 N. 590 Fairview St 13790. **Fax:** 607/729-8949. **Terms:** Pets. **Facility:** 107
rooms. Convenient suburban location, near Oakdale Mall. 2 stories; exterior corridors. **Dining:** Restaurant
nearby. **All Rooms:** extended cable TV. **Some Rooms:** Fee: microwaves. **Cards:** AE, CB, DI, DS, MC, VI.

——— RESTAURANTS ———

CHRISTIE'S GRILL **Lunch:** $5-$8 **Dinner:** $9-$17 **Phone:** 607/729-3100
◆◆ **Location:** SR 17, exit 70 N; in Giant Plaza. 560 Harry L Dr 13790. **Hours:** 11 am-11 pm, Fri & Sat-midnight,
merican Sun 10 am-9 pm. Closed: 11/23 & 12/25. **Reservations:** accepted. **Features:** casual dress; Sunday brunch;
children's menu; early bird specials; health conscious menu items; carryout; cocktails & lounge. The menu
onsists largely of traditionally prepared soups, sandwiches and salads, with a handful of dinner entree items. Crayon paper
apes the tables, setting a decidedly relaxed atmosphere. Casually attired servers are competent and friendly. **Cards:** AE,
I, DS, MC, VI. ⊠

DELGADO'S CAFE **Dinner:** $3-$11 **Phone:** 607/798-730
◆◆
Mexican **Location:** SR 17, exit 70 N, just n on Rt 201, 1.1 mi e. 119 Harry L Dr 13790. **Hours:** 3 pm-11 pm. Close
Sun. **Reservations:** accepted; parties of 5. **Features:** casual dress; early bird specials; carryout; cocktails
lounge; a la carte. Popular with the neighborhood crowd, the casual restaurant is a nice place to take th
family for good food. Although the menu centers on Mexican fare—burritos, enchiladas, tacos and nachos—you'll also find
number of traditional American choices. **Cards:** DI, DS, MC, VI.

POSSIBILITIES **Lunch:** $5-$14 **Dinner:** $7-$22 **Phone:** 607/729-908
◆◆
Continental **Location:** SR 17, exit 70 N, 0.5 mi e; in Small Mall. 365 Harry L Dr 13790. **Hours:** 11 am-midnight. Close
major holidays & Sun. **Reservations:** suggested; weekends. **Features:** casual dress; carryout; cocktails
lounge. The cozy dining room exudes the friendly ambience of a trendy bistro. Enticing selections incluc
such well-prepared dishes as curried clam chowder and salmon and lobster in puff pastry. The wine list includes numerou
by-the-glass choices. **Cards:** AE, DI, DS, MC, VI.

JOHNSTOWN pop. 9,100

—— LODGING ——

HOLIDAY INN **Phone:** 518/762-468
◆◆◆ Property failed to provide current rates
Motor Inn **Location:** 2 mi n on SR 30A. 308 N Comrie Ave 12095-1095. Fax: 518/762-4034. **Terms:** Package plans; pe
Facility: 100 rooms. Pleasant rooms. 2-3 stories, no elevator; interior/exterior corridors; heated poo
Services: winter plug-ins. **Some Rooms:** Fee: refrigerators, microwaves, VCR. **Cards:** AE, CB, DI, DS, MC, VI.

KINGSTON pop. 23,100

—— LODGING ——

HOLIDAY INN **Phone:** (914)338-040
(AAA) (SAVE) 8/1-10/31 & 1/1-4/30 1P: $119-$159 2P: $119-$159 XP: $10 F1
5/1-7/31 & 11/1-12/31 1P: $109-$139 2P: $109-$139 XP: $10 F1
◆◆◆ **Location:** I-87, exit 19, just e of traffic circle. 503 Washington Ave 12401. Fax: 914/340-1908. **Terms:** [B
Motor Inn meal plan; 2 night min stay, weekends 5/10-10/25; package plans; small pets only. **Facility:** 212 rooms. S
back from hwy. Holidome recreation area. Suites, $149; 2 stories; interior corridors; designated smoking are
heated pool, wading pool, sauna, whirlpool. **Dining:** Dining room; 6:30 am-2 & 5-10 pm; $9-$16; cocktails. **Recreation:** gan
room. **All Rooms:** extended cable TV. **Some Rooms:** Fee: refrigerators, VCR. **Cards:** AE, CB, DI, DS, JC, MC, VI.

—— RESTAURANTS ——

ARMADILLO BAR & GRILL **Lunch:** $6-$8 **Dinner:** $9-$14 **Phone:** 914/339-155
◆◆ **Location:** In Rondout Historic Region; just s of Broadway, 1.8 mi e of jct 587 and 28. 97 Abeel St 1240
Mexican **Hours:** 11:30 am-3 & 4:30-10:30 pm, Fri 5 pm-11:30 pm, Sat noon-3 & 5-11:30 pm, Sun noon-3 & 4-10 pr
closing hrs may vary in winter. Closed: 11/23, 12/25 & Mon. **Features:** casual dress; Sunday brunc
children's menu; carryout; cocktails & lounge; street parking. Soft colors decorate the dining room, where a wide array
regulars gather to enjoy Southwestern cuisine, particularly Tex-Mex specialties. Frozen margaritas and microbrewed beer
complement such selections as stuffed jalapenos and grilled tuna. **Cards:** AE, CB, DI, DS, MC, VI.

THE HOFFMAN HOUSE Historical **Lunch:** $7-$9 **Dinner:** $13-$19 **Phone:** 914/338-262
◆◆ **Location:** I-87, exit 19, 0.5 mi e on Washington Ave, left at bus station. 94 N Front St 12401. **Hours:** 11::
American am-10 pm, Fri & Sat-11 pm. Closed major holidays & Sun. **Reservations:** suggested. **Features:** casu
dress; children's menu; health conscious menu; cocktails & lounge; a la carte. The late-17th-century, Dut
rubble house exudes historic charm, with three fireplaces and lots of original woodwork. Representative of traditional fa
are fish and chips, as well as the Saturday special of prime rib with Yorkshire pudding. **Cards:** AE, CB, DI, DS, MC, VI.

ONTAUK HOUSE
♦◆
teak and
eafood

Dinner: $12-$22

Phone: 914/339-3474

Location: 0.8 mi n of jct W I-587 (Col George Chandler Dr). 395 Albany Ave 12401. **Hours:** 4 pm-10 pm, Sun noon-8 pm. Closed: 12/25 & Mon. **Reservations:** suggested. **Features:** casual dress; children's menu; early bird specials; carryout; cocktails. Near the scenic Catskills, the intimate restaurant has three dining rooms: one bright, one romantic and one rustic, with lots of wood and a fireplace. The menu centers on teak and fresh seafood. Much attention goes into delicious homemade desserts. **Cards:** AE, CB, DI, DS, MC, VI.   ⊠

LAKE GEORGE pop. 900—*See also ADIRONDACK MOUNTAINS.*

—— LODGINGS ——

DMIRAL MOTEL
Ⓐ
♦◆
otel

			Phone: (518)668-2097	
7/1-9/5	1P: $80-$95	2P: $80-$95	XP: $7	F10
5/1-6/30 & 9/6-10/23	1P: $55-$68	2P: $55-$68	XP: $7	F10

Location: Center; in village. 401 Canada St 12845. **Terms:** Open 5/1-10/23; weekly rates avail; 7 day cancellation notice; cancellation fee imposed; 2 night min stay, weekends in summer; package plans. **Facility:** 27 rooms. Pleasant rooms surrounded by attractively landscaped grounds. Emphasis on housekeeping. 2 stories; xterior corridors; heated pool. **Dining:** Restaurant nearby. **All Rooms:** combo or shower baths, extended cable TV. ards: AE, DS, MC, VI.

ALMORAL MOTEL
♦◆
otel

			Phone: (518)668-2673	
6/27-9/4	1P: $59-$89	2P: $79-$99	XP: $10	F16
5/1-6/26 & 9/5-4/30	1P: $39-$79	2P: $39-$79	XP: $10	F16

Location: 0.3 mi n on SR 9, at jct Rt 9 and 9 N. 444 Canada St 12845. Fax: 518/668-9248. **Terms:** 14 day ancellation notice; pets, $10 extra charge. **Facility:** 31 rooms. Variety of room styles ranging from compact to spacious. 2 tories; exterior corridors; heated pool. **Services:** area transportation. **All Rooms:** combo or shower baths. **Cards:** AE, DS, C, VI.

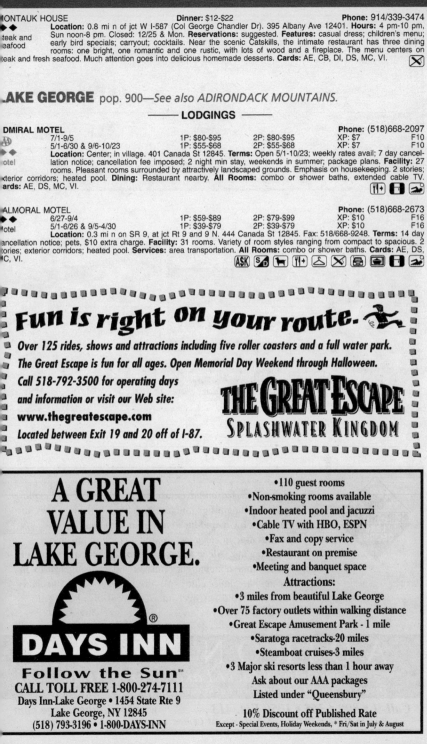

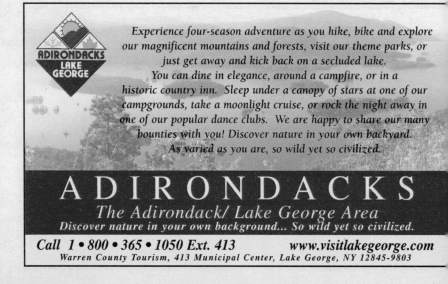

BEST WESTERN OF LAKE GEORGE

AAA SAVE
Motel

Phone: (518)668-5701

6/23-9/3	1P: $99-$145	2P: $99-$145	XP: $15	F12
9/4-10/8	1P: $79-$99	2P: $79-$99	XP: $15	F12
5/1-6/22 & 10/9-4/30	1P: $65-$91	2P: $65-$91	XP: $15	F12

Location: I-87 Northway, exit 21. Luzerne Rd 12845 (50 Canada Street). Fax: 518/668-4926. **Terms:** [BP] meal plan; weekly rates avail; 3 day cancellation notice; cancellation fee imposed; package plans. **Facility:** 87 rooms. 1 three-bedroom unit, 7 two-bedroom units. Whirlpool room, $169-$289; suites, $139-$249; 2 stories; interior/exterior corridors; small heated indoor pool, wading pool, whirlpool. **Dining:** Restaurant nearby. **Services:** winter plug-ins. **All Rooms:** extended cable TV. **Some Rooms:** 3 efficiencies, kitchen. Fee: VCR. **Cards:** AE, CB, DI, DS, MC, VI. **Special Amenities:** Free room upgrade and preferred room (each subject to availability with advanced reservations).

COLONIAL MANOR MOTOR INN

AAA
◆◆
Motel

Phone: 518/668-4884

7/29-9/4	1P: $82-$160	2P: $82-$160	XP: $20	F12
6/30-7/28	1P: $68-$140	2P: $68-$140	XP: $20	F12
5/26-6/29 & 9/5-10/9	1P: $48-$85	2P: $48-$95	XP: $10	F12

Location: 0.5 mi s on US 9, 0.5 mi n on US 9 from I-87, exit 21. 2200 State Rt 9 12845 (Rt 9, Box 528). **Terms:** Open 5/26-10/9; weekly rates avail; 14 day cancellation notice; cancellation fee imposed. **Facility:** 44 rooms. Set back from main road on spacious grounds. Family oriented. Motel rooms and cottages. 1-2 stories; exterior corridors; heated pool, whirlpool; playground. **Dining:** Restaurant nearby. **All Rooms:** combo or shower baths, extended cable TV. **Cards:** AE, DS, MC, VI.

COL. WILLIAMS RESORT

AAA
◆◆
Motel

Phone: (518)668-5727

6/23-9/4	1P: $88-$130	2P: $88-$130	XP: $10	
5/25-6/22 & 9/5-9/10	1P: $68-$98	2P: $68-$98	XP: $10	

Location: 1.5 mi s on US 9, 0.5 mi s of I-87, exit 21. Rt 9 12845 (PO Box 268). Fax: 518/668-2996. **Terms:** Open 5/25-9/10; weekly rates avail; 14 day cancellation notice; cancellation fee imposed; 2 night min stay, 7/1-8/31. **Facility:** 43 rooms. Variety of room types ranging from compact to large, some plans. Spacious, very attractive grounds. 5 two-bedroom units. 16 one- & two-bedroom suites, $130-$180 in season; 1 story; interior/exterior corridors; smoke free premises; 2 heated pools, wading pool, sauna, whirlpools; playground. **Recreation:** exercise equipment, game room, lawn games. **All Rooms:** combo or shower baths, extended cable TV. **Cards:** AE, DS, MC, VI. *(See color ad below)*

CRESTHAVEN RESORT
Phone: 518/668-333

7/8-8/25 Wkly	2P: $840-$3000	XP: $25
6/17-7/7 Wkly	2P: $900-$2400	XP: $25
8/26-10/31 Dly	2P: $85-$395	XP: $25
5/1-6/16 Dly	2P: $80-$395	XP: $25

Complex

Location: 2 mi n on SR 9 N, 1 mi n of I-87, exit 22. 3210 Lake Shore Dr 12845. Fax: 518/668-0324
Terms: Open 5/1-10/31; weekly rates avail; 30 day cancellation notice; cancellation fee imposed; 3 night min stay, 6/24-9/? package plans. **Facility:** 48 rooms. Rustic duplex cabins and cottages, some with fireplace. Sprawling property located o Lake George. 29 two-bedroom housekeeping units weekly, $695-$1050 for up to 4 persons, 6/24-9/4. Some new 2-story lo units avail, extra charge; 1-2 stories; exterior corridors; designated smoking area; beach, heated pool, wading pool; pla ground. Fee: boat dock. **Dining:** Restaurant; 11 am-10 pm; Sat & Sun from 8 am 6/15-9/6; Wed-Fri 4 pm-10 pm; Sat & Sun am-10 pm, rest of year; $13-$20; cocktails. **Recreation:** swimming, fishing, rowboats. **All Rooms:** combo or shower baths extended cable TV. **Some Rooms:** 38 kitchens. **Cards:** MC, VI.

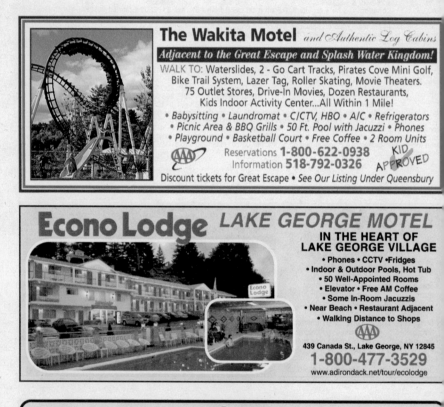

ECONO LODGE LAKE GEORGE MOTEL

Phone: (518)668-2689

6/30-9/3	1P: $89-$138	2P: $89-$138	XP: $10 F17
6/16-6/29	1P: $72-$101	2P: $72-$101	XP: $10 F17
5/1-6/15 & 9/4-10/31	1P: $46-$66	2P: $46-$66	XP: $10 F17

Motel

Location: 0.3 mi n on US 9 and SR 9 N. 0.3 mi s of I-87, exit 22; at jct US 9 and SR 9 N. 439 Canada St 12845. Fax: 518/798-3455. **Terms:** Open 5/1-10/31; weekly rates avail; 7 day cancellation notice; cancellation fee imposed; 3 night min stay, weekends 7/30-9/6. **Facility:** 50 rooms. Variety of room sizes ranging from compact to spacious; all with hair dryer. 2 whirlpool rooms, $108-$185; 2-3 stories; interior/exterior corridors; designated smoking area; 2 pools, 1 heated pools, 1 small heated indoor, whirlpool. **Recreation:** arcade games, pool table. **All Rooms:** combo or shower baths, extended cable TV. **Cards:** AE, DI, DS, MC, VI. **Special Amenities:** Free local telephone calls and preferred room (subject to availability with advanced reservations). (See color ad p 284)

FORT WILLIAM HENRY RESORT HOTEL & CONFERENCE CENTER

Phone: (518)668-3081

6/23-9/3	1P: $141-$189	2P: $141-$189	XP: $15 F12
9/4-10/8	1P: $89-$124	2P: $89-$124	XP: $15 F12
5/1-6/22	1P: $65-$124	2P: $65-$124	XP: $15 F12
10/9-4/30	1P: $69-$99	2P: $69-$99	XP: $15 F12

Historic
Resort

Location: 0.5 mi s on US 9 and SR 9 N, 1 mi n of I-87, exit 21. 48 Canada St 12845. Fax: 518/668-4926. **Terms:** [BP] meal plan; weekly rates avail; 3 day cancellation notice; cancellation fee imposed; 2 night min stay, weekends in season; package plans. **Facility:** 99 rooms. Open weekends, 4/1-4/30. Overlooking Lake George. 2 stories; interior/exterior corridors; designated smoking area; 2 pools, 1 indoor heated, sauna, whirlpool. Fee: miniature golf. **Dining:** 2 dining rooms, restaurant; 7 am-10 pm; $10-$17; cocktails. **Services:** gift shop. **Recreation:** Fee: bicycles, fort museum & movies. **All Rooms:** combo or shower baths, extended cable TV. **Some Rooms:** kitchen. **Cards:** AE, CB, DI, DS, MC, VI. **Special Amenities:** Free room upgrade and preferred room (each subject to availability with advanced reservations).

GENTLEMAN JOHNNY'S INN

Phone: 518/668-2096

7/1-9/5		2P: $55-$65	XP: $5
5/1-6/30 & 9/6-11/1		2P: $35-$45	XP: $5

Motel

Location: 1.5 mi n on SR 9 N, 0.5 mi n of I-87, exit 22. 3057 Lake Shore Dr 12845. Fax: 518/668-0168. **Terms:** Open 5/1-11/1; [CP] meal plan; 7 day cancellation notice, 30 day for housekeeping units; cancellation fee imposed. **Facility:** 17 rooms. Pleasant rooms, modestly furnished. 3 two-bedroom units. 4 housekeeping units, $455-$575 weekly in season for 2-4 persons; 1 story; exterior corridors; playground. **Dining:** Restaurant nearby. **Recreation:** grills, picnic tables. **All Rooms:** combo or shower baths, extended cable TV. **Some Rooms:** Fee: refrigerators. **Cards:** AE, DS, MC, VI.

THE GEORGIAN

Phone: (518)668-5401

6/24-9/4	1P: $129-$229	2P: $129-$229	XP: $10 F5
5/1-6/23 & 9/5-4/30	1P: $69-$169	2P: $69-$169	XP: $10 F5

Motor Inn

Location: Just n on Rt 9 and SR 9 N; 0.5 mi se of I-87 Northway, exit 22. 384 Canada St 12845. Fax: 518/668-5870. **Terms:** [BP] & [MAP] meal plans; weekly & monthly rates avail; 3 day cancellation notice; 2 night min stay, some weekends; package plans. **Facility:** 164 rooms. Located on Lake George. Variety of different room styles. 1 two-bedroom unit. Suites, $229-$329 for up to 2 persons; 31 whirlpool rooms; 1-3 stories; exterior corridors; beach, heated pool. **Dining:** Cocktails; dining room, see separate listing. **Recreation:** swimming. **All Rooms:** extended cable TV. **Cards:** AE, CB, DI, DS, MC, VI. (See color ad p 287)

GREEN HAVEN
◆◆
Motel

8/1-8/31	2P: $64-$114	XP: $10	D16
7/1-7/31	2P: $54-$109	XP: $10	D16
5/1-6/30 & 9/1-4/30	2P: $39-$89	XP: $10	D16

Phone: (518)668-2489

Location: 1.8 mi n on SR 9 N, 0.8 mi n of I-87, exit 22. 3136 Lake Shore Dr 12845. Fax: 518/668-2575. **Terms:** [CP] mea plan; 10 day cancellation notice; package plans; pets, off season. **Facility:** 20 rooms. Family oriented. Landscaped grounds Community room with kitchen use avail. 3 two-bedroom units. 1-2 stories; exterior corridors; playground. **All Rooms:** combo or shower baths. **Some Rooms:** efficiency. **Cards:** AE, CB, DI, DS, MC, VI.

(ASK) (S🅙) (⬆️🚭) (🐾) (✕) (🎥) (VCR) (⬛) (🖥️) (🗄️) (DATA PORT) (🏊) (✕)

HERITAGE OF LAKE GEORGE
ⒶⒶⒶ
◆◆
Motel

6/16-9/4	1P: $65-$140	2P: $65-$140	XP: $15	F16
5/12-6/15 & 9/5-10/15	1P: $45-$90	2P: $45-$90	XP: $15	F16

Phone: 518/668-3357

Location: 0.3 mi n on US 9 and SR 9 N, 0.3 mi s of I-87, exit 22. 419 Canada St 12845. Fax: 518/668-9784 **Terms:** Open 5/12-10/15; weekly rates avail; 14 day cancellation notice; cancellation fee imposed; 2 night mir stay, 7/1-8/31 weekends; package plans. **Facility:** 38 rooms. Variety of room styles. 1-2 stories; exterior corridors; designated smoking area; heated pool. **Dining:** Restaurant nearby. **Services:** area transportation, bus station **Recreation:** basketball, grills, picnic tables, shuffleboard. **All Rooms:** combo or shower baths, extended cable TV. **Cards:** AE DS, MC, VI.

(🚭) (✕) (⬛) (🖥️) (🗄️) (🏊)

Lake Haven Motel
Canada Street Lake George, NY (Exit 22-I-87)
518-668-2260
For Reservations Only 1-800-347-0543
• Two Time Beautification Award Winner •
A Modern Family Motel in the Heart of Lake George Village
All Rooms Include: • Color Cable TV Remote - Free HBO
• Refrigerators • Direct Dial Phones • Air Conditioning • Heat
• Outdoor Heated Pool • Adjacent Restaurant
• 300 ft. to Beach • Free Morning Coffee
• **Off Season + Group Rates Available**

★ Family oriented motel
★ Clean attractive motel and cottages
★ Located on five acres
★ Heated outdoor pool
★ Non-Efficiency Two Bedroom Cottages
★ Picnic-playground area with BBQ grills
★ Free in-room coffee
★ All units air conditioned
★ Remote control color cable TV

★ Telephones and refrigerators
★ No-smoking units
★ 500 yard walk to Great Escape
★ Great Escape discount tickets
★ Adjacent to Sutton's Marketplace & Cafe
★ Across from Pirate's Cove Miniature Golf & Go-Karts
★ Near several golf courses, bike trails, restaurants and factory outlet shopping

Three miles south of Lake George with trolley service directly in front of motel during season

1082 LAKE GEORGE ROAD • QUEENSBURY, NEW YORK 12804
Exit 19 or 20 off Interstate I-87
(518) 792-0223
See listing under Queensbury

Graycourt
MOTEL
ⒶⒶⒶ
"Your Home Away From Home"
...at affordable rates.

Minimum stay not required. Free local calls. Free room upgrade (subject to availability). All credit cards accepted

HOLIDAY INN TURF AT LAKE GEORGE
Phone: (518)668-5781

AAA SAVE

◆◆◆

Motor Inn

	5/26-10/15	1P: $84-$229	2P: $84-$229	XP: $10	F19
	10/16-4/30	1P: $84-$129	2P: $84-$129	XP: $10	F19
	5/1-5/25	1P: $84-$110	2P: $84-$110	XP: $10	F19

Location: 0.8 mi s on US 9 and SR 9 N; 0.8 mi n of I-87 Northway, exit 21. Canada St 12845 (Rt 9, Box 231). Fax: 518/668-9213. **Terms:** 3 day cancellation notice; package plans, 10/15-5/15. **Facility:** 105 rooms. Located on hill top, many rooms with view of the lake. 2 stories; interior corridors; miniature golf; 2 pools, 1 indoor heated, wading pool, sauna; playground. **Dining:** Restaurant; 6:30 am-2 & 5-10 pm; $10-$20; cocktails; dinner theatre Mon-Sat 6/18-10/16. **Services:** gift shop; winter plug-ins. **Recreation:** some exercise equip avail near pool. **All Rooms:** extended cable TV. **Cards:** AE, CB, DI, DS, JC, MC, VI. **Special Amenities:** Early check-in/late check-out and free newspaper.

INN ON THE HILL
Phone: (518)668-2572

◆◆

Motel

| | 6/30-9/3 | 1P: $65-$85 | 2P: $65-$85 | XP: $20 | F16 |
| | 5/25-6/29 & 9/4-10/10 | 1P: $50-$65 | 2P: $50-$65 | XP: $15 | F16 |

Location: 1 mi n on SR 9 N, just n of I-87, exit 22 to SR 9 N. 3007 Lake Shore Dr 12845. Fax: 518/668-3728. **Terms:** Open 5/25-10/10; 7 day cancellation notice; cancellation fee imposed. **Facility:** 20 rooms. Located on small hillside with view of Lake George. 2 two-bedroom units. 2 stories; exterior corridors; smoke free premises; heated pool. **Cards:** AE, MC, VI.

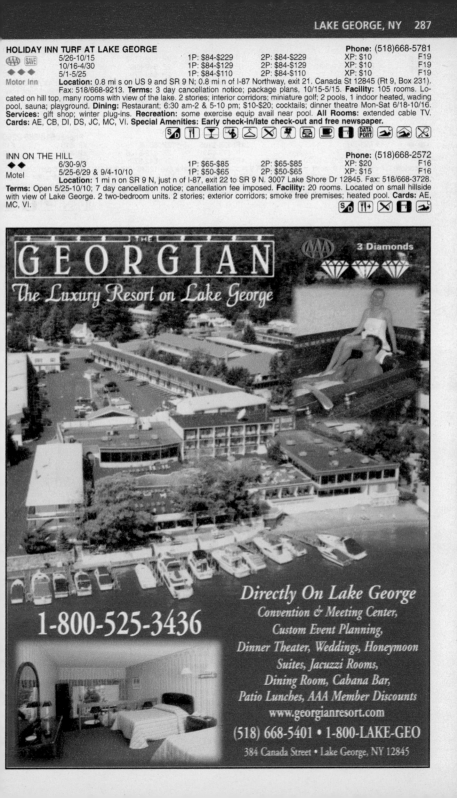

KNIGHT'S INN
◆◆
Motel

	6/23-9/4	1P: $89-$129	2P: $99-$139	XP: $10	F17
	5/1-6/22 & 9/5-10/9	1P: $49-$89	2P: $49-$99	XP: $10	F17
	10/10-4/30	1P: $45-$79	2P: $49-$79	XP: $10	F17

Phone: 518/668-2143

Location: Jct US 9 and SR 9 N, 0.3 mi s of I-87, exit 22. 435 Canada St 12845. Fax: 518/668-3025. **Terms:** 14 day cancellation notice. **Facility:** 39 rooms. Newest motel in town with well-kept rooms. 2 stories; exterior corridors; heated pool; playground. **Some Rooms:** Fee: refrigerators. **Cards:** DS, MC, VI.

LAKE HAVEN MOTEL
◆◆
Motel

	7/21-9/7	1P: $78-$105	2P: $85-$125	XP: $10	F12
	7/1-7/20	1P: $75-$98	2P: $78-$105	XP: $10	F12
	5/1-6/30 & 9/8-10/20	1P: $42-$70	2P: $42-$75	XP: $7	F12

Phone: 518/668-2260

Location: 0.4 mi n on SR 9, at jct of US 9 and SR 9 N. Canada St & Lake Ave 12845 (PO Box 581). **Terms:** Open 5/1-10/20; 10 day cancellation notice; cancellation fee imposed; 2 night min stay, Sat & Sun in season; package plans, off season. **Facility:** 31 rooms. Rooms range from small to large. 2 stories; exterior corridors; designated smoking area; heated pool. **Services:** area transportation. **All Rooms:** combo or shower baths. **Cards:** AE, MC, VI. *(See color ad p 286)*

Mohican Resort

A Family Resort Motel In The Beautiful Adirondacks

➤ **Indoor Heated Pool**
➤ Two Jacuzzis
➤ Outdoor Pool
➤ 2 Kiddie Pools
➤ Coffee Shop
➤ Sauna
➤ Extra Large Playground
➤ Game Room
➤ Basketball Court
➤ Picnic Area
➤ A/C and Heat
➤ Color TV, Cable & HBO
➤ Phones
➤ Microwave
   & Refrigerators

Enjoy all that Lake George has to offer . . .

Golf Courses
Biking & Hiking Trails
Lake George Boat Cruises
Outlet Mall Shopping
Amusement Parks
And Much Much More!!!

1545 State Route 9 • Lake George, NY • 12845-3438
Phone (518) 792-0474 • Fax (518) 761-4089

www.themohicanresort.com

TALL PINES MOTEL

Outstanding Pool Complex with Heated Pool, Jacuzzi, Slide and Kiddie Pool
Indoor Spa Pool and Sauna, In-room phones
Non-Smoking Rooms
Halfway Between Lake George Village and The Great Escape
Near the Factory Outlets

Large clean rooms with balconies, refrigerators, climate control, ceramic tile
baths with tub & shower, cable TV w/remote & telephones.

FOR RESERVATIONS OR FREE BROCHURE
Call 1-518-668-5122   8 AM-10 PM
P.O. Box 506 Lake George, NY 12845

LYN AIRE MOTEL

Phone: (518)668-4612

7/21-9/5	1P: $99-$139	2P: $99-$149	XP: $10 F12
6/23-7/20	1P: $79-$119	2P: $89-$129	XP: $10 F12
5/26-6/22	1P: $59-$99	2P: $69-$99	XP: $10 F12
9/6-10/10	1P: $59-$99	2P: $59-$99	XP: $10 F12

(AAA) [SAVE] ◆◆ Motel

Location: I-87, exit 21, 1 mi s. 1872 SR 9 12845. **Fax:** 518/668-5804. **Terms:** Open 5/26-10/10; 14 day cancellation notice; pets, pet on premises. **Facility:** 27 rooms. Pleasant rooms. Several buildings spread out on spacious grounds. 1 story; exterior corridors; heated pool, whirlpool; playground. **Recreation:** basketball, game pavilion, volleyball. **All Rooms:** combo or shower baths, extended cable TV. **Some Rooms:** Fee: microwaves. **Cards:** AE, DS, MC, VI. **Special Amenities:** Early check-in/late check-out and free local telephone calls. *(See color ad below)*

MARINE VILLAGE RESORT

Phone: (518)668-5478

7/21-9/3	1P: $113-$173	2P: $113-$173	XP: $10
6/23-7/20	1P: $99-$154	2P: $99-$154	XP: $10
5/1-6/22	1P: $70-$108	2P: $70-$108	XP: $10
9/4-10/31	1P: $56-$80	2P: $56-$80	XP: $10

(AAA) ◆◆ Motel

Location: On Lake George; in center of village, 0.5 mi s of I-87, exit 22. 370 Canada St 12845. **Fax:** 518/668-5546. **Terms:** Open 5/1-10/31; 7 day cancellation notice; cancellation fee imposed; 3 night min stay, some summer weekends. **Facility:** 100 rooms. All rooms with voice mail. Suites, $205-$215; 1-2 stories; exterior corridors; beach, heated pool. Fee: boat dock. **Dining:** Restaurant; 6:30-11 am; snack bar 11 am-5 pm seasonal. **Recreation:** swimming, fishing, rowboats; game room, grill, picnic tables, shuffleboard. Rental: paddleboats. **All Rooms:** extended cable TV. **Cards:** AE, CB, DI, DS, MC, VI. *(See color ad below)*

MOHAWK MOTEL & COTTAGES

◆◆
Motel

	6/23-9/4	1P: $89-$129	2P: $99-$139	XP: $10	F17
	5/1-6/22 & 9/5-10/9	1P: $49-$89	2P: $49-$99	XP: $10	F17
	10/10-4/30	1P: $45-$79	2P: $49-$79	XP: $10	F17

Phone: 518/668-2143

Location: Jct US 9 and SR 9 N, 0.3 mi s of I-87, exit 22. 435 Canada St 12845. Fax: 518/668-3025. **Terms:** 14 day cancellation notice, 21 day in housekeeping units; 3 night min stay, efficiencies. **Facility:** 23 rooms. Variety of different styles, from motel rooms to cabins, a few with fireplace. 4 two-bedroom units. 2 stories; exterior corridors; designated smoking area; heated pool; playground. **All Rooms:** combo or shower baths. **Some Rooms:** 5 efficiencies. Fee: refrigerators. **Cards:** DS, MC, VI. *(See color ad below)*

MOTEL MONTREAL

Phone: (518)668-5439

7/1-9/5	1P: $65-$89	2P: $65-$109	XP: $10	F15
6/2-6/30	1P: $49-$75	2P: $49-$85	XP: $10	F15
5/1-6/1 & 9/6-10/10	1P: $42-$75	2P: $42-$85	XP: $10	F15

Motel **Location:** 0.3 mi s of I-87, exit 22, just e on Lake Ave at jct US 9 and SR 9 N. 3 Lake Ave 12845. **Terms:** Open 5/1-10/10; weekly rates avail; 7 day cancellation notice; cancellation fee imposed; 3 night min stay, in 2-bedroom unit. **Facility:** 40 rooms. Excellent housekeeping. 1 two-bedroom unit, $145; $115 off season; 1-2 stories; exterior corridors; beach access, heated pool. **Dining:** Restaurant nearby. **Recreation:** grills, picnic tables, shuffleboard. **All Rooms:** combo or shower baths, extended cable TV. **Some Rooms:** kitchen. Fee: refrigerators. **Cards:** DS, MC, VI. **Special Amenities:** Free room upgrade and preferred room (each subject to availability with advanced reservations). *(See color ad p 292)*

NASSAU MOTEL

Phone: (518)668-5356

7/1-9/6	1P: $65-$85	2P: $75-$125	XP: $8	F12
5/1-6/30 & 9/7-4/30	1P: $50-$70	2P: $50-$75	XP: $8	F12

Motel **Location:** I-87, exit 21, 0.8 mi s. 1881 SR 9 12845. **Fax:** 518/668-3671. **Terms:** Weekly & monthly rates avail; 10 day cancellation notice. **Facility:** 21 rooms. Variety of room types ranging from modest cabins to a spacious 2-bedroom unit. 1 two-bedroom unit. 5 cabins, $40-$50; kitchenettes & 2-bedroom unit, $500-$650 weekly, daily rate avail; 1-2 stories; exterior corridors; playground. **Services:** winter plug-ins. **Recreation:** basketball, small video game room. **All Rooms:** combo or shower baths, extended cable TV. **Some Rooms:** 3 efficiencies, 6 kitchens. **Cards:** DS, MC, VI. **Special Amenities:** Preferred room (subject to availability with advanced reservations).

THE NOMAD MOTEL

Phone: (518)668-4697

7/1-9/4	2P: $52-$125	XP: $10	F12
5/1-6/30 & 9/5-10/15	2P: $42-$86	XP: $10	F12

Motel **Location:** Jct of US 9 and Birch Ave, 0.5 mi s. 2199 SR 9 12845-6124. **Fax:** 518/668-4697. **Terms:** Open 5/1-10/15; 7 day cancellation notice. **Facility:** 18 rooms. Very good housekeeping and maintenance. 1 story; exterior corridors. **Dining:** Restaurant nearby. **Services:** winter plug-ins. **Recreation:** grills, picnic tables. **All Rooms:** combo or shower baths, extended cable TV. **Cards:** AE, DI, MC, VI. **Special Amenities:** Free local telephone calls.

NORTHLAND MOTOR LODGE

Phone: (518)668-2470

5/26-9/15	1P: $45-$125	2P: $45-$125	XP: $10 F12
5/1-5/25 & 9/16-4/30	1P: $38-$85	2P: $38-$85	XP: $10 F12

(AAA) [SAVE]
◆◆
Motel

Location: 0.8 mi s. 2159 SR 9 12845 (PO Box 747). **Fax:** 518/668-4338. **Terms:** Weekly rates avail, in winter; cancellation fee imposed. **Facility:** 54 rooms. 1-2 stories; exterior corridors. **Dining:** Restaurant nearby. **Recreation:** small playground area, small barbecue area. **All Rooms:** extended cable TV. **Some Rooms:** 2 efficiencies. Fee: refrigerators. **Cards:** AE, CB, DI, DS, MC, VI.

ROARING BROOK RANCH & TENNIS RESORT

Phone: (518)668-5767

6/23-9/3	2P: $162-$172	XP: $50 D8
5/15-6/22 & 9/4-10/15	2P: $142-$152	XP: $50 D8

(AAA)
◆◆◆
Resort

Location: 2.5 mi s on SR 9 N; 1 mi w of I-87, exit 21. (Lake George 3, 12845). **Fax:** 518/668-4019. **Terms:** Open 5/15-10/15; [MAP] meal plan; weekly rates avail; 10 day cancellation notice; 2 night min stay; package plans. **Facility:** 136 rooms. Sprawling complex on spacious grounds in mountain setting. Family oriented atmosphere. Open weekends 2/1-2/28, $120. Suites for up to 2 persons. Rental mini-fridge avail; suites, $192-$212; 1-2 stories; interior/exterior corridors; designated smoking area; 3 pools, 1 indoor heated, saunas; 5 tennis courts (2 lighted), tennis clinic; playground. **Dining:** Dining room, coffee shop; 8 am-7:30 pm; cocktails; entertainment. **Services:** gift shop. Fee: massage. **Recreation:** children's counselor 7/1-8/31; hiking trails, archery, basketball, horseshoes, shuffleboard. Fee: horseback riding, riding instruction. **Some Rooms:** Fee: VCR. **Cards:** MC, VI. *(See color ad p 291)*

SURFSIDE ON THE LAKE

Phone: (518)668-2442

6/23-8/26	1P: $65-$75	2P: $85-$160	XP: $10 F12
8/27-9/3	1P: $55	2P: $65-$130	XP: $10 F12
5/1-6/22	1P: $45	2P: $49-$120	XP: $10 F12
9/4-11/5	1P: $43	2P: $45-$90	XP: $10 F12

(AAA)
◆◆
Motor Inn

Location: 0.3 mi n on US 9 and SR 9 N, 0.3 m s of I-87, exit 22. 400 Canada St 12845. **Fax:** 518/668-3202. **Terms:** Open 5/1-11/5; weekly rates avail; 10 day cancellation notice; cancellation fee imposed; 3 night min stay, some summer wknds; package plans. **Facility:** 143 rooms. Variety of rooms ranging from modest to spacious suites. Located on Lake George. 15 two-bedroom units. Efficiencies, suites with kitchenettes, $85-$215; 1-2 stories; interior/exterior corridors; designated smoking area; beach, heated pool; playground. **Dining:** Restaurant; 7:30-11 am 7/1-8/31; cocktails. **Recreation:** swimming; barbecue grills. **All Rooms:** combo or shower baths, extended cable TV. **Some Rooms:** 15 kitchens. **Cards:** AE, CB, DI, MC, VI. *(See color ad below)*

TALL PINES MOTEL   **Phone:** (518)668-5122
△△△ SAVE   6/23-9/4   1P: $85-$125   2P: $85-$125   XP: $10
            5/1-6/22   1P: $50-$70   2P: $50-$70   XP: $10
◆◆   9/5-10/20 & 4/1-4/30 1P: $50-$60   2P: $50-$60   XP: $10
Motel   **Location:** 2 mi s on US 9, 1.5 mi n of I-87, exit 20. 1747 SR 9 S 12845 (PO Box 506). **Terms:** Open 5/1-10/20
& 4/1-4/30; [CP] meal plan; 7 day cancellation notice; cancellation fee imposed. **Facility:** 26 rooms. Attractively
landscaped grounds. Well-maintained, comfortable rooms. 1-2 stories; exterior corridors; heated pool, wading pool, sauna,
whirlpools; basketball; playground. **Recreation:** picnic tables & gas grills. **All Rooms:** extended cable TV. **Cards:** DS, MC, VI.
Special Amenities: Free room upgrade and preferred room (each subject to availability with advanced reservations).
(See color ad p 288)   (icons)

WYANA MOTEL & CABINS   **Phone:** 518/668-4860
◆◆   5/10-9/20   1P: $70   2P: $70-$76   XP: $10   F17
Motel   **Location:** 0.8 mi n on SR 9 N from I-87, exit 22. 3142 Lake Shore Dr 12845. **Terms:** Open 5/10-9/20; 10 day
cancellation notice, 60 day in housekeeping units. **Facility:** 12 rooms. Housekeeping cottages and motel
rooms located on spacious grounds. Picnic tables and grills. 1 story; exterior corridors; playground. **All Rooms:** shower baths.
Cards: AE, MC, VI.   (icons)

——— **RESTAURANTS** ———

EAST COVE RESTAURANT   **Dinner:** $10-$24   **Phone:** 518/668-5265
△△△   **Location:** 0.8 mi e on US 9L. Rt 9L 12845. **Hours:** 5 pm-10 pm, Sun from 11 am. Closed: Mon & Tues
◆◆   11/1-4/30. **Reservations:** suggested. **Features:** casual dress; Sunday brunch; children's menu; early bird
American   specials; carryout; cocktails & lounge. Turn-of-the-20th-century photographs of Lake George decorate the
walls of the informal dining room, which has the atmosphere of a rustic log cabin. The menu delivers fresh
seafood, succulent steaks and traditional preparations of chicken and veal. **Cards:** AE, CB, DI, DS, MC, VI.
                                                                              (icon)

THE GEORGIAN DINING ROOM   **Lunch:** $6-$14   **Dinner:** $17-$24   **Phone:** 518/668-5401
◆◆   **Location:** 0.3 mi n on US 9 and SR 9 N; 0.5 mi se of I-87 Northway, exit 22; in The Georgian. 384 Canada
American   St 12845. **Hours:** Open 5/19-10/21; 7:30 am-10 pm; 7:30 am-1 & 5:30-9 pm, 5/19-7/1.
Reservations: suggested; in season. **Features:** dressy casual; children's menu; early bird specials; health
conscious menu; carryout; cocktails & lounge; a la carte. The attractive dining room—as well as the luncheon patio—
overlooks Lake George. In addition to tableside-carved chateaubriand and thick-cut prime rib, the restaurant serves tasty
breakfast selections. Entertainers perform on summer nights. **Cards:** AE, DI, DS, MC, VI.   (icon)

MARIO'S RESTAURANT   **Dinner:** $10-$18   **Phone:** 518/668-2665
△△△   **Location:** 0.3 mi n on US 9 and SR 9 N, 0.3 mi s of I-87 Northway, exit 22. 429 Canada St 12845.
◆◆   **Hours:** 3:30 pm-11 pm; also 8 am-noon, 7/1-8/31; 4:30 pm-11 pm, also Sun 1 pm-10 pm, 12/15-4/30.
Italian   **Closed:** 11/1-12/15, Tues & Wed 12/15-4/30. **Reservations:** suggested. **Features:** casual dress; children's
menu; carryout; cocktails & lounge; a la carte. Family-operated since 1954, the friendly neighborhood
restaurant serves a good variety of steak, chops, chicken, pasta, seafood and veal—all dished up in
generous portions. The laid-back mood is inviting to families. Servers are knowledgeable. **Cards:** AE, CB, DI, MC, VI. (icon)

SHORELINE RESTAURANT   **Lunch:** $8-$11   **Dinner:** $14-$20   **Phone:** 518/668-2875
◆◆   **Location:** Center, on lake at foot of Kurosaka Ln. 4 Kurosaka Ln 12845. **Hours:** 11 am-10 pm, Fri & Sat-11
American   pm, Sun 10 am-9 pm; hrs may vary slightly off season. **Closed:** 11/1-3/31. **Reservations:** suggested;
evenings. **Features:** casual dress; children's menu; health conscious menu; carryout; salad bar; cocktails &
lounge; minimum charge-$10. Overlooking the lake, the contemporary dining room is handsome and casual, while the
seasonal terrace is warm and breezy. Among oven-cooked and grilled entrees are inventive chicken selections. The Sunday
breakfast buffet is particularly popular. Smoke free premises. **Cards:** AE, DI, DS, MC, VI.   (icon)

TROLLEY STEAK & SEAFOOD   **Dinner:** $14-$18   **Phone:** 518/668-3165
◆◆   **Location:** US 9 and SR 9 N; 1 mi n of I-87 Northway, exit 21. 50 Canada St 12845. **Hours:** Open
Steak and   5/15-10/15; 5 pm-9 pm; to 10 pm 7/1-9/1. **Closed:** Mon, Tues & 5/15-6/22. **Reservations:** accepted.
Seafood   **Features:** casual dress; children's menu; carryout; cocktails & lounge. Quality ingredients go into such
delicious selections as French onion soup and stuffed sole. The muted decor comprises hardwood floors,
brick accent walls and black-and-white historic photographs of the area. Relax on the breezy, comfortable terrace.
Cards: AE, CB, DI, DS, MC, VI.   (icon)

LAKE LUZERNE pop. 2,800—*See also ADIRONDACK MOUNTAINS.*

——— **LODGINGS** ———

THE LAMPLIGHT INN BED & BREAKFAST   **Phone:** (518)696-5294
△△△   7/27-9/4   2P: $110-$225   XP: $25
            5/1-7/26 & 9/5-10/31   2P: $98-$189   XP: $25
◆◆◆   11/1-4/30   2P: $89-$179   XP: $25
Historic Bed **Location:** I-87, exit 21, 10.2 mi s on SR 9 N. 231 Lake Ave 12846 (PO Box 70). **Terms:** [BP] meal plan; age
& Breakfast restrictions may apply; 21 day cancellation notice; package plans. **Facility:** 15 rooms. Restored 1890's home.
Individually decorated rooms, some with fireplace. Owner pet on premises. Closed 12/24 & 12/25; 4 whirlpool
rooms, $165-$225; 1-2 stories; interior corridors; smoke free premises. **Dining:** Breakfast open to the public Sun 10:30 am-
12:30 pm; wine/beer only. **Services:** gift shop. **All Rooms:** combo or shower baths, extended cable TV. **Some Rooms:** color
TV. **Cards:** AE, MC, VI.   (icons)

LUZERNE COURT

Phone: 518/696-2734

AAA ◆ Motel

5/25-10/10 | 1P: $50-$65 | 2P: $65-$90 | XP: $10 | F12

Location: 1.1 mi ne on SR 9 N; from I-87, exit 21, 8.7 mi sw on Rt 9N. 508 Lake Ave 12846. **Fax:** 518/696-3204. **Terms:** Open 5/25-10/10; weekly rates avail; 14 day cancellation notice; 2 night min stay, weekends 7/1-8/31; pets. **Facility:** 10 rooms. 1 story; exterior corridors. **Dining:** Coffee shop; 7:30-11 am 7/1-8/31. **All Rooms:** combo or shower baths. **Some Rooms:** 2 efficiencies. Fee: refrigerators. **Cards:** AE, DS, MC, VI.

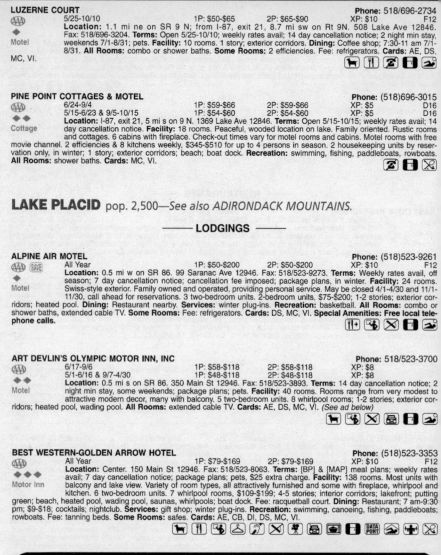

PINE POINT COTTAGES & MOTEL

Phone: (518)696-3015

AAA ◆ ◆ Cottage

6/24-9/4 | 1P: $59-$66 | 2P: $59-$66 | XP: $5 | D16
5/15-6/23 & 9/5-10/15 | 1P: $54-$60 | 2P: $54-$60 | XP: $5 | D16

Location: I-87, exit 21, 5 mi s on 9 N. 1369 Lake Ave 12846. **Terms:** Open 5/15-10/15; weekly rates avail; 14 day cancellation notice. **Facility:** 18 rooms. Peaceful, wooded location on lake. Family oriented. Rustic rooms and cottages. 6 cabins with fireplace. Check-out times vary for motel rooms and cabins. Motel rooms with free movie channel. 2 efficiencies & 8 kitchens weekly, $345-$510 for up to 4 persons in season. 2 housekeeping units by reservation only, in winter; 1 story; exterior corridors; beach; boat dock. **Recreation:** swimming, fishing, paddleboats, rowboats. **All Rooms:** shower baths. **Cards:** MC, VI.

LAKE PLACID pop. 2,500—*See also ADIRONDACK MOUNTAINS.*

———— LODGINGS ————

ALPINE AIR MOTEL

Phone: (518)523-9261

AAA SAVE ◆ Motel

All Year | 1P: $50-$200 | 2P: $50-$200 | XP: $10 | F12

Location: 0.5 mi w on SR 86. 99 Saranac Ave 12946. **Fax:** 518/523-9273. **Terms:** Weekly rates avail, off season; 7 day cancellation notice; cancellation fee imposed; package plans, in winter. **Facility:** 24 rooms. Swiss-style exterior. Family owned and operated, providing personal service. May be closed 4/1-4/30 and 11/1-11/30, call ahead for reservations. 3 two-bedroom units. 2-bedroom units, $75-$200; 1-2 stories; exterior corridors; heated pool. **Dining:** Restaurant nearby. **Services:** winter plug-ins. **Recreation:** basketball. **All Rooms:** combo or shower baths, extended cable TV. **Some Rooms:** Fee: refrigerators. **Cards:** DS, MC, VI. **Special Amenities:** Free local telephone calls.

ART DEVLIN'S OLYMPIC MOTOR INN, INC

Phone: 518/523-3700

AAA ◆ ◆ Motel

6/17-9/6 | 1P: $58-$118 | 2P: $58-$118 | XP: $8
5/1-6/16 & 9/7-4/30 | 1P: $48-$118 | 2P: $48-$118 | XP: $8

Location: 0.5 mi s on SR 86. 350 Main St 12946. **Fax:** 518/523-3893. **Terms:** 14 day cancellation notice; 2 night min stay, some weekends; package plans; pets. **Facility:** 40 rooms. Rooms range from very modest to attractive modern decor, many with balcony. 5 two-bedroom units. 8 whirlpool rooms; 1-2 stories; exterior corridors; heated pool, wading pool. **All Rooms:** extended cable TV. **Cards:** AE, DS, MC, VI. *(See ad below)*

BEST WESTERN-GOLDEN ARROW HOTEL

Phone: (518)523-3353

AAA ◆ ◆ ◆ Motor Inn

All Year | 1P: $79-$169 | 2P: $79-$169 | XP: $10 | F12

Location: Center. 150 Main St 12946. **Fax:** 518/523-8063. **Terms:** [BP] & [MAP] meal plans; weekly rates avail; 7 day cancellation notice; package plans; pets, $25 extra charge. **Facility:** 138 rooms. Most units with balcony and lake view. Variety of room types, all attractively furnished and some with fireplace, whirlpool and kitchen. 6 two-bedroom units. 7 whirlpool rooms, $109-$199; 4-5 stories; interior corridors; lakefront; putting green; beach, heated pool, wading pool, saunas, whirlpools; boat dock. Fee: racquetball court. **Dining:** Restaurant; 7 am-9:30 pm; $9-$18; cocktails; nightclub. **Services:** gift shop; winter plug-ins. **Recreation:** swimming, canoeing, fishing, paddleboats; rowboats. Fee: tanning beds. **Some Rooms:** safes. **Cards:** AE, CB, DI, DS, MC, VI.

ECONO LODGE
6/23-10/15
12/22-4/30
10/16-12/21
5/1-6/22
Motel

Phone: (518)523-2817

1P: $60-$100	2P: $60-$100	XP: $5	F18
1P: $50-$100	2P: $50-$100	XP: $5	F18
1P: $50-$80	2P: $50-$80	XP: $5	F18
1P: $50-$75	2P: $50-$75	XP: $5	F18

Location: 1 mi s on Rt 73. Cascade Rd 12946 (PO Box 527). Fax: 518/523-2817. **Terms:** 2 night min stay, some weekends. **Facility:** 61 rooms. 2 stories; interior/exterior corridors; heated pool, whirlpool. **Services:** winter plug-ins. **Recreation:** video game room. **All Rooms:** extended cable TV. **Some Rooms:** Fee: refrigerators. **Cards:** AE, CB, DI, DS, JC, MC, VI. **Special Amenities:** Free local telephone calls and free room upgrade (subject to availability with advanced reservations).

EDGE OF THE LAKE MOTEL
6/23-10/21 & 12/22-4/30
5/1-6/22 & 10/22-12/21
Motel

Phone: (518)523-9430

1P: $61-$100	2P: $69-$109	XP: $8	F12
1P: $39-$81	2P: $39-$89	XP: $8	F12

Location: 0.5 mi w on SR 86. 56 Saranac Ave 12946. Fax: 518/523-7886. **Terms:** Weekly rates avail; cancellation fee imposed; 2 night min stay, weekends in season; package plans; pets, $10 fee. **Facility:** 25 rooms. Small to large, well-furnished rooms. Family suite, $10 extra charge; 2-3 stories, no elevator; interior/exterior corridors; beach; playground. Fee: boat dock. **Dining:** Restaurant nearby. **Services:** winter plug-ins. **Recreation:** canoeing, paddleboats; rowboats. **All Rooms:** combo or shower baths, extended cable TV. **Some Rooms:** 9 efficiencies. Fee: refrigerators. **Cards:** AE, DS, MC, VI.

HILTON LAKE PLACID RESORT
7/1-9/4
9/5-12/31
5/1-6/30 & 1/1-4/30
Hotel

Phone: (518)523-4411

1P: $119-$199	2P: $119-$199	XP: $12	F18
1P: $89-$199	2P: $89-$199	XP: $12	F18
1P: $69-$199	2P: $79-$199	XP: $12	F18

Location: 0.3 mi w on SR 86. 1 Mirror Lake Dr 12946. Fax: 518/523-1120. **Terms:** 7 day cancellation notice; cancellation fee imposed; package plans; pets, $25 extra charge, $50 dep req. **Facility:** 179 rooms. Spacious rooms. Rooms located in 3 buildings, some lakeside, most with lake view. 2-5 stories; interior corridors; 4 heated pools, 2 indoor. **Recreation:** fishing, paddleboats. **Some Rooms:** Fee: refrigerators. **Cards:** AE, CB, DI, DS, MC, VI. *(See color ad p 297 & p 57)*

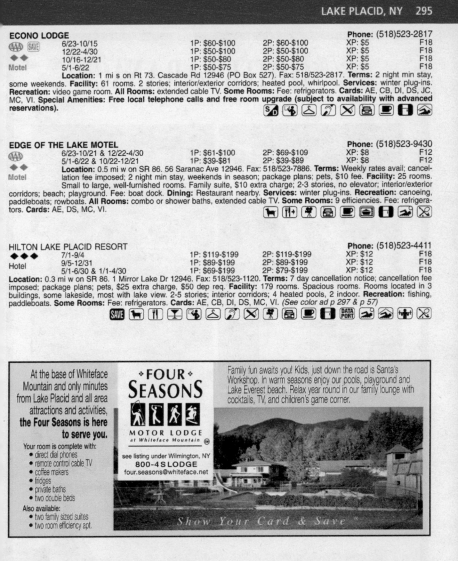
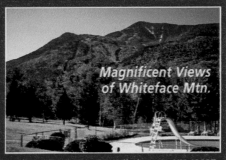

HOWARD JOHNSON RESORT INN

Phone: (518)523-9555

(AAA) (SAVE) — All Year — 1P: $70-$130 — 2P: $70-$130 — XP: $10 — F18

◆◆◆ Motor Inn

Location: 90 Saranac Ave 12946. Fax: 518/523-4765. **Terms:** [MAP] meal plan; 3 day cancellation notice; package plans; pets. **Facility:** 92 rooms. Lakeside location, lovely mountain views. Many rooms with balcony. Attractive indoor pool area. 1-2 stories; interior/exterior corridors; heated pool, whirlpool; 2 tennis courts; boat dock. **Dining:** Restaurant; 6:15 am-10 pm, Fri & Sat-11 pm; $7-$13; cocktails. **Services:** winter plug-ins. **Recreation:** canoeing, fishing, paddleboats, row boats; cross country skiing. **All Rooms:** extended cable TV. **Cards:** AE, CB, DI, DS, MC, VI.

LAKE PLACID RAMADA INN

Phone: (518)523-2587

(AAA) (SAVE) — All Year — 1P: $59-$130 — 2P: $69-$140 — XP: $10 — F18

◆◆◆ Motor Inn

Location: 0.3 mi w on SR 86. 8-12 Saranac Ave 12946. Fax: 518/523-2328. **Terms:** [BP] & [MAP] meal plans; 3 day cancellation notice; cancellation fee imposed; package plans; pets. **Facility:** 90 rooms. Greenhouse lounge with lake view. Average to spacious rooms. 2-3 stories; interior/exterior corridors; 2 pools, 1 indoor heated, whirlpool. **Dining:** Restaurant; 7-11 am, 11:30-1:30 & 5-9 pm; $8-$18; cocktails. **Services:** winter plug-ins. **Recreation:** limited exercise equipment. **All Rooms:** extended cable TV. **Some Rooms:** Fee: refrigerators, VCR. **Cards:** AE, CB, DI, DS, JC, MC, VI. *(See color ad below)*

LAKE PLACID RESORT/HOLIDAY INN

Phone: (518)523-2556

◆◆◆ — All Year — 1P: $69-$229 — 2P: $69-$229 — XP: $10 — F19

Motor Inn

Location: Center. 1 Olympic Dr 12946. Fax: 518/523-9410. **Terms:** Check-in 4 pm; 7 day cancellation notice; cancellation fee imposed; package plans; pets, $100 dep req. **Facility:** 205 rooms. On hill overlooking Mirror Lake. Beautiful mountain views. Most rooms with balcony. Some suites with fireplace. 11 two-bedroom units. 2-4 stories; interior corridors; putting green; heated pool; 4 tennis courts; playground. Fee: 45 holes golf. **Services:** gift shop; winter plug-ins. **Recreation:** swimming, paddleboats; cross country skiing. **Some Rooms:** 2 kitchens. **Cards:** AE, CB, DI, DS, MC, VI. *(See color ad p 298)*

MAPLE LEAF INN

Phone: (518)523-2471

(AAA) (SAVE) — 5/1-11/1 & 11/30-3/26 — 1P: $48-$125 — 2P: $48-$125 — XP: $15 — F12

◆◆ Motel

Location: 0.5 mi w on SR 86. 53-55 Saranac Ave 12946. Fax: 518/523-5378. **Terms:** Open 5/1-11/1 & 11/30-3/26; weekly rates avail; 7 day cancellation notice; cancellation fee imposed. **Facility:** 15 rooms. 1 two-bedroom unit. 3 kitchen units, $125-$170 in season. 2-3 night min stay, in season; 1-2 stories; exterior corridors. **Dining:** Restaurant nearby. **Recreation:** picnic & charcoal grill area, ski-waxing room. **All Rooms:** extended cable TV. **Cards:** AE, MC, VI. **Special Amenities:** Early check-in/late check-out and free local telephone calls.

MIRROR LAKE INN RESORT AND SPA

				Phone: (518)523-2544
5/1-10/8 & 12/18-1/3	1P: $205-$285	2P: $205-$285	XP: $40	F18
1/4-4/30	1P: $170-$215	2P: $170-$215	XP: $40	F18
10/9-12/17	1P: $130-$180	2P: $130-$180	XP: $40	F18

Complex   **Location:** 0.5 mi w, just off SR 86. 5 Mirror Lake Dr 12946. Fax: 518/523-2871. **Terms:** [BP] & [MAP] meal plans; 14 day cancellation notice; cancellation fee imposed; 3 night min stay, some weekends; package plans. **Facility:** 128 rooms. Most rooms with balcony overlooking Mirror Lake. Beautiful mountain and traditional atmosphere. 1 two-bedroom unit, 1 three-bedroom unit. Specialty themed suites, $170-$650; 18 whirlpool rooms, $400-$685; 1-4 stories; interior/exterior corridors; beach, 2 heated pools, sauna, whirlpool, swim dock; 1 tennis court; boat dock. **Dining:** Dining room, restaurant, coffee shop; 7:30 am-9 pm; $16-$25; health conscious menu; afternoon tea; also, Averil Conwell Dining Room, see separate listing. **Services:** gift shop; winter plug-ins. Fee: massage. **Recreation:** swimming, canoeing, fishing, paddleboats, fishing dock, row boats; cross country skiing, ice skating, guided snowshoe hikes; hiking trails, aerobic instruction, spa activities. Fee: spa treatments. **All Rooms:** extended cable TV. **Cards:** AE, CB, DI, DS, MC, VI. *(See color ad p 299)*

MOUNTAIN VIEW INN

Phone: (518)523-2439

	12/26-3/29	1P: $95-$105	2P: $95-$105	XP: $15	F13
◆◆	6/27-11/1	1P: $85-$105	2P: $85-$105	XP: $15	F13
Motel	5/12-6/26	1P: $68-$87	2P: $68-$87	XP: $15	F13

Location: On SR 86. 140 Main St 12946. Fax: 518/523-8974. **Terms:** Open 5/12-11/1 & 12/26-3/29; 14 day cancellation notice. **Facility:** 18 rooms. Some rooms with balcony. Open weekends & some mid-weeks in winter, by reservation only; 2-3 stories, no elevator; interior/exterior corridors. **Dining:** Restaurant nearby. **Recreation:** use of Lake Placid Club Beach. **All Rooms:** extended cable TV. **Cards:** AE, MC, VI.

⊕ ✕ 📭 🍽 📠

THE NORTHWAY MOTEL

Phone: (518)523-3500

	12/15-4/30	1P: $55-$70	2P: $70-$90	XP: $8	F16
◆◆	6/16-10/21	1P: $55-$65	2P: $70-$85	XP: $8	F16
Motel	5/1-6/15 & 10/22-12/14	1P: $45-$55	2P: $52-$65	XP: $5	F16

Location: 0.5 mi e, jct SR 73 and 86. 5 Wilmington Rd 12946. **Terms:** [CP] meal plan; weekly rates avail; 3 day cancellation notice; 2 night min stay, weekends; package plans. **Facility:** 14 rooms. Modest to large rooms. Open weekends and holidays, in winter season. 2 two-bedroom units. 1-2 stories; exterior corridors. **Services:** winter plug-ins. **All Rooms:** extended cable TV. **Some Rooms:** Fee: refrigerators. **Cards:** AE, DS, MC, VI. **Special Amenities:** Free local telephone calls and preferred room (subject to availability with advanced reservations).

✕ 🛢 📠 📠 🐾

SWISS ACRES INN & RESTAURANT

Phone: (518)523-3040

	6/16-10/15 & 12/24-4/30		2P: $50-$85	XP: $8	F16
◆	5/1-6/15 & 10/16-12/23		2P: $42-$60	XP: $8	F16

Location: 1 mi w on SR 86. 189 Saranac Ave 12946. Fax: 518/523-2196. **Terms:** [BP] meal plan, 6/15-10/12 midweek only; weekly & monthly rates avail; 7 day cancellation notice; package plans; pets, with prior approval. **Facility:** 40 rooms. Variety of different style guest rooms, modestly furnished. Efficiencies, $79-$129; 1-2 stories; interior/exterior corridors; sauna, whirlpool. **Dining:** Dining room; 7:30 am-10 & 5-9 pm 6/1-10/15; hrs vary in winter; $10-$17; cocktails. **Services:** winter plug-ins. **Recreation:** basketball. **All Rooms:** combo or shower baths, extended cable TV. **Some Rooms:** 8 efficiencies. Fee: refrigerators. **Cards:** AE, MC, VI. **Special Amenities:** Free room upgrade and preferred room (each subject to availability with advanced reservations).

🛏 🐾 🍴 🍸 ✕ 📭 📠 🐾

TOWN & COUNTRY MOTOR INN
Phone: 518/523-9268

(AAA) [SAVE]

◆◆

Motel

12/22-3/18		2P: $86	XP: $8	F10
5/1-10/15		2P: $56-$83	XP: $8	F10
10/16-12/21 & 3/19-4/30		2P: $72	XP: $8	F10

Location: 0.8 mi w on SR 86. 67 Saranac Ave 12946. Fax: 518/523-8058. **Terms:** Weekly rates avail; 10 day cancellation notice. **Facility:** 24 rooms. Average to large rooms, 2 with fireplace. 1 two-bedroom unit. 2-3 night min stay some weekends. Apartment & housekeeping cottage with fireplace, $140; 2 stories; exterior corridors; heated pool. **Services:** winter plug-ins. **Recreation:** picnic area with grills. **All Rooms:** combo or shower baths, extended cable TV. **Cards:** AE, DS, MC, VI.

TOWN HOUSE LODGE BY THE LAKE
Phone: (518)523-2532

(AAA)

◆◆

Motel

All Year	1P: $50-$88	2P: $52-$110	XP: $10	F12

Location: 0.5 mi w on SR 86. 40 Saranac Ave 12946. Fax: 518/523-2533. **Terms:** 15 day cancellation notice; cancellation fee imposed; 2 night min stay, summer weekends. **Facility:** 25 rooms. Some modest rooms with cozy Adirondack decor, other larger rooms with more modern look. 2 kitchens, $10 extra charge. 3 two-bedroom units, $68-$104 for up to 4 persons; 1-2 stories; exterior corridors; heated pool, wading pool. **Services:** winter plug-ins. **Recreation:** canoeing; picnic tables. Fee: pool table. **All Rooms:** combo or shower baths, extended cable TV. **Cards:** AE, MC, VI.

—— RESTAURANTS ——

ALPINE CELLAR RESTAURANT
Dinner: $13-$25
Phone: 518/523-2180

◆◆

German

Location: 0.8 mi e on SR 86; just e of traffic light from jct SR 73. SR 86 12946. **Hours:** Open 5/15-10/22 & 12/20-3/25; 5 pm-10 pm. Closed: 12/25, Mon & Tues. **Reservations:** suggested. **Features:** casual dress; children's menu; carryout; cocktails & lounge; a la carte. Such specialties as schnitzel, sauerbraten and roladen make up a menu that also includes American and Swiss cuisine. The open dining room has Bavarian overtones. The selection of imported beers is impressive. Homemade breads and desserts are wonderful. **Cards:** AE, CB, DI, DS, MC, VI.

AVERIL CONWELL DINING ROOM Historical
Dinner: $15-$30
Phone: 518/523-2544

(AAA)

◆◆◆

Regional American

Location: 0.5 mi w, just off SR 86; in Mirror Lake Inn Resort and Spa. 5 Mirror Lake Dr 12946. **Hours:** 7:30 am-10 & 5:30-9 pm, Sat & Sun 7:30 am-11 & 5:30-9 pm. **Reservations:** suggested. **Features:** casual dress; children's menu; health conscious menu; cocktails & lounge; a la carte. Every day, the restaurant goes through about 20 dozen of its signature chocolate chip cookies, a recipe that has been passed down for years. Mahogany walls and fieldstone fireplaces decorate the cozy, candlelit dining room, which overlooks Mirror Lake. Smoke free premises. **Cards:** AE, DI, DS, MC, VI.

THE CHARCOAL PIT
Dinner: $14-$33
Phone: 518/523-3050

(AAA)

◆◆

American

Location: 1 mi w. SR 86 12946. **Hours:** 5 pm-10 pm. Closed: Mon-Fri 4/1-4/30 & 11/1-11/30. **Reservations:** accepted. **Features:** casual dress; children's menu; cocktails & lounge; a la carte. At the edge of the picturesque Lake Placid village, the restaurant has been family-owned since 1957. Nearly any craving can be satisfied with the interesting variety of dishes on the menu. Don't pass up the mouthwatering homemade breads and pastries. **Cards:** AE, CB, DI, DS, MC, VI.

THE GREAT ADIRONDACK STEAK & SEAFOOD COMPANY & GREAT ADIRONDACK BREWING CO
Lunch: $5-$15   Dinner: $8-$20   Phone: 518/523-1629

(AAA)

◆◆

Steak and Seafood

Location: Center. 34 Main St 12946. **Hours:** 11:30 am-10 pm; hrs may vary slightly off season. **Features:** casual dress; children's menu; carryout; cocktails & lounge; street parking. In the heart of the village, the casual restaurant offers a little something for everyone—ranging from flavorful French onion soup to exquisite flatbreads. An interesting story is behind the name of every beer made at the on-site microbrewery. **Cards:** AE, CB, DI, DS, MC, VI.

LA VERANDA
Dinner: $11-$25
Phone: 518/523-3339

◆◆◆

Continental

Location: Center; in Lake Placid Resort/Holiday Inn. 1 Olympic Dr 12946. **Hours:** Open 6/15-9/5; 5:30 pm-9:30 pm. Closed: Mon. **Reservations:** suggested. **Features:** casual dress; cocktails; a la carte. The beautifully restored house boasts intimate dining rooms with tasteful decor. Thought is given to food arrangement and garnishes in such excellent dishes as shrimp scampi over angel hair pasta. The strawberry custard tart is simply delicious. **Cards:** AE, CB, DI, DS, MC, VI. *(See color ad p 298)*

LANSING pop. 3,300

—— LODGINGS ——

ECONO LODGE
Phone: (607)257-1400

(AAA) [SAVE]

◆◆

Motel

All Year	1P: $46-$95	2P: $55-$125	XP: $10	F18

Location: 3.5 mi n on SR 13, Triphammer Rd exit; adjoining Cayuga Mall. 2303 N Triphammer Rd 14850 (2303 N Triphammer Rd, ITHACA). Fax: 607/257-6359. **Terms:** [CP] meal plan; 7 day cancellation notice; pets, $10 extra charge. **Facility:** 72 rooms. Nice rooms. Close to Ithaca shopping malls. 2 whirlpool rooms, $82-$150; 2 stories; interior corridors. **Dining:** Restaurant nearby. **Services:** winter plug-ins. **Some Rooms:** Fee: refrigerators, microwaves. **Cards:** AE, CB, DI, DS, JC, MC, VI. **Special Amenities:** Free breakfast and free room upgrade (subject to availability with advanced reservations).

RAMADA INN-AIRPORT
Phone: (607)257-3100

◆◆

Motor Inn

5/1-11/15	1P: $95-$179	2P: $95-$179	XP: $10
11/16-4/30	1P: $95-$149	2P: $95-$149	XP: $10

Location: Jct SR 13 and 34, 3.5 mi n on SR 13, Triphammer Rd exit, just w. 2310 N Triphammer Rd 14850 (2310 N Triphammer Rd, ITHACA). Fax: 607/257-4425. **Terms:** 10 day cancellation notice; pets, $50 dep req. **Facility:** 121 rooms. Executive training center featured. Modest rooms. Close to shopping mall. 2 stories; interior corridors; 2 pools, 1 indoor heated. **Services:** area transportation; winter plug-ins. **All Rooms:** combo or shower baths. **Some Rooms:** Fee: refrigerators, microwaves, VCR. **Cards:** AE, CB, DI, DS, JC, MC, VI.

——— RESTAURANT ———

ROGUE'S HARBOR STEAK & ALE INC
◆◆
American
Lunch: $5-$10   **Dinner:** $8-$20   **Phone:** 607/533-3535
Location: US 34, 6 mi n of Ithaca, at corner US 34 and 34B. 2079 East Shore Dr 14882. **Hours:** 11 am-10 pm, Sun 10 am-9 pm. Closed: Mon. **Features:** casual dress; Sunday brunch; early bird specials; carryout; cocktails & lounge. Antiques, local memorabilia and 13 fireplaces add to the ambience of the 19th-century, historic landmark. The menu centers on prime rib, fresh seafood and interesting pasta combinations. Beverages include many local wines and draft beers. **Cards:** AE, DS, MC, VI. ⊠

LATHAM pop. 10,100 (See map p. 193; index p. 192)

——— LODGINGS ———

CENTURY HOUSE RESTAURANT & HOTEL   **Phone:** (518)785-0931   [30]

7/26-9/4	1P: $109-$129	2P: $129	XP: $15	F12
5/1-7/25 & 9/5-4/30	1P: $95	2P: $105	XP: $12	F12

◆◆◆ Motor Inn
Location: 9 mi n on US 9; 1.5 mi n of jct SR 7. 997 New Loudon Rd 12047 (RD 1, Box 287, COHOES). Fax: 518/785-3274. **Terms:** [BP] meal plan; weekly & monthly rates avail; cancellation fee imposed; pets, $10 extra charge. **Facility:** 68 rooms. Attractive well appointed rooms with Colonial theme. 2 two-bedroom units. 2 stories; interior corridors; 1 tennis court. **Dining:** 6:30-9:30 am, Sat & Sun 8-11 am; restaurant, see separate listing. **Services:** area transportation; winter plug-ins. **All Rooms:** extended cable TV. **Some Rooms:** 4 kitchens. **Cards:** AE, CB, DI, DS, MC, VI.

(ASK) 🔗 🐾 🍴 🎎 🛎 ⊠ 🎦 📠 💻 📺 🛏 [DATA PORT] 🏊 🛗 ⊠

COMFORT INN AT ALBANY AIRPORT   **Phone:** (518)783-1900   [28]

7/26-9/4	1P: $79-$89	2P: $89-$99	XP: $10	F18
5/1-7/25 & 9/5-4/30	1P: $74-$79	2P: $79-$89	XP: $10	F18

◆◆◆ Motor Inn
Location: 1.8 mi nw of jct I-87, exit 4. 866 Albany Shaker Rd 12110. Fax: 518/783-4085. **Terms:** [CP] meal plan. **Facility:** 96 rooms. Whirlpool room, $99-$125; 2 stories; interior corridors. **Dining:** Dining room; 11:30 am-10 pm; $9-$16; cocktails. **All Rooms:** extended cable TV. **Cards:** AE, CB, DI, DS, MC, VI.
Special Amenities: Free breakfast and free local telephone calls.

[SD] 🔗 🍴 🎎 🛎 ⊠ 🎦 📠 💻 📺 🛏 [DATA PORT] 🛗

HAMPTON INN-LATHAM   **Phone:** (518)785-0000   [32]

7/21-9/5	1P: $109-$129	2P: $114-$134	XP: $5	F18
9/6-4/30	1P: $89-$129	2P: $94-$134	XP: $5	F18
6/2-7/20	1P: $99-$109	2P: $104-$114	XP: $5	F18
5/1-6/1	1P: $89-$99	2P: $94-$104	XP: $5	F18

◆◆◆ Motel
Location: US 9, just n of jct Rt 7 and I-87, exit 7. (981 New Loudon Rd, COHOES, 12047). Fax: 518/785-1285. **Terms:** [CP] meal plan; pets. **Facility:** 126 rooms. 4 stories; interior corridors. **Services:** winter plug-ins. **Cards:** AE, DI, DS, JC, MC, VI.

[SD] 🔗 🐾 🎎 🛎 🐶 ⊠ 🎦 📠 💻 🛏 [DATA PORT] 🏊 🛗

MICROTEL INN   **Phone:** (518)782-9161   [34]

5/1-11/16	1P: $47-$80	2P: $47-$80	XP: $4	F18
11/17-4/30	1P: $45-$55	2P: $45-$55	XP: $4	F18

◆◆ Motel
Location: Just w of I-87, exit 6. 7 Rensselaer Ave 12110. Fax: 518/782-9162. **Terms:** 7 day cancellation notice; cancellation fee imposed; pets. **Facility:** 100 rooms. Compact rooms. 2 stories; interior corridors. **Dining:** Restaurant nearby. **All Rooms:** combo or shower baths, extended cable TV. **Some Rooms:** Fee: refrigerators, microwaves. **Cards:** AE, CB, DI, DS, MC, VI. *(See ad p 194)*

[SD] 🐾 🍴 🎎 🛎 ♿ ⊠ 🎦 📠 💻 🛏 [DATA PORT]

RESIDENCE INN BY MARRIOTT ALBANY AIRPORT   **Phone:** (518)783-0600   [27]

7/25-9/5	1P: $155	2P: $205	
9/6-11/16	1P: $129	2P: $159	
5/1-7/24	1P: $123	2P: $153	
11/17-4/30	1P: $109	2P: $139	

◆◆◆ Apartment
Location: On SR 7, 2 mi w of jct I-87, exit 6. 1 Residence Inn Dr 12110. Fax: 518/783-0709. **Terms:** [CP] meal plan; pets, $5 extra charge. **Facility:** 112 rooms. Studio, 1-bedroom and bi-level loft units with fireplace. 2 stories; exterior corridors. **Services:** area transportation. **Recreation:** sports court. **All Rooms:** kitchens. **Cards:** AE, CB, DI, DS, MC, VI.

(ASK) [SD] 🔗 🐾 🎎 🛎 🌀 ⊠ 🎦 📠 💻 📺 🛏 [DATA PORT] 🏊 🛗 ⊠

WINGATE INN   **Phone:** (518)869-9100   [29]

All Year	1P: $125	2P: $135	XP: $10 F18

◆◆◆ Motor Inn
Location: I-87, exit 4, just w on Albany Shaker Rd. 254 Old Wolf Rd 12110. Fax: 518/869-0114. **Terms:** [CP] meal plan. **Facility:** 106 rooms. Contemporary property near airport. 5 stories; interior corridors. **All Rooms:** combo or shower baths, safes. **Cards:** AE, CB, DI, DS, MC, VI.

(ASK) [SD] 🔗 🍴 🍸 🎎 🛎 🐶 ♿ ⊠ 📠 💻 🛏 [DATA PORT] 🛗

——— RESTAURANTS ———

CENTURY HOUSE
◆◆
Regional
American
Lunch: $6-$10   **Dinner:** $14-$20   **Phone:** 518/785-0834   [25]
Location: 9 mi n on US 9; 1.5 mi n of jct SR 7; in Century House Restaurant and Hotel. 997 New Loudon Rd 12047. **Hours:** 11 am-3 & 4-9 pm, Fri-10 pm, Sat 4 pm-10 pm, Sun noon-9 pm. Closed: 12/25. **Reservations:** suggested. **Features:** casual dress; children's menu; early bird specials; carryout; cocktails & lounge; a la carte. Early American furnishings decorate the casual dining room of the well-established restaurant. Garlic beef—flaked roast sirloin brushed with garlic butter—is the specialty on a menu of mostly steaks and seafood. Death by chocolate cake is decadent. **Cards:** AE, CB, DI, DS, MC, VI. ⊠

(See map p. 193)

DAKOTA   **Dinner:** $9-$18   **Phone:** 518/786-1234 ②④
◆◆   **Location:** Just e of I-87, exit 6; in Latham Circle Farms. 579 Troy-Schenectady Rd 12110. **Hours:** 4:30
Steak and   pm-10 pm, Fri & Sat-11 pm, Sun 1 pm-9 pm. Closed: 11/23 & 12/25. **Reservations:** accepted.
Seafood   **Features:** casual dress; children's menu; carryout; salad bar; cocktails & lounge. Hand-cut steaks and fresh
seafood make up the bulk of the relaxed restaurant's menu. The rustic dining room has the feel of an
Adirondack mountain lodge, with wood beams, two fireplaces and American Indian artifacts. Try the yummy
mud pie. **Cards:** AE, DI, DS, MC, VI.

LEEDS pop. 700

—— LODGING ——

CARL'S RIP VAN WINKLE MOTOR LODGE   **Phone:** 518/943-3303
   5/1-11/15 & 4/15-4/30   1P: $48-$65   2P: $48-$65   XP: $15
◆◆   **Location:** CR 23B, 0.3 mi w of I-87, exit 21. CR 23B 12451 (PO Box 849, CATSKILL, 12414).
Complex   Fax: 518/943-2309. **Terms:** Open 5/1-11/15 & 4/15-4/30; weekly rates avail; 7 day cancellation notice, 30 day
for efficiencies. **Facility:** 37 rooms. Well established family run property for 3 generations. Large motel rooms
and also log cabins on peaceful wooded hillside. 6 efficiencies, weekly in season, $425-$450 for up to 4 persons; 1 story; exterior corridors; wading pool; playground. **Dining:** Restaurant nearby. **Recreation:** fishing; hiking trails.
All Rooms: combo or shower baths, extended cable TV. **Cards:** AE, MC, VI. *(See ad p 232)*

—— RESTAURANT ——

LOGSIDER CAFE   **Dinner:** $9-$19   **Phone:** 518/943-2581
◆◆   **Location:** CR 23B, 0.3 mi w of I-87, exit 21. 12451. **Hours:** Open 5/1-12/31 & 3/3-4/30; 4:30 pm-9 pm, Sun
American   noon-8 pm; 7 am-11 & 4:30-9 pm 5/1-10/31. Closed: Mon 9/4-10/31. **Reservations:** suggested; weekends.
Features: casual dress; children's menu; health conscious menu items; carryout; cocktails & lounge. The
1934 log cabin has an Adirondack atmosphere, with timbers, massive stone fireplaces and varied antique
appointments. Well-seasoned dishes include traditional preparations of black Angus beef and fresh seafood.
The barbecue ribs are outstanding. **Cards:** AE, DS, MC, VI.

LEONARDSVILLE pop. 700

—— RESTAURANT ——

THE HORNED DORSET INN Historical   **Dinner:** $18-$28   **Phone:** 315/855-7898
◆◆◆◆   **Location:** Center; 4 mi s of jct SR 8 and 20. Rt 8 13364. **Hours:** 6 pm-9 pm, Sun 3 pm-8 pm. Closed: 1/1,
French   12/25 & Mon 9/1-6/30. **Reservations:** suggested. **Features:** dressy casual; health conscious menu; cocktails
& lounge; street parking. On a village main street tucked away in the countryside, the hidden restaurant is a
bona fide treat. Elaborate wood trim and a heavy stone hearth decorate the upscale dining room. Fish, red meat and fowl
are prepared with both care and flair. **Cards:** AE, MC, VI.

LE ROY pop. 5,000

—— LODGING ——

EDSON HOUSE BED & BREAKFAST   **Phone:** (716)768-8579
(SAVE)   All Year   1P: $69-$79   2P: $79-$99   XP: $10   F10
◆◆   **Location:** SR 19, just s of I-90 (New York Thruway), exit 47. 7863 Griswold Circle Rd 14482-0296.
Bed &   Fax: 716/768-2063. **Terms:** [CP] meal plan; weekly rates avail; 10 day cancellation notice; cancellation fee imposed. **Facility:** 4 rooms. Attractive individually decorated rooms. Owner pet on premises. 2 stories; interior
Breakfast   corridors; smoke free premises. **All Rooms:** extended cable TV. **Cards:** DS, MC, VI. **Special Amenities:** Free
breakfast.

—— RESTAURANTS ——

THE CREEKSIDE INN   **Lunch:** $4-$7   **Dinner:** $7-$25   **Phone:** 716/768-7846
◆◆   **Location:** Center. 1 Main St 14482. **Hours:** 11 am-9 pm, Fri & Sat-10 pm, Sun 1 pm-8 pm. Closed major
American   holidays. **Reservations:** suggested. **Features:** casual dress; children's menu; carryout; cocktails & lounge.
The casual, tavern-style restaurant overlooks the mill stream and pretty waterfalls. Among selections on the
extensive menu are lots of finger foods, as well as seafood, prime rib, pork, chicken, soups, salads and sandwiches. Servers
are pleasant. **Cards:** AE, DI, MC, VI.

D & R DEPOT RESTAURANT   **Lunch:** $4-$8   **Dinner:** $6-$17   **Phone:** 716/768-6270
◆◆   **Location:** Just n from jct SR 5 and 19. 63 Lake St (SR 19) 14482. **Hours:** 7 am-9 pm. Closed major
American   holidays. **Reservations:** accepted; suggested wknds. **Features:** casual dress; children's menu; health
conscious menu; carryout; beer & wine only. The restored, turn-of-the-20th-century train depot is a
memorable spot in which to enjoy a traditional breakfast; a salad or sandwich lunch; or a dinner of steak,
seafood or chicken. Homemade breads, pastries and desserts are mouthwatering temptations. **Cards:** AE,
DS, MC, VI.

LEWISTON —See Niagara Falls p. 396.

LIBERTY pop. 4,100

——— LODGINGS ———

DAYS INN LIBERTY   Phone: (914)292-7600
AAA SAVE   7/1-9/4   1P: $52-$95   2P: $57-$95   XP: $6   F12
◆ ◆   5/26-6/30   1P: $47-$75   2P: $52-$75   XP: $6   F12
Motel   5/1-5/25 & 9/5-4/30 1P: $47-$52   2P: $52-$57   XP: $6   F12
Location: SR 17, exit 100, 0.3 mi e. 25 Sullivan Ave 12754. Fax: 914/292-3303. **Terms:** [CP] meal plan; pets, $100 dep req. **Facility:** 118 rooms. 2 stories; interior corridors; 2 pools, 1 indoor heated. **Services:** winter plug-ins. **All Rooms:** extended cable TV. **Cards:** AE, CB, DI, DS, MC, VI. **Special Amenities:** Free newspaper and preferred room (subject to availability with advanced reservations).

RAMADA LIMITED   Phone: (914)292-7171
AAA SAVE   7/1-9/30   1P: $99-$120   2P: $110-$120   XP: $10   F12
◆   5/1-6/30 & 10/1-4/30 1P: $60-$70 2P: $60-$70   XP: $10   F12
Motel   **Location:** SR 17, exit 100, just e. 7 Rt 52 E 12754. Fax: 914/292-0203. **Terms:** [CP] meal plan; pets, $5 extra charge. **Facility:** 70 rooms. Large rooms. 2 stories; interior corridors; designated smoking area. **Dining:** Restaurant nearby. **All Rooms:** extended cable TV. **Some Rooms:** Fee: refrigerators. **Cards:** AE, CB, DI, DS, MC, VI. **Special Amenities:** Early check-in/late check-out and free breakfast.

——— RESTAURANT ———

——— *The following restaurant has not been inspected by AAA* ———
but is listed for your information only.

VILLAGE SQUARE CAFE   Phone: 914/292-2233
fyi   Not inspected. **Location:** 70 New York 52 E. **Features:** This casual, non-smoking restaurant is open for lunch only. Outdoor dining is available in season.

LITTLE FALLS pop. 5,800

——— LODGING ———

BEST WESTERN LITTLE FALLS MOTOR INN   Phone: (315)823-4954
AAA   5/1-9/5   1P: $60-$70   2P: $65-$75   XP: $6   F12
◆ ◆   9/6-4/30   1P: $55-$65   2P: $60-$70   XP: $6   F12
Motor Inn **Location:** On SR 5 and 167. 20 Albany St 13365. Fax: 315/823-4507. **Terms:** Pets, $10 dep req. **Facility:** 56 rooms. 2 stories; interior corridors. **Dining:** Dining room; 6:30 am-2 & 5-9 pm, Sun 7 am-1 & 5-9 pm; $8-$15; cocktails. **Services:** winter plug-ins. **Recreation:** Fee: movie theaters. **All Rooms:** extended cable TV.
Cards: AE, CB, DI, DS, MC, VI.

——— RESTAURANTS ———

BEARDSLEE CASTLE   Dinner: $12-$23   Phone: 315-823-3000
◆ ◆ ◆   **Location:** On SR 5, just w of East Canada Creek. 123 Old State Rd 13365. **Hours:** 5 pm-9 pm, Fri & American   Sat-9:30 pm, Sun 2:30 pm-8 pm; hrs may vary in winter. Closed: 1/1, 12/25, Tues & Wed. **Reservations:** suggested. **Features:** dressy casual; cocktails; a la carte. Read through the written history of the castle as you enjoy the quaint surroundings. Stone walls and fireplaces enhance the ambience of the dining room. The innovative, daily changing menu dabbles in steak, seafood and lamb, just to name a few. **Cards:** AE, DS, MC, VI.

BELLA VISTA RESTAURANT   Dinner: $10-$18   Phone: 315-823-2861
◆ ◆   **Location:** On SR 167, 1.3 mi s of jct SR 167 and 5 S. 3622 SR 167 13365. **Hours:** 5 pm-9 pm, Fri & Sat-10 Italian   pm, Sun 1 pm-7 pm. Closed: 1/1, 12/24, 12/25, Mon & Tues. **Reservations:** suggested. **Features:** dressy casual; cocktails & lounge; a la carte. Enjoy hearty, tasty food—such as the pleasantly presented chicken Christina, a chicken breast stuffed with crabmeat, spinach and cheese—in this casual, friendly restaurant. Look across the street for beautiful views of Shoemaker Mountain. **Cards:** AE, MC, VI.

CANAL SIDE INN Historical   Dinner: $15-$21   Phone: 315/823-1170
AAA   **Location:** Just s of SR 5, following SR 167 S. 395 S Ann St 13365. **Hours:** 5 pm-9 pm, Fri & Sat-10 pm. ◆ ◆ ◆   Closed major holidays, Sun, Mon & 2/1-3/20. **Reservations:** suggested. **Features:** casual dress; health French   conscious menu; carryout; cocktails & lounge; street parking. An extensive wine list complements the owner/chef's thoughtful preparations of traditional French cuisine, including well-presented swordfish. The converted structure, decorated with attractive art and pretty table settings, exudes a historic charm. **Cards:** DI, MC, VI.

OVERLOOK MANSION   Dinner: $15-$24   Phone: 315/823-4222
◆ ◆ ◆   **Location:** From SR 169 (W Monroe St), just e on Lewis St, then just s on Douglas St to end follow signs. 1 Continental Overlook Ln 13365. **Hours:** Open 5/1-1/3 & 2/1-4/30; 6 pm-9 pm, Sun 2 pm-4 pm. Closed: 12/24, 12/25 & Mon-Wed. **Reservations:** suggested. **Features:** semi-formal attire; cocktails & lounge; a la carte. The lovely hilltop setting and elegantly decorated dining room combine to offer a sophisticated experience. Attractive presentation marks such dishes as cappellini pasta with crabmeat, scallops, mushrooms and vegetables. Service is attentive. Smoke free premises. **Cards:** AE, MC, VI.

LIVERPOOL pop. 2,600 (See map p. 478; index p. 477)

—— LODGINGS ——

DAYS INN-NORTH
◆◆
Motor Inn
Phone: (315)451-1511 **24** F18
All Year 1P: $69-$210 2P: $69-$210 XP: $10
Location: 4 mi n, w of I-81, exit 7th North St, at jct I-90 (New York Thruway), exit 36 and I-81. 400 7th North St 13088. Fax: 315/457-6897. **Terms:** [CP] meal plan; 5 day cancellation notice; small pets only. **Facility:** 126 rooms. 3 stories; interior/exterior corridors. **Cards:** AE, CB, DI, DS, MC, VI.

HAMPTON INN
◆◆◆
Motel
Phone: (315)457-9900 **27**
5/22-4/30 1P: $67-$95 2P: $74-$105
5/1-5/21 1P: $65-$95 2P: $72-$105
Fax: 315/457-6600. **Terms:** [CP] meal plan; cancellation fee imposed; small pets only, $25 extra charge. **Facility:** 105 rooms. Contemporary styled rooms. 3 stories; interior corridors. **All Rooms:** combo or shower baths. **Some Rooms:** Fee: refrigerators, microwaves. **Cards:** AE, CB, DI, DS, JC, MC, VI.

HOLIDAY INN SYRACUSE/LIVERPOOL
◆◆◆
Motor Inn
Phone: (315)457-1122 **32** F18
All Year 1P: $120-$150 2P: $120-$150 XP: $10
Location: I-90 (New York Thruway), exit 37, 1.3 mi w of I-81, exit 25, 7th N St at Electronics Pkwy. 441 Electronics Pkwy 13088. Fax: 315/451-1269. **Terms:** Package plans; pets. **Facility:** 277 rooms. Fresh contemporary rooms and public areas all well-appointed. Modest space in rooms. Easy interstate access. 2-7 stories; interior corridors; heated pool. **Cards:** AE, CB, DI, DS, JC, MC, VI.

HOMEWOOD SUITES
◆◆◆
Suite Motel
Phone: 315/451-3800 **25**
All Year 1P: $119-$199
Location: 1 mi w of jct I-81, exit 7th N St. 275 Elwood Davis Rd 13088. Fax: 315/451-5838. **Terms:** [CP] meal plan; 7 day cancellation notice; cancellation fee imposed; pets, $75 dep req. **Facility:** 72 rooms. Spacious comfortable suites, few with gas fireplace. 3 stories; interior corridors. **Services:** gift shop; area transportation. **All Rooms:** kitchens. **Cards:** AE, CB, DI, DS, JC, MC, VI.

KNIGHTS INN
◆◆ SAVE ◆◆
Motel
Phone: (315)453-6330 **30** F17
All Year 1P: $35-$89 2P: $40-$99 XP: $6
Location: Just s of I-90 (New York Thruway), exit 37 (Electronics Pkwy). 430 Electronics Pkwy 13088. Fax: 315/457-9240. **Terms:** Weekly rates avail, in winter; pets, $5 extra charge. **Facility:** 78 rooms. 1 story; exterior corridors. **Dining:** Restaurant nearby. **All Rooms:** extended cable TV. **Cards:** AE, CB, DI, DS, MC, VI. **Special Amenities:** Early check-in/late check-out and preferred room (subject to availability with advanced reservations).

SUPER 8 MOTEL ROUTE 57
◆◆◆ SAVE
Motel
Phone: 315/451-8550 **29** F12
All Year 1P: $55-$110 2P: $60-$150 XP: $5
Location: I-90, exit 38, 1 mi n on CR 57. 7360 Oswego Rd 13090. Fax: 315/451-6205. **Terms:** [CP] meal plan. **Facility:** 43 rooms. 2 stories; interior corridors. **All Rooms:** extended cable TV. **Cards:** AE, DI, DS, MC, VI.

SUPER 8 MOTEL SYRACUSE/LIVERPOOL
◆◆
Motel
Phone: (315)451-8888 **31**
All Year 1P: $45-$52 2P: $54-$59
Location: 4 mi n, off I-81, exit 7th N St, at jct I-90 (New York Thruway), exit 36. 421 7th N St 13088. Fax: 315/451-0043. **Terms:** [CP] meal plan. **Facility:** 99 rooms. In commercial location. 4 stories; interior corridors. **Cards:** AE, CB, DI, DS, JC, MC, VI.

LIVINGSTON MANOR pop. 1,500

—— LODGING ——

THE MAGICAL LAND OF OZ B & B
◆◆
Bed & Breakfast
Phone: (914)438-3418
1P: $75-$85 2P: $75-$85
Location: SR 17, exit 96, 4 mi s following signs. 455 Shandelee Rd 12758. Fax: 914/439-3446. **Terms:** [BP] meal plan; pets, with prior approval. **Facility:** 7 rooms. 2 stories; interior corridors. **Recreation:** canoeing, fishing, paddleboats. **Cards:** AE, MC, VI.

LOCKPORT pop. 24,400

—— LODGING ——

COMFORT INN
◆◆◆
Motel
Phone: (716)434-4411
5/26-9/3 1P: $89-$119 2P: $99-$139 XP: $10 F18
9/4-11/2 1P: $75-$95 2P: $85-$105 XP: $10 F18
11/3-4/30 1P: $72-$92 2P: $82-$102 XP: $10 F18
5/1-5/25 1P: $69-$89 2P: $79-$99 XP: $10 F18
Location: 1 mi s on SR 78. 551 S Transit St 14094. Fax: 716/434-9649. **Terms:** [CP] meal plan; 3 day cancellation notice; package plans. **Facility:** 50 rooms. Spacious rooms with contemporary decor. 2 stories; interior corridors. **Cards:** AE, CB, DI, DS, JC, MC, VI.

LONG ISLAND (See map p. 305)

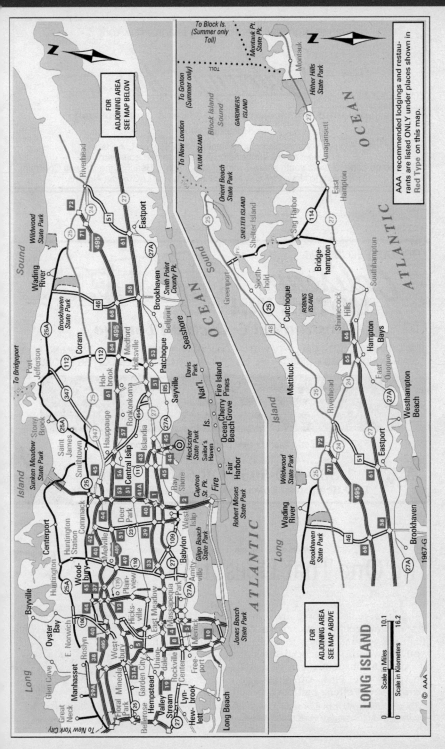

To Block Is.
(Summer only
Toll)

FOR
ADJOINING AREA
SEE MAP BELOW

AAA recommended lodgings and restaurants are listed ONLY under places shown in
Red Type on this map.

LONG ISLAND

FOR
ADJOINING AREA
SEE MAP ABOVE

Scale in Miles
Scale in Kilometers

© AAA

1967-G

The One That Does It All

AAA

*F*or years, people have turned to AAA for their emergency road service needs. But AAA is more than just towing. Access to AAA's travel services can give you the world. Its financial services can help you pay for it. And AAA insurance can give you the peace of mind to enjoy the ride. Plus, AAA gives you exclusive Show Your Card & Save® offers, bail bond benefits, and much more.

Discover the ways AAA can simplify your life. Call or stop by your nearest AAA office today. And make AAA the one for you.

LONG LAKE pop. 900—See also ADIRONDACK MOUNTAINS.

——— LODGINGS ———

JOURNEY'S END COTTAGES
Phone: 518/624-5381

6/21-9/10 Wkly	1P: $625-$700	2P: $625-$700	
5/1-6/20 & 9/11-11/1 Wkly	1P: $500-$600	2P: $500-$600	

Location: 1 mi s on SR 30 and 28 N. Deerland Rd, Rt 30 12847 (PO Box 96). **Terms:** Open 5/1-11/1; 60 day cancellation notice; 3 night min stay, off season; pets, in spring & fall only. **Facility:** 4 rooms. Peaceful location on lake. 1-, 2- and 3-bedroom fully equipped housekeeping cottages. Additional charge for housekeeping services. 1 two-bedroom unit. 3-bedroom unit, $500-$650 for up to 6 persons; 1 story; exterior corridors; beach. **Recreation:** swimming, canoeing, fishing. Fee: floatboat. **All Rooms:** kitchens, combo or shower baths, extended cable TV. **Cards:** DS, MC, VI.

Cottage

LONG VIEW LODGE
Phone: (518)624-2862

5/26-10/10	2P: $65-$85	XP: $10
5/1-5/25 & 10/11-4/30	2P: $55-$70	XP: $10

Location: 2.3 mi s on SR 30 and 28 N. Rt 28 N & 30 12847 (HCO1 Box 32). Fax: 518/624-2862. **Terms:** [BP] & [CP] meal plans, 7/1-8/31; check-in 4 pm; 7 day cancellation notice; cancellation fee imposed; package plans, off season; pets, cottages only. **Facility:** 15 rooms. 4 two-bedroom units. 2 cottages, $85; 2 stories; interior corridors; designated smoking area; beach; boat dock. **Dining:** Dining room; 5 pm-9 pm; $12-$17; cocktails. **Recreation:** swimming, canoeing, fishing. **All Rooms:** combo or shower baths, extended cable TV. **Cards:** DS, MC, VI.

Historic Country Inn

MOTEL LONG LAKE & COTTAGES
Phone: (518)624-2613

5/15-10/15	1P: $65-$95	2P: $65-$95

Location: 200 yds from SR 30 traffic lights, follow signs. Boat Landing Rd 12847 (PO Box 578). Fax: 518/624-2576. **Terms:** Open 5/15-10/15; weekly rates avail; 10 day cancellation notice. **Facility:** 17 rooms. Quiet lakefront motel with screened patios. 1- to 2-room cottages. Extensive wooded grounds. Housekeeping services not provided in cottages. 1 three-bedroom unit. 7 housekeeping cottages, $500-$950 weekly 6/1-10/1 for up to 4 persons. 3 night min stay on advance reservations for motel rooms, 7/1-8/31; 1 story; exterior corridors; beach; boat dock. **Recreation:** swimming, fishing. **All Rooms:** combo or shower baths. **Cards:** AE, MC, VI.

Motel

SANDY POINT MOTEL
Phone: (518)624-3871

5/1-10/28 & 4/14-4/30	2P: $50-$80	

Location: 2 mi s on SR 30 and 28 N. Rt 30 12847 (PO Box 8). **Terms:** Open 5/1-10/28 & 4/14-4/30; weekly rates avail; 10 day cancellation notice; cancellation fee imposed. **Facility:** 11 rooms. Quiet, beautiful lakefront views. Sandy beach. Modest guest rooms with nice screened in patio or balcony. 5 efficiencies, $12 extra charge; 2 stories; exterior corridors; beach, sauna; boat dock. **Recreation:** swimming, fishing. Rental: boats, canoes. **Cards:** AE, DS, MC, VI. **Special Amenities:** Free local telephone calls and preferred room (subject to availability with advanced reservations).

Motel

SHAMROCK MOTEL AND COTTAGES
Phone: (518)624-3861

7/1-9/15	1P: $60	2P: $75	XP: $10 F12
5/1-6/30 & 9/16-10/15	1P: $50	2P: $60	XP: $10 F12

Location: 1 mi s on SR 30 and 28 N. (PO Box 205, 12847). Fax: 518/624-9803. **Terms:** Open 5/1-10/15; weekly rates avail. **Facility:** 17 rooms. Peaceful location. Lakefront motel, 2-bedroom cottages also avail. Weekly rental only for housekeeping cottages 7/1-8/31, $475-$600 for up to 6 persons. 2 efficiencies, $10 extra charge; 1 story; exterior corridors; beach; boat dock; playground. **Recreation:** swimming, fishing. **All Rooms:** combo or shower baths. **Cards:** AE, DS, MC, VI. **Special Amenities:** Free local telephone calls and preferred room (subject to availability with advanced reservations).

Motel

LOUDONVILLE pop. 10,800   (See map p. 193; index p. 192)

——— RESTAURANT ———

PEARL OF THE ORIENT
Lunch: $6-$7   **Dinner:** $7-$17   Phone: 518/459-0903   (40)

Chinese

Location: Kimberly Square; just w of jct Albany Shaker and Osborn rds, 1.7 mi e, I-87, exit 4. 471 Albany Shaker Rd 12211. **Hours:** 11 am-10 pm, Fri-11 pm, Sat noon-11 pm, Sun noon-10 pm. Closed: 11/23 & 12/25. **Reservations:** accepted. **Features:** casual dress; carryout; cocktails; a la carte. Traditional preparations of Hunan, Szechwan and Cantonese fare line the menu. Oriental decorations, including artwork and rich colors, add to the relaxed atmosphere of the dining room. The weekday lunch buffet is well-stocked and popular. **Cards:** AE, MC, VI.

LOWMAN

——— LODGING ———

RED JACKET MOTOR INN
Phone: (607)734-1616

5/1-11/30	1P: $39-$75	2P: $45-$75	XP: $10 F12
12/1-4/30	1P: $35-$50	2P: $40-$55	XP: $10 F12

Location: SR 17, just e from CR 8 (between MM 195 and 196). Rt 17 14902 (PO Box 489, ELMIRA). Fax: 607/732-0848. **Terms:** Weekly & monthly rates avail; 3 day cancellation notice; small pets only, $10 extra charge. **Facility:** 48 rooms. Rural location; attractive lobby with slate floor and brick fireplace. 1 story; exterior corridors; playground. **Dining:** Restaurant; 5 am-9 pm; $7-$13. **All Rooms:** combo or shower baths, extended cable TV. **Some Rooms:** Fee: refrigerators, microwaves. **Cards:** AE, CB, DI, DS, MC, VI. **Special Amenities:** Free breakfast and free local telephone calls. (See color ad p 253)

Motor Inn

LOWVILLE pop. 3,600

——— LODGING ———

RIDGE VIEW MOTOR LODGE   **Phone:** 315/376-2252
◆◆   All Year   1P: $47-$65   2P: $57-$72   XP: $10   F12
Motel   **Location:** 1.5 mi n on SR 12. Rt 12 13367 (Rt 1 Box 14M). Fax: 315/376-2977. **Terms:** [CP] meal plan; 6 day cancellation notice, winter weekends. **Facility:** 40 rooms. Quiet and peaceful country surroundings. Picnic tables out back. Comfortable rooms with a home-like atmosphere. 1 story; interior corridors; playground. **Services:** winter plug-ins. **Some Rooms:** Fee: refrigerators, microwaves, VCR. **Cards:** AE, MC, VI.

MALONE pop. 6,800

——— LODGINGS ———

FOUR SEASONS MOTEL   **Phone:** (518)483-3490
(AAA) (SAVE)   5/1-10/1   1P: $45-$52   2P: $48-$59   XP: $5   F10
   10/2-4/30   1P: $38-$45   2P: $40-$52   XP: $5   F10
◆◆   **Location:** 1 mi w on SR 11. 236 W Main St 12953. Fax: 518/483-3490. **Terms:** Cancellation fee imposed;
Motel   package plans; pets. **Facility:** 26 rooms. 1 large suite kitchenette room. 1 story; exterior corridors.
   Services: winter plug-ins. **All Rooms:** combo or shower baths, extended cable TV. **Cards:** AE, DI, DS,
MC, VI.

SUPER 8 MOTEL AT JONS   **Phone:** (518)483-8123
(AAA) (SAVE)   5/19-10/31   1P: $60   2P: $66   XP: $6   F12
   4/1-4/30   1P: $55   2P: $61   XP: $6   F12
◆◆   5/1-5/18 & 11/1-3/31   1P: $53   2P: $59   XP: $6   F12
Motel   **Location:** SR 30 S, just s of jct SR 11 and 30. Finny Blvd, Rt 30 12953 (17 Rockland St). Fax: 518/483-8058. **Terms:** 5 day cancellation notice; small pets only, in designated rooms. **Facility:** 44 rooms. Modern rooms. 2 stories; interior corridors. **Dining:** Restaurant nearby. **Services:** winter plug-ins. **Recreation:** Fee: movie rentals. **All Rooms:** extended cable TV. **Some Rooms:** Fee: VCR. **Cards:** AE, CB, DI, DS, MC, VI. **Special Amenities:** Early check-in/late check-out and free local telephone calls.

——— RESTAURANT ———

JONS FAMILY RESTAURANT   **Lunch:** $2-$10   **Dinner:** $2-$10   **Phone:** 518/483-6230
(AAA)   **Location:** On SR 30 S, just s of jct SR 11/30/37. Finney Blvd 12953. **Hours:** 5:30 am-9 pm, Fri & Sat-10
◆   pm. Closed: 11/23 & 12/25. **Features:** casual dress; carryout; salad bar; cocktails; a la carte. Every member
American   of the family is welcomed at the casual restaurant, which is decorated with local artwork and seasonal motifs. The menu is all about traditional comfort foods that are tasty and filling. For dessert, choose from a variety of pies and sundaes. **Cards:** AE, DS, MC, VI.

MANCHESTER pop. 1,600—*See also FINGER LAKES.*

——— LODGING ———

ROADSIDE INN   **Phone:** (716)289-3811
(AAA) (SAVE)   7/1-8/31   1P: $45-$70   2P: $50-$75   XP: $8   F12
   5/1-6/30   1P: $45-$60   2P: $50-$65   XP: $8   F12
◆   9/1-10/31   1P: $40-$60   2P: $45-$65   XP: $8   F12
Motel   11/1-4/30   1P: $40-$50   2P: $40-$60   XP: $8   F12
   Location: I-90 (New York Thruway), exit 43. Rts 21 & 96 14504 (4078 Rt 96). Fax: 716/289-3811. **Facility:** 38 rooms. Rooms range from modest decor to pleasant. 1-2 stories; interior/exterior corridors. **Dining:** Dining room nearby. **Cards:** AE, CB, DI, DS, JC, MC, VI. **Special Amenities:** Free local telephone calls and free newspaper.

MARGARETVILLE pop. 600

——— LODGING ———

MARGARETVILLE MOUNTAIN INN BED & BREAKFAST   **Phone:** (914)586-3933
◆◆   All Year   1P: $65-$145   2P: $65-$145   XP: $15   F12
Historic Bed   **Location:** 2 mi n on Walnut St/Margaretville Mountain Rd. Margaretville Mountain Rd 12455 (Box 16).
& Breakfast   Fax: 914/586-1699. **Terms:** [BP] meal plan; check-in 4 pm; 10 day cancellation notice; cancellation fee imposed; 2 night min stay, some wkends 7/1-8/31; package plans; pet on premises. **Facility:** 7 rooms. Attractively restored 1886 Queen Anne Victorian home located in peaceful rural area. 2 stories; interior corridors; smoke free premises. **Some Rooms:** combo or shower baths, shared bathrooms. **Cards:** AE, MC, VI.

MASSAPEQUA PARK pop. 18,000

——— LODGING ———

BEST WESTERN BAR HARBOUR MOTEL   **Phone:** (516)541-2000
(AAA)   All Year   1P: $88-$110   2P: $88-$110   XP: $10   F12
◆◆   **Location:** SR 27 E, 2.5 mi e of SR 135. 5080 Sunrise Hwy (SR 27 E) 11762. Fax: 516/541-2004. **Terms:** [CP]
Motel   meal plan. **Facility:** 51 rooms. Guest rooms are average sized offering good, budget-oriented accommodations. 2 stories; exterior corridors. **Dining:** Restaurants nearby. **All Rooms:** extended cable TV. **Cards:** AE, CB, DI, DS, MC, VI.

MASSENA pop. 11,700

—— LODGINGS ——

ECONO LODGE　　　　　　　　　　　　　　　　　　　　**Phone:** (315)764-0246

(AAA) (SAVE)

6/16-10/15	1P: $68-$90	2P: $75-$95	XP: $5	F18
5/1-6/15	1P: $68-$90	2P: $73-$95	XP: $5	F18
10/16-4/30	1P: $68-$90	2P: $73-$95	XP: $10	F18

♦♦♦

Motor Inn　**Location:** 2.7 mi sw on SR 37. 15054 SR 37 13662. Fax: 315/764-9615. **Facility:** 52 rooms. Attractive, well furnished rooms. Few smaller units. 1 two-bedroom unit. 2 stories; interior/exterior corridors. **Dining:** Restaurant; 6 am-10:30 & 5-10 pm, Mon 5 pm-10 pm, Sun 7 am-2 pm 5/1-10/31; $8-$20; cocktails. **Services:** winter plug-ins. **All Rooms:** extended cable TV. **Cards:** AE, DI, DS, JC, MC, VI. **Special Amenities:** Free local telephone calls and free room upgrade (subject to availability with advanced reservations).

SUPER 8 MOTEL　　　　　　　　　　　　　　　　　　　**Phone:** 315/764-1065

♦♦

All Year	1P: $55-$75	2P: $60-$80	XP: $10	F12

Motel　**Location:** SR 37, 2 mi e of jct Hwy 56. 84 Grove St 13662. Fax: 315/764-9710. **Facility:** 42 rooms. Close to some food outlets. 3 stories, no elevator; interior corridors. **Services:** winter plug-ins. **Cards:** AE, DI, DS, MC, VI.

MAYVILLE pop. 1,600

—— RESTAURANT ——

WEBB'S CAPTAINS TABLE　　**Lunch:** $6-$10　　**Dinner:** $12-$30　　**Phone:** 716-753-3960

♦♦♦

American　**Location:** 115 W Lake Rd 14757. **Hours:** 11 am-11 pm. **Closed:** 11/23, 12/24 & 12/25. **Reservations:** suggested; on weekends. **Features:** dressy casual; children's menu; carryout; cocktails & lounge. Many tables in the interestingly decorated dining room overlook Lake Chautauqua. Regional dishes—as well as weekend specials and vegetarian choices—line the menu. Half portions are available. The neatly dressed wait staff provides attentive service. **Cards:** AE, DS, MC, VI.

MCGRAW

—— LODGING ——

ECONO LODGE OF CORTLAND　　　　　　　　　　　　　**Phone:** (607)753-7594

(AAA) (SAVE)

7/1-8/31	1P: $54-$95	2P: $64-$95	XP: $10	F18
5/1-6/30	1P: $49-$95	2P: $59-$95	XP: $10	F18
9/1-10/31	1P: $49-$89	2P: $59-$89	XP: $10	F18
11/1-4/30	1P: $45-$69	2P: $55-$69	XP: $10	F18

♦

Motel　**Location:** I-81, exit 10. 3775 US Rt 11 13101. Fax: 607/753-6508. **Terms:** 30 day cancellation notice; cancellation fee imposed; pets, in second floor smoking rooms. **Facility:** 72 rooms. Ground floor rooms have been renovated. Older style rooms on 2nd floor. Whirlpool room, $79-$125; 2 stories; interior corridors. **Cards:** AE, DI, DS, JC, MC, VI. **Special Amenities:** Early check-in/late check-out and free breakfast.

MEDFORD pop. 21,300

—— LODGING ——

THE INN AT MEDFORD　　　　　　　　　　　　　　　　**Phone:** 631/654-3000

♦♦♦

Motel　Property failed to provide current rates

Location: I-495, exit 64, just s. 2695 Rt 112 11763. Fax: 631/654-1281. **Terms:** [ECP] meal plan. **Facility:** 76 rooms. Southwest decor in lobby. Nicely landscaped fenced backyard. 2 stories; interior/exterior corridors. **Some Rooms:** 32 efficiencies. **Cards:** AE, DI, DS, MC, VI.

MELVILLE pop. 12,600

—— LODGINGS ——

HUNTINGTON HILTON　　　　　　　　　　　　　　　　**Phone:** 631/845-1000

♦♦♦

Hotel　Property failed to provide current rates

Location: 1 mi s of I-495, exit 49, on SR 110. 598 Broad Hollow Rd (SR 110) 11747. Fax: 631/845-5287. **Terms:** Check-in 4 pm; package plans, weekends. **Facility:** 302 rooms. Garden atrium and indoor pool with rock ponds and waterfalls. 5 stories; interior corridors; 2 pools, 1 indoor heated; 1 lighted tennis court. **Services:** gift shop. Fee: massage. **All Rooms:** combo or shower baths. **Some Rooms:** Fee: VCR. **Cards:** AE, CB, DI, DS, JC, MC, VI. *(See color ad p 57)*

MELVILLE MARRIOTT LONG ISLAND　　　　　　　　　**Phone:** 631/423-1600

♦♦♦

All Year	1P: $229-$259	2P: $229-$259

Hotel　**Location:** I-495 E (Long Island Expwy), exit 49 S, just n; I-495 W, exit 49 N, off n service road, just w of SR 110. 1350 Old Walt Whitman Rd 11747. Fax: 631/423-1790. **Terms:** Package plans. **Facility:** 370 rooms. Executive level rooms are offered. Sunny atrium public areas. 4 stories; interior corridors; heated pool. **Services:** gift shop; area transportation. **All Rooms:** combo or shower baths. **Some Rooms:** Fee: refrigerators. **Cards:** AE, CB, DI, DS, MC, VI.

MERRICK pop. 23,000

——— LODGING ———

GATEWAY INN
Phone: 516/378-7100
All Year   1P: $84-$103   2P: $84-$103   XP: $7   F12
Location: 1780 Sunrise Hwy 11566. Fax: 516/378-5745. **Terms:** [CP] meal plan; weekly & monthly rates avail.
Motel   **Facility:** 60 rooms. Attractive yet simple guest rooms; some featuring a large bay window that overlooks a lush courtyard setting. 1 two-bedroom unit. 2 stories; interior/exterior corridors. **All Rooms:** combo or shower baths.
Some Rooms: Fee: refrigerators. **Cards:** AE, DI, DS, MC, VI. *(See color ad p 306)*

MEXICO pop. 1,600

——— RESTAURANT ———

ARENA'S EIS HOUSE
Dinner: $8-$20   Phone: 315/963-3830
Location: 1 mi n on CR 16. Academy St & Watson 13114. **Hours:** 5 pm-10 pm. Closed: Mon & Sun.
Continental   **Reservations:** suggested. **Features:** casual dress; children's menu; carryout; cocktails & lounge; a la carte.
On the Little Salmon River, the restaurant sits in the midst of a lovely setting, with lots of beautiful landscaping. The informal dining room welcomes families to enjoy fellowship and well-prepared food. Entertainers perform two nights a week. **Cards:** AE, CB, DI, MC, VI.

MIDDLETOWN pop. 24,200

——— LODGINGS ———

HAMPTON INN
Phone: (914)344-3400
All Year   1P: $86-$100   2P: $89-$110
Motel   **Location:** SR 17, exit 122. 20 Crystal Run Crossing 10941. Fax: 914/344-3403. **Terms:** [ECP] meal plan.
Facility: 127 rooms. Scheduled to open May, 1999. 4 stories; interior corridors. **Cards:** AE, CB, DI, DS,
MC, VI.

HOLIDAY INN
Phone: (914)343-1474
12/31-4/30   1P: $80-$115   2P: $90-$125   XP: $10   F18
Motor Inn   5/1-12/30   1P: $80-$105   2P: $90-$115   XP: $10   F18
Location: SR 17, exit 122, 0.3 mi n. 68 Crystal Run Rd 10941. Fax: 914/692-7155. **Facility:** 102 rooms. Contemporary and attractive decor in large units. Pleasant recreational areas, with exercise room overlooking the pool. 2 stories; interior corridors; 2 pools, 1 indoor heated. **Services:** winter plug-ins. **Cards:** AE, CB, DI, DS, JC, MC, VI.

MIDDLETOWN MOTEL
Phone: (914)342-2535
5/1-11/1   1P: $50-$90   2P: $50-$90   XP: $10   F12
Motel   11/1-4/30   1P: $45-$70   2P: $45-$70   XP: $10   F12
Location: At jct SR 17, exit 120 and SR 211. 501 Rt 211 E 10941. Fax: 914/342-0892. **Terms:** [BP] meal plan; 7 day cancellation notice; pets. **Facility:** 101 rooms. Set on hilltop with steep driveway. Many spacious rooms. 2 stories; interior/exterior corridors; heated pool. **Some Rooms:** Fee: refrigerators, microwaves, VCR. **Cards:** AE, CB, DI, DS, MC, VI.

SUPER 8 MOTEL
Phone: (914)692-5828
All Year   1P: $65-$75   2P: $85-$95   XP: $5   F12
Motel   **Location:** SR 211, 0.3 mi e of jct SR 17, exit 120; 0.5 mi n of I-84, exit 4 W. 563 Rt 211 E 10940.
Fax: 914/692-5828. **Terms:** Pets, $25 dep req. **Facility:** 82 rooms. Set back from main road. 2 stories; interior corridors. **Cards:** AE, CB, DI, DS, MC, VI.

——— RESTAURANT ———

HANA
Lunch: $8-$17   **Dinner:** $12-$26   Phone: 914/342-6634
Location: On SR 211; SR 17, exit 120 W and follow 1 mi; 2 mi w of I-84, exit 4 W. 339 Rt 211 10940.
Ethnic   **Hours:** noon-10:30 pm, Fri & Sat-11 pm, Sun-10 pm. Closed: 11/23. **Reservations:** suggested; weekends.
Features: casual dress; carryout; cocktails & lounge; a la carte. A red brick base lines the bottom of this attractive, stone-sided building. Soft Japanese music plays in the background as diners enjoy traditional Japanese and Korean cuisine, including a nice array of sushi. The tatami room is available by reservation. **Cards:** AE, MC, VI.

MILTON pop. 1,100

——— RESTAURANT ———

SHIP LANTERN INN
Lunch: $8-$15   **Dinner:** $15-$23   Phone: 914/795-5400
Location: On US 9 W; 4.3 mi s of jct US 44 and SR 55 at Mid-Hudson Bridge. 1725 Rt 9 W 12547.
Continental   **Hours:** noon-2 & 4:30-9:30 pm, Sat 5 pm-10:30 pm, Sun 1 pm-8 pm. Closed: 12/24, 12/25, Mon & 1/1-1/15.
Reservations: suggested. **Features:** casual dress; carryout; cocktails & lounge; a la carte. Representative of sophisticated seafood preparations are such dishes as Parmesan-crusted swordfish with a citrus beurre blanc or porcini-dusted sea bass with olive and pepper salsa. Nautical decor, including many ship models, punctuates the dining room. **Cards:** AE, DS, MC, VI.

MINEOLA

—— RESTAURANT ——

LA CISTERNA RESTAURANT **Lunch:** $13-$16   **Dinner:** $18-$24   **Phone:** 516/248-2112
◆◆◆ **Location:** From SR 25, 1 mi s, just n of train station. 109 Mineola Blvd 11501. **Hours:** noon-3:30 & 5:30-10
Italian pm. Closed: 1/1, 7/4 & 12/25. **Reservations:** suggested. **Features:** casual dress; cocktails; street parking; a
la carte. Dine on heavenly Italian food while angel dolls watch from above in the dining room, which is
tastefully appointed with Renaissance-type, faux oil paintings. The creative menu lists great dishes prepared with fresh
ingredients. Service is unobtrusive. Smoke free premises. **Cards:** AE, CB, DI, DS, MC, VI. ⊠

MONTAUK pop. 3,000

—— LODGINGS ——

GURNEY'S INN RESORT & SPA **Phone:** 631/668-2345
(AAA) 10/17-4/30   1P: $200-$225   2P: $300-$410   XP: $80   F3
      5/16-10/16   1P: $270-$305   2P: $325-$395   XP: $98   F3
◆◆◆ 5/1-5/15   1P: $180-$205   2P: $280-$390   XP: $80   F3
Complex **Location:** 3 mi w. 290 Old Montauk Hwy 11954 (PO Box 5073). **Fax:** 631/668-3576. **Terms:** [MAP] meal plan;
check-in 3:30 pm; 14 day cancellation notice; cancellation fee imposed; 4 night min stay, 5/22-9/7; package
plans. **Facility:** 109 rooms. Overlooking ocean. Full service spa and beachfront accommodations. Cottages avail for families.
1- to 3-bedroom cottages, $450-$1330 for up to 6 persons; 4 stories, no elevator; interior/exterior corridors; oceanfront; beach,
heated pool, saunas, steamrooms, whirlpools, heated seawater pools & lifeguards on beach. **Dining:** Restaurant, coffee shop;
cocktails; also, Sea Grill at Gurney's Inn, see separate listing. **Services:** gift shop. Fee: massage. **Recreation:** swimming,
fishing; full service beauty salon & spa. **All Rooms:** extended cable TV. **Some Rooms:** 5 efficiencies, no utensils. **Cards:** AE,
CB, DI, DS, MC, VI. ⊞ ⍻ ⊡ 🛆 🅥 🏌 📷 ⊡ VCR 🖨 ▣ 🖥 DATA PORT ⤬ ⤬ ♿ ⊠

MONTAUK YACHT CLUB RESORT & MARINA **Phone:** (631)668-3100
◆◆◆ 7/1-9/4   1P: $199-$369   2P: $199-$369   XP: $25   F16
      5/16-6/30 & 3/17-4/30   1P: $49-$259   2P: $49-$259   XP: $25   F16
      9/5-1/1   1P: $69-$219   2P: $69-$219   XP: $25   F16
Resort **Location:** 1 mi e on SR 27, 1.8 mi n on W Lake Dr (CR 77), then just e. 32 Star Island Rd 11954 (PO Box 5048).
Fax: 631/668-3303. **Terms:** Open 5/1-1/1 & 3/17-4/30; 10 day cancellation notice; 2 night min stay, weekends; package plans.
Facility: 107 rooms. Splendid view of marina. Nicely renovated rooms feature bright, cheerful decor, most units with a bal-
cony. 2 stories; interior corridors; 3 pools, 1 indoor, 2 heated; boat ramp. Fee: 9 tennis courts (4 lighted); marina. **Services:** gift
shop; area transportation. Fee: massage. **Recreation:** Fee: canoeing; bicycles. Rental: paddleboats. **All Rooms:** safes.
Cards: AE, CB, DI, DS, MC, VI. ASK S🅓 ⍻ ⊡ 🛆 🏌 ⊠ 🖨 🖥 🖥 DATA PORT ⤬ ⤬ ♿ ⊠

—— RESTAURANTS ——

GOSMAN'S DOCK **Dinner:** $10-$30   **Phone:** 631/668-5330
◆◆ **Location:** 1 mi e on SR 27, 2.5 mi n. 500 W Lake Dr 11954. **Hours:** Open 5/1-10/15; noon-10 pm.
Seafood **Features:** casual dress; cocktails & lounge; a la carte. From the flower-filled patio to the open dining dock,
the setting here is perfect for a summer meal. The menu offers the sea's bounty—particularly excellent local
lobster and Long Island produce—in traditional and modern dishes. Expect a wait for seatin. Smoke free premises.
Cards: AE, MC, VI. ⊠

SEA GRILL AT GURNEY'S INN **Dinner:** $18-$30   **Phone:** 631/668-2660
(AAA) **Location:** 3 mi w; in Gurney's Inn Resort & Spa. Old Montauk Hwy 11954. **Hours:** 5:30 pm-10 pm.
◆◆ **Reservations:** suggested; in season. **Features:** semi-formal attire; early bird specials; cocktails & lounge;
Italian entertainment; valet parking; a la carte, also prix fixe. Mouthwatering aromas hang in the air as the on-site
bakery produces tempting fresh bread. Enjoy breathtaking views of the ocean from the modestly decorated
dining room. The menu lists internationally influenced entrees of fresh seafood and prime meat. Smoke free
premises. **Cards:** AE, DI, DS, MC, VI. ⊠

MONTICELLO pop. 6,600

—— LODGINGS ——

BEST WESTERN MONTICELLO **Phone:** (914)796-4000
(AAA) 5/1-9/16   1P: $85-$125   2P: $145   XP: $10   F12
      9/17-4/30   1P: $75-$105   2P: $115   XP: $10   F12
◆◆◆ **Location:** SR 17, exit 104, 0.3 mi s on SR 17B. 21 Raceway Rd 12701. **Fax:** 914/796-4000. **Terms:** [CP] meal
Motel plan; 3 day cancellation notice; 2 night min stay, summer weekends. **Facility:** 62 rooms. Nice hillside location.
8 whirlpool rooms, $105-$145; suites, $150-$200; 2 stories; interior corridors; designated smoking area; small
heated indoor pool, sauna. **Dining:** Restaurant nearby. **Services:** winter plug-ins. **All Rooms:** extended cable TV.
Some Rooms: 3 efficiencies. Fee: refrigerators, microwaves. **Cards:** AE, CB, DI, DS, MC, VI.
⍻ 🛆 🛆 ⊠ 🏌 🖨 ▣ 🖥 🖥 ⤬

ECONO LODGE **Phone:** (914)794-8800
(AAA) SAVE 5/1-9/10   1P: $55-$135   2P: $65-$150   XP: $10   F18
      9/11-4/30   1P: $45-$125   2P: $55-$125   XP: $10   F18
◆◆ **Location:** Center. 190 Broadway 12701. **Fax:** 914/794-8800. **Terms:** [CP] meal plan. **Facility:** 47 rooms. 5
Motel whirlpool rooms, $135-$150; 2 stories; exterior corridors. **Dining:** Restaurant nearby. **Services:** winter plug-ins.
All Rooms: combo or shower baths, extended cable TV. **Some Rooms:** 4 efficiencies, no utensils. Fee: mi-
crowaves, VCR. **Cards:** AE, CB, DI, DS, JC, MC, VI. **Special Amenities:** Free breakfast and free local telephone calls.
S🅓 ⍻ ⊠ 🏌 VCR 🖨 ▣ 🖥 🖥 ⤬

MONTOUR FALLS pop. 1,800—*See also FINGER LAKES.*

——— LODGINGS ———

FALLS MOTEL
◆
Motel
5/1-11/30	1P: $65-$125	2P: $65-$125	XP: $10

Phone: (607)535-7262
F16
Location: SR 14 S, just w; SR 14 N, just w, then just e. 239 N Genesee St 14865 (PO Box 631). Fax: 607/535-2977. **Terms:** Open 5/1-11/30; 14 day cancellation notice; pets, $8 extra charge. **Facility:** 12 rooms. Quiet, off street location. 1 story; exterior corridors. **Cards:** AE, DS, MC, VI.

(A$K) 🐾 ⊗ 🖨 📷 🔒

RELAX INN
(AAA) (SAVE)
◆
Motel
5/1-10/31	1P: $44-$78	2P: $54-$89	XP: $5
11/1-4/30	1P: $36-$44	2P: $36-$44	XP: $5

Phone: (607)535-7183
F8
F8
Location: Jct SR 14 and 224. 100 Clawson Blvd 14865. Fax: 607/535-6199. **Terms:** 3 day cancellation notice; pets, $10 extra charge. **Facility:** 12 rooms. Simple rooms in residential area at junction of two hwys. 1 story; exterior corridors. **Services:** winter plug-ins. **All Rooms:** combo or shower baths, extended cable TV. **Cards:** AE, DS, MC, VI. **Special Amenities:** Early check-in/late check-out and free local telephone calls.

(S/D) 🐾 ⊗ 🖨 🔒

——— RESTAURANT ———

CHEF'S DINER
◆
American
Lunch: $4-$7	**Dinner:** $4-$14	Phone: 607/535-9975

Location: 1 mi n on Rt 14; or 2.4 mi s on Rt 14 from Watkins Glen State Park entrance. Rt 14 Montour-Watkins Rd 14865. **Hours:** 6 am-11 pm; to 10 pm off season. Closed: 12/25. **Features:** casual dress; children's menu; senior's menu; health conscious menu items; carryout. The family-style restaurant—an area institution since the late 1940s—delivers a diverse menu of traditional favorites, ranging from salads, sandwiches and quiche to meatloaf and pork chops. Big portions and reasonably prices mean excellent value.

MOUNT KISCO —*See New York p. 373.*

MOUNT MORRIS

——— LODGING ———

COUNTRY INN AND SUITES
◆◆◆
Motel
All Year	1P: $80-$119	2P: $80-$119	XP: $10

Phone: (716)658-4080
F18
Location: Center; on SR 36. 130 N Main St 14510. Fax: 716/658-4020. **Terms:** [CP] meal plan; cancellation fee imposed. **Facility:** 60 rooms. 2 stories; interior corridors; small heated indoor pool. **Services:** winter plug-ins. **All Rooms:** combo or shower baths. **Cards:** AE, DI, DS, MC, VI. *(See color ad below)*

(A$K) (S/D) 🎿 ♿ 🌀 ⊗ 🍴 🖨 🖥 📷 🔒 (DATA PORT) 🏊 🏊 🛗

MOUNT UPTON pop. 500

——— RESTAURANT ———

THE OLD MILL
◆◆
American
Dinner: $14-$20	Phone: 607/764-8300

Location: SR 8, 1.5 mi n from jct Rt 51. Rt 8 13809. **Hours:** 4:30 pm-9 pm, Sun noon-7:30 pm. Closed: 11/23, Mon, Tues & Wed 11/1-11/24. **Reservations:** suggested. **Features:** casual dress; children's menu; early bird specials; senior's menu; cocktails. The converted old mill—featuring tables set with hand-painted china—sits alongside the river and affords beautiful views. Such dishes as the signature chicken Old Mill are well-prepared, tasty and served in ample portions. Service is prompt and pleasant. **Cards:** AE, DI, DS, MC, VI.

⊗

MUMFORD pop. 900

——— LODGING ———

GENESEE COUNTRY INN
◆◆◆   All Year   2P: $114-$150   XP: $15   **Phone:** (716)538-2500
Historic Bed   **Location:** Just w from SR 36. 948 George St 14511-0340. **Fax:** 716/538-4565. **Terms:** [BP] meal plan; 7 day
& Breakfast   cancellation notice; cancellation fee imposed; package plans. **Facility:** 9 rooms. Restored old stone mill circa
1833, in setting by waterfall. 3 rooms with fireplace and 2 with balcony. 3 stories, no elevator; interior corridors;
smoke free premises. **Services:** gift shop. **Recreation:** fishing. **All Rooms:** combo or shower baths. **Cards:** AE, DI, DS,
MC, VI.

⊠ [VCR] [🖨] ⊠

NANUET —See New York p. 373.

NAPLES pop. 1,200—See also FINGER LAKES.

——— RESTAURANT ———

REDWOOD RESTAURANT   **Lunch:** $4-$8   **Dinner:** $7-$15   **Phone:** 716/374-6360
◆   **Location:** 0.5 mi s on SR 21. 6 Cohocton St 14512. **Hours:** noon-1:30 & 4:30-8 pm, Fri & Sat 4:30 pm-9
American   pm, Sun noon-8 pm. Closed: 12/25. **Reservations:** suggested; weekends. **Features:** children's menu;
carryout; salad bar; cocktails & lounge. Many windows let in lots of light at the bright, family-oriented
restaurant. The menu includes seafood and steaks, as well as soups, sandwiches and Italian entrees. The Friday fish fry is
popular, as are the delicious—and tempting—homemade desserts. **Cards:** AE, DS, MC, VI.

⊠

NEWBURGH pop. 26,500

——— LODGINGS ———

COMFORT INN NEWBURGH   **Phone:** (914)567-0567
◆◆◆   5/1-9/1   1P: $86-$125   2P: $96-$125
Motel   9/2-4/30   1P: $76-$125   2P: $86-$125
Location: I-84, exit 6, just w. 5 Lakeside Rd 12550. **Fax:** 914/567-0582. **Terms:** 7 day cancellation notice.
Facility: 130 rooms. Spacious, very clean rooms. Pleasant staff. 3 stories; interior corridors. **Services:** winter plug-ins.
Cards: AE, CB, DI, DS, MC, VI.

[SAVE] [S/D] [✈] [¶†] [🚭] [△] [⟳] ⊠ [📷] [🖨] [💻] [DATA PORT] [~]

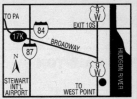

HAMPTON INN-NEWBURGH
◆◆◆ All Year   1P: $86-$150   2P: $92-$150   **Phone:** (914)567-9100
Motel   **Location:** I-87, exit 17, w to SR 300 (Union Ave), just n; I-84, exit 7 S. 1292 SR 300 12550. **Fax:** 914/567-6331. **Terms:** [CP] meal plan; 14 day cancellation notice; cancellation fee imposed. **Facility:** 116 rooms. New property. Attractive public areas. 2 stories; interior corridors; designated smoking area; heated pool. **All Rooms:** combo or shower baths. **Some Rooms:** Fee: refrigerators. **Cards:** AE, CB, DI, DS, MC, VI.

HOLIDAY INN-WEST POINT
◆◆◆   Property failed to provide current rates   **Phone:** 914-564-9020
Motor Inn   **Location:** I-87, exit 17, then w; I-84, exit 6, 2 mi e. 90 Rt 17K 12550. **Fax:** 914/564-9040. **Facility:** 122 rooms. Average sized guest rooms. 2 stories; interior/exterior corridors; designated smoking area. **Services:** winter plug-ins. **Some Rooms:** Fee: refrigerators. **Cards:** AE, CB, DI, JC, MC, VI.

HOWARD JOHNSON INN
AAA **SAVE**
◆◆◆
Motor Inn

7/1-11/1	1P: $79-$99	2P: $79-$99	XP: $8
5/1-6/30	1P: $69-$99	2P: $69-$99	XP: $8
11/2-4/30	1P: $53-$89	2P: $53-$89	XP: $8

     Phone: (914)564-4000

Location: I-87, exit 17, just w on 17K W; I-84 W, exit 7S to 17K W; I-84 E, exit 6, 2 mi e. 95 Rt 17K 12550. **Fax:** 914/564-0620. **Terms:** [CP] meal plan. **Facility:** 74 rooms. Large guest rooms with attractive decor. 2 stories; interior corridors; designated smoking area; wading pool; 1 tennis court. **Dining:** Restaurant nearby. **Some Rooms:** Fee: refrigerators, microwaves. **Cards:** AE, CB, DI, DS, MC, VI. **Special Amenities:** Free breakfast and free local telephone calls.

NEWBURGH COURTYARD BY MARRIOTT
◆◆◆   Property failed to provide current rates   **Phone:** 914/567-4800
Motel   **Location:** I-84, exit 6; at Stewart International Airport Industrial Park. 4 Governor Dr 12550. **Fax:** 914/567-9550. **Terms:** 2 night min stay, some weekends. **Facility:** 78 rooms. Comfortably furnished spacious guest rooms. 3 stories; interior corridors; designated smoking area; small heated indoor pool. **All Rooms:** combo or shower baths. **Cards:** AE, CB, DI, DS, MC, VI.

RAMADA INN
◆◆◆   Property failed to provide current rates   **Phone:** 914/564-4500
Motor Inn   **Location:** I-87, exit 17, 17K W to SR 300 (Union Ave), just n; I-84, exit 7 S. 1289 Rt 300 12550. **Fax:** 914/564-4524. **Terms:** Package plans. **Facility:** 164 rooms. Property newly renovated. Contemporary decor. 2 stories; interior corridors. **Some Rooms:** Fee: refrigerators. **Cards:** AE, CB, DI, DS, MC, VI.

—— RESTAURANTS ——

IL CENA'COLO
◆◆◆   **Lunch:** $8-$22   **Dinner:** $16-$28   **Phone:** 914/564-4494
Northern Italian   **Location:** On Rt 52, just w of jct Rt 300 and 52. 228 Rt 52 12550. **Hours:** noon-2:30 & 5-9 pm, Fri & Sat 6 pm-11 pm, Sun 4 pm-9 pm. Closed major holidays & Tues. **Reservations:** suggested. **Features:** casual dress; cocktails & lounge; a la carte. An outstanding example of true Tuscan cuisine is the ravioli, which is stuffed with cheese and spinach, with pureed mushrooms in cream sauce. The wine list concentrates exclusively on Italian selections. Melt-in-your-mouth desserts are homemade. **Cards:** AE, DI, MC, VI.

YOBO ORIENTAL RESTAURANT
◆◆◆   **Lunch:** $5-$10   **Dinner:** $10-$23   **Phone:** 914/564-3848
Ethnic   **Location:** I-87, exit 17, to SR 300 via 17K W, just n. 1297 SR 300 12550. **Hours:** 11:30 am-9:30 pm, Fri-10:30 pm, Sat 12:30 pm-10:30 pm, Sun from 12:30 pm. Closed: 11/23. **Reservations:** accepted. **Features:** casual dress; carryout; cocktails & lounge; a la carte. Despite covering broad territory, the menu does a good job with cuisines of China, Japan, Thailand, Korea and Indonesia. Among selections are sushi, sashimi, tempura, dim sum and Korean bolgogi. The wait staff provides capable, well-executed service. **Cards:** AE, DI, MC, VI.

NEWFANE —See Niagara Falls p. 396.

NEW HAMPTON pop. 1,300

—— LODGING ——

DAYS INN-MIDDLETOWN
◆◆
Motel

5/1-10/31	1P: $49-$89	2P: $59-$89	XP: $7	F10
11/4-4/30	1P: $49-$89	2P: $59-$79	XP: $7	F10

     Phone: (914)374-2411

Location: On US 6 and SR 17M, 0.8 mi s of jct I-84, exit 3 E. Rt 17M 10958 (PO Box 279). **Fax:** 914/374-0011. **Terms:** [CP] meal plan; pets. **Facility:** 45 rooms. Nicely landscaped grounds with spacious back yard. Variety of rooms ranging from very small to large and well-appointed. 2 stories; interior/exterior corridors. **Services:** winter plug-ins. **All Rooms:** combo or shower baths. **Some Rooms:** Fee: refrigerators, microwaves. **Cards:** AE, CB, DI, DS, MC, VI.

NEW HARTFORD pop. 2,100

—— LODGINGS ——

HOLIDAY INN UTICA
◆◆◆ All Year
Motor Inn
Phone: (315)797-2131
1P: $89-$159   2P: $89-$159
Location: I-90 (New York Thruway), exit 31, 4.5 mi w on SR 5 W, exit on Burrstone Rd, 1 mi nw. 1777 Burrstone Rd 13413. Fax: 315/797-5817. **Terms:** Package plans; small pets only. **Facility:** 100 rooms. Large comfortable guest rooms. 2 stories; interior corridors. **Dining:** nightclub. **Services:** winter plug-ins. **All Rooms:** combo or shower baths. **Some Rooms:** 4 kitchens. Fee: refrigerators, microwaves. **Cards:** AE, CB, DI, DS, JC, MC, VI.

RAMADA INN
◆◆◆
Motor Inn
Phone: (315)735-3392
5/1-10/31   1P: $96-$103   2P: $103-$110   XP: $10   F16
11/1-4/30   1P: $81-$88   2P: $88-$95   XP: $10   F16
Location: Rt 8, just n of Rts 5 and 12 (New York Mills exit). 141 New Hartford St 13413. Fax: 315/738-7642.
Terms: 3 day cancellation notice; package plans. **Facility:** 104 rooms. Small rooms. 2 stories; interior corridors; heated pool. **Some Rooms:** Fee: refrigerators. **Cards:** AE, DI, DS, MC, VI.

—— RESTAURANTS ——

CARMELLA'S CAFE
◆◆
American
Lunch: $5-$11   **Dinner:** $6-$14   **Phone:** 315/797-3350
Location: 0.5 mi w on SR 5. 8530 Seneca Tpke 13413. **Hours:** 11 am-1 am, Sun from 9 am. Closed: 11/23 & 12/25. **Reservations:** accepted. **Features:** casual dress; Sunday brunch; children's menu; early bird specials; carryout; cocktails & lounge. A festive mood prevails in the energized dining room, which is decorated with eclectic antiques. Chicken riggies—which blends rigatoni noodles, charbroiled chicken, mushrooms, peppers, olives and onions—has long been a favorite dinner selection. **Cards:** AE, CB, DI, DS, MC, VI.

MICHAEL T'S
ⒶⒶ
◆◆
Italian
Dinner: $6-$15   **Phone:** 315/724-4882
Location: 1 mi w of jct SR 12 and 5 W on SR 5. 8390 Seneca Tpke 13413. **Hours:** 4 pm-9 pm, Fri & Sat-10 pm, Sun 3 pm-9 pm. Closed major holidays & Mon. **Reservations:** accepted. **Features:** casual dress; children's menu; carryout; cocktails & lounge. Family-owned and operated, this restaurant is known for fresh haddock preparations as well as such regional favorites as greens trunfio and chicken riggies. Collectible Jim Beam bottles line the dining room shelves. Service is friendly and prompt. **Cards:** AE, DS, MC, VI.

—— *The following restaurant has not been inspected by AAA but is listed for your information only.* ——

HOOK, LINE & SINKER PUB
(fyi)
Phone: 315/732-3636
Not inspected. **Location:** 0.8 mi w of jct SR 12 and 5 W on SR 5. 8471 Seneca Tpke 13413. **Features:** As the name implies, this is casual family dining in a nautical atmosphere.

NEW LEBANON

—— LODGING ——

VALLEY REST MOTEL
ⒶⒶ SAVE
◆
Motel
Phone: (518)794-7551
5/1-9/8   1P: $50-$78   2P: $60-$85   XP: $10   F11
9/9-4/30   1P: $49-$55   2P: $59-$65   XP: $10   F11
Location: 1 mi w on US 20. 776 Rt 20 12125. Fax: 518/794-7125. **Terms:** Weekly & monthly rates avail; 7 day cancellation notice; 2 night min stay, weekends 6/28-9/3. **Facility:** 14 rooms. Very modest guest rooms. Limited rooms open winter and spring. 1 story; exterior corridors. **Services:** winter plug-ins. **All Rooms:** combo or shower baths, extended cable TV. **Some Rooms:** efficiency, no utensils. **Cards:** AE, MC, VI.

—— RESTAURANT ——

MARIO'S RESTAURANT
◆◆
Northern
Italian
Dinner: $14-$22   **Phone:** 518/794-9495
Location: Just n on SR 22 N of jct SR 20 and 22. Rt 20 & 22 12125. **Hours:** 4 pm-10 pm, Sun noon-9:30 pm. Closed: 11/23, 12/25 & Tues. **Reservations:** suggested. **Features:** casual dress; carryout; cocktails & lounge; a la carte. The restaurant's pleasant wait staff serves a fine selection of traditional and seasonal Northern Italian dishes, including preparations of pasta, veal, seafood and chicken. Enjoy the serene mountain setting and the elegant surroundings. **Cards:** AE, CB, DI, DS, MC, VI.

NEW PALTZ pop. 5,500

—— LODGINGS ——

ECONO LODGE
ⒶⒶ SAVE
◆◆
Motel
Phone: (914)255-6200
5/1-10/31   1P: $67-$99   2P: $67-$99   XP: $6   F17
11/1-4/30   1P: $57-$90   2P: $57-$90   XP: $6   F17
Location: 0.5 mi e on Rt 299 E, I-87 Thruway exit 18. 530 Main St 12561. Fax: 914/256-0675. **Terms:** [CP] meal plan; weekly rates avail, off season. **Facility:** 34 rooms. Set back from road. Variety of room styles. 1 two-bedroom unit. 2 stories; interior/exterior corridors; designated smoking area. **Services:** winter plug-ins. **All Rooms:** combo or shower baths, extended cable TV. **Cards:** AE, CB, DI, DS, MC, VI. **Special Amenities:** Free breakfast.

SUPER 8 MOTEL OF NEW PALTZ
Phone: 914/255-8865
◆◆   5/1-10/31   1P: $66-$125   2P: $71-$125
Motel   11/1-4/30   1P: $58-$125   2P: $63-$125
Location: Just w of I-87 Thruway, exit 18. 7 Terwilliger Ln 12561. Fax: 914/255-1629. **Facility:** 68 rooms. 2 stories; interior corridors; designated smoking area. **Services:** winter plug-ins. **Cards:** AE, CB, DI, DS, MC, VI.

(ASK) (S🛏) (🍽→) (✕) (📹) (🖨) (🖼) (📀) (DATA PORT)

─────── *The following lodging was either not inspected or did not* ───────
meet AAA rating requirements but is listed for your information only.

MOHONK MOUNTAIN HOUSE
Phone: 914/255-1000
(fyi)   Not inspected. **Location:** 1000 Mountain Rest Rd 12561. Facilities, services, and decor characterize a mid-range property.

─────── **RESTAURANTS** ───────

DOMINICK'S   **Lunch:** $4-$8   **Dinner:** $9-$17   **Phone: 914/255-0120**
◆◆   **Location:** I-87 Thruway, exit 18, 1.5 mi w on Rt 299, just n on SR 32. 30 N Chestnut, Rt 32 N 12561.
Italian   **Hours:** 11:30 am-10 pm, Sat from noon, Sun 11 am-9 pm. Closed: 11/23, 12/24, 12/25, Mon & Tues. **Reservations:** suggested; weekends. **Features:** casual dress; Sunday brunch; children's menu; health conscious menu items; carryout; cocktails & lounge; a la carte. The menu's focus is on traditional Italian fare, such as rich fettuccine Alfredo, although American favorites also are listed. The atmosphere is pleasant and casual, making this place a nice spot for families. The Friday evening buffet is popular. **Cards:** AE, DI, DS, MC, VI.   (✕)

THE LOCUST TREE INN   Historical   **Lunch:** $5-$9   **Dinner:** $15-$21   **Phone: 914/255-7888**
(AAA)   **Location:** I-87 Thruway, exit 18, 1.5 mi w on Rt 299, n just before bridge, 1.3 mi on Huguenot St; on public
◆◆◆   golf course. 215 Huguenot St 12561. **Hours:** 11:30 am-2:30 & 5:30-10 pm, Sat from 5:30 pm, Sun 11 am-2
American   & 3:30-8 pm. Closed: 1/1, 12/25, Mon & 1/25-2/10. **Reservations:** suggested. **Features:** casual dress; Sunday brunch; cocktails; a la carte. The 1759 stone house has a sophisticated, upscale ambience. Not only is the summer patio a nice spot for leisurely dining, it also has seen many weddings, parties and other events. The menu lists a good variety of dishes, including vegetarian choices. **Cards:** AE, DI, DS, MC, VI.   (✕)

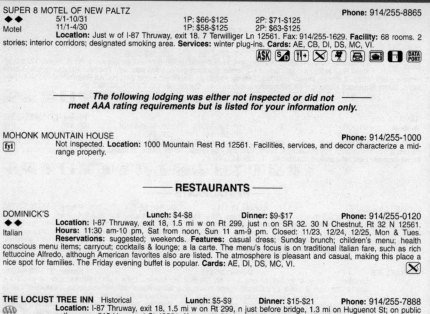

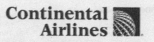

NEWPORT

—— RESTAURANT ——

WEST SIDE SALOON
◆
American
Lunch: $4-$20   **Dinner:** $4-$20   **Phone:** 315/845-8822
Location: On SR 28. 7591 Main St 13416. **Hours:** 11 am-9 pm, Fri-10 pm, Sat 4 pm-10 pm, Sun noon-7 pm. Closed major holidays, Mon & Tues 1/1-3/1. **Reservations:** accepted. **Features:** casual dress; carryout; cocktails & lounge; a la carte. Casual, river front dining. **Cards:** AE, DI, DS, MC, VI.
[X]

NEW ROCHELLE —See New York p. 373.

NEW WINDSOR pop. 8,900

—— LODGINGS ——

DAYS INN
[AAA] [SAVE]
◆ ◆
Motel
Phone: (914)564-7550
5/1-10/31   1P: $50-$65   2P: $55-$80   XP: $6   F12
11/1-4/30   1P: $40-$55   2P: $45-$60   XP: $6   F12
Location: On SR 300, s following signs for Stewart Airport, from jct I-84, exit 7 S; I-87 Thruway, exit 17 via 17K W to SR 300, 2 mi s. 915 Union Ave (SR 300) 12553. Fax: 914/564-7560. **Terms:** Weekly & monthly rates avail; 14 day cancellation notice. **Facility:** 88 rooms. Elevated site overlooking Washington Lake. Some small guest rooms. 2 stories; interior corridors; designated smoking area; heated indoor pool open 5/30-9/1. **Dining:** Restaurant nearby. **Services:** winter plug-ins. **All Rooms:** combo or shower baths, extended cable TV. **Some Rooms:** Fee: refrigerators, microwaves. **Cards:** AE, CB, DI, DS, MC, VI. **Special Amenities:** Early check-in/late check-out and free breakfast. *(See ad p 313)*
[S] [||•] [⊛] [△] [X] [※] [▣] [目] [⊸]

WINDSOR MOTEL
[AAA] [SAVE]
◆ ◆
Motel
Phone: (914)562-7777
4/1-4/30   1P: $39-$129   2P: $39-$139
5/1-11/30   1P: $39-$129   2P: $39-$139   XP: $10   F12
12/1-3/31   1P: $35-$99   2P: $35-$109   XP: $10   F12
Location: US 9 W, 2.4 mi s of jct SR 17 K and 32. 2976 Rt 9 W 12553. Fax: 914/562-7889. **Terms:** [CP] meal plan; weekly & monthly rates avail; 7 day cancellation notice. **Facility:** 30 rooms. Clean, contemporary rooms. 1 story; exterior corridors; designated smoking area. **All Rooms:** shower baths. **Cards:** AE, DS, MC, VI. **Special Amenities:** Early check-in/late check-out. *(See ad p 313)*
[S] [X] [※] [▣] [目]

—— RESTAURANTS ——

JADE ALOHA
◆ ◆
Chinese
Lunch: $5-$6   **Dinner:** $8-$12   **Phone:** 914/561-8400
Location: 3 mi s of jct SR 32 and 17K. 335 Windsor Hwy 12553. **Hours:** 11:30 am-10 pm. Closed: 11/23. **Reservations:** suggested. **Features:** casual dress; carryout; cocktails & lounge; also prix fixe. An extensive menu of home-style Chinese dishes includes several cuisine types: Hunan, Mandarin, Cantonese and Szechwan. The atmosphere is simple and casual, enhanced by colorful Oriental paintings. Banana and ice cream desserts are delicious. **Cards:** AE, MC, VI.
[X]

JOHNNY D'S
◆ ◆
American
Lunch: $3-$8   **Dinner:** $7-$15   **Phone:** 914/567-1600
Location: I-87, exit 17 via 17K w to SR 300, 2 mi s. 909 Union Ave (SR 300) 12553. **Hours:** 24 hrs. **Features:** casual dress; children's menu; health conscious menu; carryout; salad bar; cocktails & lounge; a la carte. The charming 1950s-style diner is all chrome and neon, with Coca Cola memorabilia and lots of windows that overlook the lake. The 15-page menu includes a little bit of everything—from eggs to lobster tail. Tempting desserts are made on the premises. **Cards:** AE, DI, DS, MC, VI.
[X]

SCHLESINGER'S STEAK HOUSE
◆ ◆
Steak and
Seafood
Lunch: $6-$20   **Dinner:** $7-$30   **Phone:** 914/561-1762
Location: 2 mi s on Rt 300. 475 Temple Hill, SR 300 12553. **Hours:** 11:30 am-3 & 4:30-9:30 pm, Sat 4:30 pm-10 pm & Sun 3 pm-9 pm. Closed: 11/23 & 12/25. **Features:** casual dress; children's menu; carryout; cocktails & lounge. Built in 1762, this stone house welcomes families to enjoy a diverse menu that lists everything from burgers and pasta to ribs, steak and seafood. Rocky Mountain mashed potatoes, which are prepared with roasted garlic and herbs, are outstanding. **Cards:** AE, DI, MC, VI.
[X]

Destination New York City

*F*rom pastrami and corned beef on rye to spicy Indian curry, the Big Apple dishes up varied cuisine.

*T*ake a bite out of New York and visit Little Italy for eggplant *parmigiana*, or Chinatown for dim sum. While in Harlem, stop for some soul food, or grab a slice of pizza at one of the city's many pizzerias. Don't forget about New York's favorite street fare–jumbo hot dogs, giant soft pretzels and bags of roasted chestnuts–all served from pull-carts.

Skyline, New York City. Growing up rather than out, the tiny island city is home to some 200 lofty skyscrapers.

Lincoln Center, New York. The plaza fountain is a great place to people watch during the opera intermission. (See listing page 122)

*P*laces included in this AAA Destination City:

Armonk	370	Nyack	374
Brooklyn	370	Orangeburg	374
Carmel	371	Ossining	374
Chappaqua	371	Pearl River	375
Congers	371	Peekskill	375
Croton-On-		Port Chester	375
Hudson	371	Pound Ridge	375
Elmsford	372	Rye	376
Hartsdale	372	Rye Brook	376
Hawthorne	372	Staten Island	377
Jamaica	372	Suffern	377
Mount Kisco	373	Tarrytown	377
Nanuet	373	White Plains	378
New Rochelle	373	Yonkers	379

Suffern   Nanuet

NEW YORK
NEW JERSEY

Staten Island

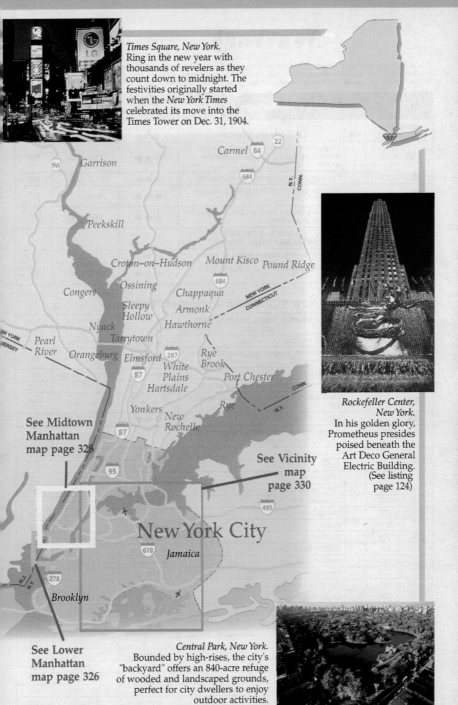

Times Square, New York.
Ring in the new year with
thousands of revelers as they
count down to midnight. The
festivities originally started
when the *New York Times*
celebrated its move into the
Times Tower on Dec. 31, 1904.

Rockefeller Center,
New York.
In his golden glory,
Prometheus presides
poised beneath the
Art Deco General
Electric Building.
(See listing
page 124)

Central Park, New York.
Bounded by high-rises, the city's
"backyard" offers an 840-acre refuge
of wooded and landscaped grounds,
perfect for city dwellers to enjoy
outdoor activities.
(See listing page 119)

See Midtown
Manhattan
map page 328

See Vicinity
map
page 330

See Lower
Manhattan
map page 326

Carmel

Garrison

Peekskill

Croton–on–Hudson   Mount Kisco   Pound Ridge

Congers   Ossining   Chappaqua

Sleepy   Armonk
Hollow
Nyack   Hawthorne
Pearl   Tarrytown
River   Orangeburg   Elmsford
White   Rye
Plains   Brook
Hartsdale   Port Chester

Yonkers   New   Rye
Rochelle

New York City

Jamaica

Brooklyn

NEW YORK
CONNECTICUT

New York *pop. 7,322,600*

This index helps you "spot" where approved accommodations are located on the detailed maps that follow. Rate ranges are for comparison only and show the property's high season. Turn to the listing page for more detailed rate information and consult display ads for special promotions. Restaurant rate range is for dinner unless only lunch (L) is served.

✈ Airport Accommodations

Spotter/Map Page Number	OA	LA GUARDIA AIRPORT	Diamond Rating	Rate Range High Season	Listing Page
144 / p. 330		Courtyard by Marriott New York/Laguardia Airport, Opposite La Guardia International Airport	◆◆◆	$129-$209	364
146 / p. 330		La Guardia Marriott Hotel, opposite airport	◆◆◆	$129-$239	365
141 / p. 330		Sheraton La Guardia East Hotel, 3 mi se of airport	◆◆◆	$225-$250	367
145 / p. 330		Wyndham Garden Hotel at La Guardia Airport, opposite airport entrance	◆◆◆	$125-$165	367
		JOHN F. KENNEDY INTERNATIONAL AIRPORT			
133 / p. 330	⏣	**Holiday Inn-JFK Airport, just n of airport**	◆◆◆	$169-$179	365
138 / p. 330		Ramada Plaza Hotel at JFK, at entrance to airport	◆◆◆	$199-$259	366

NEW YORK (LOWER MANHATTAN)

Spotter/Map Page Number	OA	NEW YORK (LOWER MANHATTAN) - Lodgings	Diamond Rating	Rate Range High Season	Listing Page
❶ / p. 326		Marriott Financial Center Hotel	◆◆◆	$195-$369	331
❸ / p. 326	⏣	**Best Western Seaport Inn, New York - see color ad p 331**	◆◆◆	$179-$219 🗲	331
❹ / p. 326		Holiday Inn Downtown	◆◆◆	Failed to provide	331
❺ / p. 326	⏣	**The Millenium Hilton - see color ad p 57**	◆◆◆◆	$135-$495	332
❻ / p. 326	⏣	**Manhattan Seaport Suites - see color ad p 331**	◆◆	$109-$249	331
❼ / p. 326		Marriott World Trade Center	◆◆◆	$205-$369	332
		NEW YORK (LOWER MANHATTAN) - Restaurants			
① / p. 326		Il Cortile	◆◆◆	$25-$40	333
② / p. 326		Cyclo	◆◆	$8-$14	333
③ / p. 326		I Trulli	◆◆	$18-$29	333
④ / p. 326	⏣	**The Yankee Clipper**	◆◆	$15-$23	336
⑤ / p. 326		Ristorante S P Q R	◆◆◆	$16-$25	335
⑥ / p. 326		The Old Homestead	◆◆	$16-$33	334
⑦ / p. 326		Babbo	◆◆◆◆	$16-$28	332
⑧ / p. 326		Montrachet	◆◆◆	$22-$32	334
⑨ / p. 326		Gotham Bar & Grill	◆◆◆◆	$27-$33	333
⑩ / p. 326		Hudson River Club	◆◆◆◆	$29-$36	333
⑬ / p. 326		Periyali	◆◆◆	$17-$26	335
⑭ / p. 326		One If By Land, Two If By Sea	◆◆◆◆	$27-$39	334
⑮ / p. 326		Savoy Restaurant	◆◆◆	$18-$26	335
⑯ / p. 326	⏣	Il Bocconcino	◆◆	$10-$18	333
⑰ / p. 326		L'Ecole, the Restaurant of the French Culinary Institute	◆◆◆	$25	334
⑱ / p. 326	⏣	**Monte's Restaurant**	◆◆	$8-$22	334
⑲ / p. 326		Il Mulino	◆◆◆	$10-$45	333
⑳ / p. 326		Pacifica	◆◆	$15-$25	335
㉑ / p. 326		Canton	◆◆	$16-$25	332
㉒ / p. 326	⏣	**Villa Mosconi Restaurant**	◆◆	$15-$30	336
㉓ / p. 326	⏣	**Zoe Restaurant**	◆◆◆	$16-$26	336
㉔ / p. 326		Rosemaries	◆◆◆	$15-$30	335
㉕ / p. 326		Windows-On-The-World	◆◆◆	$23-$35	336

Spotter/Map Page Number	OA	**NEW YORK (LOWER MANHATTAN) - Restaurants (continued)**	Diamond Rating	Rate Range High Season	Listing Page
26 / p. 326		Au Troquet	◆◆	$17-$22	332
27 / p. 326		Balthazar	◆◆◆	$15-$24	332
28 / p. 326		Chelsea Bistro & Bar	◆◆◆	$18-$23	333
30 / p. 326		El Quijote Restaurant	◆◆	$10-$30	333
32 / p. 326		le Madri	◆◆◆	$16-$30	334
34 / p. 326		Mesa Grill	◆◆◆	$18-$29	334
35 / p. 326	🌐	**Old Town Bar Restaurant**	◆	$5-$7	334
36 / p. 326		Patria	◆◆◆	$54	335
38 / p. 326		Rincon de Espana Restaurant	◆◆	$12-$20	335
39 / p. 326		Sonia Rose	◆◆◆	$41	335
40 / p. 326		Second Avenue Kosher Deli	◆◆	$15-$25	335
41 / p. 326		Alva	◆◆	$13-$26	332
43 / p. 326		Nobu	◆◆◆◆	$12-$25	334
44 / p. 326		Tribeca Grill	◆◆◆	$19-$29	336
45 / p. 326		Chanterelle	◆◆◆◆	$75-$89	332
46 / p. 326		Verbena	◆◆◆	$23-$29	336
47 / p. 326		Novita	◆◆	$12-$21	334
48 / p. 326		Tony May's Gemelli Restaurant	◆◆	$17-$29	335
49 / p. 326		Gramercy Tavern	◆◆◆◆	$62	333

NEW YORK (MIDTOWN MANHATTAN)

Spotter/Map Page Number	OA	**NEW YORK (MIDTOWN MANHATTAN) - Lodgings**	Diamond Rating	Rate Range High Season	Listing Page
25 / p. 328		Lyden House - see ad p 337	◆◆	$304-$364	347
26 / p. 328		Omni Berkshire Place	◆◆◆◆	$239-$509	348
30 / p. 328	🌐	**Hotel Beacon - see color ad p 343**	◆◆	$185-$215 🆂	344
31 / p. 328	🌐	**The Shoreham Hotel**	◆◆◆	$325-$875	350
32 / p. 328	🌐	**Travel Inn - see color ad p 350**	◆◆	$150-$190 🆂	351
33 / p. 328	🌐	**Hotel Lucerne - see color ad p 345**	◆◆◆	$200-$240 🆂	344
34 / p. 328		Regal UN Plaza Hotel	[fyi]	$429	351
35 / p. 328		Lyden Gardens Hotel - see ad p 337	◆◆◆	$334-$364	346
36 / p. 328		Hotel Wales	◆◆	Failed to provide	344
37 / p. 328		Plaza Fifty Hotel - see ad p 337	◆◆	$302-$332	349
39 / p. 328		Holiday Inn Midtown-57th Street	◆◆	$189-$259	343
41 / p. 328	🌐	**Le Parker Meridien New York**	◆◆◆◆	$365-$435	345
42 / p. 328		Eastgate Tower Hotel - see ad p 337	◆◆◆	$331-$361	341
43 / p. 328		Dumont Plaza Suite Hotel - see ad p 337	◆◆◆	$321-$351	341
44 / p. 328	🌐	**The New York Palace - see color ad p 348**	◆◆◆◆◆	$540-$690 🆂	347
45 / p. 328		Shelburne Murray Hill Hotel - see ad p 337	◆◆◆	$321-$351	349
46 / p. 328		Sheraton Russell Hotel	◆◆◆	Failed to provide	350
47 / p. 328	🌐	**The Roosevelt Hotel**	◆◆◆	$269 🆂	349
49 / p. 328	🌐	**The St Regis-New York**	◆◆◆◆◆	$575-$750	349
50 / p. 328		Beekman Tower Suite Hotel - see ad p 337	◆◆◆	$345-$375	337
53 / p. 328	🌐	**Grand Hyatt New York**	◆◆◆	$250-$275 🆂	342
54 / p. 328	🌐	**Hotel Newton - see color ad p 344**	◆	$1-$145 🆂	344
58 / p. 328		Loews New York Hotel - see ad p 346	◆◆◆	$219-$319	346
59 / p. 328		The Peninsula New York	◆◆◆◆◆	$550-$1750	348
60 / p. 328	🌐	**The Waldorf-Astoria - see color ad p 57**	◆◆◆◆	$229-$690	351
62 / p. 328		Swissotel New York-The Drake	◆◆◆	Failed to provide	351
65 / p. 328		The Lowell Hotel	◆◆◆◆	Failed to provide	346
66 / p. 328		Hotel Plaza Athenee	◆◆◆◆	$430-$620	344
67 / p. 328		The Pierre	◆◆◆◆	Failed to provide	348
68 / p. 328		The Regency Hotel	◆◆◆	Failed to provide	349
70 / p. 328		Surrey Hotel - see ad p 337	◆◆◆	$450-$480	351
71 / p. 328		The Carlyle	◆◆◆◆	Failed to provide	339
72 / p. 328	🌐	**The Stanhope**	◆◆◆◆	$300-$380 🆂	350
75 / p. 328	🌐	**Comfort Inn-Manhattan**	◆◆	$179-$409 🆂	340
76 / p. 328		Southgate Tower Suite Hotel - see ad p 337	◆◆◆	$278-$308	350

Spotter/Map Page Number	OA	NEW YORK (MIDTOWN MANHATTAN) - Lodgings (continued)	Diamond Rating	Rate Range High Season	Listing Page
77 / p. 328	◈	**Best Western Woodward - see ad p 339**	◆◆	$193-$450 ⛟	339
78 / p. 328		The Kitano New York Hotel	◆◆◆	Failed to provide	345
79 / p. 328		Sheraton Manhattan Hotel	◆◆◆	Failed to provide	350
80 / p. 328		The Avalon	◆◆◆	Failed to provide	337
81 / p. 328		Sheraton New York Hotel & Towers	◆◆◆	Failed to provide	350
82 / p. 328		The Mark	◆◆◆◆	$500-$530	347
86 / p. 328	◈	**The Warwick New York**	◆◆◆	$245-$260	351
88 / p. 328		Clarion Hotel Fifth Avenue	◆◆	$169-$325	340
89 / p. 328		Novotel New York	◆◆	$119-$249	348
90 / p. 328	◈	**New York Marriott Marquis**	◆◆◆	$335-$520	347
91 / p. 328	◈	**The Best Western Manhattan Hotel**	◆◆	$149-$799 ⛟	339
92 / p. 328		Holiday Inn Broadway - see color ad p 343	◆◆◆	$269-$399	343
93 / p. 328	◈	**Days Hotel-Midtown**	◆◆	$182-$230 ⛟	340
95 / p. 328	◈	**Belvedere Hotel - see color ad p 337**	◆◆	$125-$260 ⛟	339
96 / p. 328		Trump International Hotel & Tower	◆◆◆◆	$475-$1500	351
100 / p. 328	◈	**Delmonico's**	◆◆	$292-$535 ⛟	340
101 / p. 328	◈	**The Gorham Hotel - see color ad p 342**	◆◆◆	$205-$475 ⛟	342
103 / p. 328		Hotel Salisbury	◆◆	$259-$289	344
104 / p. 328	◈	**The Mayflower Hotel On The Park**	◆◆	$190-$250	347
105 / p. 328		Royalton	◆◆◆	Failed to provide	349
106 / p. 328	◈	**Howard Johnson Plaza Hotel**	◆◆	$182-$230 ⛟	344
107 / p. 328		The Carnegie Hotel	◆◆◆	Failed to provide	339
109 / p. 328		New York Marriott Eastside	◆◆◆	$249-$375	347
111 / p. 328		Crowne Plaza Manhattan	◆◆◆	Failed to provide	340
112 / p. 328		Millennium Broadway	◆◆◆	$290-$410	347
113 / p. 328		Courtyard by Marriott/Manhattan-Times Square South	◆◆◆	Failed to provide	340
114 / p. 328	◈	**RIHGA Royal Hotel**	◆◆◆◆	$475-$3100 ⛟	349
115 / p. 328	◈	**The Essex House-A Westin Hotel**	◆◆◆◆	Failed to provide	341
116 / p. 328		Central Park Inter Continental New York	◆◆◆◆	$299-$525	339
117 / p. 328	◈	**Doubletree Guest Suites - see color ad p 341**	◆◆◆	$219-$319 ⛟	341
118 / p. 328		Four Seasons Hotel, New York	◆◆◆◆◆	$535-$665	341
121 / p. 328		Fitzpatrick Manhattan Hotel	◆◆◆	$325-$480	341
122 / p. 328		Midtown East Courtyard by Marriott	◆◆◆	$219-$299	347
123 / p. 328	◈	**Renaissance New York Hotel**	◆◆◆◆	$299-$415 ⛟	349
124 / p. 328	◈	**The Kimberly A Boutique Suite Hotel & Spa**	◆◆◆	$289-$449	345
127 / p. 328		Crowne Plaza at the United Nations	◆◆◆	$379-$399	340
		NEW YORK (MIDTOWN MANHATTAN) - Restaurants			
51 / p. 328		Cafe Fiorello	◆◆	$15-$26	353
52 / p. 328		Wally's & Joseph's Restaurant	◆◆	$11-$30	362
53 / p. 328	◈	**Gallagher's Steak House**	◆◆	$25-$40	356
54 / p. 328		Patsy's Italian Restaurant	◆◆	$15-$28	359
55 / p. 328		Tavern on the Green	◆◆	$16-$34	361
56 / p. 328		Shun Lee	◆◆	$12-$26	361
57 / p. 328		Jean Georges Restaurant	◆◆◆◆◆	$85	356
58 / p. 328		Tapika	◆◆◆	$17-$29	361
59 / p. 328		La Caravelle	◆◆◆	$44-$65	357
60 / p. 328		Palio	◆◆◆◆	$19-$34	359
61 / p. 328	◈	**San Domenico**	◆◆◆◆	$19-$35	360
62 / p. 328	◈	**Cafe Pierre**	◆◆◆◆	$25-$37	353
63 / p. 328		Docks Oyster Bar & Seafood Grill	◆◆	$25-$35	355
64 / p. 328		Ciao Europa	◆◆◆	$15-$27	354
65 / p. 328		Docks Oyster Bar & Seafood Grill	◆◆	$9-$22	355
66 / p. 328		American Festival Cafe	◆◆	$20-$30	352
67 / p. 328		The Sea Grill	◆◆◆	$22-$32	361
68 / p. 328		La Grenouille	◆◆◆◆	$80	357
69 / p. 328		An American Place	◆◆◆◆	$23-$29	352

Spotter/Map Page Number	OA	NEW YORK (MIDTOWN MANHATTAN) - Restaurants (continued)	Diamond Rating	Rate Range High Season	Listing Page
(70) / p. 328	⊕	The Water Club	◆ ◆ ◆	$23-$35	362
(71) / p. 328		Adrienne	◆ ◆ ◆ ◆	$20-$28	352
(72) / p. 328		21 Club	◆ ◆ ◆	$27-$41	362
(73) / p. 328		Shun Lee Palace	◆ ◆ ◆	$14-$39	361
(74) / p. 328		Aureole	◆ ◆ ◆ ◆ ◆	$65	352
(75) / p. 328	⊕	Cite	◆ ◆ ◆	$20-$30	354
(76) / p. 328		Petrossian	◆ ◆ ◆	$28-$33	360
(78) / p. 328		Orso	◆ ◆	$15-$21	359
(84) / p. 328		Fifty-Seven Fifty-Seven Restaurant & Bar	◆ ◆ ◆ ◆	$18-$34	355
(85) / p. 328		Il Menestrello	◆ ◆ ◆	$17-$30	356
(87) / p. 328		La Reserve	◆ ◆ ◆	$40-$54	357
(88) / p. 328		Peacock Alley	◆ ◆ ◆ ◆	$27-$36	360
(89) / p. 328		Plaza Espana Restaurant	◆	$13-$23	360
(90) / p. 328	⊕	San Martin Restaurant	◆ ◆	$13-$24	360
(91) / p. 328	⊕	Siam Inn Too	◆ ◆	$9-$16	361
(92) / p. 328		Victor's Cafe 52	◆	$10-$32	362
(93) / p. 328		Angelo's Pizza	◆ ◆	$9-$14	352
(94) / p. 328		The View	◆ ◆ ◆	$25-$55	362
(95) / p. 328	⊕	Le Perigord	◆ ◆ ◆	$52	358
(96) / p. 328	⊕	Giambelli 50th	◆ ◆	$20-$35	356
(97) / p. 328	⊕	Sardi's	◆ ◆	$19-$30	361
(98) / p. 328		Il Monello	◆ ◆ ◆	$16-$25	356
(99) / p. 328	⊕	Barbetta	◆ ◆ ◆	$25-$29	352
(100) / p. 328		Felidia	◆ ◆ ◆	$18-$32	355
(101) / p. 328		Il Nido	◆ ◆ ◆	$19-$30	356
(102) / p. 328	⊕	Dish of Salt	◆ ◆	$17-$29	355
(103) / p. 328		Restaurant Nippon	◆ ◆	$32-$45	360
(104) / p. 328		Mimi's Macaroni	◆	$8-$15	359
(105) / p. 328		Bangkok Cuisine	◆	$7-$16	352
(106) / p. 328		Churrascaria Plataforma	◆ ◆	$33	354
(107) / p. 328		Costa del Sol Restaurant	◆	$11-$23	354
(108) / p. 328		Vong Restaurant	◆ ◆ ◆ ◆	$21-$35	362
(109) / p. 328	⊕	Lespinasse	◆ ◆ ◆ ◆ ◆	$34-$46	358
(110) / p. 328		Fred's at Barney's	◆ ◆	$20-$28	355
(111) / p. 328		Oceana	◆ ◆ ◆ ◆	$65	359
(112) / p. 328		Ess-a-Bagel	◆ ◆	$3-$8	355
(115) / p. 328		Sarabeth's	◆ ◆	$12-$20	361
(117) / p. 328		Toledo Restaurant	◆ ◆ ◆	$17-$36	361
(118) / p. 328		Aquavit	◆ ◆ ◆	$48-$62	352
(119) / p. 328		Bolivar	◆ ◆ ◆	$14-$25	353
(120) / p. 328		The Coach House	◆ ◆ ◆	$20-$35	354
(121) / p. 328		Cibo	◆ ◆ ◆	$15-$30	354
(122) / p. 328		Bello Restaurant	◆ ◆	$11-$21	352
(123) / p. 328		Cafe Botanica	◆ ◆ ◆	$22-$32	353
(125) / p. 328		Cafe Europa	◆	$7-$13	353
(126) / p. 328		Chiam	◆ ◆ ◆	$16-$26	354
(127) / p. 328		Chin Chin	◆ ◆ ◆	$12-$21	354
(128) / p. 328		dawat	◆ ◆ ◆	$13-$23	355
(130) / p. 328		Fresco by Scotto	◆ ◆	$15-$30	355
(131) / p. 328		Harley-Davidson Cafe	◆ ◆	$8-$20	356
(132) / p. 328		Jo Jo	◆ ◆ ◆	$19-$35	356
(133) / p. 328	⊕	Julian's Cuisine	◆ ◆	$7-$26	357
(135) / p. 328		La Mangeoire	◆ ◆	$15-$26	357
(136) / p. 328		La Strada Restaurant	◆ ◆	$11-$20	357
(137) / p. 328		Le Colonial	◆ ◆ ◆	$13-$20	358
(138) / p. 328		March	◆ ◆ ◆	$90-$125	358
(140) / p. 328		Matthew's	◆ ◆ ◆	$12-$18	358
(142) / p. 328		Michael's	◆ ◆ ◆	$23-$32	359

Spotter/Map Page Number	OA	NEW YORK (MIDTOWN MANHATTAN) - Restaurants (continued)	Diamond Rating	Rate Range High Season	Listing Page
(144) / p. 328		Bombay Palace Restaurant	◆◆	$9-$30	353
(145) / p. 328		Park Bistro	◆◆	$18-$22	359
(146) / p. 328		Restaurant Charlotte	◆◆◆	$17-$28	360
(147) / p. 328		Mark's	◆◆◆◆	$24-$34	358
(148) / p. 328	⊕	**Le Bernardin**	◆◆◆◆	$70	358
(149) / p. 328		Restaurant Quince	◆◆◆	$55	360
(151) / p. 328		Virgil's Real Barbecue	◆	$13-$22	362
(152) / p. 328		Zarela	◆◆	$14-$17	362
(154) / p. 328	⊕	**The Four Seasons**	◆◆◆◆	$27-$42	355
(155) / p. 328		Lutece	◆◆◆	$65	358
(157) / p. 328		Cinquanta Ristorante	◆◆	$13-$25	354
(159) / p. 328		The Post House	◆◆◆	$22-$43	360
(161) / p. 328		La Cote Basque	◆◆◆◆	$63	357
(163) / p. 328		Ben Benson's Steak House	◆◆◆	$16-$33	353
(165) / p. 328	⊕	**Le Cirque 2000 - see color ad p 348**	◆◆◆◆◆	$26-$36	358
(166) / p. 328		Zen Palate	◆◆	$11-$18	362
(168) / p. 328		Becco	◆◆	$25-$30	352
(169) / p. 328		Bryant Park Grill	◆◆	$15-$23	353
(170) / p. 328		Cafe Centro	◆◆	$16-$24	353
(171) / p. 328		Cafe Trevi	◆◆	$15-$24	353
(172) / p. 328		Caviarteria	◆◆	$11-$20	354
(173) / p. 328		Frico Bar	◆◆	$14-$24	356
(174) / p. 328		Coco Cafe	◆◆◆	$16-$28	354
(175) / p. 328		Isabella's	◆◆	$11-$19	356
(176) / p. 328		Joe Allen	◆	$9-$20	356
(177) / p. 328		Judson Grill	◆◆◆	$18-$34	357
(178) / p. 328		Kokachin	◆◆◆◆	$20-$34	357
(179) / p. 328		Korea Palace	◆	$25-$30	357
(181) / p. 328		Match Uptown	◆◆	$24-$32	358
(182) / p. 328		Monkey Bar	◆◆◆	$22-$31	359
(185) / p. 328		Ollie's	◆	$8-$18	359
(186) / p. 328		Park Avenue Cafe	◆◆◆	$20-$34	359
(187) / p. 328		Restaurant 222	◆◆◆	$22-$42	360
(188) / p. 328		Shaan	◆◆	$30-$40	361
(189) / p. 328		Trattoria Dell'Arte	◆◆◆	$16-$28	362
(190) / p. 328		Carnegie Delicatessen & Restaurant	◆	$9-$17	353

NEW YORK

Spotter/Map Page Number	OA	NEW YORK - Lodgings	Diamond Rating	Rate Range High Season	Listing Page
(133) / p. 330	⊕	**Holiday Inn-JFK Airport**	◆◆◆	$169-$179	365
(134) / p. 330	⊕	**Executive Motor Inn**	◆	$85-$98	364
(135) / p. 330	⊕	**Best Western City View - see ad p 363**	◆◆◆	$110-$160	363
(138) / p. 330		Ramada Plaza Hotel at JFK - see ad p 367	◆◆◆	$199-$259	366
(140) / p. 330	⊕	**Adria Hotel and Conference Center**	◆◆	$119-$159	363
(141) / p. 330		Sheraton La Guardia East Hotel	◆◆◆	$225-$250	367
(142) / p. 330	⊕	**Anchor Motor Inn - see color ad p 363**	◆	$101-$120	363
(144) / p. 330		Courtyard by Marriott New York/Laguardia Airport	◆◆◆	$129-$209	364
(145) / p. 330		Wyndham Garden Hotel at La Guardia Airport - see color ad p 367	◆◆◆	$125-$165	367
(146) / p. 330		La Guardia Marriott Hotel	◆◆◆	$129-$239	365
(147) / p. 330	⊕	**Pan American Hotel - see color ad p 366, p 336**	◆◆	$99-$160	365
(148) / p. 330	⊕	**Best Western Eden Park - see color ad p 364**	◆◆	$119-$209	363
(149) / p. 330	⊕	**Ramada Inn Adria**	◆◆	$119-$159	366
(150) / p. 330		Holiday Inn Wall Street Hotel	◆◆◆	$219	365

Spotter/Map Page Number	OA	**NEW YORK** - Restaurants	Diamond Rating	Rate Range High Season	Listing Page
(197) / p. 330		Jaiya Thai-Oriental Restaurant	◆	$6-$17	368
(198) / p. 330		River Cafe	◆◆◆◆	$70	368
(199) / p. 330		**Water's Edge**	◆◆◆◆	$20-$30	368
(202) / p. 330		Peter Luger's	◆◆◆	$45-$55	368

New York Vicinity

Spotter/Map Page Number	OA	**FLORAL PARK** - Lodgings	Diamond Rating	Rate Range High Season	Listing Page
(153) / p. 330		**Floral Park Motor Lodge - see color ad p 364**	◆◆	$150-$210 [SAVE]	260
		FLORAL PARK - Restaurants			
(209) / p. 330		Arturo's	◆◆	$14-$30	260
(210) / p. 330		Poppy's Place	◆	$7-$11	260
		BROOKLYN - Lodgings			
(156) / p. 330		New York Marriott Brooklyn	◆◆◆	$149-$289	370
(157) / p. 330		**Comfort Inn Bay Ridge - see color ad p 330**	◆◆	$165-$205 [SAVE]	370
(158) / p. 330		Bed & Breakfast on the Park	◆◆◆	$125-$275	370
		BROOKLYN - Restaurants			
(214) / p. 330		Grimaldi's Pizzeria	◆◆	$12-$18	370
(215) / p. 330		Aunt Suzie's Restaurant	◆	$10-$15	370
(216) / p. 330		Tommaso's	◆◆	$13-$27	371

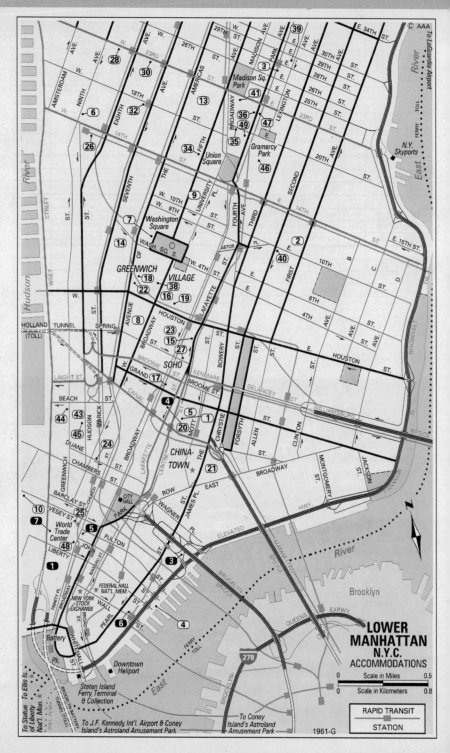

© AAA

To LaGuardia Airport

N.Y. Skyports

LOWER
MANHATTAN
N.Y.C.
ACCOMMODATIONS

Scale in Miles   0.5
0   Scale in Kilometers   0.8

RAPID TRANSIT
STATION

GREENWICH
VILLAGE

SOHO

CHINA-
TOWN

Brooklyn

Madison Sq.
Park

Union
Square

Gramercy
Park

Washington
Square

World
Trade
Center

City
Hall

New York
Stock
Exchange

Federal Hall
Nat'l. Mem.

Battery
Pk.

Downtown
Heliport

Staten Island
Ferry Terminal
& Collection

To Statue
of Liberty
Nat'l. Mon.

To Ellis Is.

To J.F. Kennedy Int'l. Airport & Coney
Island's Astroland Amusement Park

To Coney
Island's Astroland
Amusement Park

1961-G

IF YOU HAVEN'T SEEN DOWNTOWN, YOU HAVEN'T SEEN NEW YORK.

It's the birthplace of the nation. It's Wall Street. It's the World Trade Center, South Street Seaport and the Brooklyn Bridge. It's breathtaking views of the harbor and Statue of Liberty. It's narrow winding streets and skyscraper canyons. It's parks, plazas and esplanades. It's museums, concerts and outdoor sculpture. It's unexpected and refreshing. Best of all, it's a short walk from one great attraction to the next.

DOWNTOWN NEW YORK
IT ALL STARTS HERE

For more information call 800-887-0532

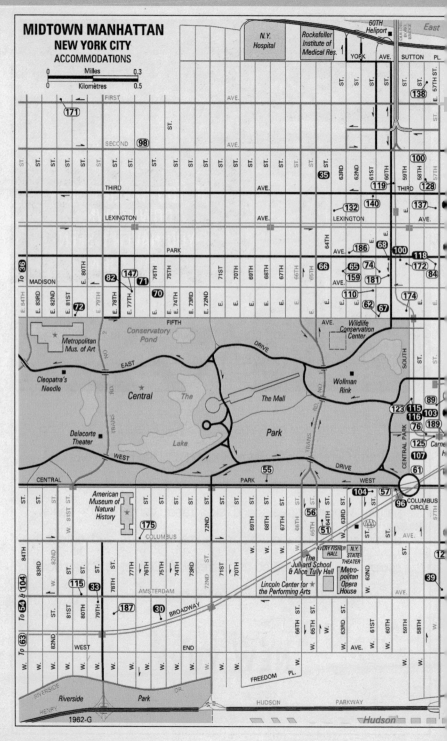

MIDTOWN MANHATTAN
NEW YORK CITY
ACCOMMODATIONS

Milles
0   0.3
0   0.5
Kilomètres

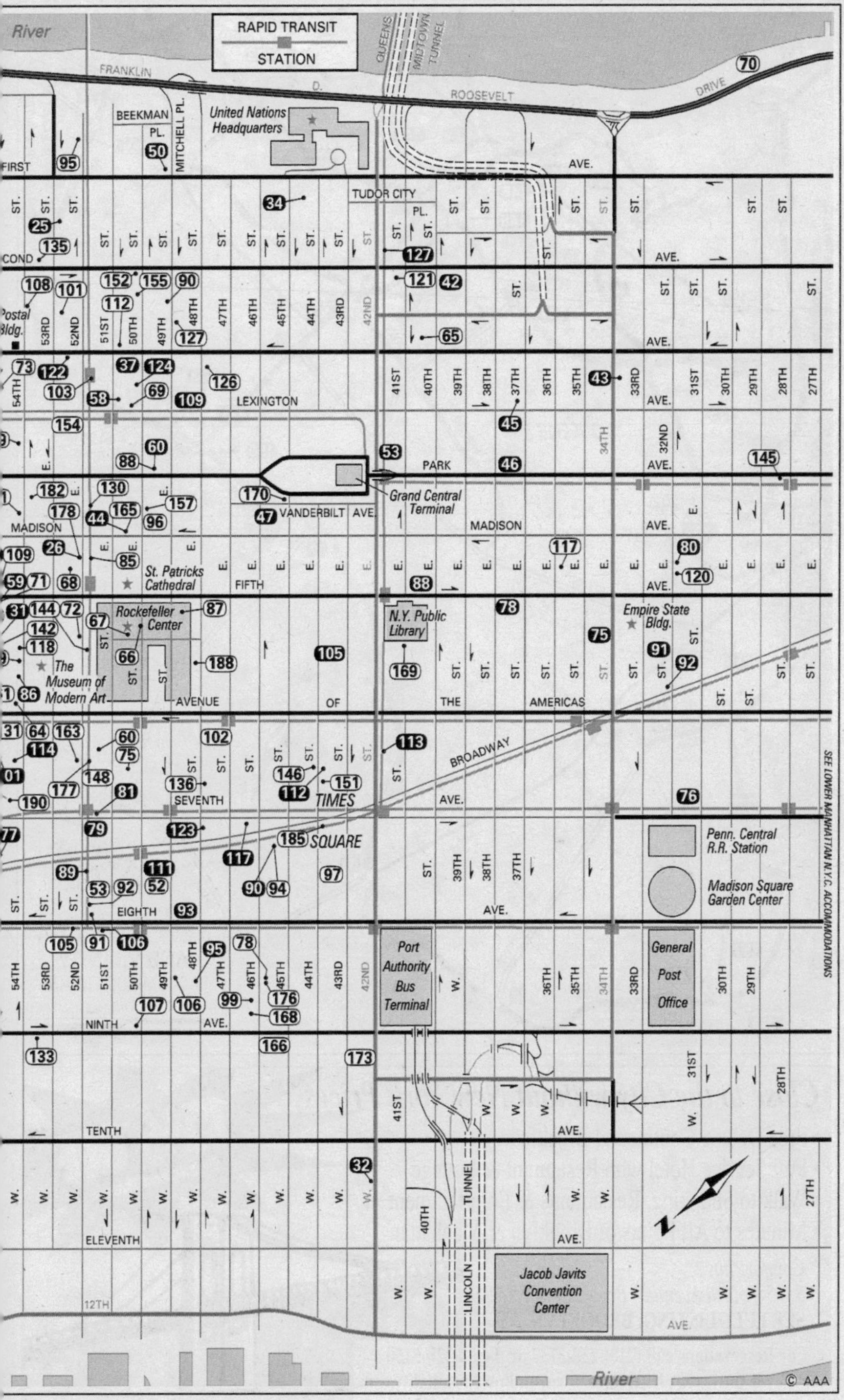
RAPID TRANSIT
STATION
River
FRANKLIN D. ROOSEVELT DRIVE
QUEENS MIDTOWN TUNNEL
BEEKMAN PL.
MITCHELL PL.
United Nations Headquarters
TUDOR CITY PL.
FIRST AVE.
SECOND AVE.
Postal Bldg.
LEXINGTON AVE.
PARK AVE.
Grand Central Terminal
VANDERBILT AVE.
MADISON AVE.
FIFTH AVE.
St. Patricks Cathedral
Rockefeller Center
The Museum of Modern Art
N.Y. Public Library
Empire State Bldg.
AVENUE OF THE AMERICAS
BROADWAY
SEVENTH AVE.
TIMES SQUARE
Penn. Central R.R. Station
Madison Square Garden Center
EIGHTH AVE.
Port Authority Bus Terminal
General Post Office
NINTH AVE.
TENTH AVE.
ELEVENTH AVE.
LINCOLN TUNNEL
Jacob Javits Convention Center
12TH AVE.
River
SEE LOWER MANHATTAN N.Y.C. ACCOMMODATIONS
© AAA

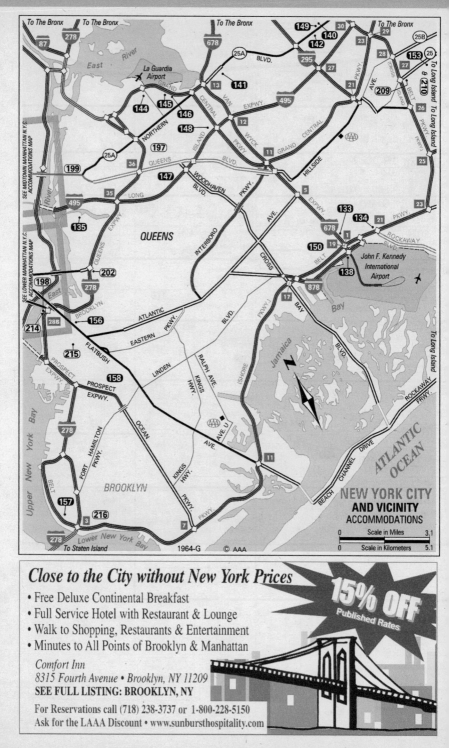

NEW YORK (LOWER MANHATTAN) (See map p. 326; index p. 320)
—— LODGINGS ——

BEST WESTERN SEAPORT INN, NEW YORK   **Phone:** (212)766-6600   **3**
All Year   1P: $179-$219   2P: $179-$219   XP: $10   F18
Location: N end of South St Seaport. 33 Peck Slip 10038. Fax: 212/766-6615. **Terms:** [CP] meal plan.
Facility: 72 rooms. 19th-century guesthouse. Some rooms with terrace offering breathtaking views of the seaport. 8 whirlpool rooms, $199-$229; 7 stories; interior corridors. **Dining:** Restaurant nearby.
Some Rooms: safes. **Cards:** AE, CB, DI, DS, MC, VI. **Special Amenities:** Free breakfast and free newspaper. *(See color ad below)*

HOLIDAY INN DOWNTOWN   **Phone:** 212/966-8898   **4**
♦♦♦   Property failed to provide current rates
Hotel   **Location:** Corner of Howard St, just n Canal St; in Chinatown. 138 LaFayette St 10013. Fax: 212/966-3933.
Terms: Package plans. **Facility:** 227 rooms. Located within walking distance of Chinatown, Greenwich Village,
Little Italy, SoHo, TriBeCa and Wall Street. 1 blk from mass transit. 14 stories; interior corridors. **Some Rooms:** Fee: refrigerators. **Cards:** AE, CB, DI, DS, MC, VI.

MANHATTAN SEAPORT SUITES   **Phone:** (212)742-0003   **6**
All Year   1P: $109-$249   2P: $109-$249   XP: $20   F12
Location: Between Pine and Wall sts. 129 Front St 10005. Fax: 212/742-0124. **Terms:** [BP] & [CP] meal plans;
cancellation fee imposed. **Facility:** 56 rooms. Most rooms are studio or 1-bedroom apartments. 8 stories; interior corridors. **Dining:** Restaurant nearby. **All Rooms:** safes. **Some Rooms:** 14 efficiencies, 30 kitchens.
Suite Motel   **Cards:** AE, DI, DS, MC, VI. *(See color ad below)*

MARRIOTT FINANCIAL CENTER HOTEL   **Phone:** (212)385-4900   **1**
♦♦♦   9/3-12/31   1P: $195-$369
Hotel   1/1-4/30   1P: $155-$309
5/1-9/2   1P: $145-$299
Location: Between Albany and Carlyle sts; at Brooklyn Battery tunnel entrance. 85 West St 10006. Fax: 212/227-8136.
Terms: Check-in 4 pm; package plans. **Facility:** 504 rooms. Centrally located in the World Financial District; many rooms with harbor views. 38 stories; interior corridors; heated pool. **Services:** gift shop. **All Rooms:** combo or shower baths, safes, honor bars. **Some Rooms:** Fee: VCR. **Cards:** AE, CB, DI, DS, MC, VI.

(See map p. 326)

MARRIOTT WORLD TRADE CENTER

◆◆◆   9/3-12/31   1P: $205-$369   **Phone:** (212)938-9100   **7**
Hotel   1/1-4/30   1P: $169-$309
         5/1-9/2   1P: $159-$299
Location: West St, between Liberty and Vesey sts; at the World Trade Center. Three World Trade Center 10048.
Fax: 212/444-3444. **Terms:** Check-in 4 pm; package plans. **Facility:** 818 rooms. Located amidst the buildings which make up
the World Trade Center. Guest rooms are comfortable and nicely decorated. Some rooms face the Trade Center courtyard. 22
stories; interior corridors; heated pool. Fee: parking. **Services:** gift shop. Fee: massage. **All Rooms:** combo or shower baths,
safes, honor bars. **Some Rooms:** Fee: VCR. **Cards:** AE, CB, DI, DS, JC, MC, VI.

THE MILLENIUM HILTON

⊚   All Year   1P: $135-$450   2P: $180-$495   XP: $45   **Phone:** (212)693-2001   **5**
◆◆◆◆   **Location:** E of World Trade Center, between Day and Fulton sts. 55 Church St 10007. Fax: 212/571-2316.   F12
Hotel   **Terms:** Weekly rates avail; cancellation fee imposed; package plans, weekends. **Facility:** 561 rooms. Magnifi-
cent city views; some river views. 5 two-bedroom units. Some suites with cassette/CD player; 15 whirlpool
rooms; 55 stories; interior corridors; heated pool, sauna. **Dining:** Dining room, restaurant; 6:30 am-10 pm; $15-
$35; health conscious menu items; cocktails; entertainment. **Services:** gift shop. Fee: massage. **All Rooms:** safes, honor bars.
Some Rooms: 3 kitchens. Fee: VCR. **Cards:** AE, CB, DI, DS, MC, VI. *(See color ad p 57)*

---

*The following lodgings were either not inspected or did not
meet AAA rating requirements but are listed for your information only.*

ABINGDON GUEST HOUSE   **Phone:** 212/243-5384
[fyi]   Not inspected. **Location:** 13 8th Ave. Facilities, services, and decor characterize a basic property.

THE ROGER WILLIAMS HOTEL   **Phone:** 212/448-7000
[fyi]   Not inspected. **Location:** 131 Madison Ave. Facilities, services, and decor characterize a mid-range property.

——— RESTAURANTS ———

ALVA   **Lunch:** $10-$18   **Dinner:** $13-$26   **Phone:** 212/228-4399   **41**
◆◆   **Location:** Between Park Ave S and Broadway. 36 E 22nd St 10010. **Hours:** noon-3 & 5:30-midnight. Sat
American   from 5:30 pm. Closed major holidays & Sun. **Reservations:** suggested. **Features:** casual dress; cocktails; a
la carte. The contemporary American bistro is appointed in the art deco style. Thomas Alva Edison is at the
heart of the dining room's theme: Antique light bulbs are al over the place. Grilled marinated portobello is among
well-prepared, creative dishes. Smoke free premises. **Cards:** AE, DI, MC, VI.

AU TROQUET   **Dinner:** $17-$22   **Phone:** 212/924-3413   **26**
◆◆   **Location:** Corner of W 12th and Greenwich sts. 328 W 12th St 10014. **Hours:** 5:30 pm-11 pm.
Provincial   **Reservations:** required; weekends. **Features:** casual dress; cocktails; a la carte. The owner-chef prepares
French   such classic fare as herb-roasted rack of lamb, breast of duck in currant sauce and grilled salmon with
ginger and basil. The ambience is decidedly romantic, with lace curtains, fresh flowers and relaxing
background music. **Cards:** AE, DI, DS, MC, VI.

BABBO   **Dinner:** $16-$28   **Phone:** 212/777-0303   **7**
◆◆◆◆   **Location:** Between 6th Ave and MacDougal St, just w of Washington Square Park. 110 Waverly Pl 10012.
Italian   **Hours:** 5:30 pm-11:30 pm, Sun 5 pm-11 pm. **Reservations:** required. **Features:** dressy casual; cocktails &
lounge; street parking; a la carte. The inviting restaurant boasts a warm, cozy ambience and a wise,
gracious staff. The cuisine is a showcase for innovative, new Italian fare, which uses only fresh local products. Try the
seven-course or pasta tasting menus, both of which are exciting. Smoke free premises. **Cards:** AE, DI, MC, VI.

BALTHAZAR   **Lunch:** $15-$24   **Dinner:** $15-$24   **Phone:** 212/965-1414   **27**
◆◆◆   **Location:** Between Broadway and Lafayette St; in Soho. 80 Spring St 10012. **Hours:** 7:30-11:30 am, noon-5
French   & 6-midnight, Sat & Sun 11:30 am-5 & 6-midnight. **Reservations:** required. **Features:** casual dress; Sunday
brunch; cocktails & lounge; street parking; a la carte. The trendy hot spot has become a favorite hangout in
which to see and be seen. Styled as a traditional French brasserie, it feels warm and authentic. Savory dishes—such as
steak fries, striped bass and diver scallops—are both traditional and modern. Smoke free premises. **Cards:** AE, MC, VI.

CANTON   **Lunch:** $14-$25   **Dinner:** $16-$25   **Phone:** 212/226-4441   **21**
◆◆   **Location:** In Chinatown; between Bowery and Market sts. 45 Division St 10002. **Hours:** noon-9:30 pm, Fri &
Chinese   Sat-10:30 pm. Closed: Mon, Tues & 7/15-8/15. **Reservations:** suggested. **Features:** casual dress; carryout;
beer & wine only; a la carte. Subdued lighting gives the moderately upscale restaurant—a well-established
local favorite—an air of romance. The seasonal menu centers on creative preparations of Cantonese cuisine, bathed in
piquant, distinctive sauces. Servers are knowledgeable. Smoke free premises.

CHANTERELLE   **Lunch:** $19-$25   **Dinner:** $75-$89   **Phone:** 212/966-6960   **45**
◆◆◆◆   **Location:** In TriBeCa, at Hudson St. 2 Harrison St 10013. **Hours:** noon-2:30 & 5:30-11 pm. Closed: Sun;
French   Mon for lunch. **Reservations:** suggested. **Features:** dressy casual; cocktails; street parking; prix fixe.
Elaborate architecture distinguishes the sophisticated dining room. The monthly changing menu showcases
fresh seasonal inspirations and innovative combinations, which are complemented by an extensive wine book. The specialty
seafood sausage is divine. Smoke free premises. **Cards:** AE, DI, DS, MC, VI.

(See map p. 326)

CHELSEA BISTRO & BAR   Dinner: $18-$23   Phone: 212/727-2026 ㉘
◆◆◆   **Location:** Between 8th and 9th aves. 358 W 23rd St 10011. **Hours:** 5:30 pm-11 pm, Fri & Sat-midnight, Sun
French   5 pm-10:30 pm. Closed: 7/4, 9/4 & Sun in summer. **Reservations:** suggested. **Features:** cocktails & lounge;
a la carte. The classic French bistro focuses on delivering modernized classic entrees. Warm tones and an
inviting brick hearth lend to the cozy ambience of the relaxed dining room. The glass conservatory has a more romantic
appeal. The wine book is comprehensive. **Cards:** AE, MC, VI.

CYCLO   Dinner: $8-$14   Phone: 212/673-3957 ②
◆◆   **Location:** Between 12th and 13th sts. 203 1st Ave 10003. **Hours:** 5:30 pm-10:45 pm, Fri & Sat-11:45 pm.
Vietnamese   **Reservations:** suggested. **Features:** casual dress; cocktails; street parking; a la carte. A rickshaw sits in
front of the upbeat restaurant, which has great seating on the sidewalk in good weather. Light and flavorful
dishes are highlighted by fresh mint, cilantro and tropical flavors. Specialties include crispy snapper and green papaya salad.
Smoke free premises. **Cards:** AE, MC, VI.

EL QUIJOTE RESTAURANT   Lunch: $7-$12   Dinner: $10-$30   Phone: 212/929-1855 ㉚
◆◆   **Location:** Between 7th and 8th aves; in Chelsa. 226 W 23rd St 10011. **Hours:** noon-midnight, Fri & Sat-1
Ethnic   am. **Reservations:** suggested; weekends. **Features:** casual dress; health conscious menu items; cocktails &
lounge; a la carte. This place is the city's oldest Spanish restaurant, and little has changed since its
inception. Older decor is accentuated with colorful murals and windmills. Lobster is brought in straight from the owner's
fishing fleet. Paella and sangria are divine. Smoke free premises. **Cards:** AE, DI, DS, MC, VI.

GOTHAM BAR & GRILL   Lunch: $16-$22   Dinner: $27-$33   Phone: 212/620-4020 ⑨
◆◆◆◆   **Location:** Between 5th Ave and University Pl. 12 E 12th 10003. **Hours:** noon-2 & 5:30-10 pm, Fri-11 pm,
American   Sat 5:30 pm-11:30 pm, Sun from 5:30 pm. Closed major holidays. **Reservations:** suggested.
Features: casual dress; health conscious menu items; cocktails; a la carte. Soaring ceilings and raised
dining areas characterize the modern, sophisticated setting. Contemporary American cuisine with strong European
influences showcases the chef's artistry. Warm chocolate cake with espresso ice cream is wonderful. Smoke free premises.
Cards: AE, DI, MC, VI.

GRAMERCY TAVERN   Dinner: $62   Phone: 212/477-0777 ㊾
◆◆◆◆   **Location:** Between Park Ave S and Broadway. 42 E 20th St 10003. **Hours:** noon-2 & 5:30-10 pm, Fri & Sat
Continental 5:30 pm-11 pm, Sun 5:30 pm-10 pm. Closed major holidays. **Reservations:** suggested.
Features: semi-formal attire; cocktails & lounge; prix fixe. The warm, charming dining room is decorated with
hand-crafted furniture from Maine. Unusual and interesting hand-picked wines complement clever preparations of seafood,
rack of lamb and roasted chicken. Servers are cordial and knowledgeable. Smoke free premises. **Cards:** AE, DI, DS,
MC, VI.

HUDSON RIVER CLUB   Lunch: $24-$28   Dinner: $29-$36   Phone: 212/786-1500 ⑩
◆◆◆◆   **Location:** Battery Park City, World Financial Center 4, lobby level. 4 World Financial Center 10281.
American   **Hours:** 11:30 am-2:30 & 5-9:30 pm, Fri & Sat-10 pm, Sun noon-2:30 pm. Closed major holidays.
Reservations: suggested. **Features:** Sunday brunch; health conscious menu items; cocktails & lounge; a la
carte. Views of the harbor and the Statue of Liberty are exceptional from the richly appointed dining room, which features
plenty of Hudson River Valley art. The menu centers on exciting and creative New American cuisine. Service is fittingly
attentive. Smoke free premises. **Cards:** AE, CB, DI, DS, MC, VI.

IL BOCCONCINO   Lunch: $10-$18   Dinner: $10-$18   Phone: 212/982-0329 ⑯
⚐⚐⚐   **Location:** Sullivan St at Houston St; in Greenwich Village. 168 Sullivan St 10012. **Hours:** noon-11 pm.
◆◆   Closed major holidays. **Features:** casual dress; carryout; cocktails; a la carte. The relaxing, warm and casual
Italian   dining room exudes a subtle, Old World charm. While enjoy selections from an extensive menu of pasta,
seafood, veal and chicken, diners can watch food being prepared in the open kitchen. Service is friendly and
efficient. **Cards:** AE, CB, DI, MC, VI.

IL CORTILE   Lunch: $15-$20   Dinner: $25-$40   Phone: 212/226-6060 ①
◆◆◆   **Location:** Between Canal and Hester sts; in Little Italy. 125 Mulberry St 10013. **Hours:** noon-midnight, Fri &
Italian   Sat-1 am. Closed: 11/23, 12/24 & 12/25. **Reservations:** suggested. **Features:** casual dress; health
conscious menu items; carryout; cocktails & lounge; a la carte. The restaurant—in the bustling heart of Little
Italy—has the inviting feel of a terrace garden, with open skylights, natural wood tables and brick walls. Specialties center on
seafood, veal and homemade pasta. Seating is available on the seasonal patio. Smoke free premises. **Cards:** AE, DI, DS,
MC, VI.

IL MULINO   Lunch: $10-$45   Dinner: $10-$45   Phone: 212/673-3783 ⑲
◆◆◆   **Location:** Between Sullivan and Thompson sts; in Greenwich Village. 86 W Third St 10012.
Italian   **Hours:** noon-2:30 & 5-11:30 pm, Sat from 5 pm. Closed major holidays, Sun & 7/1-7/31.
Reservations: required. **Features:** semi-formal attire; health conscious menu; cocktails & lounge; a la carte.
If you hope to dine here, call well in advance. The charming haven is quite small and extremely popular. The magnificent
cuisine is pure Old World Italian—rich, bountiful and among the city's finest. The specialty rack of lamb is accented by fresh
sage. Smoke free premises. **Cards:** AE, MC, VI.

I TRULLI   Lunch: $15-$29   Dinner: $18-$29   Phone: 212/481-7372 ③
◆◆   **Location:** Between Park and Lexington aves. 122 E 27th St 10016. **Hours:** noon-3 & 5:30-10:30 pm, Sat
South Italian 5:30 pm-11 pm. Closed major holidays & Sun. **Reservations:** suggested. **Features:** casual dress; cocktails
& lounge; a la carte. Flavorful Southern Italian meat and poultry dishes are prepared on the rotisserie or in
the wood-burning oven. The walled garden, with a lovely waterfall, has a romantic, relaxed appeal. It's difficult to choose a
dessert from the list of savory choices. Smoke free premises. **Cards:** AE, DI, MC, VI.

(See map p. 326)

L'ECOLE, THE RESTAURANT OF THE
FRENCH CULINARY INSTITUTE   Lunch: $18   Dinner: $25   Phone: 212/219-3300   ⑰
◆◆◆   **Location:** At Grand St. 462 Broadway 10013. **Hours:** 12:15 pm-2:30 & 6-9:30 pm, Fri & Sat-10 pm. Closed
Nouvelle   major holidays & Sun. **Reservations:** suggested; for dinner. **Features:** casual dress; cocktails; prix fixe.
French   Students of the institute prepare the innovative, daily changing menu, which includes a prix-fixe lunch as well
    as four- and five-course prix fixe menus at dinner. Set in the trendy SoHo environment, the restaurant
displays an elegant simplicity. Smoke free premises. **Cards:** AE, DI, DS, MC, VI.   ✕

LE MADRI   Lunch: $13-$22   Dinner: $16-$30   Phone: 212/727-8022   ㉜
◆◆◆   **Location:** At 7th Ave. 168 W 18th St 10011. **Hours:** noon-3 & 5:30-11:30 pm, Sun 11:45 am-2:45 & 5-10:30
Northern   pm. Closed major holidays. **Reservations:** required. **Features:** dressy casual; Sunday brunch; health
Italian   conscious menu; carryout; cocktails & lounge; a la carte. The warm, roomy dining room is appointed with
    Tuscan decor. Osso bucco, roasted salmon and the specialty baby artichoke salad are outstanding menu
selections. The wine list emphasizes imported Italian varieties. The homemade tiramisu is light and fluffy. Smoke free
premises. **Cards:** AE, DI, DS, MC, VI.   ✕

MESA GRILL   Lunch: $10-$18   Dinner: $18-$29   Phone: 212/807-7400   ㉞
◆◆◆   **Location:** Between 15th and 16th. 102 5th Ave 10011. **Hours:** noon-2:30 & 5:30-10:30 pm, Sat & Sun 11:30
Regional   am-3 & 5:30-10:30 pm. Closed: 12/25. **Reservations:** suggested. **Features:** casual dress; Sunday brunch;
American   cocktails; a la carte. Among the chef's Southwest-inspired cuisine are such creations as blue corn skillet fried
    chicken, red pepper-crusted tuna steak and shrimp and roasted garlic corn tamales. The dining room is
infused with a spirited ambience. Savor the weekend brunch. Smoke free premises. **Cards:** AE, DI, DS, MC, VI.   ✕

MONTE'S RESTAURANT   Lunch: $8-$22   Dinner: $8-$22   Phone: 212/228-9194   ⑱
ᗉᗉᗉ   **Location:** Between Bleeker and W 3rd sts; in Greenwich Village. 97 MacDougal St 10012. **Hours:** noon-11
◆◆   pm, Fri & Sat-11:30 pm. Closed: 11/23, 12/25 & Tues. **Reservations:** suggested. **Features:** casual dress;
Italian   carryout; cocktails; a la carte. The charming owner-host delights in welcoming every guest to the
    family-oriented restaurant. Enjoy home-cooking like Mama made—traditional pasta, veal and seafood
    dishes—in an old New York setting. Walls are lined with maps and celebrity pictures. Smoke free premises.
Cards: AE, DI, DS, MC, VI.   ✕

MONTRACHET   Lunch: $18-$29   Dinner: $22-$32   Phone: 212/219-2777   ⑧
◆◆◆   **Location:** In TriBeCa; between White St and Walker. 239 W Broadway 10013. **Hours:** Fri
French   noon-2:15 & 5:30-10:30 pm, Sat 5:30 pm-10:30 pm. Closed major holidays & Sun. **Reservations:**
    suggested. **Features:** casual dress; cocktails; a la carte, also prix fixe. Settle in at the unpretentious bistro, in
the heart of Tribeca, to enjoy modern French cuisine and excellent wines. The dining room is small and intimate, the perfect
place to begin a romantic night on the town. The wait staff is focused and professional. Smoke free premises. **Cards:** AE,
MC, VI.   ✕

NOBU   Lunch: $12-$20   Dinner: $12-$25   Phone: 212/219-0500   ㊸
◆◆◆◆   **Location:** In Tribeca; at Franklin St. 105 Hudson St 10013. **Hours:** 11:45 am-2:15 & 5:45-10:15 pm, Sat &
Japanese   Sun from 5:45 pm. Closed major holidays. **Reservations:** required. **Features:** casual dress; cocktails; a la
    carte. Innovative and exciting, the popular haunt for celebrities showcases the renowned chef's exquisite
"new style" Japanese cuisine. Fabulous fresh fish and seafood—including many variations of sushi—are presented both
imaginatively and traditionally. Smoke free premises. **Cards:** AE, DI, MC, VI.   ✕

NOVITA   Lunch: $12-$21   Dinner: $12-$21   Phone: 212/677-2222   ㊼
◆◆   **Location:** Between Park Ave S and Lexington; in Grammercy Park. 102 E 22nd St 10010. **Hours:** noon-3 &
Italian   6-11 pm, Fri & Sat 5:30 pm-midnight, Sun 5 pm-10 pm. Closed major holidays. **Reservations:** suggested.
    Features: casual dress; carryout; cocktails. Porcini mushroom ravioli, Australian leg of lamb with mustard
and rosemary, and breast of duck are among modern dishes on a menu of Northern Italian fare. The delicious flourless
chocolate torte is served with pistachio sauce and homemade vanilla gelati. Smoke free premises. **Cards:** AE, DI, MC, VI.   ✕

THE OLD HOMESTEAD   Lunch: $12-$25   Dinner: $16-$33   Phone: 212/242-9040   ⑥
◆◆   **Location:** Between 14th and 15th sts. 56 Ninth Ave 10011. **Hours:** 11 am-3:30 & 4-10:45 pm, Sat 1
Steakhouse   pm-11:45 pm, Sun 1 pm-9:45 pm. **Reservations:** suggested. **Features:** casual dress; carryout; cocktails &
    lounge; a la carte, also prix fixe. In the historic Chelsea meat market district, the restaurant has specialties
that range from succulent prime sirloin steak, filet mignon and prime rib to creamed spinach and cottage fries. The
restaurant has been operated by the same family since 1954. Smoke free premises. **Cards:** AE, CB, DI, MC, VI.   ✕

OLD TOWN BAR RESTAURANT   Historical   Lunch: $5-$7   Dinner: $5-$7   Phone: 212/529-6732   ㉟
ᗉᗉᗉ   **Location:** Between Park Ave and Broadway. 45 E 18th St 10003. **Hours:** 11:30 am-midnight. Closed major
◆   holidays. **Features:** casual dress; cocktails; a la carte. Housed in an 1892 structure, the old, New
American   York establishment still features many of historic architectural elements, including a pressed-tin ceiling,
    magnificent bar and beveled glass mirrors. Expect generous portions of hearty tavern food. **Cards:** AE,
MC, VI.   ✕

ONE IF BY LAND, TWO IF BY SEA   Dinner: $27-$39   Phone: 212/228-0822   ⑭
◆◆◆◆   **Location:** Just off 7th Ave between w 4th St and 7th Ave. 17 Barrow St 10014. **Hours:** 5:30 pm-midnight.
Continental   Closed major holidays. **Reservations:** suggested. **Features:** semi-formal attire; health conscious menu
    items; cocktails & lounge; entertainment; a la carte. Overlooking a small courtyard garden, the beautifully
restored, 18th-century carriage house offers candlelight dining in a room filled with the sounds of piano music. Beef
Wellington and souffles are specialties on a menu of classic and creative cuisine. Smoke free premises. **Cards:** AE, CB, DI,
DS, MC, VI.   ✕

(See map p. 326)

PACIFICA
◆◆
Chinese

Lunch: $10-$20   **Dinner:** $15-$25   **Phone:** 212/966-8898   ⑳
Location: Corner of Howard St, just n Canal St; in Chinatown; in Holiday Inn Downtown. 138 LaFayette St 10013. **Hours:** 6:30 am-11 pm. **Reservations:** suggested. **Features:** casual dress; health conscious menu items; carryout; cocktails & lounge; fee for parking & valet parking. Enjoy many exotic alternatives to "American Chinese" cuisine at the relaxing, second-floor restaurant, which overlooks the bustling street. The menu centers on Cantonese-style preparations. Oriental paintings in lacquered frames hang on the walls. Smoke free premises.
Cards: AE, DI, DS, JC, MC, VI.   ✗

PATRIA
◆◆◆
Ethnic

Lunch: $14-$19   **Dinner:** $54   **Phone:** 212/777-6211   ㊱
Location: 20th St, sw corner. 250 Park Ave S 10003. **Hours:** noon-2:30 & 6-11 pm, Fri noon-2:30 & 5-midnight, Sun 5:30 pm-10:30 pm. **Closed:** 11/23. **Reservations:** suggested; strongly advise.
Features: dressy casual; cocktails & lounge; fee for parking; prix fixe. The trend-setting spot offers nuevo Latino cuisine, which blends unusual ingredients, vibrant flavors and stunning presentations. The multilevel dining room is charged with high energy. Premium wines from Spain, Chile and Argentina are featured. Smoke free premises. **Cards:** AE, DI, MC, VI.   ✗

PERIYALI
◆◆◆
Greek

Lunch: $17-$22   **Dinner:** $17-$26   **Phone:** 212/463-7890   ⑬
Location: Between 5th and 6th aves. 35 W 20th St 10011. **Hours:** noon-3 & 5:30-11 pm, Fri-11:30 pm, Sat 5:30 pm-11:30 pm. Closed major holidays & Sun. **Reservations:** suggested. **Features:** casual dress; cocktails; a la carte. Enjoy gourmet entrees in a relaxed, gentrified Mediterranean dining room. Of particular interest are the octopus appetizer, sauteed sweetbread, barbecue quail, moussaka and the lengthy list of Greek wines. Homemade desserts are delicious. Smoke free premises. **Cards:** AE, CB, DI, MC, VI.   ✗

RINCON DE ESPANA RESTAURANT
◆◆
Ethnic

Lunch: $12-$20   **Dinner:** $12-$20   **Phone:** 212/260-4950   ㊳
Location: Between Bleeker and W 3rd sts. 226 Thompson St 10012. **Hours:** noon-11 pm, Fri & Sat-midnight. **Reservations:** suggested. **Features:** casual dress; cocktails & lounge; entertainment. The long-established, neighborhood restaurant is a local favorite for authentic Spanish fare. Shrimp a la Carlos is prepared with garlic, onions, butter, paprika and olive oil. Paintings and other decorations reflect the feel of a Spanish tavern. Smoke free premises. **Cards:** AE, DI, DS, MC, VI.   ✗

RISTORANTE S P Q R
◆◆◆
Italian

Lunch: $10-$15   **Dinner:** $16-$25   **Phone:** 212/925-3120   ⑤
Location: Between Hester and Grand sts; in Little Italy. 133 Mulberry St 10013. **Hours:** noon-11 pm, Fri & Sat-midnight. **Reservations:** suggested. **Features:** casual dress; health conscious menu items; cocktails & lounge; a la carte, also prix fixe. The turn-of-the-20th-century dining room is appointed with fresh flowers, artwork and an attractive wall mural. Representative of traditional fare are such dishes as fusilli con escarole and prosciutto- and mozzarella-stuffed chicken breast. Smoke free premises. **Cards:** AE, DI, MC, VI.   ✗

ROSEMARIES
◆◆◆
Northern
Italian

Lunch: $15-$19   **Dinner:** $15-$30   **Phone:** 212/285-2610   ㉔
Location: In TriBeCa; between W Broadway and Church St. 145 Duane St 10013. **Hours:** noon-2:30 & 5:30-10 pm, Fri & Sat-10:30 pm. Closed major holidays & Sun. **Reservations:** suggested. **Features:** casual dress; cocktails; a la carte. Quaint and homey with sparse decor and wide-spaced tables, the Tribeca restaurant affords delightful dining. Representative of creative entrees is grilled skate with lemon fettuccine—although plenty of more traditional offerings also are available. Smoke free premises. **Cards:** AE, MC, VI.   ✗

SAVOY RESTAURANT
◆◆◆
American

Lunch: $9-$14   **Dinner:** $18-$26   **Phone:** 212/219-8570   ⑮
Location: In SoHo; corner Prince and Crosby sts. 70 Prince St 10012. **Hours:** noon-3 & 6-10:30 pm, Fri & Sat-11 pm, Sun 6 pm-10 pm. Closed major holidays. **Features:** casual dress; cocktails; a la carte, also prix fixe. Three working fireplaces add to the cozy, country-cottage ambience. Such Mediterranean-inspired cuisine as salt-crust baked duck and ravioli emphasizes fresh, regional ingredients. Tasty creme brulee is made in the chef's dining room fireplace. **Cards:** AE, DS, MC, VI.   ✗

SECOND AVENUE KOSHER DELI
◆◆
American

Lunch: $8-$25   **Dinner:** $15-$25   **Phone:** 212/677-0606   ㊵
Location: At 10th St. 156 2nd Ave 10003. **Hours:** 7:30 am-midnight, Fri & Sat-3 am. Closed major holidays & Jewish Holidays. **Features:** casual dress; health conscious menu; carryout; beer & wine only; street parking; a la carte. In the older area of Manhattan, this old family deli is surprisingly warm and comfortable. The menu centers on outstanding kosher food, including magnificent chopped liver and tasty chicken soup. The thick and chewy chocolate bagka is sure to please. Smoke free premises. **Cards:** AE, DI, DS, MC, VI.   ✗

SONIA ROSE
◆◆◆
French

Lunch: $27   **Dinner:** $41   **Phone:** 212/545-1777   ㊴
Location: Between Lexington and 3rd Ave; in Dumont Plaza Suite Hotel. 150 E 34th St 10016. **Hours:** 7 am-10:30, noon-2 & 5:30-10, Fri-11 pm, Sat 8 am-11, noon-2 & 5:30-11 pm, Sun 8 am-11, noon-2 & 5:30-10 pm. **Reservations:** suggested. **Features:** dressy casual; fee for parking; prix fixe, a la carte. The ever-changing, eclectic menu reveals a classical French foundation. Overlooking a small, landscaped courtyard with a vivid mural and architectural waterfall, the dining room is a serene spot for romantic candlelight dining. Service is unobtrusive. Smoke free premises. **Cards:** AE, DI, MC, VI.   ✗

TONY MAY'S GEMELLI RESTAURANT
◆◆
South Italian

Lunch: $17-$28   **Dinner:** $17-$29   **Phone:** 212/488-2100   ㊽
Location: Between Liberty and Church sts. Four World Trade Center 10048. **Hours:** 11:30 am-2:30 & 5-9 pm. Closed major holidays & Sun. **Reservations:** suggested. **Features:** casual dress; cocktails; a la carte. In the center courtyard of the World Trade Center, the restaurant delivers a menu of traditional Southern Italian fare—such as rabbit stew with tomato and marjorane. The interior decor is simple and nicely put together. Service is casual. **Cards:** AE, DI, DS, MC, VI.   ✗

(See map p. 326)

TRIBECA GRILL
◆◆◆
American
Lunch: $12-$22   **Dinner:** $19-$29   **Phone:** 212/941-3900 ㊹
Location: In Tribeca; at Franklin. 375 Greenwich St 10013. **Hours:** 11:30 am-3 & 5:30-11 pm, Fri & Sat-11:30 pm, Sun-10 pm. Closed major holidays & Sat lunch. **Reservations:** required. **Features:** casual dress; Sunday brunch; cocktails; a la carte. Many celebrities are lured to this famous spot, which is owned by Robert DeNiro in partnership with noted restaurateur Drew Nieporent. The unpretentious setting radiates energy. A contemporary, bistrolike feel punctuates the renovated warehouse. **Cards:** AE, DI, DS, MC, VI.

VERBENA
◆◆◆
American
Lunch: $9-$11   **Dinner:** $23-$29   **Phone:** 212/260-5454 ㊻
Location: Between 18th and 19th sts. 54 Irving Place 10003. **Hours:** 5:30 pm-10:30 pm, Sun 11:30 am-2:30 & 5:30-10 pm. Closed major holidays. **Reservations:** required. **Features:** semi-formal attire; Sunday brunch; health conscious menu; cocktails; a la carte. On the lower level of a brownstone townhouse, the restaurant has dining rooms appointed in a sleek, simple style. The candlelit courtyard has an inviting charm all its own. Mediterranean influences infuse preparations of contemporary American cuisine. Smoke free premises. **Cards:** AE, DI, MC, VI.

VILLA MOSCONI RESTAURANT
AAA
◆◆
Italian
Lunch: $12-$18   **Dinner:** $15-$30   **Phone:** 212/673-0390 ㉒
Location: Between Bleeker and Houston sts. 69 MacDougal St 10012. **Hours:** noon-11 pm. Closed: 12/25 & Sun. **Reservations:** suggested. **Features:** casual dress; health conscious menu items; carryout; cocktails & lounge; a la carte. Special requests are handled expediently at the casual restaurant, which is known for flavorful, traditional preparations of homemade pasta. The down-to-earth atmosphere is reminiscent of an Old World setting. Servers are prompt and efficient. Smoke free premises. **Cards:** AE, DI, DS, MC, VI.

WINDOWS-ON-THE-WORLD
◆◆◆
American
Lunch: $15-$23   **Dinner:** $23-$35   **Phone:** 212/524-7000 ㉕
Location: On West St, between Liberty and Vesey sts; 107th Floor. 1 World Trade Center 10048. **Hours:** 11:30 am-2 & 5-10:30 pm, Fri & Sat-11:30 pm; Sun 11 am-2 & 5-10 pm. **Reservations:** suggested. **Features:** semi-formal attire; Sunday brunch; cocktails & lounge; fee for valet parking; a la carte. Floor-to-ceiling windows allow magnificent views of Manhattan and the rivers. Shades of sky blue and sunshine yellow contribute to the whimsical feel of the dining room. International influences punctuate such dishes as grilled salmon and filet mignon. Smoke free premises. **Cards:** AE, DI, DS, MC, VI.

THE YANKEE CLIPPER Historical
AAA
◆◆
Seafood
Lunch: $15-$23   **Dinner:** $15-$23   **Phone:** 212/344-5959 ④
Location: In South Street Seaport; overlooking Peking Wavertree berths. 170 John St 10038. **Hours:** 11:30 am-10 pm, Sun-9 pm. Closed: 11/23 & 12/25. **Reservations:** suggested. **Features:** casual dress; children's menu; health conscious menu items; cocktails & lounge; a la carte. The menu draws its inspiration from its location near the former fish markets. Fresh seafood items—such as lobster ravioli, crab cakes and daily catches—are prevalent, although some landlubber items are listed. Warm oak decor helps to set a clublike moo. **Cards:** AE, DI, DS, MC, VI.

ZOE RESTAURANT
AAA
◆◆◆
American
Lunch: $8-$15   **Dinner:** $16-$26   **Phone:** 212/966-6722 ㉓
Location: Between Broadway and Mercer sts. 90 Prince St 10012. **Hours:** noon-3 & 6-10:30 pm, Fri-11 pm; Sat-11:30 pm; Sun 5:30 pm-10 pm, Sat & Sun brunch. **Reservations:** suggested. **Features:** casual dress; health conscious menu items; cocktails & lounge; minimum charge-$12 lunch/$20 dinner; a la carte. Crispy calamari with Vietnamese dipping sauce and the grilled tuna club with wasabi mayonnaise are representative of flavorful dishes on the varied menu. Terra cotta columns and tile work in the cast-iron SoHo building date back to the 1890s. Smoke free premises. **Cards:** AE, CB, DI, MC, VI.

NEW YORK (MIDTOWN MANHATTAN)   (See map p. 328; index p. 321)

LODGINGS

THE AVALON
◆◆◆
Hotel
Property failed to provide current rates
Phone: 212/299-7000   80
Location: Between 5th and Madison Ave. 16 E 32nd St 10024. **Fax:** 212/299-7001. **Terms:** [CP] meal plan; package plans. **Facility:** 100 rooms. A unique European style boutique hotel just minutes away from the Empire State Building, Madison Square Garden and Macy's. The guest rooms are very spacious, even their standard rooms, exquisite decor, a lot of attention to detail. 12 stories; interior corridors. Fee: parking. **All Rooms:** safes, honor bars. **Some Rooms:** Fee: VCR. **Cards:** AE, DI, DS, MC, VI.

BEEKMAN TOWER SUITE HOTEL
◆◆◆
Hotel

1/1-4/30	1P: $345-$355	2P: $365-$375	XP: $20	F12
9/11-12/31	1P: $335-$345	2P: $355-$365	XP: $20	F12
5/1-9/10	1P: $293-$303	2P: $313-$323	XP: $20	F12

Phone: (212)355-7300   50

Location: 49th St and 1st Ave. 3 Mitchell Pl 10017. **Fax:** 212/753-9366. **Terms:** Package plans. **Facility:** 174 rooms. Beautiful views of the midtown area. Panoramic, romantic top floor lounge with balcony. 4 two-bedroom units. 26 stories; interior corridors. **Dining:** entertainment. **All Rooms:** kitchens, combo or shower baths, safes. **Cards:** AE, DI, DS, MC, VI.
(See ad below)

BELVEDERE HOTEL

Phone: (212)245-7000 95

All Year   1P: $125-$250   2P: $125-$250   XP: $10   F12

AAA SAVE
◆ ◆
Motor Inn

Location: Between 8th and 9th aves. 319 W 48th St 10036. Fax: 212/245-4455. **Terms:** Cancellation fee imposed. **Facility:** 420 rooms. Historic hotel. 17 stories; interior corridors. Fee: parking. **Dining:** Cocktails; also, Churrascaria Plataforma, see separate listing. **All Rooms:** efficiencies. **Cards:** AE, DI, DS, MC, VI.
(See color ad p 337)

THE BEST WESTERN MANHATTAN HOTEL

Phone: (212)736-1600 91

9/1-12/31	1P: $149-$699	2P: $149-$799	XP: $20	F12
5/1-8/31 & 3/1-4/30	1P: $139-$329	2P: $139-$329	XP: $20	F12
1/1-2/28	1P: $89-$199	2P: $89-$199	XP: $20	F12

AAA SAVE
◆ ◆
Hotel

Location: Between 5th and Broadway. 17 W 32nd St 10001. Fax: 212/563-4007. **Terms:** [CP] meal plan; 7 day cancellation notice; cancellation fee imposed. **Facility:** 176 rooms. Located just one block from the Empire State Building and close to Madison Square Garden. Designed as theme accommodations reflecting Manhattan's three most famous neighborhoods: Central Park, Fifth Ave and trendy SoHo. 14 stories; interior corridors. Fee: parking. **Dining:** 2 restaurants; 7 am-11 pm; $9-$25; cocktails. **Services:** gift shop. **All Rooms:** combo or shower baths, extended cable TV. **Cards:** AE, CB, DI, DS, JC, MC, VI. **Special Amenities: Free breakfast and free newspaper.**

BEST WESTERN WOODWARD

Phone: (212)247-2000 77

9/5-12/31	1P: $193-$450	2P: $223-$450	XP: $30	F12
1/1-4/30	1P: $109-$289	2P: $119-$299	XP: $10	F12
5/1-6/30	1P: $169-$279	2P: $179-$289	XP: $20	F12
7/1-9/4	1P: $119-$279	2P: $143-$289	XP: $10	F12

AAA SAVE
◆ ◆
Historic Hotel

Location: Between Broadway and 7th Ave. 210 W 55th St 10019. Fax: 212/581-2248. **Facility:** 141 rooms. 4 two-bedroom units. 14 stories; interior corridors. **Dining:** Restaurants nearby. **All Rooms:** combo or shower baths. **Cards:** AE, CB, DI, DS, JC, MC, VI. **Special Amenities: Free newspaper and preferred room (subject to availability with advanced reservations).** *(See ad below)*

THE CARLYLE

Phone: 212/744-1600 71

◆ ◆ ◆ ◆
Hotel

Property failed to provide current rates

Location: At Madison Ave. 35 E 76th St 10021. Fax: 212/717-4682. **Terms:** Pets. **Facility:** 196 rooms. Charming and gracious, reflecting subdued sophistication and old world elegance with a residential air. All rooms with fax machine. World-class cabaret style entertainment most nights in the famous Cafe' Carlyle. Lovely formal dining. 20 two-bedroom units. 34 stories; interior corridors. **Dining:** entertainment. **Services:** gift shop. Fee: massage. **All Rooms:** combo or shower baths, safes, honor bars. **Cards:** AE, DI, MC, VI.

THE CARNEGIE HOTEL

Phone: 212/245-4000 107

◆ ◆ ◆
Hotel

Property failed to provide current rates

Location: Between 7th Ave and Broadway. 229 W 58th St 10019. Fax: 212/245-6199. **Terms:** [CP] meal plan. **Facility:** 20 rooms. 5 stories; interior corridors. **All Rooms:** kitchens, safes. **Cards:** AE, DI, DS, MC, VI.

CENTRAL PARK INTER CONTINENTAL NEW YORK

Phone: (212)757-1900 116

◆ ◆ ◆ ◆
Hotel

9/5-12/31	1P: $299-$525	2P: $299-$525	XP: $50	F17
5/1-6/30	1P: $259-$475	2P: $259-$475	XP: $50	F17
7/1-9/4 & 1/1-4/30	1P: $209-$395	2P: $209-$395	XP: $50	F17

Location: Between 6th (Ave of the Americas) and 7th aves. 112 Central Park S 10019. Fax: 212/757-9620. **Terms:** Cancellation fee imposed; package plans, weekends & seasonal. **Facility:** 210 rooms. Intimate hotel opposite Central Park. Fine European decor, lavish art work and creative floral pieces. Rooms and baths range from compact to spacious. 25 stories; interior corridors. **Services:** Fee: massage. **All Rooms:** safes, honor bars. **Cards:** AE, DI, DS, MC, VI.

CLARION HOTEL FIFTH AVENUE
◆◆ All Year   1P: $169-$325   2P: $169-$325   XP: $15   **Phone:** (212)447-1500   [88]
Motel   **Location:** Between Madison Ave and 5th. 3 E 40th St 10016. **Fax:** 212/213-0972. **Facility:** 189 rooms. 30 stories; interior corridors. **Cards:** AE, CB, DI, DS, MC, VI.

COMFORT INN-MANHATTAN   **Phone:** (212)947-0200   [75]
(AAA) (SAVE)   9/1-12/31   1P: $179-$394   2P: $194-$409   XP: $15   F1
◆◆   5/1-6/30   1P: $179-$225   2P: $194-$240   XP: $15   F18
  7/1-8/31   1P: $149-$199   2P: $164-$214   XP: $15   F18
Motel   1/1-4/30   1P: $129-$179   2P: $144-$194   XP: $15   F18
   Location: Between 5th and 6th, just e of Herald Sq. 42 W 35th 10001. **Fax:** 212/594-3047. **Terms:** [CP] meal plan. **Facility:** 130 rooms. Built in 1905, this hotel features compact to above average sized guest rooms and priced accordingly. Located just blocks from the Empire State Building. Discounted off-site parking in pay garage; 13 stories; interior corridors. Fee: parking. **All Rooms:** Fee: safes. **Cards:** AE, DI, DS, JC, MC, VI. **Special Amenities:** Free breakfast and free local telephone calls.

COURTYARD BY MARRIOTT/MANHATTAN-TIMES SQUARE SOUTH   **Phone:** 212/391-0088   [113]
◆◆◆   Property failed to provide current rates
Motel   **Location:** Between Broadway and 6th Ave. 114 W 40th St 10018. **Fax:** 212/391-6023. **Terms:** Pets, on approval extra charge. **Facility:** 244 rooms. Compact high-rise with some views of the Empire State Building. 33 stories; interior corridors. **Some Rooms:** 4 efficiencies. **Cards:** AE, DI, DS, MC, VI.

CROWNE PLAZA AT THE UNITED NATIONS   **Phone:** 212/986-8800   [127]
◆◆◆   9/5-12/16   1P: $379-$399
Hotel   5/1-6/23   1P: $279-$299
  6/24-9/4 & 12/17-4/30   1P: $259-$279
Location: Between 1st and 2nd aves. 304 E 42nd St 10017. **Fax:** 212/986-1758. **Terms:** Package plans; pets, $500 dep req kennels nearby. **Facility:** 300 rooms. Located one block from the United Nations. Offering several different types of accommodations from standard rooms to various sized suites. State-of-the-art exercise room. 16-20 stories; interior corridors. Fee: parking. **Services:** Fee: massage. **All Rooms:** safes, honor bars. **Some Rooms:** Fee: VCR. **Cards:** AE, CB, DI, DS, JC, MC, VI.

CROWNE PLAZA MANHATTAN   **Phone:** 212/977-4000   [111]
◆◆◆   Property failed to provide current rates
Hotel   **Location:** 49th and Broadway. 1605 Broadway 10019. **Fax:** 212/333-7393. **Terms:** Package plans; small pets only, waiver req. **Facility:** 770 rooms. In the heart of the theater district and Times Square. 46 stories; interior corridors; heated pool. **Services:** gift shop. Fee: massage. **All Rooms:** combo or shower baths, safes, honor bars. **Cards:** AE, CB, DI, DS, MC, VI.

DAYS HOTEL-MIDTOWN   **Phone:** (212)581-7000   [93]
(AAA) (SAVE)   9/1-12/31   1P: $182-$218   2P: $195-$230   XP: $20   F14
◆◆   5/1-6/30   1P: $165-$201   2P: $177-$213   XP: $20   F14
  1/1-4/30   1P: $153-$189   2P: $165-$201   XP: $20   F14
Motor Inn   7/1-8/31   1P: $143-$179   2P: $155-$191   XP: $20   F14
   Location: Between 48th and 49th sts. 790 8th Ave 10019. **Fax:** 212/974-0291. **Terms:** 30 day cancellation notice; package plans. **Facility:** 367 rooms. 15 stories; interior corridors. Fee: parking. **Dining:** Restaurant; 6 am-midnight; $10-$20; health conscious menu items; cocktails. **Services:** gift shop. **All Rooms:** combo or shower baths, extended cable TV, safes. **Cards:** AE, CB, DI, DS, MC, VI.

DELMONICO'S   **Phone:** (212)486-0508   [100]
(AAA) (SAVE)   All Year   1P: $292-$535   2P: $292-$535
◆◆   **Location:** At 59th St. 502 Park Ave 10022. **Fax:** 212/755-3779. **Terms:** Monthly rates avail; package plans
Suite Hotel   **Facility:** 158 rooms. Spacious suites, many home touches. All rooms with hair dryer, in-room fax, iron and ironing board. 28 two-bedroom units. 30 stories; interior corridors. **Recreation:** in-room video games. **All Rooms:** kitchens, extended cable TV. **Some Rooms:** Fee: VCR. **Cards:** AE, DI, DS, MC, VI.
Special Amenities: Free newspaper and preferred room (subject to availability with advanced reservations).

DOUBLETREE GUEST SUITES

Phone: (212)719-1600   **117**

AAA **SAVE** All Year   1P: $219-$319   2P: $219-$319   XP: $20   F17
Location: 47th St and 7th Ave. 1568 Broadway 10036. Fax: 212/921-5212. **Terms:** Package plans.
Suite Hotel **Facility:** 460 rooms. Unique children's club. Time's Square location. Rooms with child safety features. 2 two-bedroom units. 43 stories; interior corridors. **Dining:** Restaurant; 6:30 am-11 pm; pre-theatre prix-fixe 5:30 pm-7:30 pm; $8-$25; health conscious menu items; cocktails. **Services:** gift shop. **Recreation:** TV video games.
All Rooms: efficiencies, combo or shower baths, extended cable TV, safes, honor bars. **Some Rooms:** Fee: VCR. **Cards:** AE, CB, DI, DS, MC, VI. *(See color ad below)*

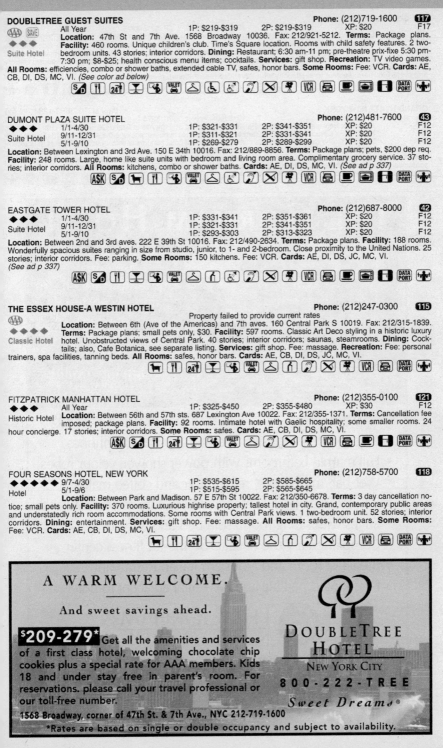

DUMONT PLAZA SUITE HOTEL

Phone: (212)481-7600   **43**

♦♦♦ 1/1-4/30   1P: $321-$331   2P: $341-$351   XP: $20   F12
Suite Hotel 9/11-12/31   1P: $311-$321   2P: $331-$341   XP: $20   F12
5/1-9/10   1P: $269-$279   2P: $289-$299   XP: $20   F12
Location: Between Lexington and 3rd Ave. 150 E 34th 10016. Fax: 212/889-8856. **Terms:** Package plans; pets, $200 dep req. **Facility:** 248 rooms. Large, home like suite units with bedroom and living room area. Complimentary grocery service. 37 stories; interior corridors. **All Rooms:** kitchens, combo or shower baths. **Cards:** AE, DI, DS, MC, VI. *(See ad p 337)*

EASTGATE TOWER HOTEL

Phone: (212)687-8000   **42**

♦♦♦ 1/1-4/30   1P: $331-$341   2P: $351-$361   XP: $20   F12
Suite Hotel 9/11-12/31   1P: $321-$331   2P: $341-$351   XP: $20   F12
5/1-9/10   1P: $293-$303   2P: $313-$323   XP: $20   F12
Location: Between 2nd and 3rd aves. 222 E 39th St 10016. Fax: 212/490-2634. **Terms:** Package plans. **Facility:** 188 rooms. Wonderfully spacious suites ranging in size from studio, junior, to 1- and 2-bedroom. Close proximity to the United Nations. 25 stories; interior corridors. Fee: parking. **Some Rooms:** 150 kitchens. Fee: VCR. **Cards:** AE, DI, DS, JC, MC, VI.
(See ad p 337)

THE ESSEX HOUSE-A WESTIN HOTEL

Phone: (212)247-0300   **115**

Property failed to provide current rates
AAA **Location:** Between 6th (Ave of the Americas) and 7th aves. 160 Central Park S 10019. Fax: 212/315-1839.
♦♦♦ **Terms:** Package plans; small pets only, $30. **Facility:** 597 rooms. Classic Art Deco styling in a historic luxury
Classic Hotel hotel. Unobstructed views of Central Park. 40 stories; interior corridors; saunas, steamrooms. **Dining:** Cocktails; also, Cafe Botanica, see separate listing. **Services:** gift shop. Fee: massage. **Recreation:** Fee: personal trainers, spa facilities, tanning beds. **All Rooms:** safes, honor bars. **Cards:** AE, CB, DI, DS, JC, MC, VI.

FITZPATRICK MANHATTAN HOTEL

Phone: (212)355-0100   **121**

♦♦♦ All Year   1P: $325-$450   2P: $355-$480   XP: $30   F12
Historic Hotel **Location:** Between 56th and 57th sts. 687 Lexington Ave 10022. Fax: 212/355-1371. **Terms:** Cancellation fee imposed; package plans. **Facility:** 92 rooms. Intimate hotel with Gaelic hospitality; some smaller rooms. 24 hour concierge. 17 stories; interior corridors. **Some Rooms:** safes. **Cards:** AE, CB, DI, DS, MC, VI.

FOUR SEASONS HOTEL, NEW YORK

Phone: (212)758-5700   **118**

♦♦♦♦ 9/7-4/30   1P: $535-$615   2P: $585-$665
Hotel 5/1-9/6   1P: $515-$595   2P: $565-$645
Location: Between Park and Madison. 57 E 57th St 10022. Fax: 212/350-6678. **Terms:** 3 day cancellation notice; small pets only. **Facility:** 370 rooms. Luxurious highrise property; tallest hotel in city. Grand, contemporary public areas and understately rich room accommodations. Some rooms with Central Park views. 1 two-bedroom unit. 52 stories; interior corridors. **Dining:** entertainment. **Services:** gift shop. Fee: massage. **All Rooms:** safes, honor bars. **Some Rooms:** Fee: VCR. **Cards:** AE, CB, DI, DS, MC, VI.

THE GORHAM HOTEL
Phone: (212)245-1800 [101]
(AAA) (SAVE)   All Year   1P: $205-$475   2P: $215-$275   XP: $25   F16
◆◆◆   **Location:** Between 6th and 7th aves; across from City Center. 136 W 55th St 10019. Fax: 212/582-8332.
Hotel   **Terms:** [BP] & [CP] meal plans; cancellation fee imposed; package plans. **Facility:** 115 rooms. Boutique-style hotel centrally located to entertainment centers and cultural attractions. Contemporary accommodations. 33 whirlpool rooms; 17 stories; interior corridors. Fee: parking. **Dining:** Restaurant nearby. **All Rooms:** efficiencies, extended cable TV, safes. **Some Rooms:** Fee: VCR. **Cards:** AE, CB, DI, MC, VI. **Special Amenities:** Free newspaper and preferred room (subject to availability with advanced reservations). *(See color ad below)*

🆂🅳 🍴 🐕 🏊 🅐 🕙 ✖ 📷 VCR 🖨 💻 🗄 🎏 📠 🛗

GRAND HYATT NEW YORK
Phone: (212)883-1234 [53]
(AAA) (SAVE)   All Year   1P: $250   2P: $275   XP: $25   F18
◆◆◆   **Location:** Between Lexington and Park aves, at E 42nd St. Park Ave at Grand Central 10017 (109 E 42nd St,
Hotel   NEW YORK). Fax: 212/697-3772. **Terms:** Cancellation fee imposed; package plans. **Facility:** 1347 rooms. Adjacent to Grand Central Station this convention oriented hotel features various boutique shops in their expansive lobby area. Walk the streets of famous 5th, Madison or Park avenues, all close by. 5 whirlpool rooms; suites avail; 34 stories; interior corridors. Fee: parking. **Dining:** Dining room, 2 restaurants; 6:30 am-midnight; $12-$40; health conscious menu items; cocktails. **Services:** gift shop. **All Rooms:** combo or shower baths. **Some Rooms:** Fee: VCR. **Cards:** AE, DI, DS, JC, MC, VI.

🍴 24ʰ 🍸 🐕 🏊 🚗 🏊 ♿ 🕙 ✖ 📷 VCR 🖨 📠

HOLIDAY INN BROADWAY

◆◆◆
Motor Inn

9/7-12/31	1P: $269-$389	2P: $279-$399	XP: $15	F19
5/1-6/30	1P: $229-$289	2P: $239-$299	XP: $15	F19
1/1-4/30	1P: $199-$289	2P: $209-$299	XP: $15	F19
7/1-9/6	1P: $199-$245	2P: $209-$255	XP: $15	F19

Phone: (212)736-3800 [92]

Location: Corner of Broadway and 32nd St. 49 W 32nd St 10001. Fax: 212/631-0449. **Terms:** Cancellation fee imposed; pets, $50 extra charge, dep req. **Facility:** 532 rooms. Located across from Greeley Square and close to Javits Center, Madison Square Garden and Empire State Building. Hotel features many French Renaissance inspired details. 18 stories; interior corridors. Fee: parking. **Services:** gift shop. Fee: massage. **All Rooms:** safes, honor bars. **Cards:** AE, DI, DS, JC, MC, VI. (See color ad below)

HOLIDAY INN MIDTOWN-57TH STREET

◆◆
Motor Inn

10/1-1/1	1P: $189-$259	2P: $189-$259	XP: $15	F18
5/1-9/30	1P: $179-$209	2P: $179-$209	XP: $15	F18
1/2-4/30	1P: $159-$189	2P: $159-$189	XP: $15	F18

Phone: (212)581-8100 [39]

Location: Between 9th and 10th aves. 440 W 57th St 10019. Fax: 212/581-7739. **Terms:** Check-in 4 pm; cancellation fee imposed; package plans. **Facility:** 596 rooms. 1 two-bedroom unit. 18 stories; interior corridors. **Services:** gift shop. **Some Rooms:** 2 efficiencies. Fee: refrigerators. **Cards:** AE, DI, DS, MC, VI.

HOTEL BEACON

AAA [SAVE]

◆◆

Hotel

Phone: (212)787-1100 ③⓪ F12

All Year   1P: $185-$195   2P: $195-$215   XP: $15
Location: At 75th St. 2130 Broadway 10023. Fax: 212/724-0839. **Terms:** Cancellation fee imposed. **Facility:** 230 rooms. Just blks away from Central Park, limited facilities. 7 two-bedroom units. Rates for up to 4 persons; suites, $250-$490; 25 stories; interior corridors. Fee: parking. **Dining:** Coffee shop nearby. **Recreation:** Fee: health club privledges. **All Rooms:** efficiencies, safes. **Cards:** AE, CB, DI, DS, JC, MC, VI.
(See color ad p 343)

HOTEL LUCERNE

AAA [SAVE]

◆◆◆

Hotel

Phone: 212/875-1000 ③③

9/11-12/28   1P: $200-$240   2P: $200-$240   XP: $15   F16
3/1-4/30   1P: $160-$225   2P: $160-$225   XP: $15   F16
5/1-9/10   1P: $160-$215   2P: $160-$215   XP: $15   F16
12/29-2/28   1P: $150-$200   2P: $150-$200   XP: $15   F16
Location: Between Amsterdam and Broadway. 201 W 79th St 10024. Fax: 212/362-7251. **Terms:** [BP] meal plan; check-in 4 pm; cancellation fee imposed. **Facility:** 179 rooms. In unique turn-of-the-century building featuring carved red stone. All rooms with contemporary decor. Rooftop sundeck. All rooms with hair dryer, iron and ironing board. Coffee makers on request; whirlpool room; 13 stories; interior corridors. Fee: parking. **Dining:** Restaurant; 7 am-10 & 5-midnight; $11-$18; cocktails; entertainment. **Recreation:** Fee: in-room video games. **All Rooms:** extended cable TV. **Cards:** AE, DI, DS, MC, VI. *(See color ad p 345)*

HOTEL NEWTON

AAA [SAVE]

◆

Hotel

Phone: (212)678-6500 ⑤④ F15

All Year   1P: $85-$145   2P: $1-$145   XP: $15
Location: Between 94th and 95th sts. 2528 Broadway 10025. Fax: 212/678-6758. **Facility:** 110 rooms. Limited facilities. Rates for up to 4 persons; 9 stories; interior corridors. **Dining:** Restaurant nearby. **All Rooms:** combo or shower baths. **Some Rooms:** Fee: refrigerators. **Cards:** AE, CB, DI, MC, VI.
(See color ad below)

HOTEL PLAZA ATHENEE

◆◆◆◆

Hotel

Phone: (212)734-9100 ⑥⑥ F

All Year   1P: $430-$590   2P: $460-$620   XP: $35
Location: Between Madison and Park aves. 37 E 64th St 10021. Fax: 212/772-0958. **Terms:** Package plans; small pets only. **Facility:** 153 rooms. Boutique hotel with traditional Old World style. 17 stories; interior corridors. **Services:** Fee: massage. **All Rooms:** safes, honor bars. **Some Rooms:** 61 efficiencies. **Cards:** AE, DI, DS, MC, VI.

HOTEL SALISBURY

◆◆

Hotel

Phone: (212)246-1300 ⑩③ F15

All Year   1P: $259-$269   2P: $279-$289   XP: $20
Location: Between 6th (Ave of the Americas) and 7th aves. 123 W 57th St 10019. Fax: 212/977-7752. **Terms:** [ECP] meal plan. **Facility:** 320 rooms. 17 stories; interior corridors. **All Rooms:** combo or shower baths, safes. **Some Rooms:** Fee: VCR. **Cards:** AE, CB, DI, MC, VI.

HOTEL WALES

◆◆

Historic Hotel

Phone: 212/876-6000 ③⑥

Property failed to provide current rates

Location: Between 92 E and 93 E sts. 1295 Madison Ave 10128. Fax: 212/860-7000. **Terms:** [ECP] meal plan; check-in 4 pm. **Facility:** 92 rooms. Beautifully appointed, boutique style hotel. Some smaller rooms. Close to museums. All rooms with CD player and hair dryer. Limited facilities. 10 stories; interior corridors. **Services:** Fee: massage. **All Rooms:** combo or shower baths, safes. **Cards:** AE, DI, MC, VI.

HOWARD JOHNSON PLAZA HOTEL

AAA [SAVE]

◆◆

Hotel

Phone: (212)581-4100 ⑩⑥

9/1-12/31   1P: $182-$218   2P: $195-$230   XP: $20   F14
5/1-6/30   1P: $165-$201   2P: $177-$213   XP: $20   F14
1/1-4/30   1P: $153-$189   2P: $165-$201   XP: $20   F14
7/1-8/31   1P: $143-$179   2P: $155-$191   XP: $20   F14
Location: Between 51st and 52nd. 851 8th Ave 10019. Fax: 212/974-7502. **Facility:** 300 rooms. 11 stories; interior corridors. Fee: parking. **Dining:** Restaurant; 7 am-11 pm; Fri & Sat-11:30 pm, daily breakfast buffet; $15-$20. **Services:** gift shop. **All Rooms:** combo or shower baths. **Cards:** AE, CB, DI, DS, MC, VI.

THE KIMBERLY A BOUTIQUE SUITE HOTEL & SPA

Phone: (212)755-0400 **124**

9/11-4/30	1P: $289-$449	2P: $289-$449
5/1-9/10	1P: $279-$439	2P: $279-$439	XP: $25	F17

Suite Hotel

Location: Between 3rd and Lexington Ave. 145 E 50th St 10022. **Fax:** 212/486-6915. **Terms:** Monthly rates avail; cancellation fee imposed; package plans. **Facility:** 186 rooms. 14 two-bedroom units. Whirlpool suite, full dining & living rm; 31 stories; interior corridors. **Dining:** 2 restaurants; 6:30 am-11 pm; $15-$30; health conscious menu items; cocktails; entertainment, nightclub. **All Rooms:** extended cable TV, honor bars. **Some Rooms:** Fee: VCR. **Cards:** AE, CB, DI, DS, MC, VI.

THE KITANO NEW YORK HOTEL

Phone: 212/885-7000 **78**

Property failed to provide current rates

Hotel

Location: At 38th St. 66 Park Ave 10016. **Fax:** 212/885-7100. **Terms:** Package plans. **Facility:** 149 rooms. Boutique hotel. Nicely appointed guest rooms with a soothing sophisticated decor. All rooms with in-room fax and internet access. 18 stories; interior corridors. **All Rooms:** safes, honor bars. **Some Rooms:** Fee: VCR. **Cards:** AE, CB, DI, DS, MC, VI.

LE PARKER MERIDIEN NEW YORK

Phone: (212)245-5000 **41**

9/5-12/31	1P: $365-$435	2P: $395-$435	XP: $30	F17
5/1-6/29 & 1/1-4/30	1P: $350-$425	2P: $380-$425	XP: $30	F17
6/30-9/4	1P: $325-$395	2P: $355-$395	XP: $30	F17

Hotel

Location: Between 6th and 7th aves, (vehicle entrance on 56th St). 118 W 57th St 10019. **Fax:** 212/307-1776. **Terms:** Cancellation fee imposed; package plans; small pets only. **Facility:** 698 rooms. In-room fax machines. 2 whirlpool rooms; suites, $450-$2500; 42 stories; interior corridors; 2 pools, 1 heated, 1 small heated, saunas. Fee: swimming classes; racquetball courts. **Dining:** 2 restaurants; 6:30 am-1 am; $20-$28; cocktails. **Services:** gift shop. Fee: massage. **Recreation:** aerobics classes. Fee: basketball, nutritionist & personal trainers avail. **All Rooms:** extended cable TV, safes, honor bars. **Some Rooms:** 123 kitchens. **Cards:** AE, CB, DI, DS, JC, MC, VI.

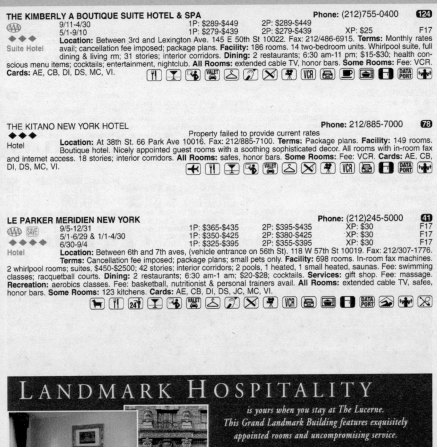

LOEWS NEW YORK HOTEL
◆◆◆   All Year   1P: $219-$319
Hotel   **Location:** Lexington Ave at E 51st St. 569 Lexington Ave 10022. Fax: 212/758-6311. **Terms:** Package plans; small pets only. **Facility:** 722 rooms. 20 stories; interior corridors. Fee: parking. **Services:** gift shop. **All Rooms:** combo or shower baths, safes. **Some Rooms:** Fee: VCR. **Cards:** AE, CB, DI, DS, MC, VI. *(See ad below)*
Phone: (212)752-7000   58
XP: $20   F17

THE LOWELL HOTEL
◆◆◆◆   Property failed to provide current rates
Hotel   **Location:** Between Park and Madison aves. 28 E 63rd St 10021. Fax: 212/319-4230. **Terms:** Package plans; small pets only. **Facility:** 67 rooms. Luxurious, intimate accommodations in a charming European-style boutique hotel. Some units with fireplace. 1 suite with separate fully equipped exercise room, all rooms with fax machine. 1 three-bedroom unit, 8 two-bedroom units. 17 stories; interior corridors. **Services:** Fee: massage. **All Rooms:** honor bars. **Cards:** AE, CB, DI, DS, JC, MC, VI.
Phone: (212)838-1400   65

LYDEN GARDENS HOTEL
◆◆◆   1/1-4/30   1P: $334-$344   2P: $354-$364
Apartment   9/11-12/31   1P: $324-$334   2P: $344-$354
5/1-9/10   1P: $314-$324   2P: $334-$344
Location: Between 3rd and 2nd aves. 215 E 64th St 10021. Fax: 212/758-7858. **Facility:** 132 rooms. Suite hotel with limited services. Quiet, residential area. Close proximity to shops and restaurants. 4 two-bedroom units. 13 stories; interior corridors. Fee: parking. **All Rooms:** kitchens, combo or shower baths, safes. **Some Rooms:** Fee: VCR. **Cards:** AE, DI, DS, JC, MC, VI. *(See ad p 337)*
Phone: (212)355-1230   35
XP: $20   F12
XP: $20   F12
XP: $20   F12

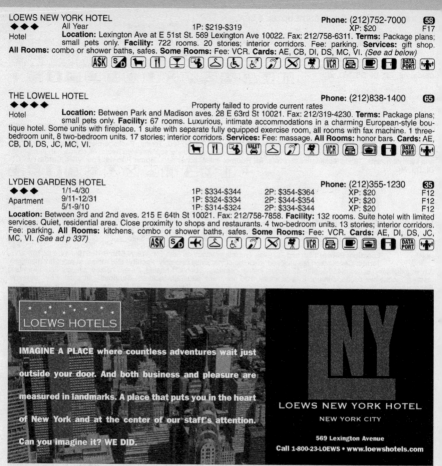

LYDEN HOUSE
◆◆
Suite Hotel

Phone: (212)888-6070   **25**
XP: $20   F12

All Year   1P: $304-$344   2P: $324-$364
Location: Between 1st and 2nd. 320 E 53rd St 10022. Fax: 212/935-7690. **Terms:** Package plans, seasonal. **Facility:** 81 rooms. Studio and 1- or 2-bedroom suites with living rooom and kitchen. Limited hotel services. 2 two-bedroom units. 11 stories; interior corridors. **All Rooms:** combo or shower baths. **Some Rooms:** Fee: VCR. **Cards:** AE, DI, DS, MC, VI. *(See ad p 337)*

THE MARK
◆◆◆◆
Historic Hotel

Phone: (212)744-4300   **82**

9/5-4/30   1P: $500   2P: $530   XP: $35   F16
5/1-9/4   1P: $470   2P: $500   XP: $35   F16
Location: Madison Ave at E 77th St. 25 E 77th St 10021. Fax: 212/744-2749. **Terms:** Cancellation fee imposed; package plans, weekends. **Facility:** 180 rooms. In the quiet neighborhood of New York's exclusive Upper East side, this charming boutique hotel features large guest rooms, many with fully equipped kitchenettes. Just half a block from famous Central Park. 5 two-bedroom units. 16 stories; interior corridors. Fee: parking. **Services:** Fee: massage. **All Rooms:** safes, honor bars. **Some Rooms:** 140 efficiencies, 40 kitchens. **Cards:** AE, DI, DS, JC, MC, VI.

THE MAYFLOWER HOTEL ON THE PARK
AAA
◆◆
Hotel

Phone: (212)265-0060   **104**

All Year   1P: $190-$230   2P: $210-$250   XP: $20   F16
Location: At 61st St. 15 Central Park W 10023. Fax: 212/265-5098. **Terms:** Package plans; small pets only. **Facility:** 365 rooms. Spacious, traditional accommodations with a European flair. Many rooms with views of Central Park. Walking distance to theaters and shopping. 11 two-bedroom units. 18 stories; interior corridors. **Dining:** Restaurant; 6:30 am-1 am; Sat & Sun brunch; $16-$22; health conscious menu items; cocktails. **All Rooms:** extended cable TV. **Some Rooms:** Fee: VCR. **Cards:** AE, CB, DI, DS, JC, MC, VI.

MIDTOWN EAST COURTYARD BY MARRIOTT
◆◆◆
Motor Inn

Phone: (212)644-9600   **122**

9/5-12/16   1P: $219-$299
12/17-4/30   1P: $159-$279
5/1-7/1   1P: $169-$259
7/2-9/4   1P: $159-$239
Location: Between 52nd and 53rd sts. 866 3rd Ave 10022. Fax: 212/813-1945. **Terms:** Cancellation fee imposed. **Facility:** 306 rooms. 31 stories; interior corridors. **All Rooms:** combo or shower baths, safes. **Cards:** AE, DI, DS, MC, VI.

MILLENNIUM BROADWAY
◆◆◆
Hotel

Phone: (212)768-4400   **112**

9/11-12/10   1P: $290-$410   2P: $290-$410   XP: $20   F12
5/1-9/10 & 12/11-4/30   1P: $265-$355   2P: $265-$355   XP: $20   F12
Location: Between 6th and 7th aves. 145 W 44th St 10036. Fax: 212/768-0847. **Terms:** Check-in 4 pm; package plans; pets. **Facility:** 752 rooms. In the heart of the Broadway Theater District and just half a block from Times Square. Offering 3 levels of accommodations from stylish guest rooms, club rooms and the newest premiere level. 52 stories; interior corridors; off site parking only. **Services:** gift shop. Fee: massage. **All Rooms:** safes, honor bars. **Some Rooms:** Fee: VCR. **Cards:** AE, DI, DS, JC, MC, VI.

NEW YORK MARRIOTT EASTSIDE
◆◆◆
Hotel

Phone: (212)755-4000   **109**

9/5-12/16   1P: $249-$375
12/17-4/30   1P: $179-$315
5/1-7/1   1P: $179-$299
7/2-9/4   1P: $179-$279
Location: Between 48th and 49th sts. 525 Lexington Ave 10017. Fax: 212/751-3440. **Terms:** Cancellation fee imposed. **Facility:** 643 rooms. Traditional style public areas and guest rooms. 6 two-bedroom units. 33 stories; interior corridors. **Services:** gift shop. **All Rooms:** combo or shower baths, honor bars. **Some Rooms:** safes. Fee: VCR. **Cards:** AE, DI, DS, MC, VI.

NEW YORK MARRIOTT MARQUIS
AAA SAVE
◆◆◆
Hotel

Phone: (212)398-1900   **90**

9/9-12/31   1P: $335-$500   2P: $355-$520   XP: $15   F18
1/1-4/30   1P: $275-$395   2P: $295-$415   XP: $15   F18
5/1-7/1   1P: $275-$375   2P: $295-$395   XP: $15   F18
7/2-9/8   1P: $250-$375   2P: $270-$395   XP: $15   F18
Location: Between 45th and 46th sts, motor entrance on 46th St. 1535 Broadway 10036. Fax: 212/704-8930. **Terms:** Package plans; small pets only. **Facility:** 1944 rooms. This large, convention oriented hotel is situated in the heart of Times Square. Revolving restaurant on top floor with spectacular view of the river. Limited on-site pay parking. 48 stories; interior corridors; saunas, whirlpool. Fee: parking. **Dining:** 2 dining rooms, restaurant; 6 am-midnight; sushi bar in lobby; $15-$35; health conscious menu items; cocktails; entertainment. **Services:** gift shop. **All Rooms:** combo or shower baths, safes, honor bars. **Some Rooms:** Fee: VCR. **Cards:** AE, CB, DI, DS, JC, MC, VI. **Special Amenities:** Free newspaper.

THE NEW YORK PALACE
AAA SAVE
◆◆◆◆◆
Historic Hotel

Phone: (212)888-7000   **44**

9/5-4/30   1P: $540-$665   2P: $565-$690   XP: $25   F18
5/1-6/22   1P: $490-$615   2P: $515-$640   XP: $25   F18
6/23-9/4   1P: $440-$565   2P: $465-$595   XP: $25   F18
Location: Between 50th and 51st (valet parking access on 50th). 455 Madison Ave 10022. Fax: 212/303-6000. **Terms:** Cancellation fee imposed; package plans; pets. **Facility:** 896 rooms. Neo-Italian Reniassance public areas featuring a grand staircase and marble fireplaces. 6 two-bedroom units. Tower suites & apartments with kitchen; 6 whirlpool rooms; 55 stories; interior corridors; steamrooms. **Dining:** Restaurant; 6:30 am-11 pm; $14-$45; health conscious menu items; cocktails; also, Le Cirque 2000, see separate listing; entertainment. **Services:** gift shop. Fee: massage. **Recreation:** spa services. **All Rooms:** combo or shower baths, extended cable TV, safes, honor bars. **Some Rooms:** 48 kitchens. **Cards:** AE, CB, DI, DS, MC, VI. **Special Amenities:** Free newspaper. *(See color ad p 348)*

NOVOTEL NEW YORK
◆◆
Hotel
Phone: (212)315-0100 [89]

9/6-12/31	1P: $119-$249	2P: $199-$249	XP: $20	F16
5/1-9/5 & 1/1-4/30	1P: $189-$229	2P: $189-$229	XP: $20	F16

Location: At Broadway; motor access on 52nd. 226 W 52nd St 10019. Fax: 212/765-5365. **Terms:** Package plans; pets, $100 dep req. **Facility:** 479 rooms. Times Square location, multi-lingual staff. 33 stories; interior corridors. **Fee:** parking. **Dining:** entertainment. **Services:** gift shop. **All Rooms:** safes, honor bars. **Some Rooms:** Fee: refrigerators. **Cards:** AE, CB, DI, MC, VI.

OMNI BERKSHIRE PLACE
◆◆◆◆
Hotel
Phone: (212)753-5800 [26]

9/17-12/31	1P: $239-$479	2P: $239-$509	XP: $30	F17
5/1-6/24	1P: $219-$419	2P: $219-$449	XP: $30	F17
6/25-9/16 & 1/1-4/30	1P: $199-$369	2P: $199-$399	XP: $30	F17

Location: Between Madison and 5th. 21 E 52nd St 10022. Fax: 212/754-5037. **Terms:** Cancellation fee imposed; package plans. **Facility:** 396 rooms. Premiere luxury hotel. 18th century inspired carpets, marble and chandeliers. 22 stories; interior corridors. **Services:** gift shop. **Fee:** massage. **All Rooms:** combo, shower or tub baths, safes, honor bars. **Cards:** AE, DI, DS, MC, VI.

THE PENINSULA NEW YORK
◆◆◆◆◆
Hotel
Phone: (212)956-2888 [59]

1/1-4/30	1P: $550-$1750	2P: $550-$1750	XP: $35	F12
5/1-12/31	1P: $535-$650	2P: $535-$650	XP: $35	F12

Location: 5th Ave at 55th St. 700 5th Ave 10019. Fax: 212/903-3949. **Terms:** Cancellation fee imposed; package plans; small pets only. **Facility:** 241 rooms. Turn-of-the-century landmark Beaux Arts building. Complete rooftop health spa. Average to luxurious sized classic contemporary rooms. All rooms with fax machine. 1 two-bedroom unit. 23 stories; interior corridors; heated pool. **Services:** Fee: massage. **All Rooms:** safes, honor bars. **Cards:** AE, CB, DI, DS, MC, VI.

THE PIERRE
◆◆◆◆
Hotel
Phone: 212/838-8000 [67]

Property failed to provide current rates

Location: At 5th Ave. 2 E 61st St 10021. **Terms:** Package plans; pets. **Facility:** 202 rooms. A Grande Dame 1930's Old New York style hotel of and stately elegance. Complete with white-gloved elevator operators. Directly opposite Central Park. Valet parking on 61st St. 7 two-bedroom units. 39 stories; interior corridors. **Dining:** entertainment. **Services:** gift shop. **Fee:** massage. **All Rooms:** safes, honor bars. **Some Rooms:** 2 efficiencies. **Fee:** VCR. **Cards:** AE, CB, DI, DS, MC, VI.

PLAZA FIFTY HOTEL
Phone: (212)751-5710 [37]

◆◆
Hotel

1/1-4/30	1P: $302-$312	2P: $322-$332	XP: $20	F12
9/11-12/31	1P: $292-$302	2P: $312-$322	XP: $20	F12
5/1-9/10	1P: $252-$262	2P: $272-$282	XP: $20	F12

Location: Between 3rd and Lexington aves. 155 E 50th St 10022. **Fax:** 212/753-1468. **Terms:** Package plans, in summer. **Facility:** 211 rooms. 3 two-bedroom units. 22 stories; interior corridors. **All Rooms:** safes. **Some Rooms:** 137 kitchens. Fee: VCR. **Cards:** AE, DI, DS, MC, VI. *(See ad p 337)*

THE REGENCY HOTEL
Phone: 212/759-4100 [68]

◆◆◆
Hotel

Property failed to provide current rates

Location: At 61st. 540 Park Ave 10021. **Fax:** 212/826-5674. **Terms:** Package plans, weekends; pets. **Facility:** 351 rooms. Located on trendy Park Ave, offering wonderfully spacious guest rooms and suites. 14 two-bedroom units. 21 stories; interior corridors. Fee: parking. **Services:** gift shop. **All Rooms:** safes, honor bars. **Some Rooms:** 80 kitchens. **Cards:** AE, DI, DS, MC, VI.

RENAISSANCE NEW YORK HOTEL
Phone: (212)765-7676 [123]

(AAA) SAVE
◆◆◆◆
Hotel

9/9-12/31	1P: $299-$395	2P: $319-$415	XP: $20	F18
5/1-7/1 & 1/1-4/30	1P: $245-$325	2P: $265-$345	XP: $20	F18
7/2-9/8	1P: $215-$280	2P: $225-$300	XP: $20	F18

Location: Times Square, Broadway and 7th Ave; auto access from 7th Ave. 714 7th Ave at 48th St 10036. **Fax:** 212/765-1962. **Terms:** Cancellation fee imposed; package plans; pets, $60 fee. **Facility:** 305 rooms. This richly decorated luxury hotel is in the center of Times Square. Large standard-style guest rooms or spacious suites with separate bedroom. No on-site parking, pay lot located on 45th St, use valet services. Suites, $525-$525; 26 stories; interior corridors. Fee: parking. **Dining:** Restaurant; 6:30 am-10:30 pm; $19-$38; health conscious menu items; cocktails; entertainment. **All Rooms:** extended cable TV, safes, honor bars. **Cards:** AE, DI, DS, JC, MC, VI. **Special Amenities:** Free newspaper.

RIHGA ROYAL HOTEL
Phone: (212)307-5000 [114]

(AAA) SAVE
◆◆◆◆
Suite Hotel

9/8-4/30	1P: $475-$3100	2P: $475-$3100
5/1-9/7	1P: $475-$3000	2P: $475-$3000

Location: Between 6th and 7th aves. 151 W 54th St 10019. **Fax:** 212/765-6530. **Terms:** Cancellation fee imposed; package plans. **Facility:** 500 rooms. Rich, understated luxury. Spacious suites provide privacy, residential feel, many amenities. Stylish art decor throughout. All room offer fax machine and CD player. 40 two-bedroom units. 4 whirlpool rooms; 54 stories; interior corridors; saunas. **Dining:** Dining room; 6:30-11 am, 11:30-2:30 & 5:30-10:30 pm; $16-$35; entertainment. **Services:** area transportation, Wall St. Fee: massage. **All Rooms:** combo or shower baths, safes, honor bars. **Some Rooms:** 4 kitchens. **Cards:** AE, CB, DI, DS, JC, MC, VI. **Special Amenities:** Free newspaper.

THE ROOSEVELT HOTEL
Phone: (212)661-9600 [47]

(AAA) SAVE
Hotel

9/5-12/31	1P: $269	2P: $269	XP: $20	F12
5/1-6/30 & 1/1-4/30	1P: $179	2P: $179	XP: $20	F12
7/1-9/4	1P: $159	2P: $159	XP: $20	F12

Location: Between Madison and Vanderbilt aves. 45 E 45th St 10017. **Fax:** 212/885-6161. **Terms:** Weekly & monthly rates avail; cancellation fee imposed. **Facility:** 1014 rooms. Restored 1926 hotel. 2 two-bedroom units, 2 three-bedroom units. 19 stories; interior corridors. **Dining:** Restaurant; 6:30 am-11 pm; $11-$20; cocktails; entertainment. **Services:** gift shop. **All Rooms:** combo or shower baths, extended cable TV, safes. **Some Rooms:** 13 efficiencies. Fee: refrigerators, VCR. **Cards:** AE, DI, DS, MC, VI. **Special Amenities:** Free newspaper.

ROYALTON
Phone: 212/869-4400 [105]

◆◆◆
Hotel

Property failed to provide current rates

Location: Between 5th and 6th Sts. 44 W 44th St 10036. **Fax:** 212/869-8965. **Facility:** 169 rooms. An avant-garde property with a stylized futuristic design. 16 stories; interior corridors. Fee: parking. **Services:** Fee: massage. **All Rooms:** combo or shower baths, honor bars. Fee: safes. **Cards:** AE, DI, MC, VI.

THE ST REGIS-NEW YORK
Phone: (212)753-4500 [49]

(AAA)
◆◆◆◆◆
Historic Hotel

1/1-4/30	1P: $575-$750	2P: $575-$750		
5/1-12/31	1P: $545-$695	2P: $545-$695	XP: $95	F

Location: Between Madison and 5th aves. 2 E 55th St 10022. **Fax:** 212/787-3447. **Terms:** Cancellation fee imposed. **Facility:** 313 rooms. Impressive architectural landmark built in the beaux-arts tradition. Ornate European styling throughout. Spacious rooms combine historic grandeur and state of the art technology. Personal butler service. 2 two-bedroom units. Suites, $950-$9000; 19 stories; interior corridors; saunas. **Dining:** Restaurant; cocktails; afternoon tea; also, Lespinasse, see separate listing; entertainment. **Services:** gift shop. Fee: massage. **Recreation:** personal trainers; hair salon. **All Rooms:** extended cable TV, safes, honor bars. **Some Rooms:** 16 efficiencies, 10 kitchens. **Cards:** AE, DI, DS, MC, VI. Sheraton Hotels & Motor Inns.

SHELBURNE MURRAY HILL HOTEL
Phone: (212)689-5200 [45]

◆◆◆
Suite Hotel

1/1-4/30	1P: $321-$331	2P: $341-$351	XP: $20	F12
9/11-12/31	1P: $311-$321	2P: $331-$341	XP: $20	F12
5/1-9/10	1P: $269-$279	2P: $289-$299	XP: $20	F12

Location: Between 38th and 37th sts. 303 Lexington Ave 10016. **Fax:** 212/779-7068. **Facility:** 263 rooms. Open the door to any of the studio, 1 or 2-bedroom suites and discover just how spacious these rooms really are. Conveniently located and minutes away form the Empire State Building, Grand Central Station, Madison and 5th ave. 15 two-bedroom units. 16 stories; interior corridors. Fee: parking. **All Rooms:** kitchens, combo or shower baths, safes. **Some Rooms:** Fee: VCR. **Cards:** AE, DI, DS, JC, MC, VI. *(See ad p 337)*

SHERATON MANHATTAN HOTEL   Phone: 212/581-3300   **79**
◆◆◆   *Property failed to provide current rates*
Hotel   **Location:** Between 51st and 52nd sts. 790 7th Ave 10019. Fax: 212/541-9219. **Terms:** Package plans; small pets only, $100 dep req. **Facility:** 660 rooms. A few blocks from famous Times Square. Lovely lobby area with many comfortable guest seating areas. Modern guest rooms with Club Level rooms on top floors. 22 stories; interior corridors; heated pool. Fee: parking. **Services:** gift shop. Fee: massage. **All Rooms:** safes, honor bars. **Some Rooms:** Fee: VCR. **Cards:** AE, CB, DI, DS, MC, VI.

SHERATON NEW YORK HOTEL & TOWERS   Phone: 212/581-1000   **61**
◆◆◆   *Property failed to provide current rates*
Hotel   **Location:** At 52nd St. 811 7th Ave 10019. **Terms:** Package plans; pets. **Facility:** 1756 rooms. A mega-hotel in the heart of Midtown with easy access to Central Park, the theater district, Carnegie Hall. 50 stories; interior corridors. **Dining:** entertainment. **Services:** gift shop. Fee: massage. **All Rooms:** combo or shower baths, safes, honor bars. **Some Rooms:** Fee: VCR. **Cards:** AE, CB, DI, DS, MC, VI.

SHERATON RUSSELL HOTEL   Phone: 212/685-7676   **46**
◆◆◆   *Property failed to provide current rates*
Hotel   **Location:** At 37th St. 45 Park Ave 10016. Fax: 212/889-3193. **Terms:** [CP] meal plan; package plans. **Facility:** 146 rooms. Classic traditions, club-like hotel. 10 stories; interior corridors. **Services:** gift shop. **All Rooms:** safes, honor bars. **Some Rooms:** Fee: refrigerators, VCR. **Cards:** AE, CB, DI, DS, MC, VI.

THE SHOREHAM HOTEL   Phone: (212)247-6700   **31**
(AAA) (SAVE)   5/1-6/30 & 9/1-4/30   1P: $325-$875   2P: $325-$875
◆◆◆   7/1-8/31   1P: $275-$675   2P: $275-$675
Hotel   **Location:** Between 5th and 6th aves. 33 W 55th St 10019. Fax: 212/765-9741. **Terms:** [CP] meal plan; cancellation fee imposed. **Facility:** 176 rooms. Unique combination of modernistic decor melds metal, glass, lighting, textures and serene colors to create an affordable boutique-style hotel. Guest rooms designed for no more than two people. Whirlpool room; suites, $397-$879; 11 stories; interior corridors. Fee: parking. **Dining:** Restaurant; $15-$25; cocktails. **Recreation:** CD & video library. **All Rooms:** combo or shower baths, extended cable TV, safes. **Cards:** AE, DI, JC, MC, VI. **Special Amenities:** Free local telephone calls and free room upgrade (subject to availability with advanced reservations).

SOUTHGATE TOWER SUITE HOTEL   Phone: (212)563-1800   **78**
◆◆◆   1/1-4/30   1P: $278-$288   2P: $298-$308   XP: $20   F12
Extended   9/11-12/31   1P: $268-$278   2P: $288-$298   XP: $20   F12
Stay Hotel   5/1-9/10   1P: $234-$244   2P: $254-$264   XP: $20   F12
               Location: At 31st St. 371 7th Ave 10001-3984. Fax: 212/643-8028. **Terms:** Pets. **Facility:** 524 rooms. Opposite Madison Square Garden, lobby accented by ornate plaster ceiling and grand crystal chandelier. Comfortable suites with refined residential feel decor. 9 two-bedroom units. 28 stories; interior corridors. Fee: parking. **Some Rooms:** 504 kitchens. **Cards:** AE, DI, DS, MC, VI. *(See ad p 337)*

THE STANHOPE   Phone: (212)288-5800   **72**
(AAA) (SAVE)   All Year   1P: $300-$380   2P: $300-$380   XP: $35   F16
◆◆◆◆   **Location:** At 81st St. 995 5th Ave 10028. Fax: 212/517-0088. **Terms:** Monthly rates avail; cancellation fee imposed; package plans, weekend. **Facility:** 185 rooms. Opposite Metropolitan Museum of Art and Central Park.
Hotel   A grand hotel, finely appointed rooms and suites. Luxury suites avail; 4 whirlpool rooms; 17 stories; interior corridors; sauna. **Dining:** Restaurant; 7 am-10:30 pm; $17-$27; cocktails; afternoon tea. **Services:** area transportation. Fee: massage. **All Rooms:** extended cable TV, safes, honor bars. **Some Rooms:** 30 efficiencies. **Cards:** AE, CB, DI, DS, JC, MC, VI. **Special Amenities:** Free newspaper. A Preferred Hotel.

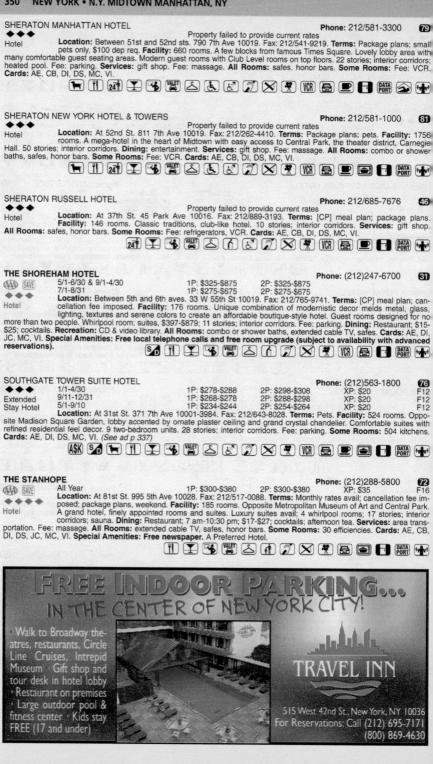

SURREY HOTEL
◆◆◆
Hotel

Phone: (212)288-3700 [70]

	1P: $450-$460	2P: $470-$480	XP: $20	F12
1/1-4/30				
9/11-12/31	1P: $440-$450	2P: $460-$470	XP: $20	F12
5/1-9/10	1P: $395-$405	2P: $415-$425	XP: $20	F12

Location: 76th and Madison. 20 E 76th 10021. **Fax:** 212/628-1549. **Terms:** Pets, $200 dep req. **Facility:** 131 rooms. 1- and 2-bedroom units with living room and kitchen. All rooms with hair dryer, iron and ironing board. 16 stories; interior corridors. **Fee:** parking. **All Rooms:** safes. **Some Rooms:** 30 efficiencies, 101 kitchens. **Cards:** AE, DI, DS, JC, MC, VI.
(See ad p 337)

SWISSOTEL NEW YORK-THE DRAKE
◆◆◆
Hotel

Phone: 212/421-0900 [62]

Property failed to provide current rates

Location: At 56th St, between Park and Madison aves. 440 Park Ave 10022. **Fax:** 212/752-4593. **Terms:** Package plans; pets, signed release mandatory. **Facility:** 495 rooms. Luxurious European style boutique hotel in the heart of midtown offers the business and leisure traveler an oasis of comfort while away from home. 6 two-bedroom units. 21 stories; interior corridors. **Services:** gift shop. **Fee:** massage. **All Rooms:** combo or shower baths, safes, honor bars. **Cards:** AE, CB, DI, DS, MC, VI.

TRAVEL INN
(AAA) SAVE
◆◆
Motor Inn

Phone: (212)695-7171 [32]

| | 1P: $150-$180 | 2P: $160-$190 | XP: $15 | F16 |

Location: Between 10th and 11th aves. 515 W 42nd St 10036. **Fax:** 212/967-5025. **Terms:** Cancellation fee imposed. **Facility:** 160 rooms. Located a few blks from bus terminal, convention center, Times Square and the theater district. Grey line tour ticket office off lobby. 7 stories; interior corridors. **Dining:** Deli; 6 am-8 pm; $6-$10; wine/beer only. **Services:** gift shop. **All Rooms:** extended cable TV. **Cards:** AE, DI, DS, MC, VI.
(See color ad p 350)

TRUMP INTERNATIONAL HOTEL & TOWER
◆◆◆◆
Hotel

Phone: (212)299-1000 [96]

| | 1P: $475-$1500 | 2P: $475-$1500 |
| All Year | | |

Location: At Columbus Cir; jct Central Park S. 1 Central Park W 10023. **Fax:** 212/299-1150. **Terms:** Check-in 4 pm; cancellation fee imposed; package plans. **Facility:** 167 rooms. Magnificent Central Park views avail. Luxurious decor; outstanding amenities. 40 two-bedroom units. 17 stories; interior corridors; heated pool. **Services:** Fee: massage. **All Rooms:** kitchens, safes, honor bars. **Cards:** AE, DI, MC, VI.

THE WALDORF-ASTORIA
(AAA)
◆◆◆◆
Classic Hotel

Phone: (212)872-4800 [60]

| | 1P: $229-$650 | 2P: $269-$690 | XP: $40 | F18 |
| All Year | | | | |

Location: Between E 49th and 50th sts. 301 Park Ave 10022. **Fax:** 212/872-4875. **Terms:** Cancellation fee imposed; package plans. **Facility:** 1341 rooms. Classic accommodations in world famous hotel, circa 1932. Magnificent lobby with optimal people watching facilities. Elegant and comfortably appointed guest rooms. 40 two-bedroom units, 24 three-bedroom units. 42 stories; interior corridors; steamrooms. **Dining:** Dining room, 2 restaurants, coffee shop; 6:30 am-midnight; $12-$45; health conscious menu items; cocktails; afternoon tea; also, Peacock Alley, see separate listing; entertainment. **Services:** gift shop. Fee: massage. **All Rooms:** combo or shower baths, extended cable TV, honor bars. **Cards:** AE, CB, DI, DS, MC, VI. A Hilton Hotel. *(See color ad p 57)*

THE WARWICK NEW YORK
(AAA) SAVE
◆◆◆
Historic Hotel

Phone: (212)247-2700 [86]

9/11-12/31	1P: $245-$260	2P: $245-$260	XP: $30	F12
1/1-4/30	1P: $220-$250	2P: $220-$250		
5/1-9/10	1P: $210-$235	2P: $210-$235	XP: $30	F12

Location: Corner of 54th St and 6th Ave. 65 W 54th St 10019. **Fax:** 212/713-1751. **Terms:** Package plans; pets, $100 dep req. **Facility:** 425 rooms. Originally built in 1927 by William Randolph Hearst and centered in midtown Manhattan close to all the famous shops and Central Park. 1 two-bedroom unit. Whirlpool room; 33 stories; interior corridors. **Fee:** parking. **Dining:** 6:30 am-11 pm; cocktails; also, Ciao Europa, see separate listing. **Services:** gift shop. **All Rooms:** combo or shower baths, extended cable TV, safes, honor bars. **Cards:** AE, DI, JC, MC, VI. **Special Amenities:** Free newspaper and preferred room (subject to availability with advanced reservations).

The following lodgings were either not inspected or did not meet AAA rating requirements but are listed for your information only.

THE BENJAMIN HOTEL
[fyi]
Hotel

Phone: 212/715-2500

9/11-12/31	1P: $384-$550	2P: $384-$550
1/1-4/30	1P: $340-$500	2P: $340-$500
5/1-9/10	1P: $320-$475	2P: $320-$475

Too new to rate. **Location:** Between Lexington Ave and 3rd St. 125 E 50th St 10022. **Fax:** 212/715-2525. **Terms:** Cancellation fee imposed. **Amenities:** 209 rooms, pets, restaurant, radios, coffeemakers, microwaves, exercise facilities. **Cards:** AE, DI, DS, JC, MC, VI.

THE FRANKLIN
[fyi]

Phone: 212/369-1000

Not inspected. **Location:** Between 3rd and Lexington Aves. 164 E 87th St 10128. Facilities, services, and decor characterize a mid-range property.

REGAL UN PLAZA HOTEL
[fyi]
Hotel

Phone: (212)758-1234 [34]

9/5-12/31	1P: $429	2P: $429	XP: $35	F16
1/1-4/30	1P: $319-$399	2P: $319-$399	XP: $35	F16
5/1-6/15	1P: $319	2P: $319	XP: $35	F16
6/16-9/4	1P: $299	2P: $299	XP: $35	F16

Under major renovation, scheduled to be completed July 2000. **Last rated:** ◆◆◆◆ **Location:** Between 1st and 2nd aves. One UN Plaza, 44th St 10017-3575. **Fax:** 212/702-5051. **Terms:** Cancellation fee imposed; package plans. **Facility:** 427 rooms. Opposite the United Nations and overlooking East River. 40 stories; interior corridors; heated pool. **Fee:** parking; 1 indoor tennis court. **Services:** gift shop; area transportation. Fee: massage. **All Rooms:** combo or shower baths, safes, honor bars. **Some Rooms:** 40 efficiencies. **Cards:** AE, CB, DI, JC, MC, VI.

W NEW YORK
(fyi)
Not inspected. **Location:** Lexington Ave at E 49th St. 541 Lexington Ave 10022. Facilities, services, and decor characterize a mid-range property.
Phone: 212/755-1200

——— RESTAURANTS ———

ADRIENNE
◆◆◆◆
American
Lunch: $20-$28   **Dinner:** $20-$28   **Phone:** 212/903-3918   (71)
Location: At 55th St; in The Peninsula New York. 700 5th Ave 10019. **Hours:** 7 am-10:30, noon-2:30 & 6-10 pm, Sat 7 am-10:30 & 5:30-10 pm, Sun 11:30-2:30 pm. Closed: Sun, 8/1-8/31 & Mon for dinner. **Reservations:** suggested. **Features:** semi-formal attire; health conscious menu; cocktails & lounge; entertainment; fee for valet parking; a la carte. Padded silk walls, fresh-cut flowers and a grand piano just away from the main area lend an air of sophistication to the classically elegant dining room. Try the chef's amuse to get a wonderful taste of exceptional culinary talent. Service is flawless. Smoke free premises. **Cards:** AE, CB, DI, DS, MC, VI.
✕

AMERICAN FESTIVAL CAFE
◆◆
American
Lunch: $15-$25   **Dinner:** $20-$30   **Phone:** 212/332-7620   (66)
Location: On concourse level, at Rockefeller Center Skating Rink between 5th and 6th aves. 20 W 50th 10020. **Hours:** 7:30 am-11 pm, Sat & Sun from 9 am. **Reservations:** suggested. **Features:** No A/C; casual dress; Sunday brunch; children's menu; health conscious menu items; cocktails & lounge; fee for parking; a la carte. Overlooking Rockefeller Center, the restaurant is a favorite for relaxed dining. Nicely garnished dishes, such as fettuccine primavera, are colorful, tasty and served in ample portions. Servers exhibit good menu knowledge and communication skills. Smoke free premises. **Cards:** AE, CB, DI, JC, MC, VI.
✕

AN AMERICAN PLACE
◆◆◆◆
American
Lunch: $16-$21   **Dinner:** $23-$29   **Phone:** 212/684-2122   (69)
Location: Between Park and Madison aves. 2 Park Ave at 32nd St 10016. **Hours:** 11:45 am-3 & 5:30-9:30 pm, Sat from 5:30 pm. Closed major holidays & Sun. **Reservations:** suggested. **Features:** casual dress; health conscious menu items; cocktails; a la carte. Regal cedar sentinels welcome diners at the glass entry door. The chef is insistent on using only American ingredients, which are blended to creative wonderfully innovative interpretations. The wine list, too, shows only American selections. Smoke free premises. **Cards:** AE, DI, DS, MC, VI.
✕

ANGELO'S PIZZA
◆◆
Italian
Lunch: $9-$14   **Dinner:** $9-$14   **Phone:** 212/333-4333   (93)
Location: Between 6th and 7th aves. 117 W 57th St 10019. **Hours:** 11:30 am-11 pm, Fri & Sat-midnight. Closed: 12/25. **Features:** casual dress; carryout; cocktails; a la carte. Tried-and-true family recipes are used to create delicious dishes, such as pasta fagiole and pizzas baked in a coal-fired brick oven. Black-and-white photographs of old New York street scenes and celebrities line the walls. Service is efficient. Smoke free premises. **Cards:** AE, MC, VI.
✕

AQUAVIT
◆◆◆
Swiss
Lunch: $18-$24   **Dinner:** $48-$62   **Phone:** 212/307-7311   (118)
Location: Between 5th and 6th aves. 13 W 54th St 10019. **Hours:** noon-2:30 & 5:30-10:30 pm, Sat 5:30 pm-10:30 pm. Closed major holidays & Sun. **Reservations:** suggested. **Features:** casual dress; cocktails; fee for parking; prix fixe. The stunning dining room features as its focal point a soaring atrium with a soft, two-story waterfall. Scandinavian, mostly Swedish, seafood and meat preparations make up the bulk of the menu. Try an "aquavit," a refreshing house-made drink. **Cards:** AE, DI, MC, VI.
✕

AUREOLE
◆◆◆◆◆
American
Lunch: $18-$29   **Dinner:** $65   **Phone:** 212/319-1660   (74)
Location: Between Park & Madison. 34 E 61st St 10021. **Hours:** noon-2:30 & 5:30-11 pm, Sat 5 pm-11:30 pm. Closed major holidays & Sun. **Reservations:** required. **Features:** semi-formal attire; health conscious menu items; cocktails; prix fixe. Operated by the owner/chef, this absolute jewel of a restaurant wraps you in elegant comfort. Imaginative cuisine harmoniously blends flavors and textures. Service is delivered with impeccable precision. The prix fixe lunch is a great value. Smoke free premises. **Cards:** AE, CB, DI, DS, MC, VI.
✕

BANGKOK CUISINE
◆
Ethnic
Lunch: $7-$15   **Dinner:** $7-$16   **Phone:** 212/581-6370   (105)
Location: Between 52nd and 53rd sts. 885 8th Ave 10019. **Hours:** noon-11:30 pm, Sun from 5 pm. **Reservations:** suggested; weekends. **Features:** casual dress; carryout; cocktails & lounge; a la carte. Mee grob, pad Thai and spring rolls are representative of offerings on the traditional menu. The lunch buffet, served Wednesday through Friday, affords a good general introduction to Thai food. The restaurant has been family owned since 1975. Smoke free premises. **Cards:** AE, DS, MC, VI.
✕

BARBETTA
(AAA)
◆◆◆
Northern
Italian
Lunch: $17-$25   **Dinner:** $25-$29   **Phone:** 212/246-9171   (99)
Location: Between 8th and 9th aves; on Restaurant Row. 321 W 46th St 10036. **Hours:** noon-2 & 5-midnight. Closed major holidays & Sun. **Reservations:** suggested. **Features:** dressy casual; cocktails & lounge; entertainment; a la carte. Opulence abounds in the sophisticated dining room, which is appointed with 18th-century decor. The lovely patio is bright and relaxed. Such preparations as salmon over lentils in tomato broth are unequivocally Italian. Service is attentive. Smoke free premises. **Cards:** AE, DI, DS, JC, MC, VI.
✕

BECCO
◆◆
Regional
Italian
Lunch: $16-$18   **Dinner:** $25-$30   **Phone:** 212/397-7597   (168)
Location: Between 8th and 9th aves. 355 W 46th St 10036. **Hours:** noon-3 & 5-midnight, Wed-Sat noon-3 & 4:30-midnight, Sun noon-10 pm. Closed: 11/23 & 12/25. **Reservations:** required. **Features:** casual dress; cocktails; a la carte. Symphony de pasta is the signature dish on a menu of farmhouse-style, countrified Northern Italian cuisine. Portions are ample, and dishes are reasonably priced. Three dining areas deliver distinct, but altogether pleasant, experiences. Smoke free premises. **Cards:** AE, DI, DS, MC, VI.
✕

BELLO RESTAURANT
◆◆
Northern
Italian
Lunch: $11-$21   **Dinner:** $11-$21   **Phone:** 212/246-6773   (122)
Location: At 56th St. 863 9th Ave 10019. **Hours:** 11:30 am-11 pm, Fri-midnight, Sat 3:30-midnight. Closed: 1/1, 7/4 & Sun. **Reservations:** suggested. **Features:** casual dress; health conscious menu items; cocktails & lounge; a la carte. The restaurant clearly does things right, as it's packed even at 10 o'clock on a Friday evening. Most notably, you'll find ample quantities of consistently flavorful food: pasta pomodoro, boiled salmon and light, fluffy, homemade tiramisu. Smoke free premises. **Cards:** AE, DI, DS, MC, VI.
✕

BEN BENSON'S STEAK HOUSE   **Lunch:** $16-$33   **Dinner:** $16-$33   **Phone:** 212/581-8888 163
◆◆◆   **Location:** Between 6th and 7th aves. 123 W 52nd St 10019. **Hours:** 11:45 am-11 pm, Fri-midnight, Sat 5
Steak and   pm-midnight, Sun 5 pm-10 pm. Closed major holidays. **Reservations:** suggested. **Features:** casual dress;
Seafood   carryout; cocktails & lounge; a la carte. In addition to succulent, well-aged steaks, the restaurant delivers
veal, lamb and seafood, including outstanding crab cakes. The seasonal outdoor cafe is warm and inviting.
Although the place is often busy, servers remain attentive and prompt. **Cards:** AE, DI, MC, VI.

BOLIVAR   **Lunch:** $12-$15   **Dinner:** $14-$25   **Phone:** 212/838-0440 119
◆◆◆   **Location:** Between 2nd and 3rd aves. 206 E 60th St 10022. **Hours:** noon-3 & 5:30-10:30 pm, Sat-11 pm,
Latino   Sun 5:30 pm-10 pm. Closed: 11/23. **Reservations:** suggested. **Features:** casual dress; health conscious
menu items; cocktails & lounge; a la carte, also prix fixe. Wildly creative and satisfying Pan American cuisine
picks up broad influences from Peru, Argentina and Brazil. Latin details are evident in cozy dining rooms. Ethnically dressed
servers show good menu knowledge and timely follow-up skills. Smoke free premises. **Cards:** AE, DI, DS, MC, VI.

BOMBAY PALACE RESTAURANT   **Lunch:** $9-$30   **Dinner:** $9-$30   **Phone:** 212/541-7777 144
◆◆   **Location:** Between 5th and 6th aves. 30 W 52nd St 10019. **Hours:** noon-3 & 5:30-11 pm.
Indian   **Reservations:** suggested. **Features:** dressy casual; health conscious menu items; cocktails & lounge; a la
carte, also prix fixe. Tandoori chicken and vegetable curry are representative of authentic Indian cuisine. The
all-you-can-eat lunch buffet, which lays out a nice assortment of choices, is offered daily. Chandeliers and etched glass lend
an upscale feel to the dining room. Smoke free premises. **Cards:** AE, DI, MC, VI.

BRYANT PARK GRILL   **Lunch:** $13-$19   **Dinner:** $15-$23   **Phone:** 212/840-6500 169
◆◆   **Location:** Between 5th and 6th aves. 25 W 40th St 10018. **Hours:** 11:30 am-10 pm, Fri & Sat-10:30 pm,
American   Sat & Sun brunch 11:30 am-3:30 pm. **Reservations:** suggested. **Features:** casual dress; Sunday brunch;
cocktails & lounge; a la carte. Tempting selections include the succulent filet mignon, lobster salad and pork
tenderloin. The large, glorious building—which overlooks the park for which the restaurant is named—offers seasonal
seating on the rooftop. Servers exhibit good menu knowledg. **Cards:** AE, DI, MC, VI.

CAFE BOTANICA   **Lunch:** $16-$27   **Dinner:** $22-$32   **Phone:** 212/484-5120 123
◆◆◆   **Location:** Between 6th (Ave of the Americas) and 7th aves; in The Essex House-A Westin Hotel. 160
French   Central Park S 10019. **Hours:** 6:30 am-10:30, noon-2:30 & 5:30-10:30 pm. **Reservations:** suggested.
Features: dressy casual; health conscious menu items; cocktails & lounge; fee for valet parking; a la carte.
A warm, relaxed ambience settles in the lush, almost magical, dining room of the upscale restaurant. Enjoy first-rate gourmet
cuisine on the prix fixe and pre- and post-theater menus. Set aside time to visit for the Sunday champagne brunch. Smoke
free premises. **Cards:** AE, DI, DS, MC, VI.

CAFE CENTRO   **Lunch:** $15-$22   **Dinner:** $16-$24   **Phone:** 212/818-1222 170
◆◆   **Location:** Between Lexington and Vanderbilt. 200 Park Ave on 45th 10166. **Hours:** 11:30 am-3 & 5-10:30
French   pm, Sat 5 pm-10:30 pm. Closed major holidays & Sun. **Reservations:** suggested. **Features:** casual dress;
cocktails & lounge; a la carte. A massive stone fireplace encloses eight rotisserie spits laden with roasting
chicken, rack of lamb, pork and filet mignon. The warm, comfortable dining room resembles a Parisian brasserie. Dishes
reflect North African and Mediterranean influences. Smoke free premises. **Cards:** AE, DI, MC, VI.

CAFE EUROPA   **Lunch:** $7-$13   **Dinner:** $7-$13   **Phone:** 212/977-4030 125
◆   **Location:** At 7th Ave. 205 W 57th St 10019. **Hours:** 7 am-1 am, Fri & Sat-3 am. **Features:** carryout; a la
American   carte. The unpretentious bakery sticks to a menu of mostly lighter fare—pasta, sandwiches, salads and
pizza—as well as exceptional European pastries and desserts. Bright lighting adds to the energetic, upbeat
mood of the dining room. Gourmet coffees are a trea. Smoke free premises. **Cards:** AE, DI, DS, MC, VI.

CAFE FIORELLO   **Lunch:** $14-$19   **Dinner:** $15-$26   **Phone:** 212/595-5330 51
◆◆   **Location:** At 64th St. 1900 Broadway 10023. **Hours:** 11:30 am-11 pm, Fri & Sat-12:45 am, Sat & Sun
Italian   brunch 11 am-3 pm. Closed: 12/25. **Features:** casual dress; Sunday brunch; health conscious menu items;
carryout; cocktails; a la carte. Settle into the colorful, festive dining room to enjoy award-winning, gourmet
pizzas, as well as antipasto, salads, soups and traditional entrees. Such desserts as New York cheesecake, which is topped
with strawberries and whipped cream, are tempting. Smoke free premises. **Cards:** AE, DI, MC, VI.

CAFE PIERRE   **Lunch:** $18-$36   **Dinner:** $25-$37   **Phone:** 212/940-8195 62
AAA   **Location:** At 5th Ave; in The Pierre. 5th Ave at 61st St 10021. **Hours:** 7 am-10:30, noon-2:30 & 6-10 pm.
◆◆◆◆   **Reservations:** suggested. **Features:** semi-formal attire; Sunday brunch; health conscious menu items;
French   cocktails & lounge; entertainment; fee for valet parking; a la carte, also prix fixe. An old New York style
punctuates the richly opulent dining room, in which both creative contemporary and traditional classic entrees
are served. Enjoy light lunches and high tea on the trompe l'oeil Queen's Court rotunda. The tasting menu is
exquisite. Smoke free premises. **Cards:** AE, DI, DS, MC, VI.

CAFE TREVI   **Dinner:** $15-$24   **Phone:** 212/249-0040 171
◆◆   **Location:** Between 81st and 82nd sts. 1570 First Ave 10028. **Hours:** 5:30 pm-midnight. Closed major
Italian   holidays & Sun. **Reservations:** suggested. **Features:** casual dress; cocktails & lounge; a la carte. Flickering
candles, Florentine prints and brick walls enhance the intimate ambience of the neighborhood restaurant.
The menu lists honest, simply great food. For dessert, it's tough to choose with such selections as tiramisu and pumpkin
cheesecake. Smoke free premises. **Cards:** AE, DI, MC, VI.

CARNEGIE DELICATESSEN & RESTAURANT   **Lunch:** $9-$17   **Dinner:** $9-$17   **Phone:** 212/757-2245 190
◆   **Location:** At 55th St. 854 7th Ave 10019. **Hours:** 6:30 am-4 am. **Features:** casual dress; carryout; minimum
American   charge-$10; a la carte. The 1937 landmark is the quintessential New York deli. In addition to wonderful
pastrami sandwiches and matzo ball soup, the restaurant serves a cheesecake that gives your sweet tooth a
knockout punch. Servers are gruff, but with a twinkle in their eyes. Smoke free premises.

CAVIARTERIA Lunch: $11-$20 Dinner: $11-$20 Phone: 212/759-7410 (172)
◆◆ **Location:** Between Park and Madison sts on 59th St. 502 Park Ave 10022. **Hours:** 9 am-7 pm. Sun noon-5
Ethnic pm. Closed major holidays. **Reservations:** suggested. **Features:** casual dress; early bird specials; health
conscious menu; carryout; cocktail lounge; beer & wine only. One of the nation's foremost importers of caviar
opened this tasting bar, which invites haughty palates to distinguish among beluga, oscetra and sevruga varieties. The
greatly varied selections are fresh and held to high standards of quality. Smoke free premises. **Cards:** AE, MC, VI. ✕

CHIAM Lunch: $14-$19 Dinner: $16-$26 Phone: 212/371-2323 (126)
◆◆◆ **Location:** Between Lexington and 3rd aves. 160 E 48th St 10017. **Hours:** 11:30 am-11:30 pm. Closed:
Chinese 11/23. **Reservations:** suggested. **Features:** casual dress; carryout; cocktails & lounge; minimum
charge-$10; a la carte. Carefully selected wines complement creative preparations of Cantonese food. Crispy
sea bass, served in a spicy sauce, is unusual and tasty. The restaurant, which got its name from combining Chinese and
American, is a favorite for dim sum. Smoke free premises. **Cards:** AE, DI, DS, MC, VI. ✕

CHIN CHIN Lunch: $9-$18 Dinner: $12-$21 Phone: 212/888-4555 (127)
◆◆◆ **Location:** Between 2nd and 3rd aves. 216 E 49th St 10017. **Hours:** noon-midnight, Sat & Sun from 5 pm.
Nouvelle Closed: 11/23. **Reservations:** suggested. **Features:** casual dress; cocktails & lounge; a la carte. Gracious,
Chinese knowledgeable servers enhance the overall experience at the chic, sophisticated restaurant. Grand Marnier
shrimp and steamed salmon with black bean sauce are representative of outstanding cuisine. The
atmosphere is relaxed and refined. Smoke free premises. **Cards:** AE, DI, MC, VI. ✕

CHURRASCARIA PLATAFORMA Lunch: $28 Dinner: $33 Phone: 212/245-0505 (106)
◆◆ **Location:** Between 8th and 9th aves; in Belvedere Hotel. 316 W 49th St 10019. **Hours:** noon-midnight.
Brazilian Closed: 1/1 & 12/25. **Reservations:** required. **Features:** dressy casual; cocktails & lounge; prix fixe. This
lively and elegant Brazilian-style steakhouse offers several meat selections, including pork, ribeye, sirloin,
chicken and sausage, all cut off a skewer and carried to the table by experienced staff. The wine list covers all prominent
regions. **Cards:** AE, CB, DI, DS, MC, VI. ✕

CIAO EUROPA Lunch: $14-$21 Dinner: $15-$27 Phone: 212/247-1200 (64)
◆◆◆ **Location:** Corner of 54th St and 6th Ave; in The Warwick New York. 63 W 54th St 10019. **Hours:** 6:30
Northern am-11:30 pm. Closed major holidays. **Reservations:** suggested. **Features:** casual dress; carryout; cocktails
Italian & lounge; a la carte, also prix fixe. Fresh ingredients go into preparations on a seasonally changing menu.
Ravioli with lobster and herbs, garlic confit with braised radicchio and roast rack of lamb with shallots are
favorite choices. In-house desserts and ice cream are tasty extras. Smoke free premises. **Cards:** AE, DI, DS, MC, VI. ✕

CIBO Lunch: $15-$30 Dinner: $15-$30 Phone: 212/681-1616 (121)
◆◆◆ **Location:** At 41st St. 767 Second Ave 10017. **Hours:** 11:30 am-3 & 5:30-10 pm, Fri & Sat-11 pm. Closed:
Italian 12/24 & 12/25. **Reservations:** suggested. **Features:** Sunday brunch; health conscious menu; cocktails &
lounge; a la carte. A romantic aura punctuates the modern dining room, which is filled with floral
arrangements and dramatic, fresh-cut branches. The seasonal menu centers on Tuscan-American cuisine. Weekend
brunches are popular, as are the pastry chef's decadent creations. Smoke free premises. **Cards:** AE, DI, DS, MC, VI. ✕

CINQUANTA RISTORANTE Lunch: $12-$22 Dinner: $13-$25 Phone: 212/759-5050 (157)
◆◆ **Location:** Between Madison and Park aves. 50 E 50th St 10022. **Hours:** noon-11:30 pm, Fri & Sat-midnight,
Italian Sun 5 pm-11 pm. **Reservations:** suggested. **Features:** casual dress; health conscious menu items; carryout;
cocktails; a la carte, also prix fixe. The bright dining room has an art deco feel. Representative of dishes is
the bass, which is encrusted with shredded potatoes and served in thickened fish broth. Outfitted in black and white attire,
the wait staff delivers old-school, professional service. **Cards:** AE, CB, DI, DS, MC, VI. ✕

CITE Lunch: $20-$30 Dinner: $20-$30 Phone: 212/956-7100 (75)
AAA **Location:** Between 6th and 7th aves. 120 W 51st 10020. **Hours:** 11:30 am-11:30 pm. Closed major
◆◆◆ holidays. **Reservations:** suggested. **Features:** casual dress; health conscious menu; cocktails &
American lounge; a la carte, also prix fixe. The Parisian-style brasserie has an upscale casual atmosphere that pleases
theatergoers and the professional crowd. An extensive wine list complements colorful, interestingly combined
selections of steak, chicken, seafood and pasta. Desserts are superb. Smoke free premises. **Cards:** AE, CB,
DI, DS, MC, VI. ✕

THE COACH HOUSE Lunch: $20-$24 Dinner: $20-$35 Phone: 212/696-1800 (120)
◆◆◆ **Location:** Between 5th and Madison Ave. 16 E 32nd St 10016. **Hours:** 11:30 am-3 & 5:30-9:30 pm, Sat &
American Sun from 5:30 pm. **Reservations:** suggested. **Features:** casual dress; early bird specials; cocktails &
lounge; a la carte. Adjacent to the Avalon Hotel, the intimate dining room has a limited number of tables and
a menu of fresh seafood and free-range organic game and meats. The lengthy wine list focuses heavily on California
selections. The atmosphere simply bustles. **Cards:** AE, DI, DS, MC, VI. ✕

COCO CAFE Lunch: $16-$28 Dinner: $16-$28 Phone: 212/935-3535 (174)
◆◆◆ **Location:** Between 5th and Park Ave. 7 E 59th St 10022. **Hours:** 11:30 am-3 & 5:30-11:30 pm. Closed
Italian major holidays. **Reservations:** suggested. **Features:** casual dress; cocktails & lounge; a la carte. A colorful,
flavorful example of Tuscan country cuisine is the wild sea bass filet, which is served atop a pool of pureed
chickpeas with roasted red peppers and red-skinned potatoes, which are caramelized and browned. The mood is warm and
inviting. Smoke free premises. **Cards:** AE, DI, DS, MC, VI. ✕

COSTA DEL SOL RESTAURANT Lunch: $8-$17 Dinner: $11-$23 Phone: 212/541-8382 (107)
◆ **Location:** Corner 9th Ave and W 50th St. 369 W 50th St 10019. **Hours:** noon-11 pm, Fri & Sat-midnight.
Spanish **Features:** casual dress; carryout; cocktails & lounge. A local favorite for authentic Spanish cuisine, the
restaurant delivers such specialties as tapas, seafood paella, homemade flan and mussels vinaigrette. The
dining room has a casual, contemporary feel. Service is friendly and well-timed. **Cards:** AE, DI, DS, MC, VI. ✕

DAWAT   Lunch: $13-$23   Dinner: $13-$23   Phone: 212/355-7555   128
◆◆◆   **Location:** Between 2nd and 3rd aves. 210 E 58th St 10022. **Hours:** 11:30 am-2:45 & 5:30-10:45 pm,
Ethnic   Fri-11:15 pm, Sun 5:30 pm-10:45 pm. **Reservations:** suggested. **Features:** semi-formal attire; carryout;
cocktails & lounge; a la carte. Reserved formality is evident in the every aspect of the restaurant—from its
menu of creatively prepared dishes to its servers in crisp uniform. Wonderful ground lamb meatballs are served in a thick
puree of onions, tomatoes, and chilis. Smoke free premises. **Cards:** AE, DI, MC, VI.   ✕

DISH OF SALT   Lunch: $17-$29   Dinner: $17-$29   Phone: 212/921-4242   102
⚅⚅   **Location:** Between 6th and 7th aves. 133 W 47th St 10036. **Hours:** 11:30 am-midnight, Sat from 4 pm; Sun
◆◆   4 pm-10 pm. **Reservations:** suggested. **Features:** casual dress; carryout;
Chinese   cocktails & lounge; a la carte. Piano music drifts through the multi-level dining room which has high ceilings,
well-spaced tables and an ethnic, almost whimsical decor. Peking duck is the specialty on a menu of mostly
Cantonese fare. Macadamia nut ice cream is simple but delicious. **Cards:** AE, DI, MC, VI.   ✕

DOCKS OYSTER BAR & SEAFOOD GRILL   Lunch: $14-$22   Dinner: $9-$22   Phone: 212/986-8080   65
◆◆   **Location:** Between 40th and 41st sts. 633 Third Ave 10017. **Hours:** 11:30 am-11 pm, Fri-midnight, Sat 5
Seafood   pm-midnight, Sun 11:30 am-3 & 5-11 pm. Closed: 12/25. **Reservations:** suggested. **Features:** casual dress;
Sunday brunch; health conscious menu items; cocktails & lounge; minimum charge-$10; a la carte. Shellfish
are at the heart of a varied menu that includes selections of chicken, pasta, steak and—of course—seafood. Sconces and
artwork add to the appeal of the lively, noisy dining room. The wait staff, in casual dress, delivers knowledgeable service.
Smoke free premises. **Cards:** AE, DI, DS, MC, VI.   ✕

DOCKS OYSTER BAR & SEAFOOD GRILL   Lunch: $15-$18   Dinner: $25-$35   Phone: 212/724-5588   63
◆◆   **Location:** Between 89th and 90th sts. 2427 Broadway 10024. **Hours:** 11:30 am-11 pm, Fri-midnight, Sat 5
Seafood   pm-midnight, Sun 11:30 am-3 & 5-11 pm. Closed: 12/25. **Reservations:** suggested. **Features:** casual dress;
Sunday brunch; health conscious menu items; cocktails & lounge; a la carte. Shellfish are at the heart of a
varied menu that includes selections of chicken, pasta, steak and—of course—seafood. Sconces and artwork add to the
appeal of the lively, noisy dining room. The wait staff, in casual dress, delivers knowledgeable service. Smoke free premises.
Cards: AE, DI, DS, MC, VI.   ✕

ESS-A-BAGEL   Lunch: $3-$8   Dinner: $3-$8   Phone: 212/980-1010   112
◆◆   **Location:** Between 50th and 51st sts. 831 3rd Ave 10022. **Hours:** 6:30 am-10 pm, Sat & Sun 8 am-5 pm.
American   Closed major holidays. **Features:** casual dress; carryout; a la carte. The unpretentious spot is a local favorite
for classic New York bagels, which are served with myriad spreads, including some vegetarian, tofu and fish,
such as sturgeon. Also on the menu are reasonably priced prepared salads and homemade desserts. Smoke free premises.
Cards: AE, DI, DS, MC, VI.   ✕

FELIDIA   Lunch: $18-$27   Dinner: $18-$32   Phone: 212/758-1479   100
◆◆◆   **Location:** Between 2nd and 3rd aves. 243 E 58th St 10022. **Hours:** noon-3 & 5-11 pm, Sat from 5 pm.
Northern   Closed major holidays & Sun. **Reservations:** suggested. **Features:** casual dress; cocktails; a la carte. A
Italian   wonderful oasis in hectic Manhattan, the cozy, skylit dining room provides authentic regional Italian food and
fine, attentive service. An extensive wine list represents several regions of Italy. Breads—including long, thin
breadsticks—are excellent. Smoke free premises. **Cards:** AE, DI, DS, MC, VI.   ✕

FIFTY-SEVEN FIFTY-SEVEN
   RESTAURANT & BAR   Lunch: $17-$26   Dinner: $18-$34   Phone: 212/758-5757   84
◆◆◆◆   **Location:** Between Madison and Park; in Four Seasons Hotel. 57 E 57th St 10022. **Hours:** 7 am-10:30 pm;
American   Sat & Sun brunch 11 am-2:30 pm. **Reservations:** suggested. **Features:** Sunday brunch; health conscious
menu items; cocktails & lounge; entertainment; fee for valet parking; a la carte. Representative of
exceptional, inventive cuisine is the pan-seared salmon, which is caramelized until nearly crispy on the exterior and silky and
moist on the inside. The stylish dining room and technically proficient servers enhance the experience. Smoke free
premises. **Cards:** AE, CB, DI, DS, MC, VI.   ✕

THE FOUR SEASONS   Lunch: $24-$39   Dinner: $27-$42   Phone: 212/754-9494   154
⚅⚅   **Location:** Between Park and Lexington aves. 99 E 52nd St 10022. **Hours:** noon-2 & 5-11 pm, Sat from 5
◆◆◆◆   pm. Closed major holidays & Sun. **Reservations:** suggested. **Features:** semi-formal attire; health conscious
American   menu; cocktails & lounge; a la carte, also prix fixe. A landmark for 40 years, the restaurant broke new ground
when it opened for its creative cuisine and striking, post-modern decor. The menu changes seasonally but
continually offers such famed specialties as duck and Dover sole. Service is smooth. Smoke free premises.
Cards: AE, CB, DI, DS, MC, VI.   ✕

FRED'S AT BARNEY'S   Lunch: $16-$22   Dinner: $20-$28   Phone: 212/833-2200   110
◆◆   **Location:** Madison Ave at 61st St. 10 E 61st St 10021. **Hours:** 11:30 am-9 pm, Sun noon-6 pm. Closed
American   major holidays. **Reservations:** suggested. **Features:** casual dress; health conscious menu items; carryout;
cocktails; a la carte. A separate entrance leads you into the chic market/wine bar/restaurant of Barney's
department store. More than 50 varieties of international cheeses, as well as fresh bakery items, are among offerings. Light
lunches are served in the marketplace. Smoke free premises. **Cards:** AE, CB, DI, JC, MC, VI.   ✕

FRESCO BY SCOTTO   Lunch: $15-$30   Dinner: $15-$30   Phone: 212/935-3434   130
◆◆   **Location:** Between Madison and Park aves. 34 E 52nd St 10022. **Hours:** 11:30 am-3 & 5:30-11 pm, Sat
Northern   from 5:30 pm. Closed major holidays & Sun. **Reservations:** suggested. **Features:** health conscious menu
Italian   items; cocktails; a la carte. The mood is upbeat in the inviting dining room, which is appointed in such
visually stimulating decor as wall frescoes. Modern Tuscan menu selections include well-prepared veal chops
and ribeye steak. Sidewalk seating is nice during the season. **Cards:** AE, DI, MC, VI.   ✕

FRICO BAR
◆◆
Italian

Lunch: $12-$17   **Dinner:** $14-$24   **Phone:** 212/564-7272   [173]
Location: Between 9th and 10th. 402 W 43rd St 10036. **Hours:** 11 am-3 & 5-11:30 pm, Sat from 4:30 pm, Sun 4 pm-10 pm. **Closed:** 12/25. **Reservations:** required; pre-theatre. **Features:** casual dress; carryout; cocktails & lounge; minimum charge-$20 food order; a la carte. The small dining room has a cozy feel, enhanced with partial walls, indirect lighting and opaque sheets draped from the ceiling. Penne pasta with eggplant and rich marinara is an excellent example of authentic Northeast Italian (Friuli) cuisine. **Cards:** AE, DI, DS, MC, VI.

GALLAGHER'S STEAK HOUSE
(AAA)
◆◆
Steakhouse

Lunch: $20-$35   **Dinner:** $25-$40   **Phone:** 212/245-5336   [53]
Location: Between Broadway and 8th Ave. 228 W 52nd St 10019. **Hours:** noon-midnight. **Reservations:** suggested. **Features:** casual dress; cocktails & lounge; a la carte. A New York landmark since 1927, the steakhouse is known for its succulent, aged prime beef and seafood. An excellent selection of wines is available. The restaurant has catered to celebrities for so many years that servers are fazed by nothing. **Cards:** AE, CB, DI, DS, MC, VI.

GIAMBELLI 50TH
(AAA)
◆◆
Northern
Italian

Lunch: $25-$35   **Dinner:** $20-$35   **Phone:** 212/688-2760   [96]
Location: Between Madison and Park aves. 46 E 50th St 10022. **Hours:** noon-midnight. **Reservations:** suggested. **Features:** dressy casual; health conscious menu items; cocktails & lounge; minimum charge-$19; a la carte, also prix fixe. An interesting collection of art decorates the moderately upscale restaurant. On the menu is a wide variety of selections, ranging from seafood and pasta to veal and beef. Many wines serve as fitting complements. Servers are knowledgeable. **Cards:** AE, CB, DI, DS, MC, VI.

HARLEY-DAVIDSON CAFE
◆◆
American

Lunch: $8-$20   **Dinner:** $8-$20   **Phone:** 212/245-6000   [131]
Location: At 56th St. 1370 Ave of the Americas 10019. **Hours:** 11:30 am-midnight, Fri & Sat-1 am. **Reservations:** accepted. **Features:** cocktails & lounge; a la carte. The themed restaurant showcases 90 years of Harley-Davidson history, with memorabilia ranging from celebrity motorcycles to pictures. In addition to enjoy traditional comfort foods, diners can have kitschy souvenir photographs taken on a "hog.". Smoke free premises. **Cards:** AE, DI, MC, VI.

IL MENESTRELLO
◆◆◆
Northern
Italian

Lunch: $17-$30   **Dinner:** $17-$30   **Phone:** 212/421-7588   [85]
Location: Between 5th and Madison aves. 14 E 52nd St 10022. **Hours:** noon-11 pm, Fri & Sat-midnight. Closed major holidays. **Reservations:** suggested. **Features:** dressy casual; health conscious menu items; cocktails & lounge; minimum charge-$20 per person; a la carte. Aromatic herbs and spices wake up the flavors in such dishes as Dover sole. The dining room atmosphere is sophisticated and contemporary, with modern artwork and nice flowers. Professional basketball players have been known to frequent the establishment. Smoke free premises. **Cards:** AE, DI, MC, VI.

IL MONELLO
◆◆◆
Northern
Italian

Lunch: $16-$25   **Dinner:** $16-$25   **Phone:** 212/535-9310   [98]
Location: Between 76th and 77th sts. 1460 2nd Ave 10021. **Hours:** noon-3 & 5-11 pm, Fri & Sat 5 pm-midnight, Sun noon-10 pm. Closed major holidays. **Reservations:** suggested. **Features:** dressy casual; cocktails; a la carte. Elegant table settings and attractive artwork lend to the sophisticated appeal of the comfortably refined dining room. The menu centers on Northern Italian dishes, which are well complemented by an assortment of wines. Desserts are delicious. Smoke free premises. **Cards:** AE, CB, DI, MC, VI.

IL NIDO
◆◆◆
Northern
Italian

Lunch: $18-$27   **Dinner:** $19-$30   **Phone:** 212/753-8450   [101]
Location: Between 2nd and 3rd aves. 251 E 53rd St 10022. **Hours:** noon-3 & 5:30-11 pm. Closed major holidays & Sun. **Reservations:** suggested. **Features:** semi-formal attire; health conscious menu items; cocktails; a la carte. An extensive selection of Italian wines complements selections of Northern Italian cuisine. Subtle lighting helps to give the quiet, Tuscan-influenced dining room a warm, intimate feel. Among the wonderful desserts are classic tiramisu and zabaglione. Smoke free premises. **Cards:** AE, CB, DI, MC, VI.

ISABELLA'S
◆◆
American

Lunch: $11-$19   **Dinner:** $11-$19   **Phone:** 212/724-2100   [175]
Location: At 77th St. 359 Columbus Ave 10024. **Hours:** 11:30 am-12:30 am, Fri-1 am, Sat 11 am-1 am, Sun 10:30 am-midnight. **Closed:** 12/25. **Reservations:** accepted. **Features:** casual dress; carryout; cocktails & lounge; a la carte. Value and variety are a cornerstone of the big sidewalk cafe. Herb-crusted salmon, striped bass wrapped in prosciutto and well-prepared sirloin are among American dishes that exhibit Mediterranean influences. Save room for the decadent desserts. Smoke free premises. **Cards:** AE, MC, VI.

JEAN GEORGES RESTAURANT
◆◆◆◆◆
French

Lunch: $29-$42   **Dinner:** $85   **Phone:** 212/299-3900   [57]
Location: At Columbus Cir; jct Central Park S; in Trump International Hotel & Tower. 1 Central Park W 10023. **Hours:** noon-2:30 & 5:30-11 pm. Closed major holidays & Sun. **Reservations:** suggested. **Features:** semi-formal attire; cocktails & lounge; fee for valet parking; prix fixe. Smoke free premises. **Cards:** AE, DI, MC, VI.

JOE ALLEN
◆
Regional
American

Lunch: $9-$20   **Dinner:** $9-$20   **Phone:** 212/581-6464   [176]
Location: Between 8th and 9th aves. 326 W 46th St 10036. **Hours:** noon-11:45 pm, Fri-midnight, Sat 11:30 am-midnight, Sun & Wed 11:30 am-11:45 pm. **Closed:** 11/23 & 12/25. **Reservations:** required. **Features:** casual dress; Sunday brunch; cocktails & lounge; a la carte. A theater district classic, the cheerful pub delivers unpretentious, home-style staples, such as meatloaf, liver and roasted chicken. Apple pie is stuffed full of fruit and served warm. Broadway stars are known to gather here for light night meals. **Cards:** MC, VI.

JO JO
◆◆◆
French

Lunch: $19-$35   **Dinner:** $19-$35   **Phone:** 212/223-5656   [132]
Location: Between 3rd and Lexington aves. 160 E 64th St 10021. **Hours:** noon-2:30 & 6-11 pm, Sat noon-2 & 5:30 pm-11 pm. Closed major holidays & Sun. **Reservations:** suggested. **Features:** casual dress; health conscious menu items; cocktails; a la carte. The dining room exudes the lively ambience of an upscale bistro. Mostly French wines complement selections of creative cuisine, such as salmon in rice wrappers. Desserts— especially the caramelized apple slices over toasted brioche—are exquisite. Smoke free premises. **Cards:** AE, DI, MC, VI.

JUDSON GRILL Lunch: $16-$24 Dinner: $18-$34 Phone: 212/582-5252 [177]
◆◆◆
American
Location: Between 6th and 7th aves. 152 W 52nd St 10019. Hours: noon-2:30 & 5:30-11 pm, Fri-11:30 pm, Sat 5 pm-11:30 pm. Closed major holidays & Sun. Reservations: suggested. Features: dressy casual; cocktails & lounge; a la carte. Convenient to the theater district, the dining room is a big, open space decorated in an elegant style. Eclectic, contemporary dishes, which are touched by Mediterranean influences, are well complemented by a selection of more than 160 wines. Smoke free premises. Cards: AE, DI, DS, MC, VI. ✕

JULIAN'S CUISINE Lunch: $6-$16 Dinner: $7-$26 Phone: 212/262-4800 [133]
ⒶⒶⒶ
◆◆
Italian
Location: Between 53rd and 54th sts. 802 9th Ave 10019. Hours: noon-11 pm, Fri & Sat-midnight, Sun 11:30 am-11 pm. Closed major holidays. Reservations: suggested. Features: casual dress; Sunday brunch; carryout; cocktails; a la carte. The menu covers broad territory, with Northern and Southern Italian dishes as well as Mediterranean cuisine. Shelves with European decorations line the comfortable dining room. The seasonal garden and relaxed sidewalk area invite diners to unwind. Cards: AE, DI, DS, MC, VI. ✕

KOKACHIN Lunch: $18-$28 Dinner: $20-$34 Phone: 212/753-5800 [178]
◆◆◆◆
American
Location: Between Madison and 5th; in Omni Berkshire Place. 21 E 52nd St 10022. Hours: 6:30 am-11 pm, Sat & Sun 7 am-midnight. Reservations: suggested. Features: dressy casual; health conscious menu items; cocktails & lounge; entertainment; fee for valet parking; a la carte. The dining room is elegant, yet comfortable—inviting you to relax and enjoy such dishes as Dover sole and veal chop with sauce. The well-chosen wine list is lined with selections to appropriately complement any selection. Service is technically sound. Smoke free premises. Cards: AE, DI, DS, MC, VI. ✕

KOREA PALACE Lunch: $13-$18 Dinner: $25-$30 Phone: 212/832-2350 [179]
◆
Korean
Location: Between Park and Lexington. 127 E 54th St 10022. Hours: 10:30 am-10:30 pm. Closed: 11/23. Reservations: suggested. Features: casual dress; carryout; cocktails & lounge. Duck, Pajeon seafood pancake and Korean barbecue are favorite offerings from the restaurant's varied menu. The relaxed dining room is appropriately appointed in ethnic decor. Servers in black-and-white uniforms are friendly and efficient. Smoke free premises. Cards: AE, DI, MC, VI. ✕

LA CARAVELLE Lunch: $25-$38 Dinner: $44-$65 Phone: 212/586-4252 [59]
◆◆◆
French
Location: Between 5th and 6th aves. 33 W 55th St 10019. Hours: noon-2:30 & 5:30-10:30 pm, Sat from 5:30 pm. Closed major holidays, Sun & first week of July. Reservations: required. Features: semi-formal attire; cocktails; prix fixe, a la carte. Colorful wall murals with Parisian scenes and fresh flowers decorate the bright, yet intimate, dining room. Dover sole, truffled pike with lobster sauce and roasted duck are representative of outstanding innovations. Service is polished and professional. Cards: AE, DI, MC, VI. ✕

LA COTE BASQUE Lunch: $35 Dinner: $63 Phone: 212/688-6525 [161]
◆◆◆◆
French
Location: Between 5th and 6th aves. 60 W 55th St 10019. Hours: noon-2:30 & 5:30-10:30 pm, Fri & Sat-11:30 pm, Sun 5 pm-10 pm. Closed major holidays. Reservations: suggested. Features: semi-formal attire; cocktails; prix fixe. Basque Coast murals wrap around the warm, colorful dining room, a delightful spot for upscale dining. The menu samples both classical and nouvelle cuisine, all of which is served in great amounts. Impeccably groomed servers are professional in every way. Smoke free premises. Cards: AE, CB, DI, DS, MC, VI. ✕

LA GRENOUILLE Lunch: $45 Dinner: $80 Phone: 212/752-1495 [68]
◆◆◆◆
French
Location: Between 5th and Madison aves. 3 E 52nd 10022. Hours: noon-2:30 & 5:45-11:15 pm. Closed major holidays, Sun, Mon & 8/1-8/31. Reservations: required. Features: semi-formal attire; cocktails; prix fixe. A romantic ambience pervades the lovely dining room, which is appointed with abundant floral arrangements. The restaurant is a long-standing city favorite for classic French cuisine, including such seasonal items as venison in caranqueneur sauce. Smoke free premises. Cards: AE, DI, MC, VI. ✕

LA MANGEOIRE Lunch: $8-$23 Dinner: $15-$26 Phone: 212/759-7086 [135]
◆◆
French
Location: Between 53rd and 54th sts. 1008 Second Ave 10022. Hours: noon-2:30 & 5:30-10:30 pm, Fri & Sat-11 pm, Sun 11:30 am-3 pm & 5-9 pm. Closed major holidays & Sun 7/4-9/2. Reservations: suggested. Features: Sunday brunch; cocktails; a la carte, also prix fixe. Representative of excellent food is the grilled striped bass, served with herb-roasted vegetables and sweet pepper coulis. A country decor prevails in the quaint, two-level restaurant. The wine list carefully combines French and Californian selections. Smoke free premises. Cards: AE, DI, MC, VI. ✕

LA RESERVE Lunch: $32 Dinner: $40-$54 Phone: 212/247-2993 [87]
◆◆◆
French
Location: Between 5th and 6th aves, Rockefeller Center. 4 W 49th St 10020. Hours: noon-3 & 5:30-10:30 pm, Fri & Sat-11 pm, Sun noon-3 & 5-8 pm. Closed major holidays. Reservations: suggested. Features: semi-formal attire; health conscious menu items; cocktails & lounge; prix fixe. The refined restaurant emphasizes the classics, such as baguettes, salmon mousse and asparagus vinaigrette. Fennel sauce adds zest to the bass. A romantic feel hangs over the lovely dining room. Servers are gracious, knowledgeable and professional. Smoke free premises. Cards: AE, CB, DI, DS, MC, VI. ✕

LA STRADA RESTAURANT Lunch: $11-$20 Dinner: $11-$20 Phone: 212/869-7188 [136]
◆◆
South Italian
Location: Between 6th and 7th aves. 134 W 46th St 10036. Hours: noon-10:45 pm, Fri & Sat-11:45 pm, Sat brunch noon-3:30 pm. Closed major holidays & Sun. Reservations: suggested. Features: casual dress; cocktails & lounge; fee for parking; a la carte. Cannelloni Alfredo, lasagna and veal marsala are representative of traditional, reasonably priced entrees on the long-established restaurant's menu. The cozy, warm atmosphere makes for an inviting pre- or post-theater stop. Desserts are made in-house. Cards: AE, DI, DS, MC, VI. ✕

LE BERNARDIN
◆◆◆◆
Seafood
Lunch: $32-$42 **Dinner:** $70 **Phone:** 212/489-1515 (148)
Location: Between 6th and 7th aves; in the Equitable Center. 155 W 51st St 10019. **Hours:** noon-2:30 & 5:30-10:30 pm, Fri-11 pm, Sat 5:30 pm-11 pm. Closed major holidays & Sun. **Reservations:** required. **Features:** semi-formal attire; cocktails; fee for parking; prix fixe, a la carte. Splurge on the six-course tasting menu, which gives a wonderful overview of contemporary French cuisine. Rich woods, autumn tones and high ceilings lend to the sophisticated elegance of the dining room. The thoughtfully chosen wine list is extensive. Smoke free premises. **Cards:** AE, DI, DS, MC, VI.

LE CIRQUE 2000
◆◆◆◆◆
French
Lunch: $25-$30 **Dinner:** $26-$36 **Phone:** 212/303-7788 (165)
Location: Between 50th and 51st (valet parking access on 50th); in The New York Palace. 455 Madison Ave 10022. **Hours:** 11:45 am-2:45 & 5:30-11 pm; Sun 5:30 pm-10:30 pm. Closed major holidays. **Reservations:** required. **Features:** semi-formal attire; health conscious menu items; cocktails & lounge; a la carte. The grand rooms are pulled colorfully into the future with strings of neon, whimsical deep purple and teal chairs and eclectic fusion cuisine. Top awards consistently go to the restaurant, which is known for formal service and its classic creme brulee. Smoke free premises. **Cards:** AE, DI, MC, VI. *(See color ad p 348)*

LE COLONIAL
◆◆◆
Ethnic
Lunch: $13-$20 **Dinner:** $13-$20 **Phone:** 212/752-0808 (137)
Location: Between 2nd and 3rd aves. 149 E 57th St 10022. **Hours:** noon-2:15 & 5:30-11:30 pm, Fri-midnight, Sat & Sun 5:30 pm-11 pm. Closed: 11/23 & 12/25. **Reservations:** suggested. **Features:** health conscious menu; cocktails & lounge; a la carte. Twirling fans, tall ferns and an original tin ceiling painted deep, brick red with a black border give the dining room the feel of 1940s Vietnam. The menu centers on excellent Vietnamese cuisine, all priced reasonably. Servers are gentle and efficient. Smoke free premises. **Cards:** AE, DI, MC, VI.

LE PERIGORD
◆◆◆
French
Lunch: $32 **Dinner:** $52 **Phone:** 212/755-6244 (95)
Location: E of 1st Ave. 405 E 52nd St 10022. **Hours:** noon-3 & 5:30-10:30 pm, Sat from 5:30 pm, Sun 5 pm-10:30 pm. Closed: 1/1 & 12/25. **Reservations:** required. **Features:** casual dress; cocktails; prix fixe, a la carte. In a residential area near the United Nations building, the established restaurant boasts an open, spacious dining room with an elegant edge. The broad menu centers on classic French cuisine, which is nicely complemented by the fine wine list. Smoke free premises. **Cards:** AE, DI, DS, MC, VI.

LESPINASSE
◆◆◆◆◆
French
Lunch: $44 **Dinner:** $34-$46 **Phone:** 212/339-6719 (109)
Location: Between Madison and 5th aves; in The St Regis New York. 2 E 55th St 10022. **Hours:** 7 am-10:30, noon-2 & 6-10 pm, Sun 7 am-10 am. Closed major holidays, lunch & dinner Sun & Mon. **Reservations:** required. **Features:** semi-formal attire; cocktails & lounge; fee for valet parking; a la carte. Luxurious Louis XV furnishings decorate the opulent, spacious dining room. Asian and French influences fuse in exquisite menu selections, which are as pleasing to the eye as to the palate. Service is impeccable—and markedly unobtrusive—in every aspect. Smoke free premises. **Cards:** AE, CB, DI, DS, MC, VI.

LUTECE
◆◆◆
French
Lunch: $38 **Dinner:** $65 **Phone:** 212/752-2225 (155)
Location: Between 2nd and 3rd aves. 249 E 50th St 10022. **Hours:** noon-2 & 5:30-10 pm, Mon & Sat from 5:30 pm. Closed major holidays & Sun. **Reservations:** suggested. **Features:** cocktails & lounge; prix fixe. Tender, caramelized short ribs—garnished with minced chives, accompanied by pureed, butter-laden potatoes and resting in a pool of reduced au jus—are a delicious representation of modern French fare. The large, professional staff is attentive. Smoke free premises. **Cards:** AE, DI, DS, MC, VI.

MARCH
◆◆◆
American
Lunch: $68-$93 **Dinner:** $90-$125 **Phone:** 212/754-6272 (138)
Location: Between 1st Ave and Sutton Place. 405 E 58th St 10022. **Hours:** 6 pm-11 pm, Sun-10:30 pm. Closed major holidays. **Reservations:** required. **Features:** semi-formal attire; health conscious menu; cocktails; fee for parking; prix fixe. An unpretentious ambience prevails in the quietly elegant dining room, which is well attended by a welcoming, professional staff. An award-winning wine list complements dishes of many ethnic influences. The rooftop terrace is cozy and relaxed. **Cards:** AE, DI, MC, VI.

MARK'S
◆◆◆◆
Continental
Lunch: $15-$26 **Dinner:** $24-$34 **Phone:** 212/879-1864 (147)
Location: At Madison Ave; in The Mark. 25 E 77th St 10021. **Hours:** 7 am-10 pm, Sun from 8 am. **Reservations:** suggested. **Features:** dressy casual; Sunday brunch; health conscious menu; cocktails & lounge; fee for valet parking; a la carte, also prix fixe. Roman prints decorate the walls of the plush, tri-level dining room. The atmosphere is refined and comfortable, welcoming diners to unwind. The menu presents traditional choices, such as barbecue hangar steak and onion rings on corn cakes. Smoke free premises. **Cards:** AE, DI, DS, MC, VI.

MATCH UPTOWN
◆◆
American
Lunch: $15-$25 **Dinner:** $24-$32 **Phone:** 212/906-9177 (181)
Location: Between Madison and Park aves. 33 E 60th St 10022. **Hours:** 11:30 am-3:30 & 6-2 am, Sun 6 pm-11 pm. Closed: 7/4, 11/23 & 12/25. **Reservations:** suggested. **Features:** dressy casual; cocktails & lounge; a la carte. Particularly popular with the locals who frequent the place, the restaurant is decorated in a funky, nouveau spirit. Pacific Rim influences are evident in preparations of seafood, meat and poultry. The sushi bar delivers a wide variety of good choices. **Cards:** AE, DI, MC, VI.

MATTHEW'S
◆◆◆
American
Lunch: $10-$15 **Dinner:** $12-$18 **Phone:** 212/838-4343 (140)
Location: At 61st St. 1030 Third Ave 10021. **Hours:** noon-5 & 6-11 pm, Sun noon-5 & 5:45-10 pm. Closed major holidays. **Reservations:** suggested. **Features:** Sunday brunch; health conscious menu items; cocktails & lounge; a la carte. A Moroccan flair punctuates creative American entrees, such as crispy red snapper, chicken roasted with lemon and spiced lamb shanks. The decor reflects a Casablanca mood—light, airy and romantic. Desserts are as colorful as they are delicious. **Cards:** AE, CB, DI, DS, MC, VI.

MICHAEL'S
◆◆◆
American

Lunch: $23-$26   **Dinner:** $23-$32   **Phone:** 212/767-0555   (142)
Location: Between 5th and 6th aves. 24 W 55th St 10019. **Hours:** 7:30 am-9:30, noon-3 & 5:30-10:30 pm, Sat 5:30 pm-10:30 pm. Closed major holidays & Sun. **Reservations:** suggested. **Features:** casual dress; cocktails & lounge; a la carte. The emphasis is on modern creative cuisine, such as the intensely flavorful tuna nicoise. California choices are the focus of the award-winning wine list. The butterscotch/chocolate dessert—a rich, crunchy delight—expertly blends tastes and textures. Smoke free premises. **Cards:** AE, DI, MC, VI.   ☒

MIMI'S MACARONI
◆
Italian

Lunch: $7-$9   **Dinner:** $8-$15   **Phone:** 212/866-6311   (104)
Location: 95th St. 718 Amsterdam Ave 10025. **Hours:** 11:30 am-11 pm. Closed: 11/23 & 12/25. **Features:** casual dress; Sunday brunch; children's menu; carryout; cocktails & lounge; a la carte. The homey, neighborhood eatery focuses on delivering wholesome, family fare. Many choices involve pasta, such as Jophus, which is named for the owner. Tasty tartuffo coats vanilla ice cream with hard chocolate and fills it with the flavor of raspberries. Smoke free premises. **Cards:** CB, DI, DS, MC, VI.   ☒

MONKEY BAR
◆◆◆
American

Lunch: $16-$28   **Dinner:** $22-$31   **Phone:** 212/838-2600   (182)
Location: Between Madison and Park aves. 60 E 54th St 10022. **Hours:** noon-2:30 & 5:30-10:30 pm; Fri-11:15 pm, Sat 5:30 pm-11:15 pm, Sun 6 pm-10 pm; Sun hrs may vary. Closed: 1/1 & 12/25. **Reservations:** suggested. **Features:** semi-formal attire; cocktails & lounge; a la carte. The unusually decorated dining area resembles a nightclub during the "golden years" of movies. Black-and-white photographs of the stars of yesteryear—such as the inimitable Joan Crawford—adorn the walls. The food is delightful; save room for dessert. Smoke free premises. **Cards:** AE, CB, DI, MC, VI.   ☒

OCEANA
◆◆◆◆
Seafood

Lunch: $40   **Dinner:** $65   **Phone:** 212/759-5941   (111)
Location: Between Madison and Park aves. 55 E 54th St 10022. **Hours:** noon-2:30 & 5:30-10:30 pm. Closed major holidays & Sun. **Reservations:** suggested. **Features:** semi-formal attire; cocktails; prix fixe. Creative New American cuisine—such as seared striped wild bass over truffled mashed potatoes—exhibits outstanding visual and flavor combinations. The staff is welcoming and gracious. Tasty sticky pudding with praline ice cream is loaded with pecans. Smoke free premises. **Cards:** AE, DI, DS, MC, VI.   ☒

OLLIE'S
◆
Chinese

Lunch: $8-$18   **Dinner:** $8-$18   **Phone:** 212/921-5988   (185)
Location: Between 7th and 8th aves. 200 W 44th St 10036. **Hours:** 11:30 am-midnight, Fri & Sun 1 am, Sun 11:30 am-11:30 pm. **Reservations:** required. **Features:** casual dress; carryout; cocktails; a la carte. Known for dumplings, barbecue and a good variety of soups, the Times Square restaurant is a favorite for traditional food. The Chinese monkey story is depicted on the wall. Servers in red shirts and black slacks are efficient and no-nonsense. Smoke free premises. **Cards:** AE, MC, VI.   ☒

ORSO
◆◆
Northern
Italian

Lunch: $15-$21   **Dinner:** $15-$21   **Phone:** 212/489-7212   (78)
Location: Between 8th and 9th aves; on Restaurant Row. 322 W 46th St 10036. **Hours:** noon-11:45 pm, Wed & Sat from 11:30 am; Sun closing hrs may vary. Closed: 11/23 & 12/25. **Reservations:** suggested. **Features:** dressy casual; cocktails; a la carte. The intimate restaurant is appointed with the warm, rustic decor of a trattoria. The frequently changing menu includes light-crusted pizzas, seafood and pasta, all of which are complemented by a carefully selected Italian wine list. Service is pleasant. Smoke free premises. **Cards:** MC, VI.   ☒

PALIO
◆◆◆◆
Northern
Italian

Lunch: $19-$29   **Dinner:** $19-$34   **Phone:** 212/245-4850   (60)
Location: In the atrium of Equitable Center; between 6th and 7th aves. 151 W 51st St 10019. **Hours:** noon-2:30 & 5:30-11 pm, Sat from 5:30 pm. Closed major holidays & Sun. **Reservations:** suggested. **Features:** semi-formal attire; health conscious menu items; cocktails & lounge; a la carte. Save time for a drink in the bar to view the spectacular overhead mural depicting the Sienese races. The dining room affords a more subdued and elegant setting, the perfect backdrop in which to enjoy fine Northeast Italian cuisine. Service is unobtrusive. Smoke free premises. **Cards:** AE, DI, DS, MC, VI.   ☒

PARK AVENUE CAFE
◆◆◆
American

Lunch: $16-$25   **Dinner:** $20-$34   **Phone:** 212/644-1900   (186)
Location: At Park Ave. 100 E 63rd St 10021. **Hours:** 11:30 am-2:30 & 5:30-10:30 pm, Sat 5:30 pm-11:30 pm, Sun 11:45 am-2:30 & 5-9:30 pm. Closed: 1/1 & 12/25. **Reservations:** suggested. **Features:** casual dress; Sunday brunch; health conscious menu items; cocktails & lounge; a la carte, also prix fixe. Ingenuity and consistency are hallmarks of the nightly changing menu, which focuses on contemporary cuisine. The pastry chef creates such sinful temptations as honey-roasted pecan Napoleon and raspberry tartlette with creme fraiche and lemon thyme. Smoke free premises. **Cards:** AE, DI, DS, JC, MC, VI.   ☒

PARK BISTRO
◆◆
French

Lunch: $15-$20   **Dinner:** $18-$22   **Phone:** 212/689-1360   (145)
Location: Between 28th and 29th sts. 414 Park Ave S 10016. **Hours:** noon-3 & 5:30-11 pm, Sat 5:30 pm-11 pm, Sun 5:30 pm-10:30 pm. Closed major holidays. **Reservations:** suggested. **Features:** cocktails; a la carte. The wonderful food fits the description of bistro cooking—bold, colorful, flavorful and hearty. Meaty hangar steak is topped with a highly seasoned cream sauce. An excellent homemade caramel sauce is drizzled over the luscious apple dessert. Smoke free premises. **Cards:** AE, DI, MC, VI.   ☒

PATSY'S ITALIAN RESTAURANT
◆◆
Northern
Italian

Lunch: $12-$22   **Dinner:** $15-$28   **Phone:** 212/247-3491   (54)
Location: Between Broadway and 8th Ave. 236 W 56th St 10019. **Hours:** noon-10:30 pm, Fri & Sat-11:30 pm, Sun noon-10:30 pm. Closed major holidays. **Reservations:** suggested. **Features:** casual dress; health conscious menu items; cocktails & lounge; fee for parking; a la carte. A landmark since 1944, the restaurant delivers traditional Southern Italian fare, such as spaghetti in a delicious marinara sauce. The two dining rooms are casual and familiar, welcoming to families and theatergoers alike. Service is professional. Smoke free premises. **Cards:** AE, CB, DI, DS, MC, VI.   ☒

PEACOCK ALLEY **Dinner;** $27-$36 **Phone:** 212/872-4895 (88)
◆◆◆◆ **Location:** Between E 49th and 50th sts; in The Waldorf Astoria and Towers. 301 Park Ave 10022. **Hours:** 7
French am-10:30 & 5:30-10 pm, Sat 5:30 pm-10:30 pm, Sun brunch 10 am-2 pm. Closed: for dinner Sun, Mon &
8/1-8/31. **Reservations:** suggested. **Features:** semi-formal attire; health conscious menu items; cocktails &
lounge; fee for valet parking; a la carte. Nestled away from the hustle of the city, the serene setting is decorated with elegant
murals that depict regal peacocks in a fanciful land. Although the menu centers on seafood preparations with delicate
sauces, you'll also find lamb, beef and chicken. Smoke free premises. **Cards:** AE, CB, DI, DS, MC, VI.

PETROSSIAN **Lunch:** $19 **Dinner:** $28-$33 **Phone:** 212/245-2214 (76)
◆◆◆ **Location:** At 7th Ave. 182 W 58th St 10019. **Hours:** 11:30 am-3 & 5:30-11:30 pm, Sun-10:30 pm.
Continental **Reservations:** suggested. **Features:** semi-formal attire; cocktails & lounge; a la carte, also prix fixe. Caviar,
smoked salmon and foie gras are specialties at the elegant, upscale restaurant. The dining room is
appointed in the art deco style, with sandblasted mirrors, attractive sculpture and striking chandeliers. Service is professional
and attentive. Smoke free premises. **Cards:** AE, CB, DI, JC, MC, VI.

PLAZA ESPANA RESTAURANT **Lunch:** $13-$23 **Dinner:** $13-$23 **Phone:** 212/757-6434 (89)
◆ **Location:** Between 6th and 7th aves. 130 W 58th St 10019. **Hours:** noon-11 pm, Sun-10 pm. Closed major
Spanish holidays. **Reservations:** suggested. **Features:** casual dress; a la carte. The simple dining room
provides an intimate setting in which to savor authentic Spanish dishes, such as paella with assorted
seafood, fish prepared Basque-style and veal in sherry wine. The restaurant is frequented by a solid base of regulars.
Cards: AE, DI, MC, VI.

THE POST HOUSE **Lunch:** $16-$29 **Dinner:** $22-$43 **Phone:** 212/935-2888 (159)
◆◆◆ **Location:** Between Park and Madison aves; in The Lowell Hotel. 28 E 63rd St 10021. **Hours:** noon-11 pm,
American Sat & Sun from 5:30 pm. Closed major holidays. **Reservations:** suggested. **Features:** semi-formal attire;
cocktails; a la carte. Although the atmosphere is bustling and vibrant, you'll enjoy a relaxed, unhurried meal
of well-prepared steak or fresh seafood. Choose from an award-winning wine list, and browse irresistible selections on the
dessert cart until one strikes your fancy. Smoke free premises. **Cards:** AE, CB, DI, DS, JC, MC, VI.

RESTAURANT CHARLOTTE **Lunch:** $16-$22 **Dinner:** $17-$28 **Phone:** 212/768-4400 (146)
◆◆◆ **Location:** Between 6th and 7th aves; in Millennium Broadway. 145 W 44th St 10036. **Hours:** noon-2:30 &
American 5:15-10:30 pm, Sun 10 am-2:30 pm. **Reservations:** suggested. **Features:** dressy casual; Sunday brunch;
health conscious menu items; cocktails & lounge; a la carte. Food quality is sharp in such dishes as grilled
salmon over riced rutabagas with cream and nutmeg. The atmosphere in the art deco-appointed dining room is refined and
comfortable. Delicious macadamia cake is topped with caramelized fresh bananas. Smoke free premises. **Cards:** AE, DI,
DS, MC, VI.

RESTAURANT NIPPON **Lunch:** $20-$29 **Dinner:** $32-$45 **Phone:** 212/758-0226 (103)
◆◆ **Location:** Between 3rd and Lexington aves. 155 E 52nd St 10022. **Hours:** noon-2:30 & 5:30-10 pm,
Japanese Fri-10:30 pm, Sat 5:30 pm-10:30 pm, major holidays 5:30 pm-10 pm. Closed: Sun.
Reservations: suggested. **Features:** semi-formal attire; health conscious menu; carryout; cocktails; a la
carte. Homemade buckwheat noodles are among quality ingredients that flavor dishes of traditional Japanese cuisine. The
dessert menu includes such wonderful choices as yokan (red bean cake), seasonal fruit and green tea ice cream. Service is
attentive. Smoke free premises. **Cards:** AE, CB, DI, JC, MC, VI.

RESTAURANT QUINCE **Lunch:** $18-$24 **Dinner:** $55 **Phone:** 212/582-8993 (149)
◆◆◆ **Location:** Between 5th and 6th aves. 33 W 54th St 10019. **Hours:** noon-2:30 & 5:30-10 pm. Closed major
American holidays, Sat & Sun. **Reservations:** required. **Features:** casual dress; cocktails; prix fixe. Geared for adult
dining, the restaurant delivers a prix fixe menu of contemporary American cuisine, including preparations of
seafood and game. The garden patio, a favorite seating option during temperate weather, is comfortable and inviting. Smoke
free premises. **Cards:** AE, DI, DS, MC, VI.

RESTAURANT 222 **Dinner:** $22-$42 **Phone:** 212/799-0400 (187)
◆◆◆ **Location:** Between Broadway and Amsterdam; on the Upper West Side. 222 W 79th St 10024. **Hours:** 5
American pm-11 pm. **Reservations:** required. **Features:** casual dress; cocktails. The cozy, romantic restaurant has the
look of an English library, with oak-paneled walls and subtle lighting. Known for culinary extravagance, the
chef prepares rare and high-priced delicacies. In-house desserts include the exquisite tuille. **Cards:** AE, CB, DI, DS, MC, VI.

SAN DOMENICO **Lunch:** $17-$30 **Dinner:** $19-$35 **Phone:** 212/265-5959 (61)
ⓐⓐⓐ **Location:** W 59th St between Broadway and 7th Ave. 240 Central Park S 10019. **Hours:** noon-2:30 &
◆◆◆◆ 5:30-11 pm, Sat 5:30 pm-11 pm, Sun 5:30 pm-10 pm. Closed: 1/1, 11/23 & 12/25. **Reservations:** suggested.
Northern **Features:** semi-formal attire; cocktails & lounge; a la carte, also prix fixe. A seasonal art collection enhances
Italian the sophisticated, contemporary dining room. The building was designed by Italian architects and constructed
of Italian materials. Risotto Parmigiano with beef glaze is an outstanding choice. Service is exemplary.
Smoke free premises. **Cards:** AE, CB, DI, MC, VI.

SAN MARTIN RESTAURANT **Lunch:** $11-$18 **Dinner:** $13-$24 **Phone:** 212/832-0888 (90)
ⓐⓐⓐ **Location:** Between Lexington and 3rd aves. 143 E 49th St 10017. **Hours:** noon-midnight.
Reservations: suggested. **Features:** semi-formal attire; health conscious menu items; cocktails & lounge; a
◆◆ la carte, also prix fixe. Relax in the unpretentious dining room and enjoy preparations of traditional Italian
Continental cuisine, such as penne pasta with porcini mushrooms, sun-dried potatoes, green peas and cream sauce. A
good-size staff in crisp uniforms is trained to be attentive. Smoke free premises. **Cards:** AE, DI, DS, MC, VI.

SARABETH'S
◆◆
American

Lunch: $8-$12   **Dinner:** $12-$20   **Phone:** 212/496-6280   (115)
Location: Between 80th and 81st sts. 423 Amsterdam St 10024. **Hours:** 8 am-10:30 pm, Fri-11 pm, Sat 9 am-11 pm, Sun 9 am-9:30 pm. Closed: 12/25. **Features:** casual dress; Sunday brunch; cocktails; a la carte. Menu offerings include goldi lox, which blends smoked salmon and cream cheese; pumpkin waffles; and Popeye eggs, which are served on homemade English muffins. The homelike atmosphere is reminiscent of a country inn. Baked goods are delicious. Smoke free premises. **Cards:** AE, DI, MC, VI.   ✕

SARDI'S
AAA
◆◆
Continental

Lunch: $14-$24   **Dinner:** $19-$30   **Phone:** 212/221-8440   (97)
Location: Between Broadway and 8th Ave. 234 W 44th St 10036. **Hours:** 11:30 am-12:30 am, Fri & Sat-1 am. Closed: Sun. **Reservations:** required. **Features:** casual dress; health conscious menu items; cocktails & lounge; a la carte. In the historic theater district, the restaurant is interestingly decorated with hundreds of caricatures of stage and screen stars. Cannelloni au gratin, shrimp Sardi and veal cutlet Vincent are local favorites. Flashily dressed servers are prompt. **Cards:** AE, DI, MC, VI.   ✕

THE SEA GRILL
◆◆◆
Seafood

Lunch: $19-$28   **Dinner:** $22-$32   **Phone:** 212/332-7610   (67)
Location: On concourse level; at Rockefeller Center Skating Rink. 19 W 49th St 10020. **Hours:** noon-2:45 & 5-10 pm, Sat from 5 pm. Closed major holidays & Sun. **Reservations:** suggested. **Features:** health conscious menu items; cocktails & lounge; a la carte. Menu selections show great innovation. A good choice is the crispy-skinned salmon, cooked until opaque and juicy and hidden beneath a stack of potato strings. The subtly lighted, elegantly appointed dining room exudes cozy, romantic ambience. Smoke free premises. **Cards:** AE, CB, DI, MC, VI.   ✕

SHAAN
◆◆
Indian

Lunch: $15-$25   **Dinner:** $30-$40   **Phone:** 212/977-8400   (188)
Location: Between 5th and 6th aves. 57 W 48th St 10020. **Hours:** noon-3 & 5:30-11 pm. **Reservations:** suggested. **Features:** casual dress; carryout; cocktails & lounge; a la carte. The vast menu includes many selections prepared in the tandoori oven. Lavish decorating lends the dining room an upscale feel and comfy ambience, which is further enhanced on weekends by live sitar music. A daily lunch buffet lays out many choices. Smoke free premises. **Cards:** AE, DI, MC, VI.   ✕

SHUN LEE
◆◆
Chinese

Lunch: $10-$24   **Dinner:** $12-$26   **Phone:** 212/595-8895   (56)
Location: Between Columbus Ave and Central Park W. 43 W 65th St 10023. **Hours:** noon-midnight, Sun-10:30 pm. Closed: 11/23. **Reservations:** suggested. **Features:** casual dress; health conscious menu items; cocktails & lounge; a la carte. Often packed with people, this friendly, casual restaurant is a favorite of the neighborhood. The dining room exudes a chic, trendy ambience. A good selection of wines complement traditional preparations of authentic Hunan and Szechwan cuisine. Smoke free premises. **Cards:** AE, CB, DI, MC, VI.   ✕

SHUN LEE PALACE
◆◆◆
Chinese

Lunch: $12-$24   **Dinner:** $14-$39   **Phone:** 212/371-8844   (73)
Location: Between Lexington and 3rd. 155 E 55th 10022. **Hours:** noon-11:30 pm, Sun-11 pm. Closed: 11/23. **Reservations:** suggested. **Features:** semi-formal attire; carryout; cocktails & lounge; a la carte, also prix fixe. Plants, flowers and pictures of trees are elements of the dining room's soft, inviting decor. A gentle ambience, enhanced by subtle lighting, settles over the room. The menu centers on well-prepared gourmet Szechwan and Cantonese selections. Smoke free premises. **Cards:** AE, DI, MC, VI.   ✕

SIAM INN TOO
AAA
◆◆
Ethnic

Lunch: $7-$10   **Dinner:** $9-$16   **Phone:** 212/757-4006   (91)
Location: Between W 51st and W 52nd sts. 854 8th Ave 10019. **Hours:** 11:45 am-11:30 pm, Sat & Sun from 4 pm. Closed major holidays. **Reservations:** suggested. **Features:** casual dress; health conscious menu; cocktails; a la carte, also prix fixe. The decor is soft and inviting, welcoming diners to relax and unwind. Delicious pad Thai and green papaya salad are among authentic dishes prepared with fresh ingredients and served in generous portions. Servers exhibit good follow-up skills. Smoke free premises. **Cards:** AE, CB, DI, MC, VI.   ✕

TAPIKA
◆◆◆
Southwest
American

Lunch: $13-$17   **Dinner:** $17-$29   **Phone:** 212/397-3737   (58)
Location: At 56th St. 950 8th Ave 10019. **Hours:** noon-2:30 & 5:30-11 pm, Sat 5 pm-11:30 pm, Sun 11:30 am-2:30 & 5-10 pm. Closed major holidays. **Reservations:** suggested. **Features:** carryout; cocktails & lounge; a la carte. Creativity is at the forefront of everything the restaurant does. The decor is fun, with an overgrown white picket fence in the plate glass window. Southwestern influences are evident in such dishes as rare tuna under spicy shrimp on a bed of Swiss chard. Smoke free premises. **Cards:** AE, DI, DS, MC, VI.   ✕

TAVERN ON THE GREEN
◆◆
American

Lunch: $13-$30   **Dinner:** $16-$34   **Phone:** 212/873-3200   (55)
Location: Central Park at W 67th St 10023. **Hours:** 11:30 am-3:30 & 5-11 pm, Fri-11:30 pm, Sat 10 am-3:45 & 5-11:30 pm, Sun 10 am-3:45 & 5-11 pm. **Reservations:** suggested. **Features:** casual dress; Sunday brunch; cocktails & lounge; entertainment; a la carte. One of the city's most famous restaurants, the restaurant delivers a seasonally changing menu of traditional American cuisine. The fabulous decor of the Crystal dining room reflects a rococo whimsy, with its topiary menagerie and paper lanterns. Smoke free premises. **Cards:** AE, CB, DI, DS, MC, VI.   ⟨👤⟩ ✕

TOLEDO RESTAURANT
◆◆◆
Ethnic

Lunch: $17-$36   **Dinner:** $17-$36   **Phone:** 212/696-5036   (117)
Location: Between 5th and Madison Ave. 6 E 36th St 10016. **Hours:** noon-10:30 pm, Fri & Sat-11 pm. Closed major holidays & Sun. **Reservations:** suggested. **Features:** dressy casual; children's menu; cocktails & lounge; a la carte. Elegant, upscale appointments decorate the sophisticated dining room, which is illuminated by sconces, opaque globes and spot lighting. Soft background music contributes to the romantic ambience. The classic Spanish menu delivers seafood and prime beef. Smoke free premises. **Cards:** AE, DI, MC, VI.   ✕

TRATTORIA DELL'ARTE   **Lunch:** $16-$28   **Dinner:** $16-$28   **Phone:** 212/245-9800   (189)
◆◆◆   **Location:** Between 56th and 57th sts. 900 Seventh Ave 10019. **Hours:** 11:45 am-2:30 & 5-11:30 pm, Sat 11
Northern   am-3:15 & 5-11:30 pm, Sun 11 am-3:15 & 5-10:30 pm. Closed: 11/23 & 12/25. **Reservations:** suggested.
Italian   **Features:** dressy casual; carryout; cocktails & lounge; a la carte. Convenient to Carnegie Hall, the
          whimsical, artsy restaurant bustles with energy. A complete line of vegetables and seafood makes up the
antipasto bar. The thin-crusted pizza margarita is tasty. Desserts, especially tiramisu and cannoli, are outstanding.
Cards: AE, DI, DS, MC, VI.

21 CLUB   **Lunch:** $24-$39   **Dinner:** $27-$41   **Phone:** 212/582-7200   (72)
◆◆◆   **Location:** Between 5th and 6th aves (Ave of the Americas). 21 W 52nd St 10019. **Hours:** noon-2:15 &
American   5:30-10:15 pm, Fri & Sat-11:15 pm. Closed major holidays, Sat for lunch & Sun. **Reservations:** suggested.
          Features: semi-formal attire; cocktails & lounge; a la carte. The restaurant is noticeable from the street
because of colorful miniature statuary and black, wrought-iron fencing surrounding the entrance. Toys hanging from the
ceiling lend to the whimsical decor. Peppercorn-coated sirloin is a wonderful choice. Smoke free premises. **Cards:** AE, CB,
DI, DS, MC, VI.

VICTOR'S CAFE 52   **Lunch:** $8-$19   **Dinner:** $10-$32   **Phone:** 212/586-7714   (92)
◆   **Location:** Between Broadway and 8th Ave. 236 W 52nd St 10019. **Hours:** noon-midnight, Fri & Sat-1 am.
Cuban   **Reservations:** suggested. **Features:** casual dress; health conscious menu items; cocktails & lounge; a la
          carte. Argentinean flank steak with chimichurri sauce is representative of selections on the restaurant's
menu. Wildly colorful wall murals lend energy and boldness to the upbeat dining room and colorful atrium area. Servers with
ethnic accents are personable. Smoke free premises. **Cards:** AE, CB, DI, MC, VI.

THE VIEW   **Dinner:** $25-$55   **Phone:** 212/398-1900   (94)
◆◆◆   **Location:** Between 45th and 46th sts; in Marriott Marquis. 1535 Broadway 10036. **Hours:** 5:30 pm-11, Fri &
American   Sat 5 pm-midnight. **Reservations:** suggested. **Features:** No A/C; dressy casual; Sunday brunch; cocktails; a
          la carte. The city's only revolving rooftop restaurant, The View got its name for obvious reasons. Chilean sea
bass and seared veal chop are among appetizing dishes on a menu of creative fare. In addition to being tasty, desserts are
showy and fun. **Cards:** AE, DI, DS, MC, VI.

VIRGIL'S REAL BARBECUE   **Lunch:** $13-$25   **Dinner:** $13-$22   **Phone:** 212/921-9663   (151)
◆   **Location:** Between Broadway and 6th. 152 W 44th St 10036. **Hours:** 11:30 am-midnight, Sun & Mon-11 pm.
American   Closed: 12/25. **Reservations:** accepted. **Features:** children's menu; carryout; cocktails & lounge. The menu
          centers on mostly hickory-smoked pork barbecue—prepared Southern style. Also offered are grilled and
smoked ham, grilled catfish, pulled chicken and delicious ribs. The dining room has the bustling ambience of a fun and
rowdy roadhouse. Smoke free premises. **Cards:** AE, MC, VI.

VONG RESTAURANT   **Lunch:** $21-$35   **Dinner:** $21-$35   **Phone:** 212/486-9592   (108)
◆◆◆◆   **Location:** Between 2nd and 3rd aves. 200 E 54th St 10022. **Hours:** noon-2:30 & 6-11 pm, Sat 5:30
Thai   pm-11:30 pm, Sun 5:30 pm-10 pm. Closed major holidays. **Reservations:** suggested. **Features:** dressy
          casual; cocktails & lounge; a la carte, also prix fixe. Orchids and warm shades of brown, red and gold lend a
soft, fantasylike feel to the dining room, which is appointed in an almost-templelike decor. French accents infuse striking
dishes of Thai cuisine, including the delicious lobster with herbs. **Cards:** AE, DI, MC, VI.

WALLY'S & JOSEPH'S RESTAURANT   **Lunch:** $10-$23   **Dinner:** $11-$30   **Phone:** 212/582-0460   (52)
◆◆   **Location:** Between Broadway and 8th Ave. 249 W 49th St 10019. **Hours:** noon-11:30 pm, Sat from 4:30
Steakhouse   pm. Closed major holidays & Sun 6/29-7/21. **Reservations:** suggested. **Features:** casual dress; cocktails &
          lounge; a la carte. Big names in Broadway and other entertainment visit this popular steakhouse for sizzling,
juicy sirloin; fresh seafood; and well-prepared Northern Italian fare, such as filet mignon pizzaiole. The wait staff functions as
a well-oiled machine. **Cards:** AE, DI, MC, VI.

THE WATER CLUB   **Lunch:** $17-$34   **Dinner:** $23-$35   **Phone:** 212/683-3333   (70)
(AAA)   **Location:** On E end of 23rd St to FDR service road, n. 500 E 30th St 10016. **Hours:** noon-2:30 & 5:30-10
          pm, Fri & Sat-10:30 pm, Sun 11 am-3 & 5:45-9:30 pm. **Reservations:** suggested. **Features:** casual dress;
◆◆◆   Sunday brunch; cocktails; entertainment; valet parking; a la carte. On a barge on the East River, the
American   restaurant affords distinctive views of the city. The menu emphasizes seafood and game, with such tempting
          entrees as steamed Chilean sea bass, rack of lamb and wood-grilled filet mignon. The apple tart is delicious.
Smoke free premises. **Cards:** AE, DI, MC, VI.

ZARELA   **Lunch:** $10-$15   **Dinner:** $14-$17   **Phone:** 212/644-6740   (152)
◆◆   **Location:** Between 50th and 51st sts. 953 Second Ave 10022. **Hours:** noon-3 & 5-11 pm, Fri-11:30 pm, Sat
Mexican   5 pm-11:30 pm, Sun 5 pm-10 pm. Closed major holidays. **Reservations:** suggested. **Features:** health
          conscious menu items; cocktails & lounge; minimum charge-$15; a la carte. Step inside the lively restaurant
and you'll feel as if you're inside a pinata. Wild colors and "stuff" are everywhere. Creative, well-prepared choices include
sole in green olive sauce and spicy calamari. Traditional Mexican dishes also are listed. **Cards:** AE, DI, MC, VI.

ZEN PALATE   **Lunch:** $7-$9   **Dinner:** $11-$18   **Phone:** 212/582-1669   (166)
◆◆   **Location:** At 46th St (sw corner). 663 9th Ave 10036. **Hours:** 11:30 am-10:45 pm, Fri & Sat-11 pm, Sun
Vegetarian   noon-10:30 pm. Closed: 7/4. **Reservations:** suggested; pre-theatre. **Features:** dressy casual; minimum
          charge-$10(dinner); a la carte. The restaurant affords diners a moment of calm in the midst of the Midtown
rush. Warm sconce lighting and skylights are among features of the soothing decor. Dishes creatively blend Asian and
Western influences. The key lime pie is satisfying. Smoke free premises. **Cards:** AE, DI, MC, VI.

NEW YORK pop. 7,322,600   (See map p. 330; index p. 324)

———— LODGINGS ————

ADRIA HOTEL AND CONFERENCE CENTER **Phone:** (718)631-5900 **140**
All Year 1P: $119-$149 2P: $129-$159 XP: $10 F12
Location: SR 25A, from Cross Island Pkwy, exit 31 W. 221-17 Northern Blvd 11361. Fax: 718/279-9080.
Terms: Weekly rates avail. **Facility:** 57 rooms. 4 stories; interior corridors. **Dining:** Restaurant nearby.
Motel **Cards:** AE, CB, DI, DS, JC, MC, VI.

ANCHOR MOTOR INN **Phone:** (718)428-8000 **142**
All Year 1P: $101-$120 2P: $101-$120
Location: SR 25A, 0.8 mi w of Cross Island Pkwy, exit 31 W. 215-34 Northern Blvd 11361. Fax: 718/428-7001.
Terms: [CP] meal plan; cancellation fee imposed. **Facility:** 66 rooms. Rates for up to 4 persons; 12 whirlpool
Motel rooms, $111-$129; 2 stories; interior corridors. **Dining:** Restaurant nearby. **Some Rooms:** 8 efficiencies,
utensil deposit. **Cards:** AE, CB, DI, DS, MC, VI. *(See color ad below)*

BEST WESTERN CITY VIEW **Phone:** (718)392-8400 **135**
All Year 1P: $110-$140 2P: $120-$160 XP: $10 F12
Location: West Long Island Expwy, just s of Greenpoint Ave exit; eastbound Long Island Expwy, right after toll,
Borden Ave to Greenpoint. 33-17 Greenpoint Ave 11101. Fax: 718/392-2110. **Terms:** [CP] meal plan; weekly &
Motel monthly rates avail. **Facility:** 71 rooms. Some rooms with view of Manhattan skyline. 2 rooms with canopy bed.
In former public school building; interesting architecture. 8 whirlpool rooms, $140-$160; 5 stories; interior cor-
ridors. **Services:** area transportation, shops & subway. **Some Rooms:** Fee: refrigerators. **Cards:** AE, CB, DI, DS, MC, VI.
Special Amenities: Free breakfast and free newspaper. *(See ad below)*

BEST WESTERN EDEN PARK **Phone:** (718)699-4500 **148**
9/13-12/31 1P: $119-$199 2P: $129-$209 XP: $10 F17
8/30-9/12 1P: $149-$179 2P: $159-$189 XP: $10 F17
1/1-4/30 1P: $119-$169 2P: $129-$179 XP: $10 F17
Motor Inn 5/1-8/29 1P: $109-$159 2P: $119-$169 XP: $10 F17
Location: Grand Central Pkwy, exit 10, just w via n service rd for Long Island Expwy. 113-10 Corona Ave
11368. Fax: 718/760-3916. **Terms:** Cancellation fee imposed. **Facility:** 74 rooms. 5 stories; interior corridors. **Dining:** Restaurant; 6 am-11 & 6-11 pm; $7-$20; health conscious menu; cocktails. **Cards:** AE, DI, DS, MC, VI. **Special Amenities:** Early
check-in/late check-out and free room upgrade (subject to availability with advanced reservations).
(See color ad p 364)

(See map p. 330)

COURTYARD BY MARRIOTT NEW YORK/LAGUARDIA AIRPORT   **Phone:** (718)446-4800   [144]
◆◆◆   9/2-12/31   1P: $129-$209   2P: $129-$209
Motor Inn   5/1-7/1   1P: $119-$189   2P: $119-$189
            1/1-4/30   1P: $119-$179   2P: $119-$179
            7/2-9/1   1P: $109-$179   2P: $109-$179
Location: 0.5 mi w of Grand Central Pkwy, exit 94th St. 90-10 Grand Central Pkwy 11369. Fax: 718/446-5733. **Terms:** Package plans. **Facility:** 288 rooms. 1-6 stories; interior corridors. **All Rooms:** combo or shower baths. **Cards:** AE, CB, DI, DS, MC, VI.

EXECUTIVE MOTOR INN   **Phone:** 718/341-0800   [134]
(AAA)   All Year   1P: $85-$98   2P: $85-$98   XP: $10   F12
◆   **Location:** Belt Pkwy, exit 21A (Rockaway Blvd), just w on n service road (Conduit Ave). 151-67 N Conduit Ave
Motel   11434. Fax: 718/712-2079. **Terms:** [CP] meal plan; weekly rates avail. **Facility:** 44 rooms. Convenient location to JFK airport. 3 stories; interior corridors. **Some Rooms:** Fee: refrigerators. **Cards:** AE, DS, MC, VI.

(See map p. 330)

HOLIDAY INN-JFK AIRPORT
Phone: (718)659-0200 **133**
All Year 1P: $169-$179 2P: $169-$179
Location: From Van Wyck Expwy, exit 2 (Rockaway Blvd), just e to 143rd St, then just s. 144-02 135th Ave 11436. Fax: 718/322-2533. **Terms:** Package plans. **Facility:** 360 rooms. Access to JFK International Airport. 12 stories; interior corridors; heated pool, whirlpool. **Dining:** Restaurant; 6 am-1 am; $8-$25. **Services:** gift shop. **Cards:** AE, CB, DI, DS, MC, VI.

HOLIDAY INN WALL STREET HOTEL
Phone: (212)232-7700 **150**
5/1-6/30 & 9/6-4/30 1P: $219 2P: $219 XP: $25 F18
7/1-9/5 1P: $209 2P: $209 XP: $25 F18
Location: Corner of Gold and Platt sts. 15 Gold St 10038. Fax: 212/425-0330. **Terms:** 21 day cancellation notice; cancellation fee imposed; package plans; small pets only. **Facility:** 138 rooms. In the heart of Wall Sreet, this truly "business class" hotel features a large working desk with internet access. Quiet location away from the traffic. 17 stories; interior corridors. Fee: parking. **All Rooms:** safes, honor bars. **Cards:** AE, DI, DS, JC, MC, VI.

LA GUARDIA MARRIOTT HOTEL
Phone: (718)565-8900 **146**
8/27-12/16 1P: $129-$239
5/1-6/30 & 12/17-4/30 1P: $129-$229
7/1-8/26 1P: $119-$219
Location: 0.3 mi e of 94th St exit of Grand Central Pkwy. 102-05 Ditmars Blvd 11369. Fax: 718/898-4955. **Terms:** Cancellation fee imposed; package plans; small pets only, $100 dep req. **Facility:** 436 rooms. 9 stories; interior corridors; heated pool. **Services:** gift shop. **All Rooms:** combo or shower baths. **Some Rooms:** Fee: refrigerators, VCR. **Cards:** AE, DI, DS, MC, VI.

PAN AMERICAN HOTEL
Phone: (718)446-7676 **147**
All Year 1P: $99-$160 2P: $99-$160 XP: $6 F12
Location: 1 mi e of I-278. 79-00 Queens Blvd (SR 25) 11373. Fax: 718/446-7991. **Facility:** 216 rooms. Proximity to LaGuardia Airport. Free car storage for 1 week; 7 stories; interior corridors. **Dining:** Restaurant; 7 am-midnight; $10-$25; health conscious menu items; cocktails. **Cards:** AE, CB, DI, DS, MC, VI. **Special Amenities:** Early check-in/late check-out. (See color ad p 366 & p 336)

(See map p. 330)

RAMADA INN ADRIA   Phone: (718)631-4900   **149**
All Year   1P: $119-$149   2P: $129-$159   XP: $10   F12
Location: 25A (Northern Blvd) 0.3 w of Cross Island Pkwy, exit 31 W. 220-33 Northern Blvd 11361.
Fax: 718/631-7501. **Terms:** Weekly rates avail. **Facility:** 48 rooms. 4 stories; interior corridors. **Dining:** Res-
Motor Inn   taurant; 6 am-midnight, Fri & Sat-1 am; $12-$24; health conscious menu items; cocktails. **Cards:** AE, CB, DI,
DS, JC, MC, VI. **Special Amenities:** Free newspaper and free room upgrade (subject to availability with
advanced reservations).

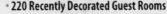

RAMADA PLAZA HOTEL AT JFK   Phone: (718)995-9000   **138**
All Year   1P: $199-$259   2P: $199-$259   XP: $10   F12
Hotel   **Location:** Van Wyck Expwy (I-678) at jct Belt Pkwy; sw corner. Bldg 144 11430-1613 (Bldg 144/JFK Intl Air-
port, JAMAICA, 11430-1630). Fax: 718/224-8962. **Terms:** [BP] meal plan; cancellation fee imposed; package
plans. **Facility:** 477 rooms. Airport property with large public areas; some smaller rooms. 6 stories; interior corridors.
Services: gift shop. **Some Rooms:** color TV. **Cards:** AE, CB, DI, DS, MC, VI. *(See ad p 367)*

(See map p. 330)

SHERATON LA GUARDIA EAST HOTEL   Phone: (718)460-6666   **141**
◆◆◆   1/1-4/30   1P: $225-$235   2P: $240-$250   XP: $15   F17
Hotel   5/1-12/31   1P: $215-$225   2P: $230-$240   XP: $15   F17
      Location: Grand Central Pkwy to Northern Blvd, 1 mi e to Main St, 0.3 mi s to 39th Ave, just w. 135-20 39th Ave 11354. Fax: 718/445-2655. **Facility:** 173 rooms. Some rooms offer distant views of Manhattan skyline and Flushing Meadows attractions. Oriental art in public areas. 16 stories; interior corridors. **Services:** gift shop. **All Rooms:** honor bars.
Cards: AE, CB, DI, DS, MC, VI.

WYNDHAM GARDEN HOTEL AT LA GUARDIA AIRPORT   Phone: (718)426-1500   **145**
◆◆◆   All Year   1P: $125-$165   XP: $20   F18
Motel   **Location:** Grand Central Pkwy, exit 6, 94th St, just e. 100-15 Ditmars Blvd 11369. Fax: 718/205-5853.
      Terms: Cancellation fee imposed; package plans. **Facility:** 229 rooms. 6-8 stories; interior corridors.
All Rooms: combo or shower baths. **Cards:** AE, CB, DI, DS, MC, VI. *(See color ad below)*

One Perfect Gift

Give the gift of security, service, and savings — buy someone you care about a AAA gift membership. AAA memberships provide your loved ones more than emergency road service.

AAA members also have access to travel services, insurance, financial services, exclusive Show Your Card & Save® discounts, bail bond services, and more.

Give them more than a gift. Give them AAA. And let them discover how AAA can simplify their lives. Call or stop by your nearest AAA office today. And make AAA the one for you.

(See map p. 330)

——— RESTAURANTS ———

JAIYA THAI-ORIENTAL RESTAURANT   **Lunch:** $5-$9   **Dinner:** $6-$17   **Phone:** 718/651-1330   197
◆   **Location:** 81st and Broadway; in East Elmhurst section. 81-11 Broadway 11373. **Hours:** 11:30 am-midnight,
Thai   Sat & Sun from noon. **Features:** casual dress; cocktails; street parking; a la carte. In the heart of the
Chinatown area of Queens, the cozy restaurant delivers piquant Thai dishes that employ seafood, tropical
fruits and spices, chili peppers and vegetables. The atmosphere is casual and relaxed, while servers are friendly and
efficient. **Cards:** AE, DI, MC, VI.

PETER LUGER'S   **Lunch:** $15-$30   **Dinner:** $45-$55   **Phone:** 718/387-7400   202
◆◆◆   **Location:** From Manhattan outside lane of Williamsburg Bridge, 1st exit, then sharp right. 178 Broadway
Steakhouse   11211. **Hours:** 11:45 am-9:45 pm, Fri & Sat-10:45 pm; Sun & major holidays 1 pm-9:45 pm.
Reservations: suggested. **Features:** casual dress; cocktails & lounge; a la carte. Succulent prime
porterhouse steaks, which are dry-aged on premise, are this sophisticated restaurant's specialty—and they are exceptional.
Many by-the-glass selections line the excellent wine list. The dining room exudes an elegant, Old World charm. Smoke free
premises.

RIVER CAFE   **Lunch:** $18-$30   **Dinner:** $70   **Phone:** 718/522-5200   198
◆◆◆◆   **Location:** At base of Brooklyn Bridge. 1 Water St 11201. **Hours:** noon-3 & 6-11 pm, Sun 11:30 am-2:30 &
American   6-11 pm. **Reservations:** required; for dinner. **Features:** Sunday brunch; cocktails & lounge; valet parking;
prix fixe. Twinkling lights in the floating restaurant's gardenlike entryway guide you inside to the dining room,
which affords spectacular views of the Manhattan skyline. Satisfying short ribs, resting on a pool of hominy and au jus, are
rich in flavor and texture. Smoke free premises. **Cards:** AE, DI, MC, VI.

WATER'S EDGE   **Lunch:** $12-$18   **Dinner:** $20-$30   **Phone:** 718/482-0033   199
ⒶⒶⒶ   **Location:** In Long Island City (Queens); from Manhattan, take 59th St Queensborough bridge upper level to
21st St exit, left on 21st to 44th Dr 2nd light, right to river. 44th Dr at the East River 11101. **Hours:** noon-3 &
◆◆◆◆   6-11 pm, Sat 6 pm-11:30 pm. Closed: Sun. **Reservations:** suggested. **Features:** semi-formal attire; health
American   conscious menu items; cocktails & lounge; entertainment; valet parking; a la carte. Across the East River, the
restaurant affords a spectacular view of Manhattan. An extensive selection of wines complements such
dishes as roasted chicken with nutmeg-spiked potato galette. White chocolate mousse resembles a piece of modern art.
Smoke free premises. **Cards:** AE, DI, MC, VI.

——— *The following restaurants have not been inspected by AAA* ———
but are listed for your information only.

BARNEY'S GREENGRASS   **Phone:** 212/724-4707
fyi   Not inspected. **Location:** Upper west side, by 86th and 87th sts. 541 Amsterdam Ave 10024. **Features:**
Since 1908, the "sturgeon king" has offered varieties of smoked fish including sable, lob, nova, and pickled
herring. A popular breakfast spot, it serves eggs and bagels, as well deli sandwiches and salads. A wait occurs often. No
credit cards.

BYBLOS   **Phone:** 212/687-0808
fyi   Not inspected. **Location:** 200 E 39th St. **Features:** This casual, informal restaurant serves a of variety of
Lebanese dishes.

CANYON ROAD   **Phone:** 212/734-1600
fyi   Not inspected. **Location:** 1470 Second Ave. **Features:** Canyon's Southwestern cuisine is imaginative and
slightly nouvelle, and dependably good—served in two serene, upscale settings.

CHINATOWN ICE CREAM FACTORY   **Phone:** 212/608-4170
fyi   Not inspected. **Location:** In Chinatown at jct Mott St. 65 Bayard St 10013. **Features:** If you are looking for a
great spot for dim sum, look no further. And you can choose from 42 flavors of ice cream, from the traditional
to exotic such as green tea, red bean, lychee and ginger. They close 30 minutes earlier in the fall and winter.

DELPHINI   **Phone:** 212/579-1145
fyi   Not inspected. **Location:** 519 Columbus Ave. **Features:** Delphini serves very unusual Mediterranean dishes
in a remarkable atmosphere.

EL POLLO   **Phone:** 212/996-7810
fyi   Not inspected. **Location:** 1746 Second Ave. **Features:** The only meat on the menu is chicken, delightfully
marinated in Peruvian spices and baked until crisp and flavorful; choose a quarter, half or whole chicken.
This is a small casual closely spaced restaurant, where wine is the only alcohol served.

EVERGREEN CAFE   **Phone:** 212/744-3266
fyi   Not inspected. **Location:** 1288 First Ave. **Features:** This is a comfortable place to come with children to
have a good Chinese meal.

FERRARA PASTICCERIA BAKERY & CAFE   **Phone:** 212/226-6150
fyi   Not inspected. **Location:** Just e of jct Mulberry St; in Little Italy. 195 Grand St 10013. **Features:** Since 1892,
cafe has offered a bustling European-feeling spot in which to savor great pastry, sweets, gelato, and
Italian   ny your delicacy with espresso or cappuccino.

Phone: 718/875-5181
ected. **Location:** On Fulton pedestrian mall, between Boerum Pl and Smith St. 372 Fulton (Jay) St
eatures: This 1870s American steak and seafood restaurant has a warm, original decor with a
remises.

Phone: 212/799-0243
d. **Location:** At jct 72nd St. 2090 Broadway 10025. **Features:** These corner counter spots offer
most popular grilled hot dogs around with your favorite toppings, and accompanied by fresh
n seen in movies and TV shows. They are a great bargain.

Phone: 212/260-3532
cation: At jct 8th St. 402 Avenue of the Americas. **Features:** These corner counter spots
most popular grilled hot dogs around with your favorite toppings, and accompanied by
n seen in movies and TV shows. They are a great bargain.

(See map p. 330)

JASMINE
fyi   Phone: 212/517-8054
Not inspected. **Location:** 1619 Second Ave. **Features:** The bamboo entrance leads you into a charming, dimly lit world where unusual and traditional Thai dishes are served.

JOHN'S PIZZERIA
fyi   Phone: 212/243-1680
Not inspected. **Location:** Just e of jct 6th Ave (Ave of the Americas). 278 Bleecker St 10014. **Features:** A Greenwich Village institution for 70 years, John's offers traditional coal-fired pizza with a charred and chewy crust. They are known for their sweet sausage. No slices are served, nor are credit cards accepted.

KATZ DELI
fyi   Phone: 212/254-2246
Not inspected. **Location:** 205 E Houston. **Features:** This is a typical New York style deli offering large portions of good quality food.

LINDY'S
fyi   Phone: 212/767-8343
Not inspected. **Location:** 825 7th Ave. **Features:** Excellent, authentic New York cheesecake is the reason to visit this basic restaurant. Take out is recommended.

MOLYVOS
fyi   Phone: 212/582-7500
Not inspected. **Location:** 871 Seventh Ave. **Features:** This attractive, casual restaurant features tasty Greek dishes.

MYRTOS TAVERNA
fyi   Phone: 718/357-6596
Not inspected. **Location:** On 25A/Northwestern Blvd, w of Cross Island Expwy; in Flushing. 196-29 Northern Blvd 11358. **Features:** Enjoy regional Greek cuisine from Cephalunia Island. A good selection of fish and meat dishes is prepared daily. Many interesting, authentic appetizers and salads and traditional Greek desserts, such as yummy baklava, grace the menu. Ethnic staff.

NOBU NEXT DOOR
fyi   Phone: 212/334-4445
Not inspected. **Location:** In Tribeca; at Franklin St. 105 Hudson. **Features:** Reservations are difficult to come by. A first-come, first-served option is offered in a more casual manner. Many exciting and innovative dishes are available, along with an extensive raw bar, market and sake bar. Whole fish are cooked to order.

OYSTER BAR
fyi   Phone: 212/490-6650
Not inspected. **Location:** Lower level of Grand Central Station. 42nd St. **Features:** The Oyster Bar offers an extensive seafood menu, including more than 50 kinds of fresh fish.

PAYARD PATISSERIE BISTRO
fyi   Phone: 212/717-5252
Not inspected. **Location:** 1032 Lexington Ave. **Features:** The extensive menu of bistro food includes numerous daily specials. The wonderful desserts arre made on the premises.

PICHOLINE
fyi   Phone: 212/724-8585
Not inspected. **Location:** 35 W 64th St. **Features:** This is upscale dining offering unusual and creative dishes.

RUBY FOO'S DIM SUM & SUSHI PALACE
fyi   Phone: 212/724-6700
Not inspected. **Location:** 2182 Broadway. **Features:** Pan Asian a work of Asian art in itself. The family style dishes are portioned for sharing.

SIAM SQUARE
fyi   Phone: 212/505-1240
Not inspected. **Location:** 92 Second Ave. **Features:** This is a small, casual, family-run Thai restaurant.

UNION PACIFIC
fyi   Phone: 212/995-8500
Not inspected. **Location:** 111 E 22nd St. **Features:** A variety of delightful dishes is served in casual, upscale elegance.

(See map p. 330)

The New York Vicinity

ARMONK pop. 2,700

———— LODGING ————

RAMADA INN
AAA SAVE
◆◆◆
Motor Inn

All Year   1P: $109-$169   2P: $119-$179   XP: $10   F18
Phone: (914)273-9090
Location: I-684, northbound exit 3S; southbound exit 3, 0.3 mi w on SR 22 to business park. 94 Business Park Dr 10504. Fax: 914/273-4105. **Terms:** Monthly rates avail. **Facility:** 140 rooms. 2 stories; interior corridors. **Dining:** Restaurant; 6:30 am-11 pm; $11-$22; cocktails. **Services:** area transportation, local businesses. **All Rooms:** combo or shower baths. **Cards:** AE, CB, DI, DS, JC, MC, VI.

BROOKLYN (See map p. 330; index p. 325)

———— LODGINGS ————

BED & BREAKFAST ON THE PARK
◆◆◆
Historic Bed
& Breakfast

All Year   2P: $125-$275   XP: $35
Phone: 718/499-6115   158
Location: Between 6th and 7th sts; opposite Prospect Park. 113 Prospect Park W 11215. Fax: 718/499-1385. **Terms:** [BP] meal plan; 10 day cancellation notice; cancellation fee imposed; 2 night min stay. **Facility:** 7 rooms. Opulent Victorian brownstone (Circa 1892), lavishly furnished with period antiques and extraordinary family art collection provides a romantic setting opposite large natural park. 4 stories, no elevator; interior corridors; smoke free premises. **Cards:** AE, MC, VI.

COMFORT INN BAY RIDGE
AAA SAVE
◆◆
Motor Inn

9/7-4/30   1P: $165-$195   2P: $175-$205   XP: $10   F18
5/1-9/6   1P: $159-$189   2P: $169-$199   XP: $10   F18
Phone: (718)238-3737   157
Location: I-278, southbound 86th St exit; northbound 92nd St exit, w to 4th Ave, just n. 8315 Fourth Ave, Bay Ridge 11209. Fax: 718/680-0827. **Terms:** [ECP] meal plan; weekly & monthly rates avail. **Facility:** 70 rooms. Nice setting in area with many shops, restaurants and residences. 3 whirlpool rooms, $209-$299; 4 stories; interior corridors. **Dining:** Restaurant; 11 am-10 pm; $14-$20; cocktails. **All Rooms:** safes. **Cards:** AE, CB, DI, DS, MC, VI. **Special Amenities:** Early check-in/late check-out. *(See color ad p 330)*

NEW YORK MARRIOTT BROOKLYN
◆◆◆
Hotel

All Year   1P: $149-$289   2P: $149-$289
Phone: (718)246-7000   156
Location: I-278 (Brooklyn-Queens Expwy), Tillary St exit, s then just e. 333 Adams St 11201. Fax: 718/246-0563. **Terms:** Check-in 4 pm. **Facility:** 376 rooms. Located across the Brooklyn Bridge from Manhattan in a commercial downtown area. Plush lobby, cozy lounge, upscale rooms. 7 stories; interior corridors; heated pool. Fee: parking. **Services:** gift shop. **All Rooms:** combo or shower baths, safes, honor bars. **Cards:** AE, DI, DS, MC, VI.

———— RESTAURANTS ————

AUNT SUZIE'S RESTAURANT
◆
South Italian

Dinner: $10-$15   **Phone:** 718/788-2868   215
Location: Between Carroll St and Garfield Pl. 247 5th Ave 11215. **Hours:** 5 pm-10 pm, Fri & Sat-11:30 pm. Closed: 11/23 & 12/25. **Features:** casual dress; carryout; beer & wine only. The neighborhood restaurant delivers one of the best bargains in the metro area, with its enormous portions of hearty, reasonably priced food. The tasty penne is served in a rich, satisfying pink sauce studded with dried tomatoes and peppercorns. Smoke free premises. **Cards:** MC, VI.

GRIMALDI'S PIZZERIA
◆◆
American

Lunch: $12-$18   **Dinner:** $12-$18   **Phone:** 718/858-4300   214
Location: Adjacent to base of Brooklyn Bridge; between Water and Front sts. 19 Old Fulton St 11201. **Hours:** 11:30 am-11 pm; Fri-midnight, Sat noon-midnight, Sun noon-11 pm. Closed: 9/9-9/30. **Features:** casual dress; carryout; beer & wine only; fee for parking; a la carte. Although the lively restaurant serves calzones, antipasto and pasta, it is known for great, brick-oven pizza. Lamps and sconces provide subtle, romantic lighting. The dessert menu tempts with such selections as cannoli, spumoni, tortini and tartufo. Smoke free premises.

(See map p. 330)

TOMMASO'S
◆◆ Italian
Lunch: $7-$11   **Dinner:** $13-$27   **Phone:** 718/236-9883   216
Location: Belt Pkwy, Bay 8th St exit, 0.6 mi ne. 1464 86th St 11228. **Hours:** 11:30 am-11 pm, Mon-4 pm, Sat noon-midnight, Sun noon-11 pm. Closed: 12/25 & Mon. **Reservations:** suggested. **Features:** casual dress; health conscious menu items; carryout; cocktails; a la carte. A warm, cozy atmosphere pervades this friendly neighborhood restaurant. The menu offers pasta, chicken and fish, as well as well-prepared quail, veal and lamb. Many desserts are made in-house. Family pictures and crystal figurines adorn the dining room. Smoke free premises. **Cards:** AE, DI, MC, VI.

The following restaurant has not been inspected by AAA but is listed for your information only.

LA BOUILLABAISE
fyi
Phone: 718/522-8275
Not inspected. **Location:** 145 Atlantic Ave. **Features:** If you've been in a stew looking for a cozy, casual French restaurant, try La Bouillabaise.

CARMEL pop. 4,800

——— RESTAURANT ———

CUTILLO'S RESTAURANT
◆◆ Continental
Lunch: $6-$11   **Dinner:** $13-$30   **Phone:** 914/225-8903
Location: I-84, exit 17, 1 mi e on SR 52, just n. 1196 Farmers Mill Rd, RD 3 10512. **Hours:** 11:30 am-10:30 pm. Closed: 12/25. **Reservations:** suggested. **Features:** casual dress; children's menu; carryout; cocktails. The Cutillo family home is decorated with many family furnishings and pictures. On the menu are many dishes named after family members, such as clams Camille, chicken Lucille, shrimp Patricia and caratelli Pasquale. Homemade cheesecake is decadent. **Cards:** DS, MC, VI.

CHAPPAQUA pop. 6,400

——— RESTAURANT ———

CRABTREES KITTLE HOUSE
◆◆◆ American
Lunch: $10-$16   **Dinner:** $18-$28   **Phone:** 914/666-8044
Location: Saw Mill Pkwy, exit 33, 0.5 mi se on Readers Digest Rd to Roaring Brook Rd (CR 117), 0.5 mi n on CR 117. 11 Kittle Rd 10514. **Hours:** noon-2:30 & 5:30-9:30 pm, Fri-10:30 pm, Sat 5:30 pm-11 pm, Sun noon-2:30 & 3-9 pm. Closed: 12/25. **Reservations:** suggested. **Features:** semi-formal attire; Sunday brunch; health conscious menu items; cocktails & lounge; valet parking; a la carte, a la carte. An award-winning list of wines complements such colorfully prepared choices as seafood stew and free-range chicken with couscous, vegetables and rice vermici. A woodsy setting and large, white pillars distinguish the stately, Colonial-style building. **Cards:** AE, DI, DS, MC, VI.

CONGERS pop. 8,000

——— RESTAURANTS ———

RESTAURANT X
◆◆◆ American
Lunch: $10-$15   **Dinner:** $17-$25   **Phone:** 914/268-6555
Location: 1 mi s on SR 303 from jct US 9 W; 4.5 mi n exit 12, I-87 (I-287). 117 N SR 303 10920. **Hours:** noon-2:30 & 5-9:30 pm, Sat from 5 pm, Sun 2 pm-9 pm. Closed major holidays & Mon. **Reservations:** suggested. **Features:** dressy casual; health conscious menu items; cocktails & lounge; a la carte. A relaxed country charm envelops the leisurely restaurant, which overlooks a duck pond. Grilled squab and crispy salmon roll tempura stand out on a menu of contemporary American cuisine. For dessert, savor warm coconut cake or rum raisin ice cream. **Cards:** AE, MC, VI.

ROMOLO'S
◆◆◆ Italian
Lunch: $11-$14   **Dinner:** $12-$22   **Phone:** 914/268-3770
Location: I-87 (I-287), exit 12, 3.5 mi n. 77 Rt 303 10920. **Hours:** 11:30 am-2:30 & 5-9:30 pm, Fri-10:30 pm, Sat 5 pm-10:30 pm, Sun 3 pm-8:30 pm. Closed major holidays. **Reservations:** suggested. **Features:** casual dress; cocktails & lounge; a la carte. Excellently seasoned dishes include ravioli stuffed with goat cheese and grilled chicken salad with endive and arugula leaves. Photographs of celebrities line the entry area. Polished servers exhibit solid menu knowledge and timely follow-up. **Cards:** AE, DI, DS, MC, VI.

CROTON-ON-HUDSON pop. 7,000

——— LODGING ———

ALEXANDER HAMILTON HOUSE
◆◆ Historic Bed & Breakfast
Phone: (914)271-6737
All Year   **1P:** $75-$150   **2P:** $95-$250   **XP:** $25   D18
Location: US 9, exit Rt 129, e to light, n on Riverside, e on Grand, then n on Hamilton to Van Wyck St. 49 Van Wyck St 10520. Fax: 914/271-3927. **Terms:** [BP] meal plan; 7 day cancellation notice; cancellation fee imposed; 2 night min stay, weekends. **Facility:** 7 rooms. Located in a quiet residential neighborhood. This historic home, built in 1889, has many modern amenities. Some rooms offer a wood burning fireplace. 2 suites with whirlpool. 3 stories, no elevator; interior corridors; designated smoking area. **All Rooms:** combo or shower baths. **Cards:** AE, DI, DS, MC, VI.

ELMSFORD pop. 3,900

------- LODGINGS -------

HAMPTON INN WHITE PLAINS/TARRYTOWN　　　　　　　　　　　　　　　**Phone:** (914)592-5680
◆◆◆　　All Year　　　　　　1P: $117-$127　　2P: $119-$129
Motel　　**Location:** SR 119 W (Tarrytown Rd); I-287, exit 1; I-87, exit 8, just s. 200 Tarrytown Rd 10523.
　　Fax: 914/592-6727. **Terms:** [CP] meal plan; small pets only. **Facility:** 156 rooms. 7 stories; interior corridors.
All Rooms: combo or shower baths. **Some Rooms:** Fee: refrigerators. **Cards:** AE, DI, DS, MC, VI. *(See color ad p 378)*

[ASK] [SD] [icons]

RAMADA INN　　　　　　　　　　　　　　　　　　　　　　　**Phone:** (914)592-3300
ⓐⓐⓐ [SAVE]　All Year　　　　　　1P: $89-$139　　2P: $99-$149　　XP: $10　　F18
◆◆　　**Location:** SR 9A, 1.5 mi n of SR 119; 1 mi n of I-287, westbound exit 2, eastbound exit 1, at jct SR 100C. 540
Motor Inn　Sawmill River Rd 10523. Fax: 914/592-3381. **Terms:** Monthly rates avail; package plans. **Facility:** 101 rooms.
　　Convenient location to major hwys, semi-rural area. 4 stories; interior corridors; heated pool. **Dining:** Restau-
　　rant; 7 am-10 pm; $11-$17; cocktails. **Recreation:** Fee: in room video game. **All Rooms:** combo or shower
baths. **Cards:** AE, CB, DI, DS, JC, MC, VI.

[SD] [icons]

------- RESTAURANT -------

ICHI RIKI RESTAURANT　　　　**Lunch:** $9-$19　　　**Dinner:** $15-$25　　**Phone:** 914/592-2220
◆◆　　**Location:** Downtown; from jct Rt 119 (Main St or Tarrytown Rd) and Rt 9A, just e on Rt 119. 1 E Main St
Ethnic　10523. **Hours:** 11:45 am-2:30 & 5:30-10 pm; Fri-11 pm; Sat noon-2:30 & 5-11 pm; Sun 5 pm-9:30 pm.
　　Closed: Mon. **Reservations:** suggested. **Features:** casual dress; carryout; cocktails; a la carte. Japanese
music and art, tatami rooms and servers in kimonos lend to the authentic feel of the comfortable restaurant. The menu lists
varied sushi and sashimi, as well as wonderfully seasoned preparations of seafood, beef, pork and chicken. Smoke free
premises. **Cards:** AE, CB, DI, MC, VI.　　　　　　　　　　　　　　　　　　　　　[X]

HARTSDALE pop. 9,600

------- RESTAURANT -------

CAFE MEZE'　　　　　　　　　　**Dinner:** $16-$24　　　　　　**Phone:** 914/428-2400
◆◆◆　　**Location:** Just n of jct Hartsdale and Central aves. 20 N Central Ave 10530. **Hours:** 5:30 pm-10 pm, Fri &
Ethnic　Sat-10:30 pm, Sun 9:30 pm. Closed: 7/4 & 12/25. **Reservations:** suggested; weekends. **Features:** casual
　　dress; health conscious menu items; cocktails & lounge; a la carte. Lobster bisque with shiitake mushrooms
and black Angus steak with broccoli and mushrooms are representative of fare on the upscale restaurant's menu. Dark
wood millwork and spot lighting enhance the dining room. In-house desserts are outstanding. Smoke free premises.
Cards: AE, DI, DS, MC, VI.　　　　　　　　　　　　　　　　　　　　　　　　[X]

HAWTHORNE pop. 4,800

------- LODGING -------

The following lodging was either not inspected or did not
meet AAA rating requirements but is listed for your information only.

COMFORT INN & SUITES　　　　　　　　　　　　　　　　　　　**Phone:** (914)592-8600
ⓐⓐⓐ [SAVE]　All Year　　　　　　1P: $105-$115　　2P: $120-$130　　XP: $15　　F18
[fyi]　　Under major renovation, scheduled to be completed June 2000. **Last rated:** ◆ **Location:** Sawmill River Pkwy
Motel　northbound, Hawthorne 9A-100, exit 25; southbound, from Eastview exit, left under overpass, to Sawmill Pkwy
　　N; 2.5 mi n of I-287 W, exit 2. 20 Sawmill River Rd 10532. Fax: 914/592-7457. **Terms:** Check-in 3:30 pm; 3
day cancellation notice. **Facility:** 85 rooms. 2 stories; exterior corridors. **Dining:** Restaurant nearby.
Cards: AE, DI, DS, MC, VI. **Special Amenities:** Free local telephone calls and free newspaper.

[SD] [icons]

JAMAICA

------- LODGING -------

RADISSON HOTEL-JFK AIRPORT　　　　　　　　　　　　　　　**Phone:** (718)322-2300
◆◆◆　　6/1-10/31 & 1/1-4/30　　1P: $159　　2P: $159　　XP: $15　　F16
Hotel　5/1-5/31 & 11/1-12/31　　1P: $149　　2P: $149　　XP: $15　　F16
　　Location: From Van Wyck Expwy, exit 2 (Rockaway Blvd), just e to 140th St, then s. 135-30 140th St 11436.
Fax: 718/322-6894. **Facility:** 386 rooms. Stylish modern decor. Large well-equipped exercise room overlooks runway. 12 sto-
ries; interior corridors. **Services:** gift shop. **Cards:** AE, CB, DI, DS, MC, VI.

[icons]

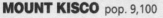

MOUNT KISCO pop. 9,100

―――― LODGING ――――

HOLIDAY INN
[AAA] [SAVE]
◆◆◆
Motor Inn

All Year   1P: $145-$160   **Phone:** (914)241-2600
Location: Sawmill Pkwy, exit 37, just e. 1 Holiday Inn Dr 10549. Fax: 914/241-4742. **Terms:** Monthly rates avail; package plans; pets, $25 extra charge. **Facility:** 122 rooms. Whirlpool room; 2 stories; interior corridors. **Dining:** Restaurant; 6 am-10:30 pm; $12-$20; cocktails. **All Rooms:** extended cable TV. **Some Rooms:** Fee: refrigerators. **Cards:** AE, DI, DS, MC, VI. **Special Amenities:** Free room upgrade and preferred room (each subject to availability with advanced reservations).
XP: $10   F18

(SD) 🐾 🛏 🍴 🍸 🐕 ⬇ 🔥 📷 ✕ 🎥 🖨 💻 🖥 🔋 [DATA PORT] 🚗 [handicap]

NANUET pop. 14,100

―――― LODGING ――――

COMFORT INN
[AAA] [SAVE]
◆◆◆
Motor Inn

All Year   1P: $96-$150   2P: $101-$150   **Phone:** (914)623-6000
Location: Jct SR 59/304, just e. 425 Rt 59 E 10954. Fax: 914/623-9338. **Terms:** [ECP] meal plan; weekly & monthly rates avail; 3 day cancellation notice. **Facility:** 100 rooms. 2 whirlpool rooms, $115-$170; 2-3 stories; interior corridors. **Dining:** Restaurant; 7 am-11 & 5-10 pm; $12-$18; health conscious menu items; cocktails. **Some Rooms:** Fee: refrigerators. **Cards:** AE, CB, DI, DS, JC, MC, VI. **Special Amenities:** Free breakfast and free newspaper.
XP: $10   F18

(SD) 🍴 🍸 🐕 ⬇ 🔥 ✕ 🎥 🖨 💻 🖥 🔋 [DATA PORT] 🚗 [handicap]

NEW ROCHELLE pop. 67,700

―――― LODGING ――――

RAMADA PLAZA HOTEL
[AAA] [SAVE]
◆◆
Hotel

All Year   1P: $109   2P: $119   **Phone:** (914)576-3700
Location: I-95, exit 16, via Cedar St. 1 Ramada Plaza 10801. Fax: 914/576-5864. **Terms:** Package plans. **Facility:** 130 rooms. 10 stories; interior corridors. **Dining:** Restaurant; 6:30 am-10 pm; $10-$17; cocktails. **Cards:** AE, CB, DI, DS, MC, VI. **Special Amenities:** Free local telephone calls. *(See color ad below)*
XP: $10   F18

🍴 🍸 🐕 ⬇ 🔥 ✕ 🎥 [VCR] 🖨 💻 🖥 🔋 [DATA PORT] 🚗 [handicap]

Stop! Savings Ahead

[AAA]

When you see the red [SAVE] icon next to listings in this book, you know these establishments offer at least a 10% savings to AAA members!

So, as you're turning the pages, remember to stop when you see [SAVE]. It's your guarantee of savings.

Travel With Someone You Trust

NYACK pop. 6,600

———— LODGINGS ————

BEST WESTERN NYACK ON HUDSON
Phone: (914)358-8100
AAA SAVE
All Year 1P: $99-$119 2P: $99-$119 XP: $5 F17
◆ ◆
Location: I-87, exit 11, New York Thrwy northbound exit on right; southbound exit to light, left on Rt 59, 0.3 mi
Motor Inn on left. 26 Rt 59 10960. Fax: 914/338-3644. **Facility:** 80 rooms. 2 stories; exterior corridors. **Dining:** Restaurant; 6 am-1 am; $8-$12; cocktails. **Services:** winter plug-ins. **All Rooms:** extended cable TV. **Cards:** AE, CB, DI, DS, MC, VI. **Special Amenities:** Early check-in/late check-out and free newspaper.
(See color ad below)

SUPER 8 MOTEL
Phone: 914/353-3880
◆ ◆
Property failed to provide current rates
Motel **Location:** I-287, exit 11; SR 59, just w. 47 Rt 59 10960. Fax: 914/353-0271. **Facility:** 43 rooms. 2 stories; interior corridors. **Cards:** AE, CB, DI, DS, MC, VI.

———— RESTAURANTS ————

THE HUDSON HOUSE OF NYACK **Lunch:** $7-$9 **Dinner:** $14-$19 Phone: 914/353-1355
◆ ◆
Location: Downtown; jct Franklin and Main sts, just e. 134 Main St 10960. **Hours:** 11:30 am-2:30 & 5:30-10
American pm, Fri & Sat-11 pm, Sun 11:30 am-2:30 & 4:30-9:30 pm. Closed: 12/25 & Mon. **Reservations:** suggested; Fri & Sat. **Features:** casual dress; carryout; cocktails; a la carte. The restaurant delivers complex cuisine, such as blackened catfish over artichoke hearts, radicchio, Belgian endive, mesclun, red potatoes and orange slices. The restored storefront building exudes a quaint, comfortable charm. Desserts are homemade. **Cards:** AE, MC, VI.

ICHI RIKI **Lunch:** $8-$15 **Dinner:** $15-$25 Phone: 914/358-7977
◆ ◆
Location: Downtown; on continuation of SR 59. 110 Main St 10960. **Hours:** noon-2:30 & 5:30-10 pm, Fri-11
Ethnic pm, Sat 5 pm-11 pm, Sun 5 pm-9:30 pm. Closed: Mon. **Reservations:** suggested; weekends. **Features:** casual dress; health conscious menu; carryout; cocktails & lounge; street parking. Japanese music and art, tatami rooms and servers in kimonos lend to the authentic feel of the comfortable restaurant. The menu lists varied sushi and sashimi, as well as wonderfully seasoned preparations of seafood, beef, pork and chicken. **Cards:** AE, CB, DI, MC, VI.

ORANGEBURG pop. 3,600

———— LODGING ————

ORANGEBURG HOLIDAY INN & REGISTRY HOTEL Phone: (914)359-7000
◆ ◆ ◆
1/1-4/30 1P: $119-$159 2P: $119-$159 XP: $10 F18
Motor Inn 5/1-12/31 1P: $114-$149 2P: $114-$149 XP: $10 F18
Location: SR 303, 4 mi s of I-87 (287), exit 12; 1 mi n of Palisades Interstate Pkwy, exit 5N northbound, 1 mi e of exit 6E. 329 Rt 303 10962. Fax: 914/359-7196. **Facility:** 167 rooms. 2-3 stories; interior corridors. **Services:** area transportation. **All Rooms:** combo or shower baths. **Some Rooms:** Fee: refrigerators. **Cards:** AE, CB, DI, DS, JC, MC, VI.

OSSINING pop. 22,600

———— RESTAURANT ————

GUIDA'S **Lunch:** $10-$15 **Dinner:** $20-$30 Phone: 914/941-2662
◆ ◆ ◆
Location: Downtown, corner of Rt 9 and Main St. 199 Main St 10562. **Hours:** 11:30 am-10 pm, Fri & Sat-11
Italian pm, Sun 1 pm-10 pm. Closed: 11/23 & 12/25. **Reservations:** suggested. **Features:** casual dress; carryout; cocktails; street parking & valet parking; a la carte. Sconce lighting, ornately framed mirrors and upscale table settings enhance the sophisticated appeal of the downtown restaurant. The spaghetti, served with tomatoes and a spicy sauce sprinkled with sliced olives, is fresh and colorfully presented. **Cards:** AE, DI, MC, VI.

PEARL RIVER pop. 15,300

—— LODGING ——

HILTON PEARL RIVER
♦♦♦ All Year   1P: $129-$189   2P: $145-$205   XP: $16   F18
Hotel   **Location:** Palisades Interstate Pkwy, exit 6 W, 2.5 mi w. 500 Veterans Memorial Dr 10965. Fax: 914/735-9005.
Terms: Cancellation fee imposed. **Facility:** 150 rooms. Beautiful chateau-style building nestled on 17 pictur-
esque acres, adjoining golf course. Spacious accommodations. 5 stories; interior corridors; heated pool. **Dining:** entertain-
ment. **Services:** area transportation. **Cards:** AE, CB, DI, DS, JC, MC, VI. *(See color ad p 57)*

Phone: (914)735-9000

PEEKSKILL pop. 19,500

—— LODGING ——

PEEKSKILL INN   **Phone:** (914)739-1500
All Year   1P: $95-$120   2P: $95-$120
♦♦   **Location:** Rt 9 and jct Rt 6, e to top of Main St. 634 Main St 10566. Fax: 914/739-7067. **Terms:** [CP] meal
Motor Inn   plan; small pets only. **Facility:** 53 rooms. Located on hilltop with pleasant views of the Hudson Valley and
water. 2 stories; exterior corridors. **Dining:** Restaurant; 11:30 am-10 pm; $12-$18; cocktails. **Cards:** AE, DI,
DS, MC, VI.

—— RESTAURANT ——

—— **The following restaurant has not been inspected by AAA** ——
but is listed for your information only.

MONTEVERDE AT OLDSTONE   **Phone:** 914/739-5000
[fyi]   Not inspected. **Location:** Rt 6 & 202 W. **Features:** This 18th-century mansion overlooks the Hudson River
and features a Continental menu.

PORT CHESTER pop. 24,700

—— RESTAURANT ——

THE WILLETT HOUSE   **Lunch:** $9-$21   **Dinner:** $15-$33   **Phone:** 914/939-7500
♦♦   **Location:** Corner of Willett Ave and Main St. 20 Willett Ave 10573. **Hours:** 11:45 am-10 pm, Sat 4 pm-11
Steak and   pm, Sun 4 pm-9 pm. Closed: 1/1. **Reservations:** suggested. **Features:** casual dress; children's menu;
Seafood   cocktails & lounge; fee for parking; a la carte. The large and attractive red-brick restaurant welcomes families
to enjoy well-prepared selections of prime steak, plus lobster and grilled seafood. Lighter lunch fare includes
such tasty sandwiches as the BLT, which comes with homemade potato chips. **Cards:** AE, DI, MC, VI.

POUND RIDGE pop. 900

—— RESTAURANT ——

THE INN AT POUND RIDGE Historical   **Lunch:** $10-$14   **Dinner:** $19-$30   **Phone:** 914/764-5779
♦♦♦ **Location:** In the hamlet; just n of jct 172 on SR 137. 258 Westchester Ave (SR 137) 10576.
American   **Hours:** noon-2:30 & 6-9:30 pm, Fri-10:30 pm, Sat 6 pm-10:30 pm, Sun noon-9 pm. Closed: 1/1, 12/25 &
Mon. **Reservations:** suggested. **Features:** semi-formal attire; health conscious menu items; cocktails &
lounge; a la carte. Nestled amid beautifully landscaped grounds, the historic inn features extensive accents of wood and
stone. Rack of lamb is the signature dish on a menu of contemporary American cuisine. An accomplished pianist performs
on Saturday nights. **Cards:** AE, DI, MC, VI.

RYE pop. 14,900

------ LODGING ------

COURTYARD BY MARRIOTT
◆◆◆   All Year   1P: $169   2P: $169   **Phone:** (914)921-1110
Motel   **Location:** I-95 N, exit 22, 0.3 mi n; I-95 S, exit 21, just right, stay right thru light; I-95 N, exit 22; I-287, exit 11,
just right; left at 2nd set of lights. 631 Midland Ave 10580. Fax: 914/921-2446. **Facility:** 145 rooms. 4 stories;
interior corridors; heated pool. **All Rooms:** combo or shower baths. **Cards:** AE, DI, DS, MC, VI.

------ RESTAURANTS ------

BLACK BASS GRILLE   **Dinner:** $14-$27   **Phone:** 914/967-6700
◆◆   **Location:** I-95, exit 20, 0.5 mi s on US 1 (Central Ave). 2 Central Ave 10580. **Hours:** 5:30 pm-9:30 pm, Fri
American & Sat-10:30 pm, Sun 5 pm-9 pm. Closed major holidays. **Features:** carryout; cocktails & lounge; a la carte.
The charming restaurant is decorated in the motif of a rustic fishing lodge, with plenty of nautical accents
and a cozy fireplace as a focal point. Menu selections—such as fresh seafood, veal and pasta—are prepared with a
creative, contemporary flair. **Cards:** AE, DI, MC, VI.

LA PANETIERE   **Lunch:** $17-$27   **Dinner:** $25-$34   **Phone:** 914/967-8140
◆◆◆◆   **Location:** I-95, exit 19, 0.8 mi e to Milton Rd, 0.5 mi s. 530 Milton Rd 10580. **Hours:** noon-2:30 & 6-9:30
French   pm, Sat from 6 pm, Sun 1 pm-2:30 & 5-8:30 pm. Closed: 1/1. **Reservations:** required.
Features: semi-formal attire; cocktails & lounge; a la carte. Clay figurines are stationed around the formal
dining room, which is decorated with country French furnishings. Pumpkin soup and veal osso bucco are representative of
the fantastic cuisine. The tasting menu is a showcase for the chef's creativity. Smoke free premises. **Cards:** AE, DI, DS,
MC, VI.

RYE BROOK pop. 7,800

------ LODGING ------

HILTON RYE TOWN   **Phone:** (914)939-6300
      5/1-7/1 & 9/3-4/30   1P: $109-$269   2P: $129-$289   XP: $20   F18
      7/2-9/2   1P: $129-$259   2P: $149-$279   XP: $20   F18
◆◆◆◆   **Location:** I-287, exit 10, 0.3 mi n. 699 Westchester Ave 10573. Fax: 914/939-5328. **Terms:** Monthly rates
Hotel   avail; cancellation fee imposed; package plans. **Facility:** 440 rooms. Landscaped grounds in secluded wooded
area. Country elegance. 4 stories; interior corridors; 2 pools, 1 indoor heated, saunas, whirlpool. Fee: 3 tennis
courts (3 indoor, 3 lighted). **Dining:** Dining room, coffee shop; 6:30 am-10:30 pm; $21-$42; cocktails; seasonal summer restaurant & pool bar; entertainment. **Services:** gift shop. **Recreation:** basketball, shuffleboard. **All Rooms:** combo or shower
baths, honor bars. **Cards:** AE, CB, DI, DS, JC, MC, VI. **Special Amenities:** Free newspaper and preferred room (subject
to availability with advanced reservations). (See color ad p 57 & below)

STATEN ISLAND

──── RESTAURANTS ────

THE OLD BERMUDA INN
◆◆◆ **Location:** SR 440, exit 4, just sw. 2512 Arthur Kill Rd 10309. **Hours:** 4 pm-10 pm, Fri & Sat-11 pm. Closed:
Continental   12/25 & Sun-Tues. **Reservations:** suggested. **Features:** dressy casual; Sunday brunch; early bird specials;
cocktails & lounge; valet parking. The 1830s mansion, restored to resemble a Henry VIII pub, has a cozy,
intimate ambience. Eggplant Napoleon and chicken chasseur stand out on a menu of well-prepared choices. Bananas
Hamilton, served on a bed of creme anglaise, is exquisite. Smoke free premises. **Cards:** AE, DI, DS, MC, VI.
Dinner: $14-$26   **Phone:** 718/948-7600
☒

───── *The following restaurant has not been inspected by AAA* ─────
but is listed for your information only.

GOOD FELLA'S OLD WORLD BRICK OVEN PIZZA   **Phone:** 718/987-2422
fyi   Not inspected. **Location:** I-278, 2 mi s Bayst/Hylan Blvd, Hylan Blvd and Garretson Ave. 1716 Hylan Blvd.
Features: Their prize winning, signature pizza—Pizza A'la Vodka—salads, pasta and variety of desserts are
offered at this traditional New York pizza parlor.

SUFFERN pop. 11,100

──── LODGINGS ────

HOLIDAY INN-SUFFERN   **Phone:** (914)357-4800
AAA SAVE   All Year   1P: $120   2P: $120
◆◆◆   **Location:** I-287, exit 14B, just n. 3 Executive Blvd 10901. Fax: 914/368-0471. **Terms:** [AP] meal plan; monthly
Motor Inn   rates avail; check-in 4 pm; cancellation fee imposed; package plans, weekends. **Facility:** 240 rooms. Suites
with microwave, coffeemaker & refrigerator; 6 whirlpool rooms; 3 stories; interior corridors; heated pool, sauna,
whirlpool. **Dining:** Restaurant; 6:30 am-10, noon-2 & 5-10 pm, Fri-11 pm, Sat 7 am-10:30, noon-2 & 5-11 pm;
Sun 7 am-11 & 5-10 pm; $12-$25; health conscious menu items; cocktails. **Some Rooms:** Fee: refrigerators. **Cards:** AE, CB,
DI, DS, MC, VI. *(See color ad p 365)*

WELLESLEY INN & SUITES   **Phone:** (914)368-1900
AAA SAVE   All Year   1P: $71-$103   2P: $76-$103   XP: $8
◆◆   **Location:** I-87 (287), exit 14B, just s. 17 N Airmont Rd 10901. Fax: 914/368-1927. **Terms:** [CP] meal plan;
Motel   monthly rates avail; small pets only. **Facility:** 95 rooms. 4 stories; interior corridors. **Dining:** Restaurant nearby.
All Rooms: combo or shower baths. **Cards:** AE, CB, DI, DS, JC, MC, VI. **Special Amenities:** Free breakfast
and free newspaper. *(See color ad p 4)*

──── RESTAURANT ────

MARCELLO'S OF SUFFERN   **Lunch:** $11-$14   **Dinner:** $18-$27   **Phone:** 914/357-9108
AAA   **Location:** Center; between Orange and Chestnut aves. 21 Lafayette Ave 10901. **Hours:** noon-2 & 5-9:30
◆◆◆   pm, Sat 5 pm-9:30 pm, Sun 4:30 pm-8:30 pm. Closed major holidays. **Reservations:** suggested.
Italian   **Features:** casual dress; health conscious menu items; cocktails; street parking; a la carte. Autographed
photographs of celebrities line the reception area of the attractively upscale dining room. The menu is classic
Italian, with such delicious dishes as pasta with sea scallops and cherry tomatoes. Opt for the chocolate
torte for dessert. **Cards:** AE, CB, DI, DS, MC, VI.
☒

TARRYTOWN pop. 10,700

──── LODGINGS ────

THE CASTLE AT TARRYTOWN   **Phone:** 914/631-1980
◆◆◆◆   11/2-4/30   1P: $275-$295   2P: $275-$295   XP: $50   F3
Historic   5/1-11/1   1P: $255-$275   2P: $255-$275   XP: $50   F3
Country Inn   **Location:** I-287, exit 1, 0.3 mi on 119 W to Benedict Ave, 0.6 mi; opposite entrance to Hackley School. 400
Benedict Ave 10591. Fax: 914/631-4612. **Terms:** Check-in 4 pm; 7 day cancellation notice; cancellation fee
imposed; package plans. **Facility:** 31 rooms. Turn-of-the-century stone castle overlooking Hudson River. Luxurious public
areas and rooms furnished in antiques and reproductions. Some rooms with fireplace. 3-4 stories; interior corridors; 1 tennis
court. **Services:** Fee: massage. **Recreation:** hiking trails, jogging. Fee: bicycles. **All Rooms:** safes, honor bars. **Cards:** AE,
DI, MC, VI.

COURTYARD BY MARRIOTT   **Phone:** (914)631-1122
◆◆◆   All Year   1P: $159-$179   2P: $159-$179
Motel   **Location:** I-287, exit 1, 1 mi n. 475 White Plains Rd 10591. Fax: 914/631-1357. **Terms:** Cancellation fee imposed. **Facility:** 139 rooms. Situated atop a scenic hillside. 3 stories; interior corridors; small heated indoor
pool. **All Rooms:** combo or shower baths. **Cards:** AE, DI, DS, MC, VI.

HILTON OF TARRYTOWN   **Phone:** (914)631-5700
AAA SAVE   12/17-4/30   1P: $109-$259   2P: $129-$279   XP: $20   F18
◆◆◆   5/1-7/1 & 9/3-12/16   1P: $109-$249   2P: $129-$269   XP: $20   F18
Motor Inn   7/2-9/2   1P: $129-$229   2P: $149-$249   XP: $20   F18
Location: US 9 S thruway, I-287/87, exit 9. 455 S Broadway 10591. Fax: 914/631-0075. **Terms:** Weekly &
monthly rates avail; cancellation fee imposed; package plans; pets dep req. **Facility:** 246 rooms. Spacious
landscaped grounds located in the Hudson River Valley. Traditional room decor. 2 stories; interior corridors; valley view; 2
pools, 1 indoor heated, wading pool, saunas, whirlpool; 2 tennis courts; playground. **Dining:** Restaurant; outdoor terrace in
season; 6:30 am-10 pm; $15-$25; health conscious menu items; cocktails. **Services:** gift shop. **Recreation:** jogging.
All Rooms: honor bars. **Some Rooms:** Fee: refrigerators. **Cards:** AE, CB, DI, DS, JC, MC, VI. **Special Amenities:** Free
newspaper and preferred room *(subject to availability with advanced reservations)*. *(See color ad p 57 & p 376)*

TARRYTOWN HOUSE
◆ ◆ ◆
Motel

			Phone: (914)591-8200
5/1-6/30 & 9/1-10/31	1P: $145-$195	2P: $145-$195	XP: $15 F11
7/1-8/31 & 11/1-4/30	1P: $135-$185	2P: $135-$185	XP: $15 F11

Location: 1 mi s of Tappan Zee Bridge; off SR 9, opposite Sunnyside. E Sunnyside Ln 10591 (PO Box 222). Fax: 914/591-3131. **Terms:** [BP] meal plan; check-in 4 pm; package plans. **Facility:** 148 rooms. 26 acre estate. 2 historic mansions with modern facilities and accommodations. Many rooms with scenic views of the Hudson Valley; professional, courteous staff in a tranquil setting. 5 stories; interior corridors; 2 pools, 1 indoor heated; racquetball court, 2 tennis courts. **Services:** gift shop. **Some Rooms:** Fee: refrigerators. **Cards:** AE, DI, DS, MC, VI.

WESTCHESTER MARRIOTT HOTEL
◆ ◆ ◆
Hotel

			Phone: (914)631-2200
1/1-4/30	1P: $220-$260	2P: $220-$260	
5/1-12/31	1P: $205-$245	2P: $205-$245	

Location: SR 119, 0.3 mi w of I-287, exit 1; I-87, exit 8, 1.3 mi e on 119. 670 White Plains Rd 10591. Fax: 914/631-7819. **Terms:** Check-in 4 pm; package plans. **Facility:** 444 rooms. Stylish rooms; some with balcony. 10 stories; interior corridors; heated pool. **Dining:** nightclub. **Services:** gift shop. Fee: massage. **Recreation:** sports court. **All Rooms:** combo or shower baths. **Cards:** AE, CB, DI, DS, JC, MC, VI.

RESTAURANTS

EQUUS
◆ ◆ ◆ ◆
French

Lunch: $10-$16	**Dinner:** $14-$32	**Phone:** 914/631-1980

Location: I-287, exit 1, 0.3 mi on 119 W to Benedict Ave, 0.6 mi; opposite entrance to Hackley School; in The Castle at Tarrytown. 400 Benedict Ave 10591. **Hours:** 7 am-10, noon-2:30 & 6-10 pm. **Reservations:** suggested. **Features:** semi-formal attire; Sunday brunch; health conscious menu; cocktails & lounge; valet parking; a la carte, also prix fixe. In a veritable stone castle atop a hill overlooking the Hudson River, the restaurant is as noted for its setting as for its impressive contemporary French cuisine. Grilled salmon, for example, is simply superb—perfectly seasoned, yet moist and opaque. Smoke free premises. **Cards:** AE, DI, MC, VI.

HORSEFEATHERS
◆ ◆
American

Lunch: $7-$12	**Dinner:** $10-$20	**Phone:** 914/631-6606

Location: Downtown. 94 N Broadway (SR 9) 10591. **Hours:** 11:30 am-10 pm, Fri-11:30 pm, Sun Noon-9 pm. Closed major holidays. **Features:** children's menu; health conscious menu items; carryout; cocktails & lounge; fee for parking. Decor is reflective of the 1700s in this quaint, casual restaurant. A literary theme— with books and murals of authors—ties it all together. The menu centers on wholesome, home-style fare, such as burgers, steaks and pasta. Weekend brunch is popular. **Cards:** AE, DI, DS, MC, VI.

WHITE PLAINS pop. 48,700

LODGINGS

CROWNE PLAZA WHITE PLAINS
◆ ◆ ◆
Hotel

			Phone: (914)682-0050
All Year	1P: $169-$189	2P: $169-$189	

Location: Cross Westchester Expwy, I-287, exit 8 westbound to Rt 119 via Bloomingdale Rd, right on Maple Ave; exit 8W eastbound, left on Bloomingdale Rd, right on Maple. 66 Hale Ave 10601. Fax: 914/682-0405. **Terms:** Cancellation fee imposed; package plans. **Facility:** 400 rooms. Contemporary design, spacious accommodations. Adjacent to Westchester Mall. 14 stories; interior corridors; heated pool. **Services:** gift shop; area transportation. **All Rooms:** combo or shower baths, safes. **Some Rooms:** Fee: refrigerators. **Cards:** AE, DI, DS, MC, VI.

RENAISSANCE WESTCHESTER HOTEL
◆ ◆ ◆
Hotel

			Phone: (914)694-5400
4/2-4/30	1P: $209-$219	2P: $209-$219	XP: $10
9/3-12/31	1P: $205-$215	2P: $205-$215	XP: $10
5/1-9/2 & 1/1-4/1	1P: $199-$209	2P: $199-$209	XP: $10

Location: I-287 W, exit 9 N-S, 0.8 mi w on Westchester Ave, I-287 E, exit 9N-S, left to Kenilworth Rd, left to Westchester Ave then 0.5 mi to Red Oak Ln, follow signs. 80 W Red Oak Ln 10604. Fax: 914/694-5616. **Terms:** Package plans. **Facility:** 350 rooms. Spacious, attractive grounds. Rural setting, large rooms. 6 stories; interior corridors; heated pool. Fee: 2 lighted tennis courts. **Services:** gift shop. **Recreation:** hiking trails. **All Rooms:** honor bars. **Some Rooms:** Fee: refrigerators, VCR. **Cards:** AE, DI, DS, JC, MC, VI.

——— RESTAURANTS ———

DAWAT
◆◆
Ethnic

Lunch: $10   **Dinner:** $12-$20   **Phone:** 914/428-4411
Location: Downtown; from intersection of Mamaroneck Ave and E Post Rd, just ne. 230 E Post Rd 10601.
Hours: noon-2:45 & 5:30-10:15 pm, Fri & Sat-10:45 pm, Sun noon-2:45 & 5-10 pm.
Reservations: suggested. **Features:** casual dress; carryout; cocktails; a la carte. Indian music plays in the background of the dining room, which is decorated with artwork of carved wood and painted faces. The daily luncheon buffet lays out piquant selections of beef, chicken, rice and lamb. Service is consistent and thorough. **Cards:** AE, DI, MC, VI.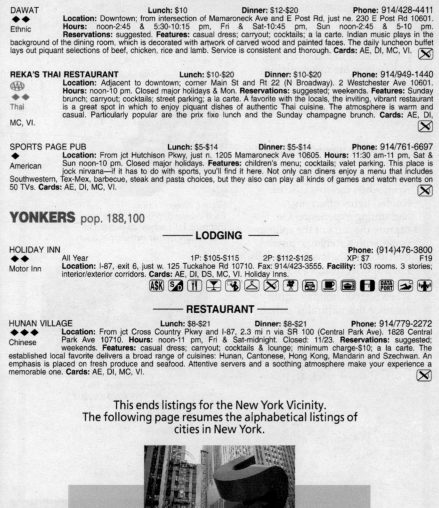

REKA'S THAI RESTAURANT
ΔΔΔ
◆◆
Thai

MC, VI.

Lunch: $10-$20   **Dinner:** $10-$20   **Phone:** 914/949-1440
Location: Adjacent to downtown; corner Main St and Rt 22 (N Broadway). 2 Westchester Ave 10601.
Hours: noon-10 pm. Closed major holidays & Mon. **Reservations:** suggested; weekends. **Features:** Sunday brunch; carryout; cocktails; street parking; a la carte. A favorite with the locals, the inviting, vibrant restaurant is a great spot in which to enjoy piquant dishes of authentic Thai cuisine. The atmosphere is warm and casual. Particularly popular are the prix fixe lunch and the Sunday champagne brunch. **Cards:** AE, DI,

SPORTS PAGE PUB
◆
American

Lunch: $5-$14   **Dinner:** $5-$14   **Phone:** 914/761-6697
Location: From jct Hutchison Pkwy, just n. 1205 Mamaroneck Ave 10605. **Hours:** 11:30 am-11 pm, Sat & Sun noon-10 pm. Closed major holidays. **Features:** children's menu; cocktails; valet parking. This place is jock nirvana—if it has to do with sports, you'll find it here. Not only can diners enjoy a menu that includes Southwestern, Tex-Mex, barbecue, steak and pasta choices, but they also can play all kinds of games and watch events on 50 TVs. **Cards:** AE, DI, MC, VI.

YONKERS pop. 188,100

——— LODGING ———

HOLIDAY INN
◆◆
Motor Inn

Phone: (914)476-3800
All Year   1P: $105-$115   2P: $112-$125   XP: $7   F19
Location: I-87, exit 6, just w. 125 Tuckahoe Rd 10710. Fax: 914/423-3555. **Facility:** 103 rooms. 3 stories; interior/exterior corridors. **Cards:** AE, DI, DS, MC, VI. Holiday Inns.

——— RESTAURANT ———

HUNAN VILLAGE
◆◆◆
Chinese

Lunch: $8-$21   **Dinner:** $8-$21   **Phone:** 914/779-2272
Location: From jct Cross Country Pkwy and I-87, 2.3 mi n via SR 100 (Central Park Ave). 1828 Central Park Ave 10710. **Hours:** noon-11 pm, Fri & Sat-midnight. Closed: 11/23. **Reservations:** suggested; weekends. **Features:** casual dress; carryout; cocktails & lounge; minimum charge-$10; a la carte. The established local favorite delivers a broad range of cuisines: Hunan, Cantonese, Hong Kong, Mandarin and Szechwan. An emphasis is placed on fresh produce and seafood. Attentive servers and a soothing atmosphere make your experience a memorable one. **Cards:** AE, DI, MC, VI.

This ends listings for the New York Vicinity.
The following page resumes the alphabetical listings of
cities in New York.

Destination Niagara Falls

*W*elcome to Niagara Falls, where the mesmerizing cataracts will capture your heart forever. The Honeymoon Capital attracts some 50,000 newlyweds yearly.

*T*here are more ways than one to view the plunging water. Take an evening stroll along the river, when the spectacle of colored lights offers an enchanting experience. Or capture the aura of the rolling water with a romantic picnic overlooking the marvelous falls. For a special treat, visit in early winter for the Festival of Lights, when 500,000 holiday lights enhance this natural wonder.

Skyline, Niagara Falls.
Each year, millions visit these awe inspiring falls where 20 percent of the world's freshwater supply flows.

Niagara Reservation State Park.
Stop by New York's oldest state park and view the electronic displays at the visitor center. (See listing page 148)

Niagara Falls

CANADA | U.S.A.

QEW

Lewiston   **See**   *Newfane*   104

Vicinity map page 384

405

Sanborn

Niagara Falls   ✈

20

See Vicinity map page 385   ONT. | N.Y.   190   *Wheatfield*

QEW   290

Touring Niagara Falls.
Whether you hike to the bottom of the falls via footpaths, ride aboard a double-decker trolley, or buzz over them in a helicopter, touring this majestic site is the thing to do.
(See listing page 149)

*P*laces included in this AAA Destination City:

Niagara Falls......386
Lewiston.............396
Newfane..............396
Sanborn..............396
Wheatfield...........396
Youngstown........397

Nearby Ontario
Niagara Falls....397

NIAGARA FALLS
including Niagara Falls, Ontario
Niagara Falls, New York *pop. 61,800*

Accommodations for the Canadian Side are listed under Niagara Falls, Ontario.

This index helps you "spot" where approved accommodations are located on the detailed maps that follow. Rate ranges are for comparison only and show the property's high season. Turn to the listing page for more detailed rate information and consult display ads for special promotions. Restaurant rate range is for dinner unless only lunch (L) is served.

Spotter/Map Page Number	OA	NIAGARA FALLS, NEW YORK - Lodgings	Diamond Rating	Rate Range High Season	Listing Page
❶ / p. 384	⬨	Travelers Budget Inn	◆	$29-$109 SAVE	395
❸ / p. 384	⬨	Howard Johnson Hotel at the Falls - see color ad p 391	◆◆	$100-$150 SAVE	392
❹ / p. 384	⬨	Days Inn at the Falls - see color ad p 388	◆◆	$89-$200 SAVE	389
❺ / p. 384	⬨	Holiday Inn Select-Niagara Falls	◆◆◆	$89-$159 SAVE	392
❻ / p. 384	⬨	Thriftlodge - see color ad p 386	◆◆	$45-$139 SAVE	395
❾ / p. 384	⬨	Ramada By the Falls - see color ad p 390	◆◆	$59-$179 SAVE	393
⓫ / p. 384	⬨	Hospitality Inn	◆◆	$79-$120 SAVE	392
⓬ / p. 384	⬨	Comfort Inn The Pointe - see color ad p 388	◆◆◆	$89-$159 SAVE	386
⓭ / p. 384	⬨	Best Western Inn on the River - see color ad p 387	◆◆◆	$89-$169 SAVE	386
⓮ / p. 384	⬨	Howard Johnson Inn-Niagara - see color ad p 393	◆◆	$55-$149 SAVE	393
⓰ / p. 384	⬨	Riviera Motel	◆◆	$29-$99 SAVE	394
⓲ / p. 384	⬨	Knights Inn	◆◆	$68-$89 SAVE	393
⓳ / p. 384		Ramada Inn at the Falls	◆◆	$65-$145	393
⓴ / p. 384	⬨	Red Maple Inn-Niagara Falls	◆◆	$49-$199 SAVE	394
㉒ / p. 384	⬨	Driftwood Motel - see color ad p 389	◆	$34-$99 SAVE	390
㉕ / p. 384	⬨	Days Inn Riverview at the Falls - see color ad p 389	◆◆	$65-$185	389
㉖ / p. 384	⬨	The Red Coach Inn	◆◆◆	$99-$149 SAVE	394
㉗ / p. 384	⬨	Holiday Inn at the Falls - see color ad p 391	◆◆◆	$99-$269	392
㉘ / p. 384		Holley Rankine House	◆◆	$60-$120	392
㉚ / p. 384		Econo Lodge - see color ad p 390	◆◆	$55-$159	390
㉛ / p. 384	⬨	Bel Aire Motel	◆	$58-$62	386
㉞ / p. 384	⬨	Best Western Summit Inn - see color ad p 387	◆◆◆	$89-$139 SAVE	386
㊲ / p. 384	⬨	Scottish Inns - see color ad p 394	◆◆	$49-$140 SAVE	394
		NIAGARA FALLS, NEW YORK - Restaurants			
① / p. 384	⬨	Como Restaurant & Deli	◆◆	$7-$18	395
② / p. 384		John's Flaming Hearth	◆◆	$12-$19	395
③ / p. 384		Pete's Market House Restaurant	◆	$4-$12	395
④ / p. 384	⬨	The Red Coach Inn Restaurant	◆◆◆	$7-$20	395
⑥ / p. 384		Top of the Falls Restaurant	◆	$5-$8	395
⑦ / p. 384		Goose's Roost	◆	$7-$12	395
⑧ / p. 384		Timber Lodge Steakhouse	◆◆	$8-$19	395

Nearby Ontario

NIAGARA FALLS, ONTARIO

Spotter/Map Page Number	OA	NIAGARA FALLS, ONTARIO - Lodgings	Diamond Rating	Rate Range High Season	Listing Page
❶ / p. 385	⬨	Oakes Inn Fallsview - see color ad p 420	◆◆◆	Failed to provide	420
❷ / p. 385	⬨	Renaissance Fallsview Hotel - see color ad p 428	◆◆◆	$205-$444 SAVE	429
❸ / p. 385	⬨	Cascade Inn - see color ad p 405	◆	$95-$185 SAVE	406

Spotter/Map Page Number	OA	NIAGARA FALLS, ONTARIO - Lodgings (continued)	Diamond Rating	Rate Range High Season	Listing Page
4 / p. 385	⊛	Holiday Inn-By The Falls - see color ad p 414, p 435	◆◆◆	$115-$255 ⓢ	412
5 / p. 385	⊛	Hampton Inn North of the Falls	◆◆◆	$79-$299	411
6 / p. 385	⊛	Niagara Family Inn	◆	$55-$89 ⓢ	417
7 / p. 385	⊛	Cadillac Motel	◆	$59-$120	402
8 / p. 385	⊛	Chalet Motor Inn	◆◆◆	$89-$139	406
9 / p. 385	⊛	Travelodge Near The Falls - see color ad p 432	◆◆	$89-$229 ⓢ	434
10 / p. 385	⊛	Quality Hotel-Near the Falls - see color ad p 423	◆◆◆	$129-$299 ⓢ	421
11 / p. 385	⊛	Best Western Fallsview Motor Hotel - see color ad p 402	◆◆	$129-$249 ⓢ	401
12 / p. 385	⊛	Days Inn Near the Falls - see color ad p 408	◆◆	$90-$300 ⓢ	410
13 / p. 385	⊛	Howard Johnson By The Falls - see color ad p 415	◆◆◆	$99-$219	412
14 / p. 385	⊛	Imperial Hotel & Suites	◆◆◆	$129-$249 ⓢ	414
15 / p. 385	⊛	Camelot Inn - see color ad p 429	◆◆	$49-$229 ⓢ	402
16 / p. 385	⊛	Days Inn Clifton Hill/Casino - see color ad p 407	◆◆	Failed to provide	406
17 / p. 385	⊛	Hampton Inn at the Falls - see color ad starting on p 412	◆◆◆	$149-$339	411
18 / p. 385	⊛	Comfort Inn Fallsway - see color ad starting on p 425	◆◆	$79-$279 ⓢ	406
19 / p. 385	⊛	Quality Inn Fallsway - see color ad starting on p 425	◆◆	$79-$279 ⓢ	421
20 / p. 385	⊛	Budgetel Motor Inn	◆	$59-$149	402
21 / p. 385	⊛	Brock Plaza - see color ad p 403	◆◆◆	$99-$669	402
22 / p. 385	⊛	Michael's Inn-By The Falls - see color ad p 437, starting on p 418	◆◆◆	$88-$298 ⓢ	416
23 / p. 385	⊛	Comfort Inn North of the Falls	◆◆	$69-$269 ⓢ	406
24 / p. 385	⊛	Days Inn North of the Falls - see color ad p 409	◆◆	$88-$298 ⓢ	410
25 / p. 385	⊛	Crystal Motel	◆◆	$69-$149 ⓢ	406
26 / p. 385	⊛	Skyline Foxhead - see color ad p 403	◆◆◆	$99-$669	429
27 / p. 385	⊛	Canuck Motel	◆◆	$59-$149	402
28 / p. 385		Glengate Motel	◆	$50-$130	411
29 / p. 385	⊛	Sunset Inn - see color ad p 429	◆◆	$59-$169 ⓢ	430
30 / p. 385	⊛	Best Western Fireside Hotel	◆◆◆	$89-$299 ⓢ	401
31 / p. 385	⊛	Fallsview Inn - see color ad p 407	◆◆◆	$99-$189 ⓢ	410
32 / p. 385	⊛	Melody Motel	◆	$48-$88 ⓢ	416
33 / p. 385	⊛	Days Inn Fallsview District - see color ad p 409	◆◆	$75-$325 ⓢ	406
34 / p. 385	⊛	Vacation Inn - see color ad inside front cover	◆◆	$104-$225 ⓢ	434
35 / p. 385	⊛	Horseshoe Falls Motor Inn - see color ad p 413	◆◆	$69-$169 ⓢ	412
36 / p. 385	⊛	Comfort Hotel & Suites-Fallsview - see color ad p 398	◆◆◆	$129-$503 ⓢ	406
37 / p. 385	⊛	Sheraton Fallsview Hotel & Conference Centre - see color ad p 430	◆◆◆◆	$225-$270 ⓢ	429
38 / p. 385	⊛	Aurora Motel - see color ad p 400	◆	$59-$125	400
39 / p. 385	⊛	Niagara Falls Marriott Fallsview - see color ad p 417	◆◆◆◆	$259-$850	417
40 / p. 385	⊛	The President Motor Inn - see color ad p 422	◆	$59-$130	421
41 / p. 385	⊛	Lincoln Motor Inn - see color ad p 415	◆◆	$89-$199 ⓢ	416
42 / p. 385	⊛	Stanley Motor Inn	◆◆	$65-$150 ⓢ	429
43 / p. 385	⊛	Victoria Motor Inn	◆	$79-$139 ⓢ	434
44 / p. 385	⊛	Impala Motel	◆	$59-$149	414
45 / p. 385	⊛	Best Western Cairn Croft Hotel - see color ad p 401	◆◆◆	$134-$169 ⓢ	400
46 / p. 385	⊛	Knights Inn On Lundy's Lane	◆◆	$69-$239 ⓢ	416
47 / p. 385	⊛	Days Inn-Lundy's Lane - see color ad p 407	◆◆	Failed to provide	407

Spotter/Map Page Number	OA	NIAGARA FALLS, ONTARIO - Lodgings (continued)	Diamond Rating	Rate Range High Season	Listing Page
48 / p. 385	(CAA)	The Village Inn - see color ad p 433	◆	$79-$399	434
49 / p. 385		Ramada Suites Niagara - see color ad p 424	◆◆◆	$119-$219	428
50 / p. 385	(CAA)	Hilton Niagara Falls - see color ad p 409	◆◆◆	$199-$999 ⬛	411
51 / p. 385		Thriftlodge	◆◆	$80-$220	433
52 / p. 385	(CAA)	Stardust Inn	◆◆	$79-$199 ⬛	429
53 / p. 385	(CAA)	Ashbury Motel	◆	$79-$149 ⬛	400
54 / p. 385	(CAA)	Carriage House Motor Lodge - see color ad p 404	◆◆	$69-$130	403
55 / p. 385		HoJo Inn	◆◆	$60-$200 ⬛	411
56 / p. 385	(CAA)	Ameri-Cana Resort & Conference Centre - see color ad p 399	◆◆◆	$89-$199 ⬛	397
58 / p. 385	(CAA)	Four Points Hotel, Niagara Falls, By-the-Falls - see color ad p 411	◆◆◆	$109-$349 ⬛	411
61 / p. 385	(CAA)	A-1 Motel	◆	$48-$150 ⬛	397
62 / p. 385	(CAA)	Travelodge Bonaventure - see color ad p 432	◆◆◆	$89-$199 ⬛	433
63 / p. 385	(CAA)	Park Plaza - see color ad p 421	◆◆◆	$99-$199 ⬛	421
64 / p. 385	(CAA)	Flamingo Motor Inn - see color ad p 410	◆◆	$69-$169 ⬛	410
65 / p. 385	(CAA)	Ramada Coral Resort - see color ad p 424	◆◆◆	$84-$199 ⬛	424
66 / p. 385	(CAA)	Super 8 Lodge - see color ad p 431	◆◆◆	$59-$289 ⬛	430
67 / p. 385		Rodeway Inn & Suites - see color ad p 428	◆◆	$100-$150	429
68 / p. 385		Marco Polo Inn	◆◆	$69-$149	416
69 / p. 385		Kings Inn Near the Falls	◆◆	$89-$199	416
72 / p. 385	(CAA)	Midtown Lodge	◆◆	$59-$149	416
73 / p. 385	(CAA)	Niagara Parkway Court Motel	◆◆	$49-$149 ⬛	417
74 / p. 385		Surfside Inn - see ad p 431	◆◆◆	$89-$149	432
75 / p. 385	(CAA)	Niagara Falls Motor Lodge	◆◆	$88-$138	417
76 / p. 385	(CAA)	Peninsula Inn & Resort	◆◆◆	$109-$199 ⬛	421
77 / p. 385	(CAA)	Inn On The Niagara Parkway	◆	$69-$189	416
		NIAGARA FALLS, ONTARIO - Restaurants			
1 / p. 385		Minolta Tower Centre/Pinnacle Restaurant	◆◆◆	$19-$48	437
2 / p. 385	(CAA)	Victoria Park Restaurant	◆◆	$15-$21	438
3 / p. 385	(CAA)	The Skylon Tower Dining Rooms - see color ad p 156, p 437	◆◆◆	$33-$54	438
4 / p. 385		Fine Kettle 'O' Fish	◆◆	$8-$30	435
6 / p. 385	(CAA)	Hard Times	◆◆	$10-$23	436
7 / p. 385	(CAA)	The Beef Baron	◆◆	$11-$25	434
8 / p. 385	(CAA)	Mama Mia's	◆◆	$7-$22	436
10 / p. 385	(CAA)	The Last Resort Prime-Steaks-Seafood-Italian - see color ad p 436	◆◆	$8-$18	436
12 / p. 385		Frank's Tomato Pie	◆◆	$10-$20	435
13 / p. 385		Fallsview Dining Room - see color ad p 430	◆◆◆	$20-$31	435
14 / p. 385	(CAA)	Delduca's	◆◆	$10-$20	435
15 / p. 385	(CAA)	Whirlpool Restaurant	◆◆	$12-$18	438
16 / p. 385	(CAA)	Queenston Heights Restaurant	◆◆	$20-$26	438
17 / p. 385	(CAA)	Table Rock Restaurant	◆◆	$12-$21	438
18 / p. 385		The Love Boat II	◆	$5-$25	436
19 / p. 385		Farfalle	◆◆◆◆	$18-$34	435
20 / p. 385	(CAA)	Capri Restaurant	◆◆◆	$8-$25	435
21 / p. 385		La Hacienda Restaurant	◆	$7-$20	436
22 / p. 385		The Rainbow Room	◆◆◆	$15-$35	438
23 / p. 385		Mick and Angelo's Eatery and Bar	◆◆	$7-$14	437
25 / p. 385		Betty's Restaurant	◆	$7-$14	434
26 / p. 385		Happy Wanderer	◆	$10-$25	436
27 / p. 385		Penthouse Restaurant	◆◆◆	$24-$30	437
28 / p. 385		Luna Eurogrille & Lounge	◆◆	$5-$19	436
29 / p. 385		Terrapin Grille	◆◆◆	$19-$40	438

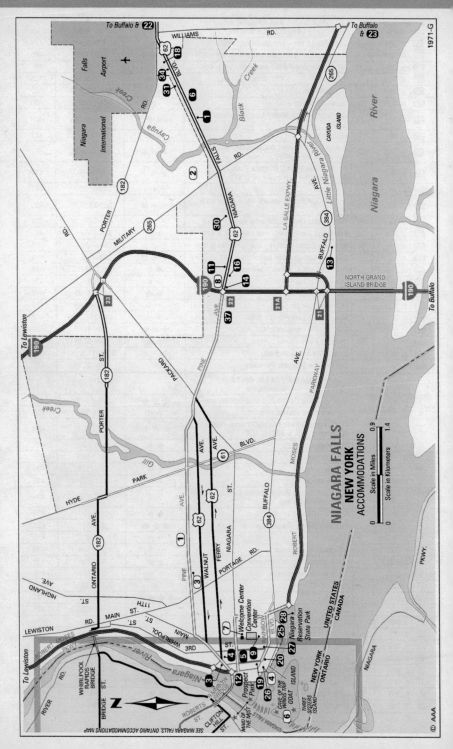

NIAGARA FALLS
NEW YORK
ACCOMMODATIONS

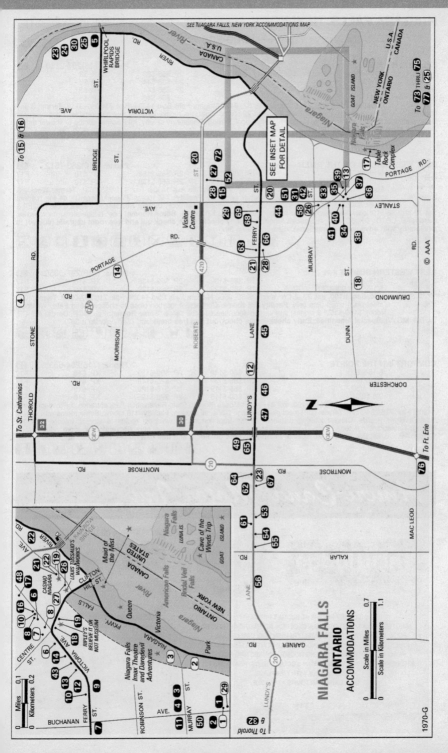

SEE NIAGARA FALLS, NEW YORK ACCOMMODATIONS MAP

NIAGARA FALLS
ONTARIO
ACCOMMODATIONS

Scale in Miles
Scale in Kilometers

1970-G

© AAA

NIAGARA FALLS, NEW YORK pop. 61,800 (See map p. 384; index p. 381)

———— LODGINGS ————

BEL AIRE MOTEL

(AAA) ◆ Motel

Phone: (716)297-2250 **31**

6/19-9/6	2P: $58-$62	XP: $8
9/7-10/13	2P: $38-$44	XP: $8
5/1-6/18	2P: $36-$44	XP: $5
10/14-4/30	2P: $36-$40	XP: $5

Location: I-190, exit 22, 1 mi s on US 62. 9470 Niagara Falls Blvd 14304. Fax: 716/297-8712. **Terms:** 3 day cancellation notice; cancellation fee imposed. **Facility:** 22 rooms. Spacious rooms, pleasant and comfortable. 3 two-bedroom units. Whirlpool room; 1 story; exterior corridors; heated pool. **Dining:** Restaurant nearby. **All Rooms:** combo or shower baths, extended cable TV. **Cards:** AE, MC, VI.

BEST WESTERN INN ON THE RIVER

(AAA) [SAVE] ◆◆◆ Motor Inn

Phone: (716)283-7612 **13**

5/19-9/4	1P: $89-$169	2P: $89-$169	XP: $10 F17
5/1-5/18 & 9/5-4/30	1P: $69-$139	2P: $69-$139	XP: $10 F17

Location: I-190, exit 21, just s on SR 384. 7001 Buffalo Ave 14304. Fax: 716/283-7631. **Terms:** Weekly & monthly rates avail; package plans; small pets only. **Facility:** 150 rooms. Peaceful location on the Niagara River. 8 stories; interior corridors; heated pool, sauna; boat dock. **Dining:** Restaurant; 7 am-2 & 5-9 pm, Fri & Sat-10 pm; $8-$19; cocktails. **Recreation:** fishing; game room, fun center. **Some Rooms:** Fee: refrigerators, microwaves. **Cards:** AE, CB, DI, DS, JC, MC, VI. **Special Amenities: Early check-in/late check-out and free room upgrade (subject to availability with advanced reservations).** *(See color ad p 387)*

BEST WESTERN SUMMIT INN

(AAA) [SAVE] ◆◆◆ Motel

Phone: (716)297-5050 **34**

5/19-9/4	1P: $89-$139	2P: $89-$139	XP: $10 F17
5/1-5/18 & 9/5-4/30	1P: $69-$129	2P: $69-$129	XP: $10 F17

Location: I-190, exit 22, 2.1 mi e on US 62. 9500 Niagara Falls Blvd 14304. Fax: 716/297-0802. **Terms:** [CP] meal plan; small pets only. **Facility:** 88 rooms. Convenient location close to shopping and Falls. Whirlpool room, $109-$159; 2 stories; interior corridors; heated pool, sauna. **Some Rooms:** Fee: VCR. **Cards:** AE, CB, DI, DS, MC, VI. **Special Amenities: Early check-in/late check-out and free breakfast.** *(See color ad p 387)*

COMFORT INN THE POINTE

(AAA) [SAVE] ◆◆◆ Motor Inn

Phone: (716)284-6835 **12**

6/16-9/5	1P: $89-$149	2P: $99-$159	XP: $10 F17
5/1-6/15	1P: $65-$139	2P: $75-$149	XP: $10 F17
11/1-4/30	1P: $65-$119	2P: $75-$129	XP: $10 F17
9/6-10/31	1P: $69-$115	2P: $79-$125	XP: $10 F17

Location: I-290 W to I-190, exit 21 Robert Moses Pkwy to State Reservation Park entrance. 1 Prospect Pointe 14303. Fax: 716/284-5177. **Terms:** [CP] meal plan; package plans, off season. **Facility:** 118 rooms. Some rooms with view of Niagara River Rapids. Closest walking distance to falls from lodging. 4 whirlpool rooms; 6 stories; interior corridors. **Dining:** Restaurant, cafeteria; 7 am-11 pm; hrs vary off season; $9-$13; wine/beer only. **Recreation:** in-room video games. **Cards:** AE, CB, DI, DS, JC, MC, VI. **Special Amenities: Free breakfast and free newspaper.** *(See color ad p 388)*

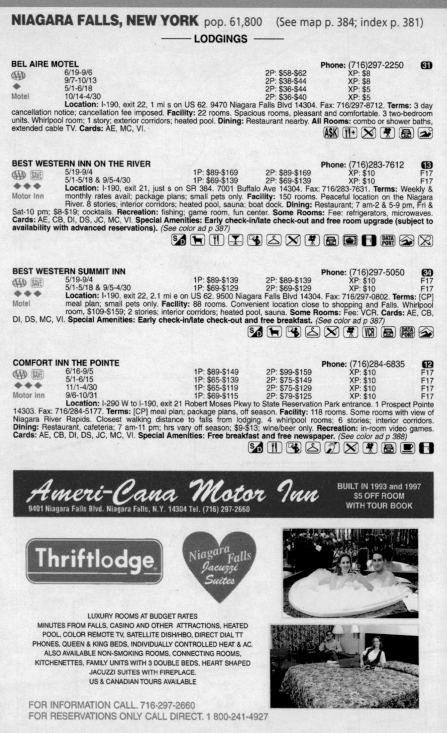

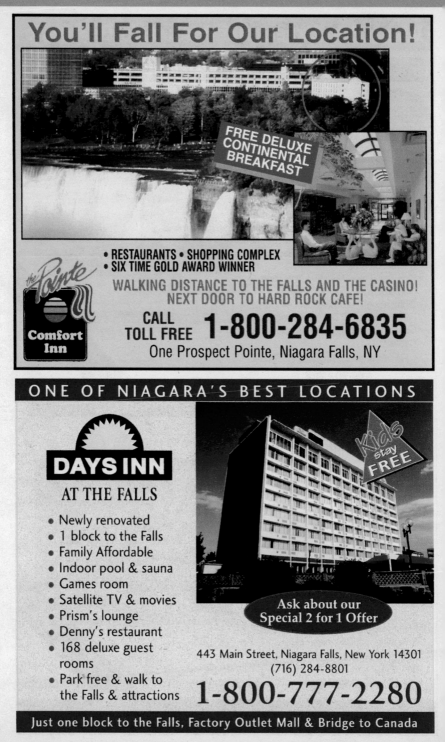

(See map p. 384)

DAYS INN AT THE FALLS Phone: (716)284-8801 4

5/1-9/30	1P: $89-$200	2P: $89-$200	XP: $10	F17
10/1-4/30	1P: $49-$99	2P: $49-$99	XP: $10	F17

◆ ◆
Hotel

Location: SR 104, facing entrance to Rainbow Bridge to Canada. 443 Main St 14301. Fax: 716/284-8633. **Terms:** Cancellation fee imposed; package plans. **Facility:** 168 rooms. Downtown, close to the falls. 7 king rooms with fireplace & whirlpool, $99-$250; 7 whirlpool rooms; 9 stories; interior corridors; heated pool, sauna. **Dining:** Restaurant; 24 hrs; $4-$12; cocktails. **Recreation:** in-room video games. **Cards:** AE, DS, MC, VI.
(See color ad p 388)

DAYS INN RIVERVIEW AT THE FALLS Phone: (716)285-2541 25

5/1-9/4	1P: $65-$185	2P: $65-$185	XP: $10	F16
10/29-4/30	1P: $40-$150	2P: $40-$150	XP: $10	F16
9/5-10/28	1P: $60-$145	2P: $60-$145	XP: $10	F16

Motor Inn

Location: Robert Moses Pkwy, exit 4th St. 401 Buffalo Ave 14303. Fax: 716/285-6108. **Terms:** [BP] meal plan; 7 day cancellation notice; package plans. **Facility:** 197 rooms. Spacious restaurant and conference rooms overlooking upper river rapids. 4 stories; interior corridors; heated pool. **Services:** gift shop. **Recreation:** playroom. **Some Rooms:** Fee: refrigerators. **Cards:** AE, DI, DS, MC, VI. *(See color ad below)*

(See map p. 384)

DRIFTWOOD MOTEL
Phone: (716)692-6650 **22**

All Year   1P: $34-$99   2P: $34-$99   XP: $10   D4

Motel   **Location:** I-190, exit 22, 5 mi s on US 62. 2754 Niagara Falls Blvd 14304. Fax: 716/695-6928. **Terms:** Weekly & monthly rates avail; 5 day cancellation notice. **Facility:** 20 rooms. Spacious, well-maintained rooms. Family owned since 1959. Shopping nearby. 1 story; exterior corridors. **Dining:** Restaurant nearby. **Cards:** AE, DS, MC, VI. **Special Amenities:** Free room upgrade (subject to availability with advanced reservations).

(See color ad p 389)

ECONO LODGE
Phone: (716)283-0621 **30**

6/15-9/4   1P: $55-$149   2P: $59-$159   XP: $10   F16

Motel   5/1-6/14 & 9/5-10/31   1P: $45-$99   2P: $49-$129   XP: $7   F16

11/1-4/30   1P: $35-$79   2P: $39-$99   XP: $7   F16

Location: I-190, exit 22, 0.8 mi e on US 62. 7708 Niagara Falls Blvd 14304. Fax: 716/283-2121. **Terms:** 3 day cancellation notice. **Facility:** 70 rooms. Within a few miles/minutes to the Falls and convention center. 2 stories; interior corridors; heated pool. **Services:** gift shop. **Some Rooms:** Fee: VCR. **Cards:** AE, CB, DI, DS, JC, MC, VI. *(See color ad below)*

(See map p. 384)

HOLIDAY INN AT THE FALLS

				Phone: (716)282-2211	27
AAA	7/1-9/3	1P: $99-$269	2P: $99-$269	XP: $10	F18
◆◆◆	5/1-5/31 & 9/4-4/30	1P: $59-$249	2P: $59-$249	XP: $10	F18
	6/1-6/30	1P: $69-$199	2P: $69-$199	XP: $10	F18

Hotel **Location:** Downtown; just s of Rainbow Mall; 2 blks from the falls. 231 Third St 14303. Fax: 716/282-2748. **Terms:** Package plans. **Facility:** 161 rooms. Spacious modern rooms. Fireplace in some whirlpool rooms. 23 whirlpool rooms, $89-$319; 8 stories; interior corridors; heated pool, sauna, whirlpool; playground. **Dining:** Restaurant; 24 hrs; $6-$14; cocktails. **Recreation:** in-room video games. **Some Rooms:** Fee: refrigerators. **Cards:** AE, CB, DI, DS, JC, MC, VI.
(See color ad p 391)

HOLIDAY INN SELECT-NIAGARA FALLS

				Phone: (716)285-3361	5
AAA SAVE	5/26-9/5	1P: $89-$159	2P: $89-$159	XP: $10	F18
◆◆◆	5/1-5/25	1P: $69-$99	2P: $69-$99	XP: $10	F18
	9/6-10/31	1P: $69-$99		XP: $10	F18
Hotel	11/1-4/30	1P: $49-$89		XP: $10	F18

Location: Downtown; at Third and Niagara sts, between the convention center and shopping outlet. 300 Third St 14303 (PO Box 845, NIAGARA FALLS). Fax: 716/285-3900. **Terms:** [BP] meal plan; weekly & monthly rates avail; package plans. **Facility:** 386 rooms. Tastefully decorated rooms. 4 whirlpool rooms, $200-$300; suites, $175-$275; 6 stories; interior corridors; heated pool, sauna, whirlpool. **Dining:** Restaurant; 6:30 am-10 pm; to 11 pm in summer; $13-$20; cocktails. **Services:** gift shop. **Recreation:** video arcade. **All Rooms:** combo or shower baths. **Some Rooms:** Fee: refrigerators, microwaves. **Cards:** AE, DI, DS, MC, VI.

HOLLEY RANKINE HOUSE

| | | | | Phone: 716/285-4790 | 28 |
| ◆◆ | All Year | 1P: $60 | 2P: $120 | | |

Historic Bed & Breakfast **Location:** I-90, exit 21 Robert Moses Pkwy (Moses-City exit), just w (Buffalo Ave); just s. 525 Riverside Dr 14303. **Terms:** [BP] meal plan; age restrictions may apply. **Facility:** 5 rooms. A historic property in a quiet residential neighborhood close to Niagara Falls. 3 stories; interior corridors; designated smoking area. **Some Rooms:** color TV. **Cards:** MC, VI.

HOSPITALITY INN

				Phone: (716)283-8611	11
AAA SAVE	7/1-9/15	1P: $79-$110	2P: $89-$120	XP: $10	F8
◆◆	5/1-6/30 & 4/1-4/30	1P: $35-$40	2P: $45-$55	XP: $10	F8
	9/16-3/31	1P: $30-$35	2P: $35-$45	XP: $10	F8

Motel **Location:** US 62, 0.3 mi e of jct I-190, exit 22. 6734 Niagara Falls Blvd 14304. Fax: 716/283-6097. **Terms:** Weekly rates avail; 3 day cancellation notice. **Facility:** 28 rooms. Nicely decorated rooms beyond concealed entry. Whirlpool room, $85-$170; 1-2 stories; exterior corridors; heated pool. **Dining:** Restaurant nearby. **All Rooms:** extended cable TV. **Some Rooms:** 2 efficiencies, kitchen. **Cards:** AE, CB, DI, DS, MC, VI. **Special Amenities:** Free local telephone calls and preferred room (subject to availability with advanced reservations).

HOWARD JOHNSON HOTEL AT THE FALLS

				Phone: (716)285-5261	3
AAA SAVE	6/1-9/3	1P: $100-$140	2P: $110-$150	XP: $10	F18
◆◆	9/4-10/31	1P: $65-$100	2P: $75-$105	XP: $8	F18
	5/1-5/31	1P: $55-$85	2P: $65-$95	XP: $8	F18
Hotel	11/1-4/30	1P: $50-$80	2P: $55-$90	XP: $8	F18

Location: I-190 N, exit 21, 2 mi e on Robert Moses Pkwy (1st exit), just n to Rainbow Blvd, just s. 454 Main St 14301. Fax: 716/285-8536. **Terms:** [BP] meal plan; check-in 4 pm; 3 day cancellation notice; 2 night min stay, in summer; package plans; small pets only, $10 extra charge. **Facility:** 80 rooms. Within walking distance to the Falls, area attractions and Casino Niagara. 2 whirlpool rooms, $159-$259; 5 stories; interior corridors; heated pool, sauna. **Dining:** Restaurant; 7 am-11 pm; $8-$20; cocktails. **Services:** gift shop. **Some Rooms:** Fee: refrigerators, microwaves. **Cards:** AE, CB, DI, DS, MC, VI. **Special Amenities:** Free room upgrade and preferred room (each subject to availability with advanced reservations).
(See color ad p 391)

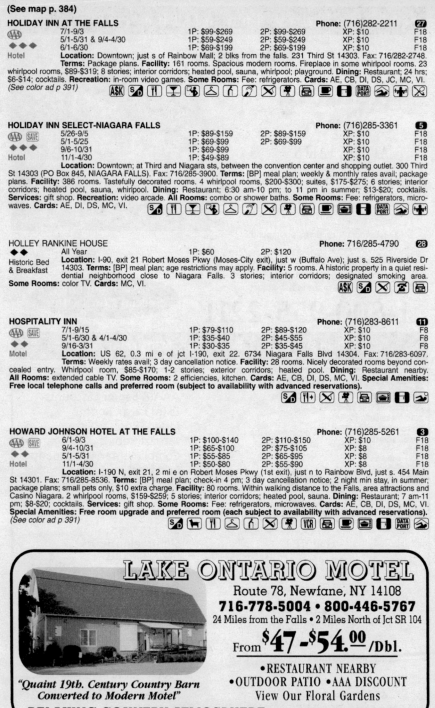

(See map p. 384)

HOWARD JOHNSON INN-NIAGARA

Phone: (716)283-8791   **14**

	6/15-9/15	1P: $55-$135	2P: $59-$149	XP: $10	F16
AAA SAVE	5/1-6/14 & 9/16-10/31	1P: $45-$95	2P: $49-$129	XP: $10	F16
◆◆	11/1-4/30	1P: $35-$75	2P: $39-$79	XP: $10	F16

Motel   **Location:** Jct I-190 and US 62, exit 22, just e. 6505 Niagara Falls Blvd 14304. Fax: 716/283-9313. **Terms:** Weekly rates avail. **Facility:** 88 rooms. Pleasant decor. 9 whirlpool rooms; 2 stories; interior corridors; heated pool. **Dining:** Restaurant nearby. **Some Rooms:** Fee: refrigerators, VCR. **Cards:** AE, DI, DS, JC, MC, VI. **Special Amenities:** Early check-in/late check-out and free newspaper. *(See color ad below)*

KNIGHTS INN

Phone: (716)297-3647   **18**

	7/1-8/31	1P: $68-$89	2P: $68-$89	XP: $8	F14
AAA SAVE	5/1-6/30 & 9/1-11/30	1P: $48-$68	2P: $48-$68	XP: $6	F14
◆◆	12/1-4/30	1P: $38-$58	2P: $38-$58	XP: $6	F14

Motel   **Location:** I-190, exit 22, 2.5 mi s on US 62 (Niagara Falls Blvd); I-290, exit 3, 10 mi n on US 62 (Niagara Falls Blvd). 9900 Niagara Falls Blvd 14304. Fax: 716/297-6558. **Terms:** Weekly & monthly rates avail; 7 day cancellation notice; package plans; pets. **Facility:** 22 rooms. Clean attractive accommodations located across from Niagara Falls International Airport. 2 whirlpool rooms, $89-$125; 1 story; exterior corridors. **Dining:** Restaurant nearby. **Some Rooms:** Fee: refrigerators, VCR. **Cards:** AE, DS, MC, VI. **Special Amenities:** Free local telephone calls.

RAMADA BY THE FALLS

Phone: (716)282-1734   **9**

	6/23-9/3	1P: $59-$169	2P: $59-$179	XP: $10	F18
AAA SAVE	9/4-10/15	1P: $49-$89	2P: $49-$99	XP: $10	F18
◆◆	5/1-6/22	1P: $39-$89	2P: $39-$99	XP: $10	F18
Motor Inn	10/16-4/30	1P: $39-$59	2P: $39-$79	XP: $10	F18

Location: I-190, exit 21, 3.5 mi w on Robert Moses Pkwy, just s of Rainbow Mall. 219 4th St 14303. Fax: 716/282-1881. **Terms:** [AP], [BP], [CP] & [MAP] meal plans; weekly & monthly rates avail; package plans. **Facility:** 112 rooms. Walking distance from the falls. 12 whirlpool rooms; 2 stories; interior corridors; heated pool, whirlpool. **Dining:** Restaurant; 6:30 am-11 pm; $10-$16; cocktails. **Services:** gift shop. **Some Rooms:** Fee: refrigerators. **Cards:** AE, CB, DI, DS, MC, VI. **Special Amenities:** Early check-in/late check-out. *(See color ad p 390)*

RAMADA INN AT THE FALLS

Phone: (716)282-1212   **19**

	6/26-9/15	1P: $65-$135	2P: $75-$145	XP: $10	F18
◆◆	5/1-6/25 & 9/16-10/15	1P: $55-$95	2P: $55-$95	XP: $10	F18
Motor Inn	10/16-4/30	1P: $50-$90	2P: $50-$90	XP: $10	F18

Location: Downtown; adjoining Rainbow Shopping Center. 240 Rainbow Blvd N 14303. Fax: 716/282-1216. **Terms:** Pets, $25 dep req. **Facility:** 217 rooms. Close to shopping and falls. 4 stories; interior corridors; heated pool. **Services:** gift shop. **Some Rooms:** Fee: VCR. **Cards:** AE, CB, DI, DS, MC, VI.

(See map p. 384)

THE RED COACH INN Phase: Phone: (716)282-1459 🆖

6/30-9/4	1P: $99-$149	2P: $99-$149	XP: $20
5/1-6/29	1P: $89-$129	2P: $89-$129	XP: $20
9/5-12/31	1P: $79-$129	2P: $79-$129	XP: $20
1/1-4/30	1P: $69-$119	2P: $69-$119	XP: $20

(AAA) (SAVE) ◆◆◆ Suite Country Inn

Location: Downtown. 2 Buffalo Ave 14303. Fax: 716/282-2650. **Terms:** [CP] meal plan; weekly & monthly rates avail; 10 day cancellation notice; cancellation fee imposed; package plans. **Facility:** 14 rooms. Uniquely decorated suites and 18th-century decor. 2 rooms avail with laundry. Most rooms with view of Niagara River Rapids. 4 two-bedroom units. 14 whirlpool rooms, $69-$149; 3 stories, no elevator; interior/exterior corridors; designated smoking area. **Dining:** Restaurant, see separate listing. **All Rooms:** extended cable TV. **Some Rooms:** 9 kitchens. **Cards:** DS, MC, VI. **Special Amenities:** Free breakfast and free newspaper.

RED MAPLE INN-NIAGARA FALLS Phone: (716)285-7316 🆖

5/1-9/30	1P: $49-$199	2P: $59-$199	XP: $10 F12
10/1-4/30	1P: $39-$159	2P: $39-$159	XP: $10 F12

(AAA) (SAVE) ◆◆ Motel

Location: Downtown; just s of Rainbow Mall. 200 Rainbow Blvd 14303. Fax: 716/285-8541. **Terms:** 3 day cancellation notice; pets, $10 extra charge. **Facility:** 48 rooms. Nicely decorated rooms. 2 whirlpool rooms, $85-$299; 3 stories; interior/exterior corridors. **Dining:** Restaurant nearby. **All Rooms:** combo or shower baths. **Some Rooms:** Fee: VCR. **Cards:** AE, DI, DS, MC, VI. **Special Amenities:** Free local telephone calls and preferred room (subject to availability with advanced reservations).

RIVIERA MOTEL Phone: (716)283-3839 🆖

All Year	1P: $29-$99	2P: $36-$99	XP: $6 F6

(AAA) (SAVE) ◆◆ Motel

Location: I-190, exit 22, just s on US 62 (Niagara Falls Blvd). 6621 Niagara Falls Blvd 14304. Fax: 716/283-3675. **Terms:** Weekly & monthly rates avail; cancellation fee imposed. **Facility:** 30 rooms. Modernized guest rooms, strong in decor. 1 story; exterior corridors. **Dining:** Restaurant nearby. **All Rooms:** extended cable TV. **Cards:** AE, CB, DI, DS, MC, VI. **Special Amenities:** Free local telephone calls.

SCOTTISH INNS Phone: (716)283-1100 🆖

7/1-8/31	1P: $49-$120	2P: $49-$140	XP: $5 F16
9/1-10/31	1P: $40-$80	2P: $40-$90	XP: $5 F16
5/1-6/30	1P: $49-$79	2P: $54-$89	XP: $5 F16
11/1-4/30	1P: $39-$59	2P: $44-$69	XP: $5 F16

(AAA) (SAVE) ◆◆ Motel

Location: I-190, exit 22, 0.3 mi n on US 62. 5919 Niagara Falls Blvd 14304. Fax: 716/283-2150. **Terms:** [BP] & [CP] meal plans; weekly & monthly rates avail. **Facility:** 37 rooms. Nicely decorated some rooms. Whirlpool room, $89-$199; 1 story; exterior corridors; playground. **Dining:** Restaurant nearby. **All Rooms:** extended cable TV. **Cards:** AE, DI, DS, MC, VI. **Special Amenities:** Early check-in/late check-out and free breakfast. (See color ad below)

(See map p. 384)

THRIFTLODGE Phone: (716)297-2660 6

6/24-9/4	1P: $45-$119	2P: $50-$139	XP: $10	F12
9/5-10/21	1P: $39-$75	2P: $45-$79	XP: $8	F12
5/1-6/23	1P: $39-$75	2P: $39-$79	XP: $8	F12
10/22-4/30	1P: $36-$59	2P: $40-$65	XP: $6	F12

AAA SAVE
◆◆
Motel

Location: I-190, exit 22, 1.8 mi e on US 62. 9401 Niagara Falls Blvd 14304. Fax: 716/297-7675.
Terms: Weekly & monthly rates avail; 5 day cancellation notice; cancellation fee imposed. **Facility:** 45 rooms. Nice appearance to room decor. 6 whirlpool rooms, $79-$179; 1 story; exterior corridors; heated pool. **Dining:** Restaurant nearby.
All Rooms: extended cable TV. **Some Rooms:** 6 efficiencies, no utensils. **Cards:** AE, CB, DI, DS, MC, VI.
(See color ad p 386)

TRAVELERS BUDGET INN Phone: (716)297-3228 1

AAA SAVE
◆
Motel

All Year	1P: $29-$99	2P: $32-$109	XP: $6	F12

Location: I-190 exit 22, 1.7 mi e on US 62. 9001 Niagara Falls Blvd 14304. Fax: 716/775-0604.
Terms: Weekly rates avail; 3 day cancellation notice; cancellation fee imposed; pets, $6 extra charge.
Facility: 24 rooms. Nice look to average size rooms. 7 whirlpool rooms, $52-$129; 1 story; exterior corridors.
Dining: Restaurant nearby. **All Rooms:** combo or tub baths, extended cable TV. **Some Rooms:** kitchen.
Fee: refrigerators, VCR. **Cards:** DS, MC, VI. **Special Amenities:** Early check-in/late check-out and free local telephone calls.

─── RESTAURANTS ───

COMO RESTAURANT & DELI Lunch: $4-$8 Dinner: $7-$18 Phone: 716/285-9341 1

AAA
◆◆
Italian

Location: US 62A, 1 mi s of jct SR 104. 2220 Pine Ave 14301. **Hours:** 11:30 am-10 pm, Fri & Sat-11 pm. Closed: 12/25. **Reservations:** suggested. **Features:** casual dress; Sunday brunch; children's menu; early bird specials; senior's menu; carryout; cocktails & lounge. Family-owned since 1927, the restaurant consistently delivers tasty homemade pasta and traditional American dishes. Generous portions and reasonable prices make this place a good choice for the value-conscious diner. Servers are friendly and prompt. **Cards:** AE, DS, MC, VI.

GOOSE'S ROOST Lunch: $3-$7 Dinner: $7-$12 Phone: 716/282-6255 7

◆
American

Location: Downtown; just e of convention center. 343 4th & Niagara St 14303. **Hours:** 7 am-10 pm, Fri & Sat-11 pm. Closed: 12/25. **Reservations:** accepted. **Features:** casual dress; children's menu; health conscious menu items; carryout; cocktails. Next to the convention center, the cozy restaurant is a favorite for its home-style menu of salads, sandwiches and sides, as well as breakfast selections and Italian dinners. Families appreciate the good value. Service is pleasant and prompt. **Cards:** AE, DS, MC, VI.

JOHN'S FLAMING HEARTH Lunch: $5-$8 Dinner: $12-$19 Phone: 716/297-1414 2

◆◆
American

Location: I-190, exit 22, 1.2 mi e on US 62, 0.5 mi n on SR 265. 1965 Military Rd 14304. **Hours:** 11:30 am-3 & 4-10 pm, Fri & Sat-11 pm, Sun noon-9 pm. **Reservations:** suggested. **Features:** casual dress; children's menu; early bird specials; cocktails & lounge. Chicken marsala, New York strip steak and Polynesian chicken are representative of tried-and-true menu selections. The dining room is cozy and casual. Desserts—such as the specialty pumpkin ice cream pie and homemade apple pie—melt in your mouth. **Cards:** AE, DI, DS, MC, VI.

PETE'S MARKET HOUSE RESTAURANT Lunch: $3-$6 Dinner: $4-$12 Phone: 716/282-7225 3

◆
Traditional
Steak and
Seafood

Location: US 62A, 0.8 mi s of jct SR 104. 1701 Pine Ave 14301. **Hours:** 11:15 am-2:15 & 4:30-10:30 pm, Fri 11:15 am-midnight, Sat 3:30 pm-midnight, Sun 1 pm-10 pm. **Features:** casual dress; children's menu; early bird specials; health conscious menu items; cocktails & lounge; a la carte. Steaks and lobster tail are specialties on a varied menu of satisfying selections, all priced reasonably. An easy, relaxed atmosphere prevails in the informal dining areas. Service is diner-style in many aspects—friendly without formality.

THE RED COACH INN RESTAURANT Lunch: $4-$9 Dinner: $7-$20 Phone: 716/282-1459 4

AAA
◆◆◆
American

Location: Downtown; in The Red Coach Inn. 2 Buffalo Ave 14303. **Hours:** 11:30 am-10 pm, Fri & Sat-11 pm, Sun noon-10 pm; to 9 pm 11/1-4/30. Closed: 12/25. **Reservations:** suggested. **Features:** casual dress; children's menu; senior's menu; carryout; cocktails & lounge; a la carte. The Tudor-style, tavernlike dining room has an Old World feel. Selections on the varied menu display creative preparation and nice presentation. The house specialty is succulent prime rib. Servers exhibit good menu knowledge and timely follow-up. **Cards:** DS, MC, VI.

TIMBER LODGE STEAKHOUSE Dinner: $8-$19 Phone: 716/283-2548 8

◆◆
Steakhouse

Location: I-190, exit 22. 6560 Niagara Falls Blvd 14304. **Hours:** 4 pm-10 pm, Fri-11 pm, Sat 3 pm-11 pm, Sun 3 pm-10 pm. Closed: 11/23 & 12/25. **Features:** casual dress; children's menu; early bird specials; carryout; cocktails & lounge. The casual steakhouse, decorated in a lodgelike motif, emphasizes plentiful portions and value prices. In addition to numerous selections of quality beef, the menu features chicken, shrimp and fresh fish. Be sure to come with a healthy appetite. **Cards:** AE, DI, DS, MC, VI.

TOP OF THE FALLS RESTAURANT Lunch: $5-$8 Dinner: $5-$8 Phone: 716/278-0337 6

◆
American

Location: On Goat Island; at Terrapin Point, overlooking Horseshoe Falls. Goat Island-Amer Falls Pk 14302. **Hours:** Open 5/28-9/6; 11 am-7 pm, hrs may vary. **Features:** children's menu; health conscious menu items; cocktails & lounge; minimum charge-15% service charge; fee for parking; a la carte. The stark decor of the second-floor dining room serves to accentuate all the more the excellent, Horseshoe Falls views—which are afforded from every table. Simple menu offerings include sandwiches, burgers, salads and finger foods. Servers are pleasant. **Cards:** AE, DS, MC, VI.

The Niagara Falls Vicinity

LEWISTON pop. 3,000

——— LODGING ———

PORTAGE HOUSE MOTEL
Phone: (716)754-8295

◆

| | 5/1-10/31 | 1P: $57 | 2P: $64 | XP: $7 | F18 |
| Motel | 11/1-4/30 | 1P: $42 | 2P: $49 | XP: $7 | F18 |

Location: 0.3 mi w from jct SR 18F and Robert Moses Pkwy; opposite entrance to Artpark. 280 Portage Rd 14092. Fax: 716/754-1613. **Facility:** 21 rooms. Rooms with vintage to more contemporary decor. All with 2 double beds. Office closed 11 pm-7 am. 2 stories; interior/exterior corridors. **Cards:** AE, DS, MC, VI.

——— RESTAURANTS ———

CLARKSON HOUSE   Historical
Dinner: $12-$30
Phone: 716/754-4544

◆◆

American

Location: 0.4 mi w on SR 104 from jct Robert Moses Pkwy. 810 Center St 14092. **Hours:** 11:30 am-2:30 & 5-10:30 pm, Sat from 5 pm, Sun 3 pm-9 pm. Closed: 12/25. **Reservations:** suggested; weekend. **Features:** casual dress; children's menu; health conscious menu items; cocktails & lounge. Since the 1940s, the restaurant has listed steak, live lobster and baked Alaska on its traditional menu. Over the years, such dishes as swordfish with lime salsa, thickly cut lamb chops and cherries jubilee have become welcomed additions. **Cards:** AE, DI, MC, VI.

FOUR 90 CENTER BAR & GRILLE
Lunch: $5-$12
Dinner: $12-$13
Phone: 716/754-4904

◆◆◆

American

Location: 490 Center St 14092. **Hours:** 11:30 am-3 & 4-9 pm, Fri & Sat-10 pm; after Labor Day closed Sun & open Mon, same hrs as above. Closed: 11/23 & 12/25. **Reservations:** suggested. **Features:** casual dress; carryout; cocktails & lounge. In the center of the historic area, the restaurant is an area favorite for creative cuisine, such as Cajun catfish. Well-done desserts include the wonderful lemon poppy seed sponge cake with berries. Comfortable surroundings contribute to relaxed dining. **Cards:** AE, MC, VI.

NEWFANE pop. 3,000

——— LODGING ———

LAKE ONTARIO MOTEL
Phone: 716/778-5004

◆◆

| Motel | 5/1-10/31 & 4/20-4/30 | 1P: $37-$84 | 2P: $46-$84 | XP: $7 | F12 |

Location: 2.2 mi n of jct SR 104 on SR 78. 3330 Lockport-Olcott Rd 14108. **Terms:** Open 5/1-10/31 & 4/20-4/30; 5 day cancellation notice; pets. **Facility:** 11 rooms. Turn-of-the-century barn with new contemporary rooms. 2 stories; interior corridors. **All Rooms:** shower baths. **Cards:** AE, DS, MC, VI. (See ad p 392)

——— RESTAURANT ———

RIB HOUSE RESTAURANT
Dinner: $8-$20
Phone: 716/778-7910

◆

American

Location: 3.4 mi n of jct SR 104 on SR 78. 2990 Lockport-Olcott Rd (NY Rt 78) 14108. **Hours:** 4 pm-9 pm, Fri & Sat-10 pm, Sun 4 pm-8 pm. Closed: 12/25. **Reservations:** suggested; weekends. **Features:** casual dress; children's menu; early bird specials; health conscious menu items; carryout; cocktails & lounge. The rustic country dining room at this restaurant is charming. Prime rib and the signature ribs—which actually are only a small portion of the menu—stand out among selections of seafood, poultry, steak and pork. The chocolate swirl cheesecake is great. **Cards:** AE, CB, DI, DS, MC, VI.

SANBORN pop. 800

——— RESTAURANT ———

THE NEW SCHIMSCHACK'S RESTAURANT
Dinner: $10-$32
Phone: 716/731-4111

◆◆

American

Location: 1.3 mi n from jct SR 425 and 31, 2.3 mi w. 2943 Upper Mountain Rd 14132. **Hours:** 4 pm-9 pm, Sat-10 pm, Sun noon-8 pm. Closed: 12/24, 12/25 & Mon 1/1-3/31. **Reservations:** suggested. **Features:** dressy casual; children's menu; early bird specials; cocktails. Charbroiled baby back ribs stand out on a menu of traditional favorites. The three-tired dining room, which affords lovely panoramic views of the vineyards, exudes an informal, romantic ambiance. Tempting desserts are prepared on the premises. **Cards:** AE, CB, DI, DS, MC, VI.

WHEATFIELD pop. 11,100

——— LODGING ———

ANCHOR MOTEL
Phone: 716/693-0850

◆

	6/9-9/17	1P: $46-$65	2P: $52-$84
Motel	5/1-6/8 & 9/18-10/22	1P: $38-$52	2P: $46-$62
	10/23-4/30	1P: $30-$48	2P: $42-$56

Location: I-90 (New York Thruway) to I-290, exit 1 (Delaware Ave), 5.8 mi n on SR 384. 2332 River Rd 14304. **Facility:** 21 rooms. Quiet location with grounds on Niagara River. 1 story; exterior corridors. **All Rooms:** combo or shower baths. **Cards:** AE, DS, MC, VI.

——— RESTAURANT ———

SUZANNE'S FINE DINING
Dinner: $10-$22
Phone: 716/694-6562

◆◆◆

American

Location: 2843 Niagara Falls Blvd 14304. **Hours:** 3 pm-10 pm. Closed: 12/25, Sun & Mon. **Reservations:** suggested. **Features:** casual dress; children's menu; health conscious menu items; cocktails. Decorated in peach tones, the dining room features fresh flowers and angel pictures. The menu lists such well-prepared items as veal Edward with artichoke hearts, mushrooms and sun-dried tomatoes and bacon-wrapped shrimp stuffed with crab meat. **Cards:** AE, DS, MC, VI.

YOUNGSTOWN pop. 2,100
—— LODGING ——

CAMEO MANOR BED & BREAKFAST
◆◆
Bed & Breakfast

All Year 1P: $70-$170 2P: $75-$175 XP: $20 **Phone:** (716)745-3034

Location: SR 18F (Seaway Tr), 4.5 mi w and n from jct Robert Moses Pkwy and SR 104. 3881 Lower River Rd 14174. Fax: 716/745-7444. **Terms:** [BP] meal plan; age restrictions may apply; 3 day cancellation notice; cancellation fee imposed; 2 night min stay; 7/1-8/31 weekends; package plans. **Facility:** 4 rooms. 1840s stately English manor featuring a fine wooden staircase, extensive parlors with fireplace, large dining room, 2 suites with enclosed porches, and compact regular rooms. Quiet location. 1 two-bedroom unit. 2 stories; interior corridors; smoke free premises. **Some Rooms:** color TV. **Cards:** DS, MC, VI. 🐾 ✕ ☎ VCR 🖨

Nearby Ontario
NIAGARA FALLS pop. 76,900 (See map p. 385; index p. 381)
—— LODGINGS ——

AMERI-CANA RESORT & CONFERENCE CENTRE **Phone:** (905)356-8444 **56**
(AAA) (SAVE)
◆◆◆
Motor Inn

6/16-8/26	1P: $89-$179	2P: $99-$199	XP: $10
8/27-10/8	1P: $69-$139	2P: $79-$159	XP: $10
5/1-6/15 & 10/9-4/30	1P: $59-$129	2P: $69-$139	XP: $10

Location: 5.5 km w on Hwy 20, 0.5 km off QEW, Hwy 20 W exit. 8444 Lundy's Ln L2H 1H4. Fax: 905/356-8576. **Terms:** 7 day cancellation notice; cancellation fee imposed; package plans. **Facility:** 160 rooms. Very spacious tastefully decorated rooms; some with balcony or patio. 10 two-bedroom units. 17 whirlpool rooms, $99-$299; 2 stories; interior corridors; 2 heated pools, saunas, whirlpool; 1 lighted tennis court; playground. **Dining:** Restaurant; 7 am-11 pm, Fri & Sat-midnight; $6-$18; cocktails. **Services:** gift shop. Fee: area transportation, local shuttle. **Recreation:** jogging, basketball, shuffleboard, squash court, volleyball. **Some Rooms:** Fee: refrigerators, VCR. **Cards:** AE, DI, DS, JC, MC, VI. **Special Amenities:** Preferred room **(subject to availability with advanced reservations).** *(See color ad p 399)*

🍴 🍸 🐾 🛎 🏋 📹 VCR 🖨 📠 DATA PORT 🚗 🏖 ✕

A-1 MOTEL **Phone:** (905)354-6038 **61**
(AAA) (SAVE)
◆
Motel

6/23-9/3	1P: $48-$70	2P: $54-$150	XP: $10	F14
5/5-6/22 & 9/4-10/10	1P: $36-$48	2P: $38-$72	XP: $10	F14

Location: 4.7 km w on Hwy 20, from QEW, Hwy 20 W. 7895 Lundy's Ln L2H 1H3. **Terms:** Open 5/5-10/10; weekly & monthly rates avail; 7 day cancellation notice. **Facility:** 29 rooms. Compact to large units. 1 two-bedroom unit. 1 story; exterior corridors; heated pool. **Dining:** Restaurant nearby. **Services:** Fee: area transportation, casino in season. **Recreation:** sliding board. **All Rooms:** combo or shower baths. **Some Rooms:** kitchen. **Cards:** AE, MC, VI. **Special Amenities:** Early check-in/late check-out and free local telephone calls.

🅢 🛗 ✕ 🖨 📠 📶 🚗

(See map p. p. 385)

ASHBURY MOTEL Phone: (905)356-8280 🔢53

CAA SAVE | 6/1-9/15 | 1P: $79-$149 | 2P: $79-$149 | XP: $10 | F5
◆ | 5/1-5/31 | 1P: $49-$99 | 2P: $49-$99 | XP: $10 | F5
Motor Inn | 9/16-4/30 | 1P: $39-$79 | 2P: $39-$79 | XP: $5 | F5

Location: 4.6 km w on Hwy 20, from QEW, Hwy 20 W. 7800 Lundy's Ln L2H 1H1. Fax: 905/356-6948. **Terms:** Cancellation fee imposed. **Facility:** 67 rooms. Abundant flowers on nicely kept grounds with pool. 1 three-bedroom unit, 3 two-bedroom units. 17 efficiencies, $89-$98 for up to 2 persons, utensil dep req; 2 whirlpool rooms, $99-$199; 2 stories; exterior corridors; heated pool. **Dining:** Restaurant; 6 am-midnight; $5-$10. **Cards:** AE, MC, VI. **Special Amenities: Early check-in/late check-out and free room upgrade (subject to availability with advanced reservations).**

AURORA MOTEL Phone: 905/356-4490 🔢38

CAA | 6/23-9/3 | 1P: $59-$125 | 2P: $59-$125 | XP: $6 | F12
◆ | 5/1-6/22 & 4/1-4/30 | 1P: $39-$59 | 2P: $39-$59 | XP: $6 | F12
Motel | 9/4-11/5 | 1P: $39-$45 | 2P: $39-$45 | XP: $6 | F12

Location: Just w of Minolta Tower. 5630 Dunn St L2G 2N7. **Terms:** Open 5/1-11/5 & 4/1-4/30; 3 day cancellation notice; cancellation fee imposed. **Facility:** 29 rooms. Well kept rooms in quiet, residential type area yet convenient access to falls area and attractions. 2 stories; exterior corridors; heated pool. **Dining:** Restaurant nearby. **All Rooms:** extended cable TV. **Cards:** AE, CB, DI, DS, MC, VI. *(See color ad below)*

BEST WESTERN CAIRN CROFT HOTEL Phone: (905)356-1161 🔢45

CAA SAVE | 6/16-9/3 | 1P: $134-$164 | 2P: $139-$169 | XP: $10 | F16
◆◆◆ | 9/4-10/28 | 1P: $89-$94 | 2P: $94-$99 | XP: $10 | F16
Motor Inn | 10/29-4/30 | 1P: $84-$89 | 2P: $94-$99 | XP: $10 | F16
 | 5/1-6/15 | 1P: $84-$89 | 2P: $89-$94 | XP: $10 | F16

Location: 2.4 km w on Hwy 20. 6400 Lundy's Ln L2G 1T6. Fax: 905/356-8664. **Terms:** Package plans. **Facility:** 165 rooms. Variety of rooms and facilities catering to families and business people alike. 8 whirlpool rooms, $169-$189; 2-5 stories; interior/exterior corridors; heated pool. **Dining:** Dining room; 7 am-2 & 5-9 pm; to 8 pm off season except weekends; $7-$19; cocktails. **Services:** winter plug-ins. **Recreation:** arcade game area, in-room video games. **All Rooms:** extended cable TV. **Cards:** AE, DI, DS, MC, VI. *(See color ad p 401)*

(See map p. p. 385)

BEST WESTERN FALLSVIEW MOTOR HOTEL   Phone: (905)356-0551   **11**

CAA SAVE

◆ ◆
Motor Inn

	6/9-9/4	1P: $129-$249	2P: $129-$249	XP: $10	F12
	9/5-10/31	1P: $99-$199	2P: $99-$199	XP: $10	F12
	5/1-6/8 & 11/1-4/30	1P: $79-$149	2P: $79-$149	XP: $10	F12

Location: Just n on Murray St from jct Niagara Pkwy. 5551 Murray St L2G 2J4. Fax: 905/356-7773. **Terms:** 3 day cancellation notice; package plans; small pets only. **Facility:** 244 rooms. Ample parking and within walking distance to Falls and Victoria Park. Many extra large family rooms and upscale decor. 20 whirlpool rooms, $179-$399; 4-6 stories; interior/exterior corridors; heated pool, sauna, whirlpool; playground. **Dining:** Restaurant; 7 am-10 & 5-10 pm; weekends only 8 am-9 pm 10/13-5/14; $7-$16; cocktails. **Services:** gift shop. **All Rooms:** combo or shower baths. **Cards:** AE, DI, DS, MC, VI. (See color ad p 402)

BEST WESTERN FIRESIDE HOTEL   Phone: (905)374-2027   **30**

CAA SAVE

◆ ◆ ◆
Motor Inn

| | 5/1-9/30 | 1P: $89-$299 | 2P: $89-$299 | XP: $10 | F12 |
| | 10/1-4/30 | 1P: $59-$229 | 2P: $89-$229 | XP: $10 | F12 |

Location: 3 km n of Rainbow Bridge. 4067 River Rd L2E 3E5. Fax: 905/374-7746. **Terms:** 3 day cancellation notice; package plans. **Facility:** 96 rooms. All rooms with gas fireplace. Some rooms with view of Niagara River Gorge. 12 whirlpool rooms; 4 stories; interior corridors; heated pool, sauna, whirlpool. **Dining:** Restaurant; 8 am-10 pm; $7-$18; cocktails. **Some Rooms:** Fee: VCR. **Cards:** AE, CB, DI, DS, JC, MC, VI. **Special Amenities:** Free local telephone calls and free newspaper.

(See map p. p. 385)

BROCK PLAZA

6/1-10/15	1P: $99-$669	XP: $10	F18
5/1-5/31	1P: $99-$379	XP: $10	F18
10/16-4/30	1P: $69-$379	XP: $10	F18

Phone: (905)374-4444 **21**

Historic Hotel **Location:** At entrance to Rainbow Bridge on Hwy 20, just n from the falls. 5685 Falls Ave L2E 6W7. Fax: 905/371-8349. **Terms:** [BP] & [MAP] meal plans; cancellation fee imposed; package plans. **Facility:** 233 rooms. 140 rooms with falls view. Superior public areas in this grand old hotel built in 1929. Some especially attractive upgraded rooms. Indoor walkway to Casino Niagara. 9 whirlpool rooms, $119-$799; 12 stories; interior corridors; heated pool, wading pool, sauna, whirlpool. Fee: parking. **Dining:** The Rainbow Room, see separate listing. **Services:** gift shop. **All Rooms:** combo or shower baths, extended cable TV. **Cards:** AE, CB, DI, DS, JC, MC, VI. *(See color ad p 403)*

BUDGETEL MOTOR INN

7/10-8/20	1P: $59-$149	2P: $69-$149	XP: $10 F12
8/21-11/30	1P: $49-$99	2P: $49-$99	XP: $10 F12
5/1-7/9 & 3/1-4/30	1P: $39-$99	2P: $49-$99	XP: $10 F12

Phone: (905)354-5814 **20**

Motel **Location:** Corner of Hwy 420 and Stanley Ave. 5410 Buchanan Ave L2E 5A9. Fax: 905/358-2795. **Terms:** Open 5/1-11/30 & 3/1-4/30; 3 day cancellation notice. **Facility:** 46 rooms. Modest rooms near residential area and reasonably close to falls and attractions. Whirlpool room, $99-$299; 1-2 stories; exterior corridors. **Dining:** Coffee shop nearby. **All Rooms:** extended cable TV. **Cards:** AE, DS, MC, VI.

CADILLAC MOTEL

6/20-9/8	1P: $59-$99	2P: $69-$120	XP: $10 F10
5/1-6/19	1P: $40-$65	2P: $50-$70	XP: $8 F10
9/9-4/30	1P: $40-$60	2P: $50-$65	XP: $8 F10

Phone: (905)356-0830 **7**

Motel **Location:** On Hwy 20, 0.6 km from the falls. 5342 Ferry St L2G 1R7. Fax: 905/356-5624. **Terms:** Cancellation fee imposed. **Facility:** 23 rooms. Simple rooms in commercial area close to falls and attractions. 1 two-bedroom unit. 1 story; exterior corridors. **Dining:** Restaurant nearby. **Cards:** AE, DS, MC, VI.

CAMELOT INN

6/17-9/3	1P: $49-$179	2P: $49-$229	XP: $10 F12
5/1-6/16 & 9/4-4/30	1P: $39-$129	2P: $39-$149	XP: $10 F12

Phone: 905/354-3754 **15**

Motel **Location:** Just n of Hwy 20, n on Stanley Ave; just s of Hwy 420. 5640 Stanley Ave L2G 3X5. Fax: 905/354-6683. **Terms:** Package plans, off season; small pets only. **Facility:** 53 rooms. Modern rooms within reasonable proximity of commercial area, falls and attractions. 8 two-bedroom units. 6 whirlpool rooms, $79-$279; 2 stories; exterior corridors; heated pool. **Dining:** Restaurant nearby. **Some Rooms:** Fee: refrigerators. **Cards:** AE, DS, MC, VI. *(See color ad p 429)*

CANUCK MOTEL

6/9-9/4	1P: $59-$129	2P: $69-$149	XP: $10
5/1-6/8, 9/5-10/31 & 3/21-4/30	1P: $49-$99	2P: $59-$129	XP: $10

Phone: (905)374-7666 **27**

Motel **Location:** Just s of Hwy 420 and Stanley Ave, just e. 5334 Kitchener St L2G 1B5. Fax: 905/358-8221. **Terms:** Open 5/1-10/31 & 3/21-4/30; 7 day cancellation notice; cancellation fee imposed; package plans. **Facility:** 75 rooms. Well maintained rooms in quiet residential type neighborhood yet convenient to falls and attractions. 11 whirlpool rooms, $99-$299; 2 stories; interior/exterior corridors; heated pool, saunas. **Dining:** Restaurant nearby. **Some Rooms:** Fee: refrigerators. **Cards:** AE, MC, VI.

(See map p. 385)

CARRIAGE HOUSE MOTOR LODGE

(See map p. p. 385)

CASCADE INN
ⓒⓐⓐ ⓢⓐⓥⒺ
◆
Motor Inn

Phone: (905)354-2796 ❸

6/23-9/3	1P: $95-$185	2P: $95-$185	XP: $5	F14
5/1-6/22	1P: $55-$145	2P: $55-$145	XP: $5	F14
10/9-4/30	1P: $49-$125	2P: $49-$125	XP: $5	F14
9/4-10/8	1P: $65-$115	2P: $65-$115	XP: $5	F14

Location: Just n of the falls; adjacent to Skylon Tower. 5305 Murray St L2G 2J3. Fax: 905/354-2797. **Facility:** 65 rooms. Short walking distance to falls. 2 whirlpool rooms, $85-$225; 2-6 stories; interior/exterior corridors; heated pool, whirlpool. **Dining:** Restaurant; 7-11 am 5/1-10/15. **Services:** gift shop. **Cards:** AE, DS, MC, VI. **Special Amenities:** Free newspaper and preferred room (subject to availability with advanced reservations). (See color ad p 405)

CHALET MOTOR INN
ⓒⓐⓐ
◆◆◆
Motel

Phone: (905)374-1921 ❽

6/15-9/5	1P: $89	2P: $139	XP: $10	F16
9/6-9/30	1P: $69	2P: $99	XP: $10	F16
5/1-6/14 & 10/1-4/30	1P: $59	2P: $79	XP: $10	F16

Location: 0.6 km from the falls, n on Clifton, then just e. 5577 Ellen Ave L2G 3P5. Fax: 905/374-1868. **Facility:** 44 rooms. A comfortable and restful atmosphere. 9 new rooms, all with gas fireplace and whirlpool. 3 two-bedroom units. 15 whirlpool rooms, $139-$225; 3 stories, no elevator; interior/exterior corridors; heated pool, sauna. **Dining:** Restaurant nearby. **Cards:** AE, CB, DI, DS, MC, VI.

COMFORT HOTEL & SUITES-FALLSVIEW
ⓒⓐⓐ ⓢⓐⓥⒺ
◆◆◆
Hotel

Phone: (905)356-1944 ㊱

7/1-8/31	1P: $129-$503	2P: $129-$503	XP: $10	F12
9/1-10/31	1P: $79-$503	2P: $79-$503	XP: $10	F12
5/1-6/30 & 11/1-4/30	1P: $69-$449	2P: $69-$449	XP: $10	F12

Location: Across from Minolta Tower; corner of Stanley Ave and Dunn St. 6733 Oakes Dr L2G 3W6. Fax: 905/356-8245. **Terms:** [CP] meal plan; cancellation fee imposed. **Facility:** 98 rooms. 33 whirlpool rooms, $94-$503; heated pool. **Dining:** Dining room nearby. **Services:** Fee: area transportation, casino. **Some Rooms:** safes. **Cards:** AE, CB, DI, DS, JC, MC, VI. (See color ad p 398)

COMFORT INN FALLSWAY
ⓒⓐⓐ ⓢⓐⓥⒺ
◆◆◆
Motor Inn

Phone: (905)358-3293 ⓲

5/1-10/31	1P: $79-$279	2P: $79-$279	XP: $10	F18
11/1-4/30	1P: $49-$189	2P: $49-$189	XP: $10	F18

Location: Just s of jct Victoria Ave and Clifton Hill. 4960 Clifton Hill L2E 6S8 (PO Box 60, NIAGARA FALLS, ON). Fax: 905/358-3818. **Terms:** [CP] meal plan; package plans, 9/7-6/8. **Facility:** 180 rooms. Nice rooms in midst of Clifton Hill tourist attractions; walking distance to Victoria Park, falls and casino. 7 two-bedroom units. 2 whirlpool rooms, $109-$329; 3 stories, no elevator; interior corridors; heated pool, whirlpool. Fee: miniature golf. **Dining:** Restaurant; 11 am-2 am; $7-$20; cocktails. **Recreation:** arcade. **Cards:** AE, CB, DI, DS, JC, MC, VI. **Special Amenities:** Free breakfast and free local telephone calls. (See color ad starting on p 425)

COMFORT INN NORTH OF THE FALLS
ⓒⓐⓐ ⓢⓐⓥⒺ
◆◆
Motel

Phone: (905)356-0131 ㉓

5/1-9/30	1P: $69-$269	2P: $69-$269	XP: $10	F12
10/1-4/30	1P: $49-$199	2P: $49-$199	XP: $10	F12

Location: 3 km n Rainbow Bridge. 4009 River Rd L2E 3E9. Fax: 905/356-3306. **Terms:** 3 day cancellation notice; package plans. **Facility:** 66 rooms. All whirlpool rooms. 5 whirlpool rooms, 2 stories; exterior corridors. **Dining:** Coffee shop; 7 am-10 pm; closed 12/1-4/30; $8-$14. **Services:** Fee: area transportation. **Some Rooms:** Fee: VCR. **Cards:** AE, DI, DS, JC, MC, VI. **Special Amenities:** Free local telephone calls and free newspaper.

CRYSTAL MOTEL
ⓒⓐⓐ ⓢⓐⓥⒺ
◆◆
Motel

Phone: (905)354-0460 ㉕

6/28-9/5	1P: $69-$139	2P: $79-$149	XP: $10	F12
5/1-6/27 & 9/6-10/31	1P: $49-$89	2P: $49-$99	XP: $6	F12
11/1-4/30	1P: $45-$69	2P: $49-$79	XP: $6	F12

Location: 2.8 km n of falls on Niagara River Pkwy. 4267 River Rd L2E 3E7. Fax: 905/374-4972. **Terms:** 3 day cancellation notice; cancellation fee imposed. **Facility:** 38 rooms. Some rooms with balcony overlooking Niagara River Gorge; 10 with fireplace. 7 whirlpool rooms, $89-$199; 2 stories; exterior corridors; heated pool. **Dining:** Restaurant nearby. **Cards:** AE, DS, MC, VI. **Special Amenities:** Free local telephone calls and preferred room (subject to availability with advanced reservations).

DAYS INN CLIFTON HILL/CASINO
ⓒⓐⓐ
◆◆
Motor Inn

Phone: (905)356-2461 ⓰

Property failed to provide current rates

Location: Just e on Hwy 20. 5657 Victoria Ave L2G 3L5. Fax: 905/356-2467. **Terms:** Cancellation fee imposed; package plans. **Facility:** 88 rooms. Rooms close to casino and local attraction. 5 two-bedroom units. 2 stories; exterior corridors; heated pool. **Dining:** 10:30 am-2:30 & 3-11:30 pm; 4 pm-9:30 pm off season; $10-$18. **Cards:** AE, CB, DI, DS, JC, MC, VI. (See color ad p 407)

DAYS INN FALLSVIEW DISTRICT
ⓒⓐⓐ ⓢⓐⓥⒺ
◆◆
Motor Inn

Phone: (905)356-5877 ㉝

5/1-9/30	1P: $75-$325	2P: $75-$325	XP: $10	F12
10/1-4/30	1P: $55-$225	2P: $55-$225	XP: $10	F12

Location: Between Minolta and Skylon Towers, just w of the falls via Murray St. 6408 Stanley Ave L2G 3Y5. Fax: 905/356-9452. **Terms:** [BP] meal plan; 3 day cancellation notice; package plans. **Facility:** 102 rooms. 3 two-bedroom units. 3 stories; interior/exterior corridors; heated pool, sauna. **Dining:** Restaurant; 7 am-10 & 5-8 pm; $8-$20; cocktails. **All Rooms:** combo or shower baths. **Cards:** AE, DI, DS, JC, MC, VI. (See color ad p 409)

(See map p. p. 385)

DAYS INN-LUNDY'S LANE

Phone: (905)358-3621 **47**

Property failed to provide current rates

CAA
◆ ◆
Motor Inn

Location: 3.8 km w on Hwy 20; from QEW, Hwy 20 W. 7280 Lundy's Ln L2G 1W2. Fax: 905/358-0277. **Terms:** [BP] meal plan; 3 day cancellation notice; cancellation fee imposed; package plans. **Facility:** 135 rooms. 2-5 stories; interior/exterior corridors; miniature golf seasonal; heated pool, sauna, whirlpool, playground. **Dining:** Restaurant; 24 hrs; $6-$13; wine/beer only. **Cards:** AE, DI, DS, JC, MC, VI.

(See color ad below)

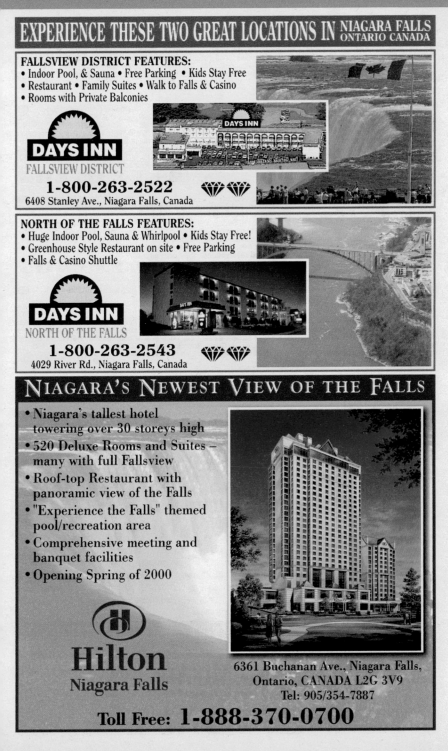

(See map p. p. 385)

DAYS INN NEAR THE FALLS

(CAA) (SAVE) ◆ ◆   Motel

| 5/1-9/30 | 1P: $90-$300 | 2P: $90-$300 | XP: $20 |
| 10/1-4/30 | 1P: $80-$280 | 2P: $80-$280 | XP: $20 |

Phone: (905)374-3333   12
F12
F12

Location: On Hwy 20, 0.6 km from the falls. 5943 Victoria Ave L2G 3L8. Fax: 905/374-0669. **Terms:** Cancellation fee imposed; package plans, off season. **Facility:** 117 rooms. In popular commercial area. 16 whirlpool rooms; 7 stories; interior corridors; heated pool, sauna, whirlpool. **Dining:** Restaurant nearby. **Services:** gift shop. **Recreation:** game rooms. **Cards:** AE, DI, DS, MC, VI. *(See color ad p 408)*

DAYS INN NORTH OF THE FALLS

(CAA) (SAVE) ◆ ◆   Motor Inn

| 5/1-9/30 | 1P: $88-$298 | 2P: $88-$298 | XP: $10 |
| 10/1-4/30 | 1P: $48-$198 | 2P: $48-$198 | XP: $10 |

Phone: (905)356-6666   24
F12
F12

Location: 3 km n of Rainbow Bridge. 4029 River Rd L2E 3E5. Fax: 905/356-1800. **Terms:** 3 day cancellation notice; package plans. **Facility:** 94 rooms. Some rooms overlooking Niagara Gorge. All rooms with gas fireplace. 7 whirlpool rooms; 4 stories, no elevator; interior/exterior corridors; heated pool, sauna, whirlpool. **Dining:** Restaurant; 7 am-10 pm; $8-$14; cocktails. **Some Rooms:** Fee: refrigerators, VCR. **Cards:** AE, CB, DI, DS, JC, MC, VI. **Special Amenities:** Free local telephone calls and free newspaper. *(See color ad p 409)*

FALLSVIEW INN

(CAA) (SAVE) ◆ ◆ ◆   Motor Inn

| 6/22-9/4 | 1P: $99-$189 | 2P: $99-$189 | XP: $10 |
| 5/1-6/21 & 9/5-4/30 | 1P: $48-$189 | 2P: $48-$189 | XP: $10 |

Phone: (905)374-4244   31
F18
F18

Location: 1.2 km w on Hwy 20, just s. 6170 Stanley Ave L2G 3Y4. Fax: 905/374-6142. **Terms:** Package plans. **Facility:** 65 rooms. Spacious rooms in short walking distance to the falls. 8 whirlpool rooms, $79-$229; 5 stories; interior corridors; heated pool, sauna. **Dining:** Restaurant; 7 am-11 & 5-9 pm; $6-$13; cocktails. **Some Rooms:** Fee: refrigerators. **Cards:** AE, DS, MC, VI. **Special Amenities:** Free room upgrade (subject to availability with advanced reservations). *(See color ad p 407)*

FLAMINGO MOTOR INN

(CAA) (SAVE) ◆ ◆   Motel

6/23-9/3	1P: $69-$139	2P: $79-$169	XP: $10
5/1-6/22 & 9/4-10/14	1P: $49-$99	2P: $52-$109	XP: $10
10/15-4/30	1P: $39-$69	2P: $49-$79	XP: $10

Phone: (905)356-4646   64
F14
F14
F14

Location: 3.4 km w on Hwy 20 from QEW. 7701 Lundy's Ln L2H 1H3. Fax: 905/356-9373. **Terms:** Weekly rates avail; 7 day cancellation notice. **Facility:** 93 rooms. Variety of room sizes avail, in a commercial area. 3 two-bedroom units. 11 whirlpool rooms, $89-$209; 2 stories; exterior corridors; heated pool. **Dining:** Restaurant nearby. **Services:** winter plug-ins. **All Rooms:** extended cable TV. **Some Rooms:** efficiency. **Cards:** AE, CB, DI, DS, MC, VI. **Special Amenities:** Free local telephone calls and free newspaper. *(See color ad below)*

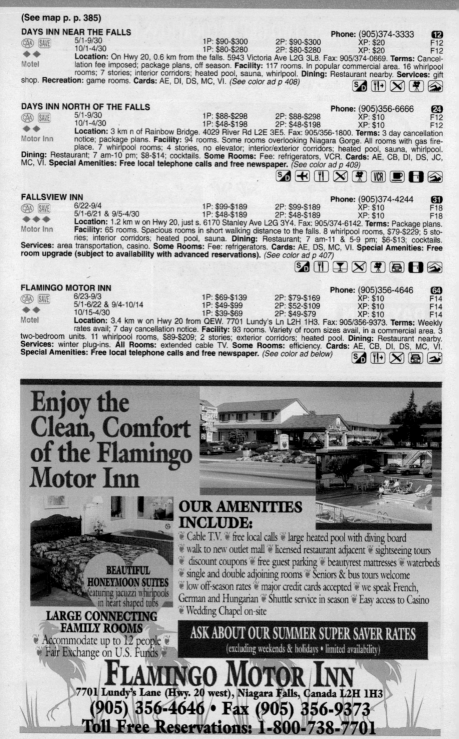

(See map p. p. 385)

FOUR POINTS HOTEL, NIAGARA FALLS, BY-THE-FALLS   Phone: (905)374-4142   [58]

6/16-9/16	1P: $109-$339	2P: $119-$349	XP: $12 F16
9/17-10/28	1P: $89-$319	2P: $99-$319	XP: $12 F16
5/1-6/15	1P: $89-$319	2P: $99-$319	XP: $12 F16
10/29-4/30	1P: $69-$309	2P: $79-$319	XP: $12 F16

CAA SAVE / ◆◆◆ / Motor Inn

Location: 1.2 km w on Hwy 20, then s. 6045 Stanley Ave L2G 3Y3. Fax: 905/358-3430. **Terms:** [BP] & [MAP] meal plans; package plans. **Facility:** 112 rooms. Nicely appointed rooms at location convenient to falls and commercial areas. Fireplace suites, $149-$399; 21 whirlpool rooms, $135-$449; 8 stories; interior corridors; heated pool, sauna, whirlpool. **Dining:** Restaurant; 7 am-noon & 5-11 pm; $10-$15; cocktails. **Services:** Fee: area transportation, local shuttle. **Recreation:** small game room. **All Rooms:** extended cable TV. **Cards:** AE, CB, DI, DS, MC, VI. **Special Amenities:** Free newspaper and preferred room (subject to availability with advanced reservations). *(See color ad below)*

GLENGATE MOTEL   Phone: (905)357-1333   [28]

5/1-9/6	1P: $50-$120	2P: $50-$130	XP: $10 F12
9/7-4/30	1P: $40-$99	2P: $45-$105	XP: $10 F12

◆ / Motel

Location: Just s of Hwy 420 and Stanley Ave. 5534 Stanley Ave L2G 3X2. Fax: 905/357-1341. **Terms:** 3 day cancellation notice; cancellation fee imposed; small pets only, $8 extra charge. **Facility:** 31 rooms. 10 minute walk to Clifton Hill and the falls. 3 stories, no elevator; exterior corridors; heated pool. **Some Rooms:** 3 efficiencies. **Cards:** AE, CB, DI, DS, MC, VI.

HAMPTON INN AT THE FALLS   Phone: (905)357-1626   [17]

7/1-9/3	1P: $149-$339	2P: $149-$339	XP: $10 F18
5/1-6/30 & 9/4-10/9	1P: $99-$279	2P: $99-$279	XP: $10 F18
10/10-4/30	1P: $69-$199	2P: $69-$199	XP: $10 F18

CAA / ◆◆◆ / Motel

Location: At top of Clifton Hill; ne of the falls. 5591 Victoria Ave L2G 3L4. Fax: 905/357-5869. **Terms:** [BP] & [CP] meal plans; weekly & monthly rates avail; cancellation fee imposed. **Facility:** 127 rooms. Spacious, family oriented accommodations. 11 rooms with fireplace. 22 two-bedroom units. 6 stories; interior corridors; heated pool, sauna, whirlpool. **Dining:** Restaurant nearby. **Services:** gift shop. **Some Rooms:** Fee: refrigerators. **Cards:** AE, CB, DI, DS, JC, MC, VI. *(See color ad starting on p 412)*

HAMPTON INN NORTH OF THE FALLS   Phone: (905)358-5555   [5]

5/1-9/30	1P: $79-$299	2P: $79-$299	XP: $10
10/1-4/30	1P: $59-$199	2P: $59-$199	

CAA / ◆◆◆ / Motor Inn

Location: 2.8 km n of the falls. 4357 River Rd L2E 3E8. Fax: 905/358-0140. **Terms:** [CP] meal plan; package plans. **Facility:** 105 rooms. Some rooms with fireplace. Rates for up to 4 persons; 15 whirlpool rooms; 5 stories; interior corridors; heated pool, sauna, whirlpool. **Dining:** Restaurant; 6 am-10 & 5-10 pm; 6 am-10 & noon-10 pm 7/1-8/31; $7-$14; wine/beer only. **Services:** Fee: area transportation, falls/casino (in season). **Recreation:** game room. **Cards:** AE, DI, DS, MC, VI.

HILTON NIAGARA FALLS   Phone: (905)354-7887   [50]

6/30-9/3	1P: $199-$999	2P: $199-$999	XP: $10
5/1-6/29 & 9/4-4/30	1P: $99-$999	2P: $99-$999	XP: $10

CAA SAVE / ◆◆◆ / Motel

Location: Hwy 20, just s. 6361 Buchanan Ave L2G 3V9. Fax: 905/357-9300. **Terms:** 3 day cancellation notice; package plans. **Facility:** 520 rooms. Many rooms with view of the falls. 82 whirlpool rooms, $129-$1299; 36 stories; interior corridors; heated pool, sauna, whirlpool. **Dining:** Cocktails; restaurant nearby. **Services:** gift shop. **Cards:** AE, CB, DI, DS, JC, MC, VI. *(See color ad p 409)*

HOJO INN   Phone: (905)358-9777   [55]

6/23-9/3	1P: $60-$200	2P: $60-$200	XP: $10 F12
9/4-4/30	1P: $39-$200	2P: $39-$200	XP: $10 F12
5/1-6/22	1P: $39-$150	2P: $39-$150	XP: $10 F12

CAA SAVE / ◆◆ / Motel

Location: 5 km w on Hwy 20, from QEW, Hwy 20 W. 8100 Lundy's Ln L2H 1H1. Fax: 905/358-0575. **Terms:** Weekly rates avail; cancellation fee imposed. **Facility:** 84 rooms. Family oriented accommodations in commercial area. 24 whirlpool rooms, $70-$300; 2 stories; exterior corridors; heated pool. **Dining:** Coffee shop; 7 am-1 pm; open weekends off season. **Services:** winter plug-ins. Fee: area transportation, casino. **Cards:** AE, CB, DI, DS, JC, MC, VI.

(See map p. p. 385)

HOLIDAY INN-BY THE FALLS

CAA SAVE
◆◆◆
Motor Inn

			Phone: (905)356-1333	
6/16-9/3	1P: $115-$255	2P: $115-$255	XP: $10	F14
9/4-10/8	1P: $85-$199	2P: $85-$199	XP: $10	F14
5/1-6/15	1P: $69-$185	2P: $69-$185	XP: $5	F14
10/9-4/30	1P: $59-$175	2P: $59-$175	XP: $5	F14

Location: Just w from the falls on Murray St; adjacent to Skylon Tower. 5339 Murray Hill at Buchanan Ave L2G 2J3. Fax: 905/356-7128. **Terms:** Package plans; pets, $50 dep req. **Facility:** 122 rooms. Not a member of Holiday Inns; well appointed, spacious rooms. 6 whirlpool rooms, $140-$350; 6 stories; interior corridors; 2 heated pools, sauna, whirlpool. **Dining:** Restaurant; 8 am-10 pm; 7 am-11 pm 6/14-10/15; $10-$19; cocktails; patio entertainment 6/14-9/5. **Services:** gift shop. Fee: area transportation, casino. **Cards:** AE, CB, DI, DS, JC, MC, VI. **Special Amenities:** Free newspaper and free room upgrade (subject to availability with advanced reservations). (See color ad p 414 & p 435)

HORSESHOE FALLS MOTOR INN

CAA SAVE
◆◆
Motor Inn

			Phone: (905)358-9353	
6/23-9/4	1P: $69-$169	2P: $69-$169	XP: $10	F12
5/1-6/22 & 9/5-10/9	1P: $49-$139	2P: $49-$139	XP: $7	F12
10/10-4/30	1P: $39-$109	2P: $39-$109	XP: $7	F12

Location: Opposite Minolta Tower. 5481 Dunn St L2G 2N6. Fax: 905/356-7298. **Terms:** 4 day cancellation notice. **Facility:** 64 rooms. 1 poolside section and 1 mid-rise building. 2 whirlpool rooms, $100-$400; 2-4 stories; interior/exterior corridors; heated pool, whirlpool. **Dining:** Restaurant; 8 am-midnight; closed 5/1-10/31; $7-$18; cocktails. **Some Rooms:** Fee: refrigerators. **Cards:** AE, CB, DI, DS, JC, MC, VI. **Special Amenities:** Free local telephone calls. (See color ad p 413)

HOWARD JOHNSON BY THE FALLS

CAA
◆◆◆
Motel

			Phone: 905/357-4040	
6/25-9/6	1P: $99-$219	2P: $99-$219	XP: $10	F16
5/1-6/24 & 9/7-10/31	1P: $69-$159	2P: $69-$159	XP: $10	F16
11/1-4/30	1P: $59-$139	2P: $59-$139	XP: $10	F16

Location: On Hwy 20, 0.6 km from the falls. 5905 Victoria Ave L2G 3L8. Fax: 905/357-6202. **Terms:** Package plans. **Facility:** 199 rooms. Downtown high-rise building with combined indoor/outdoor pools. 6 two-bedroom units. 68 whirlpool rooms, $99-$199; 7 stories; interior corridors; 2 heated pools, sauna, whirlpool. **Dining:** Restaurant nearby. **Services:** gift shop. **Cards:** AE, CB, DI, DS, JC, MC, VI. (See color ad p 415)

(See map p. p. 385)

IMPALA MOTEL　　　　　　　　　　　　　　　　　　　　**Phone:** (905)358-6567　**44**

(CAA)	7/10-8/20	1P: $59-$149	2P: $69-$149	XP: $10	F12
	8/21-10/31	1P: $49-$99	2P: $49-$99	XP: $10	F12
◆	5/1-7/9 & 4/1-4/30	1P: $39-$99	2P: $49-$99	XP: $10	F12

Motel   **Location:** Corner of Ferry St and Stanley Ave, then just s. 5923 Stanley Ave L2G 3Y2. Fax: 905/374-4602. **Terms:** Open 5/1-10/31 & 4/1-4/30; 3 day cancellation notice. **Facility:** 38 rooms. Nice rooms set back from street and concealed by plain exterior wall. 8 whirlpool rooms, $99-$299; 2 stories; interior/exterior corridors; heated pool. **Dining:** Restaurant nearby. **Some Rooms:** kitchen, no utensils. **Cards:** AE, DI, DS, MC, VI.　⊞✕☎⊟☄

IMPERIAL HOTEL & SUITES　　　　　　　　　　　　　　**Phone:** (905)356-2648　**14**

(CAA) SAVE	6/17-9/4	1P: $129-$249	2P: $129-$249	XP: $15	F14
◆◆◆	5/1-6/16 & 9/5-10/28	1P: $79-$159	2P: $79-$159	XP: $15	F14
	10/29-4/30	1P: $59-$139	2P: $59-$139	XP: $15	F14

Motor Inn   **Location:** On Hwy 20, 0.5 km from the falls. 5851 Victoria Ave L2G 3L6. Fax: 905/356-4068. **Terms:** [BP] meal plan; check-in 4 pm; package plans. **Facility:** 104 rooms. Spacious, nicely appointed suites, some with partial view of falls. 8 whirlpool rooms, $189-$309; 10 stories; interior corridors; heated pool, whirlpool. **Dining:** Coffee shop; 7 am-2 am. **Services:** gift shop. **Recreation:** game room. **Some Rooms:** Fee: microwaves. **Cards:** AE, DI, DS, MC, VI. **Special Amenities:** Free breakfast and free local telephone calls.　⑤ⓘ⊟✕☄

(See map p. p. 385)

INN ON THE NIAGARA PARKWAY

			Phone: (905)295-4371	**77**
7/1-9/3	1P: $69-$189	2P: $69-$189	XP: $10	F12
5/5-6/30 & 9/4-10/30	1P: $49-$149	2P: $49-$149	XP: $10	F12

CAA ◆ Motel

Location: 2 km s of Horseshoe Falls. 7857 Niagara River Pkwy L2G 6R5. Fax: 905/295-0630. **Terms:** Open 5/5-10/30; [CP] meal plan; small pets only. **Facility:** 53 rooms. Quiet location on the Niagara River. Whirlpool room; 1 story; exterior corridors; heated pool. **Cards:** AE, DS, JC, MC, VI.

KINGS INN NEAR THE FALLS

			Phone: (905)356-1233	**69**
6/23-9/3	1P: $89-$199	2P: $89-$199	XP: $15	F12
5/1-6/22 & 9/4-9/30	1P: $59-$149	2P: $59-$149	XP: $10	F12
10/1-4/30	1P: $44-$89	2P: $44-$89	XP: $10	F12

◆◆ Motel

Location: On Hwy 20, 1 km from the falls. 5525 Ferry St L2G 1S3. Fax: 905/374-6412. **Terms:** Package plans. **Facility:** 44 rooms. Well kept rooms in commercial area close to the falls and attractions. 3 stories, no elevator; exterior corridors; heated pool. **Cards:** AE, CB, DI, DS, JC, MC, VI.

KNIGHTS INN ON LUNDY'S LANE

			Phone: (905)354-6939	**46**
6/30-9/3	1P: $69-$219	2P: $69-$239	XP: $8	F12
5/1-6/29	1P: $45-$195	2P: $45-$215	XP: $5	F12
9/4-4/30	1P: $45-$195	2P: $45-$205	XP: $5	F12

CAA SAVE ◆◆ Motel

Location: 3.4 km w on Hwy 20. 7034 Lundy's Ln L2G 1V9. Fax: 905/354-3699. **Facility:** 64 rooms. Family oriented facility on nice lot in commercial area near attractions. 2 two-bedroom units. 2 stories; exterior corridors; heated pool. **Dining:** Restaurant nearby. **All Rooms:** extended cable TV. **Some Rooms:** Fee: refrigerators. **Cards:** AE, DI, DS, MC, VI. **Special Amenities:** Free local telephone calls and free newspaper.

LINCOLN MOTOR INN

			Phone: (905)356-1748	**41**
6/23-8/26	1P: $89-$199	2P: $89-$199	XP: $10	F15
5/26-6/22 & 8/27-4/30	1P: $55-$159	2P: $55-$159	XP: $7	F15
5/1-5/25	1P: $49-$119	2P: $49-$119	XP: $7	F15

CAA SAVE ◆◆ Motor Inn

Location: By Minolta Tower; 0.3 mi w of the falls via Murray St. 6417 Main St L2G 5Y3. Fax: 905/356-7531. **Terms:** [AP] & [BP] meal plans; weekly rates avail; cancellation fee imposed; package plans. **Facility:** 60 rooms. Nicely maintained facility near many area attractions. 3 two-bedroom units. 5 whirlpool rooms, $105-$255; 2 stories; exterior corridors; heated pool, whirlpool. **Dining:** Restaurant; 7 am-9:30 pm; to 10 pm 6/19-9/4; 7:30-11:30 am 11/1-3/31; $6-$14; health conscious menu items; cocktails; Reservations accepted for groups. **Cards:** AE, DI, DS, MC, VI. **Special Amenities:** Free local telephone calls and free newspaper. *(See color ad p 415)*

MARCO POLO INN

			Phone: (905)356-6959	**68**
6/30-9/4	1P: $69-$129	2P: $79-$149	XP: $10	F12
9/5-4/30	1P: $49-$69	2P: $59-$79	XP: $10	F12
5/1-6/29	1P: $49-$69	2P: $49-$69	XP: $10	F12

◆◆ Motel

Location: On Hwy 20, 1 km from the falls. 5553 Ferry St L2G 1S3. Fax: 905/356-8298. **Terms:** Cancellation fee imposed. **Facility:** 38 rooms. Spacious accommodations in commercial area. 3 stories, no elevator; interior corridors; heated pool. **Cards:** AE, DI, DS, JC, MC, VI.

MELODY MOTEL

			Phone: (905)227-1023	**32**
6/26-9/6	1P: $48-$78	2P: $48-$88	XP: $8	F12
5/1-6/25	1P: $38-$68	2P: $48-$78	XP: $8	F12
9/7-4/30	1P: $34-$64	2P: $42-$68	XP: $6	F12

CAA SAVE ◆ Motel

Location: 9.2 km w on Hwy 20. 13065 Lundy's Ln L2E 6S4. Fax: 905/227-3712. **Terms:** 3 day cancellation notice; cancellation fee imposed. **Facility:** 19 rooms. Simple lodging in country setting on outskirts of Niagara Falls. 1 story; exterior corridors; heated pool. **Services:** winter plug-ins. **Cards:** AE, DS, MC, VI. **Special Amenities:** Free local telephone calls.

MICHAEL'S INN-BY THE FALLS

			Phone: (905)354-2727	**22**
6/9-9/11	1P: $88-$298	2P: $88-$298	XP: $10	F12
5/1-6/8 & 9/12-11/4	1P: $58-$178	2P: $58-$178	XP: $10	F12
11/5-4/30	1P: $49-$118	2P: $49-$118	XP: $10	F12

CAA SAVE ◆◆◆ Motor Inn

Location: Just n of Rainbow Bridge and QEW. 5599 River Rd L2E 3H3. Fax: 905/374-7706. **Terms:** Package plans. **Facility:** 130 rooms. Overlooking Niagara River and the Gorge, many rooms with view of the falls. 13 whirlpool rooms, $125-$495; 4 stories; interior corridors; heated pool, wading pool, sauna, whirlpool. **Dining:** Restaurant; 7 am-11 pm; 8 am-9 pm 11/1-4/30; $10-$26; cocktails. **Services:** gift shop. **All Rooms:** extended cable TV. **Cards:** AE, CB, DI, MC, VI. *(See color ad p 437 & starting on p 418)*

MIDTOWN LODGE

			Phone: (905)357-2723	**72**
6/9-9/4	1P: $59-$129	2P: $69-$149	XP: $10	
5/1-6/8, 9/5-10/31 & 3/21-4/30	1P: $49-$99	2P: $59-$129	XP: $10	

CAA ◆◆ Motel

Location: Corner of Lorne Ave and Slater St. 5265 Lorne Ave L2G 1G7. Fax: 905/358-8221. **Terms:** Open 5/1-10/31 & 3/21-4/30; 7 day cancellation notice; cancellation fee imposed. **Facility:** 25 rooms. Spacious rooms in residential type neighborhood, yet convenient to falls and attractions. 5 whirlpool rooms, $99-$299; 2 stories; exterior corridors. **Dining:** Restaurant nearby. **Some Rooms:** Fee: refrigerators. **Cards:** AE, MC, VI.

(See map p. p. 385)

NIAGARA FALLS MARRIOTT FALLSVIEW

Phone: (905)357-7300 **39**

7/1-8/31	1P: $259-$850	2P: $259-$850	XP: $10
9/1-11/30	1P: $169-$850	2P: $169-$850	XP: $10
5/1-6/30 & 12/1-4/30	1P: $129-$850	2P: $129-$850	XP: $10

Hotel   **Location:** Next to Minolta Tower. 6740 Oakes Dr L2G 3W6. Fax: 905/357-0490. **Facility:** 285 rooms. 75 whirlpool rooms, $149-$599; 20 stories; interior corridors; heated pool, saunas, whirlpool. **Dining:** Terrapin Grille, see separate listing. **Some Rooms:** color TV. **Cards:** AE, CB, DI, DS, JC, MC, VI. *(See color ad below)*

NIAGARA FALLS MOTOR LODGE

Phone: (905)295-3569 **75**

6/24-9/5	1P: $88-$138	2P: $88-$138	XP: $10 F12
5/1-6/23 & 9/6-4/30	1P: $48-$98	2P: $48-$98	XP: $10

Motel   **Location:** 2 km s of Horseshoe Falls on Niagara Pkwy to Portage Rd S, just to the right; 1.2 km s of Marineland. 7950 Portage Rd S L2G 5Y8. Fax: 905/295-0022. **Terms:** 3 day cancellation notice. **Facility:** 20 rooms. Spacious, well kept rooms in quiet neighborhood close to Niagara River. 2 stories; exterior corridors; heated pool. **Dining:** Restaurant nearby. **Cards:** AE, MC, VI.

NIAGARA FAMILY INN

Phone: (905)354-9844 **6**

7/1-9/4	1P: $55-$69	2P: $69-$89	XP: $10 F
5/1-6/30 & 9/5-4/30	1P: $39-$59	2P: $49-$69	XP: $10 F

Motor Inn   **Location:** Clifton Ave, just e. 5612 Ellen Ave L2G 3P6. Fax: 905/354-6691. **Terms:** Weekly rates avail; 5 day cancellation notice. **Facility:** 36 rooms. Family oriented accommodations close to area attractions. 2 stories; interior/exterior corridors; heated pool, sauna, whirlpool. **Dining:** Restaurant; 11 am-1 am; $6-$15; cocktails; banquet facilities avail, hrs vary off season. **Cards:** AE, DS, MC, VI. **Special Amenities:** Preferred room (subject to availability with advanced reservations).

NIAGARA PARKWAY COURT MOTEL

Phone: (905)295-3331 **73**

6/16-9/16	1P: $49-$99	2P: $59-$149	XP: $20 F10
5/1-6/15 & 9/17-4/30	1P: $49-$69	2P: $59-$99	XP: $15 F10

Motel   **Location:** 2.5 km s of the falls on the Niagara Pkwy. 3708 Main St L2G 6B1. Fax: 905/295-0543. **Terms:** [CP] meal plan; cancellation fee imposed; small pets only, $10 extra charge; in 1 room. **Facility:** 19 rooms. Quiet section located close to scenic river. Whirlpool room, $99-$199; 2 stories; exterior corridors; golf course nearby. **Dining:** Restaurant nearby. **Recreation:** playground & wading pool along nearby river. **Some Rooms:** 4 efficiencies. **Cards:** AE, DI, MC, VI. **Special Amenities:** Early check-in/late check-out and free breakfast.

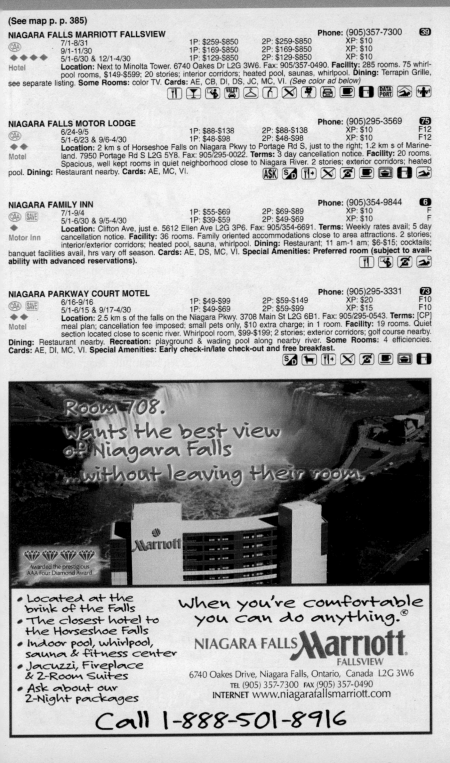

(See map p. p. 385)

OAKES INN FALLSVIEW   **Phone:** (905)356-4514 ❶

(CAA)   Property failed to provide current rates

◆◆◆   **Location:** By Minolta Tower. 6546 Buchanan Ave L2G 3W2. **Fax:** 905/356-3651. **Facility:** 167 rooms. Top

Motor Inn   floors of hotel section overlook falls; observation deck for guests. Older section of property is a motel. 2-12 sto-ries; interior/exterior corridors; 2 heated pools, sauna, whirlpool. **Dining:** Dining room; 7 am-midnight; 8 am-10 pm, 9/16-5/1; $7-$16; cocktails. **Services:** gift shop. Fee: area transportation, casino. **Some Rooms:** Fee: re-frigerators. **Cards:** AE, DI, DS, JC, MC, VI. *(See color ad below)*

(See map p. p. 385)

PARK PLAZA
Phone: (905)353-1010   63
(CAA) (SAVE)

	6/23-9/3	1P: $99-$199	2P: $99-$199	XP: $10	F12
◆◆◆	5/1-6/22 & 9/4-10/28	1P: $79-$179	2P: $79-$179	XP: $10	F12
Hotel	10/29-4/30	1P: $69-$169	2P: $69-$169	XP: $10	F12

Location: Just s of jct Main and Ferry sts. 5807 Ferry St L2G 1S8. Fax: 905/358-7131. **Terms:** [CP] meal plan; check-in 4 pm; cancellation fee imposed; package plans. **Facility:** 145 rooms. Elegantly appointed guest rooms with eye catching teal wrought iron furnishings. 28 whirlpool rooms, $89-$249; 11 stories; interior/exterior corridors; 2 heated pools, sauna, whirlpool. **Dining:** Restaurant; 6 am-2 am; $8-$15; cocktails. **Services:** area transportation, casino & falls. Fee: massage. **All Rooms:** combo or shower baths, extended cable TV. **Some Rooms:** honor bars. **Cards:** AE, DI, DS, JC, MC, VI. **Special Amenities:** Free newspaper and preferred room (subject to availability with advanced reservations). *(See color ad below)*

PENINSULA INN & RESORT
Phone: (905)354-8812   76
(CAA) (SAVE)

	6/24-9/4		2P: $109-$199	XP: $10	F12
◆◆◆	5/1-6/23		2P: $79-$129	XP: $10	F12
Hotel	9/5-4/30		2P: $69-$129	XP: $10	F12

Location: QEW, exit McLeod Rd, just w. 7373 Niagara Square Dr L2E 6S5. Fax: 905/354-7174. **Terms:** Cancellation fee imposed; package plans; pets, $10 fee, restrictions apply. **Facility:** 95 rooms. Oversized corridor areas lead to tastefully decorated guest rooms in peaceful setting. 13 whirlpool rooms, $149-$349; 5 stories; interior corridors; heated pool, sauna, whirlpool. **Dining:** Restaurant; 7 am-2 & 5-11 pm, Sat & Sun 7 am-11 pm; cocktails. **Services:** gift shop; area transportation, casino & downtown. **Cards:** AE, DI, MC, VI.

THE PRESIDENT MOTOR INN
Phone: 905/358-7272   40
(CAA)

| | 6/23-8/19 | 1P: $59-$130 | 2P: $59-$130 | XP: $10 | F12 |
| ◆ | 5/1-6/22 & 8/20-12/31 | 1P: $30-$69 | 2P: $30-$69 | XP: $10 | F12 |

Motel   **Location:** Just w of Minolta Tower, corner of Stanley and Dixon aves. 6503 Stanley Ave L2G 7L2. Fax: 905/356-0392. **Terms:** Open 5/1-12/31. **Facility:** 42 rooms. Budget accommodations in reasonably close proximity to the falls. 2 two-bedroom units, $120; $60, off season for up to 6 persons; 2 stories; exterior corridors; heated pool. **Dining:** Restaurant nearby. **All Rooms:** extended cable TV. **Cards:** AE, DS, MC, VI. *(See color ad p 422)*

QUALITY HOTEL-NEAR THE FALLS
Phone: (905)356-2842   10
(CAA) (SAVE)

| | 7/1-8/31 | 1P: $129-$299 | 2P: $129-$299 | XP: $25 | F16 |
| ◆◆◆ | 5/1-6/30 & 9/1-4/30 | 1P: $69-$249 | 2P: $69-$249 | XP: $25 | F16 |

Motor Inn   **Location:** On Hwy 20, 0.7 km from the falls. 5257 Ferry St L2G 1R6. Fax: 905/356-6629. **Terms:** Cancellation fee imposed; package plans, off season. **Facility:** 120 rooms. Walking distance to the falls, casino and local attractions. All rooms with hair dryer. 14 whirlpool rooms, $129-$389; 11 stories; interior corridors; heated pool, wading pool, sauna, whirlpool. **Dining:** Restaurant; 7 am-noon, buffet. **Services:** gift shop. **Recreation:** sun deck. **Cards:** AE, CB, DI, DS, JC, MC, VI. *(See color ad p 423)*

QUALITY INN FALLSWAY
Phone: (905)358-3601   19
(CAA) (SAVE)

| | 5/1-10/31 | 1P: $79-$279 | 2P: $79-$279 | XP: $10 | F18 |
| ◆◆ | 11/1-4/30 | 1P: $49-$189 | 2P: $49-$189 | XP: $10 | F18 |

Motor Inn   **Location:** Just s of jct Victoria Ave and Clifton Hill. 4946 Clifton Hill L2E 6S8 (PO Box 60, NIAGARA FALLS, ON). Fax: 905/358-3818. **Terms:** Package plans, 9/7-6/8. **Facility:** 275 rooms. Within walking distance of falls and major attractions. 7 two-bedroom units, 7 whirlpool rooms, $109-$329; 2-3 stories, no elevator; interior/exterior corridors; arcade; 2 pools, 1 indoor heated, wading pool, whirlpool. Fee: miniature golf. **Dining:** Restaurant; 6:30 am-11 pm; $5-$15; cocktails. **Services:** gift shop. **Recreation:** Dazzleland Arcade. **Cards:** AE, CB, DI, DS, JC, MC, VI. **Special Amenities:** Free local telephone calls. *(See color ad starting on p 425)*

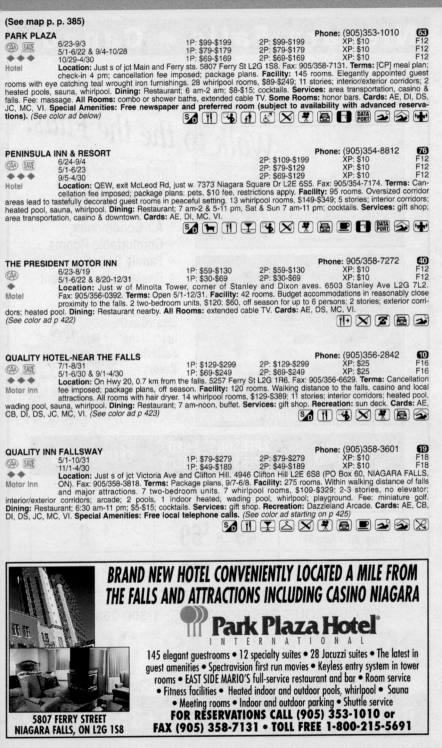

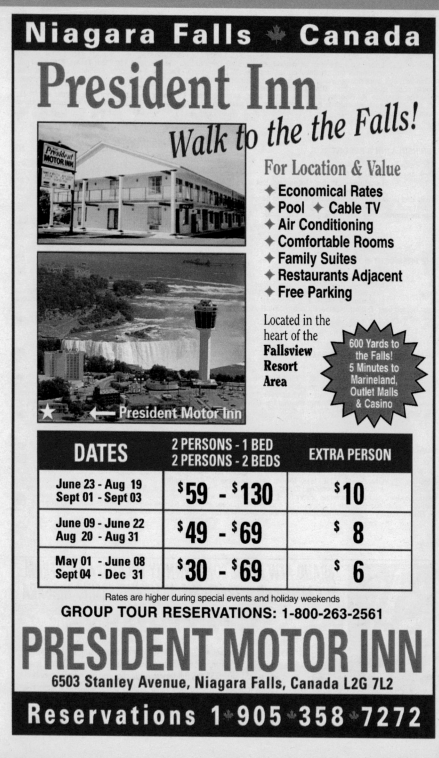

(See map p. p. 385)

RAMADA CORAL RESORT

[CAA] [SAVE]
◆◆◆
Motor Inn

			Phone: (905)356-6116	**65**
6/16-9/3	1P: $84-$199	2P: $84-$199	XP: $10	F18
9/4-10/21	1P: $64-$139	2P: $64-$139	XP: $10	F18
5/1-6/15	1P: $64-$119	2P: $64-$119	XP: $10	F18
10/22-4/30	1P: $59-$109	2P: $59-$109	XP: $10	F18

Location: From QEW, exit Lundy's Lane (Hwy 20 W); from downtown 4 km w. 7429 Lundy's Ln L2H 1G9. Fax: 905/356-7204. **Terms:** Cancellation fee imposed; package plans, 11/1-4/30. **Facility:** 130 rooms. Well appointed and tastefully decorated spacious rooms with shared facilities with adjoining Ramada Suites. 1 two-bedroom unit. 4 whirlpool rooms, $109-$259; 4 stories; interior corridors; 2 heated pools, sauna, whirlpool. Fee: miniature golf. **Dining:** Restaurant; 7 am-9 pm; $7-$17; cocktails. **Services:** gift shop; winter plug-ins. Fee: area transportation, attractions/casino. **Recreation:** indoor playground area, game room, in-room video games. **Cards:** AE, CB, DI, DS, JC, MC, VI. **Special Amenities:** Free local telephone calls. *(See color ad below)*

Clifton Hill, the street of fun at the Falls, Niagara Falls, Canada

Discover the fun exploring the great attractions and amusements on Clifton Hill
- Ripley's Believe It or Not
- Ripley's Moving Theatre
- Maid of the Mist
- Dazzleland Family Fun Center
- Movieland Museum of Stars
- Dinosaur Park Miniature Golf
- Guinness World of Records
- Casino Niagara

And just minutes away:
- Marineland
- Minolta Tower
- Niagara Parks
- Skylon Tower
- Imax Theatre
- Butterfly Conservatory

Clifton Hill has a selection of some of the best restaurants in Niagara Falls.

www.cliftonhill.com

(See map p. p. 385)

RAMADA SUITES NIAGARA
◆◆◆
Suite Motor
Inn

	6/16-9/3	1P: $119-$219	2P: $119-$219	XP: $10
	9/4-4/30	1P: $84-$159	2P: $84-$159	XP: $10
	5/1-6/15	1P: $84-$139	2P: $84-$139	XP: $10

Phone: (905)356-6119 **49**
F18
F18
F18

Location: From QEW, exit Lundy's Ln (Hwy 20 W); from downtown 4 km w. 7389 Lundy's Ln L2H 2W9. Fax: 905/356-7204. **Terms:** Cancellation fee imposed; package plans, 11/30-4/30. **Facility:** 73 rooms. Well appointed suites. Superior meeting facilities. 2 TVs in each suite. 7 stories; interior corridors; 2 pools, 1 indoor heated. Fee: miniature golf. **Services:** Fee: area transportation. **Cards:** AE, CB, DI, DS, JC, MC, VI. *(See color ad p 424)*

Picture this...

RENAISSANCE.
FALLSVIEW HOTEL
NIAGARA FALLS, ONTARIO

• *Affordable Luxury* • *Walking Distance to Falls*
• *Shuttle available to Casino Niagara*
• *Indoor Pool, Sauna & Health Club*

CAA and AAA SPECIAL RATES
from $89 *to* $179 CDN

based on availability of cityview
or riverview rooms only - sgl/dbl occ.

1-800-363-3255

6455 Buchanan Ave., Niagara Falls, ON Canada L2G 3V9
Tel: (905)357-5200 Fax: (905)357-3422

www.niagara.com/nf-renaissance

RODEWAY INN & SUITES

7720 Lundy's Lanes, Niagara Falls, ON, Canada L2H 1H1
(905) 358-9833
Toll Free: 1-800-228-2000
from Toronto to Buffalo, follow QEW highway to Niagara Falls, take Lundy's Lane exit. Turn left on Montrose Road, next light turn right, Inn on left

ACCOMMODATIONS / FEATURES
* 94 modern rooms with air-conditioning
* Honeymoon Suites with in-room heart shaped jacuzzis
* Family Rooms
* Complimentary Tea/Coffee
* Direct Dial Phones
* Colour Cable T.V. (35+channels)
* Heated indoor pool and hot tub
* Non-Smoking Rooms
* City shuttle bus to area attractions (May-October)

AREA ATTRACTIONS
(within 3 miles of Inn)
* Niagara Falls-Maid of the Mist
* Casino Niagara
* Marineland-Botanical Gardens
* Niagara Parks Greenhouse - Floral Clock
* Shopping Malls
* 10 miles to Welland Canal
* 15 miles to historic Niagara-on-the-Lake & Wine Region
* Various Restaurants
Lounges within walking distance

(See map p. p. 385)

RENAISSANCE FALLSVIEW HOTEL
Phone: (905)357-5200 **2**

CAA SAVE

◆◆◆

Hotel

6/17-9/30	1P: $205-$444	2P: $205-$444		
5/1-6/16 & 10/1-10/31	1P: $155-$380	2P: $155-$380	XP: $20	F17
11/1-4/30	1P: $129-$285	2P: $129-$285	XP: $20	F17

Location: Just n of Minolta Tower, corner Buchanan and Dixon aves. 6455 Buchanan Ave L2G 3V9. Fax: 905/357-3422. **Terms:** Cancellation fee imposed; package plans. **Facility:** 262 rooms. Luxurious rooms and furnishings. Top 7 floors with view of the falls. 91 whirlpool rooms, $205-$444; 18 stories; interior corridors; heated pool, saunas, whirlpool; squash-1 court. Fee: racquetball court. **Dining:** Dining room, restaurant; 6:30 am-midnight; $8-$40; cocktails. **Services:** gift shop. **All Rooms:** honor bars. **Cards:** AE, CB, DI, DS, JC, MC, VI. *(See color ad p 428)*

RODEWAY INN & SUITES
Phone: (905)358-9833 **67**

◆◆

Motel

7/1-9/5	1P: $100-$150	2P: $110-$150	XP: $10	F18
9/6-10/31	1P: $60-$100	2P: $60-$100	XP: $10	F18
5/1-6/30 & 11/1-4/30	1P: $50-$90	2P: $60-$100	XP: $10	F18

Location: 4 km w on Hwy 20 from QEW. 7720 Lundy's Ln L2H 1H1. Fax: 905/358-3090. **Terms:** 3 day cancellation notice; cancellation fee imposed. **Facility:** 89 rooms. Recently remodeled rooms in the midst of Lundy's Ln commercial areas. 4 two-bedroom units. 2 stories; interior/exterior corridors; 2 pools, 1 indoor heated. **Services:** Fee: area transportation. **Some Rooms:** 18 efficiencies, color TV. **Cards:** AE, DI, DS, MC, VI. *(See color ad p 428)*

SHERATON FALLSVIEW HOTEL & CONFERENCE CENTRE
Phone: (905)374-1077 **37**

CAA SAVE

◆◆◆◆

Hotel

5/26-9/30	1P: $225-$270	2P: $225-$270	XP: $20	F17
10/1-10/28	1P: $170-$215	2P: $170-$215	XP: $20	F17
5/1-5/25	1P: $145-$210	2P: $145-$210	XP: $20	F17
10/29-4/30	1P: $155-$200	2P: $155-$200	XP: $20	F17

Location: Near Minolta Tower. 6755 Oaks Dr L2G 3W7. Fax: 905/374-6224. **Terms:** [BP] meal plan; package plans. **Facility:** 295 rooms. Excellent furnishings. 146 rooms with a view of the falls. All rooms with hair dryer, iron and ironing board. 34 whirlpool rooms, $335-$455; 20 stories; interior corridors; heated pool, sauna, whirlpool. **Dining:** Restaurant; also, Fallsview Dining Room, see separate listing. **Services:** gift shop; area transportation, casino. **Recreation:** playroom/nursery. **Some Rooms:** Fee: VCR. **Cards:** AE, CB, DI, DS, JC, MC, VI. **Special Amenities:** Free local telephone calls. *(See color ad p 430)*

SKYLINE FOXHEAD
Phone: (905)374-4444 **26**

CAA

◆◆◆

Hotel

6/1-10/15	1P: $99-$669	XP: $10	F18
5/1-5/31	1P: $99-$379	XP: $10	F18
10/16-4/30	1P: $69-$379	XP: $10	F18

Location: At entrance to Rainbow Bridge on Hwy 20. 5875 Falls Ave L2E 6W7. Fax: 905/371-8349. **Terms:** Package plans. **Facility:** 388 rooms. 147 rooms overlooking the Falls. Other rooms with city view. Adjacent gift mall. Neighbors Casino Niagara. 14 stories; interior corridors. Fee: parking. **Dining:** Restaurant; cocktails; also, Penthouse Restaurant, see separate listing. **Recreation:** shared facilities with adjacent hotel. **Some Rooms:** Fee: refrigerators. **Cards:** AE, CB, DI, DS, JC, MC, VI. *(See color ad p 403)*

STANLEY MOTOR INN
Phone: (905)358-9238 **42**

CAA SAVE

◆◆

Motel

6/25-9/25	1P: $65-$120	2P: $95-$150	XP: $10	F10
5/1-6/24	1P: $60-$70	2P: $70-$85	XP: $10	F10
9/26-4/30	1P: $46-$60	2P: $60-$70	XP: $10	F10

Location: 2 blks from the falls, w of Skylon Tower. 6220 Stanley Ave L2G 3Y4. Fax: 905/358-2840. **Terms:** Pets, $10 extra charge. **Facility:** 49 rooms. Well-kept rooms near commercial area. 9 whirlpool rooms, $100-$170; 2 stories; exterior corridors. **Dining:** Restaurant nearby. **All Rooms:** combo or shower baths, extended cable TV. **Some Rooms:** Fee: refrigerators. **Cards:** AE, CB, DI, DS, JC, MC, VI. **Special Amenities:** Free local telephone calls and preferred room (subject to availability with advanced reservations).

STARDUST INN
Phone: (905)354-5773 **52**

CAA SAVE

◆◆

Motel

5/16-10/15	1P: $79-$199	XP: $10	F5
5/1-5/15 & 10/16-4/30	1P: $59-$129	XP: $10	F5

Location: Directly e of Kitchener St. 5528 Buchanan Ave L2G 3T8. Fax: 905/354-0935. **Facility:** 24 rooms. 9 whirlpool rooms, $149-$299; 2 stories; exterior corridors. **All Rooms:** extended cable TV. **Cards:** AE, MC, VI. **Special Amenities:** Free breakfast and free local telephone calls.

(See map p. p. 385)

SUNSET INN

CAA SAVE

♦♦ Motel

	6/16-9/3	1P: $59-$169	2P: $59-$169	XP: $10	F12
	5/1-6/15 & 9/4-10/11	1P: $49-$139	2P: $49-$139	XP: $10	F12
	10/12-4/30	1P: $39-$99	2P: $39-$99	XP: $10	F12

Phone: 905/354-7513 **29**

Location: 1.2 km w on Hwy 20, n on Stanley Ave, just s of Hwy 420. 5803 Stanley Ave L2G 3X8. Fax: 905/354-4766. **Terms:** Package plans. **Facility:** 32 rooms. Nice rooms on small lot close to commercial area and falls attractions. 2 two-bedroom units. 5 whirlpool rooms; 2 stories; exterior corridors; heated pool. **Dining:** Restaurant nearby. **Services:** winter plug-ins. **All Rooms:** extended cable TV. **Some Rooms:** Fee: refrigerators. **Cards:** AE, DI, DS, MC, VI. *(See color ad p 429)*

SUPER 8 LODGE

CAA SAVE

♦♦♦ Motor Inn

All Year	1P: $59-$289	2P: $59-$289	XP: $5	F12

Phone: (905)356-0052 **66**

Location: On Hwy 20, 1.5 km from the falls. 5706 Ferry St L2G 1S7. Fax: 905/356-7760. **Terms:** Package plans. **Facility:** 121 rooms. Nicely furnished rooms in courtyard section; tastefully appointed rooms in tower building. 12 whirlpool rooms, $109-$399; 2-7 stories; interior/exterior corridors; 2 pools, 1 indoor heated, sauna, whirlpool. **Dining:** Restaurant; 7 am-2 pm. **Services:** gift shop. **Recreation:** game room. **Some Rooms:** Fee: refrigerators. **Cards:** AE, CB, DI, DS, MC, VI. **Special Amenities:** Free local telephone calls. *(See color ad p 431)*

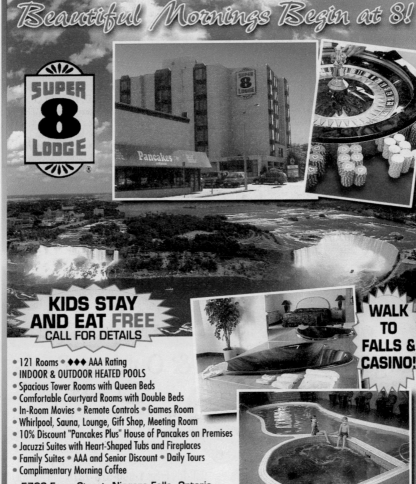

(See map p. p. 385)

SURFSIDE INN
◆◆◆   6/20-9/9   1P: $89-$149   2P: $89-$149   Phone: (905)295-4354   **74**
Motel   5/1-6/19 & 9/10-4/30 1P: $49-$99   2P: $49-$99   XP: $10   F12
                                                                        XP: $10   F12
Fax: 905/295-4374. **Terms:** 3 day cancellation notice; cancellation fee imposed; package plans. **Facility:** 31 rooms. Charming
Location: 3.5 km s of Horseshoe Falls on Niagara River Pkwy. 3665 Macklem St L2G 6C8.
accommodations in quiet location near Niagara River. 1 story; exterior corridors; heated pool. **Some Rooms:** 3 efficiencies.
Cards: AE, CB, DI, DS, JC, MC, VI. *(See ad p 431)*

(See map p. p. 385)

THRIFTLODGE
Phone: (905)358-6243 **51**

◆◆
6/24-9/4   1P: $80-$195   2P: $90-$220   XP: $15   F16
9/5-4/30   1P: $60-$190   2P: $60-$190   XP: $15   F16
Motel
5/1-6/23   1P: $50-$90   2P: $60-$120   XP: $15   F16

Location: 1.3 km w on Hwy 20, just s. 6000 Stanley Ave L2G 3Y1. Fax: 905/358-1864. **Terms:** Pets. **Facility:** 80 rooms. Residential look to building near light commercial area with convenient access to falls and attractions. 2 stories; interior/exterior corridors; heated pool. **Cards:** AE, CB, DI, DS, MC, VI.

TRAVELODGE BONAVENTURE
Phone: (905)374-7171 **62**

6/23-9/3   1P: $89-$189   2P: $99-$199   XP: $10   F17
5/1-6/22 & 9/4-10/14   1P: $59-$129   2P: $64-$139   XP: $10   F17
◆◆◆
10/15-4/30   1P: $49-$99   2P: $49-$109   XP: $10   F17

Motor Inn   **Location:** 4.5 km w on Hwy 20, from QEW, Hwy 20 W. 7737 Lundy's Ln L2H 1H3. Fax: 905/374-1151. **Terms:** 7 day cancellation notice; package plans. **Facility:** 118 rooms. Nice rooms in complex with residential look. 17 whirlpool rooms, $99-$259; 3 stories; interior/exterior corridors; 2 heated pools, sauna, whirlpool. **Dining:** Coffee shop; 7:30 am-noon; weekends only off season. **All Rooms:** extended cable TV. **Cards:** AE, CB, DI, DS, JC, MC, VI. **Special Amenities:** Free local telephone calls and free newspaper. *(See color ad p 432)*

(See map p. p. 385)

TRAVELODGE NEAR THE FALLS

(CAA) [SAVE]
♦ ♦
Motor Inn

			Phone: (905)374-7771	**9**
6/16-8/15	1P: $89-$229	2P: $89-$229	XP: $10	F12
8/16-9/30	1P: $89-$199	2P: $89-$199	XP: $10	F12
5/1-6/15 & 10/1-4/30	1P: $59-$199	2P: $59-$199	XP: $10	F12

Location: On Hwy 20, 0.8 km from the falls. 5234 Ferry St L2G 1R5. Fax: 905/374-7771. **Terms:** 14 day cancellation notice; cancellation fee imposed; package plans. **Facility:** 79 rooms. Tastefully appointed rooms with good floor space in commercial area close to the falls. 22 whirlpool rooms, $169-$399; 2-4 stories; interior/exterior corridors; heated pool, sauna, whirlpool. **Dining:** Restaurant; 7 am-2 pm. **All Rooms:** combo or shower baths. **Cards:** AE, DI, MC, VI. *(See color ad p 432)*

VACATION INN

(CAA) [SAVE]
♦ ♦ ♦
Motor Inn

			Phone: (905)356-1722	**34**
All Year	1P: $104-$225	2P: $104-$225	XP: $10	F11

Location: At corner of Dixon, 2 blks from Minolta Tower. 6519 Stanley Ave L2G 7L2. Fax: 905/356-0392. **Terms:** [BP] & [MAP] meal plans; package plans. **Facility:** 95 rooms. 3 stories, no elevator; interior corridors; heated pool. **Dining:** Restaurant; 8 am-11:30 & 5-9 pm; $5-$30; cocktails. **All Rooms:** extended cable TV. **Cards:** AE, DS, MC, VI. *(See color ad inside front cover)*

VICTORIA MOTOR INN

(CAA) [SAVE]
♦
Motel

			Phone: (905)374-6522	**43**
6/15-9/4	1P: $79-$139	2P: $79-$139	XP: $15	F16
5/1-6/14	1P: $69-$99	2P: $69-$99	XP: $15	F16
9/5-4/30	1P: $59-$99	2P: $59-$99	XP: $15	F16

Location: Just w on Victoria Ave from Clifton St. 5869 Victoria Ave L2G 3L6. Fax: 905/374-3038. **Facility:** 33 rooms. Simple accommodations in commercial area near falls attractions. 6 whirlpool rooms, $199-$299; 3 stories, no elevator; exterior corridors; heated pool. **Dining:** Coffee shop; 6 am-noon. **Services:** gift shop. **Cards:** AE, DS, MC, VI. **Special Amenities:** Early check-in/late check-out and free newspaper.

THE VILLAGE INN

(CAA)
♦
Motel

		Phone: (905)374-4444	**48**
5/1-10/15	1P: $79-$399	XP: $10	F18
10/16-4/30	1P: $69-$299	XP: $10	F18

Location: At the Ontario end of the Rainbow Bridge. 4800 Bender Hill L2E 6W7. Fax: 905/371-8349. **Terms:** Cancellation fee imposed; package plans. **Facility:** 206 rooms. Pleasant looking rooms close to falls and attractions. 2 stories; interior/exterior corridors. Fee: parking. **Dining:** Restaurants nearby. **Recreation:** privileges to facilities at Skyline Foxhead, Brock Plaza & Hampton Inn. **All Rooms:** extended cable TV. **Cards:** AE, DI, DS, JC, MC, VI. *(See color ad p 433)*

The following lodgings were either not inspected or did not meet AAA rating requirements but are listed for your information only.

COURTYARD NIAGARA FALLS

[fyi]
Motel

			Phone: 905-358-3083
6/25-9/6	1P: $129-$249	2P: $129-$249	
5/1-6/24 & 9/7-10/31	1P: $99-$189	2P: $99-$189	
11/1-4/30	1P: $89-$169	2P: $89-$169	

Too new to rate, opening scheduled for May 2000. **Location:** 5950 Victoria Ave L2G 3L7. **Terms:** Cancellation fee imposed. **Amenities:** 256 rooms, restaurant, radios, coffeemakers, pool, exercise facilities. **Cards:** AE, CB, DI, DS, JC, MC, VI.

FALLSVIEW PLAZA HOTEL & SUITES

[fyi]
Motor Inn

			Phone: 905/356-0014	
6/16-9/4	1P: $129-$329	2P: $129-$329	XP: $10	F12
5/1-6/15 & 9/5-10/28	1P: $89-$269	2P: $89-$269	XP: $10	F12
10/29-4/30	1P: $79-$239	2P: $79-$239	XP: $10	F12

Too new to rate, opening scheduled for May 2000. **Location:** Hwy 420 to Stanley Ave; across from The Minolta Tower. 6733 Oakes Dr L2G 3W6. Fax: 905/374-2555. **Amenities:** 99 rooms, radios, coffeemakers, microwaves, refrigerators, pool, exercise facilities. **Cards:** AE, DI, DS, JC, MC, VI.

SKYLINE FALLSVIEW

[fyi]
Hotel

Phone: 905/374-4444

Property failed to provide current rates

Too new to rate, opening scheduled for November 1999. **Location:** At entrance to Rainbow Bridge on Hwy 20 (located above the Skyline Foxhead on the top 9 floors). 5875 Falls Ave L2E 6W7. Fax: 905/371-0157. **Terms:** Check-in 4 pm. **Amenities:** 288 rooms, restaurant, radios, pool, exercise facilities. **Cards:** AE, CB, DI, DS, JC, MC, VI.

RESTAURANTS

THE BEEF BARON

(CAA)
♦ ♦
Steakhouse

	Lunch: $4-$8	**Dinner:** $11-$25	Phone: 905/356-6110	**7**

Location: At top of Clifton Hill. 5019 Centre St L2G 3N5. **Hours:** 4 pm-midnight, Sat & Sun noon-11:30 pm; noon-11:30 pm, 6/15-9/15. Closed: 12/24 & 12/25. **Reservations:** suggested; in season. **Features:** casual dress; children's menu; carryout; fee for parking. Hungry? Really hungry? Order Baron's 26 oz. porterhouse. Prime rib and seafood are two more house favorites. Three dining rooms, trimmed in cherry wood, brass and Italian prints, mix well in the bustling summer atmosphere and quieter ambience of winter. **Cards:** AE, CB, DI, DS, JC, MC, VI.

BETTY'S RESTAURANT

♦
Seafood

	Lunch: $4-$9	**Dinner:** $7-$14	Phone: 905/295-4436	**25**

Location: In Chippawa district; Niagara Pkwy s to Main St, just w. 8921 Sodom Rd L2E 6S6. **Hours:** 7 am-8 pm. Closed: 12/25. **Features:** casual dress; Sunday brunch; children's menu; senior's menu; carryout; cocktails. Betty's pleasantly appointed, spacious dining room highlights the good-value home cooking served here. Seafood and fish are what they do best, but many other tasty dishes are offered. The fish and chips keeps regular patrons coming back for more. **Cards:** AE, MC, VI.

(See map p. p. 385)

CAPRI RESTAURANT   Lunch: $4-$13   Dinner: $8-$25   Phone: 905/354-7519   [20]
Location: On Hwy 20, 1 km from the falls. 5438 Ferry St L2G 1S1. **Hours:** 11 am-11 pm. Closed: 12/24-12/26. **Reservations:** accepted. **Features:** casual dress; children's menu; health conscious menu items; carryout; cocktails & lounge; a la carte, a la carte. The dining room offers an elegant yet relaxed atmosphere for special occasion or family dining. The menu emphasizes Southern Italian cuisine and features a wide selection of homemade pasta as well as a full array of steak, seafood and poultry selections.
Italian
Cards: AE, CB, DI, MC, VI.

DELDUCA'S   Dinner: $10-$20   Phone: 905/357-3638   [14]
Location: Hwy 420, just n on Stanley Ave, just w on Morrison St to jct with Portage Rd. 4781 Portage Rd L2E 6B1. **Hours:** 5 pm-10 pm. Closed: 12/25. **Features:** casual dress; carryout; cocktails; a la carte. Enjoy the spacious, modern bistro-style atmosphere and featured fare of homemade pasta, ravioli and savory appetizers. Large portions are prepared fresh and presented attractively. Pleasant Mediterranean background music adds to the European ambience. Smoke free premises. **Cards:** AE, MC, VI.
Italian

FALLSVIEW DINING ROOM   Lunch: $6-$13   Dinner: $20-$31   Phone: 905/374-1077   [13]
Location: Near Minolta Tower; in Sheraton Fallsview Hotel & Conference Center. 6755 Oaks Dr L2G 3W7. **Hours:** 7 am-10 pm. **Reservations:** suggested. **Features:** casual dress; Sunday brunch; children's menu; early bird specials; senior's menu; cocktails & lounge; a la carte. Diners are awed by the spectacular views overlooking the falls and upper river—that and the wonderful selection of salad, appetizers, entrees and dessert on the daily buffet. A full a la carte menu is also offered with creative international items. **Cards:** AE, DI, DS, JC, MC, VI.
Continental
(See color ad p 430)

FARFALLE   Lunch: $11-$14   Dinner: $18-$34   Phone: 905/374-3598   [19]
Location: Just n of Rainbow Bridge; in Casino Niagara, 2nd floor. 5705 Falls Ave L2G 7M9. **Hours:** 11:30 am-4 & 5:30-11 pm, Fri & Sat-midnight. **Reservations:** suggested. **Features:** casual dress; cocktails; fee for parking; valet parking; a la carte. The setting is elegant and quiet yet comfortably casual with a view of the falls and away from the casino bustle. A Mediterranean-influenced menu features delightful items such as Thai shrimp and smoked salmon. Select and taste from a plethora of wines. **Cards:** AE, CB, DI, DS, JC, MC, VI.
Continental

FINE KETTLE 'O' FISH   Lunch: $6-$9   Dinner: $8-$30   Phone: 905/357-3474   [4]
Location: At jct of Huggins in far back section of strip mall. 3641 Portage Rd L2J 2K8. **Hours:** 11:30 am-10 pm. Closed: 12/25 & 12/26. **Features:** casual dress; children's menu; carryout; a la carte. The casual, nautical setting at this popular eatery is enhanced by cozy corners and fish aquariums throughout. Good menu selections offer a wide range of fresh seafood—from fish and chips to lobster as well as steak, chicken and stir-fry options. **Cards:** AE, MC, VI.
Seafood

FRANK'S TOMATO PIE   Lunch: $6-$10   Dinner: $10-$20   Phone: 905/371-9111   [12]
Location: At jct of Dorchester Rd. 6889 Lundys Lane L2G 1V7. **Hours:** 11 am-midnight, Fri & Sat-1 am. Closed: 12/25. **Reservations:** suggested. **Features:** children's menu; cocktails; a la carte. Fresh salad and bread accompany all of Frank's entrees including popular pizza, pasta, beef, veal, poultry and seafood meals. Enjoy the fun, casual atmosphere with brick walls, mosaic tile and lots of greenery. The outdoor patio area is open in season. **Cards:** AE, MC, VI.
Italian

(See map p. p. 385)

HAPPY WANDERER
◆
German

Lunch: $5-$12 **Dinner:** $10-$25 **Phone:** 905/354-9825 26
Location: Near Minolta Tower. 6405 Stanley Ave L2G 3Y6. **Hours:** 8 am-11 pm. **Closed:** 12/24. **Reservations:** accepted. **Features:** casual dress; children's menu; carryout; cocktails; minimum charge-$15. Imagine a heaping helping of sauerkraut and home fries with your grilled sausage. Or how about hand-grated German potato pancakes? The Happy Wanderer has it all, including a distinctive Bavarian decor and Canadian and American steak and seafood dishes. **Cards:** AE, MC, VI.

HARD TIMES
CAA
◆ ◆
American

Lunch: $5-$8 **Dinner:** $10-$23 **Phone:** 905/374-3650 6
Location: At top of Clifton Hill. 5759 Victoria Ave L2G 3L6. **Hours:** 11:30 am-midnight; 4 pm-10 pm 11/1-12/31. **Closed:** 12/23-12/25. **Reservations:** suggested; weekends/summer. **Features:** casual dress; children's menu; health conscious menu items; carryout; salad bar; cocktails & lounge; fee for parking; a la carte. Hard Times does chicken seven different ways yet still has the time to create a plethora of other specialties such as prime rib, Alaskan crab, white fish fillet and baby back ribs. The dining room has a nautical air with a mock ship as a decoration. **Cards:** AE, DI, DS, JC, MC, VI.

LA HACIENDA RESTAURANT
◆
Ethnic

Dinner: $7-$20 **Phone:** 905/356-8051 21
Location: 1.6 km e on Hwy 20 from QEW intersection. 5991 Lundy's Ln L2G 1T2. **Hours:** 4 pm-midnight; from 11 am, 7/1-8/31. Closed major holidays & Wed off season. **Reservations:** accepted. **Features:** casual dress; children's menu; carryout; cocktails; minimum charge-per table. La Hacienda offers the best of two worlds: Tex-Mex and Italian fare. So don't be surprised to find veal parmigiana on one side of the menu and fajitas-for-two on the other. And what a wonderful way to blend both cuisines—in a creative Mexican cannoli. **Cards:** AE, DI, MC, VI.

THE LAST RESORT PRIME-STEAKS-
SEAFOOD-ITALIAN
CAA
◆ ◆
American

(See color ad below)

Lunch: $4-$18 **Dinner:** $8-$18 **Phone:** 905/357-4888 10
Location: Just e of jct Clifton Hill and Victoria Ave. 5645 Victoria Ave L2G 3L5. **Hours:** noon-11 pm, Fri & Sat-midnight. **Closed:** 12/24 & 12/25. **Reservations:** suggested; Sat. **Features:** children's menu; carryout; cocktails & lounge; a la carte. The Last Resort sports a fun, bustling atmosphere in a casual setting of Tiffany lights, brick and log cabin walls—creating a cozy feeling. The varied menu emphasizes lots of finger food and a good selection of steak, ribs, chicken and Mexican specials. **Cards:** AE, CB, DI, JC, MC, VI.

THE LOVE BOAT II
◆
South French

Lunch: $5-$25 **Dinner:** $5-$25 **Phone:** 905/358-0660 18
Location: 1.1 km w of Minolta Tower. 6130 Dunn St L2G 2P1. **Hours:** 11:30 am-11 pm; 4 pm-9 pm 10/1-4/30. **Closed:** 12/25. **Reservations:** accepted. **Features:** casual dress; children's menu; carryout; cocktails & lounge. A collection of seafaring articles such as anchors, portholes and nets adds to this eatery's pleasant nautical ambience. Bouillabaisse with a light tomato broth and seafood, linguine with clam sauce and strawberry-topped cheesecake are house favorites. **Cards:** AE, DI, MC, VI.

LUNA EUROGRILLE & LOUNGE
◆ ◆
Continental

Lunch: $5-$10 **Dinner:** $5-$19 **Phone:** 905/357-3876 28
Location: Downtown; at jct Ferry and Main sts. 5890 Main St L2G 5Z8. **Hours:** 11 am-midnight. **Closed:** 12/25. **Reservations:** suggested; wknds/holidays. **Features:** casual dress; children's menu; carryout; cocktails & lounge; street parking; a la carte. The modern, bi-level dining room with an open kitchen complements Luna's bright, trendy, contemporary decor. The fun menu boasts a variety of creative appetizers, gourmet pizza, pasta, salad and sandwiches, all freshly and colorfully prepared. **Cards:** AE, MC, VI.

MAMA MIA'S
CAA
◆ ◆
Italian

Lunch: $5-$9 **Dinner:** $7-$22 **Phone:** 905/354-7471 8
Location: At top of Clifton Hill. 5719 Victoria Ave L2G 3L5. **Hours:** 11:30 am-11 pm; hrs vary seasonally. **Closed:** 12/23-12/25, Wed & Thurs 1/1-2/28. **Features:** casual dress; children's menu; health conscious menu items; cocktails; fee for parking; a la carte. What would an Italian eatery be without a good menu selection of lasagna, manicotti and cannelloni? You'll never find out because Mama Mia's serves all these house specialties and more in its quaint dining room. Steak and seafood also make an appearance. **Cards:** AE, DI, DS, JC, MC, VI.

(See map p. p. 385)

MICK AND ANGELO'S EATERY AND BAR   Lunch: $4-$7   Dinner: $7-$14   Phone: 905/357-6543   [23]
♦♦   **Location:** From QEW, exit Lundy's Ln, corner of Lundy's Ln and Montrose Rd. 7600 Lundy's Ln L2H 1H1.
Continental   **Hours:** 11 am-12:30 am. Closed: 12/25. **Reservations:** accepted. **Features:** casual dress; children's menu; health conscious menu items; carryout; cocktails & lounge. A diverse crowd patronizes this popular eatery and bar where an extensive menu, large portions and reasonable prices prevail. The specialty white pizza (sans tomato sauce) consists of oil, garlic and three cheeses. Entertainment is offered in season. **Cards:** AE, MC, VI.   ⊠

MINOLTA TOWER CENTRE/PINNACLE
RESTAURANT   Lunch: $10-$26   Dinner: $19-$48   Phone: 905/356-1501   ①
♦♦♦   **Location:** In Minolta Tower Centre. 6732 Oakes Dr L2G 3W6. **Hours:** 11 am-10 pm; extended hrs, in
Continental   summer. **Reservations:** suggested. **Features:** casual dress; children's menu; early bird specials; cocktails; a la carte. Enjoy a bird's-eye view of the falls from atop the Minolta Tower while relaxing in an upscale atmosphere. The menu features a variety of traditional fare served in ample portions and attractively plated. Full a la carte or prix fixe specials are served. **Cards:** AE, DI, DS, JC, MC, VI.   ⊠

PENTHOUSE RESTAURANT   Lunch: $8-$14   Dinner: $24-$30   Phone: 905/374-4444   [27]
♦♦♦   **Location:** At entrance to Rainbow Bridge on Hwy 20; in Skyline Foxhead. 5875 Falls Ave L2E 6W7.
American   **Hours:** 6:30-10:30 am, 11:30-2 & 5:30-10 pm, Fri & Sat-11 pm; 7-10:30 am, 11:30-1:30 & 5:30-10 pm, Fri & Sat 7-10:30 am, 11:30-1:30 & 5-10 pm in winter. **Reservations:** suggested. **Features:** casual dress; children's menu; early bird specials; salad bar; cocktails & lounge; valet parking. There's always something to tempt all tastes on the all-you-can-eat breakfast, lunch and dinner buffet. Besides a spectacular view of the falls, the Penthouse offers daily entertainment in season; weekends off season. An a la carte menu is also available. **Cards:** AE, CB, DI, DS, JC, MC, VI.   ⊠

(See map p. p. 385)

QUEENSTON HEIGHTS RESTAURANT   Lunch: $9-$13   Dinner: $20-$26   Phone: 905/262-4274   ⑯
CAA
◆◆
American
Location: 10.4 km n of Rainbow Bridge, on scenic route, Niagara Pkwy. 14184 Niagara Pkwy L2E 6T2. **Hours:** 11 am-3 & 5-9 pm; summer tea 3 pm-5 pm, hrs vary off season. Closed: 4/13, 12/25, 12/26 & 1/1-3/31. **Reservations:** suggested. **Features:** Sunday brunch; children's menu; health conscious menu items; cocktails; a la carte. Enjoy a panoramic view of the lower Niagara River and surrounding fruit lands from your table, while scanning a varied menu of such specialties as Atlantic salmon, Black Angus prime rib and seasonal fruit dessert. Patio lounge dining is offered in season. **Cards:** AE, DI, MC, VI.   ✕

THE RAINBOW ROOM   Lunch: $8-$16   Dinner: $15-$35   Phone: 905/374-4444   ㉒
◆◆◆
American
Location: At entrance to Rainbow Bridge on Hwy 20, just n from the falls; in the Brock Plaza. 5685 Falls Ave L2E 6W7. **Hours:** 7 am-2 & 5:30-10 pm. **Reservations:** suggested. **Features:** casual dress; children's menu; early bird specials; salad bar; cocktails & lounge; fee for parking. Creative food presentation and good menu variety are hallmarks at The Rainbow Room. Poultry, beef, seafood, fresh vegetables, dessert and a full buffet keep excellent company in a casually elegant dining room with a fine view of the falls. **Cards:** AE, CB, DI, DS, JC, MC, VI.   ✕

THE SKYLON TOWER DINING ROOMS   Lunch: $21-$29   Dinner: $33-$54   Phone: 905/356-2651   ③
CAA
◆◆◆
American
Location: In Skylon Tower. 5200 Robinson St L2G 2A3. **Hours:** 8-10 am, 11:30-3 & 4:30-10 pm. **Reservations:** suggested. **Features:** casual dress; children's menu; early bird specials; cocktails; a la carte, a la carte. Most tables have a good view of the falls in this revolving eatery and Summit Suite Buffet atop the Skylon Tower. Breakfast and lunch buffets are offered as well as an a la carte menu; dinner buffet in season. There's an extra $2 charge for the elevator. **Cards:** AE, DI, DS, JC, MC, VI. *(See color ad p 156 & p 437)*   ✕

TABLE ROCK RESTAURANT   Lunch: $7-$12   Dinner: $12-$21   Phone: 905/354-3631   ⑰
CAA
◆◆
American
Location: At Canadian Horseshoe Falls. 6400 Niagara Pkwy L2E 6T2. **Hours:** 11:30 am-8 pm, Sat-9 pm. Closed: 12/25. **Reservations:** accepted. **Features:** casual dress; children's menu; early bird specials; health conscious menu items; cocktails & lounge; fee for parking. It's difficult to take your eyes off the outstanding view of Horseshoe Falls and the upper rapids long enough to make a choice from the menu featuring traditional fare and some Canadian dishes. Attentive and friendly service is the norm. Hrs may vary.
Cards: AE, DI, MC, VI.   ✕

TERRAPIN GRILLE   Lunch: $8-$18   Dinner: $19-$40   Phone: 905/357-7300   ㉙
◆◆◆
Continental
Location: Next to Minolta Tower; in Niagara Falls Marriott Fallsview. 6740 Oaks Dr L2G 3W6. **Hours:** 6 am-11 pm. **Reservations:** suggested. **Features:** dressy casual; children's menu; health conscious menu; cocktails & lounge; a la carte. Terrapin Grille has capitalized on relaxed sophistication, elegant Continental cuisine and a marvelous view of the falls. Of note is the tasty appetizer sampler of calamari, grilled shrimp and portobello mushrooms with several flavorful side sauces. **Cards:** AE, CB, DI, DS, MC, VI.   ✕

VICTORIA PARK RESTAURANT   Lunch: $7-$11   Dinner: $15-$21   Phone: 905/356-2217   ②
CAA
◆◆
American
Location: In Queen Victoria Park, on scenic route. 6345 Niagara Pkwy L2E 6T2. **Hours:** Open 5/8-10/10; 11:30 am-10 pm; 11:30 am-3:30 & 4-9 pm 5/5-6/18 & 9/5-10/10. **Reservations:** suggested; in summer. **Features:** No A/C; casual dress; children's menu; early bird specials; health conscious menu; cocktails; fee for parking; a la carte. What better way to enjoy a breathtaking view of the falls than from an open-air balcony while dining on an array of items, including some Canadian fare, prepared with fresh ingredients. A year-round cafeteria with more formal dining in season. **Cards:** AE, MC, VI.   ✕

WHIRLPOOL RESTAURANT   Lunch: $6-$10   Dinner: $12-$18   Phone: 905/356-7221   ⑮
CAA
◆◆
American
Location: 5.3 km n of Rainbow Bridge, on scenic route, Niagara Pkwy; in the Public Whirlpool Golf Complex. 3351 Whirlpool Golf Complex L2E 6T2. **Hours:** 7 am-3 pm 4/1-10/31; 6 am-8 pm 6/19-9/6. **Reservations:** suggested. **Features:** casual dress; children's menu; health conscious menu items; carryout; cocktails & lounge; a la carte. Canadian dishes, snacks and daily seasonal featured fare are served in this casual, golf-course-view restaurant across from a whirlpool gorge. Try the very good chicken teriyaki atop angel hair pasta and an eye-appealing fruit plate for dessert. **Cards:** AE, DS, MC, VI.   ✕

This ends listings for the Niagara Falls Vicinity.
The following page resumes the alphabetical listings of
cities in New York.

NIAGARA FALLS, NEW YORK —*See Niagara Falls p. 386.*

NIAGARA FALLS, ONTARIO —*See Niagara Falls p. 397.*

NORTH CREEK pop. 900—*See also ADIRONDACK MOUNTAINS.*

——— LODGINGS ———

THE COPPERFIELD INN
Phone: (518)251-2500
AD SAVE All Year   1P: $140-$250   2P: $140-$250   XP: $20   F11
◆◆◆◆ **Location:** Center; just e of SR 28. 307 Main St 12853 (PO Box 28). Fax: 518/251-4143. **Terms:** [BP] & [MAP]
Country Inn meal plans; 30 day cancellation notice; cancellation fee imposed; 3 night min stay, some wknds in season;
package plans. **Facility:** 31 rooms. Large, individually furnished rooms in contemporary country inn. Property
closed 11/1-11/30. 7 whirlpool rooms & suites, $210-$375; 2 stories; interior corridors; heated pool, saunas,
whirlpool, full service salon, tanning beds; 1 lighted tennis court. **Dining:** Dining room, see separate listing. **Services:** area
transportation, ski area. Fee: massage. **Recreation:** Fee: bicycles. **All Rooms:** safes, honor bars. **Cards:** AE, CB, DI, DS,
MC, VI. **Special Amenities:** Free breakfast and free newspaper.

MOOSE POND INN
Phone: (518)251-3434
◆◆◆ All Year   1P: $65-$95   2P: $80-$115   XP: $20
Historic Bed **Location:** SR 28, 1 mi e, 0.9 mi n. 196 Main St 12853 (PO Box 273). Fax: 518/251-3434. **Terms:** [BP] meal
Breakfast plan; age restrictions may apply; 14 day cancellation notice; 2 night min stay, weekends; package plans; pets
on premises. **Facility:** 4 rooms. Renovated 1894 inn. Individually decorated rooms. Many antiques. 2 stories;
interior corridors; designated smoking area. **Services:** area transportation. **All Rooms:** combo or shower baths.

——— RESTAURANT ———

GARDENS Country Inn   **Lunch:** $6-$14   **Dinner:** $8-$29   **Phone:** 518/251-2500
◆◆ **Location:** Center; just e of SR 28, in The Copperfield Inn. 307 Main St 12853. **Hours:** Open 6/14-10/16 &
American 12/17-4/1; 7-11 am, 11:30-3 & 5:30-9 pm, Fri & Sat-11 pm. Closed: 4/1-6/30, for breakfast.
Reservations: suggested. **Features:** casual dress; children's menu; cocktails & lounge; a la carte. The a la
carte menu lists mainly well-prepared steak and seafood specialties. An elegant atmosphere is prevalent in the dining room,
which is appointed with original artwork and large, French doors that open onto a relaxed, courtyard dining area. **Cards:** AE,
CB, DI, DS, MC, VI.

NORTH HUDSON pop. 300—*See ADIRONDACK MOUNTAINS.*

NORTH LANSING

——— LODGING ———

ROSE INN
Phone: (607)533-7905
AD SAVE 5/1-11/30 & 4/1-4/30   1P: $105-$190   2P: $115-$200   XP: $25
◆◆◆ 12/1-3/31   1P: $105-$165   2P: $115-$175   XP: $25
Historic **Location:** 3.3 mi n from jct SR 34 and 34 B. 813 Auburn Rd, Rt 34 N 14851 (PO Box 6576, ITHACA).
Country Inn Fax: 607/533-7908. **Terms:** [BP] meal plan; age restrictions may apply; 14 day cancellation notice; cancellation fee imposed; 2 night min stay, weekends; dog on premises. **Facility:** 23 rooms. An 1850s farm home featuring a stunning circular staircase of Honduran Mahogany. Carriage house executive conference center, all
situated on 20 acres of grounds. 11 whirlpool rooms, $230-$320; suites, $275; 2 stories; interior corridors; smoke free prem-
ises. **Dining:** Dining room; prix fixe gourmet dinner Tues-Sat, $45 per person; $18-$28; cocktails; reservations req; entertain-
ment. **Some Rooms:** color TV. **Cards:** MC, VI. **Special Amenities:** Free breakfast and free local telephone calls.

NORTH SYRACUSE pop. 7,400   (See map p. 478; index p. 477)—

——— LODGINGS ———

BEST WESTERN SYRACUSE AIRPORT INN
Phone: (315)455-7362   [36]
AD SAVE All Year   1P: $71-$90   2P: $78-$98   XP: $8   F12
◆◆ **Location:** 5.5 mi n at Hancock Airport, I-81 exit 27. Hancock Airport 13212. Fax: 315/455-6840. **Terms:** 7 day
Motor Inn cancellation notice. **Facility:** 95 rooms. Modest size single rooms. 2 stories; interior corridors. **Dining:** Dining
room; 7 am-2 & 5-10 pm; Sun 4 pm-midnight; $10-$14; cocktails. **All Rooms:** extended cable TV. **Cards:** AE,
CB, DI, DS, MC, VI. **Special Amenities:** Free room upgrade (subject to availability with advanced
reservations).

THE CLUB HOTEL BY DOUBLETREE AIRPORT AREA
Phone: (315)457-4000   [34]
◆◆ 5/1-12/31 & 4/1-4/30   1P: $99   2P: $99
Motor Inn 1/1-3/31   1P: $94   2P: $94
Location: 0.8 mi w of jct I-81 (7th North St) and I-90, exit 36. 6701 Buckley Rd 13212. Fax: 315/453-7877.
Terms: 3 day cancellation notice; small pets only. **Facility:** 187 rooms. Good size comfortable rooms. 2 stories; interior corri-
dors; heated pool. **Some Rooms:** Fee: refrigerators. **Cards:** AE, CB, DI, DS, MC, VI.

(See map p. 478)

RAMADA INN ◆◆◆
Motor Inn
Phone: (315)457-8670 [35]

1/1-4/30	1P: $79	2P: $139	XP: $15 F18
5/1-12/31	1P: $79	2P: $119	XP: $10 F18

Location: 0.5 mi w of jct I-81 (7th North St) and I-90, exit 36. 1305 Buckley Rd 13212. Fax: 315/457-8633. **Terms:** [BP] meal plan. **Facility:** 150 rooms. 2 stories; interior corridors. **Services:** winter plug-ins. **All Rooms:** combo or shower baths. **Cards:** AE, CB, DI, DS, JC, MC, VI.

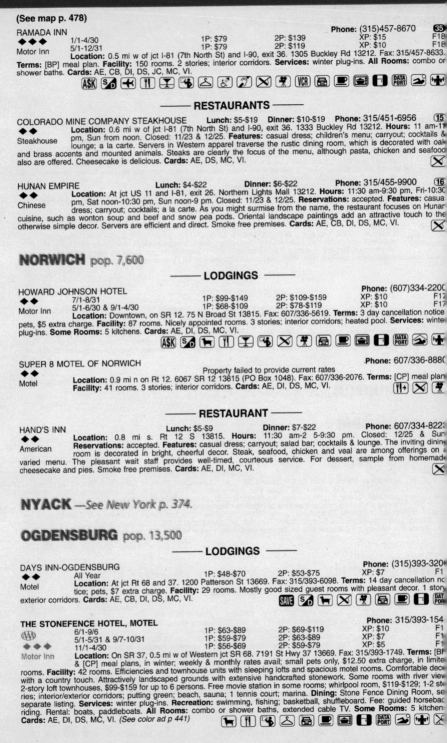

———— RESTAURANTS ————

COLORADO MINE COMPANY STEAKHOUSE ◆◆
Steakhouse
Lunch: $5-$19 **Dinner:** $10-$19 **Phone:** 315/451-6956 [15]
Location: 0.6 mi w of jct I-81 (7th North St) and I-90, exit 36. 1333 Buckley Rd 13212. **Hours:** 11 am-11 pm, Sun from noon. Closed: 11/23 & 12/25. **Features:** casual dress; children's menu; carryout; cocktails & lounge; a la carte. Servers in Western apparel traverse the rustic dining room, which is decorated with oak and brass accents and mounted animals. Steaks are clearly the focus of the menu, although pasta, chicken and seafood also are offered. Cheesecake is delicious. **Cards:** AE, DS, MC, VI.

HUNAN EMPIRE ◆◆
Chinese
Lunch: $4-$22 **Dinner:** $6-$22 **Phone:** 315/455-9900 [16]
Location: At jct US 11 and I-81, exit 26. Northern Lights Mall 13212. **Hours:** 11:30 am-9:30 pm, Fri-10:30 pm, Sat noon-10:30 pm, Sun noon-9 pm. Closed: 11/23 & 12/25. **Reservations:** accepted. **Features:** casual dress; carryout; cocktails; a la carte. As you might surmise from the name, the restaurant focuses on Hunan cuisine, such as wonton soup and beef and snow pea pods. Oriental landscape paintings add an attractive touch to the otherwise simple decor. Servers are efficient and direct. Smoke free premises. **Cards:** AE, CB, DI, DS, MC, VI.

NORWICH pop. 7,600

———— LODGINGS ————

HOWARD JOHNSON HOTEL ◆◆
Motor Inn
Phone: (607)334-2200

7/1-8/31	1P: $99-$149	2P: $109-$159	XP: $10 F17
5/1-6/30 & 9/1-4/30	1P: $68-$109	2P: $78-$119	XP: $10 F17

Location: Downtown, on SR 12. 75 N Broad St 13815. Fax: 607/336-5619. **Terms:** 3 day cancellation notice pets, $5 extra charge. **Facility:** 87 rooms. Nicely appointed rooms. 3 stories; interior corridors; heated pool. **Services:** winter plug-ins. **Some Rooms:** 5 kitchens. **Cards:** AE, DI, DS, MC, VI.

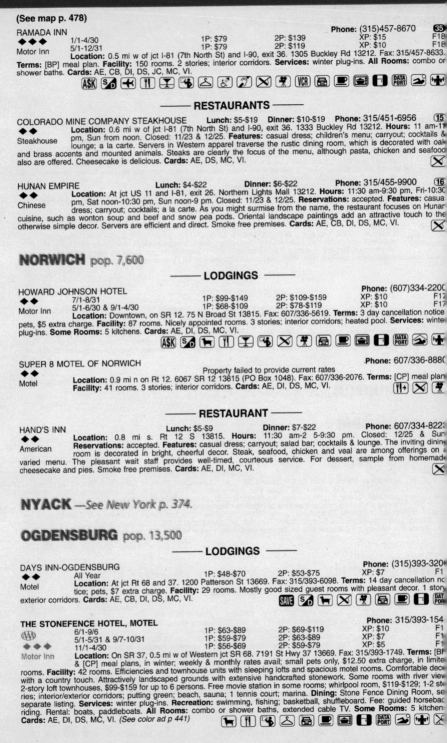

SUPER 8 MOTEL OF NORWICH ◆◆
Motel
Phone: 607/336-8880
Property failed to provide current rates
Location: 0.9 mi n on Rt 12. 6067 SR 12 13815 (PO Box 1048). Fax: 607/336-2076. **Terms:** [CP] meal plan; **Facility:** 41 rooms. 3 stories; interior corridors. **Cards:** AE, DI, DS, MC, VI.

———— RESTAURANT ————

HAND'S INN ◆◆
American
Lunch: $5-$9 **Dinner:** $7-$22 **Phone:** 607/334-8223
Location: 0.8 mi s. Rt 12 S 13815. **Hours:** 11:30 am-2 5-9:30 pm. Closed: 12/25 & Sun **Reservations:** accepted. **Features:** casual dress; carryout; salad bar; cocktails & lounge. The inviting dining room is decorated in bright, cheerful decor. Steak, seafood, chicken and veal are among offerings on a varied menu. The pleasant wait staff provides well-timed, courteous service. For dessert, sample from homemade cheesecake and pies. Smoke free premises. **Cards:** AE, DI, MC, VI.

NYACK — See New York p. 374.

OGDENSBURG pop. 13,500

———— LODGINGS ————

DAYS INN-OGDENSBURG ◆◆
Motel
Phone: (315)393-3200
All Year 1P: $48-$70 2P: $53-$75 XP: $7 F1
Location: At jct Rt 68 and 37. 1200 Patterson St 13669. Fax: 315/393-6098. **Terms:** 14 day cancellation notice; pets, $7 extra charge. **Facility:** 29 rooms. Mostly good sized guest rooms with pleasant decor. 1 story exterior corridors. **Cards:** AE, CB, DI, DS, MC, VI.

THE STONEFENCE HOTEL, MOTEL
Motor Inn ◆◆◆
Phone: 315/393-1545

6/1-9/6	1P: $63-$89	2P: $69-$119	XP: $10 F1
5/1-5/31 & 9/7-10/31	1P: $59-$79	2P: $63-$89	XP: $7 F1
11/1-4/30	1P: $56-$69	2P: $59-$79	XP: $5 F1

Location: On SR 37, 0.5 mi w of Western jct SR 68. 7191 St Hwy 37 13669. Fax: 315/393-1749. **Terms:** [BP] & [CP] meal plans, in winter; weekly & monthly rates avail; small pets only, $12.50 extra charge, in limited rooms. **Facility:** 42 rooms. Efficiencies and townhouse units with sleeping lofts and spacious motel rooms. Comfortable decor with a country touch. Attractively landscaped grounds with extensive handcrafted stonework. Some rooms with river views. 2-story loft townhouses, $99-$159 for up to 6 persons. Free movie station in some rooms; whirlpool room, $119-$129; 1-2 stories; interior/exterior corridors; putting green; beach, sauna; 1 tennis court; marina. **Dining:** Stone Fence Dining Room, see separate listing. **Services:** winter plug-ins. **Recreation:** swimming, fishing, basketball, shuffleboard. Fee: guided horseback riding. **Rental:** boats, paddleboats. **All Rooms:** combo or shower baths, extended cable TV. **Some Rooms:** 5 kitchens. **Cards:** AE, DI, DS, MC, VI. *(See color ad p 441)*

—— RESTAURANTS ——

GRAN-VIEW **Lunch:** $5-$12 **Dinner:** $11-$29 **Phone:** 315/393-4550
◆◆ **Location:** SR 37, 1.5 mi w of Western jct SR 68; in Quality Inn Gran-View. 6765 State Hwy 37 13669.
Continental **Hours:** 7 am-10 pm, Fri & Sat-11 pm, Sun 8 am-9 pm; Sun 10:30 am-1:30 pm 11/1-3/31. Closed: 12/24 &
12/25. **Reservations:** suggested. **Features:** casual dress; Sunday brunch; children's menu; senior's menu;
carryout; cocktails & lounge; a la carte. Overlooking the St. Lawrence River, the restaurant affords stunning views of the
Canadian sunset. Italian influences touch selections of Continental cuisine, such as chicken cordon bleu with burgundy
currant sauce. The chocolate cheesecake is decadent. **Cards:** AE, CB, DI, DS, JC, MC, VI. ⊠

STONE FENCE DINING ROOM **Lunch:** $4-$10 **Dinner:** $8-$17 **Phone:** 315/393-1545
◆ **Location:** On SR 37, 0.5 mi w of Western jct SR 68; in The Stonefence Hotel, Motel. 7191 Riverside Dr
American 13669. **Hours:** 7 am-2:30 & 4:30-9 pm; winter hrs may vary. Closed: 1/1, 12/24 & 12/25.
Reservations: suggested. **Features:** casual dress; children's menu; carryout; salad bar. The inviting,
seasonal patio—as well as both levels of the dining room—overlooks beautifully landscaped grounds and the waterway.
London broil is representative of traditionally prepared menu selections. Service is attentive throughout the meal. **Cards:** AE,
DI, DS, MC, VI. (See color ad below) ⊠

OLD FORGE pop. 1,500—See also ADIRONDACK MOUNTAINS.

—— LODGINGS ——

BEST WESTERN SUNSET INN **Phone:** (315)369-6836
◆◆◆

6/30-9/3	1P: $99-$189	2P: $99-$189	XP: $10	F12
9/4-4/30	1P: $49-$119	2P: $59-$129	XP: $10	F12
5/1-6/29	1P: $49-$99	2P: $59-$109	XP: $10	F12

Location: 0.3 mi s. Rt 28 13420 (Rt 28, PO Box 261). Fax: 315/369-2607. **Terms:** [CP] meal plan; 7 day cancellation notice;
cancellation fee imposed; 2 night min stay, weekends in season; pets, in smoking rooms, dogs only. **Facility:** 52 rooms. Attractive indoor pool area. Many spacious rooms, pleasant decor. 1-2 stories; interior/exterior corridors; heated pool; 1 tennis
court. **Services:** winter plug-ins. **Cards:** AE, CB, DI, DS, MC, VI.

BLUE SPRUCE MOTEL **Phone:** 315/369-3817

7/1-11/1	1P: $50-$90	2P: $50-$90	XP: $5
12/1-3/31	1P: $50-$75	2P: $50-$75	XP: $5
5/1-6/30	1P: $45-$60	2P: $45-$60	XP: $5

Motel **Location:** 2898 SR 28 13420 (PO Box 604). **Terms:** Open 5/1-11/1 & 12/1-3/31; weekly rates avail. in winter;
14 day cancellation notice; cancellation fee imposed; 2 night min stay, weekends in season. **Facility:** 13 rooms.
Modern, comfortable rooms. 1 efficiency, $10 extra charge; 1 story; exterior corridors; heated pool. **Dining:** Restaurant nearby.
Services: winter plug-ins. **All Rooms:** extended cable TV. **Cards:** AE, MC, VI.

COUNTRY CLUB MOTEL **Phone:** 315/369-6340

6/23-9/4	1P: $75-$85	2P: $75-$85	XP: $5	F12
5/1-6/22	1P: $40-$85	2P: $40-$85	XP: $5	F12
12/25-4/30	1P: $35-$85	2P: $35-$85	XP: $5	F12
9/5-12/24	1P: $45-$65	2P: $45-$65	XP: $5	F12

Location: 0.3 mi s. 2747 SR 28 13420 (PO Box 419). **Terms:** Weekly rates avail. off season; 14 day cancellation notice; 2 night min stay, weekends in season. **Facility:** 27 rooms. Adjacent to Thendara golf course, with spacious
grounds. Some larger rooms. 1 story; exterior corridors; heated pool. **Dining:** Restaurant nearby. **Services:** winter plug-ins.
All Rooms: extended cable TV. **Cards:** AE, DI, DS, MC, VI.

19TH GREEN MOTEL **Phone:** 315/369-3575

6/26-9/5		2P: $55-$80	XP: $5	F4
12/26-4/30		2P: $50-$80	XP: $5	F4
9/6-12/25		2P: $40-$55	XP: $5	F4
5/1-6/25		2P: $38-$55	XP: $5	F4

Location: 0.3 mi s. 2761 SR 28 13420 (PO Box 37). **Terms:** Weekly rates avail; 14 day cancellation notice;
cancellation fee imposed. **Facility:** 13 rooms. 1 story; exterior corridors; heated pool. **Dining:** Restaurant nearby.
Services: winter plug-ins. **Recreation:** cross country skiing. **All Rooms:** combo or shower baths, extended cable TV.
Cards: AE, CB, DI, DS, MC, VI.

WATER'S EDGE INN & CONFERENCE CENTER
◆◆◆   5/1-12/31
Motor Inn   1/1-4/30
Phone: 315/369-2484
2P: $92-$250   XP: $10   F9
2P: $45-$150   XP: $10   F9
Location: Center; on SR 28, opposite Enchanted Forest. SR 28 13420 (PO Box 1141). Fax: 315/369-6782
Terms: 7 day cancellation notice; cancellation fee imposed. **Facility:** 61 rooms. Some rooms with balcony overlooking the lake. 2-3 stories, no elevator; interior corridors; heated pool; boat dock. **Recreation:** fishing. 🍴 🍸 💆 🛏 🏊 ✕

—————— RESTAURANT ——————

THE OLD MILL RESTAURANT   Dinner: $12-$20   Phone: 315/369-3662
◆◆   **Location:** 0.3 mi sw on SR 28. Main St 13420. **Hours:** Open 5/10-11/1 & 12/26-3/15; 4:30 pm-9:30 pm, Fr
American & Sat-10 pm, Sun 1 pm-9 pm. **Features:** casual dress; children's menu; cocktails & lounge; a la carte. Resembling a rustic Adirondack log cabin, the dining room is an ideal, casual spot for family dining. Expec
large portions of everything from salad to steak. The restaurant often is packed, and it's not unusual to have
to wait during peak times. **Cards:** MC, VI.   ✕

OLEAN pop. 16,900

—————— LODGINGS ——————

HAMPTON INN   Phone: 716/375-1000
◆◆◆   Property failed to provide current rates
Motor   **Location:** Downtown; on Main St at Union St (SR 16). 101-109 Main St 14760. Fax: 716/375-1279
Terms: [CP] meal plan; pets, $20 dep req. **Facility:** 76 rooms. Recently opened facility close to downtown and
convenient to St. Bonaventure University. 3 stories; interior corridors. **All Rooms:** combo or shower baths. **Some Rooms**
Fee: refrigerators, microwaves. **Cards:** AE, DI, DS, MC, VI.
🐾 💆 🛎 🏠 🔕 ✕ 🎥 VCR 🖨 💻 🖥 🛏 📠

OLD LIBRARY INN BED & BREAKFAST   Phone: 716/373-980
◆◆◆   All Year   1P: $65-$75   2P: $65-$75   XP: $10   F1
Historic Bed **Location:** Downtown; just s of jct SR 16 and 417. 120 S Union St 14760. Fax: 716/373-2462. **Terms:** [BF
& Breakfast   meal plan; cancellation fee imposed; package plans. **Facility:** 8 rooms. Rooms with varying antique appoint
ments in a beautifully restored Victorian home built in 1895. Public areas with lots of beautiful oak woodwork
2 stories; interior corridors; designated smoking area. **All Rooms:** combo or shower baths. **Cards:** AE, DS, MC, VI.
ASK 💆 🍴 💆 🛎 ✕ 🎥 VCR 🖨 🛏

—————— RESTAURANTS ——————

BEEF N' BARREL RESTAURANT   Lunch: $4-$8   Dinner: $5-$16   Phone: 716/372-2985
◆◆   **Location:** Downtown; at jct SR 16 and 417. 146 N Union St 14760. **Hours:** 11 am-10 pm, Fri & Sat-11 pm
American Closed major holidays & Sun. **Features:** casual dress; children's menu; carryout; cocktails & lounge. The
restaurant is locally popular and with good reason. Selections of choice grade beef, especially the
hand-carved roast beef, are succulent and well-prepared. Aromatic baked goods—breads, rolls, pastries
cakes and the like—are made on the premises. **Cards:** AE, DI, DS, MC, VI.   ✕

OLD LIBRARY RESTAURANT   Historical   Lunch: $5-$10   Dinner: $8-$26   Phone: 716/372-2220
◆◆   **Location:** Adjacent to Old Library Inn Bed & Breakfast. 116 S Union St 14760. **Hours:** 11 am-11 pm, Sun-10
American pm. Closed: 12/25. **Reservations:** accepted. **Features:** casual dress; Sunday brunch; children's menu; early
bird specials; health conscious menu items; carryout; cocktails & lounge. The renovated 1910 library serve
as a relaxed setting in which to enjoy such creatively prepared dishes as pasta Louis. Homemade dessert
are rich and satisfying. The Friday seafood buffet is particularly popular. Servers show good menu
knowledge. **Cards:** AE, DS, MC, VI.   ✕

ONEIDA CASTLE pop. 700

—————— LODGING ——————

GOVERNOR'S HOUSE BED & BREAKFAST   Phone: 315/363-564
◆◆◆   Property failed to provide current rates
Historic Bed **Location:** I-90, exit 33, then 4 mi s on Rt 365 at jct of Rt 365 and SR 5. 50 Seneca Ave 13421. **Terms:** [BF
& Breakfast   meal plan; 3 day cancellation notice. **Facility:** 4 rooms. Restored 1848 federal brick mansion. 3 stories, no e
evator; interior corridors. **All Rooms:** combo or shower baths. **Cards:** AE, DI, DS, MC, VI.   ✕ 🎥 🖨

ONEONTA pop. 14,000

—————— LODGINGS ——————

HOLIDAY INN ONEONTA/COOPERSTOWN AREA   Phone: (607)433-2250
◆◆◆ SAVE   6/30-8/31   1P: $149-$199
◆◆◆   5/1-6/29 & 9/1-4/30   1P: $89-$129
Motor Inn **Location:** On SR 23, 1.5 mi e of jct I-88, exit 15. Rt 23 Southside 13820-0634 (PO Box 634)
Fax: 607/432-7028. **Terms:** [BP] meal plan; cancellation fee imposed; package plans; small pets onl
Facility: 120 rooms. On outskirts of town yet close to commercial areas and interstate access. Rates for up t
5 persons; 2 stories; interior corridors; wading pool; playground. **Dining:** Restaurant; 6:30 am-10 pm; $11-$18; cocktails; er
tertainment. **Recreation:** basketball, volleyball. **Some Rooms:** Fee: refrigerators. **Cards:** AE, CB, DI, DS, JC, MC, V
Special Amenities: Early check-in/late check-out and free local telephone calls. *(See color ad p 241)*
💆 🐾 🍴 🍸 💆 🛎 🏊 ✕ 🎥 🖨 💻 🖥 🛏 📠 🛒 📠 ✕

COUNTRY LIVING-THE SISTERS B & B
Phone: 607/432-0186
Historic Bed Breakfast
All Year   1P: $70   2P: $70   XP: $15
Location: I-88 E, exit 14, just s; I-88 W, exit 15, 1 mi s. 576 SR 28 13820. **Terms:** [BP] meal plan; age restrictions may apply; 14 day cancellation notice; cancellation fee imposed; Owner has dog. **Facility:** 4 rooms. Country atmosphere yet near commercial area with very cordial and accommodating owner sisters. 2 stories; exterior corridors; designated smoking area.

RAINBOW INN ONEONTA/COOPERSTOWN AREA
Phone: (607)432-1280

6/30-9/2	1P: $119-$169	2P: $139-$173	XP: $10 F12
5/1-6/29 & 9/3-10/28	1P: $68-$99	2P: $79-$99	XP: $10 F12
10/29-4/30	1P: $58-$79	2P: $79-$99	XP: $10 F12

Motel
Location: On SR 7, 0.3 mi e of jct I-88, exit 16. 5690 SR 7 13820. Fax: 607/433-2972. **Terms:** [CP] meal plan; 30 day cancellation notice; cancellation fee imposed. **Facility:** 28 rooms. Spacious grounds with picnic area. Variety of room types from small to spacious; very attractive. 8 whirlpool rooms, $175-$250; 1 story; interior/exterior corridors. **Dining:** Restaurant nearby. **Services:** winter plug-ins. **All Rooms:** extended cable TV. **Cards:** AE, CB, DI, DS, MC, VI. **Special Amenities:** Free breakfast and preferred room (subject to availability with advanced reservations). (See color ad p 239)

SUPER 8 MOTEL
Phone: 607/432-9505
Motel
Property failed to provide current rates
Location: SR 23, 0.3 mi e of I-88, exit 15. 4973 SR 23 13820. Fax: 607/432-9505. **Terms:** Pets. **Facility:** 60 rooms. 2 two-bedroom units. 2 stories; interior corridors. **Services:** winter plug-ins. **Some Rooms:** Fee: VCR. **Cards:** AE, DI, DS, JC, MC, VI.

RESTAURANTS

BROOKS HOUSE OF BAR-B-Q
Lunch: $4-$10   Dinner: $5-$15   Phone: 607/432-1782
American
Location: 2 mi e on SR 7, Eastend; 0.3 mi w of I-88, Emmons/Davenport exit 16. 5560 State Hwy 7 13820. **Hours:** 11 am-9 pm. Closed: 1/1, 11/23, 12/24, 12/25 & 12/31. **Features:** casual dress; children's menu; carryout; salad bar, Delicious chicken, ribs, pork, beef and seafood are prepared over a charcoal pit barbecue. The family-oriented restaurant is large and open, while the summer picnic areas encourage you to kick back and enjoy time among friends. Servers are pleasant. **Cards:** MC, VI.

FARMHOUSE Historical
Dinner: $11-$17   Phone: 607/432-7374
American
Location: 2 mi e on SR 7; at jct I-88, exit 16. SR 1 13820. **Hours:** 3 pm-9 pm, Fri & Sat-9 pm, Sun noon-8 pm. Closed: 12/25. **Reservations:** suggested. **Features:** casual dress; Sunday brunch; children's menu; senior's menu; health conscious menu items; carryout; salad bar; cocktails. The former farmhouse has a quaint, homey feeling, with a blue room, wood stove, plants and a greenhouse that affords pretty views of the outdoors. Traditionally prepared dishes of beef, chicken, veal and seafood make up the bulk of the menu. **Cards:** AE, DI, MC, VI.

NNELLI'S RISTORANTE
Lunch: $4-$7   Dinner: $7-$17   Phone: 607/433-5230
Regional Italian
Location: SR 7 and 23, 0.4 mi w of jct with Main St. 99 Chestnut St 13820. **Hours:** 11:30 am-10 pm, Sun 11:30 am-9 pm. Closed major holidays. **Reservations:** suggested. **Features:** casual dress; children's menu; health conscious menu items; carryout; cocktails & lounge. The popular restaurant deserves its popularity for distinctive cuisine. Ample, reasonably priced meals are prepared in the nouveau style—affording diners a refreshing change from typical Italian fare. Tiramisu and cheesecake are good dessert choices. **Cards:** AE, DS, MC, VI.

SABATINI'S LITTLE ITALY
Lunch: $7-$8   Dinner: $10-$15   Phone: 607/432-3000
Italian
Location: I-88, exit 15, just s then just w. Rt 23 Southside 13856. **Hours:** 11:30-3 & 4-9 pm, Fri-10 pm, Sat 4 pm-10 pm, Sun 4 pm-9 pm. Closed: 12/25. **Reservations:** accepted. **Features:** casual dress; children's menu; health conscious menu items; carryout; cocktails & lounge; a la carte. The charming dining room is set up to remind diners of old Italy. Wrought-iron lamps and a suspended ceiling add to the look. The menu centers on large portions of pasta, veal, beef, chicken and seafood, as well as flavorful, brick-oven pizzas. **Cards:** AE, DI, DS, MC, VI.

ORANGEBURG —See New York p. 374.

OSSINING —See New York p. 374.

OSWEGO pop. 19,200

LODGINGS

BEST WESTERN CAPTAIN'S QUARTERS
Phone: (315)342-4040
Motor Inn
Property failed to provide current rates
Location: Just n on SR 481. 26 E 1st St 13126. Fax: 315/342-5454. **Facility:** 93 rooms. Located on the banks of the Oswego River. Many rooms with harbor view. 4 stories; interior corridors. **All Rooms:** combo or shower baths, honor bars. **Cards:** AE, CB, DI, DS, MC, VI.

ECONO LODGE RIVERFRONT HOTEL
Phone: (315)343-1600

7/2-9/3	1P: $68-$98	2P: $80-$190	XP: $12 F16
5/1-7/1 & 9/4-4/30	1P: $63-$93	2P: $75-$185	XP: $12 F16

Motel
Location: Just n on SR 481. 70 E First St 13126. Fax: 315/343-1222. **Terms:** Cancellation fee imposed. **Facility:** 93 rooms. Modern, well furnished guest rooms. 5 stories; interior corridors. **Services:** winter plug-ins. **All Rooms:** combo or shower baths. **Cards:** AE, CB, DI, DS, MC, VI.

------ RESTAURANT ------

CANALE'S RISTORANTE **Lunch:** $5-$7 **Dinner:** $7-$18 **Phone:** 315/343-354
◆◆ **Location:** At jct Utica and Herrick sts; 0.8 mi w of jct Rt 481. 156 W Utica St 13126. **Hours:** 11:30 am-1
Italian pm, Fri & Sat-11 pm; closed for lunch Sat & Sun in summer. Closed major holidays
Reservations: suggested. **Features:** casual dress; children's menu; carryout; cocktails. Vintage artwork
overhead lighting and lots of windows add to the casual warmth of the informal dining room. Diners enjoy good-size portion
of steaks, veal, pizza, sandwiches and seafood. Servers in attractive uniforms are pleasant and prompt. **Cards:** AE, CB, D
DS, MC, VI.

OWEGO pop. 4,400

------ LODGINGS ------

HOLIDAY INN EXPRESS **Phone:** (607)687-900
(AAA) [SAVE] 5/1-10/31 1P: $85-$100 2P: $85-$100 XP: $10 F1
11/1-4/30 1P: $69-$89 2P: $69-$89 XP: $10 F1
◆◆◆ **Location:** At foot of exit 65, ramp from SR 17. 20 Hickory Park Rd 13827. Fax: 607/687-3034. **Terms:** [ECP
Motel meal plan; check-in 4 pm. **Facility:** 74 rooms. On shore of river. Spacious rooms. 2 whirlpool rooms; 2 stories
interior corridors. **Dining:** Breakfast bar; restaurant nearby. **Recreation:** fishing. **All Rooms:** extended cabl
TV. **Some Rooms:** 35 efficiencies, no utensils. **Cards:** AE, CB, DI, DS, JC, MC, VI. **Special Amenities:** Free breakfast an
free local telephone calls.

SUNRISE MOTEL **Phone:** 607/687-566
(AAA) [SAVE] All Year 1P: $43 2P: $47-$49 XP: $5 F1
◆◆ **Location:** SR 17, exit 64, SR 96 across river w to 17C, then 2 mi on left. 3778 Waverly Rd 1382
Motel Fax: 607/687-5666. **Terms:** Weekly rates avail; pets, $5 extra charge, small dogs only. **Facility:** 20 rooms. R
cently remodeled rooms with fine furniture and decor enhancements in a quiet, rural setting. Community kitch
enette. 1 story; exterior corridors. **All Rooms:** combo or shower baths, extended cable TV. **Cards:** AE, CB, D
DS, MC, VI.

PAINTED POST pop. 2,000—*See also FINGER LAKES.*

------ LODGINGS ------

BEST WESTERN LODGE ON THE GREEN **Phone:** (607)962-245
(AAA) [SAVE] 5/23-10/22 1P: $80 2P: $80 XP: $8 F1
5/1-5/22 & 10/23-4/30 1P: $60 2P: $60 XP: $8 F1
◆◆◆ **Location:** SR 17, exit 44, s to Gang Mills exit, then n. 3171 Canada Rd 14870. Fax: 607/962-176
Motor Inn **Terms:** [AP] & [CP] meal plans; weekly & monthly rates avail; package plans; pets. **Facility:** 135 rooms. A lus
campus of 8 buildings shaded by mature trees. 1-2 stories; exterior corridors. **Dining:** Dinin
room; 6:30 am-9 pm, Sun-8 pm; $10-$22; cocktails. **Services:** area transportation, within 30 mi; winter plug-in
All Rooms: extended cable TV. **Some Rooms:** 3 efficiencies. Fee: refrigerators, microwaves. **Cards:** AE, DI, DS, MC, V
Special Amenities: Free newspaper and free room upgrade (subject to availability with advanced reservations).

ECONO LODGE **Phone:** (607)962-444
◆ 5/1-10/11 1P: $65-$95 2P: $75-$125
Motel 10/12-4/30 1P: $59-$85 2P: $64-$95
Location: Jct US 15 and SR 17, exit 44, s to Gang Mills exit. 200 Robert Dann Dr 14870. Fax: 607/937-539
Terms: [CP] meal plan. **Facility:** 62 rooms. Suburban property. 2 stories; interior corridors. **Services:** winter plug-in
Cards: AE, CB, DI, DS, JC, MC, VI.

HAMPTON INN **Phone:** (607)936-334
◆◆◆ 5/20-9/5 1P: $79-$125 2P: $79-$150
Motel 5/1-5/19 & 9/6-10/31 1P: $69-$125 2P: $79-$150
11/1-4/30 1P: $61-$85 2P: $70-$95
Location: SR 17, exit 43. 9775 Victory Hwy 14870. Fax: 607/936-3393. **Terms:** [ECP] meal plan. **Facility:** 67 rooms. New
facility near light commercial area with convenient hwy access. 3 stories; interior corridors; heated pool. **Services:** winter plu
ins. **All Rooms:** combo or shower baths. **Some Rooms:** Fee: refrigerators, microwaves. **Cards:** AE, CB, DI, DS, MC, VI.

HOLIDAY INN **Phone:** (607)962-502
◆◆◆ 7/7-10/28 1P: $89-$95 2P: $89-$95 XP: $5 F1
Motor Inn 5/1-7/6 & 10/29-4/30 1P: $85-$90 2P: $85-$90 XP: $5 F1
Location: SR 17, exit 44, s on SR 15 to Gang Mills exit, then s. 304 S Hamilton St 14870. Fax: 607/937-408
Terms: 3 day cancellation notice; cancellation fee imposed; package plans. **Facility:** 105 rooms. Traditional motor inn desi
on nice grounds in light commercial area. 2 stories; interior corridors; heated pool. **Cards:** AE, CB, DI, DS, JC, MC, VI.

SUPER 8 MOTEL **Phone:** 607/937-538
◆◆ All Year 1P: $55-$75 2P: $60-$80 XP: $5 F
Motel **Location:** SR 17, exit 44, on SR 15 S to Gang Mills exit. 255 S Hamilton St 14870. Fax: 607/962-711
Terms: [CP] meal plan. **Facility:** 61 rooms. Standard rooms close to small shopping center and with conve
ient access to nearby hwy. 2 stories; interior corridors. **Services:** winter plug-ins. **All Rooms:** combo or shower bath
Cards: AE, DI, DS, MC, VI.

PALENVILLE pop. 900

——— LODGING ———

CATSKILL MOUNTAIN LODGE
Phone: (518)678-3101

AAA	11/21-3/17	1P: $70-$95	2P: $75-$105	XP: $10	F5
◆◆	5/1-9/3	1P: $70-$95	2P: $75-$100	XP: $10	F5
Motor Inn	9/4-11/20	1P: $65-$90	2P: $70-$95	XP: $10	F5
	3/18-4/30	1P: $65-$85	2P: $70-$90	XP: $10	F5

Location: 1 mi se. 334 Rt 32A 12463. Fax: 518/678-3103. **Terms:** Weekly rates avail; 14 day cancellation notice; cancellation fee imposed; 2 night min stay, summer weekends. **Facility:** 42 rooms. Variety of rooms, some spacious. Kitchenettes & cottages, $495-$625; $495-$255 weekly in summer; 1-2 stories; interior/exterior corridors; heated pool, wading pool. **Dining:** Restaurant; 7 am-3 pm, Wed-Sun 5 pm-9 pm; $12-$15; cocktails. **Services:** winter plug-ins. **Recreation:** lawn games. **All Rooms:** combo or shower baths, extended cable TV. **Some Rooms:** 2 efficiencies, kitchen. Fee: refrigerators. **Cards:** AE, CB, DI, DS, MC, VI.

PARKSVILLE pop. 800

——— LODGING ———

BEST WESTERN PARAMOUNT
Phone: (914)292-6700

AAA SAVE	All Year	1P: $45-$220	2P: $55-$220	XP: $10

◆◆◆
Resort

Location: 0.3 mi n following signs, SR 17, exit 98. Tanzman Rd 12768. Fax: 914/292-8203. **Terms:** [AP], [BP], [CP] & [MAP] meal plans; weekly & monthly rates avail; cancellation fee imposed; package plans; small pets only, $100 dep req. **Facility:** 183 rooms. Senior citizen and group tour oriented property. Transient overnight room availability may be limited. Family run resort since 1905. 2 stories; interior corridors; designated smoking area; miniature golf; 2 pools, 1 indoor heated, wading pool, sauna; 1 tennis court. **Dining:** Dining room; single seating meals; 8 am, 1 pm & 7 pm; $20-$25; cocktails; entertainment, nightclub. **Recreation:** fishing, paddleboats, rowboats; ice skating; shuffleboard, bocce ball, basketball & volleyball. **Cards:** AE, DI, DS, MC, VI. **Special Amenities: Free breakfast and free room upgrade (subject to availability with advanced reservations).**

——— RESTAURANT ———

TUMBLEWEED RESTAURANT   **Lunch:** $5-$13   **Dinner:** $9-$17   **Phone:** 914/292-2492
◆

American

Location: SR 17, exit 98. Main St 12768. **Hours:** Open 5/1-11/30 & 4/1-4/30; 4 pm-9 pm, Fri-Sat 11:30 am-9 pm, Sun 7:30 am-9 pm 5/30-9/7. Closed: Mon-Wed 10/1-4/30. **Features:** casual dress; carryout; minimum charge-$2. The casual restaurant delivers variety, with such dishes as tangy Texas barbecue chicken, gold ribs in honey-mustard sauce and the might Mex platter, which includes a taco, burrito, enchilada and chimichanga. The decor shows a Southwestern flair. **Cards:** AE, CB, DI, DS, MC, VI.

PEARL RIVER —*See New York p. 375.*

PEEKSKILL —*See New York p. 375.*

PEMBROKE pop. 4,200

——— LODGING ———

DARIEN LAKES ECONOLODGE
Phone: (716)599-4681

◆◆	7/1-9/7	1P: $60-$80	2P: $65-$80	XP: $5	F18
Motel	5/16-6/30	1P: $45-$60	2P: $50-$60	XP: $5	F18
	5/1-5/15 & 9/8-4/30	1P: $39-$50	2P: $45-$50	XP: $5	F18

Location: On SR 77, 0.3 mi s of I-90, exit 48A. 8493 SR 77 14036. Fax: 716/599-3040. **Terms:** Pets. **Facility:** 73 rooms. Well coordinated guest rooms with simple appointments. 2 stories; interior corridors. **Some Rooms:** Fee: refrigerators, VCR. **Cards:** AE, CB, DS, MC, VI.

PENFIELD pop. 6,300   (See map p. 456; index p. 455)

——— LODGING ———

COURTYARD BY MARRIOTT
Phone: (716)385-1000

◆◆◆	1/1-4/30	1P: $74-$114	2P: $74-$114	
Motel	5/1-12/31	1P: $74-$104	2P: $74-$104	

Location: Rt 441 to Washington Rd exit, just s to Linden Park, just w. 1000 Linden Park 14625. Fax: 716/385-1005. **Terms:** Cancellation fee imposed. **Facility:** 95 rooms. 5 stories; interior corridors; heated pool. **All Rooms:** combo or shower baths. **Cards:** AE, DI, DS, MC, VI.

(See map p. 456)

—————— RESTAURANT ——————

DAISY FLOUR MILL   Historical   **Dinner: $11-$25**   **Phone:** 716/381-1880   ⑲
◆◆◆   **Location:** 1.5 mi e of I-590, exit 6 (Blossom Rd); in Ellison Park. 1880 Blossom Rd 14625. **Hours:** 5 pm-9
American   pm, Fri & Sat-10 pm, Sun 4 pm-8 pm. Closed major holidays & Super Bowl Sun. **Reservations:** suggested.
             Features: casual dress; children's menu; early bird specials; cocktails & lounge; valet parking; a la carte.
The 1848 restored grist mill is decorated with lots of wood and interesting furnishings, including a 1919 Ford Model T
Huckster in the foyer. Beef, seafood and game dishes are the focus of the menu. Delicious desserts are prepared with the
mill's flour. **Cards:** AE, CB, DI, DS, MC, VI.   ⊠

PENN YAN pop. 5,200—See also FINGER LAKES.

—————— LODGING ——————

MERRITT HILL MANOR BED & BREAKFAST   **Phone:** 315/536-7682
◆◆◆   All Year   1P: $110-$125   2P: $110-$125   XP: $25
Historic Bed   **Location:** 3 mi s on SR 54A, 1 mi w on Merritt Hill Rd. 2756 Coates Rd 14527. **Terms:** [BP] meal plan; age
& Breakfast   restrictions may apply; 7 day cancellation notice; 2 night min stay, weekends, 5/1-10/31. **Facility:** 5 rooms.
             Renovated 1822 Federal era farmhouse. 2 stories; interior corridors; smoke free premises. **All Rooms:** combo
or shower baths. **Cards:** MC, VI.   ⊠ Ⓚ ☎

PERTH

—————— RESTAURANT ——————

RAINDANCER STEAK PARLOUR   **Lunch:** $5-$10   **Dinner:** $12-$20   **Phone:** 518/842-2606
◆◆   **Location:** On SR 30, 3.8 mi n of jct SR 67, 4.5 mi n of jct I-90, exit 27. 4582 SR 30 12010. **Hours:** 11:30
Steak and   am-10 pm, Sun 1 pm-9 pm. Closed: 12/24 & 12/25. **Reservations:** suggested. **Features:** casual dress;
Seafood   children's menu; early bird specials; carryout; salad bar; cocktails & lounge. Prime rib and Alaskan king crab
             legs are specialties on a menu of mostly steak, seafood and pasta dishes, which are served in generous
portions. Fireplaces and antiques decorate the rustic dining room. The casual atmosphere is welcoming to families.
Cards: AE, DS, MC, VI.   ⊠

PINE VALLEY

—————— LODGING ——————

BEST WESTERN MARSHALL MANOR   **Phone:** (607)739-3891
Ⓐ SAVE   6/30-10/14   1P: $57-$62   2P: $66-$71   XP: $5   F18
◆◆◆   5/1-6/29 & 10/15-11/26   1P: $45   2P: $52-$56   XP: $5   F18
Motel   11/27-4/30   1P: $39   2P: $43-$47   XP: $5   F18
             Location: SR 14, 5 mi n of jct SR 17, exit 52. 3527 Watkins Rd 14845. Fax: 607/739-3891. **Terms:** [ECP] meal
plan; weekly rates avail; pets, $4 extra charge. **Facility:** 40 rooms. Charming rural location with a wooded hill
behind a bucolic gazebo in front. Classic brick construction in traditional design. 1 story; exterior corridors; heated pool.
Dining: Restaurant nearby. **All Rooms:** extended cable TV. **Some Rooms:** Fee: VCR. **Cards:** AE, CB, DI, DS, MC, VI.
Special Amenities: Free breakfast and free local telephone calls. *(See ad below)*

⚤ 🛏 🏋 ⊠ 📽 VCR 🖨 💻 📠 🔌 🗖 🌊

PITTSFORD pop. 1,500   (See map p. 456; index p. 455)

—— LODGINGS ——

BROOKWOOD INN   **Phone:** (716)248-9000 26
(AAA) (SAVE) 5/1-10/31   1P: $99-$135   2P: $99-$135   XP: $10 F18
◆◆◆ 11/1-4/30   1P: $79-$125   2P: $79-$125   XP: $10 F18
Motor Inn **Location:** I-490 (Bushnell's Basin), exit 27, just n. 800 Pittsford/Victor Rd 14534. **Fax:** 716/248-8569.
Terms: Package plans. **Facility:** 108 rooms. 19 whirlpool rooms, $115-$169; 5 stories; interior corridors; heated pool, sauna, whirlpool. **Dining:** Dining room; 6:30 am-10 pm, Sat & Sun from 7:30 am; $10-$21; cocktails. **Recreation:** Fee: bicycles, in-room video games. **Cards:** AE, CB, DI, DS, MC, VI. *(See ad below)*

OLIVER LOUD'S INN   **Phone:** (716)248-5200 27
◆◆◆◆ All Year   1P: $125-$135   2P: $135-$145   XP: $10
Historic **Location:** I-490, exit Bushnell's Basin (Rt 96 N), 3 mi from New York Thruway exit 45 to I-490 W, exit Bush-
Country Inn nell's Basin (Rt 96 N) to Marsh Rd. 1474 Marsh Rd 14534. **Fax:** 716/248-9970. **Terms:** [CP] meal plan; age restrictions may apply; 7 day cancellation notice; cancellation fee imposed. **Facility:** 8 rooms. 1810 stagecoach inn moved to the shoreline of The Erie Canal. Elegant period decor. Some canal view rooms. 2 stories; interior corridors; smoke free premises. **Recreation:** cross country skiing; jogging. **Cards:** AE, CB, DI, MC, VI.

—— RESTAURANTS ——

RICHARDSON'S CANAL HOUSE   Historical   **Dinner:** $35   **Phone:** 716/248-5000 15
◆◆◆ **Location:** I-490, exit Bushnell's Basin (Rt 96 N), 3 mi from New York Thruway exit 45 to I-490 W, exit
American Bushnell's Basin (Rt 96 N) to Marsh Rd; in Oliver Loud's Inn. 1474 Marsh Rd 14534. **Hours:** 6 pm-8 pm; lighter fare avail in lounge Mon-Fri 5 pm-9 pm. Closed major holidays & Sun. **Reservations:** suggested.
Features: semi-formal attire; cocktails & lounge; prix fixe, a la carte. Sophisticated furnishings decorate the refurbished 1818 Erie Canal tavern, a favorite romantic spot for couples. Freshly prepared American country and French regional cuisine is complex and flavorful. Creme caramel is beautifully presented. Smoke free premises. **Cards:** AE, CB, DI, MC, VI.

SPRING HOUSE   Historical   **Lunch:** $5-$12   **Dinner:** $14-$18   **Phone:** 716/586-2300 14
(AAA) **Location:** 4.8 mi s on I-590, exit 2 (SR 310), 4 mi s. 3001 Monroe Ave 14618. **Hours:** 11:30 am-3 & 5-9 pm,
◆◆ Sun noon-8 pm. Closed: 12/25 & Mon. **Reservations:** suggested. **Features:** casual dress; children's menu;
American early bird specials; carryout; cocktails & lounge. The 1829 Colonial inn is fittingly appointed with antiques, fireplaces and Early American art. The varied menu includes preparations of prime rib, fish, roasts and lamb tenderloin. During summer, the cozy patio affords a relaxed experience. **Cards:** AE, DI, MC, VI.

PLAINVIEW pop. 26,200

—— LODGINGS ——

HOLIDAY INN   **Phone:** 516/349-7400
◆◆   Property failed to provide current rates
Motor Inn **Location:** I-495, exit 46 N, ne corner. 215 Sunnyside Blvd 11803. **Fax:** 516/349-7491. **Terms:** Package plans, weekends. **Facility:** 125 rooms. All guest rooms with contemporary appeal. 2 stories; interior/exterior corridors.
All Rooms: combo or shower baths. **Some Rooms:** Fee: refrigerators. **Cards:** AE, CB, DI, DS, JC, MC, VI.

RESIDENCE INN BY MARRIOTT   **Phone:** (516)433-6200
◆◆◆ All Year   1P: $189-$199   2P: $189-$199
Motor Inn **Location:** Off Old Country Rd, opposite Central General Hospital; I-495 (Long Island Expwy), exit 44 S, exit 10, just e. 9 Gerhard Rd 11803. **Fax:** 516/433-2569. **Terms:** [ECP] meal plan; check-in 4 pm; cancellation fee imposed; pets, $20 extra charge, $100 cleaning fee. **Facility:** 165 rooms. Nightly hospitality activities. Studio and 1-bedroom suites offer comfort and convenience. 2-3 stories; interior corridors; 2 pools, 1 indoor heated. **All Rooms:** combo or shower baths. **Some Rooms:** 110 efficiencies, 55 kitchens. **Cards:** AE, CB, DI, DS, JC, MC, VI.

RODEWAY INN

1/1-4/30	1P: $98-$108	2P: $98-$108	XP: $10	F18
5/1-10/31	1P: $100-$105	2P: $100-$105	XP: $10	F18
11/1-12/31	1P: $95-$100	2P: $95-$100	XP: $10	F18

Phone: (516)694-6500

Motor Inn   **Location:** I-495, exit 48, sw corner. 333 S Service Rd 11803. Fax: 516/694-4718. **Facility:** 84 rooms. 4 whirlpool rooms; 3 stories; interior/exterior corridors; 1 tennis court. **Dining:** Restaurant; noon-8 pm; $6-$10; cocktails. **All Rooms:** extended cable TV. **Cards:** AE, DS, MC, VI. **Special Amenities:** Free breakfast and free newspaper.

PLATTSBURGH pop. 21,300

—— LODGINGS ——

BAYMONT INN & SUITES-PLATTSBURGH

5/1-9/3	1P: $67-$72	2P: $72-$77	XP: $5	F18
9/4-4/30	1P: $60-$65	2P: $65-$70	XP: $5	F18

Phone: (518)562-4000

Motel   **Location:** I-87, exit 37. 16 Plaza Blvd 12901-6439. Fax: 518/561-3234. **Terms:** [CP] meal plan; pets, in limited rooms. **Facility:** 104 rooms. Comfortable rooms with modern decor. 4 stories; interior corridors; heated pool. **Services:** winter plug-ins. **All Rooms:** combo or shower baths. **Cards:** AE, CB, DI, DS, MC, VI. *(See color ad below)*

COMFORT INN

9/22-10/15	1P: $100-$160	2P: $110-$170	XP: $10	F18
6/19-9/21	1P: $97-$160	2P: $107-$170	XP: $10	F18
10/16-4/30	1P: $87-$150	2P: $97-$160	XP: $10	F18
5/1-6/18	1P: $84-$150	2P: $94-$160	XP: $10	F18

Phone: (518)562-2730

Motor Inn   **Location:** I-87 Northway, exit 37. 411 Rt 3 12901. Fax: 518/563-1562. **Terms:** [CP] meal plan; 3 day cancellation notice; cancellation fee imposed; package plans. **Facility:** 111 rooms. Large rooms, few 2 room suites. Family oriented atmosphere. 2 stories; interior corridors; miniature golf; heated pool; playground. Fee: racquetball courts. **Services:** winter plug-ins. **Recreation:** ice skating. **Some Rooms:** 4 efficiencies. Fee: VCR. **Cards:** AE, DS, MC, VI.

DAYS INN

5/1-10/21	1P: $65-$75	2P: $75-$85	XP: $10	F17
10/22-4/30	1P: $55-$65	2P: $65-$75	XP: $10	F17

Phone: (518)561-0403

Motel   **Location:** I-87 Northway, exit 37. 8 Everleth Dr 12901. Fax: 518/561-4192. **Terms:** [CP] meal plan; 3 day cancellation notice; cancellation fee imposed; package plans. **Facility:** 112 rooms. Nestled among pine trees back from main road. Good size rooms with pleasant decor. 3 stories; interior corridors; 2 pools, 1 indoor heated. **Services:** winter plug-ins. **Cards:** AE, CB, DI, DS, MC, VI.

THE INN AT SMITHFIELD BY BEST WESTERN

6/27-10/13	1P: $79-$99	2P: $89-$99	XP: $12	F18
5/1-6/26	1P: $69-$89	2P: $79-$89	XP: $10	F18
10/14-4/30	1P: $64-$84	2P: $74-$84	XP: $10	F18

Phone: (518)561-7750

Motor Inn   **Location:** Jct I-87 Northway, exit 37. 446 Rt 3 12901 (PO Box 1278). Fax: 518/561-9431. **Terms:** Pets. **Facility:** 120 rooms. Variety of room types and decor. 2 stories; interior corridors; heated pool. **Dining:** Restaurant; 6 am-11 pm, Fri & Sat-midnight; $7-$12; cocktails. **Services:** winter plug-ins. **Recreation:** small playground area. Fee: in-room video games. **All Rooms:** extended cable TV. **Cards:** AE, CB, DI, DS, MC, VI. **Special Amenities:** Free local telephone calls and free newspaper.

POINT AUROCHE LODGE A BED & BREAKFAST

5/16-10/15	1P: $60-$100	2P: $82-$137	XP: $20	F5
1/1-4/30	1P: $70-$100	2P: $85-$135	XP: $15	F5
5/1-5/15 & 10/16-12/31	1P: $60-$100	2P: $75-$125	XP: $20	F5

Phone: (518)563-8714

Bed & Breakfast   **Location:** I-87 Northway, exit 40, just s on Rt 9, 2.2 mi e. 463 Point Au Roche Rd 12901. Fax: 518/563-6310. **Terms:** [BP] meal plan; 7 day cancellation notice; cancellation fee imposed. **Facility:** 9 rooms. TV and phone avail on request. Owner pets on premises. Located in a very quiet rural area adjacent to Point Au Roche State Park. Attractive individually themed guest rooms. 2 stories; interior corridors; smoke free premises. **Recreation:** bicycles. **All Rooms:** combo or shower baths. **Some Rooms:** color TV. **Cards:** AE, MC, VI.

STONEHELM LODGE

Phone: (518)563-4800

5/1-9/6 & 9/23-10/15	1P: $35-$55	2P: $40-$60	XP: $5	F10
9/7-9/22 & 10/16-4/30	1P: $35	2P: $40	XP: $5	F10

[AAA] [SAVE]

Motor Inn

Location: At I-87 Northway, exit 40. 72 Spellman Rd 12901. **Fax:** 518/562-1380. **Terms:** Weekly & monthly rates avail. **Facility:** 40 rooms. Quiet rural location. Picnic area with barbecue grills. Good sized modestly furnished guest rooms. 1 story; interior/exterior corridors. **Dining:** Coffee shop; 7:30 am-2 pm, Sun 7:30 am-noon; closed Mon; wine/beer only. **Services:** winter plug-ins. **Cards:** AE, DS, MC, VI. **Special Amenities:** Early check-in/late check-out and free room upgrade (subject to availability with advanced reservations).

--------- RESTAURANTS ---------

ANTHONY'S RESTAURANT & BISTRO   **Lunch:** $6-$10   **Dinner:** $10-$30   **Phone:** 518/561-6420

[AAA]

◆◆◆

Continental

Location: W of jct I-87 Northway, exit 37. 538 Rt 3 12901. **Hours:** 11:30 am-2:30 & 5-9 pm, Sat & Sun 5 pm-10 pm. Closed major holidays. **Reservations:** suggested. **Features:** casual dress; children's menu; cocktails & lounge. An extensive wine list complements such well-prepared dishes as Atlantic salmon with hollandaise sauce. The split-level dining room exudes rustic, understated charm. Formally uniformed servers exhibit good menu knowledge and technical skill. **Cards:** AE, CB, DI, MC, VI.

BUTCHER BLOCK STEAK & SEAFOOD   **Lunch:** $6-$8   **Dinner:** $11-$20   **Phone:** 518/563-0920

◆◆

Steak and Seafood

Location: I-87 Northway, exit 37. 15 Booth Dr 12901. **Hours:** 11:30 am-2:30 & 5-9:30 pm, Sun 5 pm-9 pm. Closed: 11/23 & 12/25. **Reservations:** suggested. **Features:** casual dress; children's menu; carryout; salad bar; cocktails & lounge; a la carte. As its name might suggest, the restaurant centers the menu on seafood and steak, particularly the succulent prime rib. The atmosphere of the dining room is rustic and cozy, welcoming to families. Decadent desserts appeal to both eyes and palate. **Cards:** AE, DI, DS, MC, VI.

DOMENIC'S RESTAURANT & LOUNGE   **Dinner:** $8-$17   **Phone:** 518/563-6980

[AAA]

◆◆

Italian

MC, VI.

Location: 2 mi n on Rt 9 N; just s of I-87, exit 39 E. 7081 Rt 9 N 12901. **Hours:** 4 pm-9 pm, Fri & Sat-10 pm. Closed major holidays. **Reservations:** suggested. **Features:** casual dress; children's menu; senior's menu; carryout; cocktails & lounge. The atmosphere is casual and festive inside the upbeat dining room, which is decorated in bold shades of red, white and green. Homemade Italian-American fare centers heavily on surf and turf selections. Spumoni and tiramisu satisfy a sweet tooth. **Cards:** AE, CB, DI, DS,

IRISES CAFE AND WINE BAR   **Lunch:** $4-$10   **Dinner:** $10-$20   **Phone:** 518/566-7000

◆◆

American

Location: Downtown; jct Court St and City Hall Pl. 20-22 City Hall Pl 12901. **Hours:** 11:30 am-2:30 & 4:30-9:30 pm, Fri-10 pm, Sat 4:30 pm-10 pm, Sun 10 am-2 & 4-9 pm. Closed: 5/30, 9/4 & 12/25. **Reservations:** accepted. **Features:** casual dress; cocktails & lounge; street parking; a la carte. Representative of creatively made dishes are such selections as Long Island duckling with sliced pears and cognac; Cajun, tomato-herb-crusted chicken over fettuccine Alfredo; and goat cheese salad with pears, pecans and a warm sherry-shallot dressing. **Cards:** AE, DS, MC, VI.

PORTAGEVILLE pop. 300

--------- RESTAURANT ---------

GLEN IRIS INN   **Lunch:** $5-$10   **Dinner:** $15-$25   **Phone:** 716/493-2622

◆◆

American

Location: In Letchworth State Park; 1 mi n off SR 19A and 436. 7 Letchworth State Park 14427. **Hours:** Open 5/1-10/31 & 4/13-4/30; 8 am-10, noon-4 & 5:30-8 pm, Fri & Sat-9 pm. **Reservations:** suggested. **Features:** casual dress; children's menu; cocktails. Victorian furnishings decorate the former country estate, which is near a waterfall in Letchworth State Park. Although the steaks, seafood and chicken are well-prepared and tasty, what you'll remember is the Berry Hill dessert, which is made tableside. Smoke free premises. **Cards:** AE, MC, VI.

PORT CHESTER —See New York p. 375.

PORT JEFFERSON pop. 7,500

--------- RESTAURANT ---------

25 EAST AMERICAN BISTRO   Country Inn   **Lunch:** $8-$17   **Dinner:** $16-$30   **Phone:** 631/928-5200

◆◆

American

Location: In village center; adjacent to ferry dock; in Danford's Inn Marina and Conference Center. 25 E Broadway 11777. **Hours:** 7 am-10:30 & 11:30-10 pm, Sat & Sun 8 am-10:30 & 11:30-11 pm. **Reservations:** suggested. **Features:** casual dress; Sunday brunch; children's menu; health conscious menu items; carryout; cocktails & lounge; a la carte. Overlooking the marina and ferry terminal, the restaurant is decorated with lots of ship memorabilia and nautical accents. Seafood is clearly the focus, with such choices as clams and broiled fish. The casual dining dock has a relaxed, comfortable feel. Smoke free premises. **Cards:** AE, DI, DS, MC, VI.

PORT JERVIS pop. 9,100

—— LODGING ——

COMFORT INN
Phone: (914)856-6611

AAA SAVE

6/1-10/31   1P: $69-$119   2P: $69-$119   XP: $7   F12
5/1-5/31 & 11/1-4/30   1P: $39-$89   2P: $39-$89   XP: $7   F12

Motor Inn
Location: I-84, exit 1, follow signs. 40 Greenville Tpke 12771. **Fax:** 914/856-5299. **Terms:** [CP] meal plan; pets. **Facility:** 103 rooms. This property has a very good hillside location with a steak house and brewery on premises also. 2 stories; interior corridors; heated pool. **Dining:** Restaurant; 11 am-9 pm, Fri-10 pm, Sat & Sun 8 am-10 pm; cocktails. **All Rooms:** extended cable TV. **Some Rooms:** Fee: refrigerators, microwaves. **Cards:** AE, CB, DI, DS, MC, VI. **Special Amenities:** Free breakfast and free local telephone calls.

—— RESTAURANT ——

FLO-JEAN RESTAURANT
Lunch: $6-$20   **Dinner:** $6-$20   **Phone:** 914/856-6600

American
Location: On US 6 and 209 at Delaware River Bridge. 2 Pike St 12771. **Hours:** 11:30 am-10 pm. Closed: Mon, Tues & 12/1-3/30. **Reservations:** suggested. **Features:** casual dress; children's menu; carryout; cocktails & lounge; a la carte. Overlooking the Delaware River, this intimate restaurant specializes in fresh steaks and seafood—although the menu includes plenty of other selections. Victorian charm punctuates the dining areas of the 1850s tollhouse. Service is attentive. **Cards:** AE, MC, VI.

POTSDAM pop. 10,300

—— LODGINGS ——

THE CLARKSON INN
Phone: 315/265-3050

Motel
All Year   1P: $75-$120   2P: $85-$120   XP: $5
Location: Center; at jct SR 11 and 56. 1 Main St 13676. Fax: 315/265-5848. **Terms:** 14 day cancellation notice; cancellation fee imposed. **Facility:** 40 rooms. Victorian inn atmosphere with elegantly appointed spacious rooms. Located on the Racquette River. 2 stories; interior corridors. **Services:** winter plug-ins. **Cards:** AE, MC, VI.

THE SMALLING MOTEL
Phone: 315/265-4640

Motel
All Year   1P: $43   2P: $48-$53   XP: $5   F5
Location: 2.3 mi n on SR 56. 6775 State Hwy 56 13676. Fax: 315/265-4614. **Facility:** 15 rooms. Set back from road on spacious, nicely landscaped grounds. Some larger rooms. 1 story; exterior corridors.
Services: winter plug-ins. **Cards:** AE, MC, VI.

POUGHKEEPSIE pop. 28,800—See also RED OAKS MILL.

—— LODGINGS ——

BEST INN
Phone: (914)454-1010

AAA SAVE

All Year   1P: $65-$100   2P: $75-$110   XP: $6   F16

Motel
Location: 2 mi e of Mid Hudson Bridge on US 44 and SR 55. 62 Haight Ave 12603. Fax: 914/454-0127. **Terms:** [CP] meal plan; 7 day cancellation notice. **Facility:** 41 rooms. Rooms vary in size. 1-2 stories; exterior corridors. **Dining:** Restaurant nearby. **Services:** winter plug-ins. **All Rooms:** shower baths, extended cable TV. **Some Rooms:** Fee: refrigerators, microwaves. **Cards:** AE, CB, DI, DS, MC, VI. **Special Amenities:** Free breakfast and free newspaper.

BEST WESTERN INN & CONFERENCE CENTER
Phone: (914)462-4600

Motor Inn
All Year   1P: $90-$110   2P: $90-$110   XP: $10   F16
Location: On US 9, 5 mi s of jct US 44 and SR 55. 679 South Rd-US 9 12601. Fax: 914/462-3228. **Terms:** Package plans. **Facility:** 153 rooms. Variety of room types. Attractive pond area by swimming pool. 3 stories, no elevator; interior corridors; designated smoking area. **Some Rooms:** Fee: refrigerators, microwaves. **Cards:** AE, CB, DI, DS, MC, VI.

HOLIDAY INN EXPRESS
Phone: (914)473-1151

Motor Inn
All Year   1P: $109-$169   2P: $109-$169   XP: $10   F19
Location: US 9, 1.8 mi s of jct US 44 and SR 55. 341 South Rd 12601. Fax: 914/485-8127. **Terms:** [ECP] meal plan; small pets only. **Facility:** 121 rooms. Located back from main hwy. Large lobby with breakfast area. 4 stories; interior corridors; designated smoking area. **All Rooms:** combo or shower baths. **Some Rooms:** Fee: refrigerators. **Cards:** AE, CB, DI, DS, JC, MC, VI.

—— RESTAURANT ——

CAPPUCINO BY COPPOLA'S
Lunch: $6-$16   **Dinner:** $6-$20   **Phone:** 914/462-4545

Italian
Location: On US 9; 4 mi s of jct US 44 and SR 55. 568 South Rd 12601. **Hours:** 11 am-10 pm, Fri & Sat-11 pm, Sun 10 am-9 pm. Closed: 11/23 & 12/25. **Reservations:** suggested. **Features:** casual dress; Sunday brunch; children's menu; carryout; cocktails & lounge; a la carte. In operation since the late 1960s, the casual restaurant is a favorite for home-style, bistro fare. Six small dining rooms offer warmth and cozy comfort. The extensive menu includes several lighter items. Sunday brunch draws a hungry crowd.
Cards: AE, DI, DS, MC, VI.

POUND RIDGE —See New York p. 375.

QUEENSBURY pop. 800—See also ADIRONDACK MOUNTAINS.

———— LODGINGS ————

ALPENHAUS MOTEL
Phone: (518)792-6941

(AAA)	7/26-9/4	1P: $85	2P: $90	XP: $5
◆◆	6/30-7/25	1P: $65-$70	2P: $70-$80	XP: $5
Motel	5/1-6/29 & 9/5-4/30	1P: $45-$50	2P: $50-$60	XP: $5

Location: 2 mi n on US 9, 0.5 mi ne of I-87 Northway, exit 19. 851 Lake George Rd, Rt 9 12804. **Terms:** 3 day cancellation notice; cancellation fee imposed. **Facility:** 15 rooms. Quaint alpine appearance. Well-maintained rooms. 1 story; exterior corridors. **Dining:** Restaurant nearby. **Services:** winter plug-ins. **All Rooms:** combo or shower baths, extended cable TV. **Cards:** AE, MC, VI.

BROWN'S WELCOME INN MOTEL
Phone: (518)792-9576

(AAA) [SAVE]	6/25-9/6	1P: $75-$95	2P: $75-$98	XP: $5
◆◆	5/12-6/24 & 9/7-10/23	1P: $49-$59	2P: $49-$69	XP: $5
Motel				

Location: 2.3 mi n on US 9, 0.8 mi ne of I-87 Northway, exit 19. 932 Rt 9, Lake George Rd 12804. **Fax:** 518/792-8072. **Terms:** Open 5/12-10/23; 7 day cancellation notice. **Facility:** 20 rooms. Pleasant rooms. 1 story; exterior corridors; heated pool; playground. **Dining:** Restaurant nearby. **All Rooms:** combo or shower baths, extended cable TV. **Some Rooms:** Fee: refrigerators. **Cards:** AE, DS, MC, VI. **Special Amenities:** Free local telephone calls and preferred room (subject to availability with advanced reservations). (See color ad p 282)

DAYS INN OF LAKE GEORGE
Phone: (518)793-3196

◆◆	6/17-9/4	1P: $68-$146	2P: $68-$146	XP: $10	F16
Motor Inn	9/5-10/21	1P: $58-$96	2P: $58-$96	XP: $10	F16
	5/1-6/16 & 10/22-4/30	1P: $58-$86	2P: $58-$86	XP: $10	F16

Location: Just n on US 9, I-87 exit 20; at jct US 149 and 9. 1454 SR 9 12845. **Fax:** 518/793-6028. **Terms:** 14 day cancellation notice; cancellation fee imposed; 2 night min stay, weekends 6/1-9/5. **Facility:** 104 rooms. Located among many shopping outlets. 2 stories; interior corridors; heated pool. **Some Rooms:** Fee: refrigerators. **Cards:** AE, CB, DI, DS, MC, VI. (See color ad p 281)

DUNHAM'S BAY LODGE ON LAKE GEORGE
Phone: (518)656-9242

(AAA) [SAVE]	6/23-9/4	1P: $140-$150	2P: $155-$200	XP: $25	D18
◆◆◆	5/26-6/22 & 9/5-10/9	1P: $75	2P: $85	XP: $20	D18
Complex				

Location: 5 mi ne of jct US 9. 2999 SR 9L 12845. **Fax:** 518/656-9250. **Terms:** Open 5/26-10/9; [CP] meal plan; weekly rates avail; 14 day cancellation notice; cancellation fee imposed. **Facility:** 54 rooms. Motel and housekeeping units. Spacious grounds with picnic tables and grills. Rooms located across from Lake George. 1- & 2-bedroom suite units with kitchen. 7 night min stay in season for suites; 1-3 stories, no elevator; exterior corridors; beach, heated pool, wading pool, whirlpool; 1 tennis court; marina; playground. Fee: boat dock, boat ramp. **Dining:** Coffee shop; snack bar at beach, weather permitting; 8:30 am-10:30 & 11-1 pm. **Recreation:** swimming, charter fishing, fishing, snorkeling, fishing poles; hiking trails, jogging, game room, lawn games, surf bikes. Fee: sailboating, waterskiing, rental rowboats, jet boats. Rental: canoes, paddleboats. **All Rooms:** extended cable TV. **Some Rooms:** Fee: refrigerators, microwaves, coffeemakers. **Cards:** AE, MC, VI. **Special Amenities:** Early check-in/late check-out and preferred room (subject to availability with advanced reservations). (See color ad p 285)

ECONO LODGE OF GLENS FALLS/LAKE GEORGE
Phone: (518)793-3491

◆◆	6/30-9/3	1P: $70-$90	2P: $75-$95	XP: $10	F16
Motel	5/1-6/29 & 9/4-11/2	1P: $50-$70	2P: $55-$75	XP: $10	F16
	11/3-4/30	1P: $35-$55	2P: $40-$60	XP: $10	F16

Location: I-87, exit 19, just e. 543 Aviation Rd 12801. **Fax:** 518/793-8678. **Facility:** 48 rooms. Some small rooms. 2 stories; exterior corridors. **Cards:** AE, DS, MC, VI.

GRAYCOURT MOTEL
Phone: 518/792-0223

(AAA)	6/24-9/4	1P: $75-$85	2P: $110	XP: $5
◆◆	5/26-6/23 & 9/5-9/17	1P: $50-$65	2P: $75	XP: $5
Motel				

Location: 3 mi n on US 9, 1.3 mi ne of I-87 Northway, exit 19. 1082 St Rt 9 12804. **Terms:** Open 5/26-9/17; 7 day cancellation notice. **Facility:** 25 rooms. Pleasant rooms, modest size cottages. 3 two-bedroom cottages, $120 for up to 6 persons in season; 1 story; exterior corridors; heated pool. **Recreation:** small playground area, picnic area with barbecue grill. **All Rooms:** combo or shower baths, extended cable TV. **Cards:** AE, DS, MC, VI. (See color ad p 286)

MOHICAN MOTEL
Phone: (518)792-0474

(AAA) [SAVE]	6/23-9/4	1P: $85	2P: $140	XP: $10	F12
◆◆◆	5/1-6/22 & 9/5-4/30	1P: $48	2P: $88	XP: $10	F12
Motel				

Location: 3.5 mi s of village on US 9, 0.8 mi n of I-87, exit 20. 1545 SR9 12845-3438. **Fax:** 518/761-4089. **Terms:** Weekly rates avail; 21 day cancellation notice; cancellation fee imposed. **Facility:** 43 rooms. Spacious attractive grounds. Pleasant rooms. 22 two-bedroom housekeeping units, $130-$225; $88-$130 off season. 3-night min stay for efficiency & kitchen units; 7 whirlpool rooms, $48-$120; 1-2 stories; exterior corridors; 2 pools, 1 indoor heated, wading pools, sauna, whirlpools, indoor pool closed 11/1-4/1; playground. **Dining:** Coffee shop; 7:30 am-2 pm 4/1-11/1. **Services:** winter plug-ins. **Recreation:** sports court, game room. **All Rooms:** extended cable TV. **Cards:** AE, CB, DI, MC, VI. **Special Amenities:** Free room upgrade and preferred room (each subject to availability with advanced reservations). (See color ad p 288)

RAMADA INN GLENS FALLS
◆◆
Motor Inn
All Year   1P: $59-$139   2P: $69-$149   XP: $10   F16
Phone: (518)793-7701
Location: I-87, exit 19, just w. 1 Abby Ln 12804. Fax: 518/792-5463. **Facility:** 110 rooms. Convienent to inter-state exit. 2 stories; interior corridors; heated pool. **Services:** winter plug-ins. **Some Rooms:** 3 efficiencies.
Cards: AE, CB, DI, DS, JC, MC, VI.

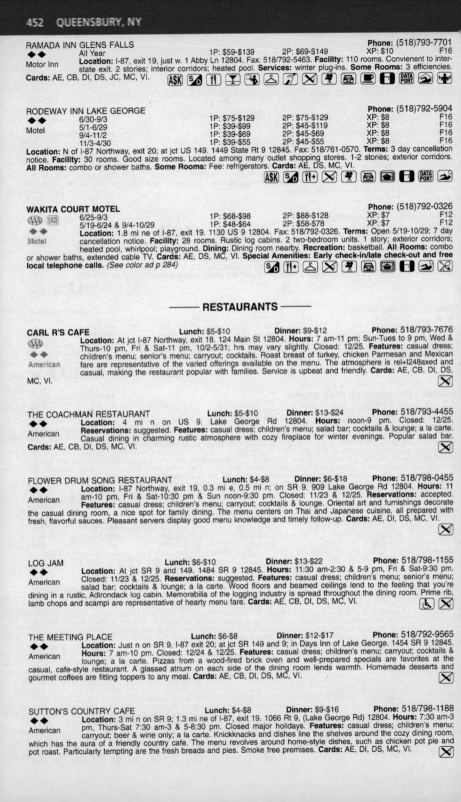

RODEWAY INN LAKE GEORGE
◆◆
Motel
Phone: (518)792-5904
6/30-9/3	1P: $75-$129	2P: $75-$129	XP: $8	F16
5/1-6/29	1P: $39-$99	2P: $45-$119	XP: $8	F16
9/4-11/2	1P: $39-$69	2P: $45-$69	XP: $8	F16
11/3-4/30	1P: $39-$55	2P: $45-$55	XP: $8	F16

Location: N of I-87 Northway, exit 20; at jct US 149. 1449 State Rt 9 12845. Fax: 518/761-0570. **Terms:** 3 day cancellation notice. **Facility:** 30 rooms. Good size rooms. Located among many outlet shopping stores. 1-2 stories; exterior corridors. **All Rooms:** combo or shower baths. **Some Rooms:** Fee: refrigerators. **Cards:** AE, DS, MC, VI.

WAKITA COURT MOTEL
(AAA) SAVE
◆◆
Motel
Phone: (518)792-0326
| 6/25-9/3 | 1P: $68-$98 | 2P: $88-$128 | XP: $7 | F12 |
| 5/19-6/24 & 9/4-10/29 | 1P: $48-$64 | 2P: $58-$78 | XP: $7 | F12 |

Location: 1.8 mi ne of I-87, exit 19. 1130 US 9 12804. Fax: 518/792-0326. **Terms:** Open 5/19-10/29; 7 day cancellation notice. **Facility:** 28 rooms. Rustic log cabins. 2 two-bedroom units. 1 story; exterior corridors; heated pool, whirlpool; playground. **Dining:** Dining room nearby. **Recreation:** basketball. **All Rooms:** combo or shower baths, extended cable TV. **Cards:** AE, DS, MC, VI. **Special Amenities:** Early check-in/late check-out and free local telephone calls. (See color ad p 284)

RESTAURANTS

CARL R'S CAFE
(AAA)
◆◆
American
Lunch: $5-$10   Dinner: $9-$12   Phone: 518/793-7676
Location: At jct I-87 Northway, exit 18. 124 Main St 12804. **Hours:** 7 am-11 pm; Sun-Tues to 9 pm, Wed & Thurs-10 pm, Fri & Sat-11 pm, 10/2-5/31; hrs may vary slightly. **Closed:** 12/25. **Features:** casual dress; children's menu; senior's menu; carryout; cocktails. Roast breast of turkey, chicken Parmesan and Mexican fare are representative of the varied offerings available on the menu. The atmosphere is rel+l248axed and casual, making the restaurant popular with families. Service is upbeat and friendly. **Cards:** AE, CB, DI, DS, MC, VI.

THE COACHMAN RESTAURANT
◆◆
American
Lunch: $5-$10   Dinner: $13-$24   Phone: 518/793-4455
Location: 4 mi n on US 9. Lake George Rd 12804. **Hours:** noon-9 pm. **Closed:** 12/25. **Reservations:** suggested. **Features:** casual dress; children's menu; salad bar; cocktails & lounge; a la carte. Casual dining in charming rustic atmosphere with cozy fireplace for winter evenings. Popular salad bar. **Cards:** AE, CB, DI, DS, MC, VI.

FLOWER DRUM SONG RESTAURANT
◆◆
American
Lunch: $4-$8   Dinner: $6-$18   Phone: 518/798-0455
Location: I-87 Northway, exit 19, 0.3 mi e, 0.5 mi n; on SR 9. 909 Lake George Rd 12804. **Hours:** 11 am-10 pm, Fri & Sat-10:30 pm & Sun noon-9:30 pm. **Closed:** 11/23 & 12/25. **Reservations:** accepted. **Features:** casual dress; children's menu; carryout; cocktails & lounge. Oriental art and furnishings decorate the casual dining room, a nice spot for family dining. The menu centers on Thai and Japanese cuisine, all prepared with fresh, flavorful sauces. Pleasant servers display good menu knowledge and timely follow-up. **Cards:** AE, DI, DS, MC, VI.

LOG JAM
◆◆
American
Lunch: $6-$10   Dinner: $13-$22   Phone: 518/798-1155
Location: At jct SR 9 and 149. 1484 SR 9 12845. **Hours:** 11:30 am-2:30 & 5-9 pm, Fri & Sat-9:30 pm. **Closed:** 11/23 & 12/25. **Reservations:** suggested. **Features:** casual dress; children's menu; senior's menu; salad bar; cocktails & lounge; a la carte. Wood floors and beamed ceilings lend to the feeling that you're dining in a rustic, Adirondack log cabin. Memorabilia of the logging industry is spread throughout the dining room. Prime rib, lamb chops and scampi are representative of hearty menu fare. **Cards:** AE, CB, DI, DS, MC, VI.

THE MEETING PLACE
◆◆
American
Lunch: $6-$8   Dinner: $12-$17   Phone: 518/792-9565
Location: Just n on SR 9, I-87 exit 20; at jct SR 149 and 9; in Days Inn of Lake George. 1454 SR 9 12845. **Hours:** 7 am-10 pm. **Closed:** 12/24 & 12/25. **Features:** casual dress; children's menu; carryout; cocktails & lounge; a la carte. Pizzas from a wood-fired brick oven and well-prepared specials are favorites at the casual, cafe-style restaurant. A glassed atrium on each side of the dining room lends warmth. Homemade desserts and gourmet coffees are fitting toppers to any meal. **Cards:** AE, CB, DI, DS, MC, VI.

SUTTON'S COUNTRY CAFE
◆◆
American
Lunch: $4-$8   Dinner: $9-$16   Phone: 518/798-1188
Location: 3 mi n on SR 9; 1.3 mi ne of I-87, exit 19. 1066 Rt 9, (Lake George Rd) 12804. **Hours:** 7:30 am-3 pm, Thurs-Sat 7:30 am-3 & 5-8:30 pm. **Closed** major holidays. **Features:** casual dress; children's menu; carryout; beer & wine only; a la carte. Knickknacks and dishes line the shelves around the cozy dining room, which has the aura of a friendly country cafe. The menu revolves around home-style dishes, such as chicken pot pie and pot roast. Particularly tempting are the fresh breads and pies. Smoke free premises. **Cards:** AE, DI, DS, MC, VI.

RAYMERTOWN pop. 500

———— RESTAURANT ————

TAVERN AT STERUP SQUARE
◆◆
American
Location: 10.1 mi e of jct I-787. 2113 SR 7. **Lunch:** $8-$17   **Dinner:** $13-$23   **Phone:** 518/663-5800   **Hours:** 11 am-11 pm, Sun from 10 am. Closed: 12/25. **Reservations:** suggested. **Features:** casual dress; Sunday brunch; children's menu; health conscious menu; carryout; cocktails. Representative of internationally influenced, new American cuisine are such dishes as roasted rack of lamb and fresh salmon. The dining room has the atmosphere of an upscale European pub. Save room for the yummy Sterup Square berry patch dessert. **Cards:** AE, DI, DS, MC, VI.

RED CREEK pop. 600

———— LODGING ————

BLACK CREEK FARM B & B
◆◆◆
Bed &
Breakfast

5/1-10/31 & 12/20-4/30	1P: $60	2P: $85	**Phone:** (315)947-5282 XP: $20	
11/1-12/19	1P: $60	2P: $75	XP: $20	

Location: 0.8 mi w of 104A. 13615 Mixer Rd 13143 (PO Box 390, FAIR HAVEN, 13064). Fax: 315/947-5282. **Terms:** [BP] meal plan; age restrictions may apply; 14 day cancellation notice. **Facility:** 4 rooms. 2 stories; interior corridors; designated smoking area. **Recreation:** fishing; bicycles. **Cards:** AE, MC, VI.

RED OAKS MILL pop. 4,900—*See also POUGHKEEPSIE.*

———— LODGING ————

INN AT THE FALLS
AAA
◆◆◆◆
Bed &
Breakfast

All Year	1P: $155-$160	2P: $155-$160	**Phone:** (914)462-5770 XP: $10 F12

Location: 5 mi s of Poughkeepsie on US 44 and SR 55, on CR 44 at jct SR 376, 1.5 mi nw of Dutchess County Airport. 50 Red Oaks Mill Rd 12603. Fax: 914/462-5943. **Terms:** [CP] meal plan; 3 day cancellation notice; cancellation fee imposed. **Facility:** 36 rooms. A contemporary mansion with country inn personality, serene location overlooking Mill Pond. Individually and beautifully furnished rooms. 9 whirlpool rooms, $190-$195; 2 stories; interior corridors; designated smoking area. **Dining:** 7-10 am. **Services:** complimentary evening beverages. **Recreation:** fishing. **All Rooms:** extended cable TV, safes. **Cards:** AE, DI, DS, MC, VI.

RHINEBECK pop. 2,700

———— LODGING ————

BEEKMAN ARMS & DELAMATER HOUSE AND CONFERENCE CENTER
◆◆◆
Historic
Country Inn

All Year	1P: $85-$150	2P: $85-$150	**Phone:** 914/876-7077 XP: $10

Location: At jct SR 9 and 308. 6387 Mill St 12572. Fax: 914/876-7077. **Terms:** [ECP] meal plan; 7 day cancellation notice; 2 night min stay, 5/1-10/31 weekends; pets, in motel units. **Facility:** 64 rooms. Some rooms in original inn, majority in guest house buildings. Few motel units avail. Variety of individually decorated, beautifully furnished guest rooms. 1 two-bedroom unit. 2-3 stories, no elevator; interior/exterior corridors; designated smoking area. **Some Rooms:** kitchen, color TV. **Cards:** AE, DI, MC, VI.

———— RESTAURANT ————

BEEKMAN 1766 TAVERN   Historical
◆◆
Regional
American
Location: At jct SR 9 and 308; in Beekman Arms & Delamater House and Conference Center. 4 Mill St 12572. **Lunch:** $9-$13   **Dinner:** $19-$26   **Phone:** 914/871-1766   **Hours:** 11:30-3 & 5:30-9 pm, Fri & Sat-9:30 pm, Sun 10 am-2 & 3:30-8:30 pm. **Reservations:** suggested; weekends. **Features:** casual dress; Sunday brunch; children's menu; carryout; cocktails & lounge. Cedar-plank salmon stands out as the signature dish among selections of seafood, duck, pork, chicken and beef. The 1766 inn has the feel of a cozy tavern, with Colonial furnishings and a charming pewter room. The creative menu changes seasonally. **Cards:** AE, CB, DI, MC, VI.

RICHFIELD SPRINGS pop. 1,600

———— LODGINGS ————

FOUNTAIN VIEW MOTEL
AAA
◆◆
Motel

6/15-9/4	1P: $70-$80	2P: $70-$80	**Phone:** 315/858-1360 XP: $5
9/5-12/1	1P: $45-$70	2P: $45-$70	XP: $5
4/1-4/30	1P: $50-$60	2P: $50-$60	XP: $5
5/1-6/14	1P: $45-$55	2P: $45-$55	XP: $5

Location: 1 mi e. 3607 US 20 13439. **Terms:** Open 5/1-12/1 & 4/1-4/30; 3 day cancellation notice; cancellation fee imposed. **Facility:** 16 rooms. On hillside overlooking lake with illuminated fountain. Large rooms with pleasant simple decor. 1 story; exterior corridors; smoke free premises. **All Rooms:** extended cable TV. **Cards:** AE, DS, MC, VI.
(See color ad p 239)

STONY BROOK MOTEL

Phone: 315/858-9929

6/16-9/5	1P: $67	2P: $72	XP: $5
9/6-10/31	1P: $40-$50	2P: $45-$55	XP: $5
11/1-4/30	1P: $40	2P: $45	
5/1-6/15	1P: $40	2P: $45	XP: $5

Motel **Location:** 0.5 mi e on US 20. 232 Main St 13439 (PO Box 1466). **Terms:** 3 day cancellation notice. **Facility:** 7 rooms. Simple guest rooms with pleasant front deck. 1 story; exterior corridors. **Services:** winter plug-ins. **All Rooms:** shower baths, extended cable TV. **Cards:** DS, MC, VI.

VILLAGE MOTEL

Phone: 315/858-1540

6/15-9/11	1P: $70-$75	2P: $75-$80	XP: $5
9/12-10/31	1P: $45-$50	2P: $55-$65	XP: $5
5/1-6/14	1P: $40-$45	2P: $55-$65	XP: $5
11/1-4/30	1P: $40-$45	2P: $50-$60	XP: $5

Motel **Location:** Center. 168 Main St (Rt 20) 13439 (PO Box 766). **Terms:** 3 day cancellation notice. **Facility:** 11 rooms. Modest exterior, pleasant guest rooms. 1 story; exterior corridors. **Services:** winter plug-ins. **All Rooms:** extended cable TV. **Cards:** DS, MC, VI.

RIPLEY pop. 1,200

—— **LODGING** ——

BUDGET HOST COLONIAL SQUIRE

Phone: (716)736-8000

5/1-10/31	1P: $49	2P: $55	XP: $5
11/1-4/30	1P: $40	2P: $45	

Motel **Location:** I-90, exit 61. 6151 Shortman Rd 14775. **Terms:** 7 day cancellation notice; pets. **Facility:** 28 rooms. Spacious guest rooms. 1 story; exterior corridors. **All Rooms:** extended cable TV. **Cards:** AE, DS, MC, VI. *(See color ad p 194)*

RIVERHEAD pop. 8,800

—— **LODGINGS** ——

BUDGET HOST INN

Phone: (631)727-6200

6/19-9/11	1P: $71-$108	2P: $76-$128	XP: $10 F16
5/1-6/18 & 9/12-4/30	1P: $71-$81	2P: $76-$86	XP: $10 F16

Motel **Location:** I-495, exit 71. 4.4 mi s on SR 24 to jct CR 63 (E Moriches Rd). 30 E Moriches Rd 11901. Fax: 631/727-6466. **Facility:** 68 rooms. 2 stories; interior corridors; 1 tennis court. **Some Rooms:** 12 efficiencies. **Cards:** AE, CB, DI, DS, MC, VI. *(See color ad p 194)*

RAMADA INN-EAST END

Phone: (631)369-2200

5/1-10/31	1P: $149-$189	2P: $149-$189	XP: $10 F16
11/1-4/30	1P: $129-$149	2P: $129-$149	XP: $10 F16

Motor Inn **Location:** I-495, exit 72 (SR 25 E). 1830 SR 25 11901. Fax: 631/369-1202. **Terms:** Package plans, seasonal; pets, $50 dep req. **Facility:** 100 rooms. 2 stories; interior corridors. **Some Rooms:** Fee: refrigerators, microwaves. **Cards:** AE, CB, DI, DS, MC, VI.

ROCHESTER pop. 231,600 (See map p. 456; index below)

This index helps you "spot" where approved accommodations are located on the detailed maps that follow. Rate ranges are for comparison only and show the property's high season. Turn to the listing page for more detailed rate information and consult display ads for special promotions. Restaurant rate range is for dinner unless only lunch (L) is served.

✈ Airport Accommodations

Spotter/Map Page Number	OA	ROCHESTER	Diamond Rating	Rate Range High Season	Listing Page
14 / p. 456	AAA	Comfort Inn Central, 0.3 mi n of airport	◆◆	$64-$79	261
15 / p. 456		Fairfield Inn by Marriott-Airport, at airport	◆◆◆	$80-$90	262
13 / p. 456		Holiday Inn-Airport, 0.5 mi e of airport	◆◆◆	$115	262

ROCHESTER

Spotter/Map Page Number	OA	ROCHESTER - Lodgings	Diamond Rating	Rate Range High Season	Listing Page
1 / p. 456		428 Mt. Vernon	◆◆◆	$95-$115	457
2 / p. 456		A Bed and Breakfast at Dartmouth House Inn	◆◆◆	$85-$125	457
4 / p. 456	AAA	Crowne Plaza Rochester	◆◆◆	$89-$129	457
5 / p. 456		Sheraton Four Points Rochester Riverside	◆◆	$59-$139	459
6 / p. 456	AAA	Hyatt Regency Rochester	◆◆◆	$129-$154	458
9 / p. 456	AAA	Strathallan - see color ad p 459	◆◆◆	$159-$169	459
10 / p. 456	AAA	The Best Western Diplomat Hotel	◆◆	$54-$80	457
11 / p. 456	AAA	Radisson Hotel Rochester Airport - see color ad p 459	◆◆◆	$89-$169	459

Spotter/Map Page Number	OA	ROCHESTER - Restaurants	Diamond Rating	Rate Range High Season	Listing Page
② / p. 456		The Grill at Water Street	◆◆◆	$19-$30	460
③ / p. 456		Cutler's Restaurant at the Gallery	◆◆	$16-$25	460
④ / p. 456		Five 50 Pub	◆◆◆	$12-$28	460
⑤ / p. 456	ⒶⒶⒶ	**India House Restaurant**	◆◆	$8-$16	460
⑥ / p. 456		Palladio	◆◆◆	$15-$25	460
⑧ / p. 456		The Rio	◆◆◆	$18-$27	460
⑨ / p. 456		Raj Mahal	◆	$7-$15	460

Nearby Accommodations

Spotter/Map Page Number	OA	GATES - Lodgings	Diamond Rating	Rate Range High Season	Listing Page
⓭ / p. 456		Holiday Inn-Airport - see color ad p 457	◆◆◆	$115	262
⓮ / p. 456	ⒶⒶⒶ	**Comfort Inn Central - see ad p 261**	◆◆	$64-$79 ⓢ	261
⓯ / p. 456		Fairfield Inn by Marriott-Airport	◆◆◆	$80-$90	262
		BRIGHTON - Lodgings			
⓰ / p. 456		Hampton Inn-South	◆◆◆	$99	209
⓱ / p. 456	ⒶⒶⒶ	**Wellesley Inn & Suites - see color ad p 458 & color ad p 4**	◆◆	$60-$105 ⓢ	209
⓲ / p. 456		Courtyard by Marriott Brighton	◆◆◆	$89-$114	209
⓳ / p. 456	ⒶⒶⒶ	**Towpath Motel**	◆	$35-$75 ⓢ	209
		BRIGHTON - Restaurant			
⑪ / p. 456		Mario's Via Abruzzi	◆◆	$13-$17	209
		GREECE - Lodgings			
⓴ / p. 456		Courtyard by Marriott-Rochester West	◆◆◆	$109	265
㉑ / p. 456	ⒶⒶⒶ	**Comfort Inn-West - see ad p 457**	◆◆	$74-$89 ⓢ	264
㉒ / p. 456		Marriott Airport Hotel	◆◆◆	$160	265
㉓ / p. 456	ⒶⒶⒶ	**Wellesley Inn & Suites - see color ad p 458 & color ad p 4**	◆◆	$60-$105 ⓢ	265
㉔ / p. 456		Hampton Inn-Rochester North	◆◆◆	$78-$96	265
㉕ / p. 456		Residence Inn by Marriott-West	◆◆◆	$84-$169	265
		PITTSFORD - Lodgings			
㉖ / p. 456	ⒶⒶⒶ	**Brookwood Inn - see ad p 447**	◆◆◆	$99-$135 ⓢ	447
㉗ / p. 456		Oliver Loud's Inn	◆◆◆◆	$125-$145	447
		PITTSFORD - Restaurants			
⑭ / p. 456	ⒶⒶⒶ	**Spring House**	◆◆	$14-$18	447
⑮ / p. 456		Richardson's Canal House	◆◆◆	$35	447
		FAIRPORT - Lodgings			
㉘ / p. 456		The Lodge At Woodcliff	◆◆◆	$99-$135	254
㉙ / p. 456	ⒶⒶⒶ	**Trail Break Motor Inn**	◆	$35-$69	254
		HENRIETTA - Lodgings			
㉛ / p. 456		Fairfield Inn by Marriott	◆◆◆	$84	269
㉜ / p. 456	ⒶⒶⒶ	**Econo Lodge-Rochester South - see ad p 458**	◆◆	$64-$79 ⓢ	269
㉟ / p. 456		Microtel	◆◆	Failed to provide	269
㊱ / p. 456	ⒶⒶⒶ	**Super 8 Motel**	◆◆	$50-$67 ⓢ	269
㊲ / p. 456		Rochester Marriott Thruway Hotel	◆◆◆	$105	269
㊳ / p. 456		Holiday Inn South	◆◆◆	$116	269
㊴ / p. 456	ⒶⒶⒶ	**Red Roof Inn-Henrietta**	◆◆	$48-$83	269
㊵ / p. 456		Residence Inn by Marriott - see color ad p 458	◆◆◆	$97-$130	269
		PENFIELD - Lodgings			
㊽ / p. 456		Courtyard By Marriott	◆◆◆	$74-$114	445
		PENFIELD - Restaurant			
⑲ / p. 456		Daisy Flour Mill	◆◆◆	$11-$25	446
		WEST HENRIETTA - Restaurant			
㉒ / p. 456	ⒶⒶⒶ	**The Cartwright Inn**	◆◆	$10-$20	491

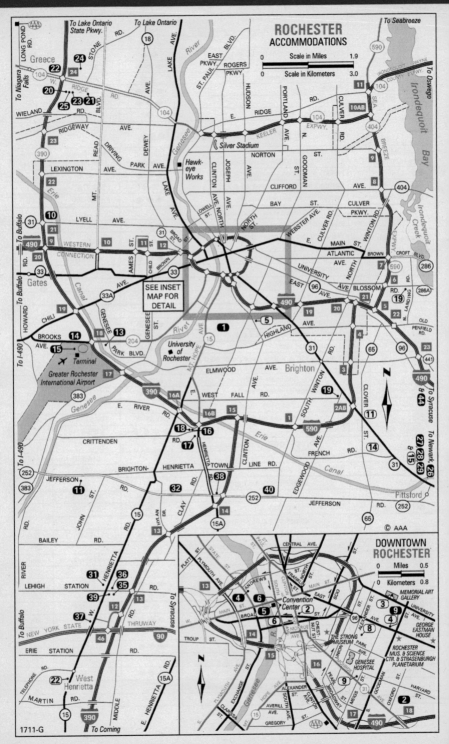

ROCHESTER
ACCOMMODATIONS

Scale in Miles

Scale in Kilometers

DOWNTOWN
ROCHESTER

Miles

Kilometers

© AAA

1711-G

ROCHESTER pop. 231,600 (See map p. 456; index p. 454)

LODGINGS

A BED AND BREAKFAST AT DARTMOUTH HOUSE INN
Phone: (716)271-7872 **2**
◆◆◆ All Year 1P: $85-$99 2P: $110-$125 XP: $25
Historic Bed **Location:** I-490, exit 18, just w on SR 31 W (Monroe Ave), just n. 215 Dartmouth St 14607. Fax: 716/473-0778.
& Breakfast **Terms:** [BP] meal plan; age restrictions may apply; 7 day cancellation notice; cancellation fee imposed.
Facility: 4 rooms. 1905 renovated English Tudor home. Located close to area museums. 5 course gourmet
candlelight breakfast. Free movie library. 2 stories; interior corridors; smoke free premises. **All Rooms:** combo or shower
baths. **Cards:** AE, CB, DI, MC, VI.

THE BEST WESTERN DIPLOMAT HOTEL
Phone: (716)254-1000 **10**
◆◆◆ 〔SAVE〕 All Year 1P: $54-$80 2P: $54-$80 XP: $10 F16
◆◆ **Location:** I-390, exit 21; just e (SR 31). 1956 Lyell Ave 14606. Fax: 716/254-1510. **Terms:** 3 day cancellation
Motel notice, weekends only; cancellation fee imposed. **Facility:** 90 rooms. 6 whirlpool rms with refrigerator & micro-
wave, $90-$126; 5 stories; interior corridors. **Dining:** Restaurant nearby. **Recreation:** health club privileges for
adults. **All Rooms:** extended cable TV. **Cards:** AE, CB, DI, DS, MC, VI. **Special Amenities:** Early check-
in/late check-out and free breakfast.

CROWNE PLAZA ROCHESTER
Phone: (716)546-3450 **4**
◆◆◆ 〔SAVE〕 All Year 1P: $89-$129 2P: $89-$129
◆◆◆ **Location:** Downtown. 70 State St 14614. Fax: 716/546-8712. **Terms:** Package plans; small pets only.
Hotel **Facility:** 362 rooms. 7 stories; interior corridors; heated pool, sauna. Fee: parking. **Dining:** Dining room; 6
am-2 & 5-10 pm; $13-$25; cocktails. **Services:** gift shop; area transportation, train & bus stations.
Some Rooms: honor bars. **Cards:** AE, CB, DI, DS, MC, VI. **Special Amenities:** Free newspaper and pre-
ferred room (subject to availability with advanced reservations).

428 MT. VERNON
Phone: (716)271-0792 **1**
◆◆◆ All Year 1P: $95 2P: $115
Historic Bed **Location:** 1 mi s on South Ave, just e on Rockingham, then just s. 428 Mt. Vernon Ave 14620.
& Breakfast Fax: 716/271-0946. **Terms:** Age restrictions may apply. **Facility:** 7 rooms. Beautifully restored 1917 home set
on 2 wooded acres. Attractive individually decorated rooms. 3 stories; interior corridors. **All Rooms:** combo or
shower baths. **Cards:** AE, DI, MC, VI.

(See map p. 456)

HYATT REGENCY ROCHESTER

🔺🔺🔺 Hotel

⬛⬛

All Year — 1P: $129 — 2P: $154

Phone: (716)546-1234 — XP: $25 — **6** — F18

Location: Downtown. 125 E Main St 14604. Fax: 716/546-6777. **Terms:** Cancellation fee imposed; package plans. **Facility:** 336 rooms. Connected by skywalk to convention center. 2 whirlpool rooms; 25 stories; interior corridors; heated pool, whirlpool, accessible pool lift for the handicapped. Fee: parking. **Dining:** Palladio, see separate listing. **Services:** gift shop. **All Rooms:** combo or shower baths, extended cable TV. **Some Rooms:** Fee: refrigerators, VCR. **Cards:** AE, DI, DS, JC, MC, VI.

⊞ 🍴 ▼ 🔌 ⬛ 🛗 ♿ 📷 ✕ 📹 VCR 🗄 ⬛ 🖥 🔲 DATA PORT 🏊 ♿

(See map p. 456)

RADISSON HOTEL ROCHESTER AIRPORT

Phone: (716)475-1910   **11**

AAA SAVE
◆◆◆
Motor Inn

| | 5/1-10/31 & 4/1-4/30 | 1P: $89-$169 | 2P: $89-$169 |
| | 11/1-3/31 | 1P: $69-$169 | 2P: $69-$169 |

Location: 1.6 mi w on SR 252 from jct SR 15. 175 Jefferson Rd 14623. Fax: 716/475-9633. **Terms:** [BP] meal plan; cancellation fee imposed; package plans. **Facility:** 171 rooms. 4 stories; interior corridors; heated pool, sauna. **Dining:** Restaurant; 6 am-10 pm; $10-$18; cocktails. **Services:** area transportation, within 5 mi. **All Rooms:** extended cable TV. **Cards:** AE, CB, DI, DS, MC, VI. **Special Amenities:** Early check-in/late check-out and free room upgrade (subject to availability with advanced reservations). (See color ad below)

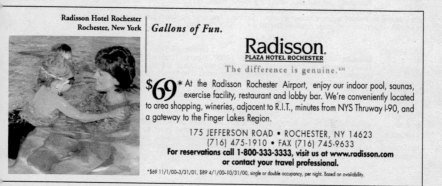

SHERATON FOUR POINTS ROCHESTER RIVERSIDE

Phone: (716)546-6400   **5**

◆◆
Hotel

| | All Year | 1P: $59-$129 | 2P: $69-$139 | XP: $10 | F16 |

Location: Downtown. 120 E Main St 14604. Fax: 716/546-1341. **Terms:** 30 day cancellation notice; cancellation fee imposed; package plans. **Facility:** 466 rooms. Riverside location, opposite convention center. 15 stories; interior corridors; heated pool. Fee: parking. **Services:** gift shop; area transportation. **All Rooms:** combo or shower baths. **Cards:** AE, CB, DI, DS, MC, VI.

STRATHALLAN

Phone: (716)461-5010   **9**

AAA SAVE
◆◆◆
Suite Hotel

| | All Year | 1P: $159-$169 | 2P: $159-$169 | XP: $10 | F18 |

Location: I-490, exit 17, 0.9 mi n on Goodman, just w. 550 East Ave 14607. Fax: 716/461-3387. **Terms:** Weekly & monthly rates avail; package plans. **Facility:** 156 rooms. Conveniently located near Memorial Art Gallery and other attractions. All rooms with hair dryer, iron and ironing board. 1- & 2-bedroom suites; many with balcony; whirlpool room; 9 stories; interior corridors; sauna. **Dining:** Restaurant; $8-$25; cocktails; also, Five 50 Pub, see separate listing. **All Rooms:** extended cable TV. **Some Rooms:** 87 efficiencies, 59 kitchens, safes. Fee: VCR. **Cards:** AE, DI, DS, MC, VI. (See color ad below)

(See map p. 456)

——— **RESTAURANTS** ———

CUTLER'S RESTAURANT AT THE GALLERY　**Lunch:** $8-$11　**Dinner:** $16-$25　**Phone:** 716/473-6380　③
◆◆　**Location:** I-490, University/Main St exit, 1.8 mi ne. 500 University Ave 14607. **Hours:** 11:30 am-2:30 &
American　5-8:30 pm, Sun 11 am-2 pm. Closed major holidays & Mon. **Reservations:** suggested. **Features:** casual
dress; Sunday brunch; cocktails; a la carte. In the Memorial Art Gallery, the restaurant is fittingly decorated
with gallery artwork. The inside dining room is warm and cozy, while the terrace—enveloped by fountains and statues—has
a more casual aura. The menu of well-prepared fare changes daily. Smoke free premises. **Cards:** AE, MC, VI.　☒

FIVE 50 PUB　**Lunch:** $7-$15　**Dinner:** $12-$28　**Phone:** 716/461-5010　④
◆◆◆　**Location:** I-490, exit 17, 0.9 mi n on Goodman, just w; in Strathallan. 550 East Ave 14607. **Hours:** 6:30-9:30
American　am, 11:30-2 & 6:30-10 pm, Sat 7 am-11 & 6-10 pm, Sun 7 am-11 & 5:30-9 pm. **Reservations:** suggested.
Features: casual dress; carryout; cocktails & lounge; valet parking. Local art depicting area festivals
decorates the upscale dining room, where professionals and couples dine together in cozy elegance. Such selections as
shellfish bouillabaisse are flavorful and satisfying. Personable servers show good technical skill. Smoke free premises.
Cards: AE, DI, DS, MC, VI.　☒

THE GRILL AT WATER STREET　**Lunch:** $8-$14　**Dinner:** $19-$30　**Phone:** 716/454-1880　②
◆◆◆　**Location:** Center. 175 N Water St 14604. **Hours:** 11:30 am-2:30 & 5-10 pm, Sat from 5 pm. Closed major
American　holidays & Sun. **Reservations:** accepted. **Features:** dressy casual; cocktails & lounge; street parking & valet
parking; a la carte. The decor is funky yet sophisticated, and the menu offers a good selection of traditional
American red meat and fish dishes. Pleasing creative twists enhance both the preparation and presentation. The extensive
wine list is carefully culled. **Cards:** AE, DI, DS, MC, VI.　☒

INDIA HOUSE RESTAURANT　**Lunch:** $8-$9　**Dinner:** $8-$16　**Phone:** 716/461-0880　⑤
ⓐⓐⓐ　**Location:** I-490, exit 17, sw to Clinton, just s. 998 S Clinton Ave 14620. **Hours:** 11:30 am-2:30 & 5-9:30 pm,
◆◆　Fri & Sat-10 pm. Closed: 7/4, 11/23 & 12/25. **Reservations:** suggested. **Features:** casual dress; carryout;
Ethnic　cocktails. Piquant flavors, pungent aromas and distinctive spices combine to create delicious dishes, such as
aloo samosa and curried lamb. Tapestries, paintings and carvings are examples of Indian art in the large, but
intimate, dining room. Servers are attentive. Smoke free premises. **Cards:** AE, DI, DS, MC, VI.　♿ ☒

PALLADIO　**Lunch:** $6-$12　**Dinner:** $15-$25　**Phone:** 716/423-6767　⑥
◆◆◆　**Location:** Downtown; in Hyatt Regency Rochester. 125 E Main St 14604. **Hours:** 6:30 am-2:30 & 5-10:30
Northern　pm, Fri-10 pm, Sat 7 am-2 & 5-10 pm, Sun 7 am-2 & 5-10:30 pm. **Reservations:** suggested.
Italian　**Features:** casual dress; children's menu; health conscious menu items; carryout; cocktails; fee for parking;
area transportation; a la carte, buffet. Italian architecture is the focus of artwork in the sophisticated dining
room, where restaurant regulars gather to enjoy creatively prepared Southern Italian dishes. A good choice is bow tie pasta
with fresh vegetables and grilled chicken. **Cards:** AE, CB, DI, DS, MC, VI.　♿ ☒

RAJ MAHAL　**Lunch:** $8　**Dinner:** $7-$15　**Phone:** 716/546-2315　⑨
◆　**Location:** 0.5 mi e. 324 Monroe Ave 14607. **Hours:** 11:30 am-2:30 & 5-10 pm. Closed major holidays.
Ethnic　**Reservations:** suggested; weekends. **Features:** casual dress; carryout; cocktails. Paintings and statues
decorate the comfortable, laid-back dining room. The menu centers on traditional preparations of beef,
seafood, lamb and chicken, including a good array of baked entrees. The lunch buffet is loaded with tempting choices.
Cards: AE, DI, DS, MC, VI.　☒

THE RIO　**Dinner:** $18-$27　**Phone:** 716/473-2806　⑧
◆◆◆　**Location:** 0.5 mi via East Ave, just s. 282 Alexander St 14607. **Hours:** 5 pm-10 pm. Closed major holidays
Continental　& Sun. **Reservations:** suggested. **Features:** semi-formal attire; cocktails & lounge; valet parking; a la carte.
Popular and long-established, the restaurant delivers attractively presented dishes, such as salmon tornedos.
The converted house is elegantly appointed with upscale furnishings. For dessert, splurge on the wonderful caramel-fudge
cheesecake. **Cards:** AE, DI, DS, MC, VI.　☒

ROCKVILLE CENTRE　pop. 24,700

——— **LODGING** ———

HOLIDAY INN　**Phone:** (516)678-1300
ⓐⓐⓐ SAVE　1/1-4/30　　1P: $155-$165　2P: $155-$165　XP: $15　F19
5/1-12/31　1P: $145-$155　2P: $145-$155　XP: $15　F19
◆◆◆　**Location:** On SR 27. 173 Sunrise Hwy 11570. Fax: 516/678-5657. **Terms:** [BP] meal plan; package plans;
Motor Inn　pets, $15 extra charge. **Facility:** 100 rooms. Centrally located, adjacent to train station. 5 stories; exterior cor-
ridors. **Dining:** Restaurant; 6:30 am-2:30 & 5-10 pm; closed Sun evenings; $8-$15; health conscious menu
items; cocktails. **Some Rooms:** Fee: refrigerators. **Cards:** AE, CB, DI, DS, MC, VI. **Special Amenities:** Free newspaper and
free room upgrade (subject to availability with advanced reservations).

ⓢⓓ 🛏 🍴 ⛶ 🚲 🏋 🎦 ☒ 🎥 🖨 🖥 🎱 DATAPORT 🏃 ♨

——— **RESTAURANTS** ———

TAIKO　**Lunch:** $6-$10　**Dinner:** $11-$15　**Phone:** 516/678-6149
◆◆　**Location:** Just s of jct Sunrise Hwy. 15 S Village Ave 11570. **Hours:** noon-2:30 & 5:30-10:30 pm, Fri-11 pm,
Japanese　Sat 5:30 pm-11 pm. Closed major holidays. **Features:** casual dress; carryout; cocktails; street parking; a la
carte. Rice paper screens and tatami tables decorate the simple dining room. Sushi and sashimi choices are
excellent, and more timid palates will find plenty of cooked choices, such as teriyaki, tempura and noodle dishes. Ice cream
flavors are exquisite. Smoke free premises. **Cards:** AE, CB, DI, MC, VI.　☒

TOMATOES
American

Dinner: $15-$25
Phone: 516/594-2977
Location: Center; between N Park & N Village aves. 242 Sunrise Hwy 11570. **Hours:** 5 pm-10 pm, Fri & Sat-11 pm, Sun 3 pm-9:30 pm. **Features:** casual dress; carryout; cocktails; street parking; a la carte. Sesame-crusted, seared ahi tuna and the vegetable tower are two shining examples of interesting, California-Italian cuisine. Dishes exhibit interesting and complex flavors, as well as fun shapes. The energized dining room has a bright, upbeat feel. Smoke free premises. **Cards:** AE, DS, MC, VI.

ROME pop. 44,400

———— LODGINGS ————

ADIRONDACK THIRTEEN PINES MOTEL
Motel

Phone: 315/337-4930

6/1-10/1	1P: $40-$45	2P: $45-$50	XP: $5	F18
5/1-5/31 & 10/2-4/30	1P: $35-$40	2P: $40-$45	XP: $5	F18

Location: SR 365 E, 0.5 mi e of jct Hwy 49. 7353 River Rd 13440. **Terms:** 3 day cancellation notice; pets. **Facility:** 11 rooms. Modestly furnished roadside motel in rural area. 1 story; exterior corridors; heated pool; playground. **Services:** winter plug-ins. **All Rooms:** combo or shower baths. **Some Rooms:** Fee: refrigerators. **Cards:** AE, DS, MC, VI.

AMERICAN HERITAGE MOTOR INN
Motel

Phone: (315)339-3610

5/1-10/31	1P: $35-$45	2P: $45-$55	XP: $5	F8
11/1-4/30	1P: $35-$40	2P: $45-$50	XP: $5	F8

Location: Hwy 49, 69 and 26, Lawrence St exit. 799 Lower Lawrence St 13440. Fax: 315/336-4577. **Terms:** [CP] meal plan; weekly & monthly rates avail; pets, $5 extra charge. **Facility:** 27 rooms. Modest roadside property. 2 stories; exterior corridors. **Services:** winter plug-ins. **All Rooms:** extended cable TV. **Cards:** AE, DI, DS, MC, VI. **Special Amenities:** Free local telephone calls and free room upgrade (subject to availability with advanced reservations).

BEECHES-PAUL REVERE MOTOR LODGE
Motor Inn

Phone: (315)336-1776

All Year	1P: $56-$62	2P: $63-$69	XP: $5	F16

Location: SR 26, 2 mi n of jct SR 46. 7900 Turin Rd 13440. Fax: 315/339-2636. **Terms:** Weekly & monthly rates avail; package plans; weekends; small pets only, $5 extra charge. **Facility:** 66 rooms. Sprawling property on 52 acre estate. Whirlpool suite, $150 for up to 2 persons; whirlpool room, $150-$200; 1 story; exterior corridors. **Dining:** Restaurant; 6 am-10 & 11:30-10 pm, Sat 8 am-11 pm, Sun 8 am-2 pm, closed Mon; $9-$15; cocktails. **All Rooms:** combo or shower baths, extended cable TV. **Cards:** AE, CB, DI, DS, MC, VI. **Special Amenities:** Preferred room (subject to availability with advanced reservations).

GREEN LANTERN MOTOR COURT
Motel

Phone: (315)336-5200

All Year	1P: $45	2P: $55

Location: SR 26, 2.5 mi n of jct SR 46. 8189 Turin Rd 13440. Fax: 315/336-5203. **Terms:** 3 day cancellation notice. **Facility:** 11 rooms. All rooms with hair dryer. Pleasant decor. 3 efficiencies, $65-$75 for up to 4 persons; 1 story; exterior corridors. **Services:** winter plug-ins. **All Rooms:** combo or shower baths, extended cable TV. **Cards:** AE, MC, VI.

———— RESTAURANT ————

SAVOY RESTAURANT
Italian

Lunch: $4-$7 **Dinner:** $6-$15 **Phone:** 315/339-3166
Location: Just s of jct Rt 26 and 46. 255 E Dominick St 13440. **Hours:** 11:30 am-10 pm, Fri & Sat-11 pm, Sun 4 pm-9 pm. **Closed:** 11/23 & 12/25. **Reservations:** suggested. **Features:** casual dress; children's menu; carryout; cocktails & lounge. In operation since 1908, the family restaurant has a warm, casual atmosphere. El cicco—a seasoned steak with wine, garlic and spices—is particularly flavorful on a menu of mostly Italian choices. Some American specialties also are offered. **Cards:** AE, CB, DI, DS, MC, VI.

RONKONKOMA pop. 20,400

———— LODGINGS ————

ECONO LODGE LONG ISLAND ISLIP MACARTHUR AIRPORT
Motel

Phone: (631)588-6800

All Year	1P: $69-$99	2P: $78-$119	F18

Location: I-495, exit 57, 3 mi se. 3055 Veterans Memorial Hwy 11779. Fax: 631/588-6815. **Terms:** [CP] meal plan. **Facility:** 59 rooms. Some smaller rooms. 2 stories; interior/exterior corridors. **All Rooms:** combo or shower baths, extended cable TV. **Cards:** AE, CB, DI, DS, MC, VI.

HOLIDAY INN
Motor Inn

Phone: (631)585-9500

1/1-4/30	1P: $185	2P: $195	XP: $10	F18
5/1-12/31	1P: $175	2P: $185	XP: $10	F18

Location: I-495, exit 57, 4.5 mi se (signs to MacArthur Airport). 3845 Veterans Memorial Hwy 11779. Fax: 631/585-9550. **Terms:** 3 day cancellation notice; package plans. **Facility:** 287 rooms. 2 stories; interior corridors. **Services:** gift shop; area transportation. **All Rooms:** combo or shower baths. **Some Rooms:** Fee: refrigerators. **Cards:** AE, CB, DI, DS, MC, VI.

ROSCOE pop. 1,000

—— LODGING ——

ROSCOE MOTEL
Phone: (607)498-5220
All Year 1P: $45 2P: $50-$65 XP: $10 F5
Location: SR 17, exit 94, 0.5 mi n on SR 206, just w. Old Rt 17 12776 (PO Box 609). Fax: 607/498-4643.
Motel **Terms:** 2 night min stay, weekends 4/1-10/31; small pets only, $5 extra charge. **Facility:** 18 rooms. Quiet setting along river. Some rooms with expanded cable. Very well-kept property. 1 story; exterior corridors; designated smoking area. **Recreation:** trout fishing. **All Rooms:** combo or shower baths. **Some Rooms:** 2 efficiencies. **Cards:** AE, MC, VI.

ROSLYN pop. 2,000

—— RESTAURANT ——

BRYANT & COOPER STEAKHOUSE Lunch: $7-$18 Dinner: $17-$29 Phone: 516/627-7270
Location: I-495, exit 36 (Searingtown Rd), n to Northern Blvd (25A), e to first light. 2 Middle Neck Rd 11576.
Steakhouse **Hours:** noon-3:30 & 5-10 pm, Fri-11 pm, Sat 5 pm-midnight, Sun 3 pm-10 pm. Closed: 12/25.
Reservations: suggested. **Features:** casual dress; health conscious menu items; cocktails & lounge; valet parking; a la carte. Hardwood floors, earth tones and paneling add to the rich, clublike ambience of the upscale dining room. A comprehensive selection of wines complements preparations of prime rib, chicken, seafood and ribeye steak. Servers are knowledgeable. Smoke free premises. **Cards:** AE, DI, MC, VI.

ROTTERDAM pop. 21,200

—— LODGING ——

SUPER 8 SCHENECTADY
Phone: 518/355-2190
Property failed to provide current rates
Motel **Location:** At jct Curry and Carman rds; I-90, exit 25. 3083 Carman Rd 12303. Fax: 518/355-3843.
Terms: Small pets only, $10 extra charge. **Facility:** 99 rooms. Compact guest rooms. 2 stories; interior corridors. **Services:** winter plug-ins. **Some Rooms:** Fee: refrigerators. **Cards:** AE, CB, DI, DS, MC, VI.

—— RESTAURANT ——

MALLOZZI'S RESTAURANT Dinner: $11-$18 Phone: 518/355-0340
Location: Jct Altamont Ave and Curry Rd from I-90, exit 25, 2 mi nw. 1930 Curry Rd 12303. **Hours:** 4:30
Italian pm-9 pm, Sat from 5 pm, Sun 2 pm-8 pm. Closed: 7/4, 12/25 & Mon. **Reservations:** suggested.
Features: casual dress; carryout; cocktails. Well-prepared offerings include steaks, chops, veal and such tempting seafood selections as the fisherman's delight platter—a combination of fresh clams, New Zealand mussels, lobster tail, shrimp and scallops over linguine in marinara sauce. **Cards:** AE, MC, VI.

RYE —See New York p. 376.

RYE BROOK —See New York p. 376.

SACKETS HARBOR pop. 1,300

—— RESTAURANTS ——

OLD STONE ROW RESTAURANT Historical Dinner: $10-$17 Phone: 315/646-2923
Location: 336 Brady Rd 13685. **Hours:** 5 pm-9 pm. Closed: 11/23, 12/24, 12/25, Sun & Mon.
American **Reservations:** suggested; wkends 7/1-8/31. **Features:** casual dress; health conscious menu items; carryout; cocktails; a la carte. In restored army barracks built from 1816 to 1819, the restaurant is decorated in muted, tasteful decor. Flavorful rack of lamb is pleasingly presented with thought to food placement and arrangement. The sophisticated atmosphere caters to couples. **Cards:** AE, CB, DI, DS, MC, VI.

SACKETS HARBOR BREWING CO Lunch: $6-$7 Dinner: $9-$22 Phone: 315/646-2739
Location: Center. 212 Main St 13685. **Hours:** 11:30 am-3 & 5-10 pm, Mon-Wed from 5 pm; hrs vary off
American season. Closed: 4/23, 11/23 & 12/25. **Reservations:** suggested. **Features:** casual dress; children's menu; cocktails & lounge; a la carte. In a former train station, the waterfront brew pub offers seating in the bileve dining room and on the patio. The eclectic menu puts a new spin on old favorite dishes, such as chicken pasta pilaf. Custom-prepared microbrewed beers are a nice touch. **Cards:** AE, MC, VI.

SAG HARBOR pop. 2,100

—— LODGING ——

BARON'S COVE INN
◆◆
Motel

7/1-8/31	1P: $155-$425	2P: $155-$425	XP: $15	F
5/1-6/30 & 9/1-10/31	1P: $95-$245	2P: $95-$245	XP: $15	F
11/1-4/30	1P: $71-$110	2P: $71-$110	XP: $15	F

Phone: (631)725-2100

Location: W on Long Island Ave to W Water St. 31 W Water St 11963 (PO Box 869). Fax: 631/725-2144. **Terms:** 10 day cancellation notice; 2 night min stay, weekends 6/1-9/30; package plans. **Facility:** 66 rooms. Pleasant settings, adjacent to the marina. Some loft rooms. 2 stories; exterior corridors; 1 tennis court. **Some Rooms:** Fee: VCR. **Cards:** AE, DI, DS, MC, VI. *(See ad below)*

—— RESTAURANTS ——

B SMITH'S
◆◆
Seafood

Lunch: $9-$15   **Dinner:** $13-$15   **Phone:** 631/725-5858
Location: At end of Bay St. Long Wharf Promenade 11963. **Hours:** Open 6/1-9/30; noon-4 & 6-11 pm. Closed major holidays. **Features:** casual dress; Sunday brunch; cocktails & lounge; street parking; a la carte. Relax in the brightly lit dining room and enjoy views of yachts and boats sailing into and out of the harbor. Mediterranean and Southern influences infuse preparations of new American cuisine, such as caramelized diver scallops over orrechiette pasta. Smoke free premises. **Cards:** AE, DS, MC, VI.

SEN
◆
Ethnic

Lunch: $6-$17   **Dinner:** $9-$18   **Phone:** 631/725-1774
Location: Center; just w of SR 114 from s side of bridge. 23 Main St 11963. **Hours:** 6 pm-10 pm, Fri & Sat noon-2:30 & 6-10 pm, Sun from 6 pm; hrs vary seasonally. Closed: Weds off season. **Features:** casual dress; beer & wine only; street parking; a la carte. Expect ultra-modern, sparse decor and a bustling atmosphere at the highly popular spot. The menu delivers sushi, a wide assortment of traditional and unusual rolls, fun appetizers, noodle soup and steamed fish. Saki varieties are extensive. Smoke free premises. **Cards:** AE, MC, VI.

ST. JAMES pop. 12,700

—— RESTAURANT ——

MIRABELLE
◆◆◆
French

Lunch: $11-$22   **Dinner:** $21-$30   **Phone:** 631/584-5999
Location: 1.6 mi on SR 25A (N Country Rd) from jct SR 25. 404 N Country Rd (SR 25A) 11788. **Hours:** noon-2 & 6-10 pm, Sat from 6 pm, Sun 5 pm-10 pm. Closed: 1/1, 12/25 & Mon. **Reservations:** suggested. **Features:** casual dress; health conscious menu; cocktails & lounge; a la carte. In a small house in a small town, the trendy dining room has bright yellow walls, low ceilings and a large painting that is reprinted on the menu cover. Foie gras mousse roulade and eggplant-goat cheese terrine are representative appetizers. Smoke free premises. **Cards:** AE, DI, DS, MC, VI.

ST. JOHNSVILLE pop. 1,800

—— LODGING ——

INN BY THE MILL
◆◆◆
Historic Bed
& Breakfast

5/1-1/2 & 4/1-4/30	1P: $100-$125	2P: $100-$150

Phone: (518)568-2388
XP: $30

Location: 1 mi w on SR 5, 0.5 mi n. 1679 Mill Rd 13452. Fax: 518/568-2388. **Terms:** Open 5/1-1/2 & 4/1-4/30; age restrictions may apply; 7 day cancellation notice; cancellation fee imposed. **Facility:** 5 rooms. Relaxing location on extensively landscaped grounds. Beautifully restored 1835 Grist Mill and home. 2 stories; interior corridors; smoke free premises. **Services:** gift shop; area transportation. **Some Rooms:** shower baths, shared bathrooms. **Cards:** DS, MC, VI.

SANBORN —See Niagara Falls p. 396.

SARANAC LAKE pop. 5,400—See also ADIRONDACK MOUNTAINS.

—— LODGINGS ——

ADIRONDACK COMFORT INN
(AAA) (SAVE)
♦♦♦
Motor Inn

6/19-10/15	1P: $75-$120	2P: $75-$120	XP: $5	F18
12/25-4/30	1P: $65-$95	2P: $65-$95	XP: $5	F18
5/1-6/18 & 10/16-12/24	1P: $65-$90	2P: $65-$90	XP: $5	F18

Phone: (518)891-1970

Location: 0.8 mi e on SR 86. 148 Lake Flower Ave 12983. Fax: 518/891-6195. **Terms:** [BP] meal plan; package plans; pets, $30 dep req. **Facility:** 69 rooms. Well-furnished, large rooms. 2 stories; interior corridors; designated smoking area; heated pool, sun deck. **Dining:** Restaurant; 6 am-2 pm; $4-$7; cocktails. **All Rooms:** extended cable TV. **Cards:** AE, CB, DI, DS, JC, MC, VI. **Special Amenities: Free local telephone calls and free newspaper.** (See color ad below)

ADIRONDACK MOTEL
(AAA)
♦
Motel

All Year	1P: $50-$135	2P: $50-$135	XP: $10	F10

Phone: 518/891-2116

Location: 0.5 mi e on SR 86. 23 Lake Flower Ave 12983. Fax: 518/891-0380. **Terms:** [CP] meal plan; 7 day cancellation notice; cancellation fee imposed; 2 night min stay, for fireplace units; pets, $5 extra charge 2nd pet. **Facility:** 13 rooms. 2 rooms with fireplace. Lovely view of the Adirondack Mountains. Efficiencies & kitchen units, $75-$95; $48-$58 off season; 1-2 stories; exterior corridors; beach; boat dock. **Recreation:** swimming, canoeing, fishing, paddleboats. **All Rooms:** combo or shower baths, extended cable TV. **Cards:** AE, DS, MC, VI.

THE HOTEL SARANAC OF PAUL SMITH'S COLLEGE
(AAA) (SAVE)
♦♦♦
Historic Motor Inn

6/15-10/14	1P: $75-$105	2P: $75-$105	XP: $10	F18
5/1-6/14 & 10/15-4/30	1P: $69-$99	2P: $69-$99	XP: $10	F18

Phone: (518)891-2200

Location: Center. 101 Main St 12983. Fax: 518/891-5664. **Terms:** [BP] & [MAP] meal plans; 3 day cancellation notice; cancellation fee imposed; package plans; pets. **Facility:** 92 rooms. Restored 1927 hotel. Training facility for hotel management students. Variety of room types, many on the small side, all well-lighted. 6 stories; interior corridors; designated smoking area. **Dining:** Bakery on premises; also, A.P. Smith Restaurant, see separate listing. **Services:** gift shop. Fee: massage. **Recreation:** Fee: videos. **All Rooms:** extended cable TV. **Some Rooms:** Fee: refrigerators, VCR. **Cards:** AE, DI, DS, MC, VI. **Special Amenities: Free newspaper and free room upgrade (subject to availability with advanced reservations).** (See color ad p 296)

LAKE FLOWER INN
◆
Motel

	6/23-10/16	1P: $68-$78	2P: $72-$92	XP: $6	F16
	12/26-4/30	1P: $58-$78	2P: $72-$92	XP: $6	F16
	5/1-6/22 & 10/17-12/25	1P: $40-$50	2P: $42-$62	XP: $6	F16

Phone: 518/891-2310

Location: 0.6 mi se on SR 86. 15 Lake Flower Ave 12983. **Terms:** 14 day cancellation notice; cancellation fee imposed; pets. **Facility:** 14 rooms. Pleasant guest rooms. Located on small lake with lovely moutain view. 1 story; exterior corridors; designated smoking area. **Recreation:** canoeing. **All Rooms:** combo or shower baths. **Cards:** AE, MC, VI.

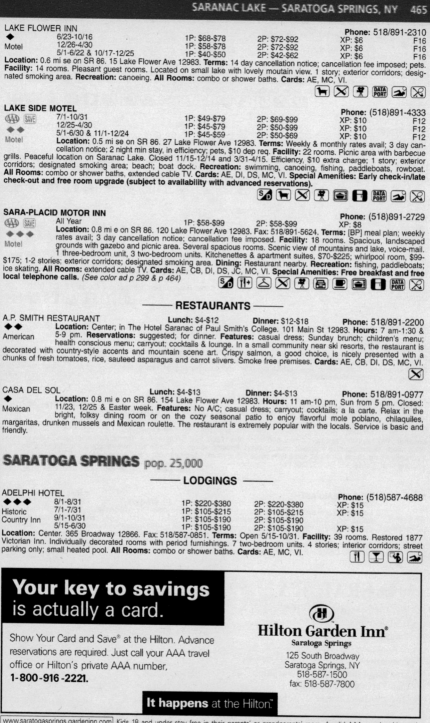

LAKE SIDE MOTEL
(AAA) (SAVE)
◆ ◆
Motel

	7/1-10/31	1P: $49-$79	2P: $69-$99	XP: $10	F12
	12/25-4/30	1P: $45-$79	2P: $50-$99	XP: $10	F12
	5/1-6/30 & 11/1-12/24	1P: $45-$59	2P: $50-$69	XP: $10	F12

Phone: (518)891-4333

Location: 0.5 mi se on SR 86. 27 Lake Flower Ave 12983. **Terms:** Weekly & monthly rates avail; 3 day cancellation notice; 2 night min stay, in efficiency; pets, $10 dep req. **Facility:** 22 rooms. Picnic area with barbecue grills. Peaceful location on Saranac Lake. Closed 11/15-12/14 and 3/31-4/15. Efficiency, $10 extra charge; 1 story; exterior corridors; designated smoking area; beach; boat dock. **Recreation:** swimming, canoeing, fishing, paddleboats, rowboat. **All Rooms:** combo or shower baths, extended cable TV. **Cards:** AE, DI, DS, MC, VI. **Special Amenities:** Early check-in/late check-out and free room upgrade (subject to availability with advanced reservations).

SARA-PLACID MOTOR INN
(AAA) (SAVE)
◆ ◆ ◆
Motel

All Year   1P: $58-$99   2P: $58-$99   XP: $8

Phone: (518)891-2729

Location: 0.8 mi e on SR 86. 120 Lake Flower Ave 12983. Fax: 518/891-5624. **Terms:** [BP] meal plan; weekly rates avail; 3 day cancellation notice; cancellation fee imposed. **Facility:** 18 rooms. Spacious, landscaped grounds with gazebo and picnic area. Several spacious rooms. Scenic view of mountains and lake, voice-mail. 1 three-bedroom unit, 3 two-bedroom units. Kitchenettes & apartment suites; $70-$225; whirlpool room, $99-$175; 1-2 stories; exterior corridors; designated smoking area. **Dining:** Restaurant nearby. **Recreation:** fishing, paddleboats; ice skating. **All Rooms:** extended cable TV. **Cards:** AE, CB, DI, DS, JC, MC, VI. **Special Amenities:** Free breakfast and free local telephone calls. (See color ad p 299 & p 464)

RESTAURANTS

A.P. SMITH RESTAURANT
◆ ◆
American

Lunch: $4-$12   Dinner: $12-$18   Phone: 518/891-2200

Location: Center; in The Hotel Saranac of Paul Smith's College. 101 Main St 12983. **Hours:** 7 am-1:30 & 5-9 pm. **Reservations:** suggested; for dinner. **Features:** casual dress; Sunday brunch; children's menu; health conscious menu; carryout; cocktails & lounge. In a small community near ski resorts, the restaurant is decorated with country-style accents and mountain scene art. Crispy salmon, a good choice, is nicely presented with a chunks of fresh tomatoes, rice, sauteed asparagus and carrot slivers. Smoke free premises. **Cards:** AE, CB, DI, DS, MC, VI.

CASA DEL SOL
◆
Mexican

Lunch: $4-$13   Dinner: $4-$13   Phone: 518/891-0977

Location: 0.8 mi e on SR 86. 154 Lake Flower Ave 12983. **Hours:** 11 am-10 pm, Sun from 5 pm. Closed: 11/23, 12/25 & Easter week. **Features:** No A/C; casual dress; carryout; cocktails; a la carte. Relax in the bright, folksy dining room or on the cozy seasonal patio to enjoy flavorful mole poblano, chilaquiles, margaritas, drunken mussels and Mexican roulette. The restaurant is extremely popular with the locals. Service is basic and friendly.

SARATOGA SPRINGS pop. 25,000

LODGINGS

ADELPHI HOTEL
◆ ◆ ◆
Historic
Country Inn

	8/1-8/31	1P: $220-$380	2P: $220-$380	XP: $15
	7/1-7/31	1P: $105-$215	2P: $105-$215	XP: $15
	9/1-10/31	1P: $105-$190	2P: $105-$190	
	5/15-6/30	1P: $105-$190	2P: $105-$190	XP: $15

Phone: (518)587-4688

Location: Center. 365 Broadway 12866. Fax: 518/587-0851. **Terms:** Open 5/15-10/31. **Facility:** 39 rooms. Restored 1877 Victorian Inn. Individually decorated rooms with period furnishings. 7 two-bedroom units. 4 stories; interior corridors; street parking only; small heated pool. **All Rooms:** combo or shower baths. **Cards:** AE, MC, VI.

HILTON GARDEN INN-SARATOGA SPRINGS

Phone: (518)587-1500

◆◆◆
Motor Inn

7/23-9/4	1P: $159-$279	2P: $169-$289	XP: $10	F18
5/1-7/22 & 9/5-10/31	1P: $79-$209	2P: $89-$219	XP: $10	F18
11/1-4/30	1P: $79-$179	2P: $89-$189	XP: $10	F18

Location: I-87, exit 13 (Northway), 3.4 mi on SR 9 N. 125 S Broadway 12866. Fax: 518/587-7800. **Terms:** 3 day cancellation notice; cancellation fee imposed; 2 night min stay, weekends; package plans. **Facility:** 112 rooms. Stylish rooms and public areas in walking distance of downtown historic Saratoga Springs. 4 stories; interior corridors; small heated indoor pool. **All Rooms:** combo or shower baths, safes. **Cards:** AE, DI, DS, JC, MC, VI. *(See ad p 465)*

HOLIDAY INN

Phone: (518)584-4550

◆◆◆
Motor Inn

7/26-9/3	1P: $219-$279	2P: $219-$279	XP: $10	F19
5/1-7/25 & 9/4-11/18	1P: $120-$169	2P: $120-$169	XP: $10	F19
11/19-4/30	1P: $89-$129	2P: $89-$129	XP: $10	F19

Location: Just s on US 9, at jct SR 50. 232 Broadway, Rt 9 12866. Fax: 518/584-4417. **Terms:** 3 day cancellation notice; package plans; pets. **Facility:** 168 rooms. Nicely landscaped grounds and courtyard. 4 stories; interior corridors; heated pool. **Services:** winter plug-ins. **Some Rooms:** safes. **Cards:** AE, CB, DI, DS, JC, MC, VI.

THE INN AT SARATOGA

Phone: (518)583-1890

(AAA) [SAVE]
◆◆◆
Historic Motor Inn

7/28-9/3	1P: $230-$280
7/1-7/27	1P: $125-$150
5/1-6/30	1P: $95-$130
9/4-4/30	1P: $75-$130

Location: On w side at jct SR 50 and US 9. 231 Broadway 12866. Fax: 518/583-2543. **Terms:** [CP] meal plan; 30 day cancellation notice; cancellation fee imposed; 2 night min stay, weekends in season; package plans. **Facility:** 38 rooms. Restored inn dating from 1890. Spacious, well-appointed rooms. 2 room suites, $95-$145; $240-$340, 7/27-9/4; 3 stories; interior corridors. **Dining:** Dining room; 5 pm-9 pm, Fri & Sat-10 pm; $16-$21; cocktails; Sun brunch 10 am-2 pm with live jazz music. **All Rooms:** extended cable TV. **Some Rooms:** Fee: refrigerators. **Cards:** AE, CB, DI, DS, JC, MC, VI.

THE LOMBARDI FARM BED & BREAKFAST

Phone: (518)587-2074

◆◆
Bed & Breakfast

9/10-4/30	1P: $150	2P: $150	XP: $20	F12
5/1-9/9	1P: $100	2P: $150	XP: $20	F12

Location: 2.3 mi nw on US 9 N (Church St), 0.5 mi ne. 41 Locust Grove Rd 12866. Fax: 518/587-2074. **Terms:** [BP] meal plan; 14 day cancellation notice; pet on premises. **Facility:** 6 rooms. Restored 1850's farmhouse. Home-like atmosphere. Age restrictions may apply during August racing season. 2 stories; interior corridors. **All Rooms:** combo or shower baths.

LONGFELLOWS INN AND RESTAURANT

Phone: (518)587-0108

◆◆◆
Country Inn

7/27-9/6	1P: $145-$495	2P: $145-$495	XP: $10	F17
5/1-7/26	1P: $85-$295	2P: $85-$295	XP: $10	F17
9/7-4/30	1P: $75-$295	2P: $75-$295	XP: $10	F17

Location: I-87 Northway, exit 14, 1.4 mi e. 500 Union Ave 12866. Fax: 518/587-6649. **Terms:** [CP] meal plan; 14 day cancellation notice; cancellation fee imposed; package plans. **Facility:** 18 rooms. Stylish and modern rooms and amenities found in a converted barn. Some loft suites and a full service dining room. 1 two-bedroom unit. 2 stories; interior corridors; designated smoking area. **Cards:** AE, DI, DS, MC, VI.

SARATOGA BED & BREAKFAST

Phone: (518)584-0920

(AAA)
◆◆◆
Historic Bed & Breakfast

All Year	1P: $75-$225	2P: $75-$225	XP: $25	D8

Location: 2.3 m nw on US 9 N (Church St). 434 Church St 12866. Fax: 518/584-4500. **Terms:** [BP] meal plan; weekly rates avail, off season; age restrictions may apply; check-in 4 pm; 14 day cancellation notice; package plans. **Facility:** 9 rooms. Small to spacious rooms located in a 1850 restored red brick Federal home and 1860 wood framed farmhouse. Some with fireplace. 2 stories; interior corridors; smoke free premises. **Services:** winter plug-ins. **Recreation:** bicycles. **All Rooms:** combo or shower baths, extended cable TV. **Some Rooms:** color TV. **Cards:** AE, DS, MC, VI.

SARATOGA DOWNTOWNER MOTEL

(AAA) [SAVE]
◆ ◆
Motel

Phone: (518)584-6160

7/26-9/4	1P: $137-$167	2P: $137-$167	XP: $10	F17
9/5-10/31	1P: $75-$85	2P: $75-$85	XP: $10	F17
5/1-7/25	1P: $59-$85	2P: $59-$85	XP: $10	F17
11/1-4/30	1P: $59-$69	2P: $59-$69	XP: $10	F17

Location: Center. 413 Broadway 12866-2245. Fax: 518/584-2907. **Terms:** [CP] meal plan; weekly rates avail, off season; 7 day cancellation notice, in season; 2 night min stay, 7/28-9/5; package plans. **Facility:** 41 rooms. Pleasant guest rooms. 2 stories; interior/exterior corridors; heated pool. **Dining:** Restaurant nearby. **Services:** winter plug-ins. **All Rooms:** extended cable TV. **Cards:** AE, DI, DS, MC, VI. **Special Amenities:** Free breakfast and free local telephone calls.

SARATOGA MOTEL

◆
Motel

Phone: (518)584-0920

All Year	1P: $55-$150	2P: $55-$150	XP: $25	F8

Location: 2.3 mi nw on US 9 N (Church St). 440 Church St 12866. **Terms:** Check-in 4 pm; 14 day cancellation notice; 2 night min stay, weekends in summer; pets. **Facility:** 9 rooms. Rural location. Modestly furnished guest rooms. 1 story; exterior corridors. **All Rooms:** combo or shower baths. **Some Rooms:** 2 efficiencies. **Cards:** AE, DS, MC, VI.

SHERATON SARATOGA SPRINGS HOTEL & CONFERENCE CENTER

(AAA) [SAVE]
◆ ◆ ◆
Hotel

Phone: (518)584-4000

7/26-9/4	1P: $315-$420	2P: $315-$420	XP: $15	F17
9/5-11/19	1P: $157-$224	2P: $172-$239	XP: $15	F17
5/1-7/25	1P: $155-$222	2P: $170-$237	XP: $15	F17
11/20-4/30	1P: $110-$177	2P: $125-$192	XP: $15	F17

Location: Downtown on SR 50; I-87, exit 15. 534 Broadway 12866. Fax: 518/584-7430. **Terms:** 14 day cancellation notice, in season; cancellation fee imposed; package plans. **Facility:** 240 rooms. Elegant public areas with traditional decor. Prepayment required, in season; 10 whirlpool rooms; suites, $295-$1200; 5 stories; interior corridors; heated pool, sauna. **Dining:** Restaurant; 7 am-10 pm; $10-$19; cocktails. **Services:** gift shop; area transportation, within 2 mi. **Recreation: Fee:** in-room video games. **All Rooms:** combo or shower baths, extended cable TV. **Some Rooms:** 16 efficiencies. **Cards:** AE, CB, DI, DS, MC, VI.

THE SPRINGS MOTEL

(AAA)
◆ ◆
Motel

Phone: (518)584-6336

7/26-9/4	1P: $160	2P: $160	XP: $10	F16
5/1-7/25 & 9/5-10/1	1P: $70	2P: $75	XP: $5	F16
10/2-4/30	1P: $50	2P: $55	XP: $5	F16

Location: Just s on US 9. 165 Broadway 12866. Fax: 518/587-8164. **Terms:** 7 day cancellation notice; cancellation fee imposed. **Facility:** 28 rooms. Comfortable rooms with pleasant decor. 2-3 night min stay, 8/1-8/31; 2 stories; exterior corridors. **Services:** winter plug-ins. **All Rooms:** extended cable TV. **Cards:** AE, MC, VI.

TURF AND SPA MOTEL

◆ ◆
Motel

Phone: 518/584-2550

7/26-9/3	1P: $140-$160	2P: $140-$160	XP: $5	F18
6/30-7/25	1P: $70-$80	2P: $70-$80	XP: $5	F18
5/1-6/29	1P: $50-$65	2P: $55-$65		
9/4-4/30	1P: $40-$65	2P: $45-$65		

Location: Just s on US 9. 140 Broadway 12866. Fax: 518/584-2550. **Terms:** [CP] meal plan; weekly rates avail, off season; 14 day cancellation notice; cancellation fee imposed. **Facility:** 43 rooms. 2-3 night min, 7/1-9/6; 2 stories; exterior corridors; heated pool, 2 mineral water whirlpools. **Dining:** Restaurant nearby. **Services:** winter plug-ins. **Fee:** massage. **All Rooms:** extended cable TV. **Cards:** AE, MC, VI. *(See color ad p 466)*

UNION GABLES BED & BREAKFAST

(AAA)
◆ ◆ ◆
Historic Bed
& Breakfast

Phone: 518/584-1558

7/26-9/5	1P: $240-$290	2P: $240-$300	XP: $50	F12
5/1-7/25 & 9/6-10/31	1P: $135-$165	2P: $135-$165	XP: $25	F12
11/1-4/30	1P: $125-$155	2P: $125-$155	XP: $25	F12

Location: I-87 Northway, exit 14, 1.8 mi s. 55 Union Ave 12866. Fax: 518/583-0649. **Terms:** [CP] meal plan; 14 day cancellation notice; 2 night min stay, weekends 7/1-8/31; pets. **Facility:** 10 rooms. Graciously restored 1901 Victorian home. Beautifully furnished rooms, each individually decorated. Owner has pet on premises. 1 two-bedroom unit. 3 stories, no elevator; interior corridors; whirlpool; 1 tennis court. **Recreation:** bicycles. **All Rooms:** combo or shower baths. **Cards:** AE, DS, MC, VI.

Home Away from Home

Visit a bygone era of romance and elegance by spending a romantic evening or weekend away from home at one of the B&Bs located in the *Bed & Breakfast Ad Index* of this TourBook® guide.

THE WESTCHESTER HOUSE BED & BREAKFAST   Phone: (518)587-7613

7/25-9/4	1P: $225-$300	2P: $225-$300	
5/1-7/24 & 9/5-11/30	1P: $95-$150	2P: $110-$185	
3/1-4/30	1P: $85-$150	2P: $95-$165	

Historic Bed & Breakfast **Location:** 1 mi s on US 9 (Broadway); 0.3 mi e on Lincoln Ave; I-87, exit 13 N, 3.5 mi nw on US 9, 0.3 mi e. 102 Lincoln Ave 12866 (PO Box 944). Fax: 518/583-9562. **Terms:** Open 5/1-11/30 & 3/1-4/30; [ECP] meal plan; age restrictions may apply; check-in 4 pm; 14 day cancellation notice; package plans. **Facility:** 7 rooms. Gracious 1885 Queen Ann Victorian inn. Old World ambiance with up-to-date comforts. TV's avail. 2 night min stay, summer & fall weekends; 2 stories; interior corridors; smoke free premises. **All Rooms:** combo or shower baths. **Cards:** AE, MC, VI. **Special Amenities:** Free local telephone calls and preferred room (subject to availability with advanced reservations). *(See color ad p 500)*

─────── **RESTAURANTS** ───────

LILLIAN'S   Lunch: $5-$8   Dinner: $12-$20   Phone: 518/587-7766
American **Location:** Center. 408 Broadway 12866. **Hours:** 11 am-10 pm, Fri & Sat-11 pm, Sun noon-9 pm. Closed: 11/23 & 12/25. **Reservations:** suggested; weekends. **Features:** casual dress; children's menu; carryout; cocktails & lounge; street parking; a la carte. Named after actress Lillian Russell, the restaurant is appointed in turn-of-the-20th-century style, with Tiffany-style lamps, stained glass and Victorian accents. Prime rib and grilled salmon stand out on a menu of steak and seafood selections. **Cards:** AE, CB, DI, MC, VI.

THE OLDE BRYAN INN Historical   Lunch: $5-$9   Dinner: $10-$19   Phone: 518/587-2990
American **Location:** 1.5 mi s on Rt 50, I-87 exit 15. 123 Maple Ave 12866. **Hours:** 11 am-11 pm, Fri & Sat-midnight; winter hrs may vary. Closed: 11/23, 12/24 for dinner & 12/25. **Features:** casual dress; Sunday brunch; children's menu; carryout; cocktails & lounge; a la carte. Originally established as an inn in 1773, the Victorian restaurant is quaintly decorated with red globe lamps and wood accents. Menu selections are tried and true—prime rib, old-fashioned turkey dinner, homemade apple crisp and chocolate chip pie. **Cards:** AE, CB, DI, DS, MC, VI.

PANZA'S RESTAURANT   Dinner: $12-$18   Phone: 518/584-6882
Continental **Location:** Rt 9P, s end of Saratoga Lake. RD 1, Saraatoga Lake 12866. **Hours:** 5 pm-10 pm, Fri & Sat-11 pm. Closed: 12/25, Mon & Tues 9/1-6/30. **Reservations:** suggested. **Features:** casual dress; children's menu; carryout; cocktails; a la carte. Family-owned since 1938, the restaurant is decorated in the art deco style, with black linens and striking artwork. Chicken Tuscany and shrimp Sorrentino, which blends shrimp, eggplant, mozzarella cheese and butter, are outstanding choices. **Cards:** AE, CB, DI, MC, VI.

PROFESSOR MORIARTY'S DINING & DRINKING SALON   Lunch: $5-$9   Dinner: $12-$18   Phone: 518/587-5981
American **Location:** Center. 430 Broadway 12866. **Hours:** 11:30 am-10 pm, Sun from 11 am. Closed: 11/23 & 12/25. **Reservations:** suggested; in season. **Features:** casual dress; Sunday brunch; children's menu; carryout; cocktails & lounge; street parking. Representative of well-prepared fare are filet mignon; smoked salmon snow crab chowder; and Watson's scallops, which are sauteed with mushrooms, scallions and melted cheese. The setting is reminiscent of an English pub, with antiques and paintings. **Cards:** AE, CB, DI, DS, MC, VI.

SPRING WATER INN Historical   Lunch: $6-$10   Dinner: $15-$22   Phone: 518/584-6440
Continental **Location:** Corner Union Ave and Nelson, opposite thoroughbred racetrack; I-87, exit 14, 1.5 mi w. 139 Union Ave 12866. **Hours:** 11:30 am-3 & 5-10 pm. Closed: 1/1, 11/23 & 12/25. **Reservations:** suggested. **Features:** casual dress; carryout; cocktails & lounge. Attractively restored Victorian home. Valet parking 8/1-8/31. **Cards:** AE, CB, DI, MC, VI.

WEATHERVANE SEAFOOD RESTAURANT   Lunch: $4-$10   Dinner: $4-$18   Phone: 518/584-8157
Seafood **Location:** 1.5 mi s on US 9, 2.5 mi n of I-87 Northway, exit 13 N. 3368 S Broadway 12866. **Hours:** 11 am-9:30 pm; to 9 pm in winter. Closed: 11/23, 12/24 & 12/25. **Features:** casual dress; children's menu; carryout; cocktails & lounge. Fresh seafood is the menu's clear focus, with such tempting choices as fish and chips and Maine lobster. Dark wood and seascapes decorate the dining room, a warm spot in which families are welcomed. For dessert, savor the Cape Cod apple crisp. **Cards:** MC, VI.

WHEATFIELDS   Lunch: $7-$8   Dinner: $8-$19   Phone: 518/587-0534
Italian **Location:** Center. 440 Broadway 12866. **Hours:** 11:30 am-10 pm, Fri & Sat-10:30 pm; hrs may vary off season. Closed: 11/23 & 12/25. **Reservations:** accepted; 6 or more. **Features:** casual dress; carryout; cocktails; street parking. The moderately upscale restaurant delivers an excellent variety of homemade pasta dishes, as well as preparations of fresh veal and seafood. The inviting dining room, with candlelit tables, is a nice contrast to the more casual seasonal patio. Smoke free premises. **Cards:** AE, DS, MC, VI.

SAUGERTIES pop. 3,900

─────── **LODGING** ───────

COMFORT INN   Phone: (914)246-1565

5/1-10/31	1P: $70-$99	2P: $70-$99	XP: $6	F17
11/1-4/30	1P: $65-$85	2P: $65-$85	XP: $6	F17

Motel **Location:** Just n of I-87 Thruway, exit 20. 2790 SR 32 12477. Fax: 914/246-1631. **Terms:** [CP] meal plan; 3 day cancellation notice. **Facility:** 65 rooms. Attractive, well-furnished rooms. 3 whirlpool rooms, $80-$120; 2 stories; interior corridors. **Services:** winter plug-ins. **Recreation:** small playground area, exercise equipment avail. **All Rooms:** extended cable TV. **Some Rooms:** efficiency. **Cards:** AE, CB, DI, JC, MC, VI. **Special Amenities:** Free breakfast and free local telephone calls.

———— RESTAURANTS ————

CAFE TAMAYO Historical
◆◆◆
Regional
American

Lunch: $5-$9   **Dinner:** $14-$18   **Phone:** 914/246-9371
Location: Center; on SR 32 and 9 W s. 89 Partition St 12477. **Hours:** 5 pm-9:30 pm, Fri-10 pm, Sat noon-3 & 5-10 pm, Sun 11:30 am-9:30 pm. Closed: 1/1, 12/25, Mon & Tues. **Reservations:** suggested. **Features:** casual dress; Sunday brunch; cocktails; a la carte. The attractively restored 1864 building has an original walnut bar, belt-driven paddle fans and plaster on canvas ceilings. Representative of complex preparations is the confit of duck, which is served with wild rice and red onion marmalade. **Cards:** DS, MC, VI. ☒

EMILIANI RISTORANTE
◆◆◆
Italian

Dinner: $13-$24   **Phone:** 914/246-6169
Location: Center. 147-149 Ulster Ave 12477. **Hours:** 4:30 pm-10 pm, Fri & Sat-11 pm, Sun 3 pm-9 pm. Closed: 11/23, 12/25 & Wed. **Reservations:** suggested; weekends. **Features:** casual dress; carryout; cocktails. Stenciled and decorated by the owner, the cozy restaurant has a quaint, homey atmosphere. The menu is undeniably sophisticated, with thoughtful preparations of chicken, veal, steak, seafood and pasta. The breads and desserts will make your mouth water. **Cards:** AE, DS, MC, VI.

SCHENECTADY pop. 65,600

———— LODGINGS ————

DAYS INN
◆◆
Motel

			Phone: (518)370-3297	
5/1-12/31	1P: $79-$89	2P: $89-$99	XP: $10	F17
1/1-4/30	1P: $79-$89	2P: $79-$89	XP: $10	F17

Location: 2 blks n of jct State St (SR 5) and Nott Terr. 167 Nott Terr 12308. Fax: 518/370-5948. **Terms:** [CP] meal plan; cancellation fee imposed; small pets only, $10 extra charge. **Facility:** 68 rooms. Good sized rooms with pleasant decor. 3 stories; interior corridors. **Services:** winter plug-ins. **Cards:** AE, CB, DI, DS, JC, MC, VI.

🆂🅰🆅🅴 🆂🅳 🐾 🍴 ⬛ 🔔 ☒ 🎥 🖨 💻 🗂 DATA PORT

HOLIDAY INN-DOWNTOWN SCHENECTADY
◆◆◆
Motor Inn

		Phone: (518)393-4141
All Year	1P: $89-$119	2P: $89-$129

Location: Center; 2 blks n of jct Nott Terr and State St (SR 5). 100 Nott Terr 12308. Fax: 518/393-4174. **Terms:** Small pets only. **Facility:** 184 rooms. Contemporary lobby with holidome and indoor recreation area. 4 stories; interior corridors; putting green; heated pool. **Cards:** AE, CB, DI, DS, JC, MC, VI.

A$K 🆂🅳 ✚ 🐾 🍴 🍸 🦆 🗜 ☒ 🎥 🖨 💻 🗂 DATA PORT 🏊 🐾 ☒

RAMADA INN
◆◆
Motor Inn

			Phone: (518)370-7151	
5/1-6/30	1P: $91-$149	2P: $101-$159	XP: $10	F18
7/1-9/30	1P: $81-$149	2P: $91-$159	XP: $10	F18
10/1-4/30	1P: $71-$91	2P: $81-$101	XP: $10	F18

Location: Just e of jct Erie Blvd and Nott St. 450 Nott St 12308. Fax: 518/370-0441. **Terms:** 7 day cancellation notice; small pets only, $59-$99 dep req. **Facility:** 170 rooms. Large guest rooms. 7 stories; interior corridors; heated pool. **All Rooms:** Fee: safes. **Some Rooms:** Fee: VCR. **Cards:** AE, CB, DI, DS, JC, MC, VI.

A$K 🆂🅳 🐾 🍴 🍸 🦆 🗜 ☒ 🎥 VCR 🖨 💻 🗂 DATA PORT 🏊 🐾

———— RESTAURANT ————

THE CARLTON RESTAURANT
◆◆◆
Continental

Lunch: $7-$10   **Dinner:** $12-$28   **Phone:** 518/393-0707
Location: SR 7, 1.5 mi w on SR 5 (State St), just n on McClellan St to Becker St. 1605 Becker St 12304. **Hours:** 11:30 am-1:30 & 4:30-9:30 pm, Fri-10 pm, Sat 4:30 pm-10 pm, Sun 4:30 pm-9:30 pm. Closed major holidays & Tues. **Reservations:** suggested. **Features:** dressy casual; health conscious menu; carryout; cocktails; a la carte. Prime rib and Delmonico steak stand out on a menu of classic cuisine. The sinful, mocha-butter-frosted Carlton cassata dessert stacks five layers of triple sec-soaked pound cake with sweetened ricotta cheese, chocolate chips and dried apricots. **Cards:** AE, CB, DI, DS, MC, VI.

SCHOHARIE pop. 1,000

———— LODGING ————

———— *The following lodging was either not inspected or did not* ————
meet AAA rating requirements but is listed for your information only.

HOLIDAY INN EXPRESS & SUITES SCHOHARIE
[fyi]
Motel

			Phone: 518/295-6088	
6/23-9/3	1P: $89-$109	2P: $99-$119	XP: $10	F19
5/1-6/22 & 9/4-10/21	1P: $69-$89	2P: $79-$99	XP: $10	F19
10/22-4/30	1P: $69-$89	2P: $69-$89		

Too new to rate, opening scheduled for July 1999. **Location:** I-88, exit 23. Rt 30A 12157 (RD 2, Box 330B). Fax: 518/295-6099. **Terms:** [CP] meal plan. **Amenities:** 56 rooms, radios, coffeemakers, microwaves, refrigerators, exercise facilities. **Cards:** AE, CB, DI, DS, JC, MC, VI.

———— RESTAURANTS ————

GEORGE MANN'S TORY TAVERN Historical
🆎🅰🅰
◆◆◆
American

Dinner: $30-$35   **Phone:** 518/295-7128
Location: Center; 1.2 mi n on SR 30; I-88, exit 23, 2.2 mi s on 30, just e Rt 443. Vroman Rd 12157. **Hours:** 5 pm-9 pm, Sun 1 pm-7 pm. Closed: 1/1-2/1. **Reservations:** suggested. **Features:** casual dress; cocktails; prix fixe, a la carte. Colonial furnishings decorate the restored 1700s tavern. The daily changing menu might include such dishes as veal-mushroom pate, rabbit-white bean soup and flavorful veal gruyere with fresh, al dente vegetables. Desserts are almost irresistible. **Cards:** AE, MC, VI. ☒

THE PARROTT HOUSE   Historical   **Lunch:** $4-$6   **Dinner:** $9-$16   **Phone:** 518/295-7111
◆ ◆   **Location:** Downtown; on SR 30. 280 Main St 12157. **Hours:** 11 am-2 & 5-9 pm. Closed: 1/1, 5/31, 9/6,
American   12/25 & Sun. **Reservations:** suggested; weekends. **Features:** casual dress; early bird specials; cocktails &
           lounge. The 1870s inn boasts the rustic ambience of a tavern. Home-style specialties of steak, seafood and
game pepper a menu that also includes Italian fare. Chilled strawberry soup is a delightful surprise on a warm day. Service
is well-timed and efficient. **Cards:** AE, CB, DI, DS, MC, VI.   [X]

SCHROON LAKE pop. 1,700—See also ADIRONDACK MOUNTAINS.

———— LODGING ————

BLUE RIDGE MOTEL   **Phone:** (518)532-7521
[AAA] [SAVE]   5/19-10/15   1P: $55-$65   2P: $65-$75   XP: $10   F17
◆   **Location:** 6 mi n on US 9, exit 28, 4 mi n on US 9. (RR 1, Box 260, 12870). Fax: 518/532-9235. **Terms:** Open
Motel   5/19-10/15; [CP] meal plan; pets, $5 extra charge. **Facility:** 17 rooms. Modest accommodations located out-
           side town. 1 story; interior/exterior corridors; small pool. **Recreation:** kiddie playground. **All Rooms:** combo or
           shower baths. **Cards:** MC, VI. **Special Amenities: Early check-in/late check-out and free breakfast.**
                                                           [S/D] [icons] [X] [Z] [icons]

———— RESTAURANT ————

DRAKE'S RESTAURANT   **Lunch:** $3-$14   **Dinner:** $8-$18   **Phone:** 518/532-9040
[AAA]   **Location:** 1 mi n on US 9; in Drakes Motel. US 9 12870. **Hours:** Open 5/28-10/10; 11:30 am-3 & 4:30-9 pm;
◆ ◆   7:30 am-3 & 4:30-7:30 pm in summer. **Reservations:** suggested. **Features:** casual dress;
American   children's menu; cocktails & lounge. In a seasonal resort town, the cheerful restaurant is appointed with
           nautical decor. Reasonably priced selections of standard American favorites make this place popular with
           families. Breakfasts and light lunches also are served. Service is friendly. **Cards:** AE, DS, MC, VI.   [X]

SCHUYLERVILLE pop. 1,400

———— LODGING ————

BURGOYNE MOTOR INN   **Phone:** 518/695-3282
◆   7/25-9/4   1P: $95-$105   2P: $105-$120   XP: $10   D12
Motel   5/1-7/24 & 9/5-4/30   1P: $50-$55   2P: $55-$65   XP: $10   D12
           Location: US 4 and SR 32, just n of jct SR 29. 220 Broad St 12871. **Terms:** 7 day cancellation notice.
Facility: 11 rooms. Modestly furnished rooms. 2 stories; exterior corridors. **Cards:** AE, MC, VI.   [ASK] [S/D] [icons]

SCOTIA pop. 7,400

———— RESTAURANT ————

GLEN SANDERS MANSION   **Lunch:** $7-$14   **Dinner:** $17-$28   **Phone:** 518/374-7262
◆ ◆ ◆   **Location:** Just sw on Glen Ave from SR 5, 1 mi from I-890. 1 Glen Ave 12302. **Hours:** 11:30 am-2 & 5-10
Continental   pm, Sat 5 pm-10 pm, Sun 10:30 am-1:30 & 4-9 pm. **Reservations:** suggested. **Features:** dressy casual;
           Sunday brunch; carryout; cocktails & lounge; a la carte. The elegantly restored 1658 inn sits on the banks of
the river. Fresh flowers and decorative candles dress up the tables. Pan-seared sea bass is garnished with fresh herbs. The
attractively presented peanut butter-chocolate torte is deliciously sinful. Smoke free premises. **Cards:** AE, CB, DI, DS,
MC, VI.   [X]

SENECA FALLS pop. 7,400—See also FINGER LAKES.

———— LODGING ————

THE GUION HOUSE   **Phone:** 315/568-8129
◆ ◆ ◆   All Year   1P: $75-$95   2P: $75-$95   XP: $20
Historic Bed   **Location:** Center; on US 20 and 5. 32 Cayuga St 13148. **Terms:** [BP] meal plan; age restrictions may apply;
& Breakfast   3 day cancellation notice; cancellation fee imposed. **Facility:** 6 rooms. Beautifully restored 1876 home. Attrac-
           tive, individually decorated rooms. 3 stories, no elevator; interior corridors; smoke free premises. **Services:** gift
shop. **Cards:** MC, VI.   [X] [Z] [icons]

SHELTER ISLAND pop. 1,200

———— LODGING ————

DERING HARBOR INN   **Phone:** (631)749-0900
◆ ◆   5/26-9/5   1P: $180-$415   2P: $180-$415   XP: $20   F12
Motor Inn   5/12-5/25 & 9/6-10/15   1P: $145-$340   2P: $145-$340   XP: $20   F12
           Location: North ferry, 0.5 mi s on SR 114; just e of jct SR 114 and Winthrop Rd. 13 Winthrop Rd 11965 (PO
Box 3028). Fax: 631/749-2045. **Terms:** Open 5/12-10/15; 14 day cancellation notice; cancellation fee imposed; 2 night min
stay, 6/1-10/15 weekends. **Facility:** 20 rooms. Most rooms are 1-bedroom suites and a few motel units. Most offer water views,
many on wooded grounds are spectacular. Well spaced rooms off a lot of privacy. 3 two-bedroom units. 2 stories; exterior corridors; 2 tennis courts. Fee: boat dock. **Recreation:** fishing. **Some Rooms:** 16 kitchens. **Cards:** AE, DS, MC, VI.
                                          [icons row]

SHERRILL pop. 2,900

—— RESTAURANTS ——

COLOSSEO ITALIAN & AMERICAN RESTAURANT **Lunch:** $3-$5   **Dinner:** $6-$12   **Phone:** 315/363-9075
◆ **Location:** SR 5 13461. **Hours:** 11 am-10 pm, Fri & Sat-11 pm. Closed major holidays.
Italian **Reservations:** suggested. **Features:** casual dress; children's menu; carryout; cocktails & lounge. A casual ease is evident in the relaxed dining room of the family-oriented restaurant. Traditional entrees are split among American and Italian selections. The manicotti is particularly tasty, as is the scrumptious blueberry pie, served a la mode. **Cards:** AE, MC, VI.   ✉

ROSS'S GINGERBREAD HOUSE
  FAMILY RESTAURANT **Lunch:** $4-$7   **Dinner:** $7-$14   **Phone:** 315/363-6644
◆◆ **Location:** On SR 5, just e of Main St. Rt 5 & Betsinger Rd 13461. **Hours:** 11 am-9 pm, Mon-3 pm, Fri &
American Sat-9:30 pm. Closed major holidays & Sun. **Reservations:** accepted. **Features:** casual dress; children's menu; carryout; cocktails & lounge. Three daughters help with the cooking at the charming restaurant. Country crafts and Victorian appointments decorate the inviting dining room. Chicken in lemon butter and haddock with white wine sauce are tasty choices, as are splendid homemade desserts. **Cards:** AE, DI, DS, MC, VI.   ✉

SHINNECOCK HILLS

—— LODGING ——

OCEAN VIEW TERRACE MOTEL   **Phone:** 631/728-4036
◆ 5/19-9/10   1P: $115-$275   2P: $115-$275   XP: $50   F12
Motel 5/1-5/18 & 9/11-4/30   1P: $80-$175   2P: $80-$175   XP: $25   F12
  Location: Just e of jct SR 24 on CR 80. 285 E Montauk Hwy 11946 (285 E Montauk Hwy, HAMPTON BAYS).
Fax: 631/723-3287. **Terms:** 10 day cancellation notice; cancellation fee imposed; 2 night min stay, in season weekends.
Facility: 16 rooms. Attractive comfortable rooms, some with patio, nice grassy areas. Views of the bay. 1 two-bedroom unit. 1 story; exterior corridors. **All Rooms:** combo or shower baths. **Some Rooms:** 4 efficiencies, 2 kitchens. **Cards:** AE, CB, DI, DS, MC, VI.
ASK SD ᵀⁱ⁺ 🛏 💻 📷 🔒 🏊

SKANEATELES pop. 2,700—*See also FINGER LAKES.*

—— LODGINGS ——

HI-WAY HOST MOTEL   **Phone:** (315)685-7633
◆ 6/1-12/31   1P: $48-$52   2P: $52-$56   XP: $5   F10
Motel 5/1-5/31 & 4/1-4/30   1P: $48   2P: $48-$52   XP: $5   F10
  Location: 0.8 mi w on US 20. 834 W Genesee St 13152. **Terms:** Open 5/1-12/31 & 4/1-4/30. **Facility:** 12
rooms. Pleasant rooms with cozy decor. 1 story; exterior corridors. **Services:** winter plug-ins. **Cards:** MC, VI.
ᵀⁱ⁺ ✉

HOBBIT HOLLOW FARM BED AND BREAKFAST   **Phone:** 315/685-2791
◆◆◆ 5/1-12/31   2P: $120-$270
Historic Bed 1/1-4/30   2P: $100-$250
& Breakfast **Location:** 1.7 mi s on SR 41A from US 20. 3061 W Lake Rd 13152. Fax: 315/685-3426. **Terms:** [BP] meal plan; age restrictions may apply; 10 day cancellation notice. **Facility:** 4 rooms. Lovely public area and well appointed rooms. Short drive to village. 2 stories; interior corridors; smoke free premises. **Services:** Fee: massage. **Recreation:** cross country skiing. **Cards:** AE, DI, MC, VI.
✉ 🖨 DATA PORT ✉

—— RESTAURANTS ——

DOUG'S FISH FRY **Lunch:** $6-$12   **Dinner:** $6-$12   **Phone:** 315/685-3288
◆ **Location:** Center. 8 Jordan St 13152. **Hours:** Open 5/1-12/31 & 1/15-4/30; 11 am-10 pm; to 8 pm 9/3-5/26.
Seafood Closed major holidays. **Features:** casual dress; carryout; beer & wine only; a la carte. There's a good reason people flock to the "hole-in-the-wall" restaurant—the food is great. Fried just right, the fish fry is lightly browned, with the fish turning out light and flaky. Crispy, golden fries and tangy slaw are delicious accompaniments.   ✉

THE KREBS Country Inn   **Dinner:** $32-$37   **Phone:** 315/685-5714
◆◆◆ **Location:** On US 20. 53 W Genesee St 13152. **Hours:** Open 5/1-10/30; 6 pm-9 pm, Fri & Sat-10 pm, Sun
American 10:30 am-2 & 4-9 pm. **Reservations:** suggested. **Features:** casual dress; Sunday brunch; children's menu; cocktails & lounge; prix fixe, a la carte. The long-established restaurant delivers a seven-course prix fixe meal that includes country-style entrees of lobster Newburg, prime rib and fried chicken. Early American decor pulls together the dining room in a tidy, cohesive theme. Service is prompt. **Cards:** AE, CB, DI, DS, MC, VI.   ✉

MANDANA INN   **Dinner:** $12-$25   **Phone:** 315/685-7798
AAA **Location:** 6 mi s on SR 41A. 1937 W Lake Rd 13152. **Hours:** Open 5/1-1/1 & 4/2-4/30; 5 pm-10 pm, Sun 3
◆◆ pm-8:30 pm. Closed: 4/1-5/31, 9/3-1/1, Mon & Tues; 11/1-1/1, Mon-Thurs. **Reservations:** suggested.
Seafood **Features:** casual dress; children's menu; cocktails & lounge; street parking; a la carte. Near Skaneateles Lake, the former stagecoach tavern is decorated with antique grandfather clocks and local artwork. The menu centers on well-prepared entrees of flavorful seafood and steak. The homemade desserts here have been popular for many years. **Cards:** AE, DI, MC, VI.   ✉

ROSALIE'S CUCINA   **Dinner:** $10-$28   **Phone:** 315/685-2200
◆◆◆   **Location:** 0.6 mi w. 841 W Genessee St 13152. **Hours:** 5 pm-9 pm; Fri & Sat-10 pm. Closed major
Italian   holidays. **Reservations:** accepted; 6 or more. **Features:** casual dress; cocktails. Scampi Rosalie—a
delicious choice with shrimp, garlic butter, angel hair pasta, artichokes and oven-cured tomatoes—is just one
of the creative dishes on the tempting menu. Tuscan furnishings and warm, wood ceilings decorate the dining room. Smoke
free premises. **Cards:** AE, MC, VI.   ✖

SHERWOOD INN DINING ROOM   Country Inn   **Lunch:** $7-$12   **Dinner:** $12-$25   **Phone:** 315/685-3405
◆◆   **Location:** US 20; in Sherwood Inn. 26 W Genesee St 13152. **Hours:** 11:30 am-9 pm, Fri & Sat-10 pm, Sun
American   5 pm-9 pm. Closed: 12/25 & for dinner 12/24. **Reservations:** suggested. **Features:** casual dress; children's
menu; carryout; cocktails & lounge. Enjoy beautiful views of the water from most seats in the comfortable
dining room. The menu centers on generous portions of standard tavern fare—fish, chicken, red meat, salad, sandwiches
and pizza. The historic inn was established in 1807. **Cards:** AE, DI, MC, VI.   ✖

SMITHTOWN pop. 25,600

—— LODGING ——

SHERATON LONG ISLAND HOTEL   **Phone:** (631)231-1100
AAA   5/1-12/31   1P: $199-$225   2P: $199-$255   XP: $20   F18
   1/1-4/30   1P: $209-$235   2P: $209-$235   XP: $20   F18
◆◆◆   **Location:** I-495, exit 53 (Wicks Rd), 0.3 mi e. 110 Vanderbilt Motor Pkwy 11788. **Fax:** 631/231-1143.
Hotel   **Terms:** [BP] meal plan; monthly rates avail; cancellation fee imposed; package plans, weekends. **Facility:** 209
rooms. Spacious contemporary accommodations. All rooms with hair dryer, iron and ironing board. Concierge
level rooms avail. 6 stories; interior corridors; small heated indoor pool, sauna, steamroom, whirlpool. **Dining:** Restaurant; 6:30
am-11 pm, Sat 7 am-1 am, Sun 7 am-midnight; $9-$19; cocktails. **Services:** gift shop. **Recreation:** in-room video games.
All Rooms: extended cable TV. **Some Rooms:** Fee: refrigerators. **Cards:** AE, CB, DI, DS, MC, VI.

(ASK) (S/D) (✈) (♨) (🍴) (Y) (🛏) (△) (ᵛ) (♿) (🔌) (✖) (🎦) (📠) (💻) (🏋) (DATA PORT) (🛄) (△) (🖥)

—— RESTAURANTS ——

CASA RUSTICA   **Lunch:** $11-$16   **Dinner:** $15-$25   **Phone:** 631/265-9265
◆◆◆   **Location:** 0.5 mi e of jct 25 and 25A. 175 W Main St 11787. **Hours:** noon-3 & 5-10 pm, Fri noon-11 pm, Sat
Northern   5 pm-11 pm, Sun 2 pm-9 pm. Closed: 1/1, 11/23 & 12/25. **Reservations:** suggested; for dinner.
Italian   **Features:** dressy casual; cocktails & lounge; a la carte. Representative of mouthwatering fare are two
specialties: vitello Casa Rustica, which is a breaded rack of veal covered with mozzarella in herb and garlic
sauce, and pesce in crosta di sale, a flavorful preparation of the fresh catch of the day. **Cards:** AE, DI, DS, MC, VI.   ✖

The following restaurant has not been inspected by AAA
but is listed for your information only.

IL VIOLINO RESTAURANT   **Phone:** 631/382-9744
(fyi)   Not inspected. **Location:** 53 W Main St 11787. **Features:** Il Violino offers fine dining in an intimate
atmosphere.

SOUTHAMPTON pop. 4,000

—— LODGING ——

EVERGREEN ON PINE BED & BREAKFAST   **Phone:** 631/283-0564
◆◆◆   7/1-8/31   2P: $180-$275   XP: $25
Bed &   5/1-6/30   2P: $125-$195   XP: $25
Breakfast   9/1-10/31   2P: $140-$165   XP: $25
   11/1-4/30   2P: $100-$150   XP: $25
Location: Center; from jct Main St and Meeting House Ln, just e. 89 Pine St 11968. **Fax:** 631/283-0564. **Terms:** [CP] meal
plan; age restrictions may apply; 10 day cancellation notice; cancellation fee imposed; 2 night min stay, weekends, holidays;
package plans. **Facility:** 5 rooms. Bright, cheerful, contemporary guest rooms featuring hardwood floors, duvets and some antiques. Inviting outdoor patio. 2 stories; interior corridors; smoke free premises. **Services:** area transportation.
All Rooms: combo or shower baths. **Some Rooms:** color TV. **Cards:** AE, DS, MC, VI.   (ASK) (✈) (✖) (📠)

—— RESTAURANTS ——

BARRISTER'S   **Lunch:** $7-$9   **Dinner:** $13-$20   **Phone:** 631/283-6206
◆   **Location:** Center. 36 Main St 11968. **Hours:** 11:30 am-5 & 5:30-11 pm, Fri & Sat-midnight, Sun 11:30 am-4
American   & 5-11 pm. Closed: 11/23. **Features:** No A/C; Sunday brunch; children's menu; carryout; cocktails & lounge;
a la carte. The casual tavern is a favorite haunt in which neighbors dine and chat over simply prepared,
flavorful dishes. Penne pasta, pepper-rubbed tuna steak and grilled pork loin medallions are representative of menu
fare. The covered terrace is relaxing. **Cards:** AE, DI, DS, MC, VI.   ✖

BASILICO   **Lunch:** $8-$15   **Dinner:** $14-$25   **Phone:** 631/283-7987
◆◆◆   **Location:** Just w of Main St via Jobs Ln. 10 Windmill Ln 11960. **Hours:** 5:30 pm-10 pm, Fri 6 pm-11 pm,
American   Sat noon-3 & 6-11 pm, Sun noon-3 pm. Closed: 1/1, 11/23, 12/24 & 12/25. **Reservations:** suggested; for
dinner. **Features:** dressy casual; Sunday brunch; health conscious menu items; cocktails; street parking; a la
carte. A country trattoria ambience punctuates the chic cafe, which presents a menu of dishes prepared with subtle
Mediterranean influences. Fresh ingredients flavor such dishes as spaghetti with broccoli, grilled vegetable pizza and
marinated, grilled fish. Smoke free premises. **Cards:** AE, DI, DS, MC, VI.   ✖

DRIVERS SEAT RESTAURANT   Lunch: $7-$13   Dinner: $14-$19   Phone: 631/283-6606
◆
American   **Location:** Center. 62 Jobs Lane 11968. **Hours:** 11:30 am-11 pm, Fri & Sat-midnight. Closed: 12/25. **Features:** No A/C; Sunday brunch; children's menu; carryout; cocktails & lounge; a la carte. Known for steak and seafood specials, the casual family restaurant serves traditional American fare with a twist. An inviting patio—dotted with nicely spaced tables covered by umbrellas—sits out back. Service is basic, prompt and friendly. **Cards:** AE, MC, VI.

SOUTH GLENS FALLS pop. 3,500—*See also GLENS FALLS.*

—— LODGING ——

LANDMARK MOTOR INN   Phone: 518/793-3441
7/24-9/3	1P: $100	2P: $105	XP: $5	F18
5/1-7/23	1P: $55	2P: $60-$67	XP: $3	F18
9/4-10/8	1P: $50	2P: $55-$60	XP: $3	F18
10/9-4/30	1P: $44	2P: $46-$50	XP: $3	F18

Motel   **Location:** 4.8 mi s on US 9, jct SR 197; 1.3 mi n of I-87 Northway, exit 17 N. US 9 12803 (PO Box 376, GLENS FALLS, 12801). Fax: 518/761-6909. **Facility:** 74 rooms. Spacious beautifully landscaped grounds. 1 story; exterior corridors; designated smoking area; putting green; 2 pools, 1 indoor heated, whirlpool; playground. **Dining:** Restaurant nearby. **Services:** winter plug-ins. **All Rooms:** extended cable TV. **Some Rooms:** Fee: refrigerators. **Cards:** AE, CB, DI, DS, MC, VI.

SOUTH KORTRIGHT pop. 100

—— RESTAURANT ——

THE HIDDEN INN Historical   Dinner: $9-$20   Phone: 607/538-9259
◆◆
American   **Location:** CR 18, just s of SR 10, following signs. Main St 13842. **Hours:** 5 pm-9 pm, Sun noon-7 pm. Closed: 12/25. **Reservations:** required; weekends. **Features:** casual dress; Sunday brunch; children's menu; senior's menu; carryout; salad bar; cocktails & lounge. The 1890s restored Colonial home is decorated in a French country motif, with fresh flowers, chandeliers and tableside lighting. The bottomless bowl of shrimp is a favorite offering on a menu of lamb, veal, duck, beef and seafood choices. **Cards:** AE, CB, DI, DS, MC, VI.

SOUTHOLD pop. 5,200

—— RESTAURANT ——

ROSS' NORTH FORK RESTAURANT   Lunch: $14-$19   Dinner: $18-$22   Phone: 631/765-2111
◆◆◆
American   **Location:** On CR 48; w of Young Ave. PO Box 560 11971. **Hours:** noon-2:30 & 5-9 pm, Sun 1 pm-9 pm. Closed: 12/25, Mon. & 1/1-2/14. **Reservations:** suggested. **Features:** casual dress; health conscious menu items; cocktails & lounge; a la carte. A large selection of Long Island wines complements selections of regional cuisine that employs local produce, duckling and seafood. A wonderful choice, grilled salmon, is bathed in a flavorful dill sauce. Peach flan is among the homemade desserts. Smoke free premises. **Cards:** AE, DI, MC, VI.

SOUTHPORT

—— LODGING ——

COACHMAN MOTOR LODGE   Phone: (607)733-5526
5/1-10/31	1P: $55-$65	2P: $65-$90	XP: $5	F16
11/1-4/30	1P: $40-$50	2P: $50-$60	XP: $5	F16

Motel   **Location:** SR 17, exit 56, follow signs 1.8 mi s on SR 14. (908 Pennsylvania Ave, ELMIRA, 14904). Fax: 607/733-0961. **Terms:** Weekly & monthly rates avail; small pets only. **Facility:** 18 rooms. All rooms with separate living room. 2 stories; exterior corridors. **Services:** winter plug-ins. **All Rooms:** kitchens, extended cable TV. **Cards:** AE, CB, DS, MC, VI. **Special Amenities:** Early check-in/late check-out and free local telephone calls.

SOUTH WORCESTER

—— LODGING ——

CHARLOTTE VALLEY INN BED & BREAKFAST   Phone: (607)397-8164
5/1-10/31 & 4/1-4/30	1P: $115-$120	2P: $120-$125	XP: $25	F7
11/1-3/31	1P: $85-$90	2P: $90-$95	XP: $20	F7

Historic Bed & Breakfast   **Location:** SR 23, 0.5 mi n on Deleware CR 9/40. 480 CR 40 12197. **Terms:** [BP] meal plan; 7 day cancellation notice; cancellation fee imposed; small pets only. **Facility:** 5 rooms. Restored 1832 period home with many antiques and peaceful view over Charlotte Valley. 2 stories; interior corridors. **Some Rooms:** combo or shower baths, shared bathrooms. **Cards:** MC, VI.

SPECULATOR pop. 400—See also ADIRONDACK MOUNTAINS.

—— RESTAURANT ——

ZEISER'S
◆◆
American

Lunch: $4-$6   **Dinner:** $14-$21   **Phone:** 518/548-7021
Location: Center; on SR 30. NYS Rt 30 12164. **Hours:** noon-4 & 5:30-8 pm, Fri & Sat-9 pm, Sun 1 pm-7 pm. Closed: 12/25 & usually Tues (Dec-May). **Reservations:** suggested. **Features:** casual dress; cocktails & lounge. Chicken Genevieve—braised chicken served with white wine sauce—is representative of tasty choices on the restaurant's limited menu. Wood and marble accents, as well as horse prints, decorate the modestly upscale dining room. Service is gracious. Smoke free premises. **Cards:** AE, MC, VI.   ✉

SPENCERTOWN pop. 500

—— LODGING ——

SPENCERTOWN COUNTRY HOUSE
◆◆◆
Historic Bed
& Breakfast

MC, VI.

Phone: 518/392-5292
All Year   1P: $70-$175   2P: $85-$195   XP: $25
Location: CR 9, 0.9 mi n of jct SR 203. 1909 CR 9 12165 (PO Box 279). Fax: 518/392-7453. **Terms:** [BP] meal plan; age restrictions may apply. **Facility:** 9 rooms. Federalist style mansion built in 1803, located in Berkshires. 2 stories; interior corridors; smoke free premises. **All Rooms:** combo or shower baths. **Cards:** AE,

SPRINGFIELD CENTER —See also COOPERSTOWN.

—— LODGINGS ——

BAYSIDE INN & MARINA
⬨
◆◆
Motel

Phone: 607/547-2371
6/16-9/4   1P: $119-$159   2P: $119-$159   XP: $10
5/1-6/15 & 9/5-10/31   1P: $59-$109   2P: $59-$109   XP: $10
Location: 3 mi s on SR 80. 7090 State Hwy 80 13326. Fax: 607/547-5856. **Terms:** Open 5/1-10/31; weekly rates avail; 3 day cancellation notice; cancellation fee imposed. **Facility:** 19 rooms. In wooded area on Lake Otsego. Attractive lobby with game room and outdoor deck. The higher rate range applies to weekends; 1-2 stories; interior/exterior corridors; beach, children's swimming area; playground. Fee: marina. **Recreation:** canoeing, fishing, paddleboats. **All Rooms:** extended cable TV. **Some Rooms:** Fee: refrigerators. **Cards:** DS, MC, VI. *(See ad p 240)*

COOPERTOWN'S LAKE 'N PINES MOTEL
⬨ SAVE
◆◆◆
Motel

Phone: (607)547-2790
6/9-9/3   1P: $100-$135   2P: $100-$135   XP: $7
5/1-6/8   1P: $65-$80   2P: $65-$80   XP: $7
9/4-11/26   1P: $50-$80   2P: $50-$80   XP: $7
3/25-4/30   1P: $50-$60   2P: $50-$60   XP: $7
Location: SR 80, 3 mi s at jct SR 20. 7102 State Hwy 80 13326 (7102 State Hwy 80, COOPERSTOWN). Fax: 607/547-5671. **Terms:** Open 5/1-11/26 & 3/25-4/30; [CP] meal plan; 5 day cancellation notice. **Facility:** 33 rooms. On Lake Otsego. Variety of different room styles, some with lake view and balcony. 1-2 stories; exterior corridors; 2 heated pools, sauna, whirlpool; boat dock, boat ramp. **Recreation:** fishing, paddleboats, rowboats; game room. **All Rooms:** combo or shower baths, extended cable TV. **Some Rooms:** Fee: refrigerators. **Cards:** AE, DS, MC, VI. *(See color ad p 239)*

HICKORY GROVE MOTOR INN
⬨ SAVE
◆◆
Motel

Phone: (607)547-9874
6/16-9/3   1P: $98-$110   2P: $100-$120   XP: $5
5/1-6/15, 9/4-10/29 & 4/16-4/30   1P: $50-$80   2P: $50-$88   XP: $5
Location: On SR 80, 4.7 mi sw of jct SR 20. (6854 State Hwy 80, COOPERSTOWN, 13326). Fax: 607/547-8567. **Terms:** Open 5/1-10/29 & 4/16-4/30; [CP] meal plan; 3 day cancellation notice; cancellation fee imposed. **Facility:** 12 rooms. Pleasant guest rooms. Overlooking Otsego Lake. Lake privileges. 1 story; exterior corridors; beach; boat dock. **Dining:** Restaurant nearby. **Recreation:** fishing, paddleboats, small stone beach area. **All Rooms:** shower baths, extended cable TV. **Cards:** AE, DS, MC, VI. **Special Amenities:** Free local telephone calls and free room upgrade (subject to availability with advanced reservations).

STAATSBURG pop. 1,100

—— RESTAURANT ——

PORTOFINO RISTORANTE
⬨
◆◆
Italian

Dinner: $10-$16   **Phone:** 914/889-4711
Location: Center. 57 Old Post Rd 12580. **Hours:** 4 pm-9:30 pm, Fri & Sat-10:30 pm, Sun-9 pm. Closed major holidays. **Features:** casual dress; carryout; cocktails & lounge. Regional Italian dishes mingle with daily changing specials that show piquant influences from the Pacific Rim. Art deco prints decorate the walls of the dining room; soft music, ranging from jazz to easy listening pop, plays in the background. **Cards:** AE, DI, MC, VI.   ✉

STAFFORD pop. 600

―――― RESTAURANT ――――

RED OSIER LANDMARK RESTAURANT   Dinner: $10-$30   Phone: 716/343-6972
◇◇◇
Steak and
Seafood
Location: On SR 5, 1 mi e of jct SR 237; between I-90, exit 47 and 48. 6492 Main Rd 14143. **Hours:** 4 pm-10 pm, Sun 1 pm-9 pm; closing hours may vary. Closed: 11/23, 12/24, 12/25 & Mon. **Reservations:** accepted. **Features:** dressy casual; children's menu; early bird specials; carryout; cocktails & lounge. Several local awards have been bestowed on the popular country restaurant, a clear favorite for semicasual dining. Succulent prime rib—the house specialty—is carved tableside. The dessert of brownie, ice cream, fudge and whipped cream is incredible. **Cards:** AE, MC, VI.

STATEN ISLAND—See New York p. 377.

STEPHENTOWN pop. 700

―――― LODGING ――――

MILL HOUSE INN   Phone: 518/733-5606
◇◇◇
Bed &
Breakfast
5/15-10/31 & 12/15-3/15   1P: $75-$85   2P: $90-$109   XP: $15
Location: 1.1 mi e of jct SR 22. Rt 43 12168 (PO Box 477). Fax: 518/733-6025. **Terms:** Open 5/15-10/31 & 12/15-3/15; [CP] meal plan; 14 day cancellation notice; 2 night min stay, weekends 7/1-8/31. **Facility:** 12 rooms. Alpine chalet inn on wooded site. Variety of different room types. 2 rooms with fireplace. 2 stories; interior/exterior corridors; smoke free premises; small pool. **Services:** winter plug-ins. **All Rooms:** combo or shower baths. **Some Rooms:** color TV. **Cards:** AE, MC, VI.

STONY BROOK pop. 13,700

―――― LODGINGS ――――

HOLIDAY INN EXPRESS STONY BROOK   Phone: (631)471-8000
◇◇◇
Motel
5/1-10/31 & 4/1-4/30   1P: $139   2P: $139
11/1-3/31   1P: $129   2P: $129
Location: I-495, exit 62, 8 mi n on Nichols Rd (CR 97), then e. US 347 -3131 Nesconset Hwy 11720. Fax: 631/471-8623. **Terms:** [ECP] meal plan; cancellation fee imposed. **Facility:** 142 rooms. Small garden and pond stocked with gold fish and 2 resident ducks. Gazebo and benches. 6 stories; interior corridors; heated pool. **Some Rooms:** Fee: refrigerators, microwaves. **Cards:** AE, CB, DI, DS, MC, VI.

THREE VILLAGE INN   Phone: (631)751-0555
◇◇◇◇ SAVE All Year   1P: $115-$139   2P: $125-$159   XP: $10   F12
◇◇◇
Historic
Country Inn
Location: Opposite Village Green; overlooking Stony Brook Harbor, just n of jct 25A and Main St. 150 Main St 11790. Fax: 631/751-0593. **Terms:** Package plans. **Facility:** 26 rooms. The Jonas Smith Homestead of 1751 and cottages facing marina. Quaint yet modernized accommodations. Colonial decor, shaded brick patio at some cottages. Rooms with fireplace, $25 extra charge; 2 stories; interior/exterior corridors; smoke free premises. **Dining:** Dining room; restaurant, see separate listing. **All Rooms:** combo or shower baths, extended cable TV. **Cards:** AE, CB, DI, MC, VI. **Special Amenities:** Free room upgrade and preferred room (each subject to availability with advanced reservations).

―――― RESTAURANT ――――

THREE VILLAGE INN Country Inn   Lunch: $9-$18   Dinner: $26-$35   Phone: 631/751-0555
◇◇◇
Regional
American
Location: Opposite Village Green; overlooking Stony Brook Harbor, 0.3 mi n of jct 25A and Main St, in Three Village Inn. 150 Main St 11790. **Hours:** 7 am-11, noon-4 & 5-9 pm, Fri & Sat 8 am-11 pm, Sun 8 am-11, noon-3 & 4-9 pm. Closed: 12/25. **Reservations:** suggested. **Features:** dressy casual; Sunday brunch; children's menu; health conscious menu items; cocktails & lounge. A Colonial theme weaves through the converted 1751 homestead. Enjoy panoramic views of the village and harbor from the charming dining rooms. Yankee pot roast, roast duckling and seafood pie are examples of traditional New England dishes. Smoke free premises. **Cards:** AE, DI, MC, VI.

STORMVILLE pop. 400

―――― RESTAURANT ――――

HARRALDS   Dinner: $65   Phone: 914/878-6595
◇◇◇◇
Continental
Location: On SR 52, 2.5 mi w of I-84, exit 17. 3110 SR 52 12582. **Hours:** 6 pm-9 pm, Sat seatings at 5:30 pm-9 pm. Closed: 12/24, 12/25, 1/1-2/15, 9/1-9/10 & Sun-Tues. **Reservations:** required. **Features:** semi-formal attire; cocktails & lounge; prix fixe. Take a drive into the Hudson Valley area to dine with Harrald, your host at Harralds. The chef's exceptional six-course meal, complemented by a comprehensive wine list, is an experience in Old World elegance. Service is attentive, yet unobtrusive.

SUFFERN —See New York p. 377.

SYLVAN BEACH pop. 1,100

—— RESTAURANTS ——

CANAL VIEW CAFE   Lunch: $3-$7   Dinner: $6-$11   Phone: 315/762-5623
◆   **Location:** On n side of Erie Canal; w of SR 13. 9 Canal St 13157. **Hours:** Open 5/1-11/19 & 3/15-4/30;
American   11:30 am-9 pm, Fri & Sat-10 pm; 11:30 am-8 pm Fri & Sat-9 pm off season. Closed: Tues 5/1-5/29 &
                     Mon-Wed after 9/4. **Reservations:** suggested. **Features:** casual dress; children's menu; carryout; beer &
wine only; a la carte. As you might guess from the name, the restaurant overlooks Erie Canal, as well as Oneida Lake. The
casual environment is welcoming to families. Menu favorites are broiled haddock and chicken caprice, which is served in
wine sauce over angel hair pasta. **Cards:** AE, DS, MC, VI.   ☒

CAPTAIN JOHN'S PRIME RIB-PASTA & SEAFOOD HOUSE   Dinner: $7-$20   Phone: 315/762-9949
ⒶⒶⒶ   **Location:** Center; on SR 13. 1424 N Beach Blvd 13157. **Hours:** Open 5/1-11/1 & 2/14-4/30; 3 pm-11 pm,
◆ ◆   Sun from noon. Closed: Tues; Wed 3/1-5/30 & 9/8-11/1. **Features:** casual dress; children's menu; early bird
Steak and   specials; carryout; cocktails & lounge. If you've got a big appetite to tame, this is the place to go. Specialties
Seafood   include two-pound prime rib cuts and one-pound lobster tails. Nautical appointments help to set a seafaring
                     tone in the casual dining room. Scrumptious desserts are homemade. **Cards:** AE, DI, DS, MC, VI.   ☒

CINDERELLA CAFE   Lunch: $3-$5   Dinner: $6-$15   Phone: 315/762-4280
ⒶⒶⒶ   **Location:** On SR 13. 1208 Main St 13157. **Hours:** 8 am-9 pm; to 10 pm 6/1-8/31. Closed: 12/1-1/15.
◆   **Reservations:** accepted. **Features:** casual dress; children's menu; senior's menu; carryout; cocktail lounge;
American   beer & wine only. Pictures of Cinderella decorate the walls of the whimsical restaurant. Wholesome,
                     home-cooked meals include such dishes as the specialty haddock. For dessert, enjoy a fresh-baked pie or
                     choose from an array of more than 30 flavors of ice cream and yogurt. **Cards:** AE, DI, DS, MC, VI.

EDDIE'S RESTAURANT   Lunch: $5-$12   Dinner: $5-$12   Phone: 315/762-5430
◆   **Location:** 901 Main St 13157. **Hours:** Open 5/1-11/30 & 3/15-4/30; 11 am-11 pm. **Features:** casual dress;
American   children's menu; carryout. Run by the Stewarts since 1934, the family-oriented restaurant is a local favorite
                     for seafood, steaks and pasta. Surrounded by windows, the bright, friendly dining room is decorated with
works by local artists. Servers are pleasant and attentive. **Cards:** MC, VI.

YESTERDAY'S ROYAL-ABBY'S RESTAURANT   Lunch: $3-$5   Dinner: $8-$15   Phone: 315/762-4677
◆ ◆   **Location:** On the canal; beside amusement park. 13 Canal St 13157. **Hours:** Open 5/1-9/30; 11:30 am-10
American   pm. Closed: Mon-Thurs 9/8-9/30. **Features:** casual dress; children's menu; early bird specials; carryout;
                     cocktails & lounge; a la carte. Portions are generous at the old-fashioned family restaurant, a favorite for
familiar preparations of fish, beef, chicken and pasta. Servers are knowledgeable and good with follow-up. Children of all
ages enjoy the ice cream bar and in-house desserts. **Cards:** AE, DI, DS, MC, VI.   ☒

SYRACUSE pop. 163,900   (See map p. 478; index below)

*This index helps you "spot" where approved accommodations are located on the detailed maps that follow. Rate ranges are
for comparison only and shwo the property's high season. Turn to the listing page for more detailed rate information and consult display ads for special promotions. Restaurant rate range is for dinner unless only lunch (L) is served.*

✈ Airport Accommodations

Spotter/Map Page Number	OA	SYRACUSE	Diamond Rating	Rate Range High Season	Listing Page

SYRACUSE

Spotter/Map Page Number	OA	SYRACUSE - Lodgings	Diamond Rating	Rate Range High Season	Listing Page
❷ / p. 478	ⒶⒶⒶ	**Red Roof Inn**	◆ ◆	$56-$73	480
❸ / p. 478		The Dickenson House on James	◆ ◆ ◆	$95-$120	480
❹ / p. 478	ⒶⒶⒶ	**Ramada Limited-University/Carrier Circle**	◆ ◆	$59-$99 [⚡]	480
❽ / p. 478		Days Inn Syracuse East	◆ ◆	$55-$85	479
⓫ / p. 478	ⒶⒶⒶ	**Holiday Inn/Farrell Road**	◆ ◆ ◆	$89 [⚡]	480
		SYRACUSE - Restaurants			
② / p. 478		China Pavilion	◆ ◆	$6-$13	481
③ / p. 478		Mimi's Bakery & Cafe	◆	$2-$7(L)	481
④ / p. 478	ⒶⒶⒶ	**Coleman's Authentic Irish Pub & Restaurant**	◆ ◆	$11-$18	481
⑤ / p. 478		Pascale Wine Bar and Restaurant	◆ ◆ ◆ ◆	$16-$24	481
⑥ / p. 478		Dinosaur Bar-B-Q Express	◆	$5-$15	481
⑦ / p. 478		Bistro 238	◆ ◆ ◆	$12-$20	481
⑧ / p. 478		Lemon Grass	◆ ◆ ◆	$9-$20	481
⑩ / p. 478	ⒶⒶⒶ	**Danzer's Restaurant**	◆	$10-$14	481

Spotter/Map Page Number	OA	**SYRACUSE** - Restaurants (continued)	Diamond Rating	Rate Range High Season	Listing Page
⑪ / p. 478		Phoebe's Garden Cafe	◆ ◆	$10-$18	481

Nearby Accommodations

Spotter/Map Page Number	OA	**EAST SYRACUSE** - Lodgings	Diamond Rating	Rate Range High Season	Listing Page
⑭ / p. 478		Courtyard by Marriott - see color ad p 479	◆ ◆ ◆	$80-$140	251
⑮ / p. 478		Residence Inn By Marriott	◆ ◆ ◆	$115-$131	251
⑯ / p. 478		Candlewood Suites	◆ ◆ ◆	$110	251
⑰ / p. 478	⏣	Holiday Inn East-Carrier Circle - see color ad p 480	◆ ◆ ◆	$94-$109 ⭤	251
⑱ / p. 478		East Syracuse Super 8	◆ ◆	$45-$66	251
⑲ / p. 478	⏣	Embassy Suites - see ad p 479	◆ ◆ ◆	$149-$169 ⭤	251
⑳ / p. 478		Microtel Inn Syracuse	◆ ◆	$44-$59	251
㉑ / p. 478		Wyndham Syracuse - see color ad p 479	◆ ◆ ◆	$79-$129	251
㉒ / p. 478	⏣	Hampton Inn-Carrier Circle - see ad p 480	◆ ◆ ◆	$82-$95	251
		EAST SYRACUSE - Restaurant			
⑬ / p. 478		Carmella's Cafe	◆ ◆	$6-$14	252
		LIVERPOOL - Lodgings			
㉔ / p. 478		Days Inn-North	◆ ◆	$69-$210	304
㉕ / p. 478		Homewood Suites	◆ ◆ ◆	$119-$199	304
㉗ / p. 478		Hampton Inn	◆ ◆ ◆	$67-$105	304
㉙ / p. 478	⏣	Super 8 Motel Route 57	◆ ◆ ◆	$55-$150 ⭤	304
㉚ / p. 478	⏣	Knights Inn	◆ ◆	$35-$99 ⭤	304
㉛ / p. 478		Super 8 Motel Syracuse/Liverpool	◆ ◆	$45-$59	304
㉜ / p. 478		Holiday Inn Syracuse/Liverpool	◆ ◆ ◆	$120-$150	304
		NORTH SYRACUSE - Lodgings			
㉞ / p. 478		The Club Hotel by DoubleTree Airport Area	◆ ◆ ◆	$99	439
㉟ / p. 478		Ramada Inn	◆ ◆ ◆	$79-$139	440
㊱ / p. 478	⏣	Best Western Syracuse Airport Inn	◆ ◆	$71-$98 ⭤	439
		NORTH SYRACUSE - Restaurants			
⑮ / p. 478		Colorado Mine Company Steakhouse	◆ ◆	$10-$19	440
⑯ / p. 478		Hunan Empire	◆ ◆	$6-$22	440
		CAMILLUS - Lodgings			
㊵ / p. 478		Green Gate Inn	◆ ◆	$60-$175	229
		CAMILLUS - Restaurants			
⑲ / p. 478		Inn Between Restaurant	◆ ◆ ◆	$18-$22	229
⑳ / p. 478		Green Gate Inn	◆ ◆	$8-$26	229
		DE WITT - Restaurants			
㉒ / p. 478		Saratoga Steaks and Seafood	◆ ◆	$12-$20	247
㉓ / p. 478		Scotch N' Sirloin	◆ ◆	$10-$30	247
		JAMESVILLE - Restaurant			
㉔ / p. 478	⏣	Glen Loch Restaurant	◆ ◆ ◆	$11-$20	279

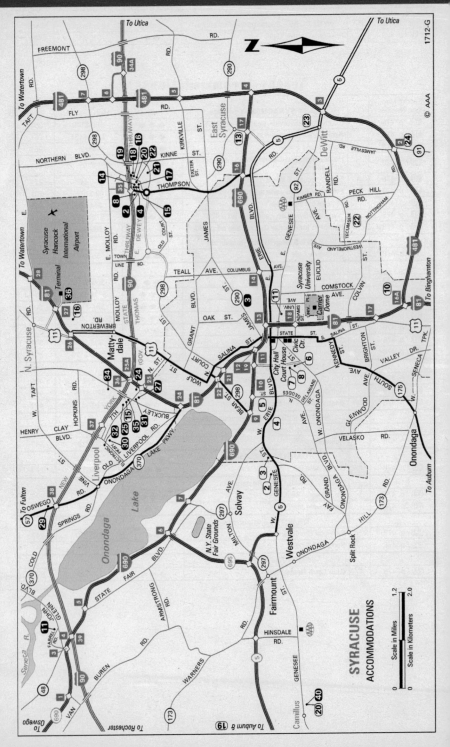

SYRACUSE
ACCOMMODATIONS

Scale in Miles
Scale in Kilometers

SYRACUSE pop. 163,900   (See map p. 478; index p. 476)

─── LODGINGS ───

DAYS INN SYRACUSE EAST
◆◆   5/1-11/1   1P: $55-$75   2P: $65-$85   **Phone:** (315)437-5998   [8]
                                                                          XP: $5   F17
Motel   11/2-2/28   1P: $45-$65   2P: $55-$80
          3/1-4/30   1P: $50-$65   2P: $60-$75   XP: $5   F17
Location: I-90, exit 35, at Carrier Cir. 6609 Thompson Rd 13206. Fax: 315/437-5965. **Terms:** [CP] meal plan; 7 day cancellation notice; pets, $10 extra charge. **Facility:** 97 rooms. 4 stories; interior corridors. **All Rooms:** combo or shower baths. **Some Rooms:** Fee: refrigerators, microwaves. **Cards:** AE, CB, DI, DS, MC, VI.

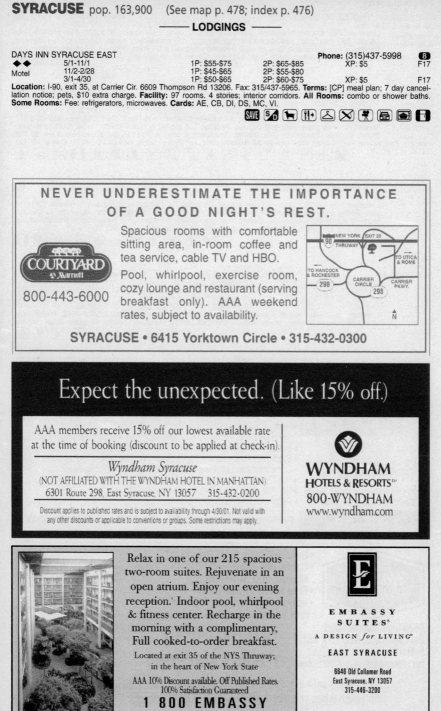

(See map p. 478)

THE DICKENSON HOUSE ON JAMES
◆◆◆   All Year   1P: $95-$120   2P: $95-$120   **Phone:** (315)423-4777   **3**
Historic Bed   XP: $20
& Breakfast   **Location:** I-90, exit 35, 1 mi s on Thompson Rd S, 2 mi w. 1504 James St 13203. Fax: 315/425-1965.
Terms: [BP] meal plan; age restrictions may apply; 7 day cancellation notice; cancellation fee imposed.
Facility: 4 rooms. Dataport hook up avail. Beautifully restored 1920 home. 3 stories, no elevator; interior corridors; smoke free premises. **All Rooms:** combo or shower baths. **Cards:** AE, DI, DS, MC, VI.

HOLIDAY INN/FARRELL ROAD
(AAA) (SAVE)   5/1-11/20 & 3/1-4/30   1P: $89   2P: $89   **Phone:** (315)457-8700   **11**
◆◆◆   11/21-2/28   1P: $69   2P: $69   XP: $15   F
Motor Inn   XP: $15   F
Location: Exit 39 Thruway to I-690 E to John Glenn Blvd exit. 100 Farrell Rd 13209. Fax: 315/457-2379.
Terms: Package plans; pets, $50 dep req. **Facility:** 152 rooms. Attractive cherry veneer furniture in guest rooms. 2 stories; interior corridors. **Dining:** Restaurant; 6 am-2 & 5-10 pm, Sat & Sun from 7 am; $9-$19; cocktails. **Recreation:** Fee: in-room video games. **All Rooms:** combo or shower baths, extended cable TV. **Cards:** AE, CB, DI, DS, JC, MC, VI.

RAMADA LIMITED-UNIVERSITY/CARRIER CIRCLE
(AAA) (SAVE)   All Year   1P: $59-$99   2P: $69-$99   **Phone:** (315)463-0202   **4**
◆◆   XP: $15   F16
Motel   **Location:** I-90, exit 35 (Carrier Cir), just w. 6590 Thompson Rd 13206. Fax: 315/463-9270. **Terms:** [CP] meal plan; weekly rates avail; cancellation fee imposed; pets, $10 extra charge. **Facility:** 73 rooms. 13 whirlpool rooms; 2 stories; interior corridors. **Dining:** Restaurant nearby. **Services:** area transportation. **Recreation:** limited exercise equipment. **All Rooms:** extended cable TV. **Cards:** AE, DI, DS, MC, VI.

RED ROOF INN
(AAA)   7/1-10/31   1P: $56-$66   2P: $63-$73   **Phone:** (315)437-3309   **2**
◆◆   4/1-4/30   1P: $51-$61   2P: $56-$66   XP: $7   F18
Motel   5/1-6/30   1P: $50-$60   2P: $55-$65   XP: $5   F18
   11/1-3/31   1P: $43-$53   2P: $48-$58   XP: $5   F18
   XP: $5   F18
Location: At Thruway exit 35 (Carrier Cir). 6614 N Thompson Rd 13206. Fax: 315/437-7865. **Terms:** Pets.
Facility: 115 rooms. Few compact rooms. 3 stories; exterior corridors. **Dining:** Restaurant nearby. **Services:** winter plug-ins.
Cards: AE, CB, DI, DS, MC, VI.

(See map p. 478)

——— RESTAURANTS ———

BISTRO 238   **Lunch:** $5-$10   **Dinner:** $12-$20   **Phone:** 315/475-9463   (7)
◆ ◆ ◆   **Location:** Center; across from the Armory. 238 W Jefferson St 13202. **Hours:** 11:30 am-2:30 & 5-10 pm,
Continental   Fri-11 pm, Sat 5 pm-11 pm. Closed: 1/1, 12/25 & Sun. **Reservations:** suggested. **Features:** dressy casual;
carryout; cocktails & lounge; street parking; a la carte. An award-winning wine list complements selections of
creative and eclectic Continental cuisine. Duck is a particularly outstanding choice. Low lighting, soft music and plush,
burgundy carpeting lend to the serene ambience of the relaxed dining room. **Cards:** AE, DI, DS, MC, VI.

CHINA PAVILION   **Lunch:** $4-$5   **Dinner:** $6-$13   **Phone:** 315/488-2828   (2)
◆ ◆   **Location:** In Westvale Plaza; I-81 exit on I-690 W to Geddes St exit 10, s on Geddes, then w. 2318 W
Chinese   Genesee St 13219. **Hours:** 11:30 am-9 pm, Fri & Sat-10 pm, Sun 11:30-9 pm. Closed: major holidays.
Features: casual dress; carryout; cocktail lounge; beer & wine only. Among cuisines sampled on the
extensive menu are Hunan, Cantonese, Peking and Szechwan. Tangerine beef and the treasure of the sea casserole are
particularly flavorful. A luncheon buffet is served on weekends; dim sum lunch is a Sunday feature. **Cards:** AE, DS, MC, VI.
🗙

COLEMAN'S AUTHENTIC IRISH PUB &
RESTAURANT   **Lunch:** $5-$9   **Dinner:** $11-$18   **Phone:** 315/476-1933   (4)
AAA   **Location:** On Tipperary Hill. 100 S Lowell Ave 13204. **Hours:** 11:30 am-10 pm, Fri & Sat-11 pm, Sun noon-9
◆ ◆   pm. Closed: 12/25. **Reservations:** suggested. **Features:** casual dress; children's menu; carryout; cocktails &
American   lounge; a la carte. Corned beef and cabbage, Guinness beef stew and fish and chips are among Irish and
Celtic items on the traditional menu. An Irish pub decor prevails, with mahogany wood, stained glass and
antique lanterns and lamps. Lively music plays all day. **Cards:** AE, DI, DS, MC, VI.
🗙

DANZER'S RESTAURANT   **Lunch:** $3-$7   **Dinner:** $10-$14   **Phone:** 315/422-0089   (10)
AAA   **Location:** I-81, exit 17, 0.7 mi s on E Brighton Ave, just e. 153 Ainsley Dr 13210. **Hours:** 11 am-11 pm, Fri &
◆   Sat-midnight, Sun noon-11 pm. Closed major holidays. **Reservations:** suggested; weekends.
German   **Features:** casual dress; children's menu; carryout; cocktails & lounge; a la carte. German and American
specialties, ranging from steaks and seafood to frankfurters and Wiener schnitzel, line the menu. The
family-oriented restaurant, in business since 1946, resembles an alpine Bavarian chalet. Service is casual,
but capable. **Cards:** AE, DI, DS, MC, VI.
🗙

DINOSAUR BAR-B-Q EXPRESS   **Lunch:** $5-$15   **Dinner:** $5-$15   **Phone:** 315/476-4937   (6)
◆   **Location:** Downtown; at jct Willow and Franklin. 246-248 Willow 13202. **Hours:** 11 am-2 am, Sun 4 pm-2
American   am. Closed major holidays. **Features:** casual dress; carryout; cocktails & lounge; entertainment; street
parking; a la carte. Start with a plate of tortilla chips topped with pulled pork, hot peppers, black beans and
melted cheese, and then dig in to the barbecue sampler, which includes chicken, pork ribs and beef. The atmosphere is
relaxed, informal and great for families. **Cards:** AE, DI, DS, MC, VI.
🗙

LEMON GRASS   **Lunch:** $6-$8   **Dinner:** $9-$20   **Phone:** 315/475-1111   (8)
◆ ◆ ◆   **Location:** Center; across from the Armory. 238 W Jefferson St 13202. **Hours:** 11:30 am-2:30 & 5-9 pm,
Thai   Fri-11 pm, Sat 11:30 am-3 & 5-11 pm, Sun 4:30 pm-9:30 pm. Closed: 1/1 & 12/25.
Reservations: suggested. **Features:** dressy casual; carryout; cocktails; street parking; a la carte.
Outstanding Thai food is what this place is all about. The seafood medley blends shrimp, scallops, clams and chunks of
squid in a spicy chili sauce over while rice. Desserts are attractively presented, with chocolate slices, powdered sugar and
fruit. Smoke free premises. **Cards:** AE, DI, DS, MC, VI.
🗙

MIMI'S BAKERY & CAFE   **Lunch:** $2-$7   **Phone:** 315/422-6630   (3)
◆   **Location:** Across from the Clinton Exchange; I-81 S, exit West and Franklin sts follow to downtown; I-81 N,
American   exit Adam St to State, just w on Erie Blvd. 260 W Genesee St 13202. **Hours:** 6:30 am-5 pm, Sat-3 pm.
Closed major holidays & Sun. **Features:** casual dress; health conscious menu items; carryout. Baked goods
are outstanding at the comfortable restaurant, a favorite for lighter, deli fare. Sandwiches, soups, salads and daily specials
are what have brought this place its devoted clientele. Sidewalk seating lets you engage in people-watching. **Cards:** MC, VI.
🗙

PASCALE WINE BAR AND RESTAURANT   **Lunch:** $6-$15   **Dinner:** $16-$24   **Phone:** 315/471-3040   (5)
◆ ◆ ◆ ◆   **Location:** Downtown; corner of Clinton and W Fayette St. 204 W Fayette St 13202. **Hours:** 11:30 am-2:30 &
American   5:30-11 pm, Sat from 5:30 pm. Closed: 1/1, 12/25 & Sun. **Reservations:** suggested. **Features:** dressy
casual; children's menu; cocktails; street parking & valet parking; a la carte. An extensive wine list with rare
vintages complements such savory choices as filet mignon in Madeira sauce, which is served with roast garlic mashed
potatoes. Stucco walls, an open kitchen and marble finishes lend to the contemporary atmosphere. **Cards:** AE, DI, DS,
MC, VI.
🗙

PHOEBE'S GARDEN CAFE   **Lunch:** $7-$10   **Dinner:** $10-$18   **Phone:** 315/475-5154   (11)
◆ ◆   **Location:** 0.5 mi e of I-81, exit 18; on SR 92. 900 E Genesee St 13210. **Hours:** 11:30 am-9 pm, Fri &
American   Sat-11 pm. Closed major holidays. **Reservations:** suggested. **Features:** casual dress; Sunday brunch;
carryout; cocktails & lounge; street parking. A sunny skylight sheds light on the bright atrium, which is filled
with plants, satisfied diners and casual, friendly ambience. Fresh seafood and steaks are at the heart of the bistrolike menu.
For dessert, savor the specialty creme brulee. **Cards:** AE, DI, MC, VI.
🗙

TANNERSVILLE pop. 500

—— LODGING ——

THE EGGERY INN
AAA SAVE
◆◆
Bed &
Breakfast

All Year   1P: $99-$108   2P: $120-$140   XP: $40   **Phone:** (518)589-5363
Location: CR 16, 1.3 mi s of jct SR 23A. (PO Box 4, CR 16, 12485). Fax: 518/589-5774. **Terms:** [BP] meal plan; weekly rates avail; 14 day cancellation notice; cancellation fee imposed; 2 night min stay, weekends; package plans; pets on premises. **Facility:** 15 rooms. Peaceful mountain setting with picturesque view. Variety of individually decorated rooms. 3 stories, no elevator; interior corridors; smoke free premises. **All Rooms:** combo or shower baths. **Cards:** AE, MC, VI. **Special Amenities:** Free breakfast. ✕ (DATA PORT)

TARRYTOWN —See New York p. 377.

THENDARA

—— RESTAURANT ——

VAN AUKEN'S INNE
◆◆
American

Lunch: $3-$8   **Dinner:** $11-$24   **Phone:** 315/369-3033
Location: Just behind Thendara train station on SR 28. 108 Forge St 13472. **Hours:** Open 5/12-10/22 & 12/8-3/18; 11 am-2:30 & 5-9 pm, Fri & Sat-10 pm. Closed: 12/25, Tues & Weds in winter. **Reservations:** suggested. **Features:** casual dress; carryout; cocktails & lounge; a la carte. The tastefully restored, turn-of-the-20th-century inn has hardwood floors, molded ceilings and an understated decor. Veal Milanese is representative of flavorful, well-prepared food. The wine list offers a nice selection. Service is attentive. **Cards:** MC, VI. ✕

TICONDEROGA pop. 2,800—See also ADIRONDACK MOUNTAINS.

—— LODGING ——

CIRCLE COURT MOTEL
AAA SAVE
◆
Motel

6/16-10/28	1P: $54-$59	2P: $59-$64	XP: $5 F12
5/1-6/15	1P: $48-$53	2P: $53-$58	XP: $5 F12
10/29-4/30	1P: $41-$46	2P: $46-$51	XP: $5 F12

Phone: (518)585-7660
Location: SR 9 N; at Liberty Monument traffic circle. 440 Montcalm St 12883. **Terms:** Weekly rates avail, off season; cancellation fee imposed; pets. **Facility:** 14 rooms. Modest to spacious rooms. 1-2 stories; exterior corridors. **Services:** winter plug-ins. **All Rooms:** combo or shower baths, extended cable TV. **Cards:** AE, MC, VI. **Special Amenities:** Free local telephone calls and preferred room (subject to availability with advanced reservations). (S/D) 🐕 🖨 🛗

TONAWANDA —See Buffalo p. 226.

TROY pop. 54,300   (See map p. 193; index p. 192)

—— LODGINGS ——

BEST WESTERN-RENSSELAER INN
AAA SAVE
◆◆
Motor Inn

All Year   1P: $59-$89   2P: $69-$89   XP: $5   F12   **Phone:** (518)274-3210 43
Location: I-787 N, exit 9E; SR 7 E, downtown exit, just on left. 1800 6th Ave 12180. Fax: 518/274-3294. **Terms:** [BP] meal plan; package plans. **Facility:** 152 rooms. Well-furnished guest rooms. 4 stories; interior corridors. **Dining:** Dining room; 7 am-10 & 5-10 pm; Sat & Sun 7 am-11 & 5-10 pm; $10-$13; cocktails. **Services:** winter plug-ins. **All Rooms:** extended cable TV. **Some Rooms:** Fee: refrigerators, VCR. **Cards:** AE, DI, DS, MC, VI. **Special Amenities:** Free breakfast and free newspaper.

(S/D) ✈ 🍽 24⏰ ▷ 🚭 ⬛ ✕ (VCR) 🖨 ▭ 🖥 🛗 (DATA PORT) 🐾 ☂

SUPER 8 MOTEL-TROY
◆◆
Motel

10/1-4/30	1P: $55-$75	2P: $60-$80	XP: $5 F17
5/1-9/30	1P: $53-$73	2P: $58-$78	XP: $5 F17

Phone: (518)274-8800 42
Location: I-787, exit 8, just e on 23rd to Federal, just e to 4th St, then just s. 1 4th St 12180. Fax: 518/274-0427. **Facility:** 74 rooms. Pleasant rooms in downtown setting. 3 stories; interior corridors. **Cards:** AE, DI, MC, VI.

(ASK) (S/D) 🍽 ✕ ☂

—— RESTAURANT ——

HOLMES & WATSON, LTD Historical
◆
American

Lunch: $4-$6   **Dinner:** $8-$12   **Phone:** 518/273-8526 32
Location: Downtown. 450 Broadway 12180. **Hours:** 11 am-1 am, Sun 5 pm-1 am. Closed: 12/25. **Features:** casual dress; children's menu; carryout; cocktails & lounge; street parking; a la carte. As the name may lead you to expect, the charming pub revolves around a Sherlock Holmes theme. Simple food, such as burgers and salads, is well complemented by more than 200 beers from around the world and 70 malt scotches. The seasonal patio is cozy. **Cards:** AE, DI, DS, MC, VI. ✕

TRUMANSBURG pop. 1,600—See also FINGER LAKES.

———— LODGING ————

TAUGHANNOCK FARMS INN
◆◆◆ 5/1-1/1 & 4/1-4/30 1P: $70-$150 2P: $95-$195 XP: $25 **Phone: 607/387-7711** D10
Historic **Location:** 10 mi n on SR 89 from Ithaca. 2030 Gorge Rd 14886. Fax: 607/387-7721. **Terms:** Open 5/1-1/1 &
Country Inn 4/1-4/30; [CP] meal plan; 10 day cancellation notice; cancellation fee imposed. **Facility:** 11 rooms. 1873 Victorian mansion with 2 guest houses. Adjacent to Taughannock Falls State Park overlooking Cayuga Lake. 1 two-bedroom unit, 1 three-bedroom unit. 1-2 stories; interior/exterior corridors; smoke free premises. **All Rooms:** combo or shower baths. **Some Rooms:** color TV. **Cards:** AE, DS, MC, VI.

———— RESTAURANT ————

TAUGHANNOCK FARMS INN Historical **Dinner:** $19-$27 **Phone: 607/387-7711**
◆◆◆ **Location:** 10 mi n from Ithaca on SR 89; in Taughannock Farms Inn. 2030 Gorge Rd 14886. **Hours:** Open
Regional 5/1-11/30 & 4/1-4/30; 5 pm-9 pm, Sun 3 pm-8 pm. **Reservations:** suggested. **Features:** dressy casual;
American children's menu; cocktails; prix fixe. Overlooking Cayuga Lake, the 1873 Victorian estate is loaded with quaint charm. In addition to such flavorful entrees as prime rib, roast duck, fresh fish and roast turkey, the restaurant serves an excellent chilled strawberry soup. Dinner is prix fixe. Smoke free premises. **Cards:** AE, DS, MC, VI.

TULLY pop. 900

———— LODGING ————

BEST WESTERN MARSHALL MANOR
All Year 1P: $49-$109 2P: $49-$109 XP: $5 **Phone: (315)696-6061** F12
◆◆ **Location:** SR 11 at I-81, exit 14. 5779 Rt 80 13159 (PO Box 156). Fax: 315/696-6406. **Facility:** 44 rooms.
Motel Good size guest rooms. 3 whirlpool rooms, $99-$109; 2 stories; interior corridors. **Dining:** Restaurant; 6 am-9 pm, Fri & Sat-10 pm, Sun-8 pm; $7-$11; cocktails. **All Rooms:** extended cable TV. **Cards:** AE, DI, DS, MC, VI.
Special Amenities: Free newspaper.

TUPPER LAKE pop. 4,100—See also ADIRONDACK MOUNTAINS.

———— LODGINGS ————

RED TOP INN
All Year 1P: $40-$50 2P: $45-$55 XP: $5 **Phone: 518/359-9209** D12
◆◆ **Location:** 3 mi s on SR 30. 90 Moody Rd 12986. **Terms:** Weekly & monthly rates avail, off season; package
Motel plans. **Facility:** 17 rooms. Overlooking Big Tupper Lake. Pleasant rooms with rustic charm. 4 two-bedroom units. 4 cabins, $45 for up to 2 persons in summer. Apartments, $75; effiencies, $60; 2 stories; interior/exterior corridors; beach; boat dock. **Dining:** Coffee shop; 7-11 am 7/1-9/30. **Services:** winter plug-ins.
Recreation: swimming, fishing, rowboats. **All Rooms:** combo or shower baths, extended cable TV. **Cards:** AE, MC, VI.

SHAHEEN'S MOTEL **Phone: 518/359-3384**
6/16-10/22 1P: $45-$67 2P: $52-$71 XP: $5 F5
12/20-4/30 1P: $42-$61 2P: $47-$69 XP: $5 F5
◆◆ 5/1-6/15 1P: $42-$56 2P: $46-$57 XP: $5 F5
Motel 10/23-12/19 1P: $42-$47 2P: $46-$57 XP: $5 F5
Location: 0.8 mi e on SR 3 and 30. 314 Park St 12986. Fax: 518/359-3384. **Terms:** [CP] meal plan; 3 day cancellation notice. **Facility:** 31 rooms. Large rooms. Family room, $75-$85; 2 stories; exterior corridors; playground. Fee: miniature golf. **Dining:** Restaurant nearby. **Services:** winter plug-ins. **Recreation:** picnic area. **All Rooms:** extended cable TV. **Cards:** AE, CB, DI, DS, MC, VI.

TUPPER LAKE MOTEL **Phone: (518)359-3381**
6/18-10/11 1P: $50 2P: $55-$63 XP: $5 F3
10/12-4/30 1P: $42-$43 2P: $45-$54 XP: $5 F3
◆◆ 5/1-6/17 1P: $42 2P: $45-$51 XP: $5 F3
Motel **Location:** 0.5 mi e on SR 3 and 30. 259 Park St 12986. Fax: 518/359-8549. **Terms:** [CP] meal plan; 3 day cancellation notice; cancellation fee imposed; package plans. **Facility:** 18 rooms. Comfortable guest rooms, a few are smaller. 1 story; exterior corridors. **Services:** winter plug-ins. **All Rooms:** shower baths, extended cable TV. **Cards:** AE, DS, MC, VI.

UNIONDALE pop. 20,300

———— LODGING ————

LONG ISLAND MARRIOTT HOTEL & CONFERENCE CENTER **Phone: (516)794-3800**
◆◆◆ All Year 1P: $179-$215 2P: $179 XP: $15 F18
Hotel **Location:** Meadowbrook Pkwy, exit M4 (follow signs to coliseum), exit Hempstead Tpke W; adjacent to Nassau Coliseum. 101 James Doolittle Blvd 11553. Fax: 516/794-5936. **Terms:** Check-in 4 pm; package plans; pets, $15 extra charge. **Facility:** 611 rooms. Full service hotel in the heart of the mid Long Island business district. 11 stories; interior corridors; heated pool. Fee: racquetball courts. **Services:** gift shop. Fee: massage. **All Rooms:** combo or shower baths.
Cards: AE, CB, DI, DS, MC, VI.

UTICA pop. 68,600

------ LODGINGS ------

A-1 MOTEL
Phone: (315)735-6698
⬤⬤⬤ SAVE
| | | | |
5/1-10/31 1P: $50-$55 2P: $55-$60 XP: $5 F8
◆
11/1-4/30 1P: $35-$38 2P: $42-$46 XP: $5 F8
Motel
Location: Just s of Thruway, exit 31. 238 N Genesee St 13502. **Terms:** Weekly rates avail, off season; 5 day cancellation notice; pets, cats not permitted. **Facility:** 20 rooms. Modest roadside motel. 2 stories; interior corridors. **All Rooms:** extended cable TV. **Cards:** AE, CB, DI, DS, MC, VI. **Special Amenities:** Early check-in/late check-out and free local telephone calls. *(See ad below)*

BEST WESTERN GATEWAY ADIRONDACK INN
Phone: (315)732-4121
◆◆◆ All Year 1P: $75-$170 2P: $80-$170 XP: $10 F12
Motel
Location: 0.5 mi s of I-90 Thruway, exit 31. 175 N Genesee St 13502. Fax: 315/797-8265. **Terms:** Pets. **Facility:** 89 rooms. Set back from main road on landscaped grounds. 1 two-bedroom unit. 2 stories; interior corridors. **Services:** gift shop; winter plug-ins. **Cards:** AE, CB, DI, DS, MC, VI. *(See ad below)*

COUNTRY MOTEL
Phone: 315/732-4628
⬤⬤⬤
6/13-10/19 1P: $36-$38 2P: $46-$55 XP: $5 F12
◆◆
5/1-6/12 & 10/20-4/30 1P: $32 2P: $42-$46 XP: $5 F12
Motel
Location: 2 mi e on SR 5 from I-90, exit 31. 1477 Herkimer Rd 13502. Fax: 315/733-8801. **Terms:** Weekly rates avail, off season; cancellation fee imposed. **Facility:** 25 rooms. Quiet setting. Attractive grounds, picnic tables set up in summer. 1 story; exterior corridors. **Services:** winter plug-ins. **All Rooms:** combo or shower baths, extended cable TV. **Cards:** AE, DS, MC, VI.

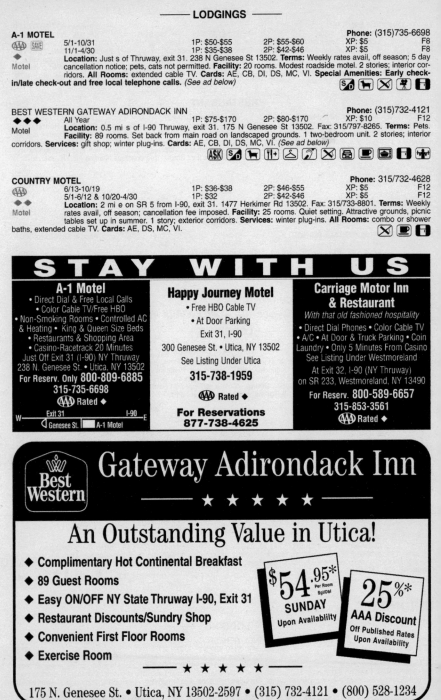

HAPPY JOURNEY MOTEL

(AAA) (SAVE)

◆

Motel

				Phone: (315)738-1959
5/1-10/31	1P: $50-$55	2P: $55-$60	XP: $5	F8
11/1-4/30	1P: $35-$38	2P: $42-$46	XP: $5	F8

Location: Just s of Thruway, exit 31. 300 N Genesee St 13502. **Terms:** Weekly rates avail, off season; 5 day cancellation notice; pets, cats not permitted. **Facility:** 18 rooms. Modest roadside motel. 2 stories; exterior corridors. **All Rooms:** combo or shower baths, extended cable TV. **Cards:** AE, CB, DI, DS, MC, VI.
Special Amenities: Early check-in/late check-out and free local telephone calls. (See p 484)

THE IRIS STONEHOUSE BED & BREAKFAST

◆◆

Bed &
Breakfast

				Phone: 315/732-6720
All Year	1P: $50-$70	2P: $60-$90	XP: $15	

Location: Jct Holland Ave and Derbyshire Pl; I-90 exit 31, 2.8 mi s on Genesee St, just e. 16 Derbyshire Pl 13501-4706. Fax: 315/797-5134. **Terms:** [BP] meal plan; age restrictions may apply; 7 day cancellation notice; cancellation fee imposed. **Facility:** 4 rooms. 1930s English stone tudor with leaded glass windows. Located in residental area. 2 stories; interior corridors; smoke free premises. **Some Rooms:** color TV. **Cards:** AE, DS, MC, VI.

RADISSON HOTEL-UTICA CENTRE

◆◆◆

Hotel

				Phone: (315)797-8010
All Year	1P: $119-$159	2P: $119-$159	XP: $10	F17

Location: Downtown. 200 Genesee St 13502. Fax: 315/797-1490. **Terms:** Package plans; small pets only, $30 dep req. **Facility:** 158 rooms. 6 stories; interior corridors; heated pool. Fee: parking. **Services:** gift shop.
Some Rooms: Fee: refrigerators. **Cards:** AE, DI, DS, MC, VI. (See color ad below)

RED ROOF INN

(AAA)

◆◆

Motel

				Phone: (315)724-7128
7/1-10/31	1P: $65-$95	2P: $75-$105	XP: $10	F18
5/1-6/30	1P: $52-$83	2P: $60-$91	XP: $8	F18
4/1-4/30	1P: $53-$73	2P: $61-$81	XP: $8	F18
11/1-3/31	1P: $49-$64	2P: $56-$71	XP: $7	F18

Location: I-90, exit 31. 20 Weaver St 13502. Fax: 315/724-7158. **Terms:** Small pets only. **Facility:** 112 rooms. Few compact rooms. 2 stories; exterior corridors. **Recreation:** Fee: in-room video games. **All Rooms:** extended cable TV. **Cards:** AE, CB, DI, DS, MC, VI.

ROSEMONT INN BED & BREAKFAST

◆◆◆

Historic Bed
& Breakfast

				Phone: 315/792-8852
All Year	1P: $89-$135	2P: $99-$145	XP: $15	

Location: I-90 Thruway, exit 31, 2.5 mi s. 1423 Genessee St 13501. Fax: 315/792-8852. **Terms:** [BP] meal plan; age restrictions may apply; 7 day cancellation notice. **Facility:** 7 rooms. An 1860 Italianate Victorian listed on the National Register of Historic Places. 3 stories, no elevator; interior corridors; smoke free premises.
Cards: MC, VI.

Savings at Your Fingertips

When you have a AAA TourBook® guide in your hand, you have a world of savings right at your fingertips. Lodgings that display the bright-red AAA emblem beside their listing want AAA member business, and many of them offer special amenities and discounts.

Also, keep your eye out for the familiar (SAVE) symbol. This icon represents a 10 percent savings off published room rates to AAA members.

So, when planning your next vacation, be sure to consult your AAA TourBook.

Travel With Someone You Trust

——— RESTAURANTS ———

BABE'S MACARONI GRILL & BAR **Lunch:** $5-$10 **Dinner:** $6-$12 **Phone:** 315/735-0777
◆◆ **Location:** 0.8 mi s of I-90 Thruway, exit 31. 80 N Genesee St 13501. **Hours:** 11 am-1 am. Closed: 11/23 &
American 12/25. **Reservations:** accepted. **Features:** casual dress; children's menu; early bird specials; carryout;
cocktails & lounge. The atmosphere is often boisterous at the bustling restaurant, which is decorated with a
wide array of memorabilia and movie posters. The broad menu includes chicken, beef and fish dishes, as well as Mexican
fare. Service is casual and friendly. **Cards:** AE, CB, DI, DS, MC, VI. ✖️

THORNBERRY'S RESTAURANT **Lunch:** $3-$8 **Dinner:** $9-$20 **Phone:** 315/735-1702
◆◆ **Location:** 1011 King St 13501. **Hours:** 11:30 am-2:30 & 4:30-10 pm. Closed: 12/25 & Sun.
American **Reservations:** suggested; on weekends. **Features:** casual dress; children's menu; cocktails &
lounge. Authentic antiques grace the walls of the casual, cottagelike restaurant, an established downtown
favorite. Quality ingredients go into the preparation of such filling selections as the muffuletta sandwich. Pleasant servers
show good menu knowledge. **Cards:** AE, DS, MC, VI. ✖️

VALATIE pop. 1,500

——— LODGING ———

BLUE SPRUCE INN & SUITES **Phone:** 518/758-9711
(AAA) [SAVE] 5/15-12/1 1P: $55-$75 2P: $65-$80 XP: $4 F3
◆◆ 12/2-4/30 1P: $47-$55 2P: $60-$70
Motel 5/1-5/14 1P: $47-$55 2P: $60-$70 XP: $4 F3
Location: 1 mi n. 3093 Route 9 12184. Fax: 518/758-1638. **Terms:** Weekly & monthly rates avail; 7 day can-
cellation notice; 2 night min stay, weekends 6/1-10/31; pets. **Facility:** 28 rooms. Small to good sized rooms.
Efficiencies, $70-$75 for up to 2 persons; 2 stories; exterior corridors; wading pool. **Dining:** Coffee shop; 7-10:30 am 5/1-11/30.
All Rooms: combo or shower baths, extended cable TV. **Some Rooms:** Fee: refrigerators. **Cards:** AE, DS, MC, VI.
(See color ad p 195) 🐾 🍽️ 🗄️ ✖️ 🐾 📠 🔌 🛶

VERNON pop. 1,300

——— RESTAURANTS ———

MASON JAR RESTAURANT **Lunch:** $4-$6 **Dinner:** $8-$15 **Phone:** 315/829-9999
◆ **Location:** On SR 5, 0.3 mi e of jct SR 31. SR 5 13476. **Hours:** 6 am-8 pm, Tues-Sat to 9 pm. Closed:
American 12/25. **Features:** casual dress; children's menu; carryout; salad bar; beer & wine only. Enjoy a nostalgic
diversion in the charming, old-fashioned dining room, which is decorated in a country style with pictures from
the 1950s. The restaurant is known for home-style cooking, such as roast pork and casseroles, and great baked goods.
Cards: AE, MC, VI. ✖️

TOWN & COUNTRY RESTAURANT **Lunch:** $3-$8 **Dinner:** $9-$26 **Phone:** 315/829-2450
◆◆ **Location:** SR 5, 0.3 mi w of jct SR 31. 5366 E Seneca St 13476. **Hours:** 7:30 am-10 pm, Sun-8 pm, Wed &
American Thurs 11:30 am-3:30 & 4-10 pm. Closed: 7/4, 12/25, Mon & Tues. **Reservations:** accepted.
Features: casual dress; children's menu; carryout; cocktails & lounge. No one will leave this restaurant
hungry, as it dishes up generous portions of such well-prepared food as steamed clams with kale and lemon and the
cooked-to-order filet. Latticework and plants throughout the dining room point to a homey atmosphere. **Cards:** MC, VI. ✖️

VERONA pop. 6,500

——— LODGING ———

TURNING STONE CASINO RESORT **Phone:** (315)361-7711
(AAA) [SAVE] 7/1-8/31 1P: $124-$174 2P: $124-$174 XP: $10 F16
◆◆◆ 5/1-6/30 1P: $109-$161 2P: $109-$161 XP: $10 F16
Resort 9/1-4/30 1P: $96-$150 2P: $96-$150 XP: $10 F16
Location: I-90, exit 33, follow signs. 5218 Patrick Rd 13478 (PO Box 126). Fax: 315/361-7665.
Terms: Package plans. **Facility:** 285 rooms. New York's only casino offers a wide variety of gaming activities
as well as spa and recreational facilities. All rooms with hair dryer, iron and ironing board. 4 stories; interior corridors; designated smoking area; putting green; heated pool, saunas, steamrooms, whirlpools, outdoor pool privileges. Fee: 9 hole executive course & lessons. **Dining:** Variety of dining outlets include ethnic, buffet, diner, American & formal; 24 hrs; $5-$35; health
conscious menu items; name entertainment, nightclub. **Services:** gift shop; area transportation, RV Park. Fee: massage.
Recreation: in-room video games, salon services, tanning bed. **All Rooms:** combo or shower baths. **Cards:** AE, CB, DI, DS,
MC, VI. [S] [icons] [24] [icons] [VALET] [icons] [DATA PORT] [icons]

VERONA BEACH pop. 900

——— RESTAURANT ———

SPAGHETTI FACTORY **Lunch:** $4-$7 **Dinner:** $10-$17 **Phone:** 315/762-9948
◆◆ **Location:** 6800 SR 13 13162. **Hours:** 11 am-9 pm, Sun noon-8 pm (5/31-9/7). Closed: 11/14-3/23.
Italian **Reservations:** accepted. **Features:** casual dress; children's menu; carryout; cocktails; a la carte. Prime
steaks and chops stand out on an Italian-American menu with about 40 generously portioned pasta dishes.
Skylights and vines hanging from beams give the dining room the atmosphere of a vineyard. Neatly uniformed servers are
pleasant. **Cards:** AE, DS, MC, VI. ✖️

VESTAL pop. 5,500

———— LODGINGS ————

HOLIDAY INN AT THE UNIVERSITY
Phone: (607)729-6371
AAA SAVE ◆◆◆ Motor Inn
All Year — 1P: $99 — 2P: $99 — XP: $10 — F12
Location: SR 17, exit 70 S, 2.5 mi s on US 201 to SR 434 W, right on Bunn Hill Rd into parking lot. 4105 Vestal Pkwy 13850. Fax: 607/729-6407. **Terms:** Weekly & monthly rates avail; check-in 4 pm; package plans. **Facility:** 145 rooms. 2 stories; interior/exterior corridors. **Dining:** Restaurant; 6:30 am-11 & 5-10 pm, Sun from 7 am; Sun brunch; $7-$15; cocktails. **All Rooms:** extended cable TV. **Cards:** AE, CB, DI, DS, JC, MC, VI.
Special Amenities: Early check-in/late check-out and preferred room (subject to availability with advanced reservations). *(See color ad p 205)*

HOWARD JOHNSON EXPRESS INN (SUNY)
Phone: (607)729-6181
◆◆ Motel
All Year — 1P: $45-$80 — 2P: $55-$90 — XP: $10 — F17
Location: SR 17, exit 70 S, 1 mi s on Rt 201 S, 0.5 mi w on Rt 434 W. 3601 Vestal Pkwy E 13850. Fax: 607/797-0309. **Terms:** [CP] meal plan; 3 day cancellation notice; pets, $10 fee. **Facility:** 58 rooms. Nicely decorated rooms in commercial area near SUNY Binghampton. 2 stories; interior corridors. **Some Rooms:** Fee: refrigerators, microwaves, VCR. **Cards:** AE, CB, DI, DS, MC, VI.

PARKWAY MOTEL
Phone: (607)785-3311
AAA SAVE ◆ Motel
All Year — 1P: $30-$45 — 2P: $45-$68 — XP: $15 — D12
Location: SR 17, exit 67 S to SR 434, then e. 900 Vestal Pkwy E 434 13851 (PO Box 363, 13850-0363). Fax: 607/785-8117. **Terms:** Weekly & monthly rates avail; 3 day cancellation notice; small pets only, $10 fee. **Facility:** 58 rooms. Some larger rooms. 1-2 stories; exterior corridors; smoke free premises. **Dining:** Restaurant nearby. **All Rooms:** combo or shower baths, extended cable TV. **Some Rooms:** 10 efficiencies.
Cards: AE, CB, DI, DS, MC, VI.

RESIDENCE INN BY MARRIOTT
Phone: (607)770-8500
◆◆◆ Apartment
All Year — 1P: $99-$150 — 2P: $99-$150
Location: SR 17, exit 70 S, 2.5 mi s on US 201, 1 mi e on SR 434 E, right on Plaza Dr to access road. 4610 Vestal Pkwy 13850. Fax: 607/770-6216. **Terms:** [CP] meal plan; pets, $10 extra charge, $250 dep req. **Facility:** 72 rooms. 18 two-bedroom units. 2 stories; exterior corridors; designated smoking area; heated pool. **Services:** area transportation. **Recreation:** sports court. **All Rooms:** kitchens. **Some Rooms:** Fee: VCR. **Cards:** AE, CB, DI, DS, JC, MC, VI.

———— RESTAURANT ————

THE VESTAL STEAKHOUSE & SEAFOOD GRILL
Dinner: $10-$25 — **Phone:** 607/798-7871
AAA ◆◆ Steakhouse
Location: 5 mi w on SR 434, 3 mi e of jct SR 17, exit 67 S. 3401 Vestal Pkwy 13850. **Hours:** 4 pm-9:30 pm, Fri & Sat-10:30 pm, Sun 4 pm-9 pm. **Reservations:** suggested. **Features:** casual dress; early bird specials; cocktails & lounge. The independently owned restaurant is as popular for its casual, eclectic decor—ranging from ceramic animal heads to Mexican art—as for its seasoned preparations of black Angus beef and fresh seafood. Servers are knowledgeable and attentive. **Cards:** AE, CB, DI, DS, MC, VI.

VICTOR pop. 2,300—*See also FINGER LAKES.*

———— LODGINGS ————

EXIT 45 MOTEL
Phone: (716)924-2121
AAA SAVE ◆ Motel
All Year — 1P: $36-$54 — 2P: $43-$70 — XP: $8 — F8
Location: SR 96, 0.8 mi s of I-90, exit 45. 7463 SR 96 14564. Fax: 716/924-0468. **Facility:** 34 rooms. Simple rooms. 1 two-bedroom unit. 1 story; exterior corridors. **Dining:** Restaurant nearby. **Cards:** AE, DI, DS, MC, VI.

HAMPTON INN AND SUITES-ROCHESTER/VICTOR
Phone: (716)924-4400
◆◆◆ Motel
5/1-8/31 — 1P: $99-$119 — 2P: $109-$129
9/1-4/30 — 1P: $95-$110 — 2P: $105-$120
Location: Just n of I-90, exit 45. 7637 NY SR 96 14564. Fax: 716/924-4478. **Terms:** [CP] meal plan; 3 day cancellation notice; cancellation fee imposed. **Facility:** 123 rooms. 3 stories; interior corridors; heated pool. **All Rooms:** combo or shower baths. **Some Rooms:** 55 kitchens. **Cards:** AE, DI, DS, MC, VI.

MICROTEL
Phone: (716)924-9240
AAA SAVE ◆◆
Motel
5/1-8/31 — 1P: $54-$64 — 2P: $54-$64 — XP: $5 — F18
9/1-10/26 — 1P: $49-$59 — 2P: $49-$59 — XP: $5 — F18
10/27-4/30 — 1P: $44-$54 — 2P: $44-$54 — XP: $5 — F18
Location: Just off SR 96, s of I-90, exit 45. 7498 Main St Fishers 14564. Fax: 716/924-9241. **Terms:** 7 day cancellation notice; cancellation fee imposed; pets. **Facility:** 99 rooms. Small single rooms. Suite avail with microwave, coffeemaker, refrigerator & room safe; 2 stories; interior corridors. **Dining:** Restaurant nearby. **Recreation:** Fee: in room video games. **All Rooms:** combo or shower baths. **Some Rooms:** safes. **Cards:** AE, DI, DS, MC, VI. *(See ad p 256)*

—— RESTAURANT ——

LOLIS FAMILY RESTAURANT   **Lunch:** $3-$7   **Dinner:** $5-$8   **Phone:** 716/924-5025
◆   **Location:** Downtown; 2.5 mi s of I-90, exit 45. 34 E Main St 14564. **Hours:** 5:30 am-9 pm, Sun-3 pm.
American   Closed: 12/25. **Reservations:** accepted. **Features:** casual dress; children's menu; carryout. Locals frequent
the casual, neighborhood restaurant for friendly service and home-style meals. Homemade soups change
daily, as do lunch and dinner specials of modest—but good—food. The warm, inviting atmosphere is particularly appealing
to families. **Cards:** AE, DS, MC, VI.   ✕

WARRENSBURG pop. 4,200—See also ADIRONDACK MOUNTAINS.

—— LODGING ——

ALYNN'S BUTTERFLY INN BED & BREAKFAST   **Phone:** 518/623-9390
◆◆   All Year   1P: $89-$129   2P: $99-$139   XP: $15
Bed &   **Location:** I-87, exit 23, 3.3 mi n on SR 9, just w. Rt 28 W 12885 (PO Box 248). Fax: 518/623-9396.
Breakfast   **Terms:** [BP] meal plan; 14 day cancellation notice; 2 night min stay, 7/1-8/31; package plans; pets, pet on
premises. **Facility:** 4 rooms. In rural area on 176 acres. Individually decorated guest rooms. 2 stories; interior
corridors; smoke free premises. **Recreation:** cross country skiing; hiking trails. **Cards:** AE, DS, MC, VI.

ASK ⬛ ⬛ ✕ ⬛ ⬛ ⬛ ⬛ ✕

—— RESTAURANT ——

MERRILL MAGEE HOUSE   Country Inn   **Dinner:** $15-$27   **Phone:** 518/623-2449
◆◆   **Location:** Center; opposite bandstand. 2 Hudson St 12885. **Hours:** 5 pm-9 pm. Closed: 12/25.
Continental   **Reservations:** suggested. **Features:** casual dress; carryout; cocktails & lounge. Rack of lamb and beef
Wellington are house specialties at the casual, Victorian inn. Soft background music and attractive table
settings lend to a romantic and modestly elegant ambience. The apple crisp dessert is a lightly sweet end to a nice meal.
Cards: AE, CB, DI, DS, MC, VI.   ✕

WARWICK pop. 6,000

—— RESTAURANTS ——

CHATEAU HATHORN   Country Inn   **Dinner:** $18-$24   **Phone:** 914/986-6099
◆◆◆   **Location:** 1 mi sw on SR 94 from jct SR 17A. 33 Hathorn Rd 10990. **Hours:** 5 pm-9 pm, Sat-10 pm, Sun 3
Continental   pm-8 pm. Closed: 12/24, 12/25, Mon & Tues. **Reservations:** suggested. **Features:** dressy casual; health
conscious menu items; cocktails & lounge; a la carte. On a small hill surrounded by impressive landscaping,
the remarkable mansion features cathedral ceilings and windows that afford beautiful views. Thoughtfully presented seafood,
chicken and steak dishes are complemented by a superior wine list. **Cards:** AE, MC, VI.   ✕

WARWICK INN   Historical   **Dinner:** $13-$24   **Phone:** 914/986-3666
◆◆◆   **Location:** Center; on SR 94 and 17A. 36 Oakland Ave (SR 94 & 17A) 10990. **Hours:** 5 pm-9 pm, Sun 1
American   pm-7 pm. Closed: 12/24, 12/25, Mon, Tues & 1/19-2/3. **Reservations:** suggested; weekends.
Features: casual dress; children's menu; health conscious menu items; salad bar; cocktails & lounge. A
turn-of-the-20th-century ambience infuses the old Victorian home, which is decorated with antiques, crown molding and
stained glass. The restaurant's signature is fresh seafood, such as the delicious pistachio-encrusted salmon with honey
glaze. **Cards:** AE, DI, MC, VI.   ✕

WATERLOO pop. 5,100—See also FINGER LAKES.

—— LODGING ——

HOLIDAY INN WATERLOO-SENECA FALLS   **Phone:** (315)539-5011

7/1-9/30	1P: $119-$139	2P: $119-$139
5/1-6/30	1P: $79-$129	2P: $79-$129
3/1-4/30	1P: $79-$119	2P: $79-$119
10/1-2/28	1P: $69-$99	2P: $69-$99

Motor Inn   **Location:** SR 414, 0.5 mi n at jct US 20 and 5, 4 mi s of I-90, exit 41. 2468 SR 414 13165 (PO Box 149).
Fax: 315/539-8355. **Terms:** Pets. **Facility:** 148 rooms. Very well kept. 4 whirlpool rooms, $139-$229; 2 stories; interior corridors; heated pool, sauna, whirlpool; 1 tennis court. **Dining:** Dining room; 6:30 am-10 pm; to 9 pm, in winter; $9-$20; cocktails.
All Rooms: extended cable TV. **Cards:** AE, CB, DI, DS, JC, MC, VI. **Special Amenities:** Early check-in/late check-out and
free local telephone calls. (See color ad p 257)

⬛ ⬛ ⬛ ⬛ ⬛ ⬛ ✕ ⬛ ⬛ ⬛ ⬛ ⬛ ⬛ ⬛ ✕

WATERTOWN pop. 29,400

—— LODGINGS ——

DAVIDSON'S MOTEL   **Phone:** (315)782-3861

5/1-10/31	1P: $35-$39	2P: $45-$49	XP: $5 F12
11/1-4/30	1P: $32-$37	2P: $39-$42	XP: $5 F12

Motel   **Location:** 3.5 mi e on SR 3 from Town Square. 26177 NYS Rt 3 13601. Fax: 315/786-0599. **Terms:** Weekly
rates avail, off season. **Facility:** 19 rooms. Spacious wooded grounds with 2 beaver ponds. Modestly furnished
1 story; exterior corridors; heated pool. **Recreation:** hiking trails, grills, picnic tables.
All Rooms: combo or shower baths. **Some Rooms:** Fee: refrigerators, microwaves. **Cards:** AE, DS, MC, VI.

DAYS INN
◆◆ Motor Inn

Phone: (315)782-2700

	7/4-10/1	1P: $78	2P: $83
	5/1-7/3	1P: $66	2P: $71
	10/2-4/30	1P: $64	2P: $69

Location: I-81, exit 45, 0.5 mi e. 110 Commerce Park Dr 13601. Fax: 315/782-7691. **Terms:** 30 day cancellation notice; cancellation fee imposed; package plans. **Facility:** 135 rooms. 20 three-bedroom units. 6 stories; interior corridors; heated pool. **Services:** area transportation. **Some Rooms:** 20 efficiencies. **Cards:** AE, DI, DS, JC, MC, VI.

THE INN
◆◆ Motel

Phone: (315)788-6800

| | All Year | 1P: $50-$56 | 2P: $60-$70 | XP: $6 | F16 |

Location: I-81, exit 45, 0.3 mi e. 1190 Arsenal St 13601. Fax: 315/788-5366. **Terms:** Pets. **Facility:** 96 rooms. 2 stories; interior corridors; heated pool. **Services:** winter plug-ins. **Cards:** AE, DI, DS, MC, VI.

RAMADA INN
◆◆ Motor Inn

Phone: (315)788-0700

| | 5/1-10/31 | 1P: $64 | 2P: $64 | XP: $10 | F18 |
| | 11/1-4/30 | 1P: $51 | 2P: $51 | XP: $10 | F18 |

Location: I-81, exit 45. 6300 Arsenal St 13601. Fax: 315/785-9875. **Terms:** Package plans; pets, $200 dep req. **Facility:** 145 rooms. 4 stories; interior corridors. **Cards:** AE, DI, DS, MC, VI.

--- **RESTAURANT** ---

PARTRIDGE BERRY INN   Country Inn
◆◆ American

Dinner: $8-$20   **Phone:** 315/788-4610

Location: 4.5 mi e on SR 3 from Public Square; Black River Rd. 26561 SR 3 13601. **Hours:** 4:30 pm-9 pm, Sun 11:30 am-2:30 & 4-8 pm. Closed: 12/24. **Reservations:** suggested. **Features:** casual dress; Sunday brunch; children's menu; cocktails & lounge; a la carte. Sunday brunch and succulent prime rib are favorite offerings at the rustic inn, which is tidily appointed with antiques. The signature veal a la Partridge Berry Inn is well-prepared and flavorful. Casually uniformed servers provide skilled attention. **Cards:** AE, MC, VI.

WATKINS GLEN   pop. 2,200—*See also FINGER LAKES.*

--- **LODGINGS** ---

BELLEVUE MOTEL
◆◆ Motel

Phone: (607)535-4232

| | 5/26-9/17 | 1P: $55-$75 | 2P: $65-$85 | XP: $10 | F7 |
| | 5/1-5/25 & 9/18-11/25 | 1P: $45-$65 | 2P: $65-$75 | XP: $10 | F7 |

Location: 3 mi on SR 14, at jct SR 14A. 3812 SR 14 14891. Fax: 607/535-4669. **Terms:** Open 5/1-11/25; [CP] meal plan; weekly rates avail; 5 day cancellation notice; cancellation fee imposed. **Facility:** 13 rooms. 1940s era motor court motel on rural hillside but near town, overlooking Seneca Lake. 1 three-bedroom unit, 2 two-bedroom units. Efficiency units, $15 extra charge; gas grills, $2 extra charge; 1 story; exterior corridors. **All Rooms:** combo or shower baths. **Cards:** AE, DS, MC, VI. **Special Amenities: Free breakfast and preferred room (subject to availability with advanced reservations).**

CHIEFTAIN MOTEL
◆ Motel

Phone: (607)535-4759

| | 5/26-9/10 | 1P: $49-$69 | 2P: $49-$69 | XP: $5 | F5 |
| | 5/1-5/25 & 9/11-10/31 | 1P: $39-$69 | 2P: $39-$69 | XP: $5 | F5 |

Location: 3 mi n on SR 14, at jct SR 14A. 3815 SR 14 14891. Fax: 607/535-6091. **Terms:** Open 5/1-10/31; weekly & monthly rates avail; 5 day cancellation notice; cancellation fee imposed; small pets only, $25 dep req. **Facility:** 14 rooms. Scenic valley view. Open weekends 11/1-11/30. 2 two-bedroom units. 1 efficiency, $10 extra charge; 1 story; exterior corridors. **All Rooms:** combo or shower baths. **Some Rooms:** Fee: refrigerators, microwaves, VCR. **Cards:** AE, DS, MC, VI. **Special Amenities: Early check-in/late check-out and preferred room (subject to availability with advanced reservations).**

LONGHOUSE LODGE MOTEL
◆◆◆ Motel

Phone: 607/535-2565

| | 5/1-10/31 | 1P: $59-$129 | 2P: $69-$139 | XP: $5 | F17 |
| | 11/1-4/30 | 1P: $49-$119 | 2P: $59-$129 | XP: $5 | F17 |

Location: 2 mi n on SR 14 at Abrams Rd. 3625 SR 14 14891. Fax: 607/535-5415. **Terms:** [CP] meal plan; 7 day cancellation notice; cancellation fee imposed. **Facility:** 21 rooms. Scenic valley view; very tastefully decorated. 1 efficiency, $10 extra charge; 1 story; exterior corridors. **Recreation:** exercise equipment. **All Rooms:** combo or shower baths. **Some Rooms:** Fee: VCR. **Cards:** AE, DS, MC, VI.

LONGHOUSE MANOR
◆◆◆ Bed & Breakfast

Phone: 607/535-2565

| | All Year | 1P: $110-$150 | 2P: $110-$150 | XP: $15 |

Location: 2 mi n on SR 14 at Abrams Rd. 3137 Abrams Rd 14891 (PO Box 111). **Terms:** [BP] meal plan; age restrictions may apply; 10 day cancellation notice. **Facility:** 4 rooms. Finely appointed spacious rooms, grounds enjoy beautiful view overlooking Seneca Lake. 1 story; interior corridors; heated pool. **Recreation:** billiards, board games, ping pong. **All Rooms:** extended cable TV. **Cards:** AE, DS, MC.

QUEEN CATHERINE MOTEL
◆ Motel

Phone: (607)535-2441

| | 5/1-10/31 | 1P: $45-$65 | 2P: $55-$75 | XP: $5 | F16 |
| | 11/1-4/30 | 1P: $35-$55 | 2P: $45-$65 | XP: $5 | F16 |

Location: On SR 14, just s from jct SR 14 and 414 W. 436 S Franklin St 14891. Fax: 607/535-4340. **Terms:** [CP] meal plan; 7 day cancellation notice. **Facility:** 15 rooms. Quiet relaxing atmosphere close to downtown attractions. 1 story; exterior corridors. **Dining:** Restaurant nearby. **Services:** winter plug-ins. **All Rooms:** extended cable TV. **Cards:** AE, DS, MC, VI. **Special Amenities: Free breakfast and free local telephone calls.**

THE SENECA LAKE WATCH BED & BREAKFAST
◆◆◆
Bed &
Breakfast

5/1-11/30	1P: $85-$115	2P: $85-$115
12/1-4/30	1P: $65-$95	2P: $65-$95

Phone: 607/535-4490
XP: $20

Location: On SR 14, 0.6 mi n from jct SR 14, 414 E and 329. 104 Seneca St 14891. **Terms:** [BP] meal plan; age restrictions may apply; 14 day cancellation notice; 2 night min stay, weekends in season. **Facility:** 5 rooms. Completely restored circa 1890 Victorian mansion with wraparound porch featuring view of Seneca Lake. 2 stories; interior corridors; designated smoking area. **All Rooms:** shower baths. **Cards:** AE, MC, VI.

——— RESTAURANTS ———

FRANKLIN STREET GRILLE   Lunch: $4-$8   Dinner: $8-$25   Phone: 607/535-2007
◆
American
Location: Downtown; SR 14. 413 N Franklin St 14891. **Hours:** 11:30 am-9 pm, Fri & Sat-10 pm. Closed: 11/23 & 12/25. **Reservations:** accepted. **Features:** casual dress; children's menu; health conscious menu items; carryout; cocktails & lounge. Louisiana crab dip and juicy steaks are divine at the friendly family restaurant, an established favorite with the locals. A distinctive mural details 50 years of racing in the streets of Watkins Glen. A pianist performs on Friday and Saturday nights. **Cards:** AE, MC, VI.

SEASONS   Dinner: $15-$30   Phone: 607/535-4619
◆◆
American
Location: Center; on SR 14. 108 N Franklin St 14891. **Hours:** 5:30 pm-9:30 pm 4/1-10/31; 5:30 pm-9 pm, Sun & Mon 5:30 pm-8:30 pm. Closed: 1/1, 11/23, 12/24-12/26, Tues & Wed off season. **Reservations:** suggested. **Features:** casual dress; children's menu; health conscious menu items; carryout; cocktails & lounge. The late-19th-century building stretches three stories and is decorated with granite trim, racing pictures and local memorabilia. The seasonal menu delivers regional American fare, which is complemented by a wine list that emphasizes New York choices. **Cards:** AE, DI, DS, MC, VI.

WILDFLOWER CAFE   Lunch: $5-$8   Dinner: $12-$22   Phone: 607/535-9797
◆◆
American
Location: Downtown; on SR 14. 301 N Franklin St 14891. **Hours:** 11 am-2 & 5-9 pm. Closed: 1/1, 11/23, 12/25, Mon & Tues. **Reservations:** accepted. **Features:** casual dress; children's menu; health conscious menu items; carryout; cocktails & lounge; street parking. Fine art hangs throughout the moderately upscale dining room, a favorite spot for out-of-towners. The broad menu centers on Northern Italian cuisine, with assorted game selections as well as Cajun entrees. Homemade desserts provide much temptation. Smoke free premises. **Cards:** AE, MC, VI.

——— *The following restaurant has not been inspected by AAA* ———
but is listed for your information only.

JERLANDO'S RISTORANTE   Phone: 607/535-4254
[fyi]
Not inspected. **Location:** 400 N Franklin St 14891. **Features:** This is casual, family-style dining in a smoke-free atmosphere with a variety of seafood, steak, veal and Italian dishes on the menu. Pizza also is popular.

WEBSTER pop. 5,500

——— LODGINGS ———

FAIRFIELD INN ROCHESTER EAST/WEBSTER   Phone: (716)671-1500
◆◆◆
Motel
All Year   1P: $79-$89   2P: $79-$89
Location: Just s on Hard Rd from SR 104, exit Hard Rd. 915 Hard Rd 14580. Fax: 716/671-1610. **Terms:** [CP] meal plan. **Facility:** 63 rooms. 3 stories; interior corridors; heated pool. **All Rooms:** combo or shower baths. **Cards:** AE, DI, DS, MC, VI.

WEBSTER SUPER 8 MOTEL   Phone: 716/671-6990
(AAA)
◆◆
Motel
All Year   1P: $43-$60   2P: $48-$65   XP: $5   F12
Location: I-590, exit 8, 3.7 mi e on SR 404. 2450 Empire Blvd 14580. Fax: 716/671-7494. **Terms:** [CP] meal plan; cancellation fee imposed. **Facility:** 42 rooms. Neatly kept rooms furnished with white wood furniture. 10 rooms with sleeper sofa. 4 whirlpool rooms, $55-$70; 2 stories; interior corridors. **All Rooms:** extended cable TV. **Cards:** AE, DI, DS, MC, VI.

WEEDSPORT pop. 2,000—See also FINGER LAKES.

——— LODGINGS ———

BEST WESTERN WEEDSPORT INN   Phone: (315)834-6623
◆◆
Motel

5/1-8/31	1P: $59-$99	2P: $69-$110	XP: $10	F11
9/1-10/31	1P: $54-$99	2P: $54-$99
4/1-4/30	1P: $45-$50	2P: $50-$55
11/1-3/31	1P: $40-$45	2P: $45-$50

Location: 0.3 mi w on SR 31 from jct SR 34; 0.5 mi sw of I-90, exit 40. 2709 Erie Dr 13166. Fax: 315/834-6626. **Terms:** [CP] meal plan; small pets only, $10 extra charge. **Facility:** 34 rooms. Comfortable guest rooms with pleasant decor. 1 story; exterior corridors. **Cards:** AE, CB, DI, DS, MC, VI.

DAYS INN-WEEDSPORT   Phone: 315/834-6198
(AAA)
◆◆
Motel
All Year   1P: $59-$99   2P: $64-$125   XP: $5   F12
Location: Just s of I-90, exit 40; at jct SR 31 and 34. 9050 SR 34 13166. Fax: 315/834-9849. **Terms:** [CP] meal plan. **Facility:** 40 rooms. Modern guest rooms. 2 whirlpool suites, $75-$150 for up to 2 persons; 2 stories; exterior corridors. **All Rooms:** combo or shower baths, extended cable TV. **Cards:** AE, DS, MC, VI.

WELLSVILLE pop. 5,200

——— LODGING ———

LONG-VUE MOTEL
Phone: (716)593-2450

(AAA) (SAVE) All Year 1P: $55-$85 2P: $65-$100 XP: $10 F11
◆◆ **Location:** 3 mi w on SR 417 from jct SR 19. 5081 Rt 417 W 14895 (PO Box 287). Fax: 716/593-2450.
Motel **Terms:** Weekly rates avail; 30 day cancellation notice. **Facility:** 19 rooms. Modest, traditional motel with spectacular views of the valley below. 1 story; exterior corridors. **Services:** winter plug-ins. **Recreation:** video tapes. **All Rooms:** combo or shower baths, extended cable TV. **Some Rooms:** Fee: refrigerators, microwaves.
Cards: AE, MC, VI.

[icons]

WESTFIELD pop. 3,500

——— LODGING ———

THE WILLIAM SEWARD INN
Phone: (716)326-4151
◆◆◆ All Year 1P: $60-$155 2P: $70-$165 XP: $25 D10
Historic **Location:** SR 394, 4 mi s of I-90, exit 60. 6645 S Portage Rd 14787. Fax: 716/326-4163. **Terms:** [BP] meal
Country Inn plan; age limitations may apply; 3 day cancellation notice; package plans. **Facility:** 12 rooms. Historic mansion. Rooms individually appointed with period antiques, many with highpost beds. 2 stories; interior corridors; smoke free premises. **All Rooms:** combo or shower baths. **Some Rooms:** color TV. **Cards:** AE, DS, MC, VI.

[icons]

WEST HENRIETTA pop. 700   (See map p. 456; index p. 455)—

——— RESTAURANT ———

THE CARTWRIGHT INN **Lunch:** $5-$9 **Dinner:** $10-$20 **Phone:** 716/334-4444 (22)
(AAA) **Location:** On SR 15; at jct SR 253, 0.8 mi s of I-90 Thruway overpass. 5691 W Henrietta Rd 14586.
◆◆ **Hours:** 11:30 am-10 pm, Sat-10:30 pm, Sun 12:30 pm-9:30 pm. **Reservations:** suggested. **Features:** casual
American dress; children's menu; early bird specials; carryout; cocktails & lounge; a la carte. The well-established restaurant caters to a varied clientele that includes everyone from business travelers to families. Prime rib and New England clam chowder stand out on a menu of mostly surf and turf choices. Service is prompt and efficient. **Cards:** AE, DI, DS, MC, VI.

[icon]

WEST ISLIP pop. 29,500

——— RESTAURANT ———

LA GRANGE INN **Lunch:** $11 **Dinner:** $15-$25 **Phone:** 631/669-0765
(AAA) **Location:** 1 mi e on SR 27A (Montauk Hwy) at Higbie Ln, 1 mi w of Robert Moses Cswy, exit 2. 499
◆◆◆ Montauk Hwy 11795. **Hours:** noon-9 pm, Wed & Thurs-10 pm, Fri-11 pm, Sat 2 pm-11 pm. Closed: 12/24 &
Continental Tues. **Reservations:** suggested. **Features:** semi-formal attire; Sunday brunch; children's menu; early bird specials; cocktails & lounge. Sauerbraten is among delicious German specialties on the restaurant's traditional menu. The atmosphere is serene and welcoming, with bright, homelike decor. Twice a week, on Monday and Thursday, a lunch buffet lays out a great assortment of dishes. **Cards:** AE, DI, DS, MC, VI.

[icon]

WESTMORELAND pop. 5,700

——— LODGING ———

CARRIAGE MOTOR INN
Phone: (315)853-3561
(AAA) (SAVE) 5/1-10/31 1P: $38-$42 2P: $45-$48 XP: $5 F8
◆ 11/1-4/30 1P: $33-$36 2P: $42-$45 XP: $5 F8
Motel **Location:** SR 233, just n at exit 32, I-90 Thruway. SR 233 13490 (PO Box 379). Fax: 315/853-3563.
Terms: Weekly rates avail; 5 day cancellation notice; small pets only, $5 extra charge, $5 dep req. **Facility:** 24 rooms. Variety of rooms, set back on spacious grounds. 1 two-bedroom unit. 1-2 stories; exterior corridors.
Services: winter plug-ins. **All Rooms:** shower baths, extended cable TV. **Cards:** AE, CB, DI, DS, MC, VI. **Special Amenities:** Free breakfast and free local telephone calls. *(See ad p 484)*

[icons]

WEST POINT pop. 8,000

WHEATFIELD —See Niagara Falls p. 396.

WHITEHALL pop. 3,100—See also ADIRONDACK MOUNTAINS.

——— **LODGING** ———

FINCH & CHUBB INN
Phone: (518)499-2049
◆   All Year   1P: $39-$59   2P: $69-$89   XP: $15   F7
Motor Inn   **Location:** From Rt 4, 0.7 mi ne. 82 N William St 12887. Fax: 518/499-2049. **Terms:** Cancellation fee imposed.
Facility: 6 rooms. Located near Lock 12, overlooking the entrance to Lake Champlain. Small modestly furnished guest rooms to spacious suites with lovely view. Wine shop. 2 two-bedroom units. 2 stories; interior corridors; designated smoking area. Fee: marina. **Services:** gift shop. **Recreation:** fishing. Rental: canoes. **All Rooms:** combo or shower baths. **Some Rooms:** efficiency, kitchen. **Cards:** AE, CB, DI, DS, MC, VI.

------ RESTAURANT ------

FINCH & CHUBB INN & RESTAURANT   **Lunch:** $5-$10   **Dinner:** $9-$24   **Phone:** 518/499-2049
(AAA)   **Location:** From Rt 4, 0.7 mi ne. 82 N Williams St 12887. **Hours:** 11:30 am-2 & 4:30-9 pm. Closed: Mon &
◆◆   lunch in winter. **Reservations:** suggested. **Features:** casual dress; children's menu; early bird specials;
Continental   cocktails & lounge. The owner/chef prepares such down-home favorites as French onion soup, fresh seafood
          and homemade apple crisp a la mode. Tables in the dining room afford great views of the lock and Lake
          Champlain. The sounds of classical music hang in the air. **Cards:** AE, CB, DS, MC, VI.   ⊠

WHITE PLAINS —See New York p. 378.

WHITNEY POINT pop. 1,100

------ LODGING ------

POINT MOTEL   **Phone:** (607)692-4451
(AAA) [SAVE]   All Year   1P: $33-$40   2P: $37-$45   XP: $4   D14
◆   **Location:** US 11, just e of I-81, exit 8. 2961 US 11 13862 (PO Box 468). Fax: 607/692-4450. **Facility:** 13
Motel   rooms. Small, but attractive, comfortable rooms. 1 story; exterior corridors. **Dining:** Restaurant nearby.
          Recreation: Whitney Point Reservoir nearby. **All Rooms:** combo or shower baths. **Cards:** AE, DS, MC, VI.
          Special Amenities: Free local telephone calls.   [S⊘] [ⁱ‖⁺] [△] [⊠] [📽] [📠]

------ RESTAURANT ------

AIELLO'S RESTAURANT/PIZZERIA   **Lunch:** $2-$5   **Dinner:** $7-$15   **Phone:** 607/692-4114
◆◆   **Location:** I-81, exit 8, 1 mi s; downtown. SR 11 & Main St 13862. **Hours:** 11 am-10 pm, Fri & Sat-10:30 pm.
American   Closed: 11/23 & 12/25. **Reservations:** suggested. **Features:** casual dress; children's menu; health
          conscious menu items; carryout; cocktails. The established restaurant does a booming business with the
locals who have come here for years. Seafood-stuffed mushrooms are a favorite appetizer, while homemade tiramisu is sure
to tame a sweet tooth. Interesting pictures hang on the walls. **Cards:** AE, DS, MC, VI.   ⊠

WILLIAMSVILLE —See Buffalo p. 226.

WILLISTON PARK pop. 7,500

------ RESTAURANT ------

RIVERBAY SEAFOOD BAR & GRILL   **Lunch:** $8-$13   **Dinner:** $12-$22   **Phone:** 516/742-9191
◆◆   **Location:** L I E exit 37, NSP exit 28 S, 1.5 mi s. 700 Willis Ave 11596. **Hours:** noon-4 & 5-10 pm, Fri-11 pm,
Seafood   Sat 5 pm-11 pm, Sun 11:30 am-9:30 pm. Closed: 11/23 & 12/25. **Features:** casual dress; Sunday brunch;
          health conscious menu; cocktails & lounge; a la carte. Rich, mahogany beams, antique light fixtures and
beveled glass add to the comfortable charm of the relaxed dining room. Many varieties of oysters are among well-prepared
selections of fresh seafood, nicely complemented by a lengthy wine list. **Cards:** AE, DI, MC, VI.   ⊠

WILMINGTON pop. 1,000—See also ADIRONDACK MOUNTAINS.

------ LODGINGS ------

FOUR SEASONS MOTOR LODGE AT WHITEFACE MOUNTAIN   **Phone:** (518)946-2247
(AAA) [SAVE]   11/18-3/31   1P: $74-$104   2P: $74-$104
◆◆   5/1-9/4   1P: $56-$104   2P: $56-$104
Motel   9/5-11/17 & 4/1-4/30   1P: $56-$87   2P: $56-$87
          Location: Jct SR 86 and Whiteface Mt Hwy (SR 431). SR 86 12997 (HCR 2 Box 12). Fax: 518/946-7158.
          Terms: Package plans. **Facility:** 26 rooms. Variety of room styles. 2 two-bedroom units. Max rate for up to 4
persons. 2 two-room suites, $20 extra charge. Kitchenette, $30 extra charge; 2 stories; interior/exterior corridors; wading pool;
playground. **Dining:** Restaurant; 6:30 am-9 pm; cocktails. **All Rooms:** combo or shower baths, extended cable TV.
Some Rooms: kitchen. **Cards:** DS, MC, VI. **Special Amenities:** Early check-in/late check-out and free local telephone
calls. (See color ad p 295)   [S⊘] [‖] [⊠] [▭] [▤] [🛏] [🛆] [⊠]

GRAND VIEW MOTEL   **Phone:** (518)946-2209
(AAA) [SAVE]   12/26-3/26   1P: $62-$82   2P: $69-$89
◆   5/26-10/10   1P: $52-$72   2P: $62-$82
Motel   **Location:** 1 mi e. SR 86 12997. **Terms:** Open 5/26-10/10 & 12/26-3/26; weekly rates avail; small pets only.
          Facility: 17 rooms. Scenic view of Whiteface Mountain. Well kept rooms. 1 story; exterior corridors; designated
          smoking area; playground. **All Rooms:** shower baths. **Cards:** MC, VI. **Special Amenities:** Free room up-
grade and preferred room (each subject to availability with advanced reservations).   [S⊘] [🛏] [⊠] [▤] [🛆] [⊠]

HUNGRY TROUT MOTOR INN

Phone: (518)946-2217

(AAA) [SAVE]
◆ ◆
Motor Inn

7/1-8/31	1P: $69-$89	2P: $89-$139
9/1-10/31	1P: $59-$89	2P: $69-$139
12/20-3/31	1P: $49-$89	2P: $59-$139
5/1-6/30	1P: $59-$79	2P: $69-$89

Location: 2 mi w. SR 86 12997. Fax: 518/946-7418. **Terms:** Open 5/1-10/31 & 12/20-3/31; [BP] & [MAP] meal plans; 7 day cancellation notice; cancellation fee imposed; package plans; pets. **Facility:** 20 rooms. On the Ausable River. Scenic mountain views. 2 two-bedroom units. 2 efficiencies, $89-$139; 1 story; exterior corridors; designated smoking area; wading pool; playground. **Dining:** Cocktails; restaurant, see separate listing. **Recreation:** fishing, fly shop, private fly fishing waters & hunting. **All Rooms:** extended cable TV. **Some Rooms:** Fee: refrigerators. **Cards:** AE, DS, MC, VI. **Special Amenities:** Early check-in/late check-out and free local telephone calls.

LEDGE ROCK AT WHITEFACE MOUNTAIN

Phone: (518)946-2379

(AAA) [SAVE]
◆ ◆
Motel

6/16-10/13 & 11/16-4/30	1P: $79-$120	2P: $79-$120
5/1-6/15	1P: $56-$120	2P: $56-$120
10/14-11/15	1P: $56-$110	2P: $56-$110

Location: 3 mi sw on SR 86. Placid Rd, SR 86 12997 (HCR 1, Box 34). Fax: 518/946-7594. **Terms:** [MAP] meal plan; 10 day cancellation notice; cancellation fee imposed; package plans; pets. **Facility:** 19 rooms. Set back from main road on small hill. Magnificent view, directly facing Whiteface Mountain. Some rooms with balcony. A few modest rooms, most are good sized units. 3 two-bedroom units & efficiency, $100-$159; 2 stories; exterior corridors; playground. **Recreation:** paddleboats; cross country skiing, ice skating, tobogganing; game room with VCR, movies avail. **All Rooms:** extended cable TV. **Some Rooms:** kitchen. **Cards:** AE, DS, MC, VI. **Special Amenities:** Early check-in/late check-out and free local telephone calls. *(See color ad p 295)*

NORTH POLE MOTOR INN

Phone: (518)946-7733

(AAA) [SAVE]
◆ ◆
Motel

All Year	1P: $59-$79	2P: $59-$79	XP: $5 F15

Location: 1 mi sw. SR 86 12997 (PO Box 68). Fax: 518/946-7705. **Terms:** Weekly rates avail; 7 day cancellation notice; cancellation fee imposed; package plans; pets. **Facility:** 20 rooms. Few modest rooms. TV room with fireplace. Family room, $79-$89; housekeeping cottages with full kitchen & gas fireplace; 1-2 stories; exterior corridors; heated pool, wading pool; playground. Fee: miniature golf. **Services:** winter plug-ins. **Recreation:** fishing; shared recreational facilities with adjacent campground. **All Rooms:** combo or shower baths, extended cable TV. **Cards:** DS, MC, VI. **Special Amenities:** Early check-in/late check-out and free room upgrade (subject to availability with advanced reservations).

------ RESTAURANT ------

HUNGRY TROUT RESTAURANT

Dinner: $14-$19   **Phone:** 518/946-2217

◆ ◆
Seafood

Location: 2 mi w; in Hungry Trout Motor Inn. SR 86 12997. **Hours:** Open 5/1-10/21 & 12/26-4/15; 5 pm-10 pm. **Reservations:** suggested. **Features:** casual dress; children's menu; health conscious menu; carryout; cocktails & lounge; a la carte. Overlooking the west branch of the Ausable River, the dining room has large windows that accentuate the view. Although mountain trout is the specialty, the menu also includes poultry, beef, game and other seafood. Servers are prompt and courteous. **Cards:** AE, CB, DS, MC, VI.

WILTON pop. 10,600

------ RESTAURANT ------

CHEZ PIERRE RESTAURANT

Dinner: $14-$23   **Phone:** 518/793-3350

◆ ◆
French

Location: 3 mi w of jct I-87 Northway, exit 17 S. 340 Rt 9 12831. **Hours:** 5 pm-10 pm, Sun 4 pm-9 pm. Closed: 12/24 & 12/25. **Reservations:** suggested. **Features:** casual dress; children's menu; carryout; cocktails & lounge. Family-owned and operated since the mid-1960s, the restaurant delivers provincial French cuisine, such as pepper steak flambe, veal Oscar and chateaubriand. An Eiffel tower sign out front, as well as Parisian bistro furnishings, help to set the mood. **Cards:** AE, MC, VI.

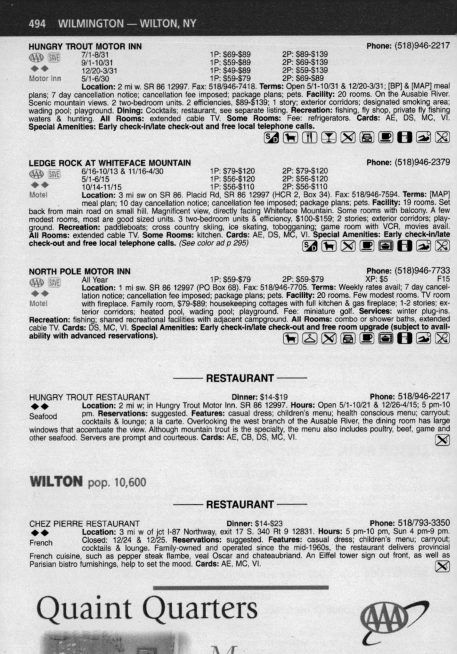

WINDHAM pop. 1,700

—— LODGING ——

ALBERGO ALLEGRIA HISTORIC BED & BREAKFAST **Phone:** (518)734-5560

9/16-4/30	1P: $73-$183	2P: $73-$183	XP: $25
5/1-9/15	1P: $73-$133	2P: $73-$133	XP: $25

Bed &
Breakfast

Location: SR 23, just s on SR 296. (Rt 296, Box 267, 12496). Fax: 518/734-5570. **Terms:** [BP] meal plan; 14 day cancellation notice; cancellation fee imposed; 2 night min stay, weekends; package plans; pets on premises. **Facility:** 21 rooms. A variety of individually decorated large rooms. Near ski slopes. 1 two-bedroom unit. 8 rooms with fireplace, extra charge.; 6 whirlpool rooms, $143-$233; 1-2 stories; interior/exterior corridors; smoke free premises; golf driving net. **Services:** gift shop; winter plug-ins. **Recreation:** shuffleboard. **Cards:** MC, VI.
(See color ad p 500)   [X] [VCR]

—— RESTAURANT ——

LAGRIGLIA   **Lunch:** $8-$12   **Dinner:** $14-$20   **Phone:** 518/734-4499

Northern
Italian

Location: SR 23, just s on SR 296. 38 Rt 296 12496. **Hours:** 5 pm-9 pm, Fri-10 pm, Sat 11:30 am-3 & 4-10 pm, Sun 11 am-9 pm. Closed: Some Mon & Tues 4/1-5/31 & 11/1-11/30. **Reservations:** suggested; weekends. **Features:** casual dress; Sunday brunch; children's menu; early bird specials; carryout; cocktails & lounge; a la carte. In the Catskills, the moderately upscale restaurant serves traditional and seasonal Northern Italian preparations of pasta, veal and seafood. The serene mountain setting, pleasant wait staff and elegant, country surroundings add to the dining experience. **Cards:** AE, CB, DI, DS, MC, VI.   [X]

WOODBURY pop. 8,000

—— LODGING ——

BEST WESTERN WOODBURY INN   **Phone:** (516)921-6900

All Year	1P: $99-$129	2P: $99-$129	XP: $5 F18

Motel

Location: I-495, exit 44 N, exit 14 E off SR 135, 1.5 mi n on SR 135, then 1 mi e. 7940 Jericho Tpke 11797. Fax: 516/921-6908. **Terms:** [CP] meal plan. **Facility:** 85 rooms. Close to area shopping centers. Set back from road, quiet spot surrounded by woods. 2 stories; exterior corridors. **Dining:** Restaurant nearby. **All Rooms:** combo or shower baths, extended cable TV. **Cards:** AE, CB, DI, DS, MC, VI. **Special Amenities:** Free breakfast and free newspaper.   [S][D] [Y+] [≡] [X] [⟲] [VCR] [▤] [▯] [DATA PORT] [≈] [⊕]

WYOMING pop. 500

—— RESTAURANT ——

GASLIGHT VILLAGE CAFE   **Lunch:** $5-$8   **Dinner:** $8-$19   **Phone:** 716/495-6695

American

Location: Center; in the Gaslight Commons, corner SR 19 and Main St. 1 Main St 14591. **Hours:** Open 5/1-1/15 & 3/15-4/30; 11:30 am-5 pm, Fri & Sat-8:30 pm, Sun-5 pm. Closed: 1/1, 11/23 & 12/25. **Reservations:** accepted. **Features:** casual dress; children's menu; carryout; cocktails & lounge; street parking; a la carte. Built in 1846, the building is appointed in charming country decor. The menu center primarily on comfort foods, along the lines of meatloaf and seafood. The adjacent pub features automotive memorabilia collected by the founder of Car & Driver magazine. **Cards:** AE, DI, DS, MC, VI.   [X]

YONKERS —See New York p. 442.

YORKVILLE pop. 3,000

—— RESTAURANT ——

SYMEON'S   **Lunch:** $5-$8   **Dinner:** $8-$17   **Phone:** 315/736-4074

Greek

Location: On SR 5A, 0.5 mi e of Sangertown Square Shopping Center. 4941 Commercial Dr 13495. **Hours:** 11 am-10 pm, Fri & Sat-11 pm, Sun noon-9 pm. Closed: 4/23, 11/23, 12/24 & 12/25. **Features:** casual dress; children's menu; carryout; beer & wine only; a la carte. Greek artwork, posters and pottery decorate the five, intimate dining rooms. Among well-prepared traditional Greek dishes are the specialty souvlaki, spanakopita and crisp, tasty salad. Casually uniformed servers are pleasant and efficient. **Cards:** DS, MC, VI.   [X]

YOUNGSTOWN —See Niagara Falls p. 397.

⚠️ *Offices*

Cities with main offices are listed in **BOLD TYPE** and toll-free member service numbers in *ITALIC TYPE*.
All are closed Saturdays, Sundays and holidays unless otherwise indicated.
The type of service provided is designated below the name of the city where the office is located:
Auto travel services, including books/maps, marked maps and on-demand Triptik maps ✛
Auto travel services, including books/maps, marked maps, but no on-demand Triptik maps ●
Provides books/maps only. No marked maps or on-demand Triptik maps available ■
Travel agency services ▲

NEW YORK

ALBANY—AAA HUDSON VALLEY, 618 DELAWARE AVE, 12209-1096. MON-FRI 9-5, THU 9-7, SAT 9-1. (518) 426-1000.✛▲

AUBURN—AAA WESTERN AND CENTRAL NEW YORK, 15-17 DILL ST, 13021-0416. MON-FRI 9-5:30, THU 9-7, SAT 9-1. (315) 253-8661.✛▲

BATAVIA—AAA WESTERN AND CENTRAL NEW YORK, 25 LIBERTY ST #6, 14020. MON-FRI 9-5:03, SAT 9-1. (716) 344-1910.✛▲

BINGHAMTON—AAA SOUTHERN NEW YORK, 21 WASHINGTON ST, 13901. MON-FRI 8:30-5, MON & THU 8:30-6. (607) 722-7255.✛▲

BROOKLYN—AUTOMOBILE CLUB OF NEW YORK, 2334 RALPH AVE, 11234. MON-FRI 8:45-5:30, SAT 9-5. (718) 224-2222.✛▲

BUFFALO—AAA WESTERN AND CENTRAL NEW YORK, 100 INTERNATIONAL DR, 14221. MON-FRI 9-5:30, MON & TUE & THU 9-7, SAT 9-2. (716) 633-9860.✛▲

BUFFALO—AAA WESTERN AND CENTRAL NEW YORK, 2640 DELAWARE AVE, 14216. MON-FRI 9-8, FRI 9-5, SAT 9-4. (716) 873-0111.✛▲

BUFFALO—AAA WESTERN AND CENTRAL NEW YORK, 307 CAYUGA RD #100, 14225. (716) 633-9860.

CAMILLUS——AAA WESTERN AND CENTRAL NEW YORK W GENESEE ST., 13031. MON-FRI 8:30-5:30, THU 8:30-7, SAT 8:30-1,(315) 487-2700. ✛▲

CANANDAIGUA—AAA ROCHESTER, 119 EASTERN BLVD, 14424. MON-FRI 9-5:30, THU 9-8. (716) 396-9000, *(800) 836-2582.*✛▲

CANTON—AAA ST LAWRENCE, VILAS HALL, 13617. MON-FRI 8:30-5. (315) 229-5662, *(800) 814-4430.*●▲

CHEEKTOWAGA—AAA WESTERN AND CENTRAL NEW YORK, 4095 GENESEE ST, 14225-1902. MON-FRI 8-8, MON & FRI 8-5:30, SAT 9-2. (716) 631-3771.●▲

COOPERSTOWN—AAA TRI COUNTY MOTOR CLUB, 72 ELM ST, 13326. MON-FRI 8:30-5:30, SAT 9-4, MEMORIAL DAY - COLUMBUS DAY SUN 9-4. (607) 547-2519.✛▲

CORNING—AAA WESTERN AND CENTRAL NEW YORK, 273 W PULTENEY ST, 14830. MON-FRI 8:30-5:30, SAT 9-1. (607) 936-4166.✛▲

DELHI—AAA TRI COUNTY MOTOR CLUB, 102 ALUMNI HAL/ SUNY[@00DE]LHI, 13753. MON-FRI 8-5. (607) 746-4222.✛▲

DUNKIRK—AAA WESTERN AND CENTRAL NEW YORK, 3968 VINEYARD DR, 14048. MON-FRI 9-7, FRI 9-5, SAT 9-2. (716) 366-3599.✛▲

ELMIRA HEIGHTS—AAA SOUTHERN NEW YORK, 99 W MCCANNS BLVD, 14903. MON-FRI 8:30-5, THU 8:30-6. (607) 734-5246.✛

ENDICOTT—AAA SOUTHERN NEW YORK, 124 WASHINGTON AVE, 13760. MON-FRI 9-5, MON & THU 9-6. (607) 754-1060. ✛▲

GARDEN CITY—AUTOMOBILE CLUB OF NEW YORK, 1415 KELLUM PL, 11530-1690. MON-FRI 8:45-5:30. (516) 746-7730.

THIS IS AN ADMINISTRATIVE OFFICE. FOR TRAVEL INFORMATION IN GARDEN CITY, CONTACT THE FOLLOWING OFFICE:

GARDEN CITY—AUTOMOBILE CLUB OF NEW YORK, 229 SEVENTH ST, 11530. MON-FRI 8:45-5:30, SAT 9-5. (516) 746-7730.✛▲

HERKIMER—AAA UTICA & CENTRAL NEW YORK, 246 N MAIN ST, 13350-1956. MON-FRI 8-6. (315) 866-1830, *(800) 640-6144.*✛▲

HUDSON—AAA HUDSON VALLEY, 179 HEALY BLVD, 12534. MON-FRI 9-5, THU 9-7. (518) 828-4537.✛▲

ITHACA—AAA WESTERN AND CENTRAL NEW YORK, 303 N LINCOLN ST, 14850. MON-FRI 9-5:30, THU 9-6, SAT 9-2. (607) 273-6727.✛▲

JAMAICA—AUTOMOBILE CLUB OF NEW YORK, 186-06 HILLSIDE AVE, 11432. MON-FRI 8:45-5:30, SAT 9-5. (718) 224-2222.✛▲

JAMESTOWN—AAA JAMESTOWN, 111 W 5TH ST, 14701. MON-FRI 8:30-5, SAT 9:30-12:30. (716) 488-1981.✛▲

JOHNSTOWN—AAA NORTHWAY, 338 N COMRIE AVE, 12095-1019. MON-FRI 9-5, TUE & THU 9-7. (518) 762-4619.✛▲

LEWISTON—AAA WESTERN AND CENTRAL NEW YORK, 5927 MILITARY RD, 14092-2299. MON-FRI 9-5, TUE & THU 9-7, SAT 10-2. (716) 297-3163.✛▲

LIVERPOOL—AAA WESTERN AND CENTRAL NEW YORK, 7485 HENRY CLAY BLVD, 13088. MON-FRI 9-5:30, THU 9-7, SAT 9-3. (315) 451-1115.✛▲

LOCKPORT—AAA NIAGARA-ORLEANS AUTO CLUB, 7135 ROCHESTER RD, 14094. MON-FRI 9-5, THU 9-8. (716) 434-2865.✛▲

MASSENA—AAA ST LAWRENCE, HARTE-HAVEN SHOPPING CTR, 13662. MON-FRI 8:30-5:30. (315) 769-8873.●▲

NEW YORK—AUTOMOBILE CLUB OF NEW YORK, BROADWAY AT W 62ND ST, 10023. MON-FRI 8:45-5:30, SAT 9-5. (212) 586-1166.✛▲

NORWICH—AAA TRI COUNTY MOTOR CLUB, 1 S BROAD ST, 13815-1619. MON-FRI 8-5:30, SAT 9-2. (607) 334-9269.✛▲

OGDENSBURG—AAA ST LAWRENCE, RT 37 & PARK ST, 13669. MON-FRI 8:30-5. (315) 393-4280, *(800) 244-4280.*✛▲

OLEAN—AAA WESTERN AND CENTRAL NEW YORK, 1657 E STATE RD, 14760. MON-FRI 9-5.✛▲

ONEONTA—AAA TRI COUNTY MOTOR CLUB, 195 ONEIDA ST SUITE A, 13820. MON-FRI 8-5:30, SAT 9-2. (607) 432-4512.✛▲

ORCHARD PARK—AAA WESTERN AND CENTRAL NEW YORK, 3364 SOUTHWESTERN BLVD, 14127-1524. MON-FRI 9-5:30, TUE & WED & THU 9-7, SAT 9-2. (716) 675-4454.✛▲

PENFIELD—AAA ROCHESTER, 2156 PENFIELD RD, 14526. MON-FRI 9-5:30, THU 9-8, SAT 9-2. (716) 377-8500, *(800) 836-2582.*✛▲

PLATTSBURGH—AAA NORTHWAY, 20 BOOTH DR, 12901. MON-FRI 9-5, TUE & THU 9-7. (518) 563-3830.✛▲

POTSDAM—AAA ST LAWRENCE, 20 ELM ST, 13676. MON-FRI 8:30-5. (315) 265-1328.●▲

QUEENSBURY—AAA NORTHWAY, 740 UPPER GLEN ST, 12804. MON-FRI 9-5, TUE & THU 9-7. (518) 792-0088.✛▲

ROCHESTER—AAA ROCHESTER, 777 CLINTON AVE S, 14620. MON-FRI 8:30-5:30, THU 8:30-8. (716) 461-4660, *(800) 836-2582.*✛▲

ROCHESTER—AAA ROCHESTER, 1100 LONG POND RD, 14626. MON-FRI 9-5:30, WED 9-8, SAT 9-2. (716) 227-9600, *(800) 836-2582.*✛▲

ROME—AAA WESTERN AND CENTRAL NEW YORK, 5783 ROME-TABERG RD SR 69, 13440. MON-FRI 9-7, FRI 9-5, SAT 9-4. (315) 337-9677.✛▲

SARATOGA SPRINGS—AAA NORTHWAY, 26 WEST AVE, 12866. MON-FRI 9-5, TUE & THU 9-7. (518) 587-8449.✛▲

SCARSDALE—AUTOMOBILE CLUB OF NEW YORK, 111 BROOK ST, 10583. MON-FRI 8:45-5:30, SAT 9-5. (914) 948-4600.●▲

SCHENECTADY—AAA NORTHWAY, 112 RAILROAD ST, 12301. MON-FRI 9-5, TUE & THU 9-6. (518) 374-4575.✛▲

SENECA FALLS—AAA ROCHESTER, 73 FALL ST, 13148. MON-FRI 9-5. (315) 568-8742.✛▲

SMITHTOWN—AUTOMOBILE CLUB OF NEW YORK, 729 SMITHTOWN BY-PASS, 11787. MON-FRI 8:45-5:30, SAT 9-5. (516) 746-7730.✛▲

ST. BONAVENTURE—AAA WESTERN AND CENTRAL NEW YORK, ST BONIV ROBINSON HL #127, 14778. MON-FRI 9-5. (716) 373-3232.▲

SYRACUSE—AAA WESTERN AND CENTRAL NEW YORK, 3175 E GENESEE ST, 13224. MON-FRI 9-6:30, FRI 9-5, SAT 9-1. (315) 446-3134.✦▲

TROY—AAA HUDSON VALLEY, 514 CONGRESS ST, 12180. MON-FRI 9-5, THU 9-7, SAT 9-1. (518) 426-1000.✦▲

UTICA—**AAA UTICA & CENTRAL NEW YORK**, 409 COURT ST, 13502-4291. MON-FRI 8-6. (315) 797-5000, *(800) 640-6144.*✦▲

WATERTOWN—AAA WESTERN AND CENTRAL NEW YORK, 19482 US RT 11, 13601. MON-FRI 8:30-5:30, SAT 9-1. (315) 788-5250.✦▲

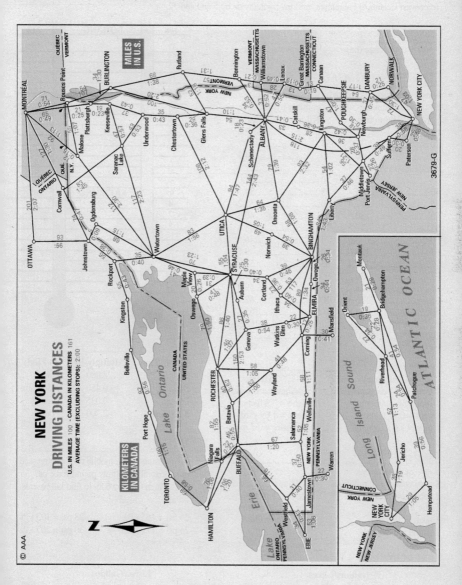

© AAA

NEW YORK
DRIVING DISTANCES
U.S. IN MILES 100 · CANADA IN KILOMETERS 161
AVERAGE TIME (EXCLUDING STOPS): 2:00

KILOMETERS IN CANADA

MILES IN U.S.

3679-G

Metric Equivalents Chart

TEMPERATURE

To convert Fahrenheit to Celsius, subtract 32 from the Fahrenheit temperature, multiply by 5 and divide by 9. To convert Celsius to Fahrenheit, multipy by 9, divide by 5 and add 32.

ACRES

1 acre = 0.4 hectare (ha)   1 hectare = 2.47 acres

MILES AND KILOMETRES

Note: A kilometre is approximately 5/8 or 0.6 of a mile. To convert kilometres to miles multiply by 0.6.

Miles/Kilometres	Kilometres/Miles
15.....................24.1	30 ....18.6
20.....................32.2	35 ....21.7
25.....................40.2	40 ....24.8
30.....................48.3	45 ....27.9
35.....................56.3	50 ....31.0
40.....................64.4	55 ....34.1
45.....................72.4	60 ....37.2
50.....................80.5	65 ....40.3
55.....................88.5	70 ....43.4
60.....................96.6	75 ....46.6
65...................104.6	80 ....49.7
70...................112.7	85 ....52.8
75...................120.7	90 ....55.9
80...................128.7	95 ....59.0
85...................136.8	100 ....62.1
90...................144.8	105 ....65.2
95...................152.9	110 ....68.3
100.................160.9	115 ....71.4

LINEAR MEASURE

Customary	Metric
1 inch = 2.54 centimetres	1 centimetre = 0.4 inches
1 foot = 30 centimetres	1 metre = 3.3 feet
1 yard = 0.91 metres	1 metre = 1.09 yards
1 mile = 1.6 kilometres	1 kilometre = .62 miles

LIQUID MEASURE

Customary	Metric
1 fluid ounce = 30 millilitres	1 millilitre = .03 fluid ounces
1 cup = .24 litres	1 litre = 2.1 pints
1 pint = .47 litres	1 litre = 1.06 quarts
1 quart = .95 litres	1 litre = .26 gallons
1 gallon = 3.8 litres	

Celsius °   Fahrenheit °

Celsius		Fahrenheit
100	BOILING	212
37		100
35		95
32		90
29		85
27		80
24		75
21		70
18		65
16		60
13		55
10		50
7		45
4		40
2		35
0	FREEZING	32
-4		25
-7		20
-9		15
-12		10
-15		5
-18		0
-21		-5
-24		-10
-27		-15

WEIGHT

If You Know:	Multiply By:	To Find:
Ounces	28.000	Grams
Pounds	0.450	Kilograms
Grams	0.035	Ounces
Kilograms	2.200	Pounds

PRESSURE

Air pressure in automobile tires is expressed in kilopascals. Multiply pound-force per square inch (psi) by 6.89 to find kilopascals (kPa).

24 psi = 165 kPa	28 psi = 193 kPa
26 psi = 179 kPa	30 psi = 207 kPa

GALLON AND LITRES

Gallons/Litres		Litres/Gallons	
5.....................19.0	12.....................45.6	10.....................2.6	40.....................10.4
6.....................22.8	14.....................53.2	15.....................3.9	50.....................13.0
7.....................26.6	16.....................60.8	20.....................5.2	60.....................15.6
8.....................30.4	18.....................68.4	25.....................6.5	70.....................18.2
9.....................34.2	20.....................76.0	30.....................7.8	80.....................20.8
10...................38.0	25.....................95.0	35.....................9.1	90.....................23.4

Border Information

FOR CANADIAN RESIDENTS

Entering the United States

PASSPORTS to enter the United States or return to Canada are not required for native-born citizens of either country. However, a Canadian passport remains the best internationally accepted evidence of Canadian citizenship. Proof of citizenship must be carried; a birth certificate, accompanied by a photo ID will usually suffice. Proof of residence also may be required.

UNITED STATES CUSTOMS permits you to bring, free of duty, for personal use and not intended for sale: clothing, personal effects and equipment appropriate to the trip. Personal effects may include 200 cigarettes, 50 cigars or 4.4 pounds (2 kgs) of tobacco or proportionate amounts of each, and 1 liter of alcoholic beverage.

If you are planning to be in the United States at least 72 hours, you may bring gifts up to a fair retail value of $100 (U.S.), provided you have not claimed this exemption within the preceding 6 months. Perfume containing alcohol and valued at more than $5 retail, tobacco products and alcoholic beverages are excluded from the gift provision.

Radio Communication Equipment: You may use your General Radio Service Station (CB) and cellular phone in the United States without any restrictions.

Returning to Canada

CANADIAN CUSTOMS allows you to bring, free of duty and taxes, goods valued up to $200 (Canadian) any number of times per year, provided you have been in the United States **48 hours or more.** All goods must accompany you; a written declaration *may* be required.

You may claim a $50 (Canadian) exemption on goods, excluding alcoholic beverages and tobacco products, if you are returning after an absence of **24 hours or more** and are not using any other exemption. If more than $50 worth of goods is brought back, the regular rate of duty and taxes will be levied on the entire value. This exemption may apply any number of times in a year.

If you are returning after **7 days or more** in the United States (not counting the day of departure from Canada), you may claim an exemption on goods valued up to $750 (Canadian). Goods, other than alcohol and tobacco products, are not required to accompany you; a written declaration *may* be required.

Permitted within the $200 and $750 exemptions are up to 50 cigars, 200 cigarettes, 400 tobacco sticks and 14 ounces (400 gm) of tobacco and up to 2 quarts (1.14 L) of liquor, 1.6 quarts (1.5 L) of wine or 9 quarts (8.5 L) of beer and/or ale (or its equivalent of 24 bottles or cans). You must meet the minimum age requirement of the province entered to claim alcohol or tobacco products.

There is nothing to prevent you from importing any quantity of goods, even if you do not qualify for any kind of personal exemption, provided the goods you are importing are not restricted and the full rate of duty and taxes is paid.

Special Tariff: When you exceed your $200 or $750 exemptions, a special rate of 7 percent combined duty and taxes is levied on the next $300 value in goods (except tobacco and alcohol) in excess of maximum exemptible amounts, provided the goods are of U.S. origin. Regular duties apply on any amount over that. For detailed information concerning specific duty rates, consult Canadian Customs before leaving on your trip.

All exemptions are individual and may not be combined with those of another person. You may be asked to verify the length of your visit; dated receipts normally constitute proof.

GIFTS to the value of $60 (Canadian) may be sent from abroad, free of duty or taxes. These may not include alcoholic beverages, tobacco products or advertising matter. Gifts valued at over $60 (Canadian) are subject to duty and taxes on the amount in excess of $60. Gifts *sent* from abroad do not count against your personal exemption, but gifts brought back *must* be included as part of your exemption.

New York

SARATOGA SPRINGS

The Westchester House
- Gracious in-town Accommodations
- Old World Ambiance - up to date Comforts
- Walk to all Attractions
- Surrounded by old-fashioned Gardens

888-834-1921
102 Lincoln Ave.
www.westcasterhousebandb.com   SARATOGA

WINDHAM

Albergo Allegria
- 1892 Victorian Mansion
- Hearty Gourmet Breakfast
- Jacuzzi & Fireplace Suites
- Catskill Mountain Forest Preserve

(518) 734-5560
RT. 296 Windham, NY 12496
www.AlbergoUSA.com

Bed & Breakfast Lodgings Index

Some bed and breakfasts listed below might have historical significance. Those properties are also referenced in the Historical index. The indication that continental [CP] or full breakfast [BP] is included in the room rate reflects whether a property is a Bed-and-Breakfast facility.

NEW YORK

ACCOMMODATIONS

428 MT. VERNON .... ROCHESTER   457
A BED AND BREAKFAST AT DARTMOUTH HOUSE INN... ROCHESTER   457
ACORN INN .... BRISTOL CENTER   209
ALBANY MANSION HILL INN & RESTAURANT .... ALBANY   194
ALBERGO ALLEGRIA HISTORIC BED & BREAKFAST ...... WINDHAM   495
ALEXANDER HAMILTON HOUSE .... CROTON-ON-HUDSON   371
ALYNN'S BUTTERFLY INN BED & BREAKFAST ...... WARRENSBURG   488
ANGELICA INN BED & BREAKFAST .... ANGELICA   199
BED & BREAKFAST ON THE PARK .... BROOKLYN   370
BLACK CREEK FARM B & B .... RED CREEK   453
BLUSHING ROSE BED & BREAKFAST .... HAMMONDSPORT   267
BREEZY ACRES FARM BED & BREAKFAST ....HOBART   272
CAMBRIDGE INN BED & BREAKFAST .... CAMBRIDGE   229
CAROLE'S BED & BREAKFAST .... EAST QUOGUE   250
CHARLOTTE VALLEY INN BED & BREAKFAST ... SOUTH WORCESTER   473
EDSON HOUSE BED & BREAKFAST .... LE ROY   302
EVERGREEN ON PINE BED & BREAKFAST .... SOUTHAMPTON   472
GENESEE COUNTRY INN .... MUMFORD   313
GOOSE POND INN .... NORTH CREEK   439
GOVERNOR'S HOUSE BED & BREAKFAST .... ONEIDA CASTLE   442
GREENWOODS BED & BREAKFAST INN .... HONEOYE   272
HOBBIT HOLLOW FARM BED AND BREAKFAST ......SKANEATELES   471
ILEX INN .... RED OAKS MILL   453
INN AT THE FALLS .... ST. JOHNSVILLE   463
INN BY THE MILL .... FILLMORE   255
JUST A "PLANE" BED & BREAKFAST .... FILLMORE   255
KOUNTRY LIVING-THE SISTERS B & B .... ONEONTA   443
LONGHOUSE MANOR .... WATKINS GLEN   489
MARGARETVILLE MOUNTAIN INN BED &
   BREAKFAST .... MARGARETVILLE   308
MERRITT HILL MANOR BED & BREAKFAST .... PENN YAN   446
MILL HOUSE INN .... STEPHENTOWN   475

OLD LIBRARY INN BED & BREAKFAST .... OLEAN   442
PEREGRINE HOUSE VICTORIAN INN .... ITHACA   277
POINT AUROCHE LODGE A BED & BREAKFAST .... PLATTSBURGH   448
ROSEMONT INN BED & BREAKFAST .... UTICA   485
ROSEWOOD INN .... CORNING   244
SANDY CREEK MANOR HOUSE .... HAMLIN   267
SARATOGA BED & BREAKFAST .... SARATOGA SPRINGS   466
SOUTH GLENORA TREE FARM BED & BREAKFAST .... GLENORA   263
SPENCERTOWN COUNTRY HOUSE .... SPENCERTOWN   474
SUGARBUSH BED AND BREAKFAST .... BARNEVELD   201
SUTHERLAND HOUSE .... CANANDAIGUA   230
THE ARTFUL LODGER .... CLINTON   235
THE BARTLETT HOUSE INN .... GREENPORT   265
THE CARRIAGE HOUSE BED AND BREAKFAST ......EAST DURHAM   249
THE DICKENSON HOUSE ON JAMES .... SYRACUSE   480
THE EGGERY INN .... TANNERSVILLE   482
THE GREAT SOUTH BAY INN .... BELLPORT   203
THE GUION HOUSE .... SENECA FALLS   470
THE HEDGES .... CLINTON   235
THE INN AT SILVER MAPLE FARM .... CANAAN   229
THE IRIS STONEHOUSE BED & BREAKFAST .... UTICA   485
THE JEFFERSON INN .... ELLICOTTVILLE   252
THE LAMPLIGHT INN BED & BREAKFAST ...... LAKE LUZERNE   293
THE LOMBARDI FARM BED & BREAKFAST ... SARATOGA SPRINGS   466
THE MAGICAL LAND OF OZ B & B .... LIVINGSTON MANOR   304
THE SENECA LAKE WATCH BED & BREAKFAST .... WATKINS GLEN   490
THE WESTCHESTER HOUSE BED & BREAKFAST.. SARATOGA SPRINGS   467
UNION GABLES BED & BREAKFAST ...... SARATOGA SPRINGS   467

ONTARIO

ACCOMMODATIONS

CAMEO MANOR BED & BREAKFAST .... YOUNGSTOWN   397
HOLLEY RANKINE HOUSE ....NIAGARA FALLS   392

Country Inns Index

Some of the following country inns can also be considered as bed-and-breakfast operations. The indication that continental [CP] or full breakfast [BP] is included in the room rate reflects whether a property is a Bed-and-Breakfast facility.

NEW YORK

ACCOMMODATIONS

ADELPHI HOTEL .... SARATOGA SPRINGS 465
ASA RANSOM HOUSE .... CLARENCE 223
BEEKMAN ARMS & DELAMATER HOUSE AND CONFERENCE
  CENTER .... RHINEBECK 453
BELHURST CASTLE .... GENEVA 262
BRAE LOCH INN .... GENEVA 262
FRIENDS LAKE INN .... CAZENOVIA 233
GENEVA-ON-THE-LAKE .... CHESTERTOWN 234
GREEN GATE INN .... GENEVA 262
HUNTER INN .... CAMILLUS 229
LA TOURELLE COUNTRY INN .... HUNTER 274
LONG VIEW LODGE .... ITHACA 276
LONGFELLOWS INN AND RESTAURANT .... SARATOGA SPRINGS 466
OLD DROVERS INN .... LONG LAKE 307
OLIVER LOUD'S INN .... DOVER PLAINS 248
PARK INN .... PITTSFORD 447
ROSE INN .... HAMMONDSPORT 267
SHERWOOD INN .... NORTH LANSING 439
TAUGHANNOCK FARMS INN .... GREENE 265
THE CASTLE AT TARRYTOWN .... TRUMANSBURG 483
THE COPPERFIELD INN .... TARRYTOWN 377
THE GREGORY HOUSE COUNTRY INN .... NORTH CREEK 439
THE ROYCROFT INN .... AVERILL PARK 200
                                                      EAST AURORA 224

THE SEDGWICK INN .... BERLIN 204
THE STEWART HOUSE .... ATHENS 199
THE WHITE INN .... FREDONIA 260
THE WILLIAM SEWARD INN .... WESTFIELD 491
THREE VILLAGE INN .... STONY BROOK 475
TUNNICLIFF INN .... COOPERSTOWN 242
VILLAGE TAVERN INN .... HAMMONDSPORT 267

RESTAURANTS

25 EAST AMERICAN BISTRO .... PORT JEFFERSON 449
ASA RANSOM HOUSE
  DINING ROOM .... CLARENCE 223
AUBERGINE .... HILLSDALE 272
AURORA INN DINING ROOM .... AURORA 200
BRAE LOCH INN .... CAZENOVIA 233
CHATEAU HATHORN .... WARWICK 488
GARDENS .... NORTH CREEK 439
MERRILL MAGEE HOUSE .... WARRENSBURG 488
OLD DROVERS INN .... DOVER PLAINS 248
PARTRIDGE BERRY INN .... WATERTOWN 489
SEDGWICK INN DINING ROOM .... BERLIN 204
SHERWOOD INN DINING ROOM .... SKANEATELES 472
THE BREWSTER INN DINING ROOM .... CAZENOVIA 233
THE KREBS .... SKANEATELES 471
THE PALM IN HUNTTING INN .... EAST HAMPTON 250
THREE VILLAGE INN .... STONY BROOK 475

Historical Lodgings & Restaurants Index

Some of the following historical lodgings can also be considered as bed-and-breakfast operations. The indication that continental [CP] or full breakfast [BP] is included in the room rate reflects whether a property is a Bed-and-Breakfast facility.

NEW YORK

ACCOMMODATIONS

428 MT. VERNON .... ROCHESTER 457
A BED AND BREAKFAST AT DARTMOUTH HOUSE INN ... ROCHESTER 457
ACORN INN .... BRISTOL CENTER 209
ADELPHI INN .... SARATOGA SPRINGS 465
ALBANY MANSION HILL INN & RESTAURANT .... ALBANY 194
ALEXANDER HAMILTON HOUSE .... CROTON-ON-HUDSON 371
ANGELICA INN BED & BREAKFAST .... ANGELICA 199
ASA RANSOM HOUSE .... CLARENCE 223
BED & BREAKFAST ON THE PARK .... BROOKLYN 370
BEEKMAN ARMS & DELAMATER HOUSE AND CONFERENCE
  CENTER .... RHINEBECK 453
BELHURST CASTLE .... GENEVA 262
BEST WESTERN SEAPORT INN, NEW YORK .... N.Y. LOWER
  MANHATTAN 331
BEST WESTERN WOODWARD .... N.Y. MIDTOWN MANHATTAN 339
BLUSHING ROSE BED & BREAKFAST .... HAMMONDSPORT 267
BREEZY ACRES FARM BED & BREAKFAST .... HOBART 272
CHARLOTTE VALLEY INN BED & BREAKFAST .... SOUTH WORCESTER 473
FITZPATRICK MANHATTAN HOTEL.... N.Y. MIDTOWN MANHATTAN 341
FRIENDS LAKE INN .... CHESTERTOWN 234
GENESEE COUNTRY INN .... MUMFORD 313
GENEVA-ON-THE-LAKE .... GENEVA 262
GOOSE POND INN .... NORTH CREEK 439
GOVERNOR'S HOUSE BED & BREAKFAST .... ONEIDA CASTLE 442
GREEN GATE INN .... CAMILLUS 229
HOBBIT HOLLOW FARM BED AND BREAKFAST .... SKANEATELES 471
HOTEL WALES .... N.Y. MIDTOWN MANHATTAN 344
INN BY THE MILL .... ST. JOHNSVILLE 463
KOUNTRY LIVING-THE SISTERS B & B .... ONEONTA 443
LONG VIEW LODGE .... LONG LAKE 307
MARGARETVILLE MOUNTAIN INN BED &
  BREAKFAST .... MARGARETVILLE 308
MERRITT HILL MANOR BED & BREAKFAST .... PENN YAN 446
OLD DROVERS INN .... DOVER PLAINS 248
OLD LIBRARY INN BED & BREAKFAST .... OLEAN 442
OLIVER LOUD'S INN .... PITTSFORD 447
PARK INN .... HAMMONDSPORT 267
PEREGRINE HOUSE VICTORIAN INN .... ITHACA 277
ROSE INN .... NORTH LANSING 439
ROSEMONT INN BED & BREAKFAST .... UTICA 485
ROSEWOOD INN .... CORNING 244
SARATOGA BED & BREAKFAST .... SARATOGA SPRINGS 466
SPENCERTOWN COUNTRY HOUSE .... SPENCERTOWN 474
ST. CHARLES HOTEL .... HUDSON 274
TAUGHANNOCK FARMS INN .... TRUMANSBURG 483
THE ARTFUL LODGER .... CLINTON 235
THE BARTLETT HOUSE INN .... GREENPORT 265
THE CASTLE AT TARRYTOWN .... TARRYTOWN 377
THE DICKENSON HOUSE ON JAMES .... SYRACUSE 480
THE GUION HOUSE .... SENECA FALLS 470
THE HOTEL SARANAC OF PAUL SMITH'S COLLEGE .... SARANAC LAKE 464
THE INN AT SARATOGA .... SARATOGA SPRINGS 466
THE LAMPLIGHT INN BED & BREAKFAST .... LAKE LUZERNE 293
THE MARK .... N.Y. MIDTOWN MANHATTAN 347
THE NEW YORK PALACE .... N.Y. MIDTOWN MANHATTAN 347
THE ROYCROFT INN .... EAST AURORA 224
THE ST REGIS-NEW YORK .... N.Y. MIDTOWN MANHATTAN 349
THE STEWART HOUSE .... ATHENS 199
THE WARWICK NEW YORK .... N.Y. MIDTOWN MANHATTAN 351
THE WESTCHESTER HOUSE BED & BREAKFAST.. SARATOGA SPRINGS 468

THE WHITE INN .... FREDONIA 260
THE WILLIAM SEWARD INN .... WESTFIELD 491
THREE VILLAGE INN .... STONY BROOK 475
TUNNICLIFF INN .... COOPERSTOWN 242
UNION GABLES BED & BREAKFAST .... SARATOGA SPRINGS 467
VILLAGE TAVERN INN .... HAMMONDSPORT 267

RESTAURANTS

ARAD EVANS INN .... FAYETTEVILLE 255
AVERIL CONWELL DINING ROOM .... LAKE PLACID 300
BEEKMAN 1766 TAVERN .... RHINEBECK 453
BENN CONGER INN .... GROTON 266
CAFE TAMAYO .... SAUGERTIES 469
CANAL SIDE INN .... LITTLE FALLS 303
CLAUDIO'S RESTAURANT
  CLAM BAR & MARINA .... GREENPORT 265
DAISY FLOUR MILL .... PENFIELD 446
DEPUY CANAL HOUSE .... HIGH FALLS 271
ENCHANTE .... BUFFALO 217
FARMHOUSE .... ONEONTA 443
GEORGE MANN'S TORY TAVERN .... SCHOHARIE 469
GLEN LOCH RESTAURANT .... JAMESVILLE 279
HANNY'S EAGLE HOUSE
  RESTAURANT .... WILLIAMSVILLE 228
HOLMES & WATSON, LTD .... TROY 482
LINCOLN HILL INN .... CANANDAIGUA 231
LORD CHUMLEY'S .... BUFFALO 218
MORETTI'S RESTAURANT .... ELMIRA 253
NUMBER 5 .... BINGHAMTON 207
OLD LIBRARY RESTAURANT .... OLEAN 442
OLD ORCHARD INN .... EAST AURORA 224
OLD STONE ROW RESTAURANT .... SACKETS HARBOR 462
OLD TOWN BAR RESTAURANT .... N.Y. LOWER MANHATTAN 334
RICHARDSON'S CANAL HOUSE .... PITTSFORD 447
SPRING HOUSE .... PITTSFORD 447
SPRING WATER INN .... SARATOGA SPRINGS 468
SPRINGSIDE INN .... AUBURN 200
TAUGHANNOCK FARMS INN .... TRUMANSBURG 483
THE 1819 HOUSE RESTAURANT & TAVERN .... INDEX 276
THE AKRON HOUSE .... AKRON 219
THE HIDDEN INN .... SOUTH KORTRIGHT 473
THE HOFFMAN HOUSE .... KINGSTON 280
THE HORNED DORSET INN .... LEONARDSVILLE 302
THE INN AT POUND RIDGE .... POUND RIDGE 375
THE LOCUST TREE INN .... NEW PALTZ 316
THE OLDE BRYAN INN .... SARATOGA SPRINGS 468
THE ORIGINAL HOLLOWAY HOUSE .... BLOOMFIELD 207
THE PARROTT HOUSE .... SCHOHARIE 470
THE ROYCROFT INN DINING ROOM .... EAST AURORA 224
THE STATION RESTAURANT .... ITHACA 278
THE WHITE INN DINING ROOM .... FREDONIA 260
THE YANKEE CLIPPER .... N.Y. LOWER MANHATTAN 336
WARWICK INN .... WARWICK 488

NEARBY ONTARIO

ACCOMMODATIONS

BROCK PLAZA .... NIAGARA FALLS 402
HOLLEY RANKINE HOUSE .... NIAGARA FALLS 392

RESTAURANT

CLARKSON HOUSE.. LEWISTON 396

Resorts Index

Many establishments are located in resort areas; however, the following places have extensive on-premises recreational facilities:

NEW YORK
ACCOMMODATIONS

BEST WESTERN PARAMOUNT .... PARKSVILLE   445
MONTAUK YACHT CLUB RESORT & MARINA .... MONTAUK   311

PEEK'N PEAK RESORT & CONFERENCE CENTER .... CLYMER   235
RIVEREDGE RESORT & HOTEL .... ALEXANDRIA BAY   198
ROARING BROOK RANCH & TENNIS RESORT.......... LAKE GEORGE   292
THE INN AT HOLIDAY VALLEY RESORT............... ELLICOTTVILLE   252
THE SAGAMORE.................................. BOLTON LANDING   207
TURNING STONE CASINO RESORT............................ VERONA   486

Points of Interest Index

AIRPORTS
BUFFALO-NIAGARA FALLS
  INTERNATIONAL AIRPORT..........................NIAGARA FALLS, NY 144
ELMIRA-CORNING REGIONAL AIRPORT.....................ELMIRA, NY 83
JOHN F. KENNEDY...................................NEW YORK, NY 109
LA GUARDIA..NEW YORK, NY 109
NEWARK AIRPORT....................................NEW YORK, NY 109
NIAGARA FALLS INTERNATIONAL AIRPORT........NIAGARA FALLS, NY 144

AMUSEMENTS & THEME PARKS
ENCHANTED FOREST/WATER SAFARI.....................OLD FORGE, ON 159
FRONTIER TOWN...................................NORTH HUDSON, ON 157
THE GREAT ESCAPE AND SPLASHWATER KINGDOM...QUEENSBURY, ON 164
LONG ISLAND GAME FARM AND FAMILY RIDE PARK.....MANORVILLE, NY 102
*MARINELAND....................................NIAGARA FALLS, NY 152
MARTIN'S FANTASY ISLAND.........................GRAND ISLAND, NY 72
MIDWAY PARK..JAMESTOWN, NY 94
PLAYLAND...RYE, NY 139
SEABREEZE PARK/RAGING RIVERS WATER PARK.......ROCHESTER, NY 167
*SIX FLAGS DARIEN LAKE........................DARIEN CENTER, NY 80

AMPHITHEATERS
OAKES GARDEN THEATRE.......................NIAGARA FALLS, ON 154

ANTIQUES
*ROSE HILL MANSION..................................GENEVA, NY 87

AQUARIUMS
AQUARIUM FOR WILDLIFE CONSERVATION ....BROOKLYN, NY 129
AQUARIUM OF NIAGARA.........................NIAGARA FALLS, NY 147
*MARINELAND................................NIAGARA FALLS, ON 152

ARBORETUMS
BAYARD CUTTING ARBORETUM......................GREAT RIVER, NY 89
CORNELL PLANTATIONS...................................ITHACA, NY 93
MONROE COUNTY ARBORETUM.........................ROCHESTER, ON 167
PARRISH ART MUSEUM AND ARBORETUM ....SOUTHAMPTON, ON 176
*PLANTING FIELDS ARBORETUM SHP.................OYSTER BAY, NY 161

ARCHEOLOGICAL SITES
FORT WILLIAM HENRY MUSEUM ....LAKE GEORGE (VILLAGE), NY 97
SACKETS HARBOR BATTLEFIELD SHS..........SACKETS HARBOR, ON 169

ART GALLERIES
ALBANY INSTITUTE OF HISTORY AND ART.................ALBANY, NY 56
*ALBRIGHT-KNOX ART GALLERY..........................BUFFALO, NY 69
ALICE AUSTEN HOUSE ....RICHMOND (STATEN ISLAND), NY 131
ANDERSON GALLERY...................................BUFFALO, NY 69
ARNOT ART MUSEUM....................................ELMIRA, NY 83
ART GALLERY..JAMESTOWN, NY 94
ART MUSEUM.......................................STONY BROOK, ON 177
ARTS CENTER/OLD FORGE............................OLD FORGE, ON 159
ASIA SOCIETY GALLERIES ....MIDTOWN MANHATTAN, NY 118
BROOKLYN MUSEUM.................................BROOKLYN, NY 130
THE BURCHFIELD-PENNEY ART CENTER..................BUFFALO, NY 69
CANAJOHARIE LIBRARY AND ART GALLERY ....CANAJOHARIE, NY 73
CASTELLANI ART MUSEUM.......................NIAGARA FALLS, NY 148
*THE CLOISTERS......................UPPER MANHATTAN, NY 126
COLUMBIA COUNTY MUSEUM.......................KINDERHOOK, NY 95
COOPER-HEWITT NATIONAL DESIGN MU SEUM-SMITHSONIAN
  INSTITUTION.....................UPPER MANHATTAN, NY 126
DONALD KENDALL SCULPTURE GARDENS.............PURCHASE, NY 139
DUNKIRK HISTORICAL MUSEUM..........................DUNKIRK, NY 81
EVERSON MUSEUM OF ART............................SYRACUSE, ON 177
*FENIMORE ART MUSEUM.........................COOPERSTOWN, NY 78
FOSDICK-NELSON GALLERY..............................ALFRED, NY 58
THE FRANCES LEHMAN LOEB ART CENTER ...POUGHKEEPSIE, NY 164
FREDERIC REMINGTON ART MUSEUM ....OGDENSBURG, ON 158
FRICK COLLECTION.................MIDTOWN MANHATTAN, NY 122
GALLERY OF SPORTING ART ....MUMFORD, NY 104
GIBSON GALLERY.....................................POTSDAM, ON 164
*GOVERNOR NELSON A. ROCKEFELLER EMPIRE STATE
  PLAZA.......................................ALBANY, NY 56
GUGGENHEIM MUSEUM SOHO.......UPPER MANHATTAN, NY 128
GUILD HALL OF EAST HAMPTON ....EAST HAMPTON, NY 84
HECKSCHER MUSEUM................................HUNTINGTON, NY 92
HERBERT F. JOHNSON MUSEUM OF ART..................ITHACA, NY 93
HISPANIC SOCIETY OF AMERICA.......UPPER MANHATTAN, NY 126
THE HORSEHEADS HISTORICAL SOCIETY MUSEUM ....HORSEHEADS, NY 91
THE HUDSON RIVER MUSEUM OF WESTCHESTER ....YONKERS, NY 141
*THE HYDE COLLECTION ART MUSEUM ....GLENS FALLS, NY 88
THE ISAMU NOGUCHI GARDEN MUSEUM................QUEENS, NY 131
ITHACA COLLEGE......................................ITHACA, NY 93
JACQUES MARCHAIS MUSEUM OF
  TIBETAN ART ....RICHMOND (STATEN ISLAND), NY 131
JAPAN SOCIETY ....MIDTOWN MANHATTAN, NY 122
KATONAH MUSEUM OF ART ....KATONAH, NY 138

MEMORIAL ART GALLERY.............................ROCHESTER, ON 167
*METROPOLITAN MUSEUM OF ART....... MIDTOWN MANHATTAN, NY 124
*MUNSON-WILLIAMS-PROCTOR ARTS INSTITUTE.............UTICA, ON 181
MUSEUM OF AMERICAN FOLK ART...... MIDTOWN MANHATTAN, NY 124
*THE MUSEUM OF MODERN ART...... MIDTOWN MANHATTAN, NY 124
THE MUSEUMS AT STONY BROOK...................STONY BROOK, ON 177
MYERS FINE ARTS GALLERY ....PLATTSBURGH, ON 163
NATIONAL ACADEMY OF DESIGN ......UPPER MANHATTAN, NY 128
NEUBERGER MUSEUM OF ART...........................HARRISON, NY 138
THE NEW MUSEUM OF CONTEMPORARY ART ....LOWER MANHATTAN
                                     AND NEW YORK HARBOR, NY 115
NEWHOUSE CENTER FOR
  CONTEMPORARY ART ....RICHMOND (STATEN ISLAND), NY 131
NIAGARA FALLS ART GALLERY/KURELEK
  COLLECTION...........................NIAGARA FALLS, ON 153
OGDEN GALLERY....................CORNWALL-ON-HUDSON, NY 79
PARRISH ART MUSEUM AND ARBORETUM ....SOUTHAMPTON, ON 176
PEPSICO SCULPTURE GARDEN ....HARRISON, NY 138
PICKER ART GALLERY.................................HAMILTON, NY 89
PIERPONT MORGAN LIBRARY .... MIDTOWN MANHATTAN, NY 124
PLATTSBURGH ART MUSEUM, SUNY.................PLATTSBURGH, ON 163
QUEENS MUSEUM OF ART..............................QUEENS, NY 131
ROBERT JENKINS HOUSE AND MUSEUM ....HUDSON, NY 91
*ROCKWELL MUSEUM..................................CORNING, NY 79
SCHWEINFURTH MEMORIAL ART CENTER ....AUBURN, NY 60
*SENATE HOUSE SHS...............................KINGSTON, NY 96
*SOLOMON R. GUGGENHEIM MUSEUM....UPPER MANHATTAN, NY 128
STORM KING ART CENTER......................MOUNTAINVILLE, NY 104
WALTER ELWOOD MUSEUM AND ART GALLERY .....AMSTERDAM, NY 59
WAVE HILL..THE BRONX, NY 129
WEST END GALLERY...................................CORNING, NY 79
WHITNEY MUSEUM OF AMERICAN ART ... MIDTOWN MANHATTAN, NY 126
WHITNEY MUSEUM OF AMERICAN ART AT
  PHILIP MORRIS.................MIDTOWN MANHATTAN, NY 126
YAGER MUSEUM.....................................ONEONTA, ON 160

ARTS & CRAFTS
AMERICAN CRAFT MUSEUM .... MIDTOWN MANHATTAN, NY 118
MADISON COUNTY HISTORICAL SOCIETY HEADQUARTERS....ONEIDA, NY 159
MARITIME CRAFTS CENTER......LOWER MANHATTAN AND NEW YORK
                                          HARBOR, NY 116
SALAMANCA ....ON 170

AUDITORIUMS
ANDERSON CENTER FOR THE PERFORMING ARTS..... BINGHAMTON, NY 62
BRUNO WALTER AUDITORIUM ...... MIDTOWN MANHATTAN, NY 122
THE JUILLIARD SCHOOL .... MIDTOWN MANHATTAN, NY 122

BATTLEFIELDS
BENNINGTON BATTLEFIELD SHS .... NORTH HOOSICK, NY 157
*FORT TICONDEROGA .... NY 86
JOHNSTOWN BATTLEFIELD...........................JOHNSTOWN, NY 95
LAKE GEORGE BATTLEFIELD PARK.....LAKE GEORGE (VILLAGE), NY 97
ORISKANY BATTLEFIELD...................................ROME, NY 169
QUEENSTON HEIGHTS PARK ....NIAGARA FALLS, ON 155
SACKETS HARBOR BATTLEFIELD SHS ....SACKETS HARBOR, ON 169
SARATOGA NHP..ON 171
STONY POINT BATTLEFIELD SHS ....STONY POINT, NY 140
SULLIVAN'S MONUMENT AT NEWTOWN BATTLEFIELD ......ELMIRA, NY 83
WHITE PLAINS NB SITE............................WHITE PLAINS, NY 141

BATTLE RE-ENACTMENTS
*FORT TICONDEROGA .... NY 86
*OLD FORT NIAGARA ....YOUNGSTOWN, NY 151

BEACHES
CONEY ISLAND BEACH AND BOARDWALK ....NEW YORK, NY 133
FIRE ISLAND NS .... NY 84
GREAT KILLS PARK ....NEW YORK, NY 133
GRIFFON ....NIAGARA FALLS, NY 150
HENNEPIN ....NIAGARA FALLS, NY 150
JACOB RIIS BEACH ....GATEWAY NRA, NY 87
JACOB RIIS PARK ....NEW YORK, NY 133
JAMAICA BAY ....NEW YORK, NY 133
JAYNE ....NIAGARA FALLS, NY 150
*JONES BEACH SP................................JONES BEACH, NY 95
JONES BEACH SP ....LONG ISLAND, NY 101
LAKE GEORGE (VILLAGE) .... NY 97
LAKE PLACID .... NY 98
LASALLE ....NIAGARA FALLS, NY 150
LONG ISLAND .... NY 100
MANHATTAN BEACH ....NEW YORK, NY 133
MILLION DOLLAR BEACH...........LAKE GEORGE (VILLAGE), NY 97
ORCHARD BEACH ....NEW YORK, NY 133
PELHAM BAY PARK ....NEW YORK, NY 133
PLAYLAND ....RYE, NY 139

INDEX ABBREVIATIONS

NB...................................national battlefield
NBP...........................national battlefield park
NC.................................national cemetery
NF.......................................national forest
NHM........... national historic(al) monument
NHP................... national historic(al) park
NHS.................... national historic(al) site
NL.................................national lakeshore
NME...............................national memorial
NMO................................national monument
NMP..........................national military park
NP......................................national park
NRA.................national recreation area

NR...................................national river
NS..............................national seashore
NWR............... national wildlife refuge
PHP............provincial historic(al) park
PHS.............provincial historic(al) site
PP.................................provincial park
SF.......................................state forest
SHM........... state historic(al) monument
SHP................... state historic(al) park
SHS.................... state historic(al) site
SME...............................state memorial
SP......................................state park
SRA................. state recreation area

PLUMB BEACH ..... GATEWAY NRA, NY 87
ROBERT MOSES SP ..... MASSENA, NY 102
ROCKAWAY BEACH AND BOARDWALK ..... NEW YORK, NY 133
SAILORS HAVEN ..... FIRE ISLAND NS, NY 85
ST. LAWRENCE ISLANDS NP ..... THOUSAND ISLANDS, ON 178
SANDY HOOK ..... GATEWAY NRA, NY 87
SOUTH BEACH AND BOARDWALK ..... NEW YORK, NY 133
SOUTHAMPTON ..... ON 175
THOUSAND ISLANDS ..... ON 178
TUPPER LAKE ..... ON 180
WOLFE'S POND PARK ..... NEW YORK, NY 134

BIRTHPLACES
BLESSED KATERI TEKAKWITHA ..... AURIESVILLE, NY 61
ELIZABETH CADY STANTON ..... JOHNSTOWN, NY 95
FREDERIC REMINGTON ..... CANTON, NY 74
GERRIT SMITH MILLER ..... CAZENOVIA, NY 74
MILLARD FILLMORE CABIN ..... MORAVIA, NY 104
THEODORE ROOSEVELT BIRTHPLACE NHS ..... LOWER MANHATTAN AND NEW YORK HARBOR, NY 117
WALT WHITMAN BIRTHPLACE SHS ..... HUNTINGTON, NY 92

BOARDWALKS
CONEY ISLAND BEACH AND BOARDWALK ..... NEW YORK, NY 133
PLAYLAND ..... RYE, NY 139
ROCKAWAY BEACH AND BOARDWALK ..... NEW YORK, NY 133
SOUTH BEACH AND BOARDWALK ..... NEW YORK, NY 133

BRIDGES
BAYONNE BRIDGE ..... NEW YORK, NY 107
BROOKLYN BRIDGE ..... NEW YORK, NY 106
DELAWARE AQUEDUCT ..... UPPER DELAWARE SCENIC AND RECREATIONAL RIVER, ON 180
HEADLESS HORSEMAN BRIDGE ..... SLEEPY HOLLOW, NY 140
KOREAN VETERANS MEMORIAL BRIDGE ..... ROUSES POINT, ON 169
PINE STREET BRIDGE ..... LOCKPORT, NY 100
TRIPHAMMER BRIDGE ..... ITHACA, NY 93
VERRAZANO-NARROWS BRIDGE ..... NEW YORK, NY 107

BRIDGES, COVERED
OLD BLENHEIM BRIDGE ..... NORTH BLENHEIM, ON 157

BUILDINGS, MASONIC
GEORGE WASHINGTON'S HEADQUARTERS AT TAPPAN ..... TAPPAN, NY 140

BUILDINGS, OFFICE
*EMPIRE STATE BUILDING ..... MIDTOWN MANHATTAN, NY 119
LEVER HOUSE ..... MIDTOWN MANHATTAN, NY 124
MANUFACTURER'S HANOVER BANK ..... MIDTOWN MANHATTAN, NY 124
METLIFE BUILDING ..... MIDTOWN MANHATTAN, NY 122
SEAGRAM BUILDING ..... MIDTOWN MANHATTAN, NY 124
WORLD FINANCIAL CENTER ..... LOWER MANHATTAN AND NEW YORK HARBOR, NY 118
*WORLD TRADE CENTER ..... LOWER MANHATTAN AND NEW YORK HARBOR, NY 118

BUILDINGS, PUBLIC; CAPITOL; CITY HALL
CENTER CITY ..... SCHENECTADY, ON 173
CITY HALL ..... BUFFALO, NY 70
CITY HALL ..... KINGSTON, NY 96
CITY HALL ..... LOWER MANHATTAN AND NEW YORK HARBOR, NY 113
CITY HALL ..... ROCHESTER, ON 165
CONFERENCE BUILDING ..... MIDTOWN MANHATTAN, NY 126
CUSTOM HOUSE ..... OGDENSBURG, ON 158
FEDERAL RESERVE BANK ..... LOWER MANHATTAN AND NEW YORK HARBOR, NY 113
GENERAL ASSEMBLY BUILDING ..... MIDTOWN MANHATTAN, NY 126
*GOVERNOR NELSON A. ROCKEFELLER EMPIRE STATE PLAZA ..... ALBANY, NY 56
NEW YORK STATE ARMORY ..... OGDENSBURG, ON 158
NEW YORK STATE CAPITOL ..... ALBANY, NY 56
SECRETARIAT BUILDING ..... MIDTOWN MANHATTAN, NY 126
*UNITED NATIONS HEADQUARTERS ..... MIDTOWN MANHATTAN, NY 126

CANALS
CAYUGA-SENECA CANAL ..... SENECA FALLS, ON 174
CHAMPLAIN CANAL ..... LAKE CHAMPLAIN, NY 96
DELAWARE & HUDSON CANAL MUSEUM ..... HIGH FALLS, NY 90
LOCKPORT ..... NY 100
LOCKPORT CAVE AND UNDERGROUND BOAT RIDE ..... LOCKPORT, NY 100
LOCKPORT LOCKS AND ERIE CANAL CRUISES ..... LOCKPORT, NY 100
OSWEGO CANAL ..... FULTON, NY 86
WELLAND CANAL ..... GREAT LAKES-ST. LAWRENCE SEAWAY SYSTEM, NY 89

CARILLONS
MANSION HOUSE ..... ONEIDA, ON 159
RAINBOW CARILLON TOWER ..... NIAGARA FALLS, ON 155
*RIVERSIDE CHURCH ..... UPPER MANHATTAN, NY 128

CAROUSELS
C. FRED JOHNSON PARK ..... BINGHAMTON, NY 62
FLUSHING MEADOWS CORONA PARK ..... QUEENS, NY 130
GEORGE W. JOHNSON PARK ..... BINGHAMTON, NY 62
THE HERSCHELL CARROUSEL FACTORY MUSEUM ..... NORTH TONAWANDA, NY 72
HIGHLAND PARK ..... BINGHAMTON, NY 62
RECREATION PARK ..... BINGHAMTON, NY 62
ROSS PARK ZOO ..... BINGHAMTON, NY 62
STEWART PARK ..... ITHACA, NY 94
WEST ENDICOTT PARK ..... BINGHAMTON, NY 62

CASINO AND RIVERBOAT GAMBLING
CASINO NIAGARA ..... NIAGARA FALLS, ON 156
TURNING STONE CASINO ..... VERONA, ON 181

CAVES
*HOWE CAVERNS ..... HOWES CAVE, NY 91
NATURAL STONE BRIDGE AND CAVES ..... POTTERSVILLE, ON 164

CEMETERIES
CYPRESS HILLS NC ..... BROOKLYN, NY 130
FOREST LAWN CEMETERY ..... BUFFALO, NY 70
FORT HILL CEMETERY ..... AUBURN, NY 60
MOUNT HOPE CEMETERY ..... ROCHESTER, ON 165
OLD DUTCH CHURCH AND CEMETERY ..... KINGSTON, NY 96
OLD MILITARY CEMETERY ..... SACKETS HARBOR, ON 169
SLEEPY HOLLOW CEMETERY ..... SLEEPY HOLLOW, NY 140
UNCLE SAM TABLET ..... TROY, ON 180
UNION CEMETERY ..... FORT EDWARD, NY 85
WOODLAWN CEMETERY ..... THE BRONX, NY 129
WOODLAWN NC ..... ELMIRA, NY 83
YOUNG MEMORIAL CEMETERY ..... OYSTER BAY, ON 162

CHILDREN'S ATTRACTIONS
BROOKLYN CHILDREN'S MUSEUM ..... BROOKLYN, NY 130
BUFFALO MUSEUM OF SCIENCE ..... BUFFALO, NY 69
BUFFALO ZOOLOGICAL GARDENS ..... BUFFALO, NY 69
BURNETT PARK ZOO ..... SYRACUSE, ON 177
*CATSKILL GAME FARM ..... CATSKILL, NY 74
CENTER AT HIGH FALLS ..... ROCHESTER, ON 167
CHILDREN'S CENTER ..... LOWER MANHATTAN AND NEW YORK HARBOR, NY 116
CHILDREN'S MUSEUM OF MANHATTAN ..... MIDTOWN MANHATTAN, NY 119
ENCHANTED FOREST/WATER SAFARI ..... OLD FORGE, ON 159
EVERETT CHILDREN'S ADVENTURE GARDEN ..... THE BRONX, NY 129
FORT RICKEY CHILDREN'S DISCOVERY ZOO ..... ROME, ON 168
FRONTIER TOWN ..... NORTH HUDSON, ON 157
THE GREAT ESCAPE AND SPLASHWATER KINGDOM ..... QUEENSBURY, ON 164
IROQUOIS INDIAN MUSEUM ..... HOWES CAVE, NY 91
JUNIOR MUSEUM ..... TROY, ON 179
*MARINELAND ..... NIAGARA FALLS, ON 152
MARTIN'S FANTASY ISLAND ..... GRAND ISLAND, NY 72
NEW YORK HALL OF SCIENCE ..... QUEENS, NY 131
NEW YORK SKYRIDE ..... MIDTOWN MANHATTAN, NY 124
NORTH WIND UNDERSEA INSTITUTE ..... THE BRONX, NY 129
ONTARIO COUNTY HISTORICAL SOCIETY MUSEUM ..... CANANDAIGUA, NY 73
PLAYLAND ..... RYE, NY 139
SANTA'S WORKSHOP ..... WILMINGTON, ON 185
SCIENCE DISCOVERY CENTER OF ONEONTA ..... ONEONTA, ON 160
THE SCI-TECH CENTER OF NORTHERN NEW YORK ..... WATERTOWN, ON 181
SEABREEZE PARK/RAGING RIVERS WATER PARK ..... ROCHESTER, ON 167
*SIX FLAGS DARIEN LAKE ..... DARIEN CENTER, NY 80
SONG MOUNTAIN ALPINE SLIDE ..... TULLY, ON 180
THE SONY IMAX THEATRE ..... MIDTOWN MANHATTAN, NY 125
SONY WONDER TECHNOLOGY LAB ..... MIDTOWN MANHATTAN, NY 125
SPLISH SPLASH WATER PARK ..... RIVERHEAD, ON 165
STATEN ISLAND CHILDREN'S MUSEUM ..... RICHMOND (STATEN ISLAND), NY 131
*THE STRONG MUSEUM ..... ROCHESTER, ON 168
THEATRE OF YOUTH (TOY) COMPANY ..... BUFFALO, NY 71

CHURCHES, CATHEDRALS & BASILICAS
BIG ROUND CHURCH ..... AURIESVILLE, NY 61
CAROLINE CHURCH OF BROOKHAVEN ..... SETAUKET, ON 175
CATHEDRAL OF ALL SAINTS ..... ALBANY, NY 56
CATHEDRAL OF ST. JOHN THE DIVINE ..... UPPER MANHATTAN, NY 126
CATHEDRAL OF THE IMMACULATE CONCEPTION ..... ALBANY, NY 56
CATHEDRAL OF THE INCARNATION ..... GARDEN CITY, NY 86
FIRST CHURCH IN ALBANY ..... ALBANY, NY 56
JOHN STREET CHURCH ..... LOWER MANHATTAN AND NEW YORK HARBOR, NY 115
"LITTLE CHURCH AROUND THE CORNER" ..... MIDTOWN MANHATTAN, NY 122
OLD DUTCH CHURCH AND CEMETERY ..... KINGSTON, NY 96
*RIVERSIDE CHURCH ..... UPPER MANHATTAN, NY 128
ST. JOHN'S EPISCOPAL CHURCH ..... BROOKLYN, NY 130
ST. MARK'S CHURCH IN THE BOWERY ..... LOWER MANHATTAN AND NEW YORK HARBOR, NY 115
ST. MARY OF THE CATARACT CHURCH ..... NIAGARA FALLS, NY 149
*ST. PATRICK'S CATHEDRAL ..... MIDTOWN MANHATTAN, NY 125
ST. PETER'S EPISCOPAL CHURCH ..... ALBANY, NY 56
TRINITY CHURCH ..... LOWER MANHATTAN AND NEW YORK HARBOR, NY 118

CHURCHES-CHAPELS
CADET CHAPEL ..... WEST POINT, ON 184
CHAPEL OF THE MOST HOLY TRINITY ..... WEST POINT, ON 184
*THE CLOISTERS ..... UPPER MANHATTAN, NY 126
JEWISH CHAPEL ..... WEST POINT, ON 184
MOUNT CARMEL SPIRITUAL CENTRE ..... NIAGARA FALLS, ON 153
NATIONAL SHRINE BASILICA OF OUR LADY OF FATIMA ..... LEWISTON, NY 151
OLD CADET CHAPEL ..... WEST POINT, ON 184
ST. PAUL'S CHAPEL ..... LOWER MANHATTAN AND NEW YORK HARBOR, NY 116
SHRINE OF OUR LADY OF THE ISLAND ..... EASTPORT, NY 82
UNION CHURCH OF POCANTICO HILLS ..... SLEEPY HOLLOW, NY 140
U.S. MERCHANT MARINE MEMORIAL CHAPEL ..... KINGS POINT, NY 96
WILLARD MEMORIAL CHAPEL ..... AUBURN, NY 60

CHURCHES-MISSONS
*LAKE GEORGE OPERA FESTIVAL ..... SARATOGA SPRINGS, ON 172
SAINTE MARIE AMONG THE IROQUOIS ..... SYRACUSE, ON 178

CHURCHES-SHRINES
GRAYMOOR CHRISTIAN UNITY CENTER ..... GARRISON, NY 138
MARIAN SHRINE ..... WEST HAVERSTRAW, NY 141
NATIONAL SHRINE BASILICA OF OUR LADY OF FATIMA ..... LEWISTON, NY 151
THE NATIONAL SHRINE OF BLESSED KATERI TEKAKWITHA AND NATIVE AMERICAN EXHIBIT ..... FONDA, NY 85
NATIONAL SHRINE OF NORTH AMERICAN MARTYRS ..... AURIESVILLE, NY 61
OUR LADY OF VICTORY BASILICA AND NATIONAL SHRINE ..... LACKAWANNA, NY 72
ST. FRANCES X. CABRINI SHRINE ..... UPPER MANHATTAN, NY 128
SHRINE OF OUR LADY OF THE ISLAND ..... EASTPORT, NY 82

CHURCHES-TEMPLES & SYNAGOGUES
GRAYMOOR CHRISTIAN UNITY CENTER ..... GARRISON, NY 138
TEMPLE EMANU-EL ..... MIDTOWN MANHATTAN, NY 125

CONVENTION CENTERS
INTERNATIONAL CONVENTION CENTER ..... NIAGARA FALLS, NY 150
MADISON SQUARE GARDEN ..... MIDTOWN MANHATTAN, NY 122

CONVENTS & MONASTERIES
GRAYMOOR CHRISTIAN UNITY CENTER ..... GARRISON, NY 138
MOUNT CARMEL SPIRITUAL CENTRE ..... NIAGARA FALLS, ON 153

COURTHOUSES
COURT OF APPEALS BUILDING ..... ALBANY, NY 56
THE TYRON COUNTY COURT HOUSE ..... JOHNSTOWN, NY 95

CULTURAL CENTERS & CIVIC CENTERS
*EARL W. BRYDGES ARTPARK ..... LEWISTON, NY 151
KENAN CENTER ..... LOCKPORT, NY 100
*LINCOLN CENTER FOR THE PERFORMING ARTS ..... MIDTOWN MANHATTAN, NY 122
MADISON SQUARE GARDEN ..... MIDTOWN MANHATTAN, NY 122
MIDDLEBURGH-SCHOHARIE RAILROAD COMPLEX ..... SCHOHARIE, ON 173
*MUNSON-WILLIAMS-PROCTOR ARTS INSTITUTE ..... UTICA, ON 181
SARATOGA PERFORMING ARTS CENTER ..... SARATOGA SPRINGS, ON 172
SNUG HARBOR CULTURAL CENTER ..... RICHMOND (STATEN ISLAND), NY 131
WAVE HILL ..... THE BRONX, NY 129

DAMS
*MOSES-SAUNDERS POWER DAM ..... MASSENA, NY 102

EVENTS-GENERAL
CHINESE NEW YEAR ..... NEW YORK, NY 137
EGG ROLLING ..... NEW YORK, NY 137
*FEDERAL HALL NME ..... LOWER MANHATTAN AND NEW YORK HARBOR, NY 113
HARLEM WEEK ..... NEW YORK, NY 137
LINCOLN CENTER OUT-OF-DOORS ..... NEW YORK, NY 137
MUSEUM MILE ..... NEW YORK, NY 137

NEW YORK IS BOOK COUNTRY DAY ... NEW YORK, NY 137
TREE LIGHTING CEREMONY AND CHRISTMAS CAROLS ... NEW YORK, NY 137

EVENTS-CRAFT SHOWS
FRIENDSHIP FESTIVAL ... BUFFALO, NY 71

EVENTS-DANCES
NIAGARA SUMMER EXPERIENCE ... NIAGARA FALLS, NY 150

EVENTS-FESTIVALS
ALLENTOWN ART FESTIVAL ... BUFFALO, NY 71
THE FEAST OF SAN GENNARO ... NEW YORK, NY 137
FESTA ITALIANA ... NEW YORK, NY 137
FESTIVAL OF LIGHTS ... NIAGARA FALLS, NY 150
FOURTH OF JULY FIREWORKS ... NEW YORK, NY 137
FRIENDSHIP FESTIVAL ... BUFFALO, NY 71
GREENWICH VILLAGE JAZZ ... NEW YORK, NY 137
HELLENIC FESTIVAL ... BUFFALO, NY 71
NINTH AVENUE INTERNATIONAL FOOD ... NEW YORK, NY 137
SAINT ANTHONY ... NEW YORK, NY 137
SCARECROW FESTIVAL ... NIAGARA FALLS, NY 150
STERLING RENAISSANCE FESTIVAL ... STERLING, ON 176
TASTE OF BUFFALO ... BUFFALO, NY 71
UKRAINIAN ... NEW YORK, NY 137
WINTERFEST ... BUFFALO, NY 71

EVENTS-MUSIC
FESTIVAL OF LIGHTS ... NIAGARA FALLS, NY 150
*GLIMMERGLASS OPERA ... SPRINGFIELD CENTER, ON 176
GREENWICH VILLAGE JAZZ ... NEW YORK, NY 137
METROPOLITAN OPERA SEASON ... NEW YORK, NY 137
NIAGARA SUMMER EXPERIENCE ... NIAGARA FALLS, NY 150

EVENTS-PAGEANTS, PARADES, DAYS
AFRICAN-AMERICAN DAY ... NEW YORK, NY 137
AMERICAN ETHNIC ... NEW YORK, NY 137
ARMED FORCES DAY ... NEW YORK, NY 137
COLUMBUS DAY ... NEW YORK, NY 137
DESFILE DE LA HISPANIDAD: COLUMBUS DAY ... NEW YORK, NY 137
EASTER ... NEW YORK, NY 137
FESTIVAL OF LIGHTS ... NIAGARA FALLS, NY 150
GREEK INDEPENDENCE DAY ... NEW YORK, NY 137
GREENWICH VILLAGE HALLOWEEN ... NEW YORK, NY 137
ISRAELI DAY ... NEW YORK, NY 137
LABOR DAY ... NEW YORK, NY 137
MEMORIAL DAY ... NEW YORK, NY 137
NORWEGIAN CONSTITUTION DAY ... NEW YORK, NY 137
PUERTO RICAN DAY ... NEW YORK, NY 137
PULASKI DAY ... NEW YORK, NY 137
ST. PATRICK'S DAY ... BUFFALO, NY 71
ST. PATRICK'S DAY ... NEW YORK, NY 137
SOLIDARITY DAY ... NEW YORK, NY 137
STEUBEN DAY ... NEW YORK, NY 137
THANKSGIVING DAY ... NEW YORK, NY 137
VETERANS DAY ... NEW YORK, NY 137
WEST INDIAN-AMERICAN DAY ... NEW YORK, NY 137

EVENTS-SHOWS
WASHINGTON SQUARE OUTDOOR ART SHOW ... NEW YORK, NY 137

EVENTS-SPORTS
LAKE ERIE CAN AM CHALLENGE WALLEYE TOURNAMENT ... BUFFALO, NY 71
U.S. OPEN TENNIS CHAMPIONSHIPS ... NEW YORK, NY 134

EXHIBITS & COLLECTIONS-GENERAL
ALBANY INSTITUTE OF HISTORY AND ART ... ALBANY, NY 56
ALUMNI HALL ... HAMILTON, NY 89
AMERICAN MAPLE MUSEUM ... CROGHAN, NY 80
CANAJOHARIE LIBRARY AND ART GALLERY ... CANAJOHARIE, NY 73
CASTLEGOULD ... PORT WASHINGTON, ON 163
CATHEDRAL OF ALL SAINTS ... ALBANY, NY 56
CATHEDRAL OF THE IMMACULATE CONCEPTION ... ALBANY, NY 56
*CORNING GLASS CENTER ... CORNING, NY 78
EAST HAMPTON TOWN MARINE MUSEUM ... AMAGANSETT, NY 59
FRICK COLLECTION ... MIDTOWN MANHATTAN, NY 122
*GEORGE EASTMAN HOUSE ... ROCHESTER, ON 167
GUINNESS WORLD OF RECORDS ... NIAGARA FALLS, ON 152
HANFORD MILLS MUSEUM ... EAST MEREDITH, NY 82
HARNESS RACING MUSEUM & HALL OF FAME ... GOSHEN, NY 88
HOYT-POTTER HOUSE ... ROCHESTER, ON 167
INTERNATIONAL BOXING HALL OF FAME ... CANASTOTA, NY 73
INTERNATIONAL CENTER OF PHOTOGRAPHY ... UPPER MANHATTAN, NY 128
THE INTERNATIONAL MUSEUM OF CERAMIC ART AT ALFRED ... ALFRED, NY 58
LUCY-DESI MUSEUM ... JAMESTOWN, NY 94
LUNDY'S LANE HISTORICAL MUSEUM ... NIAGARA FALLS, ON 152
MOVIELAND WAX MUSEUM ... NIAGARA FALLS, ON 153
MUSEUM OF TELEVISION AND RADIO ... MIDTOWN MANHATTAN, NY 124
NATIONAL BOTTLE MUSEUM ... BALLSTON SPA, NY 61
NEW YORK CITY POLICE MUSEUM ... LOWER MANHATTAN AND NEW YORK HARBOR, NY 115
NIAGARA FALLS ART GALLERY/KURELEK COLLECTION ... NIAGARA FALLS, ON 153
OLANA SHS ... HUDSON, NY 91
POTSDAM PUBLIC MUSEUM ... POTSDAM, ON 164
*RIPLEY'S BELIEVE IT OR NOT! MUSEUM ... NIAGARA FALLS, ON 155
ROGER TORY PETERSON INSTITUTE OF NATURAL HISTORY ... JAMESTOWN, NY 95
ROOSEVELT BIRD SANCTUARY AND TRAILSIDE MUSEUM ... OYSTER BAY, ON 162
*SENATE HOUSE SHS ... KINGSTON, NY 96
SOUTH STREET SEAPORT MUSEUM ... LOWER MANHATTAN AND NEW YORK HARBOR, NY 116
UIHLEIN-CORNELL SUGAR HOUSE ... LAKE PLACID, NY 98
UNICEF HOUSE ... MIDTOWN MANHATTAN, NY 125

EXHIBITS & COLLECTIONS-ANIMALS & BIRDS
*AMERICAN MUSEUM OF NATURAL HISTORY ... MIDTOWN MANHATTAN, NY 118
BAYARD CUTTING ARBORETUM ... GREAT RIVER, NY 89
CHARLES DICKERT WILDLIFE MUSEUM ... SARANAC LAKE, ON 171
CLYDE PEELING'S REPTILAND ... CATSKILL, NY 74
DELAWARE INDIAN RESOURCE CENTER ... CROSS RIVER, NY 138
MUSEUM OF THE HUDSON HIGHLANDS ... CORNWALL-ON-HUDSON, NY 79
NIAGARA PARKS BUTTERFLY CONSERVATORY ... NIAGARA FALLS, ON 154
THE PEMBER MUSEUM OF NATURAL HISTORY ... GRANVILLE, NY 89
ROGER TORY PETERSON NATURE INTERPRETIVE BUILDING ... JAMESTOWN, NY 94
ROGERS ENVIRONMENTAL EDUCATION CENTER ... SHERBURNE, ON 175
*VANDERBILT MANSION, MARINE MUSEUM, PLANETARIUM AND PARK ... CENTERPORT, NY 75

EXHIBITS & COLLECTIONS-AVIATION
NATIONAL SOARING MUSEUM ... ELMIRA, NY 83
NATIONAL WARPLANE MUSEUM ... HORSEHEADS, NY 91
OLD RHINEBECK AERODROME ... RHINEBECK, ON 165

EXHIBITS & COLLECTIONS-CIVIL WAR HISTORY
ONTARIO COUNTY HISTORICAL SOCIETY MUSEUM ... CANANDAIGUA, NY 73
SENECA FALLS HISTORICAL SOCIETY ... SENECA FALLS, ON 174

EXHIBITS & COLLECTIONS-CLOCKS
HOFFMAN CLOCK MUSEUM ... NEWARK, NY 105

EXHIBITS & COLLECTIONS-COINS
AMERICAN NUMISMATIC SOCIETY ... UPPER MANHATTAN, NY 126

EXHIBITS & COLLECTIONS-DOLLS & TOYS
GLENN H. CURTISS MUSEUM ... HAMMONDSPORT, NY 89
HERKIMER COUNTY HISTORICAL SOCIETY ... HERKIMER, NY 90
HISTORIC RICHMOND TOWN ... RICHMOND (STATEN ISLAND), NY 131
*ROCKWELL MUSEUM ... CORNING, NY 79
SCHUYLER COUNTY HISTORICAL SOCIETY MUSEUM ... MONTOUR FALLS, NY 104
TOY TOWN MUSEUM ... EAST AURORA, NY 72
VICTORIAN DOLL MUSEUM AND CHILI DOLL HOSPITAL ... NORTH CHILI, ON 157

EXHIBITS & COLLECTIONS-HISTORICAL
THE 1890 HOUSE MUSEUM ... CORTLAND, NY 79
1932 & 1980 LAKE PLACID WINTER OLYMPIC MUSEUM ... LAKE PLACID, NY 98
ADIRONDACK HISTORY CENTER ... ELIZABETHTOWN, NY 82
*ADIRONDACK MUSEUM ... BLUE MOUNTAIN LAKE, NY 63
AGRICULTURAL MUSEUM ... LA FARGEVILLE, NY 96
ALBANY INSTITUTE OF HISTORY AND ART ... ALBANY, NY 56
*THE ALICE T. MINER MUSEUM ... CHAZY, NY 76
ALLING COVERLET MUSEUM ... PALMYRA, ON 162
ALUMNI HALL ... HAMILTON, NY 89
*AMERICAN MUSEUM OF FIREFIGHTING ... HUDSON, NY 91
THE AMERICAN MUSEUM OF IMMIGRATION ... LOWER MANHATTAN AND NEW YORK HARBOR, NY 117
*AMERICAN MUSEUM OF NATURAL HISTORY ... MIDTOWN MANHATTAN, NY 118
AMHERST MUSEUM ... AMHERST, NY 71
BARTOW-PELL MANSION MUSEUM ... THE BRONX, NY 128
BOLDT CASTLE ... ALEXANDRIA BAY, NY 58
BOOK OF MORMON HISTORIC PUBLICATION SITE ... PALMYRA, ON 162
*BOSCOBEL ... GARRISON, NY 138
BOWNE AND CO. STATIONERS ... LOWER MANHATTAN AND NEW YORK HARBOR, NY 116
BRIDGEHAMPTON HISTORICAL MUSEUM ... BRIDGEHAMPTON, NY 63
BRONCK MUSEUM ... COXSACKIE, NY 80
BROOKLYN HISTORY MUSEUM ... BROOKLYN, NY 130
BUFFALO AND ERIE COUNTY HISTORICAL SOCIETY ... BUFFALO, NY 69
CAMPBELL-WHITTLESEY HOUSE MUSEUM ... ROCHESTER, ON 166
CANAJOHARIE LIBRARY AND ART GALLERY ... CANAJOHARIE, NY 73
CANAL MUSEUM ... LOCKPORT, NY 100
CANASTOTA CANAL TOWN MUSEUM ... CANASTOTA, NY 73
CAPE VINCENT HISTORICAL MUSEUM ... CAPE VINCENT, NY 74
CARRIAGE HOUSE MUSEUM ... TAPPAN, NY 140
CATHEDRAL OF ALL SAINTS ... ALBANY, NY 56
CATHEDRAL OF THE IMMACULATE CONCEPTION ... ALBANY, NY 56
CAYUGA MUSEUM/CASE RESEARCH LAB MUSEUM ... AUBURN, NY 60
CENTERS FOR NATURE EDUCATION/BALTIMORE WOODS ... MARCELLUS, NY 102
THE CHAPMAN HISTORICAL MUSEUM ... GLENS FALLS, NY 88
CHEMUNG VALLEY HISTORICAL MUSEUM ... ELMIRA, NY 83
CHERRY VALLEY MUSEUM ... CHERRY VALLEY, NY 76
CLERMONT SHS ... GERMANTOWN, NY 87
CLINTON ACADEMY ... EAST HAMPTON, NY 82
CLINTON COUNTY HISTORICAL MUSEUM ... PLATTSBURGH, ON 163
COE HALL ... OYSTER BAY, ON 161
COL. WILLIAM M. BOND HOUSE ... LOCKPORT, NY 100
COLUMBIA COUNTY MUSEUM ... KINDERHOOK, NY 95
CONSTABLE HALL ... CONSTABLEVILLE, NY 77
THE CORNING-PAINTED POST HISTORICAL SOCIETY MUSEUM COMPLEX ... CORNING, NY 78
CRAILO SHS ... RENSSELAER, ON 165
CROWN POINT SHS ... CROWN POINT, NY 80
CUSTOM HOUSE ... SAG HARBOR, ON 170
DELAWARE & HUDSON CANAL MUSEUM ... HIGH FALLS, NY 90
DELAWARE COUNTY HISTORICAL ASSOCIATION MUSEUM ... DELHI, NY 81
DUNKIRK HISTORICAL LIGHTHOUSE AND VETERANS PARK MUSEUM ... DUNKIRK, NY 81
DUNKIRK HISTORICAL MUSEUM ... DUNKIRK, NY 81
DYCKMAN HOUSE ... UPPER MANHATTAN, NY 126
EARLE-WIGHTMAN HOUSE MUSEUM ... OYSTER BAY, ON 161
ELEANOR ROOSEVELT NHS ... HYDE PARK, NY 92
*ELLIS ISLAND ... LOWER MANHATTAN AND NEW YORK HARBOR, NY 117
FALAISE ... PORT WASHINGTON, ON 163
*THE FARMERS' MUSEUM ... COOPERSTOWN, NY 77
*FENIMORE ART MUSEUM ... COOPERSTOWN, NY 78
FENTON HISTORY CENTER-MUSEUM & LIBRARY ... JAMESTOWN, NY 94
FORT DELAWARE—MUSEUM OF COLONIAL HISTORY ... NARROWSBURG, NY 104
FORT JOHNSON ... FORT JOHNSON, NY 85
FORT KLOCK HISTORIC RESTORATION ... ST. JOHNSVILLE, ON 170
*FORT TICONDEROGA ... NY 86
FORT WILLIAM HENRY MUSEUM ... LAKE GEORGE (VILLAGE), NY 97
FOUNTAIN ELMS MUSEUM ... UTICA, ON 181
FRANKLIN COUNTY HOUSE OF HISTORY ... MALONE, NY 101
*FRANKLIN D. ROOSEVELT MUSEUM AND LIBRARY ... HYDE PARK, NY 92
FULTON COUNTY MUSEUM ... GLOVERSVILLE, NY 88
GARVIES POINT MUSEUM AND PRESERVE ... GLEN COVE, NY 88
*GENESEE COUNTRY VILLAGE & MUSEUM ... MUMFORD, NY 104
GEORGE WASHINGTON'S HEADQUARTERS AT TAPPAN ... TAPPAN, NY 140
GLENN H. CURTISS MUSEUM ... HAMMONDSPORT, NY 89
GOSHEN PUBLIC LIBRARY ... GOSHEN, NY 88
GRANGER HOMESTEAD AND CARRIAGE MUSEUM ... CANANDAIGUA, NY 73
GRANT COTTAGE SHS ... WILTON, ON 185
GREAT CAMP SAGAMORE ... RAQUETTE LAKE, ON 165
H. LEE WHITE MARINE MUSEUM ... OSWEGO, ON 160
HARNESS RACING MUSEUM & HALL OF FAME ... GOSHEN, NY 88
HART-CLUETT MANSION ... TROY, ON 179
HERKIMER COUNTY HISTORICAL SOCIETY ... HERKIMER, NY 90
HERKIMER HOME SHS ... LITTLE FALLS, NY 100
HILL-HOLD MUSEUM ... MONTGOMERY, NY 103
HISTORIC BUILDINGS ... STONY BROOK, ON 177
HISTORIC CHERRY HILL ... ALBANY, NY 56
HISTORIC RICHMOND TOWN ... RICHMOND (STATEN ISLAND), NY 131
HISTORICAL SOCIETY MUSEUM ... GENEVA, NY 87
HISTORICAL SOCIETY OF ROCKLAND COUNTY ... NEW CITY, NY 139
HISTORICAL SOCIETY OF SARATOGA SPRINGS MUSEUM ... SARATOGA SPRINGS, ON 172
HISTORY MUSEUM ... STONY BROOK, ON 177
HOLLAND LAND OFFICE MUSEUM ... BATAVIA, NY 61
*HOME OF FRANKLIN D. ROOSEVELT NHS ... HYDE PARK, NY 93
"HOME SWEET HOME" ... EAST HAMPTON, NY 82
THE HORSEHEADS HISTORICAL SOCIETY MUSEUM ... HORSEHEADS, NY 91

THE HUDSON RIVER MUSEUM OF WESTCHESTER ... YONKERS, NY 141
HUDSON-MOHAWK URBAN CULTURAL PARK ... TROY, ON 179
HUNTINGTON HISTORICAL SOCIETY ... HUNTINGTON, NY 92
IRISH-AMERICAN HERITAGE MUSEUM ... EAST DURHAM, NY 81
IROQUOIS INDIAN MUSEUM ... HOWES CAVE, NY 91
JACQUES MARCHAIS MUSEUM OF TIBETAN ART ... RICHMOND (STATEN ISLAND), NY 131
JAMES VANDERPOEL HOUSE ... KINDERHOOK, NY 95
JEFFERSON COUNTY HISTORICAL SOCIETY ... WATERTOWN, ON 181
JEWISH MUSEUM ... UPPER MANHATTAN, NY 128
JOHN JAY HOMESTEAD SHS ... KATONAH, NY 138
JOHNSON HALL SHS ... JOHNSTOWN, NY 95
JOSEPH SMITH HOME ... PALMYRA, ON 162
JUNIOR MUSEUM ... TROY, ON 179
KENT-DELORD HOUSE MUSEUM ... PLATTSBURGH, ON 163
LAKE PLACID/NORTH ELBA HISTORICAL SOCIETY MUSEUM ... LAKE PLACID, NY 98
LANSING MANOR MUSEUM ... NORTH BLENHEIM, ON 157
LEFFERTS HOMESTEAD ... BROOKLYN, NY 130
LEWIS COUNTY HISTORICAL SOCIETY MUSEUM (GOULD MANSION) ... LYONS FALLS, NY 101
LITTLE FALLS HISTORICAL SOCIETY MUSEUM ... LITTLE FALLS, NY 100
LOCUST LAWN FEDERAL MANSION AND STONE HOUSE ... NEW PALTZ, NY 105
THE LOG VILLAGE GRIST MILL AND MUSEUM ... HARTFORD, NY 90
LORENZO SHS ... CAZENOVIA, NY 75
LUNDY'S LANE HISTORICAL MUSEUM ... NIAGARA FALLS, ON 152
LUYKAS VAN ALEN HOUSE AND ICHABOD CRANE SCHOOLHOUSE ... KINDERHOOK, NY 95
LYNDHURST ... TARRYTOWN, NY 140
MADAME BRETT'S HOMESTEAD ... BEACON, NY 61
MADISON COUNTY HISTORICAL SOCIETY HEADQUARTERS ... ONEIDA, ON 159
MANOR OF ST. GEORGE ... SHIRLEY, ON 175
MANSION HOUSE ... ONEIDA, ON 159
MARGARET REANEY MEMORIAL LIBRARY AND MUSEUM ... ST. JOHNSVILLE, ON 170
MARTIN VAN BUREN NHS ... KINDERHOOK, NY 95
MASSENA MUSEUM ... MASSENA, NY 102
THE MCCLURG MANSION ... WESTFIELD, ON 183
MILLARD FILLMORE CABIN ... MORAVIA, NY 104
MONTAUK POINT LIGHTHOUSE MUSEUM ... MONTAUK, NY 103
MONTGOMERY PLACE ... ANNANDALE-ON-HUDSON, NY 59
MORRIS-JUMEL MANSION ... UPPER MANHATTAN, NY 128
THE MULFORD FARMHOUSE ... EAST HAMPTON, NY 82
MUSEUM GALLERY ... LOWER MANHATTAN AND NEW YORK HARBOR, NY 116
MUSEUM OF AMERICAN FINANCIAL HISTORY ... LOWER MANHATTAN AND NEW YORK HARBOR, NY 115
MUSEUM OF JEWISH HERITAGE—A LIVING MEMORIAL TO THE HOLOCAUST ... LOWER MANHATTAN AND NEW YORK HARBOR, NY 115
MUSEUM OF THE CITY OF NEW YORK ... UPPER MANHATTAN, NY 128
MUSEUM OF THE HUDSON HIGHLANDS ... CORNWALL-ON-HUDSON, NY 79
MUSEUM VILLAGE ... MONROE, NY 103
THE MUSEUMS AT STONY BROOK ... STONY BROOK, ON 177
NEVERSINK VALLEY AREA MUSEUM ... CUDDEBACKVILLE, NY 80
NEW WINDSOR CANTONMENT SHS ... NEWBURGH, NY 105
NEW YORK CITY FIRE MUSEUM ... LOWER MANHATTAN AND NEW YORK HARBOR, NY 115
NEW YORK HISTORICAL SOCIETY ... MIDTOWN MANHATTAN, NY 124
NEW YORK STATE MUSEUM ... ALBANY, NY 56
NIAGARA COUNTY HISTORICAL SOCIETY ... LOCKPORT, NY 100
NIAGARA'S WAX MUSEUM ... NIAGARA FALLS, NY 148
NORWAY GALLERIES ... LOWER MANHATTAN AND NEW YORK HARBOR, NY 116
OLD BETHPAGE VILLAGE RESTORATION ... OLD BETHPAGE, ON 158
OLD FORT HOUSE MUSEUM ... FORT EDWARD, NY 85
OLD STONE FORT MUSEUM COMPLEX ... SCHOHARIE, ON 173
THE OLDE HALSEY HOUSE ... SOUTHAMPTON, ON 176
ONEIDA COUNTY HISTORICAL SOCIETY ... UTICA, ON 181
ONONDAGA HISTORICAL ASSOCIATION MUSEUM ... SYRACUSE, ON 178
ONTARIO COUNTY HISTORICAL SOCIETY MUSEUM ... CANANDAIGUA, NY 73
OPUS 40 AND QUARRYMAN'S MUSEUM ... SAUGERTIES, ON 173
THE PENFIELD HOMESTEAD HISTORICAL MUSEUM ... CROWN POINT, NY 80
THE PHILIP SCHUYLER HOUSE ... SARATOGA NHP, ON 172
PHILIPSBURG MANOR ... SLEEPY HOLLOW, NY 140
PRATT HOUSE ... FULTON, NY 86
RAIL CITY HISTORICAL MUSEUM ... SANDY CREEK, ON 171
REMINGTON MUSEUM ... ILION, NY 93
RICHARDSON-BATES HOUSE MUSEUM ... OSWEGO, ON 161
ROBERSON MUSEUM AND SCIENCE CENTER ... BINGHAMTON, NY 62
ROBERT JENKINS HOUSE AND MUSEUM ... HUDSON, NY 91
ROBERT LOUIS STEVENSON COTTAGE ... SARANAC LAKE, ON 171
ROCK HALL MUSEUM ... LAWRENCE, NY 99
*ROSE HILL MANSION ... GENEVA, NY 87
SACKETS HARBOR BATTLEFIELD SHS ... SACKETS HARBOR, ON 169
SAG HARBOR WHALING MUSEUM ... SAG HARBOR, ON 170
SAGAMORE HILL NHS ... OYSTER BAY, ON 162
ST. LAWRENCE COUNTY MUSEUM ... CANTON, NY 74
SAINTE MARIE AMONG THE IROQUOIS ... SYRACUSE, ON 178
SALT MUSEUM ... SYRACUSE, ON 178
SAMUEL F.B. MORSE HISTORIC SITE, LOCUST GROVE ... POUGHKEEPSIE, ON 164
SANDS POINT PRESERVE ... PORT WASHINGTON, ON 163
SCHENECTADY COUNTY HISTORICAL SOCIETY MUSEUM ... SCHENECTADY, ON 173
SCHENECTADY MUSEUM AND SCHENECTADY HERITAGE AREA VISITORS CENTER ... SCHENECTADY, ON 173
SCHUYLER COUNTY HISTORICAL SOCIETY MUSEUM ... MONTOUR FALLS, NY 104
SECOND HOUSE MUSEUM ... MONTAUK, NY 103
*SENATE HOUSE SHS ... KINGSTON, NY 96
SENECA FALLS HISTORICAL SOCIETY ... SENECA FALLS, ON 174
THE SHAKER MUSEUM AND LIBRARY ... OLD CHATHAM, ON 158
SKENESBOROUGH MUSEUM ... WHITEHALL, ON 185
SMITHSONIAN'S NATIONAL MUSEUM OF THE AMERICAN INDIAN ... LOWER MANHATTAN AND NEW YORK HARBOR, NY 116
SONNENBERG GARDENS ... CANANDAIGUA, NY 73
SOUTHAMPTON HISTORICAL MUSEUM AND COLONIAL SOCIETY ... SOUTHAMPTON, ON 176
STATEN ISLAND FERRY COLLECTION ... RICHMOND (STATEN ISLAND), NY 132
STATEN ISLAND INSTITUTE OF ARTS AND SCIENCES ... RICHMOND (STATEN ISLAND), NY 132
STONE-TOLAN HOUSE MUSEUM ... ROCHESTER, ON 168
*THE STRONG MUSEUM ... ROCHESTER, ON 168
SUFFOLK COUNTY HISTORICAL SOCIETY ... RIVERHEAD, ON 165
*SUNNYSIDE ... TARRYTOWN, NY 141
THEODORE ROOSEVELT BIRTHPLACE NHS ... LOWER MANHATTAN AND NEW YORK HARBOR, NY 117
THEODORE ROOSEVELT INAUGURAL NHS ... BUFFALO, NY 69
THOMPSON HOUSE ... SETAUKET, ON 175
THE THOUSAND ISLANDS MUSEUM ... CLAYTON, NY 77
TICONDEROGA HISTORICAL SOCIETY LIBRARY AND MUSEUM ... TICONDEROGA, ON 179
THE TIOGA COUNTY HISTORICAL SOCIETY MUSEUM ... OWEGO, ON 161
TOLLHOUSE ... UPPER DELAWARE SCENIC AND RECREATIONAL RIVER, ON 180
TOMPKINS COUNTY MUSEUM AND DEWITT HISTORICAL SOCIETY ... ITHACA, NY 94
VAN CORTLANDT MANOR ... CROTON-ON-HUDSON, NY 138
*VANDERBILT MANSION, MARINE MUSEUM, PLANETARIUM AND PARK ... CENTERPORT, NY 75
*VANDERBILT MANSION NHS ... HYDE PARK, NY 93
VOLUNTEER FIREMEN'S HALL AND MUSEUM OF KINGSTON ... KINGSTON, NY 96
WALT WHITMAN BIRTHPLACE SHS ... HUNTINGTON, NY 92
WALTER ELWOOD MUSEUM AND ART GALLERY ... AMSTERDAM, NY 59
WALWORTH MEMORIAL MUSEUM ... SARATOGA SPRINGS, ON 172
WASHINGTON'S HEADQUARTERS MUSEUM (ELIJAH MILLER HOUSE) ... WHITE PLAINS, NY 141
WATERVLIET ARSENAL MUSEUM ... WATERVLIET, ON 183
WAYNE COUNTY HISTORICAL SOCIETY MUSEUM ... LYONS, NY 101
WESTBURY HOUSE ... OLD WESTBURY, ON 159
WILDER FARM—BOYHOOD HOME OF ALMANZO WILDER ... MALONE, NY 101
WILLIAM FLOYD ESTATE ... FIRE ISLAND NS, NY 85
WILLIAM H. SEWARD HOUSE ... AUBURN, NY 60
WILLIAM PRYOR LETCHWORTH PIONEER AND INDIAN MUSEUM ... CASTILE, NY 74
WILLIAMSVILLE WATER MILLS ... WILLIAMSVILLE, NY 72
THE WINE AND GRAPE MUSEUM OF GREYTON H. TAYLOR ... HAMMONDSPORT, NY 89
WOMEN'S RIGHTS NHP ... SENECA FALLS, ON 174
WOODSIDE MANSION ... ROCHESTER, ON 168
ZADOCK PRATT MUSEUM ... PRATTSVILLE, ON 164

EXHIBITS & COLLECTIONS-INDIAN

*AMERICAN MUSEUM OF NATURAL HISTORY ... MIDTOWN MANHATTAN, NY 118
BAYARD CUTTING ARBORETUM ... GREAT RIVER, NY 89
CAYUGA COUNTY AGRICULTURAL MUSEUM ... AUBURN, NY 60
CHERRY VALLEY MUSEUM ... CHERRY VALLEY, NY 76
DELAWARE INDIAN RESOURCE CENTER ... CROSS RIVER, NY 138
FORT JOHNSON ... FORT JOHNSON, NY 85
FORT PLAIN MUSEUM ... FORT PLAIN, NY 86
GANONDAGAN SHS ... VICTOR, ON 181
IROQUOIS INDIAN MUSEUM ... HOWES CAVE, NY 91
THE NATIONAL SHRINE OF BLESSED KATERI TEKAKWITHA AND NATIVE AMERICAN EXHIBIT ... FONDA, NY 85
NATIONAL SHRINE OF NORTH AMERICAN MARTYRS ... AURIESVILLE, NY 61
NIAGARA COUNTY HISTORICAL SOCIETY ... LOCKPORT, NY 100
*ROCKWELL MUSEUM ... CORNING, NY 79
SAINTE MARIE AMONG THE IROQUOIS ... SYRACUSE, ON 178
SCHUYLER COUNTY HISTORICAL SOCIETY MUSEUM ... MONTOUR FALLS, NY 104
SENECA-IROQUOIS NATIONAL MUSEUM ... SALAMANCA, ON 170
SMITHSONIAN'S NATIONAL MUSEUM OF THE AMERICAN INDIAN ... LOWER MANHATTAN AND NEW YORK HARBOR, NY 116
THE TIOGA COUNTY HISTORICAL SOCIETY MUSEUM ... OWEGO, ON 161
WALTER ELWOOD MUSEUM AND ART GALLERY ... AMSTERDAM, NY 59

EXHIBITS & COLLECTIONS-MUSIC

MARCELLA SEMBRICH MEMORIAL STUDIO ... BOLTON LANDING, NY 63
*METROPOLITAN MUSEUM OF ART ... MIDTOWN MANHATTAN, NY 124

EXHIBITS & COLLECTIONS-REVOLUTIONARY WAR HISTORY

CROWN POINT SHS ... CROWN POINT, NY 80
FORT JOHNSON ... FORT JOHNSON, NY 85
*FORT STANWIX NMO ... NY 86
*FORT TICONDEROGA ... NY 86
GEORGE WASHINGTON'S HEADQUARTERS AT TAPPAN ... TAPPAN, NY 140
HERKIMER HOME SHS ... LITTLE FALLS, NY 100
JOHNSON HALL SHS ... JOHNSTOWN, NY 95
MORRIS-JUMEL MANSION ... UPPER MANHATTAN, NY 128
NEW WINDSOR CANTONMENT SHS ... NEWBURGH, NY 105
OLD FORT HOUSE MUSEUM ... FORT EDWARD, NY 85
ORISKANY MUSEUM ... ORISKANY, ON 160
RAYNHAM HALL MUSEUM ... OYSTER BAY, ON 162
TROPHY POINT ... WEST POINT, ON 184
*WASHINGTON'S HEADQUARTERS SHS ... NEWBURGH, NY 105

EXHIBITS & COLLECTIONS-SCIENCE

BUFFALO MUSEUM OF SCIENCE ... BUFFALO, NY 69
CHILDREN'S MUSEUM OF MANHATTAN ... MIDTOWN MANHATTAN, NY 119
THE ENERGY CENTER ... OSWEGO, ON 160
HICKSVILLE GREGORY MUSEUM ... HICKSVILLE, NY 90
THE HUDSON RIVER MUSEUM OF WESTCHESTER ... YONKERS, NY 141
JUNIOR MUSEUM ... TROY, ON 179
MILTON J. RUBENSTEIN MUSEUM OF SCIENCE AND TECHNOLOGY ... SYRACUSE, ON 178
*MOSES-SAUNDERS POWER DAM ... MASSENA, NY 102
NEW YORK HALL OF SCIENCE ... QUEENS, NY 131
NEW YORK STATE MUSEUM ... ALBANY, NY 56
NORTH WIND UNDERSEA INSTITUTE ... THE BRONX, NY 129
ROBERSON MUSEUM AND SCIENCE CENTER ... BINGHAMTON, NY 62
*ROCHESTER MUSEUM & SCIENCE CENTER ... ROCHESTER, ON 167
SCHENECTADY MUSEUM AND SCHENECTADY HERITAGE AREA VISITORS CENTER ... SCHENECTADY, ON 173
SCIENCE DISCOVERY CENTER OF ONEONTA ... ONEONTA, ON 160
SCIENCENTER ... ITHACA, NY 94
THE SCI-TECH CENTER OF NORTHERN NEW YORK ... WATERTOWN, ON 181
SONY WONDER TECHNOLOGY LAB ... MIDTOWN MANHATTAN, NY 125

EXHIBITS & COLLECTIONS-SPORTS

1932 & 1980 LAKE PLACID WINTER OLYMPIC MUSEUM ... LAKE PLACID, NY 98

EXHIBITS & COLLECTIONS-VEHICLES

*ADIRONDACK MUSEUM ... BLUE MOUNTAIN LAKE, NY 63
ANTIQUE BOAT MUSEUM ... CLAYTON, NY 77
CARRIAGE MUSEUM ... STONY BROOK, ON 177
DELAWARE AND ULSTER RAIL RIDE ... ARKVILLE, NY 59
FULTON MARKET BUILDING ... LOWER MANHATTAN AND NEW YORK HARBOR, NY 116
GLENN H. CURTISS MUSEUM ... HAMMONDSPORT, NY 89
GRANGER HOMESTEAD AND CARRIAGE MUSEUM ... CANANDAIGUA, NY 73
INTREPID SEA-AIR-SPACE MUSEUM ... MIDTOWN MANHATTAN, NY 122
LONG ISLAND MARITIME MUSEUM ... WEST SAYVILLE, ON 184
LORENZO SHS ... CAZENOVIA, NY 75
THE MUSEUM OF AUTOMOBILE HISTORY ... SYRACUSE, ON 178
MUSEUM SHIPS ... LOWER MANHATTAN AND NEW YORK HARBOR, NY 116
THE MUSEUMS AT STONY BROOK ... STONY BROOK, ON 177
NEW YORK CITY TRANSIT MUSEUM ... BROOKLYN, NY 130
NIAGARA COUNTY HISTORICAL SOCIETY ... LOCKPORT, NY 100
NORTHEAST CLASSIC CAR MUSEUM ... NORWICH, ON 158

PEDALING HISTORY BICYCLE MUSEUM ... ORCHARD PARK, NY 72
SALAMANCA RAIL MUSEUM ... SALAMANCA, ON 170
WAYNE COUNTY HISTORICAL SOCIETY MUSEUM ... LYONS, NY 101

EXHIBITS & COLLECTIONS-WARS

CLINTON COUNTY HISTORICAL MUSEUM ... PLATTSBURGH, ON 163
DUNKIRK HISTORICAL LIGHTHOUSE AND VETERANS PARK MUSEUM ... DUNKIRK, NY 81
ELDRED WWII MUSEUM ... ELDRED, NY 82
*FORT TICONDEROGA ... NY 86
LUNDY'S LANE HISTORICAL MUSEUM ... NIAGARA FALLS, ON 152
NAVAL AND MILITARY PARK ... BUFFALO, NY 69
NEW WINDSOR CANTONMENT SHS ... NEWBURGH, NY 105
ORISKANY MUSEUM ... ORISKANY, ON 160
TROPHY POINT ... WEST POINT, ON 184
*WEST POINT MUSEUM ... WEST POINT, ON 184

EXHIBITS & COLLECTIONS-WEAPONS

*FORT TICONDEROGA ... NY 86
*ROCKWELL MUSEUM ... CORNING, NY 79

FARMS

THE ANIMAL FARM ... MANORVILLE, NY 101
FARM SANCTUARY ... WATKINS GLEN, ON 183
MISTY MEADOW FARM ... ROMULUS, ON 169
THE MULFORD FARMHOUSE ... EAST HAMPTON, NY 82
MURPHY ORCHARD ... NIAGARA FALLS, NY 150

FISH HATCHERIES

SALMON RIVER FISH HATCHERY ... ALTMAR, NY 58

FORESTS

CENTERS FOR NATURE EDUCATION/BALTIMORE WOODS ... MARCELLUS, NY 102

FORESTS, NATIONAL; STATE

CATSKILL FOREST PRESERVE ... CATSKILL, NY 74
FINGER LAKES NF ... NY 84

FORTS & MILITARY INSTALLATIONS

CROWN POINT SHS ... CROWN POINT, NY 80
FORT DELAWARE—MUSEUM OF COLONIAL HISTORY ... NARROWSBURG, NY 104
FORT DRUM ... WATERTOWN, ON 181
FORT HANCOCK ... GATEWAY NRA, NY 87
FORT JOHNSON ... FORT JOHNSON, NY 85
FORT KLOCK HISTORIC RESTORATION ... ST. JOHNSVILLE, ON 170
FORT ONTARIO SHS ... OSWEGO, ON 160
*FORT STANWIX NMO ... NY 86
*FORT TICONDEROGA ... NY 86
FORT TILDEN ... GATEWAY NRA, NY 87
FORT WILLIAM HENRY MUSEUM ... LAKE GEORGE (VILLAGE), NY 97
*OLD FORT NIAGARA ... YOUNGSTOWN, NY 151
OLD STONE FORT MUSEUM COMPLEX ... SCHOHARIE, ON 173
THE SITE OF FORT CLINTON ... WEST POINT, ON 184
*UNITED STATES MILITARY ACADEMY ... WEST POINT, ON 184
WEST BATTERY FORT ... LOWER MANHATTAN AND NEW YORK HARBOR, NY 113

FOSSILS

FOSSIL TREE STUMPS ... GILBOA, NY 88

FOUNTAINS

PEACE FOUNTAIN ... UPPER MANHATTAN, NY 126

GAPS & PASSES

AUSABLE CHASM ... AUSABLE CHASM, NY 61
CHAUTAUQUA GORGE ... WESTFIELD, ON 183
HIGH FALLS GORGE ... WILMINGTON, ON 185
ROME-BOONVILLE GORGE ... ROME, ON 169

GARDENS

ADIRONDACK HISTORY CENTER ... ELIZABETHTOWN, NY 82
*THE ALICE T. MINER MUSEUM ... CHAZY, NY 76
BARTOW-PELL MANSION MUSEUM ... THE BRONX, NY 128
BIBLICAL GARDEN ... UPPER MANHATTAN, NY 126
*BROOKLYN BOTANIC GARDEN ... BROOKLYN, NY 130
BROOKLYN MUSEUM ... BROOKLYN, NY 130
BUFFALO AND ERIE COUNTY BOTANICAL GARDENS ... BUFFALO, NY 69
CASINO AND CONGRESS PARK ... SARATOGA SPRINGS, ON 172
CENTERS FOR NATURE EDUCATION/BALTIMORE WOODS ... MARCELLUS, NY 102
CENTRAL PARK ... SCHENECTADY, ON 173
CLARK BOTANIC GARDEN ... ALBERTSON, NY 57
CLERMONT SHS ... GERMANTOWN, NY 87
CONSERVATORY GARDENS ... MIDTOWN MANHATTAN, NY 119
CORNELL PLANTATIONS ... ITHACA, NY 93
DONALD KENDALL SCULPTURE GARDENS ... PURCHASE, NY 139
EAST HAMPTON TOWN MARINE MUSEUM ... AMAGANSETT, NY 59
ELEANOR ROOSEVELT NHS ... HYDE PARK, NY 92
EVERETT CHILDREN'S ADVENTURE GARDEN ... THE BRONX, NY 129
FLORAL CLOCK ... NIAGARA FALLS, ON 151
FORT DELAWARE—MUSEUM OF COLONIAL HISTORY ... NARROWSBURG, NY 104
*GEORGE EASTMAN HOUSE ... ROCHESTER, ON 167
HERKIMER HOME SHS ... LITTLE FALLS, NY 100
HIGHLAND PARK ... ROCHESTER, ON 167
HILL-HOLD MUSEUM ... MONTGOMERY, NY 103
*HOME OF FRANKLIN D. ROOSEVELT NHS ... HYDE PARK, NY 93
HOOPES MEMORIAL PARK ... AUBURN, NY 60
THE ISAMU NOGUCHI GARDEN MUSEUM ... QUEENS, NY 131
JACKSON'S GARDEN ... SCHENECTADY, ON 173
JEFFERSON COUNTY HISTORICAL SOCIETY ... WATERTOWN, ON 181
KENAN HOUSE ... LOCKPORT, NY 100
LUA A. MINNS MEMORIAL GARDENS ... ITHACA, NY 93
LYNDHURST ... TARRYTOWN, NY 140
MAPLEWOOD PARK ... ROCHESTER, ON 167
MONTGOMERY PLACE ... ANNANDALE-ON-HUDSON, NY 59
*NEW YORK BOTANICAL GARDEN ... THE BRONX, NY 129
THE NIAGARA PARKS BOTANICAL GARDENS ... NIAGARA FALLS, ON 154
NIAGARA PARKS GREENHOUSES ... NIAGARA FALLS, ON 154
OAKES GARDEN THEATRE ... NIAGARA FALLS, ON 154
OLD STONE FORT MUSEUM COMPLEX ... SCHOHARIE, ON 173
OLD WESTBURY GARDENS ... OLD WESTBURY, ON 159
THE OLDE HALSEY HOUSE ... SOUTHAMPTON, ON 176
PEPSICO SCULPTURE GARDEN ... HARRISON, NY 138
*PLANTING FIELDS ARBORETUM SHP ... OYSTER BAY, ON 161
QUEENS BOTANICAL GARDEN ... QUEENS, NY 131
ROCK HALL MUSEUM ... LAWRENCE, NY 99
SAMUEL F.B. MORSE HISTORIC SITE, LOCUST GROVE ... POUGHKEEPSIE, ON 164
SCHENECTADY COUNTY HISTORICAL SOCIETY MUSEUM ... SCHENECTADY, ON 173
SCHOELLKOPF GEOLOGICAL MUSEUM ... NIAGARA FALLS, NY 149
SENECA FALLS HISTORICAL SOCIETY ... SENECA FALLS, ON 174
SHRINE OF OUR LADY OF THE ISLAND ... EASTPORT, NY 82
SONNENBERG GARDENS ... CANANDAIGUA, NY 73
STATEN ISLAND BOTANICAL GARDEN ... RICHMOND (STATEN ISLAND), NY 131
STEWART PARK ... ITHACA, NY 94
TARGET ROCK NWR ... SHIRLEY, ON 175
WAVE HILL ... THE BRONX, NY 129
WINTERGARDEN ... NIAGARA FALLS, NY 149
YADDO ... SARATOGA SPRINGS, ON 172

GENEALOGICAL INFORMATION

CANAJOHARIE LIBRARY AND ART GALLERY ... CANAJOHARIE, NY 73
CAPE VINCENT HISTORICAL MUSEUM ... CAPE VINCENT, NY 74
COLUMBIA COUNTY MUSEUM ... KINDERHOOK, NY 95
FENTON HISTORY CENTER-MUSEUM & LIBRARY ... JAMESTOWN, NY 94
GOSHEN PUBLIC LIBRARY ... GOSHEN, NY 88
LITTLE FALLS HISTORICAL SOCIETY MUSEUM ... LITTLE FALLS, NY 100
LOWER EAST SIDE TENEMENT MUSEUM ... LOWER MANHATTAN AND NEW YORK HARBOR, NY 115
MADISON COUNTY HISTORICAL SOCIETY HEADQUARTERS ... ONEIDA, ON 159
OLD STONE FORT MUSEUM COMPLEX ... SCHOHARIE, ON 173
ONTARIO COUNTY HISTORICAL SOCIETY MUSEUM ... CANANDAIGUA, NY 73
ROBERT JENKINS HOUSE AND MUSEUM ... HUDSON, NY 91
SCHENECTADY COUNTY HISTORICAL SOCIETY MUSEUM ... SCHENECTADY, ON 173
SENECA FALLS HISTORICAL SOCIETY ... SENECA FALLS, ON 174
THE TIOGA COUNTY HISTORICAL SOCIETY MUSEUM ... OWEGO, ON 161
WOODSIDE MANSION ... ROCHESTER, ON 168

GEOLOGICAL FORMATIONS

NATURAL STONE BRIDGE AND CAVES ... POTTERSVILLE, ON 164
NIAGARA ESCARPMENT ... NIAGARA FALLS, ON 155
PANAMA ROCKS ... PANAMA, ON 162

GRAVES & TOMBS

ALEXANDER HAMILTON ... LOWER MANHATTAN AND NEW YORK HARBOR, NY 118
ANDREW CARNEGIE ... SLEEPY HOLLOW, NY 140
DUKE ELLINGTON ... THE BRONX, NY 129
ELIZABETH CADY STANTON ... THE BRONX, NY 129
FRANCIS BELLAMY ... ROME, ON 168
FREDERICK DOUGLASS ... ROCHESTER, ON 165
GEN. ZEBULON PIKE ... SACKETS HARBOR, ON 169
GEORGE CLINTON ... KINGSTON, NY 96
GRAVE OF MARK TWAIN ... ELMIRA, NY 83
HERMAN MELVILLE ... THE BRONX, NY 129
JANE MCCREA ... FORT EDWARD, NY 85
JOHN BROWN FARM SHS ... LAKE PLACID, NY 98
JOSEPH PULITZER ... THE BRONX, NY 129
LOGAN ... AUBURN, NY 60
OSSIP GABRILOWITSCH ... ELMIRA, NY 83
PRESIDENT AND MRS. ROOSEVELT ... HYDE PARK, NY 93
PRESIDENT ROOSEVELT ... OYSTER BAY, ON 162
PRESIDENT ULYSSES S. GRANT AND HIS WIFE ... UPPER MANHATTAN, NY 128
ROBERT FULTON ... LOWER MANHATTAN AND NEW YORK HARBOR, NY 118
SAMUEL WILSON ... TROY, ON 180
SUSAN B. ANTHONY ... ROCHESTER, ON 165
TOMB OF THE UNKNOWN SOLDIERS OF THE AMERICAN REVOLUTION ... ROME, ON 168
WASHINGTON IRVING ... SLEEPY HOLLOW, NY 140
WHITELAW REID ... SLEEPY HOLLOW, NY 140
WILLIAM ROCKEFELLER ... SLEEPY HOLLOW, NY 140
WILLIAM SEWARD ... AUBURN, NY 60

HALLS OF FAME

DANCE HALL OF FAME ... SARATOGA SPRINGS, ON 172
HALL OF FAME FOR GREAT AMERICANS ... THE BRONX, NY 129
INTERNATIONAL BOXING HALL OF FAME ... CANASTOTA, NY 73
MAPLE INDUSTRY HALL OF FAME ... CROGHAN, NY 80
*NATIONAL BASEBALL HALL OF FAME AND MUSEUM ... COOPERSTOWN, NY 78
NATIONAL MUSEUM OF RACING AND HALL OF FAME ... SARATOGA SPRINGS, ON 172
NATIONAL SOCCER HALL OF FAME ... ONEONTA, ON 160
NATIONAL WOMEN'S HALL OF FAME ... SENECA FALLS, ON 174

HISTORIC BUILDINGS & HOUSES

BEVIER HOUSE ... KINGSTON, NY 96
BOLDT CASTLE ... ALEXANDRIA BAY, NY 58
*BOSCOBEL ... GARRISON, NY 138
COBBLESTONE SOCIETY MUSEUM ... CHILDS, NY 76
COL. WILLIAM M. BOND HOUSE ... LOCKPORT, NY 100
COXSACKIE ... NY 80
CUSTOM HOUSE ... OGDENSBURG, ON 158
CUSTOM HOUSE ... SAG HARBOR, ON 170
DELONG HOUSE ... GLENS FALLS, NY 88
DYCKMAN HOUSE ... UPPER MANHATTAN, NY 126
EARLE-WIGHTMAN HOUSE MUSEUM ... OYSTER BAY, ON 161
FALAISE ... PORT WASHINGTON, ON 163
*FENIMORE ART MUSEUM ... COOPERSTOWN, NY 78
FIRST CHURCH IN ALBANY ... ALBANY, NY 56
FORT JOHNSON ... FORT JOHNSON, NY 85
FORT PLAIN MUSEUM ... FORT PLAIN, NY 86
FRAUNCES TAVERN MUSEUM ... LOWER MANHATTAN AND NEW YORK HARBOR, NY 113
GREAT CAMP SAGAMORE ... RAQUETTE LAKE, ON 165
HARRIETT TUBMAN HOME ... AUBURN, NY 60
HEMPSTEAD HOUSE ... PORT WASHINGTON, ON 163
"HOME SWEET HOME" ... EAST HAMPTON, NY 82
JAMES VANDERPOEL HOUSE ... KINDERHOOK, NY 95
JAMESTOWN ... NY 94
JOHN LLOYD MANOR HOUSE ... HUNTINGTON, NY 91
JOSEPH SMITH HOME ... PALMYRA, ON 162
KENAN HOUSE ... LOCKPORT, NY 100
KYKUIT ... SLEEPY HOLLOW, NY 140
LE ROY HOUSE MUSEUM AND JELL-O GALLERY ... LE ROY, NY 99
LOCUST LAWN FEDERAL MANSION AND STONE HOUSE ... NEW PALTZ, NY 105
LUYKAS VAN ALEN HOUSE AND ICHABOD CRANE SCHOOLHOUSE ... KINDERHOOK, NY 95
MANOR OF ST. GEORGE ... SHIRLEY, ON 175
MARK TWAIN STUDY ... ELMIRA, NY 83
MARTIN VAN BUREN NHS ... KINDERHOOK, NY 95
THE MCCLURG MANSION ... WESTFIELD, ON 183
MILLARD FILLMORE CABIN ... MORAVIA, NY 104
MORRIS-JUMEL MANSION ... UPPER MANHATTAN, NY 128
MOUNT LEBANON SHAKER VILLAGE ... NEW LEBANON, NY 105
THE MULFORD FARMHOUSE ... EAST HAMPTON, NY 82
NEAR WESTSIDE ... ELMIRA, NY 83
NEW PALTZ ... NY 105
NEW YORK STATE ARMORY ... OGDENSBURG, ON 158
*NEW YORK STOCK EXCHANGE ... LOWER MANHATTAN AND NEW YORK HARBOR, NY 115
NEWBURGH ... NY 105
NIELSON HOUSE ... SARATOGA NHP, ON 171
OLD FORT HOUSE MUSEUM ... FORT EDWARD, NY 85
THE OLD HOUSE ... CUTCHOGUE, NY 80

THE OLDE HALSEY HOUSE ... SOUTHAMPTON, ON 176
PALATINE HOUSE ... SCHOHARIE, ON 173
PETER WHITMER FARM ... PALMYRA, ON 162
THE PHILIP SCHUYLER HOUSE ... SARATOGA NHP, ON 172
RAYNHAM HALL MUSEUM ... OYSTER BAY, ON 162
ROBERT INGERSOLL MUSEUM ... DRESDEN, NY 81
ROBERT LOUIS STEVENSON COTTAGE ... SARANAC LAKE, ON 171
*ROSE HILL MANSION ... GENEVA, NY 87
SAGAMORE HILL NHS ... OYSTER BAY, ON 162
SAMUEL F.B. MORSE HISTORIC SITE, LOCUST GROVE ... POUGHKEEPSIE, ON 164
SCHOHARIE ... ON 173
*SCHUYLER MANSION SHS ... ALBANY, NY 56
SHERWOOD-JAYNE HOUSE ... SETAUKET, ON 175
*SUNNYSIDE ... TARRYTOWN, NY 141
THE SUSAN B. ANTHONY HOUSE ... ROCHESTER, ON 168
THOMAS PAINE COTTAGE ... NEW ROCHELLE, NY 139
THE TYRON COUNTY COURT HOUSE ... JOHNSTOWN, NY 95
*VANDERBILT MANSION, MARINE MUSEUM, PLANETARIUM AND PARK ... CENTERPORT, NY 75
WASHINGTON'S HEADQUARTERS MUSEUM (ELIJAH MILLER HOUSE) ... WHITE PLAINS, NY 141
*WASHINGTON'S HEADQUARTERS SHS ... NEWBURGH, NY 105
WHITE PINE CAMP ... PAUL SMITHS, ON 162
WILDER FARM—BOYHOOD HOME OF ALMANZO WILDER ... MALONE, NY 101
WILLIAM FLOYD ESTATE ... FIRE ISLAND NS, NY 85
WILLIAM H. SEWARD HOUSE ... AUBURN, NY 60
WINTER OLYMPICS ... LAKE PLACID, NY 98

HISTORIC DOCUMENTS, MANUSCRIPTS & RARE BOOKS
MUSEUM OF AMERICAN FINANCIAL HISTORY ... LOWER MANHATTAN AND NEW YORK HARBOR, NY 115
PIERPONT MORGAN LIBRARY ... MIDTOWN MANHATTAN, NY 124
ROBERT INGERSOLL MUSEUM ... DRESDEN, NY 81
STATEN ISLAND INSTITUTE OF ARTS AND SCIENCES ... RICHMOND (STATEN ISLAND), NY 132
WALT WHITMAN BIRTHPLACE SHS ... HUNTINGTON, NY 92

HISTORIC SITES
BENNINGTON BATTLEFIELD SHS ... NORTH HOOSICK, ON 157
BOOK OF MORMON HISTORIC PUBLICATION SITE ... PALMYRA, ON 162
CLERMONT SHS ... GERMANTOWN, NY 87
CRAILO SHS ... RENSSELAER, ON 165
CROWN POINT SHS ... CROWN POINT, NY 80
ELEANOR ROOSEVELT NHS ... HYDE PARK, NY 92
*ELLIS ISLAND ... LOWER MANHATTAN AND NEW YORK HARBOR, NY 117
FORT ONTARIO SHS ... OSWEGO, ON 160
FORT PLAIN MUSEUM ... FORT PLAIN, NY 86
FRAUNCES TAVERN MUSEUM ... LOWER MANHATTAN AND NEW YORK HARBOR, NY 113
GANONDAGAN SHS ... VICTOR, ON 181
GRANT COTTAGE SHS ... WILTON, ON 185
HERKIMER HOME SHS ... LITTLE FALLS, NY 100
HILL CUMORAH ... PALMYRA, ON 162
*HOME OF FRANKLIN D. ROOSEVELT NHS ... HYDE PARK, NY 93
JOHN BROWN FARM SHS ... LAKE PLACID, NY 98
JOHN JAY HOMESTEAD SHS ... KATONAH, NY 138
JOHNSON HALL SHS ... JOHNSTOWN, NY 95
LORENZO SHS ... CAZENOVIA, NY 75
MARTIN VAN BUREN NHS ... KINDERHOOK, NY 95
*MILLS MANSION SHS ... HYDE PARK, NY 93
MOUNT DEFIANCE ... FORT TICONDEROGA, NY 86
NATHAN HALE MEMORIAL MONUMENT ... HUNTINGTON, NY 92
NEW WINDSOR CANTONMENT SHS ... NEWBURGH, NY 105
OLANA SHS ... HUDSON, NY 91
ROOSEVELT FIELD ... GARDEN CITY, NY 86
SACKETS HARBOR BATTLEFIELD SHS ... SACKETS HARBOR, ON 169
SAGAMORE HILL NHS ... OYSTER BAY, ON 162
SAMUEL F.B. MORSE HISTORIC SITE, LOCUST GROVE ... POUGHKEEPSIE, ON 164
SARATOGA NHP ... ON 171
SCHOHARIE CROSSING SHS ... FORT HUNTER, NY 85
*SENATE HOUSE SHS ... KINGSTON, NY 96
STONY POINT BATTLEFIELD SHS ... STONY POINT, NY 140
SULLIVAN'S MONUMENT AT NEWTOWN BATTLEFIELD ... ELMIRA, NY 83
THEODORE ROOSEVELT BIRTHPLACE NHS ... LOWER MANHATTAN AND NEW YORK HARBOR, NY 117
THEODORE ROOSEVELT INAUGURAL NHS ... BUFFALO, NY 69
*VANDERBILT MANSION NHS ... HYDE PARK, NY 93
WALT WHITMAN BIRTHPLACE SHS ... HUNTINGTON, NY 92
*WASHINGTON'S HEADQUARTERS SHS ... NEWBURGH, NY 105
WHITE PLAINS NB SITE ... WHITE PLAINS, NY 141
WOMEN'S RIGHTS NHP ... SENECA FALLS, ON 174

INDIAN MOUNDS, REMAINS & RUINS
THE NATIONAL SHRINE OF BLESSED KATERI TEKAKWITHA AND NATIVE AMERICAN EXHIBIT ... FONDA, NY 85

INDUSTRIAL TOURS
BLENHEIM-GILBOA PUMPED STORAGE POWER PROJECT ... NORTH BLENHEIM, ON 157
THE MATT BREWING CO. ... UTICA, ON 181
THE ORIGINAL AMERICAN KAZOO CO. ... EDEN, NY 72
QRS MUSIC TECHNOLOGY ... BUFFALO, NY 70
REMINGTON PLANT TOUR ... ILION, NY 93

ISLANDS
*ELLIS ISLAND ... LOWER MANHATTAN AND NEW YORK HARBOR, NY 117
FIRE ISLAND NS ... NY 84
*GOAT ISLAND ... NIAGARA FALLS, NY 148
LONG ISLAND ... NY 100
LUNA ISLAND ... NIAGARA FALLS, NY 148
ST. LAWRENCE ISLANDS NP ... THOUSAND ISLANDS, ON 178
THOUSAND ISLANDS ... ON 178
THREE SISTERS ISLANDS ... NIAGARA FALLS, NY 148

JAILS
HERKIMER COUNTY HISTORICAL SOCIETY ... HERKIMER, NY 90

LAKES, PONDS & RESERVOIRS
ADIRONDACK PARK ... NY 54
ASHOKAN RESERVOIR ... KINGSTON, NY 96
CANANDAIGUA LAKE ... CANANDAIGUA, NY 73
CAYUGA ... FINGER LAKES, NY 84
FINGER LAKES ... NY 84
LAKE CHAMPLAIN ... LAKE CHAMPLAIN, NY 96
LAKE GEORGE ... LAKE GEORGE (VILLAGE), NY 97
ONONDAGA LAKE PARK ... SYRACUSE, ON 178
SENECA ... FINGER LAKES, NY 84
SENECA LAKE ... GENEVA, NY 87
SENECA LAKE ... MONTOUR FALLS, NY 104

LIBRARIES, ARCHIVES
AMERICAN NUMISMATIC SOCIETY ... UPPER MANHATTAN, NY 126
BROOKLYN HISTORY MUSEUM ... BROOKLYN, NY 130
BROOME COUNTY HISTORICAL SOCIETY RESEARCH LIBRARY ... BINGHAMTON, NY 62
CANAJOHARIE LIBRARY AND ART GALLERY ... CANAJOHARIE, NY 73
CASE LIBRARY ... HAMILTON, NY 89
COLUMBIA COUNTY MUSEUM ... KINDERHOOK, NY 95
DELAWARE COUNTY HISTORICAL ASSOCIATION MUSEUM ... DELHI, NY 81
DUNKIRK HISTORICAL MUSEUM ... DUNKIRK, NY 81
FENTON HISTORY CENTER-MUSEUM & LIBRARY ... JAMESTOWN, NY 94
*FRANKLIN D. ROOSEVELT MUSEUM AND LIBRARY ... HYDE PARK, NY 92
GOSHEN PUBLIC LIBRARY ... GOSHEN, NY 88
HAMMARSKJOLD LIBRARY ... MIDTOWN MANHATTAN, NY 126
IMMIGRATION LIBRARY ... LOWER MANHATTAN AND NEW YORK HARBOR, NY 117
MADISON COUNTY HISTORICAL SOCIETY HEADQUARTERS ... ONEIDA, ON 159
MARGARET REANEY MEMORIAL LIBRARY AND MUSEUM ... ST. JOHNSVILLE, ON 170
MCKINNEY LIBRARY ... ALBANY, NY 56
NEW YORK HISTORICAL SOCIETY ... MIDTOWN MANHATTAN, NY 124
NEW YORK PUBLIC LIBRARY ... MIDTOWN MANHATTAN, NY 124
NEW YORK PUBLIC LIBRARY FOR THE PERFORMING ARTS ... MIDTOWN MANHATTAN, NY 122
OLIN LIBRARY ... ITHACA, NY 93
THE PEMBER MUSEUM OF NATURAL HISTORY ... GRANVILLE, NY 89
PIERPONT MORGAN LIBRARY ... MIDTOWN MANHATTAN, NY 124
PLATTSBURGH ART MUSEUM, SUNY ... PLATTSBURGH, ON 163
ST. LAWRENCE COUNTY MUSEUM ... CANTON, NY 74
SANDY HOOK ... GATEWAY NRA, NY 87
THE SHAKER MUSEUM AND LIBRARY ... OLD CHATHAM, ON 158
STATEN ISLAND INSTITUTE OF ARTS AND SCIENCES ... RICHMOND (STATEN ISLAND), NY 132
*THE STRONG MUSEUM ... ROCHESTER, ON 168
SUFFOLK COUNTY HISTORICAL SOCIETY ... RIVERHEAD, ON 165
TICONDEROGA HISTORICAL SOCIETY LIBRARY AND MUSEUM ... TICONDEROGA, ON 179
WALT WHITMAN BIRTHPLACE SHS ... HUNTINGTON, NY 92
WOODSIDE MANSION ... ROCHESTER, ON 168

LIGHTHOUSES
BARCELONA HARBOR ... WESTFIELD, ON 183
CHAMPLAIN MEMORIAL LIGHTHOUSE ... CROWN POINT, NY 80
DUNKIRK HISTORICAL LIGHTHOUSE AND VETERANS PARK MUSEUM ... DUNKIRK, NY 81
FIRE ISLAND LIGHTHOUSE ... FIRE ISLAND NS, NY 84
THE LOG VILLAGE GRIST MILL AND MUSEUM ... HARTFORD, NY 90
MONTAUK POINT LIGHTHOUSE MUSEUM ... MONTAUK, NY 103
STONY POINT BATTLEFIELD SHS ... STONY POINT, NY 140

LOCKS
BERTRAND SNELL ... MASSENA, NY 102
DELAWARE & HUDSON CANAL MUSEUM ... HIGH FALLS, NY 90
DWIGHT D. EISENHOWER ... MASSENA, NY 102
LOCKPORT ... NY 100
LOCKPORT CAVE AND UNDERGROUND BOAT RIDE ... LOCKPORT, NY 100
LOCKPORT LOCKS AND ERIE CANAL CRUISES ... LOCKPORT, NY 100
OSWEGO CANAL ... FULTON, NY 86
WILEY-DONDERO SHIP CHANNEL ... GREAT LAKES-ST. LAWRENCE SEAWAY SYSTEM, NY 89

MARINE ATTRACTIONS
AQUARIUM OF NIAGARA ... NIAGARA FALLS, NY 147
*MARINELAND ... NIAGARA FALLS, ON 152
*NEW YORK STOCK EXCHANGE ... LOWER MANHATTAN AND NEW YORK HARBOR, NY 115

MARKETS
BROADWAY MARKET ... BUFFALO, NY 71
FULTON MARKET ... LOWER MANHATTAN AND NEW YORK HARBOR, NY 116

MEMORIALS
AMERICAN IMMIGRANT WALL OF HONOR ... LOWER MANHATTAN AND NEW YORK HARBOR, NY 117
CIVIL WAR HEROES ... BROOKLYN, NY 130
EAST COAST WAR MEMORIAL ... LOWER MANHATTAN AND NEW YORK HARBOR, NY 113
*FEDERAL HALL NME ... LOWER MANHATTAN AND NEW YORK HARBOR, NY 113
FULTON MARKET BUILDING ... LOWER MANHATTAN AND NEW YORK HARBOR, NY 116
GENERAL GRANT NME ... UPPER MANHATTAN, NY 128
JOHN F. KENNEDY ... BROOKLYN, NY 130
LAKE GEORGE BATTLEFIELD PARK ... LAKE GEORGE (VILLAGE), NY 97
ROOSEVELT BIRD SANCTUARY AND TRAILSIDE MUSEUM ... OYSTER BAY, ON 162
STRAWBERRY FIELDS ... MIDTOWN MANHATTAN, NY 119
UNCLE SAM TABLET ... TROY, ON 180
WASHINGTON IRVING MEMORIAL ... TARRYTOWN, NY 141

MILLS
THE LOG VILLAGE GRIST MILL AND MUSEUM ... HARTFORD, NY 90
PANTIGO WINDMILL ... EAST HAMPTON, NY 82
PHILIPSBURG MANOR ... SLEEPY HOLLOW, NY 140
STONY BROOK GRIST MILL ... STONY BROOK, ON 177
WILLIAMSVILLE WATER MILLS ... WILLIAMSVILLE, NY 72

MINES & MINERALS
GORE MOUNTAIN GARNET MINE ... NORTH CREEK, ON 157
HERKIMER ... NY 90

MONUMENTS, GENERAL
BATTLE MONUMENT ... WEST POINT, ON 184
CAPTORS' MONUMENT ... TARRYTOWN, NY 141
GEN. SIR ISAAC BROCK ... NIAGARA FALLS, ON 155
JOHN BROWN FARM SHS ... LAKE PLACID, NY 98
LAKE GEORGE BATTLEFIELD PARK ... LAKE GEORGE (VILLAGE), NY 97
LIBERTY MONUMENT ... TICONDEROGA, ON 179
MARTYRS' MONUMENT ... BROOKLYN, NY 130
MASSACRE OF 1778 ... CHERRY VALLEY, NY 76
NATHAN HALE MEMORIAL MONUMENT ... HUNTINGTON, NY 92
SARATOGA MONUMENT ... SARATOGA NHP, ON 171
SARATOGA MONUMENT ... SCHUYLERVILLE, ON 174
SULLIVAN'S MONUMENT AT NEWTOWN BATTLEFIELD ... ELMIRA, NY 83
TOWER OF VICTORY MONUMENT ... NEWBURGH, NY 105

MONUMENTS, NATIONAL; STATE
CASTLE CLINTON NMO ... LOWER MANHATTAN AND NEW YORK HARBOR, NY 113
*FORT STANWIX NMO ... NY 86
*STATUE OF LIBERTY NMO AND ELLIS ISLAND ... LOWER MANHATTAN AND NEW YORK HARBOR, NY 117

MOUNTAINS
BEAR MOUNTAIN ... WEST POINT, ON 184
BLUE MOUNTAIN ... BLUE MOUNTAIN LAKE, NY 63
MOUNT MARCY ... ADIRONDACK PARK, NY 54
SLIDE MOUNTAIN ... CATSKILL, NY 74
WHITEFACE MOUNTAIN ... LAKE PLACID, NY 98
WHITEFACE MOUNTAIN ... WILMINGTON, ON 185

MURALS & MOSAICS
*NIAGARA POWER PROJECT VISITOR CENTER ... NIAGARA FALLS, NY 148

MUSEUMS

THE 1890 HOUSE MUSEUM ... CORTLAND, NY 79
1932 & 1980 LAKE PLACID WINTER OLYMPIC MUSEUM ... LAKE PLACID, NY 98
ADIRONDACK HISTORY CENTER ... ELIZABETHTOWN, NY 82
★ADIRONDACK MUSEUM ... BLUE MOUNTAIN LAKE, NY 63
AGRICULTURAL MUSEUM ... LA FARGEVILLE, NY 96
ALBANY INSTITUTE OF HISTORY AND ART ... ALBANY, NY 56
ALICE AUSTEN HOUSE ... RICHMOND (STATEN ISLAND), NY 131
ALLING COVERLET MUSEUM ... PALMYRA, ON 162
AMERICAN CRAFT MUSEUM ... MIDTOWN MANHATTAN, NY 118
AMERICAN MAPLE MUSEUM ... CROGHAN, NY 80
AMERICAN MERCHANT MARINE MUSEUM ... KINGS POINT, NY 96
★AMERICAN MUSEUM OF FIREFIGHTING ... HUDSON, NY 91
THE AMERICAN MUSEUM OF IMMIGRATION ... LOWER MANHATTAN AND NEW YORK HARBOR, NY 117
★AMERICAN MUSEUM OF NATURAL HISTORY ... MIDTOWN MANHATTAN, NY 118
AMERICAN MUSEUM OF THE MOVING IMAGE ... QUEENS, NY 130
AMHERST MUSEUM ... AMHERST, NY 71
ANTIQUE BOAT MUSEUM ... CLAYTON, NY 77
ARNOT ART MUSEUM ... ELMIRA, NY 83
ART MUSEUM ... STONY BROOK, ON 177
AUDUBON TERRACE MUSEUM GROUP ... UPPER MANHATTAN, NY 126
BARTOW-PELL MANSION MUSEUM ... THE BRONX, NY 128
BRIDGEHAMPTON HISTORICAL MUSEUM ... BRIDGEHAMPTON, NY 63
BRONCK MUSEUM ... COXSACKIE, NY 80
BROOKLYN CHILDREN'S MUSEUM ... BROOKLYN, NY 130
BROOKLYN HISTORY MUSEUM ... BROOKLYN, NY 130
BROOKLYN MUSEUM ... BROOKLYN, NY 130
BUFFALO MUSEUM OF SCIENCE ... BUFFALO, NY 69
CAMPBELL-WHITTLESEY HOUSE MUSEUM ... ROCHESTER, ON 166
CANAL MUSEUM ... LOCKPORT, NY 100
CANASTOTA CANAL TOWN MUSEUM ... CANASTOTA, NY 73
CAPE VINCENT HISTORICAL MUSEUM ... CAPE VINCENT, NY 74
CARRIAGE HOUSE MUSEUM ... TAPPAN, NY 140
CARRIAGE MUSEUM ... STONY BROOK, ON 177
CAYUGA COUNTY AGRICULTURAL MUSEUM ... AUBURN, NY 60
CAYUGA MUSEUM/CASE RESEARCH LAB MUSEUM ... AUBURN, NY 60
THE CHAPMAN HISTORICAL MUSEUM ... GLENS FALLS, NY 88
CHARLES DICKERT WILDLIFE MUSEUM ... SARANAC LAKE, ON 171
CHEMUNG VALLEY HISTORICAL MUSEUM ... ELMIRA, NY 83
CHERRY VALLEY MUSEUM ... CHERRY VALLEY, NY 76
CHILDREN'S MUSEUM OF MANHATTAN ... MIDTOWN MANHATTAN, NY 119
CLINTON COUNTY HISTORICAL MUSEUM ... PLATTSBURGH, ON 163
★THE CLOISTERS ... UPPER MANHATTAN, NY 126
COBBLESTONE SOCIETY MUSEUM ... CHILDS, NY 76
COL. WILLIAM M. BOND HOUSE ... LOCKPORT, NY 100
COLD SPRING HARBOR WHALING MUSEUM ... COLD SPRING HARBOR, NY 77
COLUMBIA COUNTY MUSEUM ... KINDERHOOK, NY 95
COOPER-HEWITT NATIONAL DESIGN MUSEUM-SMITHSONIAN INSTITUTION ... UPPER MANHATTAN, NY 126
THE CORNING-PAINTED POST HISTORICAL SOCIETY MUSEUM COMPLEX ... CORNING, NY 78
DAHESH MUSEUM ... MIDTOWN MANHATTAN, NY 119
DELAWARE & HUDSON CANAL MUSEUM ... HIGH FALLS, NY 90
DELAWARE COUNTY HISTORICAL ASSOCIATION MUSEUM ... DELHI, NY 81
DUNKIRK HISTORICAL LIGHTHOUSE AND VETERANS PARK MUSEUM ... DUNKIRK, NY 81
DUNKIRK HISTORICAL MUSEUM ... DUNKIRK, NY 81
EAST HAMPTON TOWN MARINE MUSEUM ... AMAGANSETT, NY 59
ELDRED WWII MUSEUM ... ELDRED, NY 82
★ELLIS ISLAND ... LOWER MANHATTAN AND NEW YORK HARBOR, NY 117
ERIE CANAL MUSEUM ... SYRACUSE, ON 177
EVERSON MUSEUM OF ART ... SYRACUSE, ON 177
★THE FARMERS' MUSEUM ... COOPERSTOWN, NY 77
FENTON HISTORY CENTER-MUSEUM & LIBRARY ... JAMESTOWN, NY 94
FORT DELAWARE—MUSEUM OF COLONIAL HISTORY ... NARROWSBURG, NY 104
FORT PLAIN MUSEUM ... FORT PLAIN, NY 86
★FORT TICONDEROGA ... NY 86
FORT WILLIAM HENRY MUSEUM ... LAKE GEORGE (VILLAGE), NY 97
THE FRANCES LEHMAN LOEB ART CENTER ... POUGHKEEPSIE, ON 164
FRANKLIN COUNTY HOUSE OF HISTORY ... MALONE, NY 101
★FRANKLIN D. ROOSEVELT MUSEUM AND LIBRARY ... HYDE PARK, NY 92
FRAUNCES TAVERN MUSEUM ... LOWER MANHATTAN AND NEW YORK HARBOR, NY 113
★FREDERIC REMINGTON ART MUSEUM ... OGDENSBURG, ON 158
FULTON COUNTY MUSEUM ... GLOVERSVILLE, NY 88
GARVIES POINT MUSEUM AND PRESERVE ... GLEN COVE, NY 88
★GENESEE COUNTRY VILLAGE & MUSEUM ... MUMFORD, NY 104
★GEORGE EASTMAN HOUSE ... ROCHESTER, ON 167
GLENN H. CURTISS MUSEUM ... HAMMONDSPORT, NY 89
GRANGER HOMESTEAD AND CARRIAGE MUSEUM ... CANANDAIGUA, NY 73
GUGGENHEIM MUSEUM SOHO ... UPPER MANHATTAN, NY 128
GUILD HALL OF EAST HAMPTON ... EAST HAMPTON, NY 82
H. LEE WHITE MARINE MUSEUM ... OSWEGO, ON 160
HANFORD MILLS MUSEUM ... EAST MEREDITH, NY 82
HARNESS RACING MUSEUM & HALL OF FAME ... GOSHEN, NY 88
HARRIETT TUBMAN HOME ... AUBURN, NY 60
HECKSCHER MUSEUM ... HUNTINGTON, NY 92
THE HERSCHELL CARROUSEL FACTORY MUSEUM ... NORTH TONAWANDA, NY 72
HICKSVILLE GREGORY MUSEUM ... HICKSVILLE, NY 90
HILL-HOLD MUSEUM ... MONTGOMERY, NY 103
HISTORICAL SOCIETY MUSEUM ... GENEVA, NY 87
HISTORICAL SOCIETY OF ROCKLAND COUNTY ... NEW CITY, NY 139
HISTORICAL SOCIETY OF SARATOGA SPRINGS MUSEUM ... SARATOGA SPRINGS, ON 172
HISTORY MUSEUM ... STONY BROOK, ON 177
HOFFMAN CLOCK MUSEUM ... NEWARK, NY 105
HOLLAND LAND OFFICE MUSEUM ... BATAVIA, NY 61
THE HORSEHEADS HISTORICAL SOCIETY MUSEUM ... HORSEHEADS, NY 91
THE HUDSON RIVER MUSEUM OF WESTCHESTER ... YONKERS, NY 141
HUNTINGTON HISTORICAL SOCIETY ... HUNTINGTON, NY 92
THE INTERNATIONAL MUSEUM OF CERAMIC ART AT ALFRED ... ALFRED, NY 58
INTERNATIONAL MUSEUM OF PHOTOGRAPHY AND FILM ... ROCHESTER, ON 167
INTREPID SEA-AIR-SPACE MUSEUM ... MIDTOWN MANHATTAN, NY 122
IRISH-AMERICAN HERITAGE MUSEUM ... EAST DURHAM, NY 81
IROQUOIS INDIAN MUSEUM ... HOWES CAVE, NY 91
THE ISAMU NOGUCHI GARDEN MUSEUM ... QUEENS, NY 131
JACQUES MARCHAIS MUSEUM OF TIBETAN ART ... RICHMOND (STATEN ISLAND), NY 131
JEFFERSON COUNTY HISTORICAL SOCIETY ... WATERTOWN, ON 181
JEWISH MUSEUM ... UPPER MANHATTAN, NY 128
JUNIOR MUSEUM ... TROY, ON 179
KATONAH MUSEUM OF ART ... KATONAH, NY 138
LAKE PLACID/NORTH ELBA HISTORICAL SOCIETY MUSEUM ... LAKE PLACID, NY 98
LE ROY HOUSE MUSEUM AND JELL-O GALLERY ... LE ROY, NY 99
LEFFERTS HOMESTEAD ... BROOKLYN, NY 130
LEWIS COUNTY HISTORICAL SOCIETY MUSEUM (GOULD MANSION) ... LYONS FALLS, NY 101
LITTLE FALLS HISTORICAL SOCIETY MUSEUM ... LITTLE FALLS, NY 100
THE LOG VILLAGE GRIST MILL AND MUSEUM ... HARTFORD, NY 90
LONG ISLAND MARITIME MUSEUM ... WEST SAYVILLE, ON 184
LONG ISLAND REPTILE MUSEUM ... HICKSVILLE, NY 90
★LOUIS TUSSAUD'S WAXWORKS ... NIAGARA FALLS, ON 152
LOWER EAST SIDE TENEMENT MUSEUM ... LOWER MANHATTAN AND NEW YORK HARBOR, NY 115
LUCY-DESI MUSEUM ... JAMESTOWN, NY 94
LUNDY'S LANE HISTORICAL MUSEUM ... NIAGARA FALLS, ON 152
MARGARET REANEY MEMORIAL LIBRARY AND MUSEUM ... ST. JOHNSVILLE, ON 170
MASSENA MUSEUM ... MASSENA, NY 102
★METROPOLITAN MUSEUM OF ART ... MIDTOWN MANHATTAN, NY 124
THE MIKE WEAVER DRAIN TILE MUSEUM ... GENEVA, NY 87
MILTON J. RUBENSTEIN MUSEUM OF SCIENCE AND TECHNOLOGY ... SYRACUSE, ON 178
MONTAUK POINT LIGHTHOUSE MUSEUM ... MONTAUK, NY 103
MUSEUM GALLERY ... LOWER MANHATTAN AND NEW YORK HARBOR, NY 116
MUSEUM OF AMERICAN FINANCIAL HISTORY ... LOWER MANHATTAN AND NEW YORK HARBOR, NY 115
MUSEUM OF AMERICAN FOLK ART ... MIDTOWN MANHATTAN, NY 124
THE MUSEUM OF AUTOMOBILE HISTORY ... SYRACUSE, ON 178
MUSEUM OF JEWISH HERITAGE—A LIVING MEMORIAL TO THE HOLOCAUST ... LOWER MANHATTAN AND NEW YORK HARBOR, NY 115
★THE MUSEUM OF MODERN ART ... MIDTOWN MANHATTAN, NY 124
MUSEUM OF TELEVISION AND RADIO ... MIDTOWN MANHATTAN, NY 124
MUSEUM OF THE CITY OF NEW YORK ... UPPER MANHATTAN, NY 128
MUSEUM OF THE HUDSON HIGHLANDS ... CORNWALL-ON-HUDSON, NY 79
MUSEUM VILLAGE ... MONROE, NY 103
THE MUSEUMS AT STONY BROOK ... STONY BROOK, ON 177
★NATIONAL BASEBALL HALL OF FAME AND MUSEUM ... COOPERSTOWN, NY 78
NATIONAL BOTTLE MUSEUM ... BALLSTON SPA, NY 61
NATIONAL MUSEUM OF DANCE ... SARATOGA SPRINGS, ON 172
NATIONAL MUSEUM OF RACING AND HALL OF FAME ... SARATOGA SPRINGS, ON 172
NATIONAL SOARING MUSEUM ... ELMIRA, NY 83
NATIONAL WARPLANE MUSEUM ... HORSEHEADS, NY 91
NEUBERGER MUSEUM OF ART ... HARRISON, NY 138
NEVERSINK VALLEY AREA MUSEUM ... CUDDEBACKVILLE, NY 80
THE NEW MUSEUM OF CONTEMPORARY ART ... LOWER MANHATTAN AND NEW YORK HARBOR, NY 115
NEW YORK CITY FIRE MUSEUM ... LOWER MANHATTAN AND NEW YORK HARBOR, NY 115
NEW YORK CITY POLICE MUSEUM ... LOWER MANHATTAN AND NEW YORK HARBOR, NY 115
NEW YORK CITY TRANSIT MUSEUM ... BROOKLYN, NY 130
NEW YORK HISTORICAL SOCIETY ... MIDTOWN MANHATTAN, NY 124
NEW YORK STATE MUSEUM ... ALBANY, NY 56
NIAGARA COUNTY HISTORICAL SOCIETY ... LOCKPORT, NY 100
NIAGARA FALLS ART GALLERY/KURELEK COLLECTION ... NIAGARA FALLS, ON 153
NORTHEAST CLASSIC CAR MUSEUM ... NORWICH, ON 158
OLD FORT HOUSE MUSEUM ... FORT EDWARD, NY 85
OLD ORCHARD MUSEUM ... OYSTER BAY, ON 162
OLD STONE FORT MUSEUM COMPLEX ... SCHOHARIE, ON 173
ONONDAGA HISTORICAL ASSOCIATION MUSEUM ... SYRACUSE, ON 178
OPUS 40 AND QUARRYMAN'S MUSEUM ... SAUGERTIES, ON 173
ORISKANY MUSEUM ... ORISKANY, ON 160
PALATINE HOUSE ... SCHOHARIE, ON 173
PARRISH ART MUSEUM AND ARBORETUM ... SOUTHAMPTON, ON 176
PEDALING HISTORY BICYCLE MUSEUM ... ORCHARD PARK, NY 72
THE PEMBER MUSEUM OF NATURAL HISTORY ... GRANVILLE, NY 89
THE PENFIELD HOMESTEAD HISTORICAL MUSEUM ... CROWN POINT, NY 80
PLATTSBURGH ART MUSEUM, SUNY ... PLATTSBURGH, ON 163
POTSDAM PUBLIC MUSEUM ... POTSDAM, ON 164
QUEENS MUSEUM OF ART ... QUEENS, NY 131
RAIL CITY HISTORICAL MUSEUM ... SANDY CREEK, ON 171
RAYNHAM HALL MUSEUM ... OYSTER BAY, ON 162
REMINGTON MUSEUM ... ILION, NY 93
RICHARDSON-BATES HOUSE MUSEUM ... OSWEGO, ON 161
★RIPLEY'S BELIEVE IT OR NOT! MUSEUM ... NIAGARA FALLS, ON 155
ROBERSON MUSEUM AND SCIENCE CENTER ... BINGHAMTON, NY 62
ROBERT INGERSOLL MUSEUM ... DRESDEN, NY 81
ROBERT JENKINS HOUSE AND MUSEUM ... HUDSON, NY 91
★ROCHESTER MUSEUM & SCIENCE CENTER ... ROCHESTER, ON 167
ROCK HALL MUSEUM ... LAWRENCE, NY 99
★ROCKWELL MUSEUM ... CORNING, NY 79
ROOSEVELT BIRD SANCTUARY AND TRAILSIDE MUSEUM ... OYSTER BAY, ON 162
★ROSE HILL MANSION ... GENEVA, NY 87
ROSE MUSEUM ... NEW YORK, NY 136
SACKETS HARBOR BATTLEFIELD SHS ... SACKETS HARBOR, ON 169
SAG HARBOR WHALING MUSEUM ... SAG HARBOR, ON 170
ST. LAWRENCE COUNTY MUSEUM ... CANTON, NY 74
SALAMANCA RAIL MUSEUM ... SALAMANCA, ON 170
SALT MUSEUM ... SYRACUSE, ON 178
SCHENECTADY COUNTY HISTORICAL SOCIETY MUSEUM ... SCHENECTADY, ON 173
SCHENECTADY MUSEUM AND SCHENECTADY HERITAGE AREA VISITORS CENTER ... SCHENECTADY, ON 173
SCHOELLKOPF GEOLOGICAL MUSEUM ... NIAGARA FALLS, NY 149
SCHUYLER COUNTY HISTORICAL SOCIETY MUSEUM ... MONTOUR FALLS, NY 104
SCIENCENTER ... ITHACA, NY 94
SECOND HOUSE MUSEUM ... MONTAUK, NY 103
SENECA FALLS HISTORICAL SOCIETY ... SENECA FALLS, ON 174
SENECA-IROQUOIS NATIONAL MUSEUM ... SALAMANCA, ON 170
THE SHAKER MUSEUM AND LIBRARY ... OLD CHATHAM, ON 158
SKENESBOROUGH MUSEUM ... WHITEHALL, ON 185
SMITHSONIAN'S NATIONAL MUSEUM OF THE AMERICAN INDIAN ... LOWER MANHATTAN AND NEW YORK HARBOR, NY 116
SOCIETY OF ILLUSTRATORS MUSEUM OF AMERICAN ILLUSTRATION ... MIDTOWN MANHATTAN, NY 125
★SOLOMON R. GUGGENHEIM MUSEUM ... UPPER MANHATTAN, NY 128
SONY WONDER TECHNOLOGY LAB ... MIDTOWN MANHATTAN, NY 125
SOUTH STREET SEAPORT MUSEUM ... LOWER MANHATTAN AND NEW YORK HARBOR, NY 116
SOUTHAMPTON HISTORICAL MUSEUM AND COLONIAL SOCIETY ... SOUTHAMPTON, ON 176
SPENCE CREST NATURE CENTER ... CORNING, NY 78
STATEN ISLAND CHILDREN'S MUSEUM ... RICHMOND (STATEN ISLAND), NY 131
STATEN ISLAND INSTITUTE OF ARTS AND SCIENCES ... RICHMOND (STATEN ISLAND), NY 132
STORM KING ART CENTER ... MOUNTAINVILLE, NY 104
★THE STRONG MUSEUM ... ROCHESTER, ON 168
TACKAPAUSHA MUSEUM AND PRESERVE ... SEAFORD, ON 174
THIRD HOUSE MUSEUM ... MONTAUK, NY 103
THE THOUSAND ISLANDS MUSEUM ... CLAYTON, NY 77

TICONDEROGA HISTORICAL SOCIETY LIBRARY AND MUSEUM .... TICONDEROGA, ON 179
THE TIOGA COUNTY HISTORICAL SOCIETY MUSEUM .... OWEGO, ON 161
TOMPKINS COUNTY MUSEUM AND DEWITT HISTORICAL SOCIETY .... ITHACA, NY 94
TOY TOWN MUSEUM .... EAST AURORA, NY 72
TRAILSIDE MUSEUM AND ZOO .... WEST POINT, ON 184
TRAILSIDE NATURE MUSEUM .... CROSS RIVER, NY 138
ULSTER COUNTY HISTORICAL SOCIETY HEADQUARTERS AND MUSEUM .... KINGSTON, NY 96
VAN CORTLANDT HOUSE MUSEUM .... THE BRONX, NY 129
*VANDERBILT MANSION, MARINE MUSEUM, PLANETARIUM AND PARK .... CENTERPORT, NY 75
VICTORIAN DOLL MUSEUM AND CHILI DOLL HOSPITAL .... NORTH CHILI, ON 157
VOLUNTEER FIREMEN'S HALL AND MUSEUM OF KINGSTON .... KINGSTON, NY 96
WALTER ELWOOD MUSEUM AND ART GALLERY .... AMSTERDAM, NY 59
WALWORTH MEMORIAL MUSEUM .... SARATOGA SPRINGS, ON 172
WASHINGTON'S HEADQUARTERS MUSEUM (ELIJAH MILLER HOUSE) .... WHITE PLAINS, NY 141
*WASHINGTON'S HEADQUARTERS SHS .... NEWBURGH, NY 105
WATERVLIET ARSENAL MUSEUM .... WATERVLIET, ON 183
WAYNE COUNTY HISTORICAL SOCIETY MUSEUM .... LYONS, NY 101
*WEST POINT MUSEUM .... WEST POINT, ON 184
WHITNEY MUSEUM OF AMERICAN ART .... MIDTOWN MANHATTAN, NY 126
WHITNEY MUSEUM OF AMERICAN ART AT PHILIP MORRIS .... MIDTOWN MANHATTAN, NY 126
WILLIAM PRYOR LETCHWORTH PIONEER AND INDIAN MUSEUM .... CASTILE, NY 74
THE WINE AND GRAPE MUSEUM OF GREYTON H. TAYLOR .... HAMMONDSPORT, NY 89
YAGER MUSEUM .... ONEONTA, ON 160
ZADOCK PRATT MUSEUM .... PRATTSVILLE, ON 164

MUSIC HALLS & OPERA HOUSES

ALICE TULLY HALL .... MIDTOWN MANHATTAN, NY 122
AVERY FISHER HALL .... MIDTOWN MANHATTAN, NY 122
CARNEGIE HALL .... NEW YORK, NY 136
CITY CENTER .... NEW YORK, NY 136
METROPOLITAN OPERA HOUSE .... MIDTOWN MANHATTAN, NY 122
RADIO CITY MUSIC HALL .... MIDTOWN MANHATTAN, NY 125
TOWN HALL .... NEW YORK, NY 137

MYTHICAL PERSONS & ANIMALS

CHAMP .... LAKE CHAMPLAIN, NY 96
UNCLE SAM .... TROY, ON 179

NATURAL BRIDGES

NATURAL STONE BRIDGE AND CAVES .... POTTERSVILLE, ON 164

NATURAL PHENOMENA

CENTER AT HIGH FALLS .... ROCHESTER, ON 167

NATURE CENTERS

BEAVER LAKE NATURE CENTER .... BALDWINSVILLE, NY 61
BEAVER MEADOW NATURE CENTER .... JAVA CENTER, NY 95
CUMMING NATURE CENTER .... NAPLES, NY 104
JAMESTOWN AUDUBON NATURE CENTER .... JAMESTOWN, NY 94
MINER INSTITUTE .... CHAZY, NY 76
MINNA ANTHONY COMMON NATURE CENTER .... ALEXANDRIA BAY, NY 58
NIAGARA PARKS BUTTERFLY CONSERVATORY .... NIAGARA FALLS, ON 154
PEMBER NATURE PRESERVE .... GRANVILLE, NY 89
ROGER TORY PETERSON INSTITUTE OF NATURAL HISTORY .... JAMESTOWN, NY 95
ROGER TORY PETERSON NATURE INTERPRETIVE BUILDING .... JAMESTOWN, NY 94
ROGERS ENVIRONMENTAL EDUCATION CENTER .... SHERBURNE, ON 175
TACKAPAUSHA MUSEUM AND PRESERVE .... SEAFORD, ON 174
TEATOWN LAKE RESERVATION .... OSSINING, NY 139
TIFFT NATURE PRESERVE .... BUFFALO, NY 69
WARD POUND RIDGE RESERVATION .... CROSS RIVER, NY 138
WILLOW LAKE NATURE AREA .... QUEENS, NY 131

NATURE TRAILS

ADIRONDACK HISTORY CENTER .... ELIZABETHTOWN, NY 82
BARGE CANAL TRAIL .... ROCHESTER, ON 166
BEAVER LAKE NATURE CENTER .... BALDWINSVILLE, NY 61
BEAVER MEADOW NATURE CENTER .... JAVA CENTER, NY 95
BRUCE TRAIL .... NIAGARA FALLS, ON 155
CENTERS FOR NATURE EDUCATION/BALTIMORE WOODS .... MARCELLUS, NY 102
CHAUTAUQUA GORGE .... WESTFIELD, ON 183
CLERMONT SHS .... GERMANTOWN, NY 87
CORNELL PLANTATIONS .... ITHACA, NY 93
CORNING PRESERVE .... ALBANY, NY 55
CUMMING NATURE CENTER .... NAPLES, NY 104
ELEANOR ROOSEVELT NHS .... HYDE PARK, NY 92
FIRE ISLAND NS .... NY 84
GARVIES POINT MUSEUM AND PRESERVE .... GLEN COVE, NY 88
GRIFFIS SCULPTURE PARK .... ASHFORD HOLLOW, NY 59
HAVANA GLEN .... MONTOUR FALLS, NY 104
HIGH FALLS PARK .... CHATEAUGAY, NY 75
IROQUOIS INDIAN MUSEUM .... HOWES CAVE, NY 91
JAMAICA BAY WILDLIFE REFUGE .... QUEENS, NY 131
JAMESTOWN AUDUBON NATURE CENTER .... JAMESTOWN, NY 94
*LETCHWORTH SP .... CASTILE, NY 74
LONG ISLAND GAME FARM AND FAMILY RIDE PARK .... MANORVILLE, NY 102
LONG ISLAND NWR COMPLEX .... SHIRLEY, ON 175
MINNA ANTHONY COMMON NATURE CENTER .... ALEXANDRIA BAY, NY 58
MONTEZUMA NWR .... SENECA FALLS, ON 174
MORTON NWR .... SOUTHAMPTON, ON 176
MOUNT LEBANON SHAKER VILLAGE .... NEW LEBANON, NY 105
MUSEUM OF THE HUDSON HIGHLANDS .... CORNWALL-ON-HUDSON, NY 79
NEWCOMB CENTER .... ADIRONDACK PARK, NY 54
NIAGARA RESERVATION SP .... NIAGARA FALLS, NY 148
NIAGARA RIVER RECREATIONAL TRAIL .... NIAGARA FALLS, ON 155
PAUL SMITHS .... ADIRONDACK PARK, NY 54
PROSPECT PARK .... BROOKLYN, NY 130
ROCK CITY PARK .... OLEAN, ON 159
ROGERS ENVIRONMENTAL EDUCATION CENTER .... SHERBURNE, ON 175
SAMUEL F.B. MORSE HISTORIC SITE, LOCUST GROVE .... POUGHKEEPSIE, ON 164
SANDS POINT PRESERVE .... PORT WASHINGTON, ON 163
SAPSUCKER WOODS .... ITHACA, NY 93
SARATOGA SPA SP .... SARATOGA SPRINGS, ON 172
SCHOELLKOPF GEOLOGICAL MUSEUM .... NIAGARA FALLS, NY 149
SCHOHARIE CROSSING .... FORT HUNTER, NY 85
SCHOHARIE CROSSING SHS .... FORT HUNTER, NY 85
SPENCE CREST NATURE CENTER .... CORNING, NY 78
TACKAPAUSHA MUSEUM AND PRESERVE .... SEAFORD, ON 174
*TAUGHANNOCK FALLS SP .... ITHACA, NY 94
TEATOWN LAKE RESERVATION .... OSSINING, NY 139
TIFFT NATURE PRESERVE .... BUFFALO, NY 69
TRAILSIDE MUSEUM AND ZOO .... WEST POINT, ON 184
WHIRLPOOL SP .... NIAGARA FALLS, NY 149

OBSERVATORIES

KELLOGG OBSERVATORY .... BUFFALO, NY 69
LYMAN K. STUART OBSERVATORY .... ITHACA, NY 94
PLANETARIUM .... CENTERPORT, NY 75

PAINTINGS

THE PASSION OF CHRIST .... NIAGARA FALLS, ON 153
SAPSUCKER WOODS .... ITHACA, NY 93

PARKS, CITY; STATE; PROVINCIAL

ADIRONDACK PARK .... NY 54
ALLEGANY SP .... ELLICOTTVILLE, NY 82
BATTERY PARK .... LOWER MANHATTAN AND NEW YORK HARBOR, NY 113
BEAR MOUNTAIN SP .... WEST POINT, ON 184
BUTTERMILK FALLS .... ITHACA, NY 93
C. FRED JOHNSON PARK .... BINGHAMTON, NY 62
CANAL PARK .... FULTON, NY 86
CASINO AND CONGRESS PARK .... SARATOGA SPRINGS, ON 172
*CENTRAL PARK .... MIDTOWN MANHATTAN, NY 119
CENTRAL PARK .... SCHENECTADY, ON 173
CENTRE COURT .... NIAGARA FALLS, NY 150
CLERMONT SHS .... GERMANTOWN, NY 87
COBB'S HILL PARK .... ROCHESTER, ON 165
CONNETQUOT RIVER SP PRESERVE .... OAKDALE, ON 158
DELAWARE PARK .... BUFFALO, NY 69
DEVIL'S HOLE .... NIAGARA FALLS, NY 150
DURAND-EASTMAN PARK .... ROCHESTER, ON 167
DWYER MEMORIAL PARK .... CORTLAND, NY 79
EDWARD A. HANNA PARK .... UTICA, ON 180
EMERSON PARK .... AUBURN, NY 60
FILLMORE GLEN SP .... MORAVIA, NY 104
FLUSHING MEADOWS CORONA PARK .... QUEENS, NY 130
FORT GREENE PARK .... BROOKLYN, NY 130
FORT NIAGARA SP .... YOUNGSTOWN, NY 151
GARVIES POINT MUSEUM AND PRESERVE .... GLEN COVE, NY 88
GEORGE W. JOHNSON PARK .... BINGHAMTON, NY 62
GRAMERCY PARK .... LOWER MANHATTAN AND NEW YORK HARBOR, NY 113
GREAT KILLS PARK .... GATEWAY NRA, NY 87
GREAT KILLS PARK .... NEW YORK, NY 133
GRIFFON .... NIAGARA FALLS, NY 150
HENNEPIN .... NIAGARA FALLS, NY 150
HIGH FALLS PARK .... CHATEAUGAY, NY 75
HIGHLAND PARK .... BINGHAMTON, NY 62
HIGHLAND PARK .... ROCHESTER, ON 167
HITHER HILL SP .... MONTAUK, NY 103
HOOPES MEMORIAL PARK .... AUBURN, NY 60
HUDSON-MOHAWK URBAN CULTURAL PARK .... TROY, ON 179
HYDE PARK .... NIAGARA FALLS, NY 150
JACOB RIIS BEACH .... GATEWAY NRA, NY 87
JACOB RIIS PARK .... NEW YORK, NY 133
JAYNE .... NIAGARA FALLS, NY 150
*JONES BEACH SP .... JONES BEACH, NY 95
JONES BEACH SP .... LONG ISLAND, NY 101
LAKE ERIE SP .... DUNKIRK, NY 81
LAKE GEORGE BATTLEFIELD PARK .... LAKE GEORGE (VILLAGE), NY 97
LASALLE .... NIAGARA FALLS, NY 150
*LETCHWORTH SP .... CASTILE, NY 74
MANHATTAN SQUARE PARK .... ROCHESTER, ON 165
MAPLEWOOD PARK .... ROCHESTER, ON 167
MENDON PONDS PARK .... ROCHESTER, ON 165
MONTAUK COUNTY PARK .... MONTAUK, NY 103
MONTAUK POINT SP .... MONTAUK, NY 103
NIAGARA PARKS BUTTERFLY CONSERVATORY .... NIAGARA FALLS, ON 154
NIAGARA RESERVATION SP .... NIAGARA FALLS, NY 148
OGDEN AND RUTH LIVINGSTON MILLS MEMORIAL PARK .... HYDE PARK, NY 93
ONONDAGA LAKE PARK .... SYRACUSE, ON 178
PATRIOTS' PARK .... TARRYTOWN, NY 141
PELHAM BAY PARK .... NEW YORK, NY 133
PLUMB BEACH .... GATEWAY NRA, NY 87
PROSPECT PARK .... BROOKLYN, NY 130
*QUEEN VICTORIA PARK .... NIAGARA FALLS, ON 155
QUEENSTON HEIGHTS PARK .... NIAGARA FALLS, ON 155
RECREATION PARK .... BINGHAMTON, NY 62
RECREATION PARK .... FULTON, NY 86
RIVERSIDE PARK .... COXSACKIE, NY 80
ROBERT H. TREMAN .... ITHACA, NY 93
ROBERT MOSES SP .... FIRE ISLAND NS, NY 85
ROBERT MOSES SP .... MASSENA, NY 102
SARATOGA SPA SP .... SARATOGA SPRINGS, ON 172
SENECA PARK ZOO .... ROCHESTER, ON 168
SMITH POINT COUNTY PARK .... FIRE ISLAND NS, NY 84
STEWART PARK .... ITHACA, NY 94
SULLIVAN'S MONUMENT AT NEWTOWN BATTLEFIELD .... ELMIRA, NY 83
*TAUGHANNOCK FALLS SP .... ITHACA, NY 94
THOMPSON PARK .... WATERTOWN, ON 181
TIFFT NATURE PRESERVE .... BUFFALO, NY 69
UNITY .... NIAGARA FALLS, NY 150
UPPER DELAWARE SCENIC AND RECREATIONAL RIVER .... ON 180
UPPER FALLS PARK .... ROCHESTER, ON 165
WARD POUND RIDGE RESERVATION .... CROSS RIVER, NY 138
WASHINGTON SQUARE PARK .... NEW YORK, NY 133
*WATKINS GLEN SP .... WATKINS GLEN, ON 183
WEST ENDICOTT PARK .... BINGHAMTON, NY 62
WHIRLPOOL SP .... NIAGARA FALLS, NY 149
WINTERGREEN PARK .... CANAJOHARIE, NY 73
WOLFE'S POND PARK .... NEW YORK, NY 134

PARKS, NATIONAL

FIRE ISLAND NS .... NY 84
GATEWAY NRA .... NY 86
SARATOGA NHP .... ON 171
WOMEN'S RIGHTS NHP .... SENECA FALLS, ON 174

PIERS

CHELSEA PIERS .... NEW YORK, NY 134

PLANETARIUMS

ANDRUS PLANETARIUM .... YONKERS, NY 141
HENRY HUDSON PLANETARIUM .... ALBANY, NY 55
MILTON J. RUBENSTEIN MUSEUM OF SCIENCE AND TECHNOLOGY .... SYRACUSE, ON 178
PLANETARIUM .... CENTERPORT, NY 75
ROBERSON MUSEUM AND SCIENCE CENTER .... BINGHAMTON, NY 62
SCHENECTADY MUSEUM AND SCHENECTADY HERITAGE AREA VISITORS CENTER .... SCHENECTADY, ON 173
STRASENBURGH PLANETARIUM .... ROCHESTER, ON 167
*VANDERBILT MANSION, MARINE MUSEUM, PLANETARIUM AND PARK .... CENTERPORT, NY 75

RACETRACKS-AUTO

WATKINS GLEN INTERNATIONAL .... WATKINS GLEN, ON 183

RACETRACKS-HORSE

AQUEDUCT RACE TRACK .... NEW YORK, NY 134

BELMONT PARK RACE TRACK ... NEW YORK, NY 134
BUFFALO RACEWAY ... BUFFALO, NY 70
FINGER LAKES RACE TRACK ... CANANDAIGUA, NY 73
HISTORIC GOSHEN TRACK ... GOSHEN, NY 88
MEADOWLANDS ... NEW YORK, NY 134
SARATOGA HARNESS RACING ... SARATOGA SPRINGS, ON 172
SARATOGA RACE COURSE ... SARATOGA SPRINGS, ON 172
YONKERS RACEWAY ... NEW YORK, NY 134

RADIO & TV STATIONS
NBC STUDIO TOURS ... MIDTOWN MANHATTAN, NY 124

RAILROADS
ARCADE AND ATTICA RAILROAD ... ARCADE, NY 59
THE BATTEN KILL RAMBLER SCENIC TRAIN ... SALEM, ON 171
DELAWARE AND ULSTER RAIL RIDE ... ARKVILLE, NY 59

RAILROADS-LOCOMOTIVES & CARS
RAIL CITY HISTORICAL MUSEUM ... SANDY CREEK, ON 171

RAILROADS & SKI LIFTS, CABLE; COG; INCLINE; NARROW GAUGE
FALLS INCLINE RAILWAY ... NIAGARA FALLS, ON 151
*NIAGARA SPANISH AERO CAR ... NIAGARA FALLS, ON 154
SKI WINDHAM ... WINDHAM, ON 185

RECREATION-SUMMER ACTIVITIES
ADIRONDACK PARK ... NY 54
ALLEGANY SP ... ELLICOTTVILLE, NY 82
BARGE CANAL TRAIL ... ROCHESTER, ON 166
BEAVER LAKE NATURE CENTER ... BALDWINSVILLE, NY 61
BIG TUPPER LAKE ... TUPPER LAKE, ON 180
BUTTERMILK FALLS ... ITHACA, NY 93
CANANDAIGUA LAKE ... CANANDAIGUA, NY 73
CATHARINE CREEK ... MONTOUR FALLS, NY 104
CATSKILL FOREST PRESERVE ... CATSKILL, NY 74
*CENTRAL PARK ... MIDTOWN MANHATTAN, NY 119
*CHAUTAUQUA INSTITUTION ... CHAUTAUQUA, NY 75
CHELSEA PIERS ... NEW YORK, NY 134
CORNING PRESERVE ... ALBANY, NY 55
DELAWARE PARK ... BUFFALO, NY 69
DURAND-EASTMAN PARK ... ROCHESTER, ON 167
*EARL W. BRYDGES ARTPARK ... LEWISTON, NY 151
ELLICOTTVILLE ... NY 82
EMERSON PARK ... AUBURN, NY 60
FILLMORE GLEN SP ... MORAVIA, NY 104
FINGER LAKES NF ... NY 84
FIRE ISLAND NS ... NY 84
FLUSHING MEADOWS CORONA PARK ... QUEENS, NY 130
GATEWAY NRA ... NY 86
HAVANA GLEN ... MONTOUR FALLS, NY 104
HITHER HILL SP ... MONTAUK, NY 103
HOLIDAY VALLEY RESORT ... ELLICOTTVILLE, NY 83
*JONES BEACH SP ... JONES BEACH, NY 95
LAKE ERIE SP ... DUNKIRK, NY 81
LAKE ONTARIO ... ROCHESTER, ON 166
LAKE PLACID ... NY 98
LAKE SIMOND ... TUPPER LAKE, ON 180
LONG ISLAND NWR COMPLEX ... SHIRLEY, ON 175
MCCAULEY MOUNTAIN ... OLD FORGE, ON 159
MIDWAY PARK ... JAMESTOWN, NY 94
MILLION DOLLAR BEACH ... LAKE GEORGE (VILLAGE), NY 97
MONTAUK POINT SP ... MONTAUK, NY 103
MONTEZUMA NWR ... SENECA FALLS, ON 174
NIAGARA RESERVATION SP ... NIAGARA FALLS, NY 148
OGDEN AND RUTH LIVINGSTON MILLS MEMORIAL PARK ... HYDE PARK, NY 93
OLANA SHS ... HUDSON, NY 91
OLD FORGE ... ON 159
OLYMPIC SPORTS COMPLEX AT MOUNT VAN HOEVENBERG ... LAKE PLACID, NY 99
ONONDAGA LAKE PARK ... SYRACUSE, ON 178
PROSPECT PARK ... BROOKLYN, NY 130
QUEENSTON HEIGHTS PARK ... NIAGARA FALLS, ON 155
RAQUETTE POND ... TUPPER LAKE, ON 180
RAQUETTE RIVER ... TUPPER LAKE, ON 180
ROBERT H. TREMAN ... ITHACA, NY 93
ROBERT MOSES SP ... FIRE ISLAND NS, NY 85
ROBERT MOSES SP ... MASSENA, NY 102
ROGERS ENVIRONMENTAL EDUCATION CENTER ... SHERBURNE, ON 175
SARATOGA SPA SP ... SARATOGA SPRINGS, ON 172
SARATOGA SPRINGS ... ON 172
SENECA LAKE ... MONTOUR FALLS, NY 104
SKI WINDHAM ... WINDHAM, ON 185
SPENCE CREST NATURE CENTER ... CORNING, NY 78
SPLISH SPLASH WATER PARK ... RIVERHEAD, ON 165
*TAUGHANNOCK FALLS SP ... ITHACA, NY 94
THOMPSON PARK ... WATERTOWN, ON 181
TIFFT NATURE PRESERVE ... BUFFALO, NY 69
THE TOWN TINKER TUBE RENTAL ... PHOENICIA, ON 163
TUPPER LAKE ... ON 180
UPPER DELAWARE SCENIC AND RECREATIONAL RIVER ... ON 180
WARD POUND RIDGE RESERVATION ... CROSS RIVER, NY 138

RECREATION-WINTER ACTIVITIES
ADIRONDACK PARK ... NY 54
ALLEGANY SP ... ELLICOTTVILLE, NY 82
ALPINE RECREATION AREA ... NIAGARA FALLS, NY 150
BEAVER LAKE NATURE CENTER ... BALDWINSVILLE, NY 61
BUTTERMILK FALLS ... ITHACA, NY 93
CATHARINE CREEK ... MONTOUR FALLS, NY 104
CENTER CITY ... SCHENECTADY, ON 173
*CENTRAL PARK ... MIDTOWN MANHATTAN, NY 119
CHELSEA PIERS ... NEW YORK, NY 134
CUMMING NATURE CENTER ... NAPLES, NY 104
ELLICOTTVILLE ... NY 82
FILLMORE GLEN SP ... MORAVIA, NY 104
FINGER LAKES NF ... NY 84
GARNET HILL ... NORTH CREEK, ON 157
GORE MOUNTAIN ... NORTH CREEK, ON 157
HIGHMOUNT ... NY 90
HOLIDAY VALLEY ... BUFFALO, NY 70
HOLIDAY VALLEY RESORT ... ELLICOTTVILLE, NY 83
*HOWE CAVERNS ... HOWES CAVE, NY 91
KISSING BRIDGE ... BUFFALO, NY 70
KISSING BRIDGE ... NIAGARA FALLS, NY 150
LAKE ERIE SP ... DUNKIRK, NY 81
LAKE ONTARIO ... ROCHESTER, ON 166
LAKE PLACID ... NY 98
MCCAULEY MOUNTAIN ... OLD FORGE, ON 159
MERRITT ESTATE WINERY ... FORESTVILLE, NY 85
OGDEN AND RUTH LIVINGSTON MILLS MEMORIAL PARK ... HYDE PARK, NY 93
OLANA SHS ... HUDSON, NY 91
OLD FORGE ... ON 159
OLYMPIC SPORTS COMPLEX AT MOUNT VAN HOEVENBERG ... LAKE PLACID, NY 99
ROBERT H. TREMAN ... ITHACA, NY 93
ROBERT MOSES SP ... MASSENA, NY 102
ROGERS ENVIRONMENTAL EDUCATION CENTER ... SHERBURNE, ON 175
SARATOGA SPRINGS ... ON 172
SKI PLATTEKILL ... ROXBURY, ON 169
SKI WINDHAM ... WINDHAM, ON 185
SPENCE CREST NATURE CENTER ... CORNING, NY 78
TAMARACK RIDGE ... NIAGARA FALLS, NY 150
*TAUGHANNOCK FALLS SP ... ITHACA, NY 94
TIFFT NATURE PRESERVE ... BUFFALO, NY 69
WARD POUND RIDGE RESERVATION ... CROSS RIVER, NY 138
WHITEFACE MOUNTAIN ... LAKE PLACID, NY 98
WHITEFACE MOUNTAIN SKI CENTER ... WILMINGTON, ON 185

RELIGIOUS COLONIES
MOUNT LEBANON SHAKER VILLAGE ... NEW LEBANON, NY 105

RESEARCH ORGANIZATIONS
CORNELL LABORATORY OF ORNITHOLOGY ... ITHACA, NY 94

RESTORED VILLAGES & SETTLEMENTS
ERIE CANAL VILLAGE ... ROME, ON 168
*GENESEE COUNTRY VILLAGE & MUSEUM ... MUMFORD, NY 104
HISTORIC RICHMOND TOWN ... RICHMOND (STATEN ISLAND), NY 131
MUSEUM VILLAGE ... MONROE, NY 103
OLD BETHPAGE VILLAGE RESTORATION ... OLD BETHPAGE, ON 158

RIVERS
CENTER AT HIGH FALLS ... ROCHESTER, ON 167

ROCKS
PANAMA ROCKS ... PANAMA, ON 162

SCENIC DRIVES
ASHOKAN RESERVOIR ... KINGSTON, NY 96
CATSKILL ... NY 74
CAYUGA WINE TRAIL ... SENECA FALLS, ON 174
GEORGE W. PERKINS MEMORIAL DRIVE ... WEST POINT, ON 184
LAKE SHORE DRIVE ... LAKE GEORGE (VILLAGE), NY 97
PROSPECT MOUNTAIN VETERANS MEMORIAL HIGHWAY ... LAKE GEORGE (VILLAGE), NY 97
SR 23 ... CATSKILL, NY 74
SR 23B ... CATSKILL, NY 74
SR 89 ... ITHACA, NY 93
US 9 ... ELIZABETHTOWN, NY 82
*WHITEFACE MOUNTAIN VETERANS' MEMORIAL HIGHWAY ... WILMINGTON, ON 185

SCHOOLS
THE JUILLIARD SCHOOL ... MIDTOWN MANHATTAN, NY 122
LILY DALE ASSEMBLY ... DUNKIRK, NY 81
NIAGARA PARK SCHOOL OF HORTICULTURE ... NIAGARA FALLS, ON 154
THE NIAGARA PARKS BOTANICAL GARDENS ... NIAGARA FALLS, ON 154
SCHWEIZER SOARING SCHOOL ... ELMIRA, NY 83
THEOLOGICAL SEMINARY ... AUBURN, NY 60
THOUSAND ISLANDSCRAFT SCHOOL ... CLAYTON, NY 76

SCHOOLS-ACADEMIES
AMERICAN ACADEMY OF ARTS AND LETTERS ... UPPER MANHATTAN, NY 126
CLINTON ACADEMY ... EAST HAMPTON, NY 82
*UNITED STATES MILITARY ACADEMY ... WEST POINT, ON 184
U.S. MERCHANT MARINE ACADEMY ... KINGS POINT, NY 96

SCHOOLS-COLLEGES & UNIVERSITIES
BRONX COMMUNITY COLLEGE ... THE BRONX, NY 128
BUFFALO STATE COLLEGE ... BUFFALO, NY 69
COLGATE UNIVERSITY ... HAMILTON, NY 89
COLUMBIA UNIVERSITY ... UPPER MANHATTAN, NY 126
CORNELL UNIVERSITY ... ITHACA, NY 93
D'YOUVILLE COLLEGE ... BUFFALO, NY 65
FORDHAM UNIVERSITY ... THE BRONX, NY 129
HOBART AND WILLIAM SMITH COLLEGE ... GENEVA, NY 87
ITHACA COLLEGE ... ITHACA, NY 93
NEW YORK UNIVERSITY ... LOWER MANHATTAN AND NEW YORK HARBOR, NY 115
PLATTSBURGH ART MUSEUM, SUNY ... PLATTSBURGH, ON 163
ST. LAWRENCE UNIVERSITY ... CANTON, NY 74
STATE UNIVERSITY OF NEW YORK ... BINGHAMTON, NY 62
STATE UNIVERSITY OF NEW YORK ... HARRISON, NY 138
STATE UNIVERSITY OF NEW YORK AT BUFFALO ... AMHERST, NY 71
STATE UNIVERSITY OF NEW YORK AT BUFFALO ... BUFFALO, NY 65
SYRACUSE UNIVERSITY ... SYRACUSE, ON 177
UNION COLLEGE ... SCHENECTADY, ON 173
UNIVERSITY OF ROCHESTER ... ROCHESTER, ON 165

SCHOOLS-INSTITUTES
AMERICAN ACADEMY OF ARTS AND LETTERS ... UPPER MANHATTAN, NY 126
*CHAUTAUQUA INSTITUTION ... CHAUTAUQUA, NY 75
CULINARY INSTITUTE OF AMERICA ... HYDE PARK, NY 92
EASTMAN SCHOOL OF MUSIC ... ROCHESTER, ON 166
NATIONAL TECHNICAL INSTITUTE FOR THE DEAF ... ROCHESTER, ON 165
RENSSELAER POLYTECHNIC INSTITUTE ... TROY, ON 179
ROCHESTER INSTITUTE OF TECHNOLOGY ... ROCHESTER, ON 165

SELF-GUIDING TOURS
ALBANY ... NY 54
ALLENTOWN ... BUFFALO, NY 70
BINGHAMTON ... NY 61
CAYUGA WINE TRAIL ... ITHACA, NY 93
DOWNTOWN HISTORIC DISTRICTS AND NEIGHBORHOODS ... TROY, ON 179
ELMIRA ... NY 83
FOREST LAWN CEMETERY ... BUFFALO, NY 70
GANONDAGAN SHS ... VICTOR, ON 181
GENEVA ... NY 87
HISTORIC GOSHEN TRACK ... GOSHEN, NY 88
HOBART AND WILLIAM SMITH COLLEGE ... GENEVA, NY 87
HUDSON-MOHAWK URBAN CULTURAL PARK ... TROY, ON 179
JAMESTOWN ... NY 94
JOHN BROWN FARM SHS ... LAKE PLACID, NY 98
KINGSTON ... NY 96
LITTLE FALLS ... NY 99
MENDON PONDS PARK ... ROCHESTER, ON 165
MONTEZUMA NWR ... SENECA FALLS, ON 174
MORTON NWR ... SOUTHAMPTON, ON 176
NYACK ... NY 139
OYSTER BAY ... ON 161
S. MAIN STREET ... GENEVA, NY 87
SACKETS HARBOR ... ON 169
SACKETS HARBOR BATTLEFIELD SHS ... SACKETS HARBOR, ON 169
SAINTE MARIE AMONG THE IROQUOIS ... SYRACUSE, ON 178
SARATOGA NHP ... ON 171
SARATOGA SPRINGS ... ON 172
SCHENECTADY ... ON 173
SETAUKET ... ON 175
SOUTHAMPTON ... ON 175

STONY BROOK ... ON 176
SYRACUSE ... ON 177
TROY ... ON 179
UNITED STATES OLYMPIC TRAINING CENTER ... LAKE PLACID, NY 98
WALT WHITMAN BIRTHPLACE SHS ... HUNTINGTON, NY 92
WHITEHALL ... ON 184

SHIPS & BOATS
CHELSEA PIERS ... NEW YORK, NY 134
COLD SPRING HARBOR WHALING MUSEUM ... COLD SPRING HARBOR, NY 77
INTREPID SEA-AIR-SPACE MUSEUM ... MIDTOWN MANHATTAN, NY 122
STATEN ISLAND FERRY COLLECTION ... RICHMOND (STATEN ISLAND), NY 132
USS CROAKER ... BUFFALO, NY 69
USS LITTLE ROCK ... BUFFALO, NY 69
USS SLATER ... ALBANY, NY 56
USS THE SULLIVANS ... BUFFALO, NY 69

SHOPS, FIRMS & STORES
A. SULKA & CO. ... NEW YORK, NY 135
ADIRONDACK FACTORY ... LAKE GEORGE (VILLAGE), NY 97
ALFRED DUNHILL OF LONDON ... NEW YORK, NY 135
ALLENTOWN ... BUFFALO, NY 71
AMERICAN BRIDGE PLAZA ... MASSENA, NY 102
AMMEX TAX & DUTY FREE SHOP ... BUFFALO, NY 71
AMMEX TAX & DUTY FREE SHOP ... OGDENSBURG, ON 158
AMMEX TAX & DUTY FREE SHOP ... ROUSES POINT, ON 169
ANTIQUES SHOPS ... WESTFIELD, ON 183
ARMORY SQUARE DISTRICT ... SYRACUSE, ON 177
ARNOT MALL ... ELMIRA, NY 83
ARTISANS ALLEY ... NIAGARA FALLS, NY 150
AVIATION MALL ... GLENS FALLS, NY 88
BARNEY'S ... NEW YORK, NY 135
BERGDORF GOODMAN ... NEW YORK, NY 135
BLOOMINGDALE'S ... NEW YORK, NY 135
BOLTON'S ... NEW YORK, NY 135
THE BON-TON ... BUFFALO, NY 71
BRITISH AMERICAN HOUSE ... NEW YORK, NY 135
BROOKS BROTHERS ... NEW YORK, NY 135
BUFFALO PLACE ... BUFFALO, NY 71
CAMILLUS MALL ... SYRACUSE, ON 177
CAROUSEL CENTER ... SYRACUSE, ON 177
CHAMPLAIN CENTERS MALL ... PLATTSBURGH, ON 163
CHAUTAUQUA MALL ... JAMESTOWN, NY 94
CHELSEA PIERS ... NEW YORK, NY 134
COLONIE CENTER ... ALBANY, NY 56
COURTYARD ... LOWER MANHATTAN AND NEW YORK HARBOR, NY 118
CRAFT COMPANY NO. 6 ... ROCHESTER, ON 166
CROSS COUNTY SHOPPING CENTER ... YONKERS, NY 141
CROSSGATES MALL ... ALBANY, NY 56
DELAWARE AVENUE ... BUFFALO, NY 71
EASTVIEW MALL ... ROCHESTER, ON 166
FAYETTEVILLE MALL ... SYRACUSE, ON 177
F.R. TRIPLER & CO. ... NEW YORK, NY 135
FRENCH MOUNTAIN COMMONS ... LAKE GEORGE (VILLAGE), NY 97
GALLERIA MALL ... WHITE PLAINS, NY 141
GATEWAY CENTRE ... OGDENSBURG, ON 158
GRAND CENTRAL TERMINAL ... MIDTOWN MANHATTAN, NY 122
GREAT NORTHERN MALL ... SYRACUSE, ON 177
HERTEL ... BUFFALO, NY 71
IRONDEQUOIT MALL ... ROCHESTER, ON 166
JAY STREET PEDESTRIAN WALKWAY ... SCHENECTADY, ON 173
JOB'S LANE ... SOUTHAMPTON, ON 175
KAUFMANN'S ... BUFFALO, NY 71
KINGS PLAZA SHOPPING CENTER ... NEW YORK, NY 135
LAKE GEORGE PLAZA ... LAKE GEORGE (VILLAGE), NY 97
LANE BRYANT ... NEW YORK, NY 135
LITTLE FALLS ANTIQUE CENTER ... LITTLE FALLS, NY 100
LOCKPORT MALL ... LOCKPORT, NY 100
LOEHMANN'S ... NEW YORK, NY 135
LOG JAM ... LAKE GEORGE (VILLAGE), NY 97
LORD AND TAYLOR ... NEW YORK, NY 135
MACY'S ... NEW YORK, NY 135
MAIN PLACE MALL ... BUFFALO, NY 71
MAIN STREET SHOPPING AREA ... NIAGARA FALLS, NY 150
THE MALL AT GREECE RIDGE CENTER ... ROCHESTER, ON 166
THE MARKET ... NEW YORK, NY 135
MARKETPLACE MALL ... ROCHESTER, ON 166
MCDONALD'S ... NEW YORK, NY 135
MOHAWK MALL ... SCHENECTADY, ON 173
MURPHY ORCHARD ... NIAGARA FALLS, NY 150
MUSEUM BLOCK ... LOWER MANHATTAN AND NEW YORK HARBOR, NY 116
NIAGARA DUTY FREE SHOP ... NIAGARA FALLS, NY 150
NIAGARA FACTORY OUTLET MALL ... NIAGARA FALLS, NY 150
NORTH MAIN STREET ... BUFFALO, NY 71
OAKDALE MALL ... BINGHAMTON, NY 62
OUTLET CENTRE AT SOUTHTOWN PLAZA ... ROCHESTER, ON 166
PANORAMA OUTLET MALL AND PLAZA ... ROCHESTER, ON 166
PAUL STUART ... NEW YORK, NY 135
PLANET HOLLYWOOD ... NEW YORK, NY 135
QUEENS CENTER ... NEW YORK, NY 135
RAINBOW CENTRE FACTORY OUTLET ... NIAGARA FALLS, NY 150
RIVERSIDE ... BUFFALO, NY 71
*ROCKEFELLER CENTER ... MIDTOWN MANHATTAN, NY 124
ROOSEVELT FIELD SHOPPING CENTER ... GARDEN CITY, NY 86
ROTTERDAM SQUARE ... SCHENECTADY, ON 173
ST. LAWRENCE CENTRE MALL ... MASSENA, NY 102
SAKS ... NEW YORK, NY 135
SCHERMERHORN ROW ... LOWER MANHATTAN AND NEW YORK HARBOR, NY 116
SEAWAY SHOPPING CENTER ... OGDENSBURG, ON 158
SOUTH STREET SEAPORT MUSEUM ... NEW YORK, NY 135
STATEN ISLAND MALL ... NEW YORK, NY 135
STERNS ... NEW YORK, NY 135
SUMMIT PARK MALL ... NIAGARA FALLS, NY 150
TRUMP TOWER ... NEW YORK, NY 135
UNITED NATIONS GIFT CENTER ... NEW YORK, NY 135
UPPER UNION STREET ... SCHENECTADY, ON 173
VILLAGE GATE SQUARE ... ROCHESTER, ON 166
WALDEN GALLERIA ... BUFFALO, NY 71
WALLACH'S ... NEW YORK, NY 135
WALT WHITMAN MALL ... HUNTINGTON, NY 92
WARREN STREET ... HUDSON, NY 91
WASHINGTON STREET ... ELLICOTTVILLE, NY 83
WILTON MALL ... SARATOGA SPRINGS, ON 172
WORLD FINANCIAL CENTER ... LOWER MANHATTAN AND NEW YORK HARBOR, NY 118

SIGHTSEEING-AIRCRAFT RIDES & TOURS
ADIRONDACK BALLOON FLIGHTS ... GLENS FALLS, NY 88
HARRIS HILL SOARING CORPORATION ... ELMIRA, NY 83
OLD RHINEBECK AERODROME ... RHINEBECK, ON 165
RAINBOW AIR INC. HELICOPTER TOURS ... NIAGARA FALLS, NY 149

SIGHTSEEING TOURS
92ND STREET YMCA ... NEW YORK, NY 133
AFT TOURS INC. ... BUFFALO, NY 70
APEX TRANSPORTATION SERVICES ... BUFFALO, NY 70
ARCADE AND ATTICA RAILROAD ... ARCADE, NY 59
AUSABLE CHASM ... AUSABLE CHASM, NY 61
THE BATTEN KILL RAMBLER SCENIC TRAIN ... SALEM, ON 171
BEDORE TOURS ... NIAGARA FALLS, NY 147
BEDORE TOURS INC. ... BUFFALO, NY 70
BLUE BIRD ... NIAGARA FALLS, NY 149
*CAVE OF THE WINDS TRIP ... NIAGARA FALLS, NY 148
COLGATE UNIVERSITY ... HAMILTON, NY 89
CORNELL UNIVERSITY ... ITHACA, NY 93
DELAWARE AND ULSTER RAIL RIDE ... ARKVILLE, NY 59
GAVIN TRAVEL SERVICE INC. ... NIAGARA FALLS, NY 149
*GOVERNOR NELSON A. ROCKEFELLER EMPIRE STATE PLAZA ... ALBANY, NY 56
GRAND ISLAND TRANSIT ... NIAGARA FALLS, NY 149
GRAY LINE ... NEW YORK, NY 132
GRAY LINE OF BUFFALO & NIAGARA FALLS ... BUFFALO, NY 70
GRAY LINES OF NIAGARA FALLS ... NIAGARA FALLS, NY 149
HARLEM, YOUR WAY! TOURS UNLIMITED ... NEW YORK, NY 133
HISTORIC DISTRICT ... NEWBURGH, NY 105
HUGUENOT HISTORICAL SOCIETY TOURS ... NEW PALTZ, NY 105
LAKE PLACID SIGHTSEEING TOURS ... LAKE PLACID, NY 98
LOCKPORT CAVE AND UNDERGROUND BOAT RIDE ... LOCKPORT, NY 100
MOTHERLAND CONNEXTIONS INC. ... BUFFALO, NY 70
MUNICIPAL ART SOCIETY ... NEW YORK, NY 132
MUSEUM OF THE CITY OF NEW YORK ... NEW YORK, NY 133
NBC STUDIO TOURS ... MIDTOWN MANHATTAN, NY 124
NEW YORK CITY CULTURAL WALKING TOURS ... NEW YORK, NY 133
NIAGARA MAJESTIC TOURS ... NIAGARA FALLS, NY 149
NIAGARA SCENIC BUS LINES ... NIAGARA FALLS, NY 149
NIAGARA VIEWMOBILES ... NIAGARA FALLS, NY 149
OVER THE FALLS TOURS ... NIAGARA FALLS, NY 148
RADIO CITY MUSIC HALL ... MIDTOWN MANHATTAN, NY 125
RAINBOW TOURS OF NIAGARA ... NIAGARA FALLS, NY 149
SARATOGA NHP ... ON 171
SHORT LINE ... NEW YORK, NY 132
TALK-A-WALK ... NEW YORK, NY 133
TROLLEY TOURS ... ELMIRA, NY 83
*UNITED NATIONS HEADQUARTERS ... MIDTOWN MANHATTAN, NY 126

SIGHTSEEING TOURS-BOATS
ALEX BAY BOAT TOURS ... ALEXANDRIA BAY, NY 57
AUSABLE CHASM ... AUSABLE CHASM, NY 61
BEDORE TOURS ... NIAGARA FALLS, NY 147
CAPTAIN BILL'S SENECA LAKE CRUISES ... WATKINS GLEN, ON 183
CAPTAIN GRAY'S BOAT TOURS ... CANANDAIGUA, NY 73
*CHAUTAUQUA BELLE ... MAYVILLE, NY 103
CIRCLE LINE CRUISES ... NEW YORK, NY 132
DISCOVERY WETLANDS CRUISE ... STONY BROOK, ON 176
DUTCH APPLE RIVER CRUISES ... ALBANY, NY 56
ERIE CANAL VILLAGE ... ROME, ON 168
HUDSON RIVER CRUISES ... KINGSTON, NY 96
JUNIPER BOAT TOURS ... PLATTSBURGH, ON 163
KEUKA MAID DINNER BOAT ... HAMMONDSPORT, NY 89
LAKE CHAMPLAIN FERRIES ... LAKE CHAMPLAIN, NY 96
LAKE GEORGE STEAMBOAT CO. ... LAKE GEORGE (VILLAGE), NY 97
LAKE OTSEGO BOAT TOURS ... COOPERSTOWN, NY 78
LAKE PLACID BOAT RIDES ... LAKE PLACID, NY 98
LOCKPORT LOCKS AND ERIE CANAL CRUISES ... LOCKPORT, NY 100
*MAID OF THE MIST ... NIAGARA FALLS, NY 148
*MAID OF THE MIST ... NIAGARA FALLS, ON 152
MID-LAKES NAVIGATION CO. ... SKANEATELES, ON 175
MID-LAKES NAVIGATION CO. LTD. ... SYRACUSE, ON 178
MISS APPLE GROVE ... MEDINA, NY 103
MISS BUFFALO CRUISE BOATS ... BUFFALO, NY 70
OLD FORGE LAKE CRUISES ... OLD FORGE, ON 159
RAINBOW TOURS OF NIAGARA ... NIAGARA FALLS, NY 149
SHORELINE CRUISES OF LAKE GEORGE ... LAKE GEORGE (VILLAGE), NY 97
SPIRIT CRUISES ... NEW YORK, NY 132
STATEN ISLAND FERRY ... NEW YORK, NY 132
SUMMER WIND RIVER AND LAKE CRUISES ... CELORON, NY 75
UNCLE SAM BOAT TOURS ... ALEXANDRIA BAY, NY 58
UNCLE SAM BOAT TOURS ... CLAYTON, NY 77
WORLD YACHT ... NEW YORK, NY 132

SIGHTSEEING TOURS-HOUSE & GARDEN
OLD WESTBURY GARDENS ... OLD WESTBURY, ON 159

SIGHTSEEING TOURS-RAFTING & CANOEING
ARO ADVENTURES ... WATERTOWN, ON 181
HUDSON RIVER RAFTING CO. ... LAKE LUZERNE, NY 97
HUDSON RIVER RAFTING CO. ... NORTH CREEK, ON 157
HUDSON RIVER RAFTING CO. ... WATERTOWN, ON 183

SOUND & LIGHT PRESENTATIONS
ADIRONDACK HISTORY CENTER ... ELIZABETHTOWN, NY 82
CENTER AT HIGH FALLS ... ROCHESTER, ON 167
*NIAGARA FALLS IMAX THEATRE AND DAREDEVIL ADVENTURE ... NIAGARA FALLS, ON 153
STRASENBURGH PLANETARIUM ... ROCHESTER, ON 167
UNICEF HOUSE ... MIDTOWN MANHATTAN, NY 125

SPORTS ARENAS
CARRIER DOME ... SYRACUSE, ON 177
DUNN TIRE PARK ... BUFFALO, NY 70
GIANTS STADIUM ... NEW YORK, NY 134
LOUIS ARMSTRONG MEMORIAL STADIUM ... NEW YORK, NY 134
MADISON SQUARE GARDEN ... MIDTOWN MANHATTAN, NY 122
MARINE MIDLAND ARENA ... BUFFALO, NY 70
NASSAU COLISEUM ... NEW YORK, NY 134
OLYMPIC CENTER ... LAKE PLACID, NY 98
OLYMPIC JUMPING COMPLEX ... LAKE PLACID, NY 99
THE RALPH WILSON STADIUM ... BUFFALO, NY 70
SHEA STADIUM ... NEW YORK, NY 134
YANKEE STADIUM ... NEW YORK, NY 134

SPRINGS
SALT SPRING ... SYRACUSE, ON 178

STATUES
CASINO AND CONGRESS PARK ... SARATOGA SPRINGS, ON 172
GRIFFIS SCULPTURE PARK ... ASHFORD HOLLOW, NY 59
HILL CUMORAH ... PALMYRA, ON 162
NATIONAL SHRINE BASILICA OF OUR LADY OF FATIMA ... LEWISTON, NY 151
OPUS 40 AND QUARRYMAN'S MUSEUM ... SAUGERTIES, ON 173
PARRISH ART MUSEUM AND ARBORETUM ... SOUTHAMPTON, ON 176
SHRINE OF OUR LADY OF THE ISLAND ... EASTPORT, NY 82
*STATUE OF LIBERTY NMO AND ELLIS ISLAND ... LOWER MANHATTAN AND NEW YORK HARBOR, NY 117
STEPOVA BABA ... NIAGARA FALLS, ON 153

STREETS, PLAZAS, SQUARES, CITY AREAS
THE BOWERY ... LOWER MANHATTAN AND NEW YORK HARBOR, NY 113

CANAL SQUARE ... SCHENECTADY, ON 173
*CHINATOWN ... LOWER MANHATTAN AND NEW YORK HARBOR, NY 113
EAST INDIAN NEIGHBORHOOD ... NEW YORK, NY 132
GARMENT DISTRICT ... MIDTOWN MANHATTAN, NY 122
G.E. REALTY PLOT ... SCHENECTADY, ON 173
*GOVERNOR NELSON A. ROCKEFELLER EMPIRE STATE PLAZA ... ALBANY, NY 56
GRAND CENTRAL TERMINAL ... MIDTOWN MANHATTAN, NY 122
GREENWICH VILLAGE ... LOWER MANHATTAN AND NEW YORK HARBOR, NY 113
HISTORIC CANAL PLACE ... LITTLE FALLS, NY 99
JAY STREET ... SCHENECTADY, ON 173
JEWISH SECTOR ... NEW YORK, NY 132
LITTLE ITALY ... NEW YORK, NY 132
MIDDLE EASTERN ENCLAVE ... NEW YORK, NY 132
NIAGARA SQUARE ... BUFFALO, NY 68
PARK AVENUE ... MIDTOWN MANHATTAN, NY 124
SOHO ... LOWER MANHATTAN AND NEW YORK HARBOR, NY 116
STOCKADE DISTRICT ... SCHENECTADY, ON 173
VILLAGE GREEN ... CUTCHOGUE, NY 80
WALL STREET ... LOWER MANHATTAN AND NEW YORK HARBOR, NY 118
WASHINGTON SQUARE ... LOWER MANHATTAN AND NEW YORK HARBOR, NY 118

THEATERS-BUILDINGS
ALICE BUSCH OPERA THEATER ... SPRINGFIELD CENTER, ON 176
ALLEYWAY THEATRE ... BUFFALO, NY 71
ANDERSON CENTER FOR THE PERFORMING ARTS ... BINGHAMTON, NY 62
CAPITAL REPERTORY THEATRE ... ALBANY, NY 55
CHERRY LANE THEATER ... NEW YORK, NY 136
CLEMENS PERFORMING ARTS CENTER ... ELMIRA, NY 83
DELACORTE THEATER ... MIDTOWN MANHATTAN, NY 119
DRYDEN THEATER ... ROCHESTER, ON 167
*EARL W. BRYDGES ARTPARK ... LEWISTON, NY 151
EASTMAN THEATER ... ROCHESTER, ON 165
THE FORUM ... BINGHAMTON, NY 62
FRANKLIN STREET THEATRE ... BUFFALO, NY 71
GEVA THEATRE ... ROCHESTER, ON 165
GUILD HALL OF EAST HAMPTON ... EAST HAMPTON, NY 82
IRISH CLASSICAL THEATRE CO. ... BUFFALO, NY 71
KAVINOKY THEATRE-D'YOUVILLE COLLEGE ... BUFFALO, NY 71
THE NEW PHOENIX THEATRE ... BUFFALO, NY 71
NEW YORK SKYRIDE ... MIDTOWN MANHATTAN, NY 124
NEW YORK STATE THEATER ... MIDTOWN MANHATTAN, NY 122
*NIAGARA FALLS IMAX THEATRE AND DAREDEVIL ADVENTURE ... NIAGARA FALLS, ON 153
NIAGARA FESTIVAL THEATER ... NIAGARA FALLS, NY 148
PALACE THEATRE ... ALBANY, NY 55
PARK PLAYHOUSE ... ALBANY, NY 55
PAVILION THEATRE ... CORTLAND, NY 79
PFEIFER THEATRE ... BUFFALO, NY 71
PROCTOR'S THEATER ... SCHENECTADY, ON 173
PROVINCETOWN PLAYHOUSE ... NEW YORK, NY 136
QUEENS THEATRE IN THE PARK ... NEW YORK, NY 136
RIDE NIAGARA ... NIAGARA FALLS, ON 155
RIPLEY'S BELIEVE IT OR NOT! MOVING THEATER ... NIAGARA FALLS, ON 155
SHEA'S PERFORMING ARTS CENTER ... BUFFALO, NY 71
THE SONY IMAX THEATRE ... MIDTOWN MANHATTAN, NY 125
SPA LITTLE THEATRE ... SARATOGA SPRINGS, ON 172
STRASENBURGH PLANETARIUM ... ROCHESTER, ON 167
STUDIO ARENA THEATER ... BUFFALO, NY 71
SULLIVAN STREET PLAYHOUSE ... NEW YORK, NY 136
THE TAYLOR THEATER ... LOCKPORT, NY 100
UJIMA THEATRE ... BUFFALO, NY 71
UNIVERSITY THEATER ... HAMILTON, NY 89
VETERANS HALL ... RICHMOND (STATEN ISLAND), NY 131

THEATERS-PLAYS, DRAMAS & MUSICALS
CORTLAND REPERTORY THEATRE ... CORTLAND, NY 79

TOWERS
1000 ISLANDS SKYDECK ... ALEXANDRIA BAY, NY 58
MANHATTAN SQUARE PARK ... ROCHESTER, ON 165
MINOLTA TOWER CENTRE ... NIAGARA FALLS, ON 153
MONTEZUMA NWR ... SENECA FALLS, ON 174
OLYMPIC JUMPING COMPLEX ... LAKE PLACID, NY 99
PROSPECT POINT OBSERVATION TOWER ... NIAGARA FALLS, NY 148
RAINBOW CARILLON TOWER ... NIAGARA FALLS, ON 155
SKYLON TOWER ... NIAGARA FALLS, ON 156
UNIVERSITY CLOCK TOWER ... ITHACA, NY 93

TREES
LLOYD NECK BLACK OAK ... HUNTINGTON, NY 91

TUNNELS
BROOKLYN BATTERY TUNNEL ... NEW YORK, NY 107
HOLLAND TUNNEL ... NEW YORK, NY 107
*TABLE ROCK COMPLEX ... NIAGARA FALLS, ON 156

VIEWS
1000 ISLANDS SKYDECK ... ALEXANDRIA BAY, NY 58
ADIRONDACK BALLOON FLIGHTS ... GLENS FALLS, NY 88
ADIRONDACK PARK ... NY 54
BATTERY PARK ... LOWER MANHATTAN AND NEW YORK HARBOR, NY 113
BLUE MOUNTAIN ... BLUE MOUNTAIN LAKE, NY 63
CANAL PARK ... FULTON, NY 86
CITY HALL ... BUFFALO, NY 70
COBB'S HILL PARK ... ROCHESTER, ON 165
CORNING TOWER BUILDING ... ALBANY, NY 56
*EMPIRE STATE BUILDING ... MIDTOWN MANHATTAN, NY 119
FRASER HILL ... SARATOGA NHP, ON 171
*GOAT ISLAND ... NIAGARA FALLS, NY 148
*GREAT GORGE ADVENTURE ... NIAGARA FALLS, ON 151
HARRIS HILL SOARING CORPORATION ... ELMIRA, NY 83
MINOLTA TOWER CENTRE ... NIAGARA FALLS, ON 153
MOUNT DEFIANCE ... FORT TICONDEROGA, NY 86
OLYMPIC JUMPING COMPLEX ... LAKE PLACID, NY 99
ORISKANY BATTLEFIELD ... ROME, ON 169
PROMENADE HILL ... HUDSON, NY 91
PROSPECT MOUNTAIN VETERANS MEMORIAL HIGHWAY ... LAKE GEORGE (VILLAGE), NY 97
PROSPECT POINT OBSERVATION TOWER ... NIAGARA FALLS, NY 148
*QUEEN VICTORIA PARK ... NIAGARA FALLS, ON 155
QUEENSTON HEIGHTS PARK ... NIAGARA FALLS, ON 155
RIVERSIDE PARK ... COXSACKIE, NY 80
ROCK CITY PARK ... OLEAN, ON 159
SKYLON TOWER ... NIAGARA FALLS, ON 156
STONY POINT BATTLEFIELD SHS ... STONY POINT, NY 140
*TABLE ROCK COMPLEX ... NIAGARA FALLS, ON 156
TOP OF THE WORLD ... LOWER MANHATTAN AND NEW YORK HARBOR, NY 118
TRIPHAMMER BRIDGE ... ITHACA, NY 93
WHITEFACE MOUNTAIN ... WILMINGTON, ON 185
*WORLD TRADE CENTER ... LOWER MANHATTAN AND NEW YORK HARBOR, NY 118

VISITOR CENTERS
ALBANY HERITAGE AREA VISITOR CENTER ... ALBANY, NY 55
BINGHAMTON VISITOR CENTER ... BINGHAMTON, NY 62
BLENHEIM-GILBOA PUMPED STORAGE POWER PROJECT ... NORTH BLENHEIM, ON 157
CASTLEGOULD ... PORT WASHINGTON, ON 163
CUMMING NATURE CENTER ... NAPLES, NY 104
FIRE ISLAND LIGHTHOUSE ... FIRE ISLAND NS, NY 84
FRASER HILL ... SARATOGA NHP, ON 171
HERKIMER HOME SHS ... LITTLE FALLS, NY 100
JAMAICA BAY WILDLIFE REFUGE ... QUEENS, NY 131
*MOSES-SAUNDERS POWER DAM ... MASSENA, NY 102
NEWCOMB CENTER ... ADIRONDACK PARK, NY 54
*NIAGARA POWER PROJECT VISITOR CENTER ... NIAGARA FALLS, NY 148
NIAGARA RESERVATION SP ... NIAGARA FALLS, NY 148
PAUL SMITHS ... ADIRONDACK PARK, NY 54
PETER WHITMER FARM ... PALMYRA, ON 162
RIVERSPARK VISITOR CENTER ... TROY, ON 179
ST. LAWRENCE ISLANDS NP ... THOUSAND ISLANDS, ON 178
SARATOGA SPRINGS HERITAGE AREA AND VISITOR CENTER ... SARATOGA SPRINGS, ON 172
*UNITED STATES MILITARY ACADEMY ... WEST POINT, ON 184
URBAN CULTURAL PARK'S VISITOR CENTER ... KINGSTON, NY 96

VISITOR INFORMATION
ALBANY ... NY 54
AMHERST ... NY 71
AMSTERDAM ... NY 59
ARCADE ... NY 59
AUBURN ... NY 59
BALDWINSVILLE ... NY 61
BATAVIA ... NY 61
BINGHAMTON ... NY 61
BLUE MOUNTAIN LAKE ... NY 63
BOLTON LANDING ... NY 63
BOONVILLE ... NY 63
CANANDAIGUA ... NY 73
CANASTOTA ... NY 73
CANTON ... NY 74
CAPE VINCENT ... NY 74
CATSKILL ... NY 74
CAZENOVIA ... NY 74
CLAYTON ... NY 76
COOPERSTOWN ... NY 77
CORNING ... NY 78
CORTLAND ... NY 79
CROTON-ON-HUDSON ... NY 138
CUTCHOGUE ... NY 80
DELHI ... NY 81
DUNKIRK ... NY 81
EAST AURORA ... NY 71
EAST HAMPTON ... NY 82
ELLICOTTVILLE ... NY 82
ELMIRA ... NY 83
FORT EDWARD ... NY 85
FULTON ... NY 86
GARDEN CITY ... NY 86
GENEVA ... NY 87
GLEN COVE ... NY 88
GLENS FALLS ... NY 88
GLOVERSVILLE ... NY 88
GOSHEN ... NY 88
GRAND ISLAND ... NY 72
GREATER BUFFALO CONVENTION AND VISITORS BUREAU ... BUFFALO, NY 66
HAMILTON ... NY 70
HARRISON ... NY 138
HERKIMER ... NY 90
HICKSVILLE ... NY 90
HUDSON ... NY 91
HUNTINGTON ... NY 91
HYDE PARK ... NY 92
ITHACA ... NY 93
JAMESTOWN ... NY 94
KINGSTON ... NY 96
LACKAWANNA ... NY 72
LAKE GEORGE (VILLAGE) ... NY 97
LAKE PLACID ... NY 98
LOCKPORT ... NY 100
LONG ISLAND ... NY 100
LYONS ... NY 101
MALONE ... NY 101
MASSENA ... NY 102
MAYVILLE ... NY 103
MEDINA ... NY 103
NEW CITY ... NY 138
NEW PALTZ ... NY 105
NEW ROCHELLE ... NY 139
NEW YORK CONVENTION AND VISITORS BUREAU ... NEW YORK, NY 108
NEWARK ... NY 137
NEWBURGH ... NY 105
NIAGARA FALLS CONVENTION AND VISITORS BUREAU ... NIAGARA FALLS, NY 144
NORTH CREEK ... ON 157
NORTH TONAWANDA ... NY 72
NYACK ... NY 139
OGDENSBURG ... ON 158
OLD FORGE ... ON 159
OLEAN ... ON 159
ONEIDA ... ON 159
ONEONTA ... ON 159
ORCHARD PARK ... NY 72
OSSINING ... NY 139
OSWEGO ... ON 160
OWEGO ... ON 161
OYSTER BAY ... ON 161
PLATTSBURGH ... ON 163
PORT WASHINGTON ... ON 163
POTSDAM ... ON 163
POUGHKEEPSIE ... ON 164
RHINEBECK ... ON 165
RIVERHEAD ... ON 165
ROCHESTER ... ON 165
ROME ... ON 168
ROUSES POINT ... ON 169
SAG HARBOR ... ON 169
SALAMANCA ... ON 170
SARANAC LAKE ... ON 171
SARATOGA SPRINGS ... ON 172
SCHENECTADY ... ON 173
SCHOHARIE ... ON 173
SENECA FALLS ... ON 174
SKANEATELES ... ON 175
SOUTHAMPTON ... ON 175

SYRACUSE ON 177
TARRYTOWN NY 140
TICONDEROGA ON 179
TROY ON 179
TUPPER LAKE ON 180
UTICA ON 180
VICTOR ON 181
WASHINGTONVILLE ON 181
WATERTOWN ON 181
WATKINS GLEN ON 183
WHITE PLAINS NY 141
WHITEHALL ON 184
WILLIAMSVILLE NY 72
YONKERS NY 141

WALKING TOURS
92ND STREET YMCA NEW YORK, NY 133
ALBANY NY 54
BINGHAMTON NY 61
DELAWARE & HUDSON CANAL MUSEUM HIGH FALLS, NY 90
EAST INDIAN NEIGHBORHOOD NEW YORK, NY 132
GENEVA NY 87
*GREAT GORGE ADVENTURE NIAGARA FALLS, ON 151
GREENWICH VILLAGE WALKING TOUR NEW YORK, NY 133
HARLEM, YOUR WAY! TOURS UNLIMITED NEW YORK, NY 133
*HOME OF FRANKLIN D. ROOSEVELT NHS HYDE PARK, NY 93
JAMESTOWN NY 94
JEWISH SECTOR NEW YORK, NY 132
KINGSTON NY 96
LITTLE ITALY NEW YORK, NY 132
LOWER EAST SIDE TENEMENT MUSEUM LOWER MANHATTAN AND NEW YORK HARBOR, NY 115
MIDDLE EASTERN ENCLAVE NEW YORK, NY 132
MUNICIPAL ART SOCIETY NEW YORK, NY 132
MUSEUM OF THE CITY OF NEW YORK NEW YORK, NY 133
NATURAL STONE BRIDGE AND CAVES POTTERSVILLE, ON 164
NEW YORK CITY CULTURAL WALKING TOURS NEW YORK, NY 133
NYACK NY 139
OLANA SHS HUDSON, NY 91
SACKETS HARBOR BATTLEFIELD SHS SACKETS HARBOR, ON 169
SETAUKET ON 175
STONY BROOK ON 176
SYRACUSE ON 177
TALK-A-WALK NEW YORK, NY 133
TROY ON 179
WHITE PINE CAMP PAUL SMITHS, ON 162
WHITEHALL ON 184
WOMEN'S RIGHTS NHP SENECA FALLS, ON 174

WATERFALLS
AMERICAN FALLS NIAGARA FALLS, NY 142
BRIDAL VEIL NIAGARA FALLS, NY 142
CANADIAN NIAGARA FALLS, NY 142
CENTER AT HIGH FALLS ROCHESTER, ON 167
CHEQUA-GUA FALLS MONTOUR FALLS, NY 104
HAVANA GLEN MONTOUR FALLS, NY 104
HIGH FALLS PARK CHATEAUGAY, NY 75
HORSESHOE NIAGARA FALLS, NY 142
MIDDLE FALLS CASTILE, NY 74
NAPLES NY 104
NIAGARA FALLS NIAGARA FALLS, NY 142
RAINBOW FALLS WATKINS GLEN, ON 183
TAUGHANNOCK FALLS ITHACA, NY 94
UPPER FALLS PARK ROCHESTER, ON 165
*WATKINS GLEN SP WATKINS GLEN, ON 183
WINTERGREEN PARK CANAJOHARIE, NY 73

WATER PARKS
ENCHANTED FOREST/WATER SAFARI OLD FORGE, ON 159
THE GREAT ESCAPE AND SPLASHWATER KINGDOM QUEENSBURY, ON 164
SEABREEZE PARK/RAGING RIVERS WATER PARK ROCHESTER, ON 167
*SIX FLAGS DARIEN LAKE DARIEN CENTER, NY 80
SPLISH SPLASH WATER PARK RIVERHEAD, ON 165

WAX MUSEUMS
*LOUIS TUSSAUD'S WAXWORKS NIAGARA FALLS, ON 152
MOVIELAND WAX MUSEUM NIAGARA FALLS, ON 153
NIAGARA'S WAX MUSEUM NIAGARA FALLS, NY 148

WILDLIFE SANCTUARIES
*BRONX ZOO/WILDLIFE CONSERVATION PARK THE BRONX, NY 129
CONNETQUOT RIVER SP PRESERVE OAKDALE, ON 158
FARM SANCTUARY WATKINS GLEN, ON 183
FUERTES WILD FOWL PRESERVE ITHACA, NY 94
JAMAICA BAY WILDLIFE REFUGE QUEENS, NY 131
LONG ISLAND NWR COMPLEX SHIRLEY, ON 175
MINNA ANTHONY COMMON NATURE CENTER ALEXANDRIA BAY, NY 58
MONTEZUMA NWR SENECA FALLS, ON 174
MORTON NWR SHIRLEY, ON 175
MORTON NWR SOUTHAMPTON, ON 176
RENWICK BIRD SANCTUARY ITHACA, NY 94
ROOSEVELT BIRD SANCTUARY AND TRAILSIDE MUSEUM OYSTER BAY, ON 162
SAPSUCKER WOODS ITHACA, NY 93
TACKAPAUSHA MUSEUM AND PRESERVE SEAFORD, ON 174
TARGET ROCK NWR SHIRLEY, ON 175
TEATOWN LAKE RESERVATION OSSINING, NY 139
WARD POUND RIDGE RESERVATION CROSS RIVER, NY 138
WERTHEIM NWR SHIRLEY, ON 175

WINERIES
BROTHERHOOD WINERY WASHINGTONVILLE, ON 181
BULLY HILL VINEYARDS HAMMONDSPORT, NY 89
CASCADE MOUNTAIN WINERY AMENIA, NY 59
CAYUGA RIDGE ESTATE WINERY OVID, ON 161
CAYUGA WINE TRAIL ITHACA, NY 93
CHATEAU LAFAYETTE RENEAU WATKINS GLEN, ON 183
GLENORA WINE CELLARS DUNDEE, NY 81
GOOSE WATCH WINERY ROMULUS, ON 169
HARGRAVE VINEYARD CUTCHOGUE, NY 80
HUNT COUNTRY VINEYARDS BRANCHPORT, NY 63
JOHNSON ESTATE WINERY WESTFIELD, ON 183
MERRITT ESTATE WINERY FORESTVILLE, NY 85
MILLBROOK VINEYARDS & WINERY MILLBROOK, NY 103
*PLEASANT VALLEY WINE CO. HAMMONDSPORT, NY 90
ROYAL KEDEM WINERY MILTON, NY 103
SWEDISH HILL VINEYARD AND WINERY ROMULUS, ON 169
VETTER VINEYARDS WESTFIELD, ON 183
WAGNER VINEYARDS AND MICRO BREWERY LODI, NY 100
WIDMER'S WINE CELLARS INC. NAPLES, NY 104
WOODBURY VINEYARDS WINERY DUNKIRK, NY 81

ZOOLOGICAL PARKS & EXHIBITS
BERKSHIRE BIRD PARADISE AND SANCTUARY PETERSBURG, ON 162
*BRONX ZOO/WILDLIFE CONSERVATION PARK THE BRONX, NY 129
BUFFALO ZOOLOGICAL GARDENS BUFFALO, NY 69
BURNETT PARK ZOO SYRACUSE, ON 177
*CATSKILL GAME FARM CATSKILL, NY 74
CENTRAL PARK ZOO AND WILDLIFE CONSERVATION CENTER MIDTOWN MANHATTAN, NY 119
CLYDE PEELING'S REPTILAND CATSKILL, NY 74
LOLLYPOP PETTING ZOO HARTWICK, NY 90
LONG ISLAND GAME FARM AND FAMILY RIDE PARK MANORVILLE, NY 102
*MARINELAND NIAGARA FALLS, ON 152
PROSPECT PARK BROOKLYN, NY 130
ROSS PARK ZOO BINGHAMTON, NY 62
SENECA PARK ZOO ROCHESTER, ON 168
STATEN ISLAND ZOO RICHMOND (STATEN ISLAND), NY 132
TRAILSIDE MUSEUM AND ZOO WEST POINT, ON 184
UTICA ZOO UTICA, ON 181

ZOOLOGICAL PARKS & EXHIBITS-CHILDREN'S ZOOS
THE ANIMAL FARM MANORVILLE, NY 101
*BRONX ZOO/WILDLIFE CONSERVATION PARK THE BRONX, NY 129
BUFFALO ZOOLOGICAL GARDENS BUFFALO, NY 69
*CATSKILL GAME FARM CATSKILL, NY 74
ENCHANTED FOREST/WATER SAFARI OLD FORGE, ON 159
FORT RICKEY CHILDREN'S DISCOVERY ZOO ROME, ON 168
LOLLYPOP PETTING ZOO HARTWICK, NY 90
LONG ISLAND GAME FARM AND FAMILY RIDE PARK MANORVILLE, NY 102
*SIX FLAGS DARIEN LAKE DARIEN CENTER, NY 80
STATEN ISLAND ZOO RICHMOND (STATEN ISLAND), NY 132
THOMPSON PARK WATERTOWN, ON 181
UTICA ZOO UTICA, ON 181

SAVE *Attraction Admission Discount Index*

NEW YORK

ADIRONDACK BALLOON FLIGHTS GLENS FALLS 88
ADIRONDACK MUSEUM BLUE MOUNTAIN LAKE 62
ALBANY INSTITUTE OF HISTORY AND ART ALBANY 56
AQUARIUM OF NIAGARA NIAGARA FALLS 147
ARO ADVENTURES WATERTOWN 181
AUSABLE CHASM AUSABLE CHASM 61
BERKSHIRE BIRD PARADISE AND SANCTUARY PETERSBURG 162
BRONCK MUSEUM COXSACKIE 80
BURNETT PARK ZOO SYRACUSE 177
CHILDREN'S MUSEUM OF MANHATTAN MIDTOWN MANHATTAN 119
CIRCLE LINE CRUISES NEW YORK 132
THE CORNING-PAINTED POST HISTORICAL SOCIETY MUSEUM COMPLEX CORNING 78
CUMMING NATURE CENTER NAPLES 104
DELAWARE AND ULSTER RAIL RIDE ARKVILLE 59
FORT DELAWARE—MUSEUM OF COLONIAL HISTORY NARROWSBURG 104
GENESEE COUNTRY VILLAGE & MUSEUM MUMFORD 104
GRANGER HOMESTEAD AND CARRIAGE MUSEUM CANANDAIGUA 73
GRAY LINE NEW YORK 132
GRAY LINE OF BUFFALO & NIAGARA FALLS BUFFALO 70
GRAY LINES OF NIAGARA FALLS NIAGARA FALLS 149
THE GREAT ESCAPE AND SPLASHWATER KINGDOM QUEENSBURY 164
HANFORD MILLS MUSEUM EAST MEREDITH 82
HARNESS RACING MUSEUM & HALL OF FAME GOSHEN 88
THE HERSCHELL CARROUSEL FACTORY MUSEUM NORTH TONAWANDA 72
HILL-HOLD MUSEUM MONTGOMERY 103
HISTORIC CHERRY HILL ALBANY 56
HUDSON RIVER CRUISES KINGSTON 96
HUGUENOT HISTORICAL SOCIETY TOURS NEW PALTZ 105
HUNTINGTON HISTORICAL SOCIETY HUNTINGTON 92
IRISH-AMERICAN HERITAGE MUSEUM EAST DURHAM 81
LAKE OTSEGO BOAT TOURS COOPERSTOWN 78
LAKE PLACID SIGHTSEEING TOURS LAKE PLACID 98
LINCOLN CENTER FOR THE PERFORMING ARTS MIDTOWN MANHATTAN 122
LOCKPORT CAVE AND UNDERGROUND BOAT RIDE LOCKPORT 100
LUCY-DESI MUSEUM JAMESTOWN 94
MOUNT DEFIANCE FORT TICONDEROGA 86
THE MUSEUM OF AUTOMOBILE HISTORY SYRACUSE 178
THE MUSEUMS AT STONY BROOK STONY BROOK 177
NATIONAL SOARING MUSEUM ELMIRA 83
NATURAL STONE BRIDGE AND CAVES POTTERSVILLE 164
NAVAL AND MILITARY PARK BUFFALO 69
NEVERSINK VALLEY AREA MUSEUM CUDDEBACKVILLE 80
NIAGARA MAJESTIC TOURS NIAGARA FALLS 149
NIAGARA'S WAX MUSEUM NIAGARA FALLS 148
NORTHEAST CLASSIC CAR MUSEUM NORWICH 158
OLD FORT NIAGARA YOUNGSTOWN 151
ROCHESTER MUSEUM & SCIENCE CENTER ROCHESTER 167
ROCKWELL MUSEUM CORNING 79
SAMUEL F.B. MORSE HISTORIC SITE, LOCUST GROVE POUGHKEEPSIE 164
SENECA FALLS HISTORICAL SOCIETY SENECA FALLS 174
SCIENCENTER ITHACA 94
SIX FLAGS DARIEN LAKE DARIEN CENTER 80
THE STRONG MUSEUM ROCHESTER 168
SUMMER WIND RIVER AND LAKE CRUISES CELORON 75
THE SUSAN B. ANTHONY HOUSE ROCHESTER 168
WALT WHITMAN BIRTHPLACE SHS HUNTINGTON 92
WHITE PINE CAMP PAUL SMITHS 162
WHITEFACE MOUNTAIN VETERANS' MEMORIAL HIGHWAY WILMINGTON 185
WILLIAM H. SEWARD HOUSE AUBURN 60
WORLD TRADE CENTER LOWER MANHATTAN AND NEW YORK HARBOR 118

NEARBY ONTARIO

GUINNESS WORLD OF RECORDS NIAGARA FALLS 152
LOUIS TUSSAUD'S WAXWORKS NIAGARA FALLS 152
RIPLEY'S BELIEVE IT OR NOT! MOVING THEATER NIAGARA FALLS 155
RIPLEY'S BELIEVE IT OR NOT! MUSEUM NIAGARA FALLS 155
SKYLON TOWER NIAGARA FALLS 156

Comprehensive City Index

Here is an alphabetical list of all cities appearing in this TourBook® guide. Cities are presented by state/province. Page numbers under the POI column indicate where points of interest text begins. Page numbers under the L&R column indicate where lodging and restaurant listings begin.

NEW YORK

City	POI	L&R
ACRA	N/A	190
ADIRONDACK MOUNTAINS	N/A	190
ADIRONDACK PARK	54	N/A
AKRON	N/A	219
ALBANY	54	191
ALBERTSON	57	N/A
ALEXANDRIA BAY	57	197
ALFRED	58	198
ALTMAR	58	N/A
AMAGANSETT	59	199
AMENIA	59	N/A
AMHERST	71	219
AMITYVILLE	N/A	199
AMSTERDAM	59	199
ANGELICA	N/A	199
ANNANDALE-ON-HUDSON	59	N/A
ARCADE	59	N/A
ARKVILLE	59	N/A
ARMONK	N/A	370
ASHFORD HOLLOW	59	N/A
ATHENS	N/A	19
AUBURN	59	199
AURIESVILLE	61	N/A
AURORA	N/A	200
AUSABLE CHASM	61	N/A
AVERILL PARK	N/A	200
AVOCA	N/A	200
BABYLON	N/A	200
BAINBRIDGE	N/A	200
BALDWINSVILLE	61	N/A
BALLSTON LAKE	N/A	201
BALLSTON SPA	61	201
BARNEVELD	N/A	201
BATAVIA	61	201
BATH	N/A	202
BAY SHORE	N/A	203
BEACON	61	N/A
BELLEROSE	N/A	203
BELLPORT	N/A	203
BEMUS POINT	N/A	204
BERLIN	N/A	204
BIG FLATS	N/A	204
BINGHAMTON	61	204
BLASDELL	N/A	221
BLOOMFIELD	N/A	207
BLUE MOUNTAIN LAKE	63	N/A
BOLTON LANDING	63	207
BOONVILLE	63	208
BOWMANSVILLE	N/A	221
BRANCHPORT	63	N/A
BREWERTON	N/A	208
BRIDGEHAMPTON	63	N/A
BRIGHTON	N/A	209
BRISTOL CENTER	N/A	209
BROCKPORT	N/A	209
BROOKLYN	129	370
BUFFALO	64	210
CAMBRIDGE	N/A	229
CAMILLUS	N/A	229
CANAAN	N/A	229
CANAJOHARIE	73	N/A
CANANDAIGUA	73	229
CANASTOTA	73	231
CANTON	74	231
CAPE VINCENT	74	N/A
CARLE PLACE	N/A	231
CARMEL	N/A	371
CASSADAGA	N/A	232
CASTILE	74	N/A
CASTLETON-ON-HUDSON	N/A	232
CATSKILL	74	232
CAYUGA HEIGHTS	N/A	233
CAZENOVIA	74	233
CELORON	75	N/A
CENTERPORT	75	N/A
CHAPPAQUA	N/A	371
CHATEAUGAY	75	N/A
CHAUTAUQUA	75	233
CHAZY	75	N/A
CHEEKTOWAGA	N/A	221
CHERRY VALLEY	76	N/A
CHESTERTOWN	N/A	234
CHILDS	76	N/A
CICERO	N/A	234
CLARENCE	N/A	223
CLAY	N/A	234
CLAYTON	76	234
CLIFTON PARK	N/A	235
CLINTON	N/A	235
CLYMER	N/A	235
COBLESKILL	N/A	235
COLD SPRING HARBOR	77	N/A
COLLIERSVILLE	N/A	236
COLONIE	N/A	236

City	POI	L&R
COMMACK	N/A	238
CONGERS	N/A	371
CONSTABLEVILLE	77	N/A
COOPERS PLAINS	N/A	238
COOPERSTOWN	77	239
CORNING	78	242
CORNWALL-ON-HUDSON	79	N/A
CORTLAND	79	245
COXSACKIE	80	246
CROGHAN	80	N/A
CROSS RIVER	138	N/A
CROTON-ON-HUDSON	138	371
CROWN POINT	80	N/A
CUBA	N/A	246
CUDDEBACKVILLE	80	N/A
CUTCHOGUE	80	N/A
DARIEN CENTER	80	246
DE WITT	N/A	247
DELHI	81	246
DEPEW	N/A	224
DIAMOND POINT	N/A	247
DOVER PLAINS	N/A	248
DRESDEN	81	N/A
DUNDEE	81	N/A
DUNKIRK	81	248
EAGLE BAY	N/A	249
EAST AMHERST	N/A	249
EAST AURORA	71	224
EAST DURHAM	81	249
EAST GREENBUSH	N/A	249
EAST HAMPTON	82	250
EAST MEADOW	N/A	250
EAST MEREDITH	82	N/A
EAST NORWICH	N/A	250
EAST QUOGUE	N/A	250
EAST SYRACUSE	N/A	251
EASTPORT	82	N/A
EDEN	72	N/A
ELDRED	82	N/A
ELIZABETHTOWN	82	252
ELLICOTTVILLE	82	252
ELMA	N/A	225
ELMIRA HEIGHTS	N/A	253
ELMIRA	83	253
ELMSFORD	N/A	372
ENDICOTT	N/A	253
FAIRPORT	N/A	254
FALCONER	N/A	254
FARMINGTON	N/A	254
FAYETTEVILLE	N/A	254
FILLMORE	N/A	255
FINGER LAKES NF	84	N/A
FINGER LAKES	84	255
FIRE ISLAND NS	84	N/A
FISHKILL	N/A	259
FLORAL PARK	N/A	260
FONDA	85	N/A
FORESTVILLE	85	N/A
FORT EDWARD	85	N/A
FORT HUNTER	85	N/A
FORT JOHNSON	85	N/A
FORT PLAIN	86	N/A
FORT STANWIX NMO	86	N/A
FORT TICONDEROGA	86	N/A
FRANKFORT	N/A	260
FREDONIA	N/A	260
FREEPORT	N/A	261
FULTON	86	261
GARDEN CITY	86	N/A
GARRISON	138	N/A
GATES	N/A	261
GATEWAY NRA	86	N/A
GENEVA	87	262
GERMANTOWN	87	N/A
GHENT	N/A	263
GILBOA	88	N/A
GLEN COVE	88	263
GLENMONT	N/A	263
GLENORA	N/A	263
GLENS FALLS	88	264
GLOVERSVILLE	88	N/A
GOSHEN	88	N/A
GRAND ISLAND	72	225
GRANVILLE	89	N/A
GREAT LAKES-ST. LAWRENCE SEAWAY SYSTEM	89	N/A
GREAT NECK	N/A	264
GREAT RIVER	89	N/A
GREECE	N/A	264
GREENE	N/A	265
GREENPORT	N/A	265
GREENWICH	N/A	266
GROTON	N/A	266
GUILDERLAND	N/A	266
HALFMOON	N/A	266

COMPREHENSIVE CITY INDEX (CONT'D)

	POI	L&R
HAMBURG	N/A	225
HAMILTON	89	N/A
HAMLIN	N/A	267
HAMMONDSPORT	89	267
HANCOCK	N/A	267
HARRISON	138	N/A
HARTFORD	90	N/A
HARTSDALE	N/A	372
HARTWICK SEMINARY	N/A	268
HARTWICK	90	N/A
HAUPPAUGE	N/A	268
HAWTHORNE	N/A	372
HENRIETTA	N/A	269
HERKIMER	90	270
HICKSVILLE	90	270
HIGH FALLS	90	271
HIGHLAND FALLS	N/A	271
HIGHLAND	N/A	271
HIGHMOUNT	90	N/A
HILLSDALE	N/A	272
HOBART	N/A	272
HOLBROOK	N/A	272
HOLTSVILLE	N/A	272
HONEOYE FALLS	N/A	272
HONEOYE	N/A	272
HORNELL	90	273
HORSEHEADS	90	273
HOUGHTON	N/A	273
HOWES CAVE	91	N/A
HUDSON	91	274
HUNTER	N/A	274
HUNTINGTON STATION	N/A	274
HUNTINGTON	91	274
HYDE PARK	92	275
ILION	93	N/A
INDEX	N/A	276
INLET	N/A	276
ISLANDIA	N/A	276
ITHACA	93	276
JAMAICA	N/A	372
JAMESTOWN	94	278
JAMESVILLE	N/A	279
JAVA CENTER	95	N/A
JOHNSON CITY	N/A	279
JOHNSTOWN	95	280
JONES BEACH	95	N/A
KATONAH	138	N/A
KINDERHOOK	95	N/A
KINGS POINT	96	N/A
KINGSTON	96	280
LA FARGEVILLE	96	N/A
LACKAWANNA	72	N/A
LAKE CHAMPLAIN	96	N/A
LAKE GEORGE (VILLAGE)	97	N/A
LAKE GEORGE	N/A	281
LAKE LUZERNE	97	293
LAKE PLACID	98	294
LANSING	N/A	301
LATHAM	N/A	301
LAWRENCE	99	N/A
LE ROY	99	302
LEEDS	N/A	302
LEONARDSVILLE	N/A	302
LEWISTON	151	N/A
LIBERTY	N/A	303
LITTLE FALLS	99	303
LIVERPOOL	N/A	304
LIVINGSTON MANOR	N/A	304
LOCKPORT	100	304
LODI	100	N/A
LONG ISLAND	100	304
LONG LAKE	N/A	307
LOUDONVILLE	N/A	307
LOWER MANHATTAN AND NEW YORK HARBOR	113	N/A
LOWMAN	N/A	307
LOWVILLE	N/A	308
LYONS FALLS	101	N/A
LYONS	101	308
MALONE	N/A	308
MANCHESTER	N/A	308
MANORVILLE	101	N/A
MARCELLUS	102	N/A
MARGARETVILLE	N/A	308
MASSAPEQUA PARK	N/A	308
MASSENA	102	309
MAYVILLE	103	309
MCGRAW	N/A	309
MEDFORD	N/A	309
MEDINA	103	N/A
MELVILLE	N/A	309
MERRICK	N/A	310
MEXICO	N/A	310
MIDDLETOWN	N/A	310
MIDTOWN MANHATTAN	118	N/A
MILLBROOK	103	310
MILTON	103	310
MINEOLA	N/A	311
MONROE	103	N/A
MONTAUK	103	N/A
MONTGOMERY	N/A	311
MONTICELLO	103	312
MONTOUR FALLS	103	312
MORAVIA	104	N/A
MOUNT KISCO	N/A	373
MOUNT MORRIS	N/A	312
MOUNT UPTON	N/A	312
MOUNTAINVILLE	104	N/A
MUMFORD	104	313
NANUET	N/A	373
NAPLES	104	313
NARROWSBURG	104	N/A
NEW CITY	138	N/A
NEW HAMPTON	N/A	314
NEW HARTFORD	N/A	315
NEW LEBANON	105	315
NEW PALTZ	105	315
NEW ROCHELLE	139	373
NEW WINDSOR	N/A	317
NEW YORK	106	N/A
NEW YORK	132	318
NEWARK	105	N/A
NEWBURGH	105	313
NEWPORT	N/A	317
NIAGARA FALLS	142	380
NORTH CREEK	N/A	439
NORTH LANSING	N/A	439
NORTH SYRACUSE	N/A	439
NORTH TONAWANDA	72	N/A
NORWICH	N/A	440
N.Y. LOWER MANHATTAN	N/A	331
N.Y. MIDTOWN MANHATTAN	N/A	336
NYACK	139	374
OGDENSBURG	N/A	440
OLD FORGE	N/A	441
OLEAN	N/A	442
ONEIDA CASTLE	N/A	442
ONEONTA	N/A	442
ORANGEBURG	N/A	374
ORCHARD PARK	72	N/A
OSSINING	139	374
OSWEGO	N/A	443
OWEGO	N/A	444
PAINTED POST	N/A	444
PALENVILLE	N/A	445
PARKSVILLE	N/A	445
PEARL RIVER	N/A	375
PEEKSKILL	139	375
PEMBROKE	N/A	445
PENFIELD	N/A	445
PENN YAN	N/A	446
PERTH	N/A	446
PINE VALLEY	N/A	447
PITTSFORD	N/A	447
PLAINVIEW	N/A	448
PLATTSBURGH	N/A	375
PORT CHESTER	N/A	375
PORT JEFFERSON	N/A	449
PORT JERVIS	N/A	450
PORTAGEVILLE	N/A	449
POTSDAM	N/A	450
POUGHKEEPSIE	N/A	450
POUND RIDGE	N/A	375
PURCHASE	139	N/A
QUEENS	130	N/A
QUEENSBURY	N/A	451
RAYMERTOWN	N/A	453
RED CREEK	N/A	453
RED OAKS MILL	N/A	453
RHINEBECK	N/A	453
RICHFIELD SPRINGS	N/A	453
RICHMOND (STATEN ISLAND)	131	N/A
RIPLEY	N/A	454
RIVERHEAD	N/A	454
ROCHESTER	N/A	454
ROCHESTER	N/A	457
ROCKVILLE CENTRE	N/A	460
ROME	N/A	461
RONKONKOMA	N/A	461
ROSCOE	N/A	462
ROSLYN	N/A	462
ROTTERDAM	N/A	376
RYE BROOK	N/A	376
RYE	139	376
SACKETS HARBOR	N/A	462
SAG HARBOR	N/A	463
SARANAC LAKE	N/A	464
SARATOGA SPRINGS	N/A	465
SAUGERTIES	N/A	468
SCHENECTADY	N/A	469
SCHOHARIE	N/A	469
SCHROON LAKE	N/A	470
SCHUYLERVILLE	N/A	470
SCOTIA	N/A	470
SENECA FALLS	N/A	470
SHELTER ISLAND	N/A	471
SHERRILL	N/A	471
SHINNECOCK HILLS	N/A	471
SKANEATELES	N/A	471
SLEEPY HOLLOW	139	N/A
SMITHTOWN	N/A	472
SOUTH GLENS FALLS	N/A	473
SOUTH KORTRIGHT	N/A	473
SOUTH WORCESTER	N/A	473
SOUTHAMPTON	N/A	472
SOUTHOLD	N/A	473
SOUTHPORT	N/A	473

COMPREHENSIVE CITY INDEX (CONT'D)

	POI	L&R
SPECULATOR	N/A	474
SPENCERTOWN	N/A	474
SPRINGFIELD CENTER	N/A	474
ST. JAMES	N/A	463
ST. JOHNSVILLE	N/A	463
STAATSBURG	N/A	474
STAFFORD	N/A	475
STATEN ISLAND	N/A	377
STEPHENTOWN	N/A	475
STONY BROOK	N/A	475
STONY POINT	140	N/A
STORMVILLE	N/A	475
SUFFERN	N/A	377
SYLVAN BEACH	N/A	476
SYRACUSE	N/A	476
SYRACUSE	N/A	479
TANNERSVILLE	N/A	482
TAPPAN	140	N/A
TARRYTOWN	140	377
THE BRONX	128	N/A
THENDARA	N/A	482
TICONDEROGA	N/A	482
TONAWANDA	N/A	226
TROY	N/A	482
TRUMANSBURG	N/A	483
TULLY	N/A	483
TUPPER LAKE	N/A	483
UNIONDALE	N/A	483
UPPER MANHATTAN	126	N/A
UTICA	N/A	484
VALATIE	N/A	486
VERNON	N/A	486
VERONA BEACH	N/A	486
VERONA	N/A	486
VESTAL	N/A	487

	POI	L&R
VICTOR	N/A	487
WARRENSBURG	N/A	488
WARWICK	N/A	488
WATERLOO	N/A	488
WATERTOWN	N/A	488
WATKINS GLEN	N/A	489
WEBSTER	N/A	490
WEEDSPORT	N/A	490
WELLSVILLE	N/A	491
WEST HAVERSTRAW	141	N/A
WEST HENRIETTA	N/A	491
WEST ISLIP	N/A	491
WEST POINT	N/A	492
WESTFIELD	N/A	491
WESTMORELAND	N/A	491
WHITE PLAINS	141	378
WHITEHALL	N/A	492
WHITNEY POINT	N/A	493
WILLIAMSVILLE	72	226
WILLISTON PARK	N/A	493
WILMINGTON	N/A	493
WILTON	N/A	494
WINDHAM	N/A	495
WOODBURY	N/A	495
WYOMING	N/A	495
YONKERS	141	379
YORKVILLE	N/A	495
YOUNGSTOWN	151	N/A

NEARBY ONTARIO

	POI	L&R
LEWISTON	N/A	396
NEWFANE	N/A	396
NIAGARA FALLS	151	386
SANBORN	N/A	396
WHEATFIELD	N/A	396
YOUNGSTOWN	N/A	397

Photo Credit Index

Adirondack Park / P. Degginger,
H. Armstrong Roberts .... Cover, Title, Table of Contents

Hot air balloons over Hudson River, Glens Falls
Jake Rajs, Tony Stone Images .... Cover

TOURBOOK NAVIGATOR

Hotel / Hotel Royal Plaza, Lake Buena Vista, FL 20
Motel / Sea Gull Motel, Virginia Beach, VA 20
Country Inn / Greenville Inn, Greenville, ME 20
Resort / Turnberry Isle Resort & Club, Aventura, FL 20
B&B / Harbour Town Inn, Boothbay Harbor, ME 20
Condo / Sands of Kahana, Kahana, Maui, HI 20
Motor Inn / Days Inn-Hwy 192, Kissimmee, FL 20
Complex / The Beachmere Inn, Ogunquit, ME 21
Lodge / Frankenmuth Bavarian Inn,
Frankenmuth, MI 21
Apartment / Coral Beach Motel, Daytona Beach, FL 21
Cottage / Desert Rose Inn, Bluff, UT 21
Ranch / C Lazy U Ranch, Granby, CO 21

NEW YORK

North Fork Boquet River, Adirondack Park
© Jeff Gnass .... 27, 33, 187, Table of Contents

Heart Lake, Adirondack Park
© David Muench .... 28, Table of Contents

Adirondack Mountains / © David Muench 47
Letchworth State Park / © Jeff Gnass 49

East Hampton, Long Island
F. Sieb, H. Armstrong Roberts 50

Vanderbilt Mansion National Historic Site
© David Muench 51
American-Niagara Falls
W. Bertsch, H. Armstrong Roberts 53
Buffalo / Skyline from the Erie Basin Marina / J. Blank,
H. Armstrong Roberts .... 64, Table of Contents
Buffalo / Buffalo Museum
of Science / © Mark E. Gibson 65, 228
New York / Brooklyn Bridge
Koji Kitagawa, SuperStock 106
New York / Radio City Music Hall / Michael
Ventura, Folio, Inc. .... 107, 379, Table of Contents
New York / Theater Ticket Bargains / Majestic Theater
R. Kord, H. Armstrong Roberts 137
Niagara Falls / Elevated view of the American Falls
David Ball, Tony Stone Images 142
Niagara Falls / Youngsters catch water on Cave of the
Winds Walk / Richard Nowitz, Folio, Inc. 143, 438,
Table of Contents

*A special thank you to the following organizations for
their photo contributions throughout the TourBook:*
Archive Photos™
The Farmers' Museum
New York State Historical Association
Maid of the Mist
Aquarium of Niagara Falls
Niagara Falls Convention & Visitors Bureau
Greater Buffalo Convention & Visitors Bureau
New York Convention & Visitors Bureau
Niagara County Tourism Department
*New York State Office of Parks, Recreation &
Historic Presentation*
Bronx Zoo

Call on the names you trust.

Call 1-800-HOLIDAY for special AAA Rates at more than 1,000 Holiday Inn® hotels across the U.S., where kids always eat and stay free.* You'll enjoy all the amenities of a full-service hotel, along with dependable AT&T communications at most locations. AT&T helps you keep in touch with the ones who matter most.

Experience today's Holiday Inn hotels, building on a reputation you've come to trust. For AAA Rates or special discounts, visit our Web site at www.holiday-inn.com.

Holiday Inn
HOTELS · RESORTS

For reservations, call
1-800-HOLIDAY

AT&T

To learn more about AT&T services, dial 1-800 CALL ATT or visit www.att.com

Guests with hearing impairments please call 1-800-238-5544 (TDD only).